CA Chartered Accountants of Canada

Nadi Chlala, FCA, FCMA

Andrée Lavigne, CA
Maryse Vendette, CA

2009

Financial Reporting in Canada

UNDER

IFRS

Notice to Reader

The Research Studies department of the Knowledge Development Group of the Canadian Institute of Chartered Accountants (CICA) commissioned this publication as part of its continuing research program. The views and conclusions expressed in this publication are those of the authors. They have not been adopted, endorsed, approved, disapproved or otherwise acted upon by a Board, Committee, the governing body or membership of the CICA or any provincial Institute/Ordre.

Library and Archives Canada Cataloguing in Publication

Chlala, Nadi, date –

      Financial reporting in Canada under IFRS / Nadi Chlala, Andrée Lavigne, Maryse Vendette.

ISBN 978-1-55385-405-0

1. Accounting–Standards–Canada. 2. Financial statements–Standards–Canada.
I. Lavigne, Andrée II. Vendette, Maryses III. Canadian Institute of Chartered Accountaants IV. Title.

HF5626.C45 2009   657'.02'1871   C2009-900975-7

Copyright 2009
The Canadian Institute of Chartered Accountants
277 Wellington Street West
Toronto, Ontario
M5V 3H2
www.cica.ca

Printed and bound in Canada.

Table of Contents

Preface

The move to International Financial Reporting Standards (IFRS), is a big challenge for everyone involved in financial reporting in Canada: preparers, users, practitioners, auditors, professors and students. Although IFRS are in many ways similar to Canadian GAAP, they do differ in their detail and some standards are, in fact, substantially different. The CICA Research Studies department has prepared this publication as a primer for understanding IFRS and their practical application.

Financial Reporting in Canada under IFRS provides practical explanations and illustrations of the application of IFRS from a Canadian perspective. It examines and explains presentation and disclosure issues using numerous extracts of financial statements of companies – mostly in Europe – that have already adopted IFRS. It also highlights how these presentations and disclosures differ under Canadian GAAP. These extracts provide real-life illustrations of the practical implementation of IFRS, which can be, depending on the issues covered, both more or less prescriptive than Canadian GAAP. It addresses a wide variety of conversion and implementation issues and compares IFRS requirements to Canadian GAAP.

The focus of this publication is on the preparers of financial statements and the practitioners who work with them. It can, however, also serve as a valuable supplement to accounting textbooks on IFRS as it explains those standards in great detail and discuss practical applications.

This first edition of *Financial Reporting in Canada under IFRS* is a new publication and, although it may be somewhat similar to its predecessor *Financial Reporting in Canada*, it is fundamentally different. Indeed, while it provides practical examples of the application of disclosure requirements using extracts of financial statements, it mainly focuses on the discussion, explanation and illustration of IFRS measurements and recognition requirements, the differences from Canadian GAAP and practical implementation issues. Once IFRS have taken root in this country, future editions of this publication will offer more Canadian application examples, becoming a valuable reference source for all domestic preparers of financial statements.

The authors hope that this publication provides useful guidance to everyone involved in the preparation or interpretation of IFRS financial statements. Compiling the information and writing the text has been a huge undertaking; even though every effort was made to ensure the reliability of the text in this first edition, the extent of the coverage and the complexity of certain issues addressed might have resulted in errors or omissions. The authors would be grateful for comments from readers, both pointing out errors and omissions and proposing improvements.

Many people were involved in the creation of *Financial Reporting in Canada under IFRS*. The CICA would like to express its gratitude to Nadi Chlala, FCA, FCMA, the principal author of this publication, whose contribution was key to the undertaking of this first edition. Thanks also go to Andrée Lavigne, CA, project director, who initiated and lead this project, and coauthor of this publication. As well, special thanks to the many volunteers at Deloitte & Touche LLP who contributed to the review of this book: Maryse Vendette, CA, who reviewed the content of many of the chapters and provided useful practical insights; Peter Chant, FCA, for his advice in the design of the publication and his practical insight on several of the chapters; and several other Deloitte volunteers who contributed their time to the review of specific chapters. All contributors are specifically acknowledged below.

January 2009

CONTRIBUTORS TO THIS EDITION

Principal Author

Nadi Chlala, FCA, FCMA   ESG UQÀM, Accelia & DMR, divisions of Fujitsu Canada inc.

Coauthors

Andrée Lavigne, CA , also Project Director   CICA

Maryse Vendette, CA   Deloitte and Touche LLP

Contributing Technical Writers and Reviewers

Jo-Ann Lempert, CA

John Tang, CA   CICA

Louise Overbeek, CFA

Contributing Technical Reviewers

Peter Chant, FCA, also Advisor   Deloitte & Touche LLP

Chantal Leclerc, CA   Deloitte & Touche LLP

Hélène Marcil, CA   CICA

Robert Lefrançois, CA   Deloitte & Touche LLP

Mario Roy, CA   Deloitte & Touche LLP

Nick Capanna, CA   Deloitte & Touche LLP

Editorial Reviewer

Gundi Jeffrey

Desktop Publisher

Sandy Harris

Chapter 1
Introduction

OBJECTIVE AND ORGANIZATION OF THIS PUBLICATION

Objective

In early 2008, the Accounting Standards Board (AcSB) confirmed that January 1, 2011 would be the date that IFRS will replace Canadian GAAP for all Canadian publicly traded companies, non-listed financial institutions, securities dealers and many cooperative enterprises that qualify as "publicly accountable enterprises (PAE)."[1] Canadian private entities will be permitted, but not required, to adopt IFRS. Some PAEs may choose to adopt IFRS earlier.

This publication aims to help preparers of financial statements, as well practitioners and students, obtain a better understanding of IFRS. More specifically, it looks at the application of IFRS from a Canadian perspective by examining and explaining IFRS requirements and illustrating their application using extracts of financial statements of companies that have already adopted IFRS and discussing how those requirements differ under Canadian GAAP.

Organization

Each chapter discusses a particular accounting topic and includes the following sections:

- a list of the IFRS and Canadian standards discussed in the chapter;

- an introduction, providing an overview of the IFRS covered and any significant differences from Canadian GAAP as well as a list of the significant issues analyzed in the chapter;

- a high-level analysis of the impact on the financial statements of a Canadian entity adopting specific IFRS covered in the chapter;

- an analysis of relevant issues dealing with the significant aspects of the IFRS requirements including a comparison of requirements under Canadian GAAP and IFRS along with annotated illustrative disclosures on issues discussed;

- an illustration of IFRS application as a whole through comprehensive example(s);

- when applicable, future developments reflecting the status of IASB and IFRIC project(s); and

- some IFRS implementation suggestions for issues covered in the chapter, including specific transition requirements.

---

1   Entities required to apply IFRSs after January 1, 2011 are collectively referred to in the omnibus Exposure Draft *Adopting IFRSs in Canada* as "publicly accountable enterprises."

Illustrative Extracts

Since many countries have now adopted IFRS, we were able to obtain good application examples from financial reports of foreign companies that have already made the transition. Appendix C provides a list of the financial reports used for illustration purposes. As this appendix shows, many of the extracts were taken from financial statements prepared in accordance with both IFRS as adopted by the European Union (Euro-IFRS) and IFRS issued by the IASB (full IFRS).[2] In certain cases, extracts came from financial statements that conformed only to Euro-IFRS. These financial statements might have differed in certain respects from full IFRS. When that happened, every effort was made to provide only disclosures that would be no different than if the entity had applied full IFRS.

Generally, the extracts included in this publication were selected from financial statements contained in annual reports or in Form 20F for the fiscal year ending in 2007. In some cases, extracts from reports of other periods were used to illustrate the implementation of specific IFRS requirements or issues (2006 or 2008). In certain chapters, particularly in Chapter 20, extracts were taken from the management discussion and analysis (MD&A) included in financial reports.[3] All extracts were selected to illustrate issues discussed in the chapters. No attempt was made to present illustrations by industrial sector.

STRUCTURE OF IASB AND CONTEXT OF IFRS STANDARD SETTING

Structure

The IASB defines itself as an independent standard-setting board, appointed and overseen by a geographically and professionally diverse group of Trustees (IASC Foundation) who are accountable to the public interest. The IASB is supported by an external advisory council (SAC) and an interpretations committee (IFRIC) to offer guidance where divergence in practice occurs. The following diagram summarizes its structure. [4]

---

2 The most significant difference between Euro-IFRS and full IFRS pertains to IAS 39, *Financial Instruments: Recognition and Measurement*, which has proved to be controversial in some entities of certain European countries, in particular financial institutions.

3 Entities reporting under IFRS sometimes refer to MD&A as "management commentary."

4 Note that in an Exposure Draft issued in July 2008, the IASC Foundation has proposed significant changes to its constitution. The following modifications were adopted before going to press effective January 2009:
   • Significant enhancement to the organisation's public accountability by establishing a link to a Monitoring Board of public authorities;
   • IASB to be expanded from 14 to 16 members by 2012, with criteria added to ensure geographical diversity;
   • Enhanced liaison with investor groups;
   • Free availability of core standards through the public website.
   In December 2008, the IASC Foundation issued part II of the Exposure Draft which proposes additional modifications to the constitution. The comment period ends March 2009.

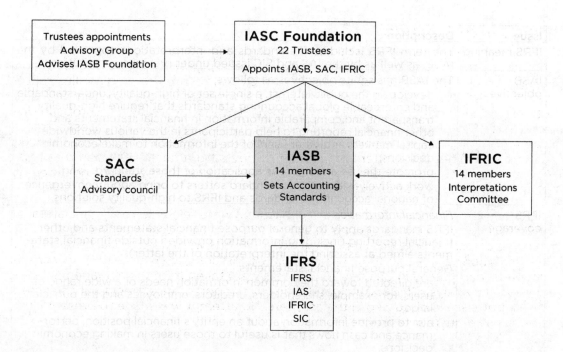

Standard-setting Process

The table below summarizes information about IASB objectives and due process and explains the scope, authority and general transition rules for IFRS application. More detailed information can be found on these aspects in IFRS *Introductory Materials*.

Issue	Description
Organization	*IASC Foundation* The governance of the International Accounting Standards Committee Foundation rests with 22 Trustees whose responsibilities include appointing the members of the IASB and associated councils and committees, as well as securing financing for the organization. *IASB* The International Accounting Standard Board was established in 2001 and currently comprises 14 voting members. IASB approves IFRS and related documents, Exposure Drafts and other discussion documents. The IASB was preceded by the Board of IASC, which came into existence on June 29, 1973, as a result of an agreement by professional accountancy bodies in Australia, Canada, France, Germany, Japan, Mexico, the Netherlands, the UK and Ireland and the US. *IFRIC* The International Financial Reporting Interpretations Committee comprises 14 voting members and a non-voting chairman, all appointed by the Trustees. The role of the IFRIC is to prepare interpretations of IFRS for approval by the IASB and, in the context of the *Framework*, to provide timely guidance on financial reporting issues.[5] The IFRIC replaced the former Standard Interpretations Committee (SIC) in 2002. *SAC* The Standards Advisory Council is appointed by the IASC Foundation Trustees. It provides a formal vehicle for participation by organizations and individuals with an interest in IFRS. The participants have diverse geographical and functional backgrounds. The SAC's objective is to give advice to the IASB on priorities and on major standard-setting projects.

---

5   The IASB *Framework* is discussed in Chapter 2 of this publication.

Issue	Description
IFRS meaning	The term IFRS includes all standards and interpretations approved by the IASB, as well as by the IAS and SIC issued under previous constitutions.
IASB objectives	The IASB has set its objectives as follows: • develop, in the public interest, a single set of high-quality, understandable and enforceable global accounting standards that require high-quality, transparent and comparable information in financial statements and other financial reporting to help participants in the various worldwide capital markets and other users of the information to make economic decisions; • promote the use and rigorous application of those standards; and • work actively with national standard setters to bring about convergence of national accounting standards and IFRS to high-quality solutions.
IFRS coverage	*Financial information* IFRS standards apply to general purpose financial statements and other financial reporting (including information provided outside financial statements aimed at assisting the interpretation of the latter). General purpose financial statements: • are directed toward the common information needs of a wide range of users, for example, shareholders, creditors, employees and the public at large; • aim to provide information about an entity's financial position, performance and cash flows that is useful to those users in making economic decisions. Under IFRS, the term "financial statements" includes a complete set of financial statements prepared for an interim or annual period and condensed financial statements for an interim period. *Requirements* IFRS standards specify recognition, measurement, presentation and disclosure requirements dealing with transactions and events that are important in general purpose financial statements. They may also set out such requirements for transactions and events that arise mainly in specific industries. *Entities* IFRS apply to all profit-oriented entities engaged in commercial, industrial, financial and similar activities, whether organized in corporate or in other forms (such as mutual insurance companies and other mutual co-operative entities that provide dividends or other economic benefits directly and proportionately to their owners, members or participants). Although IFRS are not designed to apply to not-for-profit activities in the private sector, public sector or government, entities with such activities may find them appropriate. The International Public Sector Accounting Standards Board (IPSASB) prepares accounting standards for governments and other public sector entities, other than government business entities, based on IFRS.
Standards format	IFRS standards include paragraphs in bold type and plain type, which have equal authority. Paragraphs in bold type indicate the main principles. An individual standard should be read in the context of the objective and scope stated in that standard and the IFRS Preface. The IFRIC writes interpretations of IFRS to give authoritative guidance on issues that are likely to receive divergent or unacceptable treatment were no such guidance available. Application guidance, illustrative examples and *Basis for Conclusions* that specify reasons why the IASB rejected some solutions and preferred others often accompany the standards. All such guidance states whether it is an integral part of IFRS. Only implementation guidance that is an integral part of IFRS is mandatory. Guidance that is not an integral part of IFRS does not contain requirements for financial statements.

Issue	Description
Due process – standards (See Note)	Due process for projects normally, but not necessarily, requires the IASB to carry out the following steps: • ask staff to identify and review all the issues associated with the topic and to consider the application of the *Framework* to the issues; • study national accounting requirements and practices and exchange views about the issues with national standard setters; • consult the SAC about the advisability of adding the topic to the IASB's agenda; • decide whether to conduct the project alone or jointly with another standard setter; • form a working group to give advice to the IASB on the project; • publish for public comment a discussion document; • publish for public comment an Exposure Draft approved by at least nine IASB votes; • publish a basis for conclusions within an Exposure Draft; • consider all comments received within the comment period set for discussion documents and Exposure Drafts; • consider whether to hold a public hearing and/or conduct field tests and, if considered desirable, holding such hearings and conducting such tests; • consider the need to re-expose an issue; • proceed to the approval of a standard by at least nine IASB votes and include any dissenting opinions in the published standard; and • publish a basis for conclusions within a standard, explaining, among other things, the steps in the IASB's due process and how the IASB dealt with public comments on the Exposure Draft.
Due process – interpretations	IFRS interpretations are developed through an international due process that involves various users of financial statements, the business community, regulators and other interested individuals and organizations from around the world. The IFRIC discusses technical matters in meetings that are open to the public. The due process for each project normally, but not necessarily, requires the IFRIC to carry out the following steps: • ask staff to identify and review all the issues associated with the topic and to consider the application of the *Framework* to the issues; • decide, after debate in a public meeting and a consultative period on issues not added the agenda, whether to add the issue to the agenda; • consider the implications of the hierarchy of IAS 8, *Accounting Policies, Changes in Accounting Estimates and Errors* on the issue; • publish a draft Interpretation for public comment if no more than four IFRIC members have voted against the proposal and if less than four IASB members object to it; • consider all comments received within the comment period on a draft Interpretation; • approve an Interpretation if no more than four IFRIC members have voted against the Interpretation after considering public comments on the draft Interpretation and if it is approved by at least nine IASB members.
Effective dates and transition	• effective date is specified in the document; • new or revised IFRS include transitional provisions to be applied on their initial application; • there are no general policies of exempting from the requirements of a new IFRS any transactions occurring before a specific date.

Issue	Description
Language	The approved text of any discussion document, Exposure Draft or IFRS is that approved by the IASB in the English language. The IASB may approve translations in other languages and may license other translations.
	When making the transition to IFRS, it is essential to take into account the time to convert IFRS into local law or to translate them into the local language. Copyright issues also need to be resolved early. The IASB has recently instituted a one-year delay between publication and the effective date of any significant new standard. Copyright agreements and translation arrangements have been negotiated with the IASB to permit the use of IFRSs in Canada.

Note: The process of IFRS standard setting is somewhat similar to the one followed by the AcSB.

Meaning of IFRS

Generally, IFRS constitute a principles-based set of standards that requires more judgment in applying the principles to specific situations than rules-based standards do. The disclosures required to explain the judgments made are, therefore, essential to the understanding of the accounting policies applied and estimates made in the preparation of the financial statements. Although this is an increased challenge for preparers of financial statements, who will have to provide more transparency and details in the notes, it reduces complexity in standards by avoiding detailed rules of application. In this context, it is also expected that interpretations for the standards would be issued only for areas where IFRS are not clear and have led to significantly divergent interpretations.

As indicated in the table above, when we refer to IFRS or compliance with IFRS it means compliance with the whole body of standards, including:

- IFRS: international financial reporting standards issued after 2001 by the IASB; eight have been issued so far;

- IAS: IASC standards issued prior to 2001, called International Accounting standards; there are 29 IAS;

- IFRIC: interpretations of the International Reporting Interpretations Committee issued after 2001;

- SIC: Standing Interpretations Committee, which are interpretations issued prior to the restructuring in 2001;

- interpretation guidance that is labelled as being part of a standard.

IASB Standards Projects

As with any set of standards, IFRS are not static. The IASB has many standards and research projects underway that follow the due process described above. Several of those projects have the objective of harmonizing IFRS and US GAAP and are undertaken jointly by the IASB and the US Financial Accounting Standards Board (FASB). Other standard setters around the world contribute to the projects underway; the AcSB is involved in some significant projects, notably in the revision of the *Framework*.

Annual Improvements Process

In addition to its regular projects, the IASB has adopted an annual process to deal with non-urgent but necessary amendments to IFRS called the "annual improvements process." These improvements focus on areas of inconsistency in IFRS or where clarification of wording is required. An omnibus Exposure Draft of all the proposals is published for public comment in the third or fourth quarter of the year, with a comment period of 90 days, and the final amendments are issued in the following second quarter, with an effective date of January 1 of the following year unless otherwise specified.

ADOPTION OF IFRS

Adoption of IFRS in the World

More than 100 countries now require or permit the use of IFRSs by listed companies as their basis for financial reporting. IFRSs are being used in most of the major capital markets of the world and have been the subject of evaluation by the International Organization of Securities Commissions.

Adoption in Europe

In June 2000, the European Commission (EU) announced its intention to require all listed companies throughout the EU to use IFRS beginning in 2005 as part of its initiative to build a single European financial market. This intention was made concrete in June 2002 when the European Council of Ministers (the supreme EU decision-making authority) approved the IFRS Regulation. Beginning January 1, 2005, all EU companies whose securities are listed on an EU exchange had to prepare consolidated financial statements conforming to IFRS. To regulate its relationship with the IASB, the EU created the following:

- the European Financial Reporting Advisory Group (EFRAG), which was formed in 2001 by a number of European organizations, including the European Accounting Federation (FEE). EFRAG mandates include:
  o establishing a Technical Expert Group (TEG) that performs detailed work for IASB proposals,
  o closely consulting with European national standard setters and the European Commission before drafting its views on IASB proposals (consequently, it responds formally to all IASB Discussion Papers and Exposure Drafts), and
  o providing a report when an IASB standard is issued, specifying whether the standard has the required qualities and conforms to European company law directives;
- the Accounting Regulation Committee (ARC), whose members include permanent representatives of the EU member state governments. The ARC tells the European Commission whether it endorses a newly issued IASB standard. Note that the European Parliament also has the right to comment on newly issued IASB standards. In addition, if the ARC fails to endorse an IFRS standard, the European Commission may still ask the Council of Ministers to override that decision.

The Institute of Chartered Accountants in England and Wales (ICAEW) prepared the report *EU Implementation of IFRS and the Fair Value Directive* at the request of, and with funding from, the European Commission summarizing the key findings from an on-line survey, roundtables and telephone interviews with preparers, users and auditors. Among those findings:

On the positive side:

- IFRS implementation was challenging, but successful, as evidenced by no material problems being uncovered in the 2005 numbers during the process of preparing financial information for 2006 and the absence of any general loss of confidence in financial reporting.

- There was broad agreement that the adoption of IFRS across the EU had improved the quality of financial reporting and had substantially increased comparability across countries, competitors and sectors.

- There was significant support for improving the quality of disclosures in financial statements.

On the challenges:

- In many jurisdictions, the increased amount of judgment required by IFRS as a generally principles-based set of standards presented considerable challenges, and some concerns were expressed about consistency of application.

- Some contested the value of the significantly increased disclosure requirements, noting that the disclosures required under IAS 1, *Presentation of Financial Statements* for judgments and estimates presented a challenge for preparers.

- Many participants pointed to the requirements of national legislation and national regulators and the enduring strength of national accounting traditions as factors contributing to the "local accents" found in IFRS reporting in the EU. It was thought that, over time, as the body of IFRS practice evolved in the EU, these national features of financial statements would become less evident.

Canada should, however, have an easier time with the transition to IFRS. Many European countries had to deal with more extensive change than is expected in Canada because of greater differences between IFRSs and pre-existing standards, for example, in the adoption of the standards for the recognition and measurement of financial instruments. Canada has already adopted a good number of such standards. As well, in the years following the transition year, the problems related to the increased disclosure requirements were mostly resolved.

Harmonization with US GAAP

In recent years, the IASB and the FASB have undertaken short-term convergence projects resulting in the issuance of Exposure Drafts and amended IFRS standards or amended FASB pronouncements. The two boards have also undertaken long-term joint projects such as business combinations, financial statements presentation and revenue recognition. In addition, the SEC now exempts foreign private issuers presenting financial statements complying fully with IFRS from providing IFRS-US GAPP reconciliations for earnings and equity (when preparing annual filing on Form 20-F).

The table below presents significant events in the harmonization efforts of IFRS and US GAAP:

Dates	Event
October 2002	The FASB and IASB concluded the Norwalk Agreement to (1) formalize their commitment to the development of high-quality, compatible accounting standards for domestic and cross-border financial reporting and (2) to co-ordinate their future work programs to ensure that, once achieved, compatibility is maintained. They have pledged to make their existing financial reporting standards compatible as soon as possible and to maintain that compatibility.
February 2006	The FASB and IASB issued a Memorandum of Understanding (MoU), setting out the milestones of the FASB-IASB joint work program to be reached by 2008. MoU principles include converging existing standards and replacing standards in need of improvement with jointly developed new standards.

Dates	Event
December 2007	The SEC removed the reconciliation requirement for non-US companies that are registered in the US and apply IFRS.
September 2008	The IASB and FASB issued a progress report and timetable for completion of the MoU.
November 2008	The SEC proposed a "roadmap" for phasing in mandatory IFRS filings by US public companies beginning with the years ending on or after December 15, 2014. The roadmap is conditional on progress toward "milestones" that would demonstrate improvements in both the infrastructure of international standard setting and the preparation of the US financial-reporting community. If the conditional milestones are satisfactorily achieved by 2011, the SEC would then consider rulemaking to phase in requirements for US public companies to file financial statements using IFRS as issued by the IASB. Certain US public companies operating within an "IFRS industry" would be permitted to prepare their financial statements according to IFRS as early as 2009 if the proposal is adopted unchanged. The comment period ends February 19, 2009.
December 2008	The European Commission proposed that the European Union remove the requirement for US companies with securities registered in European capital markets and reporting under US GAAP to reconcile their accounts to IFRS. This measure acknowledges that US, Japanese, Chinese, Canadian, South Korean and Indian GAAP are equivalent to the IFRS adopted by the EU. The European Commission will review the situation of some of these countries (China, Canada, South Korea, India) by 2011 at the latest. The measures will mean that foreign companies listed on EU markets will continue to be able to file their financial statements prepared in accordance with those GAAPs (the transitional provisions allowing the use of these GAAPs in the EU would otherwise have expired at the end of 2008).

IFRS ADOPTION IN CANADA
Publicly Accountable Enterprises

In early 2008, the AcSB confirmed that January 1, 2011 would be the date that IFRS will replace Canadian GAAP for all Canadian publicly traded companies as well as for non-listed financial institutions, securities dealers and many cooperative enterprises. More specifically, entities other than the following are required to apply IFRS and are referred to as "publicly accountable enterprises" (PAE)[6]:

- private enterprises, that is, profit-oriented entities that:

  o have not issued (and are not in the process of issuing) debt or equity instruments in a public market, and

  o do not hold assets in a fiduciary capacity for a broad group of outsiders. Entities with fiduciary responsibility, such as banks, credit unions, insurance companies, securities brokers/dealers, mutual funds and investment banks that stand ready to hold and manage financial resources entrusted to them by clients, customers or members not involved in the management of the entity;

- not-for-profit organizations, as defined in CICA 4400, *Financial Statement Presentation by Not-for-Profit Organizations*;

- public sector entities to which the standards in the *CICA Public Sector Accounting Handbook* apply. The introduction to that *Handbook* states that, for purposes of their financial reporting, government business enterprises and government business-type organizations are deemed to be publicly accountable enterprises and

---

6 Pension plans will continue to follow current CICA 4100, *Pension Plans*, instead of IAS 26, *Accounting and Reporting by Retirement Benefit Plans.* Issues not addressed by CICA 4100 must, however, be reported according to another IFRS (other than IAS 26).

should adhere to the standards applicable to publicly accountable enterprises in the *CICA Handbook – Accounting* unless otherwise directed to specific public sector standards. Accordingly, the changeover to IFRSs applies to these two categories of public sector entities.

Entities that are not required to apply IFRS can elect to do so.

Omnibus Exposure Drafts

In April 2008, the AcSB published the Exposure Draft *Adopting IFRSs in Canada* (Omnibus ED) which includes all 37 standards and 22 interpretations of the *IFRS 2007 Bound Volume*. Some of these standards and interpretations are similar to Canadian standards as the AcSB has worked, in recent years, toward harmonizing its requirements with those of the IASB. A second omnibus Exposure Draft is expected to be published in early 2009. This will include any new or amended standards or interpretations the IASB has issued since it released the 2007 bound volume, as well as any Exposure Drafts for which the comment deadline has passed and the IASB is re-deliberating the issues involved.

The second omnibus Exposure Draft will not contain potential future requirements issued by the time IFRS are adopted in Canada. Several projects and amendments could be added to the ever evolving IASB work plan. Despite these difficulties, the AcSB confirmed in July 2008 that none of the amendments to the IASB work plan would affect the Canadian changeover date or the AcSB's decision to adopt IFRS in full and without modification in January 2011. In December 2008, to help entities in their planning for IFRS adoption, the AcSB issued an update to a previous document entitled *Which IFRSs are Expected to Apply for Canadian Changeover in 2011?* This document outlines:

• expected IFRS standards applicable for the first year of adoption;

• IFRS standards expected to remain unchanged until adoption; and

• expected new versions of IFRS (date and impact of changes).

Other Regulations

In addition to the above, the following two documents contain certain regulatory requirements related to IFRS adoption in Canada:

• In May 2008, the Canadian Securities Administrators issued Staff Notice 52-320 *Disclosure of Expected Changes in Accounting Policies Relating to Changeover to International Financial Reporting Standards* (Staff Notice 52-320) that reflects Canadian regulators' expectations for MD&A disclosures leading up to an issuer's adoption of IFRS. The requirements cover interim and annual periods commencing three years prior to the adoption of IFRS (2008 for calendar year companies, fiscal 2009 for non-calendar year-ends). The requirements of Staff Notice 52-320 are examined in Chapter 20.

• The Office of the Superintendent of Financial Institutions Canada (OSFI) issued a letter on October 7, 2008, specifying that all federally regulated financial institutions (FRFI) considered PAE will not be permitted to adopt IFRS early. The letter requires that a progress report addressing an FRFI's transition plan be submitted to OSFI, and FRFIs that are not subject to the CSA disclosure requirements for IFRS adoption are required to submit the same disclosures directly to OSFI. There has been no similar notice of requirements for federally regulated pension plans.

Early Adoption

Some Canadian corporations, for example those with parent or subsidiary companies already reporting in accordance with IFRSs, may wish to adopt IFRSs before the mandatory changeover date. Early adoption is also likely to be affected by the elimination of the SEC requirement to reconcile financial statements prepared in accordance with IFRSs to US GAAP (see section above on "Harmonization with US GAAP"). The AcSB expects to incorporate current IFRS into the *CICA Handbook* in early 2009 to facilitate early adoption. Entities choosing to adopt the standards early would be required to adopt the full set of IFRS rather than individual standards or interpretations.

The CSA Staff Notice 52-321 "Early adoption of International Financial Reporting Standards, use of US GAAP and reference to IFRS-IASB 47" states that Staff are prepared to recommend exemptive relief on a case by case basis to permit a domestic issuer to prepare its financial statements in accordance with IFRS for financial periods beginning before January 1, 2011. They expect an issuer contemplating the possibility of adopting IFRS before 2011 would carefully assess the readiness of its staff, board of directors, audit committee, auditors, investors and other market participants to deal with the change. They also expect that an issuer will consider the implications of adopting IFRS before 2011 on its obligations under securities legislation including those relating to CEO and CFO certifications, business acquisition reports, offering documents, and previously released material forward looking information. A domestic issuer may have previously filed financial statements prepared in accordance with Canadian GAAP or US GAAP for interim periods in the first year that the issuer proposes to adopt IFRS. In such cases, Staff will recommend as a condition of the exemptive relief that the issuer file revised interim financial statements prepared in accordance with IFRS, revised interim management discussion and analysis, and new interim certificates.

AcSB Actions until Conversion

As already noted, the AcSB intends to bring IFRSs into the *Handbook* in full and without modification. The AcSB expects to incorporate the IFRS that are into the omnibus Exposure Draft into the *Handbook* in early 2009, and to expose by then any changes the IASB has made to the body of IFRS in effect at January 1, 2009.

The IASB may change IFRS both before the changeover date and afterwards, in which case the AcSB will issue corresponding Exposure Drafts to incorporate those changes into Canadian GAAP. This will ensure that, at any point in time, the most current version of IFRS is available for use by Canadian entities. At the same time, the AcSB proposes to amend CICA 1506, *Accounting Changes* to accommodate the adoption of IFRS in Canada by providing relief in respect of the requirement to disclose information about new primary sources of GAAP that have been issued but are not yet effective.

The AcSB is also working with IFRIC to resolve interpretation matters, rather than permitting local interpretations. The convergence strategy implies that Emerging Issues Committee (EIC) Abstracts will no longer be applicable to publicly accountable enterprises at the changeover date to IFRSs. The AcSB has established a group to review existing EIC to identify any issues addressed by the Abstracts that should either be referred to the IASB or the IFRIC; or the subject of guidance issued by the AcSB because the issue is affected by specific Canadian legal, tax, regulatory or other circumstances that do not apply in other countries and, therefore, will not be addressed by the IASB. The Task Force proposed that guidance should be provided on the issues addressed by EIC-111, "Determination of Substantively Enacted Tax Rates under CICA 3465," EIC-146, "Flow-Through Shares," and EIC-160, "Stripping Costs Incurred in the Production Phase of a Mining Operation." The AcSB decided that:

- the issues addressed by EIC-111 should be considered by the AcSB's planned forum for the discussion of financial reporting issues arising from the application of IFRSs;

- the issues addressed by EIC-146 should be included in staff's review of the IASB's Exposure Draft on income taxes, which is expected to be issued this summer; and

- the issues addressed in EIC-160 should be referred to the International Financial Reporting Interpretations Committee as there is a lack of guidance in IFRSs on accounting for stripping costs.

Calendar of IFRS Adoption

Canadian corporations have already started to prepare for the transition to IFRS. It involves several steps, including becoming acquainted with the new set of standards, understanding the implications for the preparation of financial statements and for the data required, offering proper training, planning the implementation and the changes to the systems, deciding on whether to adopt IFRS early for certain issues, etc. The year 2009 will be crucial in getting ready for recording the 2010 transactions that will be required for comparative information in the 2011 statements.

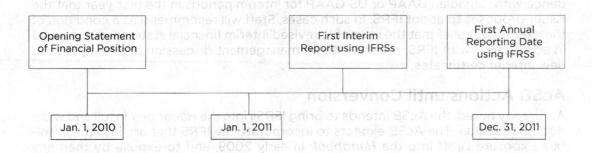

Excerpt from *Which IFRSs Are Expected to Apply for Canadian Changeover in 2011?* (Toronto: AcSB, updated December 2008)

Summary of IFRS Status and Expected Changes

The following tables provide a summary of the status of projects underway for each of the existing and proposed standards as well as for interpretations and the framework. Information on the documents issued so far and the date each new IFRS is likely to be issued are provided. The first two tables also indicate the standards and the interpretations revised or amended in 2008 that are effective in 2008 and 2009. In addition, the first table indicates whether the standards are likely to change or not before the end of 2011 as could be deducted from an analysis of IASB work plan as at December 31, 2008.

Entities can start planning their IFRS adoption by first addressing potential changes in their accounting policies in relation to IFRS standards that are unlikely to change. Entities should always keep current on any amendments and improvements to the IFRS standards and interpretations. Though the IASB work plan anticipates the completion of several projects in 2010 and 2011, it has indicated that it will consider staggering effective dates of standards to help entities moving to IFRSs make an orderly transition.

Note that the AcSB is monitoring any standards likely to change significantly before the changeover date. It points out that choices are likely to be available as to whether to adopt some new standards early, to avoid a second change in accounting policies. Entities should monitor these projects carefully and ensure that their adoption plans are flexible enough to deal with such instances.[7]

		Status of IFRS Standards			
		Revised or Amended IFRS in 2008	IFRS likely to Change Before end of 2011	Status of Projects Underway	
	IFRS Standards	Effective Date		DP and ED	Year New Standard Expected
IFRS 1	**First-time Adoption of IFRS** (updated with issuance of new standards or interpretation or amendments)		Yes		
	– Revised	Jul 2009			
	– Amendment - Cost of an Investment in a subsidiary, jointly controlled entities or associates	Jan 2009			
	– Additional Exemptions for First-time Adopters			ED 2008	2009
IFRS 2	**Share-based Payment**		Yes		
	– Amendment - Vesting conditions and cancellation	Jan 2009			
	– Group cash-settled share-based payment transactions			ED 2007	2009
IFRS 3	**Business Combinations**		Yes		
	– Revised	Jul 2009		DP or ED TBD	TBD
	– Common Control Transactions				
IFRS 4	**Insurance Contracts**		Yes		
	– DP: Preliminary Views on Insurance contracts Part 1 and 2			DP 2007, ED 2009	2011
IFRS 5	**Non-current Assets Held for Sale and Discontinued Operations**		Yes		
	– Discontinued Operations			ED 2008	2009
IFRS 6	**Exploration for and Evaluation of Mineral Resources**		Yes	DP 2009	TBD
IFRS 7	**Financial Instruments: Disclosures**		Yes		
	– Improving Disclosures about Financial Instruments			ED 2008	2009
	– Investments in Debt Instruments			ED 2008	2009
IFRS 8	**Operating Segments**	Jan 2009	No		

---

7 Adapted from *Which IFRSs Are Expected to Apply for Canadian Changeover in 2011?* (Toronto: AcSB, updated December 2008)

Status of IFRS Standards				
IFRS Standards	Revised or Amended IFRS in 2008 — Effective Date	IFRS likely to Change Before end of 2011	Status of Projects Underway — DP and ED	Year New Standard Expected
IAS 1 **Presentation of Financial Statements** – Revised in 2007 (phase A) – Preliminary Views on Financial Statement Presentation (phase B)	Jan 2009		phase B DP 2008, ED 2010	2011
IAS 2 **Inventories**		No		
IAS 7 **Cash-Flow Statements**		Yes	See IAS 1	
IAS 8 **Accounting Policies, Changes in Accounting Estimates and Errors**		No		
IAS 10 **Events After the Balance Sheet Date**		No		
IAS 11 **Construction Contracts (see IAS 18)**		Yes		
IAS 12 **Income Taxes**		Yes	ED 2009	2010
IAS 16 **Property, Plant and Equipment**		No		
IAS 17 **Leases**		Yes	DP 2009, ED 2010	2011
IAS 18 **Revenue** – Preliminary Views on Revenue Recognition in Contracts with Customers		Yes	DP 2008, ED 2010	2011
IAS 19 **Employee Benefits** – Preliminary Views on Amendments to IAS 19 Employee Benefits		Yes	DP 2008, ED 2009	2011
IAS 20 **Accounting for Government Grants and Disclosure of Government Assistance**		Yes/TBD	TBD	
IAS 21 **The Effects of Changes in Foreign Exchange Rates**		No		
IAS 23 **Borrowing Costs** – Revised 2008	Jan 2009	No		
IAS 24 **Related Party Disclosures** – State-controlled Entities and the Definition of a Related Party – Relationships with the State		Yes	ED 2007 ED 2008	2009 2009
IAS 26 **Accounting and Reporting by Retirement Benefit Plans**		No/TBD		
IAS 27 **Consolidated and Separate Financial Statements** – Amendment – Amendment: Cost of Investment in a Subsidiary, Jointly Controlled Entity or Associate – Consolidated Financial Statements	Jul 2009 Jan 2009	Yes	ED 2008	2009

Status of IFRS Standards				
IFRS Standards	Revised or Amended IFRS in 2008 — Effective Date	IFRS likely to Change Before end of 2011	Status of Projects Underway — DP and ED	Year New Standard Expected
IAS 28 — **Investments in Associates**		No		
IAS 29 — **Financial Reporting in Hyperinflationary Economies**		No		
IAS 31 — **Interests in Joint Ventures** - Joint Arrangements		Yes	ED 2007	2009
IAS 32 — **Financial Instruments: Presentation** - Amended 2008: Financial Instruments Presentation and IAS 1 - Puttable Financial Instruments and Obligations arising on liquidation - Financial Instruments with Characteristics of Equity	Jan 2009	Yes	DP 2008, ED 2009	2011
IAS 33 — **Earnings per Share** - Simplifying Earnings per Share		Yes	ED 2008	2009
IAS 34 — **Interim Financial Reporting**		No		
IAS 36 — **Impairment of Assets**		No		
IAS 37 — **Provisions, Contingent Liabilities and Contingent Assets** - Amendments to IAS 37 Provisions, Contingent Liabilities and Contingent Assets and IAS 19 Employee Benefits		Yes	ED 2005	2009
IAS 38 — **Intangible Assets**		No	DP TBD	
IAS 39 — **Financial Instruments: Recognition and Measurement** - Amendment Reclassification of Financial Assets - Amendment: Eligible Edged Items - Embedded Derivatives - Derecognition of Financial Assets - Reducing Complexities in Reporting Financial Instruments	Jul 2008 Jul 2009	Yes	ED 2008 ED 2009 DP 2008	2009 2009/2010 TBD
IAS 40 — **Investment Property**		No		
IAS 41 — **Agriculture**		No		
New — **Fair Value Measurement Guidance**		Yes	DP 2006, ED 2009	2010
New — **Emission Trading Schemes**		Yes	ED 2009	2010
New — **Extractive Activities**		Yes	DP 2009	TBD
New — **Rate-Regulated Activities**		Yes	ED 2009	TBD
New — **IFRS for Small and Medium-sized Entities**		Yes	ED 2007	2009
Annual Improvements to IFRS 2007-2009		N/A	ED 2008	2009
Annual Improvements to IFRS 2008-1010		N/A	ED 2009	2010

IFRIC - New Interpretations and Projects Underway				
		Revised or Amended IFRIC/SIC in 2008	Status of Projects Underway	
	Interpretations	Effective Date	ED	Year New IFRIC Expected
IFRIC 9	Reassessment of Embedded Derivatives		ED 2008	2009
IFRIC 12	Service Concession Arrangements	Jan 2008		
IFRIC 13	Customer Loyalty Programs	Jul 2008		
IFRIC 14	IAS 19 — The Limit on a Defined Benefit Asset, Minimum Funding Requirements, and Their Interaction	Jan 2008		
IFRIC 15	Agreements for the Construction of Real Estate	Jan 2009		
IFRIC 16	Hedges of Net Investment in a Foreign Operation	Oct 2008		
IFRIC 17	Distribution of Non-cash Assets	Jul 2009		
IFRIC 18	Transfers of Assets from Customers	Jul 2009		

Status of Projects on Conceptual Framework and Other		
	Status of Projects underway	
Conceptual Framework Projects	DP and ED	Year New Standard Expected
Conceptual framework phase A: Objective and Qualitative Characteristics. ED: *Conceptual Framework for Financial Reporting: The Objective of Financial Reporting and Qualitative Characteristics and Constraints of Decision-Useful Financial Reporting Information*	ED 2008	2009
Conceptual framework phase B: Elements and Recognition	DP 2010	TBD
Conceptual framework phase C: Measurement	DP 2009 ED 2010	TBD
Conceptual framework phase D: Reporting Entity DP: *Preliminary views, Conceptual framework for financial reporting: The reporting entity*	DP 2008 ED 2009	TBD
Conceptual framework phase E: Presentation and Disclosure		TBD
Conceptual framework phase F: Purpose and Status of Framework		TBD
Conceptual framework phase G: Applicability to NPO		TBD
Conceptual framework phase H: Remaining Issues		TBD
Other IASB projects		
Management Commentary - Guidance	DP 2005, ED 2009	2010

ED: Exposure Draft
DP: Discussion Paper
HB: Handbook
Ef: Effective date

COVERAGE OF IFRS

With a few exceptions, all IFRS standards and interpretations are discussed in this publication. Appendix B provides a table listing of IFRS standards, interpretations, Exposure Drafts and Discussion Papers with a reference to the chapters where they are covered is discussed. The discussion is based on IFRS and related developments issued by the IASB up until end of December 2008[8].

One exception to the coverage is IAS 26, *Accounting and Reporting by Retirement Benefit Plans*. The AcSB proposes that, when publicly accountable enterprises adopt IFRS, pension plans continue to prepare their financial statements in accordance with CICA 4100, *Pension Plans*, rather than IAS 26, *Accounting and Reporting by Retirement Benefit Plans*. If CICA 4100 does not deal with certain aspects of financial reporting by pension plans, those plans currently consult other primary sources of Canadian GAAP. After the changeover to IFRSs, they would look instead to an IFRS other than IAS 26 for additional guidance. The AcSB will consider whether any modifications to Section 4100 are necessary to ensure compatibility with IFRSs. The AcSB will also encourage the IASB to undertake a project to update and improve IAS 26, with a view to eventually replacing Section 4100.

Also, except for a brief summary of the three standards dealing with specific activities in Appendix A, this publication does not deal with industry specific issues; these would merit an analysis of their own.

Given the many projects now underway that will have a significant impact on the conceptual framework, coverage of the latter is limited to the issues discussed in Chapter 2.

Any significant annual IFRS improvements issued in May 2008 have been incorporated into the analysis of the issues in each of the specific chapters. The amendments to eight IFRS proposed in the omnibus Exposure Draft issued in August 2008 are discussed in the "Future Developments" section of each chapter.

Any Exposure Drafts and Discussion Papers issued before December 31, 2008 that are still relevant are also discussed in the "Future Developments" section of each chapter.

---

8   Some developments in January 2009 might have been incorporated where possible.

Chapter 2
Financial Statements Presentation and Disclosures

Standards Discussed in this Chapter

International

Framework for the Preparation and Presentation of Financial Statements
IAS 1 – Presentation of Financial Statements
IAS 7 – Statement of Cash Flows
IAS 8 – Accounting Policies, Changes in Accounting Estimates and Errors
IAS 10 – Events after the Reporting Period
IAS 33 – Earnings per Share
IAS 34 – Interim Financial Reporting
IFRS 8 – Operating Segments

Canadian[1]

CICA 1000 – Financial Statement Concepts
CICA 1100 – Generally Accepted Accounting Principles
CICA 1400 – General Standards of Financial Statement Presentation
CICA 1505 – Disclosure of Accounting Policies
CICA 1506 – Accounting Changes
CICA 1508 – Measurement Uncertainty
CICA 1510 – Current Assets and Current Liabilities
CICA 1520 – Income Statement
CICA 1530 – Comprehensive Income
CICA 1535 – Capital Disclosures
CICA 1540 – Cash Flow Statements
CICA 1701 – Segment Disclosures
CICA 1751 – Interim Financial Statements
CICA 3240 – Share Capital
CICA 3251 – Equity
CICA 3260 – Reserves
CICA 3480 – Extraordinary Items
CICA 3500 – Earnings per Share
CICA 3610 – Capital Transactions
CICA 3820 – Subsequent Events
AcG-7 – The management report
EIC-59 – Long-term debt with covenant violations
EIC-122 – Balance sheet classification of callable debt obligations and debt obligations expected to be refinanced

---

1   Only Canadian publicly accountable enterprises will have to adopt IFRS for years started January 1, 2011. This chapter does not cover CICA 1300 Differential Reporting, which scopes out publicly accountable enterprises. However, it examines certain issues related to an IASB project for private entities (see "Future Developments" section).

INTRODUCTION

This chapter discusses a number of IFRS standards related to financial statement presentation and disclosures. Conceptual considerations related to overall financial statement preparation, such as the use of accrual accounting, are covered by IAS 1. This chapter covers these considerations insofar they are considered significant from a practical point of view or might differ under IFRS and Canadian GAAP. However, it does not examine conceptual issues raised in the IASB *Framework for the Preparation and Presentation of Financial Statements* (IASB Framework). While these conceptual issues are fundamental to the preparation of financial statements under IFRS,[2] their coverage is beyond the scope of this publication. In addition, a detailed analysis of the IASB Framework might be unwarranted at this time since it is currently undergoing major revisions (see conceptual framework project in "Future Developments" section).

In addition to analyzing certain conceptual issues in IAS 1, this chapter discusses the requirements of a number of IFRS standards and compares them with their counterparts in Canadian GAAP. The following table summarizes the chapter's coverage:

IFRS coverage	Related Canadian standard and Significant differences between IFRS and Canadian Standards
IAS 1 – *Presentation of Financial Statements*	CICA 1000, CICA 1400, CICA 1505, CICA 1508, CICA 1510, CICA 1520, CICA 1530 and CICA 1535
Establishes requirements for general purpose financial statements including: • their basis of presentation (fairness, going concern, materiality and comparative information); • their components; and • structure and minimum disclosure for each component, including classification of assets and liabilities.	Canadian standards and IFRS are generally harmonized. Some of the significant differences include: • terminology used; • more detailed discussion of issues in IAS 1 than in the corresponding Canadian standards; • GAAP hierarchy; • "true and fair" override under IFRS; • classification of loans depend on their status at the end of the period under IFRS even though refinancing is concluded prior to the completion of the financial statements; • more guidance in IAS 1 in terms of classification of expenses either by nature or function in the income statements; • increased flexibility in presenting additional line items and non-GAAP subtotals in income statements under IFRS; • more transparent disclosures under IAS 1, such as judgments when applying accounting policies; • additional information required under IFRS (but only permitted and not required under Canadian GAAP), including nature of activities of the entity and dividends per share; • presentation of changes in other comprehensive income.

---

2   Under both IFRS and Canadian GAAP, entities are required to consider the framework when no standard or interpretation specifically applies.

IFRS coverage	Related Canadian standard and Significant differences between IFRS and Canadian standards
IAS 7 – *Statement of Cash Flow*	CICA 1540
Changes in cash and cash equivalents of an entity, including the classification of cash flows during the period from operating, investing and financing activities.	CICA 1540 and IAS 7 requirements are essentially the same except for relatively minor issues, including the fact that: • IAS 7 allows the classification of certain equity investments as cash equivalents (i.e., preferred shares acquired within a short period of their maturity and with a specific redemption date); and • CICA 1540 contains specific requirements for the classification of interest and dividends received or paid.
IAS 8 – *Accounting Policies, Changes in Accounting Estimates and Errors*	CICA 1506 and CICA 1100
Issues covered include: • selecting and changing accounting policies; • accounting and disclosures related to changes in accounting policies, changes in accounting estimates and corrections of errors; • GAAP hierarchy in absence of IFRS requirements.	CICA 1506 is almost a duplicate of IAS 8. The paragraph numbering in both standards is identical. There are, however, certain differences, such as: • the Canadian GAAP hierarchy, which is excluded from CICA 1506 as it is covered in CICA 1100; • a statement of financial position at the beginning of the earliest comparative period following an accounting policy change, a correction of an error, or a reclassification of items in the financial statements is required under IAS 1; • materiality is defined in IAS 8 whereas it is less well defined in CICA 1000. • impracticability exception from restatement of prior periods due to an error correction allowed under IAS 8 is not provided for under CICA 1506.
IAS 10 – *Events after the Reporting Period*	CICA 3820
Issues covered include: • accounting for events after the reporting period; • disclosures about events after the reporting period; and • going concern issues.	CICA 3820 requirements are similar to those established by IAS 10 except that: • cut-off date to reflect post-balance sheet events differs: completion of financial statements (CICA 3820) vs. their authorization for issue (IAS 10); • CICA 3820 specifically allows an entity to show the impact of a significant, non-adjusting event on its future activities by presenting pro-forma information (i.e., effect of an event would be incorporated as if it had occurred) while IAS 10 is silent on this issue; • IAS 10 has additional disclosures, including date of authorization for issue of financial statements and the update about conditions at the balance sheet date in light of new information.

IFRS coverage	Related Canadian standard and Significant differences between IFRS and Canadian standards
IAS 29 – *Financial Reporting in Hyperinflationary Economies*	None
Preparation of adjusted financial statements when an entity operates in economies where money loses purchasing power at such a rate that comparison of amounts from transactions and other events that have occurred at different times would be misleading.	Price-level adjusted financial statements are not allowed under Canadian GAAP. CICA 1651, *Foreign Currency Translation* addresses the translation of financial statements of entities operating in "hyperinflation" conditions.
IAS 33 – *Earnings per Share*	CICA 3500
Calculation and presentation of earnings per share. Focus of the standard is on the denominator of the earnings per share calculation.	Adoption of IASB and AcSB Exposure Drafts will result in harmonization of earnings per share requirements, except for extraordinary items (see "Future Developments").
IAS 34 – *Interim Financial Reporting*	CICA 1751
Minimum content of interim financial reports including recognition and measurement of items reported.	Basically equivalent IFRS and Canadian standard except that: • CICA 1751 requires a mention that interim financial statements must be read in conjunction with the most recent annual financial statements. Such a mention is not specifically required in IAS 34; • only IAS 34 uses the term "condensed financial statements"; • contrary to CICA 1751, IAS 34 does not require a cash flow statement for the current interim period with a comparable corresponding period; • IAS 34 and CICA 1751 differ on some disclosure requirements; • although segment disclosures might be more limited under IAS 34 than under CICA 1751, the former specifies that anything material to understand the current interim period should be disclosed; • IAS 34 and CICA 1751 treat the initial recognition of a previously unrecognized income tax asset in the period differently.
IFRS 8 – *Operating Segments*	CICA 1701
Reporting information about an entity's operating segments in financial statements and related disclosures about products and services, geographical areas and major customers.	Requirements under CICA 1701 and IFRS 8 are similar except for some minor differences, such as IFRS do not have the concept of extraordinary items and CICA 1701 do not require disclosure of segment liabilities. Also, in a matrix organizational structure (two or more overlapping set of components) CICA 1701 specifies that the components based on products and services would constitute the operating segments.
N/A	CICA 3480, *Extraordinary Items*
	Under Canadian GAAP, an entity could label certain gains or losses as "extraordinary" provided that certain criteria are met. IFRS specifically prohibit such labelling.

IFRS coverage	Related Canadian standard and Significant differences between IFRS and Canadian standards
N/A	AcG-7, The management report
	AcSB has a guideline providing its views on the minimum content of a management report that acknowledges management's responsibility for financial information.
N/A	CICA 1300, *Differential Reporting*
	The *CICA Handbook* contains specific differential reporting issues. Even though IFRS do not currently cover this issue, the IASB has a project on IFRS application to private entities (see "Future Developments" section).

To summarize, this chapter covers various issues related to financial statement presentation and disclosures. To illustrate some of the differences between IFRS and Canadian GAAP, this chapter analyzes the following issues:

- scope;
- IFRS and Canadian GAAP:
  - definition,
  - hierarchy;
- overall considerations:
  - general concepts related to financial statement preparation,
  - true and fair override;
- format of financial statements:
  - primary financial statements,
  - identification of financial statements,
  - notes to financial statements;
- statement of financial position (balance sheet):
  - format and structure,
  - basic line items,
  - additional line items,
  - current/non-current classification,
  - disclosures related to equity section;
- statement of comprehensive income:
  - format and structure,
  - basic line items,
  - additional line items, headings and subtotals,
  - analysis and expenses,
  - comprehensive income components;
- statement of changes in equity;
- statement of cash flows (cash flow statement):
  - key definitions,
  - cash and cash equivalents,

- o general structure,
- o establishing operating cash flows,
- o netting of cash flows,
- o foreign currency cash flows,
- o business acquisitions and disposals,
- o discontinued operations,
- o non-cash transactions;
- note disclosures:
  - o objective,
  - o contents;
- changes in accounting policies, changes in estimates and correction of errors:
  - o changes in accounting policies,
  - o changes in accounting estimates,
  - o correction of an error,
  - o impracticability for retroactive adjustments;
- events after the reporting period:
  - o scope,
  - o types of event,
  - o accounting and disclosure requirements;
- going concern issues:
  - o uncertainties,
  - o subsequent events;
- earnings per share (EPS):
  - o definitions,
  - o basic earnings per share,
  - o diluted earnings per share,
  - o restatements,
  - o presentation and disclosures,
  - o additional per share amounts;
- segment information:
  - o objective,
  - o management approach,
  - o definition,
  - o identification of operating segments,
  - o aggregation of operating segments,
  - o minimum reportable segments,
  - o measure of segment's profitability, assets and liabilities,
  - o disclosures,
  - o reconciliation;
- interim financial information:
  - o objective,

- o choices,
- o requirements;
- management commentary:
  - o current requirements,
  - o changeover to IFRS.

IMPACT ON FINANCIAL STATEMENTS

Generally, financial statements prepared according to IFRS will be similar to those prepared under Canadian GAAP, though their format, content and disclosures might vary from existing Canadian practice on some issues, such as:

- Terminology can vary from that normally used under Canadian GAAP. For example, IFRS standards and many entities applying IFRS use the term "reserves," which does not have the same meaning in CICA 3260, and "profit and loss," which refers to "net income" under current Canadian practice.[3]

- Disclosures tend to be more detailed under IFRS, possibly because IAS 1 extensively addresses "transparency" issues. For example, IAS 1 requires an entity to disclose judgments (apart from those involving estimates) when applying an accounting policy that would significantly affect amounts recognized in the financial statements. This is normally not the case in financial statements prepared in accordance with Canadian GAAP (though similar disclosures about "critical accounting policies" can be found in management's discussion and analysis (MD&A) in annual reports). The extensive financial statement disclosure under IFRS should help users understand the basis on which management makes accounting policy choices and would allow them to compare management judgments across entities.

- Format and contents might vary more significantly from one entity to another under IFRS as IAS 1 allows additional line items, subtotals and disclosures. For example, IAS 1 specifies that additional line items, headings and subtotals in the statement of financial position (balance sheet) and the statement of comprehensive income be provided when relevant. As management judgments of relevancy differ, so will the format and content of financial statements. Currently, North American regulators seem to discourage entities from presenting subtotals that are not specifically required by accounting standards because they view such subtotals as "non-GAAP" performance measures that can mislead the readers of financial statements.

- New items (such as provisions) are shown on the face of the statement of financial position (balance sheet) because their presentation is required by a specific IFRS standard.

Other differences in financial statements prepared according to IFRS and Canadian GAAP arise from:

- accounting policy choices that Canadian companies might have made in absence of specific Canadian guideline since:
  - o other sources of GAAP might differ under Canadian and IFRS, and
  - o Canadian companies that are SEC registrants might have selected an accounting policy that does not contravene with US GAAP to avoid reconciliation requirements;
- differences in specific Canadian and IFRS standard, such as:

---

3   The terms "profit or loss," which is commonly used under IFRS, as well as other equivalent ones such "earnings" and "net income" are all used is this chapter and have the same meaning in practice.

o liabilities might be reclassified as current more frequently under IFRS as IAS 1 does not permit an entity to take into consideration post-balance sheet date events as allowed under EIC-122 and EIC-59, and

o presentation of particular items (for example, IAS 7 requires that interest and dividends received be included in operating or investing activities while CICA 1540 requires that they be classified as operating activities if they are included in profit or loss.

All of the above differences between Canadian and IFRS standards and other apparently "minor" ones could, in certain circumstances, end up having a significant impact on financial reporting on IFRS adoption. Generally, Canadian companies implementing IFRS might have to: (1) provide more detailed disclosures than currently and (2) present a less favourable statement of financial position as their debt/equity ratios might increase. It is possible, however, that the additional sub-totals in the statement of comprehensive income, which are frequently presented as relevant benchmarks under IFRS, might sometimes cast a better light on an entity's "true performance."

ANALYSIS OF RELEVANT ISSUES
Scope
The following table summarizes the scope of each IFRS standard examined in this chapter, along with observations on the corresponding Canadian standard:

IFRS Standard Scope	Observations on Corresponding Canadian Standards
IAS 1 – *Presentation of Financial Statements*	CICA 1000, CICA 1400, CICA 1505, CICA 1508, CICA 1510, CICA 1520, CICA 1530 and CICA 1535
Applies to all financial statements prepared and presented in accordance with IFRS.	All CICA sections listed apply to all financial statements prepared and presented in accordance with Canadian GAAP.
IFRS apply only to the financial statements and not necessarily to other information presented in a financial report. Consequently, IAS 1 requires that financial statements be clearly identified and distinguished from other financial information published therein.	Same scope.
IAS 7 – *Statement of Cash Flow*	CICA 1540
Cash flow statement is as an integral part of all financial statements for each period presented.	CICA 1540 scopes out some entities, including pension plans, certain investment funds, and private entities when information is readily apparent from the other financial statements while IAS 7 has no exemptions.

IFRS Standard Scope	Observations on Corresponding Canadian Standards
IAS 8 – *Accounting Policies, Changes in Accounting Estimates and Errors*	CICA 1506 CICA 1100
• Applies to situations when an entity: o selects and applies an accounting policy; o changes an accounting policy or an estimate; and o corrects prior period errors.	• CICA 1506 and CICA 1100 have similar scope.
• Sets hierarchy (criteria for selection of an accounting policy) in absence of IFRS requirements.	• Hierarchy set by CICA 1100.
• Does not apply when a specific standard covers the issue (see Note).	• Similar scope.
IAS 10 – *Events after the Reporting Period*	CICA 3820
Applies both for "adjusting" and "non-adjusting" events occurring after the balance sheet date but before the date the financial statements are authorized for issue.	CICA 3820 has the same scope as IAS 10 except that the period for considering events after the balance sheet date might be shorter under the former because it extends only to the date of completion of financial statements instead of their authorization.
IAS 29 – *Financial Reporting in Hyperinflationary Economies*	None
Applies to the financial statements of any entity from the beginning of the reporting period in which it identifies the existence of "hyperinflation" in the country in whose currency it reports. Economic indicators of hyperinflation include the following: • General population prefers to keep its wealth in non-monetary assets or in a relatively stable foreign currency. Local currencies are immediately invested to maintain purchasing power. • General population regards monetary amounts not in terms of the local currency but in terms of a relatively stable foreign currency. Prices may be quoted in that currency. • Sales and purchases on credit take place at prices that compensate for the expected loss of purchasing power during the credit period, even if the period is short. • Interest rates, wages and prices are linked to a price index. • Cumulative inflation rate over three years is approaching, or exceeds, 100%.	Canadian GAAP does not allow price-level adjusted financial statements. IAS 29 provides guidance on determining when the economy of an entity's functional currency is hyperinflationary. No such guidance exists under Canadian GAAP although hyper-inflation issues are addressed in CICA 1651 (see Chapter 10).

IFRS Standard Scope	Observations on Corresponding Canadian Standards
IAS 33 – *Earnings per Share*	CICA 3500
• Applies to financial statements of an entity whose debt or equity instruments are traded in a public market or that files, or is in the process of filing, its financial statements with a securities commission or other regulatory organizations for the purpose of issuing any class of instruments in a public market. • When an entity presents both consolidated financial statements and separate financial statements prepared in accordance with IAS 27, *Consolidated and Separate Financial Statements*, the disclosures required by IAS 33 need be presented only on the basis of the consolidated information. An entity that chooses to disclose earnings per share based on its separate financial statements must present such earnings per share information only on the face of its separate income statement, not in the consolidated financial statements.	• CICA 3500 has a similar scope except that it applies only to consolidated financial statements. • Canadian accounting standards do not specifically address parent's separate financial statements issues.
IAS 34 – *Interim Financial Reporting*	CICA 1751
• Applies if an entity is required or elects to publish an interim financial report in accordance with IFRS. • It covers both financial statements in accordance with IAS 1 and condensed financial statements.	• Same. • CICA 1751 establishes minimum requirements for all financial statements prepared in an interim period. CICA 1751 does not deal with condensed financial statements.
IFRS 8 – *Operating Segments*	CICA 1701
Applies to financial statements of an entity whose debt or equity instruments are traded in a public market or that files, or is in the process of filing, its financial statements with a securities commission or other regulatory organizations for the purpose of issuing any class of instruments in a public market. Segment information would be required only for the consolidated financial statements even when a financial report also contains the parent's separate financial statements.	The scope of CICA 1701 is similar to that of IFRS 8. Canadian accounting standards do not specifically address a parent's separate financial statement issues.
N/A	CICA 3840, *Extraordinary Items*
N/A	Applies when an entity presents extraordinary gains or losses, which is extremely rare. No extraordinary items labelling is allowed under IFRS.

Note: For example, initial application of an accounting policy to carry property, plant and equipment assets or intangible assets at fair value instead of historical costs would be accounted for in accordance with IAS 16, *Property, Plant and Equipment* or IAS 38, *Intangible Assets* rather than in accordance with IAS 8.

Contrary to Canadian GAAP, IFRS do not have special standards or exemptions for private entities and for not-for-profit organizations. An examination of Canadian requirements on these issues is outside the scope of this publication.

IFRS and Canadian GAAP

Definition

IAS 1 defines IFRS as the term used to indicate the whole body of IASB authoritative literature, which includes IASB standards and interpretations comprising:

- IFRS;
- IAS;
- IFRIC; and
- SIC.

Both the bold- and plain-type paragraphs of IFRS have equal authority and must be complied with. Paragraphs in bold type indicate the main principles.

CICA 1100 defines Canadian GAAP as a term that includes broad principles, conventions of general application, rules and procedures that comprise generally accepted accounting practices in Canada. The principles are identified in italics, but the additional guidance necessary to apply those principles is equally important. Therefore all paragraphs of a standard (italicized and non-italicized) must be complied with, unless stated otherwise.

Hierarchy

Although IAS 8 sets a hierarchy for establishing an accounting policy in absence of IFRS requirements, it does not contain a hierarchy for IFRS standards and interpretations that would, consequently, be considered as equal in status. IASB clarifies in each of its standards what material constitutes the integral part of the standard; guidance that is an integral part of IFRS is mandatory, whereas guidance that is not an integral part of IFRS does not contain requirements. The term "Appendix" is retained only for material that is part of an IFRS standard or interpretation.

In the absence of an IFRS covering a transaction, other event or condition, management must develop and apply an accounting policy that would result in information that:

- is relevant to the users of financial statements; and
- results in financial statements that:
  - represent faithfully the financial position, financial performance and cash flows of the entity,
  - reflect the economic substance of transactions, other events and conditions, and not merely the legal form,
  - are neutral (i.e., free from bias),
  - are prudent, and
  - are complete in all material respects.

Management refers to the above criteria when selecting an accounting policy and:

- *Must* refer to, and consider the applicability of, the following sources in *descending* order:
  - the requirements in IFRS dealing with similar and related issues, and

o   the definitions, recognition criteria and measurement concepts for assets, liabilities, income and expenses in the IASB Framework.

- *May* consider the most recent pronouncements of other standard-setting bodies that use a similar conceptual framework to develop accounting standards, other accounting literature and accepted industry practices, as long as these sources do not conflict with IFRS standards.

Considering Exposure Drafts issued by the IASB or the IFRIC for developing accounting policies is not appropriate as these documents might be modified subsequent to their issuance. Consequently, early adoption of an Exposure Draft proposal is not permitted.

The CICA 1100 hierarchy is similar to the one established by IAS 8, except that the former:

- provides a hierarchy of "primary sources of GAAP" that lists the following in descending order:
  o   CICA sections 1300 to 4460 (including Appendices and Board Notices),
  o   AcG, including Appendices and Board Notices,
  o   EIC, including Appendices,
  o   Background Information and Basis for Conclusions documents accompanying pronouncements,
  o   illlustrative material of above pronouncements, and
  o   implementation Guides authorized by the AcSB;
- Lists certain sources that could be used in the absence of a specific requirement in "primary sources of GAAP," which might not be appropriate under IFRS (such as textbooks and articles).

Illustrative Disclosures:

Extract 2(1) – Absence of guidelines – using US GAAP

Alcatel-Lucent (AR 2007 on Form 20-F), page 162
NOTE 1 SUMMARY OF ACCOUNTING POLICIES (in part)
o/ Revenues (in part)

In the absence of a specific guidance in IAS 18 "Revenue", software revenue recognition rules, as prescribed by the AICPA's SOP 97-2, are applied for revenues generated from licensing, selling or otherwise marketing software solutions when the software is sold on a standalone basis. When the software is embedded with the Group's hardware and the software is considered more than incidental, guidance given in AICPA'S SOP 97-2 is generally applied with limited exceptions, such as determining fair value using methods other than vendor-specific objective evidence (VSOE) of fair value, if deferring revenue related to the delivered elements due to the impossibility of determining VSOE of an undelivered element is not considered as IFRS compliant (e.g. IFRS does not require VSOE of fair value). If VSOE of fair value or fair value of an undelivered element cannot be determined or any undelivered element is essential to the functionality of the delivered element, revenue is deferred until either such criteria are met or the last element is delivered, or revenue is deferred and recognized ratably over the service period if the last undelivered element is a service.

Commentary: In this extract, the company specifies that it has applied software revenue recognition rules prescribed by SOP 97-2 because no specific IFRS standard exists. Note, however, that when applying SOP 97-2 the company must omit any requirement or guidance contained in that US standard that would result in an accounting treatment that is not IFRS compliant. Note that the application of SOP 97-2 criteria will generally result in the adoption of a prudent revenue recognition policy, which also facilitates the comparison of results with those of other entities operating in the same industry and reporting under US GAAP. Many Canadian companies that apply SOP 97-2 requirements as primary sources of GAAP do not specifically address software revenue recognition issues in their financial statements.

Extract 2(2) – Absence of guidelines – using US GAAP

Deutsche Telekom AG (AR 2007), page 127
Accounting policies (in part)
Revenues (in part)

For **multiple-element arrangements**, revenue recognition for each of the elements identified must be determined separately. The framework of the Emerging Issues Task Force Issue No. 00-21 "Accounting for Revenue Arrangements with Multiple Deliverables" (EITF 00-21) was applied to account for multiple-element revenue agreements entered into after January 1, 2003, as permitted by IAS 8.12. EITF 00-21 requires in principle that arrangements involving the delivery of bundled products or services be separated into individual units of accounting, each with its own separate earnings process. Total arrangement consideration relating to the bundled contract is allocated among the different units based on their relative fair values (i.e., the relative fair value of each of the accounting units to the aggregated fair value of the bundled deliverables). If the fair value of the delivered elements cannot be determined reliably but the fair value of the undelivered elements can be determined reliably, the residual value method is used to allocate the arrangement consideration.

Payments to customers, including payments to dealers and agents (discounts, provisions) are generally recognized as a decrease in revenue. If the consideration provides a benefit in its own right and can be reliably measured, the payments are recognized as expenses.

Commentary: This extract specifies that the company has applied EITF 00-21 requirements to account for multiple-element arrangements. The adoption of these requirements will generally result in a prudent revenue recognition policy which would be acceptable under IFRS, and permit the comparison of results with those of other entities in the same industry reporting under US GAAP. EIC-142, *Revenue arrangements with multiple deliverables* contains requirements equivalent to those specified by EITF 00-21 and, accordingly, the accounting policy used would be consistent with Canadian GAAP.

Extract 2(3) – Absence of guideline – not using US GAAP

BT Group PLC (AR & Form 20-F 2007), page 135
35. UNITED STATES GENERALLY ACCEPTED ACCOUNTING PRINCIPLES (in part)
(h) Revenue

Under IFRS, long-term contracts to design, build and operate software solutions are accounted for under IAS 18 'Revenue' and IAS 11 'Construction Contracts' under which revenue is recognised as earned over the contract period.

Under US GAAP certain of these contracts are accounted for as multiple element arrangements under EITF 00-21 and SOP 97-2, 'Software Revenue Recognition'. As vendor specific objective evidence to support the fair value of the separate elements to be delivered is unavailable, revenue of £214 million under certain contracts is deferred in the 2007 financial year (2006: £109 million, 2005: £162 million). There was no impact on net income due to the deferral of costs on these contracts. Total deferred revenue and costs recorded under US GAAP at 31 March 2007 was £562 million (2006: £348 million).

Under IFRS, IAS 18 'Revenue' connection and installation services revenue is recognised when it is earned, upon activation. Under US GAAP, SAB 104 'Revenue Recognition' such revenues are recognised over the estimated customer life and the costs directly associated with the revenue are deferred. Accordingly, an adjustment has been recognised for the first time in the 2007 financial year in respect of Openreach products which have a significant connection and installation service charge.

Commentary: The company does not specify whether it has adopted the detailed guidance of (1) software revenue recognition (SOP 97-2) and (2) multiple-element arrangements (EITF 00-21) prescribed by US GAAP. In addition the company specifies that the accounting policy it used differs from rules prescribed by SAB 104. The company might have concluded that adoption of certain aspects of US GAAP is inappropriate. This differs from the previous two extracts where the companies adopted guidance under SOP 97-2 and EITF 00-21 as permitted under IAS 8.

This extract would conform to Canadian GAAP requirements except that EIC-142, *Revenue arrangements with multiple deliverables* and EIC-141, *Revenue recognition* must be applied (which are basically harmonized with EITF 00-21 and SAB 104 respectively).

Overall Considerations

General Concepts Related to Financial Statements Preparation

IAS 1 covers certain principles underpinning financial statement presentation and disclosure. CICA 1000 and CICA 1400 discuss equivalent principles. The following table summarizes some of these principles, which are essentially converged under IFRS and Canadian GAAP.

Issue	General Principles Defined or Discussed in IAS 1 and Related Observations
Fair presentation (see discussion on "true and fair" override below)	Fair presentation means that: • transactions, other events and conditions are reported in accordance with the definitions and recognition criteria for assets, liabilities, income and expenses set out in the IASB Framework; • IFRS standards and interpretations are applied, with additional disclosure when necessary; and • information is relevant, reliable, comparable and understandable. Consequently, fair presentation implies that: • appropriate accounting policies have been selected and applied in accordance with IAS 8; • titles and captions are consistent with the definitions used in the standards; • terms not defined in the standards are clear, accurate and unambiguous; and • level of disclosure is consistent for items of similar significance.
Materiality	Omissions or misstatements of items are material if they could, individually or collectively, influence the economic decisions users make based on the financial statements. Materiality depends on the size and nature of the omission or misstatement judged according to the surrounding circumstances. Specific accounting or disclosure required by an IFRS standard or interpretation might be omitted if the information is not material. The application of fair presentation would, however, prohibit an entity from making, or leaving uncorrected, immaterial departures from GAAP to achieve a particular presentation of an entity's financial position, financial performance or cash flows.
Aggregation and omission	Items of a dissimilar nature or function must be presented separately unless they are immaterial. Aggregation of a line item that is not individually material with other ones is permitted.
Offsetting of assets and liabilities	Offsetting of assets and liabilities is prohibited unless required or permitted by an IFRS standard. Note that offsetting differs from presenting an asset net of its related "contra-asset." For example, an entity would present inventories net of their related valuation allowances.
Offsetting of income and expenses	Offsetting of income and expenses is prohibited unless required or permitted by an IFRS standard. Income and related expenses are netted for transactions that are incidental to an entity's main revenue-generating activities. Examples of such netting include: • netting gains and losses on the disposal of different non-current assets; and • netting expenditures and reimbursement received under a contractual arrangement with a third party (e.g., a supplier's warranty agreement). Netting gains or losses might be required to better reflect the substance of a transaction Where transactions are of such great size or significance, however, separate disclosure is required.

Issue	General Principles Defined or Discussed in IAS 1 and Related Observations
Reporting period	A complete set of comparative financial statements must be prepared at least annually. Changes in reporting periods (longer or shorter than one year) must be justified and disclosed specifying that comparative amounts presented in the primary statements and the related notes are not entirely comparable.
Consistency of presentation	A change in presentation and classification of items from one period to the next is permitted *only* when it results from: • a significant change in the nature of the entity's operations; • a more appropriate presentation or classification meeting IAS 8 criteria; or • a new IFRS or IFRIC requirement. Note that a significant acquisition or disposal would not be a sufficient reason for a change in financial statement presentation.

Comparative information requirements	• Except when a specific IFRS requirement permits or requires otherwise, previous period comparative information must be presented for:
	  o all amounts reported in the current period's financial statements, and
	  o narrative and descriptive information when it is still relevant to users of the current financial statements.
	• Where an entity changes its presentation or classification of items, it must:
	  o conform the corresponding figures for prior periods to the new presentation, and
	  o disclose the nature, amounts and reasons for the change;
	• If comparative information is not adjusted because it is impossible or economically unreasonable to do so, the entity must disclose the reason for the impracticability and the nature of such adjustments.

True and Fair Override

Fair presentation is a fundamental principle under IFRS. IAS 1 goes as far as to exempt an entity from applying a particular standard or requirement in the extremely rare circumstances where doing so would result in information that is so misleading that it conflicts with the objective of financial statements set out in the IASB Framework.

The true and fair override is also difficult to apply since in such circumstances an entity must explain why the objective of financial statements is not achieved when the IFRS requirement is applied and how its particular circumstances differ from those of other entities that comply with the requirement. Moreover, according to IAS 1, the fact that other entities do comply with a particular IFRS requirement leads to a rebuttable presumption that such compliance would not result in information that is so misleading that it conflicts with the objective of financial statements set out in the IASB Framework.

When it opts for a "true and fair" override, an entity must disclose:

•   title of the IFRS from which the entity has departed;

•   nature of the departure (including the treatment that the IFRS would require);

•   reason why management has concluded that complying with requirement is so misleading in the circumstances that it would conflict with the objective of financial statements set out in the IASB Framework;

•   treatment adopted; and

- for each period presented, the adjustments to each item in the financial statements that management has concluded would be necessary to achieve a fair presentation.

Canadian GAAP does not permit such an exemption in any circumstances.

Illustrative Disclosures:

Disclosures in the extracts presented below provide examples of current practices related to materiality issues, aggregation of items, offsetting, consistency, reporting period and "true and fair override" under IFRS. Except for the "true and fair override" (extracts 2(16) and 2(17)), these disclosures do not contradict Canadian GAAP.

Extract 2(4) – Materiality – Historical cost deemed to equal fair value

Sampo plc (AR 2007), page 55
Summary of Significant Accounting Policies (in part)
Financial Assets and Liabilities (in part)
Fair value (in part)

If the fair value of a financial asset cannot be determined, historical cost is deemed to be a sufficient approximation of fair value. The amount of such assets in the Group balance sheet is immaterial.

Extract 2(5) – Materiality – Immaterial product warranties

Sasol Limited (Annaul Financial Statements 2007), page 162
57 Guarantees and contingent liabilities (in part)
57.2 Product warranties

The group provides product warranties with respect to certain products sold to customers in the ordinary course of business. These warranties typically provide that products sold will conform to specifications. The group generally does not establish a liability for product warranty based on a percentage of turnover or other formula. The group accrues a warranty liability on a transaction-specific basis depending on the individual facts and circumstances related to each sale. Both the liability and the annual expense related to product warranties are immaterial to the consolidated financial statements.

Extract 2(6) – Materiality – Classification of investment property

Daejan Holdings PLC (Report & Financial Statements 2007), page 27
1. Significant accounting policies (in part)
(i) Investment property (in part)

When the Group uses only part of a property it owns and retains the remainder to generate rental income or capital appreciation the extent of the Group's utilisation is considered to determine the classification of the property. If the Group's utilisation is less than five per cent, this is regarded as immaterial such that the whole property is classified as an investment property and stated at fair value.

Extract 2(7) – Materiality – Subsidiaries that are not consolidated

Bayer Aktiengesellschaft (AR 2007), page 124
6. Scope of consolidation (in part)
6.1 Changes in the scope of consolidation (in part)

Excluded from consolidation are 115 subsidiaries and 39 associates that in aggregate are immaterial to the net worth, financial position and earnings of the Bayer Group and are recognized at cost of acquisition less any impairments. These companies account for less than 0.4 percent of Group sales, less than 0.7 percent of stockholders' equity and less than 0.4 percent of total assets.

Extract 2(8) – Materiality – Subsidiaries that are not consolidated

Fiat S.p.A. (AR 2007), page 113
Scope of consolidation (in part)

Excluded from consolidation are 108 subsidiaries that are either dormant or generate a negligible volume of business: their proportion of the Group's assets, liabilities, financial position and earnings is immaterial. In particular, 73 such subsidiaries are accounted for using the cost method; and represent in aggregate 0.3 percent of Group revenues, 0.1 percent of stockholders' equity and 0.2 percent of total assets. The Ergom group, which was acquired in November 2007, has also been excluded from consolidation due to a lack of certain of the information necessary to prepare these notes in a consistent manner. For the sake of completeness a summary balance sheet of the Group at December 31, 007 in which the Ergom group, whose balances are not significant compared to those of the Group as a whole, is consolidated on a line-by-line basis is provided in Note 36.

Extract 2(9) – Materiality – Subsidiaries that are not consolidated

ENI SpA (AR 2007), page 147
Basis of presentation (in part)

Immaterial subsidiaries are not consolidated. A subsidiary is generally considered to be immaterial when it does not exceed two of the following three limits: (i) total assets or liabilities: 3,125 thousand; (ii) total revenues: 6,250 thousand; and (iii) average number of employees: 50 units. Moreover, companies for which consolidation does not produce significant economic and financial effects are not consolidated. These are usually entities acting as sole-operator in the management of oil and gas contracts on behalf of companies participating in a joint venture. These are financed proportionately based on a budget approved by the participating companies upon presentation periodical reports of proceeds and expenses. Costs and revenues and other operating data (production, reserves, etc.) of the project, as well as the obligations arising from the project, are recognized proportionally in the financial statements of the companies involved. The effects of these exclusions are immaterial.

Immaterial subsidiaries excluded from consolidation, jointly controlled entities, associates and other interests are accounted for as described below under the item "Financial fixed assets".

Extract 2(10) – Change in method of assessing materiality

Bank of Ireland (Report & Accounts 2007), page 86
Group Accounts (in part)
Change in method of Assessing Materiality

During the year, the Group changed its method of assessing materiality. The Group previously considered the materiality of misstatements based on the amount of the misstatement originating in the current year income statement. The Group has now decided to consider the effect of any misstatements based on both;

(1) the amount of the misstatement originating in the current year income statement, and;

(2) the effects of correcting the misstatement existing in the balance sheet at the end of the current year irrespective of the year in which the misstatement originated.

The Group considers that this change of policy provides more relevant financial information as it prevents the accumulation of misstatements in the balance sheet. As a result of this change, the Group has revised its prior year financial statements for the adjustments set out below, which under the previous method of quantifying misstatements, would have been considered immaterial.

Bank of Ireland (Report & Accounts 2007) (continued)

IFRS requires that Bank of Ireland shares held by the Group, including those held by BoI Life are reclassified as treasury shares and accounted for as a deduction from equity. Any changes in the value of treasury shares held are recognised in equity at the time of disposal and dividends are not recognised as income or distributions. In prior years, the Group did not apply this treatment to the investment return on shares in Bank of Ireland held by BoI Life. Rather it recognised investment return on Bank of Ireland shares held in BoI Life on the grounds that such investment legally accrues to the unit-linked policyholders and accordingly is matched by an increase in liabilities in the income statement. The Group believes that application of the requirements of IFRS for treasury shares held by BoI Life for the benefit of policyholders creates an artificial loss and does not present fairly the legal and economic consequences of such transactions. However the Group accepts that this accounting is the basis which is currently required under IFRS and consistent with the adoption of a materiality policy that considers the effect of correcting a cumulative balance sheet misstatement on the current year income statement, that it is now appropriate to adjust for this requirement under IFRS.

The adjustments below relate to the holding of Bank of Ireland shares by BoI Life for the benefit of unit-linked policyholders that must be accounted for as treasury shares under IAS 32.

In the income statement there are two adjustments to the prior year, 31 March 2006, income statement. Life assurance investment income and gains has been reduced by €26m from €625m, as previously reported to 31 March 06, to €599m. Other operating income has been reduced by €49m from €165m to €116m. As a result Profit before tax was €75m lower, down from €1,599m to €1,524m.

Basic earnings per share were reduced by 7.9c from 136.4c to 128.5c while diluted earnings per share were similarly reduced from 135.4c to 127.6c. In the balance sheet as at 31 March 2006, Assets at fair value through profit and loss were reduced by €142m from €10,580m to €10,438m and retained earnings reduced by the same amount from €3,330m to €,188m. The impact of the changes described above on retained profit as at 31 March 2005 was €90m.

Extract 2(11) – Netting finance costs and interest income

PaperlinX Limited (Full Financial Report 2007), page 9

Note 1. Accounting policies (in part)

(8) Net financing costs (in part)

Net financing costs comprise interest and other financing charges including foreign exchange gains and losses, net of interest on funds invested. These costs are brought to account in determining profit for the year, except to the extent the interest incurred relates to major capital items in which case interest is capitalised as a cost of the asset up to the time it is ready for its intended use or sale.

Interest income is recognised in the income statement as it accrues, using the effective interest method.

Extract 2(12) – Aggregation of immaterial items

Bayer Aktiengesellschaft (AR 2007), page 133

10. Other operating income

As in the previous year, total other operating income is composed of a large number of individually immaterial items within the subsidiaries.

€ million	2006	2007
Gains from sales of noncurrent assets and from divestitures	169	80
Write-backs of receivables and other assets	98	76
Reversals of unutilized provisions	55	101
Recognition of exchange rate hedges	120	192
Miscellaneous operating income	288	373
Total	730	822

11. Other operating expenses

€ million	2006	2007
Losses from sales of noncurrent assets and from divestitures	(31)	(52)
Write-downs of receivables	(138)	(98)
Expenses related to significant legal risks	(205)	(139)
Recognition of exchange rate hedges	(126)	(57)
Miscellaneous operating expenses	(719)	(1,223)
Total	(1,219)	(1,569)

The principal restructuring expenses included in other operating expenses for 2007 amount to €709 million (2006: €408 million), including €506 million related to the integration of the Schering Group (2006: €179 million). Further details of restructuring expenses are given in Note [26.4].

Other operating expenses for 2007 include a €152 million write-down of intangible assets necessitated by the findings of the beyond study on Betaferon®/Betaseron®. In the previous year, other operating expenses contained write-downs related to development and marketing agreements for the drug alfi meprase and the product Viadur® totaling €60 million and a write-down of €31 million as a result of a change in the plan to expand the chlor-alkali production facilities in Baytown, Texas, U.S.A.

An amount of €362 million (2006: €220 million) relates to a large number of individually immaterial items within the subsidiaries.

Extract 2(13) – General statement concerning consistency

ING Groep N.V. (AR 2007), page 93

Accounting policies for the consolidated balance sheet and profit and loss account of ING Group (in part)

CHANGES IN ACCOUNTING POLICIES AND PRESENTATION (in part)

The presentation of, and certain terms used in, the balance sheet, the profit and loss account, cash flow statement, statement of changes in equity and certain notes has been changed to provide additional and more relevant information. Certain comparative amounts have been reclassified to conform with the current period presentation.

Extract 2(14) – Offsetting of derivatives (positive and negative position)

ABN AMRO Holding N.V. (AR 2007), Page 107

Accounting policies (in part)

Netting and collateral

The Group enters into master netting arrangements with counterparties wherever possible, and when appropriate, obtains collateral. If the Group has the right on the grounds of either legal or contractual provisions and the intention to settle financial assets and liabilities net or simultaneously, these are offset and the net amount is reported in the balance sheet. Due to differences in the timing of actual cash flows, derivatives with positive and negative fair values are generally not netted, even if they are held with the same counterparty.

Extract 2(15) – Consistency of year ends for entities within a group

---

Delhaize Group SA (AR 2007), page 67

2. Summary of Significant Accounting Policies (in part)

Fiscal Year

Delhaize Group's fiscal year ends on December 31. However, the year-end of Delhaize Group's U.S. businesses is the Saturday closest to December 31. The Group's consolidated results of operations and balance sheet include that of the Delhaize U.S. subsidiaries based on their fiscal calendar year. No adjustment has been made for the difference in reporting date as the impact is immaterial to the consolidated financial statements taken as a whole. The consolidated results of Delhaize Group for 2007, 2006 and 2005 include the results of operations of its U.S. subsidiaries for the 52 weeks ended December 29, 2007, 52 weeks ended December 30, 2006 and 52 weeks ended December 31, 2005, respectively. The results of operations of the companies of Delhaize Group outside the United States are prepared on a calendar year basis.

Format of Financial Statements

Financial statements comprise tables (commonly referred to as primary financial statements)[4] and related notes that include a summary of significant accounting policies and other explanatory information. This section presents an overview of IAS 1 and Canadian GAAP requirements for primary financial statements and related notes. Individual primary statements and particular notes disclosures are discussed later in this chapter.

Primary Financial Statements

The presentation of primary financial statements was recently modified in Canada with the publication of CICA 1530 and CICA 3251, which are effective for fiscal years beginning on or after October 1, 2006. The IASB amended IAS 1 by introducing similar requirements in September 2007, which are effective for annual periods beginning on or after January 1, 2009 (with early adoption permitted). IAS 1 amendments form part of a larger project being undertaken jointly by the IASB and the FASB. This project seeks to establish a common standard for the presentation of information in the financial statements, including the classification and display of line items and the aggregation of line items into subtotals and totals (see "Future Developments").

All primary statements must be presented with equal prominence (i.e., a primary statement cannot be presented by way of an "appendix" in the notes). The table below summarizes the primary financial statements required by IAS 1 (current and previous requirements) and by Canadian GAAP. Each required statement is discussed in detail later in this chapter.

---

4   We will use the term "primary financial statement" to distinguish tables from notes. The term is still used in practice, though IAS 1 does not refer to it (except in the basis for conclusions).

Current IAS 1	Previous IAS 1	Canadian GAAP and Other Observations
Statement of financial position		
Statement of financial position as at the end of the period	Balance sheet	Both titles designate the same statement and could be used in practice.
Statement of financial position as at the beginning of the earliest comparative period when an entity: • applies an accounting policy retrospectively; • makes a retrospective restatement of items in its financial statements; or • reclassifies items in its financial statements. (Note 1)	Balance sheet	No equivalent requirement under Canadian GAAP.
Statement of comprehensive income		
For the period IAS 1 allows only the following two alternatives for presenting all items of comprehensive income: • a single statement of comprehensive income showing all components of profit or loss (net income) and other comprehensive income; or • two statements, one displaying components of profit or loss (i.e., a separate income statement) and a second statement beginning with profit or loss and displaying components of other comprehensive income.	Income statement and Statement of recognized income and expense (SORIE) (Note 2)	Canadian GAAP also allows both of these alternatives. In addition, entities may display other comprehensive income components in a statement of changes in shareholders' equity (see Notes 3 and 4 below) SORIE was eliminated and its components included in the statement of comprehensive income in current IAS 1.
Statement of Changes in Equity		
For the period The statement of changes in equity required under current IAS 1 would only include transactions with equity holders. Current IAS 1 requires an entity to present, in a statement of changes in equity, all owner changes in equity. All non-owner changes in equity (i.e., comprehensive income) are to be presented in one statement of comprehensive income or in two statements (a separate income statement and a statement of comprehensive income). Components of comprehensive income cannot be presented in the statement of changes in equity.	Statement of changes in equity	A statement of changes in equity is not required but a statement of retained earning is required Various titles and presentations are allowed under Canadian GAAP (Note 4). Canadian companies are allowed to present an all-inclusive statement of changes in shareholders' equity (which is no longer acceptable under current IAS 1). Some Canadian companies present additional statements, such as a statement of retained earnings.
Statement of cash flows		
New title suggested in current IAS 1 does not change the statement's content. For the period	Cash-flows statement	

Note 1: Comparative Statements of Financial Position for Retrospective Changes

Current IAS 1 requires an entity to present a statement of financial position (balance sheet) as at the beginning of the earliest comparative period in a complete set of financial statements when the entity applies an accounting policy retrospectively or makes a retrospective restatement, as defined in IAS 8, or when the entity reclassifies items in the financial statements. Under such circumstances, the entity must present three statements of financial position (with related notes) as at:

- the end of the current period (required for all entities);
- the end of the previous period (usually required for all entities); and
- the beginning of the earliest comparative period (to which the entity has applied the accounting policy retrospectively or has made a retrospective restatement of items in its financial statements, or has reclassified items in its financial statements). Canadian GAAP does not have such a requirement.

Note 2: Previous IAS 1 Requirements (SOCIE and SORIE)

Since most companies reporting under IFRS did not adopt amended IAS 1 early, it is useful to briefly describe previous IAS 1 requirements, which allowed an entity to show either:

- *all* changes in equity, including transactions with equity holders (acting in their capacity as equity holders) in a statement of changes in equity (SOCIE); or
- changes in equity *excluding* transaction with equity holders acting in their capacity as equity holders in a statement of recognized income and expense (SORIE).

Consequently, financial statements for the year ended December 31, 2007 would either (1) omit the presentation of the SORIE and include all components that would be presented in the latter in the SOCIE; or (2) present the SORIE as a primary statement. If the second alternative is adopted, a reconciliation of beginning and ending balances of share capital, "reserves" and retained earnings would be disclosed in the notes to the financial statements. In addition, where an entity elected to recognize actuarial gains and losses in defined benefit plans directly in retained earnings, that entity had to prepare a SORIE as a primary financial statement.

Note 3: Canadian GAAP for Presenting Comprehensive Income Components

Canadian companies can present comprehensive income components for the period (net income and other comprehensive income) using various formats. Below are some common formats observed in practice:

- *A single statement of comprehensive income combining net income and other comprehensive income components*: This is also permitted under IAS 1 and it is probably the most desirable presentation under both Canadian GAAP and IAS 1.
- *An income statement followed immediately by a statement of comprehensive income starting with the net income figure (as established by the income statement) and including other comprehensive income components*: This is also the other alternative permitted under IAS 1.
- *An income statement and a statement of changes in shareholder's equity that includes all changes of other comprehensive income*: IAS 1 prohibits this presentation.

Note 4: Canadian GAAP Statement of Changes in Shareholders' Equity

Under Canadian GAAP companies are allowed to present an all-inclusive statement of changes in shareholders' equity (which is no longer acceptable under current IAS 1). Statement of retained earnings is required under Canadian GAAP.

Identification of Financial Statements

Each financial statement and the notes should be clearly identified and basic information should be displayed prominently, including the name of the reporting entity (and any change since the preceding period), whether the financial statements are of an individual entity or a group of entities, the date of the end of the reporting period or the period covered by the set of financial statements or notes, the presentation currency and the level of rounding used in presenting amounts in the financial statements.

Notes to Financial Statements

Notes to financial statements provide a summary of significant accounting policies and other explanatory information. They are an essential element of a complete set of financial statements.

IAS 1 specifies that notes must provide:

- narrative descriptions or disaggregations of items presented in the primary financial statements; and
- information about items that do not qualify for recognition in those statements.

IAS 1 also specifies that notes cannot rectify inappropriate accounting policies.

CICA 1000 has equivalent requirements as it states that notes are an integral part of financial statements that provide:

- further details about items recognized in the financial statements; or
- information about items that do not meet the criteria for recognition and thus are not recognized in the financial statements.

CICA 1000 differentiates amounts disclosed in the notes from those that are recognized in the primary financial statements because it is not probable that future economic benefits will be obtained or given up or because a reasonable estimate cannot be made of the amount involved.

IAS 1 discusses some elements related to the structure and organization of the notes. The table below summarizes certain of its requirements (specific notes contents are covered later in this chapter):

Structure and Organization of the Notes	
Issue	**IAS 1 Requirements**
General contents	Disclose information: • about the basis of preparation of the financial statements and the specific accounting policies used; • required by IFRS that is not presented elsewhere in the financial statements; and • that is not presented elsewhere in the financial statements, but is relevant to an understanding of any of them.

Structure (general format)	Systematic presentation, normally in the following order, helps align disclosure practices to assists users to understand the financial statements and to compare them with financial statements of other entities:
	• statement of compliance with IFRS;
	• summary of significant accounting policies applied;
	• supporting information for items presented in the primary financial statements in the order in which each statement and each line item is presented; and
	• other disclosures, including:
	  o contingent liabilities and unrecognized contractual commitments, and
	  o non-financial disclosures, e.g., the entity's financial risk management objectives and policies (as required by IFRS 7, *Financial instruments: disclosures*).

Structure and Organization of the Notes	
Issue	**IAS 1 Requirements**
Structure (other formats)	Although a systematic presentation is required, entities could change the order of presentation of the notes when it makes sense to do so. For example, an entity may: • combine information on changes in fair value recognized in profit or loss with information on maturities of financial instruments, although the information might relate to different primary financial statements; or • present notes related to the basis of preparation of the financial statements and specific accounting policies as a separate section of the financial statements.
Cross-reference	An entity must cross-reference each item in the primary financial statements to related information included in the notes.

Illustrative Disclosures:

The illustrative disclosures presented below cover only the general organization of the notes (structure and cross reference). Individual primary financial statements and various note disclosures are illustrated later in this chapter.

Extract 2(16) – Structuring the notes

Bayer Aktiengesellschaft (AR 2007), page 96 (Part 1)		
Notes to the Consolidated Financial Statements of the Bayer Group		
1.	Key Data by Segment and Region	102
2.	General information	104
3.	Effects of new accounting pronouncements	105
4.	Basic principles, methods and critical accounting policies	107
5.	Segment reporting	121
6.	Scope of consolidation	123
6.1	Changes in the scope of consolidation	123
6.2	Business combinations and other acquisitions	127
6.3	Divestitures and discontinued operations	128

Bayer Aktiengesellschaft (AR 2007), page 96 (Part 2)		
Notes to the Statements of Income		
7.	Net sales	132
8.	Selling expenses	132
9.	Research and development expenses	132
10.	Other operating income	133
11.	Other operating expenses	133
12.	Personnel expenses / employees	134
13.	Non-operating result	134
13.1	Income (loss) from investments in affiliated companies	135
13.2	Interest expense	135
13.3	Other non-operating expense	136
14.	Income taxes	136
15.	Income / losses attributable to minority interest	138
16.	Earnings per share from continuing and discontinued operations	139

Bayer Aktiengesellschaft (AR 2007), pages 96 and 97 (Part 3)

Notes to the Balance Sheets

Bayer Aktiengesellschaft (AR 2007), page 97 (Part 4)

Notes to the Statements of Cash Flows

Bayer Aktiengesellschaft (AR 2007), pages 97 (Part 5)

Other information

Commentary: The above extract presents an example of how the notes to financial statements might be structured. The company breaks down the notes into the following six parts:

- General;
- Notes to the Statements of Income;
- Notes to the Balance Sheets;
- Notes to the Statements of Cash Flows;
- Other information.

The organization of the notes reflects the considerations on note structures described in IAS 1. Current Canadian GAAP would not prevent an entity from using a similar structure for its notes.

Extract 2(17) – Cross reference to notes

Bayer Aktiengesellschaft (AR 2007), page 99 Bayer Group Consolidated Balance Sheets			
€ million	Note	Dec. 31, 2006	Dec. 31, 2007
Noncurrent assets			
Goodwill	[17]	8,227	8,215
Other intangible assets	[17]	15,807	14,555
Property, plant and equipment	[18]	8,867	8,819
Investments in associates	[19]	532	484
Other financial assets	[20]	1,094	1,127
Other receivables	[21]	165	667
Deferred taxes	[14]	1,205	845
		35,897	34,712
Current assets			
Inventories	[22]	6,153	6,217
Trade accounts receivable	[23]	5,868	5,830
Other financial assets	[20]	401	335
Other receivables	[21]	1,512	1,461
Claims for income tax refunds		220	208
Cash and cash equivalents	[36]	2,915	2,531
Assets held for sale and discontinued operations	[6.3]	2,925	84
		19,994	16,666
Total assets		55,891	51,378
Stockholders' equity	[24]		
Capital stock of Bayer AG		1,957	1,957
Capital reserves of Bayer AG		4,028	4,028
Other reserves		6,782	10,749
		12,767	16,734
Equity attributable to minority interest		84	87
		12,851	16,821
Noncurrent liabilities			
Provisions for pensions and other post-employment benefits	[25]	6,543	5,501
Other provisions	[26]	1,464	1,166
Financial liabilities	[27]	14,723	12,911
Other liabilities	[29]	449	501
Deferred taxes	[14]	4,346	3,866
		27,525	23,945
Current liabilities			
Other provisions	[26]	3,765	3,754
Financial liabilities	[27]	5,078	1,287
Trade accounts payable	[28]	2,375	2,466
Income tax liabilities		109	56
Other liabilities	[29]	3,340	2,873
Liabilities directly related to assets held for sale and discontinued operations	[6.3]	848	176
		15,515	10,612
Total stockholders' equity and liabilities		55,891	51,378

Commentary: The above extract presents an example of cross reference to specific notes in the statement of financial position The company refers, when applicable to the specific part of the note related to an amount presented in the income statement. Nothing under current Canadian GAAP would prevent an entity from providing a similar cross reference.

Statement of Financial Position (Balance Sheet)[5]

Format and Structure

Management may choose a vertical or a horizontal format for presenting the balance sheet. Line items must be presented broadly in terms of liquidity. This may be *either* in increasing or decreasing order of liquidity. Under Canadian GAAP, the statement of financial position could also be presented either vertically or horizontally, but line items are generally presented in decreasing order of liquidity.

Basic Line Items

IAS 1 requires entities to include at least the following line items distinctly on the face of their statement of position (when applicable):

- property, plant and equipment;
- investment property;
- intangible assets;
- financial assets (other than equity investments, trade and cash);
- investments accounted for using the equity method;
- biological assets;
- inventories;
- trade and other receivables;
- cash and cash equivalents;
- trade and other payables;
- provisions;
- financial liabilities (other than trade and provisions);
- liabilities and assets for current tax;
- deferred tax liabilities and deferred tax assets;
- non-controlling interests presented within equity;
- issued capital and reserves attributable to equity holders of the parent; and
- assets held for disposal, as well as assets and liabilities held in disposal groups classified as held for sale.

Entities reporting under Canadian GAAP would present the above minimum line item amounts on their balance sheet except for investment property, biological assets and provisions which would generally not be shown because they are not covered by specific Canadian standards.

Additional Line Items

IAS 1 *requires* that additional line items, headings and subtotals be presented when they are relevant for understanding an entity's financial position. It says that the following criteria need to be considered when addressing such a requirement:

- the nature and liquidity of the assets and their materiality;
- the function of assets within the entity; and
- the amounts, nature and timing of liabilities.

---

5   Various titles are used in practice under Canadian GAAP, including "balance sheet" (which was the title IAS 1 used before its amendment in September 2007) and "statement of financial condition." Both titles are used in this publication.

In absence of specific requirements, management may *choose* the level of details to disclose on the face of the statement of financial position or in the notes as long as it can justify such level of disclosure. Circumstances when separate disclosure might be required (that might also be generally required by a specific IFRS standard or interpretation) include the following:

- A line item contains assets or liabilities that are measured using different bases. For example, financial assets measured at fair value should be disclosed separately from those carried at cost.

- A line item combines amounts expected to be realized in different periods. For example, amounts expected to be recovered in more than 12 months after the end of the reporting period should be presented distinctly from other trade receivables.

- A line item includes assets and liabilities of different functions or natures. For example, receivables from related parties should be shown distinctly from customer trade receivables.

Current/Non-current Classification[6]

IAS 1 and CICA 1510 require entities to present a classified balance sheet that distinguishes working capital from other assets and liabilities. Both standards provide an exception to current and non-current classification when an entity does not supply goods or services within a clearly identifiable operating cycle. This might be the case with financial institutions (banks and insurance companies) whose presentation of assets and liabilities in increasing or decreasing order of liquidity would be more relevant than the current/non-current classification.

The following table summarizes the classification of assets and liabilities in general as well as certain ones specified by IAS 1. All classifications are consistent with Canadian GAAP except when otherwise noted.

Classification of Components in Statement of Financial Position
All assets (Note 1)
Current assets include cash or cash equivalent (as defined in IAS 7) unless they are restricted from being exchanged or used to settle a liability for at least 12 months after the reporting period. Assets are classified as current when the entity: • expects to realize them, or intends to sell or consume them, in its normal operating cycle; • holds them primarily for the purpose of trading; or • expects to realize them within 12 months after the reporting period. The entity classifies all other assets as non-current.
All liabilities (Note 1)
Liabilities are classified as current when an entity: • expects to settle them in its normal operating cycle; • holds them primarily for the purpose of trading; • must settle them within 12 months after the reporting period; or • does not have an unconditional right to defer their settlement for at least 12 months after the reporting period. An entity would classify all other liabilities as non-current.
Financial Assets
• Assets that are held primarily for trading are generally classified as current assets. • Held-to-maturity investments and available-for-sale investments are classified as non-current assets unless realization is expected within 12 months.

---

6   IAS 1 allows both current/non-current and short/long-term assets and liabilities labelling. IFRS, however, tend to use current/non-current to describe items on the face of a classified statement of financial position and use short/long-term labelling to deal with issues other than classification, such as recognition and measurement (e.g., short-term employee benefits).

Trade Receivables, Inventories, and Prepayments

All these assets are classified as current assets because they will be realized within an entity's operating cycle (even when they are not expected to be realized within 12 months after the end of the reporting period). Note, however that related party receivables are classified as current only when there is both the ability and intention to realize those amounts within the next 12 months.

Loans – Breaching a Provision under a Long-term Loan Agreement (Note 2)

An entity that breaches a provision of a long-term loan agreement (with the effect that the liability becomes payable on demand at the balance sheet date) must classify the loan as current. It can classify the liability as non-current *only* if:
- the lender has agreed by the end of the reporting period to provide a period of grace ending at least 12 months after the reporting period;
- the entity can rectify the breach during this grace period; and
- the lender cannot demand immediate repayment during this grace period.

Loan Facilities and Refinancing (Note 3)

An entity classifies a loan as current when it is due to be settled within 12 months after the reporting period, *even* if:
- the original term was for a period longer than 12 months; and
- an agreement to refinance, or to reschedule payments, on a long-term basis is completed after the reporting period and before the financial statements are authorized for issue.

On the other hand, a loan due in the next 12 months is classified as non-current if the entity (1) expects and (2) has the discretion to refinance or roll over an obligation for at least 12 months after the reporting period under an existing loan facility. When refinancing or rolling over the obligation is not at the discretion of the entity (e.g., there is no agreement for refinancing), the potential to refinance is not considered and the obligation is classified as current.

Deferred Tax Assets (Liabilities) (Note 4)

Always classified as long term.

Equity Components (Note 5)

- Equity capital and other components must be shown separately, including the various classes of paid-in capital, share premium and reserves. Depending on the materiality and significance of equity components, details can be presented in the notes rather than on the face of the balance sheet.
- Minority interests is presented as a component of equity, separately from the parent shareholders' equity

Note 1: Operating cycle for assets is the time between their acquisition for processing and their realization in cash or cash equivalents. When an entity's normal operating cycle is not clearly identifiable, its duration is assumed to be 12 months. The same normal operating cycle applies to the classification of an entity's assets and liabilities.

Note 2: This is similar to Canadian GAAP, which requires that a loan payable on demand because certain conditions have been breached generally be classified as current. EIC-59 allows such a loan to be classified as non-current, however, when it is refinanced or renegotiated subsequent to the reporting date but prior to the financial statements being completed.

Note 3: Canadian GAAP also requires that a loan payable on demand or to be refinanced in the next 12 months be classified as current. EIC-122, however, allows such loan to not be classified as current if, subsequent to the reporting date but prior to the financial statements being completed, (1) the lender has waived its right to repayment for more than 12 months after the reporting date or (2) it is refinanced with repayment scheduled for more than 12 months after the reporting date.

Note 4: Under Canadian GAAP, deferred (future) income tax amounts reported on the balance sheet are classified consistently with the assets and liabilities with which they are associated.

Note 5: Prior to the adoption CICA 1602, *Non-controlling Interest*[7], an entity would classify non-controlling (minority) interests between total liabilities and equity, instead of being presented within equity but separate from the parent's equity.

Disclosures Related to Equity Section

IAS 1 requires entities to disclose the following, either in the statement of financial position or the statement of changes in equity, or in the notes:

- details on each class of share capital, including:
  - o   the number of shares authorized,
  - o   the number of shares issued and fully paid, and issued but not fully paid,
  - o   par value per share, or that the shares have no par value;
- reconciliations of the number of shares outstanding at the beginning and at the end of the period;
- rights, preferences and restrictions attaching to each class, including restrictions on the distribution of dividends and the repayment of capital;
- shares in the entity held by the entity or by its subsidiaries or associates; and
- shares reserved for issue under options and contracts for the sale of shares, including the terms and amounts.

In addition, entities have to provide a description of the nature and purpose of each reserve (such as accumulated other comprehensive income and other paid up capital surplus) within equity. This is not specifically required by Canadian GAAP.

Entities should disclose reclassification of some financial instruments between financial liabilities and equity, including the amount reclassified into and out of each category (financial liabilities or equity), and the timing and reason for that reclassification (See Chapter 9).

An entity without share capital (e.g., a partnership or trust) must disclose information equivalent to that required above, showing changes during the period in each category of equity interest and the rights, preferences and restrictions attached to each category of equity interest.

CICA 3240 and CICA 3610 contain equivalent disclosure requirements. In addition Canadian GAAP prescribes directions for the accounting of share capital transactions such as treatment of contributed surplus and share capital upon the issuance and redemption of shares.

Note that, prior to the adoption of CICA 1602, *Non-controlling Interest*[8], an entity would apportion non-controlling (minority) interests between total liabilities and equity, instead of presenting them within equity but separately from the parent's equity as required by IAS 1 (see further discussion in chapter 6).

Illustrative Disclosures:

All statements of financial position illustrated in the following extracts (except Extract 2 (25)) reflect requirements of IAS 1 prior to its amendment in September 2007. Amended IAS 1 is effective for fiscal years starting January 1, 2009, with early adop-

---

7   In January 2009, the AcSB issued three Handbook Sections: CICA 1582, *Business Combinations* (replacing CICA 1581 with same title), CICA 1601, *Consolidated Financial Statements* (replacing CICA 1600 with same title) and CICA 1602, *Non-controlling Interests* (a new *Handbook* Section), which provides guidance that is converged with IAS 27, *Consolidated and Separate Financial Statements* and IFRS 3, *Business Combinations*. These new CICA Sections are effective for years beginning on or after January 1, 2011, with earlier adoption permitted. Entities planning business combinations for the year beginning on or after January 1, 2010 should adopt CICA 1582, CICA 1601 and CICA 1602 in or before that year to avoid restatement on transition to IFRS in 2011.

8   See footnote 7.

tion permitted. Virtually none of the companies adopted amended IAS 1 early. The extracts would not generally contravene current Canadian GAAP.

Although amended IAS 1 necessitates calculating accumulated other comprehensive income amounts, it does not require (as does CICA 1530) its presentation separately from retained earnings and additional paid-in capital.

On IFRS adoption, Canadian companies could use the formats illustrated below, which present items by increasing liquidity, or continue to use their present format *as long as they are otherwise compliant with IAS 1 requirements.*

Extract 2(18) – Statement of financial position

Ubisoft Entertainment S.A. (AR 2008), page 52 2.1 Consolidated balance sheet			
ASSETS In thousands of euros	**Notes**	**Net** **03.31.08**	**Net (1) New** **presentation** **03.31.07**
Goodwill	1	84,376	77,374
Other intangible assets	2	398,378	301,798
Property, plant and equipment	3	22,480	25,510
Investments in associates	4	328	33,998
Other financial assets	5	2,517	2,458
Deferred tax assets	6	21,684	37,630
Non-current assets		529,763	478,768
Inventory	7	39,879	24,794
Trade receivables	8	84,226	87,857
Other receivables	9	91,683	73,959
Other current financial assets	10	39,284	19,183
Current tax assets		11,146	10,605
Cash and cash equivalents	11	228,913	126,552
Assets held for sale	10	25,058	
Current assets		520,189	342,950
Total assets		**1,049,952**	**821,718**
LIABILITIES AND EQUITY In thousands of euros	**Notes**	**03.31.08**	**03.31.07**
Capital		7,165	7,037
Premiums		459,457	435,234
Consolidated reserves		57,685	38,990
Consolidated earnings		109,844	40,558
Equity (group share)		634,151	521,819
Minority interests		-	-
Total equity	12	634,151	521,819
Provisions	13	1,861	1,952
Employee benefit	14	1,699	1,205
Long-term borrowings	15	23,323	22,706
Deferred tax liabilities	17	43,990	28,214
Non-current liabilities		70,873	54,077
Short-term borrowings	15	56,097	48,874
Trade payables	18	177,903	118,950
Other liabilities	19	95,505	75,895
Current financial liabilities	20	1,353	-
Current tax liabilities		14,070	2,103
Current liabilities		344,928	245,822
Total liabilities and equity		**1,049,952**	**821,718**

Commentary: The above extract presents a typical example of a statement of financial position. Of particular interest is the presentation of:

- minority interest in shareholder's equity presented as a line item even if balance is nil;
- deferred tax assets and liabilities in the non-current categories (which might be classified differently under Canadian GAAP); and
- assets held for sale after cash and cash equivalents (according to Canadian GAAP, these are presented as current only if proceeds are expected to be received in the next 12 months).

Note that the company presents more line items than the minimum required under IAS 1.

Presentation conforms with Canadian GAAP except that under the latter:

- a portion (or all) of the deferred tax amounts might have to be classified as a current item;
- prior to adoption of CICA 1602, *Non-controlling Interest*[9], a non-controlling interest would be presented outside equity;
- provisions would not have to be presented distinctly on the face of the statement of position;
- at least a portion of the reserves would have another label (such as accumulated other comprehensive income).

Extract 2(19) – Statement of financial position

Halfords Group plc (AR 2008), page 63
CONSOLIDATED BALANCE SHEET

	Notes	28 March 2008 £m	30 March 2007 £m
Assets			
Non-current assets			
Goodwill	9	**253.1**	253.1
Other intangible assets	9	**3.7**	4.7
Property, plant and equipment	10	**116.2**	107.5
Derivative financial instruments	18	**—**	1.3
		373.0	366.6
Current assets			
Inventories	11	**151.6**	141.6
Trade and other receivables	12	**41.6**	32.6
Derivative financial instruments	18	**1.9**	—
Cash and cash equivalents	13	**10.0**	24.8
		205.1	199.0
Total assets		**578.1**	565.6
Liabilities			
Current liabilities			
Borrowings	15	**(0.2)**	(13.3)
Derivative financial instruments	18	**(0.3)**	(2.3)
Trade and other payables	14	**(121.3)**	(113.5)
Current tax liabilities		**(12.3)**	(13.4)
Provisions	16	**(2.0)**	(1.6)
		(136.1)	(144.1)

---

9   See footnote 7.

Halfords Group plc (AR 2008) (continued)			
Net current assets		**69.0**	54.9
Non-current liabilities			
Borrowings	15	**(191.5)**	(191.5)
Derivative financial instruments	18	**—**	(0.1)
Deferred tax liabilities	17	**(1.0)**	(0.9)
Accruals and deferred income — lease incentives		**(27.8)**	(25.9)
		(220.3)	(218.4)
Total liabilities		**(356.4)**	(362.5)
Net assets		**221.7**	203.1
Shareholders' equity			
Share capital	19	**2.1**	2.2
Share premium account		**145.6**	133.2
Capital redemption reserve		**0.2**	0.1
Retained earnings		**73.8**	67.6
Total equity		**221.7**	203.1

The notes on pages 73 to 92 are an integral part of these consolidated financial statements.

The financial statements on pages 62 to 92 were approved by the Board of Directors on 4 June 2008 and were signed on its behalf by:

Nick Wharton	Paul McClenaghan
Finance Director	Director of Trading

Commentary: Similar observations made for Extract 2(20) apply here. The company uses the equity format instead of the more common balanced format. In addition, the company has presented dates and persons approving the financial statements as required by IFRS.

Note that the company presents on the statement of financial position separate line items for:

- derivatives (optional);
- provisions (required by IAS 1).

The company has segregated a "capital redemption reserve" from the retained profits, which might relate to its capital management policies or local statutory requirements. Under Canadian GAAP, such reserves are not common.

Presentation conforms with Canadian GAAP except that a portion (or all) of the deferred tax amounts might have to be classified as a current item.

Extract 2(20) – Statement of financial position

Pernod Ricard (Financial Report 2007), pages 176 and 177 Consolidated Balance Sheet Assets In euro million	30.06.2006	30.06.2007	Notes
Net amounts			
Non-current assets			
Intangible assets	8,028	**7,836**	10
Goodwill	3,527	**3,477**	10
Property, plant & equipment	1,637	**1,675**	11
Biological assets	53	**60**	
Non-current financial assets	142	**121**	12
Investments in associates	10	**2**	
Deferred tax assets	821	**839**	7
Non-current assets	14,218	**14,010**	
Current assets			
Inventories	3,327	**3,563**	13
Operating receivables	1,160	**1,228**	14
Income taxes receivable	230	**91**	
Other current assets	294	**145**	
Current derivative instruments	84	**51**	
Cash and cash equivalents	447	**383**	16
Current assets	5,542	**5,462**	
Total assets	19,760	**19,472**	

Liabilities and shareholders' equity In euro million	30.06.2006	30.06.2007	Notes
Shareholders' equity			
Share capital	292	**340**	
Additional paid-in capital	2,539	**2,053**	
Retained earnings and currency translation adjustments	2,230	**3,067**	
Net profit attributable to equity holders of the Parent	639	**831**	
Shareholders' equity - attributable to equity holders of the Parent	5,700	**6,290**	20
Minority interests	172	**168**	
Total shareholders' equity	5,872	**6,458**	
Non-current liabilities			
Non-current provisions	707	**534**	15
Provisions for pensions and other long-term employee benefits	1,009	**773**	15
Deferred tax liabilities	2,264	**2,326**	7
Bonds	1,705	**2,511**	16
Non-current derivative instruments	58	**73**	16
Other non-current financial liabilities	4,534	**3,938**	16
Total non-current liabilities	10,277	**10,155**	
Current liabilities			
Current provisions	458	**355**	15
Operating payables	1,731	**1,773**	18
Income taxes payable	795	**198**	
Other current liabilities	127	**141**	
Other current financial liabilities	500	**375**	16
Current derivative instruments		**16**	
Total current liabilities	3,610	**2,859**	
Total liabilities and shareholders' equity	19,760	**19,472**	

Pernod Ricard (Financial Report 2007) (continued)
page 195
Note 14. – Operating receivables

In euro million	30.06.2006	30.06.2007
Net carrying amounts		
Trade receivables	1,028	1,092
Other receivables	133	136
Total	**1,160**	**1,228**

Most operating receivables are due within one year.
page 205
Note 18. – Operating payables
The breakdown of operating payables is as follows:

In euro million	30.06.2006	30.06.2007
Trade payables	868	929
Tax and social security liabilities	462	442
Other operating payables	398	398
Other creditors	3	4
Total	**1,731**	**1,773**

Most operating payables are due within one year.

Commentary: The above extract is also a typical example of statement of financial position. Of particular interest are the presentation of:

- minority interest in shareholder's equity (which will conform with the Canadian GAAP requirements of CICA 1602 when adopted[10]);

- deferred tax assets and deferred tax liabilities in the non-current categories (which might be classified differently under Canadian GAAP);

- provisions – both short-term and long-term amounts (which are not required to be presented as such on the face of the statement of financial position);

- biological assets (not currently required to be disclosed under Canadian GAAP); and

- details about certain components of equity (which could be combined).

Note that the company uses the label of "operating" receivables and "operating" payables, which are detailed in the notes (also illustrated in the extract).

---

10 See footnote 7.

Extract 2(21) – Statement of financial position

Stora Enso Oyj (AR 2007), page 115
Consolidated Balance Sheet

EUR million		Note	As at 31 December 2005	2006	2007
Assets					
Fixed Assets and Non-current Investments					
Goodwill	O	14	961.8	906.8	502.7
Other intangible fixed assets	O	14	194.1	170.4	159.1
Property, plant and equipment	O	14	9 936.8	9 153.6	6 476.7
		14	11 092.7	10 230.8	7 138.5
Biological assets	O	15	76.8	111.5	88.7
Emission rights	O		43.7	98.1	5.2
Investment in associated companies	O	16	719.9	805.2	1 154.5
Available-for-Sale: Listed securities	I	17	211.6	41.2	161.8
Available-for-Sale: Unlisted shares	O	17	403.6	794.3	1 260.8
Non-current loan receivables	I	20	127.6	149.2	126.5
Deferred tax assets	T	11	72.2	53.5	63.7
Other non-current assets	O	18	28.3	61.1	22.6
			12 776.4	12 344.9	10 022.3
Current Assets					
Inventories	O	19	2 150.5	2 019.5	1 992.6
Tax receivables	T	11	85.3	66.6	34.3
Short-term operative receivables	O	20	2 186.2	2 156.6	2 063.1
Interest-bearing receivables	I	20	280.9	185.5	227.8
Cash and cash equivalents	I		351.4	609.0	970.7
			5 054.3	5 037.2	5 288.5
Total Assets			17 830.7	17 382.1	15 310.8
Equity and Liabilities					
Equity Attributable to Parent Company Shareholders					
Share capital		21	1 382.1	1 342.2	1 342.2
Share premium			545.9	528.0	525.6
Reserve fund			238.9	238.9	238.9
Treasury shares		21	-259.9	-10.5	-10.2
Other comprehensive income		27	468.0	735.6	960.4
Cumulative translation adjustment		28	-127.1	-132.0	-115.6
Retained earnings			5 083.3	4 512.4	4 749.5
Net profit for the period			-111.1	585.0	-214.7
			7 220.1	7 799.6	7 476.1
Minority Interests		22	93.6	103.5	71.9
Total Equity			7 313.7	7 903.1	7 548.0
Non-current Liabilities					
Post-employment benefit provisions	O	23	888.3	763.1	327.3
Other provisions	O	25	142.6	308.3	135.9
Deferred tax liabilities	T	11	866.0	793.0	582.0
Non-current debt	I	24	4 353.9	4 081.0	3 354.8
Other non-current operative liabilities	O	26	204.7	193.7	170.2
			6 455.5	6 139.1	4 570.2
Current Liabilities					
Current portion of non-current debt	I	24	385.0	630.2	513.1
Interest-bearing liabilities	I	24	1 114.8	217.3	482.2
Bank overdrafts	I		201.9	299.4	91.4
Current operative liabilities	O	26	2 003.6	1 992.5	1 971.3
Tax liabilities	T	11	356.2	200.5	134.6
			4 061.5	3 339.9	3 192.6
Total Equity and Liabilities			17 830.7	17 382.1	15 310.8

Items designated "O" comprise Operative Capital
Items designated "I" comprise Interest-bearing Net Liabilities
Items designated "T" comprise Net Tax Liabilities
The accompanying Notes are an integral part of these Consolidated Financial Statements

Stora Enso Oyj (AR 2007) (continued)
page 119
Note 1 Accounting Principles (in part)
Change in Accounting Policy

Share of results in Associated Companies, previously reported with financial items, are now reported in operating profit. Associated Companies supply the Group with wood, pulp and logistic services and therefore this change in accounting policy has been implemented to reflect the operational nature of these investments. The operating profit from continuing operations increases by EUR 341.4 million, EUR 88.0 million and EUR 67.1 million in 2007, 2006 and 2005, respectively, though the change has no impact on profit before tax. Comparative amounts disclosed for each prior year have been restated.

page 164
Note 20 Receivables
Short-term Operative Receivables

EUR million	As at 31 December		
	2005	2006	2007
Trade receivables	1 792.7	1 765.6	1 683.2
Provision for doubtful debts	-47.3	-42.3	-39.5
Prepaid expenses and accrued income	118.0	163.3	150.7
TRS Hedges	28.3	28.7	2.6
Other receivables	294.5	241.3	266.1
Total	**2 186.2**	**2 156.6**	**2 063.1**

Due to their short-tem nature, the carrying amounts of the above receivables are a reasonable approximation to the fair value. Any longer term Receivables, falling due after one year, are included in non-current receivables.

Currency Breakdown of Short-term Operative Receivables

EUR million	As at 31 December	
	2006	2007
EUR	1 164.1	1 175.3
USD	325.9	243.8
SEK	263.8	255.6
GBP	121.3	119.6
Other currencies	281.5	268.8
Total	**2 156.6**	**2 063.1**

The majority of the USD and GBP denominated operative receivables are held in Group companies which have EUR and SEK as their functional currencies. As at 31 December 2007, trade receivables of EUR 219.5 (EUR 212.9) million were overdue, but for which no provision had been made. These relate to number of different countries and unrelated customers for whom there is no recent history of default. The ageing analysis of these trade receivables is as follows:

Age Analysis of Trade Receivables

EUR million	As at 31 December	
	2006	2007
Less than 30 days overdue	172.6	180.9
31 to 60 days overdue	23.8	25.6
61 to 90 days overdue	7.8	6.3
91 to 180 days overdue	2.0	1.9
Over 180 days overdue	6.7	4.8
Total: Overdue Accounts	212.9	219.5
Trade Receivables within their credit terms	1 510.4	1 424.2
Total	**1 723.3**	**1 643.7**

Stora Enso Oyj (AR 2007) (continued)

page 164

Credit losses amounted to EUR 13.7 (EUR 9.2) million net of a reduction in the Doubtful Receivables Provision of EUR 1.0 (EUR 1.6) million – see Note 12 Valuation Provisions for details. All provisions for Doubtful Receivables are made on an individual basis, with no round sum allowances appropriate, and are regularly reviewed for changes in the financial position of customers. The Group credit exposure on short-term receivables, both of an operative and financial nature, is their carrying value as the Group has neither credit insurance nor holds third party guarantees. Such credit enhancements are not considered necessary as, if the Group has concerns as to the financial state of a customer, advance payment or letters of credit are required, the latter of which must be irrevocable and drawn on banks. At the year end, the total amount of Letters of Credit awaiting maturity amounted to EUR 19.5 million.

Interest-bearing Receivables

| | As at 31 December | | |
EUR million	2005	2006	2007
Derivative financial instruments (see Note 27)	167.3	147.0	185.2
Associate Company loans	127.8	136.9	116.1
Current Available-for-Sale financial asset – (see Note 17)	68.2	-	-
Other loan receivables	45.2	50.8	53.0
	408.5	334.7	354.3
Current Assets: Receivable within 12 months	280.9	185.5	227.8
Non-current Assets: Receivable after 12 months	127.6	149.2	126.5
Total	**408.5**	**334.7**	**354.3**

Annual interest rates for loan receivables at 31 December 2007 ranged from 3.0% (2.15%) to 10.0% (10.0%). Due to the nature of the Group financial assets, their carrying value is considered to approximate their fair value with the exception of the Associate Company loan to Bergvik Skog AB which has a fair value at year end currency rates of EUR 87.5 (EUR 96.6) million against a carrying value of EUR 83.4 (EUR 87.6) million. Current interest bearing receivables includes accrued interest of EUR 37.7 (EUR 34.6) million of which EUR 24.0 (EUR 24.8) million relate to interest rate swaps.

page 166

Note 22 Minority Interests

In August 2007 Stora Enso acquired 28% of the shares in Stora Enso Poland SA from the State of Poland at a price of EUR 64.3 million, thus reducing the remaining Minority holding to 5%, being shares held by current and retired employees of the company, though Stora Enso intends to purchase these as soon as feasible. Stora Enso had originally acquired 67% of the company in December 2004 when the value of the minority interest was EUR 69.4 million, though as a result of this buy-out, the current Balance Sheet value of the minority has dropped to EUR 14.2 million from EUR 78.2 million in 2006. At acquisition there was another small minority of EUR 0.5 million within the group itself, though this was disposed in 2007 when a subsidiary in Serbia was sold.

In September 2006 Stora Enso finalised its 100% acquisition of the Arapoti Group in Brazil, though the intention was to develop the business in conjunction with a local partner. Accordingly, in September 2007, Stora Enso reached agreement with Arauco, a leading forest products company in South America, to sell some of the Arapoti operations. Arauco will in future have a 20% interest in the Group's Brazilian paper business, Stora Enso Arapoti Industria de Papel SA, this interest being worth EUR 27.3 million at the end of 2007.

In June 2007 Wood Supply Sweden bought out the minority in Sydved Energileveranser for EUR 6.2 million so that the Group could further develop the business in the Swedish bio energy market.

In April 2006 Stora Enso signed an agreement with Shandong Huatai Paper to form a magazine paper company, Stora Enso Huatai (Shandong) Paper Co Ltd, in which Stora Enso holds 60%. The paper machine was ready to go into commercial production in January 2008 with an annual production capacity up to 200 000 tonnes of super-calendered (SC) magazine paper, the fixed asset investment having been some EUR 90 million. At the end of 2007 the value of the Minority Interest of Shandong Huatai Paper amounted to EUR 15.5 (EUR 7.7) million.

Stora Enso Oyj (AR 2007) (continued)

In 2005 Stora Enso acquired UPM-Kymmene Oyj's 29% minority shareholding in Corenso United Oy Ltd at a cost of EUR 22.3 million, with a charge against Retained Earnings of EUR 7.2 million. Other small Minorities still remaining within certain Corenso subsidiaries amounted to EUR 4.4 (EUR 4.2) million at the end of 2007.

In 2005 Stora Enso Timber Oy exercised its option to buy-out the 34% Minority in its Baltic subsidiary, Stora Enso Timber AS and make its Baltic operations 100% owned; other Minorities in timber businesses in Australia and Germany were also extinguished. The total purchase consideration for these buy-outs came to EUR 58.9 million, resulting in a charge of EUR 29.4 million against Retained Earnings.

In July 2005 Stora Enso China Holdings AB increased its ownership of Suzhou Mill from 80.9% to 96.5% by acquiring the 15.6% holding of the Suzhou Handicraft Co-operative in Suzhou Papyrus Paper Company Ltd. The acquisition cost was EUR 8.5 million with a charge to Retained Earnings of EUR 7.4 million. The remaining Minority of 3.5% is owned by the Suzhou New District Economic Development Group and amounted to EUR 0.4 million at the end of 2007.

Minority Interests	Year Ended 31 December		
EUR million	2005	2006	2007
At 1 January	136.1	93.6	103.5
Translation difference	4.1	0.4	4.5
Minority Interests in companies acquired, less disposed	0.9	-0.2	-0.6
Buy-out of Minority Interests	-94.2	-1.1	-71.3
Charge / (gain) to Retained Earnings on buy-outs	43.2	0.1	-4.5
Partial disposal of subsidiary company	-	-	30.9
Share of profit for the year	3.7	4.1	2.4
Dividends	-1.8	-1.1	-1.8
Equity injections	1.6	7.7	8.8
At 31 December	93.6	103.5	71.9

page 179

Principal Minority Interests	As at 31 December		
EUR million	2005	2006	2007
Intercell SA Group Poland	75.6	78.2	14.2
Stora Enso Arapoti Industria de Papel SA Brazil	-	-	27.3
Corenso United Oy Group Finland	4.9	4.2	4.4
FPB Holding GmbH & Co. KG (the former Feldmühle Group) Germany	0.8	0.6	0.6
Fortek Oy Finland	4.0	4.6	4.2
Stora Enso Huatai Paper Co Ltd China	-	7.7	15.5
Others	- 8.3	8.2	5.7
	93.6	103.5	71.9

page 179

Note 26 Operative Liabilities

Non-current Operative Liabilities	As at 31 December		
EUR million	2005	2006	2007
Provision for unrealised profit	117.7	120.5	117.5
Accruals	30.7	13.5	12.4
Share-based payments (Note 31)	30.5	47.4	26.7
Other payables	25.8	12.3	13.6
Total	**204.7**	**193.7**	**170.2**

Stora Enso Oyj (AR 2007) (continued)

The provision for unrealised profit relates to that part of the gains on sale of Tornator Oy in 2002 and Bergvik Skog AB in 2004 that were deemed to relate to the proportion of shares retained in these new Associates, being EUR 44.2 and EUR 73.3 million respectively.

Current Operative Liabilities	As at 31 December		
EUR million	2005	2006	2007
Advances received	3.5	6.2	7.0
Trade payables	962.4	913.9	803.4
Other payables	226.1	214.8	220.6
TRS Hedges	28.3	19.6	36.0
Accrued liabilities and deferred income	688.6	721.3	707.0
Current portion of provisions	94.7	116.7	197.3
Total	2 003.6	1 992.5	1 971.3

Accrued liabilities and deferred income consist mainly of personnel costs, customer discounts, and other accruals. Trade payables and payroll accruals amounting to EUR 1 057.9 (EUR 1 186.0) million are classified as financial instruments according to IAS39.

Commentary: This extract reproduces some key elements of the statement of financial position, including notes detailing:

- change in accounting policy;
- receivables;
- minority interest; and
- "operative" liabilities.

Note that the company presents:

- an additional statement of financial position at the beginning of 2005 (as might be required by IAS 1 subsequent to a change in accounting policy); and
- many additional line items on the face of statement of financial position (which would not normally appear on statements of financial position prepared under Canadian GAAP).

Presentation would not contradict Canadian GAAP except that:

- minority interest is presented in shareholder's equity (which would conform to Canadian GAAP requirements when CICA 1602 is adopted[11]);
- deferred tax assets and liabilities in the non-current categories (which might be classified differently under Canadian GAAP).

---

11   See footnote 7.

Extract 2(22) – Statement of financial position

Danfoss A/S (AR 2007), page 56 Balance sheet As per 31 December mill DKK ASSETS	Note	Parent Company		Group	
		2006	2007	2006	2007
Non-current assets					
Goodwill		10	10	2,822	2,949
Other intangible fixed assets		196	250	1,052	1,210
Intangible fixed assets	11	**206**	**260**	**3,874**	**4,159**
Land and buildings.		41	41	1,699	1,961
Machinery		501	553	2,018	2,191
Equipment		194	183	319	325
Buildings and machinery under construction . .		118	153	576	585
Tangible fixed assets	12	**854**	**930**	**4,612**	**5,062**
Investments in subsidiaries	6	3,849	3,989		
Receivables from subsidiaries	6	128			
Investments in associates and joint ventures . .	6	1,373	1,413	1,032	1,075
Other investments.	6	92	137	149	196
Defined benefit plans, net asset	20			1	
Deferred tax assets	19			464	562
Financial assets		**5,442**	**5,539**	**1,646**	**1,833**
Total non-current assets		**6,502**	**6,729**	**10,132**	**11,054**
Current assets					
Raw materials and consumables		137	145	1,075	1,288
Work in progress.		110	113	354	405
Finished goods and goods for resale.		337	449	1,370	1,670
Inventories	13	**584**	**707**	**2,799**	**3,363**
Trade receivables	14	238	236	3,670	3,748
Receivables from subsidiaries	14	3,978	4,769		
Receivables from associates and joint ventures		50	36	87	74
Receivable corporation tax	22	62	9	125	147
Other receivables		97	206	835	752
Accounts receivable		**4,425**	**5,256**	**4,717**	**4,721**
Cash and cash equivalents	21	**7**	**2**	**886**	**719**
Total current assets		**5,016**	**5,965**	**8,402**	**8,803**
Total assets		**11,518**	**12,694**	**18,534**	**19,857**

Danfoss A/S (AR 2007) (continued) page 57 As per 31 December mill DKK		Parent Company		Group	
LIABILITIES AND SHAREHOLDERS' EQUITY	Note	2006	2007	2006	2007
Shareholders' equity					
Share capital	15	1,024	1,024	1,024	1,024
Reserves		4,963	5,264	7,779	8,446
Proposed dividends		204	255	204	255
Danfoss A/S' share of equity		6,191	6,543	9,007	9,725
Minority interest				28	19
Total shareholders' equity	16	**6,191**	**6,543**	**9,035**	**9,744**
Liabilities					
Provisions for warranty and other provisions	17	123	92	483	431
Provisions for stock options and warrants	18	311	169	311	273
Deferred tax liabilities	19	206	153	511	399
Defined benefit plans	20	15	15	528	389
Bank loans, unsecured	21	1,575	1,497	1,674	1,598
Bank loans, secured	21	1		225	214
Non-current liabilities		**2,231**	**1,926**	**3,732**	**3,304**
Bank loans, unsecured	21	1,274	2,130	1,810	2,610
Bank loans, secured	21			43	34
Trade creditors		419	421	1,870	1,857
Debt to subsidiaries	21	932	1,135		
Debt to associates and joint ventures		1	1	17	16
Corporation taxes	22			138	131
Provisions for warranty and other provisions	17	35	54	265	378
Other debt		435	484	1,624	1,783
Current liabilities		**3,096**	**4,225**	**5,767**	**6,809**
Total liabilities		**5,327**	**6,151**	**9,499**	**10,113**
Total liabilities and shareholders' equity		**11,518**	**12,694**	**18,534**	**19,857**
Contingencies etc.	27				
Related parties	28				
Government grants	29				
Events after the balance sheet date	30				
Forthcoming IFRSs	31				

Danfoss A/S (AR 2007) (continued)
page 92
21. Financial instruments (in part)
The Group's debt categories and maturities

	Group 2006				Group 2007			
		Maturity				Maturity		
	Carrying amount	0-1 year	1-5 years	over 5 years	Carrying amount	0-1 year	1-5 years**)	over 5 years
Non-current debt, unsecured	3,485	1,813	1,629	43	4,208	2,610	1,451	147
Non-current debt, secured *)	200	13	67	120	170	13	49	108
Finance leases:								
Gross payment	76	21	50	5	89	23	50	16
Reduced by interest part	-9	6	-15		-11	-2	-7	-2
	3,752	1,853	1,731	168	4,456	2,644	1,543	269

*) Only Land and Buildings is set as security for the debt.
**) Maturity is evenly spread over the period.
The above debt is recorded as follows:

	Group	
	2006	2007
Current liabilities	1,853	2,644
Non-current liabilities	1,899	1,812
	3,752	4,456

Commentary: In this extract, the company presents additional line items on the face of the statement of financial position. The additional disclosure appears to provide relevant information that would not contradict Canadian GAAP.

Note that the company presents on the face of the statement of financial position:

- inventory details;
- bank loans, both secured and unsecured (note providing details is reproduced);
- references to notes of selected items.

Disclosures would not contradict Canadian GAAP, except that:

- minority interest in shareholder's equity (which would conform to Canadian GAAP requirements when CICA 1602 is adopted[12]); and
- deferred tax assets and deferred tax liabilities in the non-current categories (which might be classified differently under Canadian GAAP).

---

12   See footnote 7.

Extract 2(23) – Statement of financial position

Sasol Limited (Financial Results 2008) Statement of financial position		
at 30 June	2008 Rm	2007 Rm
Assets		
Property, plant and equipment	66 273	50 611
Assets under construction	11 693	24 611
Goodwill	874	586
Other intangible assets	964	629
Post-retirement benefit assets	571	363
Deferred tax assets	1 453	845
Other long-term assets	3 461	3 045
Non-current assets	85 289	80 690
Assets held for sale	3 833	334
Inventories	20 088	14 399
Trade and other receivables	25 323	16 987
Short-term financial assets	330	22
Cash restricted for use	814	646
Cash	4 435	5 987
Current assets	54 823	38 375
Total assets	140 112	119 065
Equity and liabilities		
Shareholders' equity	76 474	61 617
Minority interest	2 521	1 652
Total equity	78 995	63 269
Long-term debt	15 682	13 359
Long-term financial liability	37	53
Long-term provisions	4 491	3 668
Post-retirement benefit obligations	4 578	3 781
Long-term deferred income	376	2 765
Deferred tax liabilities	8 446	8 304
Non-current liabilities	33 610	31 930
Liabilities in disposal group held for sale	142	35
Short-term debt	3 496	5 621
Short-term financial liabilities	67	383
Other current liabilities	22 888	17 282
Bank overdraft	914	545
Current liabilities	27 507	23 866
Total equity and liabilities	140 112	119 065

Commentary: The above extract was obtained from the condensed financial statements. The company adopted IAS 1 (as amended in September 2007) early. The presentation differs from Canadian GAAP as accumulated other comprehensive income is not presented separately in the equity section.

Note that the company presents more line items than the minimum required under IAS 1.

Extract 2(24) – Reserves

Koninklijke Philips Electronics N.V. (AR 2007), Page 237
Stockholders' equity (in part)
Limitations distribution of stockholders' equity

Pursuant to Dutch law certain limitations exist relating to the distribution of stockholders' equity. As a further explanation it should be noted that, as of December 31, 2007, such limitations relate to common stock (EUR 228 million; 2006: EUR 228 million) as well as to legal reserves required by Dutch law included under revaluation reserves (EUR 133 million; 2006: EUR 167 million), retained earnings (EUR 1,343 million; 2006: EUR 1,291 million) and other reserves excluding currency translation losses (EUR 1,211 million; 2006: EUR 4,914 million), totaling EUR 2,915 million (2006: EUR 6,600 million).

The legal reserve required by Dutch law of EUR 1,343 million (2006: EUR 1,291 million) included under retained earnings relates to investments in affiliated companies.

Other reserves are composed of cumulative translation losses of EUR 613 million (2006: EUR 235 million gain), unrealized gains on cash flow hedges of EUR 28 million (2006: EUR 8 million gain) and unrealized gains on available-for-sale securities of EUR 1,183 million (2006: EUR 4,671 million gain). Unrealized gains on available-for-sale securities mainly relate to the Company's interest in TSMC. These unrealized gains were reduced as a result of a further reduction of our stake in TSMC in 2007.

Commentary: The company provides details on reserves and retained earnings. Reserves include "legal" revaluation reserves and cumulative translation losses. Such presentation would not contradict Canadian GAAP except that the "other reserves" would be labelled as accumulated other comprehensive income.

Extract 2(25) – Current/non-current classification

Thorntons PLC (AR 2007), pages 40 and 41
16 Borrowings (in part)

Current	Group 2007 £'000	Group 2006 £'000	Company 2007 £'000	Company 2006 £'000
Bank loans and overdrafts due within one year or on demand:				
Unsecured bank loans and overdrafts	19,000	930	19,000	12,872
Finance lease obligations	3,577	4,152	3,577	4,152
	22,577	5,082	22,577	17,024

Non-current	Group 2007 £'000	Group 2006 £'000	Company 2007 £'000	Company 2006 £'000
Unsecured bank loans	—	16,000	—	16,000
Finance lease obligations	6,692	7,421	6,692	7,421
	6,692	23,421	6,692	23,421

Bank loans and overdrafts are denominated in £ sterling and bear interest based on LIBOR or UK base rates. Non-current bank loans comprise revolving facilities where the banks cannot demand repayment within twelve months of the balance sheet date.

The effective interest rates at the balance sheet dates were as follows:

	2007 %	2006 %
Bank overdraft	—	5.30%
Bank borrowings		
— fixed interest	6.34%	5.30%
Finance leases	5.04%	5.11%

The Group's borrowings are denominated in the following currencies:

	2007 £'000	2006 £'000
Pound sterling	29,269	28,503

Thorntons PLC (AR 2007) (continued)

Maturity of financial liabilities

The maturity profile of the Group's non-current liabilities, at 30 June 2007, was as follows:

	Debt £'000	Finance leases £'000	2007 Total £'000	Debt £'000	Finance leases £'000	2006 Total £'000
Between one and two years	—	2,739	2,739	16,000	2,957	18,957
Between two and five years	—	3,953	3,953	—	4,464	4,464
	—	6,692	6,692	16,000	7,421	23,421

The Group successfully renegotiated its committed banking facilities for a three year period shortly after the balance sheet date.

Borrowing facilities

The Group has the following undrawn committed floating rate borrowing facilities available at 30 June 2007. The Group must comply with the principal lending convenants in respect of interest cover and the net debt to EBITDA ratio. At 30 June 2007 none of these convenants had been breached.

	2007 £'000	2006 £'000
Expiring within 1 year	41,400	5,400
Expiring between 1 and 2 years	—	38,070
	41,400	43,470

The facilities expiring within 1 year are three year revolving facilities due for renewal prior to August 2007, their utilisation being managed via regular review during their term. All these facilities incur commitment fees at market rates.

Commentary: The above extract shows a note providing details on the company's borrowings. Note also that the loans facilities classified as current are three-year revolving facilities due for renewal prior to August 2007 even though the company renegotiated its committed banking facilities shortly after the balance sheet date for three years. This conforms to IAS 1 requirements. Under Canadian GAAP, the company could have classified the loans in the non-current category as allowed under EIC-122.

Statement of Comprehensive Income

Format and Structure

As indicated previously, IAS 1 allows an entity to choose one of the two following structures to report total comprehensive income:

- one statement (i.e., all items of income and expense recognized in a period in a single statement of comprehensive income); or
- two statements (one displaying components of profit or loss (income statement) and the other beginning with profit or loss and displaying components of other comprehensive income (statement of comprehensive income).

Under Canadian GAAP, entities could also report comprehensive income components using one of the two options mentioned above. In addition, CICA 1530 permits entities to present comprehensive income and its components in the statement of changes in equity. IFRS does not allow this presentation.

Basic Line Items

The following is a list of the items that, at a minimum, need to be presented on the face of statement of comprehensive income (in the order listed), as required by IAS 1:

- revenue;
- finance costs;
- share of the profit or loss of associates and joint ventures accounted for using the equity method;

- tax expense (which should include current and deferred tax charges and credits);
- a single amount comprising the total of:
  o the post-tax profit or loss of discontinued operations, and
  o the post-tax gain or loss recognized on the measurement to fair value less costs to sell or on the disposal of the assets or disposal group(s) constituting the discontinued operation;
- profit or loss;
- each component of other comprehensive income classified by nature (excluding share of the other comprehensive income of associates and joint ventures);
- share of the other comprehensive income of associates and joint ventures accounted for using the equity method; and
- total comprehensive income.

In addition, IAS 1 requires that profit and loss (net income) and total comprehensive income for the period be allocated to non-controlling interests, as well as to the owners of the parent company.

All of these line items are also required by CICA 1520. The latter also requires the presentation of more line items on the face of the income statement. In addition current Canadian GAAP does not require the allocation of other comprehensive income to controlling and non-controlling interests (see chapter 6).

Additional Line Items, Headings and Subtotals

According to IAS 1 an entity considers if additional line items, headings and subtotals in the statement of comprehensive income and the separate income statement (if presented) contributes to understanding an entity's financial performance. The decision to add lines or subtotals to the statement of comprehensive income (or, alternatively, to offset or aggregate amounts) must take into consideration a number of factors.

The table below presents these factors, as well as other related issues discussed in IAS 1. All issues described and examples provided do not contravene Canadian GAAP unless specifically indicated.

Presentation Issues	
Objective/Requirements	**Examples**
Additional lines	
Must reflect entity's various activities, transactions and other events that are significant and might differ in frequency, potential for gain or loss and predictability.	• restructuring costs and their reversal; • gain or loss on disposals of equity investments; • litigation settlements.
Additional sub-totals	
Must contribute to the understanding of an entity's financial performance. (Note 1)	• operating income; • earnings before interest, depreciation, tax and amortization (EBIDTA); • earnings before interest and tax (EBIT); • earnings before unusual items.

Presentation Issues	
Objective/Requirements	**Examples**
Additional per share information	
Must contribute to the understanding of an entity's financial performance. (Note 1)	• cash flows per share; • dividend per share.
Aggregation	
When individual amounts are not significant, they may be aggregated and disclosed in a note to the financial statements.	Impairment of inventories and gains or losses on disposal of property, plant and equipment might be grouped if they result from routine events.
Offsetting	
Offsetting of income and expenses is not permitted unless required or allowed by another IFRS, or when the amounts relate to similar transactions or events that are not material. Note that IFRS permit or require offsetting if it better reflects the substance of the transaction.	Revenue is presented net in case of an agency arrangement where an entity is not exposed to the risks of a transaction (see Chapter 11).
Labels used	
Label should reflect IFRS definitions or reflect the substance of a transaction or event. (Note 2)	• Discontinued operations should only include items and activities covered by IFRS 5, *Non-current Assets Held for Sale and Discontinued Operations.* Note that the definition of what constitutes discontinued operations might differ under IFRS 5 and CICA 3475, *Disposal of Long-lived Assets and Discontinued Operations.* • Finance costs should incorporate all borrowings costs, including those related to loans and finance leases.

Note 1: Additional subtotals and per share information

Although IAS 1 does not prohibit alternative earnings measures on the face of the income statement, per-share disclosures related to such measures can be disclosed only in the notes, and not on the face of the income statement. Under Canadian GAAP, additional performance amounts are sometimes presented but not to the extent used under IFRS. Canadian GAAP also does not permit presenting per-share disclosures related to such alternative measures either on the face of the income statement or in the notes.

Note 2: Labels used – unusual and extraordinary items

IFRS and Canadian GAAP differ on labelling. First, according to IAS 1, an entity cannot present an item of income and expense as an extraordinary item in either the statement of comprehensive income or the notes. Although CICA 3480 specifically allows this, it has restricted the practice to few situations meeting the specific criteria. Second, under IAS 1, items of income or expense are presented as "unusual items" when they are significant and are necessary for fair presentation. Canadian GAAP requires separate presentation in the income statement of items characterized as "unusual items" (such items do not have all of the characteristics of an extraordinary item, but result from transactions or events that are not expected to occur frequently over several years, or do not typify normal business activities.

The additional subtotals permitted in IFRS such as profit before exceptional or non-recurring items are not used in North American practice because they could be regarded as non GAAP measures. As will be shown in the illustrations they are used to a great extent in the financial reports prepared under IFRS.

Analysis of Expenses

IAS 1 requires entities to present an analysis of expenses recognized in profit or loss (on the face of the income statement or in the notes) using a classification based on either (1) their nature or (2) their function within an entity, whichever provides information that is reliable and more relevant. A mixture of both is not allowed. Although CICA 1520 specifies that certain expenses must be disclosed, it does not have equivalent requirements to classify expenses according to their nature or function.

Note that, under both classifications of expenses, the caption "other" is often used and would generally include gains and losses related to activities that are incidental or ancillary to an entity's operations. Where the "other" caption is used, the notes should usually offer an analysis of its composition.

The following table provides certain observations on both classifications of expenses as covered by IAS 1:

Issue	Nature of Expense Method	Function of Expense or "Cost of Sales" Method
Typical expenses presented in the statement of comprehensive income	Examples: • depreciation; • transport costs; • employee benefits; • advertising costs.	Examples: • cost of sales; • general administration expenses; • sales and marketing expenses.
Application (see Note)	• No allocation of expenses to functions is required. • Method is simple to apply.	• Allocation of expenses is required. • Most difficult allocation relates to cost of sales. • Generally results in more relevant financial analysis than when expenses are presented according to their nature. • Method might require arbitrary allocations and involve considerable judgment.
Additional disclosures	No particular requirements in IAS 1.	Additional information required on the nature of expenses, including depreciation, amortization and employee benefits.

Note that many companies applying Canadian GAAP present expenses by function. As specified in the above table, this presentation often requires significant judgment for allocating costs or expenses, for example for:

- research and development, which could be allocated entirely to administrative expenses or allocated in part to another, more appropriate heading (such as costs of sales in case of the pharmaceutical industry);

- impairment, which would be allocated differently depending on the nature of the asset held, as follows:

  o inventory obsolescence would be allocated entirely to costs of sales while goodwill impairment is excluded from costs of sales,

  o property, plant and equipment impairment is allocated in accordance to how the depreciation of the particular asset is classified (i.e., it could be part of cost of sales or other expenses).

Comprehensive Income Components

Comprehensive income represents all changes in equity during a period resulting from transactions and other events, other than changes resulting from transactions with owners in their capacity as owners. It includes:

- profit or loss (or net income) that is defined as total of income less expenses, excluding the components of other comprehensive income; and

- other comprehensive income that is defined as total income less expenses (including reclassification adjustments) that are not recognized in profit or loss as required or permitted by IFRS standards.

Other Comprehensive Income Components

Other comprehensive income includes the following components:

- changes in revaluation surplus for property, plant and equipment and intangible assets when revaluation model is used;

- actuarial gains and losses on defined benefit plans recognized according to IAS 19, *Employee Benefits*;

- gains and losses arising from translating the financial statements of a foreign operation as required by IAS 21, *The Effects of Changes in Foreign Exchange Rates*;

- gains and losses on re-measuring available-for-sale financial assets as required by IAS 39, *Financial Instruments: Recognition and Measurement*; and

- the effective portion of gains and losses on hedging instruments in a cash flow hedge as specified by IAS 39.

Reclassifications adjustments must include in profit and loss amounts previously recognized in other comprehensive income. Reclassification is required for the following transactions:

- disposal of a foreign operation;

- sale of available-for-sale financial assets; and

- a hedged forecast transaction affecting profit or loss (as required by IAS 39 for cash flow hedges).

Note that reclassification adjustments do not arise on (i.e., components recognized in other comprehensive income are not reclassified to profit or loss in subsequent periods):

- changes in revaluation surplus recognized in accordance with IAS 16, *Property, Plant and Equipment*, or IAS 38, *Intangible Assets*; and

- actuarial gains and losses on defined benefit plans recognized in accordance with IAS 19, *Employee Benefits*.

Entities may present reclassification adjustments in the statement of comprehensive income or in the notes. They must disclose the amount of income tax for each component of other comprehensive income, including reclassification adjustments, either in the statement of comprehensive income or in the notes.

All the above IAS 1requirements for comprehensive income also apply to Canadian GAAP. Significant differences exits regarding the nature of components of other comprehensive income including the fact that:

- entities cannot use the revaluation model for surplus for property, plant and equipment and intangible assets;

- actuarial gains and losses on defined benefit plans cannot be recognized directly in equity.

Consequently, IFRS requirements for these elements do not apply under Canadian GAAP.

Illustrative Disclosures:

All extracts below (except Extract 2(37)) reflect IAS 1 requirements before the September 2007 amendments, which are effective for periods starting January 1, 2009. As indicated previously, almost all companies reporting under IFRS did not adopt the amended IAS 1 early.[13] Instead, they presented:

- *all* changes in equity, including transactions with equity holders (acting in their capacity as equity holders) in a statement of changes in equity (SOCIE); or

- changes in equity *excluding* transaction with equity holders acting in their capacity as equity holders in a statement of recognized income and expense (SORIE).

Consequently, the SORIE (when presented as illustrated in some of the following extracts), along with the profit and loss statement, contains all elements of other comprehensive income. Note that the separate statement including other comprehensive income components should normally follow immediately after the income statement (which might not be the case for the financial statement extracts provided below). When SORIE is not presented as a primary financial statement , the income statement would reflect only an incomplete statement of comprehensive income.

None of the presentations contradict Canadian GAAP except that:

- Although CICA 1530, like IAS 1, permits a choice of displaying comprehensive income and its components, in one or two statements of financial performance it also allows the display in a statement of changes in equity which is not permitted by IAS 1.

- IAS 1 requires the investor's share of the investee's other comprehensive income to be shown in the statement of comprehensive income. Canadian GAAP does not require the separate presentation of this Consequently, an entity could combine its proportionate share of other comprehensive income amounts with its own other comprehensive income items according to their nature and show the aggregate of those amounts in an income statement type format or in a statement of changes in equity.

- IAS 1 specifically states that the "profit or loss attributable to non-controlling interest" should be presented as an allocation of profit or loss for the period, not as an item of income or expense. Under current Canadian GAAP prior to CICA 1602, *Non-controlling Interests* adoption[14], the non-controlling interests' share of profit or loss may have been deducted from "profit or loss for the year" in a similar manner to an item of expense, to arrive at "profit attributable to the parent entity."

---

13 Because of the changes to IAS 1 that are effective January 1, 2009 there are limited examples of companies that applied the new requirements. The Guidance that accompanies IAS 1 but is not part of it provides illustration of the presentation of financial statements structure including the alternative presentations of comprehensive income, in a single statement or in two statements.

14 See footnote 7.

Extract 2(26) – Analysis of expenses by function

Vodafone Group Plc (AR 2008), page 88
Consolidated Income Statement
for the years ended 31 March

	Note	2008 £m	2007 £m	2006 £m
Revenue	3	35,478	31,104	29,350
Cost of sales		(21,890)	(18,725)	(17,070)
Gross profit		13,588	12,379	12,280
Selling and distribution expenses		(2,511)	(2,136)	(1,876)
Administrative expenses		(3,878)	(3,437)	(3,416)
Share of result in associated undertakings	14	2,876	2,728	2,428
Impairment losses	10	–	(11,600)	(23,515)
Other income and expense	29	(28)	502	15
Operating profit/(loss)	3,4	10,047	(1,564)	(14,084)
Non-operating income and expense	29	254	4	(2)
Investment income	5	714	789	353
Financing costs	5	(2,014)	(1,612)	(1,120)
Profit/(loss) before taxation		9,001	(2,383)	(14,853)
Income tax expense	6	(2,245)	(2,423)	(2,380)
Profit/(loss) for the financial year from continuing operations		6,756	(4,806)	(17,233)
Loss for the financial year from discontinued Profit/(loss) for the financial year operations	29	–	(491)	(4,588)
		6,756	(5,297)	(21,821)
Attributable to:				
– Equity shareholders	23	6,660	(5,426)	(21,916)
– Minority interests		96	129	95
		6,756	(5,297)	(21,821)
Basic earnings/(loss) per share				
Profit/(loss) from continuing operations	8	12.56p	(8.94)p	(27.66)p
Loss from discontinued operations	8, 29	–	(0.90)p	(7.35)p
Profit/(loss) for the financial year	8	12.56p	(9.84)p	(35.01)p
Diluted earnings/(loss) per share				
Profit/(loss) from continuing operations	8	12.50p	(8.94)p	(27.66)p
Loss from discontinued operations	8, 29	–	(0.90)p	(7.35)p
Profit/(loss) for the financial year	8	12.50p	(9.84)p	(35.01)p

Consolidated Statement of Recognised Income and Expense
for the years ended 31 March

	Note	2008 £m	2007 £m	2006 £m
Gains on revaluation of available-for-sale investments, net of tax	22	1,949	2,108	705
Exchange differences on translation of foreign operations, net of tax	22	5,537	(3,804)	1,494
Net actuarial (losses)/gains on defined benefit pension schemes, net of tax	22	(37)	50	(30)
Revaluation gain	22	–	–	112
Foreign exchange (gains)/losses transferred to the Consolidated Income Statement	22	(7)	838	36
Fair value gains transferred to the Consolidated Income Statement	22	(570)	–	–
Other	22	37	–	–
Net gain/(loss) recognised directly in equity		6,909	(808)	2,317
Profit/(loss) for the financial year		6,756	(5,297)	(21,821)
Total recognised income and expense relating to the year		13,665	(6,105)	(19,504)
Attributable to:				
– Equity shareholders		13,912	(6,210)	(19,607)
– Minority interests		(247)	105	103
		13,665	(6,105)	(19,504)

The accompanying notes are an integral part of these Consolidated Financial Statements.

Commentary: The company presents an income statement and a SORIE. Taken together, they could represent an illustration of a comprehensive income statement. Expenses are analyzed by function: costs of sales, selling and distribution expenses and administrative expenses are presented as separate line items.

The company presents additional line items (impairment) and sub-totals (gross profit and operating profit), which reflect common disclosures that are considered useful in assessing performance under both IFRS and Canadian GAAP.

Extract 2(27) – Analysis of expenses by function

Lafarge (AR Document de référence 2007), page F4
Consolidated statements of income

(million euros, except per share data)	Notes	YEARS ENDED DECEMBER 31,		
		2007	2006	2005*
REVENUE		17,614	16,909	14,490
Cost of sales		(12,700)	(12,385)	(10,585)
Selling and administrative expenses		(1,672)	(1,752)	(1,659)
OPERATING INCOME BEFORE CAPITAL GAINS, IMPAIRMENT, RESTRUCTURING AND OTHER		3,242	2,772	2,246
Gains on disposals, net	(5)	196	28	40
Other operating income (expenses)	(6)	(149)	(122)	(105)
OPERATING INCOME		3,289	2,678	2,181
Finance costs	(7)	(652)	(582)	(498)
Finance income	(7)	126	97	83
Income from associates	(12)	-	30	31
INCOME FROM CONTINUING OPERATIONS BEFORE INCOME TAX		2,763	2,223	1,797
Income tax	(22)	(725)	(630)	(470)
Net income from continuing operations		2,038	1,593	1,327
Net income/(loss) from discontinued operations	(3)	118	(4)	97
NET INCOME		2,156	1,589	1,424
Out of which:				
Group share		1,909	1,372	1,096
Minority interests		247	217	328
EARNINGS PER SHARE (euros)				
NET INCOME – GROUP SHARE				
Basic earnings per share		11.05	7.86	6.39
Diluted earnings per share		10.91	7.75	6.34
FROM CONTINUING OPERATIONS				
Basic earnings per share	(8)	10.37	7.88	5.82
Diluted earnings per share	(8)	10.24	7.77	5.79
FROM DISCONTINUED OPERATIONS				
Basic earnings per share	(3)	0.68	(0.02)	0.57
Diluted earnings per share	(3)	0.67	(0.02)	0.55
BASIC AVERAGE NUMBER OF SHARES OUTSTANDING (thousands)	(8)	172,718	174,543	171,491

* Figures have been adjusted as mentioned in Note 3(b) following the divestment of the Roofing Division decided in 2006 and finalized in 2007 and are therefore not comparable with those presented in the 2005 Annual Report.

The accompanying notes are an integral part of these consolidated financial statements.

Lafarge (AR Document de référence 2007) (continued)
page F9
Consolidated statement of recognized income and expense

(million euros)	DECEMBER 31,		
	2007	2006	2005
NET INCOME	2,156	1,589	1,424
Available for sale investments	(29)	145	42
Cash flow hedge instruments	12	(38)	16
Actuarial gains/(losses)	18	45*	(96)*
Deferred taxes and others	3	16	(20)
Change in translation adjustments	(354)	(682)	1,201
INCOME AND EXPENSE RECOGNIZED DIRECTLY IN EQUITY	(350)	(514)	1,143
TOTAL RECOGNIZED INCOME AND EXPENSE FOR THE PERIOD	1,806	1,075	2,567
Of which Group share	1,605	977	1,992
Of which Minority interests	201	98	575

* Figures have been adjusted after the application by the Group of the amendment of IAS 19 – Employee Benefits, allowing the recognition through equity of the actuarial gains and losses under defined-benefit pension plans (see Note 2).

The accompanying notes are an integral part of these consolidated financial statements.

page F28
Note 6 - Other operating income (expenses)
Components of other operating income (expenses) are as follows:

(million euros)	YEARS ENDED DECEMBER 31,		
	2007	2006	2005
Impairment losses on goodwill*	-	(15)	(58)
Impairment losses on property, plant and equipment	(13)	(8)	(7)
IMPAIRMENT LOSSES	(13)	(23)	(65)
Restructuring costs**	(81)	(99)	(26)
Litigations	(58)	(27)	(21)
Other income	71	73	52
Other expenses	(68)	(46)	(45)
OTHER OPERATING INCOME (EXPENSES)	(149)	(122)	(105)

* Impairment losses on goodwill are detailed in Note 9 (c).

** Restructuring costs are detailed in Note 24 (b).

2007

"Other income" includes mainly insurance proceeds to be received for 45 million euros related to the Tsunami damages that occurred on December 26, 2004.

"Other expenses" include mainly a 27 million euros loss in our insurance captives related to an unusual high loss rate in our operations in the year.

2006

"Other income" includes a 17 million euros refund to Lafarge North America Inc following the distribution to the U.S. and Mexican cement industries of unliquidated historical duties over U.S. imports of Mexican cement. The Mexican and U.S. governments came to an agreement on this subject in early 2006. In addition, an indemnity amounting to 43 million euros was received in France following a court decision in our favor.

"Other expenses" include a 29 million euros stock option expense following the buy-out of the minority interest of Lafarge North America Inc (see Note 20).

2005

"Other income" includes a 42 million euro gain as the result of the partial refund of a fine paid in 1999 to the Greek State by Heracles, under a European Union judgment related to state aid received in the mid 1980's.

The related tax effect is mentioned in the reconciliation of effective tax rate (Note 22 (a)).

Commentary: Here, too, the company presents an income statement and a SORIE that, together, could represent an illustration of a comprehensive income statement. Expenses are analyzed by function: costs of sales and selling and administrative expenses are presented as separate line items.

Note that the company presents:

- net income from continuing and discontinuing operations (which is in line with Canadian GAAP);
- did not offset finance costs and finance income as required by IAS 1. The company could have also presented finance income followed immediately by finance costs and a subtotal (e.g., "net finance costs") on the face of the income statement. Such presentations are also in line with Canadian GAAP;
- additional line items, most significantly "other operating income (expense)" detailed in a note (reproduced above);
- non-GAAP subtotal "Operating Income Before Capital Gains, Impairment, Restructuring and Other," i.e., earnings before unusual items. Although Canadian GAAP does not encourage the presentation of such subtotals, it does not forbid it.

Extract 2(28) – Analysis of expenses by nature

Royal Ten Cate (AR 2007), pages 71, 92 and 95 Consolidated profit and loss account in millions of euros	note	2007	2006
Revenues	29	886.0	770.5
Changes in inventories of finished products and work in progress		– 11.7	– 4.8
Raw materials and manufacturing supplies		463.6	402.2
Work contracted out and other external expenses		54.9	34.7
Personnel costs	31	178.3	171.2
Depreciation and impairment	37	29.1	22.1
Amortisation	38	3.6	1.0
Other operating costs	32	98.8	94.0
Total operating expenses		816.6	720.4
OPERATING RESULT		**69.4**	**50.1**
Financial income	33	0.5	0.1
Financial expenses	33	– 11.8	– 8.1
NET FINANCIAL EXPENSES		– 11.3	– 8.0
PRE-TAX RESULT		58.1	42.1
Profit tax	34	– 11.9	– 11.4
Result after tax but before divestment of activities		46.2	30.7
Result from participating interests	35	–	3.4
Result from divested operations after tax	36	0.3	42.0
RESULT AFTER TAX		**46.5**	**76.1**
ATTRIBUTABLE TO:			
Shareholders of parent company (net income)		46.4	76.0
Minority interests		0.1	0.1
Weighted average number of shares (x 1,000)	47	22,797	20,749
Weighted average number of shares after dilution (x 1,000)	47	22,967	21,264
Net profit per share (euro)		2.04	3.66
corrected to take account of result from divested activities and exceptional income*		1.89	1.64
Diluted net result per share (euro)		2.02	3.57
corrected to take account of result from divested activities and exceptional income*		1.87	1.60
* 2007: Concerns in particular income from the sale of real estate and associated expenses: € 3.1 million net.			
2006: Adjusted for comparison purposes.			

Royal Ten Cate (AR 2007) (continued)
page 92
30.3 Divestments in 2007
The following interests were sold in 2007:

	Proceeds (including cash)
• Business Key on 16 February 2007 (100% interest)	7.2
• SCI La Domitienne on 8 December 2007 (100% interest)	0.3
The following companies were closed in 2007:	
• TenCate Enbi Mexico	0.2
• TenCate Nicolon Asia	0.1
	7.8

page 95
35 RESULT FROM PARTICIPATING INTERESTS
No result from participating interests applied in 2007 (2006: € 3.4 million).
36 RESULT FROM DIVESTED OPERATIONS
See note 30.3.

	2007	2006
Business Key	0.2	–
SCI La Domitienne	0.1	–
Synbra Group	–	39.3
Plasticum Group	–	2.7
TenCate Nicolon Australia	–	– 0.1
Landscape Solutions	–	0.1
Result from divested operations	**0.3**	**42.0**

Commentary: In the above extract, the company presents an income statement. No SORIE was presented (as the SOCIE reflected amounts of other comprehensive income allocated directly to equity). IAS 1 as revised in 2007 and effective as of January 2009 would consider this presentation of results to be incomplete but Canadian GAAP would consider it acceptable since other comprehensive income amounts could be presented in a statement of changes of equity.

Expenses are analyzed by nature. No allocation to costs of sales was required. Even though nothing in Canadian GAAP prevents such a presentation, it is not frequently observed.

The company presents additional line items (depreciation and impairment) and sub-totals (operating results), reflecting common disclosures useful for assessing performance under both IFRS and Canadian GAAP.

Extract 2(29) – Details provided for "other" line items

Givaudan SA (Annual & Financial Report 2007), page 30
9. Other operating (income) expenses, net (in part)

in millions of Swiss francs	2007	2006
Restructuring expenses	-	6
Impairment of long-lived assets	14	4
(Gains) losses on fixed assets disposals	1	(16)
Business related information management projects costs	9	13
Butter flavours litigation case settlement	-	44
Quest integration expenses	194	
Other business taxes	14	12
Other (income) expenses, net	12	(4)
Total	244	59

page 31
In the year ended 31 December 2007, the Group incurred significant expenses in connection with the combination with Quest International. Integration related charges of CHF 194 million and assets impairment of CHF 14 million have been recognised in the line other operating (income) and expenses, net. Refer also to Note 18 on property, plant and equipment and Note 22 on provisions.

Commentary: This extract presents an example of note disclosures related to "other" income and expense amounts. Also included in the extract is an explanation of the "other" caption presented within the "other" income statement line item. Disclosures are in line with Canadian GAAP.

Extract 2(30) – Exceptional items

InterContinental Hotels Group PLC (AR 2007), page 55
Summary of significant accounting policies (in part)
Exceptional items

The Group discloses certain financial information both including and excluding exceptional items. The presentation of information excluding exceptional items allows a better understanding of the underlying trading performance of the Group and provides consistency with the Group's internal management reporting. Exceptional items are identified by virtue of either their size or nature so as to facilitate comparison with prior periods and to assess underlying trends in financial performance. Exceptional items can include, but are not restricted to, gains and losses on the disposal of assets, impairment charges and reversals, restructuring costs and the release of tax provisions.

Amounts that have previously been disclosed as special items have now been called exceptional items in accordance with market practice. There has been no change to the Group's accounting policy for identifying these items.

page 63
5 EXCEPTIONAL ITEMS

	Note	2007 £m	2006 £m
Exceptional operating items*			
Gain on sale of associate investments**		11	–
Gain of sale of investment in FelCor Lodging Trust, Inc.**		–	25
Gain on sale of other financial assets**		18	–
Reversal of previously recorded impairment**		3	2
Office reorganisations	a	(2)	–
		30	27
Tax*			
Tax charge on exceptional operating items		–	(6)
Exceptional tax credit	b	30	100
		30	94
Gain on disposal of assets (note 11)			
Gain on disposal of assets		20	123
Tax charge		(4)	(6)
		16	117

*   Relates to continuing operations.

**   Included within other operating income and expenses.

The above items are treated as exceptional by reason of their size or nature.

a   Profit on sale and leaseback of new head office less costs incurred to date on the office move and closure of the Group's Aylesbury facility. Costs will continue to be incurred during the first half of 2008. Costs of £7m are included in administrative expenses and £1m in depreciation and amortisation. Income of £6m is included in other operating income and expenses.

b   The exceptional tax credit relates to the release of provisions which are exceptional by reason of their size or nature relating to tax matters which have been settled or in respect of which the relevant statutory limitation period has expired, together with, in 2006, a credit in respect of previously unrecognised losses.

Commentary: The company presents details related to exceptional items (which are excluded from discontinued operations as required by IFRS 5). In addition to the exceptional items reflected in the extract above, the company presents, in Note 11 (not reproduced here), disposals that were considered to be discontinued operations. It is possible that some or all of the above exceptional items would qualify as discontinued operations under CICA 3475.

Extract 2(31) – Income statement details

Koninklijke Philips Electronics N.V. (AR 2007), pages 217 and 218

40 Income from operations

Sales composition	2005	2006	2007
Goods	22,912	24,107	24,270
Services	2,027	2,073	1,973
Licenses	506	502	550
	25,445	26,682	26,793

Salaries and wages	2005	2006	2007
Salaries and wages	4,403	4,613	4,607
Pension costs	438	461	434
Other social security and similar charges:			
- Required by law	593	636	634
- Voluntary	(145)	91	89
	5,289	5,801	5,764

See note 56 for further information on pension costs.

For remuneration details of the members of the Board of Management and the Supervisory Board, see note 34.

For information on share-based compensation, see note 33.

The Company applies IFRS 2 for recognition and measurement of share-based payments, which are similar to US GAAP-requirements.

Employees

The average number of employees by category is summarized as follows (in FTEs):

	2005	2006	2007
Production	58,466	59,955	61,447
Research & development	13,659	13,227	12,804
Other	28,338	27,694	28,469
Permanent employees	100,463	100,876	102,720
Temporary employees	15,609	16,225	16,660
Continuing operations	116,072	117,101	119,380
Discontinued operations	44,815	44,040	6,276

Depreciation and amortization

Depreciation of property, plant and equipment and amortization of intangibles are as follows:

	2005	2006	2007
Depreciation of property, plant and equipment	557	554	562
Amortization of internal-use software	78	71	76
Amortization of goodwill and other intangibles:			
- Amortization of other intangible assets	89	152	200
- Amortization of development costs	195	213	245
	919	990	1,083

Depreciation of property, plant and equipment includes an additional write-off in connection with the retirement of property, plant and equipment amounting to EUR 28 million (2006: EUR 20 million, 2005: EUR 13 million).

Included in depreciation of property, plant and equipment is an amount of EUR 22 million (2006: EUR 17 million, 2005: EUR 42 million) relating to impairment charges.

Depreciation of property, plant and equipment and amortization of software and other intangible assets are primarily included in cost of sales. Amortization of development cost is included in research and development expenses.

In 2007, no goodwill impairments were recorded (2006: EUR nil, 2005: EUR nil).

Koninklijke Philips Electronics N.V. (AR 2007) (continued)

Total depreciation and amortization

	2005	2006	2007
Medical Systems	209	232	302
DAP	128	138	135
Consumer Electronics	178	179	168
Lighting	184	255	332
Innovation & Emerging Businesses	151	107	75
Group Management & Services	69	79	71
	919	990	1,083

Other business income (expense)

Other business income (expense) consists of the following:

	2005	2006	2007
Result on disposal of business:			
- income	206	130	35
- expense	(8)	(64)	(65)
Result on disposal of fixed assets:			
- income	155	108	107
- expense	(29)	(18)	(24)
Result on remaining business:			
- income	219	90	127
- expense	(125)	(67)	(76)
	418	179	104

Results on the disposal of businesses consisted of:

	2005	2006	2007
Automotive Playback Modules	-	-	(30)
Philips Sound Solutions	-	12	-
CryptoTec	-	26	-
Connected Displays (Monitors)	158	23	-
Philips Pension Competence Center	43	-	-
Other	(3)	5	-
	198	66	(30)

2007

The result on disposal of businesses in 2007 mainly related to the sale of Automotive Playback Modules which resulted in a loss of EUR 30 million. The result on the sale of fixed assets mainly related to the sale of certain buildings in Austria and the Netherlands as well as land in the US. The other business results are mainly attributable to certain settlements and the finalization of several divestitures.

2006

The result on disposal of businesses in 2006 is related mainly to the sale of the CryptoTec activities which delivered a gain of EUR 26 million, the sale of Philips Sound Solutions PSS to D&M Holding at a gain of EUR 12 million and the sale of Connected Displays at a gain of EUR 23 million. The result on disposal of fixed assets is mainly related to the sale of certain real estate assets in Austria with a gain of EUR 31 million. Other business income consists of the settlement of certain legal claims and some releases of provisions.

2005

The result on disposal of businesses in 2005 related mainly to the sale of certain activities within Philips' monitors and flat TV business to TPV at a gain of EUR 158 million and the sale of asset management and pension administration activities to Merrill Lynch and Hewitt respectively, for an amount of EUR 43 million. In 2005, the result on disposal of fixed assets related mainly to the sale of buildings in Suresnes, France (EUR 67 million) and in the Netherlands (EUR 36 million). In 2005, other business income and expenses consists of the settlement of some legal claims and some releases of provisions.

Koninklijke Philips Electronics N.V. (AR 2007) (continued)
page 218
41 Financial income and expenses

	2005	2006	2007
Interest income	87	150	236
Interest expense	(289)	(339)	(279)
Net interest expense	(202)	(189)	(43)
Income from non-current financial assets	242	334	2,952
Foreign exchange results	1	2	(1)
Other financing income (expenses), net	67	(118)	(59)
	310	218	2,892
	108	29	2,849

Interest income increased by EUR 86 million during 2007, this was mainly as a result of higher average cash balances and higher average interest rates realized during 2007, compared to 2006.

Interest expense decreased by EUR 60 million during 2007, mainly as a result of lower average debt positions and lower interest costs on derivatives related to hedging of Philips' foreign currency denominated cash balances and inter-company funding positions.

In 2007, income from non-current financial assets totaled EUR 2,952 million, and included EUR 2,783 million from the sale of shares in TSMC, EUR 31 million gain on sale of shares in Nuance Communications, EUR 10 million loss on sale of shares in JDS Uniphase and a cash dividend of EUR 128 million from TSMC. In 2006, income from non-current financial assets totaled EUR 334 million, and included a cash dividend of EUR 223 million from TSMC and a gain of EUR 97 million upon designation of the TSMC shares received through a stock dividend as trading securities. In 2005, EUR 235 million of tax-exempt gains from the sale of the remaining shares in Atos Origin and Great Nordic were recognized.

In 2007, other financial charges included an impairment charge of EUR 36 million in relation to the investment in JDS Uniphase, a further EUR 12 million gain as a result of the fair value change in the conversion option embedded in the convertible bond received from TPV Technology. In 2006, other financial charges included an impairment charge of EUR 77 million in relation to the investment in TPO Display, a further EUR 61 million loss as a result of the fair value change in the conversion option embedded in the convertible bond received from TPV Technology and a EUR 29 million gain as a result of increases in the fair value of the trading securities held in TSMC. In 2005, other financial charges included a EUR 53 million fair value gain on the conversion option TPV Technology convertible bond.

Commentary: The company provides details on several line items presented in its income statement. Disclosures seems to be in line with Canadian GAAP.

Extract 2(32) – Analysis by function and additional sub-totals

Xstrata plc (AR 2007), pages 138 and 142
Consolidated Income Statement
For the year ended 31 December 2007

US$m	Notes	Before exceptional items	Exceptional items†	Total 2007	Before exceptional items**	Exceptional items†**	Total 2006**
Revenue		28,542	–	28,542	17,102	–	17,102
Cost of sales*		(15,544)	–	(15,544)	(8,490)	–	(8,490)
Distribution costs		(1,439)	–	(1,439)	(1,130)	–	(1,130)
Administrative expenses*		(686)	–	(686)	(502)	–	(502)
Share of results from associates	20	15	–	15	4	–	4
Income and costs of acquisition related activities		–	275	275	–	–	–
Disposal fair value adjustment		–	(25)	(25)	–	–	–
Profit on sale of available-for-sale financial assets		–	–	–	–	63	63
Profit on sale of operations		–	–	–	–	16	16
Restructuring and closure costs		–	–	–	–	(50)	(50)
Profit before interest, taxation, depreciation and amortisation	10	**10,888**	**250**	**11,138**	**6,984**	**29**	**7,013**
Depreciation and amortisation:							
– Cost of sales		(2,038)	–	(2,038)	(1,187)	–	(1,187)
– Administrative expenses		(58)	–	(58)	(32)	–	(32)
Impairment of assets:							
– Administrative expenses		–	–	–	–	(1,824)	(1,824)
Profit before interest and taxation	10	**8,792**	**250**	**9,042**	**5,765**	**(1,795)**	**3,970**
Finance income	10	142	74	216	110	170	280
Finance costs	10	(935)	(196)	(1,131)	(639)	(235)	(874)
Profit before taxation		**7,999**	**128**	**8,127**	**5,236**	**(1,860)**	**3,376**
Income tax (expense)/benefit	11	(2,301)	(10)	(2,311)	(1,545)	11	(1,534)
Profit from continuing operations		**5,698**	**118**	**5,816**	**3,691**	**(1,849)**	**1,842**
Profit after tax from discontinued operations	8	52	1	53	64	–	64
Profit for the year		**5,750**	**119**	**5,869**	**3,755**	**(1,849)**	**1,906**
Attributable to:							
Equity holders of the parent		5,424	119	5,543	3,350	(1,849)	1,501
Minority interests		326	–	326	405	–	405
		5,750	**119**	**5,869**	**3,755**	**(1,849)**	**1,906**
Earnings per share (US$)							
– basic (continuing operations)	12	5.60	0.12	5.72	4.26	(2.40)	1.86
– basic	12	5.66	0.12	5.78	4.34	(2.40)	1.94
– diluted (continuing operations)	12	5.47	0.12	5.59	3.99	(2.22)	1.77
– diluted	12	5.52	0.12	5.64	4.07	(2.22)	1.85
Dividends (US$m)							
– declared and paid	13			443			251
– proposed	13			326			281
Dividend per share (US¢)							
– declared and paid	13			46.0			34.0
– proposed	13			34.0			30.0

† Exceptional items are significant items of income and expense, presented separately due to their nature or the expected infrequency of the events giving rise to them

* Before depreciation, amortisation and impairment charges

** Restated for the revisions to the Falconbridge, Cerrejon and Tintaya acquisitions in 2006 (refer to note 7) and the disposal of the aluminium business unit (refer to note 8)

Xstrata plc (AR 2007) (continued) Consolidated Statement of Recognised Income and Expense For the year ended 31 December 2007 US$m	2007	2006*
Income and expenses recognised directly in equity:		
Actuarial gains/(losses) on defined benefit pension plans	(98)	71
Gains on available-for-sale financial assets	49	1,892
Reversal of revaluation surplus on available-for-sale financial assets	–	(2,205)
Revaluation of property, plant and equipment	22	1,418
Losses on cash flow hedges	(261)	(78)
Foreign currency translation differences	670	244
	382	1,342
Transfers to the income statement:		
Losses on cash flow hedges	121	125
Gains on sale of available-for-sale financial assets	–	(63)
Recycled foreign currency translation net losses	28	47
	531	1,451
Tax on items taken directly to or transferred from equity	(7)	15
Net income recognised directly in equity	**524**	1,466
Profit for the period	**5,869**	1,906
Total recognised income and expense for the period	**6,393**	3,372
Attributable to:		
Equity holders of the parent	**6,067**	2,967
Minority interests	**326**	405
	6,393	3,372

* Restated for the revisions to the Falconbridge, Cerrejon and Tintaya acquisitions in 2006 (refer to note 7)

page 148

6. Principal Accounting Policies (in part)

Exceptional items

Exceptional items represent significant items of income and expense which due to their nature or the expected infrequency of the events giving rise to them, are presented separately on the face of the income statement to give a better understanding to shareholders of the elements of financial performance in the year, so as to facilitate comparison with prior periods and to better assess trends in financial performance. Exceptional items include, but are not limited to, goodwill impairments, acquisition and integration costs which have not been capitalised, profits and losses on the sale of investments, profits and losses from the sale of operations, recycled gains and losses from the foreign currency translation reserve, foreign currency gains and losses on borrowings, restructuring and closure costs, loan issue costs written-off on facility refinancing and the related tax impacts of these items.

page 191

10. Revenues and Expenses (in part)

Exceptional items

Acquisition related activities

In March 2007, the Group made a cash offer to purchase the entire share capital of LionOre Mining International Limited (LionOre), a Canadian listed nickel and gold mining company. In May 2007, OJSC MMC Norilsk Nickel announced a higher cash offer and on 1 June 2007, the Group announced it would not increase its offer price. LionOre terminated the support agreement for the Group's offer and made a termination payment to the Group of CAD305 million (US$284 million) in June 2007. The Group incurred acquisition costs of US$9 million in relation to the offer for LionOre. The tax charge attributable to the termination payment and acquisition costs is US$52 million.

Xstrata plc (AR 2007) (continued)

Disposal fair value adjustment – Kagiso obligations

During the year ended 31 December 2007, a charge of US$25 million has been recorded for an increase in the fair value of the liability recognised by the Group following the black empowerment disposal to Kagiso of an interest in the Mototolo joint venture (refer to note 7 and note 28).

Restructuring and closure costs

Restructuring and redundancy costs of US$nil (2006 US$50 million) relate to the former Falconbridge Group following its acquisition.

Impairment of goodwill

The acquisition of Falconbridge was completed in two stages. The Group acquired 19.9% of Falconbridge at CAD28 per share in 2005, before acquiring the remaining 80.1% in 2006 at a price of CAD62.50 per share. The average price paid per share for the 100% interest was CAD56.44. The Group's ability to average the purchase price paid for the second tranche of shares over the full purchase provided the Group with a compelling competitive advantage and was a significant factor in the success of the transaction. Under IFRS, this advantage cannot be recognised, as goodwill is calculated separately for each transaction, regardless of the average price paid per share to acquire the 100% interest. This accounting treatment has resulted in the creation of additional goodwill of US$1,403 million.

During 2007, the Group has completed a detailed fair value assessment of the assets acquired and recognised goodwill of US$4,555 million, US$446 million more than was recorded at 31 December 2006. As required by IFRS 3, all adjustments made in finalising the acquisition accounting have been presented as if the accounting had been completed on the acquisition date. Accordingly, the additional goodwill recorded as a result of the finalisation of the acquisition accounting is subject to impairment testing at 31 December 2006. This has resulted in an additional impairment charge of US$446 million which, in accordance with IFRS 3, has been recognised in the income statement for the year ended 31 December 2006, increasing the total impairment charge to US$1,824 million. There was no other significant income statement impact arising as a result of finalising the acquisition accounting (refer to note 7).

Profit on sale of available-for-sale financial assets

US$m	2007	2006
Continuing operations:		
Unallocated	–	63
	–	63

Listed shares were sold for a consideration of US$nil in 2007 (2006 US$190 million).

Commentary: This extract presents an income statement and a SORIE. Taken together, they could represent an illustration of a comprehensive income statement. Expenses are analyzed by function: costs of sales and selling and administrative expenses are presented as separate line items.

Note that the company presents:

- net income from continuing and discontinuing operations (which is in line with Canadian GAAP);
- additional columns related to exceptional items; and
- contents of unusual items in its accounting policy note and in details provided in other notes.

None of the disclosures would contradict Canadian GAAP, although presentation of non-GAAP subtotals is not encouraged.

Extract 2(33) – Analysis of expenses by nature

ENI SpA (AR 2007), page 140
Profit and loss account

(€ million)	Note	2005 Total amount	2005 of which with related parties	2006 Total amount	2006 of which with related parties	2007 Total amount	2007 of which with related parties
REVENUES	(29)						
Net sales from operations		73,728	4,535	86,105	3,974	87,256	4,198
Other income and revenues		798		783		827	
Total revenues		**74,526**		**86,888**		**88,083**	
OPERATING EXPENSES	(30)						
Purchases, services and other		48,567	3,429	57,490	2,720	58,179	3,777
- of which non-recurring charge		290		239		91	
Payroll and related costs		3,351		3,650		3,800	
- of which non-recurring income						(83)	
Depreciation, depletion, amortization and impairments		5,781		6,421		7,236	
OPERATING PROFIT		**16,827**		**19,327**		**18,868**	
FINANCE INCOME (EXPENSE)	(31)						
Finance income		3,131	72	4,132	58	4,600	98
Finance expense		(3,497)		(3,971)		(4,683)	59
		(366)		**161**		**(83)**	
INCOME FROM INVESTMENTS	(32)						
Share of profit (loss) of equity-accounted investments		737		795		773	
Other gain (loss) from investments		177		108		470	
		914		**903**		**1,243**	
PROFIT BEFORE INCOME TAXES		**17,375**		**20,391**		**20,028**	
Income taxes	(33)	(8,128)		(10,568)		(9,219)	
Net profit		**9,247**		**9,823**		**10,809**	
Attributable to							
Eni		8,788		9,217		10,011	
Minority interest	(27)	459		606		798	
		9,247		**9,823**		**10,809**	
Earnings per share attributable to Eni (€ per share)	(34)						
Basic		2.34		2.49		2.73	
Diluted		2.34		2.49		2.73	

Commentary: Many of the comments raised in the previous extract apply here. One peculiar element of the presentation is the separate disclosures in the columns of related party amounts.

Expenses are analyzed by nature and are detailed in the notes, including the following elements (contents of these notes are not reproduced in the extract):

- operating expenses detailed in Note 30 (pages 210 to 214 of ENI AR 2007), which provides information on the following elements:
  - o purchases, services and other,
  - o payroll and related costs,
  - o average number of employees,
  - o stock-based compensation,
  - o compensation of key management,
  - o compensation of directors and statutory auditors,
  - o depreciation, amortization and impairments.

Note 30 also refer to additional information about changes in operating expenses provided in the "Financial Review" section.

- finance income (expense), detailed in Note 31 (page 215 of ENI AR 2007), which includes tables with the following reconciling items:
  - o income on investments,
  - o financial expense capitalized,
  - o net income from financial receivables,
  - o net income from securities,
  - o interest on tax credits,
  - o income (expense) on derivatives,
  - o exchange differences, net,
  - o net interest due to banks,
  - o net interest due to other financing institutions,
  - o financial expense due to passage of time (accretion discount),
  - o interest and other financial expense on ordinary bonds,
  - o other financial expense, net.

Even though certain elements related to presentation and expense analysis are uncommon under Canadian GAAP, they do not contradict it.

Extract 2(34) – Analysis of expenses by nature and other performance measures

HeidelbergCement Group (AR 2007), page 64 Group profit and loss accounts EUR '000s	Notes	2006*	2007
Turnover	1	7,997,181	**10,862,329**
Change in stock and work in progress		18,722	**-59,197**
Own work capitalised		1,368	**2,018**
Operating revenue		8,017,271	**10,805,150**
Other operating income	2	198,885	**204,973**
Material costs	3	-3,091,257	**-4,114,163**
Employee and personnel costs	4	-1,270,971	**-1,694,260**
Other operating expenses	5	-2,064,082	**-2,824,005**
Operating income before depreciation (OIBD)		1,789,846	**2,377,695**
Depreciation of tangible fixed assets	6	-451,604	**-558,504**
Amortisation of intangible assets	6	-9,408	**-14,363**
Operating income		1,328,834	**1,804,828**
Additional ordinary income	7	209,662	**1,061,762**
Additional ordinary expenses	7	-186,224	**-218,042**
Additional ordinary result		23,438	**843,720**
Result from associated companies 1)	8	185,112	**170,733**
Results from other participations	8	-6,861	**-4,125**
Earnings before interest and taxes (EBIT)		1,530,523	**2,815,156**
Interest and similar income		58,936	**73,663**
Interest and similar expenses		-283,384	**-539,565**
Foreign exchange gains and losses		4,574	**3,387**
Financial result of puttable minorities		-4,768	**-9,192**
Profit before tax		1,305,881	**2,343,449**
Taxes on income	9	-389,586	**-369,073**
Net income from continuing operations		916,295	**1,974,376**
Net income from discontinued operations		110,005	**144,404**
Profit for the financial year		1,026,300	**2,118,780**
Thereof minority interests		-75,629	**-96,998**
Thereof Group share in profit		950,671	**2,021,782**
Thereof proposed dividend	41	144,508	**162,500**
Earnings per share in EUR (IAS 33)			
Earnings per share attributable to the parent entity	10	8.22	**17.11**
Earnings per share - continuing operations		7.29	**15.92**
Earnings per share - discontinued operations		0.93	**1.19**
1) Net result from associated companies		151,955	**126,124**
* Figures have been adjusted following the presentation of maxit Group as discontinued operation (IFRS 5) and are therefore not comparable with the 2006 annual accounts			

HeidelbergCement Group (AR 2007) (continued) page 68 Statement of recognised income and expense		
EUR '000s	2006	**2007**
IAS 39 Financial Instruments: Recognition and Measurement	3,814	**-27,584**
IAS 19 Employee Benefits	5,053	**68,771**
IFRS 3 Business Combinations	32,634	
IAS 32 Financial Instruments: Presentation	-14,653	
Currency translation	-160,786	**-823,997**
Other consolidation adjustments	2,773	**7**
Income and expense directly recognised in equity	-131,165	**-782,803**
Profit for the financial year	1,026,300	**2,118,780**
Total earnings for the period	895,135	**1,335,977**
Relating to minority interests	44,318	**70,124**
Relating to HeidelbergCement AG shareholders	850,817	**1,265,853**
1) Adjustment of profit and loss reserve and minority interests at 1 January 2006		

Commentary: This extract presents an income statement and a SORIE. Taken together, they could represent an illustration of a comprehensive income statement. Expenses are analyzed by nature. Even though nothing prevents such a presentation, it is not frequently found under Canadian GAAP.

The company presents several performance measures by providing subtotals reflecting:

- operating revenues;
- operating income before depreciation (OIBD);
- operating income;
- earnings before interest and tax (EBIT).

OIBD and EBIT are considered to be "non GAAP" performance measures and Canadian regulators might well discourage such disclosures in the financial statements.

Extract 2(35) – Statement of comprehensive income (two-statement format)

Sasol Limited (Financial Results 2008)
income statement

for the year ended 30 June	2008 Rm	2007 Rm
Turnover	**129 943**	98 127
Cost of sales and services rendered	(74 634)	(59 997)
Gross profit	**55 309**	38 130
Non-trading income	635	639
Marketing and distribution expenditure	(6 931)	(5 818)
Administrative expenditure	(6 697)	(6 094)
Other operating expenditure[1]	(8 500)	(1 236)
Other expenditure	(8 800)	(1 004)
Translation gains/(losses)	300	(232)
Operating profit	**33 816**	25 621
Finance income	735	825
Finance expenses	(1 148)	(1 148)
Share of profits of associates (net of tax)	254	405
Profit before tax	**33 657**	25 703
Taxation	(10 129)	(8 153)
Profit for the year	**23 528**	**17 550**
Attributable to		
Owners of Sasol Limited	**22 417**	17 030
Minority interests in subsidiaries	**1 111**	520
	23 528	**17 550**
Earnings per share	**Rand**	**Rand**
Basic earnings per share	**37,30**	27,35
Diluted earnings per share[2]	**36,78**	27,02

1 Included in other operating expenditure is a realised loss of R2 428 million (2007 – unrealised fair value loss of R197 million) that relates to the crude oil hedge, share-based expenditure of R1 782 million (2007 – R190 million), and remeasurement items of R698 million (2007 – R1 140 million positive).

2 Diluted earnings per share is calculated taking the Sasol Share Incentive Scheme and Sasol Inzalo Employee Trusts into account.

statement of comprehensive income

for the year ended 30 June	2008 Rm	2007 Rm
Profit for the year	23 528	17 550
Other comprehensive income		
Effect of translation of foreign operations	3 452	(258)
Effect of cash flow hedges	261	–
Available-for-sale financial assets	(1)	–
Tax on other comprehensive income	(60)	–
Other comprehensive income for the year, net of tax	**3 652**	**(258)**
Total comprehensive income for the year	**27 180**	**17 292**
Attributable to		
Owners of Sasol Limited	26 062	16 772
Minority interests in subsidiaries	1 118	520
	27 180	**17 292**

Commentary: The above extract illustrates early adoption of IAS 1 as amended for a statement of comprehensive income (two-statement format). Expenses are analyzed by function. The company is one of the few that has adopted current IAS 1 early. The extract illustrates one of the presentation alternatives applicable under Canadian GAAP.

Statement of Changes in Equity

IAS 1 requires entities to present a statement of changes in equity showing:

- total comprehensive income for the period, presenting separately the total amounts attributable to owners of the parent company and to any non-controlling interests;

- for each component of equity, the effects of retrospective application or retrospective restatement recognized in accordance with IAS 8;

- for each component of equity, a reconciliation between the carrying amount at the beginning and the end of the period, separately disclosing changes resulting from:

  o profit or loss,

  o each item of other comprehensive income;

  o the amounts of transactions with owners in their capacity as owners, showing separately contributions by and distributions to owners and changes in ownership interests in subsidiaries that do not result in a loss of control.

The amount of dividends recognized as distributions to owners during the period, and the related amount per share, must be presented either in either the statement of changes in equity or the notes.

Basically, both IAS 1 and Canadian GAAP call for the same statement of changes in equity. except that under IFRS non-owner changes in equity, that is comprehensive income, cannot be presented in the statement of equity, they have to be presented in the statement of comprehensive income.

Illustrative Disclosures[15]:

All illustrations below are in line with Canadian GAAP except that, prior to CICA 1602 adoption[16], non-controlling interests would not be presented as an item in the statement of changes in equity but, rather, as an item in the income statement.

Note that "reserves" are presented as part of the statement of changes in equity. Such reserves, which can be established under an entity's capital management policies or under local statutory requirements, are segregated from the retained profits and not available for distribution. Under Canadian GAAP, the term "reserves" is rarely used in practice.

---

15 Because of the changes to IAS 1 that are effective January 1, 2009 there are limited examples of companies that applied the new requirements. Guidance accompanying IAS 1 but not part of it provides illustration of presentation of financial statements including a statement of changes in equity that comply with the new requirements.

16 See footnote 7.

Extract 2(36) – Statement of changes in equity

Sasol Limited (Financial Results 2008), page 2
statement of changes in equity

for the year ended 30 June	2008 Rm	2007 Rm
Opening balance	63 269	52 984
Shares issued during year	387	332
Repurchase of shares	(7 300)	(3 669)
Share-based payment expense	1 574	186
Acquisition of businesses	(100)	–
Change in shareholding of subsidiaries	306	1 165
Total comprehensive income for the year	27 180	17 292
Dividends paid	(5 766)	(4 613)
Dividends paid to minority shareholders	(555)	(408)
Closing balance	**78 995**	**63 269**
Comprising		
Share capital	20 176	3 628
Share repurchase programme	(10 969)	(3 669)
Sasol Inzalo share transaction	(16 161)	–
Retained earnings	77 660	61 109
Share-based payment reserve	2 540	966
Foreign currency translation reserve	3 006	(443)
Investment fair value reserve	1	2
Cash flow hedge accounting reserve	221	24
Shareholders' equity	76 474	61 617
Minority interest	2 521	1 652
Total equity	**78 995**	**63 269**

Commentary: The above extract presents an example of a statement of changes in equity under current IAS 1. This presentation is one of the allowed alternatives under Canadian GAAP.

Extract 2(37) – Statement of changes in equity

ASOS PLC (AR 2008), page 35
Statement of Changes in Equity
For the year ended 31 march 2008

Group	Share capital £'000	Share premium £'000	Retained earnings £'000	Treasury shares £'000	Total £'000
Balance as at 1 April 2007	2,544	3,128	2,949	(236)	8,385
Shares allotted in the year	20	228	—	—	248
Purchase of shares by EBT	—	—	—	(707)	(707)
Share options charge	—	—	477	—	477
Profit for the year	—	—	5,053	—	5,053
Tax on share options	—	—	2,488	—	2,488
Balance as at 31 March 2008	2,564	3,356	10,967	(943)	15,944
Balance as at 1 April 2006	2,517	3,007	(2)	—	5,522
Shares allotted in the year	27	121	—	—	148
Purchase of shares by EBT	—	—	—	(236)	(236)
Share options charge	—	—	328	—	328
Profit for the year	—	—	2,484	—	2,484
Tax on share options	—	—	139	—	139
Balance as at 31 March 2007	2,544	3,128	2,949	(236)	8,385

ASOS PLC (AR 2008) (continued)				
Company	Share capital £'000	Share premium £'000	Restated retained earnings £'000	Total £'000
Balance as at 1 April 2007 as previously reported	2,544	3,128	(4,605)	1,067
Adjustment for share options charge	—	—	554	554
Balance as at 1 April 2007 — restated	2,544	3,128	(4,051)	1,621
Shares allotted in the year	20	228	—	248
Loss for the year	—	—	(120)	(120)
Share options charge	—	—	477	477
Balance as at 31 March 2008	2,564	3,356	(3,694)	2,226
Balance as at 1 April 2006 as previously reported	2,517	3,007	(4,495)	1,029
Adjustment for share options charge	—	—	226	226
Balance as at 1 April 2006 — restated	2,517	3,007	(4,269)	1,255
Shares allotted in the year	27	121	—	148
Loss for the year	—	—	(110)	(110)
Share options charge	—	—	328	328
Balance as at 31 March 2007	2,544	3,128	(4,051)	1,621

Commentary: The above extract shows a SOCIE as required under IAS 1 before the September 2007 amendments. Note, however, that the SOCIE could be an example of a statement of changes in equity required under current IAS 1 since the company did not record any item related to other comprehensive income components. The presentation is an acceptable alternative under Canadian GAAP.

Statement of Cash Flows (Cash Flow Statement)

Key Definitions

The table below defines key IAS 7 items related to the statement of cash-flows. All definitions correspond to those in CICA 1540.

Term	IAS 7 Definition and Characteristics
Cash	• Cash in hand and deposits on demand. • Bank overdrafts that are used as part of an entity's day-to-day cash management tools rather than as financing arrangements (i.e., they regularly fluctuate from a positive balance to overdrawn) are included in the balance of cash (otherwise they are treated as part of the entity's financing).
Cash equivalents	• Short-term, highly liquid investments that are readily convertible to known amounts of cash and are subject to an insignificant risk of changes in value. • Investments with an original maturity of less than three months are considered cash equivalents unless there is doubt that the obligated entity will fully redeem the security at maturity. • The policy for determining which items are treated as cash equivalents should be consistently applied and disclosed.
Cash flows	Inflows and outflows of cash and cash equivalents.
Operating activities	Principal revenue-producing activities of the enterprise and other activities that are not investing or financing activities.
Investing activities	Acquisition and disposal of long-term assets and other investments not included in cash equivalents.
Financing activities	Activities that result in changes in the size and composition of an entity's contributed equity and borrowings.

Cash and Cash Equivalents

Components of cash and cash equivalents and reconciliation of the amounts in the statement of cash flows with the equivalent items in the statements of financial position should be disclosed. Note that under CICA 1540, cash subject to restrictions that prevent its use for current purposes would not be included in cash and cash equivalents whereas this is not specifically addressed by IAS 7. However, both standards require disclosure of significant cash and cash equivalent that are not available for use.

General Structure

According to both IAS 7 and CICA 1540, the following three main headings must be used for all cash flow statements:

- *Operating Cash Flows*, which comprise all cash flows during the period that do not qualify as either investing cash flows or financing cash flows. They are primarily derived from the principal revenue-producing activities of the entity and result from the transactions that enter into the determination of profit or loss such as cash receipts from sales, royalties, commissions, and payments made for purchase of goods and services, insurances, etc.

- *Investing Cash Flows*, which include cash payments to acquire property, plant and equipment and other long-term assets and the cash receipts from their sale. Investing activities also include cash payments and cash receipts related to acquisition and disposal of debt and equity interests in other entities and interests in joint ventures (except for these related to dealing or trading activity). Loans or advances made to other parties are classified as investing activities, as well as the cash receipts and payments related to forwards, futures, option and swaps contracts except if they are for financing purposes or they are held for dealing or trading purposes.

- *Financing Cash Flows*, which include cash flows related to obtaining, servicing and redeeming sources of finance. Those sources of finance can include loans, debentures and share capital.

Establishing Operating Cash Flows

The table below outlines certain requirements for establishing operating cash flows under IFRS and Canadian GAAP.

IFRS Requirements or Application	Related Canadian GAAP Observations
Direct method or indirect method (Note 1)	
Both methods are allowed. Direct method is preferred because the information reported would show gross cash receipts from operations instead of a net income figure (the starting point of indirect method). The indirect method is, however, more commonly used in practice.	Same.
Indirect method – starting point	
Profit or loss (after tax) although illustrative examples in IAS 7 start the reconciliation with "profit before taxation."	Under Canadian GAAP, net income (i.e., profit or loss after tax) is the usual starting point for the application of the indirect method.
Issuance or reimbursement of loans and advances	
Excluded from operating cash flows (except for financial institutions, which carry these activities in the ordinary course of their business).	Same.

IFRS Requirements or Application	Related Canadian GAAP Observations
Interest and dividends paid or received	
Accounting policy choice: classify in a consistent manner from period to period, either as operating, investing or financing activities considering the nature of the underlying cash flows.	Classify as operating activities if included in profit or loss. Otherwise, classify according to their nature (dividends and interest paid and charged to retained earnings must be presented separately as cash flows used in financing activities). Capitalised interest should be classified as investing activities.
Tax cash flows	
Classify as operating cash flows. If, however, specific cash flows can be identified as belonging to either investing activities or financing activities, an entity would classify that element of the tax cash flows as investing or financing, respectively.	Same.
Cash flows relating to derivatives such as futures and forwards	
Classify as operating cash flows unless derivatives are appropriately designated as hedges. In that case, they would be classified as the cash flows of the underlying transaction being hedged.	Same.

Note 1: Direct method, i.e., major classes of gross cash receipts and gross cash payments *or* indirect method, i.e., net profit or loss is adjusted for:

- the effects of transactions of a non-cash nature;
- any differals or accruals of past or future operating cash receipts or payments; and
- items of income or expense pertaining to investing or financing cash flows.

Under the indirect method net cash flows from operating activities may be presented by showing the revenues and expenses disclosed in the statement of comprehensive income and the changes during the period in inventories, receivables and payables.

Netting of Cash Flows

IAS 7 and CICA 1540 require an entity to report separately major classes of gross cash receipts and gross cash payments arising from investing and financing activities. Both standards further state that cash flows may be reported on a net basis *only* for:

- cash receipts and payments on behalf of customers when the cash flows reflect the activities of the customer rather than those of the entity; and
- cash receipts and payments for items in which the turnover is quick, the amounts are large and the maturities are short.

Foreign Currency Cash Flows

Under both IFRS and Canadian GAAP, foreign currency cash flows are translated at the exchange rates in place at the dates of the cash flows. A rate that approximates the actual rate, such as a weighted average rate, may be used instead. Note that the exchange rate at the end of the period cannot be used to translate foreign currency cash flows.

Reconciling differences arise between the changes in cash and cash equivalents as translated in the cash flow statement and the equivalent amounts obtained from the balance sheet. This reconciling difference, which is not a cash flow, is reported separately in the cash flow statement.

Business Acquisitions and Disposals

Under both IFRS and Canadian GAAP, the aggregate cash flows arising from obtaining or losing control of subsidiaries or other businesses must be disclosed separately and classified as an investing cash flow.

The aggregate amount of cash in the entities acquired or disposed of, over which control is obtained or lost, must be disclosed in the notes. In addition, the value of the consideration given or received should also be disclosed in the notes, together with the proportion represented by cash. Note that acquisitions and disposals cannot be aggregated. It is important to note that though IAS 1 requires the disclosure in aggregate only, disclosing cash flows related to each significant acquisition and disposal would increase transparency and would be in the spirit of IFRS.

Cash flows arising from changes in ownership in subsidiaries that do not result in change or a loss of control are classified as financing activities. This is different from CICA 1540 which requires the classification as investing activities whether or not the transaction results in obtaining or losing control of a subsidiary.

Discontinued Operations

IFRS 5 requires that the net cash flows relating to discontinued operations be disclosed and allocated among operating, investing and financing activities. CICA 3475 does not have such a requirement.

Non-cash Transactions

Both IAS 7 and CICA 1540 specify that investing and financing transactions that do not require the use of cash or cash equivalents must be excluded from the cash flow statement. Such transactions must be disclosed in the notes by providing all the relevant information about these activities.

Examples of non-cash transactions include:

- acquisition of assets by means of a finance lease;
- conversion of debt to equity; and
- acquisition of an enterprise by the issuance of equity.

Illustrative Disclosures:

Extract 2(38) – Statement of cash flows and supplemental information

Stora Enso Oyj (AR 2007), pages 116 and 117
Consolidated Cash Flow Statement

		Year Ended 31 December		
EUR million	**Note**	**2005**	**2006**	**2007**
Cash Flow from Operating Activities				
Net profit / (loss) for the period		-107.4	589.2	**-212.4**
Cash Flow from the Statement of Recognised Income & Expense				
Currency derivatives		-26.1	21.7	**-3.7**
Commodity hedges		107.2	-70.2	**11.8**
Net investment equity hedges		-56.0	-10.7	**-4.5**
Reversal of non-cash items:				
Taxes	11	-36.8	42.6	**196.1**
Depreciation, amortisation and impairment charges	13	1 427.7	1 257.7	**1 881.3**
Change in value of biological assets	15	6.7	2.2	**-7.5**
Change in fair value of options & TRS		-0.1	7.9	**23.6**
Share of results of associated companies	16	-67.2	-87.3	**-342.7**
Profits and losses on sale of fixed assets and investments	7	4.8	-201.2	**-36.0**
CTA & Equity hedges expressed	6,7,28	0.2	-5.8	**-138.8**
Net financial income	10	165.3	104.0	**266.2**
Associates company dividends received	16	11.6	5.6	**31.8**
Interest received		29.0	23.4	**21.0**
Interest paid		-175.9	-247.5	**-261.9**
Dividends received	10	4.5	1.3	**0.4**
Other financial items, net		-19.2	-11.5	**-82.4**
Income taxes paid	11	-209.0	-215.4	**-111.6**
Change in net working capital, net of businesses acquired or sold		-386.9	289.0	**-330.9**
Net Cash Provided by Operating Activities		672.4	1 495.0	**899.8**
Cash Flow from Investing Activities				
Acquisition of subsidiary shares	5	-323.9	-329.8	**-71.4**
Acquisition of shares in associated companies	16	-55.7	-19.4	**-91.6**
Acquisition of available-for-sale investments	17	-8.6	-5.2	**-14.3**
Capital expenditure	4, 14	-1 129.6	-559.1	**-770.2**
Investment in biological assets	15	-15.7	-24.3	**-50.2**
Proceeds from disposal of subsidiary shares	5	1.6	466.5	**330.1**
Proceeds from disposal of shares in associated companies	16	-	0.3	**0.4**
Proceeds from disposal of available-for-sale investments	17	97.4	209.1	**15.9**
Proceeds from sale of fixed assets	14	14.5	30.0	**83.5**
Proceeds from (payment of) non-current receivables, net		98.3	-21.3	**17.8**
Net Cash Used in Investing Activities		-1 321.7	-253.2	**-550.0**
Cash Flow from Financing Activities				
Proceeds from new long-term debt		1 258.1	775.4	**289.0**
Repayment of long-term liabilities		-453.0	-550.2	**-799.5**
Proceeds from (payment of) current borrowings, net		518.8	-869.5	**1 145.4**
Dividends paid		-365.3	-354.9	**-354.9**
Minority equity injections less dividends	22	-0.2	6.6	**7.0**
Options exercised		-	-2.0	**-2.4**
Repurchase of own shares	21	-344.7	0.3	**0.3**
Net Cash Used in Financing Activities		613.7	-994.3	**284.9**
Net Increase (Decrease) in Cash and Cash Equivalents		-35.6	247.5	**634.7**
Cash and bank in acquired companies		10.2	1.6	**0.3**
Cash and bank in divested companies		-	-20.2	**-110.8**
Translation adjustment		27.2	-68.8	**45.5**
Cash and cash equivalents at beginning of year		147.7	149.5	**309.6**
Net Cash and Cash Equivalents at Year End		149.5	309.6	**879.3**
Cash and Cash Equivalents at Year End		351.4	609.0	**970.7**
Bank Overdrafts at Year End		-201.9	-299.4	**91.4**
		149.5	309.6	**879.3**

The accompanying Notes are an integral part of these Consolidated Financial Statements.

Stora Enso Oyj (AR 2007) (continued)
Consolidated Cash Flow Statement

Supplemental Cash Flow Information		Year Ended 31 December		
EUR million	Note	2005	2006	2007
Change in Net Working Capital consists of:				
Change in inventories		-254.7	94.3	-245.7
Change in interest-free receivables: Current		-51.4	-0.2	-136.4
Non-current		-3.4	-36.6	18.3
Change in interest-free liabilities: Current		-7.1	35.7	220.8
Non-current		-12.9	105.9	-161.3
Proceeds from (payment of) short-term interest-bearing receivables		-57.4	89.9	-26.6
		-386.9	289.0	-330.9
Acquisition of Group Companies	5			
Cash Flow on Acquisitions				
Purchase consideration on acquisitions		323.9	329.8	71.4
Cash and cash equivalents in acquired companies		-10.2	-1.6	-0.3
		313.7	328.2	71.1
Non-cash Transaction				
Associate shares held	16	4.9	-	-
Total Acquisition Value		318.6	328.2	71.1
Acquired Net Assets				
Operating working capital		171.4	47.3	-9.5
Operating fixed assets	14	388.3	283.1	10.7
Tax liabilities	11	-59.8	1.2	-0.2
Interest-bearing liabilities		-274.6	-4.5	-1.2
Minority interests	22	93.3	1.1	71.3
Total Net Assets Acquired		318.6	328.2	71.1
Disposal of Group Companies	5			
Cash Flow on Disposals				
Cash flow on disposal		1.6	466.5	330.1
Cash and cash equivalents in divested companies		-	-20.2	-110.8
		1.6	446.3	219.3
Non-cash Transaction				
Available-for-Sale securities	17	-	-	377.0
Associate shares	16	-	-	24.7
Minority interest acquired	22	-	-	-30.9
Total Disposal Value		1.6	446.3	590.1
Net Assets Sold				
Operating working capital		-	59.5	-126.0
Operating fixed assets	14	-	172.4	1 695.8
Biological assets	15	-	45.5	84.1
Interest-bearing assets less cash and cash equivalents		1.6	1.2	0.6
Tax liabilities	11	-	-18.0	-49.6
Interest-bearing liabilities		-	-12.0	-1 019.2
Minority interests	22	-	-0.2	-0.6
		1.6	248.4	585.1
Gain on sale	5,7,14	-	197.9	5.0
Total Net Assets Sold		1.6	446.3	590.1

The accompanying Notes are an integral part of these Consolidated Financial Statements

Commentary: The above extract presents (1) a typical example of a statement of cash flows as required under IAS 7 and (2) a detailed schedule that relates to the statement of cash flows that provides information usually included in the notes under both IFRS and Canadian GAAP.

Note that the company has presented three comparative periods; possibly, it is an SEC registrant.

The following items are noteworthy:

- net profit is the starting point for cash flow operating activities;
- cash flows related to derivatives are included in operating activities;
- dividends from associates are included in operating activities;
- tax expense was reversed and taxes paid was included in the cash flow operating activities;
- cash flows from investments activities present distinctly:
  - o acquisition of subsidiary shares,
  - o acquisition of shares in associated companies,
  - o acquisition of available-for-sale investments,
  - o capital expenditures,
  - o investment in biological assets,
  - o proceeds from disposal of subsidiary shares,
  - o proceeds from disposal of shares in associated companies,
  - o proceeds from disposal of available-for-sale investments,
  - o proceeds from sale of fixed assets, and
  - o proceeds from (payment of) non-current receivables, net business acquisitions;
- cash flows from financing activities present distinctly:
  - o proceeds from new long-term debt,
  - o repayment of long-term liabilities,
  - o netted amounts of proceeds from (payment of) current borrowings,
  - o dividends paid,
  - o minority equity injections net of dividends paid to minority interest,
  - o options exercised, and
  - o company's repurchase of its own shares;
- other disclosures within the statement of cash flows include:
  - o cash and bank (i.e., cash equivalent) in acquired companies,
  - o cash and bank (i.e., cash equivalent) in divested companies, and
  - o translation adjustment.

All of the elements noted above are generally in line with CICA 1540, except that the acquisition of biological assets might be labeled differently and interests (borrowings costs) and dividends paid might be classified differently.

Extract 2(39) – Cash flows

Koninklijke Philips Electronics N.V. (AR 2007), page 237

64 Cash from derivatives

The Company has no trading derivatives. A total of EUR 385 million cash was received with respect to foreign exchange derivative contracts related to financing of subsidiaries (in 2006 receipt of EUR 62 million and in 2005 payment of EUR 46 million). Cash flow from interest-related derivatives is part of cash flow from operating activities. During 2007 there was a cash outflow in relation to these derivatives of EUR 2 million (in 2006 EUR 1 million cash outflow).

Commentary: In the above extract, the company specifies that cash flow from interest-related derivatives is part of the cash flow from operating activities. Depending on circumstances (for example, whether the company uses hedge accounting) and the transactions hedged, this classification would conform with Canadian GAAP.

Extract 2(40) – Bank borrowings included in cash

Vodacom Group Plc (AR 2007), page 149 31. CASH AND CASH EQUIVALENTS AT END OF YEAR	2005 Rm	2006 Rm	2007 Rm
Bank and cash balances	2,990.1	3,146.1	771.4
Short-term bank deposit	1,000.0	-	-
Bank borrowings *	(1,817.1)	(1,385.8)	(879.2)
	2,173.0	1,760.3	(107.8)

*   Bank borrowings are regarded as part of the Group's integral cash management system.

The short-term bank deposits at the end of March 31, 2005 earned interest at an effective interest rate of 7.4% and matured on April 1, 2005.

Commentary: The above extract specifies that the company includes bank borrowings, which are considered as an integral part of cash management in cash and cash equivalents. This conforms to Canadian GAAP.

Extract 2(41) – Cash flows statement

Danfoss A/S (AR 2007), page 58 Statement of cash flow As per 31 December mill DKK	Note	Parent Company		Group	
		2006	2007	2006	2007
Operating profit (EBIT). . -	14	-	82	1,601	1,616
Adjustments for non-cash transactions.	23	251	115	614	920
Changes in working capital	24	-37	-53	-399	-837
Cash flow generated from operations before interest		200	-20	1,816	1,699
Financial income		96	194	24	40
Financial expenses		-124	-302	-186	-395
Dividends received.		753	440	59	93
Cash flow from operations before tax		925	312	1,713	1,437
Paid tax		-25	28	-392	-421
Cash flow from operating activities		900	340	1,321	1,016
Acquisition of intangible fixed assets		-55	-100	-121	-238
Acquisition of tangible fixed assets		-180	-257	-1,000	-1,255
Proceeds from sale of tangible fixed assets		18	2	206	94
Acquisition of subsidiaries etc.	25	-1,343	-196	-1,995	-384
Proceeds from disposal of subsidiaries etc.	25	492	67	59	74
Acquisition (-) and sale of other investments etc. . . .	26	-1,555	-575	-169	116
Cash flow from investing activities		**-2,623**	**-1,059**	**-3,020**	**-1,593**
Free cash flow		**-1,723**	**-719**	**-1,699**	**-577**
Financing by non-shareholders:.					
Repayment of (-)/proceeds from interest-bearing debt . .		2,052	943	2,258	708
Financing by shareholders:					
Issuing of shares		10		10	
Repurchase (-)/sale of own shares.		-7	-25	-7	-25
Addition/disposal of minority interest					-43
Dividends paid		-379	-204	-384	-209
Cash flow from financing activities		**1,676**	**714**	**1,877**	**431**
Net change in cash and cash equivalents		**-47**	**-5**	**178**	**-146**
Cash and cash equivalents at 1 January		54	7	736	886
Foreign exchange adj. of cash and cash equivalents .				-28	-21
Cash and cash equivalents at 31 December		7	2	886	719
Specification: Statement of Free cash flow adjusted for acquisition and disposal of subsidiaries etc.					
Free cash flow		-1,723	-719	-1,699	-577
Acquisition of subsidiaries etc.	25	1,343	196	1,995	384
Proceeds from disposal of subsidiaries etc.	25	-492	-67	-59	-74
Purchase and sale of shares and other securities . . .	26	149	-179	159	-156
Free cash flow before M&A		**-723**	**-769**	**396**	**-423**

The cash flow statement cannot be derived on the basis of the annual financial statements alone. As part of the Group's stand-by liquid funds there are unused long-term binding credit facilities of approximately 3.9 bn DKK (2006: 2.7 bn).

Commentary: In the above extract, the company's starting amounts is a non-GAAP amount (EBIT). This would not be compatible with Canadian GAAP as the starting figure should be net income.

Extract 2(42) – Cash flows statement

Dragon Mining Limited (AR 2007), page 42
STATEMENT OF CASH FLOWS FOR THE PERIOD ENDED 31 DECEMBER 2007

	Note	Consolidated Entity 12 months to 31 Dec 2007 $'000	6 months to 31 Dec 2006 $'000	Parent Entity 12 months to 31 Dec 2007 $'000	6 months to 31 Dec 2006 $'000
Cash flows from operating activities					
Receipts from customers		42,250	16,528	-	-
Payments to suppliers and employees		(36,600)	(13,076)	(1,831)	(1,083)
Interest received		524	278	333	229
Interest expenses		(2,463)	(1,375)	(2,486)	(1,245)
Payment of government security		(589)	(236)	-	-
Net Operating Cash Flows	4	3,122	2,119	(3,984)	(2,099)
Cash flows from investing activities					
Payments for property, plant and equipment		(1,409)	(2,039)	(4)	(9)
Proceeds from sale of property, plant and equipment		413	34	2	-
Proceeds from sale of Pompously gold project		-	9,279	-	-
Proceeds from sale of shares		2,051	-	-	-
Payment for exploration, evaluation and development expenditure capitalised		(12,934)	(6,437)	-	-
Advances to controlled entities		-	-	(30,894)	(3,721)
(Loans to) / repayments from other entities		734	(734)	734	(734)
Net Investing Cash Flows		(11,145)	103	(30,162)	(4,464)
Cash flows from financing activities					
Proceeds from issue of shares		33,384	-	33,384	-
Share issue costs		(1,573)	-	(1,573)	-
Partial close-out of hedge book		(26,895)	-	-	-
Purchase of call option		(275)	-	-	-
Repayment of bank loans		(187)	(3,280)	-	-
Net Financing Cash Flows		4,454	(3,280)	31,811	-
Net decrease in cash and cash equivalents		(3,569)	(1,058)	(2,335)	(6,563)
Cash and cash equivalents at the beginning of the period		11,553	12,627	4,783	11,346
Effects of exchange rate changes on cash and cash equivalents		(9)	(16)	143	-
Cash and cash equivalents at the end of the period	4	7,975	11,553	2,591	4,783

Commentary: The above extract illustrates the application of the direct method, which is the preferred presentation under both IAS 7 and CICA 1540.

Note Disclosures

Objective

The objective of the notes is to assist users in understanding how transactions, other events and conditions are reflected in a company's reported financial performance and financial position. The notes to the financial statements typically report the following under both IFRS and Canadian GAAP:

- general information related to an entity;
- basis of the financial statements preparation;
- significant accounting policies;

- supporting information for items presented in the primary financial statements; and

- key sources of uncertainties, including contingencies, commitments and financial risks.

Contents

The emphasis on transparency in IAS 1 and other IFRS standards have prompted entities to provide significant disclosures in their notes. Even though Canadian GAAP, in particular the requirements of CICA 1400, might ask for equivalent disclosures, they are relatively brief and do not address in detail the issues raised in IAS 1. This could result in more detailed notes under IFRS than under Canadian GAAP.

IAS 1 discusses in detail disclosures in the notes related to:

- accounting policies (measurement basis and other accounting policies);

- sources of estimation uncertainty;

- capital; and

- other issues.

The table below presents a summary of IAS 1 general disclosure requirements that would be in line with Canadian GAAP (CICA 1400, CICA 1505, CICA 1506 and CICA 1508) unless specifically noted. In addition to the disclosure requirements indicated below, each IFRS standard and related Canadian standard contain specific disclosures requirements that are not presented in the table (see chapters covering the specific topic).

Specific Disclosure Requirements and Observations
Measurement Basis used and Other Accounting Policies
• Measurement basis must be disclosed (e.g., historical cost, current cost, net realizable value, fair value or recoverable amount) by specifying measurement model used for each category of assets and liabilities.
• When an entity uses more than one measurement model in the financial statements (e.g., when particular classes of assets are revalued), it is sufficient to provide an indication of the categories of assets and liabilities to which each measurement basis is applied.
• Other accounting policies that are relevant to understanding the financial statements should be disclosed.
Judgment when Selecting an Accounting Policy (Note 1)
IAS 1 requires disclosure of management judgment on accounting policies that could significantly affect amounts recognized in the financial statements (in addition to, not limited to those involving estimation). Examples of such judgments arise when determining:
• whether financial assets are held-to-maturity investments;
• when substantially all of the significant risks and rewards of ownership of financial assets and lease assets are transferred to other entities;
• whether, in substance, particular sales of goods are financing arrangements and, therefore, do not give rise to revenue; and
• whether the substance of a relationship between an entity and a special purpose entity indicates that the special purpose entity is controlled by the entity.

Specific Disclosure Requirements and Observations

Accounting Policies (Specific Requirements)

Disclosure is required when:
- policies are selected from alternatives allowed by IFRS;
- users of an entity's financial statements expect it (type of entity, nature of its operations); and
- an entity selects an accounting policy, which is not specifically required by an IFRS standard, and applies it in accordance with IAS 8, which requires that:
  - o management develops accounting policies that result in relevant and reliable financial statements,
  - o the appropriate recognition, measurement and presentation policies must be developed from (in descending order)analogy with similar requirements in IFRS, the IASB Framework, and recent pronouncements of other standard setting bodies with similar framework, other accounting literature and accepted industry practices that do not conflict with IFRS and its framework.

IAS 1 and IAS 8 elaborate on the requirements above:
- IAS 1 indicates that an accounting policy may be significant because of the nature of the entity's operations even if amounts for current and prior periods are not material.
- IAS 8 specifies that when standards provide a choice of accounting policy, an entity must choose and apply consistently one of the available accounting policies. Once adopted, an accounting policy cannot be changed unless it is required by statute or by a standard-setting body, or if the change is to a more relevant or reliable alternative.

Sources of Estimation Uncertainty

An entity must disclose the nature and carrying amount of the specific asset or liability (or class of assets or liabilities) affected by management assumptions or other source of estimation uncertainty at the end of a reporting period. It should also disclose the assumptions and other sources of measurement uncertainties related to the estimates that require management's most difficult, subjective or complex judgments.

Determining the carrying amounts of some assets and liabilities requires estimating the effects of uncertain future events on those assets and liabilities at the end of the reporting period, and therefore making assumptions about risk, discount rates, future cash flows, future changes in prices, salaries, etc. Examples of such situations include the measurement of:
- fair value in absence of recently observed market prices;
- inventories' carrying value in light of technological obsolescence;
- provisions that are subject to the future outcome of litigation in progress; and
- long-term employee benefit liabilities, such as pension obligations.

The nature and extent of the information provided vary according to the nature of the assumptions and other circumstances. Examples of the types of disclosures an entity makes are:
- the nature of the assumption or other estimation uncertainty;
- the sensitivity of carrying amounts to the methods, assumptions and estimates underlying their calculation, including the reasons for the sensitivity;
- the expected resolution of an uncertainty and the range of reasonably possible outcomes within the next financial year in respect of the carrying amounts of the assets and liabilities affected; and
- an explanation of changes made to past assumptions concerning those assets and liabilities, if the uncertainty remains unresolved.

When it is impracticable to disclose the extent of the possible effects of an assumption or another source of estimation uncertainty at the end of a reporting period, an entity must disclose that it is reasonably possible, on the basis of existing knowledge, that outcomes within the next financial year that are different from the assumption could require a material adjustment to the carrying amount of the asset or liability affected.

Note that IAS 1 does not require an entity to disclose:
- information on its budget or forecasts;
- the fact that the fair value of an asset carried at recently observed market prices will change within the next financial year as changes in fair values do not arise from assumptions or other sources of estimation uncertainty at the end of the reporting period.

Specific Disclosure Requirements and Observations

Capital Management (Note 2)

An entity must disclose information that enables users of its financial statements to evaluate the entity's objectives, policies and processes for managing capital.

More specifically, IAS 1 requires that the following information be provided (based on the information provided internally to key management personnel):

- qualitative information about its objectives, policies and processes for managing capital, including:
  - o a description of what it manages as capital,
  - o when an entity is subject to externally imposed capital requirements, the nature of those requirements and how those requirements are incorporated into the management of capital, and
  - o how it is meeting its objectives for managing capital;
- summary quantitative data about what it manages as capital. Some entities regard some financial liabilities (e.g., some forms of subordinated debt) as part of capital. Other entities regard capital as excluding some components of equity (e.g., components arising from cash flow hedges);
- any changes in qualitative information or quantitative data used for capital management from the previous period;
- whether during the period it complied with any externally imposed capital requirements to which it is subject; and
- when the entity has not complied with such externally imposed capital requirements, the consequences of such non-compliance.

Specific qualitative and quantitative disclosures about puttable financial instruments classified as equity are required.

Note that IAS 1 requires an entity to disaggregate capital information when an aggregate disclosure on capital does not provide useful information or distorts a financial statement user's understanding of an entity's capital resources.

Other Disclosures (Note 3)

IAS 1 requires the following specific disclosures in the notes:

- an explicit and unreserved statement of compliance with IFRS. An entity shall not describe financial statements as complying with IFRSs unless they comply with all the requirements of IFRSs;
- amount of dividends proposed or declared before the financial statements were authorized for issue but not recognized as a distribution to owners during the period, and the related amount per share; and
- amount of any cumulative preference dividends not recognized.

In addition, IAS 1 requires an entity to disclose the following (if not disclosed elsewhere in information published with the financial statements):

- domicile and legal form of the entity, its country of incorporation and the address of its registered office (or principal place of business, if different from the registered office);
- brief description of the nature of the entity's operations and its principal activities. This should include information about the industry(ies) in which it operates, the products or services it offers, the nature of its customers, its distribution methods and the nature of the regulatory environment, if relevant;
- name of the parent and the ultimate parent of the group; and
- information on the length of the life of a limited life entity.

IAS 10 requires entities to disclose the date when the financial statements were authorized for issue and who gave that authorization. If the enterprise's owners or others have the power to amend the financial statements after issuance, the enterprise should disclose that fact.

Note 1: Canadian GAAP does not require that judgment on the selection of accounting policy be disclosed.

Note 2: Entities must apply this IAS 1 requirement for annual periods beginning on or after January 1, 2009. CICA 1535 has essentially the same requirements, which apply to interim and annual financial statements for fiscal years beginning on or after October 1, 2007.

Note 3: Most of the information described must also be disclosed as it is also required either by Canadian GAAP or by the Canadian Securities Administrators (CSA).

The Structure and presentation of the notes are discussed in the section "Format of Financial Statements" at the beginning of the chapter.

Illustrative Disclosures:

Extract 2(43) – Compliance with IFRS, Basis of presentation and entity information

Enel SpA (AR 2007), page 124

1. Accounting policies and measurement criteria (in part)

Enel SpA, which operates in the energy utility sector, has its registered office in Rome, Italy. The consolidated financial statements of the Company for the year ending December 31, 2007 comprise the financial statements of the Company and its subsidiaries ("the Group") and the Group's holdings in associated companies and joint ventures. A list of the subsidiaries included in the scope of consolidation is reported in the annex. These financial statements were approved for publication by the Board on March 12, 2008.

Compliance with IFRS/IAS

The consolidated financial statements for the year ended December 31, 2007 have been prepared in accordance with international accounting standards (International Accounting Standards, IAS) or International Financial Reporting Standards (IFRS), the interpretations of the International Financial Reporting Interpretations Committee (IFRIC) and the Standing Interpretations Committee (SIC) endorsed by the European Union (hereinafter, "IFRS-EU"), as well as with measures issued in implementation of Article 9, paragraph 3, of Legislative Decree 38 of February 28, 2005.

Basis of presentation

The consolidated financial statements consist of the consolidated balance sheet, the consolidated income statement, the consolidated statement of cash flows, the consolidated statement of recognized income and expenses for the period and the related notes. The assets and liabilities reported in the consolidated balance sheet are classified on a "current/non-current basis", with separate reporting of assets and liabilities held for sale. Current assets, which include cash and cash equivalents, are assets that are intended to be realized, sold or consumed during the normal operating cycle of the company or in the twelve months following the balance-sheet date; current liabilities are liabilities that are expected to be settled during the normal operating cycle of the company or within the twelve months following the close of the financial year.

The consolidated income statement is classified on the basis of the nature of costs, while the indirect method is used for the cash flow statement.

The consolidated financial statements are presented in euro, the functional currency of the Parent Company Enel SpA. All figures are shown in millions of euro unless stated otherwise. The financial statements are prepared using the cost method, with the exception of items that are measured at fair value under IFRS-EU, as specified in the measurement policies for the individual items.

Commentary: The above extract presents:

- general information on the entity;
- a statement of compliance with IFRS;
- basis of presentation including:
  - "current/non-current" classification on balance sheet,
  - classification of expenses according to their nature of costs,
  - indirect method used for the cash flow statement,
  - fact that the Euro is the functional currency of the parent company and presentation currency, and
  - cost method, with the exception of items that are measured at fair value under IFRS, as specified in the measurement policies for the individual items.

None of the disclosures contradict Canadian GAAP.

Extract 2(44) – Compliance with IFRS note

Wolters Kluwer nv (AR 2007), page 90

STATEMENT OF COMPLIANCE

The consolidated financial statements have been prepared in accordance with International Financial Reporting Standards (IFRS) and its interpretations including International Accounting Standards (IAS) prevailing per December 31, 2007, as adopted by the International Accounting Standards Board (IASB) and as endorsed for use in the European Union by the European Commission. If non-IFRS compliant terminology is used in these financial statements, reference is made to Glossary.

Commentary: In the above extract, the company provides a note on its compliance with IFRS. Canadian GAAP does not require an equivalent statement in the notes.

Extract 2(45) – Note on measurement uncertainties

Dragon Mining Limited (AR 2007), page 50

1. SUMMARY OF SIGNIFICANT ACCOUNTING POLICIES (in part)

(ac) Significant Accounting Judgments, Estimates and Assumptions (in part)

(iv) Impairment of assets

The recoverable amount of each Cash Generating Unit (CGU) is determined as the higher of value in use and fair value less costs to sell.

Given the nature of the consolidated entity's mining activities, future changes in long term assumptions upon which these estimates are based, may give rise to material adjustments to the carrying value of the CGU. This could lead to a reversal of part, or all, of impairment losses recorded in the year to 31 December 2007, or the recognition of additional impairment losses in the future (refer to note 31 for details of impairment losses). The inter-relationships of the significant assumptions upon which estimated future cash flows are based, however, are such that it is impractical to disclose the extent of the possible effects of a change in a key assumption in isolation. Due to the nature of the assumptions and their significance to the assessment of the recoverable amount of each CGU, relatively modest changes in one or more assumptions could require a material adjustment to the carrying value of the related non-current assets within the next reporting period.

Write-downs of loans to controlled entities are based upon the net assets of the Company's subsidiaries.

Commentary: The above extract illustrates a note disclosure on measurement uncertainties related to asset impairment. This is in line with both IFRS and Canadian GAAP except that, under the latter, impairment would not be tested at CGU but rather at the reporting unit or assets group level.

Extract 2(46) – Note on critical accounting estimates and related assumptions and uncertainties

Deutsche Telekom AG (AR 2007), pages 130-133

Measurement uncertainties.

The presentation of the results of operations, financial position or cash flows in the consolidated financial statements is dependent upon and sensitive to the accounting policies, assumptions and estimates. The actual amounts may differ from those estimates. The following critical accounting estimates and related assumptions and uncertainties inherent in accounting policies applied are essential to understand the underlying financial reporting risks and the effects that these accounting estimates, assumptions and uncertainties have on the consolidated financial statements.

Measurement of **property, plant and equipment, and intangible assets** involves the use of estimates for determining the fair value at the acquisition date, provided they were acquired in a business combination. Furthermore, the expected useful lives of these assets must be estimated. The determination of the fair values of assets and liabilities, as well as of the useful lives of the assets is based on management's judgment.

Deutsche Telekom AG (AR 2007) (continued)

The **determination of impairments of property, plant and equipment, and intangible assets** involves the use of estimates that include, but are not limited to, the cause, timing and amount of the impairment. Impairment is based on a large number of factors, such as changes in current competitive conditions, expectations of growth in the mobile communications industry, increased cost of capital, changes in the future availability of financing, technological obsolescence, discontinuance of services, current replacement costs, prices paid in comparable transactions and other changes in circumstances that indicate an impairment exists. The recoverable amount and the fair values are typically determined using the discounted cash flow method which incorporates reasonable market participant assumptions. The identification of impairment indicators, as well as the estimation of future cash flows and the determination of fair values for assets (or groups of assets) require management to make significant judgments concerning the identification and validation of impairment indicators, expected cash flows, applicable discount rates, useful lives and residual values. Specifically, the estimation of cash flows underlying the fair values of the mobile businesses considers the continued investment in network infrastructure required to generate future revenue growth through the offering of new data products and services, for which only limited historical information on customer demand is available. If the demand for these products and services does not materialize as expected, this would result in less revenue, less cash flow and potential impairment to write down these investments to their fair values, which could adversely affect future operating results.

The **determination of the recoverable amount of a cash-generating unit** involves the use of estimates by management. Methods used to determine the fair value less costs to sell include discounted cash flow-based methods and methods that use quoted stock market prices as a basis. Key assumptions on which management has based its determination of fair value less costs to sell include ARPU, subscriber acquisition and retention costs, churn rates, capital expenditure and market share. These estimates, including the methodologies used, can have a material impact on the fair value and ultimately the amount of any goodwill impairment.

Financial assets include equity investments in foreign telecommunications service providers that are principally engaged in the mobile, fixed-network, Internet and data communications businesses, some of which are publicly traded and have highly volatile share prices. As a rule, an investment impairment loss is recorded when an investment's carrying amount exceeds the present value of its estimated future cash flows. The calculation of the present value of estimated future cash flows and the determination of whether an impairment is permanent involve judgment and rely heavily on an assessment by management regarding the future development prospects of the investee. In measuring impairments, quoted market prices are used, if available, or other valuation parameters, based on information available from the investee. To determine whether an impairment is permanent, the Company considers the ability and intent to hold the investment for a reasonable period of time sufficient for a forecasted recovery of fair value up to (or beyond) the carrying amount, including an assessment of factors such as the length of time and magnitude of the excess of carrying value over market value, the forecasted results of the investee, the regional geographic economic environment and state of the industry. Future adverse changes in market conditions, particularly a downturn in the telecommunications industry or poor operating results of investees, could result in losses or an inability to recover the carrying amount of the investments that may not be reflected in an investment's current carrying amount. This could result in impairment losses, which could adversely affect future operating results.

Management maintains an **allowance for doubtful accounts** to account for estimated losses resulting from the inability of customers to make required payments. When evaluating the adequacy of an allowance for doubtful accounts, management bases its estimates on the aging of accounts receivable balances and historical write-off experience, customer credit worthiness and changes in customer payment terms. If the financial condition of customers were to deteriorate, actual write-offs might be higher than expected.

Deutsche Telekom AG (AR 2007) (continued)

Income taxes must be estimated for each of the jurisdictions in which the Group operates, involving a specific calculation of the expected actual income tax exposure for each tax object and an assessment of temporary differences resulting from the different treatment of certain items for IFRS consolidated financial and tax reporting purposes. Any temporary differences will generally result in the recognition of deferred tax assets and liabilities in the consolidated financial statements. Management judgment is required for the calculation of actual and deferred taxes. Deferred tax assets are recognized to the extent that their utilization is probable. The utilization of deferred tax assets will depend on whether it is possible to generate sufficient taxable income in the respective tax type and jurisdiction, taking into account any legal restrictions on the length of the loss-carryforward period. Various factors are used to assess the probability of the future utilization of deferred tax assets, including past operating results, operational plans, loss-carryforward periods, and tax planning strategies. If actual results differ from these estimates or if these estimates must be adjusted in future periods, results of operations, the financial position, and cash flows may be negatively affected. In the event that the assessment of future utilization of deferred tax assets changes, the recognized deferred tax assets must be reduced and this reduction be recognized in profit or loss.

Pension obligations for benefits to non-civil servants are generally satisfied by plans which are classified and accounted for as defined benefit plans. Pension benefit costs for non-civil servants are determined in accordance with actuarial valuations which rely on assumptions including discount rates, life expectancies and, to a limited extent, expected return on plan assets. Estimations of the expected return on plan assets have a limited impact on pension cost. Other key assumptions for pension costs are based in part on actuarial valuations, which rely on assumptions, including discount rates used to calculate the amount of the pension obligation. The assumptions concerning the expected return on plan assets are determined on a uniform basis, considering long-term historical returns, asset allocation and future estimates of long-term investment returns. In the event that further changes in assumptions are required with respect to discount rates and expected returns on invested assets, the future amounts of the pension benefit costs may be affected materially.

Deutsche Telekom is obligated, under the German Federal Posts and Telecommunications Agency Reorganization Act (Gesetz zur Reorganisation der Bundesanstalt fur Post und Telekommunikation Deutsche Bundespost), to pay for its share of any operating cost shortfalls between the income of the **Civil Service Health Insurance Fund** (Postbeamtenkrankenkasse) and benefits paid. The Civil Service Health Insurance Fund provides services mainly in cases of illness, birth, or death for its members, who are civil servants employed by or retired from Deutsche Telekom AG, Deutsche Post AG and Deutsche Postbank AG, and their relatives. When Postreform II came into effect, participation in the Civil Service Health Insurance Fund was closed to new members. The insurance premiums collected by the Civil Service Health Insurance Fund may not exceed the insurance premiums imposed by alternative private health insurance enterprises for comparable insurance benefits, and, therefore, do not reflect the changing composition of ages of the participants in the fund. Deutsche Telekom recognizes provisions in the amount of the actuarially determined present value of Deutsche Telekom's share in the fund's future deficit, using a discount rate and making assumptions about life expectancies and projections for contributions and future increases in general health care costs in Germany. Since the calculation of these provisions involves long-term projections over periods of more than 50 years, the present value of the liability may be highly sensitive even to small variations in the underlying assumptions.

Deutsche Telekom exercises considerable judgment in measuring and recognizing **provisions** and the exposure to **contingent liabilities** related to pending litigation or other outstanding claims subject to negotiated settlement, mediation, arbitration or government regulation, as well as other contingent liabilities. Judgment is necessary in assessing the likelihood that a pending claim will succeed, or a liability will arise, and to quantify the possible range of the final settlement. Provisions are recorded for liabilities when losses are expected from executory contracts, a loss is considered probable and can be reasonably estimated. Because of the inherent uncertainties in this evaluation process, actual losses may be different from the originally estimated provision. In addition, significant estimates are involved in the determination of provisions related to taxes, environmental liabilities and litigation risks. These estimates are subject to change as new information becomes available, primarily with the support of internal specialists, if available, or with the support of outside consultants, such as actuaries or legal counsel. Revisions to the estimates of these losses from executory contracts may significantly affect future operating results.

Deutsche Telekom AG (AR 2007) (continued)

Revenue recognition.

Customer activation fees. The operating segments Mobile Communications Europe, Mobile Communications USA and Broadband/Fixed Network receive installation and activation fees from new customers. These fees (and related directly attributable external costs) are deferred and amortized over the expected duration of the customer relationship. The estimation of the expected average duration of the relationship is based on historical customer turnover. If management's estimates are revised, material differences may result in the amount and timing of revenue for any period.

Service contracts. T-Systems conducts a portion of its business under long-term contracts with customers. Under these contracts, revenue is recognized as performance progresses. Contract progress is estimated. Depending on the methodology used to determine contract progress, these estimates may include total contract costs, remaining costs to completion, total contract revenues, contract risks and other judgments. All estimates involved in such long-term contracts are subject to regular reviews and adjusted as necessary.

Multiple-element arrangements. The framework of the Emerging Issues Task Force Issue No. 00-21 was adopted to account for multiple-element arrangements in accordance with IAS 8.12. EITF 00-21 requires that arrangements involving the delivery of bundled products or services be separated into individual units of accounting, each with its own separate earnings process. Total arrangement consideration relating to the bundled contract is allocated among the different units based on their relative fair values (i.e., the relative fair value of each of the accounting units to the aggregated fair value of the bundled deliverables). The determination of fair values is complex, because some of the elements are price sensitive and, thus, volatile in a competitive marketplace. Revisions to the estimates of these relative fair values may significantly affect the allocation of total arrangement consideration among the different accounting units, affecting future operating results.

Commentary: The above extract presents critical accounting estimates and related assumptions and uncertainties on:

- measurement of property, plant and equipment and intangible assets (determining the fair value at acquisition and estimating expected useful lives);
- determination of impairments of property, plant and equipment, and intangible assets (use of estimates that includes cause, timing and amount of the impairment);
- financial assets measurement, including impairment loss recognition considerations;
- allowance for doubtful accounts valuation issue;
- income taxes estimation including deferred tax assets;
- employee benefits estimates (note that the company specifies that, since the calculation of the estimates involves long-term projections over periods of more than 50 years, the present value of the liability may be highly sensitive to even small variations in the underlying assumptions);
- provisions and the exposure to contingent liabilities related to pending litigation or other outstanding claims subject to negotiated settlement, mediation, arbitration or government regulation, as well as other contingent liabilities. Company specifies that significant estimates are involved in the determination of provisions related to taxes, environmental liabilities and litigation risks.

In addition, the company describes its revenue recognition accounting policy, specifying measurement uncertainties related to:

- contract progress (which is subject to regular reviews and adjusted as necessary); and
- multiple-element arrangements (for which determination of fair value of the accounting units is complex, because some of the elements are price sensitive and, thus, volatile in a competitive marketplace).

All above disclosures would not contradict Canadian GAAP.

Extract 2(47) – Management judgments on accounting policies

> **Barloworld Limited (AR 2007), pages 161 and 162**
>
> **44. Judgements made by management**
>
> Preparing financial statements in conformity with IFRS requires estimates and assumptions that affect reported amounts and related disclosures. Actual results could differ from these estimates.
>
> Certain accounting policies have been identified as involving particularly complex or subjective judgements or assessments, as follows:
>
> - *Derecognition of finance lease receivables*
>   The finance lease receivables book in the United Kingdom materials handling business was sold during the year. Management assessed that the significant risks and rewards of the book were transferred to the purchaser and the asset was derecognised.
>
> - *Asset lives and residual values*
>   Property, plant and equipment is depreciated over its useful life taking into account residual values, where appropriate. The actual lives of the assets and residual values are assessed annually and may vary depending on a number of factors. In reassessing asset lives, factors such as technological innovation, product life cycles and maintenance programmes are taken into account. Residual value assessments consider issues such as future market conditions, the remaining life of the asset and projected disposal values.
>
> - *Deferred taxation assets*
>   Deferred tax assets are recognised to the extent it is probable that taxable income will be available in future against which they can be utilised. Five-year business plans are prepared annually and approved by the boards of the company and its major operating subsidiaries. These plans include estimates and assumptions regarding economic growth, interest rates, inflation and competitive forces.
>
>   The plans contain profit forecasts and cash flows and these are utilised in the assessment of the recoverability of deferred tax assets. Deferred tax assets are also recognised on STC credits to the extent it is probable that future dividends will utilise these credits.
>
>   Management also exercises judgement in assessing the likelihood that business plans will be achieved and that the deferred tax assets are recoverable.
>
> - *Post-employment benefit obligations*
>   Post-retirement defined benefits are provided for certain existing and former employees. Actuarial valuations are based on assumptions which include employee turnover, mortality rates, the discount rate, the expected long-term rate of return of retirement plan assets, healthcare inflation cost and rates of increase in compensation costs.
>
>   Judgement is exercised by management, assisted by advisors, in adjusting mortality rates to take account of actual mortality rates within the schemes.
>
> - *Warranty claims*
>   Warranties are provided on certain equipment, spare parts and service supplied to customers. Management exercises judgement in establishing provisions required on the basis of claims notified and past experience.
>
> - *Revenue recognition*
>   The percentage of completion method is utilised to recognise revenue on long-term contracts. Management exercises judgement in calculating the deferred revenue reserve which is based on the anticipated cost of repairs over the life cycle of the equipment applied to the total expected revenue arising from maintenance and repair contracts.
>
>   In addition, management exercises judgement in assessing whether significant risks and rewards have been transferred to the customer to permit revenue to be recognised.
>
>   In cases where there is a buy-back, management considers whether the buy-back is set at a level which makes the buy-back substantive. If so, management uses the guidance from IAS 18 with regard to the transfer of risks and rewards for the purposes of revenue recognition. If the buy-back is not considered to be substantive, then it is ignored for the purposes of revenue recognition. If revenue is recognised on a transaction which includes a buy-back, then provision is made on the basis set out in repurchase commitments below as and when such provision is required.

Barloworld Limited (AR 2007) (continued)

- *Impairment of assets*

  Goodwill is considered for impairment at least annually. Property, plant and equipment, and intangible assets are considered for impairment if there is a reason to believe that an impairment may be necessary. Factors taken into consideration in reaching such a decision include the economic viability of the asset itself and where it is a component of a larger economic unit, the viability of that unit itself.

  Future cash flows expected to be generated by the assets or cash-generating units are projected, taking into account market conditions and the expected useful lives of the assets. The present value of these cash flows, determined using an appropriate discount rate, is compared to the current net asset value and, if lower, the assets are impaired to the present value. The impairment loss is first allocated to goodwill and then to the other assets of a cash-generating unit.

  Cash flows which are utilised in these assessments are extracted from formal five-year business plans which are updated annually. The company utilises the CFROI® valuation model to determine asset and cash-generating unit values supplemented, where appropriate, by discounted cash flow and other valuation techniques.

- *Repurchase commitments*

  Buy-back (repurchase) arrangements with customers are periodically concluded. The likelihood of the repurchase commitments being exercised and quantification of the possible loss, if any, on resale of the equipment is assessed at the inception of the contract and at each reporting period. Significant assumptions are made in estimating residual values. These are assessed based on past experience and take into account expected future market conditions and projected disposal values.

45. Sources of estimation uncertainty

There are no significant assumptions made concerning the future or other sources of estimation uncertainty that has been identified as giving rise to a significant risk of causing a material adjustment to the carrying amount of assets and liabilities within the next financial year.

Commentary: The above extract presents an example of note disclosures on accounting policies and measurement that the company identified as involving particularly complex or subjective judgments or assessments. These policies covered:

- derecognition of finance lease receivables;
- asset lives and residual values;
- deferred taxation assets;
- post-employment benefit obligations;
- warranty claims;
- revenue recognition (including judgment in assessing whether significant risks and rewards were transferred);
- impairment of assets;
- repurchase commitments.

Note that the company specifically states that it made no significant assumptions about the future or other sources of estimation uncertainty that gave rise to a significant risk of causing a material adjustment to the carrying amount of the assets and liabilities within the next financial year.

All the disclosures are consistent with Canadian GAAP except that judgments on accounting policy choices and risks of material adjustment to the carrying amount of assets and liabilities within the next financial year would normally be disclosed in the MD&A.

Extract 2(48) – Bases of selection of accounting policies

Royal & Sun Alliance Insurance Group plc (AR 2007), page 62
Significant accounting policies (in part)
Selection of accounting policies

The Group exercises judgement in selecting each Group accounting policy. The accounting policies of the Group are selected by the directors to present financial statements that they consider provide the most relevant information. For certain accounting policies there are different accounting treatments that could be adopted, each of which would be in compliance with IFRS and would have a significant influence upon the basis on which the financial statements are presented. The bases of selection of the accounting policies for the accounting for financial assets and for the recognition of actuarial gains and losses related to pension obligations are set out below:

- The Group designates financial assets that are held as investments on the basis on which the investment return is managed and the performance is evaluated internally. Where the investment return is managed on the basis of the periodic cashflows arising from the investment, a financial asset is designated as an available for sale financial asset with unrealised gains recognised in the statement of recognised income and expense. Where the investment return is managed on the basis of the total return on the investment (including unrealised investment gains), the financial asset is designated as at fair value through the income statement.

- The Group accounting policy is to recognise actuarial gains and losses arising from the recognition and funding of the Group's pension obligations in the statement of recognised income and expense during the period in which they arise. This policy has been adopted as it provides the most relevant basis of recognition of such gains and losses.

Commentary: The above extract presents an example of note disclosures related to judgment in selecting an accounting policy. This extract is part of a detailed note covering the following accounting policies implemented by the company (pages 62 to 69 not reproduced above):

- consolidated financial statements;
- changes in presentation and comparative information;
- selection of accounting policies (reproduced above);
- consolidation:
  - subsidiaries,
  - associates;
- translation of foreign currencies;
- goodwill and other intangible assets;
- property and equipment;
- investment property;
- financial assets;
- derivative financial instruments;
- hedging;
- estimation of the fair value of financial assets and liabilities;
- insurance contracts:
  - product classification,
  - recognition of income,
  - acquisition costs,
  - insurance liabilities,
  - reinsurance ceded;
- cash and cash equivalents;
- treasury shares;
- loan capital;
- taxation;
- employee benefits:
  - pension obligations,

- o   post-retirement benefits (including pension schemes and post retirement health schemes),
- o   termination benefits,
- o   share-based payments;
- provisions;
- dividends to equity holders;
- leases;
- operating segments;
- non-current and disposal group assets and liabilities held for sale and discontinued operations;
- current and non-current distinction;
- recently issued accounting pronouncements:
  - o   published standards and amendments to published standards that are not yet effective and have not been adopted early,
  - o   other standards and interpretations for published standards that are not relevant for the group's operations or are not expected to change accounting policies.

In addition, the company included a section on "Estimation techniques, uncertainties and contingencies" (pages 70 to 72) which covers:

- an introduction;
- estimation techniques;
- uncertainties and contingencies;
- asbestos and environmental claims;
- acquisitions and disposals;
- contracts with third parties;
- litigation, mediation and arbitration;
- reinsurance;
- impact of changes in foreign exchange rates on results;
- investment risk;
- rating agencies;
- regulatory environment.

The above disclosures would also be made under Canadian GAAP, except that the company would not be required to describe its judgment in selecting accounting policies when it has the option to adopt different accounting treatments.

Extract 2(49) – Capital management note

ALTANA Aktiengesellschaft (AR 2007), page 139

Additional Disclosures for Capital Management

The capital management of the Company comprises the management of cash and cash equivalents and marketable securities, shareholders' equity and debt. The main objectives are to ensure the availability of liquid funds within the group and the management of liquidity. The majority of ALTANA's operations are financed by the Company's operating cash flows. Excess needs of liquid funds are financed by borrowings.

In 2007, ALTANA's shareholders' equity was reduced by 80 %. This significant reduction resulted from the distribution of dividends in May 2007. At December 31, 2007, the equity ratio was 66 % after 91 % at December 31, 2006. As a result, the debt to asset ratio increased from 9 % at December 31, 2006, to 34 % at December 31, 2007. Long-term debt represented 15 % of liabilities and shareholders' equity, short-term debt represented 19 %. ALTANA has a line of credit of 400 million available as an external financing source. The agreed term of the line of credit is 2012 and may be extended for two years. This line of credit was provided by an international banking consortium and may be drawn in different currencies (see note 17).

The Company aims for a balance between equity and liabilities, which allows for further growth either through operational growth or acquisitions. Currently, the Company is not externally rated by a rating agency. The existing and the aspired balance sheet structure – including bolt-on acquisitions – shall be adequate for the requirements of an Investment Grade Rating.

Commentary: The company indicates that its capital management comprises the management of cash and cash equivalents and marketable securities, shareholders' equity and debt. It specifies that operations are financed by its operating cash flows, and that any excess requirements for liquid funds are financed by borrowings.

The company also provides an analysis of changes in capital occurring in the year and indicates that, although it is not externally rated by a rating agency, it would meet the requirements for an Investment Grade Rating.

Disclosures provided are in line with CICA 1535 requirements.

Extract 2(50) – Capital management note

AMG Advanced Metallurgical Group N.V. (AR 2007), page 103

30. Financial risk management objectives and policies (in part)

Capital management

The primary objective of the Company is to maintain strong capital ratios in order to support its business and maximise shareholder value.

The Company manages its capital structure and makes adjustments to it, in light of economic conditions. Its policy is to ensure that the debt levels are manageable to the Company and that they are not increasing at a level that is in excess of the increases that occur within equity. During the planning process, the expected cash flows of the Company are evaluated and the debt to equity and debt to total capital ratios are evaluated in order to ensure that levels are improving year over year. Debt to total capital is a more appropriate measure for the Company due to its initial equity values of the subsidiaries from the combination in 2007. Management deems total capital to include all debt (including short-term, related party debt and long-term debt) as well as the total of the equity of the Company, including minority interest.

The Company's policy is to try to maintain this ratio below 50%.

	2007	2006
Loans and borrowings	116,828	208,045
Related party loans	7,752	15,536
Short-term debt	16,202	53,180
Trade Payables	126,827	93,841
Less Cash and Cash equivalents	172,558	54,610
Net debt	95,051	315,992
Net Debt	95,051	315,992
Total Equity	309,797	(23,741)
Total capital	404,848	292,251
Debt to total capital ratio	0.23	1.08

Commentary: The extract presents capital management disclosures. Note that the company indicates that, during the planning process, it evaluated the expected cash flows, debt to equity and debt to total capital ratios to monitor business and shareholder value. At the reporting date, the company indicates that debt to total capital is a more appropriate measure and provides details about that measurement.

The disclosures are in line with CICA 1535 requirements.

Extract 2(51) – Capital management

Nokian Tyres plc (AR 2007), page 43

29. FINANCIAL RISK MANAGEMENT (in part)

Capital Management

The Group's objective of managing capital is to secure with an efficient capital structure the Group's access to capital markets at all times despite of the seasonal nature of the business. The Group monitors its capital structure on the basis of equity ratio, which has to be at least at the level of 30% in accordance with the financial covenants. Equity ratio is calculated as a ratio of total equity to total assets. Minority interest has been added to equity and advances received has been subtracted from total assets.

EUR million	2007	2006
Equity	712.8	556.6
Minority interest	0.0	0.0
Adjusted equity	712.8	556.6
Total assets	1,155.4	884.7
Advances received	2.4	1.0
Adjusted total assets	1,152.9	883.7
Equity ratio	61.8%	63.0%

Commentary: In this brief extract, the company specifies that its objective of managing capital is to secure, with an efficient capital structure, access to capital markets at all times despite the seasonal nature of the business. It monitors its capital structure using an equity ratio (set to be at a minimum of 30% per financial covenants). Actual equity ratios are significantly higher than the minimum, as detailed in the table presented in the extract.

The disclosures are in line with CICA 1535 requirements.

Extract 2(52) – Capital management

Suez (Reference Document 2007), page 274

NOTE 18 EQUITY (in part)

18.8 Capital management

SUEZ aims to optimize its financial structure at all times by pursuing an appropriate balance between net debt (see Note 14.3) and total equity, as shown in the consolidated balance sheet. The Group's key objective in managing its financial structure is to maximize value for shareholders, reduce the cost of capital and maintain a high credit rating, while at the same time ensuring the Group has the financial flexibility to leverage value-creating external growth opportunities. The Group manages its financial structure and makes any necessary adjustments in light of prevailing economic conditions. In this context it may choose to adjust the amount of dividends paid to shareholders, reimburse a portion of capital, carry out share buybacks, issue new shares, launch share-based payment plans or sell assets in order to scale back its net debt.

The Group's policy is to maintain an «A» rating with Moody's and S&P. To achieve this, it manages its financial structure in line with the indicators usually monitored by these credit rating agencies, which include the Group's operating profile, financial policy and a series of financial ratios. One of the most commonly used ratios is operating cash flow less financial expenses and taxes paid expressed as a percentage of adjusted net debt. Net debt is primarily adjusted for nuclear waste reprocessing and storage provisions, provisions for unfunded pension plans, and operating lease commitments.

The Group's objectives, policies and processes for managing capital have remained unchanged over the past few years.

SUEZ SA is not required to comply with any minimum capital requirements except those provided for by law.

Commentary: Here, the company presents a concise note on its capital management. It specifies that its policy is to maintain an A rating with Moody's and S&P and that, to achieve this credit rating, it uses a series of financial ratios including operating cash flow less financial expenses and taxes paid expressed as a percentage of adjusted net debt (adjustments concern primarily nuclear waste reprocessing and storage provisions, provisions for unfunded pension plans and operating lease commitments).

Note that the company specifies that its policies and processes for managing capital have remained unchanged over the past few years and that is not required to comply with any minimum capital requirements except those specified in law.

The disclosures are in line with CICA 1535 requirements.

Extract 2(53) – Capital management note

Centrica plc (AR 2007), page 74

5. Capital management

The Group's objective when managing capital is to maintain an optimal capital structure and strong credit rating to minimise the cost of capital. In addition, in a number of areas in which the Group operates, the Group's strong capital structure and good credit standing are important elements of the Group's competitive position.

At 31 December 2007, the Group's long-term credit rating was A3 for Moody's Investor Services Inc. (2006: A3) and A for Standard & Poor's Rating Services (2006: A).

The Group monitors capital, using a medium-term view of 3-5 years, on the basis of a number of financial ratios generally used by industry and by the rating agencies. This includes monitoring gearing ratios, interest cover and cash flow to debt ratios. The Group is not subject to externally imposed capital requirements but as is common for most companies the level of debt that can be raised is restricted by the Company's Articles of Association. Net debt is limited to the greater of £5 billion and a gearing ratio of three times adjusted capital and reserves. This restriction can be amended or removed by the shareholders of the Company passing an ordinary resolution. As a result of the volatility introduced to the Group's reserves resulting from IAS 39, Financial Instruments: Recognition and Measurement, and IAS 19, Employee Benefits, changes are being sought to the definition of reserves in the Articles of Association at this year's Annual General Meeting.

The Group's capital structure is managed against the various financial ratios as required to maintain strong credit ratings.

In order to maintain or adjust the capital structure, the Group may adjust the amount of dividends paid to shareholders, return capital to shareholders, issue new shares, repurchase shares, issue debt or repay debt.

Commentary: The above extract presents a concise note on the company's capital management. It specifies that:

- its objective when managing capital is to maintain an optimal capital structure and strong credit rating to minimize the cost of capital;
- its long-term credit rating at the reporting date;
- it monitors capital over a medium-term view of three to five years, using a number of financial ratios generally accepted by the industry and the rating agencies (which includes monitoring gearing ratios, interest cover and cash flow to debt ratios);
- it is not subject to externally imposed capital requirements (but, as with other companies, the level of debt that can be raised is restricted by the company's articles, which limit net debt and a gearing ratio;
- as a result of the volatility introduced by IAS 39, *Financial Instruments: Recognition and Measurement* and IAS 19, *Employee Benefits*, changes are being sought to the definition of reserves in the company's articles; and
- to maintain or adjust its capital structure, the company may adjust the amount of dividends paid to shareholders, return capital to shareholders, issue new shares, repurchase shares, issue debt or repay debt.

All the disclosures are in line with Canadian GAAP.

Extract 2(54) – Capital management note

Aviva plc (AR 2007), pages 214-216

53 – Group capital structure

The Group maintains an efficient capital structure from a combination of equity shareholders' funds, preference capital, subordinated debt and borrowings, consistent with our overall risk profile and the regulatory and market requirements of our business. This note describes the way we manage our capital and shows where this is employed.

(a) Capital management objectives

Aviva's capital management philosophy is focused on capital efficiency and effective risk management to support a progressive dividend policy and EPS growth. Rigorous capital allocation is one of the Group's primary strategic priorities and is ultimately overseen by the Group Executive Committee.

The Group's overall capital risk appetite is set and managed with reference to the requirements of a range of different stakeholders including shareholders, policyholders, regulators and rating agencies. In managing capital we seek to:

– maintain sufficient, but not excessive, financial strength to support new business growth and satisfy the requirements of our stakeholders

– optimise our overall debt to equity structure to enhance our returns to shareholders, subject to our capital risk appetite and balancing the requirements of the range of stakeholders

– retain financial flexibility by maintaining strong liquidity, including significant unutilised committed credit lines and access to a range of capital markets

– allocate capital rigorously across the Group, to drive value adding growth in accordance with risk appetite.

– increase the dividend on a basis judged prudent, while retaining capital to support future business growth, using dividend cover on an IFRS operating earnings after tax basis in the 1.5 to 2.0 times range as a guide.

Further detail over the management and allocation of capital resources is set out in the following sections and in note 55 on risk management.

(b) Capital resources

The primary sources of capital used by the Group are equity shareholder's funds, preference shares, subordinated debt and borrowings. We also consider and, where efficient to do so, utilise alternative sources of capital such as reinsurance and securitisation in addition to the more traditional sources of funding. Targets are established in relation to regulatory solvency, ratings, liquidity and dividend capacity and are a key tool in managing capital in accordance with our risk appetite and the requirements of our various stakeholders.

Overall, the Group has significant resources and financial strength. The ratings of the Group's main operating subsidiaries are AA/AA- ("very strong") with a stable outlook from Standard & Poor's, Aa3 ("excellent") with a stable outlook from Moody's and A+ ("Superior") with a stable outlook from AM Best. These ratings reflect the Group's strong liquidity, competitive position, capital base, increasing underlying earnings and strategic and operational management. The Group is subject to a number of regulatory capital tests and also employs economic capital measures to manage capital and risk.

(c) Capital allocation

Capital allocation is undertaken based on a rigorous analysis of a range of financial, strategic, risk and capital factors to ensure that capital is allocated efficiently to value adding business opportunities. A clear management decision making framework, incorporating ongoing operational and strategic performance review, periodic longer term strategic and financial planning and robust due diligence over capital allocation is in place, including formal oversight from the Group Executive Committee and Group Capital Management Committee. These processes incorporate various capital profitability metrics, including an assessment of return on capital employed and internal rates of return in relation to hurdle rates to ensure capital is allocated efficiently and that excess business unit capital is repatriated where appropriate.

Aviva plc (AR 2007) (continued)

(d) Different measures of capital

In recognition of the requirements of different stakeholders, the Group measures its capital on a number of different bases, all of which are taken into account when managing and allocating capital across the Group. These include measures which comply with the regulatory regimes within which the Group operates and those which the directors consider appropriate for the management of the business. The primary measures which the Group uses are:

(i) Accounting bases

The Group reports its results on both an IFRS and a European Embedded Value basis. The directors consider that the European Embedded Value principles provide a more meaningful measure of the long term underlying value of the capital employed in the Group's life and related businesses. This basis allows for the impact of uncertainty in the future investment returns more explicitly and is consistent with the way the life business is priced and managed. Accordingly, in addition to IFRS, we analyse and measure the net asset value and total capital employed for the Group on this basis. This is the basis on which Group Return on Equity is measured and against which the corresponding Group target is expressed.

(ii) Regulatory bases

Individual regulated subsidiaries measure and report solvency based on applicable local regulations, including in the UK the regulations established by the Financial Services Authority (FSA). These measures are also consolidated under the European Insurance Group's Directive ("IGD") to calculate regulatory capital adequacy at an aggregate Group level. The Group fully complied with these regulatory requirements during the year.

(iii) Rating agency bases

The Group's ratings are an important indicator of financial strength and maintenance of these ratings is one of the key drivers of capital risk appetite. Certain rating agencies have proprietary capital models which they use to assess available capital resources against capital requirements, as a component of their overall criteria for assigning ratings. In addition, rating agency measures and targets in respect of gearing and fixed charge cover are also important in evaluating the level of borrowings utilised by the Group. While not mandatory external requirements, in practice rating agency capital measures tend to act as one of the primary drivers of capital requirements, reflecting the capital strength required in relation to our target ratings.

(iv) Economic bases

The Group also measures its capital using an economic capital model that takes into account a more realistic set of financial and non-financial assumptions. This model has been developed considerably over the past few years and is increasingly relevant in the internal management and external assessment of the Group's capital resources. The economic capital model is used to assess the Group's capital strength in accordance with the Individual Capital Assessment (ICA) requirements established by the FSA. Further developments are planned to meet the emerging requirements of the Solvency II framework and other external agencies. Further details regarding the use of economic capital in risk management are set out in note 55 on "Risk Management".

(e) Group capital structure

The table below sets out the capital that is managed by the Group on an IFRS and EEV basis which, as described above, is considered as a more meaningful measure of the value of capital employed in the life and related businesses. Internally generated AVIF represents the additional value of in-force long term business recognised under the EEV basis. Further detail on the EEV basis is set out in the "Alternative method of reporting long-term business profits" section starting on page 247.

Aviva plc (AR 2007) (continued)

| | Non-GAAP measure | | | Non-GAAP measure | |
	IFRS net assets 2007 £m	Internally-generated AVIF 2007 £m	Restated EEV net assets 2007 £m	IFRS net assets 2006 £m	Internally-generated AVIF 2006 £m	Restated EEV net assets 2006 £m
Long-term savings	15,290	7,982	23,272	13,300	6,794	20,094
General insurance and health	5,487	–	5,487	5,176	–	5,176
Other business	1,056	–	1,056	1,059	–	1,059
Corporate	(31)	–	(31)	(19)	–	(19)
Total capital employed	**21,802**	**7,982**	**29,784**	19,516	6,794	26,310
Financed by						
Equity shareholders' funds and minority interests	15,402	7,982	23,384	12,874	6,794	19,668
Direct capital instrument	990	–	990	990	–	990
Preference shares	200	–	200	200	–	200
	16,592	7,982	24,574	14,064	6,794	20,858
Subordinated debt	3,054	–	3,054	2,937	–	2,937
External debt	1,257	–	1,257	1,258	–	1,258
Net internal debt	899	–	899	1,257	–	1,257
	21,802	7,982	29,784	19,516	6,794	26,310

At 31 December 2007 the Group had £29.8 billion (31 December 2006: £26.3 billion) of total capital employed, measured on an EEV basis, in its trading operations which is efficiently financed by a combination of equity shareholders' funds, preference capital, subordinated debt and borrowings.

In 2007, the total capital employed increased by £3.5 billion reflecting strong operational performance and foreign exchange impacts.

(i) "Corporate" net liabilities represent the element of the pension scheme deficit held centrally.

(ii) In addition to our external funding sources, we have certain internal borrowing arrangements in place which allow some of the assets that support technical liabilities to be invested in a pool of central assets for use across the Group. These internal debt balances allow for the capital allocated to business operations to exceed the externally sources capital resources of the Group. Although intra-group in nature, they are included as part of the capital base for the purpose of capital management. These arrangements arise in relation to the following:

– Certain subsidiaries, subject to continuing to satisfy standalone capital and liquidity requirements, loan funds to corporate and holding entities, these loans satisfy arms length criteria and all interest payments are made when due.

– Aviva International Insurance (AII) Ltd acts as both a UK general insurer and as the primary holding company for the Group's foreign subsidiaries. Internal capital management mechanisms in place allocate a portion of the total capital of the company to the UK general insurance operations. These mechanisms also allow for some of the assets backing technical liabilities to be made available for use across the Group. Balances in respect of these arrangements are also treated as internal debt for capital management purposes.

Net internal debt represents the balance of the above amounts due from corporate and holding entities, less the tangible net assets held by these entities.

Further disclosures on the Group's regulatory capital position are also set out in the capital section of the business review and in note 54, Capital Statement. The purpose of note 54, which is prepared in accordance with FRS27, is to set out the financial strength of the Group and provide an analysis of the disposition and constraints over the availability of capital to meet risks and regulatory requirements.

Commentary: The above extract presents a detailed note on capital structure and management for an insurance company. It illustrates disclosure of:
- capital management objectives;
- capital resources;
- capital allocation;
- different measures of capital which includes:
  o accounting bases,
  o regulatory bases,
  o rating agency bases,
  o economic bases;
- capital structure.

Disclosures do not contradict Canadian GAAP.

Changes in Accounting Policies, Changes in Estimates and Correction of Errors

IAS 8 covers circumstances where an entity changes its accounting policies, modifies its accounting estimates or corrects an error. CICA 1506 duplicates IAS 8 requirements except that it omits certain IAS 8 paragraphs so that it won't contravene with CICA 1100 (see GAAP hierarchy covered previously).

An entity must present at least three statements of financial position when it:

- applies an accounting policy retrospectively;
- makes a retrospective restatement of items in its financial statements; or
- reclassifies items in its financial statements.

The minimum number of three statements of financial position would apply in most circumstances when an entity presents two year comparatives financial statements and would include:

- a statement of financial position at the end of the current period;
- a statement of financial position at the end of the previous period;
- a statement of financial position at the beginning of the previous period.

Canadian GAAP does have currently this requirement.

Changes in Accounting Policies

IAS 8 defines changes in accounting policies as changes in specific principles, bases, conventions, rules and practices applied by an entity in preparing and presenting financial statements.

IAS 8 specifies that:

- a change in accounting policy is acceptable only if (1) required by an IFRS standard or interpretation; or (2) the change will result in the financial statements providing reliable and more relevant information about the effects of transactions, other events or conditions on an entity's financial position, financial performance or cash flows;
- early application of a standard or an interpretation is not a voluntary change in accounting policy;
- changing an accounting policy is permitted even if it is impracticable to apply the policy retrospectively for any prior period;
- adoption of a new accounting policy as a result of changes in facts and circumstances does not necessarily imply a change in accounting policy; and
- when it is difficult to determine whether a change is a change in accounting policy or a change in estimate, it is treated as a change in estimate.

The table below reflects IAS 8 requirements for specific contexts of changes in accounting policy:

Accounting	Disclosures
Required by a new IFRS or an amendment of an existing one.	
Refer to transitional provisions in the specific standard or guidance, which may require: • retrospective or prospective application of the change; or • an exceptional transitional accounting treatment. In the absence of specific guidance, a change in the accounting policy must be applied retrospectively by adjusting the opening balance of each affected component of equity for the earliest period presented, and the other comparative amounts disclosed, must be presented reflecting new accounting policy application unless it is impracticable to do so, as discussed below.	• Title of the standard or interpretation and, when applicable, an indication that the change in accounting policy is made in accordance with its transitional provisions. • Nature of the change in accounting policy and, when applicable, a description of the transitional provisions. • When applicable, the transitional provisions that might have an effect on future periods. • For the current period and each prior period presented, to the extent practicable, the amount of the adjustment: o for each financial statement line item affected, and o for basic and diluted earnings per share (if IAS 33 applies to the entity). • The amount of the adjustment relating to periods before those presented, to the extent practicable. • If the required retrospective application is impracticable for a particular prior period, or for periods before those presented, the entity must disclose the circumstances that led to the existence of that condition and a description of how and from when the change in accounting policy has been applied. Financial statements of subsequent periods need not repeat these disclosures.
New IFRS has been issued but is not yet effective.	
None	When an entity has not applied a new standard or interpretation that has been issued but is not yet effective, it must disclose: • this fact; and • known or reasonably estimable information relevant to assessing the possible impact that application of the new standard or interpretation will have on the entity's financial statements in the period of initial application. The entity could also consider disclosing: • title of the new standard or interpretation; • nature of the impending change or changes in accounting policy; • date by which application of the standard or interpretation is required; • date as at which it plans to apply the standard or interpretation initially and • either: o a discussion of the impact that initial application of the standard or interpretation is expected to have on the entity's financial statements, or o if that impact is not known or reasonably estimable, a statement to that effect.

Accounting	Disclosures
Voluntary change in accounting policy resulting in reliable and more relevant information.	

Apply retrospectively (i.e., adjust opening balance of each affected component of equity for the earliest prior period presented and the other comparative amounts disclosed for each prior period presented as if the new accounting policy had always been applied).	• Nature of the change in accounting policy.
	• Reasons why applying the new accounting policy provides reliable and more relevant information.
	• Amount of the adjustment for the current period and each prior period presented, to the extent practicable:
	  o for each financial statement line item affected, and
	  o for basic and diluted earnings per share (if IAS 33 applies to the entity).
	• The amount of the adjustment relating to periods before those presented, to the extent practicable.
	• If retrospective application is impracticable for a particular prior period, or for periods before those presented, the circumstances that led to the existence of that condition and a description of how and from when the change in accounting policy has been applied. Financial statements of subsequent periods need not repeat these disclosures.

Other voluntary changes in accounting policy.	
Prohibited.	N/A

Changes in Accounting Estimates

Adjustment of the carrying amount of an asset or a liability, or the amount of the periodic consumption of an asset that results from the assessment of the present status of, and expected future benefits and obligations associated with, assets and liabilities. Consequently, changes in accounting estimates result from new information or new developments and, accordingly, are not corrections of errors.

Many items in financial statements have to be estimated. Examples of estimates include bad debts, inventory obsolescence, fair value of certain financial assets or financial liabilities, useful lives of depreciable assets and warranty obligations.

The table below reflects IAS 8 requirements for changes in accounting estimates in specific contexts:

Context of changes in accounting estimates	Accounting	Disclosures
Only current period is affected.	Prospective application, recognize in income of the current period of the change by including the effect of the change in the same income statement classification as was used previously for the estimate.	Nature and amount of the change in accounting estimate.

Context of changes in accounting estimates	Accounting	Disclosures
Both current period and future periods are affected.	Prospective application, recognize in income of the current period and present the effect of the change in the estimate on the same line item as the one(s) of previous year(s) that was (were) established by reference to the original accounting estimate.	• Nature and amount of the change in accounting estimate related to current period. • Nature and expected amount to have an effect in future periods, except if it is impracticable to estimate that effect. If the amount of the effect in future periods is not disclosed because estimating it is impracticable, an entity must disclose that fact.
Last interim period (if a separate financial report is not published).	None.	Nature and amount of the change in estimate in a note to the annual financial statements for that financial year.

Correction of an Error

Omissions from, and misstatements in, an entity's financial statements for one or more prior periods arising from a failure to use, or misuse, reliable information that:

• was available when financial statements for those periods were authorized for issue; and

• could reasonably be expected to have been obtained and taken into account in the preparation and presentation of those financial statements.

Errors arise from mathematical mistakes, mistakes in applying accounting policies, oversights or misinterpretations of facts and fraud. Corrections of errors differ from changes in accounting estimates as the latter are by nature approximations that may need revision as additional information becomes known.

The table below reflects IAS 8 requirements for error correction in specific contexts:

Accounting	Disclosures
Recognition and measurement errors	
Retrospectively by restating the comparative amounts for the period(s) in which the error occurred, so that the financial statements are presented as if the error had never occurred. Consequently: • any information presented about prior periods, including any historical summaries of financial data, is restated as far back as is practicable; • when the error occurred before the earliest period presented, an entity must restate the opening balance of assets, liabilities and equity for that; • unless it is impracticable to do so, as discussed below.	• Nature of the prior period error. • Amount of correction for each prior period presented (including, if applicable, the beginning of the earliest prior period) for each financial statement line item affected. • Basic and diluted earnings per share correction for each prior period. Financial statements of subsequent periods need not repeat these disclosures. If retrospective restatement is impracticable for a particular prior period, the circumstances that led to the existence of that condition and a description of how and from when the error has been corrected.
Error of presentation of an element of financial statements	
Not applicable.	Nature of the prior period error.

Impracticability for Retroactive Adjustments

As indicated in the previous table, an entity applying a new accounting policy retrospectively must adjust comparative information of prior periods as far back as is practicable. If there has been a prior period error, the entity has to correct the amounts of the period in which the error occurred.

IAS 8 indicates that a requirement is impracticable when an entity cannot apply it after making every reasonable effort to do so. It lists circumstances when an entity could conclude that it is impracticable to apply a change in an accounting policy retrospectively or to make a retrospective restatement to correct an error:

- effects of the retrospective application or retrospective restatement are not determinable;

- retrospective application or retrospective restatement requires assumptions about what management's intent would have been in that period; or

- retrospective application or retrospective restatement requires significant estimates of amounts and it is impossible to distinguish objectively information about those estimates that:

  o provides evidence of circumstances that existed on the date(s) as at which those amounts are to be recognized, measured or disclosed, and

  o would have been available when the financial statements for that prior period were authorized for issue from other information.

When it becomes too difficult for an entity to apply a new accounting policy retrospectively, because it cannot determine the cumulative effect of applying the policy to all prior periods, it would apply the new policy prospectively from the start of the earliest period practicable. It, therefore, would disregard the portion of the cumulative adjustment to assets, liabilities and equity arising before that date.

CICA 1506 addresses impracticability issues in much the same way as IAS 8 does except that it does not provide for an impracticability exemption for a restatement involving the correction of an error.

Illustrative Disclosures:

Extract 2(55) – Accounting changes and reclassifications

> **Koninklijke Philips Electronics N.V. (AR 2007), page 205**
> **Significant IFRS accounting policies (in part)**
> **Accounting changes**
> In the absence of explicit transition requirements for new accounting pronouncements, the Company accounts for any change in accounting principle retrospectively.
> **Reclassifications**
> Certain items previously reported under specific financial statement captions have been reclassified to conform with the 2007 presentation.

Commentary: The above extract briefly mentions how accounting policy changes are recorded and the fact that certain items previously reported under specific financial statement captions have been reclassified. This general disclosure is also observed under Canadian GAAP.

Extract 2(56) – Change in accounting policy and in presentation

Alcatel-Lucent (AR 2007 on Form 20-F), page 176

NOTE 4 CHANGE IN ACCOUNTING POLICY AND PRESENTATION

a/ Change in accounting policy

On January 1, 2007, Alcatel-Lucent adopted (with retrospective effect as of January 1, 2005) the option offered by Amendment to IAS 19 "Employee benefits – Actuarial gains and losses, Group plans and Disclosures", to immediately recognize all actuarial gains and losses and any adjustment arising from an asset ceiling, net of deferred tax effects, in the period in which they occur outside the income statement in the Statement Of Recognized Income and Expense (SORIE). Management believes that the change will more fairly present the fair value of assets and liabilities related to retiree benefits in the company's balance sheet and eliminate significant volatility in its results of operations for certain plans, the participants of which are all, or almost all, fully eligible to receive benefits.

Previously, Alcatel-Lucent applied the corridor method, under which actuarial gains and losses exceeding 10% of the greater of (i) the benefit obligation or (ii) the fair value of plan assets were recognized in the income statement over the expected remaining working lives of the employees participating in the plans. The impact of the limitation in the value of plan assets to the lower of: (i) the value resulting from applying IAS 19 "Employee Benefits" prior to the Group's adoption of the option provided by the amendment to IAS 19, and (ii) the net total present value of any available refund from the plan or reduction in future contributions to the plan (arising from asset ceilings) was accounted for in the income statement.

The impact of this change in accounting policies on the balance sheet in the prior periods is as follows:

(in millions of euros)	December 31, 2006	December 31, 2005
Prepaid pension costs	701	231
Assets held for sale	10	-
Deferred tax assets (liabilities)	(291)	(80)
Pensions, retirement indemnities and other post-retirement benefits	(36)	(277)
Shareholders' equity attributable to equity holders of the parent	387	(126)
Minority interests	(3)	(2)

The impact on the income statements in the prior periods is as follows:

(in millions of euros)	Year ended December 31, 2006	Year ended December 31, 2005
Income (loss) from operating activities	(7)	(5)
Other financial income (loss)	78	(1)
Income tax (expense) income	-	-
Income (loss) from discontinued operations	(1)	(2)
NET RESULT	**70**	**(8)**
Basic earnings per share	0.05	(0.01)
Diluted earnings per share	0.05	(0.01)

b/ Change in presentation

Since January 1, 2007, the Group presents sales commissions under "administrative and selling expenses" and not in "cost of sales" as previously presented by historical Alcatel. If such a classification had been applied in 2006, "administrative and selling expenses" would have increased and "cost of sales" would have decreased by 87 million in 2006. Information for 2005 is not available.

Commentary: The company presents a detailed note describing a change in accounting policy and in presentation. The company presents the impact of the change in accounting policies on the balance sheet in the prior periods. Note that, current IAS 1, which is effective as of January 1, 2009, requires an additional complete balance sheet (at January 1, 2005 or December 31, 2004) reflecting any changes made in 2007.

The new accounting policy adopted (immediately recognize all actuarial gains and losses and any adjustment arising from an asset ceiling, net of deferred tax effects, in the period in which they occur outside the income statement) would not be acceptable under Canadian GAAP. Note that the company justifies the change by noting it is required by IAS 19.

The presentation of sales commissions under "administrative and selling expenses" and not in "cost of sales," as previously presented, might not contravene Canadian GAAP. Note that the company refers to the impracticability exception for 2005 (the company presents three years of comparatives as it is an SEC registrant).

Extract 2(57) – Change in accounting estimates

Qantas Airways Limited (AR 2007), page 85
3. Expenditure

	$M	$M	$M	$M
Finance costs				
Related parties				
– controlled entities	–	–	83.0	80.3
Other parties				
– finance leases	37.4	39.7	38.8	37.9
– other finance costs	273.9	229.8	202.9	161.0
Capitalised interest	(83.3)	(68.4)	(83.3)	(68.4)
Unwinding of discount on provisions	30.9	16.8	30.9	16.8
Total finance costs	258.9	217.9	272.3	227.6
Other				
Net foreign currency loss /(gain)	89.0	(57.8)	84.0	(57.3)
Bad and doubtful debts	3.7	1.9	3.7	1.6
Restructuring				
– redundancy costs	147.4	108.6	147.3	104.6
– other	87.7	72.9	87.7	72.9
Cancellable operating leases	170.7	163.2	157.6	149.0
Change in accounting estimates				
– Frequent Flyer deferred revenue	(41.9)	(49.1)	(41.9)	(49.1)
– long service leave provisions	–	47.7	–	47.7

Commentary: This extract presents a table that contains changes in accounting estimates related to:

• frequent Flyer deferred revenue; and
• long service leave provisions.

This disclosure would be considered to be an example of transparent disclosure under Canadian GAAP.

Extract 2(58) – Correction of errors and inconsistencies

Steinhoff International Holdings Limited (AR 2007), page 209

42. RESTATEMENTS (in part)

42.4 Notes supporting the restatements

42.4.1 Homestyle restatement

Following the acquisition and initial accounting for Homestyle Group Plc on 30 June 2005, the group has undertaken a comprehensive turnaround plan including the introduction of a largely new executive management team who have addressed a number of operational issues in the group.

In addressing certain operational issues management became aware of certain accounting inconsistencies and misstatements related to legacy issues in existence at acquisition date, 30 June 2005. In accordance with IAS 8 – *Accounting Policies, Change in Accounting Estimates and Errors*, these inconsistencies and misstatements have been corrected retrospectively by restating the comparatives for the prior periods affected.

The restatement of previously reported amounts had no effect on previously reported group earnings as they all related to acquisition balances and consequently were adjusted for in the goodwill arising on the acquisition of the Homestyle Group as follows:

	At 1 July 2005		
	As previously reported R'000	Adjustment R'000	Restated R'000
Fair value of assets and liabilities acquired	614 417	(194 614)	419 803
Minority interest	(240 483)	76 172	(164 311)
Goodwill arising on acquisition	676 163	118 442	794 605
Total consideration	1 050 097	—	1 050 097

The increase in goodwill did not give rise to any impairment based on impairment tests conducted in previous periods.

Commentary: The company indicates that it has retrospectively corrected inconsistencies and misstatements related to an acquisition by restating the comparatives for the prior periods affected.

The company presents a table detailing the restatements that have no effect on the company's previously reported earnings as they all related to acquisition balances and, consequently, were dealt with in the goodwill arising on the acquisition.

The accounting treatment and disclosures are in line with Canadian GAAP.

Extract 2(59) – Changes in accounting estimates – IFRS 3

Xstrata plc (AR 2007), pages 162 and 163

7. Acquisitions (in part)

Prior year business combinations

Falconbridge Limited

The Group obtained control of Falconbridge Limited (Falconbridge) in August 2006 for a total cash cost of US$18,819 million including transaction costs. As at 31 December 2006 the fair values of the identified assets and liabilities acquired were provisional, due to the timing and complexity of the acquisition. During 2007, these values were finalised as follows in accordance with IFRS 3 'Business Combinations':

US$m	Provisional fair value as previously reported	Fair value adjustments[a]	Fair value at acquisition
Intangible assets	267	701	968
Property, plant and equipment	18,692	(648)	18,044
Inventories	2,306	(1)	2,305
Trade and other receivables	1,372	3	1,375
Investments in associates	134	–	134
Available-for-sale financial assets	140	10	150
Derivative financial assets	56	–	56
Other financial assets	125	(83)	42
Prepayments	61	2	63
	23,153	(16)	23,137
Trade and other payables	(1,804)	(15)	(1,819)
Interest-bearing loans and borrowings	(3,800)	–	(3,800)
Derivative financial liabilities	(125)	–	(125)
Provisions	(1,239)	(164)	(1,403)
Pension deficit	(235)	(76)	(311)
Deferred tax liabilities	(3,081)	(331)	(3,412)
Income tax payable	(339)	(14)	(353)
Net assets	12,530	(616)	11,914
Minority interests	(45)	(426)	(471)
Net attributable assets	12,485	(1,042)	11,443
Goodwill*	2,859	486	3,345
Net attributable assets including goodwill	15,344	(556)	14,788

	Provisional	Adjustments	Final
Total consideration:			
Net cash acquired with the subsidiary	(879)	–	(879)
Acquisition costs	68	–	68
Cash paid for 19.9% acquired in 2005	1,715	–	1,715
Cash paid for 80.1% acquired in 2006	17,036	–	17,036
	17,940	–	17,940

| Xstrata plc (AR 2007) (continued) | | | |
US$m	Provisional	Adjustments	Final
Goodwill arising on acquisition on 19.9% interest in Falconbridge in 2005:			
Cash paid	1,715	–	1,715
Less fair value of the 19.9% share of the attributable net assets acquired**	(1,715)	–	(1,715)
Goodwill	–	–	–
Goodwill arising on acquisition on 80.1% interest in Falconbridge in 2006:			
80.1% of net cash acquired with the subsidiary	(704)	–	(704)
Acquisition costs	68	–	68
Cash paid	17,036	–	17,036
	16,400	–	16,400
Less 80.1% share of the attributable net assets acquired	(12,291)	446	(11,845)
Goodwill on 80.1% acquisition***	4,109	446	4,555
Goodwill from above*	2,859	486	3,345
Total goodwill[(b)]	6,968	932	7,900

*   This goodwill balance is the result of the requirement to recognise a deferred tax liability calculated as the difference between the tax effect of the fair value of the assets and liabilities and their tax bases.

**   In accordance with IFRS, this represents 19.9% of the fair value of the net assets at the date of acquisition in 2005.

*** Included in this goodwill are certain intangible assets that cannot be individually separated or reliably measured from the acquisition due to their nature. These items include the expected value of synergies and an assembled workforce.

(a) The fair values of identified assets and liabilities acquired have been finalised in 2007. This has resulted in updates to a number of fair values reflected at 31 December 2006.

    The main adjustments relate to:

- Intangibles increased after a review to identify such assets was undertaken, and includes long-term feed contracts and rights to a hydroelectricity development project.
- Valuations of property, plant and equipment were finalised resulting in a decrease in value.
- Provision balances have increased following a review of the level of provisioning, particularly with regard to rehabilitation and restoration obligations.
- The pension deficit obligations have increased as a result of further assessments of future obligations and actuarial assumptions.
- A net increase in tax liabilities following a thorough review of tax obligations on acquisition.
- A review of joint venture arrangements was undertaken to assess whether the Group has joint control or control over such entities. In one instance, it was determined that the Group controlled as opposed to jointly controlled the operation. Accordingly, this entity has been consolidated as opposed to proportionally consolidated. This has resulted in an increase to property, plant and equipment and minority interests.

(b) As required by IFRS 3, all adjustments made in finalising the acquisition accounting have been presented as if the accounting had been completed on the acquisition date.

    Accordingly, the additional goodwill recorded as a result of the finalisation of the acquisition accounting is subject to impairment testing at 31 December 2006. This has resulted in an additional impairment charge of US$446 million which, in accordance with IFRS 3, has been recognised in the income statement for the year ended 31 December 2006, increasing the total impairment charge to US$1,824 million. There was no other significant income statement impact arising as a result of finalising the acquisition accounting.

From the date of acquisition to 31 December 2006, Falconbridge contributed a profit of US$1,218 million to the Group prior to the impairment expense of US$1,824 million.

Commentary: The company describes details related to changes in accounting estimates. Contrary to the general requirements of IAS 8, these changes in estimates are accounted for retroactively, as required by IFRS 3. This accounting treatment is in line with Canadian GAAP.

Events after the Reporting Period

Scope

IAS 10 deals with accounting for, and disclosures of, events, both favourable and unfavourable, that occur between the date of the statement of financial position and the date the financial statements are authorized for issue.

Types of Event

IAS 10 identifies the following two types of events for financial reporting purposes:

- those that provide evidence of conditions that existed at the balance sheet date (adjusting events after the balance sheet date); and

- those that indicate conditions that arose after the balance sheet date (non-adjusting events after the balance sheet date).

CICA 3820 adopts a similar approach except that events after the balance sheet date are limited to those occurring up to the date of financial statement completion, which may be earlier than the date the financial statements are authorized for issue under IAS 10.

Accounting and Disclosure Requirements

The following table presents IAS 10 requirements related to events after balance sheet date. All requirements are in line with CICA 3820 unless identified.

Issue	IAS 10 Requirements

Adjusting events after the balance sheet date (see Note 1)	*Accounting*: The information that such events provide must therefore be reflected through adjusting amounts recognized in financial statements, or by recording items that were not previously recognized.
	
	Examples of required adjustments:
	• Adjusting a provision already recognized, or recognizing a provision instead of merely disclosing a contingent liability for the:
	  o resolution after the balance sheet date of a court case as it confirms that entity already had a present obligation at the balance sheet date,
	  o amount of profit sharing or bonus payments if it relates to present legal or constructive obligation at the balance sheet date to make such payments as a result of events before that date (see IAS 19, *Employee benefits*).
	• Record impairment related to:
	  o trade receivable subsequent to the bankruptcy of a customer which occurs after the balance sheet date as it usually confirms that a loss already existed at the balance sheet date on a trade receivable account,
	  o inventory sold after the balance sheet date which may give evidence about its net realizable value at the balance sheet date.
	• Record amounts or adjust ones already recorded related to the discovery of fraud or errors that show that the financial statements were incorrect.

Issue	IAS 10 requirements
Non-adjusting events after the balance sheet date (Note 2)	*Accounting*: Amounts in the financial statements are not adjusted. *Examples:* • Declaration of dividends after the year end (no provision required because there is no commitment to make the dividend payment at the balance date). • Decline in market value of investments after the year end (fall in market value does not normally relate to the condition of the investments at the balance sheet date but reflects circumstances that have arisen in the following period). *Disclosures*: When non-adjusting events are so material that non-disclosure would affect the ability of financial statement users to make proper evaluations and decisions, an entity must disclose (for each significant category of non-adjusting event): • the nature of the event; and • an estimate of its financial effect, or a statement that such an estimate cannot be made for a proper understanding of the financial statements. *Example of such non-adjusting events:* • A major business combination after the balance sheet date (IFRS 3, *Business Combinations* also requires specific disclosures in such cases) or disposing of a major subsidiary. • Announcing a plan to discontinue an operation, disposing of assets or settling liabilities attributable to a discontinued operation or entering into binding agreements to sell such assets or settle such liabilities (see IFRS 5, *Discontinuing Operations*). • Major purchases and disposals of assets, or expropriation of major assets by government. • Destruction of a major production plant by a fire after the balance sheet date. • Announcing, or commencing the implementation of, a major restructuring project (see IAS 37, *Provisions, Contingent Liabilities and Contingent Assets*). • Major ordinary share transactions and potential ordinary share transactions after the balance sheet date (IAS 33 requires an enterprise to disclose a description of such transactions, other than capitalization issues and share splits). • Abnormally large changes after the balance sheet date in asset prices or foreign exchange rates. • Changes in tax rates or tax laws enacted or announced after the balance sheet date that have a significant effect on current and deferred tax assets and liabilities (see IAS 12, *Income Taxes*). • Entering into significant commitments or contingent liabilities, for example by issuing significant guarantees. • Commencing major litigation arising solely out of events that occurred after the balance sheet date. Note: An entity might have to disclose, in its financial statements, information received after the balance sheet date even when that information does not affect the amounts recognized in the financial statements. One example of the need to update disclosures is when evidence becomes available after the balance sheet date about a contingent liability that existed at the balance sheet date. In addition to considering whether it should now recognize a provision under IAS 37, an enterprise would update its disclosures about the contingent liability in the light of that evidence.
Authorization for issuance of financial statements (Note 3)	*Disclosures:* • the date when the financial statements were authorized for issue; and • who gave that authorization. Moreover, if the entity's owners or others have the power to amend the financial statements after their issue, the entity must disclose that fact.

Note 1: Both IAS 1 and CICA 1510 require liabilities to be classified as current or non-current according to the circumstances existing at the reporting date. EIC-122, however, allows an entity to consider post-reporting date re-financings when determining the classification of debt at the reporting date. Also, unlike IFRS, liabilities payable on demand at the reporting date due to covenant violations might be classified as non-current in certain circumstances described in EIC-59.

Note 2: Financial statements are not modified when non-adjusting events occur after the reporting date. An exception is when post-reporting date events indicate that the financial statements should not be prepared on a going concern basis (see going concern issue below).

Note 3: CICA 3820 contains no corresponding requirement.

Illustrative Disclosures:

Extract 2(60) – Subsequent events

Koninklijke Philips Electronics N.V. (AR 2007), pages 238 and 239

70 Subsequent events (in part)

VISICU

On December 18, 2007, Philips announced a merger agreement with VISICU through which Philips is offering to acquire the entire share capital of VISICU for USD 12.00 per share.

Based in Baltimore, USA, VISICU is a leader in clinical IT systems that enable critical care medical staff to actively monitor patients in hospital intensive care units from remote locations.

Philips' cash offer represents an enterprise value of approximately EUR 200 million (approximately USD 300 million), when accounting for approximately USD 130 million in cash on VISICU's balance sheet as of September 30, 2007. Closing of the merger is subject to the terms and conditions of the merger agreement, the approval of VISICU's shareholders, and to customary regulatory clearance. The transaction is expected to close at February 20, 2008.

Set-Top Boxes and Connectivity Solutions

On December 19, 2007, Philips announced it has reached an agreement in principle to sell its Set-Top Boxes (STB) and Connectivity Solutions (CS) activities, currently part of its Home Networks business unit within the Consumer Electronics division, to Pace Micro Technology (Pace), a UK-based technology provider.

Philips agreed in principle to divest the STB and CS activities to Pace in exchange for 70 million Pace shares. The proposed transaction is subject to approvals from Pace shareholders, the relevant regulatory authorities and Philips' workers council. After its successful completion, Philips will become a shareholder of some 23% of the combined business. The transaction is expected to close at the end of the first quarter of 2008.

Share repurchase program

On December 19, 2007, the Company announced that it plans to repurchase EUR 5 billion worth of common Philips shares within the next two years. Shares repurchased under this new program will be subsequently cancelled subject to shareholder approval. In January 2008, the Company has repurchased 22,311,016 common shares for approximately EUR 587 million under this program.

Respironics

On December 21, 2007, Philips and Respironics announced a definitive merger agreement pursuant to which Philips would commence a tender offer to acquire all of the outstanding shares of Respironics for USD 66 per share, or a total purchase price of approximately EUR 3.6 billion (USD 5.1 billion) to be paid in cash upon completion.

Respironics, based in Murrysville, Pennsylvania, USA, is the leading provider of innovative solutions for the global sleep therapy and respiratory markets. The transaction is expected to close at the end of February 2008.

Koninklijke Philips Electronics N.V. (AR 2007) (continued)

Genlyte

On January 22, 2008, Philips completed the purchase of all outstanding shares of Genlyte for a total consideration of EUR 1,888 million (USD 2,747 million). This amount includes the purchase price of 331,627 shares which were already acquired in ordinary brokerage transactions by Philips from August 13, 2007 to August 23, 2007 (in total USD 23 million) and the payment with respect to Genlyte's option plan of USD 89 million. Additionally, in connection with the closing, Philips provided a loan to Genlyte of approximately USD 101 million to pay off debt.

The preliminary condensed balance sheet of Genlyte determined in accordance with IFRS, immediately before and after acquisition date:

Preliminary, unaudited	before acquisition date	after acquisition date
Assets and liabilities		
Goodwill	256	1,092
Other intangible assets	102	762
Property, plant and equipment	131	193
Working capital	90	145
Current financial assets	7	7
Deferred tax liabilities	-	(291)
Other long-term liabilities and assets (net)	(16)	(16)
Cash	75	75
	645	1,967
Financed by		
Group equity	567	1,889
Loans	78	78
	645	1,967

The goodwill recognized is related mainly to the complementary technological expertise of Genlyte's workforce and the synergies expected to be achieved from integrating Genlyte into the Lighting division.

Other intangible assets comprise:

Preliminary, unaudited	amount	amortization period in years
Core technology and developed technology/designs	100	11
Group brands	212	20
Product brands	49	10
Customer relationship	381	12
Order backlog	6	0.5
In-process R&D	14	12
	762	

Commentary: The above extract provides details on various subsequent events related to acquisitions or divestures. All disclosures are in line with Canadian GAAP.

Extract 2(61) – Dividends (non-adjusting entries)

Koninklijke Philips Electronics N.V. (AR 2007), page 236

63 Stockholders' equity (in part)

Net income and dividend

A dividend of EUR 0.70 per common share will be proposed to the 2008 Annual General Meeting of Shareholders. An amount of EUR 3,940 million is expected to be added to retained earnings.

Commentary: The company specifies that a dividend (amount specified) will be proposed at the Annual General Meeting of Shareholders. Such a disclosure does not contradict Canadian GAAP.

Going Concern Issues

Uncertainties

IAS 1 and CICA 1400 require that management assess, at each balance sheet date, an entity's ability to continue as a going concern. An entity is a going concern if it has neither the intention nor the need to liquidate or to cease its operations within at least 12 months from the balance sheet date.

The following are three possible outcomes of such an assessment and what related IFRS and Canadian GAAP require in each circumstance:

- no material uncertainties: no particular information to be provided;
- material uncertainties concerning an entity's ability to continue as a going concern: disclosures of uncertainties related to events or conditions that might cast significant doubt on the entity's ability to continue as a going concern;
- entity ceases to be a going concern:
  o prepare financial statements on a an alternative basis,
  o describe basis of financial statements preparation, and
  o disclose reason why entity is not regarded to be a going concern.

Subsequent Events

As indicated previously, the IAS 10 distinction between adjusting and non-adjusting events is not relevant for going concern issues. Consequently, any subsequent event that results in an entity ceasing to be a going concern would require the preparation of the financial statements on an alternative basis.

Illustrative Disclosures:

Extract 2(62) – Going concern issue

Rockeby biomed Limited (AR 2006), pages 53 and 54

1. SUMMARY OF ACCOUNTING POLICIES (in part)

a. Going concern

The financial report has been prepared on the going concern basis, which contemplates the continuity of normal business activity and the realisation of assets and the settlement of liabilities in the normal course of business.

The Company and consolidated entity have incurred a net loss after tax for the year ended 30 June 2006 of $7,662,118 and $7,399,069 respectively (2005: $4,305,676 and $4,393,715 respectively) and experienced net cash outflows from operating activities of $596,454 and $3,700,875 respectively (2005: $336,416 and $3,908,181 respectively). As at 30 June 2006 the Company and consolidated entity had net current asset deficiencies of $243,252 and $574,333 (2005: $17,100 and $21,445 respectively).

The directors have taken steps subsequent to 30 June 2006 to ensure the Company and the consolidated entity continue as going concerns.

These steps included:

- obtained a bank facility of $500,000 (secured by a personal guarantee of Dr. Sze Wee Tan);
- obtained the directors' agreement to defer amounts payable to them which as at 30 June 2006 represented $100,770;
- raised a further $480,000 before costs through a private placement via the issue of 32,000,000 shares at an issue price of 1.5 cents per share;
- appointed Novus Capital to provide corporate advice and assist the company in securing additional funds; and
- announced on 12 September 2006 a share purchase plan for the issue of shares to existing shareholders at an issue price of 1.5 cents per share to raise up to $1,710,000 before costs.

Rockeby biomed Limited (AR 2006) (continued)

The ability of the Company and the consolidated entity to continue as going concerns and to pay their debts as and when they fall due is dependent on the following:

- the ability of the Company and the consolidated entity to secure further funds ($1,710,000) through the share purchase plan announced on 12 September 2006;
- the ability of the Company and the consolidated entity to secure additional funding through either the issue of further shares, convertible notes or a combination. The Company has appointed an advisor with respect to raising these funds;
- securing a pan-European licensing arrangement for CanDia5 with a global pharmaceutical or biotechnology company. The Company is currently engaged in detailed discussions with three parties in this regard;
- the Company's H5N1 avian flu tests for humans and poultry continuing to generate revenues through its distribution network across Europe and the Middle East in addition to the Asia Pacific region;
- the ability to successfully and profitably market its products through existing and new markets.

Since the end of the last financial year the Company has raised $3,303,006 (net of costs) from a combination of private placements and two Entitlements issues. The directors believe that they will continue to be successful in securing additional funds through debt or equity issues.

The directors have reviewed the business outlook and are of the opinion that the use of the going concern basis of accounting is appropriate as they believe the Company and consolidated entity will achieve the matters set out above.

Notwithstanding this, there is significant uncertainty whether the Company and the consolidated entity will be able to continue as going concerns.

Should the Company and the consolidated entity be unable to continue as going concerns, they may be required to realise their assets and extinguish their liabilities other than in the normal course of business and at amounts different from those stated in the financial report.

The financial report does not include any adjustments relating to the recoverability and classification of recorded asset amounts or to the amounts and classification of liabilities that may be necessary should the Company and the consolidated entity be unable to continue as going concerns.

Commentary: The above extract presents an example of note disclosures on going concern uncertainties. The company specifies that it:

- has prepared its financial statement on a going concern basis;
- has incurred a net loss after tax and experienced net cash outflows from operating activities (amounts highlighted).

It also presents:

- steps taken by its directors to ensure that it can continue as going concern;
- discussions and amounts raised in cash.

The company indicates that the directors have reviewed the business outlook and are of the opinion that the use of the going concern basis of accounting is appropriate.

Disclosures in this extract conform to CICA 1400 requirements.

Extract 2(63) – Going concern issue

Tadpole Technology plc (AR 2007), page 37

2. Basis of preparation (in part)

The accounting policies that follow set out those policies which apply in preparing the consolidated financial statements for the year ended 30 September 2007. The consolidated financial statements are presented in Sterling and all values are rounded to the nearest thousand (£000) except where otherwise indicated.

(a) Basis of preparation and going concern

The financial statements have been prepared on the going concern basis which assumes that the Group will continue in operational existence, and will be able to meet its liabilities as they fall due, for the foreseeable future.

In concluding that it is appropriate to adopt the going concern basis in preparing the financial statements the Directors have prepared cash flow projections to September 2009 which include the impact in November 2007 of the successful placing of 20 million shares with an institutional investor, the concluding of a licensing agreement with Exent and the disposal of the Geospatial Solutions Division.

The cash flow projections to September 2009 are based on the following assumptions:

- Securing further funding by the end of March 2008, when existing cash resources will be exhausted, from a planned equity fundraising, to be notified to shareholders in February 2008 (the "Planned Fundraising"); and
- Obtaining shareholder approval in respect of the Planned Fundraising.

The Directors believe there is a reasonable prospect of the Planned Fundraising occurring before the end of March 2008. Therefore, the Directors have concluded that it is appropriate to adopt the going concern basis in preparing the financial statements.

However, until the Planned Fundraising has occurred there will remain a material uncertainty as to the future funding of the Group which would cast significant doubt on the Group's ability to continue as a going concern. In addition, if the Planned Fundraising occurs, but does not raise adequate amounts, then the Directors would need to evaluate additional sources of funding, the extent, timing and availability of which cannot be determined until the results of the Planned Fundraising are known.

In the event that the Planned Fundraising does not occur, or if the Directors are unable to obtain additional sources of funding in the event that the Planned Fundraising occurs but does not raise adequate amounts, then the Group would no longer be a going concern and adjustments to the financial statements would be necessary to reduce the carrying value of assets to their recoverable amounts, in particular to the carrying amounts of the intangibles and goodwill, to provide for any further liabilities that might arise and to reclassify fixed assets as current assets.

(b) Statement of compliance

The consolidated financial statements of Group and all its subsidiaries have been prepared in accordance with International Financial Reporting Standards (IFRSs). The parent company's financial statements have been prepared in accordance with UK generally accepted accounting practices and are included at pages 67 to 81. The consolidated financial statements of the Group have also been prepared in accordance with the IFRSs adopted for use in the European Union.

Commentary: The above extract presents an example of note disclosures on going concern issues and uncertainties. The company specifies that:

- the directors have prepared cash flow projections for two years, which include in the current year the impact of a share issue and a licensing agreement;
- two key assumptions used in preparing the cash flow projections for two years;
- clearly indicates that one of these assumption is critical; and
- in case going concern is doubtful, financial statements would have to be adjusted by:
  - o reducing the carrying value of assets to their recoverable amounts, in particular to the carrying amounts of the intangibles and goodwill,
  - o providing for any further liabilities that might arise, and
  - o reclassifying fixed assets as current assets.

The extract also presents a statement of compliance note specifying that:

- the consolidated financial statements of the group and all of its subsidiaries have been prepared in accordance with IFRS;
- the parent company's financial statements, which are included in the annual report, have been prepared in accordance with local GAAP (UK);
- the group's consolidated financial statements have also been prepared in accordance with the IFRS adopted in the European Union.

Although going concern disclosures in this extract conform to CICA 1400 requirements, no corresponding compliance statement is currently included in the notes of financial statements prepared under Canadian GAAP.

Earnings Per Share (EPS)

Earnings per share (EPS) is a benchmark often used to measure an entity's profitability. Entities that disclose EPS amounts in their financial statements prepared according to IFRS must conform to IAS 33 requirements (CICA 3500 under Canadian GAAP).

Definitions

The table below defines some of the IAS 33 terms related to EPS calculations. The definitions are in line with those described in CICA 3500 unless noted otherwise.

Term	Definition
Options and warrants	A financial instrument that gives the holder the right to purchase ordinary shares.
Contingent share agreement	Agreement to issue shares that depends on the satisfaction of specified conditions.
Contingently issuable ordinary shares	Ordinary shares issuable for little or no cash or other consideration upon the satisfaction of specified conditions in a contingent share agreement.
Dilution	Reduction in earnings per share or an increase in loss per share resulting from the assumption that convertible instruments are converted, that options or warrants are exercised, or that ordinary shares are issued upon the satisfaction of specified conditions.
Ordinary share (Note)	An equity instrument that is subordinate to all other classes of equity instruments.
Potential ordinary share	Financial instrument or other contract that may entitle its holder to ordinary shares.

Note: CICA 3500 defines the term "common share" as a share that participates in the earnings of the period only after any other types of shares, such as preferred shares. An enterprise may have more than one class of common shares.

Basic Earnings Per Share

Basic earnings per share (basic EPS) are computed by dividing net profit or loss attributable to ordinary shareholders by the weighted average number of ordinary shares outstanding during the period. The table below explains certain elements in this computation under IAS 33. All requirements conform to those in CICA 3500.

Issue	IAS 33 Requirements
Net profit or loss attributable to ordinary shareholders (Note)	Net profit or loss deducted of after-tax amount of preference dividends (includes any non-cumulative preference share dividends declared during the period, and any cumulative preference share dividends, whether or not declared).
Weighted average number of ordinary shares	• Opening balance of ordinary shares issued, adjusted for the time-weighted effect of increases and decreases in ordinary issued and bought back throughout the period. • Contingently issuable shares are included in the weighted average number of ordinary shares at the date when conditions for their issue have been satisfied. • When there is a change in the number of shares outstanding, during the period or after the reporting period, without a corresponding change in an entity's resources (for example, in case of stock dividends and stock splits), the number of shares outstanding is adjusted as if the event had occurred at the beginning of the earliest period presented.

Note: Several specific differences between IFRS and Canadian GAAP would result in a different numerator (earnings amount) being used in basic EPS calculation.

Diluted Earnings Per Share

Diluted earnings per share (diluted EPS) are calculated by adjusting basic earnings and the weighted average number of ordinary shares to give effect to all dilutive potential ordinary shares that were outstanding during the period. The table below explains certain elements in this calculation under both IAS 33 and CICA 3500.

IAS 33 Requirements	CICA 3500 Requirements
Dilution is a reduction in earnings per share or an increase in loss per share resulting from the assumption that convertible instruments are converted, options or warrants are exercized, or ordinary shares are issued upon the satisfaction of specified conditions.	In determining year-to-date diluted earnings per share using the treasury stock method for options, warrants and their equivalents, CICA 3500 requires the denominator to be calculated by taking the weighted average of the number of incremental shares included in each interim diluted earning per share computation. This difference is expected to be eliminated in the AcSB's improvements to CICA 3500.
All contracts that may be settled in shares or cash are potentially ordinary shares of the enterprise and their dilutive effects should be included in calculating diluted earnings per share. For contracts that may be settled in ordinary shares or cash at the holder's option, the more dilutive of cash settlement and share settlement is used in calculating diluted earnings per share.	CICA 3500 indicates that the presumption that shares will be used to settle the contract may be overcome if past experience or stated policy provides a reasonable basis for believing that the contract will be settled partially or wholly in cash. This difference is expected to be eliminated in the AcSB's present improvements to CICA 3500.

Restatements

Where the number of shares outstanding increases because of stock dividends, stock splits and other similar events, basic and diluted EPS for all periods presented should be restated. The EPS calculations should give effect to these changes if these events occur after the balance sheet date, but before the financial statements are issued.

When net income of a prior period is restated as a result of the retroactive application of a change in an accounting policy during the current period, or a correction of an error, earnings per share information for the prior period or periods should be restated.

Presentation and Disclosures

Basically, IAS 33 and CICA 3500 have similar requirements, except for disclosure for extraordinary item which is not required under IFRS:

- basic and diluted earnings per share for both continuing and total operations are presented on the face of the statement of comprehensive income, with equal prominence, for each class of ordinary shares;

- details of following EPS calculations must be disclosed:
    - o numerator amounts used for the calculation of basic and diluted EPS, together with a reconciliation of those amounts to profit or loss attributable to the parent entity for the period (including individual effect of each class of instruments that affects EPS),
    - o weighted average number of ordinary shares used as the denominator in calculating basic and diluted EPS, together with a reconciliation of these denominators to each other (including individual effect of each class of instruments that affects EPS);

- disclosures of the following must be provided:
    - o instruments (including contingently issuable shares) that could potentially dilute basic EPS in the future that were not included in the calculation of diluted EPS because they are anti-dilutive for the period(s) presented,
    - o if the number of ordinary or potential ordinary shares outstanding increases as a result of a capitalization, bonus issue or share split, or decreases as a result of a reverse share split, the calculation of basic and diluted earnings per share for all periods presented must be adjusted retrospectively. The fact that per share calculations reflect such changes in the number of shares must be disclosed,
    - o basic and diluted earnings per share for discontinued operation are presented either in the statement of comprehensive income or in the notes,
    - o description of significant ordinary share transactions (or potential transactions) occurring after the reporting period, if those transactions had occurred before the end of the reporting period, that result in a corresponding change in the entity's resources including:
        - an issue of shares for cash,
        - an issue of shares when the proceeds are used to repay debt or preference shares outstanding at the end of the reporting period,
        - the redemption of ordinary shares outstanding,
        - the conversion or exercise of potential ordinary shares outstanding at the end of the reporting period into ordinary shares,
        - an issue of options, warrants, or convertible instruments, and
        - the achievement of conditions that would result in the issue of contingently issuable shares.

Additional Per Share Amounts

Additional per share amounts present one significant difference between IFRS and Canadian GAAP. CICA 3500 prohibits disclosure of other income per share amounts, except when required or permitted by another Section. Cash flow per share disclosure is prohibited, while IAS 33 allows it but only under the following circumstances:

- If an entity chooses to present additional per share amounts for a reported component of income (for example, restructuring provisions), such per share amounts must be computed using the weighted average number of ordinary shares determined in accordance with IAS 33.

- If the per share amount is for a component of net profit that has not been reported as a line item on the face of the income statement, a reconciliation between the amount used and a reported amount should also be provided.

Illustrative Disclosures:

Extract 2(64) – EPS and other ratios

Stora Enso Oyj (AR 2007), page 193
Note 33 Earnings per Share and Equity per Share

Earnings per Share	Year Ended 31 December		
	2005	2006	2007
Net Profit / (Loss) for the Period, Continuing Operations, EUR million	72.0	696.2	69.2
Net Profit / (Loss) for the Period, Discontinued Operations, EUR million	-183.1	-111.2	-283.9
Net Profit / (Loss) for the Period, Total Operations, EUR million	-111.1	585.0	-214.7
Total Recognised Income & Expense, Continuing Operations, EUR million	523.2	1 044.1	336.3
Total Recognised Income & Expense, Discontinued Operations, EUR million	-175.3	-107.9	-307.3
Total Recognised Income & Expense, Total Operations, EUR million	347.9	936.2	29.0
Weighted Average Number of A and R Shares	798 686 750	788 578 383	788 599 164
Effect of warrants	530 991	284 280	151 831
Diluted Number of Shares	799 217 741	788 862 663	788 750 995
Basic Earnings / (Loss) per Share, Continuing Operations, EUR	0.09	0.88	0.09
Basic Earnings / (Loss) per Share, Discontinued Operations, EUR	-0.23	-0.14	-0.36
Basic Earnings / (Loss) per Share, Total Operations, EUR	-0.14	0.74	-0.27
Total Recognised Income & Expense per Share, Continuing Operations, EUR	0.65	1.32	0.43
Total Recognised Income & Expense per Share, Discontinued Operations EUR	-0.21	-0.13	-0.39
Total Recognised Income & Expense per Share, Total Operations, EUR	0.44	1.19	0.04

There was no difference between Basic Earnings per Shares and Diluted Earnings due to the immaterial effect of the warrants

Equity per Share	As at 31 December		
	2005	2006	2007
Shareholders' Equity, EUR million	7 220.1	7 799.6	7 476.1
Market Value, EUR million	9 304.0	9 527.9	8 076.0
Number of A and R Shares	788 565 047	788 585 872	788 619 987
Basic Shareholders' Equity per Share, EUR	9.16	9.89	9.48
Dividend per Share Paid / Declared, EUR	0.45	0.45	0.45
Market Value per Share, EUR			
A shares	11.46	12.30	10.19
R shares	11.44	12.00	10.24
Average	11.44	12.08	10.23

Commentary: This extract shows dividend per share and equity per share figures, in addition to EPS amounts. Though dividend per share might be presented, Canadian GAAP would prohibit the presentation of equity per share.

Extract 2(65) – EPS and instruments anti-dilutive

Koninklijke Philips Electronics N.V. (AR 2007), page 224

44 Earnings per share

The earnings per share (EPS) data have been calculated as follows:

	2005	2006	2007
Net income			
Income from continuing operations	3,380	654	4,728
Income (loss) from discontinued operations	(6)	4,010	(73)
Net income available to holders of common shares	3,374	4,664	4,655
Weighted average number of shares	1,249,955,546	1,174,924,579	1,086,128,418
Plus incremental shares from assumed conversions of:			
Options and restricted share rights	2,771,955 / 7,531,636		11,669,275
Convertible debentures	602,863 / 1,174,299		1,127,690
Dilutive potential common shares[1]	3,374,818	8,705,935	12,796,965
Adjusted weighted average number of shares	1,253,330,364	1,183,630,514	1,098,925,383
Basic earnings per share in euros			
Income from continuing operations	2.70	0.56	4.35
Income (loss) from discontinued operations	-	3.41	(0.06)
Net income attributable to stockholders	2.70	3.97	4.29
Diluted earnings per share in euros			
Income from continuing operations	2.70	0.55	4.30
Income (loss) from discontinued operations	-	3.39	(0.06)
Net income attributable to stockholders	2.70	3.94	4.24

1) In 2007, 27 million securities (2006: 19 million, 2005: 34 million) that could potentially dilute basic EPS were not included in the computation of dilutive EPS because the effect would have been antidilutive for the periods presented.

Commentary: The company provides details on the calculation of basic EPS and diluted EPS. Note that the company shows EPS figures from continuing operations, from discontinued operations and net income. Also the company discloses that the securities that could potentially dilute basic EPS were not included in the calculation of diluted EPS because the effect would have been anti-dilutive for the periods presented.

Disclosures are in line with CICA 3500.

Extract 2(66) – EPS and dividends per share

Vodacom Group Plc (AR 2007). page 149

32. EARNINGS AND DIVIDEND PER SHARE

32.1 Basic and diluted earnings per share

	2005 R	2006 R	2007 R
The calculation of basic earnings per ordinary share was based on earnings of R5,012.3 million (2005: R3,855.5 million) at March 31, 2006 and 10,000 issued ordinary shares (2005: 10,000) at March 31, 2006. The following adjustments were made:	385,550	501,230	
Foreign exchange gain on monetary investment in foreign operation	190	1,380	
Earnings per share – restated	385,740	502,610	
The calculation of basic diluted earnings per ordinary share is based on earnings of R6,342.4 million (2006: R5,026.1 million; 2005: R3,857.4 million) and 10,000 issued ordinary shares (2006: 10,000; 2005: 10,000).	385,740	502,610	**634,240**
Due to no dilution factors being present, basic earnings per share equals diluted earnings per share.			

32.2 Dividend per share

The calculation of the dividend per ordinary share is based on a declared ordinary dividend of R5,400.0 million (2006: R4, 500.0 million; 2005:R3, 400.0 million;) and 10,000 issued ordinary shares (2006: 10,000; 2005: 10,000). The dividends were declared as follows:

	2005 R	2006 R	2007 R
Declared March 14, 2007 to shareholders registered on April 2, 2007 and paid on April 4, 2007 (Final)	-	-	**290,000**
Declared September 7, 2006 to shareholders registered on October 2, 2006 and paid on October 4, 2006 (Interim)	-	-	**250,000**
Declared March 9, 2006 to shareholders registered on April 3, 2006 and paid on April 5, 2006 (Final)	-	280,000	-
Declared September 9, 2005 to all shareholders registered on October 1, 2005 and paid on October 3, 2005 (Interim)	-	170,000	-
Declared March 10, 2005 to shareholders registered on March 31, 2005 and paid on April 1, 2005 (Final)	180,000	-	-
Declared September 10, 2004 to shareholders registered on October 1, 2004 and paid on October 1, 2004 (Interim)	160,000	-	-
	340,000	450,000	**540,000**

Extract 2(67) – Additional per share figures

Xstrata plc (AR 2007), page 195		
12. Earnings Per Share		
US$m	**2007**	2006
Continuing operations:		
Profit before exceptional items attributable to ordinary equity holders of the parent from continuing operations	**5,372**	3,286
Exceptional items from continuing operations	**118**	(1,849)
Profit attributable to ordinary equity holders of the parent from continuing operations	**5,490**	1,437
Interest in respect of convertible borrowings	**16**	37
Profit attributable to ordinary equity holders of the parent for diluted earnings per share from continuing operations	**5,506**	1,474
Total operations:		
Profit before exceptional items attributable to ordinary equity holders of the parent from continuing operations	**5,372**	3,286
Exceptional items from continuing operations	**118**	(1,849)
Profit attributable to ordinary equity holders of the parent from continuing operations	**5,490**	1,437
Profit attributable to ordinary equity holders of the parent from discontinued operations	**53**	64
Profit attributable to ordinary equity holders of the parent	**5,543**	1,501
Interest in respect of convertible borrowings	**16**	37
Profit attributable to ordinary equity holders of the parent for diluted earnings per share	**5,559**	1,538
Weighted average number of shares (000) excluding own shares:		
For basic earnings per share	**959,549**	771,820
Effect of dilution:		
– Free shares and share options (000)	**9,196**	9,441
– Convertible borrowings	**17,418**	50,294
For diluted earnings per share	**986,163**	831,555
Basic earnings per share (US$)		
Continuing operations:		
– before exceptional items	**5.60**	4.26
– exceptional items	**0.12**	(2.40)
	5.72	1.86
Discontinued operations:		
– before exceptional items	**0.06**	0.08
– exceptional items	**–**	–
	0.06	0.08
Total:		
– before exceptional items	**5.66**	4.34
– exceptional items	**0.12**	(2.40)
	5.78	1.94
Diluted earnings per share (US$)		
Continuing operations:		
– before exceptional items	**5.47**	3.99
– exceptional items	**0.12**	(2.22)
	5.59	1.77
Discontinued operations:		
– before exceptional items	**0.05**	0.08
– exceptional items	**–**	–
	0.05	0.08
Total:		
– before exceptional items	**5.52**	4.07
– exceptional items	**0.12**	(2.22)
	5.64	1.85

Xstrata plc (AR 2007) (continued)

Basic earnings per share is calculated by dividing the net profit for the year attributable to the equity holders of the parent company by the weighted average number of ordinary shares outstanding for the year, excluding own shares. Adjustments are made for continuing and discontinued operations and before exceptional items and after exceptional items as outlined above, to present a meaningful basis for analysis.

Diluted earnings per share is based on basic earnings per share adjusted for the potential dilution if director and employee free shares and share options are exercised and the convertible bonds are converted into ordinary shares. An adjustment is also made to net profit for the interest in respect of the convertible borrowings and related hedging.

On 30 October 2006, 235,787,596 ordinary shares were issued under a rights issue which was structured as an issue of one new ordinary share at a price of GBP12.65 per share for every three existing ordinary shares held. The theoretical ex-rights price for an ordinary share was GBP19.51. The 2006 earnings per share have been calculated after applying a factor of 0.9 for the bonus element of the rights issue.

On 16 January 2008, 6,000,000 shares were issued to the ESOP at a market price of GBP34.90 per share (refer to note 26).

13. Dividends Paid and Proposed

US$m	2007	2006
Declared and paid during the year:		
Final dividend for 2006: 30 cents per ordinary share (2005: 22.4 cents per ordinary share)	**290**	159
Interim dividend for 2007: 16 cents per ordinary share (2006: 11.6 cents per ordinary share)	**153**	92
	443	251
Proposed for approval at the Annual General Meeting (not recognised as a liability as at 31 December):		
Final dividend for 2007: 34 cents per ordinary share (2006: 30 cents per ordinary share)	**326**	281

Dividends declared in respect of the year ended 31 December 2007 will be paid on 16 May 2008. The 2007 interim dividend was paid on 12 October 2007.

As stated in note 26, own shares held in the ESOP and by the ECMP have waived the right to receive dividends.

The dividends per share declared and paid prior to 30 October 2006 have been adjusted by the rights issue bonus adjustment factor of 0.9 (refer to note 12).

Commentary: The company provides details on the calculations of various performance measures of per share amounts. Disclosures are consistent with Canadian GAAP except that the latter prohibit the presentation of non-GAAP per share amounts (earnings per share before exceptional items).

Segment Information

IFRS 8 applies to annual reporting periods beginning on or after January 1, 2009. It may be adopted early, as long as that fact is disclosed in the notes to the financial statements. IFRS 8 is essentially converged with SFAS 131, *Disclosures about Segments of an Enterprise and Related Information*. CICA 1701, which is based on SFAS 131, has been applied since fiscal years beginning on or after January 1, 1998.

Objective

IFRS 8 and CICA 1701 aim to provide information that will help users of an entity's financial statements evaluate the nature and financial effects of the business activities in which it engages and the economic environments in which it operates.

Management Approach

Both IFRS 8 and CICA 1701 call for segment information disclosures based on the information management uses internally. This approach requires entities to identify and measure the financial performance of their "operating segments."

Definition

IFRS 8 and CICA 1701 define an operating segment as a component of an entity:

- that engages in business activities from which it may earn revenues and incur expenses (including revenues and expenses relating to transactions with other components of the same entity);
- whose operating results are regularly reviewed by the entity's chief operating decision maker (CODM) to make decisions about resources to be allocated to the segment and assess its performance; and
- for which discrete financial information is available.

This definition requires that both the chief operating decision maker (CODM) and operating segments be identified.

Note that IFRS 8 and CICA 1701 specify that the term CODM identifies a function, not necessarily a manager with a specific title. Often, the CODM is the chief executive officer or chief operating officer but it could also be a group of executive directors or other executive groups.

The following tables summarize IFRS 8 requirements for:

- identification of operating segments;
- aggregation of operating segments;
- minimum reportable segments;
- measure of segment's profitability, assets and liabilities;
- disclosures; and
- reconciliation.

Since IFRS 8 is almost identical to CICA 1701, all issues discussed also apply under Canadian GAAP (as required by CICA 1701). Minor differences between IFRS 8 and CICA 1701 are noted.

Identification of Operating Segments

Issue	IFRS 8 Requirements

Identification of an entity's component and CODM	• Identify:
	  o business activities (which may not necessarily earn revenue or incur expenses),
	  o CODM function that allocates resources to, and assess the performance of, the operating segments which,
	    • does not necessarily reflect a given title, and
	    • must be examined regularly, particularly following a business reorganization, acquisition or disposal.
	• Determine whether:
	  o discrete financial information is available for the business activities, and
	  o that information is regularly reviewed by the CODM.

Issue	IFRS 8 Requirements
Identification of the operating reporting (when there are matrix structures) (Note)	Entity determines which set of components constitutes the operating segments, taking account of what financial statement users would need to know to evaluate the entity's business activities and the environment it operates in. Consequently, IFRS 8 allows entities to determine their segments according to either product/services or geography. Judgment is exercised to determine which basis provides the most useful information. Under CICA 1701, entities with matrix structures must determine their segments based on products or services.
Identification of changes to the operating reporting and to the CODM	• Change in the CODM and/or the information provided to and reviewed by the CODM for the purposes of evaluating performance and allocating resources would have an impact on the identified operating segments. Judgment must be used to establish, at each reporting date, whether the current operating segment disclosure continues to be appropriate. • No specific guidance is provided. • The following should be assessed at each reporting date as they might have an impact on operating segment identification: o a restructure of reporting lines, o a modification of reporting package, o organizational chart subsequent to acquisition/disposal of business activities, o budgeting process modification, o a new line of business, and o a change from a model of geographical reporting to that of product line reporting.

Note: IFRS 8 addresses the issue of matrix structures by presenting an example where some managers are responsible for product and service lines worldwide, whereas other managers are responsible for specific geographical areas. The CODM reviews the operating results of both sets of components, and discrete financial information is available for both.

Aggregation of Operating Segments

Two or more operating segments may be combined as a single operating segment if:

- aggregation provides financial statement users with information that allows them to evaluate the business and the environment in which it operates;
- they have similar economic characteristics; and
- they are similar in each of the following respects:
  - o the nature of the products and services,
  - o the nature of the production processes,
  - o the type or class of customer for their products and services,
  - o the methods used to distribute their products or provide their services, and
  - o the nature of the regulatory environment (i.e., banking, insurance or public utilities), if applicable.

In case of operating segments represent different countries, aggregation of such operating segments should be possible if countries covered have similar exchange control regulations and underlying currency. Note that, even when such aggregation is permitted, separate disclosure of revenues and assets for each material foreign country is required. This disclosure allows financial statement users to assess the dependence of the entity on customers based in one particular country.

Minimum Reportable Segments

Issue	IFRS 8 Requirements

Quantitative thresholds	Information on an operating segment should be reported separately if one of the following quantitative thresholds is met:
	• reported revenue (external and inter-segment) is 10% or more of the combined revenue of all operating segments;
	• the absolute amount of a segment's reported profit or loss is 10% or more of the greater of:
	  o the combined reported profit of all operating segments that did not report a loss, and
	  o the combined loss of all operating segments that reported a loss;
	• the segment's assets are 10% or more of the combined assets of all operating segments.

Minimum number of reportable segments	After applying the above quantitative thresholds, an entity must ensure that the total external revenue attributable to reportable segments identified is at least 75% of the entity's total revenue. If the 75% threshold is not met, additional reportable segments must be identified (even if they do not meet the 10% thresholds) until at least 75% of the entity's total external revenue is included in its reportable segments. There is no requirement as to the maximum number of reportable segments; however IFRS 8 suggests a limit of 10.

Measure of Segment's Profitability, Assets and Liabilities

Issue	IFRS 8 Requirements
Reporting basis	• Information presented must be on the same basis as reported internally, even if the segment information does not comply with IFRS or the accounting policies used in the consolidated financial statements. • Measure of segment profitability may differ for each operating segment (must reflect reported measures of profitability to the CODM). • When the CODM receives more than one profitability measure, the measure that the CODM most relies on for assessing performance and deciding on the allocation of resources should be disclosed. • When the CODM relies on two or more measures equally, the measure most consistent with those used in measuring the corresponding amounts in the entity's financial statements should be used. *Examples of profitability measures other than the one used for consolidated financial statements:* • cash basis of accounting (as opposed to an accruals basis); • local GAAP accounting (e.g., for foreign subsidiaries); • industry benchmarks.
Allocations	• Revenues, expenses and gains or losses are included in determining reported segment profit or loss insofar that the CODM uses the resulting information. • Assets and liabilities are included in the measures of the segment's assets and liabilities if they are used by the CODM as reported for that segment. • All allocations to reported segment must be done on a reasonable basis.

Disclosures

Issue	IFRS 8 Requirements
General descriptive information for reportable segments	• factors used to identify an entity's reportable segments, including: basis of organization (for example, products and services, geographical areas, regulatory environments, or a combination of factors and whether operating segments have been aggregated); and • types of products and services from which each reportable segment derives its revenues.

Disclosures for each reportable segment (Note 1)	• Measure of profit or loss and total assets and liabilities if reviewed regularly by CODM.
	• Separate disclosure is required about each reportable segment if the specified amounts are included in the measure of segment profit or loss reviewed by the CODM, or are otherwise regularly provided to the latter, even if not included in that measure of segment profit or loss:
	  o revenues from external customers,
	  o revenues from transactions with other operating segments of the same entity,
	  o interest revenue,
	  o interest expense,
	  o depreciation and amortization,
	  o other material items of income and expense disclosed in accordance with IAS 1,
	  o entity's interest in the profit or loss of associates and joint ventures accounted for by the equity method,
	  o income tax expense or income, and
	  o material non-cash items other than depreciation and amortization.
	• Additional disclosures when the specified amounts are included in the measure of segment assets reviewed by the CODM or are otherwise regularly provided to the latter, even if not included in the measure of segment assets:
	  o amount of investment in associates and joint ventures accounted for by the equity method, and
	  o amounts of additions to non-current assets other than financial instruments, deferred tax assets, post-employment benefit assets and rights arising under insurance contracts.

Disclosures when reportable segment measures of profitability differ from the one used for consolidated financial statements	• basis of accounting for transactions between reportable segments; • nature of any differences between a segments' reported amounts and the consolidated totals (for example, those resulting from differences in accounting policies and policies for the allocation of centrally incurred costs); • nature of any changes from prior periods in the measurement methods and the effect of those changes; and • nature and effect of any asymmetrical allocations to reportable segments (for example, where an entity allocates depreciation expense to a segment without allocating the related depreciable assets to that segment).
Disclosure when changes in reporting segments (restatement)	• Corresponding information for earlier periods, including interim periods, must be restated unless the information is not available and the cost to develop it would be excessive. The determination of whether the information is not available and the cost to develop it would be excessive is made for each individual item of disclosure. • Segment information for the current period on both the old basis and the new basis of segmentation, unless the necessary information is not available and the cost to develop it would be excessive. In case of the latter, an entity specifies that it has not restated the corresponding items of segment information for earlier periods.

Issue	IFRS 8 Requirements

Entity-wide disclosures (if not provided as part of reportable segment information) (Note 2)	Unless the information is not prepared for internal use and the cost to develop it is excessive, entities are required to report:
	• revenues from external customers:
	  o for each product and service, or each group of similar products and services,
	  o attributed to the entity's country of domicile and attributed to all foreign countries from which the entity derives revenues,
	  o attributed to an individual foreign country, if material,
	  o basis for attributing revenues from external customers to individual countries.
	• non-current assets (other than financial instruments, deferred tax assets, post-employment benefit assets, and rights arising under insurance contracts) located in the entity's country of domicile and in all foreign countries in which the entity holds assets.
	• non-current assets in an individual foreign country, if material.
	• extent of reliance on major customers, including details, if any customer's revenue is greater than 10% of the entity's total revenue.

Note 1: Contrary to IFRS 8, CICA 1701 does not require the disclosure of segment liabilities. Contrary to IFRS 8, CICA 1701 requires the disclosure of extraordinary items.

Note 2: CICA 1701 requires the disclosure of "capital assets and goodwill", whereas the table above refers to "non-current assets".

Reconciliation

Issue	IFRS 8 Requirements
Specific amounts	• total of the reportable segments' revenues to the entity's revenue; • total of the reportable segments' measures of profit or loss to the entity's profit or loss before tax expense (tax income) and discontinued operations. If, however, an entity allocates to reportable segments items such as tax expense (tax income), the entity may reconcile the total of the segments' measures of profit or loss to its profit or loss after those items; • total of the reportable segments' assets to the entity's assets; • total of the reportable segments' liabilities to the entity's liabilities if segment liabilities are reported; (Note) • Total of the reportable segments' amounts for every other material item of information disclosed to the corresponding amount for the entity.
Other	All non-reportable operating segments and other business activities should be combined and disclosed in an "all other" category on a stand-alone basis. The disclosure of "other reconciling items" should be presented separately in the reconciliation of segment totals to the consolidated financial statement totals. The sources of the revenue included in the 'all other segments' category must be described.

Note: Contrary to IFRS 8, CICA 1701 does not require reconciliation for liabilities.

Illustrative Disclosures:

Extract 2(68) – Segment information

Vodafone Group Plc (AR 2008), page 96 and 97

3. Segment analysis

The Group has a single group of related services and products, being the supply of communications services and products. Segment information is provided on the basis of geographic areas, being the basis on which the Group manages its world wide interests. Revenue is attributed to a country or region based on the location of the Group company reporting the revenue. Inter-segment sales are charged at arms length prices. The Group uses adjusted operating profit for internal performance analysis and, therefore, the Group's measure of segment profit is adjusted operating profit, being operating profit excluding non-operating income of associates, impairment losses and other income and expense.

During the year ended 31 March 2008, the Group early adopted IFRS 8 "Operating Segments". The Group also changed its organisation structure such that the Group's associated undertaking in France, SFR, is now managed within the Europe region and reported within Other Europe. As a result, prior period disclosures have been amended to conform to the current year presentation.

	Segment revenue £m	Common functions £m	Intra-region revenue £m	Regional revenue £m	Inter-region revenue £m	Group revenue £m	Adjusted operating profit £m
31 March 2008							
Germany	5,397		(128)	5,269	(10)	5,259	1,265
Italy	4,435		(33)	4,402	(6)	4,396	1,573
Spain	5,063		(96)	4,967	(4)	4,963	1,282
UK	5,424		(46)	5,378	(10)	5,368	431
Arcor	1,632		(86)	1,546	(1)	1,545	225
Other Europe[1]	4,583		(64)	4,519	(3)	4,516	1,430
Europe	**26,534**		**(453)**	**26,081**	**(34)**	**26,047**	**6,206**
Eastern Europe	3,154		–	3,154	(35)	3,119	332
Middle East, Africa & Asia[2]	4,547		(1)	4,546	(24)	4,522	769
Pacific	1,645		–	1,645	(14)	1,631	181
Associates – US	–		–	–	–	–	2,447
EMAPA	**9,346**		**(1)**	**9,345**	**(73)**	**9,272**	**3,729**
Common functions[3]	–	170	–	170	(11)	159	140
Group	**35,880**	**170**	**(454)**	**35,596**	**(118)**	**35,478**	**10,075**
31 March 2007							
Germany	5,443		(123)	5,320	(9)	5,311	1,354
Italy	4,245		(44)	4,201	(5)	4,196	1,575
Spain	4,500		(106)	4,394	(3)	4,391	1,100
UK	5,124		(54)	5,070	(9)	5,061	511
Arcor	1,441		(27)	1,414	–	1,414	171
Other Europe[1]	4,275		(82)	4,193	(4)	4,189	1,448
Europe	**25,028**		**(436)**	**24,592**	**(30)**	**24,562**	**6,159**
Eastern Europe	2,477		–	2,477	(31)	2,446	184
Middle East, Africa & Asia[2]	2,565		–	2,565	(9)	2,556	694
Pacific	1,399		–	1,399	(11)	1,388	159
Associates – US	–		–	–	–	–	2,077
Associates – Other	–		–	–	–	–	130
EMAPA	**6,441**		–	**6,441**	**(51)**	**6,390**	**3,244**
Common functions[3]	–	168	–	168	(16)	152	128
Group	**31,469**	**168**	**(436)**	**31,201**	**(97)**	**31,104**	**9,531**

Vodafone Group Plc (AR 2008) (continued)	Segment revenue £m	Common functions £m	Intra-region revenue £m	Regional revenue £m	Inter-region revenue £m	Group revenue £m	Adjusted operating profit £m
31 March 2006							
Germany	5,754	(143)	5,611	(9)	5,602	1,496	
Italy	4,363	(39)	4,324	(4)	4,320	1,672	
Spain	3,995	(100)	3,895	(2)	3,893	968	
UK	5,048	(50)	4,998	(10)	4,988	698	
Arcor	1,320	(34)	1,286		1,286	139	
Other Europe[(1)]	4,697	(78)	4,619	(3)	4,616	1,452	
Europe	**25,177**	**(444)**	**24,733**	**(28)**	**24,705**	**6,425**	
Eastern Europe	1,435		1,435	(14)	1,421	176	
Middle East, Africa & Asia[(2)]	1,784		1,784	(15)	1,769	523	
Pacific	1,335		1,335	(14)	1,321	140	
Associates – US	–		–			1,732	
Associates – Other	–		–			192	
EMAPA	**4,554**		**4,554**	**(43)**	**4,511**	**2,763**	
Common functions[(3)]	–	145	–	145	(11)	134	211
Group	**29,731**	**145**	**(444)**	**29,432**	**(82)**	**29,350**	**9,399**

Notes:

(1) Adjusted operating profit includes £425 million (2007: £517 million; 2006: £479 million), representing the Group's share of results in associated undertakings.

(2) Adjusted operating profit includes £2 million (2007: £nil; 2006: £nil), representing the Group's share of results in associated undertakings.

(3) Adjusted operating profit includes £2 million (2007: £1 million; 2006: £8 million), representing the Group's share of results in associated undertakings.

A reconciliation of adjusted operating profit to operating profit/(loss) is shown below. For a reconciliation of operating profit/(loss) to profit/(loss) before taxation, see the Consolidated Income Statement on page 88.

	2008 £m	2007 £m	2006 £m
Adjusted operating profit	10,075	9,531	9,399
Impairment losses	–	(11,600)	(23,515)
Other items	(28)	505	32
Operating profit/(loss)	**10,047**	**(1,564)**	**(14,084)**

	Non-current assets[(1)] £m	Capitalised fixed asset additions[(2)] £m	Other expenditure on intangible assets £m	Depreciation and amortisation £m	Impairment of goodwill £m
31 March 2008					
Germany	18,267	392	14	1,067	–
Italy	16,215	411	1	582	–
Spain	14,589	533	–	500	–
UK	7,930	465	–	973	–
Arcor	862	221	–	100	–
Other Europe	8,303	469	11	616	–
Europe	**66,166**	**2,491**	**26**	**3,838**	**–**
Eastern Europe	6,879	633	–	665	–
Middle East, Africa & Asia	11,958	1,554	7	954	–
Pacific	1,346	212	–	245	–
EMAPA	**20,183**	**2,399**	**7**	**1,864**	**–**
Common functions	717	185	8	207	–
Group	**87,066**	**5,075**	**41**	**5,909**	**–**

Vodafone Group Plc (AR 2008) (continued)				
	Non-current assets[(1)] £m	Capitalised fixed asset additions[(2)] £m	Other expenditure on intangible assets £m	Depreciation and amortisation £m	Impairment of goodwill £m
31 March 2007					
Germany	16,233	425	–	1,063	6,700
Italy	13,722	421	26	556	4,900
Spain	12,289	547	–	449	–
UK	8,483	661	–	930	–
Arcor	627	189	–	144	–
Other Europe	7,187	489	6	586	–
Europe	**58,541**	**2,732**	**32**	**3,728**	**11,600**
Eastern Europe	6,235	435	–	349	–
Middle East, Africa & Asia	3,079	574	276	272	–
Pacific	1,249	251	–	194	–
EMAPA	**10,563**	**1,260**	**276**	**815**	**–**
Common functions	612	216	–	568	–
Group	**69,716**	**4,208**	**308**	**5,111**	**11,600**
31 March 2006					
Germany		592	–	1,167	19,400
Italy		541	1	588	3,600
Spain		502	–	395	–
UK		665	11	924	–
Arcor		129	–	140	–
Other Europe		511	4	645	515
Europe		**2,940**	**16**	**3,859**	**23,515**
Eastern Europe		280	–	231	–
Middle East, Africa & Asia		426	–	216	–
Pacific		247	–	209	–
EMAPA		**953**	**–**	**656**	**–**
Common functions		112	–	189	–
Group		**4,005**	**16**	**4,704**	**23,515**

Notes:

(1) Includes goodwill, other intangible assets and property, plant and equipment.

(2) Includes additions to property, plant and equipment and computer software, reported within intangible assets.

Vodafone Group Plc (AR 2008) (continued)
page 98
4. Operating profit/(loss)

Operating profit/(loss) has been arrived at after charging/(crediting):

	2008 £m	2007 £m	2006 £m
Net foreign exchange (gains)/losses	(27)	6	–
Depreciation of property, plant and equipment (note 11):			
Owned assets	3,400	2,994	3,069
Leased assets	27	17	10
Amortisation of intangible assets (note 9)	2,482	2,100	1,625
Impairment of goodwill (note 10)	–	11,600	23,515
Research and development expenditure	234	222	206
Staff costs (note 35)	2,698	2,466	2,310
Operating lease rentals payable:			
Plant and machinery	43	35	35
Other assets including fixed line rentals	1,117	984	933
Loss on disposal of property, plant and equipment	70	43	69
Own costs capitalised attributable to the construction or acquisition of property, plant and equipment	(245)	(244)	(256)

The total remuneration of the Group's auditor, Deloitte & Touche LLP, and its affiliates for services provided to the Group is analysed below:

	2008 £m	2007 £m	2006 £m
Audit fees:			
Parent company	1	1	1
Subsidiary undertakings	5	4	3
	6	5	4
Fees for statutory and regulatory filings[1]	1	2	–
Audit and audit-related fees	7	7	4
Other fees:			
Taxation	1	1	1
Corporate finance transactions	–	–	1
Other[2]	1	2	2
	2	3	4
Total fees	9	10	8

Notes:

(1) Amounts for 2008 and 2007 include mainly audit fees in relation to Section 404 of the US Sarbanes-Oxley Act of 2002.

(2) Amounts for 2007 and 2006 include fees mainly relating to the preparatory work required in advance of the implementation of Section 404 of the US Sarbanes-Oxley Act of 2002 and general accounting advice.

The total remuneration includes £nil (2007: £nil, 2006: £1 million) in respect of the Group's discontinued operations in Japan. In addition to the above, the Group's joint ventures and associated undertakings paid fees totalling £2 million (2007: £2 million, 2006: £2 million) and £3 million (2007: £4 million, 2006: £4 million), respectively, to Deloitte & Touche LLP and its affiliates during the year. Deloitte & Touche LLP and its affiliates have also received amounts totalling less than £1 million in each of the last three years in respect of services provided to pension schemes and charitable foundations associated to the Group.

A description of the work performed by the Audit Committee in order to safeguard auditor independence when non-audit services are provided is set out in "Corporate Governance" on page 69.

Commentary: The company says that it has adopted IFRS 8 early and specifies that it has:

- changed its organizational structure;
- amended prior period disclosures to conform to the current year presentation;
- a single group of related services and products – the supply of communications services and products;
- provided segment information on the basis of geographic areas, which is the basis on which it manages its world-wide interests;
- attributed revenue to a country or region based on the location of company reporting the revenue;
- charged inter-segment sales at arms' length prices;
- used adjusted operating profit for internal performance analysis (i.e., its segment profitability measure is adjusted operating profit, being operating profit excluding non-operating income of associates, impairment losses and other income and expense, which it reconciled to operating profit in a separate note also reproduced above.

Note that the company does not show liabilities allocated to operating segment. Non-current assets are allocated to operating segments (which include goodwill, other intangible assets and property plant and equipment).

The presentation and disclosures are in line with CICA 1701.

Extract 2(69) – Segments profitability measure

Telstra Corporation Limited (AR 2007), page 140

5.Segment information (in part)

Telstra Group

Year ended 30 June 2007	TC&C $m	TB $m	TE&G $m	TW $m	Sensis $m	TInt. $m	TO $m	Other(a) $m	Elimina-tions	Total $m
Revenue from external customers .	9,509	3,241	4,465	2,657	1,968	1,574	192	103	-	23,709
Add inter-segment revenue. . .	-	-	64	300	-	32	51	5	(452)	-
Total segment revenue	9,509	3,241	4,529	2,957	1,968	1,606	243	108	(452)	23,709
Segment result	5,593	2,592	2,572	2,867	749	52	(3,915)	(4,830)	45	5,725
Share of equity accounted net (losses)/profits.	-	-	(6)	-	(1)	-	-	-	-	(7)
Less net gain on sale of investments .	-	-	43	-	4	9	2	3	-	61
Earnings before interest and income tax expense (EBIT) . . .	5,593	2,592	2,609	2,867	752	61	(3,913)	(4,827)	45	5,779
Segment result has been calculated after charging/(crediting) the following non cash expenses:										
Impairment losses	182	8	7	6	143	21	14	14	-	395
Reversal of impairment losses .	-	(1)	-	(1)	-	-	(4)	-	-	(6)
Depreciation and amortisation .	-	-	51	-	130	325	61	3,515	-	4,082
Other significant non cash expenses	24	10	21	4	1	-	142	64		266

Commentary: The above extract presents a segment profitability measure based on EBIT (a non-GAAP measure), which would also be acceptable under Canadian GAAP.

Extract 2(70) – Segment information

Deutsche Telekom AG (AR 2007), pages 167 to 172

39 Segment reporting.

In November 2006, the International Accounting Standards Board (IASB) issued IFRS 8 "Operating Segments." IFRS 8 replaces IAS 14 "Segment Reporting" and must be applied to reporting periods beginning on or after January 1, 2009. Deutsche Telekom has opted for early adoption of IFRS 8, beginning with the financial year ending on December 31, 2007. According to IFRS 8, reportable operating segments are identified based on the "management approach." This approach stipulates external segment reporting based on the Group's internal organizational and management structure and on internal financial reporting to the chief operating decision maker. In the Deutsche Telekom Group, the Board of Management of Deutsche Telekom AG is responsible for measuring and steering the business success of the segments and is considered the chief operating decision maker within the meaning of IFRS 8.

In contrast to the former reporting structure, Deutsche Telekom reports on five operating segments, which are independently managed by bodies responsible for the respective segments depending on the nature of products and services offered, brands, sales channels, and customer profiles. The identification of Company components as business segments is based in particular on the existence of segment managers who report directly to the Board of Management of Deutsche Telekom AG and who are responsible for the performance of the segment under their charge. In accordance with IFRS 8, Mobile Communications Europe and Mobile Communications USA are reported separately as operating segments, since internal reporting and management channels in the Mobile Communications segment have been changed. Prior-year figures have been adjusted accordingly.

Information on the Group's segments is presented below.

The **Mobile Communications Europe** operating segment bundles all activities of T-Mobile International AG in Germany, the United Kingdom, the Netherlands, Austria, Poland, and the Czech Republic, as well as Deutsche Telekom's other mobile communications activities in Slovakia, Croatia, Macedonia, Montenegro, and Hungary.

The **Mobile Communications USA** operating segment combines all activities of T-Mobile International AG in the U.S. market.

All entities in the Mobile Communications Europe and Mobile Communications USA operating segments offer mobile voice and data services to consumers and business customers. The T-Mobile subsidiaries also market mobile devices and other hardware in connection with the services offered. In addition, T-Mobile services are sold to resellers and to companies that buy network services and market them independently to third parties (mobile virtual network operators, or MVNOs).

The **Broadband/Fixed Network** operating segment offers consumers and small business customers traditional fixed-network services on the basis of a state-of-the-art infrastructure, broadband Internet access, and multimedia services. This segment also conducts business with national and international network operators and with resellers (wholesale including resale). In addition, it provides wholesale telecommunications services for Deutsche Telekom's other operating segments. Outside Germany, the Broadband/Fixed Network segment has a presence in both Western and Eastern Europe: In Western Europe, it is represented by subsidiaries in Austria and Switzerland. The subsidiary T-Online France was sold in the second quarter and the subsidiary T-Online Spain in the third quarter of 2007. In Eastern Europe's markets, the operating segment has operations primarily in Hungary including Macedonia, Montenegro, Bulgaria and Romania (Magyar Telekom), Croatia (T-Hrvatski Telekom), and Slovakia (Slovak Telekom).

The **Business Customers** operating segment is divided into two operating business units: T-Systems Enterprise Services, which supports around 60 multinational corporations and large public authorities, and T-Systems Business Services, which serves around 160,000 large and medium-sized business customers. T-Systems is represented by subsidiaries in more than 20 countries, with a particular focus on the Western European countries of Germany, France, Spain, Italy, the United Kingdom, Austria, Switzerland, Belgium, and the Netherlands. The service provider offers its customers a full range of information and communication technology (ICT) from a single source. It realizes integrated ICT solutions on the basis of its extensive expertise in these two technological areas. T-Systems develops and operates infrastructure and industry solutions for its key accounts. Products and services offered to medium-sized enterprises range from low-cost standard products and high-performance networks based on the Internet Protocol (IP) to developing complete ICT solutions.

Deutsche Telekom AG (AR 2007) (continued)

Group units and subsidiaries that are not directly allocated to one of the aforementioned operating segments are included in the Group Headquarters & Shared Services segment. Group Headquarters is responsible for strategic and cross-segment management functions. All other operating functions not directly related to the aforementioned segments' core business are assumed by Shared Services. These include the Real Estate Services division, whose activities include the management of Deutsche Telekom AG's real estate portfolio, and DeTeFleetServices GmbH, a full-service provider of fleet management and mobility services. Vivento, which is also part of Shared Services, is responsible for placing employees and creating employment opportunities. Shared Services primarily has activities in Germany. Real Estate Services also has operations in Hungary and in Slovakia offering facility management services. The main Shared Services subsidiaries include DeTe Immobilien, Deutsche Telekom Immobilien und Service GmbH, GMG Generalmietgesellschaft mbH, DFMG Deutsche Funkturm GmbH, PASM Power and Air Condition Solution Management GmbH & Co. KG, DeTeFleet Services GmbH, and Vivento Customer Services GmbH. Since the beginning of the 2007 financial year, the Group Headquarters & Shared Services segment has also included the shared services and headquarters functions of Magyar Telekom. Deutsche Telekom reported these functions as part of the Broadband/Fixed Network operating segment until the end of 2006.

The reconciliation summarizes the elimination of links between segments.

The measurement principles for Deutsche Telekom's segment reporting structure are based on the IFRS principles adopted in the consolidated financial statements. Deutsche Telekom evaluates the segments' performance based on their profit/loss from operations (EBIT), among other factors. Revenue generated and goods and services exchanged between segments are calculated on the basis of market prices.

Segment assets and liabilities include all assets and liabilities that are attributable to operations and whose positive or negative results determine profit/loss from operations (EBIT). Segment assets include in particular intangible assets; property, plant and equipment; trade and other receivables; and inventories. Segment liabilities include in particular trade and other payables, and significant provisions. Segment investments include additions to intangible assets and property, plant and equipment.

Where entities accounted for using the equity method are directly allocable to a segment, their share of profit/loss after income taxes and their carrying amount is reported in this segment's accounts.

The Group's non-current assets and net revenue are shown by region. These are the regions in which Deutsche Telekom is active: Germany, Europe (excluding Germany), North America and Other countries. The Europe (excluding Germany) region covers the entire European Union (excluding Germany) and the other countries in Europe. The North America region comprises the United States and Canada. The "Other countries" region includes all countries that are not Germany or in Europe (excluding Germany) or North America. Non-current assets are allocated to the regions according to the location of the assets in question. Non-current assets encompass intangible assets; property, plant and equipment; investments accounted for using the equity method as well as other non-current assets. Net revenue is allocated according to the location of the respective customers' operations.

Deutsche Telekom AG (AR 2007) (continued)

millions of €

		Net revenue	Inter-segment revenue	Total revenue	Profit (loss) from operations (EBIT)	Interest income	Interest expense	Share of profit (loss) of associates and joint ventures accounted for using the equity method	Income taxes
Mobile Communications Europe	2007	20,000	713	20,713	2,436	208	(495)	0	635
	2006[a]	17,700	755	18,455	2,746	168	(514)	77	13
	2005[a]	16,673	945	17,618	1,487	164	(531)	131	(554)
Mobile Communications USA	2007	14,050	25	14,075	2,017	99	(457)	6	(518)
	2006[a]	13,608	20	13,628	1,756	68	(408)	3	651
	2005[a]	11,858	29	11,887	1,519	14	(271)	2	2,035
Broadband/Fixed Network	2007	19,072	3,618	22,690	3,250	522	(62)	46	(84)
	2006[b]	20,366	4,149	24,515	3,356	256	(41)	31	(241)
	2005[b]	21,447	4,395	25,842	5,264	407	(47)	54	(175)
Business Customers	2007	8,971	3,016	11,987	(323)	91	(99)	0	(47)
	2006[b]	9,301	3,568	12,869	(835)	61	(99)	(86)	(50)
	2005[b]	9,328	3,817	13,145	458	45	(107)	3	(28)
Group Headquarters & Shared Services	2007	423	3,445	3,868	(1,973)	1,015	(3,309)	2	(1,361)
	2006[b]	372	3,386	3,758	(2,138)	1,055	(3,043)	(2)	342
	2005[b]	298	3,279	3,577	(1,010)	1,033	(3,064)	(1)	(1,474)
Total	2007	62,516	10,817	73,333	5,407	1,935	(4,422)	54	(1,375)
	2006	61,347	11,878	73,225	4,885	1,608	(4,105)	23	715
	2005	59,604	12,465	72,069	7,718	1,663	(4,020)	189	(196)
Reconciliation	2007	-	(10,817)	(10,817)	(121)	(1,674)	1,647	0	1
	2006	-	(11,878)	(11,878)	402	(1,311)	1,268	1	255
	2005	-	(12,465)	(12,465)	(96)	(1,265)	1,221	25	(2)
Group	2007	62,516	-	62,516	5,286	261	(2,775)	54	(1,374)
	2006	61,347	-	61,347	5,287	297	(2,837)	24	970
	2005	59,604	-	59,604	7,622	398	(2,799)	214	(198)

a   In contrast to the previous presentation of the three strategic business areas Mobile Communications, Broadband/Fixed Network and Business Customers together with Group Headquarters & Shared Services, reporting as of December 31, 2007 is structured in five operating segments for the first time: Mobile Communications Europe, Mobile Communications USA, Broadband/Fixed Network, Business Customers, and Group Headquarters & Shared Services.

b   Since January 1, 2007, reporting of Magyar Telekom has included a further breakdown of results into the Business Customers and Group Headquarters & Shared Services segments. In previous periods these results were only reported under the Broadband/Fixed Network segment. Prior-year figures have been adjusted accordingly.

Deutsche Telekom AG (AR 2007) (continued)

		Segment assets millions of €	Segment liabilities millions of €	Segment invest- ments millions of €	Invest- ments accounted for using the equity method millions of €	Deprecia- tion and amortiza- tion millions of €	Impair- ment losses millions of €	Employees (average) millions of €
Mobile Communications	2007	35,151	5,263	2,249	0	(3,903)	(338)	30,802
Europe	2006[a]	36,950	5,187	3,231	0	(3,342)	(25)	25,345
	2005[a]	31,945	4,493	1,807	1,595	(3,004)	(1,921)	24,536
Mobile Communications	2007	30,146	3,441	2,203	10	(1,883)	(9)	31,655
USA	2006[a]	33,162	3,070	5,200	6	(1,958)	(33)	28,779
	2005[a]	33,066	3,092	4,481	4	(1,741)	(30)	24,943
Broadband/Fixed Network	2007	25,668	7,235	3,176	86	(3,605)	(70)	97,690
	2006[b]	26,913	8,106	3,251	157	(3,744)	(95)	107,006
	2005[b]	27,374	7,069	3,389	97	(3,974)	(8)	110,611
Business Customers	2007	9,352	4,699	987	9	(882)	(25)	56,566
	2006[b]	9,333	4,869	1,223	23	(939)	(7)	56,595
	2005[b]	8,893	4,010	986	18	(894)	(11)	52,591
Group Headquarters & Shared Services	2007	11,946	8,536	565	4	(708)	(259)	27,023
	2006[b]	11,882	7,608	594	2	(710)	(237)	30,755
	2005[b]	11,376	5,563	619	3	(739)	(233)	31,345
Total	2007	112,263	29,174	9,180	109	(10,981)	(701)	243,736
	2006	118,240	28,840	13,499	188	(10,693)	(397)	248,480
	2005	112,654	24,227	11,282	1,717	(10,352)	(2,203)	244,026
Reconciliation	2007	(3,201)	(3,619)	(103)	0	48	23	–
	2006	(2,963)	(3,142)	(84)	1	69	(13)	–
	2005	(1,743)	(866)	(182)	108	61	(3)	–
Group	2007	109,062	25,555	9,077	109	(10,933)	(678)	243,736
	2006	115,277	25,698	13,415	189	(10,624)	(410)	248,480
	2005	110,911	23,361	11,100	1,825	(10,291)	(2,206)	244,026

a   In contrast to the previous presentation of the three strategic business areas Mobile Communications, Broadband/Fixed Network and Business Customers together with Group Headquarters & Shared Services, reporting as of December 31, 2007 is structured in five operating segments for the first time: Mobile Communications Europe, Mobile Communications USA, Broadband/Fixed Network, Business Customers, and Group Headquarters & Shared Services.

b   Since January 1, 2007, reporting of Magyar Telekom has included a further breakdown of results into the Business Customers and Group Headquarters & Shared Services segments. In previous periods these results were only reported under the Broadband/Fixed Network segment. Prior-year figures have been adjusted accordingly.

Deutsche Telekom AG (AR 2007) (continued)					
millions of €		Net cash from (used in) operating activities	Net cash from (used in) investing activities	Of which: cash capex[c]	Net cash from (used in) financing activities
Mobile Communications Europe	2007	6,494	(3,537)	(1,938)	447
	2006[a]	4,882	(3,166)	(1,950)	(3,049)
	2005[a]	5,271	(667)	(1,717)	(3,120)
Mobile Communications USA	2007	3,622	(2,714)	(1,958)	(831)
	2006[a]	3,388	(5,291)	(5,297)	1,904
	2005[a]	2,846	(3,869)	(3,886)	(837)
Broadband/Fixed Network	2007	6,673	909	(2,805)	(2,895)
	2006[b]	8,812	(2,575)	(3,250)	(4,802)
	2005[b]	9,391	(2,201)	(2,432)	(6,022)
Business Customers	2007	553	(854)	(921)	1,191
	2006[b]	816	(1,523)	(795)	475
	2005[b]	1,575	(1,034)	(795)	(872)
Group Headquarters & Shared Services	2007	854	(3,766)	(471)	(6,933)
	2006[b]	3,208	(3,952)	(508)	(1,866)
	2005[b]	4,213	(1,246)	(475)	(6,774)
Total	2007	18,196	(9,962)	(8,093)	(9,021)
	2006	21,106	(16,507)	(11,800)	(7,338)
	2005	23,296	(9,017)	(9,305)	(17,625)
Reconciliation	2007	(4,482)	1,908	78	2,896
	2006	(6,884)	2,202	(6)	5,277
	2005	(8,238)	(1,101)	36	9,586
Group	2007	13,714	(8,054)	(8,015)	(6,125)
	2006	14,222	(14,305)	(11,806)	(2,061)
	2005	15,058	(10,118)	(9,269)	(8,039)

a   In contrast to the previous presentation of the three strategic business areas Mobile Communications, Broadband/Fixed Network and Business Customers together with Group Headquarters & Shared Services, reporting as of December 31, 2007 is structured in five operating segments for the first time: Mobile Communications Europe, Mobile Communications USA, Broadband/Fixed Network, Business Customers, and Group Headquarters & Shared Services.

b   Since January 1, 2007, reporting of Magyar Telekom has included a further breakdown of results into the Business Customers and Group Headquarters & Shared Services segments. In previous periods these results were only reported under the Broadband/Fixed Network segment. Prior-year figures have been adjusted accordingly.

c   Cash outflows for investments in intangible assets (excluding goodwill) and property, plant and equipment, as shown in the cash flow statement.

Reconciliation of the total of the segments' profit or loss to profit after income taxes.

millions of €	2007	2006	2005
Total profit (loss) of reportable segments	5,407	4,885	7,718
Reconciliation to the Group	(121)	402	(96)
Profit from operations (EBIT) of the Group	5,286	5,287	7,622
Loss from financial activities	(2,834)	(2,683)	(1,403)
Income taxes	(1,374)	970	(198)
Profit after income taxes	1,078	3,574	6,021

Deutsche Telekom AG (AR 2007) (continued)

Reconciliation of segment assets and segment liabilities.

millions of €	Dec. 31, 2007	Dec. 31, 2006	Dec. 31, 2005
Total assets of reportable segments	**112,263**	**118,240**	**112,654**
Reconciliation to the Group	(3,201)	(2,963)	(1,743)
Segment assets of the Group	**109,062**	**115,277**	**110,911**
Cash and cash equivalents	2,200	2,765	4,975
Current recoverable income taxes	222	643	613
Other current financial assets (excluding receivables from suppliers)	1,862	1,677	1,225
Investments accounted for using the equity method	109	189	1,825
Other non-current financial assets (excluding receivables from suppliers)	599	657	779
Deferred tax assets	6,610	8,952	8,140
Assets in accordance with the consolidated balance sheet	**120,664**	**130,160**	**128,468**
Total liabilities of reportable segments	**29,174**	**28,840**	**24,227**
Reconciliation to the Group	(3,619)	(3,142)	(866)
Segment liabilities of the Group	**25,555**	**25,698**	**23,361**
Current financial liabilities (excluding liabilities to customers)	8,930	7,374	10,139
Income tax liabilities	437	536	1,358
Non-current financial liabilities	33,831	38,799	36,347
Deferred tax liabilities	6,676	8,083	8,331
Other liabilities	–	–	333
Liabilities in accordance with the consolidated balance sheet	**75,429**	**80,490**	**79,869**

Information by geographic area.

millions of €	Non-current assets			Net revenue		
	Dec. 31, 2007	Dec. 31, 2006	Dec. 31, 2005	2007	2006	2005
Germany	44,808	47,449	48,661	30,694	32,460	34,183
International	52,702	57,151	54,220	31,822	28,887	25,421
Of which:						
Europe (excluding Germany)	25,238	26,786	23,568	17,264	14,823	13,272
North America	27,407	30,344	30,628	14,159	13,700	11,858
Other countries	57	21	24	399	364	291
Group	**97,510**	**104,600**	**102,881**	**62,516**	**61,347**	**59,604**

Commentary: The company indicates that it has adopted IFRS 8 early and specifies that it has:

- identified the chief operating decision maker (CODM) as the Board of Management;
- Reported Mobile Communications Europe and Mobile Communications USA separately as operating segments;
- aggregated in the Mobile Communications Europe operating segment all the activities of T-Mobile International AG in Germany, the United Kingdom, the Netherlands, Austria, Poland and the Czech Republic, as well as Deutsche Telekom's other mobile communications activities in Slovakia, Croatia, Macedonia, Montenegro and Hungary;
- aggregated in the Mobile Communications USA operating segment all activities of T-Mobile International AG in the US market.

The company also describes:

- type of products and services it sells;
- how costs are allocated to operating segments;
- measurement for segment reporting (profit/loss from operations (EBIT));
- measurement of revenue generated and goods and services exchanged between segments (calculated on the basis of market prices);
- amounts of segment assets and liabilities (including all assets and liabilities attributable to operations and whose positive or negative results determine profit/loss from operations (EBIT)). More specifically, segment:
  - o assets included in particular intangible assets; property, plant and equipment; trade and other receivables; and inventories,
  - o liabilities included in particular trade and other payables, and significant provisions,
  - o investments include additions to intangible assets and property, plant and equipment;
- directly allocable amounts to operating segments related to share of profit/loss after income taxes and carrying amount of investments accounted for using the equity method.

In addition, the company presents:

- non-current assets and net revenue by region;
- net revenue allocated according to the location of the respective customers' operations;
- reconciliation of the total of the segments' profit or loss to profit after income taxes.

All presentation and disclosures are in line with CICA 1701.

Extract 2(71) – Segment information

Deutsche Bank Aktiengesellschaft (Annual Review 2007), page 134
RECENTLY ADOPTED ACCOUNTING PRONOUNCEMENTS (in part)
IFRS 8

In November 2006, the IASB issued IFRS 8, "Operating Segments" ("IFRS 8"), which defines requirements for the disclosure of financial information of an entity's operating segments. IFRS 8 replaces IAS 14, "Segment Reporting". It follows the management approach which requires operating segments to be identified on the basis of internal reports about components of the entity that are regularly reviewed by the chief operating decision-maker, in order to allocate resources to a segment and to assess its performance. IFRS 8 is effective for fiscal years beginning on or after January 1, 2009, although earlier application is permitted. The Group adopted IFRS 8 from January 1, 2007. Therefore, the operating segment comparative information contained in the Group's consolidated financial statements for the year ending December 31, 2006 has been presented under the IFRS 8 requirements.

pages 136-145

[2] BUSINESS SEGMENTS AND RELATED INFORMATION

The following segment information has been prepared in accordance with IFRS 8, "Operating Segments," which defines requirements for the disclosure of financial information of an entity's operating segments. It follows the "management approach", which requires presentation of the segments on the basis of the internal reports about components of the entity which are regularly reviewed by the chief operating decision-maker in order to allocate resources to a segment and to assess its performance.

Deutsche Bank Aktiengesellschaft (AR 2007) (continued)

BUSINESS SEGMENTS

The business segments identified by the Group represent the organizational structure as reflected in its internal management reporting systems.

The Group is organized into three group divisions, which are further subdivided into corporate divisions. As of December 31, 2007, the group divisions and corporate divisions were:

The **CORPORATE AND INVESTMENT BANK (CIB)**, which combines the Group's corporate banking and securities activities (including sales and trading and corporate finance activities) with the Group's transaction banking activities. CIB serves corporate and institutional clients, ranging from medium-sized enterprises to multinational corporations, banks and sovereign organizations. Within CIB, the Group manages these activities in two global corporate divisions: Corporate Banking & Securities ("CB&S") and Global Transaction Banking ("GTB").

— CB&S is made up of the business divisions Global Markets and Corporate Finance. These businesses offer financial products worldwide, ranging from the underwriting of stocks and bonds to the tailoring of structured solutions for complex financial requirements.

— GTB is primarily engaged in the gathering, transferring, safeguarding and controlling of assets for its clients throughout the world. It provides processing, fiduciary and trust services to corporations, financial institutions and governments and their agencies.

PRIVATE CLIENTS AND ASSET MANAGEMENT (PCAM), which combines the Group's asset management, private wealth management and private and business client activities. Within PCAM, the Group manages these activities in two global corporate divisions: Asset and Wealth Management ("AWM") and Private & Business Clients ("PBC").

— AWM is comprised of the business divisions Asset Management ("AM"), which focuses on managing assets on behalf of institutional clients and providing mutual funds and other retail investment vehicles, and Private Wealth Management ("PWM"), which focuses on the specific needs of demanding high net worth clients, their families and selected institutions.

— PBC serves retail and affluent clients as well as small corporate customers with a full range of retail banking products.

CORPORATE INVESTMENTS (CI), which manages certain alternative assets of the bank and other debt and equity positions.

Changes in the composition of segments can arise from either changes in management responsibility, for which prior periods are restated to conform with the current year's presentation, or from acquisitions and divestitures.

Management responsibilities changed in the first quarter of 2007 for certain transaction management functions which were organizationally aligned with, and provide trading support to, the Global Markets business division in CIB. The following describes acquisitions and divestitures with a significant impact on the Group's segment operations:

— In October 2007, the Group acquired Abbey Life Assurance Company Limited, a UK company that consists primarily of unit-linked life and pension policies and annuities. The business is included within the CB&S Corporate Division.

— In July 2007, AM completed the sale of its local Italian mutual fund business and established long term distribution arrangements with the Group's strategic partner, Anima S.G.R.p.A. The business was included within the AWM Corporate Division.

— In July 2007, RREEF Private Equity acquired a significant stake in Aldus Equity, an alternative asset management and advisory boutique, which specializes in customized private equity investing for institutional and high net worth investors. The business is included within the AWM Corporate Division.

— In July 2007, the Group announced the completion of the acquisition of the institutional cross-border custody business of Türkiye Garanti Bankasi A.S. The client transition is expected to be completed in April 2008. The business will be included within the GTB Corporate Division.

— In July 2007, RREEF Infrastructure completed the acquisition of Maher Terminals LLC, a privately-held operator of port terminal facilities in North America. The acquisition was the seed asset for the North America Infrastructure Fund and is included in the AWM Corporate Division. The company was deconsolidated effective October 9, 2007 after a partial sale into the fund for which it was acquired.

— In June 2007, the Group completed the sale of the Australian Asset Management domestic manufacturing operations to Aberdeen Asset Management. The business was included within the AWM Corporate Division.

Deutsche Bank Aktiengesellschaft (AR 2007) (continued)

— In April 2007, AM reached an agreement with shareholders of Harvest Fund Management, a mutual fund manager in China, to increase its stake to 30%. The business is included within the AWM Corporate Division.

— In January 2007, the Group sold the second tranche (41%) of PBC's Italian BankAmericard processing activities to Istituto Centrale delle Banche Popolari Italiane ("ICBPI"), the central body of Italian cooperative banks. The business was part of the PBC Corporate Division.

— In January 2007, the Group completed the acquisition of MortgageIT Holdings, Inc., a residential mortgage real estate investment trust (REIT) in the U.S. The business is included in the CB&S Corporate Division.

— In January 2007, the Group completed the acquisition of Berliner Bank, which is included in the PBC Corporate Division. The acquisition expands the Group's market share in the retail banking sector of the German capital.

— In November 2006, the Group acquired norisbank from DZ Bank Group. The business is included in the PBC Corporate Division.

— In October 2006, the Group announced the acquisition of the UK wealth manager, Tilney Group Limited. The transaction was closed in December 2006. The acquisition is a key element in PWM's strategy to expand its onshore presence in dedicated core markets and to expand into various client segments, including the Independent Financial Advisors sector.

— In October 2006, the Group sold 49% of its BankAmericard operation to ICBPI.

— In July 2006, the Group deconsolidated Deutsche Wohnen AG following the termination of the control agreement with DB Real Estate Management GmbH. Deutsche Wohnen AG is a real estate investment company and was reported in the AWM Corporate Division.

— In May 2006, the Group completed the acquisition of the UK Depository and Clearing Centre business from JPMorgan Chase & Co. The business is included in the GTB Corporate Division.

— In February 2006, the Group completed the acquisition of the remaining 60% of United Financial Group (UFG), an investment bank in Russia. The business is included in CB&S Corporate Division.

— In the first quarter 2006, the Group completed its sale of EUROHYPO AG to Commerzbank AG. The business was included in the CI Group Division.

MEASUREMENT OF SEGMENT PROFIT OR LOSS

Segment reporting under IFRS 8 requires a presentation of the segment results based on management reporting methods with a reconciliation between the results of the business segments and the consolidated financial statements. The Group reports this reconciliation within the "Consolidation & Adjustments" section. The information provided about each segment is based on the internal reports about segment profit or loss, assets and other information which are regularly reviewed by the chief operating decision maker.

Management reporting for the Group is generally based on IFRS. Non-IFRS compliant accounting methods are only established on rare occasions and represent either valuation or classification differences. The largest valuation differences relate to mark-to-market accounting in management reporting versus accrual accounting under IFRS (e.g., for certain financial instruments in the Group's treasury books in CB&S and PBC) and to the recognition of trading results from own shares in revenues in management reporting (mainly in CB&S) and in equity under IFRS. The major classification difference relates to minority interest, which represents the net share of minority shareholders in revenues, provision for credit losses, noninterest expenses and income tax expenses. Minority interest is reported as a component of pre-tax income for the businesses in management reporting (with a reversal in Consolidation & Adjustments) and a component of net income appropriation under IFRS.

Revenues from transactions between the business segments are allocated on a mutually agreed basis. Internal service providers (including the Corporate Center), which operate on a nonprofit basis, allocate their noninterest expenses to the recipient of the service. The allocation criteria are generally based on service level agreements and are either determined based upon "price per unit", "fixed price" or "agreed percentages". Since the Group's business activities are diverse in nature and its operations are integrated, certain estimates and judgments have been made to apportion revenue and expense items among the business segments.

Deutsche Bank Aktiengesellschaft (AR 2007) (continued)

The management reporting systems follow the "matched transfer pricing concept" in which the Group's external net interest income is allocated to the business segments based on the assumption that all positions are funded or invested via the money and capital markets. Therefore, to create comparability with competitors who have legally independent units with their own equity funding, the Group allocates the notional interest credit on its consolidated capital to the business segments, in proportion to each business segment's allocated average active equity.

Management uses certain measures for equity and related ratios as part of its internal reporting system because it believes that these measures provide it with a more useful indication of the financial performance of the business segments. The Group discloses such measures to provide investors and analysts with further insight into how management operates the Group's businesses and to enable them to better understand the Group's results. These include:

— **AVERAGE ACTIVE EQUITY**: The Group calculates active equity to make it easier to compare it to its competitors and refers to active equity in several ratios. However, active equity is not a measure provided for in IFRS and the Group's ratios based on average active equity should not be compared to other companies' ratios without considering the differences in the calculation. The items for which the Group adjusts the average shareholders' equity are average unrealized net gains on assets available for sale, average fair value adjustments on cash flow hedges (both components net of applicable taxes), as well as average dividends, for which a proposal is accrued on a quarterly basis and for which payments occur once a year following the approval by the general shareholders' meeting. The Group's average active equity is allocated to the business segments and to Consolidation & Adjustments in proportion to their economic risk exposures, which comprise economic capital, goodwill and other unamortized intangible assets. The total amount to be allocated is the higher of the Group's overall economic risk exposure or regulatory capital demand. This demand for regulatory capital is derived by assuming a BIS Tier 1 ratio of 8.5%, which represents the mid-point of the Group's Tier 1 target range of between 8.0% and 9.0 %. If the Group's average active equity exceeds the higher of the overall economic risk exposure or the regulatory capital demand, this surplus is assigned to Consolidation & Adjustments.

— **RETURN ON AVERAGE ACTIVE EQUITY IN %** is defined as income before income taxes less minority interest as a percentage of average active equity. These returns, which are based on average active equity, should not be compared to those of other companies without considering the differences in the calculation of such ratios.

Deutsche Bank Aktiengesellschaft (AR 2007) (continued)
SEGMENTAL RESULTS OF OPERATIONS

The following tables present the results of the business segments, including the reconciliation to the consolidated results under IFRS, for the years ended December 31, 2007 and 2006.

2007

in € m. (except percentages)	Corporate Banking & Securities	Global Transaction Banking	Total	Asset and Wealth Management	Private & Business Clients	Total	Corporate Investments[5]	Total Management Reporting
	Corporate and Investment Bank			Private Clients and Asset Management				
Net revenues[1]	16,507	2,585	19,092	4,374	5,755	10,129	1,517	30,738
Provision for credit losses	102	7	109	1	501	501	3	613
Total noninterest expenses	12,169	1,633	13,802	3,453	4,108	7,561	220	21,583
therein:								
Depreciation, depletion and amortization	50	8	58	20	82	102	17	177
Severance payments	100	7	107	28	27	55	–	162
Policyholder benefits and claims	116	–	116	73	–	73	–	188
Impairment of intangible assets	–	–	–	74	–	74	54	128
Restructuring activities	(4)	(1)	(4)	(8)	(1)	(9)	–	(13)
Minority interest	34	–	34	7	–	8	(5)	37
Income before income taxes	4,201	945	5,147	913	1,146	2,059	1,299	8,505
Cost/income ratio in %	74	63	72	79	71	75	15	70
Assets[2, 3]	1,881,638	32,083	1,895,756	39,081	117,533	156,391	13,002	2,011,654
Expenditures for additions to long-lived assets	351	87	438	2	62	65	–	503
Risk-weighted positions (BIS risk positions)	218,663	18,363	237,026	15,864	69,722	85,586	4,891	327,503
Average active equity[4]	19,619	1,095	20,714	5,109	3,430	8,539	473	29,725
Pre-tax return on average active equity in %	21	86	25	18	33	24	N/M	29
1 Includes:								
Net interest income	4,362	1,106	5,467	165	3,083	3,248	(5)	8,710
Net revenues from external customers	16,691	2,498	19,189	4,615	5,408	10,023	1,492	30,703
Net intersegment revenues	(184)	87	(97)	(241)	347	106	25	34
Net income (loss) from equity method investments	51	2	52	114	2	116	184	352
2 Includes:								
Equity method investments	2,430	39	2,469	560	45	605	221	3,295

N/M – Not meaningful

3 The sum of corporate divisions does not necessarily equal the total of the corresponding group division because of consolidation items between corporate divisions, which are to be eliminated on group division level. The same approach holds true for the sum of group divisions compared to Total Management Reporting.

4 For management reporting purposes goodwill and other intangible assets with indefinite lives are explicitly assigned to the respective divisions. The Group's average active equity is allocated to the business segments and to Consolidation & Adjustments in proportion to their economic risk exposures, which comprise economic capital, goodwill and other unamortized intangible assets.

5 Net revenues in CI include gains from the sale of industrial holdings (Fiat S.p.A., Linde AG and Allianz SE) of € 626 million, income from equity method investments (Deutsche Inter-hotel Holding GmbH & Co. KG) of € 178 million, and gains from the sale of premises (sale/leaseback transaction of 60 Wall Street) of € 313 million (after group-internal fees paid).

Deutsche Bank Aktiengesellschaft (AR 2007) (continued)

| 2006 | Corporate and Investment Bank | | | Private Clients and Asset Management | | | | |
| | Corporate Banking & Securities | Global Trans-action Banking | Total | Asset and Wealth Manage-ment | Private & Business Clients | Total | Corporate Invest-ments[5] | Total Manage-ment Reporting |
in € m. (except percentages)								
Net revenues[1]	16,574	2,228	18,802	4,166	5,149	9,315	574	28,691
Provision for credit losses	(65)	(29)	(94)	(1)	391	391	2	298
Total noninterest expenses	11,236	1,552	12,789	3,284	3,717	7,000	214	20,003
therein:								
Depreciation, depletion and amortization	57	25	82	33	84	117	17	216
Severance payments	97	3	99	12	10	22	–	121
Policyholder benefits and claims	–	–	–	63	–	63	–	63
Impairment of intangible assets	–	–	–	–	–	–	31	31
Restructuring activities	77	22	99	43	49	91	1	192
Minority interest	23	–	23	(11)	–	(11)	(3)	10
Income before income taxes	5,379	705	6,084	894	1,041	1,935	361	8,380
Cost/income ratio in %	68	70	68	79	72	75	37	70
Assets[2, 3]	1,459,190	25,646	1,468,321	35,922	94,760	130,642	17,783	1,576,714
Expenditures for additions to long-lived assets	573	2	575	5	383	388	–	963
Risk-weighted positions (BIS risk positions)	177,651	14,240	191,891	12,335	63,900	76,234	5,395	273,520
Average active equity[4]	16,041	1,064	17,105	4,917	2,289	7,206	1,057	25,368
Pre-tax return on average active equity in %	34	66	36	18	45	27	34	33
1 Includes:								
Net interest income	3,097	890	3,987	162	2,767	2,928	1	6,916
Net revenues from external customers	16,894	2,060	18,954	4,435	4,724	9,159	543	28,656
Net intersegment revenues	(320)	168	(152)	(269)	425	156	31	35
Net income (loss) from equity method investments	72	1	74	142	3	145	197	416
2 Includes:								
Equity method investments	1,624	38	1,662	588	8	596	207	2,465

3 The sum of corporate divisions does not necessarily equal the total of the corresponding group division because of consolidation items between corporate divisions, which are to be eliminated on group division level. The same approach holds true for the sum of group divisions compared to Total Management Reporting.

4 For management reporting purposes goodwill and other intangible assets with indefinite lives are explicitly assigned to the respective divisions. The Group's average active equity is allocated to the business segments and to Consolidation & Adjustments in proportion to their economic risk exposures, which comprise economic capital, goodwill and other unamortized intangible assets.

5 Net revenues in CI include a gain from the sale of the bank's remaining holding in EUROHYPO AG of € 131 million and gains from the sale of industrial holdings (Linde AG) of € 92 million.

Deutsche Bank Aktiengesellschaft (AR 2007) (continued)

RECONCILIATION OF SEGMENTAL RESULTS OF OPERATIONS TO CONSOLIDATED RESULTS OF OPERATIONS

ACCORDING TO IFRS

The following table provides a reconciliation of the total results of operations and total assets of the Group's business segments under management reporting systems to the consolidated financial statements prepared in accordance with IFRS, for the years ended December 31, 2007 and 2006, respectively.

in € m.	2007 Total Management Reporting	Consolidation & Adjustments	Total Consolidated	2006 Total Management Reporting	Consolidation & Adjustments	Total Consolidated
Net revenues[1]	30,738	7	30,745	28,691	(197)	28,494
Provision for credit losses	613	(1)	612	298	(0)	298
Noninterest expenses	21,583	(200)	21,384	20,003	(147)	19,857
Minority interest	37	(37)	–	10	(10)	–
Income (loss) before income taxes	**8,505**	**244**	**8,749**	**8,380**	**(41)**	**8,339**
Assets	2,011,654	8,695	2,020,349	1,576,714	7,779	1,584,493
Risk-weighted positions (BIS risk positions)	327,503	1,315	328,818	273,520	1,939	275,459
Average active equity	29,725	121	29,846	25,368	100	25,468

1   Net interest income and noninterest income.

In 2007, income before income taxes in Consolidation & Adjustments was € 244 million. This resulted from Corporate Items of € 279 million, as well as from negative adjustments of € 35 million to reverse the impact of differences between the accounting methods used under IFRS and for the business segments in the Group's management reporting. Noninterest expenses benefited primarily from a recovery of value added tax paid in prior years, based on a refined methodology which has been agreed with the tax authorities, and also reimbursements associated with several litigation cases. The main adjustments to net revenues in Consolidation & Adjustments in 2007 were:

—   Adjustments related to positions which are marked-to-market for management reporting purposes and accounted for on an accrual basis under IFRS decreased net revenues by approximately €100 million.

—   Trading results from the Group's own shares are reflected in the CB&S Corporate Division. The elimination of such results under IFRS resulted in an increase of approximately € 30 million.

—   Decreases related to the elimination of intra-Group rental income were € 39 million.

—   Net interest income related to tax refunds and accruals increased net revenues by € 69 million.

—   The remainder of net revenues was due to other corporate items outside the management responsibility of the business segments, such as net funding expenses for nondivisionalized assets/liabilities and results from hedging the net investments in certain foreign operations.

In 2006, Consolidation & Adjustments showed a loss before income taxes of € 41 million. Negative adjustments for different accounting methods used in management reporting and IFRS were € 307 million and Corporate Items were € 267 million. Noninterest expenses benefited mainly from a provision release related to activities to restructure grundbesitz-invest, the Group's German open-ended real estate fund, and a settlement of insurance claims in respect of business interruption losses and costs related to the terrorist attacks of September 11, 2001 in the United States. Within net revenues, the main drivers in Consolidation & Adjustments were:

—   Adjustments related to financial instruments which are carried at fair value through profit or loss for management reporting purposes but accounted for on an amortized cost basis under IFRS decreased net revenues by approximately € 210 million.

—   Trading results from the Group's own shares in the CB&S Corporate Division resulted in a decrease of € 100 million.

—   The elimination of intra-Group rental income decreased net revenues by €40 million.

—   Net interest income related to tax refunds and accruals increased by € 67 million.

—   Settlement of insurance claims in respect of business interruption losses and costs related to the terrorist attacks of September 11, 2001 in the United States increased net revenues by € 125 million.

—   The remainder of net revenues was due to other corporate items outside the management responsibility of the business segments.

Deutsche Bank Aktiengesellschaft (AR 2007) (continued)

Assets and risk-weighted positions in Consolidation & Adjustments reflect corporate assets, such as deferred tax assets and central clearing accounts, outside of the management responsibility of the business segments.

Average active equity assigned to Consolidation & Adjustments reflects the residual amount of equity that is not allocated to the segments as described under "Measurement of Segment Profit or Loss" in this Note.

ENTITY-WIDE DISCLOSURES

The Group presents revenues for groups of similar products and services by group division on a standalone basis derived from the Group's management accounting systems. The following tables present the net revenue components of the CIB and PCAM Group Divisions, for the years ended December 31, 2007 and 2006, respectively.

	Corporate and Investment Bank	
in € m.	2007	2006
Sales & Trading (equity)	4,613	4,039
Sales & Trading (debt and other products)	8,407	9,016
Total Sales & Trading	**13,020**	**13,055**
Origination (equity)	861	760
Origination (debt)	714	1,331
Total Origination	**1,575**	**2,091**
Advisory	1,089	800
Loan products	974	946
Transaction services	2,585	2,228
Other products	(151)	(318)
Total	19,092	18,802

	Private Clients and Asset Management	
in € m.	2007	2006
Portfolio/fund management	3,062	3,089
Brokerage	2,172	1,910
Loan/deposit	3,173	2,774
Payments, account & remaining financial services	979	899
Other products	742	643
Total	**10,129**	**9,315**

Deutsche Bank Aktiengesellschaft (AR 2007) (continued)		
The following table presents total net revenues (before allowance for credit losses) by geographical area. The information presented for CIB and PCAM has been classified based primarily on the location of the Group's office in which the revenues are recorded. The information for Corporate Investments and Consolidation & Adjustments is presented on a global level only, as management responsibility for these areas is held centrally.		
in € m.	2007	2006
Germany:		
CIB	2,921	2,265
PCAM	5,514	4,922
Total Germany	**8,434**	**7,187**
Europe, Middle East and Africa:		
CIB	7,721	6,836
PCAM	2,816	2,661
Total Europe, Middle East and Africa[1]	**10,537**	**9,497**
Americas (primarily U.S.):		
CIB	4,628	6,810
PCAM	1,331	1,350
Total Americas	**5,959**	**8,160**
Asia/Pacific:		
CIB	3,823	2,891
PCAM	468	381
Total Asia/Pacific	**4,291**	**3,273**
CI	1,517	574
Consolidation & Adjustments	7	(197)
Consolidated net revenues[2]	**30,745**	**28,494**

1   The United Kingdom accounted for more than 60% of these revenues in 2007 and 2006, respectively.

2   Consolidated total net revenues comprise interest and similar income, interest expenses and total noninterest income (including net commission and fee income). Revenues are attributed to countries based on the location in which the Group's booking office is located. The location of a transaction on the Group's books is sometimes different from the location of the headquarters or other offices of a customer and different from the location of the Group's personnel who entered into or facilitated the transaction. Where the Group records a transaction involving its staff and customers and other third parties in different locations frequently depends on other considerations, such as the nature of the transaction, regulatory considerations and transaction processing considerations.

Commentary: In this extract, the bank has adopted IFRS 8 early and:

• presents three group divisions, which are further subdivided into corporate divisions (the bank explains composition and changes during the year and comparative period of each division);

• reports that it measures segment profit or loss generally based on IFRS (non-IFRS compliant accounting methods are established only on rare occasions);

• allocates internal service providers (including the Corporate Center) to the recipient of the service based on service level agreements (determined based on "price per unit," "fixed price" or "agreed percentages");

• follows the "matched transfer pricing concept" (external net interest income is allocated to the business segments based on the assumption that all positions are funded or invested via the money and capital markets).

The bank discloses the following measures for equity and related ratios contained in its internal reporting system because it believes that these measures provide it with a more useful indication of the financial performance of the business segments (bank indicates that these measures should not be compared to those of other companies without considering the differences in the calculation of such ratios):

• average active equity (which is not a measure provided for in IFRS); and

• return on average active equity in % (defined as income before income taxes less minority interest as a percentage of average active equity).

In addition, the bank provides detailed explanation of the reconciliation of segmental results of operations to consolidated results of operations according to IFRS and entity-wide disclosures.

All presentation and disclosures are in line with CICA 1701.

Interim Financial Information

Objective

Interim financial reports are prepared to provide timely and reliable information to investors, creditors and others to help them understand an entity's capacity to generate earnings and cash flows, as well as its financial condition and liquidity. According to IAS 34 and CICA 1751, these reports provide an update on the latest annual financial statements and, consequently, neither standard requires an entity to duplicate information previously reported but, rather, asks it to focus on new activities, events and circumstances. IAS 34 applies if an entity is required or elects to publish an interim financial report in accordance with IFRS.

Choices

Interim financial reports could be prepared according to IAS 34 by limiting the information presented to condensed financial statements and selected explanatory notes. Alternatively, an entity could, if it wants to do so, publish a complete set of interim financial statements in accordance with IAS 1.

Nothing prevents an entity reporting under Canadian GAAP from providing more details than the minimum set under CICA 1751.

Requirements

In deciding how to recognize, measure, classify, or disclose an item for interim financial reporting purposes, materiality has to be assessed in relation to the interim period financial data. In making assessments of materiality, it must be recognized that interim measurements may rely on estimates to a greater extent than measurements of annual financial data.

Recognition and Measurement

*   Recognition and measurement bases used for the interim financial information should be consistent with those that will be used for the next full financial year.
*   Requirements of a new IFRS to be adopted in the current year-end financial statements must also be adopted for the interim financial information.
*   Interim financial period should be treated as a discrete accounting period. This means that:
    o   transactions related to the period should be measured in the same way as they would at year-end,
    o   revenues should be recognized when earned and costs should be recognized when incurred,
    o   costs and revenues should be deferred only if they meet the definition of an asset or a liability,
    o   the only exception is the assessment of tax expense, which should be calculated by reference to the effective tax rate expected for the full year.

Presentation and Disclosure

The following table summarizes IAS 34 requirements, which are similar to those set out in CICA 1751 unless indicated otherwise:

Presentation or Disclosure	IAS 34 Requirements

Primary financial statements (condensed form)	• Primary financial statements condensed form include:
	  o condensed statement of financial position,
	  o condensed statement of comprehensive income (either condensed single statement, or condensed separate income statement and a condensed statement of comprehensive income),
	  o condensed statement of changes in equity (Note 1), and
	  o condensed statement of cash flows. (Note 2)
	• Condensed statements must include, at a minimum, each of the headings and subtotals that were included in an entity's most recent annual financial statements.
	• Additional line items are included if their omission would make the condensed interim financial statements misleading.

Minimum notes	• statement of compliance with IAS 34;
	• statement on accounting policies (same as most recent annual financial statements or a description of the nature and effect of the change);
	• comments about the seasonality or cyclicality of interim operations;
	• nature and amount of items affecting assets, liabilities, equity, net income, or cash flows that are unusual because of their nature, size or incidence;
	• nature and amount of changes in estimates of amounts reported in prior interim periods of the current financial year or changes in estimates of amounts reported in prior financial years (if they have a material effect in the current interim period);
	• issuances, repurchases and repayments of debt and equity securities;
	• dividends paid (aggregate or per share) separately for ordinary shares and other shares;
	• selected segment information including:
	  o revenues from external customers and inter- segment revenues, if included in the measure of segment profit or loss reviewed by the CODM or otherwise regularly provided to the latter,
	  o a measure of segment profit or loss,
	  o total assets for which there has been a material change from the amount disclosed in the last annual financial statements,
	  o a description of differences from the last annual financial statements in the basis of segmentation or in the basis of measurement of segment profit or loss,
	  o a reconciliation of the total of the reportable segments' measures of profit or loss to the entity's profit or loss before tax expense (tax income) and discontinued operations;
	• material events subsequent to the end of the interim period that have not been reflected in the financial statements for the interim period;
	• effect of changes in the composition of the entity during the interim period, including business combinations, obtaining or losing control of subsidiaries and long-term investments, restructurings, and discontinued operations;
	• changes in contingent liabilities or contingent assets since the end of the last annual reporting period;
	• additional notes are included if their omission would make the condensed interim financial statements misleading.

Presentation or Disclosure	IAS 34 Requirements
Accounting policies	Same as the ones applied at previous year end, except for those that changed since that date, which would be reflected in the next annual financial statements.
Comparatives (Note 2)	• Statement of financial position as of the end of the current interim period and a comparative statement of financial position as of the end of the immediately preceding financial year. • Statement of comprehensive income (one or two statements) for the current interim period and cumulatively for the current financial year to date, with comparative statements of comprehensive income for the comparable interim periods (current and year-to-date) of the immediately preceding financial year. • Statement of changes in equity and statement of cash flows cumulatively for the current financial year to date, with a comparative statement for the comparable year-to-date period of the immediately preceding financial year.
Basic and diluted EPS	Required when an entity is within the scope of IAS 33.

Note 1: Contrary to IFRSs, CICA 1751 does not require to present a statement of changes in equity, companies could disclose the details of equity changes in a note. CICA 1751 requires a statement of retained earnings.

Note 2: Under CICA 1751, cash flow statements also are presented for the current interim period.

Illustrative Disclosure:

Extract 2(72) – Half-yearly financial statements

Groupe Bruxelles Lambert S.A. (Half-yearly Report - June 2008), pages 12 - 19			
Consolidated balance sheet			
EUR million	Notes	30 June 2008	31 December 2007
Non-current assets		**15,902.3**	**17,519.3**
Tangible assets		17.7	23.5
Investments		15,863.6	17,478.3
Shareholdings in associated companies	1	4,057.1	599.7
Investments available-for-sale	2	11,806.5	16,878.6
Other non-current assets		20.5	17.0
Deferred tax assets		0.5	0.5
Current assets	3	**1,556.4**	**1,863.2**
Trading assets		62.3	44.6
Cash and cash equivalents		1,480.3	1,803.0
Other assets		13.8	15.6
Total assets		**17,458.7**	**19,382.5**
Shareholders' equity	7	**16,909.7**	**18,868.6**
Capital		653.1	653.1
Share premium account		3,815.8	3,815.8
Reserves		12,440.8	14,399.7
Minority interests		0.0	0.0
Non-current liabilities	3	**423.8**	**422.3**
Exchangeable bonds		418.6	416.6
Deferred tax liabilities		4.3	4.8
Provisions		0.9	0.9
Current liabilities	3	**125.2**	**91.6**
Financial debt		0.0	20.0
Tax liabilities		1.9	1.8
Derivatives		52.8	38.6
Other creditors		70.5	31.2
Total liabilities and shareholders' equity		**17,458.7**	**19,382.5**
Consolidated statement of comprehensive income			
EUR million	Notes	30 June 2008	30 June 2007
Net earnings from associated companies	1	188.7	52.4
Net dividends on investments	2	279.0	338.3
Interest income and expenses	3	30.0	11.1
Non-current assets		2.4	1.8
Current assets and financial debt		27.6	9.3
Other financial income and expenses	4	16.6	1.7
Gains on trading assets and derivatives		19.3	2.8
Other		(2.7)	(1.1)
Other operating income and expenses		(7.1)	(11.1)
Earnings on disposals and impairments of non-current assets	5	47.2	65.2
Taxes		0.5	0.5
Consolidated result of the period		**554.9**	**458.1**
Other comprehensive income			
Available-for-sale financial assets – Fair value variation	2	(1,921.2)	1,815.4
Share in other comprehensive income of associated companies		(244.1)	(8.7)
Other		0.3	0.3
Comprehensive income for the period		**(1,610.1)**	**2,265.1**
Basic earnings per share		3.56	3.23
Diluted earnings per share		3.49	3.17

Groupe Bruxelles Lambert S.A. (Half-yearly Report - June 2008) (continued) Consolidated cash flow statement EUR million	30 June 2008	30 June 2007
Cash flow from current operations	**472.4**	**459.0**
Consolidated result of the period before interest and taxes	524.4	446.5
Adjustments for:		
Net earnings from associated companies	(188.7)	(52.4)
Dividends received from associated companies	178.9	30.1
Fair value revaluation	(3.1)	6.4
Earnings on disposals and impairments of non-current assets	(47.2)	(65.2)
Other	(21.4)	(5.9)
Interest income and expenses received (paid)	21.9	9.6
Taxes received	0.0	8.5
Change in trading securities and derivatives	(3.5)	(4.5)
Change in working capital requirements	11.1	85.9
Cash flow from investing activities	**(426.3)**	**(3,136.9)**
Acquisitions of:		
Investments (associated companies)	(757.1)	(50.3)
Other financial assets	(132.1)	(3,220.4)
Other tangible and intangible assets	(6.0)	(4.1)
Disposals on investments and other financial assets	468.9	137.9
of which Iberdrola	436.0	-
Cash flow from funding activities	**(368.8)**	**333.8**
Dividends paid	(325.6)	(269.6)
Amounts received from financial debt	-	602.7
Repayment of financial debt	(20.0)	-
Net changes in treasury shares	(23.2)	0.7
Net increase (decrease) in cash and cash equivalents	**(322.7)**	**(2,344.1)**
Cash and cash equivalents at beginning of financial year	1,803.0	2,648.2
Cash and cash equivalents at end of financial year	1,480.3	304.1

Accounting methods and seasonal nature

The condensed consolidated financial statements are drawn up in accordance with the International Financial Reporting Standards (IFRS) as adopted in the European Union and the interpretations published by the International Financial Reporting Interpretations Committee of IASB (IFRIC).

The accounting and calculating methods used in the interim financial statements are identical to those used in the annual financial statements for 2007. The condensed consolidated financial statements for the half-year ended 30 June 2008 comply with IAS 34 – Interim financial reporting.

It is noteworthy that, given its percentage of ownership, its position as first shareholder and the representativeness at the Board of Directors of Lafarge in 2008, GBL considers that it exercices notable influence on this company. This investment is therefore consolidated using the equity method from 1 January 2008. On 30 June 2008, GBL owned a 19.1% stake in Lafarge.

The seasonal nature of the results is detailed in the outlook for the year 2008 as a whole.

Groupe Bruxelles Lambert S.A. (Half-yearly Report - June 2008) (continued)

1. Lafarge, Imerys and Ergon Capital Partners (ECP) consolidated using the equity method

1.1. Group share of net earnings

EUR million	30 June 2008	30 June 2007
Lafarge	174.1	-
Imerys	41.0	39.9
ECP	(26.4)	12.5
Net earnings from associated companies	**188.7**	**52.4**

Lafarge registered earnings of EUR 911 million for the half-year ended 30 June 2008. For its first period of consolidation using the equity method, it contributed EUR 174 million to GBL's result.

Imerys registered consolidated net result of EUR 144 million for the first half of 2008. Based on GBL's percentage of ownership, Imerys contributed to its half-yearly results in the amount of EUR 41 million, an increase of EUR 1 million.

ECP's contribution as of 30 June 2008 amounted to EUR - 26 million, as against EUR 13 million at end June 2007.

1.2. Share in shareholders' equity

EUR million	Lafarge	Imerys	ECP	Total
At 31 December 2007	-	486.5	113.2	599.7
Transfer from AFS	2,908.7	-	-	2,908.7
Investments	703.4	62.3	22.0	787.7
Result of the period	174.1	41.0	(26.4)	188.7
Distribution	(145.8)	(33.1)	-	(178.9)
Differences on translation	(172.5)	(24.8)	-	(197.3)
Change in revaluation reserves	(48.1)	(1.1)	-	(49.2)
Other	(2.6)	0.4	(0.1)	(2.3)
At 30 June 2008	**3,417.2**	**531.2**	**108.7**	**4,057.1**

2. Suez, Total, Pernod Ricard, Iberdrola and other investments

2.1. Net dividends on investments available-for-sale

EUR million	30 June 2008	30 June 2007
Suez	167.0	146.4
Total	96.9	91.9
Lafarge	-	91.3
Pernod Ricard	9.4	8.5
Iberdrola	3.9	-
Other	1.8	0.2
Total	**279.0**	**338.3**

During the first half of 2008, GBL accounted EUR 279 million dividends from its available-for-sale investments. Taking into account the application of the equity method on Lafarge from 1 January 2008, the dividend collected in 2008 (EUR 145.8 million) is deducted from the share in shareholders' equity. Excluding Lafarge, dividends on available-for-sale investments increased by 13%.

Groupe Bruxelles Lambert S.A. (Half-yearly Report - June 2008) (continued)

2.2. Fair value and variation

Investments in listed companies are valued on the basis of closing share prices at the end of the period.

Investments in "Funds" grouping PAI Europe III, Sagard I and Sagard II are revalued at their fair value in terms of their investment portfolio.

EUR million	31 December 2007	Acquisitions/ Disposals	Transfer	Change in revaluation reserves	Funds earnings	30 June 2008
Total	5,338.6	-	-	(247.1)	-	5,091.5
Suez	5,682.1	34.1	-	(407.9)	-	5,308.3
Lafarge	3,855.6	-	(2,908.7)	(946.9)	-	0.0
Iberdrola	723.8	(384.8)	-	(92.9)	-	246.1
Pernod Ricard	1,069.6	107.1	-	(203.4)	-	973.3
Funds	101.3	0.3	-	(0.7)	1.1	102.0
Other	107.6	-	-	(22.3)	-	85.3
Fair value	**16,878.6**	**(243.3)**	**(2,908.7)**	**(1,921.2)**	**1.1**	**11,806.5**

As a result of application of the equity method for the investment in Lafarge, the net cost of the shareholding at 1 January 2008 was transferred to associated companies. The revaluation reserve (unrealised capital gain) was cancelled under shareholders' equity.

3. Cash and debt

3.1. Current assets and liabilities

EUR million	30 June 2008	31 December 2007
Current assets	**1,556.4**	**1,863.2**
of which cash and cash equivalents	1,480.3	1,803.0
Current liabilities	**125.2**	**91.6**
of which financial debt	-	20.0
Current assets – current liabilities	**1,431.2**	**1,771.6**

3.2. Non-current financial liabilities

EUR million	30 June 2008	31 December 2007
Non-current financial debts	418.6	416.6
Exchangeable bonds	418.6	416.6

In April 2005, GBL issued bonds exchangeable for GBL shares in the amount of EUR 435 million. At 30 June 2008, the book value of those bonds amounted to EUR 419 million.

3.3. Interest income and expenses

EUR million	30 June 2008	30 June 2007
Interest on non-current assets	2.4	1.8
Interest on exchangeable loans	(8.3)	(8.2)
Nominal interest (cash earnings)	(6.4)	(6.4)
Amortized cost	(1.9)	(1.8)
Interest on treasury	35.9	17.5
Interest income and expenses	**30.0**	**11.1**

Net interest income amounted to EUR 30 million for the period, compared to EUR 11 million for the same period in 2007. This growth stems from higher interest rates than in 2007 and from the average cash position for the first half of 2008 of EUR 1.6 billion, compared to EUR 1.0 billion for the first six months of 2007.

Interest expenses were primarily made up of interest on the exchangeable bonds 2005-2012. These latter include the cost of the annual coupon (2.95%) plus the cost of reconstitution of the face value of the exchangeable bonds.

Groupe Bruxelles Lambert S.A. (Half-yearly Report - June 2008) (continued)

4. Other financial income and expenses

EUR million	30 June 2008	30 June 2007
Gains on trading assets and derivatives	19.3	2.8
Other	(2.7)	(1.1)
Total	**16.6**	**1.7**

At 30 June 2008, this heading essentially included changes in fair value on a rate swap (EUR 11 million) and results (EUR 9 million) on Total and Arkema call options and on Lafarge, Imerys and Pernod Ricard put options.

5. Earnings on disposals and impairments of non-current assets

EUR million	30 June 2008	30 June 2007
Iberdrola	47.4	-
Funds	(0.2)	45.1
Other	-	20.1
Total	**47.2**	**65.2**

At the start of 2008, GBL partially disposed of its investment in Iberdrola for a total sale price of EUR 436 million, resulting in a capital gain of EUR 47 million. This investment now amounts to 0.6%.

During the first six months of 2007, disposals by private equity funds (Sagard and PAI Europe III) resulted in earnings of EUR 45 million for GBL, mainly on the sale of Vivarte, Medi Partenaires, Saur, Provimi and the recapitalisation of Coin.

6. Transaction with related parties

EUR million	Pargesa	ECP	Other
Assets			
Non-current	-	-	0.1
Trading	15.9	-	-
Liabilities			
Derivatives	8.8	-	-
Income statement	0.3	0.3	-

The amounts listed under "Trading" and "Derivatives" relate to options on Pargesa shares as well as shares held to cover the exercise of those options.

Groupe Bruxelles Lambert S.A. (Half-yearly Report - June 2008) (continued)

7. Shareholders' equity

7.1. Capital, share premiums and reserves

EUR million	Capital	Share premium	Revalua-tion reserve	Treasury shares	Differ-ences on transla-tion	Exchange-able bonds 2005-2012	Retained earnings	Total
At 31 December 2006	595.7	2,690.7	5,716.8	(184.1)	(7.3)	17.6	6,852.6	15,682.0
Comprehensive income	-	-	1,815.9	-	(4.6)	-	453.8	2,265.1
Total transactions with equity holders	-	-	-	0.7	-	-	(269.6)	(268.9)
At 30 June 2007	595.7	2,690.7	7,532.7	(183.4)	(11.9)	17.6	7,036.8	17,678.2
Comprehensive income	-	-	(273.1)	-	(29.8)	-	309.9	7.0
Total transactions with equity holders	57.4	1,125.1	-	(0.3)	-	-	1.2	1,183.4
At 31 December 2007	653.1	3,815.8	7,259.6	(183.7)	(41.7)	17.6	7,347.9	18,868.6
Comprehensive income	-	-	(1,970.4)	-	(197.3)	-	557.6	(1,610.1)
Total transactions with equity holders	-	-	-	(24.0)	-	-	(324.8)	(348.8)
At 30 June 2008	653.1	3,815.8	5,289.2	(207.7)	(239.0)	17.6	7,580.7	16,909.7

On 15 April 2008, GBL shareholders collected a gross dividend of EUR 2.09 per share (EUR 1.90 in 2007).

On 30 June 2008, GBL held 5,576,651 treasury shares (as against 5,261,451 on 31 December 2007).

7.2. Revaluation reserve

The variations in fair value of shareholdings at the end of the period are entered in the revaluation reserve.

EUR million	Total	Suez	Lafarge	Iberdrola	Pernod Ricard	Funds	Other	Total
At 31 December 2007	3,213.4	2,865.9	946.9	58.8	83.2	12.5	78.9	7,259.6
Fair value variation	(247.1)	(407.9)	-	(92.9)	(203.4)	(0.7)	(71.5)	(1,023.5)
Equity method	-	-	(946.9)	-	-	-	-	(946.9)
At 30 June 2008	2,966.3	2,458.0	0.0	(34.1)	(120.2)	11.8	7.4	5,289.2

As a result of application of the equity method for the investment in Lafarge (from 1 January 2008), the revaluation reserve at 31 December 2007 was cancelled under shareholders' equity.

7.3. Result per share

Consolidated result

EUR million	30 June 2008	30 June 2007
Basic	554.9	458.1
Non-discontinued operations	554.9	458.1
Diluted	563.2	466.0
Non-discontinued operations	563.2	466.0

Number of shares Million	30 June 2008	30 June 2007
Outstanding shares	161.4	147.2
Treasury shares at start of the year	(5.3)	(5.3)
Weighted changes during the year	(0.2)	-
Weighted average number of shares used to determine basic result per share	155.9	141.9
Influence of the financial instruments with diluting effect:		
Exchangeable loans	5.1	5.1
Stock options	0.4	0.2
Weighted average number of shares used to determine diluted result per share	161.4	147.2

During the first half of 2008, 153,984 options on shares were issued in favour of Executive Management and personnel. Beneficiaries will have definitive entitlement to the options, which are valid for ten years, three years after the date of the offer, at the rate of one third per year. The exercise price has been set at EUR 77.40 per option.

Groupe Bruxelles Lambert S.A. (Half-yearly Report - June 2008) (continued) Summary of the result per share		
EUR	30 June 2008	30 June 2007
Basic	**3.56**	**3.23**
Non-discontinued operations	3.56	3.23
Diluted	**3.49**	**3.17**
Non-discontinued operations	3.49	3.17

8. Post balance sheet events

On 16 July 2008, the General Meetings of shareholders of GDF and Suez approved the merger of the two groups. As a result of this decision, GBL simultaneously received on 22 July shares in Suez Environnement Company and in GDF SUEZ in exchange for the Suez shares held in the portfolio until that date. These operations will not create any capital gain in GBL's accounts for 2008.

Commentary: In the above extract, the company presents primary financial statements required by IAS 34 using the condensed format. Note disclosures include the following:

- a statement that accounting and calculating methods used in the interim financial statements are identical to those used in the annual financial statements;
- a statement of compliance with IAS 34;
- share of net earnings and shareholders' equity of associates;
- details on:
  - o other investments, including fair value and its variation,
  - o current assets and liabilities and interest income and expenses,
  - o other financial income and expenses,
  - o earnings on disposals and impairments of non-current assets,
  - o transaction with related parties,
  - o shareholders' equity (including capital, share premiums, retained earnings, revaluations and translation adjustment,
  - o basic and diluted EPS, and
  - o subsequent event.

Disclosures are in line with CICA 1750.

Management Commentary

Current Requirements

Financial and operational reviews are included in the management commentary (MC). The IASB has a project on MC (see "Future Developments"). Currently, under IFRS, a financial and operational review is encouraged, but not required. Even though Canadian GAAP does not address the presentation of a financial and operational review, the Canadian Securities Administrators (CSA) have published detailed requirements for the presentation of Management Discussion and Analysis (MD&A).

IAS 1 requires the financial review to disclose and discuss known trends, commitments, events or uncertainties that are reasonably expected to have a material impact on an entity's business, financial condition or results of operations. The document should provide sufficient information on financial and non-financial risks and uncertainties, given the rapidly changing economic environment within which most entities operate. The financial information should be presented in a manner consistent with the financial statements.

In addition to the financial review, entities could also present additional reports outside the financial statements (such as environmental and corporate governance reports).

Changeover to IFRS

In Canada, the MD&A serves as the MC and its content is specified by the CSA. The CSA issued a notice providing guidance on the disclosures an issuer should be making, in its MD&A for 2008, 2009 and 2010, on the expected changes in accounting policies as a result of the changeover to IFRS. More specifically, National Instrument 51-102, *Continuous Disclosure Obligations* requires an issuer to discuss and analyze any changes in the accounting policies it has adopted or expects to adopt subsequent to the end of its most recently completed financial year, including changes resulting from a new accounting standard that the issuer does not have to adopt until a future date.

CSA Staff Notice 52-320 outlines the level of disclosures expected in interim and annual MD&A for 2008, 2009 and 2010. It also indicates that the disclosure requirements become more detailed as the date of changeover approaches and conversion plans progress.

If, at the time of preparing its MD&A, an issuer has developed an IFRS changeover plan, the interim/annual MD&A for 2008 should discuss the status of key elements and timing of the plan, which might include the impact of IFRS on:

- accounting policies, including choices among those permitted under IFRS, and implementation decisions such as whether certain changes will be applied on a retrospective or a prospective basis;
- information technology and data systems;
- internal control over financial reporting;
- disclosure controls and procedures, including investor relations and external communications plans;
- financial reporting expertise, including training requirements; and
- business activities, such as foreign currency and hedging activities, as well as matters that may be influenced by GAAP measures such as debt covenants, capital requirements and compensation arrangements.

COMPREHENSIVE EXAMPLES

This section presents two comprehensive examples.

This first illustrates the application of the IAS 1 amendment introduced in September 2007, which is effective January 1, 2009. The extracts pertain to one of the very few companies that adopted IAS 1 amendments early. The extracts reflect all the pertinent sections of the amendment introduced in September 2007 to IAS 1, including primary financial statements and related notes on the changes in accounting policies and equity reserve details (which includes accumulated other comprehensive income). All disclosures are in line with Canadian GAAP.

The second extract shows the application of IAS 1 to note disclosures of items other than those covered by specific standards examined in other chapters of this volume. All disclosures are in line with Canadian GAAP, even though it might ask for fewer disclosures.

Lihir Gold Limited – All extracts were obtained from the annual report for the year ended December 31, 2007. Note that both parent and consolidated entity financial statements are presented.

Extract 2(A1) – Lihir Gold Limited, pages 61 to 63

This extract presents the note on changes in accounting policies and new accounting standards. The company specifies that it has adopted all IAS 1 amendments, including the one on financial statement presentation, i.e., the amendment introduced in September 2007.

NOTE 3: CHANGES IN ACCOUNTING POLICIES AND NEW ACCOUNTING STANDARDS

During the period, the Board determined that in order to leverage the Company fully to movements in the price of gold, gold production and sales are no longer to be hedged. To reflect the economic consequences of this revised gold hedging policy the Consolidated Entity has changed its accounting policy in relation to the presentation and disclosure of hedging gains and losses in the Statement of Comprehensive Income. These gains and losses are now excluded from revenue and are reflected as a separate item in the Statement of Comprehensive Income. The Consolidated Entity has also determined that a change to the presentation of the Statement of Comprehensive Income, whereby the nature of costs are now consolidated into relevant categories, provides a more meaningful presentation of the financial statements.

Apart from the change to the presentation of the Statement of Comprehensive Income and changes in accounting policy noted below, the accounting policies and methods of computation are the same as those in the prior annual financial report.

Comparative figures have been adjusted to conform to the changes in presentation in the current reporting period, where necessary.

Since 1 January 2007 the Consolidated Entity has adopted the following Standards and Interpretations, for annual periods beginning on or after 1 January 2007. The following table outlines the new standards adopted by the company and the impact of the standard on the Consolidated Entity's financial report.

Reference	Title	Summary	Application date for the standard	Impact on Consolidated Entity's financial report	Application date of Consolidated Entity
IFRS 7	Financial Instruments: Disclosures	New standard replacing the disclosure requirements.	1 January 2007	IFRS 7 is a disclosure standard so has no direct impact on the measurement and recognition criteria relating to amounts included in the Consolidated Entity's financial statements, but does result in changes to the financial instrument disclosures included in the Consolidated Entity's annual report.	1 January 2007
IFRS 8	Operating Segments	New standard.	1 January 2009	IFRS 8 is a disclosure standard so has no direct impact on the measurement and recognition criteria relating to amounts included in the Consolidated Entity's financial statements, but does result in changes to the segment reporting disclosures included in the Consolidated Entity's financial report. (Refer to Note 6)	1 January 2007
IAS 1	Presentation of Financial Statements	Added disclosures about an entity's capital and changed the presentation and format of financial statements.	1 January 2007	IAS 1 is a disclosure standard so has no direct impact on the measurement and recognition criteria relating to amounts included in the Group's financial statements, but may result in changes to capital disclosures included in the Group's annual report and presentation and format of financial statements.	1 January 2007

Certain new accounting standards and interpretations have been published that are not mandatory for the 31 December 2007 reporting period. The Consolidated Entity's assessment of the impact of these new standards and interpretations on the financial report is set out below.

Reference	Title	Summary	Application date for the standard	Preliminary assessment on the impact of the Consolidated Entity's financial report	Application date of Consolidated Entity
IAS 23	Borrowing Costs	Amended to require all borrowing costs associated with a qualifying asset to be capitalised.	1 January 2009	This is consistent with the Consolidated Entity's existing accounting policy for Capitalisation of interest and financing costs and is not expected to have any additional impact.	1 January 2009
IFRIC 11	IFRS 2 – Treasury Share Transactions	This interpretation deals with accounting for share based payments issued between two entities in the same group and whether certain share based payments should be accounted for as equity-settled or cash-settled awards.	1 March 2007	This is consistent with the Consolidated Entity's existing accounting policy for Share based payments and is not expected to have any additional impact.	1 January 2008
IFRIC 12	Service Concession Arrangements	This interpretation deals with accounting for publicly owned infrastructure constructed, operated, and maintained by the private sector.	1 January 2008	Not applicable	Not applicable
IFRIC 13	Customer Loyalty Programmes	This interpretation deals with sales of goods with customer award credits should be accounted as multiple-element transactions.	1 July 2008	Not applicable	Not applicable
IFRIC 14	IAS 19 – The Limit on a Defined Benefit Asset, Minimum Funding Requirements and their Interaction	This interpretation provides Clarification of IAS 19 regarding future contributions and minimum funding requirements of defined benefit plans.	1 January 2008	Not applicable	Not applicable

Extract 2(A2) – Lihir Gold Limited, page 46

This extract presents a statement of comprehensive income that includes other comprehensive income components (i.e., single statement of comprehensive income was prepared). Expenses are analyzed by function.

STATEMENTS OF COMPREHENSIVE INCOME	Note	CONSOLIDATED ENTITY $m		COMPANY $m	
		2007	2006	2007	2006
Revenue	7	498.4	386.0	497.6	385.8
Cost of sales	9	(261.3)	(211.0)	(260.4)	(211.7)
Mine operating earnings		**237.1**	**175.0**	**237.2**	**174.1**
Corporate expense		(25.3)	(12.1)	(24.4)	(12.1)
Project studies		(7.5)	(0.8)	(7.5)	(0.8)
Exploration expense		(8.4)	(5.9)	(8.2)	(5.9)
Operating profit before other income / (expense)		**195.9**	**156.2**	**197.1**	**155.3**
Other income / (expense):					
Hedging loss	10	(97.2)	(78.3)	(97.2)	(78.3)
Other expenses	11	(13.8)	-	(13.8)	-
Financial income	12	12	4.2	7.7	4.2
Financial expenses	12	(131.6)	(6.2)	(130.6)	(5.6)
Profit / (loss) before tax		**(35.8)**	**75.9**	**(36.8)**	**75.6**
Income tax benefit / (expense)	13	**11.7**	**(22.1)**	**10.2**	**(22.0)**
Net profit / (loss) after tax		**(24.1)**	**53.8**	**(26.6)**	**53.6**
Other comprehensive income					
Exchange difference on translation of foreign operations	27	42.6	-	-	-
Cash flow hedges	27	38.7	(50.8)	38.7	(50.8)
Share based payments	27	2.9	5.5	2.9	5.5
Net change in fair value of available for sale financial assets	27	1.2	-	-	-
Income tax on other comprehensive income	13	(4.7)	20.3	(4.3)	20.4
Other comprehensive income for the period net of tax		**80.7**	**(25.0)**	**37.3**	**(24.9)**
Total comprehensive income		**56.6**	**28.8**	**10.7**	**28.7**
Earnings / (loss) per share	37				
- Basic (cents/share)		(1.4)	4.2	(1.6)	4.2
- Diluted (cents/share)		(1.4)	4.2	(1.6)	4.2

The above Statements of Comprehensive Income are to be read in conjunction with the accompanying Notes to the Financial Statements set out on pages 51–110.

Extract 2(A3) – Lihir Gold Limited, page 47 and 48

This extract presents a statement of financial position. Note that reserves that include other comprehensive income are presented distinctly from retained earnings.

STATEMENTS OF FINANCIAL POSITION		CONSOLIDATED ENTITY $m		COMPANY $m	
ASSETS	Note	2007	2006	2007	2006
CURRENT ASSETS					
Cash and cash equivalents	14	174.2	47.0	122.4	43.6
Receivables	16	14.9	4.6	15.0	4.3
Inventories	17	102.8	75.3	102.7	75.3
Derivative financial instruments	18	-	0.3	-	0.3
Other assets		2.3	5.5	2.2	5.5
Total current assets		**294.2**	**132.7**	**242.3**	**129.0**
NON-CURRENT ASSETS					
Receivables	16	0.4	0.5	0.4	2.1
Inventories	17	169.1	141.7	169.1	141.7
Derivative financial instruments	18	-	2.4	-	2.4
Deferred mining costs	19	218.3	148.3	218.3	148.3
Property plant and equipment	20	1,430.6	951.2	1,032.0	949.4
Intangible assets	21	98.4	-	7.0	-
Available-for-sale financial assets	22	2.5	33.0	-	-
Deferred income tax asset	13	92.1	86.2	92.1	86.1
Investments in subsidiaries	29	-	-	494.0	54.6
Total non-current assets		**2,011.4**	**1,363.3**	**2,012.9**	**1,384.6**
Total assets		**2,305.6**	**1,496.0**	**2,255.2**	**1,513.6**
LIABILITIES					
CURRENT LIABILITIES					
Accounts payable & accrued liabilities	23	64.0	46.6	113.9	100.1
Provisions	24	13.5	6.4	11.6	6.0
Borrowings and finance facilities	25	0.3	62.5	-	27.0
Derivative financial instruments	18	-	61.5	-	61.5
Income tax payable	13	-	0.3	-	-
Total current liabilities		**77.8**	**177.3**	**125.5**	**194.6**
NON-CURRENT LIABILITIES					
Provisions	24	15.2	14.2	14.6	14.2
Borrowings	25	0.7	218.6	-	218.6
Derivative financial instruments	18	-	274.0	-	274.0
Deferred income tax liability	13	50.8	-	-	-
Total non-current liabilities		**66.7**	**506.8**	**14.6**	**506.8**
Total liabilities		**144.5**	**684.1**	**140.1**	**701.4**
NET ASSETS		**2,161.1**	**811.9**	**2,115.1**	**812.2**
SHAREHOLDERS' EQUITY					
Share capital	26	2,319.7	1,027.1	2,319.7	1,027.5
Reserves	27	(170.0)	(250.7)	(213.3)	(250.6)
Retained earnings	27	11.4	35.5	8.7	35.3
TOTAL SHAREHOLDERS' EQUITY		**2,161.1**	**811.9**	**2,115.1**	**812.2**

The above Statements of Financial Position are to be read in conjunction with the accompanying Notes to the Financial Statements set out on pages 51–110.

Extract 2(A4) – Lihir Gold Limited, page 49

This extract presents a statement of changes in equity. All transactions with owners are shown.

STATEMENTS OF CHANGES IN EQUITY				
CONSOLIDATED ENTITY	Issued capital $m	Reserves $m	Retained Earnings $m	Total Equity $m
Balance at 1 January 2006	1,027.5	(225.7)	(18.3)	783.5
Total comprehensive income / (expense) for the period	-	(25.0)	53.8	28.8
Purchase of treasury shares	(0.4)	-	-	(0.4)
Balance at 31 December 2006	**1,027.1**	**(250.7)**	**35.5**	**811.9**
Balance at 1 January 2007	**1,027.1**	**(250.7)**	**35.5**	**811.9**
Total comprehensive income / (expense) for the period	-	80.7	(24.1)	56.6
Issue of shares – on acquisition of Ballarat	316.5	-	-	316.5
Issue of shares – rights issue / placement (net of transaction costs)	977.4	-	-	977.4
Purchase of treasury shares	(1.3)	-	-	(1.3)
Balance at 31 December 2007	**2,319.7**	**(170.0)**	**11.4**	**2,161.1**
COMPANY	Issued capital $m	Reserves $m	Retained Earnings $m	Total Equity $m
Balance at 1 January 2006	1,027.5	(225.7)	(18.3)	783.5
Total comprehensive income / (expense) for the period	-	(24.9)	53.6	28.7
Balance at 31 December 2006	**1,027.5**	**(250.6)**	**35.3**	**812.2**
Balance at 1 January 2007	**1,027.5**	**(250.6)**	**35.3**	**812.2**
Total comprehensive income / (expense) for the period	-	37.3	(26.6)	10.7
Issue of shares – on acquisition of Ballarat	316.5	-	-	316.5
Issue of shares – rights issue / placement (net of transaction costs)	977.4	-	-	977.4
Purchase of treasury shares	(1.7)	-	-	(1.7)
Balance at 31 December 2007	**2,319.7**	**(213.3)**	**8.7**	**2,115.1**
The above Statements of Changes in Equity are to be read in conjunction with the accompanying Notes to the Financial Statements set out on pages 51–110.				

Extract 2(A5) – Lihir Gold Limited, page 50

This extract presents a statement of cash flows. Note that the company has used the direct method for establishing cash flows from operating activities.

STATEMENTS OF CASH FLOWS		CONSOLIDATED ENTITY $m		COMPANY $m	
CASH FLOWS FROM OPERATING ACTIVITIES	Note	2007	2006	2007	2006
Receipts from customers		472.4	329.3	471.4	329.0
Payments arising from suppliers & employees		(365.9)	(268.7)	(359.2)	(271.5)
Cash generated from operations		**106.5**	**60.6**	**112.2**	**57.5**
Interest and finance charges paid		(8.0)	(3.3)	(7.0)	(3.3)
Net cash flow from operating activities	15	**98.5**	**57.3**	**105.2**	**54.2**
CASH FLOWS FROM INVESTING ACTIVITIES					
Interest received		9.7	1.4	6.6	1.4
Purchase of property, plant and equipment		(206.7)	(170.8)	(147.2)	(169.0)
Proceeds on disposal of property, plant and equipment		-	0.1	-	0.1
Payments for investments		(1.2)	(34.0)	(122.0)	(1.0)
Acquisition of subsidiary net of cash acquired	28	19.6	-	-	-
Net cash flow from investing activities		**(178.6)**	**(203.3)**	**(262.6)**	**(168.5)**
CASH FLOWS FROM FINANCING ACTIVITIES					
Drawdown of secured debt		22.4	65.6	22.4	30.0
Repayment of secured debt		(88.2)	-	(52.6)	-
Repayment of gold loan		(333.4)	-	(333.4)	-
Proceeds of equity issue		989.0	-	989.0	-
Underwriting expenses		(11.6)	-	(11.6)	-
Purchase of gold to close out hedge book		(648.4)	-	(648.4)	-
Receipts on close out of hedge book		279.9	-	279.9	-
Payment for treasury shares		(1.3)	(0.4)	(1.7)	-
Net cash flow from financing activities		**208.4**	**65.2**	**243.6**	**30.0**
Net increase / (decrease) in cash and cash equivalents		128.3	(80.8)	86.2	(84.2)
Cash and cash equivalents at beginning of year		47.0	127.8	43.5	127.8
Effects of exchange rates to changes in cash held		(1.1)	-	(7.3)	-
Cash and cash equivalents at end of year	14	**174.2**	**47.0**	**122.4**	**43.6**
Financing arrangements	25				

The above Statements of Cash Flows is to be read in conjunction with the accompanying Notes to the Financial Statements set out on pages 51–110.

Extract 2(A6) – Lihir Gold Limited, pages 92 to 94

This extract presents the note on the details of equity reserves as shown on the statement of financial position.

NOTE 27: RESERVES

	CONSOLIDATED ENTITY $m		COMPANY $m	
	2007	2006	2007	2006
(a) Reserves				
Hedging reserve – cash flow hedges	(221.9)	(256.1)	(221.9)	(256.1)
Employee Share based payments reserve	3.3	0.2	3.4	0.3
Landowner Share based payments reserve	5.2	5.2	5.2	5.2
Fair value reserve	0.8	-	-	-
Foreign currency translation reserve	42.6	-	-	-
	(170.0)	**(250.7)**	**(213.3)**	**(250.6)**
Movements:				
Hedging reserve – cash flow hedges				
Opening balance	(256.1)	(225.7)	(256.1)	(225.7)
Fair value of cash flow hedges	(59.1)	(40.6)	(59.1)	(40.6)
Call options sold	-	(9.4)	-	(9.4)
Deferred hedging gains / (losses)	97.8	(0.8)	97.8	(0.8)
Deferred taxation	(4.5)	20.4	(4.5)	20.4
	(221.9)	**(256.1)**	**(221.9)**	**(256.1)**

	CONSOLIDATED ENTITY $m		COMPANY $m	
	2007	2006	2007	2006
Employee share based payments reserve				
Opening balance	0.2	-	0.3	-
Share rights expensed	2.9	0.3	2.9	0.3
Deferred taxation	0.2	(0.1)	0.2	-
	3.3	**0.2**	**3.4**	**0.3**
Landowners share based payments reserve				
Opening balance	5.2	-	5.2	-
Share rights capitalised	-	5.2	-	5.2
	5.2	**5.2**	**5.2**	**5.2**
Fair value reserve				
Opening balance	-	-	-	-
Fair value of available for sale financial assets	1.2	-	-	-
Deferred tax	(0.4)	-	-	-
	0.8	**-**	**-**	**-**
Foreign currency translation reserve				
Opening balance	-	-	-	-
Currency translation differences arising during the year	42.6	-	-	-
	42.6	**-**	**-**	**-**
(b) Retained Profits				
Movements in retained profits / (losses) were as follows:				
Opening balance	35.5	(18.3)	35.3	(18.3)
Net profit for the year	(24.1)	53.8	(26.6)	53.6
	11.4	**35.5**	**8.7**	**35.3**

> **Nature and purpose of reserves**
>
> *Available-for-sale investments revaluation reserve*
>
> Changes in the fair value and exchange differences arising on translation of investments, such as equities, classified as available-for-sale financial assets, are taken to the available-for-sale investments revaluation reserve, as described in Note 1(xvii). Amounts are recognised in profit and loss when the associated assets are sold or impaired.
>
> *Hedging reserve - cash flow hedges*
>
> The hedging reserve is used to record gains or losses on a hedging instrument in a cash flow hedge that are recognised directly in equity, as described in Note 1(xvii). Amounts are recognised in profit and loss when the associated hedged transaction affects profit and loss.
>
> *Share-based payments reserve*
>
> The share-based payments reserve is used to recognise:
>
> - the fair value of options issued to employees but not exercised
> - the fair value of shares issued to employees
> - in the parent entity - the fair value of shares and options issued to employees of subsidiaries
>
> *Landowner share-based payments reserve*
>
> The landowner share-based payments reserve is used to recognise:
>
> - the fair value of shares issued to local landowners
>
> *Foreign currency translation reserve*
>
> Exchange differences arising on translation of a foreign controlled entity are taken to the foreign currency translation reserve, as described in Note 1(xxxi). The reserve is recognised in profit and loss when the net investment is disposed of.

SAP AG – All extracts were obtained from the IFRS financial reports 2007 for the year ended December 31, 2007.

Extract 2(B1) – SAP AG, page 71

This extract presents a note in which the company provides general information including:

- an affirmation that it applied all standards and interpretations that were effective and endorsed by the EU as at its year end;

- its status as an international corporation and location of its headquarters;

- fact that it classifies expenses based on their function within the entity and that various items are aggregated in the income statements and balance sheets (and that notes present details as observed in the extracts below);

- fact that functional currency is the Euro, therefore amounts included in the consolidated financial statements are reported in millions of Euro ("€ millions") unless otherwise stated;

- the activities, products and services it sells (it refers to segment information note presented in an extract below); and

- other perspectives and currency risks.

> **A. Basis of Presentation (in part)**
>
> **(1) General (in part)**
>
> We have applied all standards and interpretations that were effective and endorsed by the EU as at December 31, 2007. The effects of the adoption of IFRS on the financial position, results of operations and cash flows as presented herein are described below.
>
> Our Consolidated Statements of Income are presented using a classification of expenses based on their function within the entity.
>
> The Consolidated Balance Sheets correspond to the classification provisions contained in IAS 1 Presentation of Financial Statements. For clarity, various items are aggregated in the income statements and balance sheets. These items are disaggregated separately in the Notes. The functional currency of SAP AG is the euro, therefore amounts included in the Consolidated Financial Statements are reported in millions of euro ("€ millions") unless otherwise stated.
>
> We are an international corporation with headquarters in Walldorf, Germany. We develop, market, and sell a variety of software solutions, primarily enterprise application software products for organizations including corporations, government agencies, and educational institutions. We also offer support and other services (including consulting and training) related to our software offering. For more information, see Note 28.
>
> We operate in a dynamic and rapidly changing environment that involves numerous risks and uncertainties, many of which are beyond the Company's control. We derive a substantial portion of our revenue from software licenses and services sold to customers in Germany, the United States, the United Kingdom, and Japan (see Note 34). Our future revenue and income may be significantly adversely affected by a prolonged economic slowdown in any of these countries or elsewhere. Further, a significant portion of our business is conducted in currencies other than the euro. We continually monitor our exposure to foreign currency exchange risk and have a Company-wide foreign currency exchange risk policy under which we may hedge such risks with certain financial instruments. However, fluctuations in foreign currency exchange rates, especially the value of the U.S. dollar, pound sterling, Japanese yen, Swiss franc, Canadian dollar, and Australian dollar could significantly impact our reported financial position and results of operations.

Extract 2(B2) – SAP AG, page 79

This extract presents a note on consolidation in which the company specifies that:

- it has consolidated all of the majority-owned entities that it controls directly or indirectly (it provides a table of the changes in the number of legal entities included in the consolidated financial statements);

- it does not have any financial or non-financial interest in an SPE;

- all its entities prepare their financial statements as at December 31 and apply the same group IFRS accounting and valuation principles.

In addition, the note sets out the number of companies in which it does not have a controlling financial interest but over which it can exercise significant operating and financial policy influence.

> **(2) Scope of Consolidation**
>
> The Consolidated Financial Statements include SAP AG and all of its majority-owned entities that are controlled directly or indirectly by SAP AG. SAP does not consolidate any special-purpose entities (SPEs) as SAP does not have any financial or nonfinancial interest in an SPE.
>
> All SAP entities prepare their financial statements as at December 31. All financial statements were prepared applying the same Group IFRS accounting and valuation principles. Inter-company transactions and balances relating to consolidated entities have been eliminated.

The following table summarizes the change in the number of legal entities included in the Consolidated Financial Statements. Included in our additions to consolidated legal entities is a newly founded entity in which we hold only 49% of the voting shares. Due to the fact that the majority shareholder has entered into an agreement which provides that SAP fully controls the entity, receives all benefits, and bears all risks, we fully consolidate this entity as we would any other of our operating entities:

Number of Legal Entities Consolidated in the Financial Statements

	German	Foreign	Total
12/31/2006	21	94	115
Additions	2	24	26
Disposals	0	– 2	– 2
12/31/2007	**23**	**116**	**139**

The impact of changes in the scope of companies included in the Consolidated Financial Statements during 2007 did not have a significant effect on the comparability of the Consolidated Financial Statements presented. The additions relate to seven newly founded entities and to 19 legal entities added in connection with acquisitions. The disposals are due to mergers of consolidated legal entities.

Associates

In 2007, four companies in which we do not have a controlling financial interest but over which we can exercise significant operating and financial policy influence ("Associates"), are accounted for using the equity method (2006: five companies).

Extract 2(B3) – SAP AG, pages 79 to 91

This is an extensive extract covering different aspects of the company's significant accounting policies. The following issues are illustrated:

- use of estimates: general note indicating that financial position, income and cash flows are subject to numerous risks and uncertainties;

- different bases of measurement applied to classes of assets, liabilities or equity components;

- business combinations, including election on transition (company has not adopted IFRS 3, *Business Combinations* and IAS 27, *Consolidated and Separate Financial Statements,* which are effective July 1, 2009, early);

- foreign currencies, including a statement that the functional currency of subsidiaries is the local currency, methods used for translation and election on transition;

- a table presenting exchange rates of key currencies affecting the company;

- sources of revenues and related revenue recognition policies, notably that the company refers to US guidance on software revenue recognition issues;

- research and development costs, which are expensed because:

  o the company has determined that technological feasibility for its software products is reached shortly before the products are available for sale, and

  o the costs incurred after technological feasibility is established are generally not material;

- government grants, which are recorded when it is reasonably assured that the company will comply with the relevant conditions and that the grant will be received. Since government grants represent subsidies for activities specified in the grant, the company recognizes government grants as a reduction of the related expense when earned;

- advertising costs, which are presented as an expense or an offset to revenue;

- leases of property, plant and equipment, mainly buildings and vehicles, accounted for as operating leases that do not transfer to the company the substantive risks and rewards of ownership. Specific issues related to lessee incentives and contractually agreed future increases of rents are addressed;

- accounting for income taxes;
- accounting for share-based compensation covering both cash-settled and equity-settled awards;
- SORIE contents (note that elements indicated are now part of the statement of comprehensive income);
- definition of basic and diluted earnings per share (EPS) and cash and cash equivalents;
- accounting for investments as required by IAS 39, *Financial Instruments: Recognition and Measurement* (note that changes in the value of available-for-sale assets are part of comprehensive income as required by current IAS 1);
- accounting for investments recorded under the equity method;
- details and accounting of the "Other Financial Assets" line item presented on the statement of financial position, which includes:
  - o non-interest-bearing or below-market-rate loans to employees and to third parties that are discounted to their present value and reviewed for impairment,
  - o investments in insurance policies held for employee financed pension plans, which are recorded at their cash surrender values, including premiums paid and guaranteed interest,
  - o derivative financial instruments use and hedge accounting;
- accounts receivable details, including the allowance for doubtful accounts (that reflected a change in accounting estimate recorded in the previous year). Note that the company indicates that it presents unbilled receivables related to fixed-fee and time-and-material consulting arrangements for contract work performed to date;
- details and measurement basis of the "Other Assets" line item presented on the statement of financial position, which includes inventories (immaterial to the company);
- accounting and reporting of non-current assets and disposal groups classified as held for sale;
- goodwill treatment, including transition to IFRS election;
- accounting for other intangible assets purchased and "in-process R&D," including amortization and impairment;
- leasehold improvements and property, plant and equipment valuation and depreciation;
- impairment of long-Lived assets (the company indicates that it did not recognize any impairment charges in the years presented);
- prepaid expenses and deferred charges composition (prepayments of operating leases, support services, software royalties and discount of loans to employees);
- details of the "Accounts Payable, Financial and Other Liabilities" line presented on the statement of financial position, including a statement that the company does not designate its financial liabilities as at fair value through profit or loss on initial recognition;
- measurement of the "Other Obligations" line presented on the statement of financial position, which consists of provisions including warranties and restructuring;

- pension-benefit liabilities and other post-employment benefits, which are based on actuarial computations using the projected-unit-credit method in accordance with IAS 19, *Employee Benefits* and the accounting policy choice to recognize all actuarial gains and losses directly in other components of equity (other comprehensive income under current IAS 1);

- deferred income consisting mainly of prepayments made by customers for support, consulting and training services;

- treasury shares, which are recorded at acquisition cost and are presented as a deduction from shareholders' equity, with gains and losses on the subsequent reissuance of treasury shares being credited or charged to additional paid-in capital on an after-tax basis;

- the accounting policy choice for the classification in the consolidated statements of cash flows of:

  o interest and taxes paid, as well as interest and dividends received as cash flows from operating activities,

  o dividends paid as financing activities;

- new accounting standards adopted early in the current period (IFRS 8), presented below;

- new accounting standards not yet adopted (IAS 23, *Borrowing Costs*, IFRIC 11, IFRS 2, *Group and Treasury Share Transactions*, IFRIC 12, *Service Concession Rights*, IFRIC13, *Customer Loyalty Programmes*, IFRIC 14, IAS 19, *The Limit on a Defined Benefit Asset, Minimum Funding Requirements*, amendment to IAS 1, *Presentation of Financial Statements*, IFRS 2, (revised 2008) *Vesting Conditions and Cancellations*, IFRS 3, *Business Combinations* and IAS 27, *Consolidated and Separate Financial Statements* and amendment to IAS 32, *Financial Instruments: Disclosure and Presentation – Puttable Instruments and Obligations arising on Liquidation*.

Certain accounting policies used differ from those that would apply under Canadian GAAP including the ones related to provisions and actuarial gains and losses. Note that the statement of recognized income and expense would not be presented under current IAS 1 (as discussed previously in this chapter).

---

(3) Summary of Significant Accounting Policies

Use of Estimates

The preparation of the Consolidated Financial Statements requires us to make estimates and assumptions that affect the reported amounts of assets and liabilities, disclosure of contingent assets and liabilities at the date of the Consolidated Financial Statements, and the reported amounts of revenues and expenses during the reporting periods. In making our estimates, in particular when assessing revenues and costs, the valuation and recoverability of receivables, investments and other assets, tax positions, provisions and contingent liabilities, we consider historical and forecast information, as well as regional and industry economic conditions in which the Company or its customers operate, changes to which could adversely affect our performance. Actual results could differ from original estimates.

Our financial position, income, and cash flows are subject to numerous risks and uncertainties. Factors that could affect the Company's future financial statements and cause actual results to differ materially from current expectations include, but are not limited to, adverse changes in the global economy, consolidation and intense competition in the software industry, decline in customer demand in the most important markets in Europe, the United States, and Asia, as well as fluctuations in currency exchange rates.

Basis of Measurement

The Consolidated Financial Statements have been prepared on the historical cost basis except as follows:

- Derivative financial instruments are measured at fair value.
- Available-for-sale financial assets are measured at fair value.
- Liabilities for cash-settled share-based payment arrangements are measured at fair value.

Where applicable, information about the methods and assumptions used in determining fair values is disclosed in the Notes specific to that asset or liability.

Business Combinations

We account for all business combinations using the purchase method. As at the date of acquisition, we allocate the purchase price to the fair values of the assets acquired and liabilities assumed. Goodwill represents the excess of the cost of an acquired entity over the fair values assigned to the tangible assets acquired, to those intangible assets that are required to be recognized and reported separately from goodwill, and to the liabilities assumed.

As part of our transition to IFRS we elected to not restate our accounting for business combinations. In respect of acquisitions prior to January 1, 2006, goodwill represents the amount recognized under U.S. GAAP. The accounting treatment under U.S. GAAP is generally similar to IFRS 3. Under U.S. GAAP we ceased the periodic amortization of goodwill beginning 2002.

Foreign Currencies

The functional currency of our subsidiaries is the local currency. The assets and liabilities of our foreign operations where the functional currency is not the euro are translated into euros using period-end closing exchange rates, whereas items of income and expense are translated into euros using average exchange rates during the respective periods. The resulting foreign currency translation adjustments are included in Other components of equity. The accumulated balance of the foreign currency translation reserve reflects the differences since January 1, 2006, the date of transition to IFRS. When a foreign operation is disposed of, the foreign currency translation adjustments applicable to that entity is recognized in profit and loss.

Transactions in foreign currencies are translated to the respective functional currencies of Group entities at exchange rates at the dates of the transactions. Monetary assets and liabilities that are denominated in foreign currencies other than the functional currency are translated at the period-end closing rate with resulting gains and losses reflected in Other non-operating income/expense, net in the Consolidated Statements of Income.

Operating cash flows are translated into euros using average exchange rates during the respective periods whereas investing and financing cash flows are translated into euros using the exchange rates in effect at the time of the respective transaction. The effects on cash due to fluctuations in exchange rates are shown in a separate line in the Consolidated Statements of Cash Flows.

Exchange Rates

The exchange rates of key currencies affecting the Company are as follows:

to €1		Closing rate as at December 31,		Annual average exchange rate	
		2007	2006	2007	2006
U.S. dollar	USD	1.4721	1.3170	1.3777	1.2611
Pound sterling	GBP	0.7334	0.6715	0.6890	0.6800
Japanese yen	JPY	164.93	156.93	161.43	147.02
Swiss franc	CHF	1.6547	1.6069	1.6446	1.5757
Canadian dollar	CAD	1.4449	1.5281	1.4623	1.4296
Australian dollar	AUD	1.6757	1.6691	1.6368	1.6715

Revenue Recognition

We derive our revenues from the sale or license of our software products and of support, subscription, consulting, development, training, and other professional services. The vast majority of our software arrangements include support services and many also include professional services and other elements.

Revenue from the sale of licenses is recognized in line with the requirements for selling goods. The sale is recognized net of returns and allowances, trade discounts, and volume rebates. As authorized by IAS 8.10 to 8.11, we follow the guidance provided by the American Institute of Certified Public Accountants (AICPA) Statement of Position 97-2 as amended, Software Revenue Recognition (SOP 97-2) in order to determine the recognizable amount of license revenue in case of multi-element arrangements. Revenue on multiple-element arrangements is recognized using the residual method when company-specific objective evidence of fair value exists for all of the undelivered elements (for example, support, consulting, or other services) in the arrangement, but does not exist for one or more delivered elements (for example, software). We allocate revenue to each undelivered element based on its respective fair value which is the price charged when that element is sold separately or, for elements not yet sold separately, the price established by our management if it is probable that the price will not change before the element is sold separately. We allocate revenue to undelivered support services based on a company-wide rate charged to renewal the support services annually (such renewal rates representing a percentage of the discounted software license fee charged to the customer; the vast majority of our customers renew their annual support service contracts). We defer revenue for all undelivered elements and recognize the residual amount of the arrangement fee attributable to the delivered elements, if any, when the basic criteria in SOP 97-2 have been met.

Under SOP 97-2, provided that the arrangement does not involve significant production, modification, or customization of the software, software revenue is recognized when all of the following four criteria have been met:

1. Persuasive evidence of an arrangement exists.
2. Delivery has occurred.
3. The fee is fixed or determinable.
4. Collectibility is probable.

If at the outset of an arrangement we determine that the arrangement fee is not fixed or determinable, revenue is deferred until the arrangement fee becomes due and payable by the customer. If at the outset of an arrangement we determine that collectibility is not probable, revenue is deferred until payment is received. Substantially, none of our software license agreements includes acceptance testing provisions. If an arrangement allows for customer acceptance testing of the software, we defer revenue until the earlier of customer acceptance or when the acceptance right lapses.

We usually sell or license software on a perpetual basis. Occasionally, we license software for a specified time. Revenue from short-term time-based licenses, which generally include support services during the license period, is recognized ratably over the license term. Revenue from multi-year time-based licenses that include support services, whether separately priced or not, is recognized ratably over the license term unless a substantive support service renewal rate exists, in which case the amount allocated to software based on the residual method is recognized as software revenue once the basic criteria in SOP 97-2 have been met. Revenues from time-based licenses were not material in any of the periods presented.

Arrangements for unspecified future software updates, upgrades and enhancements and technical product support are support service contracts. Support revenues are recognized ratably over the term of the support service contract, typically one year, and are classified as support revenue in the Consolidated Statements of Income. In contrast, arrangements for unspecified future additional software products are subscriptions. Revenue from such arrangements is recognized ratably over the term of the arrangement beginning with the delivery of the first product. Revenues from subscriptions were not material in any of the periods presented.

We recognize revenue from arrangements involving resellers on evidence of sell-through by the reseller to the end customer. We have a history of honoring contingent rights if we become aware that a reseller has granted contingent rights to an end-customer, although we have no contractual obligation to do so and we therefore defer revenue recognition until a valid license agreement has been entered into without contingencies or, if applicable, until the contingencies expire.

In multiple-element arrangements involving software and consulting, training, or other professional services that are not essential to the functionality of the software, the service revenues are accounted for separately from the software revenues.

For short-term time-based licenses we allocate a portion of the arrangement fee to support revenue based on the estimated fair value of the support services.

We recognize consulting, training, and other professional service revenues when the services are performed. Consulting revenues are recognized on a time-and-material basis or using the percentage of completion method. Consulting services primarily comprise implementation support related to the installation and configuration of our software products and do not typically involve significant production, modification, or customization of our software.

Revenue for arrangements that involve significant production, modification, or customization of the software and those in which the services are not available from thirdparty vendors and are therefore deemed essential to the software, is recognized on a time-and-material basis or using the percentage of completion method of accounting, based on direct labor costs incurred to date as a percentage of total estimated project costs required to complete the project. If we do not have a sufficient basis to measure the progress of completion or to estimate the total contract revenues and costs, revenue is recognized only to the extent of contract cost incurred for which we believe recoverability to be probable. If the arrangement includes elements that do not qualify for contract accounting (for example support services and hosting) such elements are accounted for separately provided that the elements have stand-alone value and that company-specific objective evidence of fair value exists. When total cost estimates exceed revenues in an arrangement, the estimated losses are recognized immediately based on an average fully burdened daily rate applicable to the unit delivering the services, which consists of costs allocable to the arrangement.

We enter into joint development agreements with customers to leverage their industry expertise, and provide standard software solutions for selected vertical markets. These customers generally contribute cash, resources, and industry expertise in exchange for license rights for the future solution. We recognize software revenue in conjunction with these arrangements based on the percentage of completion method. If we do not have a sufficient basis to measure the progress of completion or to estimate the total contract revenues and costs, revenue is recognized when the project is complete and, if applicable, final acceptance is received from the customer.

The assumptions, risks, and uncertainties inherent in the application of the percentage of completion method affect the timing and amounts of revenues and expenses reported. Numerous internal and external factors can affect estimates, including direct labor rates, utilization, and efficiency variances. Changes in estimates of SAP's progress towards completion and of contract revenues and contract costs are accounted for as cumulative catch-up adjustments to the reported revenues for the applicable contract.

Hosting and other on-demand services are recognized ratably over the term of the individual contract. Revenues from hosting and other on-demand services are classified as Other service revenue and were not material in any of the periods presented.

We account for out-of-pocket expenses invoiced by SAP and reimbursed by customers as support, consulting, and training revenues, depending on the nature of the service for which the out-of-pocket expenses were incurred.

If a support or subscription customer is specifically identified as a bad debtor, we stop recognizing revenue except to the extent that the fees have already been collected.

We record sales net of applicable sales taxes.

Research and Development

All research and development costs are expensed as incurred. Development is the application of research findings or other knowledge to a plan or design for the production of new or substantially improved products before the start of commercial production or use. Development expenditures are capitalized only if all of the following criteria are met:

1. Development cost can be measured reliably,
2. The product is technically and commercially feasible,
3. Future economic benefits are probable, and
4. We intend to complete development and market the product.

We have determined that technological feasibility for our software products is reached shortly before the products are available for sale. Costs incurred after technological feasibility is established are generally not material.

Government Grants

We record government grants when it is reasonably assured that we will comply with the relevant conditions and that the grant will be received. Our government grants generally represent subsidies for activities specified in the grant. As a result, government grants are recognized as a reduction of the related expense when earned.

Advertising Costs

Advertising costs are included in sales and marketing expense and are expensed as incurred. Our contributions to resellers that allow our resellers to execute qualified and approved marketing activities are recognized as an offset to revenue unless we obtain a separate identifiable benefit for the contribution and the fair value of such benefit is reasonably estimable.

Lease Payments

We are a lessee of property, plant, and equipment, mainly buildings and vehicles, under operating leases that do not transfer to us the substantive risks and rewards of ownership. Rent expense on operating leases is recognized on a straight-line basis over the life of the lease including renewal terms if, at inception of the lease, renewal is reasonably assured. Some of our operating leases contain lessee incentives, such as free or reduced periods of rent. Such incentives are amortized over the life of the lease so that the rent expense is recognized on a straight-line basis over the life of the lease. The same applies to contractually agreed future increases of rents.

Income Taxes

Deferred taxes are accounted for under the asset and liability method. We recognize deferred tax assets and liabilities for the future tax consequences attributable to differences between the financial statement carrying amounts of existing assets and liabilities and their respective tax bases and on tax loss and tax credit carryforwards.

Deferred income tax assets and liabilities are measured using enacted respectively substantively enacted tax rates expected to apply to taxable income in the years in which those temporary differences are expected to be recovered or settled. The effect on deferred tax assets and liabilities of a change in tax rates is recognized in income respectively in Other components of equity in the period that includes the respective enactment date.

We reduce deferred income tax assets to the extent that it is probable that some portion or all of the deferred tax assets will not be realized.

Interest on income taxes and penalties on income taxes are classified as income tax expenses.

Share-Based Compensation

Share-based compensation covers cash-settled and equity-settled awards.

Equity-settled awards are measured at grant-date fair value and are not subsequently remeasured. The grant-date fair value is recognized over the period in which the employees become unconditionally entitled to the options with a corresponding increase in accumulated paid-in capital. The amount recognized as an expense is adjusted to reflect the actual number of share options that finally vest. The fair values are determined by using a Black-Scholes option-pricing model.

The fair value of cash-settled awards is recognized as an expense with a corresponding increase in liabilities over the period in which the employees become unconditionally entitled to payment. Cash-settled awards are remeasured to fair value at each balance sheet date until the award is settled. Any changes in the fair value of the liability are recognized as personnel expense in profit or loss. The fair values for hedged programs are based on market data reflecting current market expectations.

Statement of Recognized Income and Expense

The statement of recognized income and expense is comprised of Profit after taxes and Other components of equity.

Other components of equity include foreign currency translation adjustments, unrecognized pension cost, gains and losses from derivatives designated as cash flow hedges, gains and losses resulting from STAR hedges, and unrealized gains and losses from marketable debt and equity securities classified as available-for-sale. Other components of equity, their composition and changes are shown separately in the Statement of Recognized Income and Expense.

Earnings per Share

We present basic and diluted earnings per share (EPS). Basic earnings per share is determined by dividing Profit after taxes attributable to equity holders of the parent by the weighted average number of common shares outstanding. Diluted earnings per share reflect the potential dilution that would occur if all "in the money" securities and other contracts to issue common shares were exercised or converted.

Cash and Cash Equivalents

Cash and cash equivalents consist of cash at banks and highly liquid investments with original maturities of three months or less.

Investments

Investments with original maturities of greater than three months and remaining maturities of less than one year are classified as short-term investments.

Marketable debt and equity securities, other than investments accounted for by the equity method, are classified as available-for-sale or held-to-maturity, depending on our intent with respect to holding such investments. If it is readily determinable, marketable securities classified as available-for-sale are accounted for at fair value. Unrealized gains and losses on available-for-sale securities are excluded from earnings and reported net of tax directly in Other components of equity. Standard purchases and sales of financial assets are accounted for at trade date. We do not designate marketable debt or equity securities as financial assets at fair value through profit or loss.

Equity investments in privately held companies over which we do not have the ability to exercise significant influence and whose fair value cannot be reliably measured in absence of an active market are accounted for at cost. An impairment charge is recognized in earnings in the Financial income, net line item in the period in which objective evidence indicates that one or more events have happened that have a negative effect on the estimated future cash flows.

All marketable debt and equity securities and cost method investments are evaluated for impairment at least annually or earlier if we become aware of an event that indicates that the carrying amount of the asset may not be recoverable. These financial assets are considered impaired if there is objective evidence of a loss event that resulted in a decline of the recoverable amount below its carrying amount. Objective evidence includes but is not limited to the disappearance of an active market for that asset, a high probability of insolvency of the debtor or a material breach in contract. An impairment loss for a debt security is reversed if the reversal can be related objectively to an event occurring after the impairment loss was recognized. Impairment losses for available-for-sale equity securities are not reversed.

Net gains/losses on investments consist of impairment charges and reversals, interest income and expenses, dividends and gains and losses from the disposal of such assets. Dividend and interest income are recognized when earned and are not included in net gains/losses at the time of disposal. Investments are derecognized when all of the risks and rewards of ownership have been transferred.

At-Equity-Investments

Investments accounted for under the equity method are initially recorded at acquisition cost and are subsequently adjusted for our proportionate share of the investees' net income or losses, changes in the investees' equity and for amortization of any step-up in the value of the acquired assets over the investees' book value. The excess of our initial investment in at-equity investments over our ownership percentage in the underlying net assets of those companies is attributed to certain fair value adjustments with the remaining portion recognized as goodwill ("investor level goodwill") which is not amortized.

We recognize an impairment loss on our at-equity investments when objective evidence indicates that one or more events have had a negative effect on the higher of the value in use and fair value less cost to sell.

Other Financial Assets

Non-interest-bearing or below-market-rate loans to employees and to third parties are discounted to their present value. In the event of any delay or shortfall in payments due under employee or third-party loans, we perform an individual loan review. The same applies if we become aware of any change in the debtor's financial condition that indicates a delay or shortfall in payments may result. If it is probable that we will not be able to collect the amounts due according to the contractual terms of the loan agreement an impairment charge is recorded on an allowance account based on our best estimate of the amount that will not be recoverable. Account balances are charged off against the allowance after all collection efforts have been exhausted and the likelihood of recovery is considered remote.

Net gains/losses on Other financial assets consist of impairment charges and reversals, interest income and expenses and gains and losses from the disposal of such assets. Interest income is recognized when earned and is not included in net gains/losses at the time of disposal. Other financial assets are derecognized when all of the risks and rewards of ownership have been transferred.

Investments in insurance policies held for employee financed pension plans are recorded at their cash surrender values including premiums paid and guaranteed interest.

Included in Other financial assets are our derivative financial instruments. We use forward exchange derivative financial instruments to reduce the foreign currency exchange risk, primarily of anticipated cash flows from transactions with subsidiaries denominated in currencies other than the euro. As discussed in Note 25, the Company uses call options to hedge its anticipated cash flow exposure attributable to changes in the market value of stock appreciation rights under various plans.

We account for derivatives and hedging activities in accordance with IAS 39 Financial Instruments: Recognition and Measurement, which requires that all derivative financial instruments be recorded on the balance sheet at their fair value. If the requirements for hedge accounting as set out in IAS 39 are met, we designate and document the hedge relationship including the nature of the risk, the identification of the hedged item, the hedging instrument, and how we will assess the hedge effectiveness.

The accounting for changes in fair value of the hedging instrument depends on the effectiveness of the hedging relationship. The effective portion of the realized and unrealized gain or loss on derivatives designated as cash flow hedges is reported net of tax, within Other components of equity. We reclassify the portion of gains or losses on derivatives from equity into earnings in the same period or periods during which the hedged forecasted transaction affects earnings. The ineffective portion of gains or losses on derivatives designated as cash flow hedges are reported in earnings when the ineffectiveness occurs. In measuring the effectiveness of foreign currency-related cash flow hedges, we exclude differences resulting from time value (that is, spot rates versus forward rates for forward contracts). Changes in value resulting from the excluded component are recognized in earnings immediately.

Foreign currency exchange derivatives entered into by us to offset exposure to anticipated cash flows that do not meet the conditions for hedge accounting are recorded at fair value in the Consolidated Balance Sheets with all changes in fair value included in earnings.

Embedded derivatives are separated from the host contract and accounted for separately if the economic characteristics and risks of the host contract and the embedded derivative are not closely related, a separate instrument with the same terms as the embedded derivative would meet the definition of a derivative, and the combined instrument is not measured at fair value through profit or loss.

Accounts Receivable

Accounts receivable are non-derivative financial assets with fixed or determinable payments that are not quoted in an active market. Accounts receivable are recorded at invoiced amounts less sales allowances and an allowance for doubtful accounts. The allowance for doubtful accounts is our best estimate of the amount of probable credit losses in our existing accounts receivable portfolio. We determine the allowance for doubtful accounts using a two-step approach: First, consideration is given to the financial solvency of specific customers by assessing whether information of objective evidence of impairment is available (e.g. debtor facing serious financial difficulties, insolvency or initiated insolvency proceedings). Secondly, we evaluate homogenous portfolios of the remaining receivables according to their default risk primarily based on the age of the receivable and historical loss experience. Account balances are charged off against the allowance after all collection efforts have been exhausted and the likelihood of recovery is considered remote. As Accounts receivable do not bear interest we discount receivables with a term exceeding one year to their present value using local market interest rates. Interest effects are recognized in profit and loss.

Net gains/losses on Accounts receivable consist of impairment charges and reversals, interest income and expenses and gains and losses from the disposal of such assets. After a comprehensive review of our historical accounts receivable loss experience, in 2006 we revised our estimates of the allowance for doubtful accounts to better reflect the recoverability of the receivables within our portfolio. The effect of this change in estimate on Operating income, Profit after taxes, and earnings per share is disclosed in Note 7.

Included in Accounts receivable are unbilled receivables related to fixed-fee and time-and-material consulting arrangements for contract work performed to date. It is measured at cost plus profit recognized to date less progress billings and recognized losses. If payments received from customers exceed the income recognized, then the difference is presented as advance payments under accounts payable.

Other Assets

All Other assets are recorded at amortized cost which approximates fair value either due to their short-term nature or due to the application of interest.

Inventories, that primarily consist of costs for office supplies and documentation, are immaterial to us and are therefore included in Other assets. We record inventories at the lower of purchase or production cost or market value. Production costs consist of direct salaries, materials, and production overhead.

Assets and Liabilities Held for Sale

Noncurrent assets and disposal groups classified as held for sale are disclosed separately and reported at the lower of the carrying amount or fair value less costs to sell. Depreciation of noncurrent assets allocable to Assets held for sale ceases when the respective divestiture is announced since the assets are immediately available for sale.

Goodwill

Goodwill arises on the acquisition of subsidiaries, associates, and joint ventures.

Acquisitions prior to January 1, 2006: As part of our transition to IFRS we elected to not restate any business combinations. As a result goodwill represents the amount recognized under U.S. GAAP. Under U.S. GAAP the purchase method of accounting has been applied to acquisitions and goodwill has been amortized until 2001. Since 2002 no goodwill has been amortized anymore. Instead, goodwill has been tested for impairment at least annually.

Acquisitions on or after January 1, 2006: For acquisitions on or after January 1, 2006, goodwill represents the excess of the cost of the acquisitions over the net fair value of the identifiable assets, liabilities and contingent liabilities of the acquiree.

Subsequent measurement: We do not amortize goodwill but test it for impairment at least annually and when events occur or changes in circumstances indicate that the recoverable amount of a cash generating unit is less than its carrying value. In respect of at-equity investments, the carrying amount of goodwill is included in the carrying amount of the investment.

Other Intangible Assets

Purchased intangible assets with finite useful lives are recorded at acquisition cost, amortized on a straight-line basis over their estimated useful life of two to 12 years, and reviewed for impairment when significant events occur or changes in circumstances indicate that the carrying amount of the asset or asset group may not be recoverable. All of our intangible assets, with the exception of goodwill, have estimable useful lives and are therefore subject to amortization.

We capitalize the fair value of acquired identifiable inprocess research and development ("in-process R&D"), which represents acquired research and development efforts that have not reached technological feasibility. Amortization for these intangible assets starts when the projects are complete and are taken to the market.

Property, Plant, and Equipment

Property, plant, and equipment are valued at acquisition cost plus the fair value of related asset retirement costs, if any, and if reasonably estimable, less accumulated depreciation. Interest incurred during the construction of qualifying assets is capitalized and amortized over the related assets' estimated useful lives. Interest capitalized has not been material in any period presented.

Property, plant, and equipment is generally depreciated using the straight-line method. Certain assets with expected useful lives in excess of three years are depreciated using the declining balance method. Land is not depreciated.

	Useful lives of property, plant, and equipment
Buildings	25 to 50 years
Leasehold improvements	Based upon the lease contract
Information technology equipment	3 to 5 years
Office furniture	4 to 20 years
Automobiles	5 years

Leasehold improvements are depreciated using the straight-line method over the shorter of the term of the lease or the useful life of the asset. If a renewal option exists, the depreciation period reflects the additional time covered by the option if exercise is reasonably assured when the leasehold improvement is first placed into operation.

We do not hold property with the intention to earn capital income or for capital appreciation purposes and therefore do not classify any property as investment property.

Impairment of Long-Lived Assets

We review long-lived assets, such as property, plant, equipment, and acquired intangible assets for impairment, whenever events or changes in circumstances indicate that the carrying amount of an asset or group of assets may not be recoverable. We assess recoverability of assets to be held and used by comparing their carrying amount to the recoverable amount, which is the higher of value in use and fair value less costs to sell. If an asset or group of assets is considered to be impaired, the impairment to be recognized is measured as the amount by which the carrying amount of the asset or group of assets exceeds it's recoverable amount. In the years presented, the Company did not recognize any impairment charges on long-lived assets.

Prepaid Expenses and Deferred Charges

Prepaid expenses and deferred charges primarily comprise prepayments of operating leases, support services and software royalties which will be charged to expense in future periods as such costs are incurred. Additionally, we are capitalizing the discount of our loans to employees as prepaid expenses and releasing it ratably to employee expenses.

Accounts Payable, Financial and Other Liabilities

Trade payables and other nonderivative financial liabilities are generally measured at amortized cost using the effective interest method. We do not designate our financial liabilities as at fair value through profit or loss on initial recognition.

Derivatives with negative fair values that are not part of an effective hedging relationship as set out in IAS 39 are classified as held for trading financial liabilities and reported at fair value through profit or loss.

Other Obligations

Provisions are recorded when we have a legal or constructive obligation to third parties as a result of a past event, the amount can be reasonably estimated and it is probable that there will be an outflow of future economic benefits. We regularly adjust provisions for loss contingencies as further information develops or circumstances change. Noncurrent provisions are reported at the present value of their expected settlement amounts as at the balance sheet date. Discount rates are regularly adjusted to current market interest rates.

Our software contracts usually contain general warranty provisions guaranteeing that the software will perform according to SAP's stated specifications for six to 12 months. At the time of the sale or license of our software covered by such warranty provisions, we record an accrual for warranty costs based on historical experience.

A provision for restructuring is recognized when we have approved a detailed and formal restructuring plan and the restructuring has commenced or has been announced.

Post-Employment Benefits

We measure our pension-benefit liabilities and other postemployment benefits based on actuarial computations using the projected-unit-credit method in accordance with IAS 19 Employee Benefits. The assumptions used to calculate pension liabilities and costs are shown in Note 19. As a result of the actuarial calculation for each plan we recognize an asset or liability for the overfunded or underfunded status of the respective defined benefit plan. We classify a portion of the liability as current (determined on a plan-by-plan basis) if the amount by which the actuarial present value of benefits included in the benefit obligation payable within the next 12 months exceeds the fair value of plan assets. Changes in the amount of the defined benefit obligation or plan assets resulting from experience different than originally assumed and from changes in assumptions can result in actuarial gains and losses. We recognize all actuarial gains and losses directly in Other components of equity.

Obligations for contributions to defined contribution pension plans are recognized as an expense in profit or loss when they are due.

Deferred Income

Deferred income consists mainly of prepayments made by our customers for support, consulting and training services and deferred software license revenues. Deferred software license revenues will be recognized as software, support service, or service revenue, depending on the reasons for the deferral. Recognition of deferred revenue is possible when basic applicable revenue recognition criteria have been met. The current portion of deferred income is expected to be recognized within the next 12 months.

Treasury Stock

Treasury shares are recorded at acquisition cost and are presented as a deduction from Shareholders' equity. Gains and losses on the subsequent reissuance of treasury shares are credited or charged to Additional paid-in capital on an after-tax basis. On retirement of treasury shares any excess over the calculated par value is charged to Retained earnings.

Presentation in the Consolidated Statements of Cash Flows

We classify interest and taxes paid as well as interest and dividends received as cash flows from operating activities. Dividends paid are classified as financing activities.

New Accounting Standards Early Adopted in the Current Period

In November 2006, the IASB issued IFRS 8 Operating Segments. IFRS 8 replaces IAS 14 Segment Reporting, and aligns segment reporting with the requirements of SFAS 131 Disclosures about Segments of an Enterprise and Related Information, except for some minor differences. IFRS 8 requires an entity to report financial and descriptive information about its reportable segments. Operating segments are components of an entity for which separate financial information is available. This information is evaluated regularly by the entity's chief operating decision maker in order to make decisions about how to allocate resources and assess performance. Generally, financial information is required to be reported on the same basis as is used internally for evaluating operating segment performance and deciding how to allocate resources to operating segments. IFRS 8 will be effective for fiscal years beginning on or after January 1, 2009, with early application encouraged. The European Union adopted IFRS 8 in November 2007. SAP decided to adopt IFRS 8 early. For more information about segment reporting, see Note 28.

New Accounting Standards Not Yet Adopted

In March 2007, the IASB issued an amendment to IAS 23 Borrowing Costs. The amendment mainly relates to the elimination of the option to immediately recognize borrowing costs as an expense that are attributable to the acquisition, construction, or production of a qualifying asset. An entity is, therefore, required to capitalise borrowing costs as part of the cost of such qualifying assets defined as assets that take a substantial period of time to get ready for use or sale. IAS 23 does not require the capitalisation of borrowing costs relating to assets measured at fair value, and inventories that are manufactured or produced in large quantities on a repetitive basis, even if they take a substantial period of time to get ready for use or sale. IAS 23 applies to borrowing costs relating to qualifying assets for which the commencement date for capitalisation is on or after 1 January 2009 with earlier application permitted. The European Union has not yet endorsed the amendment to IAS 23. Due to capitalizing borrowing costs for qualifying assets in the past, the amendment to IAS 23 will have no impact our Consolidated Financial Statements.

In November 2006, the IFRIC issued IFRIC Interpretation 11 IFRS 2 Group and Treasury Share Transactions. The interpretation addresses how to apply IFRS 2 Share-based Payment to accounting for share-based payment arrangements involving an entity's own equity instruments. It also provides guidance on whether share-based payment arrangements in which suppliers of goods or services of an entity are provided with equity instruments of the entity's parent should be accounted for as cash-settled or equity-settled in the entity's financial statements. IFRIC 11 will be effective for fiscal years beginning on or after March 1, 2007 and was endorsed by the European Union in June 2007. We will be required to adopt IFRIC 11 in fiscal year 2008. We do not expect a significant impact from the adoption of IFRIC 11.

In November 2006, the IFRIC issued IFRIC Interpretation 12 Service Concession Rights, which provides guidance to private sector entities on certain recognition and measurement issues that arise in accounting for public-toprivate service concession arrangements. Service concession arrangements are arrangements whereby a government or other body grants contracts for the supply of public services such as roads, energy distribution, and transportation to private operators. IFRIC 12 will be effective for fiscal years beginning on or after January 1, 2008. The European Union has not yet endorsed IFRIC 12. Based on our analysis, we do not expect IFRIC 12 to be applicable to any of our transactions.

In June 2007, the IFRIC issued IFRIC Interpretation 13 Customer Loyalty Programmes, which addresses accounting by entities that grant loyalty award credits (such as 'points' or travel miles) to customers who buy other goods or services. Specifically, it explains how such entities should account for their obligations to provide free or discounted goods or services ('awards') to customers who redeem award credits. IFRIC 13 will be effective for fiscal years beginning on or after July 1, 2008, with early adoption permitted. The European Union has not yet endorsed IFRIC 13. We are currently in the process of determining the impact the adoption of IFRIC 13 will have on our Consolidated Financial Statements.

In July 2007, the IFRIC issued IFRIC Interpretation 14 IAS 19 – The Limit on a Defined Benefit Asset, Minimum Funding Requirements and their Interaction. IFRIC 14 addresses three issues:

- when refunds or reductions in future contributions should be regarded as 'available';
- how a minimum funding requirement might affect the availability of reductions in future contributions; and
- when a minimum funding requirement might give rise to a liability.

IFRIC 14 will be effective for fiscal years beginning on or after January 1, 2008, with early adoption permitted. The European Union has not yet endorsed IFRIC 14. We are currently in the process of determining the impact the adoption of IFRIC 14 will have on our Consolidated Financial Statements.

In September 2007, the IASB issued an amendment to IAS 1 Presentation of Financial Statements. The revision is aimed at improving users' ability to analyze and compare the information given in financial statements. IAS 1 sets overall requirements for the presentation of financial statements, guidelines for their structure and minimum requirements for their content. The revised IAS 1 resulted in consequential amendments to other statements and interpretations. The revision of IAS 1 will be effective for fiscal years beginning on or after January 1, 2009, with early adoption permitted. The European Union has not yet endorsed the amendment to IAS 1. We do not believe that the revision of IAS 1 will significantly change the current presentation in our Consolidated Financial Statements.

In January 2008, the IASB issued IFRS 2 (revised 2008) Vesting Conditions and Cancellations. IFRS 2 amends IFRS 2 Share-based Payment to clarify the terms "vesting condition" and "cancellations." IFRS 2 will be effective for fiscal years beginning on or after January 1, 2009, with early application permitted. The European Union has not yet endorsed the revised IFRS 2. We are currently evaluating the effects of IFRS 2 on our Consolidated Financial Statements.

In January 2008, the IASB issued the revised standards IFRS 3 Business Combinations and IAS 27 Consolidated and Separate Financial Statements. The revisions results in a high degree of convergence between IFRS and U.S. GAAP, although some inconsistencies remain. IFRS 3 and IAS 27 will be effective for fiscal years beginning on or after July 1, 2009, with early adoption permitted. The revised IFRS 3 and IAS 27 have not yet been endorsed by the European Union. We are currently evaluating the effects of IFRS 3 on our Consolidated Financial Statements.

In February 2008, the IASB issued an amendment to IAS 32 Financial Instruments: Disclosure and Presentation – Puttable Instruments and Obligations arising on Liquidation. The purpose for the amendment was to provide detailed guidance on the presentation of puttable financial instruments and obligations arising only on liquidation in the balance sheet. The amendment of IAS 32 will be effective for fiscal years beginning on or after January 1, 2009, with early application permitted. We do not expect any implications from the amendment to IAS 32 on our Consolidated Financial Statements.

Extract 2(B4) – SAP AG, page 95

This extract presents a note on the analysis of functional costs reflected in the income statement. Though not required by IFRS standards, the average number of employees, measured in full-time equivalents, is presented in a table.

(6) Functional Costs and Other Expenses (in part)

The information provided below is classified by the type of expense. The Consolidated Statements of Income include these amounts in various categories based on the applicable line of business.

Services and Materials

Cost of purchased development and consulting services and materials was as follows:

€ millions	2007	2006
Purchased services	862	879
Raw materials and supplies, purchased goods	37	32
	899	911

Sales and Marketing

Sales and marketing expense includes advertising costs, which amounted to € 165 million and € 174 million in 2007, and 2006 respectively.

Personnel Expenses/Number of Employees

Personnel expenses were as follows:

€ millions	2007	2006
Salaries	3,621	3,325
Social security costs	447	426
Pension expense	123	131
	4,191	3,882

Included in personnel expenses for the years ending December 31, 2007 and 2006, are expenses associated with the share-based compensation plans as described in Note 27.

The average number of employees, measured in full-time equivalents and presented according to their function within SAP, was as follows:

€ millions	2007	2006
Software and software-related services	5,764	5,017
Professional services and other services	12,325	11,363
Research and development	12,437	11,333
Sales and marketing	7,938	6,900
General and administration	2,672	2,335
Infrastructure	1,166	1,105
SAP Group	42,302	38,053

Employees who are not currently operational, who work on a part-time basis while finishing a university degree, or who are temporary are excluded from the calculation of full-time equivalents. The number of such excluded employees was not material.

Extract 2(B5) – SAP AG, page 96

This extract presents a note detailing the "Other Operating Income/Expense" line item presented in the income statement.

(7) Other Operating Income/Expense, Net		
Other operating income/expense for the years ending December 31 was as follows:		
€ millions	2007	2006
Bad debt expense	0	0
Restructuring costs	– 2	– 3
Expenses to obtain rental income	0	0
Miscellaneous other operating expenses	0	0
Other operating expense	– 2	– 3
Bad debt income	3	43
Rental income	5	5
Receipt of insurance proceeds	3	2
Miscellaneous other operating income	7	7
Other operating income	18	57
	16	54

Charges to the allowance for doubtful accounts for bad debt expense are based on a systematic, ongoing review, and evaluation of outstanding receivables that is performed every month. Specific customer credit loss risks are also included in the allowance for doubtful accounts, but are charged to the respective cost of software and support or cost of service sold. The amount of these provisions for specific customer risks charged to the respective functional cost category of software and support or cost of service approximated € 9 million and € 3 million during 2007 and 2006, respectively.

In 2006, we revised our estimate to the allowance for doubtful accounts as described in Note 3. The income from the reduction of bad debt allowance of € 43 million is primarily a result of this change in estimate. The change in estimate increased our 2006 Operating profit by € 45 million (1.8%), Profit after taxes by € 28 million (1.5%), and basic and diluted earnings per share by € 0.02 (1.5%).

For more detailed information about costs incurred in connection with exit activities, see Note 19(b).

Extract 2(B6) – SAP AG, page 96 and 97

This extract presents a note detailing "Other Non-Operating Income/Expense, Net" and "Financial Income, Net" line items presented in the income statement.

(8) Other Non-Operating Income/Expense, Net		
Other non-operating income/expense, net for the years ending December 31 was as follows:		
€ millions	2007	2006
Foreign currency losses	– 379	– 255
Other non-operating expenses	– 16	– 19
Total other non-operating expenses	– 395	– 274
Foreign currency gains	385	251
Other non-operating income	12	12
Total other non-operating income	397	263
Total other non-operating income/expenses	2	– 11

(9) Financial Income, Net

Financial income, net for the years ending December 31 was as follows:

€ millions	2007	2006
Interest and similar income	142	124
– thereof from Financial assets	142	124
Interest and similar expenses	– 7	– 4
– thereof from Financial liabilities	– 6	– 3
Income from securities, net	240	154
Expense from other financial assets and loans	– 244	– 157
Unrealized gains/losses on STAR hedge	0	7
Loss from other investments	– 6	– 1
Other financial income, net	– 10	3
Share of loss of associates accounted for using the equity method	– 1	– 1
Financial income, net	**124**	**122**
Thereof:		
Financial income (net) by financial instruments relating to categories in accordance with IAS 39		
– Loans and receivables	2	2
– Available-for-sale financial assets	131	118
– Financial liabilities measured at amortised cost	– 7	– 4

We derive interest income primarily from Cash and cash equivalents, Investments, and Other financial assets.

In the table above, income from securities and expenses for loans and other financial assets both include € 241 million in 2007 (€ 156 million in 2006) resulting from collateral held to secure capital investments made. While holding the collateral, we directly transfer to the debtor any income received on the collateral. Interest income received on the capital investment is included in interest income. We decide on a case by case basis whether to require collateral for the financial investments. We did not obtain assets by taking possession of collateral held for security purposes in 2007 or 2006.

Information on gains and losses recognized directly in Other components of equity or in profit and loss for our financial assets is given in Note 12; for our financial liabilities in Note 18. See Note 25 regarding unrealized gains on STAR hedge.

Extract 2(B7) – SAP AG, page 99

This extract presents a note detailing EPS calculations and related disclosures.

(11) Earnings per Share

Convertible bonds and stock options granted to employees under our share-based compensation programs are included in the diluted earnings per share calculations to the extent they have a dilutive effect. The dilutive impact is calculated using the treasury stock method. The computation of diluted earnings per share does not include certain convertible bonds and stock options issued in connection with the SAP AG 2000 Long Term Incentive Plan ("LTI 2000 Plan") and the SAP Stock Option Plan 2002 ("SAP SOP 2002") because their underlying exercise prices were higher than the average market prices of SAP shares in the periods presented. Such convertible bonds and stock options, if converted or exercised, represented 37.3 million SAP common shares in 2007 and 23.6 million SAP common shares in 2006. The number of outstanding stock options and convertible bonds is presented in Note 27.

€ millions	2007	2006
Profit attributable to equity holders of the parent	1,906	1,835
Weighted average shares – basic (number of shares in million)	1,207	1,226
Dilutive effect of stock options/convertible bonds (number of shares in million)	3	5
Weighted average shares – diluted (number of shares in million)	1,210	1,231
Earnings per share – basic in €	1.58	1.50
Earnings per share – diluted in €	1.58	1.49

Extract 2(B8) – SAP AG, page 100

This extract presents a note on details related to cash and cash equivalents, restricted cash and financial assets.

(12) Cash and Cash Equivalents, Restricted Cash and Financial Assets

Cash and cash equivalents, Restricted cash and Financial assets as at December 31 consisted of the following:

€ millions	Cash and cash equivalents		Restricted Cash		Short-term investments		At equity investments		Other investments	
	2007	2006	2007	2006	2007	2006	2007	2006	2007	2006
Cash	546	478								
Time deposits	376	1,598			35	19				
Money market funds	686	204								
Commercial paper	0	119								
Restricted Cash			550	0						
Fund securities (at fair value)					8	0			0	12
Auction rate securities					0	155				
Variable rate demand notes					0	34				
Other debt securities					449	268			100	448
Debt securities (at fair value)					449	457			100	448
Marketable equity securities (at fair value)					0	4			7	10
Equity securities at cost					6	3			63	55
Equity method securities							19	18		
Total	1,608	2,399	550	0	498	483	19	18	170	525

Restricted Cash

Funds classified as Restricted cash served as collateral for the credit facility entered into in connection with the acquisition of Business Objects S.A. as described in Note 4 and 18. As at December 31, 2007, the lien secured all existing and futures claims with regard to the credit facilitated by Deutsche Bank AG and could have been utilized in case we would have not complied with one of the obligations in the credit agreement. The restriction on cash was abolished in February 2008.

Debt Securities and Marketable Equity Securities

Proceeds from sales of available-for-sale financial assets in 2007 were € 45 million (2006: € 199 million). Gross gains realized from sales of available-for-sale financial assets in 2007 were € 2 million (2006: € 0 million). Gross losses realized from sales of available-for-sale financial assets in 2007 were € 1 million (2006: € 2 million). Due to these sales of available-for-sale financial assets we recognized gains of € 2 million (2006: € 0 million) and losses of € 1 million (2006: € 2 million) which had previously been recognized in Other components of equity.

Extract 2(B9) – SAP AG, pages 102 and 103

This extract presents a note on details related to other financial assets.

Other Financial Assets

Our other financial assets as at December 31 consist of the following:

€ millions	2007			2006		
	Current	Non-current	Total	Current	Non-current	Total
Fair value of STAR Hedges and other derivatives	146	1	147	117	87	204
Investments in insurance policies held for employee-financed pension plans and semi-retirement	0	107	107	0	88	88
Prepaid pension	0	56	56	0	46	46
Loans to employees	9	43	52	8	43	51
Rent deposits	0	24	24	0	26	26
Other interest receivables	15	0	15	11	0	11
Other receivables	12	0	12	11	0	11
Loans to third parties	0	4	4	1	0	1
Miscellaneous other financial assets	0	1	1	0	0	0
Total Other financial assets	182	236	418	148	290	438

Detailed information about our derivative financial instruments is presented in Note 25. Investments in insurance policies relate to the employee-financed pension plans as presented in Note 19 (a). The corresponding liability for investments in insurance policies for semiretirement and time accounts is included in employee-related obligations (see Note 19 (b)).

Loans granted to employees primarily consist of interest-free or below-market-rate building loans and amount to a nominal value of € 63 million in 2007 and € 62 million in 2006. The cumulative effect of discounting the employee loans based on the market interest rates in effect when the loans were granted was € 11 million in 2007 and € 11 million in 2006. Amortization of employee loan discounts amounted to € 3 million in 2007 and € 3 million in 2006, respectively. There have been no loans to employees or members of the Executive Board and Supervisory Board to assist them in exercising stock options or convertible bonds.

Loans to third parties are presented net of allowances for credit losses. Changes in the allowance for credit losses were as follows:

€ millions	2007	2006
Balance 1/1	1	16
Utilization	0	10
Addition	0	0
Release	1	5
Balance 12/31	0	1

We consider these Other financial assets to be individually impaired as soon as we receive information concerning debtor's financial difficulties. As at December 31, 2007, there were no Other financial assets past due but not impaired. For general information on financial risk and the nature of risk, see Note 26.

Extract 2(B10) – SAP AG, page 105

This extract presents a note on details related to other assets.

(14) Other Assets

€ millions	2007			2006		
	Current	Non-current	Total	Current	Non-current	Total
Other receivables	36	49	85	31	40	71
Other tax receivables	22	0	22	16	0	16
Advance payments	11	0	11	7	0	7
Inventories	5	0	5	4	0	4
Miscellaneous other assets	1	0	1	1	0	1
Total Other assets	75	49	124	59	40	99

Included in miscellaneous other assets are primarily salary advances and insurance claims for which the individually recognized amounts are not material.

(15) Assets and Liabilities Held for Sale

In November of 2007, the directors committed to a plan to sell the business of Tomorrow-Now, Inc., a wholly owned subsidiary of SAP America, Inc. (a wholly owned subsidiary of SAP AG) and to cease engaging in the business model of providing support services relating to third party software. Negotiations with several interested parties have subsequently taken place. The assets and liabilities of TomorrowNow, including assets and liabilities of Tomorrow - Now entities in Europe, Australia and Asia. which are expected to be sold within twelve months, have been classified as a disposal group held for sale and are presented separately in the accompanying Consolidated Balance Sheet as at December 31, 2007.

TomorrowNow is a distinct asset group that has its separable cash flows and operations, which can be separated from the rest of SAP. The operations from this disposal group are included in the Product segment. The major classes of assets and liabilities of this disposal group classified as held for sale are as follows:

€ millions	2007
Accounts receivable, net	2
Other assets	3
Current assets	5
Goodwill	7
Property, plant, and equipment, net	1
Other assets	1
Deferred tax assets	1
Noncurrent assets	10
Assets held for sale	15
Accounts payable	1
Other liabilities	3
Deferred income	5
Current liabilities	9
Liabilities held for sale	9

Extract 2(B11) – SAP AG, page 109

This extract presents a note on details on accounts payable, financial liabilities and other liabilities.

(18) Accounts Payable, Financial Liabilities and Other Liabilities

Accounts payable, Financial liabilities and Other liabilities classified based on due dates as at December 31 were as follows:

€ millions	Term				Term			
	less than 1 year	between 1 and 5 years	more than 5 years	Balance 12/31/2007	less than 1 year	between 1 and 5 years	more than 5 years	Balance 12/31/2006
Payable to suppliers	688	6	0	694	581	0	0	581
Advance payments received	27	4	0	31	29	34	0	63
Accounts payable	715	10	0	725	610	34	0	644
Bank loans and overdraft	25	2	0	27	24	0	2	26
Other financial liabilities	57	4	0	61	39	1	0	40
Financial liabilities	82	6	0	88	63	1	2	66
Other employee-related liabilities	1,060	6	49	1,115	948	0	51	999
Other taxes	262	0	0	262	220	0	0	220
Miscellaneous other liabilities	56	11	7	74	74	12	7	93
Other liabilities	1,378	17	56	1,451	1,242	12	58	1,312
	2,175	33	56	2,264	1,915	47	60	2,022

Liabilities are unsecured, except for the retention of title and similar rights customary in industry. Effective interest rates of bank loans were 8.03% in 2007 and 8.08% in 2006.

As at November 5, 2004, SAP AG entered into a €1 billion syndicated revolving credit facility agreement with an initial term of five years. The use of the facility is not restricted by any financial covenants. Borrowings under the facility bear interest of EURIBOR or LIBOR for the respective currency plus a margin ranging from 0.20% to 0.25% depending on the amount drawn. We are also required to pay a commitment fee of 0.07% per annum on the unused available credit. As at December 31, 2007 and 2006, there were no borrowings outstanding under the facility.

As at October 1, 2007, SAP AG entered into a € 5 billion credit facility agreement (subsequently reduced to € 4.45 billion as at December 31, 2007) with Deutsche Bank AG with a maturity until December 31, 2009. The credit facility was entered into in connection with the acquisition of Business Objects S.A. Initially the credit facility served as a bank guarantee to back up the tender offer. The use of the facility is not restricted by any financial covenants. Borrowings under the facility bear interest of EURIBOR plus a margin ranging from 0.25% to 0.30% depending on the amount drawn. We are also required to pay a commitment fee of 0.075% per annum on the unused available credit. As at December 31, 2007, there were no borrowings outstanding under the facility.

Within the acquisition process and with the finalization of the squeeze-out, the facility has been voluntarily cancelled to an amount of EUR 2.95 billion which corresponds to the drawdown on the facility as at February 18, 2008.

Additionally, as at December 31, 2007 and 2006, SAP AG had available lines of credit totaling € 599 million and € 599 million, respectively. As at December 31, 2007 and 2006, there were no borrowings outstanding under these lines of credit.

As at December 31, 2007 and 2006, certain subsidiaries had lines of credit available that allowed them to borrow in local currencies at prevailing interest rates up to € 44 million and € 109 million, respectively. Total aggregate borrowings under these lines of credit, which are guaranteed by SAP AG, amounted to € 27 million and € 26 million as at December 31, 2007 and 2006, respectively.

Extract 2(B12) – SAP AG, page 115

This extract presents details on the different captions of shareholders' equity, including amounts that would reflect balances of accumulated other comprehensive income under current IAS 1.

(20) Shareholders' Equity

Common Stock

As at December 31, 2007, the capital stock of SAP AG consisted of 1,246,258,408 (2006: 1,267,537,248) shares of no-par common stock (including treasury stock), with a calculated nominal value of € 1 per share.

The number of common shares was decreased by 23,000,000 shares (corresponding to € 23,000,000) in 2007 due to cancellation of shares in treasury stock, partially offset by an increase of 1,721,160 (corresponding to € 1,721,160) as a result of the exercise of awards granted under certain share-based payment plans. In 2006, the number of common shares increased by 950,652,936 (corresponding to € 950,652,936) with the issuance of bonus shares at a 1-to-3 ratio under a capital increase from corporate funds and by 426,491 shares (corresponding to € 426,491) as a result of the exercise of awards granted under certain share-based payment plans.

Shareholdings in SAP AG as at December 31, 2007, were as follows:

	2007		2006	
	Number of shares	Percent of common stock	Number of shares	Percent of common stock
	(000)	%	(000)	%
Hasso Plattner GmbH & Co. Beteiligungs-KG	113,7199.1	113,719	113,719	9.0
Dietmar Hopp Stiftung GmbH	109,869	8.8	109,869	8.7
Klaus Tschira Stiftung gGmbH	78,474	6.3	67,472	5.3
Dr. h.c. Tschira Beteiligungs GmbH & Co. KG	32,831	2.6	63,331	5.0
Hasso Plattner Förderstiftung gGmbH	15,245	1.2	16,062	1.2
DH-Besitzgesellschaft mbH & Co. KG1)	6,404	0.5	10,200	0.8
Dr. h.c. Tschira and wife	3,178	0.3	2,000	0.2
Treasury stock	48,065	3.9	49,251	3.9
Free float	838,473	67.3	835,633	65.9
	1,246,258	100.0	1,267,537	100.0

1) DH-Besitzgesellschaft mbH & Co. KG is wholly owned by Dietmar Hopp.

Authorized Capital

The Articles of Incorporation authorize the Executive Board of SAP AG (the "Executive Board") to increase the Common stock:

- Up to a total amount of € 60 million through the issuance of new common shares in return for contributions in cash until May 11, 2010 ("Authorized Capital I"). The issuance is subject to the statutory subscription rights of existing shareholders.
- Up to a total amount of € 180 million through the issuance of new common shares in return for contributions in cash until May 8, 2011 ("Authorized Capital Ia"). The issuance is subject to the statutory subscription rights of existing shareholders.
- Up to a total amount of € 60 million through the issuance of new common shares in return for contributions in cash or in kind until May 11, 2010 ("Authorized Capital II"). Subject to certain preconditions and the consent of the Supervisory Board, the Executive Board is authorized to exclude the shareholders' statutory subscription rights.
- Up to a total amount of € 180 million through the issuance of new common shares in return for contributions in cash or in kind until May 8, 2011 ("Authorized Capital IIa"). Subject to certain preconditions and the consent of the Supervisory Board, the Executive Board is authorized to exclude the shareholders' statutory subscription rights.

No authorization to increase Common stock was exercised in fiscal year 2007.

Contingent Capital

SAP AG's capital stock is subject to a contingent increase of common shares. The contingent increase may be effected only to the extent that the holders of the convertible bonds and stock options that were issued by SAP AG under certain share-based payment plans (see Note 27) exercise their conversion or subscription rights. The following table provides a summary of the changes in contingent capital for 2007 and 2006:

€ millions	Contingent capital
1/1/2006	53
Exercised	– 1
New authorized	100
Increase in consequence of capital increase	83
Reduction/cancellation	25
12/31/2006	**210**
Exercised	– 1
New authorized	0
Reduction/cancellation	0
12/31/2007	**209**

The increase in contingent capital by € 83 million in 2006 reflects the issuance of bonus shares at a 1-to-3 ratio under the capital increase described above which resulted in an increase of the contingent capital in the same proportion by operation of law.

Additional paid-in capital

Additional paid-in capital represents all capital contributed to SAP with the proceeds resulting from sale of common stock in excess of their calculated par value. Additional paid-in capital arises mainly from issuance of common stock, treasury stock transactions and share-based compensation transactions.

Retained Earnings

Retained earnings contain prior years' undistributed Profit after taxes and adjustments resulting from the first time adoption of IFRS.

Treasury Stock

By resolution of SAP AG's Annual General Meeting of Shareholders held on May 10, 2007, the Executive Board of SAP AG was authorized to acquire, on or before October 31, 2008, up to 120 million shares in the Company on the condition that such share purchases, together with any previously acquired shares, do not account for more than 10% of SAP AG's common stock. Although Treasury stock is legally considered outstanding, there are no dividend or voting rights associated with shares held in treasury. We may redeem or resell shares held in treasury or may use Treasury stock for the purpose of servicing subscription rights and conversion rights under the Company's share-based payment plans. Also, we may use the shares held in treasury as consideration in connection with the acquisition of other companies.

As at December 31, 2007, we had acquired 48 million (2006: 49 million) of our own shares, representing € 48 million (2006: € 49 million) or 3.9% (2006: 3.9%) of capital stock. In 2007, 27 million (2006: 28 million) shares in aggregate were acquired under the buyback program at an average price of approximately € 36.85 (2006: € 40.97) per share, representing € 27 million (2006: € 28 million) or 2.2% (2006: 2.2%) of Capital stock. We transferred 5 million shares to employees during the year (2006: 1 million shares) at an average price of € 28.13 (2006: € 29.83) per share. The remaining reduction in treasury stock was due to the cancellation of 23 million (corresponding to € 23 million) shares in treasury stock in 2007.

The Company purchased no SAP American Depositary Receipts ("ADRs") in 2007. (Each ADR represents one common share of SAP AG). The Company held no ADRs as at December 31, 2007, and 2006, respectively.

page 117

Other Components of Equity

Other components of equity consisted of the following as at December 31:

€ millions	Currency translation adjustments	Unrealized gains/ losses on marketable securities	Unrecog- nized pension costs	Gains/ losses on foreign currency cash flow hedges	Gains/ losses on STAR hedge	Currency effects from inter- company long-term investments	Total Other components of equity
January 1, 2006	0	11	0	– 9	24	41	67
Current-period change, net of tax	– 150	– 7	13	20	– 29	– 26	– 179
December 31, 2006	**– 150**	**4**	**13**	**11**	**– 5**	**15**	**– 112**
Current-period change, net of tax	– 191	– 3	0	10	– 6	– 5	– 195
December 31, 2007	**– 341**	**1**	**13**	**21**	**– 11**	**10**	**– 307**

- Currency translation adjustments comprise all foreign currency differences arising from the translation of the financial statements of foreign operations.
- Unrealized gains and losses on marketable securities represent the net cumulative change between fair value and cost of available-for-sale financial assets since the respective acquisition date.
- Unrecognized pension costs comprise actuarial gains and losses relating to defined benefit pension plans and similar obligations.
- Gains and losses on foreign currency cash flow hedges comprise the net change in fair value of foreign currency cash flow hedges related to hedged transactions that have not yet occurred.
- Gains and losses on STAR hedges comprise the net change in fair value of cash flow hedging instruments associated with the unrecognized potion of nonvested STARs (see Note 25).
- Currency effects from intercompany long-term investments relate to intercompany foreign currency transactions that are of long-term investments nature.

Miscellaneous

Under the German Stock Corporation Act (Aktiengesetz), the total amount of dividends available for distribution to shareholders is based on the earnings of SAP AG as reported in its statutory financial statements which are determined under the accounting rules stipulated by the German Commercial Code (Handelsgesetzbuch). For the year ending December 31, 2007, the Executive Board and the Supervisory Board of SAP AG propose a dividend in 2008 of € 0.50 per share.

Dividend per share for 2006 and 2005 were € 0.46 and € 0.36, respectively and were paid in the succeeding year.

page 118

D. Additional Information

(21) Supplemental Cash Flow Information

Interest paid in 2007 and 2006 amounted to € 6 million and € 4 million, respectively, and interest received in 2007 and 2006 amounted to € 142 million and € 124 million, respectively. Income taxes paid in 2007 and 2006, net of refunds, were € 811 million and € 866 million, respectively.

All of the items above are classified as cash flows from operating activities.

Our investing cash flows include high volumes from the purchase and sale of investments. The activities disclosed in these line items include the purchase and sale of marketable and other available-for-sale securities.

Extract 2(B13) – SAP AG, pages 134 to 137

This extract presents segment information disclosures as required by IFRS 8. The following is noteworthy:

- the executive board is the chief operating decision maker (CODM);

- a matrix structure is used as the CODM evaluates business activities in a number of different ways;

- company has determined that its lines of business (product, consulting and training) constitute operating segments;

- accounting policies applied for segment reporting purposes are based on US GAAP (which may differ from IFRS);

- inter-segment transfers are recorded as cost reductions and are not tracked as internal revenues;

- the segment result excludes development expense and management share-based compensation expense, but a one-time effect of a change in the estimate on allowance for doubtful accounts in 2006 was allocated to segments;

- the CODM does not receive segment asset information;

- external revenue by location of customers and by location of companies is provided, reflecting the location of the company's subsidiary responsible for the sale, as is information about certain long-lived assets detailed by geographic region.

Note that, due to the company's large number of customers, there is no single customer whose business accounted for a material portion of the total revenue.

---

(28) Segment and Geographic Information

Our internal reporting system produces reports in which business activities are presented in a variety of ways, for example, by line of business or by geography. Based on these reports, the Executive Board, which is responsible for assessing the performance of various company components and making resource allocation decisions as a chief operating decision maker (CODM), evaluates business activities in a number of different ways. While neither the line of business structure nor the geographic structure is identified as primary, we have determined that our lines of business constitute operating segments. We have three reportable operating segments which are organized based on products and services: Product, Consulting, and Training.

The Product segment is primarily engaged in marketing and licensing our software products, performing software development services for customers, and providing support services for our software products. The Consulting segment performs various professional services, mainly implementation of our software products. The Training segment provides educational services on the use of our software products and related topics for customers and partners.

The accounting policies applied for segment reporting purposes are based on U.S. GAAP and may differ from those described in Note 3 which are based on IFRS. Significant differences in the accounting policies are discussed in Note 1. In addition, differences in foreign currency translations result in minor deviations between the amounts reported internally for management purposes and the amounts reported in the Consolidated Financial Statements.

Our management reporting system reports our intersegment transfers as cost reduction and does not track them as internal revenues. Inter-segment transfers mainly represent utilization of manpower resources of one segment by another segment on a project-by-project basis. Inter-segment transfers are charged based on internal cost rates including certain indirect overhead costs but without profit margin.

IFRS 8 Operating Segments, applies to annual financial statements for periods beginning on or after January 1, 2009. We adopted IFRS 8 early for our fiscal year 2007, as permitted by that standard.

Segment revenue and results as well as other relevant segment information are presented below:

€ millions	Product	Consulting	Training	Total
2007				
External revenue from reportable segments	7,369	2,369	493	10,231
Other				25
Total consolidated revenues				10,256
Segment result	4,300	631	209	5,140
Unallocated corporate revenue and expenses				– 2,442
Operating profit				2,698
Other non-operating income/expense, net				2
Financial income, net				124
Profit before income taxes				2,824
Other information				
Depreciation and amortization	– 98	– 33	– 4	
2006				
External revenue from reportable segments	6,643	2,300	440	9,383
Other				19
Total consolidated revenues				9,402
Segment result	4,034	596	167	4,797
Unallocated corporate revenue and expenses				– 2,294
Operating profit				2,503
Other non-operating income/expense, net				– 11
Financial income, net				122
Profit before income taxes				2,614
Other information				
Depreciation and amortization	– 86	– 24	– 7	

Revenues

Since our segments are organized on the basis of products and services, the amounts of external revenue for the Product, Consulting, and Training segments are materially consistent with the amounts of Software and software related service revenue, Consulting revenue, and Training revenue, respectively, as reported in the Consolidated Statements of Income. The differences in revenue amounts between the three reportable segments and the corresponding captions in the Consolidated Statements of Income are due to the fact that for internal reporting purposes, revenue is generally allocated to the segment that is responsible for the related transaction regardless of revenue classification. Thus, for example, the Training segment's revenue includes certain amounts classified as software revenue.

External revenue – Other (2007: € 25 million, 2006: € 19 million) mainly represents revenue incidental to our main business activities which is generated from services provided outside the reportable segments, and minor currency translation differences.

Segment Result

Segment result reflects operating expenses directly attributable or reasonably allocable to the segments, including costs of product, costs of services, and sales and marketing expenses. Costs that are not directly attributable or reasonably allocable to the segments such as administration and other corporate expenses are not included in the segment result. Development expense is excluded from the segment result because our internal management reporting measures the segment performance without taking development expense into account. In addition, for management purposes, share-based compensation expense is not included in the segment result.

Depreciation and amortization expenses reflected in the segment result include the amounts directly attributable to each segment and the depreciation and amortization portion of the facility and IT-related expenses allocated to each segment based on headcount, facility space, and other measures.

A one-time effect of a change in estimate on allowance for doubtful accounts in 2006 was allocated to the Product segment, the Consulting segment, and the Training segment in the amounts of € 30 million, € 13 million, and € 2 million, respectively.

The following table presents a detail of unallocated corporate revenue and expenses:

€ millions	2007	2006
Unallocated corporate revenue and expenses		
External revenue from services provided outside of the reportable segments	– 11	– 10
Development expense – Management view	1,769	1,642
Administration and other corporate expenses – Management view	555	488
Share-based compensation expenses	95	99
IFRS reconciliation differences	34	75
	2,442	2,294

Development expense and administration expense above are based on a management view and do not equal the amounts under the corresponding caption in the Consolidated Statements of Income. The differences are mainly due to the fact that the management view focuses on organizational structures and cost centers rather than cost classification to functional areas.

Segment Assets

Segment asset information is not provided to the CODM. Goodwill by reportable segment is disclosed in Note 16.

Geographic Information

The following tables present external revenue by location of customers and by location of companies, which reflects the location of our subsidiary responsible for the sale, and information about certain long-lived assets detailed by geographic region.

€ millions	Revenue by location of customers		Revenue by location of SAP entities	
	2007	2006	2007	2006
Germany	2,005	1,908	2,146	2,030
Rest of EMEA[1]	3,387	2,994	3,328	2,960
Total EMEA	5,392	4,902	5,474	4,990
United States	2,717	2,617	2,702	2,597
Rest of Americas	872	776	865	753
Total Americas	3,589	3,393	3,567	3,350
Japan	447	431	443	429
Rest of Asia Pacific Japan	828	676	772	633
Total Asia Pacific Japan	1,275	1,107	1,215	1,062
	10,256	9,402	10,256	9,402

1) Europe, Middle East, Africa,

€ millions	Software and software-related service revenue by location of customers		Software and software-related service revenue by location of SAP entities	
	2007	2006	2007	2006
Germany	1,433	1,342	1,526	1,421
Rest of EMEA[1]	2,542	2,170	2,524	2,170
Total EMEA	3,975	3,512	4,050	3,591
United States	1,849	1,734	1,837	1,718
Rest of Americas	658	556	650	534
Total Americas	2,507	2,290	2,487	2,252
Japan	340	308	336	306
Rest of Asia Pacific Japan	619	495	568	456
Total Asia Pacific Japan	959	803	904	762
	7,441	6,605	7,441	6,605

1) Europe, Middle East, Africa,

€ millions	Property, plant, and equipment, net		Intangible assets, net	
	2007	**2006**	**2007**	**2006**
Germany	923	858	217	150
Rest of EMEA[1)	135	133	36	1
Total EMEA	1,058	991	253	151
United States	167	152	138	95
Rest of Americas	13	10	14	18
Total Americas	180	162	152	113
Japan	4	4	0	0
Rest of Asia Pacific Japan	74	49	0	0
Total Asia Pacific Japan	78	53	0	0
	1,316	**1,206**	**405**	**264**

1) Europe, Middle East, Africa,
Due to the large number of the customers we serve, there is no single customer whose business with us accounted for a material portion of our total revenue.

FUTURE DEVELOPMENTS

The IASB has on its agenda several projects related to the IFRS standards covered in this chapter. Below is an overview of these projects.

Annual Improvement

An Exposure Draft *Improvements to IFRSs* issued in August 2008 contains proposals that, if approved, would be effective for annual periods beginning on or after January 1, 2010, although entities would be permitted to adopt them earlier. The following two standards are affected by this Exposure Draft:

- *IFRS 8*: The basis of conclusion has been modified to clarify that only the assets and liabilities included in the chief operating decision maker's (CODM) measurement of the segment's assets and liabilities are reported for that segment. The measure for total segment assets would be nil when the CODM does not receive such information. Consequently, an entity with few physical assets would not have to present a measure of segment assets separately if the CODM does not review that information.

- IAS 7: Guidance is introduced for the classification of cash-flow expenditures incurred with the objective of generating future cash flows when those expenditures are not recognized as assets in accordance with IFRS. Currently, some entities classify such expenditures as operating activities outflows, while others classify them as outflows related to investing activities. The proposed amendment to IAS 7 would clarify that only an expenditure resulting in a recognized asset can be classified as a cash flow from investing activities.

Earnings Per Share (EPS)

In August 2008, the IASB published the Exposure Draft *Simplifying Earnings per Share*, proposing amendments to IAS 33. Subsequently, in October 2008, the AcSB issued an Exposure Draft proposing to replace CICA 3500 with IAS 33 as amended by the IASB Exposure Draft. No effective date of the proposed amendments was set, but the IASB project plan anticipates a revised standard in the second half of 2009 (the proposed new Canadian standard will be effective at the same time).

The following table presents the principal differences between the proposals in IAS 33, as modified by the IASB Exposure Draft, and current CICA 3500:

Financial Instrument/Issue	Amended IAS 33 Proposal	Observations Related to Potential Changes to CICA 3500 (Note)
Principle concerning instruments to be included in the calculation of basic EPS	Weighted average number of ordinary shares includes only those instruments that give (or are deemed to give) their holder the right to share currently in the profit or loss of the period.	Ordinary shares issuable for little or no cash or other consideration or mandatorily convertible instruments will no longer affect basic EPS.
Contracts that involve an entity receiving its own ordinary shares for cash or other financial assets (including gross, physically settled written put options and forward purchase contracts)	Treat contracts as if the entity had already repurchased the shares (mandatorily redeemable ordinary shares would be treated in the same manner).	Clarification that the shares related to the specified contracts are excluded from the denominator of the EPS calculation.
Participating instruments and two-class ordinary shares	Calculation of diluted EPS amended (test is introduced to determine whether a convertible financial instrument would have a more dilutive effect if conversion is assumed).	Amendment to the calculation of diluted EPS.
Instrument measured at fair value through profit or loss (changes in its fair value reflect the economic effect of the instrument on current equity holders for the period, i.e., the changes in fair value reflect the benefits received)	Entity does not adjust the numerator or denominator of the diluted EPS calculation.	Could change calculation as for an instrument (or the derivative component of a compound financial instrument) that is measured at fair value through profit or loss, no adjustment should be made to the numerator or denominator of the diluted EPS calculation.
Warrants and their equivalents that are not measured at fair value through profit or loss	Entity assumes the exercise of those instruments, if dilutive. To simplify the calculation of diluted EPS, ordinary shares are regarded as issued at the end-of-period market price, rather than at their average market price during the period. For year-to-date diluted earnings per share, the number of incremental shares to be included in the denominator would be calculated independently for each period presented, rather than as a year-to-date weighted average of the number of incremental shares included in each interim diluted earnings per share computation.	The ordinary shares should be regarded as issued at the end-of-period market price, rather than at their average market price during the period.

Financial Instrument/Issue	Amended IAS 33 Proposal	Observations Related to Potential Changes to CICA 3500 (Note)
Forward contracts to sell an entity's own shares	Entity calculates diluted EPS by assuming that ordinary shares relating to forward contracts are sold and the effect is dilutive, unless forward contracts are measured at fair value through profit or loss.	For the calculation of diluted EPS an entity assumes that ordinary shares relating to such a contract are sold and the effect is dilutive, unless they are measured at fair value through profit or loss.
Contracts to repurchase an entity's own shares and contracts that may be settled in ordinary shares or cash (i.e., would either be measured at fair value through profit or loss or the liability for the present value of the redemption amount).	Meet the definition of a participating instrument and hence no adjustments would be required in calculating diluted EPS or the application guidance on participating instruments and two-class ordinary shares would apply.	Deletes the calculation requirements for contracts to repurchase an entity's own shares and for contracts that may be settled in ordinary shares or cash.

Note: The IASB Exposure Draft contains no references to extraordinary items; unlike Canadian GAAP, IFRS do not permit the presentation and disclosure of such items. Therefore, the AcSB intends to require an additional disclosure to what is required by the ED — when an entity reports an extraordinary item, it should also disclose the basic and diluted amounts per share for that extraordinary item.

Financial Statement Presentation

The IASB and the FASB have a joint project on financial statement presentation that aims to improve the ability of investors and creditors to:

- understand an entity's present and past financial position;
- understand the past operating, financing and other activities that caused an entity's financial position to change and the components of those changes; and
- use that financial statement information (along with information from other sources) to assess the amounts, timing and uncertainty of an entity's future cash flows.

The standard will address the presentation of financial statement information, including the classification and display of line items and the aggregation of line items into subtotals and totals.

The project will be realized in three phases:

- Phase A: Complete set of financial statements
- Phase B: Fundamental presentation issues
- Phase C: Interim reporting

The IASB completed Phase A in September 2007 by issuing a revised IAS 1 that is effective for annual periods beginning on or after January 1, 2009, with earlier application permitted. We covered revised IAS 1 requirements in this chapter.

Phase B addresses the more fundamental issues for presentation of information on the faces of financial statements (primary financial statements). Phase B topics include:

- developing principles for aggregating and disaggregating information in each financial statement;
- defining the totals and subtotals to be reported in each financial statement (this might include categories such as business and financing); and
- reconsidering IAS 7, including whether to require the use of the direct or indirect method.

A Discussion Paper "Preliminary Views on Financial Statement Presentation" was issued in October 2008 providing preliminary views on a proposed model for presenting information in the financial statements based on three objectives: portray a cohesive financial picture of an entity's activities; disaggregate information so that it is useful in predicting an entity's future cash flows; help users assess an entity's liquidity and financial flexibility.

The proposed presentation model requires an entity to present:

- information about its business activities separately from its financing activities;
- information about its business activities segregated between operating activities and investing activities;
- information about the financing activities segregated according to the various source of financing, that is non-owner sources (and related changes) and owner sources (and related changes);
- discontinued operations separately from continuing business and financing activities. Information on income taxes is segregated from all other information in the statements of financial position and cash flows. The statement of comprehensive income should show the income tax expense (benefit) related to: (i) income from continuing operations (the total of its income or loss from business and financing activities) (ii) discontinued operations (iii) other comprehensive income items.

Each of the statement of financial position, statement of comprehensive income and statement of cash flows would present the following categories with related balances, or income and expense, or cash flows as appropriate:

- business:
  - o operating assets and liabilities (or related income and expenses, or related cash flows),
  - o investing assets and liabilities (or related income and expenses, or related cash flows),
- financing:
  - o financing assets (or related income, or related cash flows),
  - o financing liabilities (or related expenses, or related cash flows),
- income taxes;
- discontinued operations;
- equity.

Other comprehensive income would also be a category in the Statement of Comprehensive Income.

The classification of assets and liabilities into the sections and categories would be made for the statement of financial position first and determine the classification in the statements of comprehensive income and cash flows. In addition to classifying its income and expense items into the operating, investing and financing categories, an entity would disaggregate those items on the basis of their function within those categories and further disaggregate income and expense items by their nature within those functions to the extent that this disaggregation will help users in predicting the entity's future cash flows.

Presenting the statement of cash flows using the direct method is viewed as being more consistent with the proposed presentation model. This model also includes a reconciliation of cash flows to comprehensive income which disaggregates income into its cash, accrual other than remeasurements, and remeasurement components (for example, fair value changes). This information would be provided in the notes to financial statements to help users predict future cash flows and assess earnings quality.

In Phase C, the IASB will reconsider the requirements in IAS 34, including:

- financial statements required in an interim financial report;
- whether entities should be allowed to present the financial statements in an interim financial report in a condensed format; if so, whether the IASB should provide guidance on how to condense the information;
- what comparative periods, if any, should be required or allowed in interim financial reports, and when, if ever, should 12 month-to-date financial statements be required or allowed in interim financial reports; and
- whether guidance for non-public companies should differ from guidance for public companies.

Conceptual Framework

The conceptual framework is a joint project of the IASB and FASB. Its overall objective is to create a sound foundation for future accounting standards that are principles-based, internally consistent and internationally converged. Although the IASB has not reached a conclusion on the authoritative status of the common conceptual framework, it intends that the framework will not have the same status as IFRS standards and, therefore, will not override them.

The project has the following eight phases:

A. Objective and Qualitative Characteristics
B. Definitions of Elements, Recognition and Derecognition
C. Measurement
D. Reporting Entity Concept
E. Presentation and Disclosure
F. Framework Purpose and Status
G. Applicability to the Not-for-profit Sector
H. Remaining Issues

For each phase of the project, the IASB will issue an initial consultative document in the form of a Discussion Paper (DP) followed by an Exposure Draft (ED). The following paragraphs provide the status, purpose and a brief summary of four phases (A to D) that are currently active:

Phase A: Objective and Qualitative Characteristics

Status

ED issued in May 2008: *Conceptual Framework for Financial Reporting: The Objective of Financial Reporting and Qualitative Characteristics and Constraints of Decision - Useful Financial Reporting Information.*

Purpose

Establish:

- objective of financial reporting;
- qualitative characteristics of financial reporting information;
- trade-offs among qualitative characteristics and how they relate to the concepts of materiality and cost-benefit relationships.

Preliminary IASB Tentative Views

- Objective of general purpose financial reporting is to provide financial information about the reporting entity that is useful to present and potential capital providers such as equity investors, lenders, and other creditors in making decisions about whether and how to:

  o allocate their resources to a particular entity, and

  o protect or enhance their investments (which is sometimes viewed as relating to management's stewardship or accountability of the entity).

- Qualitative characteristics of financial reporting information consist of:

  o two fundamental qualitative characteristics – relevance and faithful representation,

  o four enhancing qualitative characteristics (which enhance the fundamental qualitative characteristics by distinguishing more useful information from less useful information): comparability, verifiability, timeliness and understandability, and

  o two pervasive constraints that limit the information provided by financial reporting: materiality and cost.

Note that the IASB proposes to considering faithful representation as encompassing all of aspects of reliability described in the current IASB Framework. Faithful representation is the depiction in financial reports of the economic phenomena they purport to represent, which would require that accounting representations be complete, neutral and free from error.

See also discussion below on Canadian developments

Phase B: Elements, Recognition and Derecognition

Status

- IASB Working on definitions.
- No DP issued at this time.

Purpose

- Revise and clarify the definitions of *asset* and *liability*.
- Resolve differences regarding other elements and their definitions.
- Revise the recognition criteria concepts to eliminate differences and provide a basis for resolving issues such as derecognition and unit of account.

Preliminary IASB Tentative Views

Working definitions of assets and liabilities are being developed:

- An asset of an entity is a present economic resource to which the entity has a right or other access that others do not have.

- A liability of an entity is a present economic obligation for which the entity is the obligor.

Note that existing asset and liability definitions in the IASB Framework (which are very similar to those in CICA 1000) are as follows:

An *asset* is a resource controlled by an entity as a result of past events and from which future economic benefits are expected to flow to the entity.

A *liability* is a present obligation of the entity arising from past events, the settlement of which is expected to result in an outflow from the entity of resources embodying economic benefits

Phase C: Measurement

Status

Discussions held, no DP issued at this time.

Purpose

Select a set of measurement bases that satisfy the objectives and qualitative characteristics of financial reporting.

Preliminary IASB Tentative Views (To Date)

Measurement phase will be conducted in three milestones:

- Milestone I: inventory and definition of possible measurement bases;

- Milestone II: evaluation of measurement basis candidates;

- Milestone III: conceptual conclusions and practical issues.

The IASB discussed issues related to the following primary measurement basis candidates:

- past entry price;

- past exit price;

- modified past amount;

- current entry price;

- current exit price;

- current equilibrium price;

- value in use;

- future entry price;

- future exit price.

The IASB is discussing an approach that would include considering five factors in selecting from among alternative measurement bases:

- *Value/flow weighting and separation*: the relative importance to users of information about the current value of the asset or liability versus information about the cash flows generated by the item, as well as the ease and precision with which the flows can be separated from the value changes (an indication of relevance).

- *Confidence level*: the level of confidence that can be placed on alternative measurements as representations of the asset or liability being measured (an indication of faithful representation).

- *The measurement of similar items*: items of a similar nature should be measured in similar ways (an indication of comparability).

- *The measurement of items that generate cash flows together*: items that generate cash flows as a unit should be measured the same way (an indication of understandability).

- *Cost-benefit*: An assessment of the ratio of the benefits that would be derived from alternative measurements to the costs of preparing those measurements (an indication of the primary limiting factor in financial reporting).

Phase D: Reporting Entity

Status

DP issued in May 2008: *Preliminary views, Conceptual framework for financial reporting: The reporting entity*.

Purpose

Determine what a reporting entity is, whether a definition is necessary, and other relevant issues, such as how to determine the composition of a group reporting entity.

Preliminary IASB Tentative Views (To Date)

- A reporting entity should be broadly describe (rather than precisely define) as a circumscribed area of business activity of interest to present and potential equity investors, lenders and other capital providers. It includes, but is not limited to, business activities that are structured as legal entities. Examples include a sole proprietorship, corporation, trust, partnership, association and a group of entities.

- There are three approaches for determining the composition of a group reporting entity:
  o the controlling entity model,
  o the common control model, and
  o the risks and rewards model.

- The IASB's preliminary view is that the composition of a group reporting entity should be based on control, using the controlling entity model as the primary basis. The IASB noted that:
  o the common control model may provide useful information, but the IASB would determine in specific standards when to apply that model, rather than in the framework, and
  o there is a link between control and risks and rewards as the control concept includes both power over another entity and the ability to obtain benefits (or to reduce the incidence of losses). Considering the benefits element of control typically involves considering who bears the risks and/or who receives the rewards.

Canadian Developments

In July 2008, the AcSB issued the Exposure Draft *Conceptual Framework: Objective, Qualitative Characteristics and Constraints* proposing to incorporate proposed changes to the existing IASB Framework into Canadian GAAP as follows:

- for publicly accountable enterprises, the IASB proposed conceptual frameword would become effective in Canada at the same time as required in IFRS. When the

IASB publishes the new conceptual framework in final form, the AcSB would similarly incorporate it into *CICA Handbook* with that mandatory effective date and permit early adoption. and

- for private enterprises and not-for-profit organizations , as part of the AcSB strategy of developing a "made in Canada" financial reporting system, by replacing the corresponding portions of CICA 1000 and making consequential amendments.

The AcSB identified the following principal differences between the proposals in ED *The Objective of Financial Reporting and Qualitative Characteristics and Constraints of Decision-Useful Financial Reporting Information* and CICA 1000:

- Chapter 1: The Objective of Financial Reporting:

  o The ED extends the scope of the objective of financial reporting to apply to general purpose financial reporting, including financial statements. CICA 1000 focuses only on financial statements.

  o The ED identifies the primary user group of general purpose financial reporting as current and potential capital providers, including equity investors, lenders and other creditors. CICA 1000 identifies users as investors, members, contributors, creditors and other users. The AcSB proposes to retain the material on members and contributors as users in Section 1000.

  o The ED defines the objective broadly enough to encompass all the decisions that primary users make in their capacity as capital providers, including resource allocation decisions as well as decisions to protect and enhance their investments. CICA1000 defines the objective as encompassing resource allocation decisions and/or assessing management stewardship.

- Chapter 2: Qualitative Characteristics and Constraints of Decision-useful Financial Reporting Information:

  o The ED identifies relevance and faithful representation as two fundamental characteristics and comparability, verifiability, timeliness and understand- ability as enhancing characteristics. CICA 1000 does not distinguish between fundamental and enhancing characteristics. Instead, CICA 1000 requires that trade-offs be made between qualitative characteristics.

  o The ED does not include conservatism as an aspect of faithful representation because it conflicts with the quality of neutrality and would lead to a bias in financial reporting. CICA 1000 includes both neutrality and conservatism as aspects of reliability.

  o The ED classifies timeliness and verifiability as enhancing characteristics, whereas timeliness and verifiability are included as aspects of relevance and reliability, respectively, in CICA 1000.

  o The ED identifies materiality and cost as two pervasive constraints. The cost constraint involves assessing whether the benefits of providing information justify the related costs. That is described as the benefit versus cost constraint in CICA 1000.

Management Commentary

In this project, the IASB will develop the principles and essential content elements necessary to make the management commentary (MC) useful to investors. The final work product will be issued as a non-mandatory guidance document.

Currently, the IASB is discussing certain considerations raised in its Discussion Paper *Management Commentary*, published in October 2005, which specifies that the objective of an MC is to provide information to help investors:

- interpret and assess the related financial statements in the context of the environment in which an entity operates;

- assess what management views as the most important issues facing an entity and how it intends to manage those issues; and

- assess the strategies adopted by an entity and the likelihood that those strategies will be successful.

Current discussions are considering the interaction of management commentary with the Conceptual Framework project and IFRS standards requiring certain MC-type information. For example, IAS 24, *Related Party Disclosures* and IFRS 7, *Financial Instruments: Disclosures* require certain disclosures that are found in MCs. Over the long term, once the disclosure framework is completed as part of Phase E of the Conceptual Framework project, the IASB might envisage that the placement of disclosures within IFRS (whether in the notes to the financial statements or in management commentary) needs to be revisited. An Exposure Draft is planned to be issued in the fourth quarter of 2008.

IFRS for Private Entities

In February 2007, the IASB issued the Exposure Draft *International Financial Reporting Standards for Small and Medium-sized Entities* (IFRS for SME), which is currently being re-deliberated. It is significant to note that the IASB changed the name of the proposed standard to *IFRS for Private Entities* in May 2008 as part of those redeliberations.

The objective of this project is to develop an IFRS expressly for meeting the financial reporting needs of entities that (a) do not have public accountability and (b) publish general purpose financial statements for external users, including owners who are not involved in managing the business, existing and potential creditors and credit rating agencies. The IFRS for private entities is derived from full IFRS, with appropriate modifications based on the needs of users of private entity financial statements and cost-benefit considerations. Note that CICA 1300, *Differential Reporting* has similar objectives. However, the proposed IFRS for SMEs is intended to be a stand-alone document with cross references to full IFRS when needed.

Some of the IFRS for SME proposals are presented below (no comparison is provided with current differential reporting as these requirements are still evolving):

- Topics omitted because such transactions are not likely to be encountered (with cross-references to the relevant IFRS if needed):

  o general price-level-adjusted reporting in a hyperinflationary environment,

  o equity-settled share-based payments (the computational details are in IFRS 2, *Share-based Payment*),

  o determining the fair value of agricultural assets (look to IAS 41, *Agriculture*, but the Exposure Draft also proposes to reduce the use of fair value through profit or loss for agricultural SMEs),

  o extractive industries (look to IFRS 6, *Exploration for and Evaluation of Mineral Resources*),

  o interim reporting per IAS 34,

  o lessor accounting for finance leases (finance lessors are likely to be financial institutions that would not be eligible to use the proposed IFRS for SMEs),

  o recoverable amount of goodwill (SMEs would test goodwill for impairment much less frequently than under IAS 38, *Intangible Assets* but, if required to perform such a test, would look to the calculation guidance in IAS 38); earnings per share and segment reporting (which are not presently required disclosures for private entities),

o   IAS 27, *Consolidated and Separate Financial Statements* exempts some parent entities from preparing consolidated financial statements if their debt or equity instruments are not traded in a public market. Similar exemptions are in IAS 28, *Investments in Associates* and IAS 31, *Interests in Joint Ventures*,

o   insurance contracts (insurers would not be eligible to use the proposed IFRS for SMEs).

Where full IFRS provide an accounting policy choice, only the simpler option is in the proposed IFRS for SME. However, the other option or options are permitted by cross-reference to IFRSs.

- The simpler options selected are:

  o   cost-depreciation-impairment model for investment property (fair value through profit or loss is permitted by reference to IAS 40, *Investment Property*),

  o   cost-amortization-impairment model for property, plant and equipment and intangibles (the revaluation model is allowed by references to IAS 16, *Property, Plant and Equipment* and IAS 38, *Intangible Assets*),

  o   borrowing costs treated as expense (capitalization allowed by reference to IAS 23, *Borrowing Costs*),

  o   indirect method for reporting operating cash flows (the direct method is allowed by reference to IAS 7),

  o   one method for all grants (or SMEs can use any of the alternatives in IAS 20, *Accounting for Government Grants and Disclosure of Government Assistance*);

- Some accounting recognition and measurement simplifications, including for:

  o   financial instruments:

    - two categories of financial assets rather than four; this means there is no need to deal with all of the "intent-driven," held-to-maturity rules or related "tainting," nor a need for an available-for-sale category, and many other simplifications,

    - a clear and simple principle for derecognition – if the transferor has any significant continuing involvement, do not derecognize,

    - much simplified hedge accounting,

  o   goodwill impairment – an indicator approach rather than mandatory annual impairment calculations,

  o   choice to recognize all research and development costs as expenses (IAS 38 would require capitalization after commercial viability has been assessed),

  o   cost method or fair value through profit and loss for associates and joint ventures (rather than the equity method or proportionate consolidation),

  o   explains temporary differences for recognition of deferred taxes in terms of 'timing differences,

  o   use of fair value for agriculture – only if "readily determinable without undue cost or effort",

  o   defined benefit plans – recognise actuarial gains and losses in full in profit or loss when they occur,

  o   use of intrinsic value method to record share based payments covered by IFRS 2, o finance leases – simplified measurement of lessee's rights and obligations using only the fair value of the leased property,

o first-time adoption – 'impracticability' exemption provided therefore less prior period data would have to be restated than under IFRS 1, *First-time Adoption of International Financial Reporting Standards*;

- Disclosures are substantially reduced when compared with the disclosure requirements in full IFRS (implementation guidance includes a checklist of all of the proposed disclosure requirements) as some disclosures are not included because they relate to:

  o topics covered in IFRS that are omitted from the proposed IFRS for SME,

  o recognition and measurement principles in full IFRS that have been replaced by simplifications in the proposed IFRS for SME, or

  o options that are not included in the proposed IFRS for SME.

PLANNING FOR IMPLEMENTATION

This section addresses implementation issues of IAS 1 and related standards covered in this chapter. Specific implementation considerations concerning other IFRS standards are dealt with in the following chapters.

Accounting Policies

All entities adopting IFRS will have to review each of their existing accounting policies (including those of their business units/divisions/subsidiaries) in light of the new requirements under IFRS standards and interpretations. Subsequent to this review, some companies will have to make significant changes to their existing accounting policies or consider choices provided under IFRS. Note that entities must ensure consistency of application of accounting policies across their business units/divisions/subsidiaries.

Entities will have to disclose judgments made on accounting policy choices and management estimates, which might be more significant than under Canadian GAAP. Given that such judgments will vary significantly from company to company, there can be no "model" or standard disclosure example.

IFRS requirements for judgments on the application of accounting policies are wide-ranging, as highlighted by the IAS 1 examples of judgements that may require disclosure of:

- whether financial assets are held-to-maturity investments;

- when substantially all the risks and rewards of ownership of financial assets and lease assets are transferred to other entities;

- whether sales of goods are financing arrangements in substance and, therefore, do not give rise to revenue; and

- whether the substance of the relationship between an entity and a special purpose entity indicates that the special purpose entity is controlled by the entity.

Primary Financial Statements

Even though presentation of the primary financial statements might be seen as more permissive under IFRS than under Canadian GAAP, entities must ensure that they meet specific IAS 1 requirements. For example, they should make sure that all minimum line items are presented and that presentation of additional line items and subtotals are justified.

The statement of comprehensive income is one of the most significant issues to consider when adopting IFRS. Some of the elements reported in this statement are also widely used internally for managing business. Consequently, choosing what to report externally might be impacted by choices used for internal reporting.

Under IAS 1, entities may utilize one of two formats in their presentation of comprehensive income:

- a single primary statement of income and comprehensive income; or
- a two-statement approach (a statement of income and a statement of comprehensive income).

Entities currently presenting changes in other comprehensive income in a separate category highlighted within the primary statement of changes in shareholders' equity would not be able to continue using such a presentation.

Companies must also consider carefully their presentation and disclosure alternatives. Below are certain questions they must address when preparing a statement of comprehensive income on IFRS implementation:

- Should the entity present expenses by function or nature?
- Did the entity ensure that presentation does not mix functional and natural expenses?
- If expenses are presented by function, did the entity ensure that certain expenses are not excluded from the functional classifications to which they relate?
- Should the entity add line items, headings and sub-totals and are these additions relevant to an understanding of the entity's financial performance?
- If subtotals consist of non-GAAP performance measures, did the entity ensure that they are not presented with undue prominence?
- When the term "exceptional items" is used to report significantly unusual or infrequently occurring items as components apart from continuing operations (either on the face of the income statement or in the notes to the financial statements), did the entity disclose the accounting policy it used to label such items as exceptional?
- If the entity presents operating profit as a sub-total, are the items below the operating profit line clearly non-operating in nature?

Comparative Financial Information

IAS 1 requires one year of comparatives for all numerical information in the financial statements. In certain cases, more than one year of comparative information is required to be provided by note disclosure.

In addition, IAS 1 requires a third balance sheet in situations where a restatement or reclassification has occurred because of changes in accounting policies or accounting estimates, errors, or changes in presentation of previously issued financial statements.

Transition

Entities must select their initial accounting policies cautiously when preparing their first IFRS financial statements. These policies will also have to be applied retroactively to their opening balance sheet as required by IFRS 1, *First-time adoption of International Financial Reporting Standards*. Examples of accounting policies choices under IFRS include:

- IAS 2, *Inventories*: inventories at their original cost could be determined by the weighted average unit cost method or by using FIFO method;

- IAS 16, *Property, Plant and Equipment*: property, plant and equipment could be measured at amortized historical cost or at revalued amounts;

- IAS 19, *Employee Benefits*: cumulative actuarial gains and losses on pensions and other post-employment benefit obligations could continue to be amortized according to the corridor method (as required under Canadian GAAP). Alternatively, an entity could recognize actuarial gains and losses incurred during the year in profit and loss or in other comprehensive income;

- IAS 38, *Intangible Assets*: certain intangible assets could be measured at amortized historical cost or, alternatively, at revalued amount at each closing date.

Cautious selection of accounting policies is critical since, under IAS 8 (and, more recently, under CICA 1506, which is essentially a duplicate of IAS 8), there is an underlying presumption that an accounting policy, once adopted, should not be changed. Rather, it is to be uniformly applied in accounting for events and transactions of a similar type. This consistent application of accounting policies enhances the utility of the financial statements. The presumption that an entity should not change an accounting principle may be overcome only if the reporting entity justifies the use of an alternative acceptable accounting method on the basis that it is *preferable* under the circumstances.

Renegotiation of Long-term Loans Clauses

Long-term loans should be renegotiated in light of the IAS 1 requirement that classifies debt without considering post-balance-sheet refinancing agreements. As such, more debt might be classified as current under IFRS than under Canadian GAAP. This is because, contrary to Canadian GAAP, IAS 1 would not allow an entity to classify loans due on demand at the reporting date as non-current even if, in the period between the end of the reporting period and the date the financial statements are authorized for issue, the entity has:

- refinanced the of loans on a long-term basis; or

- rectified a breach of loan agreements; or

- obtained from the lender a period of grace to rectify a breach ending more than 12 months after the reporting period.

Chapter 3

Fair Value Measurements and Disclosures

Standards Discussed in this Chapter

International
Framework for the Preparation and Presentation of Financial Statements
IAS 2 – Inventories
IAS 16 – Property, Plant and Equipment
IAS 17 – Leases
IAS 19 – Employee Benefits
IAS 26 – Accounting and Reporting by Retirement Benefit Plans
IAS 32 – Financial Instruments: Presentation
IAS 36 – Impairment of Assets
IAS 38 – Intangible Assets
IAS 39 – Financial Instruments: Recognition and Measurement
IAS 40 – Investment Property
IAS 41 – Agriculture
IFRS 1 – First-time Adoption of International Financial Reporting Standards
IFRS 2 – Share-based Payments
IFRS 3 – Business Combinations (and IFRS 3, revised 2008)

Canadian
CICA 1581 – Business Combinations (and CICA 1582 – issued in 2008)
CICA 3031 – Inventories
CICA 3063 – Impairment of Long-lived Assets
CICA 3065 – Leases
CICA 3461 – Employees Future Benefits
CICA 3831 – Non-monetary Transactions
CICA 3855 – Financial Instruments — Recognition and Measurement
CICA 3863 – Financial Instruments — Presentation
CICA 3870 – Stock-based Compensation and Other Stock-based Payments

INTRODUCTION

Canadian financial reporting standards require that a substantial portion of an entity's assets and liabilities be reported at fair value, including pension assets and liabilities, most financial assets and liabilities, tangible and intangible fixed assets acquired in a business combination, impaired assets, assets held for disposal and certain share-based compensation. IFRS standards have similar fair value reporting requirements, as well as additional ones, covering share-based liabilities, investment properties, provisions and biological assets. Almost all IFRS standards contain some considerations that *allow* or *require* fair value measurements.

Companies need to start reviewing what impact the increased use of fair value under IFRS will have on their financial statements. To help in that review, this chapter discusses the following issues:

- the fair value framework;
- meaning of fair value;
- valuation techniques;
- measurements at fair value;
- fair value option;
- value guidance; and
- fair value measurement exemptions.

IMPACT ON FINANCIAL STATEMENTS

Canadian companies adopting IFRS fair value accounting[1] will see their financial statements affected differently, some feeling little impact while others will experience major changes, depending on the characteristics of the assets and liabilities they hold and the accounting policy they select.

Fair value amounts could be difficult to establish when active market information is not available. For example, the fair value of unquoted securities requires an entity to hypothesize about its future performance. To inform financial statement readers about the uncertainties inherent in fair value measurements, standards require additional disclosures, including details of the assumptions used, the reasons they were selected and, sometimes, the impact that changes in those assumptions could have on the financial statements.

In general, it is expected that most Canadian companies adopting fair value accounting under IFRS would:

- report more uncertain amounts;
- present increased income and equity volatilities; and
- disclose more information in the notes.

ANALYSIS OF RELEVANT ISSUES

This section examines and illustrates some fair value accounting issues that will become particularly relevant as standards continue to move from a historical cost model to a fair value one.

Fair Value Framework

Neither IFRS nor Canadian GAAP have a single framework that applies to all fair value measurement methods. Instead, each standard may set preferences for fair value measurements for the specific elements it covers. This might create inconsistencies in the measurements of different elements reported on the balance sheet. In addition, since some standards allowing or requiring fair value measurements do not provide any guidance on how such measurements are to be made, different entities might look to different sources for measuring identical or similar elements, again increasing the potential for inconsistencies.

In 2005, the IASB approved a project to address concerns about potential inconsistencies in fair value measurements and issued two Discussion Papers; one in November 2005 entitled *Measurement Bases for Financial Accounting* (DP 2005) which was

---

1   We use the term "fair value reporting" and "fair value accounting" to designate standards implementation allowing or requiring fair value measurements.

prepared by the AcSB staff and the other one November 2006 entitled *Fair Value Measurements* (DP 2006). This project aims to:

- provide a single source of guidance for all fair value measurements to reduce complexity and improve consistency in their application;
- clarify the definition of fair value to establish more clearly the measurement objectives in the context of financial reporting; and
- enhance fair value disclosures.

Meaning of Fair Value

The IASB and the AcSB adopted essentially the same definition of fair value, and express it in many of their respective standards as follows: "the amount for which an asset could be exchanged, or a liability settled, between knowledgeable, willing parties in an arm's length transaction." Given the lack of precision in this definition, many standards provide more details on what fair value perspective is to be adopted for measuring the items covered by that standard.

Currently, fair value perspective can vary depending on the reason an item is measured at fair value. For example, IAS 36, which covers impairment of assets (and, hence, their possible disposal) takes the fair value perspectives of both the seller and user of an asset, while IAS 16, which examines the re-valuation method for property, plant and equipment (and its continued use), takes the fair value perspective of the purchaser of an asset.

DP 2005 discusses a number of measurement bases and their adequacy for reflecting fair values. The following paragraphs present some of these bases and provide certain comments concerning their relevance. The definitions used are those provided in the IFRS and/or in the IFRS glossary of terms.

- *Transaction price*: The fair value of the consideration given or received. Generally the transaction price is the best evidence of fair value at time of recognition, but there are exceptions, for example, transaction prices with related parties.
- *Current cost*: The amount of cash or cash equivalents that would have to be paid if the same or an equivalent asset was acquired currently. The undiscounted amount of cash or cash equivalents that would be required to settle an obligation currently.

  Commentary: Measuring an asset at current cost might not be relevant if the asset is held for sale or if the asset is not expected to yield returns to justify an investment at its current cost. Generally, current cost is not considered as a measure of fair value.
- *Net realizable value*: The estimated selling price in the ordinary course of business less the estimated costs of completion and the estimated costs necessary to make the sale. Net realisable value refers to the net amount that an entity expects to realise from the sale of inventory in the ordinary course of business. Fair value reflects the amount for which the same inventory could be exchanged between knowledgeable and willing buyers and sellers in the marketplace. The former is an entity-specific value; the latter is not. Net realisable value for inventories may not equal fair value less costs to sell.

  Commentary: This value is relevant when an asset will or may be sold in the short term. It also reflects the sacrifice an entity makes when it decides to continue to hold the asset. IFRS uses the term "fair value less cost to sell" for assets other than inventory, for example, for equipment held for sale.
- *Value in use* (VIU): This is the present value of estimated future cash flows expected to be derived from the continuing use of an asset (or a cash-generating unit) and from its disposal at the end of its useful life.

Commentary: This value is entity specific and is based on subjective management estimates rather than on market information. Reporting an asset at value in use is not relevant at the time of acquisition since it could result in an inappropriate recognition of a gain or loss. Note that, in certain circumstances, the value in use is computed by reference to an aggregation of individual assets. It recognizes that an entity may be able to recover more than the fair value, less costs to sell, through, for example, internal synergies. It is not fair value, though.

- *Recoverable amount:* This is the higher of an asset's (or cash-generating unit's) fair value less costs to sell (FVLCTS) and its value in use (VIU).

  Commentary: This value reflects the asset's "highest and best use." Management would not rationally sell an asset for less than its value in use (any lower price would fail to compensate the company for the returns expected from the asset). It really represents an impairment value as calculated under IAS 36, not a fair value.

  Canadian standards address all the fair value perspectives described above except for the "recoverable amount."

Illustrative Disclosures:

Extract 3(1) – Transaction price

> **BNP Paribas (Registration Document 2007), page 121**
> **1.c FINANCIAL ASSETS AND FINANCIAL LIABILITIES (in part)**
> **1.c.9 Determination of fair value (in part)**
> Financial assets and liabilities classified as fair value through profit or loss, and financial assets classified as available-for-sale, are measured and accounted for at fair value upon initial recognition and at subsequent dates. Fair value is defined as the amount for which an asset could be exchanged, or a liability settled, between knowledgeable, willing parties in an arm's length transaction. On initial recognition, the value of a financial instrument is generally the transaction price (i.e. the value of the consideration paid or received).

Commentary: In this extract, the company provides the general definition of fair value. It also specifies that the transaction price generally reflects the fair value at initial recognition. This is a useful disclosure for the initial recording of financial assets because banks could realize a gain on acquisition of financial instruments (referred as a "Day 1 gain"). This disclosure is in line with current Canadian GAAP.

Extract 3(2) – Recoverable amount and value in use

> **Antofagasta plc (AR 2007), page 86**
> **2 Principal Accounting Policies (in part)**
> **j) Impairment of property, plant and equipment and intangible assets (excluding goodwill) (in part)**
> Recoverable amount is the higher of fair value less costs to sell and value in use. In assessing value in use, the estimated future cash flows are discounted to their present value, using a pre-tax discount rate that reflects current market assessments of the time value of money and the risks specific to the asset for which estimates of future cash flows have not been adjusted.

Commentary: The company explains how it computed the value in use and the recoverable amount. This methodology is not used in Canadian GAAP.

Extract 3(3) – Recoverable amount

Alcatel-Lucent (AR 2007 on Form 20-F), page 53
Critical accounting policies (in part)
Impairment of property, plant and equipment (in part)

Value in use is estimated by calculating the present value of the future cash flows expected to be derived from the asset. Fair value less costs to sell is based on the most reliable information available (market statistics, recent transactions, etc.).

The planned closing of certain facilities, additional reductions in personnel and unfavorable market conditions have been considered impairment triggering events in prior years. Impairment losses of €94 million were accounted for during 2007, mainly related to the UMTS business and the planned disposal of real estate (no significant impairment losses were recorded in 2006 and 2005).

When determining recoverable value of property, plant and equipment, assumptions and estimates are made based primarily on market outlooks, obsolescence and sale or liquidation disposal values. Any change in these assumptions can have a significant effect on the recoverable amount and could lead to a revision of recorded impairment losses.

Commentary: This extract, drawn from the impairment of property, plant and equipment note, explains how the company computed the value in use and fair value less cost to sell. It also describes the factors affecting recoverable value estimates. All disclosures are in line with current Canadian GAAP, except that recoverable amount is not a recognized fair value perspective.

Extract 3(4) – Value in use (aggregate amount)

Antofagasta plc (AR 2007), pages 86 and 87
2 Principal Accounting Policies (in part)
j) Impairment of property, plant and equipment and intangible assets (excluding goodwill) (in part)

Property, plant and equipment and finite life intangible assets are reviewed for impairment if there is any indication that the carrying amount may not be recoverable. If any such indication exists, the recoverable amount of the asset is estimated in order to determine the extent of the impairment (if any). Where the asset does not generate cash flows that are independent from other assets, the Group estimates the recoverable amount of the cash-generating unit to which the asset belongs. Any intangible asset with an indefinite useful life is tested for impairment annually and whenever there is an indication that the asset may be impaired.

For mining properties, estimates of future cash flows are based on estimates of the quantities of proven and probable reserves, and assumptions as to future production levels, commodity prices, cash costs of production and capital expenditure. IAS 36 "Impairment of Assets" includes a number of restrictions on the future cash flows that can be recognised in respect of future restructurings and improvement related expenditure. When calculating value in use, it also requires that calculations should be based on exchange rates current at the time of assessment. For operations with a functional currency other than the US dollar, the impairment review is conducted in the relevant functional currency.

If the recoverable amount of an asset or cash generating unit is estimated to be less than its carrying amount, the carrying amount is reduced to the recoverable amount. An impairment charge is recognised in the income statement immediately. Where an impairment subsequently reverses, the carrying amount is increased to the revised estimate of recoverable amount, but so that the increase carrying amount does not exceed the carrying value that would have been determined if no impairment had previously been recognised. A reversal is recognised in the income statement immediately.

Commentary: This extract explains that, when it is not possible to estimate the recoverable value for an individual asset, it is grouped with other assets that form a cash generating unit (CGU). This approach is consistent with Canadian GAAP except that it does not refer to the term CGU. In addition, the extract provides an illustration of the value in use in the context of an extractive industry. Chapter 4 covers the impairment issues illustrated in this extract in more detail.

Extract 3(5) – Business combination (fair value methods)

> Danfoss A/S (AR 2007), page 62
> **2. Significant accounting policies and estimates and judgements (in part)**
> **Fair value of assets and liabilities acquired in business combinations**
> On acquisition of enterprises the acquired identifiable assets and liabilities, including contingent liabilities, are determined at fair value at the acquisition date. For a majority of the assets and liabilities acquired no active market exists which can be used to determine the fair value. This applies in particular to acquire intangible fixed assets. Other methods are then used based on Management's estimates and judgments, e.g. the income approach, which is based on the net present value of future cash flows e.g. royalty payments or other expected net cash flows associated with an asset, or the cost method, which is based on e.g. the replacement cost. The difference between the carrying amounts in acquired enterprises and the fair value of identifiable assets, liabilities and contingent liabilities is specified in note 25. Acquisition and sale of subsidiaries etc.

Commentary: This extract, which is drawn from the "Significant accounting policies and estimates and judgements" note, indicates that the company uses two fair value measurement methods namely the income approach, which is based on the net present value of future cash flows and the cost method, which is based on the replacement cost. These fair value measurement methods are acceptable under Canadian GAAP.

Valuation Techniques

Three approaches can be used for estimating the fair value of an asset or a liability:

- *Market approach*: uses prices and other relevant information generated by market transactions involving identical or comparable assets or liabilities;

- *Income approach*: uses valuation techniques to convert future amounts into a single discounted present amount;

- *Cost approach*: reflects the amount that currently would be required to replace the service capacity of an asset.

The choice of approach might be particularly significant when valuing intangible assets acquired in business combinations.

Illustrative disclosure:

Extract 3(6) – Valuation techniques for in process R&D

> Alcatel-Lucent (AR 2007 on Form 20-F), page 158
> **NOTE 1 SUMMARY OF ACCOUNTING POLICIES (in part)**
> **f/ Research and development expenses and other capitalized development costs (in part)**
> With regard to business combinations, a portion of the purchase price is allocated to in-process research and development projects that may be significant. As part of the process of analyzing these business combinations, Alcatel-Lucent may make the decision to buy technology that has not yet been commercialized rather than develop the technology internally. Decisions of this nature consider existing opportunities for Alcatel-Lucent to stay at the forefront of rapid technological advances in the telecommunications-data networking industry.
>
> The fair value of in-process research and development acquired in business combinations is usually based on present value calculations of income, an analysis of the project's accomplishments and an evaluation of the overall contribution of the project, and the project's risks.
>
> The revenue projection used to value in-process research and development is based on estimates of relevant market sizes and growth factors, expected trends in technology, and the nature and expected timing of new product introductions by Alcatel-Lucent and its competitors. Future net cash flows from such projects are based on management's estimates of such projects' cost of sales, operating expenses and income taxes.

Alcatel-Lucent (AR 2007 on Form 20-F) (continued)
NOTE 1 SUMMARY OF ACCOUNTING POLICIES (in part)
f/ Research and development expenses and other capitalized development costs (in part)

The value assigned to purchased in-process research and development is also adjusted to reflect the stage of completion, the complexity of the work completed to date, the difficulty of completing the remaining development, costs already incurred, and the projected cost to complete the projects.

Such value is determined by discounting the net cash flows to their present value. The selection of the discount rate is based on Alcatel-Lucent's weighted average cost of capital, adjusted upward to reflect additional risks inherent in the development life cycle.

Commentary: This extract describes the valuation techniques the company uses for process R&D acquired in business combinations. It discloses the variables used in its valuation model and specifies the uncertainties concerning the valuation. The information provided in this extract would be considered useful under current Canadian GAAP.

Measurements at Fair Value

Initial Measurement

Most IFRS and Canadian standards require that elements of financial statements be recorded initially at fair value, which generally corresponds to the transaction price. Some transactions are, however, concluded at a price that does not reflect the fair value of the exchange. In addition, certain contractual obligations might have to be measured at fair value at the time an entity becomes party to those contractual provisions even though no consideration was paid up front. Finally, the transaction price could cover a group of elements, each of which has to be measured at fair value. In all these circumstances, an entity would have to calculate fair value amounts that could be based on subjective assumptions.

IFRS and Canadian GAAP are generally converged on initial measurement at fair value. Below is a table showing some standards requiring the computation of a fair value estimate on initial recognition:

Topic	Standards	IFRS Basic Requirements
Finance lease (see Chapter 13)	IAS 17 and CICA 3065	At the inception of a lease, an entity would record fair value of the leased property or, if lower, the present value of the minimum lease payments (as defined in the standard).
Financial instruments (see Chapter 9)	IAS 39 and CICA 3855	When an entity becomes a party to the contractual provisions of a financial instrument, it records it at its fair value plus, in the case of a financial asset or financial liability not at fair value through profit or loss, the transaction costs that are directly attributable to the acquisition or issue of the financial asset or financial liability. (Note that the transaction price might not reflect the fair value of the financial asset or liability recorded as illustrated in the extract 3(7) below).
Business combination (see Chapter 5)	IFRS 3 and CICA 1581	Business combinations require that an entity records all acquired assets and liabilities, including contingent liabilities, at fair value, with the corresponding consideration paid also measured at fair value (see note below).
Share-based payments (see Chapter 16)	IFRS 2 and CICA 3870	An entity would establish the initial cost to equal fair value of all share-based payment arrangements with employees at the grant date. (liabilities are measured at intrinsic value under CICA 3870)

Note: According to IFRS 3 (as revised in January 2008), both the consideration transferred in a business combination (including any contingent consideration) and all assets and liabilities acquired have to be measured at fair value. However IFRS 3 provides limited exceptions for the following elements:

- leases and insurance contracts are classified on the basis of the contractual terms and other factors at the inception of the contract (or when the terms have changed) rather than on the basis of the factors that exist at the acquisition date;

- only those contingent liabilities assumed in a business combination that are a present obligation and can be measured reliably are recognized;

- certain assets and liabilities which must be recognized or measured in accordance with other IFRS standards including those within the scope of IAS 12, *Income Taxes*, IAS 19, *Employee Benefits*, IFRS 2, *Share-based Payment* and IFRS 5, *Non-current Assets Held for Sale and Discontinued Operations*;

- reacquired right for which there are special measurement requirements;

- indemnification assets which are recognized and measured on a basis that is consistent with the item that is subject to the indemnification, even if that measure is not fair value.

Illustrative Disclosures:

The extracts provided below deal with financial instruments whose transaction prices might differ from their fair value. Extracts illustrating initial measurement disclosures related to the other fair value calculations described above are found in the chapters covering the specific topic.

Extract 3(7) – Estimated fair value at recognition (derivatives)

Centrica plc (AR-2007), page 66
Financial instruments (in part)
g) Derivative financial instruments (in part)
The Group enters into certain energy derivative contracts covering periods for which observable market data does not exist. The fair value of such derivatives is estimated by reference in part to published price quotations from active markets, to the extent that such observable market data exists, and in part by using valuation techniques, whose inputs include data, which is not based on or derived from observable markets. Where the fair value at initial recognition for such contracts differs from the transaction price, a fair value gain or fair value loss will arise. This is referred to as a day-one gain or day-one loss. Such gains and losses are deferred and amortised to the Income Statement based on volumes purchased or delivered over the contractual period until such time observable market data becomes available. When observable market data becomes available, any remaining deferred day-one gains or losses are recognised within the Income Statement.

Commentary: In this extract, the company specifies that, at original recognition, the transaction prices of the derivative contracts differ from their fair value. This results in a Day 1 gain or loss. According to IFRS, this gain or loss is deferred until observable market data become available. The gain or loss deferral is in line with EITF 02-3, *Issues Involved in Accounting for Derivative Contracts Held for Trading Purposes and Contracts Involved in Energy Trading and Risk Management Activities*. Since these derivative contracts are recorded at fair value (as required by CICA 3855), the accounting policy described would also be in line with Canadian GAAP. (Since no specific Canadian standards address this issue, an entity might want to consult IFRS or US GAAP when setting its accounting policy as specified in CICA 1100, *Generally Accepted Accounting Principles*).

Extract 3(8) – Estimated fair value at recognition (complex financial instruments)

BNP Paribas (Registration Document 2007), page 122

Instruments traded in inactive markets (in part)

Products traded in inactive markets and valued using an internal valuation model based on parameters that are not observable or only partially observable

Some complex financial instruments, which are usually tailored, illiquid or have long maturities, are valued using internally-developed techniques and techniques that are based on data only partially observable on active markets.

In the absence of observable data, these instruments are measured on initial recognition in a way that reflects the transaction price, regarded as the best indication of fair value. Valuations derived from these models are adjusted for liquidity risk and credit risk.

The margin generated when these complex financial instruments are traded (day one profit) is deferred and taken to the profit and loss account over the period during which the valuation parameters are expected to remain non-observable. When parameters that were originally non-observable become observable, or when the valuation can be substantiated by comparison with recent similar transactions in an active market, the unrecognised portion of the day one profit is released to the profit and loss account.

Commentary: The company specifies that Day 1 gains on some complex financial instruments are deferred until the valuation can be substantiated by comparison with recent similar transactions in an active market. Because financial instruments have to be recorded at fair value (as required by CICA 3855), the accounting policy described would also be in line with Canadian GAAP. (Since no specific Canadian standards address the treatment of Day 1 gains, an entity might want to consult IFRS when setting its accounting policy as specified in CICA 1100.)

Subsequent Measurement

Though initial measurement requirements are basically the same under IFRS and Canadian GAAP, they may differ significantly on subsequent fair value re-measurement. The table below summarizes some of these re-measurement requirements.

Topic	Standards	IFRS Basic Requirements
Derivatives, financial assets classified as available for sale and financial assets and liabilities held for trading (see Chapter 9)	IAS 39 and CICA 3855 (basically same requirements)	All investments in equity securities, some debt securities, all derivatives and any financial asset held for trading should always be measured at fair value at each balance sheet date.
Pensions and post-retirement plan assets (see Chapter 16)	IAS 19 CICA 3461 (basically equivalent requirements)	Pension and post-retirement plan assets have to be valued at fair value at the end of each period.
Property, plant and equipment impairment (see Chapters 4 and 12)	IAS 36 CICA 3063 (equivalent requirements but *different* timing and amounts)	Property, plant and equipment impairment should be reported at no more than their recoverable amount. Note: Recoverable amount reflects a fair value measurement perspective that is defined by IAS 36 as the higher of fair value less cost to sell or value in use.
Financial asset impairment (see Chapters 4 and 9)	IAS 39 CICA 3055 and CICA 3855 (basically equivalent requirements)	Financial assets held at amortized cost have to be written down to their fair value if they are impaired.
Inventory impairment (see Chapter 11)	IAS 2 CICA 3031 (same requirements)	Inventories have to be written down to their net realizable value (fair value less costs to sell).

Topic	Standards	IFRS Basic Requirements
Agricultural assets (see Appendix A)	IAS 41 (no corresponding Canadian standard)	Animals, forests, crops and produce are recorded at fair value less estimated point of sale costs, with regular re-measurements.
Non current assets held for sale (see Chapter 12)	IFRS 5 and CICA 3475 (basically equivalent requirements)	Non current assets held for sale must be carried at the lower of cost and net realizable value (fair value less costs to sell).

Illustrative Disclosures:

Illustrations of the fair value measurements described above in the form of extracts are included in the chapters indicated covering the specific topics.

Fair Value Option

IFRS allow companies to re-measure certain assets and liabilities at fair value more frequently than Canadian GAAP does. The table below presents the fair value options permitted by both IFRS and Canadian GAAP.

Topic	Standards	IFRS Basic Requirement
IFRS adoption (see Chapters 12 and 20)	IFRS 1 (no Canadian equivalent)	Deemed cost could be designated to represent the fair value of certain assets, such as property, plant and equipment, intangible assets and investment property.
Revaluation model for property, plant and equipment (see Chapter 12)	IAS 16 (no Canadian equivalent)	Option to carry property, plant and equipment at cost, less depreciation and impairment, or to carry them at fair value less depreciation and impairment with regular re-measurement.
Revaluation model for intangible assets (see Chapter 14)	IAS 38 (no Canadian equivalent)	Option of carrying certain intangible assets at cost less amortization and impairment or at fair value (only if an active market exists for those assets, which is expected to be rare) less any subsequent accumulated amortisation and any subsequent accumulated impairment losses with regular re-evaluation.
Fair value option concerning financial assets and financial liabilities (see Chapter 9)	IAS 39 and CICA 3855 (basically equivalent requirements with less restrictions)	Option to designate certain financial assets or financial liabilities at the time of acquisition or issuance, to be carried at fair value, with gains or losses included in income.
Investment property (see Chapter 8)	IAS 40 (no Canadian equivalent)	Option to carry investments in real estate at cost, less depreciation and impairment, or to carry them at fair value, with regular re-measurements at each balance sheet date.

Illustrative Disclosures:

The extracts provided below look at fair value options for financial assets and liabilities that are more restrictive under IAS 39 than under CICA 3855. Other extracts illustrating the selection of fair value options can be found in the chapters covering the specific topic.

Extract 3(9) – Fair value option (financial liabilities)

PSA Peugeot Citroën (Registration Document 2007), page 174
C. Recognition and measurement of financial liabilities (in part)
(b) Financial liabilities accounted for using the fair value option
Exceptionally, the fair value option has been applied when it allows for a clearer presentation of the financial statements, namely because changes in the fair value of liabilities are accounted for symmetrically with any changes in the fair value of the derivatives hedging the interest rate risk on such liabilities. In such cases, the fair value of these liabilities reflects the credit risk specific to the issuer.

Commentary: The company specifies that it has applied the fair value option for certain financial liabilities to report gains and losses symmetrically with the related gain or losses of the derivatives hedging instrument. This would yield results similar to those that would have been derived had the company applied hedge accounting – which may be not permitted for non-derivative liabilities hedging non-derivative assets. The same results would be obtained under CICA 3855 when the fair value option is used.

Extract 3(10) – Fair value option (financial assets and liabilities)

BNP Paribas (Registration Document 2007), page 122
1.c FINANCIAL ASSETS AND FINANCIAL LIABILITIES (in part)
1.c.10 Financial assets and liabilities designated at fair value through profit or loss (fair value option)

The amendment to IAS 39 relating to the "fair value option" was adopted by the European Union on 15 November 2005, with effect from 1 January 2005.

This option allows entities to designate any financial asset or financial liability on initial recognition as measured at fair value, with changes in fair value recognised in profit or loss, in the following cases:

- hybrid financial instruments containing one or more embedded derivatives which otherwise would have been extracted and accounted for separately;
- where using the option enables the entity to eliminate or significantly reduce a mismatch in the measurement and accounting treatment of assets and liabilities that would arise if they were to be classified in separate categories;
- where a group of financial assets and/or financial liabilities is managed and measured on the basis of fair value, under a properly documented management and investment strategy.

BNP Paribas applies this option primarily to financial assets related to unit-linked business (in order to achieve consistency of treatment with the related liabilities), and to structured issues containing significant embedded derivatives.

Commentary: This extract specifies the restrictions on fair value option use under IAS 39. CICA 3855 does not contain any restriction on designating any financial asset or financial liability on initial recognition as measured at fair value, with changes in fair value recognized in profit or loss.

Fair Value Guidance

Some IFRS and Canadian standards offer valuation guidance by providing a hierarchy that ranges from high-level mark-to-market inputs, such as published price quotations on an active market, to entity-specific valuations. Guidance coverage varies depending on the element being measured. The table and the two related notes below summarize the principal fair value guidance included in IFRS and Canadian standards.

Topic	Guidance in IFRS	Guidance in Canadian GAAP
Share-based payments (IFRS 2 and CICA 3870) (see Chapter 16)	*Coverage*: Very extensive – Paragraphs IFRS 2.16 to IFRS 2.23 and Appendix B (paragraphs B1 to B44). *Issues addressed:* Variables to be considered when valuing shared based compensation: • vesting conditions; • reload features; • accounting after vesting date; • estimating fair value of equity instrument granted (shares, options, inputs for option pricing models, expected early exercise, expected volatility, expected dividends, risk free interest rate, capital structure effects); • modification of equity-settled share based-based payments. *Hierarchy*: Use market price and, if not available, a valuation technique taking into consideration the impact of identified variables listed above.	*Coverage*: Less extensive than IFRS – Paragraphs 3870.30 to 3870.37, 3870.53 to 3870.56 and Appendix (paragraphs A1 to A16). *Issues addressed:* Basically same IFRS variables are specified for valuing shared based compensation. *Hierarchy*: None specified.
Business combinations (IFRS 3 revised and CICA 1581) (see Chapter 5)	Coverage: Extensive – Paragraph IFRS 3.18 and Appendix B (paragraphs B41 and B49). *Issues addressed:* Measuring the fair value of particular identifiable assets and non-controlling interest in an acquiree *Hierarchy*: None (See Note 1 at the end of the table).	CICA 1582, *Business Combinations*, was issued in January 2009 and is converged with IFRS 3.
Inventories (IAS 2 and CICA 3031) (see Chapter 11)	*Coverage*: Brief – Paragraph IAS 2.7. *Issue addressed:* Interpretation of "net realizable value." *Hierarchy*: None.	*Coverage*: Identical to IFRS – same brief Paragraph 3031.7. *Issue addressed:* Same as IFRS. *Hierarchy*: None.

Topic	Guidance in IFRS	Guidance in Canadian GAAP
Property, plant and equipment (IAS 16 and CICA 3061) (see Chapter 12)	*Coverage*: Brief – Paragraphs IAS 16.32 and 16.33. *Issue addressed:* Revaluation model. *Hierarchy*: Use market based evidence and, if not available, use an income or a depreciated cost approach.	No valuation guidance (standard based on historical cost). However, paragraph 3831.09 addresses reliability issue in fair value measurement of non-monetary transactions.
Employee benefits (IAS 19 and CICA 3461) (see Chapter 16)	*Coverage*: Brief – Paragraphs IAS 19.102, 19.104 and 19.104D. *Issue addressed:* Fair value of plan assets related to post-employment defined benefit plans *Hierarchy*: Use market price and, if not available, use an estimate (e.g., discount expected future cash flows). Special rules provided for plans that include qualifying insurance policies.	*Coverage*: Very brief – Paragraph 3461.68. *Issue addressed:* Same as IFRS. *Hierarchy*: Similar to IFRS. Use market value; otherwise use a method that provides an approximation of market.
Retirement benefit plans (IAS 26 and CICA 4100)	*Coverage*: Brief – Paragraphs IAS 26.32 and 26.33. *Issue addressed:* Valuation of plan assets. Hierarchy: None as such but it specifies that investments carried at fair value means market value. Certain exemptions (with disclosures) to fair value measurements are provided.	*Coverage*: Brief – Paragraphs 4100.11 to 4100.13 and 4100.20. *Issue addressed:* Same as IFRS. *Hierarchy*: None as such but standard specifies to use for: • marketable securities: trade price and if not available, use an estimate; • real estate investments: independent appraisals Note: Actuarial asset values, i.e., adjusted market value methods, moving average market value methods and average ratio methods could be used when assumptions used in determining the actuarial value of the accrued pension benefits are developed by reference to expected long term market conditions.

Topic	Guidance in IFRS	Guidance in Canadian GAAP
Financial instruments presentation (IAS 32 and CICA 3863) (see Chapter 9)	*Coverage*: Brief – Appendix paragraph AG31. *Issue addressed:* Valuation of compound financial instruments components. *Hierarchy*: None specified, rather method to value the liability and the equity components (only acceptable method consists of valuing the debt portion and determining the value of the equity component by difference).	*Coverage*: average – Paragraph 3863.22 and Appendix paragraphs A7 and A8. *Issue addressed:* Same as IFRS. *Hierarchy*: None specified as IFRS. However, in addition to the IFRS method for the valuation of the liability and the equity components, CICA 3863 allows the valuation of both components, adjusting them subsequently on a pro rata basis so that total corresponds to the consideration obtained.
Impairment of assets (IAS 36 and CICA 3063) (see Chapter 4)	*Coverage*: Average – Paragraphs IAS 36.25 to IAS 36.29, IAS 36.78 and IAS 36.79. *Issues addressed:* Concept of recoverable amount which represents the higher of value in use (VIU) and fair value less cost to sell (FVLCTS) and other particular considerations. *Hierarchy*: Provides three levels for the measurement of fair value less cost to sell (see Note 2 below).	*Coverage*: Extensive – Appendix A1 to A 25. *Issue addressed:* Estimating fair value methods for non financial assets and liabilities including present value techniques. *Hierarchy*: • Quoted market prices in active markets are the best evidence of fair value • In absence of quoted market prices, estimates of fair value are based on the best information available, including prices for similar items and the results of other valuation techniques.
Intangible assets (IAS 38 and CICA 3064) (see Chapter 14)	*Coverage*: Average – Paragraphs IAS 38.33 and IAS 38.39 to IAS 38.41 and IAS 38.75. *Issue addressed:* Intangible assets acquired in a business combination and revaluation model for intangibles traded in active markets (need to carry revaluations regularly). *Hierarchy*: For valuation of intangible assets acquired (3 levels): • most reliable: quoted market prices in an active market; • if none, use the amount an entity would have paid for the asset, at the acquisition date, in an arm's length transaction between knowledgeable and willing parties, on the basis of the best information; • if unique and regular acquisitions are involved, use a valuation technique.	*Coverage*: No specific guidance – Paragraph 3064.65 refers to CICA 1581 for guidance. *Issue addressed:* Not applicable. *Hierarchy*: None in CICA 3064.

Topic	Guidance in IFRS	Guidance in Canadian GAAP
Financial instruments: recognition and measurement (IAS 39 and CICA 3855) (see Chapter 9)	*Coverage*: Very extensive – Paragraphs IAS 39.48, IAS 39.48A and IAS 39.49 and Appendix A (paragraphs AG64 and AG65 and AG69 to AG 79 and AG82).	*Coverage*: Same as IFRS, i.e., very extensive – Paragraphs 3855.72 and 3855.73 and Appendix A41 to A65 (very similar to IFRS).
	Issues addressed:	*Issues addressed:*
	Fair measurement considerations when referring to an active market and when using a valuation technique including the inputs to be used.	Same as IFRS.
	Hierarchy:	*Hierarchy:*
	• best evidence: quoted prices in an active market; • in absence of quoted prices in an active market, use a valuation technique.	Same as IFRS (even though CICA 3855 does not specifically make a direct reference to maximize market inputs, it specifies that the appropriate technique for estimating the fair value of a financial instrument would incorporate observable market data about the market conditions and other factors that are likely to affect the instrument's fair value).
	Note: The chosen valuation technique makes maximum use of market inputs and relies as little as possible on entity-specific inputs. It incorporates all factors that market participants would consider in setting a price and is consistent with accepted economic methodologies for pricing financial instruments.	
Investment properties (IAS 40) (see Chapter 8)	*Coverage*: Extensive Paragraphs IAS 40.36 to IAS 40.51 *Issues addressed* Fair measurement considerations *Hierarchy*: • best evidence: current prices in an active market for similar property in the same location and condition and subject to similar leases and other contracts; • in absence of an active market, consider various sources including current prices in an active market for properties of different nature, recent prices of similar properties on less active market and discounted cash flow projections. Note: Fair value related to an investment property does not include notion of value in use.	No equivalent standard

Topic	Guidance in IFRS	Guidance in Canadian GAAP
Agriculture (IAS 41) (see Appendix A)	*Coverage*: Extensive – Paragraphs IAS 41.9 and IAS 41.15 to IAS 41.25. *Issues addressed*: Fair value measurement considerations including: • grouping; • non-adjustment of fair value due to contract; • absence of market-determined prices; • whether cost could approximate fair value. *Hierarchy*: • appropriate basis: quoted market price (market expected to be used if more than one exists); • in case of absence of an active market, refer to most recent market transaction price, market prices for similar assets and/or sector benchmarks; • in case of absence of market for a biological asset in its present condition, use the present value of expected net cash flows.	No equivalent standard.

Note 1: IFRS 3 and CICA 1581 contain specific measurement requirements depending on the asset or liability being reported. Canadian and IFRS standards have different requirements for the measurement of specific assets and liabilities, mostly in that the latter emphasize the use of market price and exit price, while the former sometimes mandate the use of replacement cost of equivalent capacity as an estimate of fair value, subject to recoverability. These differences will disappear once revised IFRS 3 and new CICA 1582 (which are converged) are adopted.

IFRS 3 provides certain guidance for measuring the fair value of particular identifiable assets and a non-controlling interest in an acquiree. The guidance specifies to apply the following:

• Assets with uncertain cash flows (valuation allowances): acquirer does not recognize a separate valuation allowance as of the acquisition date for assets acquired in a business combination that are measured at their acquisition-date fair values because the effects of uncertainty about future cash flows are included in the fair value measure.

• Assets subject to operating leases in which the acquiree is the lessor: in measuring the acquisition-date fair value of an asset such as a building or a patent that is subject to an operating lease in which the acquiree is the lessor, the acquirer must take into account the terms of the lease. In other words, the acquirer does not recognise a separate asset or liability if the terms of an operating lease are either favourable or unfavourable when compared with market terms.

• Assets that the acquirer intends not to use or to use in a way that is different from the way other market participants would use them: for competitive or other reasons, the acquirer may intend not to use an acquired asset, for example, a research and development intangible asset, or it may intend to use the asset in a way that is different from the way in which other market participants would use it. Nevertheless, the acquirer shall measure the asset at fair value determined in accordance with its use by other market participants.

- Non-controlling interest in an acquiree: IFRS 3 allows the acquirer to measure a non-controlling interest in the acquiree at its fair value at the acquisition date. Sometimes an acquirer will be able to measure the acquisition-date fair value of a non-controlling interest on the basis of active market prices for the equity shares not held by the acquirer. In other situations, however, an active market price for the equity shares will not be available. In those situations, the acquirer would measure the fair value of the non-controlling interest using other valuation techniques. Note that the fair values of the acquirer's interest in the acquiree and the non-controlling interest on a per-share basis might differ. The main difference is likely to be the inclusion of a control premium in the per-share fair value of the acquirer's interest in the acquiree or, conversely, the inclusion of a discount for lack of control (also referred to as a minority discount) in the per-share fair value of the non-controlling interest.

- Measuring goodwill or a gain from a bargain purchase which necessitate the measurement at the acquisition date of fair value of the acquirer's interest in the acquiree using valuation techniques: acquirer measures the acquisition-date fair value of its interest in the acquiree using one or more valuation techniques that are appropriate in the circumstances and for which sufficient data are available. If more than one valuation technique is used, the acquirer should evaluate the results of the techniques, considering the relevance and reliability of the inputs used and the extent of the available data.

Note 2: IAS 36 contains a three-level hierarchy for measuring fair value less costs to sell as follows:

- best evidence: price in a binding sale agreement in an arm's length transaction, adjusted for incremental costs directly attributable to the disposal of the asset;

- second best evidence: asset's market price less the costs of disposal;

- lastly: fair value less costs to sell based on the best information available to reflect the amount that an entity could obtain, at the balance sheet date, from the disposal of the asset in an arm's length transaction between knowledgeable, willing parties, after deducting the costs of disposal.

Illustrative Disclosure:

The extract provided below concerns fair value guidance under IAS 39 and CICA 3855. Extracts illustrating the application of other specific guidance can be found in the chapters covering the specific topics.

Extract 3(11) – Applying fair value guidance (financial instruments)

> **BNP Paribas (Registration Document 2007), pages 121 and 122**
> **1.c FINANCIAL ASSETS AND FINANCIAL LIABILITIES (in part)**
> **1.c.9 Determination of fair value**
> **Method of determining fair value**
> Fair value is determined:
> - on the basis of quoted prices in an active market; or
> - using valuation techniques involving:
>   - mathematical calculation methods based on accepted financial theories, and
>   - parameters derived in some cases from the prices of instruments traded in active markets, and in others from statistical estimates or other quantitative methods.
>
> The distinction between the two valuation methods is made according to whether or not the instrument is traded in an active market.
>
> A market for an instrument is regarded as active, and hence liquid, if there is regular trading in that market or instruments are traded that are very similar to the instrument being valued.
>
> The Bank distinguishes between three categories of financial instruments based on the characteristics of the instrument and the measurement method used. This classification is used as the basis for the information provided in the notes to the consolidated financial statements in accordance with international accounting standards:
> - category 1: financial instruments quoted on an active market;
> - category 2: financial instruments measured using valuation models based on observable parameters;
> - category 3: financial instruments measured using valuation models based wholly or partly on non-observable parameters. A non-observable parameter is defined as a parameter whose value results from assumptions or correlations which are not based on observable current market transactions in the same instrument at the valuation date, or on observable market data at that date.
>
> **Instruments traded in active markets**
>
> If quoted prices in an active market are available, they are used to determine fair value. This method is used for quoted securities and for derivatives traded on organised markets such as futures and options.
>
> The majority of over-the-counter derivatives, swaps, forward rate agreements, caps, floors and standard options are traded in active markets. Valuations are determined using generally accepted models (discounted cash flows, Black-Scholes model, interpolation techniques) based on quoted market prices for similar instruments or underlyings.
>
> The valuation derived from these models is adjusted for liquidity and credit risk. Starting from valuations derived from median market prices, price adjustments are used to value the net position in each financial instrument at bid price in the case of short positions, or at asking price in the case of long positions. Bid price is the price at which a counterparty would buy the instrument, and asking price is the price at which a seller would sell the same instrument.
>
> A counterparty risk adjustment is included in the valuation derived from the model in order to reflect the credit quality of the derivative instrument.
>
> **Products traded in inactive markets and valued using an internal valuation model based on parameters that are not observable or only partially observable**
>
> Some complex financial instruments, which are usually tailored, illiquid or have long maturities, are valued using internally-developed techniques and techniques that are based on data only partially observable on active markets.

BNP Paribas (Registration Document 2007) (continued)

In the absence of observable data, these instruments are measured on initial recognition in a way that reflects the transaction price, regarded as the best indication of fair value. Valuations derived from these models are adjusted for liquidity risk and credit risk.

The margin generated when these complex financial instruments are traded (day one profit) is deferred and taken to the profit and loss account over the period during which the valuation parameters are expected to remain non-observable. When parameters that were originally non-observable become observable, or when the valuation can be substantiated by comparison with recent similar transactions in an active market, the unrecognised portion of the day one profit is released to the profit and loss account.

Instruments traded in inactive markets

Products traded in inactive markets and valued using an internal valuation model based on directly observable parameters or on parameters derived from observable data

Some financial instruments, although not traded in an active market, are valued using methods based on observable market data.

These models use market parameters calibrated on the basis of observable data such as yield curves, implicit volatility layers of options, default rates, and loss assumptions obtained from consensus data or from active over-the-counter markets. Valuations derived from these models are adjusted for liquidity, credit and model risk.

The margin generated when these financial instruments are traded is taken to the profit and loss account immediately.

Unlisted equity securities

The fair value of unquoted equity securities is measured by comparison with recent transactions in the equity of the company in question carried out with an independent third party on an arm's length basis. If no such reference is available, the valuation is determined either on the basis of generally accepted practices (EBIT or EBITDA multiples) or of the Group's share of net assets as calculated using the most recently available information.

Commentary: This extract describes the different methods the company uses for valuing different categories of financial instruments. Those methods satisfy the requirements of SFAS 157, *Fair Value Measurements* and are compatible with both IAS 39 and CICA 3855. Portions of this extract were also reproduced in Extract 3(8).

Fair Value Measurement Exemptions

Some IFRS standards provide exemptions to fair value measurement requirements in certain circumstances:

- *Intangible assets*: One of the criteria for recognizing intangible assets at fair value, as required by IFRS 3, is that fair value can be measured reliably. This exemption was withdrawn in the 2008 revision of IFRS 3 as the IASB is of the view that all intangible assets satisfying the identification criterion in business combinations can be measured reliably (see Chapter 14).

- *Financial instruments*: IAS 39 allows measurements other than fair value for unlisted securities whose fair value cannot be reliably measured. This differs from CICA 3855, which requires that *all* equity securities that are not traded on an active market be measured at cost (see Chapter 9).

- *Investment properties*: IAS 40 indicates that there is a rebuttable presumption that an entity can reliably determine the fair value of an investment property on a continuing basis. IAS 40 acknowledges, however, that in, exceptional cases, the fair value of an investment property is not reliably determinable on a continuing basis (see Chapter 8).

- *Biological assets*: IAS 41 contains a presumption that fair value can be measured reliably for a biological asset. That presumption can be rebutted only on initial recognition for a biological asset for which market-determined prices or values are not available and for which alternative estimates of fair value are determined to be clearly unreliable (see Appendix 1).

Illustrative Disclosure:

The extract shown below looks at the valuation of unquoted securities covered by IAS 39 and CICA 3855. Extracts illustrating the other exemptions from fair value measurement can be found in the chapters covering the specific topics.

Extract 3(12) – Unquoted securities held

> **Lafarge (AR Document de référence 2007), page F67**
> **Note 26 - Financial instruments (in part)**
> **(b) Fair values (in part)**
> **other financial assets**: for marketable securities, quoted market prices are used. Other investments, amounting to 37 million euros at December 31, 2007, for which there is no quoted price, are carried at cost because a reasonable estimate of fair value could not be made without incurring excessive costs. The investment in Cimentos de Portugal (Cimpor) is carried at market value with unrealized gains and losses recorded in a separate component of equity;

Commentary: Here, the company specifies that it carries unquoted security investments at cost, which is the only measurement acceptable under CICA 3855. Hence, the justification provided in the disclosure would not be presented under Canadian GAAP.

FUTURE DEVELOPMENTS[2]

In November 2006, the IASB published the Discussion Paper, *Fair Value Measurements* which covers many issues still being debated today. Basically, this Discussion paper seeks input on the appropriateness of converging with the FASB's SFAS 157, *Fair Value Measurements*. This SFAS establishes a measurement framework for financial and non-financial assets and liabilities that are measured at fair value under other authoritative pronouncements.

SFAS 157 raised a variety of issues that the IASB is currently considering: Below are some IASB tentative decisions reproduced from the Information for Observers prepared by the IASB staff for the IASB meeting of December 2008:

- *Single source of guidance*: The IASB has reaffirmed its preliminary view that having a single source of guidance would be an improvement over the disparate guidance in IFRS.

- *Market participant view*: The IASB has reaffirmed its preliminary view that the market participant view in SFAS 157 is generally consistent with the concepts of knowledgeable, willing parties in an arm's length transaction that are currently in IFRS.

- *Attributes specific to an asset or liability*: The IASB has reaffirmed its preliminary view that it is appropriate to consider attributes specific to the asset or liability that a market participant would consider when pricing the asset or liability. When location is an attribute of the asset or liability, the price in the principal (or most advantageous) market should be adjusted for costs that would be incurred to transport the asset or liability from its current location to the principal (or most advantageous) market. The IASB also reaffirmed its preliminary view that transaction costs are an attribute of the transaction rather than an attribute of the asset or liability. Thus, they should be considered separately from fair value. This is consistent with current IFRS.

- *Fair value hierarchy*: Because IFRS do not have a consistent hierarchy that applies to all fair value measurements, the IASB tentatively decided to introduce a single hierarchy, such as the one in SFAS 157, to reduce complexity and increase comparability.

---

2   See developments related to faifr value measurements of financial assets in Chapter 9.

- *Bid-ask spreads*: The IASB has reaffirmed its preliminary view that fair value measurements should be determined using the price within the bid-ask spread that is most representative of fair value in the circumstances. The Board also tentatively decided:

  o not to preclude the use of mid-market pricing or another pricing convention as a practical expedient for a fair value measurement within a bid-ask spread.

  o to specify that the bid-ask spread guidance applies in all levels of the fair value hierarchy.

  o not to include guidance on offsetting positions. This is because the bid-ask pricing guidance allows entities to determine, for each position, the price within the bid-ask spread that is most representative of fair value in the circumstances.

- *Definition of fair value*: the IASB tentatively decided to define fair value for assets as a current exit price. The wording of the definition of fair value will reflect the fact that an exit price considers a market participant's ability to generate economic benefit by using an asset or by selling it to a third party.

- *Highest and best use*: the IASB tentatively decided the following:

  o The fair value of an asset should reflect its highest and best use. The highest and best use is the use by market participants that would maximize the value of the asset or of the group of assets in which the asset would be used. It considers uses of the asset that are physically possible, legally permissible and financially feasible at the measurement date. The Board tentatively decided to provide a description of each criterion and an explanation of how they apply in a fair value measurement.

  o The Exposure Draft should state explicitly that an entity does not need to perform an exhaustive search to find other potential uses on which to base the valuation if there is no evidence to suggest that the current use of the asset is not its highest and best use.

  o When an entity measures an asset at fair value and currently uses the asset together with another asset in a use that differs from their highest and best use, the entity may need to split the fair value into two components: (a) the fair value of the asset assuming its current use and (b) a 'change of use option' reflecting the entity's ability to switch the asset to its highest and best use.

- *Blockage factors*: The IASB confirmed its preliminary view, as expressed in the Discussion Papers on *Fair Value Measurements* and *Reducing Complexity in Reporting Financial Instruments*,[3] that the measurement objective should be to measure fair value at the individual instrument level. The Board tentatively decided:

  o to exclude blockage factors from a fair value measurement at all levels of the fair value hierarchy.

  o that a fair value measurement should exclude other discounts or premia (such as a control premium) that apply to a holding of financial instruments and do not apply to the individual instrument.

The AcSB is monitoring the IASB Fair Value Measurement project and the issues raised by its Discussion Paper issued in 2006. The IASB expects to issue an Exposure Draft in the first quarter of 2009 and the project is expected to be completed in 2010. In the meantime, the AcSB does not expect to develop equivalent requirements for Canadian GAAP.

---

3   The Discussion Paper is discussed in Chapter 9.

COMPREHENSIVE EXAMPLE

This section presents a comprehensive example of extensive disclosures on fair value measurements. We have selected relevant extracts of the notes that might provide good examples of disclosure under both IFRS and Canadian GAAP.

ABN AMRO Holding N.V. – All extracts were obtained from the annual report for the year ended December 31, 2007.

Extract 3(A1) – ABN AMRO Holding N.V. – Summary of accounting policies, page 98

In this extract, the company describes the basis of the financial statements presentation, which were prepared using a mixed model valuation basis.

Summary significant accounting policies

Basis of preparation (in part)

The consolidated financial statements are prepared on a mixed model valuation basis as follows:

- Fair value is used for: derivative financial instruments, financial assets and liabilities held for trading or designated as measured at fair value through income, and available-for-sale financial assets,

- Other financial assets (including 'Loans and Receivables') and liabilities are valued at amortised cost,

- The carrying value of assets and liabilities measured at amortised cost included in a fair value hedge relationship is adjusted with respect to fair value changes resulting from the hedged risk,

- Non-Financial assets and liabilities are generally stated at historical cost.

Extract 3(A2) – ABN AMRO Holding N.V., page 100

This extract cites the critical accounting policies note included in the financial statements. The company describes the uncertainties inherent in the fair value measurements of financial instruments. Note that, according to CICA 3855, investments in unquoted securities would normally be measured at cost, not at fair value, unless the entity qualified as an investment company.

Critical accounting policies

Fair value of financial instruments

For financial instruments that are actively traded and for which quoted market prices or market parameters are readily available, there is little subjectivity in the determination of fair value. However, when observable market prices and parameters do not exist, management judgement is necessary to estimate fair value.

For instruments where no active liquid market exists, or quoted prices are unobtainable, recent market transactions are used or the fair value is estimated using a variety of valuation techniques — including reference to similar instruments for which market prices do exist or valuation models, such as discounted cash flow or Black & Scholes.

The Group refines and modifies its valuation techniques as markets and products develop and the pricing for such products becomes more or less transparent. Financial markets are sometimes subject to significant stress conditions where steep falls in perceived or actual asset values are accompanied by a severe reduction in market liquidity, such as recent events in the US sub prime residential mortgage market. In such cases, observable market data may become less reliable or disappear altogether. Where there is doubt over the reliability of the market data or it is no longer available, other valuation techniques are used. These alternative techniques would incorporate proprietary information as additional input and may include scenario analysis and discounted cash flow calculations.

Unobservable inputs are estimated using a combination of management judgement, historical data, market practice and benchmarking to other relevant observable market data. Where inputs to the valuation of a new transaction cannot be reliably sourced from external providers, the transaction is initially recognised at its transaction price. The difference between the transaction price and the internal valuation at inception, calculated using a model, is reserved and amortised to income at appropriate points over the life of the instrument, typically taking account of the ability to obtain reliable external data, the passage of time and the use of offsetting transactions. Subsequent changes in fair value as calculated by the valuation model are reported in income.

Fair values include appropriate adjustments to account for known inadequacies in the valuation models or to reflect the credit quality of the instrument or counterparty. Factors that could affect estimates are incorrect model assumptions, market dislocations and unexpected correlation. We believe our estimates of fair value are adequate. However, the use of different models or assumptions could result in changes in our reported results. For a further discussion on the use of fair values and the impact of applying reasonable possible alternative assumptions as inputs, see note 37 to the consolidated financial statements.

Extract 3(A3) – ABN AMRO Holding N.V., pages 172 to 175

This is an extensive note on the fair value measurements of financial instruments. The note includes:

* details on the determination of fair values, including a table that presents amounts measured at a three-level hierarchy (which is similar to the required disclosures under SFAS 157);
* sensitivity analysis of established fair values;
* fair value option election; and
* financial assets and liabilities not carried at fair value, including a table comparing carrying amounts with fair values.

---

37 Fair value of financial instruments (in part)

Assets and liabilities carried at fair value

Financial instruments classified as held for trading, designated at fair value and available-for-sale are carried at fair value on the balance sheet. Movements in fair value are recognised in the income statement, except for those relating to available-for-sale assets for which movements are taken to equity unless an impairment loss is recognised.

Determination of fair value

Fair value is defined as the amount for which an asset could be exchanged, or a liability settled, between knowledgeable and willing parties in an arm's length transaction.

The method selected to determine fair value is based on the following order of preference:

a) For instruments traded in active liquid markets, a quoted market price is used.

b) For instruments where no active liquid market exists, a recent market transaction is used.

c) For instruments for which there is neither an active market nor a recent market transaction, then a valuation technique is used.

A financial instrument is regarded as quoted in an active market if quoted prices are readily and regularly available from an exchange, dealer, broker, industry group, pricing service or regulatory agency, and those prices represent actual and regularly occurring market transactions on an arm's length basis.

Valuation techniques are generally required for the valuation of over-the-counter derivatives, unlisted trading portfolio assets and liabilities and unlisted financial investments (including private equity investments). Valuation techniques used include comparison with similar instruments for which observable market prices exist, forward pricing and swap models, using present value calculations, option models, such as Black & Scholes, Monte Carlo and binomial models and credit models such as default rate or credit spread models. The Group refines and modifies its valuation techniques as markets and products develop and the pricing for individual products becomes more transparent.

For model valuation techniques, the use of observable market data inputs is maximised over the use of unobservable inputs. Market data inputs cover foreign exchange and interest rates, volatilities, correlations, credit spreads and prepayment rates. A number of additional factors such as bid-offer spread, counterparty risk and model uncertainty are taken into account as appropriate.

Where model inputs are considered unobservable and have more than an insignificant impact on the valuation, any gains on initial recognition are deferred on the balance sheet, as a Day 1 Profit and Loss Reserve, and amortised over the life of the instruments. The table below shows the movement in the reserve:

	2007	2006
Unamortised balance at 1 January	310	300
Deferral of profit on new transactions	170	314
Recognised in the income statement during the period:		
Subsequent to observability	(73)	(80)
Amortisation	(94)	(97)
Maturity or termination	(114)	(127)
Exchange differences	(8)	–
Unamortised balance at 31 December	**191**	310

The following table presents the valuation methods used in determining the fair values of financial instruments carried at fair value*.

	2007			
	Quoted market price[1]	Valuation techniques observable market inputs[2]	Valuation techniques unobservable inputs[3]	Total
Financial assets				
Financial assets held-for-trading	74,063	165,756	2,458	242,277
Available-for-sale interest earning securities	40,188	49,932	229	90,349
Available-for-sale equities	286	387	340	1,013
Interest earning securities designated at fair value through income	–	–	100	100
Equities designated at fair value through income	1,347	5	987	2,339
Other assets-derivatives held for hedging	–	1,068	1,396	2,464
Other assets-unit-linked investments	–	4,609	–	4,609
Other assets-mortgages designated at fair value	–	1,569	–	1,569
Total assets at fair value	115,884	223,326	5,510	344,720
Financial liabilities				
Financial liabilities held for trading	28,995	124,943	1,538	155,476
Due to customers	–	42	–	42
Issued debt securities	–	39,223	5,445	44,668
Other liabilities-derivatives held for hedging	–	673	1,298	1,971
Other liabilities-unit-linked liabilities	–	4,609	–	4,609
Subordinated liabilities	–	726		726
Total liabilities at fair value	28,995	170,216	8,281	207,492

* Financial instruments recorded in assets liabilities of business held for sale are not included in this table

1 Quoted Market Price:
 • Financial assets/liabilities valued using unadjusted quoted prices in active markets for identical assets/liabilities

2 Valuation Technique – observable market inputs:
 • Quoted price for similar assets/liabilities in an active market
 • Quoted price for identical or similar assets/liabilities in inactive markets
 • Valuation model using observable inputs
 • Valuation model using inputs derived from or corroborated by observable market data
 • Financial assets/liabilities valued with a valuation model using unobservable inputs

3 Valuation Technique – unobservable market inputs:
 • Financial assets/liabilities valued with a valuation model using unobservable inputs.

	2006			
	Quoted market price[1]	Valuation techniques observable market inputs[2]	Valuation techniques unobservable inputs[3]	Total
Financial assets				
Financial assets held-for-trading	93,813	110,440	1,483	205,736
Available for sale interest earning securities	72,829	41,063	3,666	117,558
Available for sale equities	1,313	340	213	1,866
Equities designated at fair value through income	534	951	743	2,228
Other assets-derivatives held for trading	167	3,047	–	3,214
Other assets-unit-linked investments	–	5,462		5,462
Other assets-mortgages designated at fair value	–	331	–	331
Total assets at fair value	168,656	161,634	6,105	336,395
Financial liabilities				
Financial liabilities held for trading	40,280	102,969	2,115	145,364
Issued debt securities	–	25,038	4,230	29,268
Other liabilities-derivatives held for hedging	218	3,745	2	3,965
Other liabilities-unit-linked liabilities	–	5,462	–	5,462
Total liabilities at fair value	40,498	137,214	6,347	184,059

1 Quoted Market Price:
   - Financial assets/liabilities valued using unadjusted quoted prices in active markets for identical assets/liabilities
2 Valuation Technique – observable market inputs:
   - Quoted price for similar assets/liabilities in an active market
   - Quoted price for identical or similar assets/liabilities in inactive markets
   - Valuation model using observable inputs
   - Valuation model using inputs derived from or corroborated by observable market data
3 Valuation Technique – unobservable market inputs:
   - Financial assets/liabilities valued with a valuation model using unobservable inputs

Sensitivity of fair values

Included within the fair value of financial instruments carried at fair value on the balance sheet, are those estimated in full or in part using valuation techniques based on assumptions that are not fully supported by observable market data. All valuation models undergo an internal validation process before they are certified for use, and any related model valuation uncertainty is quantified and deducted from the fair values produced by the models. Whilst management believes its valuation techniques to be appropriate and the resulting estimated fair values recorded in the balance sheet to be reasonable, the use of different methodologies or assumptions could result in different estimates of fair value at the balance sheet date. The potential effect of using reasonably possible alternative assumptions as inputs to valuation models, which are fully or in part relying on unobservable inputs, has been estimated. Using less favourable assumptions would lead to a reduction of approximately EUR 261 million (2006: EUR 157 million), whilst using more favourable assumptions would lead to an increase of approximately EUR 275 million (2006: EUR 157 million).

The total amount of the change in fair value estimated using a valuation technique with unobservable inputs that was recognised in the profit and loss account for the year 2007 amounts to EUR 419 million (2006: EUR 1,516 million).

Financial assets and liabilities not carried at fair value

The following methods and significant assumptions have been applied to estimate the fair values of financial instruments carried at cost:

(i) The fair value of variable rate financial instruments and those of a fixed rate nature maturing within 6 months of the balance sheet date are assumed to approximate their carrying amounts. In the case of such loans, the fair value estimate does not reflect changes in credit quality, as the main impact of credit risk is already recognised separately through the deduction the allowances for credit losses from the carrying amounts.

(ii) The fair value of fixed rate loans and mortgages carried at amortised cost is estimated by comparing market interest rates when the loans were granted with current market rates offered on similar loans. Changes in the specific credit quality of loans within the portfolio are not taken into account in determining fair values, as the main impact of credit risk is already recognised separately through the deduction of the allowances for credit losses from the carrying amounts.

(iii) The fair value of demand deposits and savings accounts (included in due to customers) with no specific maturity is assumed to be the amount payable on demand at the balance sheet date.

The following table compares the carrying amount of financial assets and liabilities recorded at amortised cost to their estimated fair values:

	2007			2006		
	Carrying amount	Fair value	Difference	Carrying amount	Fair value	Difference
Financial assets						
Cash and balances at central banks	16,750	16,750	–	12,317	12,317	–
Interest earning securities HTM	2,634	2,599	(35)	3,729	3,763	34
Loans and receivables – banks	175,696	175,680	(16)	134,819	134,819	–
Loans and receivables – customers	396,762	393,574	(3,188)	443,255	446,589	3,334
Total	**591,842**	**588,603**	**(3,239)**	594,120	597,488	3,368
Financial liabilities						
Due to banks	239,334	239,334	–	187,989	187,982	(7)
Due to customers	330,310	330,228	(82)	362,383	362,303	(80)
Issued debt securities	130,327	129,636	(691)	172,778	171,803	(975)
Subordinated liabilities	14,890	13,695	(1,195)	19,213	19,364	151
Total	**714,861**	**712,893**	**(1,968)**	742,363	741,452	(911)

PLANNING FOR IMPLEMENTATION

The fair value "revolution" seems to be unstoppable. Fair value reporting is aimed at allowing users of financial statements to better assess an entity's performance. That assessment could, however, be clouded by the fact that reported amounts might be highly uncertain. When assets and liabilities are traded, their amounts can be observed and a fair value can be measured independently. When these assets and liabilities are not traded, however, users of financial statements must rely on a number of estimates made by management.

Many Canadian standards already require fair value measurements. Hence, the convergence to IFRS might not represent a new undertaking for most Canadian companies, although the increased fair value emphasis under IFRS might require making some adjustments. This section discusses IFRS implementation considerations related to fair value accounting.

Impact on Financial Statements

As discussed previously, IFRS calls for more fair value measurements than Canadian GAAP does. This will result in greater volatilities in reported earnings and equities.

Hence, performance measurement and disclosure have to address the additional volatility concerns.

Fair values are estimated at a specific date, using the available information and according to specific market conditions and expectations. Because these factors vary over time, the value estimated for one date may be inappropriate for another. Consequently, companies will face a greater challenge in explaining the uncertainties related to fair value measurements and the fact that changes in fair value do not indicate that the expectations were incorrect when the estimate was made but, rather, that they have changed.

Fair value measurements increase management involvement in establishing reported amounts. This could result in biased information and lack of comparability with the results obtained by other companies. To compensate for this potential reporting weakness, IFRS requires greater transparency in the disclosure of details on fair value measurement. Below is an extract that illustrates disclosures of uncertainties that might be adapted to particular circumstances:

Extract 3(13) – Informing users about limitations

> **Air France - KLM S.A. (Reference Document 2006-07), page 166**
> **Note 32 Financial instruments**
> **32.2. Market value of financial instruments (in part)**
> Market values are estimated for most of the Group's financial instruments using a variety of valuation methods, such as discounted future cash flows. However, the methods and assumptions used to provide the information set out below are theoretical in nature. They bear the following inherent limitations:
> - market values cannot take into consideration the effect of subsequent fluctuations in interest or exchange rates;
> - estimated amounts as of March 31, 2007, 2006 and 2005 are not indicative of gains and/or losses arising upon maturity or in the event of cancellation of a financial instrument.

Generating New Data and Optimizing Information Systems

Since IFRS require more fair value accounting than does Canadian GAAP, it is possible that management will require new data and reports that corporate information systems do not currently generate. These systems have to be retooled to provide the data and information management needs to:

- ensure that techniques used to estimate fair value are appropriate and consistent with economic methodologies and financial theory;
- obtain pertinent observable market data that a company should take into account;
- adjust and calibrate valuation models to ensure robustness of results; and
- document supporting fair value estimates that would include the justification of the chosen valuation method and sensitivity analysis when fair value amounts can vary significantly depending on the parameters selected.

Initial Adoption of IFRS

Generally, IFRS 1 requires that international standards be adopted retrospectively, as though an entity had always reported under IFRS. In preparing an opening balance sheet, entities will generally need to derecognize from the balance sheet all assets and liabilities not satisfying IFRS recognition criteria and recognize those that do.

On transition to IFRS, when initially measuring the recognized items, entities have to consider the available "relief" provisions. These provisions allow them to make certain elections that could change significantly the amounts reported on the opening balance sheet.

For example, an entity may elect, on transition, to measure certain fixed assets at fair value. This election is separate from the accounting policy choice under IAS 16 (i.e., the company does not have to measure the fixed asset using the revaluation model). Note that measuring fixed assets at fair value on transition (which would be their deemed cost) will have the following impact:

- post-conversion depreciation expense will be higher since it is calculated on a higher fair value amount;
- it will not be necessary for an entity to undertake the onerous task of reconstructing an asset's cost base under IFRS, including the requirements to apply component accounting.

Before making such an election, entities should determine whether the benefit of saving some effort on transition is worth the impact of higher depreciation on future reported earnings.

Selecting Accounting Policies

IFRS explicitly provide more fair value measurement options than Canadian GAAP. This creates a unique opportunity for management to select accounting policies that could potentially recast an entity's balance sheet. For example, a move to fair value revaluation for some balance sheet fixed assets may improve an entity's financial position. Should that happen, management will have to weigh this improvement against the impact of increased earnings volatility, higher depreciation expenses and increased costs related to the periodical revaluation of the fixed asset.

Keep Posted

The IASB Discussion Paper issued in 2006 *Fair Value Measurements* will eventually lead to the issuance of a new IFRS standard. If this standard is aligned with SFAS 157, it will result in a more precise definition of fair value and additional guidance for valuing hard-to-measure assets and liabilities, such as intangibles. In addition, new disclosures will be required to highlight the reliability of fair value measurements.

Chapter 4
Impairment of Assets[1]

Standards Discussed in this Chapter

International

IAS 28 – Investments in associates
IAS 36 – Impairment of assets
IFRS 6 – Exploration for and evaluation of mineral resources
IFRIC 10 – Interim financial reporting and impairment

Canadian

CICA 3051 – Investments
CICA 3063 – Impairment of long-lived assets
CICA 3064 – Intangible assets
CICA 3475 – Disposal of long-lived assets and discontinued operations

INTRODUCTION

IFRS (IAS 36) and Canadian GAAP (CICA 3063 and CICA 3064) promulgate similar principles for the recognition of impairment losses for non-financial assets. Both require:

*   entities to assess whether there is any indication that a non-financial asset may be impaired. If there is such an indication, they must carry out an impairment test and, if necessary, record a loss.

*   irrespective of whether there is any indication of impairment, entities must annually assess the impairment of any intangible assets having an indefinite useful life as well as goodwill.

Even though Canadian GAAP and IFRS espouse similar impairment principles, they differ on their application:

*   *Level at which impairment testing is performed*: IAS 36 and CICA 3063/3064 use different terminology and concepts when it is not possible to assess the impairment of an individual asset:

    o   IAS 36 requires that assets other than goodwill be tested at the lowest cash generating unit (CGU) as defined by the standard. CICA 3063 and 3064 requirements are similar except that they refer to an asset group instead of a CGU.

    o   IAS 36 requires that goodwill be allocated and tested for impairment at the lowest level at which it is managed internally (which could consist of individual CGUs or multiple CGUs). CICA 3064 requirements are similar except that it refers to the reporting unit instead of a CGU or multiple CGUs.

---

1   This chapter covers the impairment of assets covered by IAS 36 which essentially applies to the impairment of non-financial assets such as fixed assets and goodwill, although it also covers impairment issues related to investments not within the scope of IAS 39, *Financial instruments: recognition and measurement*, such as investments in associates (see scope).

- *Approaches for testing impairment*: IAS 36 uses a one-step approach for all assets, whereas Canadian GAAP requires a two-step approach for:
  o long-term tangible and intangible assets other than those with indefinite lives (CICA 3063), and
  o goodwill (CICA 3064).
- *Measuring impairment loss*: IAS 36 measures impairment loss as the excess of an asset's (CGU or group of CGUs) carrying amount over its "recoverable amount" (defined as the higher of fair value less costs to sell and value in use). CICA 3063 and 3064 differ by requiring that impairment loss be measured as the excess of an asset's (asset group or reporting unit) carrying amount over its fair value.
- *Reversal of impairment losses*: IAS 36 requires any impairment reversal to be recognized for all non-financial assets where estimates used to determine the recoverable amount have changed except for goodwill where reversals of impairment losses are prohibited. CICA 3051, CICA 3063 and CICA 3064 prohibit such impairment reversals.

To understand the magnitude of the differences between IAS 36 and the related CICA 3063 and 3064, this chapter discusses the following issues:

- scope;
- key definitions;
- basic principles;
- testing impairment:
  o frequency,
  o indicators of impairment,
  o relief from impairment test,
  o procedures for carrying out impairment tests,
  o timing;
- identifying CGU for assets other than goodwill:
  o aggregation of individual assets,
  o factors used for identifying CGU,
  o changes in CGU,
  o allocating corporate assets to CGU;
- allocating goodwill to CGU or group of CGU;
- valuation issues under IAS 36:
  o basic principle,
  o value in use (VIU),
  o fair value less costs to sell (FVLCS),
  o disclosures;
- reporting impairment losses:
  o categories of non-financial assets,
  o general disclosures;
- impairment loss reversals:
  o requirements,
  o general disclosures;

- special considerations:
  - o testing goodwill impairment in the year of acquisition,
  - o VIU established on the basis of foreign currency cash flows,
  - o VIU and foreign currency cash flows,
  - o interim reporting,
  - o reclassification as held for sale,
  - o investments in subsidiaries, associates, and joint ventures,
  - o extractive industry.

IMPACT ON FINANCIAL STATEMENTS

Even though there is an agreement on the principle of writing down non-financial assets when their carrying amounts are not expected to be recovered, the procedures for measuring and reporting such impairment differ under IFRS and Canadian standards. The impact of these differences will depend on the circumstances. For example, net income established under Canadian GAAP could decrease on IFRS adoption due to greater impairments if the CGU under IAS 36 aggregates fewer individual assets than the corresponding group of assets under CICA 3063. The decrease would result from a lower asset aggregation under IFRS which reduces the possibility of offsetting impairment losses on an individual asset with unrealized gains on another asset.

Even though the impact of IAS 36 adoption on Canadian GAAP financial statements can vary, two outcomes are expected to occur:

- net income will decrease when indications of impairment are observed. This is because IAS 36 requires the use of a one-step impairment approach while CICA 3063 requires a two-step approach. Under the latter, an entity would not write down an asset to its recoverable value (IAS 36) or fair value (CICA 3063) if the undiscounted cash flows it generates exceeds its carrying amount;

- earnings and net assets will be more volatile because IAS 36 requires a reversal of impairment losses for all non-financial assets except goodwill, whereas CICA 3051, 3063 and 3064 prohibit the reversal of such losses.

ANALYSIS OF RELEVANT ISSUES

This section discusses and illustrates IAS 36 requirements and some other related IFRS guidance, comparing them to the more significant Canadian requirements.

Scope

IAS 36 prescribes the accounting and disclosure for the impairment of all non-financial assets unless they are specifically excluded and of some financial assets not covered by IAS 39.

The assets scoped out of IAS 36 are:

- inventories (IAS 2, *Inventories*);
- assets related to construction contracts (IAS 11, *Construction contracts*);
- deferred tax assets (IAS 12, *Income taxes*);
- assets related to employee benefits (IAS 19, *Employee benefits*);
- financial assets within the scope of IAS 39, *Financial Instruments: recognition and measurement;*

- investment property carried at fair value under IAS 40, *Investment property;*
- biological assets measured at fair value less estimated costs to sell (IAS 41, *Agriculture*);
- deferred acquisition costs and intangible assets within the scope of IFRS 4, *Insurance contracts;*
- assets held for sale within the scope of IFRS 5, *Non-current assets held for sale and discontinued operations.*

Based on the above exclusions, the following would be within the scope of IAS 36:

- property, plant and equipment (IAS 16, *Property, plant and equipment*);
- intangible assets (IAS 38, *Intangible assets*);
- goodwill (IFRS 3, *Business combinations* and IAS 38, *Intangible assets*);
- investment property and biological assets carried at cost less accumulated depreciation (IAS 40 and IAS 41, respectively);
- investments in subsidiaries, associates and joint ventures (IAS 28, *Investments in associates*);
- mineral resources (IFRS 6) (note that IFRS 6 provides some different treatments for assets in the exploration and evaluation phases).

Under Canadian GAAP:

- CICA 3063 applies to non-monetary, long-lived assets, including property, plant and equipment, as well as to intangible assets with finite useful lives;
- CICA 3064 prescribes standards for impairment of goodwill and indefinite life intangible assets;
- CICA 3051, *Investments* provides recognition requirements for losses in the value of an investment in associates;
- CICA 4211, *Life insurance enterprises — specific items* provides specific guidance on the decline in the value of portfolios held by a life insurance enterprise.

Illustrative Disclosures:

Extract 4(1) – General accounting policy related to impairment

> **AMG Advanced Metallurgical Group N.V. (AR 2007) page 60**
>
> **3. Significant accounting policies (in part)**
>
> **(j) Impairment (in part)**
>
> **(i) Financial assets (in part)**
>
> A financial asset is considered to be impaired if objective evidence indicates that one or more events have had a negative effect on the estimated future cash flows of that asset. Financial assets are assessed collectively in groups that share similar credit risk characteristics.
>
> **(ii) Non-financial assets (in part)**
>
> The carrying amounts of the Company's non-financial assets, other than inventories and deferred tax assets, are reviewed at each reporting date to determine whether there is any indication of impairment. If any such indication exists, then the asset's recoverable amount is estimated.
>
> For goodwill and intangible assets that have indefinite lives or that are not yet available for use, the recoverable amount is estimated at each reporting date.
>
> **(iii) Associates (in part)**
>
> After application of the equity method, the Company determines whether it is necessary to recognize an additional impairment loss of the Company's investment in its associates. The Company determines at each balance sheet date whether there is any objective evidence that an investment in an associate is impaired.

Commentary: In the above extract, the company provides a note on the frequency of impairment testing for financial assets (as scoped in IAS 39), for non-financial assets (as covered by IAS 36) and for investments in associates (also covered by IAS 36). Under Canadian GAAP, the following would apply:

- CICA 3855, *Financial instruments: recognition and measurement* to financial assets;
- CICA 3063 and CICA 3064 to non-financial assets; and
- CICA 3051 to investments in associates.

Extract 4(2) – General accounting policy related to impairment

Auspine Limited (AR 2007) page 23

j) Impairment (in part)

i) Financial assets (in part)

A financial asset is considered to be impaired if objective evidence indicates that one or more events have had a negative impact on the estimated future cash flows of that asset. ...

Individually significant financial assets are tested for impairment on an individual basis. The remaining financial assets are assessed collectively in groups that share similar credit risk characteristics. ...

An impairment loss is reversed if the reversal can be related objectively to an event occurring after the impairment loss was recognised. ...

ii) Non-financial assets (in part)

The carrying amounts of the Group's non-financial assets, other than biological assets, investment property, inventories and deferred taxes, are reviewed at each reporting date to determine whether there is any indication of impairment. If any such indication exists then the asset's recoverable amount is estimated. For goodwill and intangible assets that have indefinite lives or that are not yet available for use, recoverable amount is estimated at each reporting date.

An impairment loss is recognised if the carrying amount of an asset or its cash-generating unit exceeds its recoverable amount. A cash-generating unit is the smallest identifiable asset group that generates cash flows that largely are independent from other assets and groups. ...

An impairment loss in respect of goodwill is not reversed. In respect of other assets, impairment losses recognised in prior periods are assessed at each reporting date for any indications that the loss has decreased or no longer exists. An impairment loss is reversed only to the extent that the asset's carrying amount does not exceed the carrying amount that would have been determined, net of depreciation or amortisation, if no impairment loss had been recognised.

Commentary: Here, the company discloses the level of asset aggregation for impairment testing purposes and when impairment/reversals are recorded. Accordingly:

- as required by IAS 39, financial assets are considered to be impaired if objective evidence indicates that one or more events have had a negative impact on the estimated future cash flows of those assets. Impairment is tested individually for significant financial assets. Otherwise, they are tested collectively by grouping assets having similar credit risk characteristics;

- as required by IAS 36, non-financial assets (other than biological assets, investment property, inventories and deferred taxes) are reviewed at each reporting date to determine whether there is any indication of impairment. If there is, the particular asset's recoverable amount is estimated. For goodwill and intangible assets that have indefinite lives or that are not yet available for use, the recoverable amount is estimated at each reporting date. An impairment loss recognized for goodwill is not reversed. For other assets, impairment losses recognized in prior periods are assessed at each reporting date for any indications that the loss has decreased or no longer exists.

The corresponding standards under Canadian GAAP are:

- CICA 3855 for financial assets; and
- CICA 3063 and 3064 for non-financial assets (note that these standards prohibit reversals of impairment losses).

Key Definitions

IAS 36 provides the following key definitions:

- *Impairment*: An asset or a cash-generating unit is impaired when its carrying amount exceeds its recoverable amount.

- *Carrying amount*: The amount at which an asset is recognized on the balance sheet after deducting accumulated depreciation and accumulated impairment losses.

- *Fair value*: The amount obtainable from the sale of an asset or a cash-generating unit in an arm's length transaction between knowledgeable, willing parties.

- *Recoverable amount*: The higher of an asset's or a cash-generating unit's fair value less costs to sell (sometimes called net selling price) and its value in use.

- *Value in use (VIU)*: The discounted present value of estimated future cash flows expected to arise from the continuing use of an asset or a cash-generating unit and from its disposal at the end of its useful life.

- *Fair value less costs to sell (FVLCS)*: The amount obtainable from the sale of an asset or cash-generating unit in an arm's length transaction between knowledgeable, willing parties, less the costs of disposal.

- *Cash-generating unit (CGU)*: The smallest identifiable group of assets that generates cash inflows largely independently of the cash inflows from other assets or groups of assets.

- *Corporate assets*: Assets other than goodwill that contribute to the future cash flows of both the cash-generating unit under review and other cash-generating units.

IAS 36 adds a measurement perspective with its use of recoverable amount than is not contemplated in Canadian GAAP. Instead the latter refer to fair value as a benchmark for impairment. Note that recoverable amount is a proxy of fair value. It is, in fact, an impairment value measure, not a fair value one.

VIU could equal fair value (although, conceptually, VIU might reflect entity-specific assumptions while fair value reflects marketplace participant assumptions). FVLCS is equivalent to "net realizable value" and requires the use of marketplace participant assumptions. It is generally used in the context of inventories valuation.

The IASB "Annual Improvements" adopted in 2008 introduced minor and non-urgent changes effective for periods starting January 1, 2009. One of the amendments concerns terminology. To improve consistency between IAS 16, IFRS 5 and IAS 36, it replaces the term "net selling price" in IAS 16 with "fair value less costs to sell."

IAS 36 uses the concept of CGU as a basis for testing the impairment of non-financial assets. Corporate assets are also allocated to and tested for impairment at the CGU level. Depending on circumstances, goodwill could be tested for impairment at an individual CGU level or at a multiple CGU level.

Even though Canadian GAAP has somewhat similar asset grouping requirements, it uses different terminology and perspectives:

- CICA 3063 refers to an "asset group" (for all non-financial assets except goodwill); and

- CICA 3064 refers to "reporting unit" (for goodwill).

An asset group could represent a CGU and a reporting unit could represent a CGU or a group of CGUs (see discussions later).

For the purposes of comparison, the following definitions are provided in the two *Handbook* sections:

Asset group (CICA 3063): The lowest level (smallest combination) of assets and liabilities for which identifiable cash flows are largely independent of the cash flows of other assets or groups of assets and liabilities.

Reporting unit (CICA 3064): The level of reporting at which goodwill is tested for impairment and is either an operating segment (as defined in CICA 1701, *Segment disclosures*) or one level below (referred to as a component). A component of an operating segment is a reporting unit when the component constitutes a business for which discrete financial information is available and segment management regularly reviews the operating results of that component. (Segment management consists of one or more segment managers, as that term is defined in CICA 1701.) Two or more components of an operating segment are aggregated and deemed a single reporting unit when the components have similar economic characteristics. An operating segment is deemed to be a reporting unit when all of its components are similar, when none of its components is a reporting unit or when it comprises only a single component.

Illustrative Disclosures:

Extract 4(3) – Key definitions provided in general accounting policy on impairment

> **Flaga Group hf. (Consolidated Financial Statements 2007) page 15**
> **3. Significant accounting policies (in part)**
> *h. Impairment* (in part)
> *ii) Non financial assets* (in part)
> The recoverable amount of an asset or cash-generating unit is the greater of its value in use and its fair value less costs to sell. In assessing value in use, the estimated future cash flows are discounted to their present value using a pre-tax discount rate that reflects current market assessments of the time value of money and the risks specific to the asset. For the purpose of impairment testing, assets are grouped together into the smallest group of assets that generates cash inflows from continuing use that are largely independent of the cash inflows of other assets or groups of assets (the "cash-generating unit"). The goodwill acquired in a business combination, for the purpose of impairment testing, is allocated to cash-generating units that are expected to benefit from the synergies of the combination.

Commentary: The above extract defines recoverable amount and CGU. It also specifies how the company calculates VIU. Such concepts do not exist under Canadian GAAP.

Basic Principles

IAS 36 aims to ensure that non-financial assets are not carried on the balance sheet at more than their recoverable amount. When required, an impairment review is performed. It involves estimating an asset's recoverable amount and comparing it with its carrying value. If the recoverable amount is lower than the carrying value, the asset is impaired and must be written down to the recoverable amount. Unlike with certain financial assets, impairment cannot be avoided by arguing that the diminution in the value of an asset is temporary.

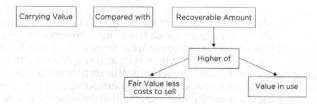

IAS 36 says that impairment of non-financial assets or CGUs is established depending on their recoverable amount, which is defined as the higher of FVLCS and VIU. Even though this definition suggests that both FVLCS and VIU must be calculated, it is not always necessary to do so. If either FVLCS or VIU exceeds the asset's or CGU's carrying amount, no impairment is recorded and it is not necessary to estimate the other amount. Moreover, if FV is greater than the carrying amount there is no need to calculate the VIU which normally requires more complex calculation.

Canadian GAAP does not use the same concept to measure recoverable amounts. Fair value is the only benchmark for measuring recoverable amounts once the impairment loss calculations have been triggered.

Where possible, assets should be tested for impairment at the individual asset level. Many assets do not generate cash inflows independently from other assets, however. In these cases, IAS 36 requires that the determination of the cash flows necessary to compute the VIU calculation be performed at the CGU level (and, possibly, at multiple CGU level for goodwill) to which the asset belongs or can be allocated.

The same principle applies under Canadian GAAP except that those principles use:

- a different grouping of assets when required for testing impairment;
- fair value as a basis of impairment measurement; and
- two-step impairment tests are used for goodwill, tangible assets and intangible assets of definite life instead of the one step impairment tests used in IAS 36.

Illustrative Disclosures:

Extract 4(4) – General accounting policy presenting an overview of IAS 36 requirements

---

Xstrata plc (AR 2007) page 151

6. Principal Accounting Policies (in part)

Impairment of assets

The carrying amounts of non-current assets are reviewed for impairment whenever events or changes in circumstances indicate the carrying amounts may not be recoverable. If there are indicators of impairment, a review is undertaken to determine whether the carrying amounts are in excess of their recoverable amounts. An asset's recoverable amount is determined as the higher of its fair value less costs to sell and its value in use. Such reviews are undertaken on an asset by asset basis, except where assets do not generate cash flows independent of other assets, in which case the review is undertaken at the cash-generating unit level.

Where a cash-generating unit, or group of cash-generating units, has goodwill allocated to it (excluding goodwill recognised as a result of the requirement to recognise deferred tax liabilities on acquisitions), or includes intangible assets which are either not available for use or which have an indefinite useful life (and which can only be tested as part of a cash-generating unit), an impairment test is performed at least annually or whenever there is an indication that the carrying amounts of such assets may be impaired.

If the carrying amount of an asset exceeds its recoverable amount, an impairment loss is recorded in the income statement to reflect the asset at the lower amount. In assessing the recoverable amount of assets, the relevant future cash flows expected to arise from the continuing use of such assets and from their disposal are discounted to their present value using a market-determined pre-tax discount rate which reflects current market assessments of the time value of money and asset-specific risks for which the cash flow estimates have not been adjusted.

An impairment loss is reversed in the income statement if there is a change in the estimates used to determine the recoverable amount since the prior impairment loss was recognised. The carrying amount is increased to the recoverable amount but not beyond the carrying amount net of depreciation or amortisation which would have arisen if the prior impairment loss had not been recognised. After such a reversal the depreciation charge is adjusted in future periods to allocate the asset's revised carrying amount, less any residual value, on a systematic basis over its remaining useful life. Goodwill impairments are not reversed.

Commentary: In the above extract, the company presents an overview of IAS 36 in its accounting policy note. Canadian GAAP differs (from IAS 36) on the following issues:

- fair value is used instead of recoverable amount;
- asset groups and reporting units (for goodwill) are used instead of CGUs or groups of CGUs (when applicable for goodwill).

Testing Impairment

Frequency

Both Canadian and IFRS standards have distinct requirements for how often impairment testing is to take place, depending on the type of non-financial assets held. The table below summarizes these requirements. However, even in the cases where there is no specific requirement for testing impairment annually (or more frequently), an entity shall at minimum assess at the end of each reporting period whether there is any indication that an asset covered by IAS 36 (as described in the table) may be impaired.

Frequency of Impairment Testing		
Type of Asset	IAS 36	CICA 3063/3064
Indefinite-life intangible assets (i.e., intangible assets not subject to amortization)	Annual testing of impairment (at the same time every year) or more frequently whether or not there is any indication that an asset may be impaired (relief available – see below)	Same as IAS 36 (no relief – see below)
Definite-life intangible assets not available for use (i.e., intangible assets not subject to amortization)	Annual testing of impairment (or more frequently but at the same time every year) whether or not there is any indication that an asset may be impaired	Whenever events or changes in circumstances indicate that asset's carrying amount may not be recoverable (i.e., there is no requirement to perform an annual test of impairment)
Goodwill	Annual testing of impairment (at the same time every year) or more frequently whenever there is an indication that the CGU or group of CGUs may be impaired ** (relief available – see below)	Annual testing of impairment (or more frequently whenever it is indicated that the reporting unit may be impaired ** (no relief – see below)
Property, plant and equipment and amortizable intangible assets	Indicators of impairment are assessed at every reporting period. When indicators of impairment exist, the carrying amount is compared with the recoverable amount	Testing of impairment when events or changes in circumstances indicate that its carrying amount may not be recoverable *

* Differences with IAS 36 might occur because indicators of impairment are assessed in relation to asset groupings that might differ from CGUs.

** If goodwill allocated to a CGU (IAS 36) or reporting unit (CICA 3064) resulted from a business combination during the current annual period, that unit must be tested for impairment before the end of the current annual period.

Note also that:

- an indication that an asset may be impaired might require a review of estimates related to asset's useful life, depreciation method or residual value;
- as the above table shows:
  - an intangible asset not yet available for use is tested for impairment differently under IFRS and Canadian GAAP;
    - IAS 36 requires an annual testing as for goodwill and intangible assets with an indefinite useful life,

- • CICA 3063 requires the same impairment testing as for property, plant and equipment and amortizable intangible assets;

  o IAS 36 provides relief from the annual impairment test for all intangible assets with an indefinite life. Conditions are the same as for goodwill (see discussion in the section "Relief from impairment test" here below). No such relief exists under Canadian GAAP.

Indicators of Impairment

One important element of all impairment testing is the determination of whether there is any indication that an asset may be impaired, which is required to be done at each reporting period for all types of assets covered by IAS 36. Indicators of impairment can be found in the external environment in which an entity operates or in the entity's own operating environment. IAS 36 (CICA 3063) lists some examples of impairment indicators (not exhaustive):

- • external indicators or sources might include:
  o a significant decline in the asset's market value,
  o adverse changes in technology, the market, the economic or legal environment,
  o increases in market interest rates, and
  o the carrying amount of the entity's net assets exceeds its market capitalization (i.e., company stock price is below book value);
- • internal indicators or sources could include:
  o evidence of obsolescence or physical damage,
  o asset is part of a restructuring or held for disposal,
  o plans to discontinue use of the asset or to dispose of it, and
  o evidence that the asset is performing less well than expected.

Relief from Impairment Test

Both IAS 36 and CICA 3064 state that entities do not need to perform an annual impairment test on goodwill, meaning that they may use the most recent previous calculation of recoverable amounts (IAS 36) or fair value (CICA 3064) if:

- • there were no significant changes in the CGU or group of CGUs (reporting unit for CICA 3064) that the goodwill belongs to;
- • calculated recoverable amount (fair value for CICA 3064) substantially exceeded the asset's carrying amount; and
- • there is only a remote chance that the recoverable amount (fair value for CICA 3064) calculation would be less than the asset's carrying amount.

In addition, as noted before, IAS 36 provides equivalent relief from the annual impairment test for all intangible assets with an indefinite life. Conditions are the same as for goodwill. This relief is not available under Canadian GAAP.

Procedures for Carrying Out Impairment Tests

IAS 36 requires that all assets be tested using a one-step impairment test. According to Canadian GAAP, a one-step or a two-step impairment test might be required depending on the type of non-financial asset involved. When a test is carried out for a group of assets, both international and Canadian standards could require an allocation of impairment loss. The table below summarizes the requirements under IAS 36 and CICA 3063/3064.

Procedures for Carrying Out Impairment Tests		
Type of Asset	IAS 36	CICA 3063/3064
Indefinite life intangible assets	One-step impairment test whereby the asset's carrying value is compared with its recoverable amount. If the former is higher, the entity records an impairment loss (equal to the difference between the carrying value and recoverable amount).	Same as IAS 36 except that the asset's carrying value is compared with its fair value. If the former is higher, the entity records an impairment loss (equal to the difference between the carrying value and fair value).
Definite-life intangible assets not available for use	One-step impairment test whereby the asset's carrying value is compared with its recoverable amount. If the former is higher, the entity records an impairment loss (equal to the difference between the carrying value and recoverable amount).	Two-step impairment test: (1) compare carrying value of the asset with the expected undiscounted cash flow; (2) if the carrying value is higher than the undiscounted cash flow, calculate fair value and record impairment loss (equal to the difference between the carrying value and fair value).
Goodwill	Impairment test is performed at the CGU or group of CGUs level that includes allocated goodwill (group of CGUs cannot be larger than a segment based on the entity's primary or secondary reporting format determined in accordance with IFRS 8, *Operating segments*). One-step impairment test: compare recoverable amount of CGU (to which goodwill was allocated) to its carrying amount. If the carrying value exceeds the recoverable amount, recognize an impairment loss.	Goodwill is tested for impairment at a reporting unit level, defined to be an operating segment or one level below (a component). A component is used where discrete financial information is available and regularly reviewed by management**. Two-step impairment process: (1) compare the carrying value of the reporting unit with its fair value; (2) if the carrying value is higher, calculate implied fair value of goodwill (which equals the goodwill that would be obtained if the reporting unit was acquired in a current business combination, i.e., it is the residual after subtracting the fair value of net identifiable net assets from the fair value of the reporting unit) and recognize impairment loss if implied fair value of goodwill is lower than its carrying value.
Property, plant and equipment and amortizable intangible assets	Impairment test is performed at an individual asset level. If this cannot be done, the test is performed at the lowest CGU level. As indicated previously, CGUs are identified on the basis of cash inflows and may also include a portion of goodwill and corporate assets. One-step impairment test whereby the asset's carrying value is compared with its recoverable amount. If the former exceeds the latter, the asset must be written down to its recoverable amount.	Impairment test is performed at the individual asset or asset group level (i.e., the lowest level of assets and liabilities for which cash inflows less related cash out flows are identifiable and independent). * Two-step impairment test: (1) compare carrying value of the asset group with the expected undiscounted cash flow; (2) if the carrying value is higher than the undiscounted cash flow, calculate fair value and record impairment loss (equal to the difference between the carrying value and the fair value).

* Asset group might correspond to CGU or differ, depending on operations and circumstances.
** Individual CGUs might be less aggregated than reporting units.

Timing

Annual impairment tests may be performed at any time during the financial year, provided that the testing is performed at the same moment in time in subsequent periods. Different intangible assets (i.e., those with an indefinite useful life or not yet available for use) and goodwill (or their respective CGUs) may be tested at different dates of the year.

The advantages of performing impairment testing before year end include:

- more resources might be available to complete the tests;
- it is possible to align tests with the budgeting process, which would generate data useful for establishing recoverable amounts;
- it permits planning the communication process related to a write down prior to year end.

The main disadvantage of performing an impairment test before the year end is that the test might need to be repeated (for example, if there is subsequent indication of further impairment).

Where individual assets within a CGU may be impaired, individual assets should be tested before testing the CGU. Similarly, where there is an indication that CGUs within a group of CGUs may be impaired, individual CGUs should be tested for impairment before the group of CGUs. Where goodwill has been allocated to a CGU (or group of CGUs) this is even more important so that any losses identified within specific asset (or CGU) are not offset in aggregating all assets (CGU) in the CGU (group of CGUs).

Illustrative Disclosures:

All the extracts presented below illustrate impairment testing which reflect the following significant differences between IAS 36 and Canadian GAAP:

- IAS 36 requires that the related CGU be tested when impairment test cannot be performed at the individual asset level. This differs from Canadian GAAP, which requires that:
    - o indefinite-life intangible assets always be tested for impairment for each asset individually,
    - o other assets be tested for impairment in asset groups when impairment cannot be performed at the individual asset level,
    - o goodwill always be tested for impairment at the reporting unit level, which may differ from the CGU level.
- IAS 36 requires that an impairment loss be recognized if an asset's (CGU) carrying amount exceeds its recoverable amount. According to Canadian GAAP:
    - o Assets or asset groups (other than for indefinite-life intangible assets and goodwill) are first assessed to establish if an impairment exists based on whether the asset's (asset group's) carrying amount exceeds the expected undiscounted future cash flows of the asset (asset group). If impairment exists, then the impairment loss is measured based on the excess of carrying amount over the fair value of the asset (asset group).
    - o For indefinite-life intangible assets, an impairment loss is assessed based on whether an asset's carrying amount exceeds its fair value and, if so, the impairment loss is measured as this excess.
    - o Goodwill is tested for impairment by comparing the carrying amount of the reporting unit(s) to which it is allocated, i.e., including the allocated goodwill, to

the fair value of the reporting unit(s). If the fair value is less than the carrying amount of the reporting unit(s), an impairment loss is calculated.

These differences are not pointed out in the commentary that follows because they will be repetitive.

On the other hand, some aspects of testing impairments under IAS 36 are quite similar to Canadian GAAP. These include indicators of impairment, as well as relief from impairment testing and timing. We will point out some of these similarities in the commentary that follows.

Also note that the disclosures related to the business combinations do not reflect IFRS 3 as revised in 2008 since it is effective only for acquisitions that occur during the first annual reporting period beginning on or after July 1, 2009.

Extract 4(5) – General disclosures related to non-financial assets impairment testing

---

InterContinental Hotels Group PLC (AR 2007) page 53

Summary of significant accounting policies (in part)

Property, plant and equipment (in part)

Property, plant and equipment are reviewed for impairment when events or changes in circumstances indicate that the carrying value may not be recoverable. Assets that do not generate independent cash flows are combined into cash-generating units. If carrying values exceed estimated recoverable amount, the assets or cash-generating units are written down to their recoverable amount. Recoverable amount is the greater of fair value less cost to sell and value in use. Value in use is assessed based on estimated future cash flows discounted to their present value using a pre-tax discount rate that reflects current market assessments of the time value of money and the risks specific to the asset.

Goodwill

Goodwill arises on consolidation and is recorded at cost, being the excess of the cost of acquisition over the fair value at the date of acquisition of the Group's share of identifiable assets, liabilities and contingent liabilities. Following initial recognition, goodwill is measured at cost less any accumulated impairment losses.

Goodwill is tested for impairment at least annually by comparing carrying values of cash-generating units with their recoverable amounts.

Intangible assets (in part)

Other intangible assets

Amounts paid to hotel owners to secure management contracts and franchise agreements are capitalised and amortised over the shorter of the contracted period and 10 years on a straightline basis.

Internally generated development costs are expensed unless forecast revenues exceed attributable forecast development costs, at which time they are capitalised and amortised over the life of the asset.

Intangible assets are reviewed for impairment when events or changes in circumstances indicate that the carrying value may not be recoverable.

Commentary: In this extract, the company describes, in general terms, its impairment testing for:

- property, plant and equipment;
- goodwill; and
- other amortizable intangible assets (consisting of amounts paid to hotel owners to secure management contracts franchise agreements).

Extract 4(6) - Timing of goodwill impairment test

Telefonaktiebolaget LM Ericsson (AR on Form 20-F 2007) pages 41 and 42

C1 Significant Accounting Policies (in part)

Business combinations

At the acquisition of a business, an allocation is made of the cost of the business combination in which fair values are assigned to acquired assets, liabilities and contingent liabilities, for example intangible assets such as customer relations, brands and patents, based upon appraisals made. Goodwill arises when the purchase price exceeds the fair value of recognizable acquired net assets.

As from the acquisition date, goodwill acquired in a business combination is allocated to each of the cash-generating units, or groups of cash-generating units, that are expected to benefit from the synergies of the combination. Corporate assets are allocated to cash-generating units in proportion to each unit's proportion of net sales. An annual impairment test for the cash-generating units to which goodwill has been allocated is performed in the fourth quarter, or when there is an indication of impairment. An impairment loss is recognized if the carrying amount of the cash-generating unit exceeds its recoverable amount. Impairment losses are recognized in the income statement. Impairment losses recognized in respect of cash-generating units are allocated first to reduce the carrying amount of the goodwill allocated to the unit and then to reduce the carrying amounts of the other assets in the unit on a pro rata basis. The recoverable amount of an asset or a cash-generating unit is the greater of its value in use and its fair value less costs to sell. In assessing value in use, the estimated future cash flows are discounted to their present value. An impairment loss in respect of goodwill is not reversed.

Commentary: Here, company describes in general terms:

- recognition of goodwill and intangible assets on business combination (same requirements exist under Canadian GAAP);
- allocation of goodwill and corporate assets to CGUs;
- impairment test for the CGU to which goodwill has been allocated;
- timing of goodwill impairment test (fourth quarter) (timing of impairment testing could also be the same under Canadian GAAP);
- recognition and allocation of impairment losses.

Extract 4(7) - Timing of goodwill impairment test

Westpac Banking Corporation (AR 2007) page 113

Note 1. Summary of significant accounting policies (in part)

b. Intangible assets (in part)

Goodwill

Goodwill represents amounts arising on the acquisition of businesses. Goodwill represents the excess of purchase consideration, including directly attributable expenses associated with the acquisition, over the fair value of the Group's share of the identifiable net assets of the acquired business.

All Goodwill is considered to have an indefinite life.

Goodwill is tested for impairment annually and whenever there is an indication that it may be impaired, and is carried at cost or deemed cost less accumulated impairment. Gains and losses on the disposal of an entity include the carrying amount of goodwill relating to the entity sold.

Goodwill is allocated to cash-generating units for the purpose of impairment testing.

Goodwill was tested for impairment at 30 September 2007.

Commentary: The company describes in general terms:

- recognition of goodwill and intangible assets after a business combination (same requirements exist under Canadian GAAP);
- timing of goodwill impairment test (date specified) (same date could be chosen under Canadian GAAP).

Identifying CGU for Assets Other than Goodwill

Aggregation of Individual Assets

To test for impairment, an entity may need to measure both VIU and FVLCS. Often, it will not be possible to isolate cash inflows related to a given asset because it is used in conjunction with others. In such instances, an entity cannot determine the VIU for a standalone asset, which means that, unless the asset's FVLCS is greater than its carrying amount, the asset's recoverable value must be tested for impairment as part of a CGU.

Factors Used for Identifying CGU

As defined previously, the CGU is the *smallest* identifiable group of assets generating cash *inflows* that are *largely independent* of the cash *inflows* from other assets or groups of assets (emphasis added).

The identification of CGU involves significant judgment in terms of the level of asset aggregation. The following should be noted when referring to CGU definition:

- The "smallest" identifiable cash inflow is a matter of fact, although the determination of what constitute "largely independent" is a matter of judgment.

- The sole determinant of CGU is the cash "inflow" (not net inflows as required for determining asset groups under CICA 3063).

Cash inflows are cash flows received from external parties. The existence of an active market for the output produced by the asset or group of assets is a determining factor for its identification as a CGU. Where this output is used internally, for example in vertically integrated operations, management should use its best estimate of future arm's length prices for which that output could be sold on an active external market.

Practically, this means that entities will have to identify CGUs by "working down" to the smallest group of assets for which cash inflows can be identified. This smallest group of assets would constitute a CGU unless its cash inflows are affected by other assets (in which case, it will be necessary to combine these assets to form a CGU that has largely independent cash inflows).

IAS 36 indicates that various factors are taken into consideration for identifying a CGU for assets other than goodwill, including the way:

- operations are managed and monitored. Consequently, a CGU could consist of product lines, businesses, individual locations, districts or regional areas;

- management makes its decisions about continuing or disposing of an entity's assets and operations.

Information about the way an entity's operations are managed and monitored only assists in the identification of CGU. Independent cash inflows depend on the way that the assets are used and not on the way management chooses to manage them.

Examples of CGU could include:

- an individual retail store or hotel would usually generate income mostly independently from the others in a group even though they might share common services such as marketing and finance;

- a factory with a single production line where there is an external market for the product at an intermediate stage; and

- a route service that a transport business provides where the assets deployed to each route, as well as the route's cash flows, can be separately identified.

The following points are noteworthy:

- Canadian GAAP refers to groups of assets, and to reporting units for goodwill, and takes into consideration many of the CGU identification factors for grouping assets;

- when the VIU of a specific asset that is part of a CGU cannot be measured, it might be possible to measure the asset's FVLCS to see if it is lower than its carrying amount. If so, the individual asset is then tested for impairment at CGU level.

Calculating the Carrying Amount of the CGU

The carrying amount of a CGU includes all relevant assets and liabilities. Many CGUs are businesses and will include property, plant and equipment, intangible assets, as well as working capital assets and liabilities. Only assets within the scope of IAS 36 are included in the carrying amount. For example, investments accounted for in accordance with IAS 39 would not be included in the carrying amount of a CGU as those investments have their separate cash flows. The carrying amount must include any allocations of corporate assets or goodwill.

Allocating Corporate Assets to CGU

Corporate assets include head office assets and research and development facilities that do not generate cash flows independently from other assets. Such assets support the activities of several CGUs. Since the recoverable value of corporate assets cannot be determined independently, those assets must be tested for impairment by being allocated to the appropriate CGUs. Such allocation must be done on a reasonable and consistent basis. If corporate assets can be allocated to individual CGUs, each CGU has its impairment test performed separately and its carrying value includes its share of the corporate assets.

If corporate assets cannot be allocated to individual CGUs on a reasonable and consistent basis, IAS 36 requires to:

- test for impairment the individual CGUs without the corporate asset and record any loss;

- identify the smallest group of CGU that includes the CGU under review to which a portion of the carrying amount of the corporate asset can be allocated on a reasonable basis;

- test for impairment the group of CGUs that incorporates the portion of the corporate assets as described above.

Change in CGU

CGUs are expected to remain constant from period to period. Any changes must be justified and disclosed in the notes to the financial statements. Examples of changes in CGU include a modification of the production or distribution channels subsequent to an acquisition.

Illustrative Disclosures:

Even though entities have to identify CGUs internally for measuring the impairment of many non-financial assets, they are not required to provide a list of such CGUs in their financial statements. Information related to CGUs contained in the financial statements is often limited to a CGU or a group of CGUs to which goodwill is allocated. Because of limited disclosures on CGUs, it is often difficult to compare asset aggregation levels under IAS 36 with those under Canadian GAAP. Many of our extracts illustrate a CGU or a group of CGUs related to goodwill impairment testing (see also illustrative disclosures in the section on goodwill allocation to CGU).

Extract 4(8) – CGU identification for measuring tangible assets impairment

Delhaize Group SA (AR 2007) page 68

2. Summary of Significant Accounting Policies (in part)

Impairment of Assets

The Group tests assets for impairment whenever events or circumstances indicate that impairment may exist. Goodwill and intangible assets with indefinite lives are tested for impairment at least annually. For impairment testing of tangible assets, the Group considers each store to be a cash generating unit. Stores for which there is potential impairment are tested for impairment by comparing the carrying value of the assets to their recoverable amount, i.e., the higher of their value in use (projected discounted cash flows) or fair value less costs to sell. If impairment exists, the assets are written down to their recoverable amount. If impairment of assets other than goodwill is no longer justified in future periods due to a recovery in fair value or value in use of the asset, the impairment is reversed.

Commentary: This is one of the few examples where an entity clearly identifies a "single" CGU. It mentions that each store consists of a CGU. Stores could represent an identifiable asset group under CICA 3063.

Extract 4(9) – General statement related to CGU identification

Danfoss A/S (AR 2007) page 63

3. Accounting policies (in part)

Business combinations (in part)

Identification of cash-generating units is based on the internal financial reporting, which in some cases do not follow the management structure. Goodwill and fair value adjustments in connection with the acquisition of a foreign entity with another functional currency than the presentation currency used in the Danfoss A/S' group accounts are treated as assets and liabilities belonging to the foreign entity and translated into the foreign entity's functional currency at the exchange rate at the transaction date.

Commentary: In the above extract, the company specifies that CGUs are identified based on internal financial reporting, which might not be representative of management structure. "Asset groups" or "reporting units," as defined by CICA 3063 and CICA 3064 respectively, could also be identified on that basis. Note also that the company explains how it accounts for assets and liabilities related to foreign acquisitions that are included in the CGU.

Extract 4(10) – Specific CGU (or group of CGUs) listed

Océ N.V. (Financial Statements 2007) page 107

[8] Intangible assets **(in part)**

Océ has designated five cash-generating units [CGU] for the purpose of impairment testing and has allocated the goodwill on acquisition to those cash-generating units.

The five cash-generating units are:

- Corporate/Commercial Printing Systems
- Océ Business Services
- Technical Document Systems
- Display Graphics Systems
- Imaging Supplies

Commentary: In this extract, the company provides a list of different CGUs consisting essentially of product lines. Though not specifically stated, the CGUs listed could consist of CGU groups. "Reporting units," as defined by CICA 3064, could also be identified on the basis of product lines.

Extract 4(11) – Considerations taken into account for CGU identification

> **Telstra Corporation Limited (AR 2007) page 123**
> **2. Summary of accounting policies (in part)**
> **2.9 Impairment (in part)**
> **(a) Non-financial assets (in part)**
>
> For assets that do not generate largely independent cash inflows, the recoverable amount is determined for the cash generating unit to which that asset belongs. Our cash generating units (CGUs) are determined according to the lowest level of aggregation for which an active market exists and the assets involved create largely independent cash inflows.
>
> We apply management judgement to establish our CGUs. We have determined that assets which form part of our ubiquitous telecommunications network work together to generate net cash flows. No one item of telecommunications equipment is of any value without the other assets to which it is connected in order to achieve the delivery of products and services. As a result, we have determined that the ubiquitous telecommunications network is a single CGU. We have referred to this CGU as the Telstra Entity CGU in our financial report.
>
> The Telstra Entity CGU excludes the hybrid fibre coaxial (HFC) cable network, which we consider not to be integrated with the rest of our telecommunications network.

Commentary: Here, the company justifies its identification of the CGU in its telecommunication operations. "Asset groups" or "reporting units," as defined by CICA 3063 and CICA 3064 respectively, could also be identified on that basis.

Extract 4(12) – Change in CGU

> **Unilever (AR on Form 20-F 2006) page 89**
> **9 Goodwill and intangible assets (in part)**
> **Impairments charges in the year**
>
> The impairments charged in 2006 principally relate to planned business disposals that will be completed during 2007.
>
> In 2006, *Slim•Fast* was fully integrated into The Americas business as part of the North American beverage operations. As a result of the integration, *Slim•Fast* is no longer evaluated on a stand-alone basis but as part of the North American beverage CGU. The 2006 impairment review on this basis and on a stand-alone basis did not result in any impairments (2005: €363 million; 2004: €791 million).

Commentary: This extract discloses the reason for a change in CGU. It also specifies that there were no impairments in 2007. Though not specifically required disclosures of a change in the asset grouping or reporting unit (as well as an indication of absence of impairment) would provide useful information.

Extract 4(13) – Allocating corporate assets to CGU based on cash flows contribution

> **TNT N.V. (AR 2007) page 111**
> **Intangible assets (in part)**
> **GOODWILL (in part)**
>
> For the purpose of assessing impairment, corporate assets are allocated to specific cash generating units before impairment testing. The basis for this allocation is to the extent in which those assets contribute to the future cash flows of the unit under review.

Commentary: The company indicates that it has allocated its corporate assets to CGUs based on the extent to which those assets contribute to the future cash flows of the latter. CICA 3063 does not deal with the allocation of corporate assets. It only specifies that these assets must be grouped with other assets to form a "group of assets" largely independent of the cash flows.

Extract 4(14) – Allocating corporate assets to CGU based on sales

Telefonaktiebolaget LM Ericsson (AR on Form 20-F 2007) page 45
C1 Significant Accounting Polices (in part)
Intangible assets other than goodwill (in part)

Corporate assets have been allocated to cash-generating units in relation to each unit's proportion of total net sales. The amount related to corporate assets is not significant. Impairment losses recognized in prior periods are assessed at each reporting date for any indications that the loss has decreased or no longer exists. An impairment loss is reversed if there has been a change in the estimates used to determine the recoverable amounts. An impairment loss is reversed only to the extent that the asset's carrying amount does not exceed the carrying amount, net of amortization, that would have been determined if no impairment loss had been recognized.

Commentary: This extract specifies that corporate assets have been allocated to CGUs on the basis of each unit's proportion of total net sales. It specifies that the amount related to corporate assets is not significant. It also explains procedures for impairment reversals. Such reversals are not allowed under CICA 3063.

Extract 4(15) – Allocating exploration assets to CGU based on geographical location

Sasol Limited (Annual Financial Statements 2007) page 57
Impairment of non-financial assets (in part)

Exploration assets are tested for impairment when development of the property commences or whenever facts and circumstances indicate impairment. An impairment is recognised for the amount by which the exploration assets' carrying amount exceeds their recoverable amount. For the purpose of assessing impairment, the relevant exploration assets are included in the existing cash-generating units of producing properties that are located in the same region.

Commentary: In this extract, the company indicates that it considers that oil and gas producing properties located in the same region to be a CGU. This grouping might reflect a higher level of assets aggregation than is normal under IAS 36 as it is allowed under IFRS 6 (discussed later). It might differ from the aggregation for an "asset group" as defined by CICA 3063. Note that the company allocated its exploration assets to CGUs as required by IFRS 6 (see later discussion on mineral resources).

Allocating Goodwill to a CGU or Group of CGUs

Similar to corporate assets, goodwill must be tested for impairment by being allocated to a CGU because it does not generate cash inflows by itself but, rather, may contribute to the cash inflows of several CGUs. Even though goodwill and corporate assets are allocated to CGUs in a similar manner, the level at which they are tested for impairment differ.

According to IAS 36, goodwill must be allocated to the lowest level within an entity at which it is monitored by management. Depending on how management monitors its investment in goodwill, this could be a single CGU level or at a higher level, involving the aggregation of several CGUs (which cannot be larger than a segment).

The way management monitors goodwill can vary from an entity to another. Such monitoring will be based on the internal structure of the management team responsible for acquisitions. For example, a company might centralize all business combination decisions at the group level or it might allow subsidiaries to decide on their own acquisitions. In the latter situation, any subsidiary making an acquisition would monitor goodwill at a lower level than in the situation where business combination decisions are made at the group level.

Goodwill cannot be allocated arbitrarily to CGU or use an allocation based on a system other than the one used internally. In all circumstances, the level of allocation cannot be higher than the primary or secondary segment level determined in accordance with

IFRS 8, *Operating Segments*, even if management monitors it at a higher level. In August 2008, the IASB proposed to clarify that the largest unit permitted is the operating segment before aggregation (aggregation of operating segments is discussed further in Chapter 2). This amendment is discussed further in the 'future developments' section of the chapter.

The requirements for the allocation of goodwill to a CGU and a group of CGUs are similar to the ones set by CICA 3064 for allocating goodwill to reporting units.

Specific Disclosure

IAS 36 has a specific requirement for the disclosure of the aggregate carrying amount of goodwill and intangible assets with indefinite useful lives allocated to a CGU (or groups of CGUs). Companies usually disclose that information using various formats. The extracts below provide an illustration of such formats and perspectives. For all extracts, a CGU (or group of CGUs) identified could correspond to reporting units under CICA 3064 and would be in line with Canadian GAAP.

Illustrative Disclosures:

Extract 4(16) – General statement on goodwill allocation to a CGU/group of CGUs

> **Unilever (AR 2007) page 75**
> **1 Accounting information and policies (in part)**
> **Goodwill (in part)**
> For the purpose of impairment testing, goodwill acquired in a business combination is, from the acquisition date, allocated to each of the Group's cash generating units, or groups of cash generating units, that are expected to benefit from the synergies of the combination, irrespective of whether other assets or liabilities of the acquired business are assigned to those units or group of units. Each unit or group of units to which the goodwill is allocated represents the lowest level within the Group at which the goodwill is monitored for internal management purposes, and is not larger than a segment based on either the Group's primary or the Group's secondary reporting format.

Commentary: In this extract, the company provides a general statement about goodwill allocation to a CGU/group of CGUs.

Extract 4(17) – CGU/group of CGUs as geographical segments

> **Vestas Wind Systems A/S (AR 2007) page 51**
> **Balance sheet (in part)**
> **Intangible assets (in part)**
> **Goodwill (in part)**
> The carrying amount of goodwill is allocated to the Group's cash-generating units at the time of acquisition. Identification of cash-generating units is based on management structure and internal financial management. Management assesses that the smallest cash-generating units to which the carrying amount of goodwill can be allocated are the Group's geographical segments, see 'Segment information'.

Commentary: Here, the company indicates that the CGU/group of CGUs consist of geographical segments based on management structure and internal financial management.

Extract 4(18) – CGU/group of CGUs as product lines

> **Elisa (AR 2007) page 25**
> **Intangible Assets (in part)**
> **Goodwill (in part)**
> ... For the purpose of testing, goodwill is allocated to cash-generating units that include Saunalahti, Mobile Communications and Fixed Network. The Saunalahti CGU (cash-generating unit) comprises mobile and fixed network services offered to Saunalahti customers. The Mobile Communications CGU comprises mobile voice and data communications services offered to Elisa's consumer, corporate and operator customers.

Extract 4(19) – Goodwill allocated to a CGU/group of CGUs following a business combination

GlaxoSmithKline (AR 2007) page 113
18 Goodwill (in part)
The cash generating units for which the carrying amount of goodwill allocated to the unit is significant in comparison with the total goodwill balance are Vaccines, Consumer Healthcare, US Pharmaceuticals, worldwide Pharmaceuticals, Japan and Poland. Total goodwill of £414 million (2006 – £362 million), principally relating to the acquisitions of ID Biomedical and Corixa, is allocated to the Vaccines unit. The recoverable value of this unit is determined using the fair value less costs to sell model. Goodwill arising on the acquisition of the minority interest in GlaxoSmithKine K.K. of £140 million (2006 – £134 million) and on the acquisition of Polfa Poznan of £111 million (2006 – £96 million) is allocated to the Japan and Poland cash generating units respectively. The recoverable value of both these units is determined using the value in use model. Goodwill arising on the acquisition of CNS, Inc. in December 2006 is allocated to the Consumer Healthcare cash generating unit. As Domantis Limited is a research operation, the goodwill arising on the acquisition has been allocated to the world- wide Pharmaceuticals cash generating unit. Goodwill arising on the acquisition of Reliant Pharmaceuticals, Inc. in December 2007 is allocated to the US Pharmaceuticals cash generating unit.

Commentary: The company explains how it allocated goodwill to a CGU/group of CGUs consisting of product lines, geographic locations or a combination of both. Note that the company shows the amounts of goodwill as a justification for such allocations.

Extract 4(20) – Goodwill and intangible assets allocation to a CGU/group of CGUs

Unilever (AR on Form 20-F 2006) page 89
Significant CGUs (in part)
The goodwill and indefinite-lived intangible assets (predominantly Knorr and Hellmann's) held in the global savoury and dressings CGU, comprising €11.6 billion (2005: €11.9 billion) and €3.4 billion (2005: €3.6 billion) respectively, are considered significant in comparison to the total carrying amounts of goodwill and indefinite-lived intangible assets at 31 December 2006. No other CGUs are considered significant in this respect.

Commentary: In this extract, the company provides some details on goodwill and indefinite-life intangible asset amounts allocated to significant CGUs/group of CGUs (which consist of product lines).

Extract 4(21) – Goodwill allocation to CGU and VIU calculations

Fugro N.V. (AR 2007) pages 101 and 102
5.37 Impairment tests for cash generating units containing goodwill (in part)
For the purpose of impairment testing, goodwill is allocated to cash generating units which represent the lowest level within the Group at which the goodwill is monitored for internal management purposes. The following cash generating units have significant carrying amounts of goodwill:

(EUR x 1,000)	2007	2006
Airborne	19,952	19,614
Survey	183,194	151,315
Jason group	73,319	73,773
Robertson group	82,745	79,011
Other	22,388	23,633
Total	381,598	347,346

Annually or when there is an indication for impairment the Group carries out impairment tests on these balances for the relevant cash-generating unit. The system and calculation method are already described in separate notes.

Extract 4(22) – Goodwill and intangible assets allocations to CGUs/group of CGUs

Telstra Corporation Limited (AR 2007) page 184

25. Impairment (in part)

Cash generating units

For the purposes of undertaking our impairment testing, we identify cash generating units (CGUs). Our CGUs are determined according to the smallest group of assets that generate cash inflows that are largely independent of the cash inflows from other assets or groups of assets.

The carrying amount of our goodwill and intangible assets with an indefinite useful life are detailed below:

	Goodwill		Intangibles with indefinite useful lives	
	As at 30 June		As at 30 June	
	2007 $m	2006 $m	2007 $m	2006 $m
CGUs				
CSL New World Mobility Group	1,100	1,246	-	-
KAZ Group	163	270	-	-
TelstraClear Group	151	137	-	-
Telstra Europe Group	108	113	-	-
Sensis Group (a) (b)	215	36	-	-
Trading Post Group (b)	-	179	-	-
Universal Publishers	15	15	10	11
Adstream Group	29	30	-	-
Telstra Business Systems	30	30	-	-
SouFun Group	293	-	-	-
1300 Australia Pty Ltd	16	4	8	8
Other	6	13	-	-
	2,126	**2,073**	**18**	19
Individual assets				
Trading Post mastheads (b)	-	-	337	447
	2,126	**2,073**	**355**	466

(a) Our assessment of the Sensis Group CGU excludes Universal Publishers, Adstream Group and SouFun Group that form part of the Sensis reportable segment.

(b) In prior years the CGU used for the purposes of testing the impairment of the goodwill acquired on the acquisition of the Trading Post business also included the Trading Post mastheads and property, plant and equipment directly attributable to the CGU. During the year, as the financial and operational functions of the Trading Post business were integrated into the Sensis Group, the goodwill has been reallocated to the Sensis Group CGU. At 30 June 2007 the Trading Post mastheads have been tested for impairment on a stand alone basis except for the inclusion of software considered integral to the generation of its largely independent cash flows.

In addition to the above CGUs, we have two further significant CGUs that are assessed for impairment. These two CGUs are:

• the Telstra Entity CGU, excluding the HFC network; and

• the CGU comprising the HFC network.

The Telstra Entity CGU consists of our ubiquitous telecommunications infrastructure network in Australia, excluding the HFC network that we consider not to be integrated with the rest of our telecommunications network. Assets that form part of the ubiquitous telecommunications network are considered to be working together to generate our net cash flows. No one item of telecommunications equipment is of any value without the other assets to which it is connected in order to achieve delivery of our products and services.

Commentary: This extract provides details on CGUs/group of CGUs, including:
- a table detailing the allocation of goodwill and intangible assets with indefinite life;
- a justified change in the grouping of assets;
- a description of its operations.

Extract 4(23) – Goodwill allocation to CGUs/group of CGUs

Pearson plc (AR 2007) page 70

11. Intangible assets (in part)

Impairment tests for cash-generating units containing goodwill

Impairment tests have been carried out where appropriate as described below. The recoverable amount for each unit tested exceeds its carrying value.

Goodwill is allocated to the Group's cash-generating units identified according to the business segment. Goodwill has been allocated as follows:

All figures in £ millions	Notes	2007	2006
Higher Education		1,031	780
School Curriculum (2006: School Book)		867	683
School Assessment and Information (2006: School Assessment and Testing)		540	342
School Technology		–	356
Other Assessment and Testing		247	490
Technology and Business Publishing (2006: Other Book)		55	56
Pearson Education total		**2,740**	**2,707**
Penguin US		155	156
Penguin UK		111	114
Pearson Australia		52	44
Penguin total		318	314
Financial Times		12	4
Mergermarket		126	97
Interactive Data		147	149
FT Group total		285	250
Total goodwill – continuing operations		3,343	3,271
Goodwill held for sale	30	96	221
Total goodwill		**3,439**	**3,492**

Goodwill has been allocated for impairment purposes to 11 cash-generating units (CGUs). During 2007, three CGUs, School Book, School Assessment and Testing and Other Book were renamed following the reorganisation of the School segment. The reorganisation resulted in the School Technology CGU being allocated between School Assessment and Information (formerly School Assessment and Testing) and School Curriculum (formerly School Book). The recoverable amount of each CGU is based on value in use calculations. Goodwill is tested for impairment annually. Other than goodwill there are no intangible assets with indefinite lives.

Commentary: The company provides a table detailing amounts of goodwill allocated to 11 CGUs/group of CGUs. It specifies that it renamed three CGUs/group of CGUs following a reorganization of a segment.

Extract 4(24) – Goodwill reconciliation and allocation to CGU/group of CGU

Helphire Group plc (AR 2007) page 40 11 GOODWILL (in part)	
	£'000
Cost	
At 1 April 2005	44,097
Recognised on acquisition of subsidiary	23,647
Other changes	761
At 1 July 2006 and 30 June 2007	68,505
Accumulated impairment losses	
1 July 2006 and 30 June 2007	(1,453)
Carrying amount	
At 1 July 2006 and 30 June 2007	67,052

Goodwill acquired in a business combination is allocated at acquisition to the cash generating units (CGUs) that are expected to benefit from that business acquisition. Before recognition of impairment losses, the carrying amount of goodwill has been allocated as follows:

	2007 £'000	2006 £'000
Albany CGU	43,405	43,405
Swift CGU	23,647	23,647
Previous Acquisitions segment (comprising several CGUs)	1,453	1,453
	68,505	68,505

Commentary: This extract presents tables explaining changes in the goodwill amount during the period, total cumulative impairment losses and amounts of goodwill allocated to two significant CGUs (or group of CGUs), as well as the amount allocated to a number of other unidentified groups of CGUs.

Extract 4(25) – Goodwill and intangible assets reconciliation and to CGUs (group of CGUs)

TeliaSonera AB (AR 2007) pages 61 and 62
Note 15 (Consolidated) Goodwill and Other Intangible Assets (in part)
The total carrying value was distributed and changed as follows.

	December 31,			
	Goodwill		Other intangible assets	
SEK in millions	2007	2006	2007	2006
---	---:	---:	---:	---:
Accumulated cost	71,515	62,957	26,350	22,327
Accumulated amortization	–	–	-12,858	-10,257
Accumulated impairment losses	-343	-319	-756	-539
Advances	–	–	1	3
Carrying value	71,172	62,638	12,737	11,534
of which work in progress	–	–	716	543
Carrying value, opening balance	62,638	62,498	11,534	11,869
Investments	4,653	3,368	3,332	1,437
of which capitalized interest	–	–	10	3
Sales and disposals	-1	-44	-13	-57
Operations acquired	3	38	248	1,206
Operations divested	–	-4	-1	1
Reclassifications	106	0	-7	-21
Amortization for the year	–	–	-2,615	-2,403
Impairment losses/reversed losses for the year	-10	-5	-212	-13
Advances	–	–	-2	-3
Exchange rate differences	3,783	-3,213	473	-482
Carrying value, closing balance	**71,172**	**62,638**	**12,737**	**11,534**

TeliaSonera AB (AR 2007) (continued)

See Note 34 "Business Combinations, etc" for more information on significant acquisitions in 2007.

Capitalized development expenses, primarily for administrative software systems, amounted to SEK 438 million in 2007 and SEK 175 million in 2006. In these years, amortization was SEK 335 million and SEK 362 million, respectively.

Goodwill is allocated between TeliaSonera's business areas as follows.

	December 31,	
SEK in millions	**2007**	**2006**
Business area Mobility Services	54,883	50,639
Business area Broadband Services	12,003	10,981
Business area Integrated Enterprise Services	398	58
Business area Eurasia	3,777	873
Other operations	111	87
Total goodwill	71,172	62,638

Goodwill as allocated in the organization existing up to the end of 2006 was to a large extent directly attributable to the new business organization. The goodwill from the acquisition of Sonera Oyj in 2002 did, however, relate to more than one part of the organization and the relative value approach was used to allocate the goodwill between business areas Mobility Services (SEK 21,297 million) and Broadband Services (SEK 8,155 million). The main part of business area Mobility Services' goodwill, in addition to the Sonera Oyj acquisition, arose in connection with the acquisitions of NetCom ASA in 2000 (SEK 21,893 million) and Orange Denmark in 2004 (SEK 3,860 million). Business area Eurasia's goodwill increased in 2007 following the acquisitions of the Uzbek and Tajik operations (SEK 3,221 million).

The total carrying value of other intangible assets was distributed by asset type as follows.

	December 31,	
SEK in millions	**2007**	**2006**
Trade names	398	594
Licenses	3,903	2,729
Customer relationships	4,694	3,306
Administrative software systems	1,584	1,572
Patents, etc.	1,324	2,465
Leaseholds, etc.	117	322
Work in progress, advances	717	546
Total other intangible assets	12,737	11,534

Commentary: In the above extract, the company presents the following:
- a reconciliation of the total carrying value of goodwill and other intangible assets;
- amounts of goodwill allocated among business areas (CGU and groups of CGU);
- amounts related to different categories of other intangible assets.

Valuation Issues under IAS 36

Introduction

As indicated in the section "basic principles," if either FVLCS or VIU exceeds the asset's or CGU's carrying amount, no impairment is recorded and it is not necessary to estimate the other amount. Moreover, if FVLCS is greater than the carrying amount there is no need to calculate the VIU which normally requires more complex calculations.

Note also that:
- often, VIU is the only reliable measurement of recoverable amount as FVLCS might not be available, for example for a specialized piece of equipment;
- the decision to dispose of a non-current asset or group of assets means that the carrying amount of the asset(s) is expected to be recovered principally through a

sale transaction rather than continuing use. Consequently, the VIU cannot be used as a measurement of recoverable amount for assets to be disposed of and the recoverable amount will, instead, correspond to FVLCS.

The following sections examine the valuation issues related to the determination of value in use and fair value less cost to sell.

Value in Use (VIU)

The following elements must be reflected in the calculation of an asset's or CGU's VIU:

- future cash-flow estimates derived from the asset in an arm's length transaction;
- expectations about possible variations in the amount or timing of future cash-flow estimates;
- time value of money (represented by the current market risk-free rate of interest);
- premium for bearing the uncertainty inherent in the asset or CGU; and
- other factors, such as illiquidity, that market participants would reflect in pricing the future cash flows the entity expects to derive from the asset or CGU.

The following considerations need to be taken into account when estimating the amount of future cash flows:

- projections must include:
  - o inflows related to use of the asset,
  - o outflows related to use of the asset that are necessarily incurred to generate the inflows including those that can be directly attributed (or allocated on a reasonable and consistent basis) to the asset, and
  - o net cash flows, if any, to be received (or paid) for the disposal of the asset at the end of its useful life;
- cash-flow projections must be based on reasonable and supportable assumptions, the most recent budgets and forecasts and extrapolation for periods beyond bud- geted projections. IAS 36 presumes that budgets and forecasts do not extend beyond five years. Management should assess the reasonableness of its assump- tions by examining the causes of differences between past cash-flow projections and actual cash flows;
- future cash flows reflect the use of the asset in its current condition. Estimates of future cash flows do not include estimated future cash inflows or outflows expected from:
  - o future restructuring to which an entity is not yet committed,
  - o improving or enhancing the asset's performance,
  - o cash inflows or outflows from financing activities, or
  - o income tax receipts or payments.

As for the discount rate to be used for VIU calculation, IAS 36 requires the pre-tax rate that reflects current market assessments of the time value of money and the risks specific to the asset for which the cash flows have not been adjusted. In addi- tion, IAS 36 specifies that:

- for impairment of an individual asset or portfolio of assets, the discount rate is the rate a company would pay in a current market transaction to borrow money to buy that specific asset or portfolio;

- if a market-determined asset-specific rate is not available, a surrogate must be used that reflects the time value of money over the asset's life as well as country risk, currency risk, price risk and cash flow risk. The following would normally be considered:
  o the enterprise's own weighted average cost of capital,
  o the enterprise's incremental borrowing rate, and
  o other market borrowing rates.

Fair Value Less Costs to Sell (FVLCS)

The following hierarchy applies under IAS 36:

1. If there is a binding sale agreement, use the price under that agreement less costs of disposal.
2. If there is no binding sale agreement but there is an active market for that type of asset, use market price less costs of disposal. Market price means current bid price if available, otherwise the price in the most recent transaction.
3. If there is no binding sale agreement or active market, use the best estimate of the asset's selling price less costs of disposal, considering the outcome of recent transactions for similar assets within the same industry.

Costs of disposal include only directly added costs. Overhead is excluded.

Disclosures

IAS 36 requires extensive disclosures. The disclosures are designed to enable readers of the financial statements to understand the valuation and impairment processes and to decide whether they would have reached the same conclusion. Disclosures related to the valuation of impairment are described below. Other disclosures are discussed in the sections on "Reporting Impairment Losses" and "Impairment loss reversals."

The following information regarding the valuation basis should be provided for each material losses recognized or reversed during the period for an individual asset, including goodwill, or a cash generating unit:

- whether the recoverable amount is the fair value less costs to sell or its value in use;
- if the recoverable amount is fair value less costs to sell, the basis used to determine the value;
- if the recoverable amount is the value in use, then the discount rate used in the current and previous estimates.

Additional disclosures are required regarding the determination of the recoverable amounts of cash-generating units containing significant amounts of allocated goodwill or intangible assets with indefinite useful lives. These disclosures are encouraged but not required for the other types of assets or CGUs. An entity should disclose:

- the carrying amount of goodwill and intangible assets with indefinite useful lives allocated to the CGU (or group of CGUs),
- the basis on which the recoverable amount of the CGU has been determined (i.e., value in use or FVLCS); and
- the assumptions used in the determination of the recoverable amount as described in the following paragraphs.

If the recoverable amount is VIU, disclosure includes:

- a description of each key assumption underlying the cash-flow projections and management's approach to determine it;

- the period over which management has projected cash flows (when more than five years, the reasons why that longer period is justified);
- the growth rate used to extrapolate cash flows;
- the discount rate applied to the cash-flow projections.

Although all the required disclosures are not listed here, significant information on some of the key disclosure elements described above include the following:

- management's approach to determining VIU should reflect the basis for estimates, for example, whether they reflect past experience or are consistent with external sources of information or why they differ from these;
- justification for using any growth rate that exceeds the long-term average growth rate for the products, industries or country or countries in which an entity operates or for the market to which the unit (group of units) is dedicated.

If the recoverable amount is based on FVLCS, disclosure includes:

- methodology used to determine FVLCS;
- if it is not determined based on market prices, the following information must be disclosed:
    - a description of each key assumption used and management's approach to determining the key assumptions,
    - whether the assumptions are consistent with past experience or external data and if not, why not.

If FVLCS is determined using discounted cash flow projections, the following information must also be disclosed:

- the period over which management has projected cash flows;
- the growth rate used to extrapolate cash flow projections; and
- the discount rate(s) applied to the cash flow projections.

The above disclosures do not apply when goodwill and intangibles with indefinite lives are allocated across multiple CGUs and the amount allocated to each specific CGUs is not significant to the entity's total goodwill or intangibles with indefinite lives. However, a description of that fact and the aggregated amounts of goodwill and intangibles with indefinite lives should be disclosed. However if the aggregate amounts are significant, and the recoverable amount of the CGUs are based on similar assumptions, the entity should provide disclosures similar to the ones described above.

Sensitivity analysis is also required. If a reasonably possible change in a key assumption underlying FVLCS or VIU would trigger an impairment, IAS 36 requires the disclosure of the following:

- the amount by which the unit's (or groups of units') recoverable amounts exceeds its carrying amount;
- the value of the key assumption;
- the amount by which key assumptions must change for the recoverable amount to be equal to its carrying amount.

Although CICA 3063 and CICA 3064 contain similar disclosure requirements to those described above, they are not nearly as extensive. For example, the disclosures relating to key assumptions for determining the recoverable amount and the sensitivity of forecast to variations in these assumptions can be quite demanding whether there is an impairment loss or not.

Illustrative Disclosures:

All of the following extracts would be in line with Canadian GAAP. Certain IAS 36 requirements might be more extensive, for example, CICA 3064 does not contain specific disclosure requirements when estimates of future cash flows used extend beyond five years.

Extract 4(26) – General statement on estimates and uncertainties

InterContinental Hotels Group PLC (AR 2007) page 56
Corporate information and accounting policies (in part)
Use of accounting estimates and judgements (in part)

The preparation of financial statements requires management to make estimates and assumptions that affect the reported amounts of assets and liabilities, disclosure of contingent assets and liabilities at the date of the financial statements and the reported amounts of revenues and expenses during the reporting period. Actual results may differ from these estimates under different assumptions and conditions.

The estimates and assumptions that have the most significant effect on the amounts recognised in the financial statements are:

Impairment – the Group determines whether goodwill is impaired on an annual basis or more frequently if there are indicators of impairment. Other non-current assets, including property, plant and equipment, are tested for impairment if there are indicators of impairment. Impairment testing requires an estimate of future cash flows and the choice of a suitable discount rate and, in the case of hotels, an assessment of recoverable amount based on comparable market transactions.

Commentary: In this extract, the company specifies uncertainties related to impairment testing. It specifies that it established recoverable amounts based on comparable market transactions.

Extract 4(27) – General valuation considerations

Eni SpA (AR 2007) pages 149 and 150
Non-current assets (in part)
Property, plant and equipment (in part)

The carrying value of property, plant and equipment is reviewed for impairment whenever events indicate that the carrying amounts for those assets may not be recoverable. The recoverability of an asset is assessed by comparing its carrying value with the recoverable amount represented by the higher of fair value less costs to sell and value in use.

If there is no binding sales agreement, fair value is estimated on the basis of market values, recent transactions, or the best available information that shows the proceeds that the company could reasonably expect to collect from the disposal of the asset.

Value in use is the present value of the future cash flows expected to be derived from the use of the asset and, if significant and reasonably determinable, the cash flows deriving from its disposal at the end of its useful life, net of disposal costs. Cash flows are determined on the basis of reasonable and documented assumptions that represent the best estimate of the future economic conditions during the remaining useful life of the asset, giving more importance to independent assumptions. Oil, natural gas and petroleum products prices (and to them which derive from the previous ones) used to quantify the expected future cash flows are estimated based on forward prices prevailing in the marketplace for the first four years and management's long-term planning assumptions thereafter.

Discounting is carried out at a rate that takes into account the implicit risk in the sectors where the entity operates.

Commentary: Here, the company provides the following information:

- calculation of FVLCS (if there is no binding sales agreement, fair value is estimated on the basis of market values, recent transactions or the best available information that shows the proceeds that the company could reasonably expect to collect from the disposal of the asset);
- calculation of VIU:
  - o cash flows are determined on the basis of reasonable and documented assumptions,
  - o discounting is carried out at a rate that takes into account the implicit risk in the sectors where the entity operates.

Extract 4(28) – Key assumptions related to VIU calculations

> **Unilever (AR 2007) page 87**
> **9 Goodwill and intangible assets (in part)**
> **Significant CGUs (in part)**
>
> During 2007, we conducted an impairment review of the carrying value of these assets. Value in use of the global savoury and dressings CGU has been calculated as the present value of projected future cash flows. A pre-tax discount rate of 10% was used.
>
> The following key assumptions were used in the discounted cash flow projections for the savoury and dressings CGU:
>
> - a longer-term sustainable growth rate of 4%, adjusted for market fade, used to determine an appropriate terminal value multiple;
> - average near-term nominal growth for the major product groups within the CGU of 4%; and
> - average operating margins for the major product groups within the CGU ranging from 15% to 18%.
>
> The growth rates and margins used to estimate future performance are based on past performance and our experience of growth rates and margins achievable in our key markets as a guide. We believe that the assumptions used in estimating the future performance of the savoury and dressings CGU are consistent with past performance.
>
> The projections covered a period of ten years as we believe this to be a suitable timescale over which to review and consider annual performance before applying a fixed terminal value multiple to the final year cash flows of the detailed projection. Stopping the detailed projections after five years and applying a terminal value multiple thereafter would not result in a value in use that would cause impairment.
>
> The growth rates used to estimate future performance beyond the periods covered by our annual planning and strategic planning processes do not exceed the long-term average rates of growth for similar products.
>
> We have performed sensitivity analysis around the base case assumptions and have concluded that no reasonably possible changes in key assumptions would cause the recoverable amount of the global savoury and dressings CGU to be less than the carrying amount.

Commentary: The company provides details on its VIU calculations, including:

- the pre-tax discount rate used;
- key assumptions, including:
  - o longer-term sustainable growth rate,
  - o average near-term nominal growth,
  - o average operating margins;
- the fact that:
  - o growth rates and margins used to estimate future performance are based on past achievable performance and experience,
  - o projections cover a period of 10 years,
  - o it performed sensitivity analysis around the base case assumptions.

Extract 4(29) – Key assumptions related to VIU calculations, including sensitivity analysis

Pearson plc (AR 2007) page 70

11. Intangible assets (in part)

Key assumptions

The value in use calculations use cash flow projections based on financial budgets approved by management covering a five year period.

The key assumptions used by management in the value in use calculations were:

Discount rate – The discount rate is based on the risk-free rate for government bonds, adjusted for a risk premium to reflect the increased risk in investing in equities. The risk premium adjustment is assessed for each specific cash-generating unit. The average pre-tax discount rates used are in the range of 10.5% to 12.0% for the Pearson Education businesses, 8.9% to 11.7% for the Penguin businesses and 10.4% to 17.2% for the FT Group businesses.

Perpetuity growth rates – The cash flows subsequent to the approved budget period are based upon the long-term historic growth rates of the underlying territories in which the CGU operates and reflect the long-term growth prospects of the sectors in which the CGU operates. The perpetuity growth rates used vary between 2.5% and 3.5%. The perpetuity growth rates are consistent with appropriate external sources for the relevant markets.

Cash flow growth rates – The cash flow growth rates are derived from forecast sales growth taking into consideration past experience of operating margins achieved in the cash-generating unit. Historically, such forecasts have been reasonably accurate.

Sensitivities

The Group's impairment review is sensitive to a change in the key assumptions used, most notably the discount rates and the perpetuity rates. Based on the Group's sensitivity analysis, a reasonable possible change in a single factor will not cause impairment in any of the Group's CGUs.

However, a significant adverse change in our key assumptions could result in an impairment in our School Curriculum and/or Penguin UK CGUs as their fair value currently exceeds their carrying value only by between 10% and 20%.

Commentary: In the above extract, the company discloses quantitative information on key assumptions used in its VIU calculations, including:

- range of discount rates by business;
- perpetuity growth rates.

In addition, the company specifies that:

- Cash-flow growth rates (reflecting forecast sales growth) have historically been reasonably accurate.
- Its impairment review is sensitive to a change in the key assumptions used, most notably the discount rates and the perpetuity rates. Based on its sensitivity analysis, a reasonably possible change in a single factor does not cause impairment in any of the CGUs. The company warns, however, that a significant adverse change in key assumptions could result in impairment for identified CGUs as their fair value is slightly higher than their carrying value.

Extract 4(30) – Key assumptions related to VIU calculations for oil and gas

---

Fugro N.V. (AR 2007) pages 101 and 102

5.37 Impairment tests for cash generating units containing goodwill (in part)

The period for the discounted cash flow calculations is in principle indefinite. However the Group has set the period at fifty years, subject to periodic evaluation, for the following reasons.

About 74% of the Group's activities relate to the oil and gas industry. The services are in principle of such a nature that our clients use us to help them to explore and extract hydrocarbon and mineral resources. Experts are without doubt that these resources will continue to be available to mankind for many decades and their reports indicate periods between fifty and hundred years.

Easily accessible places may 'dry-up' but with new techniques and means more hostile areas can also be exploited. The Group has with its high market shares and specialised techniques a solid position to continue to serve its customers.

The Group recognises that harnessing alternative means of energy, like wind, nuclear and hydro electric energy will continue. These sources however have limited output and will be difficult to transport.

The recoverable amounts of the various cash generating units that carry goodwill are determined on calculations of value in use. Those calculations use cash flow projections based on actual operating results and a five year forecast. Cash flows for further future periods are extrapolated using growth rate percentages varying from 0 to 3.5% which are deemed appropriate because of the long-term nature of the business. These growth rates are also consistent with the long-term averages in the industry based on value in use. A pre-tax discount rate of 9.5% has been used for discounting the projected cash flows. The key assumptions and the approach to determine their value are the growth rates that are based on analysis of the long-term market price trends in the oil and gas industry adjusted for actual experience.

The carrying amounts of the units remain below the recoverable amounts and as such no impairment losses are accounted for. Future adverse changes in the assumptions could however reduce the recoverable amounts below the carrying amount. As at 31 December 2007 cumulative impairment losses of EUR 442 thousand have been recognised (2006: nil).

Commentary: In this extract, the company specifies that even if the period for the discounted cash-flow calculations is, in principle, indefinite, it has set it at 50 years because:

- The majority of its activities relate to the oil and gas industry (which should continue to be available for many decades).
- Easily accessible places may dry-up but, with new techniques and means, more hostile areas can also be exploited.

The company recognizes that harnessing alternative means of energy, like wind, nuclear and hydro electric energy, will continue, but that they have signification limitations.

The company also discloses some quantitative information on the cash-flow projection period, growth rates and discount rates. It specifies that the key assumptions and the approach it uses to determine growth rates are based on an analysis of the long-term market price trends in the oil and gas industry adjusted for actual experience.

Finally, the company specifies that no impairment losses were recorded in the previous year and discloses the amount of cumulative impairment losses at the end of the current year.

Extract 4(31) – Key assumptions related to VIU calculations for goodwill and intangible assets with indefinite lives

---

Land of Leather Holdings plc (AR 2007) pages 48 and 49

21 Impairment testing of goodwill and intangible assets with indefinite lives (in part)

The Group tests annually for impairment, or more frequently if there are indications that intangible assets might be impaired.

Land of Leather Holdings plc (AR 2007) (continued)

Goodwill

Goodwill acquired has been allocated to cash generating units all associated with the UK retail operation.

Impairment testing has been conducted as follows:

Goodwill acquired through business combinations and the Land of Leather brand have been allocated for impairment testing purposes to Land of Leather Limited, the operating Company which comprises a portfolio of stores each of which is considered to be a cash generating unit. This represents the lowest level within the Group at which goodwill is monitored for internal management purposes.

The recoverable amount for the operating unit has been determined based on a value in use calculation using cash flow projections based on financial budgets approved by the board. Details of the calculation are:

	29.7.07	30.7.06
Budget period covered (months)	36	36
Discount rate applied to cash flow projections	13.4%	13.4%
Cash flow growth beyond 36 month budget period	0.0%	0.0%

This exercise has indicated that there has been no impairment of the goodwill carrying value included in the accounts at 29 July 2007.

Brand

The Group commissions an external valuation every two years, with an internal review for each intermediate year. An IAS 36 compliant valuation and impairment exercise was conduced externally by Brand Finance plc at 30 July 2006, which has been replicated internally by the Group at 29 July 2007. Both exercises have confirmed that there is no impairment of the Land of Leather brand carrying value included in the accounts at the two period ends.

For each of these review exercises, the recoverable amount for the operating unit has been determined using the 'royalty relief' approach to valuation, which takes projected future sales, applies a royalty rate to them and then discounts the projected future post tax royalties, to arrive at a net present value. Brand Finance plc has estimated the discount rate of 13.4% by using pre-tax rates that reflect current market assessments of the time-value of money, and risks specific to the asset for which the future cash flow estimates have not been adjusted.

The projected future sales are based on budgets approved by the board covering a 36 month period. Sales projections beyond the 36 month budget are extrapolated using a 0% growth rate.

The royalty rate has been determined by an analysis of the operating unit margins over the three year period preceding the valuation.

Carrying amounts of goodwill and brand

	Group	
	As at	As at
	29.7.07	30.7.06
	£000	£000
Goodwill	6,168	6,168
Brand	13,300	13,300

Commentary: The above extract describes impairment procedures for goodwill and brands. It specifies that:

- Individual stores are CGUs.
- Goodwill acquired is allocated to a group of CGUs (a portfolio of stores) for impairment purposes.
- It commissions an external valuation every two years, with an internal review for each intermediate year for its brands.
- Recoverable amount for brands have been determined using the "royalty relief" approach.

The company provides in a table setting out:

- details on VIU assumptions for goodwill impairment purposes;
- carrying amounts of goodwill and brands.

Extract 4(32) – Key assumptions related to VIU calculations including sensitivity analysis

---

Telstra Corporation Limited (AR 2007) pages 184 and 185

25. Impairment (in part)

Impairment testing

Our impairment testing compares the carrying value of an individual asset or CGU with its recoverable amount as determined using a value in use calculation.

Our assumptions for determining the recoverable amount of each asset and CGU are based on past experience and our expectations for the future. Our cash flow projections are based on five year management approved forecasts. These forecasts use management estimates to determine income, expenses, capital expenditure and cash flows for each asset and CGU.

We have used the following key assumptions in determining the recoverable amount of our CGUs to which goodwill or indefinite life intangible assets has been allocated:

	Discount rate (a)		Terminal value growth rate (b)	
	As at 30 June		As at 30 June	
	2007 %	2006 %	**2007 %**	2006 %
CSL New World Mobility Group	**11.0**	11.1	**2.0**	5.0
KAZ Group............	**15.6**	16.6	**3.0**	3.0
TelstraClear Group........	**16.5**	18.0	**3.0**	3.0
Telstra Europe Group......	**11.4**	14.9	**3.0**	3.0
Sensis Group..........	**13.1**	13.7	**3.0**	3.0
Trading Post Group (c).....	**-**	15.3	**-**	2.5
Universal Publishers......	**13.9**	14.3	**3.0**	2.5
Adstream Group.........	**14.7**	18.6	**2.5**	2.5
Telstra Business Systems....	**14.4**	15.0	**3.0**	2.5
SouFun Group..........	**18.8**	-	**5.0**	-

(a) Discount rate represents the pre tax discount rate applied to the cash flow projections. The discount rate reflects the market determined, risk adjusted, discount rate which was adjusted for specific risks relating to the CGU and the countries in which they operate.

(b) Terminal value growth rate represents the growth rate applied to extrapolate our cash flows beyond the five year forecast period. These growth rates are based on our expectation of the CGUs long term performance in their respective markets. The terminal growth rates for the Australian CGUs were aligned to three percent as part of the impairment testing conducted for the half year ended 31 December 2006.

(c) During the year the Trading Post Group was integrated into the Sensis Group and as such is no longer considered a separate CGU. As at 30 June 2007 the carrying value of the Trading Post mastheads was tested for impairment based on value in use. This test resulted in an impairment charge of $110 million being recognised in the financial statements. The impairment arose as a result of increasing competition in the traditional print classifieds market, challenges in the highly competitive on-line classified market and the risks associated with new initiatives.

As a result of the impairment, the carrying value of the Trading Post mastheads at 30 June 2007 is $337 million which is equal to its recoverable amount. Changes in the key assumptions used in determining the forecast cash flows could result in changes to these cash flows and further adjustments to the carrying value. Assuming the forecast cashflows are either surpassed or missed by 10%, the recoverable amount of the Trading Post mastheads will be higher or lower than its carrying amount by $28 million respectively.

The post tax discount rate used in determining the carrying value of the Trading Post mastheads was 12.6%. This discount rate includes a risk premium given the changing nature of the Trading Post business. Cash flows beyond year five have been extrapolated using an estimated terminal growth rate of 3%. This rate has been determined with regard to the projected growth rates for the specific market in which Trading Post participates and is not expected to exceed the long term average growth rates for this market.

Commentary: Here, the company provides detailed disclosures on:
- key assumptions in determining the recoverable amount of identified CGUs or group of CGUs to which goodwill or indefinite-life intangible assets have been allocated;
- a change in CGUs (including reason for the change) and the resulting amount of impairment loss (including reason for the impairment);
- quantitative data concerning the impairment test; and
- sensitivity analysis.

Extract 4(33) – Key assumptions related to VIU calculations, including sensitivity analysis for goodwill

Wolters Kluwer nv (AR 2007) pages 116 and 117
IMPAIRMENT TESTING FOR CASH-GENERATING UNITS OF CONTINUING OPERATIONS

Carrying amounts of goodwill and publishing rights per division	Goodwill	Publishing rights	**2007**	[1] 2006
Health	727	174	**901**	1,049
CFS	495	176	**671**	731
TAL	844	319	**1,163**	1,224
LTRE	640	214	**854**	794
• Total continuing operations	**2,706**	**883**	**3,589**	**3,798**
Discontinued operations				74
• Total	**2,706**	**883**	**3,589**	**3,872**

[1] The 2006 comparatives for the TAL and LTRE divisions have been restated to reflect the transfer of the operations in the United Kingdom from the LTRE division to the TAL division in 2007.

The Group reviews at each reporting date whether there is an indication that any of the cash-generating units that contain goodwill and publishing rights may be impaired. Furthermore, the Group carries out an annual impairment test by comparing the carrying amount of the cash-generating unit to which the goodwill and publishing rights belong, net of related deferred taxes, to the recoverable amount of the cash-generating unit. The recoverable amount is determined based on a calculation of the value in use and compared to multiples of recent transactions to estimate the net selling price. These calculations use cash flow projections based on actual operating results and the three-year Business Development Plan as approved by the Executive Board. Projections are extrapolated beyond this three-year period using an appropriate perpetual growth rate that is consistent with the long-term average market growth rate and that does not exceed 3-4.5%.

The estimated post-tax cash flows are discounted to their present value using a post-tax weighted average cost of capital (WACC). A post-tax WACC is used because this is readily available in the financial markets. Calculating the recoverable amount on a post-tax basis using a post-tax WACC should lead to the same results as pre-tax calculations. The post-tax WACC used is 8%.

The Group has decided not to apply different discount rates for different parts of the business, since its businesses serve fairly consistent markets (professional customers in developed countries), and their results are impacted in a similar and limited way by changes of the economic cycle and other significant long-term market risks.

The key assumptions used in the projections are:
- Revenue growth: based on actual experience, an analysis of market growth and the expected development of market share; and
- Margin development: based on actual experience and management's long-term projections.

The impairment test carried out in 2007 showed that the recoverable amount for each cash-generating unit exceeded the carrying amount; hence no impairment of goodwill or publishing rights was recognized in 2007. The impairment test also includes an assessment, if a reasonably possible change in a key assumption would cause the carrying amount to exceed the recoverable amount. One of the cash-generating units, with a carrying amount of .248 million of goodwill and publishing rights has a recoverable amount that exceeds the carrying amount by .23 million. Its projections include assumptions with regard to growth of net cash flows from new products, pricing, and gaining some new and retaining existing customers. The assumed long-term growth rate is 4.5%. If the cash-generating unit is unsuccessful at capitalizing on these initiatives or if the growth rate is below 4.5%, the recoverable amount would be below the carrying amount.

Commentary: The company presents assumptions related to VIU calculations, including the fact that it decided not to apply different discount rates for different parts of the business, since its businesses serve fairly consistent markets, and their results are affected in a similar and limited way by changes in the economic cycle and other significant long-term market risks.

The company indicates that it carried out an impairment test and that the recoverable amount for each CGU exceeded the carrying amount. In addition, the company presents quantitative information on its sensitivity analysis.

Extract 4(34) – Key assumptions related to VIU calculations for goodwill

TeliaSonera AB (AR 2007) pages 61 and 62

Note 15 (Consolidated) Goodwill and Other Intangible Assets (in part)

Impairment testing

Goodwill is for impairment testing purposes allocated to cash-generating units in accordance with TeliaSonera's business organization. Carrying values of all cash-generating units are annually tested for impairment. The recoverable amounts (that is, higher of value in use and fair value less cost to sell) are normally determined on the basis of value in use, applying discounted cash flow calculations. From time to time, TeliaSonera may also obtain independent appraisals of fair values to determine recoverable amounts.

As of December 31, 2007, the recoverable values of the cash-generating units were found to be in excess of their carrying values in all tests and therefore the related goodwill was not impaired. Management has used assumptions that it believes are reasonable based on the best information available as of the date of the financial statements.

The key assumptions used in the value in use calculations were sales growth, EBITDA margin development, the weighted average cost of capital (WACC), and the terminal growth rate of free cash flow. The calculations were based on 5-year forecasts approved by management, which management believes reflect past experience, forecasts in industry reports, and other externally available information. Due to the nature of the investment, the forecast period used for business area Mobility Services' Spanish operations was 10 years.

The post-tax WACC rates used in the impairment tests varied by geographic area as follows.

Geographic area	WACC rates (percent)
Nordic countries	8.5–9.1
Baltic countries	8.4–10.1
Spain	11.1
Eurasia	10.6–18.1

The growth rates used to extrapolate cash flows beyond the 5-year forecasts (in Spain 10 year forecast) varied from operation to operation. For operations within business area Mobility Services the growth rate varied between 1.0 and 2.5 percent. The corresponding rates for operations within the other business areas were 1.0 percent for Broadband Services and Integrated Enterprise Services and 1.0–3.0 percent for Eurasia. In all cases management believes the growth rates to not exceed the average growth rates for markets in which TeliaSonera operates.

Commentary: The above extract presents key assumptions underlying VIU calculations, including sales growth, EBITDA margin development, the weighted average cost of capital (WACC) per geographical area and the terminal growth rate of free cash flow. The company specifies that assumptions reflect past experience, forecasts in industry reports and other externally available information.

Extract 4(35) – Key assumptions related to VIU calculations including sensitivity analysis

Bayer Aktiengesellschaft (AR 2007) pages 120 and 121
Procedure used in global impairment testing and its impact (in part)

The recoverable amount is determined from the present value of future cash flows, based on continuing use of the asset by the strategic business entity and its retirement at the end of its useful life. The cash flow forecasts are derived from the current long-term planning for the Bayer Group, generally for a five-year planning horizon, which involves assumptions, especially regarding future selling prices, sales volumes and costs. Cash flows beyond this planning period are extrapolated using individual growth rates derived from the respective market information. The assumed growth rates, depending on the businesses valued, are zero to 4.0 percent for HealthCare, 1.4 to 5.7 percent for Crop-Science, and zero to 1.0 percent for MaterialScience.

Bayer calculates the cost of capital on the basis of the debt/equity ratio. The underlying capital structure of each subgroup is determined by benchmarking against comparable companies in the same industry sector. The cost of equity corresponds to the return expected by stockholders, while the cost of debt is based on the conditions on which the company can obtain long-term financing. Both components are derived from capital market information.

To allow for the different risk and return profiles of the Bayer Group's principal businesses, the after-tax cost of capital is calculated separately for each subgroup. The discount rates used are 8.1 percent (2006: 7.6 percent) for HealthCare, 8.1 percent (2006: 7.9 percent) for CropScience and 7.6 percent (2006: 7.3 percent) for Material-Science. The equivalent pre-tax interest rates are 8.3 percent (2006: 7.8 percent) for HealthCare, 8.5 percent (2006: 8.3 percent) for CropScience and 8.0 percent (2006: 7.8 percent) for MaterialScience. These rates are based on assumptions and estimates relating to business-specific costs of capital, which in turn depend on country risks, credit risks, and additional risks resulting from the volatility of certain businesses. The risk adjustment for each subgroup is determined by benchmarking against comparable companies in the same industry sector.

Sensitivity analysis is based on a 10 percent decline in future cash flows and a 10 percent increase in the weighted average cost of capital because changes up to this magnitude are reasonably possible. Based on the Group's experience, greater changes than this are unlikely. If the actual present value of future cash flows were 10 percent lower than the anticipated present value, the net carrying amount of goodwill in the Systems segment would have to be impaired by €31 million. If the weighted average cost of capital used for the impairment test were increased by 10 percent, assets of the Systems segment would have to be impaired by €36 million.

Page 121

In 2007 and 2006 the following write-downs were made as a result of specific events (such as restructuring) or changes in circumstances. In 2007 as in 2006, however, no impairment losses were recorded on the basis of the global annual impairment tests.

€ million	2006	2007
Impairment charges (continuing operations)	172	286
Impairment charges (discontinued operations)	18	-
Total impairment charges	190	286

Although the estimates of the useful lives of certain assets, assumptions concerning the macroeconomic environment and developments in the industries in which the Bayer Group operates and estimates of the discounted future cash flows are believed to be appropriate, changes in assumptions or circumstances could require changes in the analysis. This could lead to additional impairment charges in the future or – except in the case of goodwill – to valuation write-backs should the expected trends reverse.

Commentary: Here, the company provides details on its VIU calculations, including quantitative data on growth rates for each business, the discount rate used based on assumptions and estimates relating to business-specific costs of capital, which in turn depend on country risks, credit risks and additional risks resulting from the volatility of certain businesses. The company also provides a sensitivity analysis and describes possible impairment if any of the assumptions were to change.

Recognition of Impairment Losses

Impairment Losses on Individual Assets, CGUs or Group of CGUs

The accounting for impairment losses varies depending on whether the impairment loss is on an individual asset, on an individual CGU or on a group of CGUs. Further, there are special rules for the recognition of impairment losses on goodwill that might have been allocated to a CGU or group of CGUs.

Allocation of Impairment Losses to Individual Assets

When an asset's carrying value exceeds its recoverable amount, the carrying amount should be reduced to the recoverable amount. That reduction is an impairment loss. If the impairment loss exceeds the carrying amount of the asset, the asset should be reduced to zero. A liability for the balance of the impairment loss would be recognized only if it meets the recognition criteria of another IFRS, most likely to be IAS 37 *Provisions*, if any or the definition of a liability in the Framework.

For assets carried at amortized cost, the impairment loss is recognised in income immediately. For assets carried at revalued amount, an impairment loss is treated as a revaluation decrease.

Allocation of Impairment Losses to CGU or group of CGUs

As explained in the previous sections describing the identification of CGUs, when the recoverable amounts of assets cannot be assessed individually they need to be estimated in aggregate for the CGU to which they belong. If the recoverable amount is less than the carrying amount of the CGU, an impairment loss is recognized. The impairment loss needs to be allocated first to goodwill and then to the other assets in the CGU on a prorata basis based on the carrying amounts of each asset in the CGU. The carrying amounts of any individual asset in the CGU should not be reduced below the highest of: its FVLCS, its VIU, or zero.

Recognition of Impairment Losses for Categories of Non-financial Assets

The following table summarizes the accounting for an impairment loss for various categories of non-financial assets.

Type of Asset	IAS 36*	CICA 3063/3064
Indefinite-life intangible assets	Impairment loss is recognized in income immediately.	Same as IAS 36.
Definite-life intangible assets not available for use	Impairment loss is recognized in income immediately.	Same as IAS 36.

Type of Asset	IAS 36*	CICA 3063/3064
Property, plant and equipment and amortizable intangible assets	Impairment loss is recognized in income, unless the asset is carried at revalued amount (in accordance with IAS 16), in which case it is treated as a revaluation decrease (i.e., as a component of other comprehensive income to the extent that the impairment loss does not exceed the amount in the revaluation surplus for that same asset). When impairment losses are calculated at the CGU level, they must be allocated to reduce the carrying amount of the assets of the unit in the following order: • first, to reduce the carrying amount of any goodwill allocated to the CGU; and • then, to reduce other assets of the CGU pro rata on the basis of the carrying amount of each asset in the CGU. However, an entity cannot reduce the carrying amount of an asset below the highest of: • its FVLCS (if determinable); • its VIU (if determinable); and • zero.	Impairment loss is always recognized in income. An impairment loss of an asset group is allocated on a pro-rata basis excluding goodwill, corporate assets and indefinite-life intangible assets. The carrying amounts of the assets should not be reduced below their individual fair value (if known).
Goodwill	Impairment loss (excess of carrying value of CGU or group of CGUs over its recoverable value) is allocated to reduce the carrying amount of the assets of the CGU or group of CGUs in the following order: • first, to reduce the carrying amount of any goodwill allocated to the CGU or group of CGUs; and • then, to the other assets of the CGU or group of CGU units pro rata on the basis of the carrying amount of each asset in the CGU or group of CGUs. However, an entity cannot reduce the carrying amount of an asset below the highest of: • its FVLCS (if determinable); • its VIU (if determinable); and • zero.	Record impairment loss of goodwill as the excess of its carrying value over its implied fair value (which equals the goodwill that would be obtained if the reporting unit was acquired in a current business combination).

* Impairment can be tested either as an individual asset or as part of a CGU, except for goodwill that should be tested at the CGU or group of CGU level. When a CGU containing an intangible asset is impaired, there is no requirement to write down the intangible asset first, as required for goodwill.

General Disclosures

IAS 36 requires that impairment losses recognized during the period be disclosed separately for each class of asset and reportable segment based on the entity's primary reporting format.

All impairment losses must show distinctly the amounts recognized in income, including the line item of the statement of comprehensive income in which those impairment losses are included, and the amount of impairment losses on revalued assets recognized in other comprehensive income.

When an individual impairment loss is significant, IAS 36 requires that entities provide the following additional information (this applies to impairments of assets, CGU and goodwill):

- the circumstances giving rise to the impairment;
- the amount of impairment loss;
- the nature and description of asset or CGU (and of any changes in the way of identifying the CGU and aggregating assets);
- the primary segment to which the asset or CGU belongs;
- whether recoverable amount is FVLCS or VIU; and
    o if FVLCS, how it was determined,
    o if VIU, the discount rates used in the current assessment and in the previous one.

If impairment losses recognized are material only in aggregate to the financial statements as a whole and therefore the information described above is not provided, then IAS 36 requires the following minimal disclosures:

- main classes of assets affected; and
- main events and circumstances.

Illustrative Disclosures:

The extracts presented below illustrate the reporting of impairment losses. Under IAS 36, impairment losses equal the difference between an asset's recoverable amount and carrying amount; under Canadian GAAP, however, the impairment loss is the difference between fair value and carrying amount. The method used to allocate a loss to a group of assets differs for the two standards:

- under IAS 36, an impairment loss for a CGU is allocated first to any goodwill and then pro rata to other assets in the CGU that fall within the scope of the impairment standard (with limited exceptions);
- under Canadian GAAP, an impairment loss for an asset group is allocated on a pro-rata basis of the long-lived assets in a reporting unit that falls within the scope of CICA 3063 – which excludes goodwill and indefinite-life intangible assets;
- in case of goodwill, CICA 3064 requires that the impairment loss be measured as the difference between the implied fair value of the goodwill and its carrying amount. The implied fair value of the goodwill is determined based on the value that would be ascribed to goodwill if the reporting unit(s) were acquired in a current business combination.

On the other hand, some general disclosures under IAS 36 are quite similar to Canadian GAAP. We do not point all differences or similarities when commenting on the extracts as that would be repetitive.

Extract 4(36) – General statement concerning impairment loss allocation

Eni SpA (AR 2007) page 150
Intangible assets (in part)

When the carrying amount of the cash generating unit, including goodwill allocated thereto, exceeds the cash generating unit's recoverable amount, the excess is recognized as impairment. The impairment loss is first allocated to reduce the carrying amount of goodwill; any remaining excess to be allocated to the assets of the unit is applied pro-rata on the basis of the carrying amount of each asset in the unit. Impairment charges against goodwill are not reversed.

Commentary: In the above extract, the company describes IAS 36 requirements for CGU impairment loss allocation.

Extract 4(37) – Impairment by product group (primary segment)

Rio Tinto Group (Full Financial Statements 2007) page 32
31 PRIMARY SEGMENTAL ANALYSIS (BY PRODUCT GROUP) (in part)

	2007 Total US$m	2006 Total US$m
Impairment (charges)/reversals by product group		
Iron Ore	–	298
Energy	145	(188)
Aluminium	(9)	–
Copper	272	610
Diamonds and Industrial Minerals	(466)	(324)
	(58)	396

Commentary: Here, the company presents separately impairment losses by product group.

Extract 4(38) – Impairment by segment

Telstra Corporation Limited (AR 2007) page 140
5. Segment information (in part)
Telstra Group

	TC&C $m	TB $m	TE&G $m	TW $m	Sensis $m	TInt. $m	TO $m	Other (a) $m	Elimina-tions $m	Total $m
Year ended 30 June 2007										
Revenue from external customers	9,509	3,241	4,465	2,657	1,968	1,574	192	103	-	23,709
Add inter-segment revenue	-	-	64	300	-	32	51	5	(452)	-
Total segment revenue	9,509	3,241	4,529	2,957	1,968	1,606	243	108	(452)	23,709
Segment result	5,593	2,592	2,572	2,867	749	52	(3,915)	(4,830)	45	5,725
Share of equity accounted net (losses)/ profits	-	-	(6)	-	(1)	-	-	-	-	(7)
Less net gain on sale of investments	-	-	43	-	4	9	2	3	-	61
Earnings before interest and income tax expense (EBIT)	5,593	2,592	2,609	2,867	752	61	(3,913)	(4,827)	45	5,779
Segment result has been calculated after charging/(crediting) the following non cash expenses:										
Impairment losses	182	8	7	6	143	21	14	14	-	395
Reversal of impairment losses	-	(1)	-	(1)	-	-	(4)	-	-	(6)
Depreciation and amortisation	-	-	51	-	130	325	61	3,515	-	4,082
Other significant non cash expenses	24	10	21	4	1	-	142	64	-	266

Commentary: This extract specifies the amount of impairment loss by segment.

Extract 4(39) – Disclosure of significant impairment

Royal Ten Cate (AR 2007) page 97
37.1 Impairment and reversal of impairment
The Group recorded an impairment charge of € 2.3 million in respect of machinery in 2007. This amount is stated in the consolidated profit and loss account under depreciation and impairment. No impairment charges were reversed during the year.

Commentary: The company discloses in a separate note the amount of significant impairment.

Extract 4(40) – Disclosure of impairment losses

Givaudan SA (Annual & Financial Report 2007) pages 30 and 31
9. Other operating (income) expenses, net (in part)

in millions of Swiss francs	2007	2006
Restructuring expenses	-	6
Impairment of long-lived assets	14	4
(Gains) losses on fixed assets disposals	1	(16)
Business related information management projects costs	9	13
Butter flavours litigation case settlement	-	44
Quest integration expenses	194	
Other business taxes	14	12
Other (income) expenses, net	12	(4)
Total	244	59

In the year ended 31 December 2007, the Group incurred significant expenses in connection with the combination with Quest International. Integration related charges of CHF 194 million and assets impairment of CHF 14 million have been recognised in the line other operating (income) and expenses, net. Refer also to Note 18 on property, plant and equipment and Note 22 on provisions.

Page 36
18. Property, plant and equipment (in part)

in millions of Swiss francs – 2007	Land	Buildings and building improvements	Machinery, equipment and vehicles	Construction in progress	Total
Net book value					
Balance at 1 January	58	508	514	60	1,140
Additions		6	28	160	194
Disposals	-	-	(2)		(2)
Transfers		54	79	(133)	
Impairment	(1)	(8)	(5)		(14)
Depreciation		(27)	(93)		(120)
Acquisition of subsidiaries (see Note 4)	107	142	140	26	415
Currency translation effects	(4)	(11)	(6)	(4)	(25)
Balance at 31 December	160	664	655	109	1,588
Cost	162	1,004	1,519	109	2,794
Accumulated depreciation		(318)	(855)		(1,173)
Accumulated impairment	(2)	(22)	(9)		(33)
Balance at 31 December	160	664	655	109	1,588

Commentary: These extracts disclose the impairment loss recognized and the line item in which it is presented (other operating (income) expenses). In addition, it provides the details of the impairment loss recognized on long-lived assets by various property, plant and equipment categories.

Extract 4(41) – Disclosure of goodwill impairment

Dimension Data Holdings plc (AR 2007) page 72		
		Restated
	2007	2006
16. GOODWILL	**$'000**	$'000
Cost		
At 1 October	**73,118**	43,424
Recognised on acquisition of subsidiaries and businesses	**12,944**	5,578
Eliminated on disposal of subsidiaries	**(4,349)**	–
Arising on change in holding in subsidiary companies	**–**	34,525
Exchange differences	**8,844**	(10,409)
At end of year	**90,557**	73,118
Goodwill acquired in a business combination is allocated to the cash-generating units ('CGUs') that are expected to benefit from that business combination.		
The goodwill balance is allocated to the following regions:		
Americas	**1,988**	–
Asia	**8,738**	6,433
Australia	**2,491**	3,211
Europe	**7,166**	4,430
Middle East and Africa	**70,174**	59,044
	90,557	73,118

The Group tests goodwill annually for impairment, or more frequently if there are indications that goodwill might be impaired. There has been no impairment to goodwill.

The recoverable amounts of the CGUs are determined from value in use calculations. The key assumptions for the value in use calculations are those regarding the discount rates, growth rates and expected changes in selling prices and direct costs during the period. Management estimates discount rates using pre-tax rates that reflect current market assessments of the time value of money and risks specific to the CGUs. The growth rates are based on industry growth forecasts. Changes in selling prices and direct costs are based on past practices and expectations of future changes in the market.

The Group has prepared forecasts based on the most recent financial budgets approved by the Board of Directors. The discount rates used range between 10.1% and 15.1%. Growth factors applied to expected earnings were between 10% to 20%. These rates are consistent with growth rates of the industry in which the Group operates.

Commentary: In this extract, the company provides details on the goodwill balance and its allocation to CGU. It specifies that:

- goodwill is tested annually for impairment or more frequently if there are indications that goodwill might be impaired;
- it recorded no impairment to goodwill.

The company provides details about the recoverable amounts of the CGU (which is determined from VIU calculations) by disclosing:

- nature of key assumptions (discount rates, growth rates and expected changes in selling prices and direct costs during the period);
- how it estimates:
  - o discount rates (pre-tax rates that reflect current market assessments of the time value of money and risks specific to the CGU),
  - o growth rates (industry growth forecasts), and
  - o changes in selling prices and direct costs (past practices and expectations of future changes in the market).

Finally, the company specifies that it has prepared forecasts based on the most recent financial budgets approved by the board of directors and provides quantitative figures for discount rates and growth factors it applied.

Impairment Loss Reversals

Requirements

Reversals of impairment losses are generally recognized under IAS 36, while they are generally prohibited under Canadian GAAP:

- IAS 36 requires reversals of impairment losses where there has been a change in estimates used to determine the recoverable amount except for goodwill;
- CICA 3063 and CICA 3064 prohibit any reversals of impairment losses except for assets held for sale accounted under CICA 3475.

The prohibition of any impairment reversals for goodwill is based on the premise that any increase in recoverable amount originates from internally generated goodwill and not from an increase in the value of purchased goodwill. Hence, impairment reversal prohibition is in line with IAS 38, *Intangible assets* requirements, which prohibit the recognition of internally generated goodwill.

IAS 36 specifies that increases in VIU should not be recognized as reversals of impairment losses if they arise from the passage of time (i.e., from the unwinding of the discount rate related to the calculation of VIU). The unwinding of the discount does not trigger an impairment loss reversal because an increase in VIU due to passage of time is not the result of changes in the underlying reasons for the original impairment.

A change in an estimate requiring reversal of impairment losses may result from:

- a change in the basis for recoverable amount (VIU or FVLCS);
- a change in the amount or timing of estimated future cash flows or in the discount rate (if the recoverable amount was based on VIU);
- a change in the estimate of FVLCS.

General Disclosures

IAS 36 requires the disclosure of any amounts of impairment reversals during the period for each:

- class of asset; and
- reportable segment, based on the entity's primary reporting format.

All reversals of impairment losses must show distinctly the amounts recognized in income including the line item of the statement of comprehensive income in which those impairment losses are reversed, and the amount of reversals of impairment losses on revalued assets recognized in other comprehensive income.

When an individual impairment loss reversal is material, the following additional disclosures are required (these apply to reversals of impairments of assets, CGU and goodwill):

- the circumstances giving rise to the reversal;
- the amount of reversal;
- the nature and description of asset or CGU;
- the primary segment to which the asset or CGU belongs;
- whether recoverable amount is FVLCS or VIU; and
  - o if FVLCS, how it was determined,
  - o if VIU, the discount rates used in the current assessment and in the previous one.

If impairment loss reversals are material in aggregate to the financial statements as a whole, IAS 36 requires the following disclosures:

- main classes of assets affected; and
- main events and circumstances.

Note that:

- impairment reversal under IAS 36 is limited to an asset's carrying amount that would have been determined if no impairment loss had been recognized in prior years. This requires additional calculations of a theoretical asset's carrying amount net of amortization or depreciation in order to establish the amount of any impairment reversal;
- as a result of the goodwill reversal prohibition, an impairment loss for a CGU is allocated somewhat differently than its reversal. Reversal of an impairment loss on a CGU is recognized as follows:
  - o reversal is allocated pro rata to the assets of the unit, excluding goodwill in proportion of the assets carrying amounts,
  - o reversal is recognized in income, unless the asset is carried at a revalued amount, in which case it is treated as a revaluation increase (a component of other comprehensive income).

Extracts below illustrate the reversals of impairment losses. As indicated previously, Canadian GAAP prohibits reversals of impairments other than for assets that qualify as held for sale.

Illustrative Disclosures:

Extract 4(42) – General accounting policy on reversals

> **Sasol Limited (Annual Financial Statements 2007) page 57**
> **Impairment of non-financial assets (in part)**
> With the exception of goodwill, a previously recognised impairment will be reversed insofar as estimates change as a result of an event occurring after the impairment was recognised. An impairment is reversed only to the extent that the asset's carrying amount does not exceed the carrying amount that would have been determined had no impairment been recognised. A reversal of an impairment is charged to the income statement.

Commentary: The above extract provides a general statement reflecting IAS 36 requirements for impairment reversals.

Extract 4(43) – Impairment charges and reversals details

Rio Tinto Group (Full Financial Statements 2007) page 16 5 IMPAIRMENT (CHARGES)/REVERSALS	Pre-tax 2007 US$m	Taxation 2007 US$m	Outside interests 2007 US$m	**Net amount 2007 US$m**	Net amount 2006 US$m
Cash generating unit					
Argyle Diamonds (a)	(466)	138	–	**(328)**	(289)
Palabora (b)	272	(99)	(73)	**100**	(2)
Tarong coal mine (c)	166	(32)	–	**134**	(152)
Kennecott Utah Copper (KUC) (d)	–	–	–	**–**	381
Iron Ore Company of Canada (IOC) (e)	–	–	–	**–**	111
Other	(30)	11	–	**(19)**	(5)
	(58)	18	(73)	**(113)**	44

(a) The impairment of Argyle in 2006 followed adverse changes in assumptions about future prices, capital and operating costs. The value in use was assessed by reference to cash flows forecast in real terms and discounted at a pre-tax rate of 8 per cent. The 2006 impairment provision included goodwill of US$223 million. Further deterioration in value during the first half of 2007, relating mainly to large increases in the estimated capital cost of Argyle's underground project, triggered another assessment of its recoverable amount. Impairment of property, plant and equipment was assessed by reference to fair value less costs to sell. The determination of fair value less costs to sell was based on the estimated amount that would be obtained from sale in an arm's length transaction between knowledgeable and willing parties. This estimate was derived from discounting projections of cash flows, using valuation assumptions that a buyer might be expected to apply. The US dollar amount of the impairment is US$14 million higher than reported at the half year as a result of retranslation from Australian dollars at the average exchange rate for the full year.

(b) An increase in the Group's long term copper price assumption triggered an assessment of the recoverable amount of Palabora. The value in use was based on cash flows forecast in real terms and discounted at a pre-tax rate of 12 per cent. This led to a full reversal of the remainder of the impairment provision recognised in 2004.

(c) During 2006, a continuation of operating losses triggered an assessment of the recoverable amount of Tarong, one of the Group's coal mines in Australia. The value in use was based on cash flows forecast in real terms and discounted at a pre-tax rate of 8 per cent. During 2007, the sale of Tarong was announced for an amount that led to full reversal of the remainder of the provision recognised in the previous year.

(d) In 2006, an increase in the Group's long term copper price assumption triggered an assessment of the recoverable amount of KUC. The value in use was based on cash flows forecast in real terms and discounted at a pre-tax rate of 8 per cent. This led to a full reversal of the remainder of the impairment provision recognised in 2002.

(e) In 2006, an increase in the Group's long term iron ore price assumption triggered an assessment of the recoverable amount of IOC. The value in use was based on cash flows forecast in real terms and discounted at a pre-tax rate of 8 per cent. This led to a full reversal of the impairment provision recognised in 2002, which had aligned the carrying value with the value negotiated between shareholders during that year as part of a financial restructuring exercise.

Commentary: This extract illustrates disclosures on the amounts of impairment losses and their subsequent reversals of various CGU. Of interest is the description of factors that triggered the assessment of the recoverable amount.

Special Considerations

Testing Goodwill Impairment in the Year of Acquisition

An entity cannot allocate goodwill to a CGU or group of CGUs (IAS 36) or to reporting units (CICA 3064) until it has established the amount of acquired goodwill. Since IFRS 3 (CICA 1581, *Business combination*) allows an entity 12 months from the acquisition date to complete the purchase accounting, the goodwill number might not be determined until that time. Consequently, IAS 36 (CICA 3064) accommodates this delay by requiring that goodwill be allocated to a CGU or a group of CGUs (reporting units) at the latest by the end of the period following that in which the acquisition took place. Goodwill is tested once the allocation is completed within the imposed time limit.

VIU Established on the Basis of Foreign Currency Cash Flows

Canadian GAAP does specifically address issues related to fair value measurement based on foreign currency cash flows. IAS 36 deals specifically with this issue. Accordingly, the VIU is calculated as follows under IFRS:

- cash flows in a foreign currency are estimated in that currency;

- present value is obtained by discounting the cash flow in foreign currency using a discount rate that reflects inflation expectations and that takes into account relevant local economic data. This would yield the VIU in foreign currency;

- VIU in foreign currency is translated to the parent entity's functional currency using the spot rate at the date of the valuation.

Interim Reporting

IAS 34, *Interim financial reporting* and CICA 1751 require that an entity apply the same accounting policies in its interim financial statements as in its annual financial statements. The frequency of an entity's reporting (annual or quarterly) should not affect the measurement of its annual results (i.e., interim measurements should be on a year-to-date basis). This could be interpreted as allowing a reversal of goodwill impairment losses to be recognized in a quarter in the annual financial statements where conditions may have changed so that an impairment loss would have been less or not required at all, had the impairment assessment been made only at the year end. IFRIC 10 was issued to clarify the IFRS accounting treatment and prohibits an entity from reversing an impairment loss recognized in a previous interim period for goodwill.

Illustrative Disclosure:

Extract 4(44) – Impairments in interim periods

TeliaSonera AB (AR 2007) page 43
Note 1 (Consolidated) Basis of Preparation (in part)
New accounting standards (in part)
Standards, amendments to issued standards and interpretations, effective in 2007 or pre-adopted (in part)
IFRIC 10 "Interim Financial Reporting and Impairment" (effective for annual periods beginning on or after November 1, 2006) addresses the apparent conflict between the requirements of IAS 34 "Interim Financial Reporting" and those in other standards on the recognition and reversal of impairment losses on goodwill and certain financial assets. IFRIC 10 states that any such impairment losses recognized in an interim financial statement must not be reversed in subsequent interim or annual financial statements. TeliaSonera already in previous periods applied the principle stated by IFRIC 10.

Commentary: In this extract, the company specifies that it has already applied IFIC 10. The majority of the companies in we examined indicated that IFRIC 10 adoption did not have a significant impact on their financial statements. Note that IFRIC 10 also applies to investments classified as held for sale under IAS 39. Consequently, an entity cannot reverse an impairment loss recognized in an interim period that is related to goodwill and such investments. Canadian GAAP does not have specific guidance on that issue.

Reclassification as Held for Sale

As indicated in the scope section, non-current assets held for sale under IFRS 5 are excluded from the scope of IAS 36. According to both IFRS 5 and CICA 3475, non-current assets classified as held for sale are measured at the lower of their carrying amount and their FVLCS.

Under IFRS, two standards require this measurement at the lower of an asset's carrying amount and FVLCS:

- IAS 36 specifies that a plan to dispose of an asset or CGU is an internal indicator of impairment;
- IFRS 5 requires that an impairment test must be performed according to IAS 36 prior to classifying an asset as held for sale.

Once an asset that meets the criteria of IFRS 5 has been reviewed for impairment and is classified as held for sale, IAS 36 no longer applies. Instead, the asset is measured at fair value less costs to sell in accordance with IFRS 5 (see Chapter 12).

For an asset to be classified as held for sale, both IFRS 5 and CICA 3475 require that:

- the asset be available for immediate sale in its present condition subject only to terms that are usual and customary for sales of such assets; and
- sale of the asset must be highly probable.

Depreciation is discontinued for assets classified as held for sale. Such assets are presented distinctly on the face of the balance sheet.

Illustrative Disclosure:

Extract 4(45) – Reclassification from property, plant and equipment as held for sale and vice versa

> **InterContinental Hotels Group PLC (AR 2007) page 67**
> **11 HELD FOR SALE AND DISCONTINUED OPERATIONS (in part)**
> During the year ended 31 December 2007, the Group sold three hotels (2006 32 hotels) and two associates (2006 nil), continuing the asset disposal programme commenced in 2003. An additional three hotels were classified as held for sale during the year, whilst one hotel previously classified as held for sale was reclassified as property, plant and equipment. At 31 December 2007, three hotels (2006 four hotels and two associates) were classified as held for sale.
>
> At 31 December 2006, an impairment loss of £3m was recognised on the remeasurement of a property that was classified as held for sale. The loss, which reduced the carrying amount of the asset to fair value less costs to sell, was recognised in the income statement in gain on disposal of assets. Fair value was determined by an independent property valuation. No impairment losses have been recognised at 31 December 2007.

Commentary: In the above extract, the company indicates that it classified three hotels as held for sale during the year. It also re-classified one hotel previously classified as held for sale as property, plant and equipment. The company specifies that no impairment loss was recorded subsequent to the classification. Note that the company did incur a loss on classification as held for sale in the previous year. Similar accounting treatment and disclosures would apply under Canadian GAAP.

Investments in Subsidiaries, Associates and Joint Ventures

IAS 28 requires that an investment in an associate be tested for impairment, according to IAS 36, as a single asset by comparing its recoverable amount (higher of VIU and FVLCS) with its carrying amount. Consequently, any goodwill included as part of the carrying amount of the investment in the associate is no longer tested for impairment. Rather, it is indirectly assessed as part of the test for impairment of the investment as a whole. This treatment also applies under Canadian GAAP (according to CICA 3064, no part of the impairment write-down of an investment accounted for by the equity method can be presented in the income statement as a goodwill impairment loss).

Any impairment can be reversed if the recoverable amount of the associate increases.

To address concerns that dividends could result in inappropriate recognition of income in non-consolidated financial statements, IAS 36 introduces an additional indicator of impairment by requiring an entity to consider whether it has recognized a dividend from the investment and evidence is available that:

- the carrying amount of the investment in the separate financial statements exceeds the carrying amount in the consolidated financial statements of the investee's net assets, including associated goodwill; or
- the dividend exceeds the total comprehensive income of the subsidiary, jointly controlled entity or associate in the period in which the dividend is declared.

CICA 3051 is converged with IAS 36, except that the latter does not require evaluation at the end of every reporting date — only whenever events or changes in circumstances indicate that the carrying amount may not be recoverable. In addition, CICA 3051 specifies that an impairment loss be recognized when there has been a significant or prolonged decline in value below carrying amount.

Illustrative Disclosure:

Extract 4(46) – Impairment losses and subsequent reversals for investments in associates

---

Fiat S.p.A. (AR 2007) page 253

Measurement (in part)

Investments in subsidiaries and associated companies are stated at cost adjusted for any impairment losses.

The excess on acquisition of the purchase cost and the share acquired by the company of the investee company's net assets measured at fair value is, accordingly, included in the carrying value of the investment.

Investments in subsidiaries and associated companies are tested for impairment annually and if necessary more often. If there is any evidence that these investments have been impaired, the impairment loss is recognised directly in the income statement. If the company's share of losses of the investee exceeds the carrying amount of the investment and if the company has an obligation or intends to respond for these losses, the company's interest is reduced to zero and a liability is recognised for its share of the additional losses. If the impairment loss subsequently no longer exists it is reversed and the reversal is recognised in the income statement up to the limit of the cost of the investment.

Fiat S.p.A. (AR 2007) (continued)

2. Reversals of impairment losses (impairment losses) of investments

Reversals of impairment losses and impairment losses of investments can be analysed as follows:

(in thousands of euros)	2007	2006
Reversals of impairment losses:		
- Fiat Partecipazioni S.p.A.	1,308,000	1,388,000
- Iveco S.p.A.	–	945,814
- Fiat Netherlands Holding N.V.	–	95,536
Total Reversals of impairment losses	1,308,000	2,429,350
Impairment losses:		
- Comau S.p.A.	(60,931)	(330,000)
Total Impairment losses	(60,931)	(330,000)
Total Reversals of impairment losses (impairment losses)	1,247,069	2,099,350

This item consists of the reversals of impairment losses or impairment losses arising from the application of the cost method in accordance with IAS 27 and IAS 36.

In particular as the investments are not listed and a market value (fair value less costs to sell) cannot be reliably measured, their recoverable amount in measuring impairment losses and the reversal of impairment losses has been taken as their value in use. The value in use of an investment has been identified as the present value of the estimated cash flows expected to arise from the results of the investment and from the estimated value of a hypothetical "ultimate disposal", in line with the requirements of IAS 28 (paragraph 33). In calculating this value in use, the forecast included in the business plans of the individual Group Sectors are taken into consideration, as attributed to the investments, and increased by their terminal value, adjusted to take into account the risks and uncertainties inherent in the assumptions on which these plans are based. These results and the terminal value are then discounted to present value by applying a rate that is representative of the cost of equity, which varies between 11% and 15% (between 11% and 16% in 2006) depending on the characteristics of the Sector under consideration.

With reference to the investment in Fiat Partecipazioni S.p.A., the historical cost was impaired in previous years until 2005 mainly as a result of the losses incurred by Fiat Group Automobiles S.p.A. (at the time named Fiat Auto S.p.A.) which is held as an investment by Fiat Partecipazioni S.p.A. The residual part of the accumulated impairment loss which were available for reversal amounted to 4,015,000 thousand euros at December 31, 2006. Given the results achieved and the confirmed positive outlook for the coming years, taking into consideration the above-mentioned adjustments, at December 31, 2007 the value in use of the investment in Fiat Group Automobiles S.p.A. was estimated at 4.7 billion euros, which was then compared with the corresponding figure at December 31, 2006 of approximately 3.3 billion euros. The difference of approximately 1.4 billion euros, taken together with the operating cash flows generated during the year by Fiat Partecipazioni S.p.A. and net of the dividend distributed to Fiat S.p.A. in 2007, gave rise to a reversal of a total amount of 1,308,000 thousand euros of the previous impairment losses. The residual part of the accumulated impairment loss recognised in prior years which is available for reversal in future years amounts to 2,707,000 thousand euros at December 31, 2007, as reported in Note 11.

Considerations similar to those for Fiat Group Automobiles S.p.A. in 2007 were made in 2006 with regard to the investments in Iveco S.p.A. and Fiat Netherlands Holding N.V. (and the investment of the latter company in CNH Global N.V.) and, as a result, historic cost was fully reinstated and the impairment losses recognised in previous years for those investments were reversed.

The write-down of the investment in Comau S.p.A. has been determined using the same method.

Commentary: This extract provides detailed disclosures on impairment and the subsequent reversals of investments in subsidiaries and associated companies. The company specifies that:

- it tests impairment annually and, if necessary, more often (this differs from Canadian GAAP where impairment is tested only when events or changes in circumstances indicate that the carrying amount may not be recoverable);
- it records impairment loss in the income statement (same as would be required under Canadian GAAP);
- it might record a liability up to the level of its share of the additional losses (same as would be required under Canadian GAAP);
- the amounts of impairment losses on investments (which differ under Canadian GAAP, which uses fair value as a benchmark instead of recoverable value);
- the amount of reversals of impairment losses (which cannot be recognized under Canadian GAAP).

Extractive Industries

IFRS 6 governs the treatment of assets in the exploration and evaluation phase for extractive industries. That standard establishes which assets should be measured at cost. An entity determines its accounting policy for allocating exploration and evaluation assets to CGU or CGU groups. That level may comprise one or more CGUs.

IFRS 6 requires that exploration and evaluation assets be tested for impairment when facts and circumstances suggest that their carrying amount may exceed their recoverable amount. Indicators of impairment under IFRS 6 differ somewhat from those under IAS 36. Also, when technical feasibility and commercial viability of extracting a mineral resource become demonstrable, the assets fall outside the scope of IFRS 6 and are reclassified to be accounted for according to the pertinent IFRS standard and should be tested for impairment accordingly.

IFRS 6 includes the following examples of "facts and circumstances" that may indicate that impairment testing is required:

- period for which an entity has the right to explore in a specific area has expired or will expire in the near future, and is not expected to be renewed;
- substantive expenditure on further exploration for and evaluation of mineral resources in the specific area is neither budgeted for nor planned;
- exploration for, and evaluation of, mineral resources in a specific area have not led to the discovery of commercially viable quantities of mineral resources, and the entity has decided to discontinue such activities in the specific area; and
- sufficient data exist to indicate that, although a development in a specific area is likely to proceed, the carrying amount of the exploration and evaluation asset is unlikely to be recovered in full from either successful development or sale.

When such facts and circumstances indicate impairment, entities must assess what amount of loss to recognize. IFRS 6 allows a deferral of potential impairment loss recognition as assets might be aggregated at a level higher than the CGU. Hence, an entity can assess impairment of exploration and evaluation assets by allocating them to a CGU, or groups of CGUs, identified according to its accounting policy. The only limitation specified is that each CGU, or group of units, to which an exploration and evaluation asset is allocated cannot be larger than a segment based on either the entity's primary or secondary reporting format under IFRS 8, *Operating segments*.

This flexibility applies only to the testing of impairment. If impairment is established, losses are recognized and measured in accordance with IAS 36 requirements.

Illustrative Disclosures:

Extract 4(47) – Exploration and development costs

Eni SpA (AR 2007) page 151

Exploration and production activities[4] (in part)

Development

Development costs are those costs incurred to obtain access to proved reserves and to provide facilities for extracting, gathering and storing oil and gas. They are then capitalized within property, plant and equipment and amortized generally on a UOP basis, as their useful life is closely related to the availability of feasible reserves. This method provides for residual costs at the end of each quarter to be amortized at a rate representing the ratio between the volumes extracted during the quarter and the proved developed reserves existing at the end of the quarter, increased by the volumes extracted during the quarter. This method is applied with reference to the smallest aggregate representing a direct correlation between investments and proved developed reserves.

Costs related to unsuccessful development wells or damaged wells are expensed immediately as losses on disposal. Impairments and reversal of impairments of development costs are made on the same basis as those for tangible assets.

(4) IFRS do not establish specific criteria for hydrocarbon exploration and production activities. Eni continues to use existing accounting policies for exploration and evaluation assets previously applied before the introduction of IFRS 6 "Exploration for and evaluation of mineral resources".

Commentary: The company describes how it accounts for development costs incurred to obtain access to proved reserves and to provide facilities for extracting, gathering and storing oil and gas. It specifies that impairments and reversal of impairments of development costs are made on the same basis as those for tangible assets (i.e., according to IAS 36 requirements).

Extract 4(48) – Uncertainties related to impairment for mining activities

Dragon Mining Limited (AR 2007) page 50

1. SUMMARY OF SIGNIFICANT ACCOUNTING POLICIES (in part)

(iv) Impairment of assets (in part)

The recoverable amount of each Cash Generating Unit (CGU) is determined as the higher of value in use and fair value less costs to sell.

Given the nature of the consolidated entity's mining activities, future changes in long term assumptions upon which these estimates are based, may give rise to material adjustments to the carrying value of the CGU. This could lead to a reversal of part, or all, of impairment losses recorded in the year to 31 December 2007, or the recognition of additional impairment losses in the future (refer to note 31 for details of impairment losses). The inter-relationships of the significant assumptions upon which estimated future cash flows are based, however, are such that it is impractical to disclose the extent of the possible effects of a change in a key assumption in isolation. Due to the nature of the assumptions and their significance to the assessment of the recoverable amount of each CGU, relatively modest changes in one or more assumptions could require a material adjustment to the carrying value of the related non-current assets within the next reporting period.

Commentary: Here, the company indicates that changes in long-term assumptions related to VIU calculations may give rise to material adjustments to the carrying value of the CGU and lead to the recognition of additional impairment losses or reversals in the future. Disclosures on these measurements uncertainties are in line with Canadian GAAP except that reversals would not be a concern since they would not be allowed.

Extract 4(49) – Impairment and VIU calculations for mining operations

Rio Tinto Group (Full Financial Statements 2007) page 11

1 PRINCIPAL ACCOUNTING POLICIES (in part)

Impairment of non current assets

Property, plant and equipment and finite life intangible assets are reviewed for impairment if there is any indication that the carrying amount may not be recoverable. In addition, an impairment loss is recognised for any excess of carrying amount over the fair value less costs to sell of a non-current asset or disposal group held for sale.

When a review for impairment is conducted, the recoverable amount is assessed by reference to the higher of 'value in use' (being the net present value of expected future cash flows of the relevant cash generating unit) and 'fair value less costs to sell'. Where there is no binding sale agreement or active market, fair value less costs to sell is based on the best information available to reflect the amount the Group could receive for the cash generating unit in an arm's length transaction. The estimates used for impairment reviews are based on detailed mine plans and operating plans, modified as appropriate to meet the requirements of IAS 36 'Impairment of Assets'. Future cash flows are based on estimates of:

- the quantities of the reserves and mineral resources for which there is a high degree of confidence of economic extraction;
- future production levels;
- future commodity prices (assuming the current market prices will revert to the Group's assessment of the long term average price, generally over a period of three to five years); and
- future cash costs of production, capital expenditure, close down, restoration and environmental clean up.

The cash flow forecasts are based on best estimates of expected future revenues and costs. These may include net cash flows expected to be realised from extraction, processing and sale of mineral resources that do not currently qualify for inclusion in proved or probable ore reserves. Such non reserve material is included where there is a high degree of confidence in its economic extraction. This expectation is usually based on preliminary drilling and sampling of areas of mineralisation that are contiguous with existing reserves. Typically, the additional evaluation to achieve reserve status for such material has not yet been done because this would involve incurring costs earlier than is required for the efficient planning and operation of the mine.

The expected future cash flows of cash generating units reflect long term mine plans which are based on detailed research, analysis and iterative modelling to optimise the level of return from investment, output and sequence of extraction. The plan takes account of all relevant characteristics of the ore body, including waste to ore ratios, ore grades, haul distances, chemical and metallurgical properties of the ore impacting on process recoveries and capacities of processing equipment that can be used. The mine plan is therefore the basis for forecasting production output in each future year and the related production costs.

Rio Tinto's cash flow forecasts are based on assessments of expected long term commodity prices, which for most commodities are derived from an analysis of the marginal costs of the producers of these commodities. These assessments often differ from current price levels and are updated periodically.

In some cases, prices applying to some part of the future sales volumes of a cash generating unit are predetermined by existing sales contracts. The effects of such contracts are taken into account in forecasting future cash flows.

Cost levels incorporated in the cash flow forecasts are based on the current long term mine plan for the cash generating unit. For impairment reviews, recent cost levels are considered, together with expected changes in costs that are compatible with the current condition of the business and which meet the requirements of IAS 36. IAS 36 includes a number of restrictions on the future cash flows that can be recognised in value in use assessments in respect of future restructurings and improvement related capital expenditure.

The discount rate applied is based upon the Group's weighted average cost of capital with appropriate adjustment for the risks associated with the relevant cash flows, to the extent that such risks are not reflected in the forecast cash flows.

> **Rio Tinto Group (Full Financial Statements 2007) (continued)**
>
> For operations with a functional currency other than the US dollar, the impairment review is undertaken in the relevant functional currency. The great majority of the Group's sales are based on prices denominated in US dollars. To the extent that the currencies of countries in which the Group produces commodities strengthen against the US dollar without commodity price offset, cash flows and, therefore, net present values are reduced.
>
> When calculating 'value in use', IAS 36 requires that calculations should be based on exchange rates current at the time of the assessment.

Commentary: In this extract, the company provides detailed information on VIU measurement as it applies specifically to its mining operations. Measurements and disclosures are in line with Canadian GAAP.

Extract 4(50) – Impairment losses and their reversal for oil and gas properties

Samson Oil and Gas Limited (AR 2007) pages 68 to 70
NOTE 13. OIL AND GAS PROPERTIES

	Consolidated Entity		Parent Entity	
	2007 $	2006 $	2007 $	2006 $
Proved developed producing properties at cost	49,225,014	49,160,758	-	-
Accumulated depletion	(5,889,404)	(3,153,139)	-	-
Impairment	(9,109,694)	(6,226,352)		
	34,225,916	39,781,267	-	-
Proved undeveloped properties at cost	21,260,014	24,605,620	-	-
Impairment	(9,142,561)	(10,773,574)		
	12,117,453	13,832,046	-	-
Total	46,343,369	53,613,313	-	-

	Consolidated Entity		Parent Entity	
	2007 $	2006 $	2007 $	2006 $
Proved Developed Producing Properties				
At 1 July, net of accumulated depreciation and impairment	39,781,267	7,691,347	-	-
Additions	3,842,332	5,797,039	-	-
Fair value of assets acquired	-	32,954,704	-	-
Transfer from Proved Undeveloped Properties	-	1,545,110	-	-
Impairment	(64,824)	(6,226,352)	-	-
Depreciation charge	(3,386,181)	(2,840,529)	-	-
Exchange adjustment	(5,946,678)	859,948	-	-
At 30 June, net of accumulated depreciation and impairment	34,225,916	39,781,267	-	-
Proved Undeveloped Properties				
At 1 July, net of accumulated depreciation and impairment	13,832,046	11,218,218	-	-
Additions	322,830	-	-	-
Fair value of assets acquired	-	13,870,013	-	-
Transfer to Proved Developed Producing Properties	-	(1,545,110)	-	-
Transfer to exploration and evaluation assets	(160,656)	-	-	-
Impairment	(236,927)	(10,773,574)	-	-
Exchange adjustment	(1,639,840)	1,062,499	-	-
At 30 June, net of accumulated depreciation and impairment	12,117,453	13,832,046	-	-

Samson Oil and Gas Limited (AR 2007) (continued)

a) Assets pledged as security

In the current and prior year, Macquarie Bank Limited has a first charge mortgage over all assets (including the oil and gas properties) of the Group. This collateral has been provided as part of the funding facility provided by Macquarie Bank Limited to Samson Oil & Gas USA, Inc. Refer to Note 16 for further details relating to this facility.

	Consolidated Entity		Parent Entity	
	2007 $	2006 $	2007 $	2006 $
The written down value of assets pledged as security are:				
Producing properties	34,225,916	39,781,267	-	-
Non producing properties	12,117,453	13,832,046	-	-
	46,343,369	53,613,313	-	-

b) Impairment of oil and gas properties

At 30 June 2007, the Group reviewed the carrying value of its oil and gas properties for impairment. An independent third party was commissioned to assess the future net present value of the Group assets (by cash generating unit), determined to be value in use. The discount rate used to assess the value in use was 10%.

The value of the oil and gas properties was reviewed on a field by field basis and has resulted in net impairment expense of $301,751 (2006: $16,999,926). It is the Group's policy to use proved and probable reserves to support the carrying value of its properties.

30 June 2007

Included in this amount is a reversal of impairment losses recorded in the half year ended 31 December 2006 of $5,303,808 and a reversal of impairment losses recorded in the year ended 30 June 2006 of $1,930,579. At 30 June 2007, the Directors determined that the conditions which caused the impairments to be recorded in prior periods and the impairment was reversed in accordance with the Company's policy. This was primarily due to the installation of compression at the Lookout Wash Field which improved the production performance of that field post the reserve determination as at June 2006. In addition the existing compression system at Jonah was restaged which also improved the production performance of that field compared to that which was available at the last reserve review.

Some impairment was recognised in the current year. This primarily related to a decrease in the reserves for the Amber Field in Oklahoma. A value was assigned to undeveloped locations of this field when it was acquired by the Group from Kestrel Energy Inc. Reserves have decreased subsequent to this initial valuation and thus the field has been impaired.

30 June 2006

Impairment losses were determined based on the Consolidated Entity's proved reserves at 30 June 2006. Commodity pricing used in the Reserve Report is based on 30 June 2006 pricing, which is normally a lower pricing period for gas production. The impairment within the producing assets has been caused to some extent by the drilling results in the Jonah and Look Out Wash Fields, which in the short term have not met expectations.

The impairment of non-producing properties is, in part, due to the failure of the Greens Canyon #2 well. This well did not reach its intended target of the Muddy Formation. The stimulation of the Frontier did not reach long term economic levels, despite early flow rates that were encouraging. Accordingly reserves associated with these stratigraphic levels have been removed from a Proven Category until such time as an economic rate from these reservoirs can be achieved.

Commentary: The above extract provides details on impairment amounts for oil and gas properties. It describes in detail how the company reviews the impairment of such properties and indicates that the company reviewed the carrying value of its oil properties for impairment and commissioned an independent third party to assess the VIU of its assets by CGU. The company discloses various assumption used for VIU calculations and provides detailed information (both quantitative and qualitative) on the impairment losses it has recognized or reversed. Even though the information provided would be considered to be good disclosure, some of the accounting policies, such as ones for reversals, could not be used under Canadian GAAP.

FUTURE DEVELOPMENTS

In August 2008, the IASB proposed an amendment to IAS 36 to clarify that the largest unit permitted for allocating goodwill acquired in a business combination for the purpose of impairment testing is the operating segment as defined in IFRS 8 before the aggregation permitted by IFRS 8. The IASB proposed that this amendment be applied prospectively for annual periods beginning on or after January 1, 2010 with earlier application permitted. However, if an entity applies the amendment for an earlier period this fact should be disclosed.

COMPREHENSIVE EXAMPLES

This section presents two comprehensive examples providing extensive disclosures on asset impairment. We have selected relevant extracts of notes to the financial statements that might provide good examples of disclosure under IFRS.

Suez – All extracts 4(A) were obtained from the Reference Document for year ended December 31, 2007.

Extract 4(A1) – Suez, page 198

In this extract, the company presents impairment distinctly in the income statement as an element of income from operating activities. Note that the company elected to calculate an amount labelled as "current operating activities" that excludes impairment. The presentation of such subtotals in the income statement is allowed under IFRS.

CONSOLIDATED INCOME STATEMENTS (in part)				
In millions of euros	Notes	2007	2006	2005
Revenues		47,475.4	44,289.2	41,488.9
Purchases		(21,289.4)	(21,010.0)	(18,678.7)
Personnel costs		(8,141.5)	(7,640.8)	(7,902.9)
Depreciation, amortization and provisions		(1,912.7)	(1,684.8)	(1,701.9)
Other operating income and expenses, net		(10,956.4)	(9,457.1)	(9,303.2)
CURRENT OPERATING INCOME	4	5,175.4	4,496.5	3,902.2
Mark-to-market on commodity contracts other than trading instruments		67.8	17.1	(151.1)
Impairment of property, plant and equipment, intangible assets and financial assets		(132.0)	(150.3)	(657.9)
Restructuring costs		(42.6)	(88.8)	(101.5)
Disposals of assets, net		339.4	1,093.1	1,529.9
INCOME FROM OPERATING ACTIVITIES	5	5,408.0	5,367.6	4,521.6

Extract 4(A2) – Suez, page 204

The company describes, in general terms, the uncertainties related to the measurement of recoverable amounts for goodwill, intangible assets and property, plant and equipment.

1.3 Use of judgements and estimates (in part)
1.3.1.1 Recoverable amount of property, plant and equipment and intangible assets
The recoverable amount of goodwill, intangible assets and property, plant and equipment is based on estimates and assumptions regarding in particular the expected market outlook and future cash flows associated with the assets. Any changes in these assumptions may have a material impact on the measurement of the recoverable amount and could result in adjustments to the impairment expenses already booked.

Extract 4(A3) – Suez, pages 206 and 207

Here, the company describes IAS 36 accounting requirements for the measurement of goodwill.

1.4.4 Intangible assets (in part)

1.4.4.1.2 Measurement of goodwill

Goodwill is not amortized but tested for impairment each year, or more frequently where an indication of impairment is identified. Impairment tests are carried out at the level of cash-generating units (CGUs) which constitute groups of assets generating cash inflows that are largely independent of the cash inflows from other cash-generating units.

The methods used to carry out these impairment tests are described in section 1.4.7 "Recoverable amount of property, plant and equipment and intangible assets".

Impairment losses in relation to goodwill cannot be reversed and are shown under "Impairment" in the consolidated income statement.

Impairment losses on goodwill relating to associate companies are reported under "Share in net income of associates".

Extract 4(A4) – Suez, page 207

This extract describes IAS 36 accounting requirements for impairment testing of intangible assets other than goodwill.

1.4.4.2 Other intangible assets (in part)

1.4.4.2.3 Impairment tests

In accordance with IAS 36, impairment tests are carried out on intangible assets when there is an indication that the assets may be impaired. Such indications may be based on events or changes in the market environment, or on internal sources of information. Intangible assets that are not amortized are tested for impairment annually.

These assets are tested for impairment at the level of the individual asset or cash-generating unit as appropriate, determined in accordance with IAS 36. If the recoverable amount of an asset is lower than its carrying amount, the carrying amount is reduced to the recoverable amount by recording an impairment loss. After the recognition of an impairment loss, the amortization expense for the asset is adjusted in future periods to allocate the asset's revised carrying amount, less its residual value (if any), on a systematic basis over its remaining useful life. Impairment losses recorded in relation to intangible assets may be subsequently reversed if the recoverable amount of the assets is once again higher than their carrying amount. The increased carrying amount of an intangible attributable to a reversal of an impairment loss may not exceed the carrying amount that would have been determined (net of amortization) had no impairment loss been recognized in prior periods. The methods used for performing these impairment tests are described in section 1.4.7.

Extract 4(A5) – Suez, page 208

This extract describes IAS 36 accounting requirements for impairment testing of property, plant and equipment.

1.4.5 Property, plant and equipment (in part)

1.4.5.3 Impairment tests

In accordance with IAS 36, impairment tests are carried out on items of property, plant and equipment where there is an indication that the assets may be impaired. Such indications may be based on events or changes in the market environment, or on internal sources of information.

Items of property, plant and equipment are tested for impairment at the level of the individual asset or cash-generating unit (CGU) as appropriate, determined in accordance with IAS 36. If the recoverable amount of an asset is lower than its carrying amount, the carrying amount is reduced to the recoverable amount by recording an impairment loss. Upon recognition of an impairment loss, the depreciable amount – and possibly the useful life – of the item of property, plant and equipment concerned is revised.

Impairment losses recorded in relation to property, plant and equipment may be subsequently reversed if the recoverable amount of the assets is once again higher than their carrying value. The increased carrying amount of an item of property, plant or equipment attributable to a reversal of an impairment loss may not exceed the carrying amount that would have been determined (net of depreciation) had no impairment loss been recognized in prior periods.

The methods used for performing these impairment tests are described in section 1.4.7.

Extract 4(A6) – Suez, page 209

In this extract, the company describes IAS 36 accounting requirements for the measurement of recoverable amounts for property, plant and equipment and intangible assets.

1.4.7 Recoverable amount of property, plant and equipment and intangible assets

In order to review the recoverable amount of property, plant and equipment and intangible assets, the assets are grouped, where appropriate, into cash-generating units (CGUs) and the carrying amount of each unit is compared with its recoverable amount.

For operating entities which the Group intends to hold on a long-term and going concern basis, the recoverable amount of an asset corresponds to the higher of its fair value less costs to sell and its value in use. Value in use is primarily determined based on the present value of future operating cash flows and a terminal value. Standard valuation techniques are used based on the following main economic data:

- discount rates based on the specific characteristics of the operating entities concerned;
- terminal values in line with the available market data specific to the operating segments concerned and growth rates associated with these terminal values, limited to inflation rate.

Discount rates are determined on a post-tax basis and applied to post-tax cash flows. The recoverable amounts calculated on the basis of these discount rates are the same as the amounts obtained by applying the pre-tax discount rates to cash flows estimated on a pre-tax basis, as required by IAS 36.

For operating entities which the Group has decided to sell, the related carrying amount of the assets concerned is written down to estimated market value less costs of disposal. Where negotiations are ongoing, this value is determined based on the best estimate of their outcome as of the balance sheet date.

When impairment in value is required, the impairment loss is recorded in the consolidated income statement under «Impairment».

Extract 4(A7) – Suez, pages 216 and 217

The company provides the justification for its presentation of current operating income, which excludes impairment. This would be a non-GAAP amount that is not presented distinctly in the context of financial statements prepared according to Canadian GAAP.

1.4.17 Current operating income

Current operating income is an indicator used by the SUEZ Group to present «a level of operational performance that can be used as part of an approach to forecast recurring performance[3]». Current operating income is a sub-total which helps management to better understand the Group's performance because it excludes elements which are inherently difficult to predict due to their unusual, irregular or non-recurring nature. For SUEZ, such elements relate to asset impairments and disposals, restructuring costs and mark-to-market on commodity contracts other than trading instruments, which are defined as follows:

- impairment includes impairment losses on non-current assets;

- disposals of assets include capital gains and losses on disposals of non-current assets, consolidated companies and available-for-sale securities;

- restructuring costs concern costs corresponding to a restructuring program planned and controlled by management that materially changes either the scope of a business undertaken by an entity, or the manner in which that business is conducted, based on the criteria set out in IAS 37;

- mark-to-market on commodity contracts other than trading instruments: this item corresponds to changes in the fair value (mark-to-market) of financial instruments relating to commodities, gas and electricity, which do not qualify as either trading or hedging instruments. These contracts are used in economic hedges of operating transactions in the energy sector. Since changes in the fair value of these instruments – which must be recognized through income in IAS 39 – can be material and difficult to predict, they are presented on a separate line of the consolidated income statement.

Extract 4(A8) – Suez, page 229

In this extract, the company presents distinctly impairment amounts excluded from current operating income. This distinct presentation is generally not allowed under Canadian GAAP.

NOTE 5 INCOME FROM OPERATING ACTIVITIES (in part)			
In millions of euros	2007	2006	2005
CURRENT OPERATING INCOME	**5,175.4**	4,496.5	3,902.2
Mark-to-market on commodity contracts other than trading instruments	**67.8**	17.1	(151.1)
Impairment of property, plant and equipment, intangible assets and financial assets	**(132.0)**	(150.3)	(657.9)
Restructuring costs	**(42.6)**	(88.8)	(101.5)
Disposals of assets, net	**339.4**	1,093.1	1,529.9
INCOME FROM OPERATING ACTIVITIES	**5,408.0**	5,367.6	4,521.6

Extract 4(A9) – Suez, page 230

The company presents the details of impairment charges for various assets. It also shows how it has established the amount of impairment losses recognized.

5.2 Impairment of property, plant and equipment, intangible assets and financial assets (in part)

In millions of euros	2007	2006	2005
Asset impairment:			
Goodwill	**(1.3)**	(11.6)	(114.8)
Property, plant and equipment and other intangible assets	**(113.9)**	(131.7)	(448.0)
Financial assets	**(40.5)**	(48.6)	(117.0)
Total	**(155.7)**	(191.9)	(679.8)
Reversals of impairment losses:			
Property, plant and equipment and other intangible assets	**0.9**	8.0	10.2
Financial assets	**22.8**	33.7	11.7
Total	**23.7**	41.6	21.9
TOTAL	**(132.0)**	(150.3)	(657.9)

In the event of significant adverse events (contractual disputes, downturn in the economic environment for certain business segments or countries), the Group reviews the value in use of the assets affected and may recognize impairment losses on some of those assets. In both 2007 and 2006, impairment losses were mainly taken on SUEZ Energy International in the US amid the context of persistently unfavorable prices for certain merchant units, while in 2005 they concerned mainly the international activities of SUEZ Environment (Brazil, Argentina, etc.), SUEZ Energy International in the US, and SUEZ Energy Services in the Netherlands.

All goodwill cash-generating units (CGUs) are tested for impairment. In 2007, impairment tests were carried out by reference to data based as at end-June 2007 and to a review of events occurred in the second half of the year. The calculation of the recoverable amount of CGUs takes into account three scenarios (low, medium and high). The «medium» scenario is usually applied to compare the CGU's recoverable amount with its carrying amount.

The discount rates applied are determined on the basis of the weighted average cost of capital adjusted to reflect business, country and currency risks associated with each CGU reviewed. Discount rates correspond to a risk-free market interest rate plus a country risk premium.

The discount rates used in 2007 to calculate the present value of cash flows in the impairment test ranged from 5.2% to 15.3%, compared with discount rates between 5.1% and 12.3% in 2006 and between 5% and 14.6% in 2005.

5.2.1 Impairment of goodwill (in part)

With the exception of the Electrabel Benelux CGU, no individual amount of goodwill allocated to other CGUs represents more than 5% of the Group's total goodwill.

Electrabel Benelux CGU

The total amount of goodwill allocated to this CGU was €9.2 billion at December 31, 2007. The Electrabel Benelux CGU includes the Group's electricity production, sale and distribution activities in Belgium, the Netherlands and Luxembourg.

The annual review of this CGU's recoverable amount was based on its estimated value in use at June 30, 2007.

To estimate value in use, the Group uses cash flow projections based on financial forecasts approved by Management covering a period of six years, and a discount rate of 7%. Cash flow projections beyond this six-year period are extrapolated to obtain a terminal value.

Key assumptions used in the calculation include expected trends in long-term prices for electricity and fuel. These amounts reflect the best estimates of market prices, while fuel consumption is estimated taking into account expected changes in production assets. The risk-free rate and market risk premium represent external available sources of information.

Based on events that are reasonably likely to occur as of the balance sheet date, the Group considers that any changes in the key assumptions described above would not increase the carrying amount in excess of the recoverable amount.

Extract 4(A10) – Suez, page 231

This extract presents, in a table, the assumptions the company used to review the recoverable amount of the other main CGU. It also presented a justification of a relatively high discount rate.

5.2.1 Impairment of goodwill (in part)

Other CGUs

The table below sets out the assumptions used to review the recoverable amount of the other main cash-generating units:

Cash-generating units	Measurement method	Discount rate
Electrabel France:		
SHEM	DCF	[5.2% - 8%]
Compagnie National du Rhône (CNR)	DCF	7.10%
United Water	Multiples + DCF	5.24%
SITA UK	DCF	6.70%
Polaniec	DCF	7.90%
Agbar	Share price	
SITA Nederland BV	DCF	6.90%
SITA France	DCF	5.70%
SITA Deutschland	DCF	7%

5.2.2 Impairment of other assets

Given the regulatory environment and downbeat market conditions in the US for certain merchant units, the Group decided to carry out impairment tests on the basis of future cash flows discounted at a rate of 9% in 2007 (unchanged from 2006 and 2005). As a result of these tests, the Group recognized an impairment loss of €72 million in 2007 (€68 million in 2006 and €217 million in 2005).

Extract 4(A11) – Suez, page 241

In this extract, the company provides details of changes in goodwill balances, reflecting impairments separately.

NOTE 9 GOODWILL	
9.1 Movements in the carrying amount of goodwill (in part)	
In millions of euros	
A. GROSS AMOUNT	
At December 31, 2005	13,235.0
Acquisitions	534.4
Disposals and goodwill classified as «assets held for sale»	(226.3)
Translation adjustments	(70.6)
Other	115.2
At December 31, 2006	13,587.7
Acquisitions	2,165.3
Disposals and goodwill classified as «assets held for sale»	(364.9)
Translation adjustments	(120.0)
Other	(202.2)
At December 31, 2007	15,065.9
B. IMPAIRMENT	
At December 31, 2005	(201.8)
Impairment losses	(11.6)
Disposals and goodwill classified as «assets held for sale»	35.7
Translation adjustments	(1.1)
Other	(4.2)
At December 31, 2006	(183.1)
Impairment losses	(1.3)
Disposals and goodwill classified as «assets held for sale»	10.5
Translation adjustments	(0.6)
Other	11.4
At December 31, 2007	(163.1)
C. CARRYING AMOUNT = A + B	
At December 31, 2005	13,033.2
At December 31, 2006	13,404.6
At December 31, 2007	14,902.8

Extract 4(A12) – Suez, page 243

The company provides details on the changes in intangible assets balances, reflecting impairments separately.

NOTE 10 INTANGIBLE ASSETS, NET (in part)					
10.1 Movements in the carrying amount of intangible assets					
In millions of euros	Software	Intangible rights arising on concession contracts	Capacity entitle-ments	Other	Total
A. GROSS AMOUNT					
At December 31, 2005	536.6	3,686.0	1,163.0	1,164.9	6,550.6
Acquisitions	83.1	192.5		42.0	317.5
Disposals	(9.2)	(6.0)		(71.5)	(86.8)
Translation adjustments	(0.5)	(35.7)		(68.8)	(104.9)
Changes in scope of consolidation	(23.8)	(129.9)		15.1	(138.6)
Other	2.0	299.3	16.9	(50.5)	267.7
At December 31, 2006	588.3	4,006.1	1,179.9	1,031.2	6,805.6
Acquisitions	45.7	150.4		82.4	278.5
Disposals	(29.0)	(15.6)		(27.7)	(72.3)
Translation adjustments	0.2	(32.3)		(49.3)	(81.4)
Changes in scope of consolidation	5.1	44.5		(6.9)	42.7
Other	(51.1)	(900.1)		946.2	(5.1)
At December 31, 2007	559.2	3,253.0	1,179.9	1,975.9	6,968.0
B. Accumulated amortization and impairment					
At December 31, 2005	(392.4)	(1,701.2)	(506.3)	(497.1)	(3,097.0)
Amortization/impairment	(81.0)	(206.5)	(24.8)	(68.2)	(380.5)
Disposals	7.0	9.8		6.1	23.0
Translation adjustments	0.4	18.7		27.0	46.0
Changes in scope of consolidation	24.0	94.2		9.1	127.3
Other	7.7	(86.1)		42.3	(36.1)
At December 31, 2006	(434.4)	(1,871.1)	(531.1)	(480.8)	(3,317.5)
Amortization	(54.7)	(112.8)	(24.1)	(89.0)	(280.6)
Impairment	0.0	0.0		(2.7)	(2.7)
Disposals	29.0	14.4		23.6	67.0
Translation adjustments	(0.1)	16.8		29.4	46.1
Changes in scope of consolidation	(4.5)	(19.0)		(1.6)	(25.1)
Other	63.0	515.1		(535.8)	42.4
At December 31, 2007	(401.7)	(1,456.6)	(555.2)	(1,056.9)	(3,470.4)
C. CARRYING AMOUNT = A + B					
At December 31, 2005	144.2	1,984.7	656.7	667.9	3,453.5
At December 31, 2006	153.9	2,135.0	648.8	550.4	3,488.1
At December 31, 2007	157.5	1,796.4	624.7	919.0	3,497.7
Recognized impairment losses for 2007 amounted to €2.7 million versus €3.6 million in 2006 and €19 million in 2005 (see Note 5.2).					

Tesco PLC – All extracts 4(B) were obtained from the annual report for the year ended February 24, 2007.

Extract 4(B1) – Tesco PLC, pages 44 and 55

In this extract the company discloses separately a significant impairment loss in the income statement and a non-GAAP measurement that excludes such impairment. Under Canadian GAAP, the presentation of non-GAAP information is usually not presented in the financial statements.

Group income statement (in part)	notes	2007 £m	2006* £m
Continuing operations			
Revenue (sales excluding VAT)	2	42,641	39,454
Cost of sales		(39,401)	(36,426)
Pensions adjustment – Finance Act 2006	23	258	–
Impairment of the Gerrards Cross site		(35)	–
Gross profit		3,463	3,028
Administrative expenses		(907)	(825)
Profit arising on property-related items	2/3	92	77
Operating profit	2	2,648	2,280

Non-GAAP measure: underlying profit before tax	notes	2007 £m	2006* £m
Profit before tax (excluding discontinued operation)		2,653	2,235
Adjustments for:			
IAS 32 and IAS 39 'Financial Instruments' – Fair value remeasurements	5	4	9
Total IAS 19 Income Statement charge for pensions	23	432	303
'Normal' cash contributions for pensions	23	(321)	(270)
Exceptional items:			
Pensions adjustment – Finance Act 2006	23	(258)	–
Impairment of the Gerrards Cross site		35	–
Underlying profit before tax	1	2,545	2,277

* Results for the year ended 25 February 2006 include 52 weeks for the UK and the Republic of Ireland and 14 months for the majority of the remaining International businesses.

Note 1 Accounting policies (in part)

Use of non-GAAP profit measures – underlying profit before tax (in part)

– Impairment of the Gerrards Cross site – As detailed in the 2006 Annual Report, the Group regards each individual store as a cash-generating unit, with each store tested for impairment if there are indications of impairment at the Balance Sheet date. We are facing continuing uncertainty in respect of our Gerrards Cross site as a result of the complex legal situation following the tunnel collapse. No decision has yet been taken about the future of this site. However, at year end we have written off the carrying value of our existing asset there (an impairment of £35m). We are not yet in a position to assess any recoveries or liabilities in respect of ongoing claims.

Extract 4(B2) – Tesco PLC, page 48

This extract describes the company's accounting policy for the accounting of its investments in associates. Investment is accounted for using the equity method and impairment is deducted (when applicable) from that amount. As the carrying values of investments in joint ventures and associates include acquired goodwill, the latter would not be tested separately for impairment.

Note 1 Accounting policies (in part)

Basis of consolidation (in part)

Joint ventures and associates (in part)

The Group's share of the results of joint ventures and associates is included in the Group Income Statement using the equity method of accounting. Investments in joint ventures and associates are carried in the Group Balance Sheet at cost plus post-acquisition changes in the Group's share of the net assets of the entity, less any impairment in value. The carrying values of investments in joint ventures and associates include acquired goodwill.

If the Group's share of losses in a joint venture or associate equals or exceeds its investment in the joint venture or associate, the Group does not recognise further losses, unless it has incurred obligations to do so or made payments on behalf of the joint venture or associate.

Extract 4(B3) – Tesco PLC, page 49

In this extract, the company describes its policy for its accounting of property, plant and equipment, including the impairment review.

Note 1 Accounting policies (in part)

Property, plant and equipment (in part)

Property, plant and equipment assets are carried at cost less accumulated depreciation and any recognised impairment in value. ...

The following depreciation rates are applied for the Group:

- Freehold and leasehold buildings with greater than 40 years unexpired – at 2.5% of cost
- Leasehold properties with less than 40 years unexpired are depreciated by equal annual instalments over the unexpired period of the lease
- Plant, equipment, fixtures and fittings and motor vehicles – at rates varying from 9% to 33%.

Assets held under finance leases are depreciated over their expected useful lives on the same basis as owned assets or, when shorter, over the term of the relevant lease.

All tangible fixed assets are reviewed for impairment in accordance with IAS 36 'Impairment of Assets' when there are indications that the carrying value may not be recoverable.

Extract 4(B4) – Tesco PLC, page 49

The company describes its policy for accounting for its investment properties, which are carried at cost less accumulated depreciation and any recognized impairment in value.

Note 1 Accounting policies (in part)

Investment property

Investment property is property held to earn rental income and/or for capital appreciation rather than for the purpose of Group operating activities. Investment property assets are carried at cost less accumulated depreciation and any recognised impairment in value. The depreciation policies for investment property are consistent with those described for owner-occupied property.

Extract 4(B5) – Tesco PLC, page 50

In this extract, the company specifies that it used (as allowed by IFRS 1 – see discussion in the section "Planning for Implementation" of this chapter) amount of goodwill as established by previous GAAP.

Note 1 Accounting policies (in part)

Business combinations and goodwill (in part)

... Goodwill is reviewed for impairment at least annually by assessing the recoverable amount of each cash-generating unit to which the goodwill relates. When the recoverable amount of the cash-generating unit is less than the carrying amount, an impairment loss is recognised.

Any impairment is recognised immediately in the Income Statement and is not subsequently reversed.

On disposal of a subsidiary, joint venture or associate, the attributable amount of goodwill is included in the determination of the profit or loss on disposal.

Goodwill arising on acquisitions before 29 February 2004 (the date of transition to IFRS) was retained at the previous UK GAAP amounts subject to being tested for impairment at that date. ...

Extract 4(B6) – Tesco PLC, pages 50 and 51

Here, the company describes its accounting policy for impairment (and its reversal) of tangible and intangible assets, excluding goodwill, as required by IAS 36.

Note 1 Accounting policies (in part)

Impairment of tangible and intangible assets excluding goodwill

At each Balance Sheet date, the Group reviews the carrying amounts of its tangible and intangible assets to determine whether there is any indication that those assets have suffered an impairment loss. If such indication exists, the recoverable amount of the asset is estimated in order to determine the extent of the impairment loss (if any). Where the asset does not generate cash flows that are independent from other assets, the Group estimates the recoverable amount of the cash-generating unit to which the asset belongs.

The recoverable amount is the higher of fair value less costs to sell, and value in use. In assessing value in use, the estimated future cash flows are discounted to their present value using a pre-tax discount rate that reflects current market assessments of the time value of money and the risks specific to the asset.

If the recoverable amount of an asset (or cash-generating unit) is estimated to be less than its carrying amount, the carrying amount of the asset (or cash-generating unit) is reduced to its recoverable amount. An impairment loss is recognised as an expense immediately.

Where an impairment loss subsequently reverses, the carrying amount of the asset (or cash-generating unit) is increased to the revised estimate of the recoverable amount, but so that the increased carrying amount does not exceed the carrying amount that would have been determined if no impairment loss had been recognised for the asset (or cash-generating unit) in prior years. A reversal of an impairment loss is recognised as income immediately.

Extract 4(B7) – Tesco PLC, page 56

In this extract, the company presents the details of impairment losses (and their reversals) by segment.

Note 2 Segmental reporting (in part)				
The Board has determined that the primary segmental reporting format is geographical, based on the Group's management and internal reporting structure. Secondary information is reported by a single business segment, retail and associated activities.				
The Rest of Europe reporting segment includes the Republic of Ireland, Hungary, Poland, the Czech Republic, Slovakia and Turkey. The Asia reporting segment includes Thailand, South Korea, Malaysia, China and Japan. Following its disposal during the year, the Taiwanese business (previously included within the Asia segment) was classified as a discontinued operation in both the current and prior year.				
Geographical segments (in part)				
Year ended 24 February 2007	UK £m	Rest of Europe £m	Asia £m	Total £m
Other segment information				
Capital expenditure (including acquisitions through business combinations):				
– Property, plant and equipment	1,765	786	516	3,067
– Investment property	–	36	22	58
– Goodwill and other intangible assets	197	52	420	669*
Depreciation:				
– Property, plant and equipment	520	155	99	774
– Investment property	–	7	4	11
Amortisation of intangible assets	79	8	6	93
Impairment losses recognised in the Income Statement	(44)	(35)	(3)	(82)
Reversal of prior period impairment losses through the Income Statement	17	46	–	63
Profit/(loss) arising on property-related items	98	–	(6)	92
* Includes £166m of goodwill transferred in from joint ventures, following the acquisition of additional shares in dunnhumby and Hymall.				

Extract 4(B8) – Tesco PLC, page 66

The company provides details on its goodwill impairment measurement, including assumptions used for VIU calculations.

Note 10 Goodwill and other intangible assets (in part)

Impairment of goodwill

Goodwill arising on business combinations is not amortised but is reviewed for impairment on an annual basis or more frequently if there are indications that goodwill may be impaired. Goodwill acquired in a business combination is allocated to groups of cash-generating units according to the level at which management monitor that goodwill.

Recoverable amounts for cash-generating units are based on value in use, which is calculated from cash flow projections for five years using data from the Group's latest internal forecasts, the results of which are reviewed by the Board. The key assumptions for the value in use calculations are those regarding discount rates, growth rates and expected changes in margins. Management estimates discount rates using pre-tax rates that reflect the current market assessment of the time value of money and the risks specific to the cash-generating units. Changes in selling prices and direct costs are based on past experience and expectations of future changes in the market.

The forecasts are extrapolated beyond five years based on estimated long-term average growth rates (generally 3%-4%).

The pre-tax discount rates used to calculate value in use range from 10%-17% (2006: 9%-11%). These discount rates are derived from the Group's post-tax weighted average cost of capital as adjusted for the specific risks relating to each geographical region.

In February 2007, 2006 and 2005 impairment reviews were performed by comparing the carrying value of goodwill with the recoverable amount of the cash-generating units to which goodwill has been allocated. Management determined that there has been no impairment.

The components of goodwill are as follows:

	2007 £m	2006 £m	2005 £m
UK	501	466	463
Thailand	113	115	107
South Korea	29	32	10
Japan	115	133	135
China	346	–	–
Malaysia	64	–	–
Poland	322	331	323
Czech Republic	34	–	–
Turkey	47	55	49
Other	15	5	7
	1,586	1,137	1,094

Extract 4(B9) – Tesco PLC, pages 67 and 69

This extract provides details about property, plant and equipment impairment amounts and the assumptions used for VIU calculations.

Note 11 Property, plant and equipment (in part)	Land and buildings £m	Other (a) £m	Total £m
Cost			
At 25 February 2006	15,563	4,707	20,270
Foreign currency translation	(176)	(46)	(222)
Additions (b)	1,925	864	2,789
Acquisitions through business combinations	247	31	278
Reclassification across categories	(100)	1	(99)
Classified as held for sale	(391)	(13)	(404)
Disposals	(528)	(155)	(683)
At 24 February 2007	16,540	5,389	21,929
Accumulated depreciation and impairment losses			
At 25 February 2006	1,815	2,573	4,388
Foreign currency translation	(8)	(17)	(25)
Charge for the year	240	534	774
Reclassification across categories	2	(3)	(1)
Classified as held for sale	(40)	(7)	(47)
Disposals	(86)	(69)	(155)
Impairment losses	82	–	82
Reversal of impairment losses	(63)	–	(63)
At 24 February 2007	1,942	3,011	4,953
Net carrying value (c)(d)(e)			
At 24 February 2007	14,598	2,378	16,976
At 25 February 2006	13,748	2,134	15,882
Capital work in progress included above (f)			
At 24 February 2007	872	158	1,030

(a) Other assets consist of plant, equipment, fixtures and fittings and motor vehicles.

(b) Includes £78m (2006 – £67m) in respect of interest capitalised, principally relating to land and building assets. The capitalisation rate used to determine the amount of finance costs capitalised during the year was 5.1% (2006 – 5.1%). Interest capitalised is deducted in determining taxable profit in the year in which it is incurred.

(c) Net carrying value includes:

   (i)   Capitalised interest at 24 February 2007 of £716m (2006 – £655m).

   (ii)   Assets held under finance leases which are analysed below:

| | 2007 | | 2006 | |
	Land and buildings £m	Other (a) £m	Land and buildings £m	Other (a) £m
Cost	91	662	102	388
Accumulated depreciation and impairment losses	(16)	(480)	(14)	(367)
Net carrying value	75	182	88	21

   These assets are pledged as security for the finance lease liabilities.

(d) The net carrying value of land and buildings comprises:

	2007 £m	2006 £m
Freehold	13,267	12,616
Long leasehold – 50 years or more	657	541
Short leasehold – less than 50 years	674	591
Net carrying value	14,598	13,748

(e) Carrying value of land and buildings includes £8m (2006 – £9m) relating to the prepayment of lease premiums.

(f) Capital work in progress does not include land.

Impairment of property, plant and equipment

The Group has determined that for the purposes of impairment testing, each store is a cash-generating unit. Cash-generating units are tested for impairment if there are indications of impairment at the Balance Sheet date.

Recoverable amounts for cash-generating units are based on value in use, which is calculated from cash flow projections for five years using data from the Group's latest internal forecasts, the results of which are reviewed by the Board. The key assumptions for the value in use calculations are those regarding discount rates, growth rates and expected changes in margins. Management estimates discount rates using pre-tax rates that reflect the current market assessment of the time value of money and the risks specific to the cash-generating units. Changes in selling prices and direct costs are based on past experience and expectations of future changes in the market.

The forecasts are extrapolated beyond five years based on estimated long-term growth rates (generally 3%-4%).

The pre-tax discount rates used to calculate value in use range from 10%-17% (2006: 9%-11%) depending on the specific conditions in which each store operates. These discount rates are derived from the Group's post-tax weighted average cost of capital.

The following amounts have been (charged)/credited to operating costs in the Income Statement during the current and prior year.

	2007 £m	2006 £m
Impairment losses		
UK	(44)	(29)
Rest of Europe	(35)	(18)
Asia	(3)	–
	(82)	(47)
Reversal of impairment losses		
UK	17	29
Rest of Europe	46	23
Asia	-	–
	63	52
Net (impairment)/reversal of impairment losses	(19)	5

The impairment losses relate to stores whose recoverable amounts (either value in use or fair value less costs to sell) do not exceed the asset carrying values. In all cases, impairment losses arose due to stores performing below forecasted trading levels.

The reversal of previous impairment losses arose principally due to improvements in stores' performances over the last year which increased the net present value of future cash flows.

Extract 4(B10) – Tesco PLC, page 70

In this extract, the company provides details about its investment property. Note that no impairment was recorded.

Note 12 Investment property	2007 £m	2006 £m
Cost		
At beginning of year	785	595
Foreign currency translation	(32)	36
Additions	26	21
Acquisitions through business combinations	32	–
Transfers	101	194
Classified as held for sale	(4)	(58)
Disposals	(2)	(3)
At end of year	906	785
Accumulated depreciation and impairment losses		
At beginning of year	40	30
Foreign currency translation	(2)	2
Charge for the period	11	9
Classified as held for sale	–	(1)
Transfers	1	–
At end of year	50	40
Net carrying value	856	745

The net carrying value at 26 February 2005 was £565m.

The estimated fair value of the Group's investment property is £1,522m (2006 – £1,373m). This value has been determined by applying an appropriate rental yield to the rentals earned by the investment property. A valuation has not been performed by an independent valuer.

Extract 4(B11) – Tesco PLC, page 90

This extract describes the company's purchase accounting policy and specifies that fair values currently established for acquisitions are provisional and are consequently subject to review.

Note 26 Business combinations (in part)

The Group has made a number of acquisitions in the year, of which the material acquisitions have been disclosed separately and the remainder shown in aggregate.

The net assets and results of the acquired business are included in the consolidated accounts of the Group from the date of acquisition. Acquisition accounting has been applied and the goodwill arising has been capitalised and is subject to annual impairment testing.

The goodwill acquired in the business combinations listed below has been allocated to the single group of cash-generating units represented by the acquired businesses, as this is the lowest level within the Group at which the goodwill is monitored internally. Goodwill arising on acquisitions in the year is attributable mainly to customer loyalty, the assembled work-force and the synergies expected to be achieved.

The fair values currently established for acquisitions made in the year to 24 February 2007 are provisional. Fair values will be reviewed based on additional information up to one year from the date of acquisition. The Directors do not believe that any net adjustments resulting from such a review would have a material effect on the Group.

PLANNING FOR IMPLEMENTATION

The application of IAS 36 can be challenging because judgments and estimates have to be made for:

- assessing whether there are indications of impairment;
- identifying CGUs; and
- determining the recoverable amount of assets or CGUs.

The application of both IFRS and Canadian standards to impairment is complex. Even though the standards are similar on certain issues, IAS 36 and related interpretations use procedures for impairment testing and impairment reversals that differ significantly from Canadian GAAP.

Adapting Information Systems

The impact of adopting IAS 36 will vary depending on an entity's operations. Required changes to an entity's information systems could range from minimal to quite significant. In most cases, entities will have to collect new data on:

- the identification of CGUs;
- the allocation of corporate assets (such as research units) and goodwill to CGUs.
- the assessment at each reporting date, including interim balance sheet dates, whether there is any indication that an asset or CGU is impaired and, if there is such an indicator, the entity must test impairment using new procedures that require:
  - o the measurement of the recoverable amount (which might require calculation of both VIU and FVLCS), and
  - o the allocation of loss to assets in CGU (including goodwill);
- any impairment reversals, which requires data permitting:
  - o the assessment of whether there is any indication that an impairment loss recognized in prior periods for an asset or a CGU (other than goodwill) may no longer exist or may have decreased,
  - o the calculation of the carrying value of the asset or CGU assuming no impairment loss would have been recorded in the previous periods, and
  - o the allocation of reversals to assets in the CGU (excluding goodwill).

IAS 36 adoption might be an opportunity for entities to review their information systems, which would include business models and plans reflecting different scenarios. Information systems could allow an entity to perform a business sensitivity analysis while adjusting inputs and assumptions with goal-seeking techniques that could be useful for internal purposes as well as for providing essential data to meet disclosure requirements. For example, the data could include factors affecting an entity's business, which would help in:

- developing the extensive narrative disclosure required by IAS 36 on the impairment testing process and related key assumptions made in impairment tests and sensitivity analysis;
- drafting internal management reports on the results of a period (e.g., a month), concerning significant events in the period affecting impairments or reversals. Such events could be detailed by source, including internal factors, such as sales below budgeted levels, or external factors, such as decreases in the value of the Canadian dollar.

Initial Adoption of IFRS

At the date of transition to IFRS, an entity is required to apply IAS 36, including all disclosure requirements but excluding the transitional provisions. Therefore, on the transition date, an entity must review previously recorded impairment losses and reverse any that no longer exist at the transition date. Where the opening IFRS balance sheet reflects impairment losses made under either Canadian GAAP or IFRS, any later reversal of those impairment losses is included in income (except when IAS 36 requires the entity to treat that reversal as a revaluation).

IFRS 1, *First-time adoption of International Financial Reporting Standards* includes guidance on the estimates to be used in determining and calculating any impairment loss or its reversal. IFRS 1 requires that these estimates be consistent with those made for the same date (e.g., transition date) under previous GAAP (Canadian GAAP) after adjusting for differences in accounting policies, unless there is objective evidence that those estimates were in error. These estimates should not reflect conditions arising after transition.

The application of IFRS 1 means that estimates at the transition date must be consistent with the ones made under Canadian GAAP in absence of a change in accounting policies or objective evidence that those estimates were in error. Consequently, estimates of impairments losses are not adjusted to reflect IAS 36 measurement requirements. The estimates must, however, be increased or reduced to reflect the situation at the balance sheet date. After the date of transition to IFRS, any new information about estimates is treated in the same way as non-adjusting events after the balance sheet date under IAS 10, *Events after the balance sheet date.*

For example, assume that an entity's date of transition to IFRS is January 1, 2011. Accordingly, it will have to prepare comparative figures and establish a balance sheet at January 1, 2010. Suppose that the entity obtained new information in March 2010 that required the revision of an estimate made under Canadian GAAP at December 31, 2009. The entity cannot reflect that new information in its January 1, 2010 balance sheet. Instead, the entity will reflect that new information in its income statement for the year ended December 31, 2010 (as probably would have been required under Canadian GAAP).

An entity may need to make impairment estimates under IAS 36 at January 1, 2010 that were not required at that date by Canadian GAAP. For example, the entity must reflect conditions that existed at January 1, 2010, i.e., market prices, interest rates or foreign exchange rates existing at that date.

IFRS 1 contains an optional exemption from mandatory restatement of business combinations in order to comply with IFRS 3, *Business Combinations*, where control was obtained before the transition date. Thus, under IFRS 1, an entity that elects to use this exemption will not have to recalculate the amount of goodwill in order to reflect requirements of IFRS 3 at the date of transition (i.e., the amount of goodwill is normally frozen). Note, however, that the entity could reallocate goodwill to the CGU expected to benefit from it as the transition rules in IFRS 1 that freeze the carrying amount of goodwill do not preclude such a reallocation.

IFRS 1 contains also specific requirements relating to impairment as follows:

- Regardless of whether or not there is any indication that the goodwill may be impaired, entities must test goodwill according to IAS 36 requirements at the date of transition to IFRS which would be based on conditions at that date.

- Amount of impairment losses (and reversals) recognized during the period beginning with the date of transition to IFRS must be disclosed separately.

Informing Users of Financial Statements

Reporting impairment losses always requires good communication. Impairment and reversals are useful information to financial statements users as they provide an indication whether non-financial assets are performing in line with expectations. Users should also be told that the fact that an entity is profitable as a whole does not mean that an individual asset or a grouping of assets, such as CGUs, is not impaired.

Confusion might arise on IAS 36 adoption because its requirements, when compared with those under CICA 3063/3064, are similar on some issues and yet very different on others. In addition, depending on the circumstances, the impact of IAS 36 adoption might vary from one entity to another. For example, the grouping of assets for measuring potential impairment could be the same if the CGU under IAS 36 corresponds to "groups of assets" under CICA 3063 and if the CGU or group of CGUs under IAS 36 corresponds to "reporting unit" under CICA 3064.

IAS 36 and Canadian GAAP differ significantly in their requirements for the recognition of impairment reversals for all non-financial assets except goodwill. This has always been prohibited by Canadian GAAP and, consequently, the impact of such a reversal, including net income volatility, has to be explained to financial statements users.

Keep Posted

Even though there is no specific research project on impairment of non-financial assets on the IASB's active agenda, it is possible that the current efforts of seeking harmonization with US GAAP (on which Canadian GAAP are generally based) might lead to changes in IAS 36 requirements.

Chapter 5
Business Combinations

Standards Discussed in this Chapter

International

IFRS 3 (revised 2008) – Business Combinations

Canadian

CICA 1581 – Business Combinations
CICA 1600 – Consolidated Financial Statements
CICA 1625 – Comprehensive Revaluation of Assets and Liabilities
CICA 3064 – Goodwill and Intangible Assets
EIC-10 – Reverse takeover accounting
EIC-14 – Adjustments to the purchase equation subsequent to the acquisition date
EIC-42 – Costs incurred on business combinations
EIC-55 – Identifiable assets acquired in a business combination
EIC-66 – Transfer of a business between enterprises under common control
EIC-73 – Buy-out transactions
EIC-89 – Exchanges of ownership interests between enterprises under common control – wholly and partially owned subsidiaries
EIC-92 – Arm's length buy-out of a business followed by an amalgamation
EIC-94 – Accounting for corporation transaction costs
EIC-114 – Liability recognition for costs incurred on purchase business combinations
EIC-119 – The date of acquisition in a business combination
EIC-124 – Definition of a business
EIC-125 – Determination of the measurement date for the market price of acquirer securities issued in a business combination
EIC-127 – Accounting for contingent consideration paid to the shareholders of an acquired enterprise in a business combination
EIC-137 – Recognition of customer relationship intangible assets acquired in a business combination
EIC-140 – Accounting for operating leases acquired in either an asset acquisition or a business combination
EIC-154 – Accounting for the pre-existing relationship between the parties of a business combination
AcG-15 – Accounting for variable interest entities

INTRODUCTION

Currently, preparers of Canadian financial statements reporting on business combinations have to meet various requirements scattered throughout the *CICA Handbook*, including CICA 1581, and a number of related EICs listed above. Once they adopt IFRS, they will have to refer to only one single general standard, IFRS 3 (revised 2008).

IFRS 3 (revised 2008) is a broad standard covering many issues arising in business combination transactions. This standard, resulting from a joint project with the FASB, prompted the AcSB to issue, on January 5, 2009, CICA 1582, *Business Combinations*, CICA 1601, *Consolidated Financial Statements*, and CICA 1602 *Non-controlling Interests*, effectively replacing CICA 1581, *Business Combinations*, and CICA 1600, *Consol-*

idated Financial Statements. The issuance of CICA 1582 effectively harmonizes Canadian standards with IFRS 3 (revised 2008).

CICA 1582, CICA 1601, and CICA 1602 are mandatory for fiscal years beginning on or after January 1, 2011, with earlier adoption permitted. These three *CICA Handbook – Accounting* sections must be implemented concurrently. Non-controlling interests and transactions with non-controlling interests relating to business combinations completed prior to the implementation date of these three *CICA Handbook* sections are presented in accordance with CICA 1602, but are not to be remeasured[1].

Entities planning to adopt IFRS in 2011 and expecting to realize business combinations for the year beginning on or after January 1, 2010 should consider implementing IFRS 3 (revised 2008) starting in 2010 to avoid restatement of their comparative financial statements.

The adoption of the new *CICA Handbook* sections and IFRS 3 (revised 2008) may result in the recording of higher assets and liabilities on the balance sheet, greater equity and income and more earnings volatility than under CICA 1581, This chapter compares IFRS 3 (revised 2008) with CICA 1581.

This chapter compares IFRS 3 (revised 2008) with CICA 1581 and reviews the following topics:

- scope of application;
- accounting method:
  - o identifying the acquirer,
  - o determining the acquisition date;
- initial recognition and measurement:
  - o recognizing and measuring the identifiable assets acquired, the liabilities assumed, and any non-controlling interest in the acquiree:
    - principles,
    - conditions;
- measuring the identifiable net assets acquired at the acquisition date fair values;
- exceptions to the recognition and measurement principles:
  - o income taxes,
  - o employee benefits,
  - o indemnification assets;
- exceptions to the measurement principle:
  - o reacquired rights,
  - o share-based payments,
  - o assets held for sale;
- other considerations regarding the measurement of identifiable assets acquired and liabilities assumed:
  - o acquisition-related costs,
  - o costs to exit activities,
  - o operating leases,
  - o intangible assets;

---

1   This chapter discusses IFRS 3 (revised 2008) and consequently CICA 1582 (which is harmonized with the latter standard) as both apply to all business combinations. Discussions will only refer to IFRS 3 (revised 2008). The requirements under IAS 27 (amended) and CICA 1602 that apply to the accounting for non-controlling interests and transactions with non controlling interest holders in consolidated financial statements are further discussed in Chapter 6.

- classification or designation of identifiable assets acquired and liabilities assumed in a business combination;
- consideration paid:
  - o fair value of shares issued,
  - o transfer of assets and liabilities of the acquirer,
  - o contingent consideration;
- measurement of goodwill:
  - o bargain purchases;
- increases and decreases in ownerships:
  - o business combinations achieved in stages,
  - o business combinations achieved without the transfer of consideration,
  - o push-down accounting;
- measurement period;
- subsequent measurement of assets acquired and liabilities assumed:
  - o reacquired rights,
  - o contingent liabilities,
  - o indemnification assets,
  - o contingent consideration;
- disclosures.

IMPACT ON FINANCIAL STATEMENTS

As previously mentioned, IFRS 3 (revised 2008) introduces some significant changes to accounting for business combinations, which will impact financial statements of an entity in the year of a business combination as well as in the subsequent years.

Under IFRS 3 (revised 2008) all business combinations must be accounted for by applying the acquisition method (previously referred to as the purchase method). Companies applying this method will have to identify the acquirer; determine the acquisition date and purchase price; recognize the identifiable assets acquired and liabilities assumed of the acquiree at their fair values; and recognize goodwill or, in the case of a bargain purchase, a gain.

IFRS 3 (revised 2008) must be applied prospectively to business combinations occurring on or after 1 July 2009. It covers combinations of mutuals and combinations by contract. Common control transactions remain outside the scope of business combination.

IFRS 3 (revised 2008) amends significantly the reporting of business combination as it requires that:

- Acquirer recognizes most identifiable assets acquired and liabilities assumed of the acquiree at their full fair value on the acquisition date. Exceptions from fair-value measurement include deferred income tax assets and liabilities, employee future benefits, and leases. Assets acquired and liabilities assumed are measured at the fair value of the acquired entity at the acquisition date even if the business combination is achieved in stages or the acquirer obtains less than 100% of the equity interest in the acquiree at the acquisition date. This represents a significant change for Canadian companies as CICA 1581 requires assets acquired and liabilities assumed to be measured initially based on the cost of the purchase to the acquirer determined as of the acquisition date. Recording such interests at fair value will result in higher assets and liabilities being reflected in the balance sheet because those amounts include the fair value of the non-controlling interests' portion.

- Non controlling interests be measured, on a transaction-by-transaction basis, either at the fair value of their portion of the identifiable assets and liabilities or at their full fair value. The first option will produce a lower amount of goodwill and non-controlling interests as it reflects only the amount of goodwill attributed to the acquirer (i.e., non-controlling interest is shown at the fair value of net assets excluding goodwill). The second approach will record goodwill on the non-controlling interest as well as on the acquired controlling interest, producing a higher amount of goodwill and non-controlling interest. Recognizing full goodwill will increase reported net assets on the balance sheet. The potential downside is that any future impairment of goodwill will be greater.

- Non-controlling interests be shown as part of equity instead of being presented as a sort of "mezzanine liability'. Because non-controlling interests are treated as an element of equity, consequential changes in the presentation of consolidated financial statements would include the following changes in the periods that follow business acquisitions:

  o Consolidated net income and other comprehensive income would be shown "gross" and then are allocated proportionately between the controlling and non-controlling interests instead of being shown as an "expense" in the consolidated income statement.

  o Increases and decreases in the parent's ownership interest that leave control intact would be accounted for as capital transactions (i.e., as increases or decreases in ownership), rather than as step acquisitions or dilution gains or losses (see chapter 6).

- Measurement period (period after the acquisition date during which the acquirer may make adjustments to the "provisional" amounts recognized at the acquisition date) to end as soon as the acquirer receives the necessary information about facts and circumstances that existed at the acquisition date, or concludes that the information cannot be obtained (as under CICA 1581). This period may not exceed one year from the acquisition date (also as specified in CICA 1581). However, any adjustments to the provisional amounts during the measurement period are reflected by retrospectively adjusting the provisional amounts and recasting the prior-period information (instead of solely adjusting goodwill as required by CICA 1581 and EIC-14).

- An acquirer's unrecognized tax benefits (e.g., tax loss carry-forwards) that become more likely than not of being realized as a result of an acquisition are recorded as a reduction of income tax expense rather than as an adjustment to the acquisition accounting. Currently under CICA 1581 these tax benefits are generally recorded as a reduction of goodwill. This change will likely result in a higher goodwill amounts and, possibly, a greater risk of goodwill impairments.

- Contingent liabilities be recognized on the acquisition date and measured at fair value at that date if they relate to a present obligation of the acquiree that arises from past transactions and fair value can be measured reliably, i.e., a contingency is recognized even if it is not probable. Subsequent to the acquisition date, such contingencies are measured at the higher of (i) the amount that would be recognized under IAS 37, *Provisions, Contingent Liabilities and Contingent Assets* (i.e., best estimate) or (ii) the amount initially recorded less cumulative amortization recognized in accordance with IAS 18, *Revenue* with gains and losses recognized in profit or loss until settlement. CICA 1581 does not have this requirement.

- Purchase price represents the fair value of the consideration paid for the acquirer's interest in the acquiree at acquisition date. The consideration paid includes cash and other assets, equity interests, and contingent consideration and earn-out provisions. Note that requirement to measure the contingent consideration and earn-out provisions at fair value will result in their inclusion in purchase price even if payment is not deemed probable at the date of the acquisition. This changes significantly current practice where contingent consideration and earn-out provisions are generally recognized (often as an adjustment to goodwill) when the contingency is resolved and the consideration is paid or payable. Note that contingent consideration must be classified as equity or a liability in accordance with current GAAP. If the contingent consideration is classified as a liability, it will have to be remeasured to fair value until resolution and subsequent changes in the fair value must be recognized in profit or loss, thus introducing potential earnings volatility. Contingent consideration classified as equity is not subsequently remeasured.

- Acquisition costs associated with a business combination, (such as finder's fees, advisory, legal, accounting, valuation and other professional or consulting fees) be expensed instead of being capitalized as part of the business combination. This will decrease net income in the year of business combination and will lower the amount of reported goodwill reducing the likelihood of its impairment in the future. Costs of arranging and issuing financial liabilities or equity continue to be treated as reductions in the initial measurement of the related liability or equity.

- The only relevant date for fair value measurement acquisition be the date the acquirer obtains control of the acquiree. At that date an entity establishes fair value of consideration paid (including any equity instruments issued by the acquirer). This approach differs from CICA 1581 requirements where equity instruments are measured at fair value over a reasonable period around the date the terms of the business combination are agreed to and announced. This difference could significantly impact the amount of goodwill recognized in the context of a volatile acquirer's share prices.

- The acquirer recognize an indemnification asset equal to the recognized amount for the related contingency in case he receives an indemnity for the outcome of an uncertainty in connection with a business combination (e.g., for tax uncertainties). In measuring indemnification assets, consideration must be given to whether any valuation allowance is required due to uncertainties associated with collectibility.

Under IFRS 3 (revised 2008) the financial statements will increase in length and will be more detailed. Some of the additional disclosures requirements include:

- amount of acquisition-related costs expensed and the income statement line item in which that expense is reported;

- measurement basis selected and the recognized amount of non controlling interests in the acquiree;

- where non-controlling interest is measured at fair value, the valuation techniques and key model inputs used for determining that value;

- details of transactions that are separate from the acquisition of assets and assumption of liabilities in exchange for the acquiree;

- in a step acquisition, disclosure of the fair value of the previously held equity interest in the acquiree and the amount of gain or loss recognized in the income statement resulting from remeasurement; and

- information about receivables (fair value, gross contractual amounts receivable and best estimate of cash flows not expected to be collected at the acquisition date).

Illustrative Disclosures:

Extract 5(1) through 5(4) – Future accounting developments

Barclays PLC (AR 2007), page 174

Accounting presentation (in part)

Future Accounting Developments (in part)

– IFRS 3 – Business Combinations and IAS 27 – Consolidated and Separate Financial Statements are revised standards issued in January 2008. The revised IFRS 3 applies prospectively to business combinations first accounted for in accounting periods beginning on or after 1st July 2009 and the amendments to IAS 27 apply retrospectively to periods beginning on or after 1st July 2009. The main changes in existing practice resulting from the revision to IFRS 3 affect acquisitions that are achieved in stages and acquisitions where less than 100% of the equity is acquired. In addition, acquisition related costs – such as fees paid to advisers – must be accounted for separately from the business combination, which means that they will be recognised as expenses unless they are directly connected with the issue of debt or equity securities. The revisions to IAS 27 specify that changes in a parent's ownership interest in a subsidiary that do not result in the loss of control must be accounted for as equity transactions. Until future acquisitions take place that are accounted for in accordance with the revised IFRS 3, the main impact on Barclays will be that, from 2010, gains and losses on transactions with non-controlling interests that do not result in loss of control will no longer be recognised in the income statement but directly in equity. In 2007, gains of £23m and losses of £6m were recognised in income relating to such transactions.

BT Group PLC (AR & Form 20-F 2008), page 95

Accounting standards, interpretation and amendments to published standards not yet effective (in part)

IFRS 3 (Revised), 'Business Combinations' (effective from 1 April 2010)

IFRS 3 (Revised) amends certain aspects of accounting for business combinations set out in IFRS 3. Amendments include the requirement to expense all transaction costs as incurred and the requirement for all payments to acquire a business to be recorded at fair value at the acquisition date, with some contingent payments subsequently re-measured at fair value through the income statement. IFRS 3 (Revised) is applicable prospectively to business combinations effected on or after the effective date. The group is currently assessing the potential impact of this amendment upon the results and net assets of the group.

SABMiller plc (AR 2008), page 66

1. Accounting policies (in part)

b) Recent accounting developments (in part)

IFRS 3 (revised), 'Business combinations', (effective from 1 July 2009), is still subject to endorsement by the European Union. Among other changes it requires transaction costs to be recognised immediately in the income statement, fair value gains or losses on existing investments in an acquired company to be recognised in the income statement on the date of acquisition and adjustments to deferred tax outside of the hindsight period are recorded under IAS 12, as opposed to affecting goodwill. In addition it requires the recognition of subsequent changes in the fair value of contingent consideration in the income statement rather than against goodwill.

TeliaSonera AB (AR 2007), page 43
Note 1 (Consolidated) Basis of Preparation (in part)
Standards, amendment to issued standards and interpretations, not yet effective (in part)

Revised IFRS 3 "Business Combinations" and amended IAS 27 "Consolidated and Separate Financial Statements" (effective for annual periods beginning on or after July 1, 2009; early adoption permitted). Among other things, the changes to the standards include: transaction costs expensed as incurred; contingent consideration always recognized at fair value and for non-equity-consideration post-combination changes in fair value affects the income statement; option added to on a transaction-by-transaction basis permit recognition of 100 percent of the goodwill of the acquired entity with the increased goodwill amount also increasing the non-controlling interest; in a step acquisition, on the date that control is obtained, the fair values of the acquired entity's assets and liabilities, including goodwill, are measured and any resulting adjustments to previously recognized assets and liabilities are recognized in profit or loss; acquiring additional shares in a subsidiary after control was obtained as well as a partial disposal of shares in a subsidiary while retaining control is accounted for as an equity transaction with owners; a partial disposal of shares a subsidiary that results in loss of control triggers remeasurement of the residual holding to fair value and any difference between fair value and carrying amount is a gain or loss, recognized in profit or loss. TeliaSonera expects that applying the revised IFRS 3 and the amended IAS 27 might lead to increased volatility in the income statement.

Commentary: These extracts illustrate some of the changes made to the previous IFRS 3 to arrive at IFRS 3 (revised 2008). The differences are similar to those that Canadian companies might experienced when they will adopt the expected CICA 1582. The Barclays PLC and TeliaSonera extracts also describe the major impacts these changes will have on the reporting enterprises.

ANALYSIS OF RELEVANT ISSUES

Scope

IFRS 3 (revised 2008) and CICA 1581 are similar in scope as they both apply to a transaction or other event that meets the definition of a business combination. Some transactions now accounted under Canadian GAAP as asset acquisitions will come within the scope of business combination accounting under an expanded definition of a business as discussed below.

Business Definition

IFRS 3 (revised 2008) defines a business as follows: "An integrated set of activities and assets that is *capable* of being conducted and managed for the purpose of providing a return in the form of dividends, lower costs or other economic benefits directly to investors or other owners, members or participants." EIC-124 defines it as "a self-sustaining integrated set of activities and assets conducted and managed for the purpose of providing a return to investors. A business consists of (a) inputs, (b) processes applied to those inputs, and (c) resulting outputs that are used to generate revenues."

Consequently IFRS 3 (revised 2008) expands the concept of a business such that the integrated set of activities must only be capable of being conducted and managed to provide a return or lower costs. As a consequence, a business or group of assets must no longer be self-sustaining to be considered a business and the previous presumption that an early-stage development stage entity is not a business has been removed.

Change in Control

IFRS 3 (revised 2008) defines a business combination as a transaction or other event in which an acquirer obtains control of one or more businesses. This differs slightly from Canadian GAAP, which restricts the scope to an acquisition of net assets or equity interests that result in control. Although the definition of a business under IFRS 3 (revised 2008) is similar to that currently found in EIC-124, the slight differences can have significant implications.

It is also important to keep in mind that the control concept focuses on the relationship between two entities, in particular, whether one entity has the power to govern the financial and operating policies of another so that it can obtain benefits from its activities. Therefore, determining which of the combining entities has, as a consequence of the combination, the power to govern the financial and operating policies of the other is fundamental to identifying the acquirer, regardless of the form of the consideration given. The control approach is therefore not limited to specific acquisitions of equity interests, using the exchange of consideration, but also includes the changes in ownership interests that might result in the investor obtaining control. For example, an entity might redeem shares from one investor, effectively resulting in the remaining investor acquiring a controlling interest.

IFRS 3 (revised 2008) also specifies that it applies to business combinations involving mutual entities and business combinations achieved by contract alone. This may represent a broader application for Canadians where such arrangements are not specifically addressed by CICA 1581 and the accounting practice adopted in these circumstances might vary.

IFRS do not include specific recognition and measurement provisions for transactions among related parties the way CICA 3840, *Related Party Transactions* does. Furthermore, IFRS 3 (revised 2008) excludes from its scope combinations of entities under common control. The IASB currently has a project in its active agenda that addresses common control transactions. The project will examine the definition of common control and the methods of accounting for business combinations under common control in the acquirer's consolidated and separate financial statements. The project will also consider the accounting for demergers, such as the spin-off of a subsidiary or business. In January 2009, the IASB plans to consider whether to establish a working group for this project and whether to issue a Discussion Paper or an Exposure Draft.

Illustrative Disclosure:

Extract 5(5) – Basis of consolidation

> Libertas Capital Group plc (AR 2007), page 23
> **2 PRINCIPAL ACCOUNTING POLICIES (in part)**
> **Basis of consolidation (in part)**
> The consolidated financial statements incorporate the financial statements of the Company and entities controlled by the Company (its subsidiaries) made up to 31 December each year. Control is achieved where the Company has the power to govern the financial and operating policies of an investee entity so as to obtain benefits from its activities.

Commentary: This note describes the company's accounting policies for determining whether a subsidiary would be consolidated based on the concept of control.

Accounting Method

IFRS 3 (revised 2008) specifies that business combinations must be accounted for by applying the acquisition method. This method requires:

* identifying the acquirer;
* determining the acquisition date;

- recognizing and measuring the identifiable assets acquired, the liabilities assumed and any non-controlling interest in the acquiree; and

- recognizing and measuring goodwill or a gain from a bargain purchase.

Canadian GAAP prescribes the "purchase method." The previous IFRS 3 also used this term. Although the two methods are substantially similar, the acquisition method eliminates measuring the fair value of the acquiree as a whole and adds recognizing and measuring goodwill as a separate step. This modification focuses on measuring the components of the business combination, including any non-controlling interest in the acquiree, rather than measuring the fair value of the acquiree as a whole.

Canadian GAAP preparers are not accustomed to the concept of measuring the components of the acquired entity at their fair values and measuring goodwill as a separate step regardless of the amount of control acquired (i.e., less than 100%) and then recording the non-controlling interest at fair value . Historically, under Canadian GAAP, non-controlling interests have been recorded at cost and, if only 70% control was acquired, for example, only this amount was recorded at fair value. The IFRS 3 (revised 2008) approach represents a more transparent presentation and is considered as more faithfully representing the substance of business combination transactions.

In applying the acquisition method, IFRS 3 (revised 2008) allows an acquirer to choose to measure any non-controlling interest in the acquiree at fair value or on the basis of its proportionate interest in the acquiree's identifiable net assets. Note that this choice becomes relevant only for business combinations in which the acquirer obtains control of less than 100% of the business. Using the proportionate interest method will likely result in the following:

- The amounts recognized for non-controlling interests and goodwill are likely to be lower (and these should be the only two items affected on initial recognition).

- If a cash-generating unit is subsequently impaired, any resulting impairment of goodwill recognized through income is likely to be lower than it would have been had the non-controlling interest been measured at fair value (although it does not affect the impairment loss attributable to the controlling interest).

- If the non-controlling interests are acquired, presumably at fair value, the equity of the group is reduced by the non-controlling interests' share of any unrecognized changes in the fair value of the net assets of the business, including goodwill. If the non-controlling interest is measured initially as a proportionate share of the acquiree's identifiable net assets, rather than at fair value, the reduction in the reported equity attributable to the acquirer is likely to be larger.

If the full fair value method is selected, the value calculated might differ from the fair value of the acquirer's interest in the acquiree on a per-share basis because of the control premium of the acquirer's interest or, similarly, the inclusion of a discount for lack of control (also referred to as a minority discount) in the per-share fair value of the non-controlling interest.

Illustrative Disclosure:

Extract 5(6) – Purchase price allocation

Telstra Corporation Limited (AR 2007), page 181

24. Notes to the cash flow statement (in part)

(d) Acquisitions (in part)

SouFun Holdings Limited (SouFun)

On 31 August 2006, our controlled entity Sensis Pty Ltd acquired 55% (on an undiluted basis) of the issued capital of SouFun for a total consideration of $337 million including acquisition costs.

The effect on the Telstra Group of the acquisition is detailed below:

	SouFun 2007 $m	2007 $m
Consideration for acquisition		
Cash consideration for acquisition		333
Costs of acquisition		4
Total purchase consideration		337
Cash balances acquired		(23)
Outflow of cash on acquisition		314

	Fair value	Carrying value
Assets/(liabilities) at acquisition date		
Cash and cash equivalents	23	23
Trade and other receivables	8	8
Property, plant and equipment	1	1
Intangible assets	38	–
Other assets	1	1
Deferred tax assets	1	1
Trade and other payables	(9)	(9)
Current tax liabilities	(2)	(2)
Deferred tax liabilities	(9)	–
Revenue received in advance	(6)	(6)
Net assets	46	17
Adjustment to reflect minority interests acquired	(21)	
Goodwill on acquisition	312	
	337	

Commentary: This extract depicts how the purchase price allocation would be disclosed when a less than 100% interest is acquired yet the net assets are recognized at their full fair values. This represents a significant difference from Canadian GAAP. Under IFRS 3 (revised 2008), however, the minority interest amount (which the revised standard refers to as "non-controlling interest") will differ due to the application of either the full fair value method or the proportionate interest method. It is also important to note that the deferred tax calculations will likely change under IFRS 3 (revised 2008), and the acquisition costs would no longer be included as part of the purchase consideration.

This extract is also a good illustration of what the proportionate method of accounting for non-controlling interests might look like which is discussed in further detail below.

Identifying the Acquirer

Both IFRS 3 (revised 2008) and CICA 1581 require an acquirer to be identified for each business combination. IAS 27, *Consolidated and Separate Financial Statements* offers further guidance for identifying an acquirer, specifying the acquirer as the entity that obtains control of the acquiree. Although this wording differs slightly from the guidance found in CICA 1581, the way this concept is applied in practice should not change.

The IFRS 3 (revised 2008) provisions for identifying an acquirer also apply where difficulties arise in identifying the acquirer in combinations of two virtually equal mutual entities. Current Canadian standards do not specifically address the combination of mutual entities. IFRS guidance specifies that, since those same difficulties arise in combinations of two virtually equal investor-owned entities, those difficulties have been resolved in practice, and, therefore, the problem of accounting for business combinations among mutual entities should be resolved in the same way. Application of this guidance requires significant judgment, especially when such transactions involve reverse acquisitions, which is discussed in more detail below. Because IFRS guidance for the identification of an acquirer does not differ substantially from that currently found in Canadian GAAP, the same degree of professional judgment would be used to determine the acquirer in such cases.

Applying the IFRS 3 (revised 2008) guidance for identifying an acquirer includes considering all pertinent facts and circumstances to determine which of the combining entities has the power to govern the financial and operating policies of the other so as to obtain benefits from its activities. Pertinent facts and circumstances, which are similar to Canadian GAAP, include:

- The relative voting rights in the combined entity after the business combination. The acquirer is usually the entity whose owners, as a group retain or receive the largest portion of the voting rights in the combined entity. In determining which group of owners retains or receives the largest portion of the voting rights, an entity considers the existence of any unusual or special voting arrangements and options, warrants or convertible securities.

- The existence of a large minority voting interest in the combined entity if no other owner or organized group of owners has a significant voting interest. The acquirer is usually the entity whose single owner or organized group of owners holds the largest minority voting interest in the combined entity.

- The composition of the governing body of the combined entity. The acquirer is usually the entity whose owners have the ability to elect, appoint or remove a majority of the members of the governing body of the combined entity.

- The composition of the senior management of the combined entity. The acquirer is usually the entity whose (former) management dominates the management of the combined entity.

The following additional IFRS 3 (revised 2008) criterion is not specifically considered by Canadian GAAP:

- The terms of the exchange of equity interests. The acquirer is usually the entity that pays a premium over the pre-combination fair value of the equity interests of the other combining entity or entities.

Reverse Acquisitions

The IFRS 3 (revised 2008) guidance for identifying an acquirer is most useful in more complex transactions such as in reverse acquisitions, where it is more difficult to identify the acquirer. Reverse acquisitions commonly occur for example when a private operating entity wants to become a public entity but does not want to register its equity shares. To accomplish that, the private entity will arrange for a public entity to acquire its equity interests in exchange for the equity interests of the public entity. In this example, the public entity is the legal acquirer because it issued its equity interest, and the private entity is the legal acquiree because its equity interest was acquired. Applying the IFRS 3 (revised 2008) guidance results, however, in identifying the public entity as the acquiree and the private entity as the acquirer for accounting purposes. Canadian GAAP provides substantially the same accounting treatment in EIC-10.

Illustrative Disclosure:

Extract 5(7) – Reverse acquisition

> **Networkers International PLC (AR 2007) page 22**
>
> **1 Accounting policies (in part)**
>
> **Basis of consolidation (in part)**
>
> During 2006 Networkers International Plc formerly known as Streetnames Plc, became the legal parent of Networkers International (UK) Plc in a share for share transaction. Due to the relative size of the companies, Networkers International (UK) Plc shareholders became the majority holders of Networkers International Plc. In addition, the group's ongoing operations and executive management were those of Networkers International (UK) Plc. Accordingly, Networkers International (UK) Plc has been identified as the acquirer and the combination treated as a reverse acquisition under IFRS 3 'Business Combinations.' Consequently, although the financial statements are prepared in the name of Networkers International Plc, the legal parent, they are a continuation of those of the legal subsidiary, Networkers International (UK) Plc, with the assets and liabilities measured and recognised in the consolidated financial statements at the pre-combination carrying amounts.

Commentary: This extract describes how the acquirer was identified in a reverse acquisition. This does not differ from either IFRS 3 (revised 2008) or Canadian GAAP.

Determining the Acquisition Date

The IFRS 3 (revised 2008) guidance for determining the acquisition date is the same as that provided under Canadian GAAP, but EIC-119 spells it out in greater depth than IFRS 3 (revised 2008) does. Both specify the acquisition date as the date on which the acquirer obtains control of the acquiree. This date is generally the date the acquirer legally transfers the consideration, acquires the assets and assumes the liabilities of the acquiree – the closing date. The acquirer might, however, obtain control on a date that is either earlier or later than the closing date. For example, the acquisition date precedes the closing date if a written agreement provides that the acquirer obtains control of the acquiree on a date before the closing date.

Initial Recognition and Measurement

Recognizing and Measuring the Identifiable Assets Acquired, the Liabilities Assumed, and any Non-controlling Interest in the Acquiree

Principles

Two fundamental principles should be considered when applying IFRS 3 (revised 2008).

The recognition principle dictates that the acquirer recognizes:

- all of the identifiable assets acquired;
- all of the liabilities assumed;
- non-controlling interest, if any.

The measurement principle dictates that the acquirer measures each recognized asset acquired, each liability assumed and any non-controlling interest at its acquisition date fair value.

Conditions

Two conditions also have to be met for measuring and recognizing an item as part of applying the acquisition method: the item acquired or assumed must be:

- an asset or liability at the acquisition date (they must meet the *Framework for the Preparation and Presentation of Financial Statements* definitions of assets and liabilities at the acquisition date); and

- part of the business acquired (the acquiree) rather than the result of a separate transaction.

These principles and conditions represent significant changes for Canadian GAAP preparers since, as previously mentioned, more liabilities will likely be included in the purchase price allocation and amounts that don't meet the definition of assets – such as transaction costs and restructuring costs incurred by the acquirer to restructure the acquired company – will no longer be included in the cost of the purchase. Also, IFRS 3 (revised 2008) requires the acquirer to recognize identifiable assets acquired and liabilities assumed regardless of the degree of probability of an inflow or outflow of economic benefits. Although this will result in more assets and liabilities being recorded, the related cash-flow uncertainties will, however, be included as part of their measurement on initial recognition, likely resulting in greater revisions to these amounts once the uncertainties are resolved.

Also, EIC-127 deals with determining whether transactions among the parties to a business combination should be counted as part of the cost of the acquired business or whether they represent transactions separate from the acquisition but the concept received increased prominence in IFRS 3 (revised 2008). The objective of this condition ensures that each component is accounted for in accordance with its economic substance.

Contingent Assets and Liabilities

Contingent liabilities assumed in a business combination (such as contractual and non-contractual contingencies) that are present obligations and can be measured reliably are recognized even if it is not probable that an outflow of resources embodying economic benefits will be required to settle the obligation. Such obligations are recorded during the initial purchase price allocation at their acquisition date-fair values. This may result in liabilities being recognized sooner - when they are acquired as part of a business combination - rather than when they would be accounted for under IAS 37 or under Canadian GAAP, where preparers may apply a higher probability recognition threshold for contingent liabilities.

Subsequent measurement of contingent liabilities is covered in more detail later on in this chapter.

As for contingent assets in a business combination, the IASB concluded that they should not be recognized, even if it is virtually certain that they will become unconditional or non-contingent. If an entity determines that an asset exists at the acquisition date (i.e., that it has an unconditional right at the acquisition date), that asset is not a contingent asset and should be accounted for in accordance with the appropriate IFRS. Therefore, as in Canadian GAAP, contingent assets are not recognized.

Measuring the Identifiable Net Assets Acquired at the Acquisition Date Fair Values

As can be seen up to this point, the acquirer's perspective in business combinations has fundamentally changed. The idea that the acquirer's plans for the acquiree affect the valuation of the acquired net assets is no longer acceptable. IFRS 3 (revised

2008), defines fair value as the amount for which an asset could be exchanged, or a liability settled, between knowledgeable willing parties in an arm's length transaction. Canadian GAAP defines it as the amount of the consideration that would be agreed on in an arm's length transaction between knowledgeable willing parties who are under no compulsion to act. Thus, although the two definitions use different words, the concept is the same – fair value is a market-based measure in a transaction between unrelated parties. It is the approach to fair value, and not merely the definition, that has changed. IFRS 3 (revised 2008) makes it clearer that measuring the identifiable net assets acquired at the acquisition-date fair values is viewed from a market participant perspective which therefore disregards how or whether the acquirer intends to use those net assets. In Canada, the determination of fair value as it is applied to business combinations in practice sometimes results in the consideration of the acquirer's intentions.

IFRS 3 (revised 2008) provides guidelines for fair value measurement of particular identifiable assets that differ from Canadian GAAP although, in most cases, the differences are not significant:

- Assets with uncertain cash flows (valuation allowances): An acquirer cannot recognize a separate valuation allowance as of the acquisition date for assets acquired in a business combination that are measured at their acquisition-date fair values because the effects of uncertainty about future cash flows are included in the fair value measure. For example, the acquirer does not recognize a separate valuation allowance for receivables.

- Assets that an acquirer intends not to use or to use in a way that is different from the way other market participants would use them: For competitive or other reasons, an acquirer may not want to use an acquired asset, for example, a research and development intangible asset, or it may intend to use the asset differently from the way other market participants would use it. Nevertheless, the acquirer has to measure the asset at fair value.

Illustrative Disclosures:

Extract 5(8) – Measurement of identifiable assets and liabilities

Akzo Nobel N.V. (AR 2007), page 107
Note 1 Summary of significant accounting policies (in part)
Business combinations

In business combinations, identifiable assets and liabilities, and contingent liabilities are recognized at their fair values at the acquisition date. Determining the fair value requires significant judgments on future cash flows to be generated.

The fair value of brands, patents, trademarks, and customer lists acquired in a business combination is estimated on generally accepted valuation methods, using the discounted royalty payments that have been avoided as a result of the patent or trademark being owned or discounted cash flows expected to be derived from the use and eventual sale of the assets.

The fair value of property, plant, and equipment recognized as a result of a business combination is based on estimated market values.

The fair value of inventories acquired in a business combination is determined based on its estimated selling price in the ordinary course of business less the estimated costs of completion and sale, and a reasonable profit margin based on the effort required to complete and sell the inventories.

Commentary: This note mentions that identifiable assets and liabilities and contingent liabilities are recognized at their fair values at the acquisition date and explains how those fair values were determined. This does not differ substantially from Canadian GAAP except where an entity-specific approach might be taken.

Extract 5(9) – Measurement of identifiable assets and liabilities

Gemalto N.V. (AR 2007), page 116

Note 4 Business combination with Gemplus (in part)

Gemalto management, assisted by independent, qualified experts, identified and assigned fair values to Gemplus assets and liabilities, as part of the allocation of the value of the combination.

The final allocation of the value of the combination to the assets acquired and liabilities and contingent liabilities assumed, including those not previously recognized by the acquired entity, is as follows:

Net Assets acquired (excluding intangibles)	In millions of Euro
Gemplus net assets acquired as of the date of the acquisition	657.5
Identified intangible assets on the balance sheet	(126.9)
Net Assets acquired (excluding intangibles)	530.6
Minority Interest in Gemplus subsidiaries	(13.6)
Adjustments on Net Assets acquired	
Real estate assets	(4.0)
Inventory:	
- Revaluation to net realizable value	7.0
- Cancellation of commercial margin related to deferred revenue balance	7.8
Cancellation of commercial margin of deferred maintenance balance	0.4
Total adjustments on Net Assets acquired	11.2
Fair Value of the acquired intangible assets	
Existing Technology	81.8
In-Process R&D	20.8
Customer Relationships	22.2
Corporate Name	9.8
Fair Value of the acquired intangible assets	134.6
Deferred tax impacts	
Deferred tax liability related to the revaluation of the inventory and to amortizable intangible assets	(45.1)
Deferred tax asset related to identified intangible assets on Gemplus balance sheet, eliminated from the net assets acquired	10.1
Total adjusted net assets, including acquired intangible assets	627.8
Minority interest in adjusted net assets (56.4%)[1]	(354.5)
Gemalto share of Gemplus adjusted net assets	273.3
Goodwill	315.2

(1) Excluding minority interest in Gemplus subsidiaries and assuming all adjustments to Gemplus net assets and all identified intangible assets are allocated to wholly owned subsidiaries of Gemplus.

Compared with the preliminary valuation made as of December 31, 2006, the goodwill was increased by €3.7 million due to adjustments of the fair value of the net assets acquired from Gemplus and of acquisition costs, as required by IFRS 3.

The intangible assets listed on the balance sheet of Gemplus as of the date of acquisition consisted of €91.9 million of Goodwill, mainly related to the acquisition of Setec (€60.7 million), €20.8 million of In-Process Research & Development and €14.2 million of other intangible assets. After the elimination of those intangible assets, the book value of the acquired shareholders' equity including minority interest was €530.6 million.

IFRS 3 requires that work-in-progress and finished goods inventories assumed in connection with this transaction are recognized at net realizable value (i.e. the estimated revenue derived from the future sale of these goods, over the estimated time to sell this inventory – 2.5 to 7 months – less expected selling or distribution costs). Therefore, the value of work-in-progress and finished goods inventories in the books of Gemplus on combination date was adjusted accordingly (stepup). In accordance with this requirement, the value of Gemplus work-in-progress and finished goods inventories was increased by €14.8 million.

Gemalto N.V. (AR 2007) (continued)

Existing Technology and In-Process R&D were valued using the Relief from Royalty method under the income approach. We estimated the cost of licensing the acquired intangible asset from an independent third party using a royalty rate. Since the company owns the intangible asset, it is relieved from making royalty payments. Then the present value of the resulting cash flow savings in the context of the combined entity was calculated, and attributed to the owned intangible asset.

Customer relationships were valued using the Excess Earnings method under the income approach. It reflects the present value of the projected cash flows that are expected to be generated by the customer relationships in the context of the combined entity, less charges representing the contribution of other assets to those cash flows.

Estimated useful life of the depreciable intangible assets acquired:

Intangible Assets	Fair Value (in millions of Euro)	Amortization period
Existing Technology	81.8	64% until December 2007, 36% over 4 years
In-Process R&D	20.8	3 to 5 years
Customer Relationships	22.2	4 years
Total	124.8	

Gemplus corporate name was valued using the market approach: the appraisers analysed some recent transactions in the high-tech industry, for business-to-business products, involving trademarks and considered the price at which the trademarks had been bought. Because the Gemplus trade name ceased to be commercially used as from June 2, 2006, Gemalto Management decided to impair the asset as of that date.

Commentary: This extract illustrates the valuation techniques used to measure the assets acquired in the business combination. This would not differ from either IFRS 3 (revised 2008) or Canadian GAAP practice. Note that the level of detail included in this disclosure is not required under IFRS 3 (revised 2008). It is important to further note that the company applied the purchase method instead of the acquisition method in accounting for the business combination (which was in accordance with the previous version of IFRS 3) and, therefore, amounts may differ using this method (e.g., since IFRS 3 did not require non-controlling interests to be recorded at their acquisition-date fair values).

Extracts 5(10) – Provisions assumed at the acquisition date

Aviva plc (AR 2007), pages 134			
3 – Subsidiaries (in part)			
The assets and liabilities at the date of acquisition were:			
	Book value £m	Fair value and accounting policy adjustments £m	Fair value £m
Assets			
Acquired value of in-force business on insurance contracts	–	6	6
Intangible assets	2	18	20
Investments	411	5	416
Loans	204	16	220
Reinsurance assets	33	–	33
Receivables and other financial assets	22	–	22
Prepayments and accrued income	13	–	13
Cash and cash equivalents	35	–	35
Other assets	31	1	32
Total assets	**751**	**46**	**797**
Liabilities			
Gross insurance liabilities	(674)	(20)	(694)
Borrowings	(15)	–	(15)
Provisions	(4)	(6)	(10)
Tax liabilities	(1)	(3)	(4)
Other liabilities	(20)	–	(20)
Total liabilities	**(714)**	**(29)**	**(743)**
Total net assets acquired	**37**	**17**	**54**
Goodwill arising on acquisition			**–**

The value of Erasmus's distribution channels has been identified as a separate intangible asset and valued by an independent third party at £8 million, using estimated post-tax cash flows and discount rates. It has been assessed as having a life of 20 years and is being amortised on a straight-line basis over that period. As permitted by IFRS 4, Insurance Contracts, an intangible asset of £12 million has also been recognised for the impact of discounting the non-life insurance liabilities, to bring them to fair value. This intangible asset will be amortised over the life of the relevant non-life insurance contracts.

The assets and liabilities as at the acquisition date in the table above are stated at their provisional values, and may be amended in 2008, in accordance with paragraph 62 of IFRS 3, Business Combinations.

The results of Erasmus have been included in the consolidated financial statements of the Group with effect from 26 March 2007, and have contributed £5 million to the consolidated profit before tax.

Commentary: The acquisition of the Erasmus Group shows liabilities, such as provisions, included in the net assets acquired. Under Canadian GAAP, these might not be recognized at the acquisition date.

Extracts 5(11) – Provisions included in the liabilities assumed at the acquisition date

Networkers International PLC (AR 2007), page 60

27 Acquisitions (in part)

Acquisition of MSB International Plc (in part)

On 27 November 2006 the Group acquired MSB International Plc for £15.6m plus costs of £0.661m paid by cash and financed by a term loan for £16m. In calculating the goodwill arising on acquisition, the fair value of net assets of MSB International have been assessed and adjustments from book value have been made where necessary.

These adjustments are summarised in the following table:

	Book Value £'000	Property Provisions £'000	Intangible assets acquired £'000	Fair value £'000
Fixed assets				
Tangible	415	-	-	415
Intangible assets	-	-	929	929
Current assets				
Debtors	28,514	-	-	28,514
Cash at bank and in hand	119	-	-	119
Total assets	29,048	-	929	29,977
Creditors				
Due within one year	16,980	854	-	17,834
Net assets/(liabilities)	12,068	(854)	929	12,143

	£'000
Cash consideration (including expenses of £661,000)	16,250
Identifiable net assets acquired:	(12,143)
Goodwill arising on acquisition	4,107

Commentary: The acquisition in this extract illustrates the inclusion of a provision for an onerous contract that might not be included in the purchase price allocation under Canadian GAAP. It is also important to note that the calculation of goodwill includes transaction costs of £661,000, which were recognized under the older version of IFRS 3 but would no longer be capitalized as part of goodwill under IFRS 3 (revised 2008).

Exceptions to the Recognition and Measurement Principles

Income Taxes

IFRS 3 (revised 2008) specifies that an acquirer should recognize and measure a deferred tax asset or liability arising from the assets acquired and liabilities assumed in a business combination in accordance with IAS 12. The acquirer should also account for the potential tax effects of temporary differences and carry-forwards of an acquiree that exist at the acquisition date or arise as a result of the acquisition in accordance with IAS 12.

Initial recognition of acquired tax benefits that does not qualify as a measurement period adjustment is reflected in profit or loss. Acquired tax benefits recognized within the measurement period resulting from new information about facts and circumstances that existed at the acquisition date are reflected first as an adjustment to goodwill, and then as a bargain purchase.

Under current Canadian GAAP, initial recognition of acquired deferred tax assets subsequent to the date of acquisition increases deferred tax assets and decreases goodwill (essentially is net income neutral). There is no time limit for the recognition of this deferred tax asset.

Employee Benefits

IFRS 3 (revised 2008) specifies that the acquirer recognizes and measures a liability (or asset, if any) related to the acquiree's employee benefit arrangements in accordance with IAS 19. The main reason for this exception is because the IASB felt that it was not feasible to require all employee benefit obligations assumed in a business combination to be measured at their acquisition-date fair values. To do so would effectively require comprehensively reconsidering the relevant standards for those employee benefits as a part of the business combinations revision project. Given the complexities in accounting for employee benefit obligations under existing requirements, the IASB decided that the only practicable alternative is to require those obligations, and any related assets, to be measured in accordance with their applicable standards.

Indemnification Assets

In addition to the above exceptions, IFRS 3 (revised 2008) provides one more for indemnification assets; these are not specifically addressed by Canadian GAAP. Indemnification assets occur when the seller in a business combination contractually indemnifies the acquirer for the outcome of a contingency or uncertainty related to all or part of a specific asset or liability. For example, the seller may guarantee that the acquirer's liability from a particular contingency will not exceed a specified amount. This gives the acquirer an indemnification asset. The acquirer has to recognize an indemnification asset at the same time and on the same basis as the indemnified item, subject to the need for a valuation allowance for uncollectible amounts. For an indemnification asset measured at fair value, the effects of uncertainty about future cash flows because of collectibility considerations are included in the fair value measure, and a separate valuation allowance is not necessary.

The subsequent accounting for the exceptions detailed above is discussed below.

Exceptions to the Measurement Principle

Reacquired Rights

As part of a business combination, an acquirer may reacquire a right that it had previously granted to the acquiree to use one or more of the acquirer's recognized or unrecognized assets. Examples include the right to use the acquirer's trade name under a franchise agreement or the right to use the acquirer's technology under a technology licensing agreement. Both Canadian GAAP and IFRS treat such reacquired rights as identifiable intangible assets that the acquirer recognizes separately from goodwill. If the terms of the contract giving rise to a reacquired right are favourable or unfavourable relative to the terms of current market transactions for the same or similar items, the acquirer recognizes a settlement gain or loss.

IFRS 3 (revised 2008) permits an exception to the measurement principle: the acquirer has to measure the value of the reacquired right recognized as an intangible asset on the basis of the remaining contractual term of the related contract regardless of whether market participants would consider potential contractual renewals in determining its fair value.

Share-based Payments

Share-based payments are another IFRS 3 (revised 2008) exception to the measurement principle, mainly because initial measurement of share-based payment awards at their acquisition-date fair values would cause difficulties with the subsequent accounting for those awards in accordance with IFRS 2. Therefore, IFRS 3 (revised 2008) specifies that the acquirer measures a liability or an equity instrument related to the replacement of an acquiree's share-based payment awards with share-based payment awards of the acquirer in accordance with the method in IFRS 2, referred to [in IFRS 3 (revised 2008)] as the "market-based measure" of the award.

Assets Held for Sale

IFRS 3 (revised 2008) also includes an exception to the measurement principle for assets held for sale. The acquirer is required to measure an acquired non-current asset (or disposal group) classified as held for sale at the acquisition date in accordance with IFRS 5 at fair value less costs to sell. This exception avoids the need to recognize a loss for the selling costs immediately after a business combination (referred to as a Day 2 loss) because, in theory, it would be recognized on the day after the acquisition date. That Day 2 loss would be incurred if the assets were initially measured at fair value but the acquirer then applied IFRS 5, requiring measurement at fair value less costs to sell, for subsequent accounting. Because that loss would stem entirely from different measurement requirements for assets held for sale acquired in a business combination, and for assets already held that are classified as held for sale, the reported loss would not faithfully represent the activities of the acquirer. At its April 2008 Board meeting, the IASB decided not to amend IFRS 5 for the measurement of non-current assets held for sale. Accordingly, the exception to the measurement principle of fair value related to non-current assets held for sale in IFRS 3 (revised 2008) will remain in force.

Other Measurement of Identifiable Assets Acquired and Liabilities Assumed Considerations

Acquisition-related Costs

Acquisition-related costs are costs the acquirer incurs in a business combination, such as:

- finder's fees;

- advisory, legal, accounting, valuation and other professional or consulting fees;

- general administrative costs, including the costs of maintaining an internal acquisitions department;

- costs of registering and issuing debt and equity securities.

Under IFRS 3 (revised 2008), the acquirer accounts for acquisition-related costs as expenses in the periods in which the costs are incurred and the services are received, with one exception. The costs to issue debt or equity securities are to be recognized in accordance with IAS 32, *Financial Instruments: Presentation* and IAS 39, *Financial Instruments: Recognition and Measurement*. This is different from Canadian GAAP which permits capitalization of direct costs of the business combination, but only if they are incremental costs incurred to effect the business combination.

Costs to Exit Activities

Canadian GAAP permits the recognition of certain costs associated with an acquiree's exit activities as liability costs in the purchase equation of the business combination. Under IFRS, an acquirer recognizes liabilities for restructuring or exit activities acquired in a business combination only if they meet the definition of a liability. This would be the case, for example, when the acquiree has a restructuring provision already recorded as a liability in its records at the acquisition date. Therefore, any costs the acquirer expects but is not obliged to incur in the future to carry out its plan to exit an acquiree activity, or to terminate the employment of or relocate an acquiree's employees, are not liabilities at the acquisition date under IFRS 3 (revised 2008) but are accepted under EIC-114, *Liability recognition for costs incurred on pur-*

chase business combinations. Under IFRS 3 (revised 2008), the acquirer does not recognize those costs as part of applying the acquisition method. Instead, the acquirer recognizes those costs in its post-combination financial statements in accordance with other IFRSs.

Operating Leases

Under IFRS 3 (revised 2008), if an acquiree is a lessee, the acquirer recognizes assets or liabilities related to an operating lease only if the terms of that operating lease are favourable or unfavourable relative to market terms. This does not substantially differ from the practice adopted under Canadian GAAP.

EIC-140 specifically addresses, from the lessor perspective, the accounting for intangibles related to operating leases that are favourable or unfavourable relative to market terms. EIC-140 does not substantially differ from IFRS. IFRS 3 (revised 2008) specifies, however, that if the acquiree is the lessor, these amounts are usually embedded in the fair value of the related asset acquired and not shown as separate assets or liabilities for the portion of the leases that are favourable or unfavourable relative to market terms. This may differ from Canadian practice, where these amounts are sometimes presented separately from the value attributed to the related asset acquired on the balance sheet.

Intangible Assets

Both IFRS 3 (revised 2008) and CICA 1581 include substantially the same principles for recognizing identifiable intangible assets separately from goodwill. An intangible asset is identifiable if it meets either the separability criterion or the contractual-legal criterion. Intangible assets that are not separately identifiable are treated the same way as well, in that they are recognized as part of goodwill at the acquisition date. For example, an acquirer may attribute value to the existence of an assembled workforce or to potential contracts the acquiree is negotiating with prospective new customers. These are not identifiable assets to be recognized separately from goodwill.

Illustrative Disclosure:

Extract 5(12) – Identifiable intangible assets

> **Andritz AG (AR 2007), page 21**
> **C. Acquisitions (in part)**
> The goodwill recognized in cause of a business combination comprises acquired intangibles, which could not be recognized separately, such as experienced and trained workforce and the acquired market positions.

Commentary: This extract states that, because some intangible assets could not be recognized separately, they are included in goodwill, as under Canadian GAAP.

Classification or Designation of Identifiable Assets Acquired and Liabilities Assumed

IFRS 3 (revised 2008) specifies that, at the acquisition date, an acquirer classifies or designates the identifiable assets acquired and liabilities assumed as necessary to apply other IFRSs subsequently. The acquirer makes those classifications or designations on the basis of the contractual terms, economic conditions, its operating or accounting policies and other pertinent conditions existing at the acquisition date. Although this specific guidance is not included in Canadian GAAP, CICA 1581 does specify that the accounting of an asset or liability acquired in a business combination after acquisition is dictated by the nature of the asset acquired. Therefore, this does not represent a significant difference in application.

Consideration Paid

IFRS 3 (revised 2008) specifies that the consideration transferred in a business combination (including any contingent consideration) will be measured at fair value, which will be calculated as:

- the sum of the acquisition-date fair values of the assets transferred by the acquirer;
- the liabilities incurred by the acquirer to former owners of the acquiree; and
- the equity interests issued by the acquirer. (Any portion of the acquirer's share-based payment awards exchanged for awards held by the acquiree's employees that is included in consideration transferred in the business combination is, however, measured in accordance with IFRS 2; refer to Chapter 16 for more details.)

IFRS 3 (revised 2008) also specifies that, in a business combination in which the acquirer and the acquiree (or its former owners) exchange only equity interests, the acquisition-date fair value of the acquiree's equity interests may be more reliably measurable than the acquisition-date fair value of the acquirer's equity interests. If so, the acquirer will determine the amount of goodwill by using the acquisition-date fair value of the acquiree's equity interests. It is also important to note that this guidance applies equally to combinations of mutual entities, which Canadian GAAP does not currently address.

Although CICA 1581 does not include the same specific requirements, they both apply a fair value approach. CICA 1581 specifies that the acquirer's purchase cost should be determined by the fair value of the consideration given or the acquirer's share of the fair value of the net assets or equity interests acquired, whichever is more reliably measurable. CICA 1581, therefore, allows an approach similar to IFRS 3 (revised 2008). It is not, however, restricted to exchanges of equity interests; it applies also to exchanges of net assets. IFRS 3 (revised 2008) is also more specific about the calculation of the consideration paid, which is clearly outlined in the standard as comprising the aggregate of three components (as outlined above), whereas CICA 1581 does not include such guidance. This may represent a change in perspective for Canadian preparers exchanging net assets who are used to relying on a choice of methods when fair value measurement of the consideration paid becomes challenging.

Fair Value of Shares Issued

When shares are issued as part of the consideration given in a business combination, they are measured at fair value at the acquisition date under IFRS while, under Canadian GAAP, they are measured at their market price over a reasonable period before and after the date the terms of the business combination are agreed to and announced. This estimate may produce a different share price than the acquisition date share price required by IFRS 3 (revised 2008). Accordingly, there may be differences in the amount determined for consideration. As previously mentioned, in some cases, such as when businesses have volatile share prices, this difference can have significant implications.

Illustrative Disclosure:

Extract 5(13) – Business combinations with shares issued as consideration

Unibail-Rodamco (AR 2007), page 126

3. HIGHLIGHTS AND COMPARABILITY OF THE LAST THREE YEARS (in part)

3.3. In 2007 (in part)

Accounting for Business Combinations (in part)

In accordance with IFRS 3 – Business Combinations, the cost of the business combination is equal to the sum of the market value of the shares and the ORA Unibail-Rodamco issued in exchange for the Rodamco shares and other costs directly attributable to the acquisition.

Although in essence the transaction bears all the elements of a pure merger (pooling of interest), in accordance with accounting principles (IFRS 3 – Business Combinations) the combination was considered as a purchase of Rodamco by Unibail. The cost of the business combination was computed based on the Unibail share price (€195.80 as at June 21, 2007). This market value differed from the issue price used in the statutory financial statements of Unibail Holding which amounted to €196.60 and which was the quoted market price at the closing of the Public Exchange Offer on June 20, 2007. Taking into account the acquisition costs which amounted to €4.1 Mn, the total cost of the business combination amounts to €7,322.6 Mn.

The fees attributable to the issue of the shares and the ORA amount to respectively €34.7 Mn and €9.4 Mn and are directly accounted for in the Group shareholders' equity except for €1.2 Mn reducing the amount of ORA reclassified in 'Long term bonds' (see below 'Accounting for ORA').

At the time of the combination, Unibail and Rodamco shares were trading at a premium to net asset value, similar to the entire property sector, therefore generating a gap of more than €1.6 Bn between the value of Unibail shares issued and Rodamco's shareholders' funds.

Commentary: This extract depicts the measurement of shares exchanged as consideration in a business combination at the acquisition date. This differs from the current practice under Canadian GAAP.

Transfer of Assets or Liabilities of the Acquirer

The consideration transferred may include acquirer assets or liabilities that have carrying amounts that differ from their fair values at the acquisition date. If so, IFRS 3 (revised 2008) requires the acquirer to re-measure the transferred assets or liabilities to their fair values as of the acquisition date and to recognize the resulting gains or losses, if any, in profit or loss. This is similar to CICA 1581 recommendations, which specify the determination of the purchase cost as discussed above. IFRS 3 (revised 2008), however, specifies the accounting for transferred assets or liabilities that remain within the combined entity after the business combination (for example, because the assets or liabilities were transferred to the acquiree rather than to its former owners), and the acquirer therefore retains control over them. In that situation, IFRS 3 (revised 2008) specifies that the acquirer measures those assets and liabilities at their carrying amounts immediately before the acquisition date and does not recognize a gain or loss in profit or loss on assets or liabilities it controls both before and after the business combination. CICA 1581 does not address these specific circumstances as it does not take into account the relationship of the acquirer and its controlled assets before and after the acquisition unless the relationship is that of a related party. In that case, the application CICA 3840 may or may not result (depending on whether there is a substantive change in ownership, whether there is independent evidence to support the exchange transaction etc.) in the same treatment as that under IFRS 3 (revised 2008).

Contingent Consideration

A business combination agreement may allow for adjustments to the cost of the combination that are contingent on one or more future events. The adjustments might, for example, be contingent on a specific performance indicator, such as earnings before interests, depreciation and amortization, or working capital. These adjustments may represent the acquirer making additional payments or receiving additional amounts. IFRS 3 (revised 2008) requires the acquirer to recognize the acquisition-date fair value of contingent consideration as part of the consideration transferred.

As the basis for conclusions of IFRS 3 (revised 2008) explains, the logic behind this principle is that the acquirer's agreement to make contingent payments is the obligating event in a business combination transaction. Although the amount of the future payments the acquirer will make is conditional on future events, the obligation to make them if the specified future events occur is unconditional. The same is true for a right to the return of previously transferred consideration if specified conditions are met. Failure to recognize that obligation or right at the acquisition date would not faithfully represent the economic consideration exchanged at that date. Consequently, obligations and rights associated with contingent consideration arrangements should be measured and recognized at their acquisition-date fair values. This presents a measurement difficulty at the acquisition date because estimating the fair value of some contingent payments may be difficult. On the other hand, delaying recognition of, or otherwise ignoring, assets or liabilities that are difficult to measure would cause financial reporting to be incomplete, diminishing its usefulness for making economic decisions.

As indicated in the basis for conclusions of IFRS 3 (revised 2008), a contingent consideration arrangement is inherently part of the economic considerations in the negotiations between a buyer and seller. Buyers and sellers often reach an agreement by first agreeing to share particular specified economic risks related to uncertainties about future outcomes. Differences in their views about those uncertainties are often reconciled by their agreeing to share the risks in such a way that favourable future outcomes generally result in additional payments to the seller and unfavourable outcomes result in no or lower payments. Information used in those negotiations will often be helpful in estimating the fair value of the contingent obligation assumed by the acquirer. Most contingent consideration obligations are financial instruments, and many are derivative instruments. Reporting entities that use such instruments extensively and auditors and valuation professionals familiar with estimating the fair values of financial instruments should, therefore, be able to use valuation techniques to develop estimates of the fair values of contingent consideration obligations that are sufficiently reliable for recognition.

Under CICA 1581, however, a contingent consideration is recognized at the date of acquisition as part of the cost of the purchase only if it can be reasonably estimated and the outcome of the contingency can be determined beyond reasonable doubt. This usually results in later recognition of contingent consideration under Canadian GAAP than it would as part of the purchase price under IFRS 3 (revised 2008).

Illustrative Disclosure:

Extract 5(14) – Contingent consideration

Kewill Systems PLC (AR 2007), page 37

25. Acquisitions (in part)

During the year the Group made three acquisitions for a total consideration payable of £20,574,000. The net cash acquired with these acquisitions was £751,000. In order to present the net assets of the acquired companies at fair value, adjustments totalling £9,339,000 were made to book value of the assets and liabilities acquired. All of these transactions have been accounted for as acquisitions.

The fair value adjustments made to the acquisitions comprise valuation of the intellectual property and customer bases together with the associated deferred tax liability. Also included is the write-down of certain fixed assets and debtors in line with Group policy.

All intangible assets have been recognised at their respective fair values. The residual excess over the net assets acquired is recognised as goodwill in the financial statements.

CSF GmbH

On 16 June 2006 the Group purchased 100% of the issued share capital of CSF GmbH. An analysis of the net assets acquired is as follows;

Acquisition - fair values	Book value £000	Fair value adjustments £000	Provisional fair value £000
Intangible fixed assets	-	3,527	3,527
Tangible fixed assets	914	(570)	344
Stock & work in progress	1	-	1
Debtors	241	-	241
Cash	49		49
Creditors	(1,098)	-	(1,098)
Deferred tax	-	(1,058)	(1,058)
Net assets acquired	107	1,899	2,006
Goodwill			2,402
Consideration			4,408

Satisfied by;	
Cash	3,008
Related costs of acquisition	156
Contingent consideration	1,244
Total	4,408

Contingent consideration shown above has been discounted with regard to the notional interest payable, the full amount that we expect to pay is £1,367,000.

From the date of acquisition to 31 March 2007 CSF GmbH contributed £3,835,000 to revenue and £235,000 operating profit before amortisation to the Groups profit before tax. Amortisation of intangibles charges totalled £558,000.

CSF GmbH contributed £10,000 to the group's net operating cash flows and utilised £122,000 for capital expenditure.

Commentary: This extract shows a contingent consideration being included as part of the consideration paid at the acquisition date. This practice is not normally applied under Canadian GAAP except in situations where the outcome of the contingent consideration can be determined beyond reasonable doubt and can be reasonably estimated at the date of acquisition. It is important to note, however, that the related cost of acquisition included in the consideration paid - which is consistent with Canadian GAAP - would not satisfy IFRS 3 (revised 2008) requirements and would not be included in the cost (as previously discussed).

Measurement of Goodwill

Under IFRS 3 (revised 2008), goodwill is measured as the difference between:

- the aggregate of:
  - o the acquisition-date fair value of the consideration transferred,

o   the amount of any non-controlling interest in the acquiree, and

o   the net of the acquisition-date fair values [or, in some cases, other amounts in accordance with IFRS 3 (revised 2008)] of the identifiable assets acquired and the liabilities assumed;

- the net of the acquisition-date fair values (or, in some cases, other amounts in accordance with IFRS 3R) of the identifiable assets acquired and the liabilities assumed.

If the difference is negative, it is considered a bargain purchase, which is discussed in further detail below.

IFRS 3 (revised 2008) permits a choice of recognizing either total goodwill (full fair value method or full goodwill method) or only the acquirer's share (proportionate method or partial goodwill method), depending on which option is used for measuring the non-controlling interest (fair value or the proportionate share of the value of the net identifiable assets acquired). Under current CICA 1581, goodwill is the difference between the excess of the cost of an acquired enterprise and the net of the amounts assigned to assets acquired and liabilities assumed. These amounts reflect the fair value adjustment for the acquirer's share only.

Illustrative Example:

The purpose of this example is to illustrate, in a simplified manner, the difference between the fair value method and the proportionate method and how the goodwill and non-controlling interest amounts would differ depending on the method selected.

Example of full fair value versus proportionate method:			
ABC Company purchases 800,000 of the 1,000,000 outstanding shares (i.e. 80%) of the shares of XYZ Company for a purchase price of $5,010,000. Based on the trading price of XYZ Company at the date of gaining control, a value of $1,240,000 is assigned to the 20% non-controlling interest, indicating that ABC has paid a control premium of $50,000. The details of the net assets acquired are as follows:			
	100% FV	80% Acquired FV Method	80% Acquired Proportionate Method
Fair value / Purchase price	$6,200,000	$5,010,000	$5,010,000
Accounts receivable	1,000,000	1,000,000	1,000,000
Inventory	2,000,000	2,000,000	2,000,000
Land	1,000,000	1,000,000	1,000,000
Building	3,000,000	3,000,000	3,000,000
Equipment	2,000,000	2,000,000	2,000,000
Intangible – trademark	240,000	240,000	240,000
Accounts payable	(2,000,000)	(2,000,000)	(2,000,000)
Mortgage	(1,500,000)	(1,500,000)	(1,500,000)
Non-controlling interests	–	(1,240,000)	(1,148,000)
	$5,740,000	$4,500,000	$4,592,000
Goodwill	$460,000	$510,000	$418,000
Notes: under the "fair value method," the non-controlling interests is measured on the basis of market prices for the shares held by non-controlling shareholders or by applying another valuation technique, whereas under the "proportionate method," this amount is determined using the fair value of the net identifiable assets acquired.			

Commentary: This example illustrates the difference between using the full fair value method to measure the non-controlling interest's portion and goodwill or the proportionate interest method. It clearly illustrates the inflated amounts that result from using the full fair value method, whereas in the proportionate method, the goodwill and non-controlling interest are reflected at only the parent's portion of those amounts. It is also important to note that the proportionate method illustrates more clearly that the parent's price of the acquiree included a control premium of $50,000.

IFRS 3 (revised 2008) introduces a change in focus in the approach to measuring goodwill. Although it is still measured as a residual, IFRS 3 (revised 2008) focuses on the fair value of the consideration transferred rather than on the fair value of the acquirer's interest in the acquiree, with a presumption that the two amounts are usually equal. This was viewed as a more straightforward way of measuring goodwill as it will generally be recognized at its acquisition-date fair value. Under Canadian GAAP, the assets acquired and liabilities assumed are to be measured based on the cost of the purchase, which is measured as the more reliable of two amounts. This shift in focus will avoid unproductive disputes about whether the consideration transferred or another valuation technique provides the best evidence for measuring the acquirer's interest in the acquiree in a particular situation. The measurement of goodwill is discussed further in the next section.

As previously discussed, in a business combination in which the acquirer and the acquiree (or its former owners) exchange only equity interests, the acquisition-date fair value of the acquiree's equity interest may be more reliably measurable than the acquisition-date fair value of the acquirer's equity interests. If so, the acquirer determines the amount of goodwill by using the acquisition-date fair value of the acquiree's equity interests.

To determine the amount of goodwill in a business combination in which no consideration is transferred, the acquirer uses the acquisition-date fair-value of the acquirer's interest in the acquiree determined by using a valuation technique rather than the acquisition-date fair value of the consideration transferred. Canadian GAAP does not contain similarly restrictive guidance.

Bargain Purchases

With bargain purchases, the concept of reducing the net assets acquired to absorb negative goodwill, which is the required treatment under Canadian GAAP, is not consistent with the recognition and measurement principles in IFRS 3 (revised 2008). These amounts are recognized in earnings.

Illustrative Disclosure:

Extract 5(15) – Accounting for negative goodwill

BNP Paribas (Registration Document 2007), page 116

1.b.4 Business combinations and measurement of goodwill (in part)

Business combinations (in part)

Business combinations are accounted for by the purchase method. Under this method, the acquiree's identifiable assets, liabilities and contingent liabilities that meet the IFRS recognition criteria are measured at fair value at the acquisition date except for non-current assets classified as assets held for sale, which are accounted for at fair value less costs to sell. The Group may recognise any adjustments to the provisional accounting within 12 months of the acquisition date.

The cost of a business combination is the fair value, at the date of exchange, of assets given, liabilities assumed, and equity instruments issued to obtain control of the acquiree, plus any costs directly attributable to the combination.

Goodwill represents the difference between the cost of the combination and the acquirer's interest in the net fair value of the identifiable assets, liabilities and contingent liabilities of the acquiree at the acquisition date. Positive goodwill is recognised in the acquirer's balance sheet, and badwill is recognised immediately in profit or loss, on the acquisition date.

Goodwill is recognised in the functional currency of the acquiree and translated at the closing exchange rate.

Commentary: This extract presents the company's policies for accounting for business combinations under the previous version of IFRS 3, which will change when IFRS 3 (revised 2008) is implemented; the acquisition method will be applied instead of the purchase method. The cost of the purchase will change as well; it will be measured at the acquisition-date fair values of the assets transferred by the acquirer, the liabilities incurred by the acquirer to former owners of the acquiree and the equity interests issued by the acquirer. This amount will not include any acquisition costs. This example also illustrates the treatment of negative goodwill, which is immediately recognized in income, whereas Canadian GAAP treatment significantly differs.

Increases and Decreases in Ownership Interests

Canadian GAAP specifies the accounting for increases and decreases in ownership interests as follows: increases in investments are accounted for using the purchase method, and decreases are accounted for as sales resulting in gains or losses. This principle is used by analogy to any situation where there are changes in ownership interests. IFRS 3 (revised 2008), on the other hand, specifies guidance that applies to business combinations achieved in stages and without the transfer of consideration.

Business Combinations Achieved in Stages

IFRS 3 (revised 2008) refers to a business combination achieved in stages, sometimes also referred to as a "step acquisition," when an acquirer obtains control of an acquiree in which it held an equity interest immediately before the acquisition date. Prior to IFRS 3 (revised 2008), the old version of IFRS 3 had little guidance for such acquisitions, whereas Canadian GAAP has specific requirements under CICA 1600, *Consolidated Financial Statements*. The requirements under IFRS 3 (revised 2008), however, differ in some respects from the current guidance in Canadian GAAP.

If a business combination is achieved in stages and the acquirer obtains or loses control, this is considered a significant event that triggers re-measurement. The previously held equity interest (and equity interests retained) in the acquiree is re-measured at its acquisition-date fair value and the resulting gain or loss, if any, is recognized in profit or loss. If an acquirer increases its ownership interest before acquiring the additional controlling interest, the acquirer may have reported certain investment amounts in other comprehensive income (for example, because the investment was classified as available for sale). In these cases, the amounts previously recognized in other comprehensive income are recognized on the same basis as would be required if the acquirer had disposed directly of the previously held equity interest.

When control is retained, these transactions are not considered to be significant events. Any increases or decreases in ownership interests in the acquiree are accounted for as equity transactions and no gain or loss is recorded in income.

Illustrative Disclosure:

Extract 5(16) – Business combination achieved in stages

Deutsche Telekom AG (AR 2007), page 113 and 106

Business combinations. (in part)

On October 24, 2007 Deutsche Telekom exercised its preemptive right through Group subsidiary Scout 24 AG, Baar, Switzerland, to purchase a share of 66.22 percent in Immobilien Scout GmbH, Berlin, which was previously held by Aareal Bank, Wiesbaden, for the price of EUR 0.4 billion. The acquisition increased Scout24 AG's existing share of 33.11 percent to 99.33 percent. Immediately prior to the acquisition of the additional 66.22-percent share, the carrying amount of the existing 33.11-percent share in Immobilien Scout was EUR 7 million. Since the investment existed before Deutsche Telekom obtained control of the entity, the acquisition of the additional stake is treated as a business combination achieved in stages according to IFRS 3.

The business activities of Immobilien Scout comprise the operation of an Internet-based real estate marketing platform and associated products and services for the German market.

Immobilien Scout was included in Deutsche Telekom's consolidated financial statements as a fully consolidated subsidiary for the first time effective November 1, 2007. The existing 33.11-percent share in Immobilien Scout was carried at equity until October 31, 2007 and included in the consolidated financial statements as an associate.

The business combination resulted in total goodwill of EUR 0.3 billion. This includes around EUR 20 million from the existing 33.11-percent share that was realized in the course of the initial inclusion at equity of the Scout24 group in February 2004. The recent acquisition of the further 66.22-percent share resulted in goodwill of EUR 283 million. This amount is mainly attributable to positive future income effects and anticipated savings due to synergies. Cash and cash equivalents in the amount of EUR 1 million were acquired in conjunction with the purchase of Immobilien Scout.

The fair values of Immobilien Scout's acquired assets, liabilities and contingent liabilities recognized at the date of acquisition and their carrying amounts immediately prior to the business combination are presented in the following table:

	Immobilien Scout *	
millions of €	**Fair value at the acquisition date**	**Carrying amounts immediately prior to the business combination**
Assets	168	35
Current assets	31	31
Cash and cash equivalents	1	1
Other assets	30	30
Non-current assets	137	4
Intangible assets	133	1
Property, plant and equipment	3	3
Other assets	1	0
Liabilities	53	13
Current liabilities	13	13
Financial liabilities	–	–
Trade and other payables	–	–
Other liabilities	13	13
Non-current liabilities	40	–
Financial liabilities	–	–
Other liabilities	40	–

*   Figures excluding goodwill.

The EUR 31 million change in fair value relating to the previously held interest (33.11 percent) resulting from the complete revaluation of Immobilien Scout's assets and liabilities is recognized in the revaluation reserve. The proportion of shareholders' equity attributable to third parties is approximately EUR 1 million.

Deutsche Telekom AG (AR 2007), page 106			
Statement of recognized income and expense.			
millions of €	**2007**	**2006**	**2005**
Fair value measurement of available-for-sale securities			
– Change in other comprehensive income (not recognized in income statement)	**(1)**	3	126
– Recognition of other comprehensive income in income statement	**(1)**	(1)	(984)
Fair value measurement of hedging instruments			
– Change in other comprehensive income (not recognized in income statement)	**(118)**	385	(537)
– Recognition of other comprehensive income in income statement	**3**	(8)	(28)
Revaluation due to business combinations	**(142)**	395	(9)
Exchange differences on translation of foreign subsidiaries	**(2,510)**	(1,747)	2,878
Other income and expense recognized directly in equity	**160**	80	9
Actuarial gains and losses from defined benefit plans and other employee benefits	**923**	314	(1,099)
Deferred taxes on items in other comprehensive income	**(228)**	(275)	624
Income and expense recognized directly in equity	**(1,914)**	(854)	980
Profit after income taxes	**1,078**	3,574	6,021
Recognized income and expense	**(836)**	2,720	7,001
Minority interests	**512**	517	480
Equity attributable to equity holders of the parent	**(1,348)**	2,203	6,521

Commentary: This extract demonstrates the accounting for a business combination achieved in stages under the previous version of IFRS 3. Under IFRS 3 (revised 2008) the revaluation adjustment presented in the Statement of Recognized Income and Expense would be required to be presented in income. This represents a change from Canadian GAAP. It is also important to note that the Statement of Recognized Income and Expense (sometimes referred to as the SORIE statement) is no longer applicable and has been replaced by the Statement of Other Comprehensive Income.

Business Combinations without the Transfer of Consideration

Sometimes, an acquirer obtains control of an acquiree without transferring consideration for example when:

- The acquiree repurchases a sufficient number of its own shares for an existing investor to obtain control.

- Minority veto rights lapse that previously kept the acquirer from controlling an acquiree in which the acquirer held the majority voting rights.

- The acquirer and acquiree agree to combine their businesses by contract alone. The acquirer transfers no consideration in exchange for control of the acquiree and holds no equity interests in the acquiree, either on the acquisition date or previously. Examples of business combinations achieved by contract alone include bringing two businesses together in a stapling arrangement or forming a dual listed corporation.

The acquisition method of accounting for a business combination still applies to those combinations. It is expected that the acquisition-date fair value of the acquirer's interest in the acquiree would be used instead of the acquisition-date fair value of the consideration transferred. Such value would be determined using a valuation technique. This does not substantially differ from Canadian GAAP where the purchase method is applied in similar situations as outlined at the beginning of this section. Canadian GAAP does not, however, provide such specific measurement guidance for the approximation of the consideration transferred for the purposes of the determination of goodwill.

IFRS 3 (revised 2008) also specifies that, in business combinations achieved by contract alone, the acquirer has to attribute to the owners of the acquiree the amount of the acquiree's net assets. In other words, the equity interests in the acquiree held by parties other than the acquirer are a non-controlling interest in the acquirer's post-combination financial statements even if the result is that all of the equity interests in the acquiree are attributed to the non-controlling interest. This is substantially similar to the guidance provided by AcG-15.

Push-down Accounting

Although CICA 1625, *Comprehensive Revaluation of Assets and Liabilities* permits push-down accounting in limited circumstances, IFRS do not recognize this method of accounting. This may represent a change in practice for some financial reorganizations using this method of accounting. Due to the infrequency of such situations, this difference is not expected to have a pervasive effect.

Measurement Period

When the initial accounting for a business combination is incomplete by the end of the reporting period in which the combination occurred, both IFRS 3 (revised 2008) and Canadian GAAP require the acquirer to report, in its financial statements, provisional amounts for the items for which the accounting is incomplete. IFRS 3 (revised 2008) specifies, however, that during the measurement period, the acquirer must retrospectively adjust the provisional amounts recognized at the acquisition date to reflect new information obtained about facts and circumstances that existed as of the acquisition date and, if known, would have affected the measurement of the amounts recognized as of that date or would have resulted in the recognition of additional assets or liabilities. Under Canadian GAAP, these revisions are usually applied on a prospective basis.

IFRS 3 (revised 2008) also specifies that the measurement period ends as soon as the acquirer receives the information it was seeking about facts and circumstances that existed as of the acquisition date or learns that more information is not obtainable. The measurement period may not exceed one year from the acquisition date. CICA 1581 does not provide such detailed guidance, although EIC-14 specifies the same time limit for the measurement period.

It is sometimes difficult to distinguish between measurement period adjustments to provisional estimates of fair values at the acquisition date and subsequent changes in the fair value of a liability for contingent consideration that do not affect the acquisition-date fair value of the consideration transferred. Those subsequent changes in value are generally directly related to post-combination events and changes in circumstances related to the combined entity. Such subsequent changes in value should not affect the measurement of the consideration transferred or goodwill on the acquisition date.

Illustrative Disclosures:

Extract 5(17) – Measurement period

voestalpine AG (AR 2008), page 99		
D. Acquisitions (in part)		
A preliminary purchase price allocation effected in the 2006/07 business year following an acquisition by the Automotive Division has been restated during the reporting period in accordance with IFRS 3 less than 12 months after acquisition date. The adjustment was made as follows:		
	Assets	**Equity and liabilities**
Goodwill	3,885	
Intangible assets	–2,220	
Inventories	–930	
Deferred tax assets	1,940	
Provisions		2,675
	2,675	2,675
		In thousands of euros

Commentary: This extract depicts the retrospective application of the purchase price adjustments in the year subsequent to acquisition. Under Canadian GAAP this adjustment is usually only made prospectively.

Extract 5(18) – Measurement period

Danisco A/S (AR 2008), page 87
27 ACQUISITIONS AND DIVESTMENTS OF ENTERPRISES AND ACTIVITIES (in part)
Other adjustments of acquisitions
In 2007/08, the purchase price of Danisco (Zhangjiagang) Textural Ingredients Co., Ltd. (acquired in 2006/07) was raised by DKK 12 million while the purchase price of Danisco Sweeteners (Anyang) Co., Ltd. (acquired in 2005/06) was reduced by DKK 2 million. The adjustments have been made in consequence of the emergence of additional information.

Commentary: This extract illustrates how the purchase price is adjusted as a result of new information obtained after the acquisition date that was applied retrospectively. This can sometimes represent a difference under Canadian practice, for example when uncertain amounts are recognized at the acquisition date as part of the purchase price allocation.

Extract 5(19) – Measurement period

Alcatel-Lucent (AR 2007 on Form 20-F), page 170
NOTE 2 PRINCIPAL UNCERTAINTIES REGARDING THE USE OF ESTIMATES (in part)
I/ Purchase price allocation of a business combination

In a business combination, the acquirer shall allocate the cost of the business combination at the acquisition date by recognizing the acquiree's identifiable assets, liabilities and contingent liabilities at fair value at that date. The allocation is based upon certain valuations and other studies performed with the service of outside valuation specialists. Due to the underlying assumptions taken in the valuation process, the determination of those fair values requires estimations of the effects of uncertain future events at the acquisition date and the carrying amounts of some assets, such as fixed assets, acquired through a business combination could therefore differ significantly in the future.

As prescribed by IFRS 3, if the initial accounting for a business combination can be determined only provisionally by the end of the reporting period in which the combination is effected, the acquirer shall account for the business combination using those provisional values and has a twelve-month period to complete the purchase price allocation. Any adjustment of the carrying amount of an identifiable asset or liability made as a result of completing the initial accounting is accounted for as if its fair value at the acquisition date had been recognized from that date. Detailed adjustments accounted for in the allocation period are disclosed in note 3.

Once the initial accounting of a business combination is complete, further adjustments shall be accounted for only to correct errors.

Commentary: This note mentions that it is not always possible to arrive at definitive amounts when accounting for business combinations and explains how adjustments are treated during the measurement period and after that period.

Subsequent Measurement of Assets Acquired and Liabilities Assumed

All assets acquired, liabilities assumed and equity instruments issued in a business combination should be subsequently measured and accounted for in accordance with other applicable IFRSs for those items, depending on their nature. IFRS 3 (revised 2008) states accounting requirements for reacquired rights, contingent liabilities recognized as of the acquisition date, indemnification assets and contingent consideration that are not specifically addressed by CICA 1581, although the general requirements are the same.

Reacquired Rights

A reacquired right recognized as an intangible asset is to be amortized over the remaining contractual period of the contract in which the right was granted. An acquirer that subsequently sells a reacquired right to a third party has to include the carrying amount of the intangible asset in determining the gain or loss on the sale. This does not substantially differ from the guidance in EIC-154.

Contingent Liabilities

After initial recognition and until the liability is settled, cancelled or expires, the acquirer has to measure a contingent liability recognized in a business combination at the higher of:

- the amount that would be recognized in accordance with IAS 37, *Provisions, Contingent Liabilities and Contingent Assets*; and

- the amount initially recognized less, if appropriate, cumulative amortization recognized in accordance with IAS 18 *Revenue*.

This will likely represent a change from Canadian GAAP reporting.

Indemnification Assets

At the end of each subsequent reporting period, the acquirer must measure an indemnification asset recognized at the acquisition date on the same basis as the indemnified liability or asset, subject to any contractual limitations on its amount. And, an indemnification asset that is not subsequently measured at its fair value is measured at management's assessment of its collectibility. The acquirer would derecognize the indemnification asset only when it collects the asset, sells it or otherwise loses the right to it.

These provisions are not specified under Canadian GAAP and may represent a change for preparers.

Contingent Consideration

Under IFRS 3 (revised 2008), a contingent consideration may be adjusted after initial recognition because the acquirer got additional information after the acquisition date about facts and circumstances that existed at the acquisition date. The acquirer will then retrospectively adjust the provisional amount recognized at the acquisition date, thereby adjusting the original purchase price allocation and goodwill. Changes resulting from events happening after the acquisition date, such as meeting an earnings target, reaching a specified share price or reaching a milestone on a research and development project, will be accounted for as follows:

- Contingent consideration classified as equity is not re-measured and its subsequent settlement is accounted for within equity.

- Contingent consideration classified as an asset or a liability that:

    o is a financial instrument and is within the scope of IAS 39 is measured at fair value, with any resulting gain or loss recognized either in profit or loss or in other comprehensive income in accordance with that IFRS,

    o is not within the scope of IAS 39 will be accounted for in accordance with IAS 37 or other IFRS as appropriate.

General Business Combination Disclosures

The general disclosures specified by IFRS 3 (revised 2008) and Canadian GAAP do not differ in principle; both require that the nature and financial effect of business combinations be disclosed to the users of the financial statements. The detailed disclosure provisions required by IFRS 3 (revised 2008) are, however, more onerous than those required by Canadian GAAP. A comparison is provided in the table below.

IFRS 3 (Revised 2008)	Canadian GAAP
General information on the business combination	
The name and a description of the acquiree.	Same as under CICA 1581.
The acquisition date.	Indirectly under CICA 1581 with the disclosure of the period for which the earnings of the acquired enterprise are included in the income statement of the combined enterprise.
The percentage of voting equity interests acquired.	Same as under CICA 1581.
The primary reasons for the business combination and a description of how the acquirer obtained control of the acquiree.	This information is not required disclosure.

IFRS 3R	Canadian GAAP
Goodwill	
A qualitative description of the factors that make up the goodwill recognized, such as expected synergies from combining operations of the acquiree and the acquirer, intangible assets that do not qualify for separate recognition or other factors.	This information is not required. CICA 1581 only requires that goodwill be disclosed by reportable segment.
The total amount of goodwill that is expected to be deductible for tax purposes.	Same as under section 1581.
Consideration transferred	
The acquisition-date fair value of the total consideration transferred, and the acquisition-date fair value of each major class of consideration.	CICA 1591 requires similar disclosure, such as the cost of the purchase and, when applicable, the number of equity instruments issued or issuable, the value assigned to those equity instruments, and the basis for determining that value.
For contingent consideration arrangements and indemnification assets: • the amount recognized as of the acquisition date; • a description of the arrangement and the basis for determining the amount of the payment; and • an estimate of the range of outcomes (undiscounted) or, if a range cannot be estimated, that fact and the reasons why a range cannot be estimated. If the maximum amount of the payment is unlimited, the acquirer must disclose that fact.	Less onerous disclosure is required by CICA 1581. However, under Canadian GAAP a contingent consideration is not often recognized at the acquisition date.
Assets acquired and liabilities assumed	
The amounts recognized as of the acquisition date for each major class of assets acquired and liabilities assumed.	Same as under CICA 1581.
For acquired receivables: • the fair value of the receivables; • the gross contractual amounts receivable; and • the best estimate at the acquisition date of the contractual cash flows not expected to be collected. The disclosures must be provided by major class of receivable, such as loans, direct finance leases and any other class of receivables.	This information is not required.

IFRS 3R	Canadian GAAP
Contingent liabilities	
For each contingent liability recognized, the following information: • a brief description of the nature of the obligation and the expected timing of any resulting outflows of economic benefits; • an indication of the uncertainties about the amount or timing of those outflows. Where necessary to provide adequate information, an entity should disclose the major assumptions made concerning future events; and • the amount of any expected reimbursement, stating the amount of any asset that has been recognized for that expected reimbursement. If a contingent liability is not recognized because its fair value cannot be measured reliably, the acquirer would disclose additional information and the reasons why the liability cannot be measured reliably.	Less onerous disclosure is required by CICA 1581 and CICA 3290, *Contingencies*.
Transactions that are recognized separately	
For transactions that are recognized separately from the assets acquired and liabilities assumed: • a description of each transaction; • how the acquirer accounted for each transaction; • the amounts recognized for each transaction and the line item in the financial statements in which each amount is recognized; and • if the transaction is the effective settlement of as pre-existing relationship, the method used to determine the settlement amount.	Similar disclosures are required by EICs 127 and 154.
The disclosure of separately recognized transactions required includes the amount of acquisition-related costs and, separately, the amount of those costs recognized as an expense and the line item or items in the statement of comprehensive income in which those expenses are recognized. The amount of any issue costs not recognized as an expense and how they were recognized would also be disclosed.	This information is not required.
Bargain purchase	
In a bargain purchase the amount of any gain recognized and the line item in the statement of comprehensive income in which the gain is recognized; and a description of the reasons why the transaction resulted in a gain.	This information is not required.

IFRS 3R	Canadian GAAP
Business combination in which the acquirer holds less than 100% of the equity interests in the acquiree at the acquisition date	
For each such business combination: • the amount of the non-controlling interest in the acquiree recognized at the acquisition date and the measurement basis for that mount; and • for each non-controlling interest in an acquiree measured at fair value, the valuation techniques and key model inputs used for determining that value.	This information is not required.
Business combination achieved in stages	
• the acquisition-date fair value of the equity interest in the acquiree held by the acquirer immediately before the acquisition date; and • the amount of any gain or loss recognized as a result of re-measuring to fair value the equity interest in the acquiree held by the acquirer before the business combination and the line item in the statement of comprehensive income in which that gain or loss is recognized.	This information is not required.
Detailed information about revenue and profit or loss of the acquirees	
• the amounts of the acquiree's revenue and profit or loss since the acquisition date included in the consolidated statement of comprehensive income for the reporting period; and • the revenue and profit or loss of the combined entity for the current reporting period as though the acquisition date for all business combinations that occurred during the year had been as of the beginning of the annual reporting period. If disclosure is impracticable, that fact and an explanation should be disclosed.	This information is not required.
For individually immaterial business combinations occurring during the reporting period that are material collectively, the acquirer needs to disclose additional information that is substantially similar to the requirements listed above.	Although CICA 1581 requires similar disclosure, the requirements specified under IFRS 3 (revised 2008) are more onerous.
If the acquisition date of a business combination is after the end of the reporting period but before the financial statements are authorized for issue, the acquirer must disclose the information required above unless the initial accounting for the business combination is incomplete at the time the financial statements are authorized for issue. In that situation, the acquirer would describe which disclosures could not be made and the reasons why they could not be made.	Only disclosures required by CICA 3820, *Subsequent Events*. The disclosures required under IFRS 3 (revised 2008) are more onerous.

In addition to that listed above, IFRS 3 (revised 2008) requires the disclosure of further information to help users of financial statements evaluate the financial effects of adjustments recognized in the reporting period relating to business combinations in the current or previous reporting periods. Information is notably required about the reasons why the initial accounting for the business combination is incomplete, the details of elements and amounts for which the accounting was incomplete, details about changes in contingent considerations and models used to evaluate them, reconciliation of the carrying amount of goodwill at beginning and the end of period, as well as the amount and an explanation of any significant gain or loss relating to the identifiable assets acquired or liabilities assumed in the business combination for the current or previous period. This additional disclosure is more onerous than that currently found under Canadian GAAP.

Illustrative Disclosures:

The following examples illustrate some of the disclosure provisions described above. It is important to consider that these examples were prepared in accordance with the old version of IFRS 3 and, therefore, would require some adjustments to conform to the IFRS 3 (revised 2008) requirements (such as the capitalization of acquisition costs, for example). The disclosures included in the example below are discussed in the commentary after each example.

Extract 5(20) – Business combination disclosures

Aviva plc (AR 2007), pages 133 - 140 and page 156

3 – Subsidiaries

This note provides details of the acquisitions and disposals of subsidiaries that the Group has made during the year, together with details of businesses held for sale at the year end. The principal Group subsidiaries are listed on page 268 to 269.

(a) Acquisitions

(i) Erasmus Group

On 26 March 2007, the Group's Dutch subsidiary, Delta Lloyd, acquired 100% of the shares in Erasmus Groep BV ("Erasmus") in the Netherlands. Erasmus writes both general insurance and long-term business, and the acquisition has further strengthened Delta Lloyd's position in the Dutch insurance market.

The Erasmus acquisition has not given rise to any goodwill on acquisition. The relevant calculation is as follows:

Purchase cost:

	£m
Cash paid	53
Attributable costs	1
Total consideration	**54**

Commentary: This extract illustrates the application of all of the general information on the business combination disclosures described above.

Aviva plc (AR 2007) (continued)

3 – Subsidiaries

The assets and liabilities at the date of acquisition were:

	Book value £m	Fair value and accounting policy adjustments £m	Fair value £m
Assets			
Acquired value of in-force business on insurance contracts	–	6	6
Intangible assets	2	18	20
Investments	411	5	416
Loans	204	16	220
Reinsurance assets	33	–	33
Receivables and other financial assets	22	–	22
Prepayments and accrued income	13	–	13
Cash and cash equivalents	35	–	35
Other assets	31	1	32
Total assets	**751**	**46**	**797**
Liabilities			
Gross insurance liabilities	(674)	(20)	(694)
Borrowings	(15)	–	(15)
Provisions	(4)	(6)	(10)
Tax liabilities	(1)	(3)	(4)
Other liabilities	(20)	–	(20)
Total liabilities	**(714)**	**(29)**	**(743)**
Total net assets acquired	**37**	**17**	**54**
Goodwill arising on acquisition			**–**

The value of Erasmus's distribution channels has been identified as a separate intangible asset and valued by an independent third party at £8 million, using estimated post-tax cash flows and discount rates. It has been assessed as having a life of 20 years and is being amortised on a straight-line basis over that period. As permitted by IFRS 4, Insurance Contracts, an intangible asset of £12 million has also been recognised for the impact of discounting the non-life insurance liabilities, to bring them to fair value. This intangible asset will be amortised over the life of the relevant non-life insurance contracts.

The assets and liabilities as at the acquisition date in the table above are stated at their provisional values, and may be amended in 2008, in accordance with paragraph 62 of IFRS 3, *Business Combinations*.

The results of Erasmus have been included in the consolidated financial statements of the Group with effect from 26 March 2007, and have contributed £5 million to the consolidated profit before tax.

(ii) Bancassurance partnership with Cajamurcia

On 6 June 2007, the Group announced that it had entered into a long-term bancassurance agreement with Spanish savings bank Caja de Ahorros de Murcia (Cajamurcia) that will enhance the Group's leading position in the Spanish life market. Cajamurcia will provide exclusive access to its network of branches to Caja Murcia Vida y Pensiones, de Seguros y Reaseguros SA (Cajamurcia Vida), the newly-created life insurance company jointly-owned by the Group and Cajamurcia, to sell insurance and pension products. Regulatory approval to write new business was received on 21 November 2007 and the new company began trading on 30 November 2007.

Aviva plc (AR 2007) (continued)

3 – Subsidiaries

On signing the agreement, the Group acquired 5% of the share capital of Cajamurcia Vida and Cajamurcia granted the Group a call option over a further 45% of the shares in this company which may be exercised in the two month period following the first anniversary of the agreement being signed. Further consideration of £69 million would be payable on exercising the option, with additional amounts of up to £187 million payable, dependant on the performance of the new company. If it does not exercise this option during this period, the Group has granted a call option over its 5% holding to Cajamurcia.

The Group paid £8 million for the initial 5% holding on completion on 6 June 2007. The Group has the power to control the financial and operating policies of Cajamurcia Vida through having the majority vote at meetings of the company's board of directors. We have therefore consolidated its results and balance sheet since that date.

Commentary: This extract illustrates, in the Erasmus Group purchase, the disclosure of the assets acquired and liabilities assumed, as described above, as well as additional disclosures on the provisional amounts for initial accounting for the business combination. Also, the second acquisition of Cajamurcia illustrates the concept of control based on interests other than voting rights; under Canadian GAAP, this is considered only in the context of accounting for variable interests.

Aviva plc (AR 2007), pages 133 - 140 and page 156 (continued)

3 – Subsidiaries

The acquisition of the initial 5% shareholding has given rise to goodwill on acquisition of £2 million, calculated as follows:

Purchase cost:

	£m
Cash paid	8
Attributable costs	1
Total consideration	**9**

The book and fair values of the assets and liabilities at the date of acquisition were:

	£m
Assets	
Intangible assets	202
Other assets	–
Total assets	**202**
Liabilities	
Deferred tax on acquired assets	(60)
Total liabilities	**(60)**
Total net assets	**142**
Net assets acquired (initial 5% share)	**7**
Goodwill arising on acquisition of this holding	**2**

The value of the agreement to distribute through Cajamurcia's branch network has been identified as a separate intangible asset with a value of £202 million, using estimated post-tax cash flows and discount rates.

As noted above, the results of Cajamurcia Vida have been included in the consolidated financial statements of the Group and have contributed £nil to the consolidated profit before tax since it began trading on 30 November 2007.

Aviva plc (AR 2007) (continued)

3 – Subsidiaries

(iii) Italian transactions with Banco Popolare

During the year, the Group's Italian holding company has entered into three sets of transactions with an Italian bank, Banco Popolare Societa Cooperativa (Banco Popolare). Details of these transactions are as follows :

(a) Petunia and Banca Network

On 18 September 2007, the Group made a capital contribution of £19 million to Petunia SpA (Petunia), an investment holding company, previously held as a financial investment. The Group's holding in Petunia has increased to 40.62% but, as the Group has 51% of voting rights and management control, the Group has consolidated this company as a subsidiary. The total capitalisation of the company at this date was £47 million, which was used to purchase a 49.75% stake in Banca Bipielle Network SpA, an Italian distribution network, from Banco Popolare on 26 September 2007. The acquired company has since been renamed Banca Network Investimenti SpA (Banca Network).

The Group does not have management control of Banca Network and so accounts for it as an investment in an associate. The total consideration was £49 million, comprising cash consideration of £46 million and contingent consideration of £3 million (representing the present value of future expected performance-related consideration). The fair value of the Group's share of Banca Network's identifiable net assets at the date of acquisition was £27 million. The residual goodwill of £22 million has been included in the carrying value of the investment in associate (see note 19).

This residual goodwill has been calculated based on the provisional fair values of the net assets and liabilities of Banca Network, and may be restated in 2008, in accordance with paragraph 62 of IFRS 3, *Business Combinations*.

(b) Area Life

On 26 September 2007, the Group acquired a 55% stake in Area Life International Assurance Limited (Area Life), a life assurance company based in Ireland, selling exclusively to Italian residents, from Banco Popolare for £7 million.

This acquisition has not given rise to any goodwill on acquisition. The relevant calculation is as follows:

Purchase cost:

	£m
Cash paid	7

The assets and liabilities at the date of acquisition were:

	Book value £m	Fair value and accounting policy adjustments £m	Fair value £m
Assets			
Acquired value of in-force business on insurance contracts	–	20	20
Investments	284	–	284
Reinsurance assets	20	–	20
Cash and cash equivalents	12	–	12
Other assets	4	–	4
Total assets	**320**	**20**	**340**
Liabilities			
Gross insurance liabilities	(278)	(14)	(292)
Deferred tax liability	(5)	(1)	(6)
Payables and other financial liabilities	(26)	–	(26)
Other liabilities	(3)	–	(3)
Total liabilities	**(312)**	**(15)**	**(327)**
Total net assets	**8**	**5**	**13**
Net assets acquired (55%)	**4**	**3**	**7**
Goodwill arising on acquisition			**–**

Aviva plc (AR 2007) (continued)

3 – Subsidiaries

The assets and liabilities above have been stated at their provisional fair values and may be amended in 2008, in accordance with paragraph 62 of IFRS 3, *Business Combinations*.

The results of Petunia, Banca Network and Area Life have been included in the consolidated financial statements of the Group with effect from 26 September 2007, and have contributed £nil to the consolidated profit before tax.

(c) Bancassurance agreement via Avipop Assicurazioni

On 14 December 2007, the Group entered a long-term bancassurance partnership in protection and non-life insurance with Banco Popolare that will further strengthen the Group's bancassurance presence in Italy and creates a new opportunity in the fast-growing protection sector.

The Group paid £184 million to secure the long-term bancassurance agreement with Banco Popolare and to acquire 50% plus one share of Avipop Assicurazioni SpA (Avipop Assicurazioni), a non-life subsidiary of the bank. Life protection business will be written in a subsidiary of Avipop Assicurazioni, which will begin trading later in 2008, subject to regulatory approval. The Group has the majority of the voting rights and management control of Avipop Assicurazioni and has therefore fully consolidated it as a subsidiary.

The acquisition of Avipop Assicurazioni has given rise to goodwill on acquisition of £52 million, calculated as follows:

Purchase cost:

	£m
Cash paid	184
Attributable costs	4
Total consideration	**188**

The assets and liabilities of the company at the date of acquisition were:

	Book value £m	Fair value and accounting policy adjustments £m	Fair value £m
Assets			
Intangible assets	–	386	386
Investments	9	–	9
Other assets	3	–	3
Total assets	**12**	**386**	**398**
Liabilities			
Gross insurance liabilities	(1)	–	(1)
Deferred tax liability	–	(125)	(125)
Other liabilities	(1)	–	(1)
Total liabilities	**(2)**	**(125)**	**(127)**
Total net assets	**10**	**261**	**271**
Net assets acquired (50%)			**136**
Goodwill arising on acquisition			**52**

The value of the agreement to distribute through Banco Popolare's branch network has been identified as a separate intangible asset and has been valued by an independent third party at £386 million (100% share), using estimated post-tax cash flows and discount rates. The intangible asset has been assessed as having an indefinite useful life, subject to annual tests for impairment. The distribution agreement is initially for ten years, with five year automatic renewal periods. It is expected to be renewed indefinitely, due to the unfavourable terms of the put option for failure to renew.

The residual goodwill represents the impact of recognising a deferred tax liability on the intangible asset.

The assets and liabilities as at the acquisition date in the table opposite are stated at their provisional values, and may be amended in 2008, in accordance with paragraph 62 of IFRS 3, *Business Combinations*.

Aviva plc (AR 2007) (continued)

3 – Subsidiaries

The results of Avipop Assicurazioni have been included in the consolidated financial statements of the Group with effect from 14 December 2007, and have contributed £nil to the consolidated profit before tax.

(iv) Cyrte Investments

On 27 September 2007, the Group acquired an 85% stake in Cyrte Investments BV (Cyrte Investments), a Dutch fund management company, for £37 million. The net assets of Cyrte Investments at the date of acquisition were £nil, giving rise to residual goodwill of £37 million.

The residual goodwill represents the value of the company's workforce and a premium paid for the investment concepts developed in the company, based on Cyrte's expertise in the telecommunications, media and technology sectors. No material intangible assets were identified.

The net assets as at the acquisition date are stated at their provisional values, and may be amended in 2008, in accordance with paragraph 62 of IFRS 3, *Business Combinations*.

The results of Cyrte Investments have been included in the consolidated financial statements of the Group with effect from 27 September 2007, and have contributed £2 million to the consolidated profit before tax.

The Group has also invested £209 million in three funds, managed by Cyrte Investments, giving it an ownership interest in the three funds of between 13% and 18%. These funds have been accounted for as investments in associates, as Cyrte Investments is the general partner of the funds and the Group's holding gives it significant influence on the investment committee, the management board of the funds. The Group's investment of £209 million has been included in interests in associates in note 19.

(v) Hamilton Insurance Company Limited and Hamilton Life Assurance Company Limited

On 1 November 2007, the Group completed the acquisition of Hamilton Insurance Company Limited and Hamilton Life Assurance Company Limited (the Hamilton companies) from HFC Bank Limited, a subsidiary of HSBC Finance Corporation.

In addition, the Group's UK general insurance businesses signed a number of five-year agreements to underwrite creditor business for HFC Bank and some of its subsidiaries, and to provide home, protection and travel insurance products to 10.2 million of HSBC Bank's UK customers.

The acquisition of Hamilton Insurance Company Limited has given rise to goodwill on acquisition of £2 million, calculated as follows:

Purchase cost:

	£m
Cash paid	55
Attributable costs	2
Total consideration	**57**

The book and fair values of the assets and liabilities at the date of acquisition were:

	£m
Assets	
Investments	68
Reinsurance assets	24
Cash and cash equivalents	25
Other assets	24
Total assets	**141**
Liabilities	
Gross insurance liabilities	(67)
Other liabilities	(19)
Total liabilities	**(86)**
Total net assets acquired	**55**
Goodwill arising on acquisition	**2**

Aviva plc (AR 2007) (continued)

3 – Subsidiaries

The acquisition of Hamilton Life Assurance Company Limited (Hamilton Life) has given rise to goodwill on acquisition of £21 million, calculated as follows:

Purchase cost:

	£m
Cash paid	44
Attributable costs	1
Total consideration	**45**

The assets and liabilities at the date of acquisition were:

	Book value £m	Fair value and accounting policy adjustments £m	Fair value £m
Assets			
Acquired value of in-force business on investment contracts	–	3	3
Investments	122	–	122
Other assets	5	–	5
Total assets	**127**	**3**	**130**
Liabilities			
Gross insurance liabilities	(34)	–	(34)
Investment contract liabilities	(68)	–	(68)
Other liabilities	(4)	–	(4)
Total liabilities	**(106)**	**–**	**(106)**
Total net assets acquired	**21**	**3**	**24**
Goodwill arising on acquisition			**21**

Included in the consideration paid and goodwill arising on the Hamilton Life acquisition is £20 million in respect of unrecognised deferred tax assets, which the Group may be able to utilise in future years but cannot recognise now.

The assets and liabilities as at the acquisition date in both the tables above are stated at their provisional values, and may be amended in 2008, in accordance with paragraph 62 of IFRS 3, *Business Combinations*.

The results of the Hamilton companies have been included in the consolidated financial statements of the Group with effect from 1 November 2007, and have contributed £1 million to the consolidated profit before tax.

(vi) Material acquisitions summary

	2007 £m
Total net assets	283
Less: Minority interests	–
Net assets acquired	283
Goodwill arising on acquisition	114
Total consideration	**397**
The total consideration comprised:	
Cash paid	388
Attributable costs	9
	397

(vii) Other

In addition to the goodwill arising on the above acquisitions, the Group also made a number of smaller acquisitions, giving rise to additional goodwill of £1 million. Total goodwill arising in the year was £115 million (see note 16(a)).

Aviva plc (AR 2007) (continued)

3 – Subsidiaries

(viii) Unaudited pro forma combined revenues and profit

Shown below are unaudited pro forma figures for combined revenues and profit as though the acquisition date for all business combinations effected during the year had been 1 January 2007, after giving effect to purchase accounting adjustments and the elimination of intercompany transactions. The pro forma financial information is not necessarily indicative of the combined results that would have been attained had the acquisitions taken place at 1 January 2007, nor is it necessarily indicative of future results.

	2007 £m
Revenues (net earned premiums and fee income)	31,390
Profit before tax attributable to shareholders	1,862

Of the above pre-tax profit, £17 million has arisen since acquisition.

(ix) Non-adjusting post-balance sheet events

(a) Acquisition of UBI Assicurazioni Vita

On 17 January 2008, the Group announced that it had reached an agreement with Unione di Banche Italiane Scpa (UBI Banca) for the acquisition of 50% plus one share in UBI Assicurazioni Vita SpA., an Italian life insurance company wholly-owned by UBI Banca, for a consideration of £49 million. Completion of the transaction is subject to certain conditions and the approval of the relevant regulatory authorities, and is expected to take place in the first half of 2008.

(b) Acquisition of Swiss Life Belgium

On 21 January 2008, the Group announced that it had signed a memorandum of understanding with SNS REAAL to buy Swiss Life Belgium, a multi-line insurer, for 1135 million. By combining Swiss Life Belgium with its Belgian insurance operation, managed through its Dutch subsidiary Delta Lloyd, the Group would further strengthen its position in the Belgian group life insurance market.

The transaction is conditional upon completion of SNS REAAL's acquisition of the Dutch and Belgian activities of Swiss Life Holding, which was announced on 19 November 2007. The completion of Delta Lloyd's acquisition of Swiss Life Belgium will be subject to approval from the relevant regulators and works council, and is expected to take place in the second quarter of 2008.

(c) Investment in LIG Life Insurance Co. Ltd.

On 31 January 2008, the Group announced that it would be entering the South Korea life insurance market by agreeing to acquire jointly with Woori Finance Holdings Company Ltd ("Woori") a 91.65% stake in LIG Life Insurance Co. Ltd ("LIG Life"), a South Korean life insurance company, for KRW 137.2 billion (£73 million). After completion, the Group will hold 40.65% of LIG Life. Aviva and Woori plan to develop LIG Life's business distribution, predominantly through bancassurance via Woori's banking network and independent financial advisors.

(b) Disposal of subsidiaries, joint ventures and associates

The profit on the disposal of subsidiaries, joint ventures and associates comprises:

	2007 £m	2006 £m
United Kingdom (see note 19(b))	(7)	69
Turkey (see note 18(c))	71	–
Ireland	–	86
France	–	79
Other small operations	(15)	(12)
Profit on disposal before tax	**49**	**222**
Tax on profit on disposal	3	13
Profit on disposal after tax	**52**	**235**

Aviva plc (AR 2007) (continued)

3 – Subsidiaries

(c) Integration and restructuring costs

£153 million of integration and restructuring costs have been included in the results to 31 December 2007 (2006: £246 million). These include £45 million relating to the UK cost and efficiency programme announced in 2006.

This initiative has now been completed at a total cost of £250 million. The costs also include £82 million relating to the new savings targets announced in October 2007. Further costs of this programme are expected to be £248 million, spread over the next two years. The balance of £26 million relates to the completion of integration activity on Ark Life in Ireland and the former AmerUs business in the United States, which were both acquired in 2006.

(d) Operations classified as held for sale

(i) Assets and liabilities of operations classified as held for sale

The assets and liabilities of operations classified as held for sale as at 31 December 2007 relate to our Dutch health insurance businesses, and were as follows:

	2007 £m	2006 £m
Financial investments	316	–
Receivables and other financial assets	554	–
Prepayments and accrued income	146	–
Tax assets	16	–
Cash and cash equivalents	96	–
Total assets	**1,128**	**–**
Gross insurance liabilities	(627)	–
Borrowings	(12)	–
Payables and financial liabilities	(72)	–
Other liabilities	(220)	–
Tax liabilities and other provisions	(11)	–
Total liabilities	**(942)**	**–**
Net assets	**186**	**–**

(ii) Dutch health insurance business

On 16 July 2007, the Group announced that its Dutch subsidiary, Delta Lloyd Group (DL), had reached an agreement to sell its health insurance business to OWM CZ Groep Zorgverkeraar UA (CZ), a mutual health insurer, and create a long-term alliance for the cross-selling of insurance products. Under the terms of the agreement, CZ will purchase the DL health insurance business and take on its underwriting risk and policy administration. DL will continue to market and distribute health insurance products from CZ to its existing customers, and to provide asset management for the transferred business.

DL will also have exclusive rights to market life, general insurance and income protection products to CZ's customers. The transaction is expected to take effect on 1 January 2009, subject to regulatory, competition and other relevant approvals.

The relevant assets and liabilities of the DL health insurance business have been classified as held for sale, at their carrying values, in the consolidated balance sheet as at 31 December 2007.

(e) Other information

Principal subsidiaries at 31 December 2007 are listed on pages 268 to 269.

One of the Group's wholly-owned subsidiaries, Delta Lloyd NV, is subject to the provisions of Dutch corporate law and particularly the Dutch "structure company" regime. Under this regime, Delta Lloyd operates under a Supervisory Board which has a duty to have regard to the interests of a wide variety of stakeholders. The Supervisory Board includes two Aviva Group representatives and is responsible for advising and supervising Delta Lloyd's Executive Board. The shareholder is one of the most important stakeholders to whom the Supervisory Board has a duty.

Aviva plc (AR 2007) (continued)

3 – Subsidiaries

Dutch Law changed in October 2004 to ensure that Supervisory Board directors in Dutch companies were henceforth to be elected by a company's shareholders voting on nominations made by its Supervisory Board and the Works Council.

Under the previous system, Supervisory Board directors appointed their own successors. In 2006, Delta Lloyd commenced proceedings against Aviva plc to try to compel the Company to adhere to the system that existed prior to the change in the law, on the basis of agreements they say were entered into in 1973 when the Group acquired Delta Lloyd.

The Company disputes these claims and does not expect the litigation, whatever its outcome, to have any adverse effect on the financial or operational performance of Delta Lloyd or the Group. We expect a judgement from the court on this issue sometime in 2008, which either party will then have the ability to appeal.

page 156

16 – Goodwill (in part)

This note analyses the changes to the carrying amount of goodwill during the year, and details the results of our impairment testing on both goodwill and intangible assets with indefinite lives.

(a) Carrying amount

	2007 £m	2006 £m
Gross amount		
At 1 January	3,086	2,359
Acquisitions	115	761
Movements in contingent consideration	(5)	32
Disposals	(16)	(8)
Foreign exchange rate movements	93	(58)
At 31 December	3,273	3,086
Accumulated impairment		
At 1 January	(176)	(85)
Impairment losses	(10)	(94)
Disposals	9	–
Foreign exchange rate movements	(14)	3
At 31 December	(191)	(176)
Carrying amount at 31 December	3,082	2,910

Commentary: This extract illustrates some additional disclosures required when applying IFRS 3 (revised 2008).

In this extract, Aviva describes the different acquisitions it made during the year and mentions, for each acquisition, the name and a description of the acquiree; the acquisition date; the percentage of interests acquired; the reasons for the acquisition, including a qualitative description of the factors that make up the goodwill recognized, such as expected synergies from combining operations of the acquiree and the acquirer; intangible assets that do not qualify for separate recognition or other factors; the total consideration transferred; the assets and liabilities of the acquiree at the acquisition date, at book value and at fair value; the calculation of goodwill; the amounts of revenue and profit or loss of the acquiree since the acquisition date included in the consolidated income for the reporting period; the revenue and profit or loss of the combined entity for the current reporting period as though the acquisition date for all business combinations that occurred during the year had been as of the beginning of the year; and, for individually immaterial business combinations occurring during the year that are material collectively, a detailed reconciliation of the carrying amount of goodwill at the beginning and end of the reporting period (included in a separate note). The disclosures included additional information that is substantially similar to the requirements for material business combinations.

Additionally, as required, this extract also includes information about acquisitions for which the acquisition date of the business combinations is after the end of the reporting period but before the financial statements are authorized for issue.

Lastly, where only provisional amounts were included for the purchase price allocation, reasons why the initial accounting for the business combination was incomplete were not specifically provided.

Illustrative Disclosure:

Extract 5(21) – Acquisition after the balance sheet date

Nycomed S.C.A. SICAR (AR 2007), page 41

1. BUSINESS COMBINATION (in part)

ACQUISITIONS AFTER BALANCE SHEET DATE:

On 22 February 2008, Nycomed successfully completed the acquisition of 100% of the shares in Bradley Pharmaceuticals, Inc. (NYSE:BDY), a company focused on niche therapeutic markets in the United States. The acquisition will add further branded dermatologics to the PharmaDerm division of Nycomed US and will provide an enhanced platform for in-licensing and co-promotion of dermatology products. Nycomed plans to leverage its manufacturing and distribution capabilities to support the Bradley products line, improve customer service and optimise the cost structure. In addition, Nycomed will leverage the combined sales and marketing capabilities to enhance both the Bradley and Nycomed product lines.

The transaction has been subject to Bradley shareholder approval and approval by competition authorities. These approvals have been granted in the first quarter of 2008.

Nycomed has offered USD 20.00 per share in cash, equivalent to an equity purchase price of USD 346 million to Bradley's shareholders. The acquisition has been financed through excess cash in 2007, equity commitment by current investors and by utilisation of available credit facilities. The final costs of the combination cannot yet be determined due to uncertainties related to other costs related to the acquisition.

Acquisition of Bradley will not result in any disposals of current operations.

Nycomed intends to delist Bradley. In connection with the proposed merger, Bradley will file a proxy statement with the Securities and Exchange Commission.

Due to the fact that the acquisition has only recently been completed as well as the fact that Bradley is listed in the United States, it is not possible to incorporate the following disclosures:

1) The amounts recognised at acquisition date for each class of the acquirees assets, liabilities and contingent liabilities, and, the carrying amounts of each of those classes, determined in accordance with IFRS, immediately before the combination

2) A description of the factors that contributed to a cost that results in the recognition of goodwill

3) A description of each intangible asset that was not recognised separately from goodwill and an explanation of why the intangible asset's fair value could not be measured reliably

4) The amount of the Bradley's profit or loss since the acquisition date included in the Nycomed's profit or loss for the period

---

Commentary: This extracts illustrates the disclosure requirements for business combinations after the balance sheet date but before the financial statements were issued.

FUTURE DEVELOPMENTS

As previously mentioned, CICA 1582, *Business Combinations*, was issued on January 5, 2009 by the AcSB, and replaces CICA 1581 of the same name. CICA 1582 is effective for years beginning on or after January 1, 2011, with earlier adoption permitted. Entities transitioning to IFRS in 2011 should consider adopting the new guidance in their reporting periods beginning on or after January 1, 2010 to avoid restatement on transition.

On January 5, 2009, the AcSB also issued two new *Handbook* sections:

• CICA 1602, *Non-controlling Interests* provides guidance on the treatment of non-controlling interests after acquisition in a business combination. The guidance is converged with IAS 27 (revised 2008), *Consolidated and Separate Financial Statements.*

- CICA 1601, *Consolidated Financial Statements* carries forward existing Canadian guidance on aspects of the preparation of consolidated financial statements subsequent to acquisition and some aspects of consolidation at the date of a business combination but removes the existing guidance on non-controlling interests.

All three of these new *CICA Handbook – Accounting* sections are generally harmonized with the recently revised relevant IFRSs and, where differences exist between IFRS 3 (revised 2008) and FAS 141R (the US equivalent standard) and other related standards, the AcSB plans to align the Canadian standards with IFRS to reduce further differences upon transition.

COMPREHENSIVE EXAMPLES

It was not possible to find an illustration of the application of IFRS 3 (revised 2008) since its adoption is required only for business combinations effected on or after July 1, 2009. Earlier application is permitted but not earlier than the annual reporting period that begins on or after June 30, 2007. Consequently, no comprehensive example is provided.[2]

PLANNING FOR IMPLEMENTATION

This chapter has covered most of the IFRS 3 (revised 2008) requirements, and noted significant differences with corresponding Canadian GAAP. This section discusses suggested measures when implementing IFRSs.

Assessing New Standard Implementation

Systems, Processes and Resources Requirements

Traditionally, business combination reporting has necessitated particular data concerning fair value calculations. One of the major practical difficulties related to IFRS 3 (revised 2008) remains the recognition and measurement of intangible assets. Valuation practices have developed over time and their interpretation and implementation remains varied.

IFRS 3 (revised 2008) is a further development of the acquisition model. It applies to more transactions, as the definition of a business is expanded which could bring more transactions into acquisition accounting. Certain requirements of this standard might have new implications for systems and controls and expertise requirements. Companies must assess whether they possess the level of expertise needed and consider whether the expertise should be developed or expanded in-house or whether it will need to be sourced externally.

Below are some issues that have to be addressed when planning changes in systems and processes and assessing the need for new resources:

- existing stakes in entities acquired have to be re-measured to fair value; any resultant gain plus any previously recorded fair value movements taken to accumulated other comprehensive income should be recorded in income. This will require detailed tracking on an investment-by-investment basis, including details of carrying amount and subsequent re-measurements;

- entities must redesignate all the acquiree's hedge relationships and test them for effectiveness;

---

2   Readers can refer to the illustrative financial statements provided by accounting firms; see the CICA IFRS web portal under the heading "Implementing IFRS" at http://www.cica.ca/index.cfm/ci_id/39254/la_id/1.htm.

- contingent consideration must be measured at fair value at acquisition and, unless it is equity, is subsequently re-measured through earnings rather than the historic practice of re-measuring through goodwill. This is likely to increase the focus and attention on the opening fair value calculation and subsequent re-measurements;

- remaining interest must be valued at fair value when subsidiary becomes an investment in an associate or joint venture;

- when the full fair value method of goodwill is used, it will be necessary to measure at fair value non-controlling interests which may prove difficult in practice. However, goodwill impairment testing may be easier under this approach, as there is no need to gross-up goodwill for partially owned subsidiaries;

- new data must be collected to satisfy particular requirements including annualized revenue and profit as if deals had been completed at the start of the financial year, analysis of acquired receivables, gross contractual amounts and fair values and estimates of the range of outcomes on contingent consideration and if any part of the fair value exercise is not complete, disclosure is required of the items affected, the reasons why and any adjustments made to previously reported fair values.

Communication with Stakeholders

IFRS 3 (revised 2008) is expected to add to earnings volatility, making earnings harder to predict. It will likely result in grossed-up balance sheet figures as net assets acquired will be reflected at their full fair values in acquisitions of less than 100% of the acquiree. The effect though of contingent considerations being recognized earlier might create some volatility when those contingencies are recorded as liabilities that are subsequently re-measured to fair value through income. The presentation of the non-controlling interest on the balance sheet as part of equity and not as liabilities may affect perceptions, and the net earnings presented in the income statement will appear higher since they will include the non-controlling interest's portion. All of these changes and their resulting impacts will need to be communicated to financial statement users to ensure that they understand the financial information being provided and are interpreting and analyzing it in appropriate ways.

Other Business Considerations

In addition to changes in systems and processes, IFRS 3 (revised 2008) might have related business consequences including:

- influencing business acquisition negotiations and deal structures in an effort to mitigate unwanted earnings volatilities;

- extending scope of due diligence and data gathering needs prior to acquisition;

- influencing communication of the 'how, when and what' dealmakers and preparers of financial statements in communication to entity's stakeholders.

Initial Adoption of IFRS

On transition to IFRS, companies have to apply all relevant IFRS standards and interpretations retrospectively as if they had always applied those accounting practices in the past. But it may be extremely difficult, or even impossible, to obtain the required information to appropriately apply the standard to a business combination that may have occurred many years ago. IFRS 1, therefore, gives financial statement preparers the option to not apply IFRS 3 (revised 2008) retrospectively to past business combinations that occurred before the date of transition to IFRS. If a first-time adopter decides to restate any business combination to comply with IFRS 3 (revised 2008), however, all later business combinations are restated from that date forward.

The exemption for past business combinations also applies to past acquisitions of investments in associates and of interests in joint ventures. Therefore, when this IFRS 1 exemption is selected, it does not only apply to past business combinations, it applies also to all past acquisitions of investments in associates and joint ventures. If an entity decides to restate an acquisition of a subsidiary prior to the date of transition to IFRS, it has to restate all acquisitions of subsidiaries, associates and joint ventures after that date. Similarly, if an entity chooses to restate an acquisition of an associate at a date prior to transitioning to IFRS, all acquisitions of subsidiaries, associates and joint ventures effected after that date must also be restated.

Companies often opt to apply IFRS 3 prospectively because, by requiring few adjustments to previous balances recognized as part of past business combinations, it eases the transition to IFRS. There are instances, however, when adjustments to previous balances will be required even when the exemption is selected. Appendix B of IFRS 1 fully addresses the application of this exemption and describes the adjustments that might be required depending on the circumstances.

When an entity selects the exemption for past business combinations, it keeps, under IFRS 1, the same classification (an acquisition by the legal acquirer, a reverse acquisition by the legal acquiree, or a uniting of interests) as it used in its previous GAAP financial statements.

Also, a first-time adopter will recognize all of its assets and liabilities at the date of transition to IFRSs that were acquired or assumed in a past business combination, other than some financial assets and financial liabilities derecognized under previous GAAP.

The most commonly encountered adjustments relate to goodwill. The carrying amount of goodwill determined under previous GAAP would be adjusted on transition to IFRS in the following circumstances:

- When an item recognized as an intangible asset under previous GAAP is reclassified to goodwill (and the carrying amount is thereby increased). Conversely, an intangible asset that was subsumed in goodwill under previous GAAP, is recognized separately under IFRS, the carrying amount of goodwill is decreased accordingly (and, if applicable, adjustments may be required to deferred taxes and non-controlling interests).

- When testing goodwill for impairment in accordance with IAS 36 at the date of transition to IFRSs. Any resulting impairment loss recognized as a result of this test is accounted for in retained earnings (or, if so required by IAS 36, in revaluation surplus). The impairment test is based on conditions at the date of transition to IFRSs.

No other adjustments are made to the carrying amount of goodwill at the date of transition to IFRSs. Immediately after the business combination, the carrying amount under previous GAAP of assets acquired and liabilities assumed in that business combination will be their deemed cost under IFRSs at that date. If IFRS require a cost-based measurement of those assets and liabilities at a later date, that deemed cost will be the basis for cost-based depreciation or amortization from the date of the business combination.

IFRS require subsequent measurement of some assets and liabilities using a method that is not based on original cost, such as fair value. A first-time adopter measures these assets and liabilities on that basis in its opening IFRS statement of financial position, even if they were acquired or assumed in a past business combination. It recognizes any resulting change in the carrying amount by adjusting retained earnings (or, if appropriate, another category of equity), rather than goodwill.

There may however, be other adjustments that the first-time adopter would be required to make depending on the circumstances, which have not been discussed above, and as such, the complete guidance included in Appendix B of IFRS 1 should be considered.

Illustrative Disclosures:

Extract 5(22) – IFRS 1 exemption for business combinations

Air France – KLM S.A. (Reference Document 2006-07), pages 94 - 95

3.5. Business combinations (in part)

3.5.1. Business combinations that occurred before the transition date to IFRS (i.e. before April 1, 2004)

In accordance with the IFRS 1 exemption, business combinations that occurred prior to April 1, 2004 (essentially Air Inter and UTA) have not been accounted for in accordance with IFRS 3.

Business combinations that occurred prior to April 1, 2004 were accounted for in accordance with French GAAP. Under French GAAP certain acquired assets and liabilities were not adjusted to fair value at the time of the acquisition, or in the case of step acquisitions, the fair values of the assets acquired and liabilities assumed were assessed during the initial step of the acquisition.

Alcatel-Lucent (AR 2007 on Form 20-F), page 156

NOTE 1 SUMMARY OF ACCOUNTING POLICIES (in part)

c/ Business combinations (in part)

Regulations governing first-time adoption: Business combinations that were completed before January 1, 2004, the transition date to IFRSs, were not restated, as permitted by the optional exemption included in IFRS 1. Goodwill was therefore not recognized for business combinations occurring prior to January 1, 2004, which were previously accounted for in accordance with article 215 of Regulation No. 99-02 of the "Comité de la Réglementation Comptable". According to this regulation, the assets and liabilities of the acquired company are maintained at their carrying value at the date of the acquisition, adjusted for the Group's accounting policies, and the difference between this value and the acquisition cost of the shares is adjusted directly against shareholders' equity.

---

eXpansys PLC (IFRS Restatement Report January 2008), page 67

5. Significant changes in accounting policies (in part)

IFRS 3 Business combinations (in part)

As permitted by IFRS 1, eXpansys has applied IFRS 3 prospectively from the transition date, rather than restating all previous business combinations.

Commentary: These extracts deal with first time adoption of the previous version of IFRS 3; in each instance, the entity elected to apply the IFRS 1 exemption to not restate prior business combinations.

Keep Posted

Although IFRS 3 was recently revised, there may be further changes to this standard. And, although the IASB has added a project to its agenda to address the treatment of business combinations involving entities under common control, it has not yet announced an issuance date for an Exposure Draft.

The Fair Value Measurement Project (for which a Discussion Paper was released in December 2006 and an Exposure Draft is expected to be issued in the first half of 2009) is still in progress and might affect the definition of fair value currently contained in IFRS 3 (revised 2008). As well, other ongoing projects that are also linked to business combinations (such as IAS 37 on provisions and IAS 12 on deferred tax) may affect either the recognition and/or measurement of business combinations at the acquisition date or the subsequent accounting.

Chapter 6
Consolidated and Separate Financial Statements

Standards Discussed in this Chapter

International

IAS 27 – Consolidated and Separate Financial Statements (revised January 2008)
IFRS 3 – Business Combinations (revised January 2008)
SIC-12 – Consolidation – Special Purpose Entities
IFRIC 17 – Distributions of Non-cash Assets to Owners

Canadian

CICA 1600 – Consolidated Financial Statements
CICA 1581 – Business Combinations
CICA 1590 – Subsidiaries
AcG-15 – Consolidation of variable interest entities

INTRODUCTION

When preparing consolidated financial statements under IFRS, Canadian companies must refer to IAS 27 and, sometimes, also to IFRS 3 and SIC-12. Currently, depending on their circumstances, they have to meet various requirements set out by CICA 1600, CICA 1581, CICA 1590 and AcG-15.

IAS 27 is a standard applied in the preparation and presentation of financial statements. It describes the information a parent entity should provide in its consolidated and separate financial statements. More specifically, IAS 27 provides guidance on enhancing the relevance, reliability and comparability of the information that a parent entity provides in its separate financial statements as well as in its consolidated financial statements for a group of entities under its control. The standard specifies under what circumstances an entity must consolidate the financial statements of another entity (a subsidiary), the procedures to be applied when preparing consolidated financial statements, the accounting for changes in the level of ownership interest in a subsidiary, the accounting for the loss of control over a subsidiary, and the information that it must disclose to help users of the financial statements evaluate the nature of the relationship between the entity and its subsidiaries.

Canadian companies applying IAS 27 will be affected differently depending on their business practices and activities. At a minimum, they will need to re-examine the method they use for accounting for their investments to ensure it is still appropriate, as the application of this standard may result in the consolidation of entities that were previously accounted for using the equity or cost method. This may result in an increase in net assets and, possibly, the introduction of non-controlling interests on the balance sheet. It may also lead to greater earnings volatility resulting from the inclusion of new entities not previously reflected in the consolidated financial statements. Conversely, IFRS do not provide any accounting recommendations for variable interest entities similar to those set out in AcG-15. IFRS do provide guidance on accounting for special purpose entities in SIC-12, which may encompass some of the entities currently accounted for by the provisions of AcG-15. On transition to IFRS, they will have to carefully analyze what entities to include in their new IFRS consolidated financial statement.

In 2008, the IASB revised IAS 27 as part of a joint project with FASB. The amendments were primarily directed at the accounting for non-controlling interests and the loss of control of a subsidiary. In addition to the discussion in this chapter, the amendments are also addressed in Chapter 5, to the extent that they relate to business combinations. The revisions to IAS 27 must be applied to annual periods beginning on or after July 1, 2009, with earlier application permitted. If the revisions to IAS 27 are adopted early, however, the revised version of IFRS 3 must be adopted as well.

This chapter discusses revised IAS 27 and how it compares to Canadian GAAP.

Companies should take a close look at the impact of the current IAS 27 requirements on their financial statements since the procedures to be applied when preparing consolidated financial statements under IAS 27 differs from current Canadian GAAP in a number of areas. To help in that review, this chapter discusses the following topics:

- models used for consolidation;
- special purpose entities;
- venture capitalists, mutual funds, unit trusts and similar entities;
- presentation of consolidated and separate financial statements;
- accounting for investments in subsidiaries, jointly controlled entities and associates in separate financial statements;
- combined financial statements;
- consolidation procedures;
- non-controlling interests:
  - o   attribution of losses to non-controlling interests;
- step acquisitions and partial disposals;
- distributions of non-cash assets to owners.

IMPACT ON FINANCIAL STATEMENTS

The scope under IAS 27 would generally result in the consolidation of a greater number of entities than under Canadian GAAP. For example many qualifying special-purpose entities (QSPE) might have to be consolidated on IFRS adoption. The consolidation of additional entities will result in grossed-up balances on the balance sheet and the income statement, as well as the inclusion of non-controlling interests on the financial statements. In addition to the potential increase in entities that have to be included in IFRS consolidated financial statements, certain specific IFRS standards might impact amounts previously recorded under Canadian GAAP.

Consolidated financial statements will also be impacted by IAS 27 because it adopts the economic entity model. According to this model, all providers of equity capital are considered to be part of the entity's shareholders, even when they are not shareholders in the parent company. The current practice under Canadian GAAP is the parent company approach where financial statements are presented from the perspective of the shareholders of the parent company. Under IAS 27, all shareholders of a group - whether they are shareholders of the parent or of a part of the group (minority interest) - are providers of equity capital to that group. Consequently:

- non-controlling interest in the statement of financial position is classified in equity and is presented separately from the parent shareholders' equity. This differs from current Canadian GAAP which requires non-controlling interest to be classified between total liabilities and equity in the statement of financial position;

- non-controlling interests in profit or loss are presented as an allocation of the net profit or loss for the period below the statement of comprehensive income (or the income statement, when presented separately). Currently under Canadian GAAP, non-controlling interests in the profit or loss are presented as an item of income or expense in the income statement;

- total other comprehensive income attributable to non-controlling interests is presented as an allocation of comprehensive income for the period. Currently under Canadian GAAP, total other comprehensive income attributable to non-controlling interests is not presented as an allocation; rather, amounts are presented net of amounts attributable to non-controlling interests;

- losses applicable to the non-controlling interests in a subsidiary are allocated to non-controlling interest even if this causes it to be in a deficit position. This differs from current Canadian GAAP because losses in a subsidiary may create a debit balance in non-controlling interests only if the non-controlling interest has an obligation to fund the losses;

- all transactions with shareholders are treated in the same way. This will results in significant changes in the accounting for transactions involving changes in non-controlling interest. For example:

  o partial disposals of a participation in a subsidiary (that do not result in loss of control) or additional purchases of non-controlling interest will be recorded as equity transactions. No gain or loss would be recorded on such partial disposals and no additional goodwill would be recorded on such additional purchases. Consequently the requirements could impact financial statements negatively by a reducing net assets and equity in cases where increased participation in a subsidiary was acquired at a price greater than the carrying value of the non-controlling interest,

  o partial disposal of an interest in a subsidiary in which the parent company loses control but retains an interest (e.g., significant influence) triggers the recognition of a gain or loss on the entire interest in profit or loss: a gain or loss on the portion that has been disposed of, and a further holding gain or loss on the interest retained (i.e., the difference between the fair value and the book value of the interest retained). This differs from current Canadian GAAP because only the "realized" gain or loss is recognized in profit or loss; any retained non-controlling equity investment in the former subsidiary is not remeasured to fair value.

Note that the initial amount of non-controlling interest reported in the statement of financial position subsequent to a business combination under IFRS differs from the one established under current Canadian GAAP. Under IFRS 3 (revised in 2008), non-controlling interests are recorded initially at fair value, or at the non-controlling interests' share of the amounts recognized in the acquisition accounting excluding goodwill. This differs from current Canadian GAAP where the amount of non-controlling interest is initially based on the carrying amounts in the subsidiary's financial statements at acquisition.

In addition to changes related to IAS 27 and IFRS 3 described above, the adoption of IFRIC 17 might impact the accounting policy used by companies that distribute non-cash assets to their owners. The potential changes affect the timing of the recognition of the liability and its initial measurement and more particularly the recognition of profit after the declaration of the distributions. Basically, IFRIC 17 requires:

- the liability to be initially recognized at the fair value of the assets to be distributed. In the case where the owners have a choice of receiving either non-cash assets or cash, an estimate of the liability is calculated by assessing the fair value of each alternative and the associated probability that each alternative will be selected;

- at the end of each reporting period and immediately before settlement, the liability to be remeasured to reflect any changes in the fair value of the underlying asset. The changes are recognised in equity;

- at the settlement date, the difference between the carrying amount of the assets distributed and the liability to be recognized in profit or loss as a separate line.

Management must consider the implications of these requirements which must be applied prospectively for annual periods beginning on or after July 1, 2009 (with early application permitted) including the entity's ability to declare dividends as some jurisdictions restrict such declarations to gains that have already been earned.

Note that IFRS 5 was amended as a result of IFRIC 17. IFRS 5 now applies to non-current assets held for distribution to owners. The assets must be classified as held for distribution only when they are available for distribution in their present condition and the distribution is highly probable (taking into consideration the likelihood of shareholder approval, if required). As a result of this amendment:

- in jurisdictions where shareholder approval is required, the non-cash assets to be distributed may be reclassified as non-current assets held for distribution before the liability is recognized;

- where IFRS 5 is applicable, the non-current assets are measured at the lower of their carrying amount, or fair value less costs to distribute, whereas the liability will be measured at the fair value of the assets.

ANALYSIS OF RELEVANT ISSUES
Model Used for Consolidation Purposes
Control-based Model

Under IAS 27, consolidation is based on control which is defined as the power to govern the financial and operating policies of an entity so as to obtain benefits from its activities. Control is presumed to exist when a parent owns, directly or indirectly through subsidiaries, more than half of the voting power of an entity unless, in exceptional circumstances, it can be clearly demonstrated that such ownership does not constitute control.

An entity is determined to have control when it has the ability to exercise power, regardless of whether control is actively demonstrated or is passive in nature. Therefore, an entity's potential voting rights, such as rights that arise through share warrants, call options or conversion features in preferred shares or debt, that are currently exercisable or convertible are also considered in determining the ability to control.

Judgement is required in order to determine if an entity has control over another party particularly when assessing the facts and circumstances that affect potential voting rights. Below are some observations concerning that assessment:

- potential voting rights are considered when, in substance, they actually provide the ability to exercise power. The ability to exercise power does not exist, for example, when potential voting rights lack economic substance (e.g., the exercise price is set in a manner that precludes exercise or conversion in any feasible scenario);

- Potential voting rights held by other parties that are currently exercisable or convertible may identify one of those parties as the controlling entity. Therefore, an entity needs to consider all potential voting rights held by it and others that are currently exercisable or convertible when determining whether it controls another entity.

The definition of control under IFRS permits only one entity to have control of another. Therefore, when two or more entities each hold significant voting rights, both actual and potential, the indicators are reassessed to determine which entity has control.

Dual Consolidation Model

Canadian GAAP use a control-based model similar to IFRS though there is a slight difference as the former refers to control and the ability to obtain benefits from another entity activities and be exposed to related risks. In addition Canadian GAAP specify that a dual consolidation decision model be used by applying first a "variable interests model" as described in AcG-15 and then a "voting control model" as specified in CICA 1600.

According to AcG-15, variable interests entities ('VIEs') are entities in which the equity at risk either (1) is insufficient to finance the entity's own operations without additional subordinated financial support; or (2) lacks certain characteristics of a controlling financial interest. Under AcG-15, the assessment for consolidation is based on an analysis of economic risks and rewards. VIEs are consolidated by the primary beneficiary (i.e., the party that absorbs a majority of the expected losses or has the right to receive a majority of the expected residual returns). VIEs should have only one primary beneficiary (if any). Decision-making authority plays no role in consolidation decisions for these entities.

Consolidation based on the voting control model would apply to non-VIEs which are assessed for consolidation on the basis of voting and other decision-making rights. Under this model, control of an enterprise is the continuing power to determine its strategic operating, investing and financing policies without the cooperation of others.

De facto Control

In rare circumstances, a parent could have control over an entity even though it holds less than 50% of that entity's voting rights and lacks the legal or contractual rights for controlling the majority of the entity's voting power or board of directors (i.e., *de facto* control). An example of *de facto* control under IFRS is when a major shareholder holds a significant but not majority investment in an entity with an otherwise dispersed public shareholding. The assertion of *de facto* control is evaluated on the basis of all relevant facts and circumstances, including the legal and regulatory environment, the nature of the capital market and the ability of the majority owners of voting shares to vote together.

Canadian GAAP also considers the concept of effective control and potential voting rights under the voting interests model. Under the variable interests model, the presence of *de facto* agents (i.e., close business advisers, partners, employees, etc.) are considered when determining the primary beneficiary in a related party group.

Special Purpose Entities

Although IFRS do not specifically address the accounting for VIEs, SIC-12 does provide guidance on the accounting for special purpose entities (SPEs), which could meet the definition of a VIE in accordance with AcG-15. SPEs are created to accomplish a narrow and well-defined objective, and may take the form of a corporation, trust, partnership or unincorporated entity. SPEs are often created with legal arrangements that impose strict, and sometimes permanent, limits on the decision-making powers of their governing board, trustee or management over the operations of the SPE. The sponsor (or entity on whose behalf the SPE was created) frequently transfers assets to the SPE, obtains the right to use the SPE's assets or performs services for the SPE, while other parties (capital providers) may provide the funding to the SPE.

The provisions of SIC-12 are consistent with the control-based model of consolidation under IAS 27. The interpretation provides circumstances that there may indicate a relationship in which an entity has control over an SPE and consequently should consolidate it. These circumstances include:

- in substance, the activities of the SPE are being conducted on behalf of the entity according to its specific business needs so that the entity obtains benefits from the SPE's operation;

- in substance, the entity has the decision-making powers to obtain the majority of the benefits of the activities of the SPE or, by setting up an 'autopilot' mechanism, the entity has delegated these decision-making powers;

- in substance, the entity has rights to obtain the majority of the benefits of the SPE and therefore may be exposed to risks incident to the activities of the SPE; or

- in substance, the entity retains the majority of the residual or ownership risks related to the SPE or its assets in order to obtain benefits from its activities.

Canadian GAAP differs from IFRS because it requires the consolidation of VIEs to be based on the variable interests model, in accordance with AcG-15. Also, Canadian GAAP covers the concept of a qualifying special-purpose entity (QSPE). A QSPE is a trust or other legal vehicle that meets certain conditions (defined in AcG-12), one of which being that it holds transferred financial assets. QSPEs are not consolidated by the transferor (or its affiliate) under AcG-12. IFRS does not have the concept of a QSPE.

Venture Capitalists, Mutual Funds, Unit Trusts and Similar Entities

IAS 27 also requires venture capitalists, mutual funds, unit trusts and similar entities to consolidate investments over which they have control. This is a significant difference from Canadian GAAP since most of these entities meet the definition of an *investment company* (under AcG-18) and are required to measure their investments at fair value. Under AcG-18, investment companies are exempt from the consolidation requirements, even for majority owned investments.

The IASB decided not to scope out venture capitalists, mutual funds, unit trusts and similar entities from IAS 27 consolidation requirements because it felt that the information needs of financial statement users would not be well served if those controlling investments were measured only at fair value. This would leave a controlled entity's assets and liabilities unreported. It is conceivable that, in some circumstances, an investment in a large subsidiary would have only a small fair value. Reporting that value alone would preclude a user from being able to assess a group's financial position, results and cash flows.

Illustrative Disclosures:

Extract 6(1) – Basis of consolidation

> **Nycomed S.C.A. SICAR (AR 2007), page 26**
> **ACCOUNTING PRINCIPLES (in part)**
> **Basis of consolidation (in part)**
>
> The consolidated financial statements comprise the financial statements of Nycomed S.C.A. SICAR (the parent company) and all the companies in which Nycomed S.C.A. SICAR directly or indirectly owns more than 50% of the voting rights, or in some other way has a controlling influence (subsidiaries). Nycomed S.C.A. SICAR and these companies are referred to as the Group.
>
> The consolidated financial statements are prepared on the basis of the financial statements of the parent company and the subsidiaries, and by consolidating uniform accounting items. The consolidated financial statements are based on financial statements prepared by applying the Group's accounting policies.

Extract 6(2) – Control over an entity

> **Aviva plc (AR 2007), page 134**
> **3 – Subsidiaries (in part)**
> **(ii) Bancassurance partnership with Cajamurcia (in part)**
>
> On 6 June 2007, the Group announced that it had entered into a long-term bancassurance agreement with Spanish savings bank Caja de Ahorros de Murcia (Cajamurcia) that will enhance the Group's leading position in the Spanish life market. Cajamurcia will provide exclusive access to its network of branches to Caja Murcia Vida y Pensiones, de Seguros y Reaseguros SA (Cajamurcia Vida), the newly-created life insurance company jointly-owned by the Group and Cajamurcia, to sell insurance and pension products. Regulatory approval to write new business was received on 21 November 2007 and the new company began trading on 30 November 2007.
>
> On signing the agreement, the Group acquired 5% of the share capital of Cajamurcia Vida and Cajamurcia granted the Group a call option over a further 45% of the shares in this company which may be exercised in the two month period following the first anniversary of the agreement being signed. Further consideration of £69 million would be payable on exercising the option, with additional amounts of up to £187 million payable, dependant on the performance of the new company. If it does not exercise this option during this period, the Group has granted a call option over its 5% holding to Cajamurcia.
>
> The Group paid £8 million for the initial 5% holding on completion on 6 June 2007. The Group has the power to control the financial and operating policies of Cajamurcia Vida through having the majority vote at meetings of the company's board of directors. We have therefore consolidated its results and balance sheet since that date.

Commentary: Both extracts illustrate the consideration, in their policies for consolidation, of other interests held.

Presentation of Consolidated and Separate Financial Statements

IAS 27 requires entities to prepare consolidated financial statements but allows them to prepare separate (i.e., non-consolidated) financial statements if they so choose.

Therefore, an IFRS preparer can choose to prepare both sets of financial statements. The standard also provides an exemption to parent entities that do not wish to prepare consolidated financial statements. An entity can choose this option only if it meets the following four criteria:

- the parent is itself a wholly owned subsidiary, or is a partially owned subsidiary of another entity, and its other owners (including those not otherwise entitled to vote) have been informed about, and do not object to, the parent not presenting consolidated financial statements;

- the parent's debt or equity instruments are not traded in a public market (a domestic or foreign stock exchange or an over-the-counter market, including local and regional markets);

- the parent did not file, nor is it in the process of filing, its financial statements with a securities commission or other regulatory organization for the purpose of issuing any class of instruments in a public market; and

- the ultimate or any intermediate parent of the parent produces consolidated financial statements available for public use that comply with IFRS.

Canadian GAAP requires a parent to consolidate investments in subsidiaries and to prepare only consolidated financial statements. In practice, parent companies may prepare two sets of financial statements to meet different financial reporting requirements: one set of general purpose consolidated financial statements in accordance with Canadian GAAP for distribution to investors and lenders, and another set of non-consolidated financial statements (usually in a compilation format and without an assurance report) for filing with Canadian tax authorities.

Because CICA 1590 requires enterprises to consolidate all of their subsidiaries, separate financial statements are not prepared under Canadian GAAP.

Illustrative Disclosure:

Extract 6(3) – Accounting policy to present consolidated and separate financial statements

---

Barclays PLC (AR 2007), page 165

Significant Accounting Policies (in part)

1. Reporting entity

These financial statements are prepared for the Barclays Bank PLC Group ('Barclays' or 'the Group') under Section 227(2) of the Companies Act 1985. The Group is a major global financial services provider engaged in retail and commercial banking, credit cards, investment banking, wealth management and investment management services. In addition, individual financial statements have been prepared for the holding company, Barclays Bank PLC ('the Bank'), under Section 226(2)(b) of the Companies Act 1985. Barclays Bank PLC is a public limited company, incorporated in Great Britain and having a registered office in England.

2. Compliance with International Financial Reporting Standards (in part)

The consolidated financial statements of the Barclays Bank PLC Group, and the individual financial statements of Barclays Bank PLC, have been prepared in accordance with International Financial Reporting Standards (IFRSs) and interpretations issued by the International Financial Reporting Interpretations Committee (IFRIC), as adopted by the European Union.

Commentary: This extract illustrates the preparation of consolidated and separate financial statements included in the company's annual report. Under Canadian GAAP, if the holding company (Barclays PLC) had subsidiaries, it would be required to only prepare consolidated financial statements.

Accounting for Investments in Subsidiaries, Jointly Controlled Entities and Associates in Separate Financial Statements

When entities prepare separate financial statements under IFRS, they account for investments in subsidiaries, jointly controlled entities and associates either at cost or in accordance with IAS 39, *Financial Instruments: Recognition and Measurement* (at fair value). They would apply the same accounting for each category of investments. Investments accounted for at cost must be accounted for in accordance with IFRS 5, *Non-current Assets Held for Sale and Discontinued Operations* when they are classified as held for sale (or included in a disposal group that is classified as held for sale) in accordance with IFRS 5. The measurement of investments accounted for in accordance with IAS 39 is not changed in such circumstances.

They would also recognize a dividend from a subsidiary, jointly controlled entity or associate in profit or loss in their separate financial statements when their right to receive the dividend is established.

Cost of Investment of New Parent in a Group

The cost of the investment of a new parent in a group (in a reorganization meeting certain criteria) is measured at the carrying amount of its share of equity as shown in the separate financial statements of the previous parent.

Investments Accounted for under IAS 39 in Consolidated Financial Statements

Investments in jointly controlled entities and associates that are accounted for in accordance with IAS 39 in the consolidated financial statements must be accounted for in the same way in the parent's separate financial statements. This significantly differs from Canadian GAAP, since separate financial statements are not prepared and Canadian GAAP is silent on this issue.

Illustrative Disclosure:

Extract 6(4) – Accounting policies for consolidated and separate financial statements

---

Aviva plc (AR 2007), pages 115-116

Accounting policies (in part)

(D) Consolidation principles (in part)

Subsidiaries

Subsidiaries are those entities (including Special Purpose Entities) in which the Group, directly or indirectly, has power to exercise control over financial and operating policies in order to gain economic benefits. Subsidiaries are consolidated from the date on which effective control is transferred to the Group and are excluded from consolidation from the date of disposal. All inter-company transactions, balances and unrealised surpluses and deficits on transactions between Group companies have been eliminated.

From 1 January 2004, the date of first time adoption of IFRS, the Group is required to use the purchase method of accounting to account for the acquisition of subsidiaries. Under this method, the cost of an acquisition is measured as the fair value of assets given up, shares issued or liabilities undertaken at the date of acquisition, plus costs directly attributable to the acquisition. The excess of the cost of acquisition over the fair value of the net assets of the subsidiary acquired is recorded as goodwill (see policy N below). Any surplus of the acquirer's interest in the subsidiary's net assets over the cost of acquisition is credited to the income statement.

Aviva plc (AR 2007) (continued)

Associates and joint ventures

Associates are entities over which the Group has significant influence, but which it does not control. Generally, it is presumed that the Group has significant influence if it has between 20% and 50% of voting rights. Joint ventures are entities whereby the Group and other parties undertake an economic activity which is subject to joint control arising from a contractual agreement. In a number of these, the Group's share of the underlying assets and liabilities may be greater than 50% but the terms of the relevant agreements make it clear that control is not exercised. Such jointly-controlled entities are referred to as joint ventures in these financial statements.

Gains on transactions between the Group and its associates and joint ventures are eliminated to the extent of the Group's interest in the associates and joint ventures. Losses are also eliminated, unless the transaction provides evidence of an impairment of the asset transferred between entities.

Investments in associates and joint ventures are accounted for using the equity method of accounting. Under this method, the cost of the investment in a given associate or joint venture, together with the Group's share of that entity's post-acquisition changes to shareholders' funds, is included as an asset in the consolidated balance sheet. As explained in policy N, the cost includes goodwill identified on acquisition. The Group's share of their post-acquisition profits or losses is recognised in the income statement and its share of post-acquisition movements in reserves is recognised in reserves. Equity accounting is discontinued when the Group no longer has significant influence over the investment.

If the Group's share of losses in an associate or joint venture equals or exceeds its interest in the undertaking, the Group does not recognise further losses unless it has incurred obligations or made payments on behalf of the entity.

The Company's investments

In the Company balance sheet, subsidiaries and joint ventures are stated at their fair values, estimated using applicable valuation models underpinned by the Company's market capitalisation. These investments are classified as available for sale (AFS) financial assets, with changes in their fair value being recorded in a separate investment valuation reserve within equity.

Commentary: This extract illustrates the group's policies for accounting for investments in subsidiaries, joint ventures and associates. These policies differ from those used in the company's separate financial statements, which state that investments in subsidiaries and joint ventures are accounted for at fair value in accordance with IAS 39.

Note that companies classifying financial assets as available for sale will recognize the changes in fair value of these investments in other comprehensive income displayed in the statement of comprehensive income, for annual periods beginning on or after January 1, 2009.

Combined Financial Statements

Companies sometimes prepare combined financial statements to meet specific user needs. Although IAS 27 specifies that consolidated financial statements should include all of a parent's subsidiaries, it does not specifically address the preparation of combined financial statements. In practice, combined financial statements may be prepared in accordance with IFRS only when all of the entities concerned have been under common control during the track record period and form a "reporting entity."

CICA 1600 provides specific guidance on the preparation of combined financial statements. The circumstances permitting combined financial statements under IFRS may differ from those under Canadian GAAP, which may have a significant impact on companies accustomed to preparing them for lenders, for example, who tend to be interested only in monitoring the operations of select companies operating within a larger group. Therefore, they will have to take a close look at whether they can still prepare such statements. If not, the complexity in meeting financial reporting requirements may well increase.

Consolidation Procedures

IAS 27 and CICA 1600 suggest generally similar mechanics for the consolidation process. Both require the carrying amount of the parent's investment in each subsidiary and the parent's portion of equity of each subsidiary to be eliminated and replaced by the identifiable assets and liabilities of the subsidiary. Also, both IAS 27 and CICA 1600 require the elimination of intercompany transactions and balances. IAS 27, however, requires that intragroup balances be eliminated in full. Intragroup balances and transactions include income, expenses and dividends. Unrealized profits and losses resulting from intragroup transactions that are recognized in assets, such as inventory and fixed assets, are also eliminated in full. CICA 1600 requires that, when there is an unrealized intercompany gain or loss recognized by a subsidiary company in which there is a non-controlling interest, that gain or loss should be eliminated proportionately between the parent and the non-controlling interest in that subsidiary's income. Furthermore, for VIEs, Canadian GAAP requires that the effect of eliminating any income or expense between the primary beneficiary and the consolidated entity should be attributed in full to the primary beneficiary, and not to the non-controlling interests.

IAS 27 specifies that the consolidated financial statements should be prepared using uniform accounting policies throughout the group. Although this is usually followed in practice under Canadian GAAP, it is not a specifically stated in the *CICA Handbook*.

Furthermore, IAS 27 specifies that the consolidated financial statements should be prepared using the financial statements of the parent and its subsidiaries prepared as of the same reporting date. When the date of a subsidiary's financial statements differ from that of the parent's statements, adjustments should be made for the effects of significant transactions or events occurring between those dates. In any case, the reporting dates of a subsidiary and its parent cannot differ by more than three months.

CICA 1600 suggests (but does not require) that a subsidiary should prepare, for consolidation purposes, statements for a period that exactly or nearly coincides with the period of the parent. Furthermore, it requires that any significant transactions or events of the subsidiary that have occurred during the intervening period be recorded or disclosed. Therefore, since CICA 1600 does not require that the dates exactly coincide, it is possible that a parent entity may have consolidated subsidiaries whose reporting periods vary by more than three months from those of the parent entity.

Illustrative Disclosures:

Extract 6(5A) – Significant accounting policy on the use of uniform accounting policies

TNT N.V. (AR 2007), page 67
Summary of significant accounting policies (in part)
Consolidation (in part)
Consolidated financial information, including subsidiaries, associates and joint ventures, has been prepared using uniform accounting policies for like transactions and other events in similar circumstances. All significant intercompany transactions, balances and unrealised gains on transactions have been eliminated on consolidation. Unrealised losses are eliminated unless the transaction provides evidence of an impairment of the asset transferred.

Commentary: This extract illustrates the company's policy of using uniform accounting policies throughout the group, which is suggested but not required under Canadian GAAP. It further illustrates the elimination of intercompany balances.

Extract 6(5B) – Significant accounting policy on adjustments to ensure the use of uniform accounting policies

---

Teleset Networks Public Company Limited (AR 2007), page 25

2. Accounting policies (in part)

Basis of consolidation

The consolidated financial statements incorporate the financial statements of the Company and entities (including special purpose entities) controlled by the Company (its subsidiaries). Control is achieved where the Company has the power to govern the financial and operating policies of an entity so as to obtain benefits from its activities.

The consolidated financial statements incorporate the results of the Company and all its subsidiary undertakings for the year ended 31 December 2007 using the acquisition method of accounting as required, except as noted below for the accounting using the pooling of interests method. Profits and losses on intra-group transactions are eliminated on consolidation. The results of the subsidiary acquired during the year have been included from the date of acquisition. On acquisition of a subsidiary all the subsidiary's assets and liabilities which exist at the date of acquisition are recorded at fair value. The excess of the fair value of the consideration paid over the fair value of the identifiable net assets acquired (i.e goodwill), is capitalised net of any provision for impairment.

No income statement and balance sheet are presented for the Company as provided by the Cyprus Company Law.

The results of subsidiaries acquired or disposed of during the year are included in the consolidated income statement from the effective date of acquisition or up to the effective date of disposal, as appropriate.

Where necessary, adjustments are made to the financial statements of subsidiaries to bring their accounting policies into line with those used by other members of the Group.

All intra-group transactions, balances, income and expenses are eliminated on consolidation.

Commentary: This extract illustrates the company's policy for consolidation. It is important to note that this policy will be revised to comply with amendments to IFRS 3 and IAS 27 issued in 2008.

The pooling of interests method is specifically prohibited under IFRS 3; however, IFRS 3 does not apply to a combination of entities under common control. In the absence of guidance under IFRS, this method was applied in accordance with US and UK GAAP.

This example clearly illustrates the application of consolidation procedures, which is consistent with IAS 27, including the disclosure that adjustments are made to the financial statements of subsidiaries to ensure consistent accounting policies are applied throughout the consolidated group.

Non-controlling Interests

Initial Measurement

Under IFRS all non-controlling interests are measured initially at fair value, or at the non-controlling interest's proportionate share of the acquiree's identifiable net assets. Under Canadian GAAP initial amounts of non-controlling interest would be measured:

- at fair value when a VIE is consolidated, which is similar to IFRS except that the amounts used as the basis for the calculation would differ; and

- as a percentage of the existing carrying amounts in the subsidiary's financial statements when consolidated under the voting interests model.

Presentation

Canadian GAAP differs from IFRS because non-controlling interest is shown on the balance sheet as part of the mezzanine items between liabilities and equity. This difference in presentation can have a significant impact on users of financial statements and, possibly, key performance indicators, and can result in different amounts for net earnings and equity under IFRS.

Illustrative Disclosures:

Extract 6(6A) – Accounting policy for the presentation of non-controlling interests

Nycomed S.C.A. SICAR (AR 2007), page 26
ACCOUNTING PRINCIPLES (in part)
Basis of consolidation (in part)

On consolidation, intra-Group transactions, shareholdings, intra-Group dividend and balances and realised and unrealised gains and losses on intra-Group transactions are eliminated. Minority interests' proportional shares of profit or loss and the net assets are disclosed as separate items in the income statements and within equity in the consolidated balance sheet respectively.

Commentary: This extract illustrates the company's policy for the presentation of non-controlling interests (referred to as minority interests), which differs from Canadian GAAP.

Extract 6(6B) – Presentation of non-controlling interests

Nycomed S.C.A. SICAR (AR 2007), pages 35, 37 and 38
Consolidated income statement
1 January–31 December

Note		Nycomed S.C.A 01.01.07 31.12.07 € thousand	Nycomed S.C.A 01.01.06 31.12.06 € thousand	Proforma Unaudited 01.01.06 31.12.06 € thousand[1]
	Net turnover	3,497,415	869,949	3,394,354
2	Cost of sales	-906,619	-349,859	-852,567
	Amortisation of fair value adjustments on inventories from acquisitions	-52,970	-	-53,020
	Total cost of sales	-959,589	-349,859	-905,587
	GROSS PROFIT	2,537,826	520,090	2,488,767
	Sales and marketing expenses	-934,535	-244,525	-1,059,487
	Amortisation of fair value adjustments on patents and rights from acquisitions	-531,819	-98,400	-528,010
2	Total sales and marketing expenses	-1,466,354	-342,925	-1,587,497
2	Research and development expenses	-284,551	-37,368	-405,934
2	Administrative expenses	-259,132	-84,364	-268,721
	Integration/restructuring cost	-173,975	-9,411	-9,411
	OPERATING INCOME/(LOSS)	353,814	46,022	217,204
3	Financial income	348,935	2,269	49,454
4	Financial expenses	-425,417	-158,367	-410,433
	GAIN/LOSS BEFORE TAX	277,332	-110,076	-143,775
5	Income tax	-41,908	26,684	46,022
	NET RESULT OF THE PERIOD	235,424	-83,392	-97,753
	Attributable to:			
	Minority interest[2]	6,404	-3,387	
	Equity holders of the parent[2]	229,020	-80,005	
		235,424	-83,392	

Nycomed S.C.A. SICAR
Consolidated balance sheet 31 December 2007

Note	EQUITY AND LIABILITIES	Consolidated 31.12.07 € thousand	Consolidated 31.12.06 € thousand
9	Capital stock	16,677	16,677
	Reserves	1,326,386	1,178,480
		1,343,063	1,195,157
	Minority interest	37,553	37,279
	TOTAL STOCKHOLDERS' EQUITY	1,380,616	1,232,436

Nycomed S.C.A. SICAR (AR 2007) (continued)
Equity

STATEMENT OF CHANGES IN STOCKHOLDERS' EQUITY	Capital stock € thousand	Reserves (note 9) € thousand	Total € thousand	Minority interest (note 9) € thousand	Total equity € thousand
Stockholders' equity as of 1 January 2006	**95**	**786,186**	**786,281**	**33,103**	**819,384**
Issue of share capital (Nycomed S.C.A., SICAR)	31	-	31	1	32
Subscription of new shares by funds investors	4,808	495,193	500,001	2,634	502,635
Issue of shares in exchange for shares in Nycomed A/S	-95	95	-	-	-
Issue of shares in exchange for shares in Nycomed A/S	11,838	-11,838	-	-	-
Effect of changes in Minority share and investors contribution	-	-5,179	-5,179	5,179	-
Share Based Payments (note 16)	-	3,240	3,240	136	3,376
	16,677	1,267,696	1,284,373	41,053	1,325,427
Unrealised result on cash flow hedging, interest rate swaps	-	**-1,895**	**-1,895**	**-80**	**-1,975**
Unrealised gain/loss on investments available for sale	-	-8,275	-8,275	-348	-8,623
Change in actuarial gains and losses (note 10)	-	769	769	32	801
Tax on equity postings 2006	-	275	275	12	287
Foreign currency translation	-	1,001	1,001	42	1,043
Other direct equity postings	-	-1,086	-1,086	-46	-1,132
Total income and expense for the year recognised directly in equity	**-**	**-9,211**	**-9,211**	**-388**	**-9,599**
Net loss for the year	-	-80,005	-80,005	-3,387	-83,392
Total income and expense for the year	**-**	**-89,216**	**-89,216**	**-3,775**	**-92,991**
Stockholders' equity as of 31 December 2006	**16,677**	**1,178,480**	**1,195,157**	**37,279**	**1,232,436**
Stockholders' equity as of 1 January 2007	**16,677**	**1,178,480**	**1,195,157**	**37,279**	**1,232,436**
Share Based Payments (note 16)	**-**	**876**	**876**	**29**	**906**
Effect of changes in Minority share and investors contribution	-	3,763	3,763	-3,763	-
	16,677	1,183,119	1,199,796	33,547	1,233,342
Unrealised result on Cash Flow hedging, interests rate swaps	-	-4,194	-4,194	-117	-4,311
Unrealised gain / loss on investments available for sale	-	-317	-317	-9	-326
Change in actuarial gains and losses (note 10)	-	33,617	33,617	940	34,557
Deferred Tax of direct equity postings	-	9,257	9,257	259	9,516
Other direct equity postings	-	-1,411	-1,411	-2,313	-3,724
Foreign currency translation	-	-122,705	-122,705	-1,157	-123,862
Total income and expense for the year recognised directly in equity	**-**	**-85,753**	**-85,753**	**-2,397**	**-88,150**
Profit for the year	-	229,020	229,020	6,404	235,424
Total income and expense for the year	**-**	**143,267**	**143,267**	**4,007**	**147,274**
Stockholders' equity as of 31 December 2007	**16,677**	**1,326,386**	**1,343,063**	**37,553**	**1,380,616**

Commentary: This extract illustrates the presentation of non-controlling interest (referred to as minority interest) in the consolidated income statement, consolidated equity section of the balance sheet and consolidated statement of equity. This presentation differs from Canadian GAAP.

Note that companies are required to present all non-owner changes in equity in other comprehensive income displayed in the statement of comprehensive income, for annual periods beginning on or after January 1, 2009.

Allocation of the Profit or Loss

Under IFRS, non-controlling interests in the profit or loss are presented as an allocation of the net profit or loss for the period below the statement of comprehensive income (or the income statement, when presented separately). Under current Canadian GAAP, non-controlling interests in the profit or loss are presented as an item of income or expense in the income statement.

Attribution of Losses to Non-controlling Interests

Before its revision in 2008, IAS 27 allocated losses to both majority and minority shareholders. If, however, an investee's losses used up all of a minority shareholder's investment balance, the loss allocation to the minority shareholder would stop at zero and the minority's portion would not be shown as a deficit (i.e., it would not go negative). Any further losses that should have been attributed to the minority shareholder would then be attributed to the majority shareholder instead. Only in exceptional circumstances would the losses continue to be allocated to minority interests, for example, when a minority shareholder had a binding obligation to the investee and had the resources to make an additional investment to cover the losses. This practice was consistent with Canadian GAAP.

Currently IFRS requires an entity to attribute total comprehensive income applicable to non-controlling interests to them, even if this results in the non-controlling interests having a deficit balance. If a parent enters into an arrangement that places it under an obligation to a subsidiary or non-controlling interests, IFRS requires this parent to account for that arrangement separately and the arrangement should not affect the way the entity attributes comprehensive income to its controlling and non-controlling interests. This change is not consistent with Canadian GAAP.

Allocation of Other Comprehensive Income

Under IAS 27 as revised in 2008, total other comprehensive income attributable to non-controlling interests is presented as an allocation of comprehensive income for the period. Canadian GAAP does not specify how items in other comprehensive income should be attributed to non-controlling interests. Currently, Canadian entities do not present total other comprehensive income attributable to non-controlling interests as an allocation. Instead, they present amounts net of those attributable to non-controlling interests.

Step Acquisitions and Partial Disposals

Before IFRS 3 was revised in 2008, IFRS provided very little guidance on business combinations achieved in stages. CICA 1600 has always offered guidance, although it differs from the approach introduced in amended IFRS 3 in 2008 (see Chapter 5, "Business Combinations," for further discussion on business combinations achieved in stages).

IAS 27 provides different accounting treatments for investments where control is retained and where it is lost.

IAS 27 states that changes in ownership interests in subsidiaries that do not result in a loss of control are accounted for as equity transactions since such transactions are viewed as transactions with owners in their capacity as owners. Therefore, the carrying amounts of the controlling and non-controlling interests are adjusted to reflect the changes in their relative interests in the subsidiary. Any differences between the amount by which the non-controlling interests are adjusted and the fair value of the consideration paid or received are recognized directly in equity and attributed to the owners of the parent.

When a parent loses control of a subsidiary, it derecognizes the subsidiary's assets (including goodwill) and liabilities at their carrying amounts at the date when control is lost. It also derecognizes the carrying amount of any non-controlling interests in the former subsidiary at the date when control is lost (including any components of other comprehensive income attributable to them). The parent also recognizes the fair value of the consideration received, if any, from the transaction, and any resulting gain or loss is recorded in income. If a transaction that resulted the loss of control involves a distribution of the subsidiary's shares to owners in their capacity as owners, IAS 27 requires the parent to recognize the amount of that distribution. It further specifies that any investment retained in the former subsidiary is recorded at its fair value at the date when control is lost, and any amounts owed by or to the former subsidiary is accounted for in accordance with other pertinent IFRS from the date control is lost.

The IASB recognized that, since different accounting treatment come into play depending on whether control is kept or lost, parent entities might be persuaded to record disposals in stages so that they can manage the results. As such, IAS 27 includes guidance on how to account for loss of control in two or more arrangements. The standard, therefore, specifies circumstances that would indicate when such multiple arrangements should be accounted for as a single transaction.

In determining whether to account for multiple arrangements as a single transaction, a parent would consider all of the terms and conditions of those arrangements and their economic effects. One or more of the following may indicate that the parent should account for the multiple arrangements as a single transaction:

- they are entered into at the same time or in contemplation of each other;
- they form a single transaction designed to achieve an overall commercial effect;
- the occurrence of one arrangement depends on the occurrence of at least one other arrangement;
- one arrangement considered on its own is not economically justified, but it is economically justified when considered together with other arrangements. An example is when a disposal of shares is priced below market and is compensated for by a subsequent disposal priced above market.

The accounting for increases and decreases in ownership interests differs under Canadian GAAP, which requires that increases in investments be accounted for using the purchase method, and decreases be accounted for as sales resulting in gains or losses recorded in income. There is no distinction under Canadian GAAP for a different practice when control is kept or lost.

Canadian GAAP also does not provide guidance on the accounting for loss of control in two or more arrangements. Canadian preparers transitioning to IFRS may, therefore, experience significant changes to their financial statements as well as their internal accounting systems when undertaking step acquisitions or partial disposals.

General Disclosures for Consolidated and Separate Financial Statements

Consolidated Financial Statements

IAS 27 requires more disclosures than current Canadian GAAP does. A comparison is shown in the table below, with IAS 27 requirements shown first, followed by Canadian GAAP requirements.

The nature of the relationship between the parent and a subsidiary when the parent does not own, directly or indirectly through subsidiaries, more than half of the voting power.	Similar to Canadian GAAP requirements specified in CICA 1590.
The reasons why the ownership, directly or indirectly through subsidiaries, of more than half of the voting or potential voting power of an investee does not constitute control.	Similar to requirements specified in CICA 1590.
The end of the reporting period of the financial statements of a subsidiary when such financial statements are used to prepare consolidated financial statements and are as of a date or for a period that is different from that of the parent's financial statements, and the reason for using a different date or period.	Similar disclosure is required by CICA 1600.
The nature and extent of any significant restrictions (e.g., resulting from borrowing arrangements or regulatory requirements) on the ability of subsidiaries to transfer funds to the parent in the form of cash dividends or to repay loans or advances.	Not required under Canadian GAAP.
A schedule that shows the effects of any changes in a parent's ownership interest in a subsidiary that do not result in a loss of control over the equity attributable to owners of the parent.	Not required under Canadian GAAP.
If control of a subsidiary is lost, the parent would have to disclose the gain or loss, if any, recognized in income, and: • the portion of that gain or loss attributable to recognizing any investment retained in the former subsidiary at its fair value at the date when control is lost; and • the line item(s) in the statement of comprehensive income in which the gain or loss is recognized (if not presented separately in the statement of comprehensive income).	Not required under Canadian GAAP.

Illustrative Disclosures:

Extract 6(7A&B) – Scope and methods of consolidation

> **Unibail-Rodamco (AR 2007), page 113**
> **1. ACCOUNTING PRINCIPLES AND CONSOLIDATION METHODS (in part)**
> **1.2. Scope and methods of consolidation**
> The scope of consolidation includes all companies controlled by Unibail-Rodamco and all companies in which the Group exercises joint control or significant influence. The method of consolidation is determined by the type of control exercised.
> * Control: fully consolidated. Control is presumed if Unibail-Rodamco directly or indirectly holds an interest of more than 50%, unless there is clear evidence that this shareholding does not provide control. Full control also exists when the parent company holds 50% or less of the voting rights in a company and has authority regarding the company's financial and operational strategies and to appoint or dismiss the majority of members of the Board of Directors or an equivalent decision-making body.
> * Joint control: proportionally consolidated. This is demonstrated by the sharing of control of an economic activity under a contractual agreement. It requires the unanimous agreement of partners for operating, strategic and financial decisions.
> * Significant influence: consolidated under the equity method. Significant influence is identified when there is authority to contribute to financial and operational decision-making of the company concerned, but without exercising control over its policies. Significant influence is assumed where the Group directly or indirectly holds more than 20% of voting rights in a company.
> The consolidated financial statements are established by integrating the individual financial statements of Unibail-Rodamco with all relevant subsidiaries over which Unibail-Rodamco exercises control. Subsidiaries closing their accounts more than three months before or after that of Unibail-Rodamco prepare pro forma interim statements to December 31, determined on a 12-month basis. All inter-group balances, profits and transactions are eliminated.

Commentary: This extract illustrates how the parent determines it should consolidate its subsidiaries, including when it does not own, directly or indirectly, more than half of the voting power.

Extract 6(8) – Disclosures relating to consolidation

Barclays PLC (AR 2007), page 223
41 Other entities

There are a number of entities that do not qualify as subsidiaries under UK Law but which are consolidated when the substance of the relationship between the Group and the entity (usually a Special Purpose Entity (SPE)) indicates that the entity is controlled by the Group. Such entities are deemed to be controlled by the Group when relationships with such entities gives rise to benefits that are in substance no different from those that would arise were the entity a subsidiary.

The consolidation of such entities may be appropriate in a number of situations, but primarily when:

– the operating and financial polices of the entity are closely defined from the outset (i.e. it operates on an 'autopilot' basis) with such policies being largely determined by the Group;

– the Group has rights to obtain the majority of the benefits of the entity and/or retains the majority of the residual or ownership risks related to the entity; or

– the activities of the entity are being conducted largely on behalf of the Group according to its specific business objectives.

Such entities are created for a variety of purposes including securitisation, structuring, asset realisation, intermediation and management.

Entities may have a different reporting date from that of the parent of 31st December. Dates may differ for a variety of reasons including local reporting regulations or tax laws. In accordance with our accounting policies, for the purpose of inclusion in the consolidated financial statements of Barclays PLC, entities with different reporting dates are made up until 31st December.

Entities may have restrictions placed on their ability to transfer funds, including payment of dividends and repayment of loans, to their parent entity. Reasons for the restrictions include:

– Central bank restrictions relating to local exchange control laws.

– Central bank capital adequacy requirements.

– Company law restrictions relating to treatment of the entities as going concerns.

Although the Group's interest in the equity voting rights in certain entities exceeds 50%, or it may have the power to appoint a majority of their Boards of Directors, they are excluded from consolidation because the Group either does not direct the financial and operating policies of these entities, or on the grounds that another entity has a superior economic interest in them. Consequently, these entities are not deemed to be controlled by Barclays.

The table below includes information in relation to such entities as required by the Companies Act 1985, Section 231(5).

Country of registration or incorporation	Name	Percentage of ordinary share capital held %	Equity shareholders' funds £m	Retained profit for the year £m
UK	Oak Dedicated Limited	100	(3)	4
UK	Oak Dedicated Two Limited	100	(3)	2
UK	Oak Dedicated Three Limited	100	1	1
UK	Fitzroy Finance Limited	100	–	–
Cayman Islands	St James Fleet Investments Two Limited	100	2	–
Cayman Islands	BNY BT NewCo Limited	–	–	–

Commentary: This extract illustrates the parent's consolidation when it does not own a majority of voting interests directly. The consolidation of this entity is consistent with the guidance in SIC 12. This may or may not differ from Canadian GAAP depending on the application of AcG-15.

Separate Financial Statements

IAS 27 specifies additional disclosure requirements for separate financial statements prepared for a parent that elects not to prepare consolidated financial statements.

The additional disclosure requirements include the following:

- for the separate financial statements:
  - o the fact that the financial statements are separate financial statements,
  - o that the exemption from consolidation has been used,
  - o the name and country of incorporation or residence of the entity whose consolidated financial statements that comply with IFRS have been produced for public use, and
  - o the address where those consolidated financial statements are obtainable;
- a list of significant investments in subsidiaries, jointly controlled entities and associates, including the name, country of incorporation or residence, proportion of ownership interest and, if different, proportion of voting power held; and
- a description of the method used to account for the significant investments in subsidiaries, jointly controlled entities and associates.

When a parent, venturer with an interest in a jointly controlled entity or an investor in an associate prepares separate financial statements in addition to consolidated financial statements, those separate financial statements must disclose:

- the fact that the statements are separate financial statements and the reasons why those statements are prepared (if not required by law);
- a list of significant investments in subsidiaries, jointly controlled entities and associates, including the name, country of incorporation or residence, proportion of ownership interest and, if different, proportion of voting power held; and
- a description of the method used to account for the investments in subsidiaries, jointly controlled entities and associates.

Those separate financial statements must also identify consolidated financial statements or the financial statements prepared in accordance with IAS 28 and IAS 31 to which they relate.

Illustrative Disclosure:

Extract 6(9) – Separate and consolidated financial statements

TomTom NV (AR 2007), pages 50, 62 and 75			
2. SUMMARY OF SIGNIFICANT ACCOUNTING POLICIES (in part)			
Basis of consolidation (in part)			
Subsidiary name	Country of incorporation and residence	Place of residence	Proportion of ownership interest
TomTom International BV	NL	Amsterdam	100%
TomTom Sales BV	NL	Amsterdam	100%
TomTom Global Assets BV[1]	NL	Amsterdam	100%
TomTom Inc.	US	Concord, MA	100%
TomTom Software Ltd.	UK	London	100%
Applied Generics Ltd.	UK	Edinburgh	100%
TomTom Asia Ltd.	TW	Taipei	100%
Drivetech Inc.	TW	Taipei	100%
TomTom Work GmbH	DE	Leipzig	100%

TomTom NV (AR 2007) (Continued)

Associates

Associates are all entities over which the group has significant influence but not control, generally accompanying a shareholding of between 20% and 50% of the voting rights. Investments in associates are accounted for using the equity method of accounting, and are initially recognised at cost. The group's investment in associates includes goodwill identified on acquisition, net of any accumulated impairment loss.

The group's share of its associates' post-acquisition profits or losses is recognised in the income statement, and its share of post-acquisition movements in reserves is recognised in reserves. The cumulative post-acquisition movements are adjusted against the carrying amount of the investment. When the group's share of losses in an associate equals or exceeds its interest in the associate, including any other unsecured receivables, the group does not recognise further losses, unless it has incurred obligations or made payments on behalf of the associate. Unrealised gains on transactions between the group and its associates are eliminated to the extent of the group's interest in the associates. Unrealised losses are also eliminated, unless the transaction provides evidence of an impairment of the asset transferred. Accounting policies of associates have been changed where necessary to ensure consistency with the policies adopted by the group.

14. INVESTMENTS IN ASSOCIATES (in part)

In the fourth quarter of 2007, the Company acquired 29.9% of the shares of Tele Atlas, a leading global provider of digital maps for navigation and location-based solutions, for a total consideration of €816 million.

The movements in the investment in associate can be specified as follows:

(€ in thousands)	2007
Balance as at 31 December 2006	0
Acquisition of associate	816,030
Share of profit for the period (Nov 7 '07 – Dec 31 '07)	758
Balance as at 31 December 2007	816,788

The estimated full year revenue and net profit of the associate and its aggregated assets (excluding goodwill) and liabilities are as follows (all at 100%):

(€ in millions)

Name associate	Place of incorporation	Assets[1]	Liabilities	Revenues full year	Net profit full year	Interest held	Published fair value
Tele Atlas	The Netherlands	1,143	284	318	2	29.9%	2,598

[1] Excluding goodwill.

1. PRESENTATION OF FINANCIAL STATEMENTS AND PRINCIPLE ACCOUNTING POLICIES

The description of the activities of TomTom (the "Company") and the Company structure, as included in the notes to the consolidated financial statements, also apply to the Company financial statements.

In accordance with section 2:362 Part 8 of the Netherlands Civil Code, the Company has prepared its Company financial statements in accordance with accounting principles generally accepted in the Netherlands, applying the accounting policies as adopted in the consolidated financial statements (IFRS). Investments in subsidiaries are stated at net asset value, as the Company effectively exercises significant influence over them. For more information on the accounting policies applied, and on the notes to the consolidated financial statements, please refer to pages 49 to 55.

The total equity and profit in the Company financial statements is equal to the consolidated equity.

In accordance with section 402 of Part 9 of Book 2 of the Netherlands Civil Code, a condensed income statement is included in these financial statements.

3. INVESTMENTS IN ASSOCIATE

Please refer to notes 14, 25, 26 and 27 in the consolidated financial statements.

Commentary: The portion of this extract, which comes from the company's separate financial statements, refers to the statements having been prepared in accordance with the same policies as those applied to the consolidated financial statements, and that they are in accordance with IFRS. It states that the financial statements were prepared in accordance with section 2:362 Part 8 of the Netherlands Civil Code. The separate financial statements refer to the consolidated financial statements for the information on the list of significant investments in subsidiaries and associates, which lists their names, places of incorporation and the proportion of ownership interests held.

Distributions of Non-cash Assets to Owners[1]

Non-cash assets distributions include items of property, plant and equipment, businesses as defined by IFRS 3 or ownership interests in another entity. IFRIC 17 which covers these distributions was issued in November 2008. It is effective for annual reporting periods beginning on or after July 1, 2009. Early adoption is permitted if entity also early adopts IFRS 3 (revised in 2008), IAS 27 (revised in 2008) and IFRS 5 (amended in 2008).

The scope of IFRIC 17 is broad and is applicable to all non-reciprocal distributions of assets (i.e., distributions of non-cash assets, and distributions that give owners a choice of receiving either non-cash assets or a cash alternative). Therefore, it includes transactions other than dividends, such as those termed "returns of capital" and distributions from reserves. Management will need to consider the specific terms of distributions to determine whether it is caught by this interpretation.

IFRIC 17 does not apply to a distribution of a non-cash asset that is ultimately controlled by the same party or parties before and after the distribution. This exclusion applies to the separate, individual and consolidated financial statements of an entity that makes the distribution.

Recognition of the Liability

The liability to pay a dividend (i.e., a dividend payable) is recognized when appropriately authorized and no longer at the entity's discretion. This date will vary by jurisdiction, so IFRIC 17 further clarifies this point as follows:

- when declaration of the dividend (e.g., by management or the board of directors) is approved by the relevant authority (e.g., the shareholders) if the jurisdiction requires such approval, or

- when the dividend is declared (e.g., by management or the board of directors) if the jurisdiction does not require further approval.

Initial and Subsequent Measurements

The liability is initially recognized at the fair value of the assets to be distributed. In the case where the owners have a choice of receiving either non-cash assets or cash, an estimate of the liability is calculated by assessing the fair value of each alternative and the associated probability that each alternative will be selected.

At the end of each reporting period and immediately before settlement, the liability is remeasured to reflect any changes in the fair value of the underlying asset. The changes are recognized in equity. At the settlement date, the difference between the carrying amount of the assets distributed and the liability is recognised in profit or loss as a separate line.

---

1 IFRIC 17 does not deal with the receipt of dividends, but dividend income is recognized when the shareholder's right to receive payment is established in accordance with IAS 18, *Revenue*. Though the recognition of the right to receive payment will vary from one jurisdiction to another, its accounting should mirror the accounting in the paying entity (i.e., the dividend received should be recorded at fair value).

Non-current assets held for distribution to owners are classified as held for distribution in accordance with IFRS 5 only when they are available for distribution in their present condition and the distribution is highly probable. In this case, the non-current assets would be reported at the lower of their carrying amount, or fair value less costs to distribute, whereas the liability will be measured at the fair value of the assets.

Disclosures

The following information (if applicable) must be disclosed:

- the carrying amount of the dividend payable at the beginning and end of the period; and
- the increase or decrease in the carrying amount recognized in the period as a result of a change in the fair value of the assets to be distributed.

If, after the end of a reporting period but before the financial statements are authorized for issue, an entity declares a dividend to distribute a non-cash asset, it must disclose:

- the nature of the asset to be distributed;
- the carrying amount of the asset to be distributed as of the end of the reporting period; and
- the estimated fair value of the assets to be distributed as of the end of the reporting period, if it is different from its carrying amount, and the information about the method used to determine that fair value.

FUTURE DEVELOPMENTS

Convergence with IFRS

In January 2009, the AcSB issued CICA 1601, *Consolidated Financial Statements* and CICA 1602, *Non-controlling Interests*, which effectively replace CICA 1600.

The AcSB has decided not to adopt IAS 27 in its entirety at this time, and the requirements in CICA 1600 that do not involve non-controlling interests remain unchanged in CICA 1601.

CICA 1602 was issued in order to harmonize the accounting for non-controlling interests in a subsidiary in consolidated financial statements under Canadian GAAP with the amended IAS 27, which the IASB issued in January 2008. Except for the disclosure requirements, CICA 1602 replicates the provisions of IAS 27 applicable to non-controlling interests. These provisions are consistent with the treatment of a non-controlling interest at the date of an acquisition in CICA 1582, *Business Combinations* (discussed in Chapter 5), which was issued at the same time as CICA 1601 and CICA 1602 in January 2009.

The separation of the guidance for non-controlling interests from that of other aspects of consolidation makes it easier to distinguish the guidance that is new from the guidance that is unchanged.

CICA 1582, CICA 1601 and CICA 1602 are effective for fiscal years beginning on or after January 1, 2011, with earlier adoption permitted. Entities planning business combinations (and, therefore, consolidations) for fiscal years beginning on or after January 1, 2010 should consider adopting all of these new standards on or before the mandatory adoption date to avoid restatements on transition to IFRS in 2011.

IASB Developments

The IASB issued in December 2008 an Exposure Draft ED 10 entitled *Consolidated Financial Statements* as part of its comprehensive review of off balance sheet risk. This Exposure Draft aims to:

- strengthen and improve the requirements for identifying which entities a company controls;

- respond to the recommendations contained in a report published in April 2008 by the Financial Stability Forum, and

- address off balance sheet activities, an area cited by the G20 leaders at their November 15, 2008 meeting.

The Exposure Draft addresses the use of special structures by reporting entities, particularly banks, to manage securitisations and other more complex financial arrangements. It proposes:

- a new, principle-based, definition of *control of an entity* that would apply to a wide range of situations and be more difficult to evade by special structuring; and

- enhanced disclosure requirements that would enable an investor to assess the extent to which a reporting entity has been involved in setting up special structures and the risks to which these special structures expose the entity.

The proposed new IFRS will be the new home for the guidance on consolidated financial statements in IAS 27 and SPEs in SIC-12. A final standard is expected to be issued in the second half of 2009.

The IASB proposes to retain the requirements for the preparation of separate financial statements in IAS 27 and to rename that standard 'IAS 27, *Separate Financial Statements*'.

The proposals would apply not only to the banking sector but to any entity that uses legal entities to manage its activities. Consequently Canadian companies changing to IFRS should assess whether these proposals would impact their financial statements.

COMPREHENSIVE EXAMPLES

This section presents two comprehensive disclosure examples. Relevant extracts related to consolidation were selected, placing emphasis on potential differences between IFRS and Canadian GAAP.

voestalpine AG – All extracts were obtained from the annual report for the year ended March 31, 2008.

Extract 6(10A) – voestalpine AG, page 86

A. General information and corporate purpose

The corporate purpose of voestalpine AG and its Group companies (hereinafter referred to as the "Group") is primarily the production, processing and distribution of materials made of steel, research and development in the area of metallurgy, metal processing and materials technology.

voestalpine AG is the Group's ultimate parent company who prepares the consolidated financial statements. It is registered in the commercial register of Linz and has its registered office in Linz. voestalpine AG's company address is voestalpine-Strasse 1, 4020 Linz, Austria. The shares of voestalpine AG are listed on the stock exchange in Vienna, Austria.

The consolidated financial statements for the year ended March 31, 2008 (including comparative figures for the year ended March 31, 2007) have been prepared in accordance with International Financial Reporting Standards (IFRS) as published by the International Accounting Standard Board (IASB) and adopted by the European Union.

The consolidated financial statements are presented in euros (= functional currency of the parent company) rounded to the nearest thousand.

The consolidated income statement has been prepared using cost of sales method. The consolidated financial statements were approved by the Management Board of voestalpine AG on May 19, 2008.

Extract 6(10B) – voestalpine AG, page 80

This extract clearly presents the non-controlling interests (referred to as *minority interests*) as an allocation of profit.

Consolidated income statement 2007/08	Notes	2006/07	2007/08
Revenue	1	**6,943,850**	**10,481,204**
Cost of sales		–5,153,261	**–7,977,871**
Gross profit		**1,790,589**	**2,503,333**
Other operating income	2	188,063	**308,317**
Distribution costs		–462,474	**–866,099**
Administrative expenses		–342,666	**–468,224**
Other operating expenses	3	–162,063	**–324,749**
Profit from operations (EBIT)		**1,011,449**	**1,152,578**
Share of profit of associates	4	16,461	**28,707**
Finance income	5	65,066	**61,204**
Finance costs	6	–116,543	**–262,908**
Profit before tax (EBT)		**976,433**	**979,581**
Income tax expense	7	–221,467	**–202,485**
Profit for the period from continuing operations		**754,966**	**777,096**
Discontinued operations	8	9,930	**–25,155**
Profit for the period		**764,896**	**751,941**
Attributable to:			
Equity holders of the parent		757,403	**718,227**
Minority interest		7,493	**3,806**
Share planned for hybrid capital owners		0	**29,908**
Basic earnings per share from continuing operations (euros)	28	**4.76**	**4.69**
Diluted earnings per share from continuing operations (euros)		**4.41**	**4.56**
			In thousands of euros

Extract 6(10C) - voestalpine AG, page 83

This extract clearly presents the non-controlling interests (referred to as *minority interests*) as a component of equity.

Equity and liabilities	Notes	03/31/2007*	03/31/2008
A. Equity			
Share capital		287,784	298,756
Capital reserves		398,939	470,633
Hybrid capital		0	992,096
Reserve for own shares		-181,810	-272,304
Other reserves		-105,449	-188,720
Retained earnings		2,429,488	2,734,942
Equity attributable to equity holders of the parent		2,828,952	4,035,403
Minority interest		53,348	253,894
	17	2,882,300	4,289,297
B. Non-current liabilities			
Pensions and other employee obligations	18	566,093	839,348
Provisions	19	20,989	69,038
Deferred tax liabilities	13	85,273	361,049
Financial liabilities	20	739,583	1,262,881
		1,411,938	2,532,316
C. Current liabilities			
Provisions	19	240,608	403,090
Tax liabilities		175,884	198,650
Financial liabilities	20	629,564	3,031,674
Trade and other payables	21	1,487,220	2,146,765
		2,533,276	5,780,179
Total equity and liabilities		6,827,514	12,601,792

* Insignificant assets and liabilities from discontinued operations are separated in the Notes.   In thousands of euros

Extract 6(10D) – voestalpine AG, pages 84-85

This extract clearly presents amounts allocated to non-controlling interests (referred to as *minority interests*) on the statement of recognized income and expense and the statement of changes in equity (note that, for annual periods beginning on or after January 1, 2009, the statement of comprehensive income will replace the statement of recognized income and expense).

voestalpine AG
Statement of recognized income and expense 2007/08

2006/07	Share capital	Capital reserves	Hybrid capital	Reserve for own shares	Translation reserve	Hedging reserve	Actuarial gains (+)/ losses (−)	Retained earnings	Total attributable to equity holders of the parent	Minority interest	Total equity
Hedge Accounting	O	O	O	O	O	−1,428	O	O	−1,428	107	−1,321
Currency translation	O	O	O	O	−6,048	O	O	O	−6,048	−774	−6,822
Actuarial gains/losses (including deferred tax)	O	O	O	O	O	O	−9,217	O	−9,217	−28	−9,245
Total income and expense for the year recognized directly in equity	O	O	O	O	−6,048	−1,428	−9,217	O	−16,693	−695	−17,388
Profit for the period	O	O	O	O	O	O	O	757,403	757,403	7,493	764,896
Total income and expense for the year	O	O	O	O	−6,048	−1,428	−9,217	757,403	740,710	6,798	747,508
2007/08											
Hedge Accounting	O	O	O	O	O	−20,022	O	O	−20,022	927	−19,095
Currency translation	O	O	O	O	−64,497	O	O	O	−64,497	−7,188	−71,685
Actuarial gains/losses (including deferred tax)	O	O	O	O	O	O	1,247	O	1,247	−1,251	−4
Total income and expense for the year recognized directly in equity	O	O	O	O	−64,497	−20,022	1,247	O	−83,272	−7,512	−90,784
Profit for the period	O	O	O	O	O	O	O	748,135	748,135	3,806	751,941
Total income and expense for the year	O	O	O	O	−64,497	−20,022	1,247	748,135	664,863	−3,706	661,157

voestalpine AG
Statement of changes in equity 2007/08

	Share capital	Capital reserves	Hybrid capital	Reserve for own shares	Translation reserve	Hedging reserve	Actuarial gains (+)/ losses (−)	Retained earnings	Total attributable to equity holders of the parent	Minority interest	Total equity
Balance as of April 1, 2006	287,784	470,843	O	−831	4,353	5,084	−98,332	1,817,250	2,486,151	61,138	2,547,289
Total income and expense for the year	O	O	O	O	−6,048	−1,428	−9,217	757,403	740,710	6,798	747,508
Own shares acquired/ disposed	O	4,215	O	−180,979	O	O	O	O	−176,764	O	−176,764
Dividends	O	O	O	O	O	O	O	−122,743	−122,743	−4,363	−127,106
Convertible bond	O	−48,910	O	O	O	O	O	O	−48,910	O	−48,910
Share-based payment	O	16,727	O	O	O	O	O	−5,545	11,182	60	11,242
Other changes	O	−43,936	O	O	147	O	−8	−16,877	−60,674	−10,285	−70,959
Balance as of March 31, 2007 = Balance as of April 1, 2007	287,784	398,939	O	−181,810	−1,548	3,656	−107,557	2,429,488	2,828,952	53,348	2,882,300
Total income and expense for the year	O	O	O	O	−64,497	−20,022	1,247	748,135	664,863	−3,706	661,157
Own shares acquired/ disposed	O	−66,917	O	−90,494	O	O	O	O	−157,411	O	−157,411
Dividends	O	O	O	O	O	O	O	−234,758	−234,758	−2,744	−237,502
Hybrid capital	O	O	992,096	O	O	O	O	O	992,096	O	992,096
Capital increase	10,972	90,674	O	O	O	O	O	O	101,646	O	101,646
Share-based payment	O	17,209		O	O	O	O	O	O	17,209	132 17,341
Other changes	O	30,727	O	O	O	1	O	−207,923	−177,195	206,865	29,670
Balance as of March 31, 2008	298,756	470,633	992,096	−272,304	−66,045	−16,365	−106,310	2,734,942	4,035,403	253,894	4,289,297

In thousands of euros

Extract 6(10E) – voestalpine AG, page 87

This extract presents the significant accounting policy note on consolidation methods.

B. Summary of accounting policies (in part)

Consolidation methods

The annual financial statements of fully consolidated or proportionately consolidated entities are prepared using uniform accounting policies. For entities included using the equity method, local accounting policies and different balance sheet dates are maintained if the relevant amounts are immaterial.

In the case of initial consolidation, assets, liabilities and contingent liabilities are measured at market value on the date of acquisition. Any excess of the cost of acquisition over net asset value is recognized as goodwill. Any deficiency of the cost of acquisition below net asset value is recognized as income in the period of acquisition. Hidden reserves or charges attributable to minority shareholders are allocated as well.

All intra-group profits, receivables and payables, income and expenses are eliminated.

Extract 6(10F) – voestalpine AG, pages 96-98

This extract presents the policies for consolidation in the financial statements as well as the impact of the consolidated entities. It also presents changes to the scope of consolidation during the year.

C. Scope of consolidation

The consolidated Group (see "Investments" appendix to the notes) is established in accordance with IFRS. In addition to the annual financial statements of voestalpine AG, the consolidated financial statements also include the financial statements of entities controlled by voestalpine AG (and their subsidiaries).

Subsidiaries are entities controlled by the Group. Control exists when the Group has the direct or indirect potential to determine the financial and operating policies of an entity so as to obtain benefits from its activities. Joint ventures are included on a pro-rata basis in the consolidated financial statements. The annual financial statements of subsidiaries and joint ventures are included in the consolidated financial statements from the date that control commences until the date that control ceases.

Associates are entities over which the Group has significant influence without having control over the financial and operating policies. The annual financial statements of associates are included in the consolidated financial statements using proportionate consolidation or the equity method, from the acquisition date until disposal date. The Group's associates are listed in the "Investments" appendix to the notes.

The following table shows the pro-rata values for entities included in the financial statements by proportionate consolidation:

	03/31/2007	03/31/2008
Non-current assets	22.0	26.9
Current assets	155.2	115.9
	177.2	142.8
Equity	29.5	30.9
Non-current provisions and liabilities	11.0	11.7
Current provisions and liabilities	136.7	100.2
	177.2	142.8
	2006/07	**2007/08**
Revenue	304.5	272.9
Profit for the period	82.4	71.7
		In millions of euros

The following table shows the values (100%) for entities included in the financial statements using the equity method:

	03/31/2007	03/31/2008
Non-current assets	159.6	319.7
Current assets	469.1	722.1
	628.7	1,041.8
Equity	189.1	314.9
Non-current provisions and liabilities	28.2	130.6
Current provisions and liabilities	411.4	596.3
	628.7	1,041.8

	2006/07	2007/08
Revenue	1,778.2	2,859.7
Profit for the period	64.1	84.9
		In millions of euros

The scope of consolidation changed as follows during the business year:

	Full consolidation	Proportionate consolidation	Equity method
As of April 1, 2007	156	3	12
Change in consolidation method			
Acquisitions	1		1
Disposals			
Reorganizations	−5		−1
Divested or disposals	−5	−1	
Acquisitions	175	1	2
As of March 31, 2008	322	3	14
Of which foreign companies	265	1	5

The following entities were deconsolidated during the 2007/08 reporting year:

Name of entity	Date of deconsolidation
Fully consolidated in previous year	
voestalpine Stahlbeteiligungs GmbH	March 31, 2008
Metal Sections Limited	March 31, 2008
Nedcon Logistica Iberica S.A.	March 31, 2008
Nedcon Raktártechnikai Kft.	March 31, 2008
Uddeholm Technology AB	September 30, 2007
Reorganized	
voestalpine Automotive Finanzierungs GmbH	April 1, 2007
voestalpine Automotive GmbH	April 1, 2007
VAE SA (Pty) Ltd.	April 1, 2007
Nedcon Components B.V.	April 1, 2007
Intesy Business & IT Solutions Inc.	July 31, 2007
Proportional consolidated in previous year	
Nedcon DLS B.V.	March 31, 2008

Extract 6(10G) – voestalpine AG, pages 99-101

This extract shows the acquisitions during the year that had an impact on the consolidated financial statements. It also illustrates the accounting for increases in ownership interests in equity; however, the amounts calculated may differ under IFRS 3 and amended IAS 27.

D. Acquisitions

A preliminary purchase price allocation effected in the 2006/07 business year following an acquisition by the Automotive Division has been restated during the reporting period in accordance with IFRS 3 less than 12 months after acquisition date. The adjustment was made as follows:

	Assets	Equity and liabilities
Goodwill	3,885	
Intangible assets	-2,220	
Inventories	-930	
Deferred tax assets	1,940	
Provisions		2,675
	2,675	2,675

In thousands of euros

During business year 2007/08 a majority interest in BÖHLER-UDDEHOLM AG was acquired. This company and all its subsidiaries were initially consolidated as the new Special Steel Division on July 1, 2007. As of March 31, 2008 voestalpine´s share in BÖHLER-UDDEHOLM amounts to 90.65%. Further information on the companies of the new Special Steel Division can be found in the appendix "Investments" (p. 148 ff.).

In addition, the following entities were included in the consolidated financial statements for the first time during the business year just ended:

Name of entity	Interest in %	Date of initial consolidation
Full consolidation		
Dancke RO s.r.l.	70.000	April 1, 2007
Dancke Stanztechnik GmbH&Co. KG	70.000	April 1, 2007
Dancke Werkzeugbau GmbH&Co. KG	70.000	April 1, 2007
Meincol Distribuidora de Aços S.A.	75.000	January 1, 2008
Materiel Ferroviaire d'Arberats, S.A.S	100.000	August 16, 2007
Sharon Custom Metal Forming Inc.	100.000	January 1, 2008
BWG Services GmbH & Co KG	100.000	April 1, 2007
BWG Services Verwaltungs GmbH	100.000	April 1, 2007
Consolidation at-equity		
Rene Prinsen Spoorwegmaterialen B.V.	49.000	June 29, 2007
APK-Pensionskasse Aktiengesellschaft	29.192	July 1, 2007

These entities have contributed EUR –33.5 million to the profit for the period during the business year since initial consolidation, of which EUR –36.2 millions are attributable to the Special Steel Division.

As no separate valuations were performed for the above mentioned acquisitions on April 1, 2007, no pro-forma disclosure of figures "since the beginning of the period" is made.

The acquisitions had the following effect on the consolidated financial statements:	Recognized values	Fair value adjustments	Carrying amounts
Non-current assets	2,305.0	1,193.9	1,111.1
Current assets	2,376.7	168.5	2,208.2
Non-current provisions and liabilities	−1,248.9	−331.8	−917.1
Current provisions and liabilities	−1,080.9	−0.4	−1,080.5
Net assets	**2,351.9**	**1,030.2**	**1,321.6**
Increase in majority interest	210.8		
Increase in minority interest	−203.4		
Goodwill/badwill	1,101.4		
Costs of acquisition	3,460.7		
Cash and cash equivalents acquired	−125.1		
Net cash outflow	3,335.6		

In millions of euros

The acquired companies are included in the consolidated financial statements as of March 31, 2008, in accordance with IFRS 3 at the fair values of the acquired assets, liabilities and contingent liabilities determined as of the acquisition date, including depreciation and amortization as appropriate.

At the time of the initial consolidation of BÖHLER-UDDEHOLM AG and its subsidiaries, hidden reserves of EUR 1.112,1 million were recognized. Also recognized was a tax credit through acquisition which is stated at EUR 253.0 million and will be allocated over its residual life of 14 years. The goodwill which includes also future effects of synergies amounts to EUR 1,069.6 million and is allocated to the divisions as follows:

	2007/08
Special Steel Division	889.0
Steel Division	154.8
Railway Systems Division	25.8
	1,069.6

In millions of euros

The amounts allocated to the Steel and Railway Systems Division are based on future effects of synergies.

The goodwill also includes EUR 14.9 million in incidental costs of acquisition. In accordance with IFRS 3, the purchase price allocation is considered provisional due to its complexity.

The increase of majority interests is treated as a transaction between owners. The difference between the costs of acquisition for the additional shares and the pro-rata carrying value of the minority interests is recognized directly in equity. In the case of the BÖHLERUDDEHOLM acquisition, 79.2% of the shares (costs of acquisition EUR 2,920.6 million) had been acquired by the end of the statutory extension period of the tender offer. Any difference between cost and the pro-rata carrying amount of shares acquired after this date was charged directly in equity. Until March 31, 2008 further shares in the amount of 11.5% for EUR 397 million have been acquired. EUR 166.4 million were charged directly in equity.

Starting in business year 2007/08, put options granted to minority shareholders in exchange for their shares in Group companies are disclosed in the balance sheet as liabilities stated at fair value. If the opportunities and risks associated with ownership of a minority interest have already passed over at the time that a majority interest is acquired, an acquisition of 100% of the entity is assumed. Where the opportunities and risks have not passed over, the minority interest continues to be shown in equity. The liability is covered by a transfer from Group capital reserves with no effect on profit or loss (double credit approach).

Put options which are charged in equity had a fair value of EUR 21.2 million (2006/07: EUR 44.0 million) on March 31, 2008.

HELLENIC TELECOMMUNICATIONS ORGANISATION S.A. – All extracts were obtained from the annual report for the year ended December 31, 2007.

Extract 6(11A) – HELLENIC TELECOMMUNICATIONS ORGANISATION S.A., page 129

This extract presents the consolidated and separate balance sheet of the parent entity and the consolidated group.

	Notes	31 DECEMBER 2007		31 DECEMBER 2006	
		COMPANY	GROUP	COMPANY	GROUP
ASSETS					
Non - current assets					
Property, plant and equipment	4	2,361.9	6,371.4	2,704.4	6,583.5
Goodwill	5	-	541.5	-	540.8
Telecommunication licenses	6	3.4	396.2	3.8	384.2
Investments	7	4,104.9	158.4	1,826.4	158.7
Advances to pension funds	16	229.8	229.8	188.1	188.1
Deferred taxes	19	158.3	94.6	204.2	127.4
Other non-current assets	8	98.0	678.6	86.6	709.7
Total non - current assets		**6,956.3**	**8,470.5**	**5,013.5**	**8.692,4**
Current assets					
Inventories		34.7	201.7	36.1	205.4
Trade receivables	9	758.6	1,172.0	710.1	1,160.5
Other current assets	10	180.8	372.5	227.0	447.8
Cash and cash equivalents	11	453.1	1,316.3	814.7	2,042.5
Total current assets		**1,427.2**	**3,062.5**	**1,787.9**	**3,856.2**
TOTAL ASSETS		**8,383.5**	**11,533.0**	**6,801.4**	**12,548.6**
EQUITY AND LIABILITIES					
Equity attributable to shareholders of the Company					
Share capital	12	1,171.5	1,171.5	1,171.5	1,171.5
Share premium	12	485.9	485.9	485.9	485.9
Statutory reserve	13	312.1	312.1	283.3	283.3
Consolidation reserve	7	-	(2,533.8)	-	(580.3)
Retained earnings	13	1,596.9	2,595.8	1,309.0	2,304.4
		3,566.4	2,031.5	3,249.7	3,664.8
Minority interests		-	1,023.1	-	1,223.9
Total equity		**3,566.4**	**3,054.6**	**3,249.7**	**4,888.7**
Non - current liabilities					
Long-term loans	15	1,285.2	3,947.1	1,301.9	4,037.3
Provision for staff leaving indemnities	16	211.5	230.3	182.8	198.5
Provision for voluntary leave scheme	16	217.5	217.5	361.4	361.4
Cost of Youth account	16	273.5	273.5	277.3	277.3
Other non - current liabilities	17	41.4	233.6	79.5	126.9
Total non - current liabilities		**2,029.1**	**4,902.0**	**2,202.9**	**5,001.4**
Current liabilities					
Suppliers		608.9	931.5	562.2	938.0
Short-term loans	18	1,494.2	1,497.4	-	25.2
Short-term portion of long-term loans	15	17.5	83.3	16.1	528.0
Income tax	19	24.6	83.0	70.5	142.0
Deferred revenue		135.3	189.2	109.0	196.2
Cost of voluntary leave scheme	16	200.2	200.2	316.7	316.7
Dividends payable	14	4.0	4.0	3.7	3.7
Other current liabilities	20	303.3	587.8	270.6	508.7
Total current liabilities		**2,788.0**	**3,576.4**	**1,348.8**	**2,658.5**
TOTAL EQUITY AND LIABILITIES		**8,383.5**	**11,533.0**	**6,801.4**	**12,548.6**

Extract 6(11B) – HELLENIC TELECOMMUNICATIONS ORGANISATION S.A., page 130

This extract presents the consolidated and separate income statement of the parent entity and the consolidated group.

	Notes	2007 COMPANY	2007 GROUP	2006 COMPANY	2006 GROUP
Revenues					
Domestic telephony	21	1,495.4	2,022.2	1,596.9	2,260.6
International telephony	21	197.7	304.5	181.1	346.9
Mobile telephony	21	-	2,210.0	-	1,975.8
Other income	21	963.8	1,783.1	936.5	1,308.0
Total revenues		**2,656.9**	**6,319.8**	**2,714.5**	**5,891.3**
Operating expenses					
Employee costs		(723.8)	(1,241.3)	(764.9)	(1,241.6)
Cost of voluntary leave scheme	16	(22.1)	(22.1)	49.8	49.8
Charges from international operators		(146.8)	(216.4)	(143.9)	(208.8)
Charges from domestic operators		(323.9)	(655.3)	(366.8)	(720.9)
Depreciation and amortization		(502.2)	(1,171.8)	(528.0)	(1,128.5)
Cost of telecommunications equipment		(101.1)	(672.8)	(128.3)	(363.5)
Other operating expenses	22	(526.3)	(1,293.2)	(520.3)	(1,189.5)
Total operating expenses		**(2,346.2)**	**(5,272.9)**	**(2,402.4)**	**(4,803.0)**
Operating income before financial results		**310.7**	**1,046.9**	**312.1**	**1,088.3**
Financial Results					
Interest expense		(98.4)	(238.7)	(199.2)	(278.8)
Interest income		47.1	77.8	45.7	70.8
Foreign currency differences		(0.5)	(4.8)	2.6	4.2
Dividend income	7	242.3	16.8	196.7	23.0
Gains from investments	7	287.1	256.8	297.9	176.3
Total financial results		**477.6**	**107.9**	**343.7**	**(4.5)**
Profit before tax		**788.3**	**1,154.8**	**655.8**	**1,083.8**
Income tax	19	(211.8)	(381.8)	(124.6)	(353.0)
Profit for the year		576.5	773.0	531.2	730.8
Attributable to:					
Shareholders of the parent		576.5	662.6	531.2	574.6
Minority interests		-	110.4	-	156.2
		576.5	773.0	531.2	730.8
Basic earnings per share	23	1,1762	1,3518	1.0837	1.1723
Diluted earnings per share	23	1,1762	1,3518	1.0837	1.1723
Weighted average number of shares		490,150.389	490,150,389	490,150,389	490,150,389

Extract 6(11C) – HELLENIC TELECOMMUNICATIONS ORGANISATION S.A., page 131

This extract presents the separate statement of changes in the equity of the parent entity.

	Share Capital	Share Premium	Treasury Shares	Statutory Reserve	Retained Earnings	Total equity
Balance at 31 December 2005	**1,172.5**	**486.6**	**(5.9)**	**256.7**	**798.0**	**2,707.9**
Appropriation to statutory reserve	-	-	-	26.6	(26.6)	-
Unrealized gains on available-for-sale securities	-	-	-	-	10.6	10.6
Treasury shares cancelled	(1.0)	(0.7)	5.9	-	(4.2)	-
Net income recognized directly in equity	(1.0)	(0.7)	5.9	26.6	(20.2)	10.6
Profit for the year	-	-	-	-	531.2	531.2
Balance at 31 December 2006	**1,171.5**	**485.9**	**-**	**283.3**	**1,309.0**	**3,249.7**
Balance at 31 December 2006	**1,171.5**	**485.9**	**-**	**283.3**	**1,309.0**	**3,249.7**
Appropriation to statutory reserve	-	-	-	28.8	(28.8)	-
Dividends paid	-	-	-	-	(269.6)	(269.6)
Unrealized gains on available-for-sale securities	-	-	-	-	9.8	9.8
Net income recognized directly in equity	-	-	-	28.8	(288.6)	(259.8)
Profit for the year	-	-	-	-	576.5	576.5
Balance at 31 December 2007	**1,171.5**	**485.9**	**-**	**312.1**	**1,596.9**	**3,566.4**

Extract 6(11D) – HELLENIC TELECOMMUNICATIONS ORGANISATION S.A., page 132

This extract presents the consolidated statement of changes in the equity of the consolidated group.

	Attributable to equity holders of the parent								
	Share Capital	Share Premium	Treasury Shares	Legal Reserve	Consolidation Reserve	Retained Earnings	Total	Minority Interest	Total equity
Balance at 31 December 2005	**1,172.5**	**486.6**	**(5.9)**	**256.7**	**(238.8)**	**1,640.4**	**3,311.5**	**1,201.9**	**4,513.4**
Appropriation to statutory reserve	-	-	-	26.6	-	(26.6)	-	-	0.0
Dividends paid	-	-	-	-	-	-	-	(116.0)	(116.0)
Treasury shares cancelled	(1.0)	(0.7)	5.9	-	-	(4.2)	-	-	0.0
Unrealized gains on available-for-sale securities	-	-	-	-	-	10.6	10.6	-	10.6
Foreign currency translation	-	-	-	-	-	90.8	90.8	100.3	191.1
Net change in investment in subsidiaries	-	-	-	-	(341.5)	18.8	(322.7)	(118.5)	(441.2)
Net income recognized directly in equity	(1.0)	(0.7)	5.9	26.6	(341.5)	89.4	(221.3)	(134.2)	(355.5)
Profit for the year	-	-	-	-	-	574.6	574.6	156.2	730.8
Balance at 31 December 2006	**1,171.5**	**485.9**	**(0.0)**	**283.3**	**(580.3)**	**2,304.4**	**3,664.8**	**1,223.9**	**4,888.7**
Balance at 31 December 2006	**1,171.5**	**485.9**	**0.0**	**283.3**	**(580.3)**	**2,304.4**	**3,664.8**	**1,223.9**	**4,888.7**
Appropriation to statutory reserve	-	-	-	28.8	-	(28.8)	-	-	-
Dividends paid	-	-	-	-	-	(269.6)	(269.6)	(81.2)	(350.8)
Unrealized gains on available-for-sale securities	-	-	-	-	-	9.8	9.8	-	9.8
Foreign currency translation	-	-	-	-	-	(82.6)	(82.6)	(84.7)	(167.3)
Net change of investment in subsidiaries	-	-	-	-	(1953.5)	-	(1,953.5)	(145.3)	(2,098.8)
Net income recognized directly in equity	-	-	-	-	-	(371.2)	(2,295.9)	(311.2)	(2,607.1)
Profit for the year	-	-	-	-	(1953.5)	662.6	662.6	110.4	773.0
Balance at 31 December 2007	**1,171.5**	**485.9**	**0.0**	**312.1**	**(2,533.8)**	**2,595.8**	**2,031.5**	**1,023.1**	**3,054.6**

Extract 6(11E) – HELLENIC TELECOMMUNICATIONS ORGANISATION S.A., pages 134-136

The following extracts present the additional disclosure requirements required by IAS 27 for the preparation of separate financial statements.

---

1. COMPANY'S FORMATION AND OPERATIONS (in part)

Hellenic Telecommunications Organization S.A. (hereinafter referred to as the "Company" or "OTE"), was founded in 1949 in accordance with Law 1049/49, as a state-owned Société Anonyme and operates pursuant to Law 2246/94 (as amended), Law 2257/94 (OTE's Charter), Presidential Decree 437/95 and C.L. 2190/1920. OTE's main activities are to provide telecommunications and other related services.

The address of its registered office is: 99 Kifissias Avenue – 151 24 Maroussi Athens, Greece, while its website is www.ote.gr.

Company Name	Line of Business	Country	Ownership interest	
Indirect ownership			**31/12/2007**	**31/12/2006**
• ROMTELECOM S.A. ("ROMTELECOM")	Fixed line telephony services	Romania	54.01%	54.01%
• S.C. COSMOTE ROMANIAN MOBILE TELE-COMMUNICATIONS S.A. ("COSMOTE ROMANIA")	Mobile telecommunications services	Romania	79.71%	63.10%
• OTE MTS HOLDING B.V.	Investment holding company	Holland	90.72%	67.00%
• COSMOFON MOBILE TELECOMMUNICATIONS SERVICES A.D. – SKOPJE ("COSMOFON")	Mobile telecommunications services	Skopje	90.72%	67.00%
• COSMO BULGARIA MOBILE EAD ("GLOBUL")	Mobile telecommunications services	Bulgaria	90.72%	67.00%
• COSMO-HOLDING ALBANIA S.A. ("CHA")	Investment holding company	Albania	88.00%	64.99%
• ALBANIAN MOBILE COMMUNICATIONS Sh.a ("AMC")	Mobile telecommunications services	Albania	74.80%	55.24%
• COSMOHOLDING CYPRUS LTD ("COSMOHOLDING CYPRUS")	Investment holding company	Cyprus	81.65%	67.00%
• GERMANOS S.A.	Retail services	Greece	81.65%	66.35%
• E-VALUE S.A.	Marketing services	Greece	81.65%	46.44%
• GERMANOS TELECOM SKOPJE S.A.	Retail services	Skopje	81.65%	66.35%
• GERMANOS TELECOM ROMANIA S.A.	Retail services	Romania	81.64%	66.34%
• TEL SIM S.R.L	Retail services	Romania	81.65%	-
• SUNLIGHT ROMANIA S.R.L. -FILIALA	Retail services	Romania	81.64%	66.34%
• GERMANOS TELECOM BULGARIA A.D.	Retail services	Bulgaria	81.65%	66.35%
• MOBILBEEEP LTD	Retail services	Greece	81.65%	67.00%
• GRIGORIS MAVROMICHALIS & PARTNERS LTD	Retail services	Greece	80.82%	65.68%
• GEORGIOS PROKOPIS & PARTNERS LTD	Retail services	Greece	-	33.18%
• IOANNIS TSAPARAS & PARTNERS LTD	Retail services	Greece	41.64%	33.84%
• ALBATROS & PARTNERS LTD	Retail services	Greece	81.64%	-
• VOICENET A.E. ("VOICENET")	Telecommunications services	Greece	84.07%	79.52%
• OTENET CYPRUS LTD	Investment holding company	Cyprus	76.33%	70.02%
• OTENET TELECOMMUNICATIONS LTD	Telecommunications services	Greece	71.61%	67.14%
• HELLAS SAT S.A.	Satellite communications	Greece	99.05%	99.05%
• OTE INVESTMENT SERVICES S. A.	Investment holding company	Greece	100.00%	100.00%
• OTE PLUS BULGARIA	Consulting services	Bulgaria	100.00%	99.00%
• OTE PLUS ROMANIA	Consulting services	Romania	100.00%	99.00%

3. SIGNIFICANT ACCOUNTING POLICIES (in part)

1. Basis of Consolidation and Investments: (in part)

In the Separate Financial Statements, investments in subsidiaries and associates are accounted for at cost adjusted for any impairment where necessary.

---

7. INVESTMENTS (in part)

(a) Investments in Subsidiaries is analyzed as follows:

	Country	2007	2006
• COSMOTE	Greece	2,654.3	556.7
• OTE INTERNATIONAL INVESTMENTS LTD	Cyprus	497.9	497.9
• OTE AUSTRIA HOLDING GMBH	Austria	-	0.1
• HELLAS-SAT	Cyprus	194.7	194.7
• COSMO-ONE	Greece	3.2	3.2
• OTENET	Greece	32.1	24.7
• HELLASCOM	Greece	8.4	20.4
• OTE SAT- MARITEL	Greece	11.2	11.2
• OTE PLC	U.K.	35.0	-
• OTE PLUS	Greece	3.8	3.8
• OTE ESTATE	Greece	336.3	336.3
• INFOTE	Greece	-	12.4
• OTE-GLOBE	Greece	163.7	0.9
• OTE INSURANCE	Greece	0.6	0.6
• OTE ACADEMY	Greece	5.9	5.9
		3,947.1	1,668.8

(b) Other investments

The movement of Other Investments is as follows:

	COMPANY	GROUP
Balance at 1 January 2007	157.8	158.7
Other movements	-	(0.3)
Balance at 31 December 2007	**157.8**	**158.4**

OTE's Other Investments is analyzed as follows:

	2007	2006
TELEKOM SRBIJA	155.1	155.1
Other	2.7	2.5
	157.8	157.6

The Group has a participation stake to TELEKOM SRBIJA at 20%. The investment is stated at cost as the Group has no significant influence.

PLANNING FOR IMPLEMENTATION

Implementing IAS 27 would increase the complexity of preparing consolidated financial statements. Examples of issues that might contribute to such complexities concern data collection related to additional entities that must be consolidated under IFRS and additional procedures to ensure the alignment of accounting policies used by the parent company and all subsidiaries.

The adoption of IFRS 3 and IAS 27 must be planned well in advance to gather the necessary inputs. This planning is essential as the standards could:

- add to earnings volatility;
- make earnings harder to predict;
- influence acquisition negotiations and deal structures;
- impact the scope and extent of due diligence; and
- require new procedures to monitor and determine changes in the fair value of some assets and liabilities.

Initial Adoption of IFRS

IAS 27 Adoption

A first time adopter must apply the provisions of IAS 27 and consolidate all entities it controls (except where IAS 27 requires otherwise) as if the adopter had always applied this standard (except where IFRS 1 requires the prospective application of certain requirements under IAS 27).

In particular, first-time adopters must apply the following requirements of IAS 27, prospectively from the date of transition:

- total comprehensive income is attributed to the owners of the parent and to the non-controlling interests even if this results in the non-controlling interests having a deficit balance (paragraph 28 of IAS 27);

- accounting for changes in the parent's ownership interest in a subsidiary that do not result in a loss of control (paragraphs 30 and 31 of IAS 27); and

- accounting for a loss of control over a subsidiary (paragraphs 34-37 of IAS 27).

If a first-time adopter applies IFRS 3 retrospectively to a past business combination, it is required to:

- restate all subsequent business combinations; and

- apply the requirements (mentioned above, which would normally be applied prospectively) in IAS 27 (as amended in 2008) to that business combination and all subsequent business combinations.

Additional elections are available to subsidiaries and parent entities with different IFRS adoption dates.

If a subsidiary becomes a first-time adopter later than its parent does, the subsidiary should, in its financial statements, measure its assets and liabilities at either:

- the carrying amounts that would be included in the parent's consolidated financial statements, based on the parent's date of transition to IFRS, if no adjustments were made for consolidation procedures and for the effects of the business combination in which the parent acquired the subsidiary; or

- the carrying amounts required by IFRS, based on the subsidiary's date of transition to IFRS. These carrying amounts could differ from those described above:

  o when the exemptions in IFRS 1 result in measurements that depend on the date of transition to IFRS,

  o when the accounting policies used in the subsidiary's financial statements differ from those in the consolidated financial statements.

It is often beneficial, in terms of cost and efficiencies, to use the above IFRS 1 election because it minimizes consolidation complexities. Depending on the users of financial information, however, this election may not always be beneficial for the subsidiary.

If a parent becomes a first-time adopter later than its subsidiary does, the parent should, in its consolidated financial statements, measure the subsidiary's assets and liabilities at the same carrying amounts used in the subsidiary's financial statements, after making any consolidation and equity accounting adjustments and adjusting for the effects of the business combination in which the entity acquired the subsidiary. Similarly, if a parent becomes a first-time adopter for its separate financial statements earlier or later than for its consolidated financial statements, it should measure its assets and liabilities at the same amounts in both financial statements, except for consolidation adjustments.

When a first-time adopter prepares separate financial statements and chooses under IAS 27 to account for an investment in a subsidiary, jointly controlled entity or associate at cost (i.e., instead of in accordance with IAS 39), IFRS 1 requires the first-time adopter to measure that investment at one of the following amounts in its separate opening IFRS statement of financial position:

- cost determined in accordance with IAS 27; or
- deemed cost. The deemed cost of such an investment should be its:
  - o fair value (determined in accordance with IAS 39) at the entity's date of transition to IFRS in its separate financial statements, or
  - o previous GAAP carrying amount at that date.

A first-time adopter may choose either one of these deemed cost options to measure its investment in each subsidiary, jointly controlled entity or associate if it elects to measure that investment using a deemed cost.

If a first-time adopter uses a deemed cost in its opening IFRS statement of financial position for an investment in a subsidiary, jointly controlled entity or associate in its separate financial statements, the first-time adopter's first IFRS separate financial statements should disclose:

- the aggregate deemed cost of those investments for which deemed cost is their previous GAAP carrying amount;
- the aggregate deemed cost of those investments for which deemed cost is fair value; and
- the aggregate adjustment to the carrying amounts reported under previous GAAP.

IFRIC 17 Implementation

The measurement of the liability might create practical problems in cases where a choice is given between the owner receiving a non-cash asset or cash. In these cases, entities will have to gather information to evaluate the probability of each alternative being selected. This will mean considering past practices and other evidence of shareholder preferences. As shareholders' interests in such alternatives are usually very specific to their situation, this is likely to be a time-consuming exercise.

Obtaining Inputs from Personnel

It may be difficult to obtain the information necessary to ensure that all controlled entities are included in the consolidated financial statements. The IFRS approach to consolidation may result in more entities being included in consolidated financial statements, thus requiring additional data to be collected. Furthermore, IFRS requirements to maintain consistent accounting policies throughout a group and to prepare consolidated financial statements as of the same reporting dates may require significant adjustments and reconciliations to consolidation and year-end close procedures.

Adapting Performance Measures

In general, the IFRS approach leads to increased consolidation. Becoming responsible for reporting and explaining the performance of newly consolidated entities can have a fundamental impact on how a company portrays itself to key stakeholders. This can potentially affect debt covenants, financing arrangements, management's internal control certifications and other legal requirements.

Canadian companies that are significantly affected by the changes discussed in this chapter will have to communicate with users of their financial statements well in advance of the transition date to ensure that their information needs are met. Similarly, the presentation of non-controlling interests as an allocation of income instead of being deducted from it might affect bonus calculations. As well, the fact that non-controlling interests will be shown as a component within equity, instead of outside of it, might affect financial ratios. Communication is the key to ensuring these changes are understood and the costs are minimized on transition.

Optimizing Information Systems

Information systems may have to be adapted to collect data and information required from newly consolidated entities (which were previously not consolidated under Canadian GAAP) and to ensure that internal reconciliations are performed properly (i.e., when different reporting dates or different accounting principles are used). Information systems may also need to be adapted for changes in the accounting and presentation of non-controlling interests, and for changes in ownership interests. It is important to minimize cost inefficiencies by implementing such changes in advance of transition. Making these adjustments right before financial statement deadlines can result in costly inefficiencies and even errors in those statements.

Chapter 7
Investments in Associates and Interests in Joint Ventures

Standards Discussed in this Chapter

International
IAS 28 – Investments in Associates
IAS 31 – Interests in Joint Ventures
IASB ED 9 (September 2007) – Joint Arrangements
SIC-13 – Jointly Controlled Entities – Non-monetary Contributions by Venturers

Canadian
CICA 3051 – Investments
CICA 3055 – Interests in Joint Ventures
AcG-18 – Investment companies
EIC-8 – Recognition of an equity accounted investee's losses in excess of the investment
EIC-38 – Accounting by newly formed joint ventures
EIC-165 – Accounting by an investor upon a loss of significant influence

INTRODUCTION

This chapter discusses investments in associates and interests in joint ventures. Under IFRS, the term "associates" corresponds to what is known as "investments subject to significant influence" under Canadian GAAP. Both the IASB and the AcSB issued Exposure Drafts on this subject, the IASB publishing ED 9, *Joint Arrangements* in September 2007 and AcSB releasing corresponding ED *Joint arrangements* in November 2007. Both EDs refer to joint arrangements rather than interests in joint ventures.

Generally, IFRS and Canadian GAAP require similar accounting for investments in associates. IFRS currently permit the use of proportionate consolidation for accounting for interests in joint ventures but has proposed eliminating this option and requiring the use of the equity method only for jointly controlled entities. If adopted, the resulting accounting will differ significantly from current Canadian GAAP, which is expected to converge before the IFRS transition date. Some other noteworthy differences are explained throughout this chapter. More specifically, this chapter discusses the following topics for both associates and interests in joint ventures:

- definitions of relevant terms;
- accounting methods;
- presentation; and
- general disclosures.

IMPACT ON FINANCIAL STATEMENTS

Investments in Associates

Under IFRS, the term "investments in associates" corresponds to what is known as "investments subject to significant influence" under Canadian GAAP[1]. When accounting for investments in associates, the different approaches used to measure the impairment of such investments will have a significant impact on financial statements. IAS 28 may require an impairment to be recognized sooner than Canadian GAAP requires, and there might be more volatility in earnings because impairment losses could be reversed in future periods.

IAS 28 requires that an associate's accounting policies be consistent with those of its investor, and that the reporting dates do not differ by more than three months. Those requirements might have a significant impact on Canadian corporations that have investments in associates with different accounting polices or have reporting periods that vary by more than three months.

IFRS give venture capital organizations, mutual funds, unit trusts and similar entities, including investment-linked insurance funds, the choice of not applying IAS 28 requirements if on initial recognition they elected to carry their investments in associates at fair value through profit and loss.

Interests in Joint Ventures

IAS 31 currently permits the use of either the proportionate consolidation method or the equity method to account for jointly controlled entities, while CICA 3055 requires the use of proportionate consolidation only. It is likely, however, that Canadian companies will have to change the way they account for such entities in the near future because the option to use proportionate consolidation for jointly controlled entities is likely to be eliminated as both the IASB and AcSB Exposure Drafts are proposing the use of the equity method. The Exposure Drafts also require the disclosure of summarised financial information for each individually material joint venture and in total for all other joint ventures, which should mitigate the concern that presenting the interests in joint venture as a single line item of the balance sheet could result in a loss of information.

As in the case of investments in associates, venture capital organizations, mutual funds, unit trusts and similar entities, including investment-linked insurance funds, are exempted from applying IAS 31 requirements, if on initial recognition they chose to carry their interests in joint ventures at fair value through profit and loss.

ANALYSIS OF RELEVANT ISSUES

Scope

IAS 28 has to be applied in accounting for investments in associates, while IAS 31 is to be applied in accounting for interests in joint ventures. Neither standard, however, applies to investments in associates or in joint ventures held by:

- venture capital organizations; or
- mutual funds, unit trusts and similar entities including investment-linked insurance funds;

---

[1] In this chapter both terms "investments in associates" and "investments subject to significant influence" are used interchangeably.

that, on initial recognition, are designated as at fair value through profit or loss or are classified as held for trading and accounted for in accordance with IAS 39, *Financial Instruments: Recognition and Measurement*. When designated or classified as such, these types of investments should be measured at fair value in accordance with IAS 39, with changes in fair value recognized in profit or loss in the period of the change.

Venture capital organizations, venture trusts and similar entities, therefore, can choose to account for their investments in associates and interests in joint ventures as financial assets at fair value through profit and loss. Canadian GAAP offers no such choice. Instead, investment companies meeting certain criteria are required to account for any investments subject to significant influence at fair value, with changes in fair value recognized in profit or loss. AcG-18, *Investment companies* defines an investment company as one whose "primary business activity is buying, holding and selling investments."

Other interests in an associate such as loans, preferred shares and long-term receivables would form part of the investor's net investment in that associate and fall within the scope of IAS 28 if in substance they are an extension of the entity's investment in that associate. If not, they would fall under the scope of IAS 39 and would be accounted for according to this standard's requirements.

Investments in Associates

Definition

The definition of an associate is based on significant influence, which is the power to participate in the financial and operating policies of an entity. It is substantially converged with CICA 3051, which uses the term "investment subject to significant influence."

Both IAS 28 and CICA 3051 presume that an investor has significant influence if it holds 20% to 50% of the investee's voting power (if the investor holds more than 50%, control is presumed, requiring the preparation of consolidated financial statements). Under IFRS, potential voting rights that are exercisable currently or convertible are considered in assessing significant influence, which is not, however, the case under Canadian GAAP. As well, under both standards, should an investor have a substantial portion or majority ownership in an investee, that does not necessarily preclude a different investor from having significant influence over that same investee.

Equity Method

Both IAS 28 and CICA 3051 prescribe that associates are to be accounted for by the equity method, i.e., the investment is initially recognized at cost and the carrying amount is increased or decreased to recognize the investor's share of the profit or loss of the investee after the date of acquisition. The investor's share of the investee's profit or loss is recognized in the investor's profit or loss under both standards. In addition, distributions received from an investee reduce the carrying amount of the investment.

The carrying amount may need to be adjusted if an investor's proportionate interest in the investee changes because of changes in the investee's other comprehensive income. Such changes could arise from:

- the revaluation of property, plant and equipment; and
- foreign exchange translation differences.

The investor's share of those changes is recognized in other comprehensive income. Note, however, that revaluation of property, plant and equipment is not allowed under Canadian GAAP (refer to Chapter 12 for more details).

Illustrative Disclosure:

Extract 7(1) – Description of the accounting policy related to investments in associates and interests in joint ventures

---

Air France-KLM S.A. (Reference Document 2006-07), page 94

Note 3 Accounting policies (in part)

3.3.2. *Interest in associates and joint ventures*

Companies in which the Group has the ability to exercise significant influence on financial and operating policy decisions are accounted for using the equity method; the ability to exercise significant influence is presumed to exist when the group holds more than 20% of the voting rights.

In addition, companies in which the group exercises joint control related to a contractual agreement are accounted for using the equity method.

The consolidated financial statements include the group's share of the total recognized gains and losses of associates and joint ventures from the date that significant influence starts until the date that significant influence ceases, adjusted for any impairment loss. Adjustments to the carrying amount may also be necessary for changes in the investor's proportionate interest in the investee arising from changes in the investee's equity that have not been recognized in the investee's profit or loss. The investor's share of those changes is recognized directly in the Group's equity.

The Group's share of losses of an associate that exceed the value of the Group's interest and net investment (long term receivables) in this entity are not accounted for, unless:

• the Group has incurred contractual obligations; or

• the Group has made payments on behalf of the associate.

Any surplus of the investment cost over the Group's share in the fair value of the identifiable assets, liabilities and contingent liabilities of the associate company on the date of acquisition is accounted for as goodwill and included in the book value of the investment accounted for using the equity method.

The investments in which the Group has ceased to exercise significant influence or joint control are no longer consolidated and are valued at the carrying value on the date of withdrawal from the consolidation scope.

Commentary: This extract defines investments in associates and describes their accounting treatment. It mentions that significant influence is presumed to exist when the group holds more than 20% of the voting shares. It also describes the treatment of losses when an investment is already reduced to zero; this issue is discussed further below. Note that this disclosure does not contradict Canadian GAAP, except that under CICA 3055 would require that the company reports its interest in joint ventures using proportionate consolidation instead of the equity method.

Unrealized Profits and Losses

Under IFRS unrealised profits and losses on both upstream transactions (sales from the investee to the investor) and downstream transactions (sales from the investor to the investee) are eliminated to the extent of the investor's interest in the investee. Under Canadian GAAP upstream transactions with entities subject to significant influence are also eliminated to the extent of the investor's interest. However, unlike IFRS, Canadian GAAP require the elimination of 100% of unrealized profits and losses for downstream transactions.

Illustrative Disclosure:

Extract 7(2) – Unrealized profits and losses on transactions with associates

Aluminum Corporation of China Limited (Form 20-F 2006), page F-15
2. Summary of significant accounting policies (in part)
(b) Consolidation (in part)
(iv) Associates (in part)
Unrealized gains on transactions between the Group and its associates are eliminated to the extent of the Group's interest in the associates. Unrealized losses are also eliminated unless the transaction provides evidence of an impairment of the asset transferred. Accounting policies of associates have been changed where necessary to ensure consistency with the policies adopted by the Group.

A listing of the Group's associates is set out in Note 11(b) to the consolidated financial statements.

Commentary: This extract indicates that unrealized gains and losses on transactions with associates are eliminated to the extent of the Group's interest in the associates.

It also mentions consistency of accounting policies of associates with those adopted by the Group and the presentation of a listing of the associates (even though this information is not mandatory under IAS 28). Disclosures under Canadian GAAP would differ as requirements related to unrealized gains on transactions between the Group and its associates and consistency of accounting policies of associates differ.

Losses

Both IFRS and Canadian GAAP prescribe that, when an associate incurs losses, the carrying amount of the investor's interest is reduced only to the extent of the investor's interest in the associate, unless the investor has incurred a legal or a constructive obligation to fund losses or make payments on behalf of the associate. Unlike IFRS, however, EIC-8 requires a reduction of the investment value beyond its carrying value unless the investor would be unlikely to share in losses of the investee. Certain conditions stated in EIC-8 require the investor to continue recording its share of the investee losses.

Illustrative Disclosure:

Extract 7(3) – Losses incurred by an associate

Alma Media Corporation (AR 2007), page 51
Accounting principles used in the IFRS consolidated financial statements (in part)
Associated companies
Associated companies are those in which the Group has a significant controlling interest. A significant controlling interest arises when the Group holds 20% or more of the company's voting power or over which the Group otherwise is able to exercise significant control. Associated companies are consolidated using the equity method. Investments in associated companies include any goodwill arising from their acquisition. If the Group's share of the associated company's losses exceeds the book value of the investment, this investment is entered at zero value in the balance sheet and any losses in excess of this value are not recognized unless the Group has obligations with respect to the associated company. The Group's share of the results of its associated companies is shown as a separate item under operating profit.

Commentary: This extract defines associates and describes their accounting treatment. It specifies that losses are not recognized when the balance sheet amount is already at zero unless the Group has obligations in excess of its investment in the associate. The above disclosure does not contradict Canadian GAAP, except that amount of the investment could be accounted at an amount below zero (i.e., negative value) for example when a return to profitability is considered imminent.

Impairment

Under IAS 28, an investment in an associate is considered to be a single asset for the purpose of impairment testing. Accordingly, goodwill included in the carrying amount of an investment in an associate is not separately recognized under IAS 28 and any impairment in the investment in an associate is not separately allocated to the goodwill. The same principle would apply to an impairment reversal, which would be recorded if the recoverable amount of the investment in the associate subsequently increases (due to changes in the estimates made to determine the recoverable amount, not just because of the unwinding of the discount). Under Canadian GAAP, no reversal of impairment would be allowed.

In order to test impairment on an investment in an associate, an investor would apply the requirements of IAS 39 which requires that the investment be written down if its carrying amount is impaired. The investor also applies the requirements of IAS 39 to determine whether any additional impairment loss is recognized with respect to the investor's interest in the associate that does not constitute part of the net investment, such as loans or other interests, and determine the amount of that impairment loss. Because goodwill that forms part of the carrying amount of an investment in an associate is not separately recognised, it is not tested for impairment separately. Instead, the entire carrying amount of the investment is tested for impairment in accordance with IAS 36 as a single asset by comparing its recoverable amount with its carrying amount, whenever application of the requirements in IAS 39 indicates that the investment may be impaired.

Under Canadian GAAP, similar requirements would normally apply except that the investment in an associate is written down only if its carrying amount is impaired and the impairment is not considered to be temporary.

IFRS require that the impairment loss be calculated as the excess of the carrying amount above the recoverable amount. The recoverable amount is defined as the higher of two amounts: the fair value less costs to sell; and the value in use, which is calculated as the present value of future cash flows generated by the asset. An impairment loss recognized in those circumstances is not allocated to any asset, including goodwill, that forms part of the carrying amount of the investment in the associate. Accordingly, any reversal of that impairment loss is recognized in accordance with IAS 36 to the extent that the recoverable amount of the investment subsequently increases. Under Canadian GAAP, the impairment loss reflects the loss in value of an investment that is not considered to be temporary, and it is never reversed. Note that CICA 3051 is silent on how to measure the value of the investment (see chapter 4 for additional discussions on impairment).

Illustrative Disclosures:

Extract 7(4) – Impairment of investments in associates

Aluminum Corporation of China Limited (Form 20-F 2006), page F-24

2. Summary of significant accounting policies (in part)

(w) Impairment of investments in subsidiaries, jointly controlled entities, associates and non-financial assets

Assets that have an indefinite useful life are not subject to amortization and are tested annually for impairment. Assets that are subject to amortization or depreciation are reviewed for impairment or whenever events or changes in circumstances indicate that the carrying amount may not be recoverable. An impairment loss is recognized for the amount by which the asset's carrying amount exceeds its recoverable amount. The recoverable amount is the higher of an asset's fair value less costs to sell and value in use. For the purpose of assessing impairment, assets are grouped at the lowest levels for which there are separately identifiable cash flows (cash generating units). Assets other than goodwill that suffered an impairment are reviewed for possible reversal of the impairment at each reporting date.

Commentary: This extract indicates that investments in associates are tested annually for impairment. The company reviews the value of associates for which impairment was previously recognized for possible reversal of impairment The accounting policy described above would differ under Canadian GAAP as amount of impairment loss would be calculated differently and reversal of impairment reversal would be prohibited.

Severe Long-term Restrictions

Neither IFRS nor Canadian GAAP provide an exemption from equity accounting for an associate that operates under severe long-term restrictions.

Accounting Policies and Reporting Periods

Unlike CICA 3051, IAS 28 requires an associate's accounting policies to be consistent with those of its investor, and the reporting dates may not differ by more than three months. When the reporting dates of the investor and the associate do differ, the associate prepares, for the use of the investor, financial statements as of the same date as the investor's financial statements unless it is impracticable to do so. In that case, adjustments will be made for the effects of significant transactions or events that occur between the date of the associate's financial statements and the date of the investor's financial statements. Canadian GAAP does not require the uniformity of accounting policies and does not provide guidance on the consistency of reporting periods. CICA 3051 does mention, however, that when the fiscal periods are not co-terminous, events relating to, or transactions of, the investee that have occurred during the intervening period and significantly affect the investor's financial position or results of operations should be recorded or disclosed, as appropriate.

Illustrative Disclosures:

Extract 7(5) – Different reporting periods

Barclays PLC (AR 2007), page 223

41 Other entities (in part)

Entities may have a different reporting date from that of the parent of 31st December. Dates may differ for a variety of reasons including local reporting regulations or tax laws. In accordance with our accounting policies, for the purpose of inclusion in the consolidated financial statements of Barclays PLC, entities with different reporting dates are made up until 31st December.

Commentary: This extract mentions the reason why some associates have year-end dates differing from the reporting entity and that appropriate adjustments have been made to reflect transactions until that date. This extract would be considered consistent with Canadian GAAP as it provides elements of useful information.

Extract 7(6) – Different reporting periods

Astro All Asia Networks plc (AR 2007), page 105
12 INVESTMENTS ACCOUNTED FOR USING THE EQUITY METHOD (in part)
The financial statements of certain associates and jointly controlled entities are made up to different reporting dates from the Company. For the purpose of applying the equity method of accounting, the financial statements of these companies for the respective financial year end have been used, and appropriate adjustments have been made for the effects of significant transactions between that date and 31 January 2007.

Commentary: This extract mentions that some associates have year-end dates differing from the reporting entity and that appropriate adjustments for significant transactions have been made between the respective year-end dates. This illustration would be considered consistent with Canadian GAAP as it provides elements of useful information.

Investment Acquired for Subsequent Sale

Under IFRS, when an investment is acquired for the purpose of selling it later and it meets the criteria for classification as held for sale, the investment is not accounted for under the equity method. IFRS 5, *Non-current Assets Held for Sale and Discontinued Operations* would apply to those situations (refer to Chapter 12 for more detail). There is no such exemption under Canadian GAAP, and all investments in associates are accounted for under the equity method.

Loss of the Significant Influence

When an entity loses its significant influence over another entity, whether because it has reduced its participation or for another reason, both IFRS and Canadian GAAP stipulate that the investment does not qualify as an associate anymore and should be accounted for as a non-strategic investment (i.e., it is reported according to IAS 39 requirements).

Illustrative Disclosure:

Extract 7(7) – Loss of significant influence

Crucell NV (Form 20-F 2006), page 72
Financial income and expense, net (in part)
Financial expense (in part)
Crucell has two investments in Joint ventures (Pevion Biotech AG in Switzerland and Percivia LLC in the United States) and holds a 37% investment in the associated company Kenta Biotach AG in Switzerland. These investments have either been made in 2006 or result from the acquisition of Berna Biotech. The results of the companies are accounted for under the equity method and amount to a total loss of €1,956. In 2005 and 2004 losses of €455 and €704, respectively, reflected the investment in Galapagos B.V. in the Netherlands. In 2006, our holding in Galapagos decreased to 6.2% of its share capital. Since then, the investment has been treated as an available-for-sale-investment, as it no longer qualifies as an associate.

Commentary: This extract shows a reduction of an investment that qualified as an associate. Because the investor has lost its significant influence, the asset is now accounted for as an available-for-sale investment. Disclosures are consistent with Canadian GAAP.

Presentation

Investments in associates accounted for using the equity method must be classified as non-current assets under both IAS 28 and CICA 3051.

General Disclosures Related to Interests in Associates

IFRS require the following disclosures (which are not required under Canadian GAAP):

- the fair value of investments in associates for which there are published price quotations (only "useful" information under CICA 3051);
- the reasons why the presumption that an investor does not have significant influence is overcome if the investor holds, directly or indirectly through subsidiaries, less than 20% of the voting or potential voting power of the investee but concludes that it has significant influence;
- reasons why the presumption that an investor has significant influence is overcome if the investor holds, directly or indirectly through subsidiaries, 20% or more of the voting or potential voting power of the investee but concludes that it does not have significant influence;
- the reporting date of the financial statements of an associate, when those financial statements are used in applying the equity method and are as of a reporting date or for a period that is different from that of the investor, and the reason for using a different reporting date or different period;
- the nature and extent of any significant restrictions (e.g., resulting from borrowing arrangements or regulatory requirements) on the ability of associates to transfer funds to the investor in the form of cash dividends, or repayment of loans or advances;
- the unrecognized share of an associate's losses, both for the period and cumulatively, if an investor has discontinued recognition of its share of the associate's losses;
- the fact that an associate is not accounted for using the equity method in accordance with IAS 28; and
- summarized financial information of associates, either individually or in groups, that are not accounted for using the equity method, including the amounts of total assets, total liabilities, revenues and profit or loss.

Note that an IAS 28 amendment introduced in May 2008 (originally proposed in the Annual Improvement Exposure Draft issued in October 2007), reduces disclosure requirements in circumstances where an entity avails itself of the option to account for its investments in associates at fair value through profit or loss. According to this amendment, the only IAS 28 disclosure requirement under such circumstances is for the entity to specify the nature and extent of any significant restrictions on the ability of the associate to transfer funds to the entity in the form of cash, or repayment of loans or advances.

As under CICA 3051, the following are to be disclosed separately:
- the investor's share of the profit or loss of associates accounted for using the equity method;
- the carrying amount of those investments;
- the investor's share of any discontinued operations of such associates;
- summarized financial information of associates, including the aggregated amounts of assets, liabilities, revenues and profit or loss (required under CICA 3051 when the financial position and results of operations of companies subject to significant influence are important factors in evaluating the investor's financial position and results of operations).

As in Canadian GAAP, the investor has to recognize its share of the other comprehensive income of associates and disclose this information in the statement of changes in equity as required by IAS 1, *Presentation of Financial Statements*.

In accordance with IAS 37, *Provisions, Contingent Liabilities and Contingent Assets*, the investor also has to disclose:

- its share of an associate's contingent liabilities incurred jointly with other investors; and

- any contingent liabilities that arise because an investor is severally liable for all or part of an associate's liabilities.

Illustrative Disclosures:

Even though disclosures illustrated below are generally more detailed than under Canadian GAAP, information presented would not contravene Canadian GAAP.

Extract 7(8) – Disclosure of fair value of an investment in an associate

> **Diageo plc (AR 2007), page 154**
>
> **14. Investments in associates (in part)**
>
> **(b) Other associates (in part)**
>
> Included in other associates is a 17% effective interest held indirectly in Sichuan ShuiJingFang Joint Stock Co Ltd ('ShuiJingFang'), a manufacturer and distributor of Chinese white spirits, which is quoted on the Shanghai Stock Exchange. At 30 June 2007, ShuiJingFang's share price was RMB15 which valued the group's interest at £83 million.

Extract 7(9) – Disclosure of the reason why presumption of absence of significant influence is overcome

> **HSBC Holdings plc (Form 20-F 2006), page 361**
>
> HSBC's 15.98 per cent investment in Industrial Bank Company Limited was equity accounted with effect from May 2004, reflecting HSBC's significant influence over this associate. HSBC's significant influence was established as a result of representation on the Board of Directors, and in accordance with the Technical Support and Assistance Agreements, HSBC is assisting in the development of financial and operating policies.
>
> **International Power (AR 2007), page 163**
>
> **Evaluation of levels of control and influence (in part)**
>
> Where the Group owns between 20% and 50% of the equity of an entity and is in a position to exercise significant influence over the entity's operating and financial policies, we treat the entity as an associate. Equally, where the Group holds a substantial interest (but less than 20%) in an entity and has the power to exert significant influence over its operations, we also treat that entity as an associate. This treatment is applied to our interest in The Hub Power Company in Pakistan of which we own 17% (refer to note 38). Where the Group has the power to control the operations of an entity, and it has less than 50% of the equity, we treat the entity as a subsidiary when required.

Extract 7(10) – Disclosure of financial information of associates

Astro All Asia Networks plc (AR 2007), page 105
12 INVESTMENTS ACCOUNTED FOR USING THE EQUITY METHOD (in part)

	2007 RM'000	2006 RM'000
Investments		
At cost	87,615	64,081
Cumulative post tax results and impairment losses	(47,987)	(45,315)
	39,628	18,766
Long term advances, receivables and commitments in equity accounted investments		
Long term advances, receivables and commitments	320,234	147,293
Cumulative post tax results	(157,353)	–
	162,881	147,293

The Group's interest in the assets, liabilities, income and expenses of the investments in equity accounted units, is as follows:

	2007 RM'000	2006 RM'000
Non-current assets	250,475	49,260
Current assets	87,059	72,873
Current liabilities	(154,436)	(59,745)
Non-current liabilities	(147,195)	(49,373)
Net assets	35,903	13,015
Revenue	47,792	25,746
Expenses	(207,817)	(23,300)
	(160,025)	2,446

The Group has not recognised losses amounting to RM3,218,000 (2006: RM748,000) for the year. The accumulated losses not recognised were RM3,966,000 (2006: RM748,000).

Page 122

30 COMMITMENTS

(a) Capital commitments

Capital commitments contracted for at the balance sheet date but not recognised in the financial statements are as follows:

	2007 RM'000	2006 RM'000
Capital expenditure	43,004	34,031
Investment in an associate	17,351	18,706
Advances to associates	–	2,538
	60,355	55,275

Capital commitment for investment in an associate

The capital commitment for investment in TVB Publishing Holding Limited ("TVBPH") relates to the remaining payment for uncalled ordinary share capital following the acquisition on 20 August 2003 of an additional 10% of the issued ordinary share capital (of which 7.9% has been fully paid) ("Uncalled Shares"). These payments are to be settled in four tranches of HKD9,675,000 each, two of which were due for payment on 30 September 2004 and another two on 30 June 2005. As at 31 January 2007, the Group was negotiating for the deferment of the payments.

The Uncalled Shares rank pari passu in all respect with the existing shares except that the Uncalled Shares shall be credited when paid and voting rights shall accrue in proportion to the amounts paid and dividends shall be apportioned and paid pro-rata according to the amounts paid on the Uncalled Shares.

The shareholding in TVBPH will increase from 26.3% (2006: 26.3%) to 30.0% upon the full payment of the Uncalled Shares.

Extract 7(11) – Disclosure of financial information of associates

BOC Hong Kong Holdings Limited (AR 2007), page 190 30. Interests in associates (in part)	2007 HK$'m	2006 HK$'m
At 1 January	60	61
Investment cost addition	24	–
Share of result	4	6
Share of tax	(1)	(1)
Dividends received	(3)	(4)
Dissolution of an associate	(1)	–
Disposal of an associate	–	(2)
At 31 December	83	60

The Group's interests in its associates, all of which are unlisted, are as follows:

Name	CJM Insurance Brokers Limited		Joint Electronic Teller Services Limited		BOC Services Company Limited	
Place of incorporation	2007 and 2006 Hong Kong		2007 and 2006 Hong Kong		2007 PRC	
Particulars of issued share capital/ registered capital	6,000,000 ordinary shares of HK$1 each		100,238 ordinary shares of HK$100 each		Registered capital RMB50,000,000	
Principal activities	Insurance broker		Operation of a private inter-bank message switching network in respect of ATM services		Credit card back-end service support	
	2007 HK$'000	2006 HK$'000	**2007 HK$'000**	2006 HK$'000	**2007 HK$'000**	2006 HK$'000
Assets	64,331	66,807	354,104	350,912	53,677	–
Liabilities	51,815	52,772	77,593	75,615	–	–
Revenues	10,330	11,214	70,033	70,921	–	–
Profit after taxation	1,481	2,866	33,649	32,586	–	–
	2007	2006	**2007**	2006	**2007**	2006
Interest held	**33.33%**	33.33%	**19.96%**	19.96%	**45.00%**	–

Trilease International Limited completed winding up procedures on 7 April 2007. BOC Services Company Limited was established in Beijing in November 2007.

Extract 7(12) – Disclosure of equity variation of an associate

Cadbury Schweppes plc (AR & Accounts 2007), page 125
29. Capital and reserves
(b) Movements on capital and reserves

	Share capital £m	Share premium £m	Capital redemption reserve £m	Hedging and translation reserve £m	Acquisition revaluation reserve £m	Retained earnings £m	Total £m
At 1 January 2006	260	1,135	90	133	–	1,390	3,008
Currency translation differences (net of tax)	–	–	–	(413)	(3)	–	(416)
Revaluation reserve arising on acquisition of former associate	–	–	–	–	56	–	56
Disposal reversal of exchange in reserves	–	–	–	10	–	–	10
Share of associate reserve movements	–	–	–	–	–	(2)	(2)
Credit from share based payment and movement in own shares	–	–	–	–	–	48	48
Actuarial gains on defined benefit pension schemes (net of tax)	–	–	–	–	–	50	50
IAS 39 transfers to income or expense	–	–	–	(1)	–	–	(1)
Shares issued	2	36	–	–	–	–	38
Profit for the period attributable to equity holders of the parent	–	–	–	–	–	1,169	1,169
Dividends paid	–	–	–	–	–	(272)	(272)
At 31 December 2006	**262**	**1,171**	**90**	**(271)**	**53**	**2,383**	**3,688**
Currency translation differences (net of tax)	–	–	–	132	–	–	132
Unwind of acquisition revaluation reserve	–	–	–	–	(8)	8	–
Credit from share based payment and movement in own shares	–	–	–	–	–	24	24
Actuarial gains on defined benefit pension schemes (net of tax)	–	–	–	–	–	168	168
IAS 39 transfers to income or expense	–	–	–	–	–	–	–
Shares issued	2	54	–	–	–	–	56
Profit for the period attributable to equity holders of the parent	–	–	–	–	–	405	405
Dividends paid	–	–	–	–	–	(311)	(311)
At 31 December 2007	**264**	**1,225**	**90**	**(139)**	**45**	**2,677**	**4,162**

Commentary: In this extract the company presents its capital and reserves movements for 2006 including amounts that relate to its share of an associate reserve. Note that presentation under current IFRS (subsequent to IAS 1 amendment in September 2007 which is effective for periods starting January 1, 2009) and under Canadian GAAP would differ as certain of the reserves movements presented above would have to be included in the statement of comprehensive income.

Interests in Joint Ventures

Definition

Both IAS 31 and CICA 3055 define a joint venture as an entity, asset or operation that is subject to joint control established by a contractual arrangement.

Joint ventures can be structured in many different ways. IAS 31 and CICA 3055 identify three broad types of joint ventures: jointly controlled operations, jointly controlled assets and jointly controlled entities. The standards should be applied regardless of the structures or forms under which the joint venture activities take place.

Accounting Method

Jointly Controlled Operations

According to IAS 31, a party to jointly controlled operations recognizes in its financial statements:

- the assets it controls and the liabilities it incurs; and
- the expenses it incurs and its share of the income that the joint venture earns from the sale of goods or services.

CICA 3055 indicates that interests in jointly controlled operations should be recognized in the financial statements using the proportionate consolidation method and explains how that method is applied. Clearly, both standards call for the same accounting treatment. The IASB does not propose any change to this accounting method in its Exposure Draft.

Jointly Controlled Assets

IAS 31 asks that a party to jointly controlled assets recognizes in its financial statements:

- its share of the jointly controlled assets, classified according to the nature of the assets;
- any liabilities it has incurred;
- its share of any liabilities related to the joint venture incurred jointly with the other venturers;
- any income from the sale or use of its share of the output of the joint venture, together with its share of any expenses incurred by the joint venture; and
- any expenses it has incurred for its interest in the joint venture.

CICA 3055 indicates that interests in jointly controlled assets should be recognized in the financial statements using the proportionate consolidation method. Again, the same accounting treatment is required by both standards. The IASB does not propose any change to this accounting method in its Exposure Draft.

Jointly Controlled Entities

Under Canadian GAAP, CICA 3055 requires that proportionate consolidation be used for reporting an entity's participation in jointly controlled entities. As described further below, IFRS allows as specified in IAS 31 either the use of the proportionate consolidation method (i.e., aligned with Canadian GAAP) or the equity method (i.e., aligned with US GAAP). The IASB is proposing to remove the proportionate consolidation option. The AcSB has indicated its intention to converge with the proposed revised standard. Canadian entities will find the adoption of the equity method for accounting for jointly controlled entities a significant change.

When applying the proportionate consolidation method as required by IAS 31, an entity may:

- combine its share of each of the assets, liabilities, income and expenses of the jointly controlled entity with the similar items, line by line, in its financial statements (e.g., it may combine its share of the jointly controlled entity's inventory with its inventory, and its share of the jointly controlled entity's property, plant and equipment with its own property, plant and equipment), or alternatively;
- include separate line items for its share of the jointly controlled entity's assets, liabilities, income and expenses in its own financial statements (e.g., it may show its share of a current asset of the jointly controlled entity separately as part of its own current assets; it may show its share of the property, plant and equipment of the jointly controlled entity separately as part of its own property plant and equipment).

Valuation of Assets Contributed by Joint Ventures

EIC-38 specifies that the accounting by a joint venture for the assets contributed by the joint venturer can be measured in one of three ways commonly used in practice. Such specific guidance does not exist under IFRS.

Transactions between a Venturer and a Joint Venture

Both IFRS and Canadian GAAP require that when a venturer contributes or sells assets to a joint venture, recognition of any portion of a gain or loss from the transaction reflect the substance of the transaction. While a joint venture retains the assets, a venturer recognizes only that portion of the gain or loss attributable to the interests of the other venturers, as long as it has transferred the significant risks and rewards of ownership. The full amount of any loss is recognized when there is evidence of a reduction in net realizable value or an impairment loss. Under Canadian GAAP, however, when a contributing venturer receives cash or other assets that do not represent a claim on the assets of the joint venture, only the portion of the gain that relates to the amount of cash received, or the fair value of the other assets received, should be taken to income at the time of the transfer. Any remaining portion of the gain should be deferred and amortized to income in a rational and systematic manner over the life of the contributed asset.

Non-monetary Contributions by Venturers

SIC-13 indicates that the portion of a gain or loss attributable to the equity interests of the other venturers should be recognized, unless that portion is considered unrealized, i.e., when the significant risks and rewards of ownership of the contributed non-monetary asset(s) have not been transferred to the jointly controlled entity, the gain or loss cannot be measured reliably, or the contribution transaction lacks commercial substance. There is no concept of gain deferral based on the cash received as there is under CICA 3055 (see discussion below).

Unrealized gains or losses on non-monetary assets contributed to jointly controlled entities should be eliminated from the underlying assets under the proportionate consolidation method or from the investment under the equity method. Such unrealized gains or losses should not be presented as deferred gains or losses on the venturer's consolidated balance sheet.

Under Canadian GAAP, when joint venturers are not related parties prior to the transfer of non-monetary assets to a joint venture, the transaction will be measured at fair value if the transfer has commercial substance and is reliably measurable as per CICA 3831, *Non Monetary Transactions*. When venturers are related, the transaction should be recorded in accordance with CICA 3840, *Related Party Transactions*. In all cases, CICA 3055, requires that any loss or gain be recognized only to the extent of the interests of the other non-related venturers. However, only the portion of the gain that relates to the amount of cash received or the fair value of the other assets received should be taken to income at the time of the transfer. Any remaining portion of the gain should be deferred and amortized to income over the life of the contributed assets.

Illustrative Disclosure:

Extract 7(13) – Non-monetary contributions by venturers

Alcatel-Lucent (AR on Form 20-F 2006), page F-118

Note 38 - Summary of differences between accounting principles followed by Alcatel-Lucent and U.S. GAAP (in part)

(a) Differences in accounting for business combinations

Contribution of Space businesses by Alcatel and Alenia to two jointly controlled joint ventures

As described in Note 3 to the financial statements, on July 1, 2005, Alcatel and Finmeccanica announced the creation of two joint ventures that had been described in a memorandum of understanding signed by the parties on June 24, 2004: Alcatel Alenia Space (Alcatel holds 67% and Finmeccanica 33%) and Telespazio Holding (Finmeccanica holds 67% and Alcatel 33%). These joint ventures are jointly controlled, as defined by IAS 31 *Joint Ventures* and are therefore consolidated using the proportionate method of consolidation starting July 1, 2005.

Under IFRS, in accordance with the guidance provided by SIC 13 *Jointly Controlled Entities — Non-Monetary Contributions by Venturers*, the recognition of any portion of a gain or loss from the transaction shall reflect the substance of the transaction. While the assets are retained by the joint venture, and provided the venturer has transferred the significant risks and rewards of ownership, the venturer shall recognise only that portion of the gain or loss that is attributable to the interests of the other venturers. Therefore a gain related to the contributed business was accounted for amounting to €129 million as of December 31, 2005.

Under U.S. GAAP, contributing assets to a joint venture does not usually result in the culmination of the earnings process. However, similar to the guidance in Statement of Position 78-9, *Accounting for Investments in Real Estate Ventures*, when cash is paid to one of the joint venturers in order to balance the fair market value of assets contributed by each venturer, gain recognition is allowed insofar as such gain is limited to the lesser of the computed gain or the amount of cash received, provided the recipient has no refund or continuing support obligation. As indicated in Note 3, Alcatel received from Finmeccanica a payment of €109 million upon creation of the joint venture.

Further, the gain on contributed assets differs under U.S. GAAP from the gain accounted for under IFRS due to differences between the net book value of the contributed assets under both standards, mainly related to the amortization of goodwill (see Note 38b) and accounting treatment of pensions (see Note 38f). As a consequence of the above, the gain related to the contributed business accounted for under U.S. GAAP in 2005 amounts to €72 million.

Commentary: This extract explains the accounting treatment, pointing out that only the portion of the gain or loss that is attributable to the interests of the other venturers is recognized. In addition, it illustrates the IFRS and Canadian GAAP difference related to the amount of gain recognition (i.e., limited to the amount of cash received) where in this case US and Canadian GAAP are aligned.

Unrealized Profits and Losses

Under both IFRS and Canadian GAAP, unrealized profits and losses on transactions with jointly controlled entities are eliminated to the extent of the investor's interest in the investee.

Losses

Since IFRS provide an option to account for joint ventures using the equity method, the same guideline applies as for losses of an associate, i.e., when an associate incurs losses, the carrying amount of the investor's interest is reduced, but not below zero unless the investor has an obligation to fund losses. Since CICA 3055 requires the use of proportionate consolidation, this issue is not covered, and not relevant in that standard.

Severe Long-term Restrictions

Under CICA 3055, when an investor ceases to have joint control over a jointly controlled enterprise (for example, when severe long-term restrictions are imposed on the ability of the jointly controlled enterprise to distribute its earnings to the venturers), the investor ceases to proportionately consolidate its interest. Such interests are accounted for as investments subject to significant influence (equity accounting) or as a non strategic investment to be accounted according to CICA 3855, *Financial instruments — Recognition and Measurement*, as appropriate. Amounts reported on a proportionate consolidation basis for periods prior to the cessation of proportionate consolidation are not retroactively restated on a non-consolidated basis.

Under IFRS, there is no exemption from proportionate consolidation for a jointly controlled entity that operates under severe long-term restrictions, but IAS 31 does mention that a venturer should discontinue the use of the proportionate consolidation from the date on which it ceases to have joint control over, or have significant influence in, a jointly controlled entity.

Accounting Policies and Reporting Periods

A jointly controlled entity's accounting policies must be consistent with those of its investor, and the reporting dates may not differ by more than three months, as mentioned in the IAS 31 "Basis for conclusions." CICA 3055 does not require the uniformity of accounting policies and does not provide guidance on the consistency of reporting periods.

Illustrative Disclosure:

Extract 7(14) – Accounting policy

> **Crucell N.V. (Form 20-F 2006), page F-11**
> **1 General information (in part)**
> **1.4 Basis of consolidation**
> *Joint ventures*
> A joint venture is a contractual arrangement whereby two or more parties undertake an economic activity that is subject to joint control. A jointly controlled entity is a joint venture that involves the establishment of a separate entity in which each venturer has an interest. The Group recognizes its interest in joint ventures using the equity method. Under the equity method, the investment in the joint venture is carried in the balance sheet at cost plus post-acquisition changes in the Group's share of net assets of the associate. The income statement reflects the share of the results of operations of the associate. Periodically the Group determines whether it is necessary to recognize an impairment loss with respect to the Group's net investment in the joint venture.
>
> The reporting dates of the joint ventures are the same as those of the Group and the accounting policies of the joint ventures conform to those used by the Group.

Commentary: In this extract the company specifies that it accounts for its interest in joint ventures using the equity method and describes certain aspects when applying that method. This accounting method differs from that required under Canadian GAAP as proportionate consolidation has to be used when reporting investments in joint ventures.

Investments Acquired for Subsequent Sale

Under IFRS, when an investor invests in a jointly controlled entity for the purpose of its subsequent disposal and meets the criteria for classifying the investment as held for sale as specified in IFRS 5, *Non-current Assets Held for Sale and Discontinued Operations*, which is discussed in Chapter 12, neither the proportionate consolidation nor the equity method is used to account for the investment. The accounting for investments held for sale would be very similar under CICA 3055 and IFRS 5. The provisions of CICA 3475, *Disposal of Long-lived Assets and Discontinued Operations* would apply if the interest to be disposed of meets that *Handbook* section's criteria for being classified as held for sale. Otherwise, CICA 3055 requires that an interest in a jointly controlled enterprise intended for disposal would continue to be proportionately consolidated in the financial statements of the venturer until such time as the venturer ceases to have joint control over the jointly controlled enterprise.

General Disclosures Related to Interests in Joint Ventures

Aggregated Financial Information

CICA 3055 requires disclosure of the total amounts and the major components of each of the following joint venture items:

- current assets and long-term assets;
- current liabilities and long-term liabilities;
- revenues and expenses;
- net income;
- cash flows resulting from operating activities, from financing activities and from investing activities.

IAS 31 does not require the same disclosures. It requires disclosure of the first three items only for an interest in a jointly controlled entity not accounted for by the separate line item format (versus format that combines similar items) under proportionate consolidation.

Commitments and Contingencies

Both standards have similar requirements for the disclosure of a venturer's share of any contingencies and commitments (only capital commitment required in IAS 31) of joint ventures, as well as any contingencies that exist when the venturer is contingently liable for the liabilities of the other venturers of the joint ventures. IAS 31 also requires the disclosure of any contingent liabilities and capital commitments that a venturer has incurred for its interests in a joint venture.

Description of Interests in Joint Ventures

IAS 31 requires that a venturer disclose a listing and description of interests in significant joint ventures and the proportion of ownership interest held in jointly controlled entities. This information is desirable under CICA 3055.

Note that an IAS 31 amendment introduced in May 2008 (originally proposed in the Annual Improvements Exposure Draft issued in October 2007), reduces disclosure requirements in circumstances where an entity avails itself of the option to account for its investments in joint ventures at fair value through profit or loss. According to this amendment, the IAS 31 disclosure requirements are limited to (1) the commitments of the venturer and the joint venture and (2) the summary information about assets, liabilities, income and expenses.

Illustrative Disclosures:

Extract 7(15) – Disclosure of aggregated financial information of investments in joint ventures

Diageo plc (AR 2007), page 104

15 Investments in joint ventures

The group consolidates its attributable share of the results and net assets of joint ventures on a line-by-line basis, measured according to the terms of the arrangements. The group's principal joint ventures that are consolidated on a proportional basis are as follows:

	Country of incorporation	Country of operation	Percentage of equity owned	Principal activities
Don Julio BV	Netherlands	Mexico	50%	Production, marketing and distribution of premium drinks
Guinness Anchor Berhad	Malaysia	Malaysia	50%	Production, marketing and distribution of premium drinks
Moët Hennessy Diageo (China) Co Ltd	China	China	50%	Marketing and distribution of premium drinks
MHD Diageo Moët Hennessy KK . . .	Japan	Japan	50%	Marketing and distribution of premium drinks

In addition, the group consolidates on a proportional basis a number of other joint ventures involved in the production, marketing and distribution of premium drinks in Europe, South Africa and the Far East.

Included in the consolidated financial statements are the following amounts that represent the group's interest in the results and assets and liabilities of joint ventures:

	2007 £ million	2006 £ million	2005 £ million
Sales	479	428	365
Operating costs	(449)	(394)	(334)
Profit before tax	30	34	31

	2007 £ million	2006 £ million
Non-current assets	74	84
Current assets	208	190
Total assets.	282	274
Current liabilities.	(89)	(76)
Non-current liabilities	(68)	(84)
Total liabilities	(157)	(160)
Net assets	125	114

Alcatel-Lucent (AR 2006 on Form 20-F), page F-56

Note 16 - Share in net assets of equity affiliates and joint ventures

(d) Aggregated financial information for joint ventures

Aggregated financial information for the Group's share in the net assets of joint ventures proportionately consolidated (Alcatel Alenia Space, Telespazio, Evolium and Alda Marine in 2006 and 2005 and Alda Marine and Evolium in 2004) are as follows:

(in millions of euros)	2006	2005	2004
Balance sheet data			
Non-current assets[1]	57	1,314	209
Current assets[1]	1,723	773	6
Shareholders' equity	776	983	90
Other non-current liabilities[1]	—	135	47
Current liabilities[1]	1,004	969	78
Income statement data			
Revenues	—	2	9
Cost of sales	28	79	65
Income (loss) from operating activities before restructuring, impairment of intangible assets and capital gain on disposal of consolidated entities	21	3	(1)
Income (loss) from discontinued operations[2]	39	47	—
Net income (loss) attributable to equity holders of the parent	56	44	(5)
Cash flow statement data			
Net cash provided (used) by operating activities	28	51	60
Net cash provided (used) by investing activities	(26)	(60)	(53)
Net cash provided (used) by financing activities	(3)	9	(9)
Net cash provided (used) by operating activities of discontinued operations[2]	134	29	—
Net cash provided (used) by investing activities of discontinued operations[2]	(26)	(2)	—
Net cash provided (used) by financing activities of discontinued operations[2]	(110)	2	—

(1) *Aggregated financial information for Alcatel Alenia Space and Telespazio for 2006 are reported as assets held for sale (included in current assets) and liabilities related to disposal groups held for sale (included in current liabilities) (see Notes 3 and 10).*

(2) *Aggregated financial information for Alcatel Alenia Space and Telespazio only relates to six months of activity in 2005 and full year 2006 and has been reported as discontinued operations (see Note 3 and Note 10).*

Commentary: These extracts illustrate the disclosure of the aggregated financial information related to interests in joint ventures. As can be observed, not only are the required elements disclosed, but so are additional elements related to net income and cash flows. This presentation would be consistent with Canadian GAAP.

Extract 7(16) – Disclosure listing and describing interests in significant joint ventures

British Sky Broadcasting Group plc (AR 2007), page 81

30. Group investments (in part)

The significant investments of the Company which principally affect the consolidated results and total assets of the Group are as follows:

Name	Country of incorporation/ operation	Description and proportion of shares held (%)	Principal activity
Joint ventures and associates			
Nickelodeon UK	England and Wales	104 B Shares of £0.01 each (40%)	The transmission of children's television channels
The History Channel (UK)	England and Wales	50,000 A Shares of £1 each (50%)	The transmission of history and biography television programming
Paramount UK[(ii),(iii)]	England and Wales	Partnership interest (25%)	The transmission of general entertainment comedy channels
Australian News Channel Pty Limited	Australia	1 Ordinary Share of AUS$1 (33.33%)	The transmission of a news channel
MUTV Limited[(iv)]	England and Wales	800 B Shares of £1 each (33.33%)	The transmission, production and marketing of the Manchester United football channel
National Geographic Channel[(v)]	England and Wales	Partnership interest (50%)	The transmission of natural history and adventure channels
Attheraces Holdings Limited[(iii)]	England and Wales	1,500 Ordinary Shares of £1 each (47.50%), 20 Recoupment Shares of £0.01 each	The transmission of a horse racing channel and related on-line activities
Chelsea Digital Media Limited	England and Wales	42,648 B Shares of £0.01 each (35%) and 7m redeemable preference shares of £1 each	The transmission, production and marketing of the Chelsea Football Club football channel and website

Commentary: This extract illustrates the disclosure of listing and describing interest of significant interests in joint ventures and associates. This presentation would be consistent with Canadian GAAP.

FUTURE DEVELOPMENTS

Joint Ventures

In September 2007, the IASB issued Exposure Draft ED 9, *Joint Arrangements* (with a comment period that expired January 2008) that proposes removing the option of using proportionate consolidation for accounting for interests in jointly controlled entities and requiring the use of the equity method only. It does not propose any changes to the accounting for jointly controlled operations or jointly controlled assets. In November 2007, the AcSB issued corresponding Exposure Draft *Joint arrangements*, proposing the same revisions. The comment period also ended January 2008.

At the April 2008 IASB Meeting, comment letters received in response to the ED9 were discussed. There are differences in how many respondents have assessed the likely effect of the proposals in ED9 and how the IASB assessed the implications. On that basis, many respondents disagreed with the removal of the proportionate consolidation method. A final standard is expected in the second quarter of 2009.

COMPREHENSIVE EXAMPLES

This section presents two comprehensive disclosure examples. The first one, Extract 7 A and Extract 7 B illustrate investments in associates and interests in joint ventures respectively.

Extract 7A – Investments in Associates

The first comprehensive example shows relevant extracts of a financial statement presenting investments in associates.

Air France-KLM S.A. – All extracts 7A illustrate investments in associates and were obtained from the company's Reference document (annual report) for the year ended March 31, 2007.

Extract 7(A1) – Air France-KLM S.A., page 85

The consolidated income statements provide a distinct presentation for the "Share of profits (losses) of associates."

Year ended March 31, 2007 **Consolidated income statements (in part)**				
(In euro millions) **Period from April 1 to March 31**	**Notes**	**2007**	**2006**	**2005**
Income before tax		*1,118*	*1,200*	*1,697*
Income taxes	12	(248)	(256)	(133)
Net income of consolidated companies		**870**	**944**	*1,564*
Share of profits (losses) of associates	20	17	(23)	73
Net income from continuing operations		**887**	**921**	*1,637*
Net income from discontinued operations	13.1	-	-	59
Net income for the period		**887**	**921**	**1,696**
Group		891	913	1,710
Minority interest		**(4)**	**8**	**(14)**

Extract 7(A2) – Air France-KLM S.A., page 86

This extract shows "Investments in equity associates" presented in the non-current assets on the consolidated balance sheets.

Consolidated balance sheets (in part)				
Assets *(In euro millions)*	**Notes**	**March 31, 2007**	**March 31, 2006**	**March 31, 2005**
Goodwill	15	**204**	**208**	**205**
Intangible assets	16	424	428	437
Flight equipment	18	**11,551**	**11,017**	**10,394**
Other property, plant and equipment	18	2,007	1,955	1,895
Investments in equity associates	20	**228**	**204**	**577**
Pension assets	21	2,097	1,903	1,767
Other financial assets *(which includes €835 million of deposits related to financial leases as of March 31, 2007, €895 million as of March 31, 2006 and €875 million as of March 31, 2005)*	22	1,095	1,182	1,113
Deferred tax assets	12.5	26	7	140
Other non-current assets	25	604	1,082	336
Total non-current assets		18,236	17,986	16,864

Extract 7(A3) – Air France-KLM S.A., page 94

This extract shows Air France's note 3, *Accounting policies*, which provides various disclosures about investments in associates, including:

- a definition of interest in associates;
- a description of the equity method, including treatment of impairment losses;
- the gains and losses realized on internal sales with associates;
- the closing dates of the financial statements of the associates.

Note 3 Accounting policies

3.3.2. *Interest in associates and joint ventures*

Companies in which the Group has the ability to exercise significant influence on financial and operating policy decisions are accounted for using the equity method; the ability to exercise significant influence is presumed to exist when the group holds more than 20% of the voting rights.

In addition, companies in which the group exercises joint control related to a contractual agreement are accounted for using the equity method.

The consolidated financial statements include the group's share of the total recognized gains and losses of associates and joint ventures from the date that significant influence starts until the date that significant influence ceases, adjusted for any impairment loss. Adjustments to the carrying amount may also be necessary for changes in the investor's proportionate interest in the investee arising from changes in the investee's equity that have not been recognized in the investee's profit or loss. The investor's share of those changes is recognized directly in the Group's equity.

The Group's share of losses of an associate that exceed the value of the Group's interest and net investment (long term receivables) in this entity are not accounted for, unless:

- the Group has incurred contractual obligations; or
- the Group has made payments on behalf of the associate.

Any surplus of the investment cost over the Group's share in the fair value of the identifiable assets, liabilities and contingent liabilities of the associate company on the date of acquisition is accounted for as goodwill and included in the book value of the investment accounted for using the equity method.

The investments in which the Group has ceased to exercise significant influence or joint control are no longer consolidated and are valued at the carrying value on the date of withdrawal from the consolidation scope.

3.3.3. *Intragroup operations*

All intragroup balances and transactions, including income, expenses and dividends are eliminated in full. Profits and losses resulting from intragroup transactions that are recognized in assets are eliminated in full.

Gains and losses realized on internal sales with associates and joint control entities are eliminated, to the extent of the Group's interest in the associate or joint control entity, only when they do not represent an impairment.

3.3.4. *Closing date*

With the exception of a few non-significant subsidiaries and equity affiliates that close their books on December 31, all Group companies are consolidated based on annual financial statements closing March 31.

Extract 7(A4) – Air France-KLM S.A., pages 131-134

This extract explains the variation in the investments in associates and discloses financial information on associates.

(In euro millions)	WAM Acquisition (Amadeus GTD)	Alpha Plc	Martinair	Kenya Airways	Other	Total
Note 20 Equity affiliates						
Movements over the period						
The table below presents the movement in equity affiliates:						
Value of share in investment as at March 31, 2004	287	31	-	-	21	**339**
Share in net income of equity affiliates	50	3	9	9	2	73
Distributions	(8)	(2)	-	-	-	(10)
Changes in consolidation scope	-	-	146	22	7	175
Transfers and reclassifications	-	2	-	-	-	2
Currency translation adjustment	-	(2)	-	-	-	(2)
Value of share in investments as of March 31, 2005	329	32	155	31	30	**577**
Share in net income of equity affiliates	14	4	(59)	15	3	(23)
Distributions	-	(3)	(1)	(2)	(1)	(7)
Changes in consolidation scope	-	-	-	-	5	5
First application of IAS 32 and 39	(30)	-	-	-	-	(30)
Amadeus transaction	(313)	-	-	-	-	(313)
Transfers and reclassifications	-	-	(3)	5	(5)	(3)
Currency translation adjustment	-	-	-	-	(2)	(2)
Value of share in investment as of March 31, 2006	-	33	92	49	30	**204**
Share in net income of equity affiliates	-	-	(7)	11	13	17
Distributions	-	(3)	-	-	(1)	(4)
Change in consolidation scope	-	-	-	-	18	18
Transfers and reclassifications	-	-	(1)	-	(2)	(3)
Currency translation adjustment	-	-	-	-	(4)	(4)
Value of share in investment as of March 31, 2007	-	30	84	60	54	**228**

As of March 31, 2007, the ownership structure of WAM Acquisition is as follows: 22.08% Air France, 11.04% Iberia, 11.04% Lufthansa, 50.34% Amadelux Investments and 5.5% by the management. The ownership structure of Alpha plc is as follows: 27% Servair; the other shareholders are mainly institutional investors. The KLM and P&O Nedlloyd groups each held 50% of the capital of Martinair.

KLM held 26% of the capital of Kenya Airways.

During the Year ended March 31, 2007, the WAM General Shareholders' Meeting, held on March 28, 2007, decided on a dividend distribution of €68 million. The Group's share amounts to €16 million and has been recorded in "Other non-current income and expenses".

As of March 31, 2006, the ownership structure of WAM Acquisition was as follows: 23.4% Air France, 11.7% Iberia, 11.7% Lufthansa and 53.2% Amadelux Investments.

As of March 31, 2005, Air France-KLM owned a 23.36% interest in Amadeus, a Spanish company, which was accounted for as an equity method investment.

In July 2005, private equity funds (the "financial investors") structured a leveraged buy out of Amadeus whereby WAM Acquisition S.A. ("WAM"), a newly created and highly leveraged company tendered all Amadeus class A and class B shares in cash. Air France-KLM's portion of the total price paid in cash by the financial investors was €1,022 million at the date of the transaction.

Note 20 Equity affiliates (continued)

Simultaneously, Air France-KLM and the financial investors entered into an investing agreement, whereby Air France-KLM invested €129 million in common stock of WAM (which represented an identical stake that it had in Amadeus, i.e. 23.36%). Additionally, Air France-KLM agreed to provide a shareholder loan to WAM for an amount of €76 million. Such loan is subordinated to the senior credit agreement, bears interest and matures in 2020. There were no other equity instruments issued by WAM.

Beyond the investment and shareholder loan in WAM, the Group has not guaranteed any debt or entered into any "make-well agreements" that may require it to infuse cash into WAM under any circumstances.

Based on the above-described terms of the transaction, Air France-KLM considered that it contributed its historical stake (23.36%) in Amadeus to WAM for an identical stake in WAM plus a net cash distribution, WAM being the same company as Amadeus, only more leveraged. The Group's economic interest in the Amadeus business was not reduced. Therefore, the Group accounted for the transaction as the receipt of a large distribution from an equity affiliate, with no reduction in ownership. Consistent with IFRS, such distribution was first reflected as a reduction of the carrying value of WAM. The amount of distribution in excess of the carrying value of WAM was then recognized as income as WAM's distribution is not refundable by agreement or law and Air France-KLM is not liable for the obligations of the equity affiliate or otherwise committed to provide financial support to the affiliate.

The gain recognized by the Group during the year ended March 31, 2006 was computed as follows (in euro millions):

Cash received from WAM	1,022
Investment in cash for WAM Equity	(129)
Shareholders' loan in cash	(76)
Equity investment in Amadeus before the transaction	(313)
Gain recognized	**504**

Additionally, the Group did not recognize its earnings in WAM following the leveraged buy out transaction. The Group will resume recognizing its share of earnings in WAM in accordance with IAS 28 only when Air France-KLM's share of WAM's cumulative net income equals the gain recognized in the transaction.

The ownership structure of Alpha plc was as follows: 27% by Servair; the other shareholders were mainly institutional investors.

The KLM and P&O Nedlloyd groups each held 50% of the capital of Martinair. An impairment charge has been recorded on the Group's investment in Martinair for an amount of €59 million recorded in "Share of profits (losses) of associates".

KLM held 26% of the capital of Kenya Airways.

As of March 31, 2005, Air France held 23.4% of Amadeus GTD, Iberia 18.3%, Lufthansa 5% and the general public 53.3%. Amadeus was listed for trading on a regulated market and the market value of Amadeus shares owned by the Group amounted to €1,003 million.

The ownership structure of Alpha plc was as follows: 27% by Servair; the other shareholders were mainly institutional investors.

The KLM and P&O Nedlloyd groups each held 50% of the capital of Martinair.

KLM held 26% of the capital of Kenya Airways.

Simplified financial statements of the main equity affiliates

The equity affiliates as of March 31, 2007 mainly concerned the following companies, in which the Group has a significant influence:

* **WAM Acquisition**
  WAM Acquisition is the holding company of the Amadeus group. The Amadeus group develops booking tools and technology solutions dedicated to business and leisure travels. This expertise makes it the global partner of choice for: travel agents, rail and airlines operators, hotel chains, car rental companies. Furthermore, the Amadeus group also partners businesses involved in the reservation and management of business travel.

Note 20 Equity affiliates (continued)

- **Alpha Airport PLC (group publishing consolidated financial statements)**
  The Alpha Airports group provides retail and catering services for airlines and airports. The group operates over 200 retailing and catering outlets in 83 airports in 15 countries across five continents. The group's inflight catering business offers a comprehensive range of catering logistics, flight catering and management services for over 100 airlines.

- **Martinair (group publishing consolidated financial statements)**
  Located in the Netherlands, Martinair's core business is the air transport of passengers and freight out of Amsterdam.

- **Kenya Airways**
  Kenya Airways is a Kenyan airline based in Nairobi.

The financial information for the principal equity affiliates for the years ended March 31, 2005, 2006 and 2007 (excluding consolidation adjustments) is presented below.

(In euro millions)	WAM Acquisition (Amadeus GTD) 12/31/2004	Alpha Plc 01/31/2005	Martinair 12/31/2004	Kenya Airways 03/31/2004
% holding as of March 31, 2005	23.4%	26.2%	50.0%	25.0%
Operating revenues	2,057	715	959	313
Operating income	343	22	23	28
Net income	208	13	13	13
Stockholder's equity as of March 31, 2005	942	62	318	89
Total assets	**1,675**	**243**	**682**	**310**
Total liabilities and stockholder's equity	**1,675**	**243**	**682**	**310**
	07/31/2005 (one month)	01/31/2006	12/31/2005	03/31/2005
% holding as of March 31, 2006	23.4%	26.1%	50.0%	25.0%
Operating revenues	180	807	1,121	464
Operating income	(68)	30	22	73
Net income/loss	(89)	20	17	43
Stockholders' equity as of March 31, 2006	21	62	322	122
Total assets	**5,252**	**294**	**710**	**465**
Total liabilities and stockholders' equity	**5,252**	**294**	**710**	**465**
	12/31/2006 (5 months)	01/31/2007	12/31/2006	03/31/2006
% holding as of March 31, 2007	22.1%	26.0%	50.0%	25.0%
Operating revenues	1,076	830	1,236	580
Operating income	47	12	(17)	90
Net income/loss	(80)	5	(13)	53
Stockholders' equity as of March 31, 2007	(156)	61	281	197
Total assets	**5,577**	**288**	**703**	**791**
Total liabilities and stockholders' equity	**5,577**	**288**	**703**	**791**

Other information

The share of WAM Acquisition's loss that has not been recorded in the Group's consolidated financial statements amounted to €(18) million for the year ended March 31, 2007. Given the negative net equity after neutralization of the sum reinvested by the Air France-KLM group, its contribution to the consolidated financial statements is nil.

The closing date for the WAM Acquisition financial statements has changed. The duration of the financial year ended December 31, 2006 is, thus, five months. The loss of the previous year ended July 31, 2006 amounted to €(116) million, corresponding to a Group share of €(26) million.

Note 20 Equity affiliates (continued)			
Carrying value of listed equity affiliates			
The carrying value of the Group's stakes in listed equity affiliates is as follows at March 31, 2007:			
(In euro millions)	% interest	Net value	Market value*
Alpha Plc	26%	30	47
Kenya Airways	25%	60	130
* Based on stock price as of March 31, 2007.			

Extract 7(B) – Interests in Joint Ventures

The second comprehensive example presents relevant extracts illustrating interests in joint ventures.

British Sky Broadcasting Group plc – All extracts 7B illustrate interests in joint ventures and were obtained from the Annual Report for the year ended June 30, 2007.

Extract 7(B1) – British Sky Broadcasting Group plc, page 52

This extract shows the distinct presentation of the "Share of results of joint ventures and associates" in the consolidated income statements.

Consolidated Income Statement for the year ended 30 June 2007	Notes	2007 £m	2006 £m	2005 £m
Revenue	2	4,551	4,148	3,842
Operating expense	3	(3,736)	(3,271)	(3,020)
Operating profit		815	877	822
Share of results of joint ventures and associates	14	12	12	14
Investment income	4	46	52	29
Finance costs	4	(149)	(143)	(87)
Profit on disposal of joint venture	5	—	—	9
Profit before tax	6	724	798	787
Taxation	8	(225)	(247)	(209)
Profit for the year		499	551	578
Earnings per share from profit for the year (in pence)				
Basic	9	28.4p	30.2p	30.2p
Diluted	9	28.2p	30.1p	30.2p
The accompanying notes are an integral part of this consolidated income statement.				

Extract 7(B2) – British Sky Broadcasting Group plc, page 53

The consolidated balance sheet shows that "Investments in joint ventures and associates" are presented in the non-current assets.

Consolidated Balance Sheet as at 30 June 2007 (in part)	Notes	2007 £m	2006 £m
Non-current assets			
Goodwill	11	741	637
Intangible assets	12	261	218
Property, plant and equipment	13	670	519
Investments in joint ventures and associates	14	34	28
Available-for-sale investments	15	797	2
Deferred tax assets	16	54	100
		2,557	1,504

Extract 7(B3) – British Sky Broadcasting Group plc , page 55

This is an extract of Note 1, *Accounting policies*, which provides a description of the accounting treatment for joint ventures, including:

- a definition of joint ventures;
- a description of the equity method used for joint ventures, indicating also the treatment of impairment losses; and
- a description of the accounting method used when the disposal of interests in joint ventures is highly probable.

---

1. Accounting policies
c) Basis of consolidation
ii. Associates and joint ventures

Associates are entities where the Group has significant influence, but not control or joint control, over the financial and operating policies of the entity. Joint ventures are those entities which are jointly controlled by the Group under a contractual agreement with another party or parties.

These consolidated financial statements include the Group's share of the total recognised gains and losses of associates and joint ventures using the equity method, from the date that significant influence or joint control commences to the date that it ceases, based on present ownership interests and excluding the possible exercise of potential voting rights, less any impairment losses (see accounting policy j). When the Group's interest in an associate or joint venture has been reduced to nil because the Group's share of losses exceeds its interest in the associate or joint venture, the Group only provides for additional losses to the extent that it has incurred legal or constructive obligations to fund such losses, or where the Group has made payments on behalf of the associate or joint venture. Where the disposal of an investment in an associate or joint venture is considered to be highly probable, the investment ceases to be equity accounted and, instead, is classified as held for sale and stated at the lower of carrying amount and fair value less costs to sell.

Extract 7(B4) – British Sky Broadcasting Group plc, page 57

This extracts explains that impairments of interests in joint ventures are accounted for within the share of the profit of the joint ventures.

---

1. Accounting policies
j) Impairment

At each balance sheet date, in accordance with IAS 36 "Impairment of Assets", the Group reviews the carrying amounts of all its assets excluding inventories (see accounting policy g), non-current assets classified as held for sale, financial assets (see accounting policy h) and deferred taxation (see accounting policy p) to determine whether there is any indication that any of those assets have suffered an impairment loss.

An impairment, other than an impairment of an investment in a joint venture or associate, is recognised in the income statement whenever the carrying amount of an asset or its cash generating unit exceeds its recoverable amount. An impairment of an investment in a joint venture or associate is recognised within the share of profit from joint ventures and associates. The recoverable amount is the greater of net selling price, defined as the fair value less costs to sell, and value in use. In assessing value in use, the estimated future cash flows are discounted to their present value using a pre-tax discount rate that reflects current market assessments of the time value of money and risks specific to the asset. Where it is not possible to estimate the recoverable amount of an individual asset, the Group estimates the recoverable amount of the cash generating unit to which the asset belongs. Impairment losses recognised in respect of cash generating units are allocated first to reduce the carrying amount of any goodwill allocated to those units, and then to reduce the carrying amount of other assets in the unit on a pro-rata basis.

An impairment loss for an individual asset or cash generating unit shall be reversed if there has been a change in estimates used to determine the recoverable amount since the last impairment loss was recognised and is only reversed to the extent that the asset's carrying amount does not exceed the carrying amount that would have been determined, net of depreciation or amortisation, if no impairment loss had been recognised. Any impairment loss in respect of goodwill is irreversible.

Extract 7(B5) – British Sky Broadcasting Group plc, pages 66 and 67

This extract discloses the movements in joint ventures and associates during the year, which is not mandatory. There is also a disclosure of the Group's share of different components of the financial statement of the joint ventures.

14. Investments in joint ventures and associates

A list of the Group's significant investments in joint ventures and associates, including the name, country of incorporation and proportion of ownership interest is given in note 30 to the consolidated financial statements.

The movement in joint ventures and associates during the year was as follows:

	2007 £m	2006 £m
Share of net assets:		
At 1 July	28	23
Movement in net assets		
— Funding, net of repayments	3	2
— Dividends received	(9)	(7)
— Share of profits	12	12
Transfers to subsidiaries	—	(1)
Movement in other payables	—	(1)
At 30 June	34	28

The Group's share of any capital commitments and contingent liabilities of associates and joint ventures is shown in note 26.

a) Investments in joint ventures

Representing the Group's share of each joint venture:

	2007 £m	2006 £m
Non-current assets	4	2
Current assets	59	51
Current liabilities	(28)	(28)
Non-current liabilities	(1)	(3)
Shareholders' equity	34	22
Revenue	74	70
Expense	(60)	(56)
Taxation	(2)	(2)
Share of profit from joint ventures	12	12

Extract 7(B6) – British Sky Broadcasting Group plc, page 81

This extract lists and describes the interests in significant investments, including interests in joint ventures.

---

30. Group investments

The significant investments of the Company which principally affect the consolidated results and total assets of the Group are as follows:

Name	Country of incorporation/ operation	Description and proportion of shares held (%)	Principal activity
Subsidiaries:			
Direct holdings of the Company			
British Sky Broadcasting Limited	England and Wales	10,000,002 ordinary shares of £1 each (100%)[i]	Operation of a pay television broadcasting service in the UK and Ireland
Sky Television Limited	England and Wales	13,376,982 ordinary shares of £1 each (100%)	Holding company
Sports Internet Group Limited	England and Wales	38,432,302 ordinary shares of £0.05 each (100%)	Holding company
British Interactive Broadcasting Holdings Limited	England and Wales	651,960 ordinary shares of £1 each (100%)	The transmission of interactive services
BSkyB Investments Limited	England and Wales	100 ordinary shares of £1 each (100%)	Holding company
Sky Holdings Limited	England and Wales	100 ordinary shares of £1 each (100%)	Holding company
BSkyB Finance UK plc	England and Wales	50,000 ordinary shares of £1 each (100%)	Finance company
Subsidiaries:			
Indirect holdings of the Company			
Sky Subscribers Services Limited	England and Wales	3 ordinary shares of £1 each (100%)	The provision of ancillary functions supporting the pay television broadcasting operations of the Group
Sky In-Home Service Limited	England and Wales	1,576,000 ordinary shares of £1 each (100%)	The supply, installation and maintenance of satellite television receiving equipment
Hestview Limited	England and Wales	108 ordinary shares of £1 each (100%)	Licensed bookmakers
Sky Interactive Limited	England and Wales	3 ordinary shares of £1 each (100%)	The provision of interactive television services
Sky Ventures Limited	England and Wales	912 ordinary shares of £1 each (100%)	Holding company
British Sky Broadcasting SA	Luxembourg	12,500 ordinary shares of £12 each (100%)	Satellite transponder leasing company
Sky New Media Ventures Limited	England and Wales	12,500 ordinary shares of £1 each (100%)	Holding company
Easynet Group Limited	England and Wales	121,308,490 ordinary shares of £0.04 each (100%)	Provision of Broadband networking services in the UK and Europe
365 Media Group Plc[vi]	England and Wales	151,970,072 ordinary shares of £0.01 each (100%)	Holding company
BSkyB Publications Limited	England and Wales	2 ordinary shares of £1 each (100%)	The supply of magazines
Sky Broadband SA	Luxembourg	310 ordinary shares of £100 each (100%)	Provision of broadband services
Joint ventures and associates			
Nickelodeon UK	England and Wales	104 B Shares of £0.01 each (40%)	The transmission of children's television channels
The History Channel (UK)	England and Wales	50,000 A Shares of £1 each (50%)	The transmission of history and biography television programming
Paramount UK[ii],[iii]	England and Wales	Partnership interest (25%)	The transmission of general entertainment comedy channels
Australian News Channel Pty Limited	Australia	1 Ordinary Share of AUS$1 (33.33%)	The transmission of a news channel
MUTV Limited[iv]	England and Wales	800 B Shares of £1 each (33.33%)	The transmission, production and marketing of the Manchester United football channel
National Geographic Channel[v]	England and Wales	Partnership interest (50%)	The transmission of natural history and adventure channels
Attheraces Holdings Limited[iii]	England and Wales	1,500 Ordinary Shares of £1 each (47.50%), 20 Recoupment Shares of £0.01 each	The transmission of a horse racing channel and related on-line activities
Chelsea Digital Media Limited	England and Wales	42,648 B Shares of £0.01 each (35%) and 7m redeemable preference shares of £1 each	The transmission, production and marketing of the Chelsea Football Club football channel and website

30. Group investments (continued)

Name	Country of incorporation/ operation	Description and proportion of shares held (%)	Principal activity
Investments			
ITV	England and Wales	696,046,825 ordinary shares of £0.10 each (17.9%)	The transmission of free-to-air channels

Notes

(i) 50.00001% directly held by British Sky Broadcasting Group plc and 49.99999% held indirectly by BSkyB Investments Limited.

(ii) The registered address of Paramount UK is 180 Oxford Street, London, W1D 1DS.

(iii) These entities accounting reference date is 31 December.

(iv) MUTV Limited accounting reference date is 30 September.

(v) The registered address of National Geographic Channel is Grant Way, Isleworth, Middlesex, TW7 5QD.

(vi) Subsequent to the purchase of 365 Media by the Group, the company changed its accounting reference date from 31 December to 30 June.

PLANNING FOR IMPLEMENTATION

This chapter has covered most of the IAS 28 and IAS 31 requirements and noted significant differences with corresponding Canadian GAAP. This section discusses measures to consider when implementing these standards.

Initial Adoption of IFRS

The exemption for prior business combinations provided in IFRS 1 also applies to prior acquisitions of investments in associates and to prior interests in joint ventures. Entities may elect, at the transition date, to not apply IAS 28 and IAS 31 retrospectively to investments made before the date of transition to IFRS. The business combination exemption should be applied consistently to acquisitions of subsidiaries, investments in associates and interests in joint ventures. The date selected for the retrospective application applies equally for all such acquisitions. Refer to Chapter 5 for more details on the business combinations exemption.

IAS 28 and IAS 36 require an impairment to be recognized when the recoverable amount of an asset is less than the carrying amount, rather than when there is a significant or prolonged decline in value to below the carrying amount. Canadian companies should review the values of their investments accordingly.

When a first-time adopter accounts for an investment in associate or joint venture for the first time as a result of applying IAS 28 or IAS 31 (for example, because such investments were not regarded as an investment in an associate or joint venture) it would measure the assets and liabilities at the same carrying amounts as in the separate IFRS financial statements of the associate or joint venture, after adjusting for consolidation and equity accounting adjustments. If the associate or joint venture has not adopted IFRS in its financial statements, the carrying amounts are those that IFRS would require in those financial statements.

Finally, since IFRS permit (or might require) the reversal of an impairment losses when the recoverable amount changes, Canadian companies should review any investments that have been impaired in the past for possible reversals.

Obtaining Inputs from Personnel and Adapting Information Systems

Because IFRS mandate that an associate's and a jointly controlled entity's accounting policies be consistent with those of its investor, Canadian entities will need to review their accounting policies and adjust them if there are any differences. This may require additional training of staff and reconciliations as part of the accounting/consolidation process and year-end close.

They will also need to validate the year-end date of the associates and jointly controlled entities because reporting dates should not differ by more than three months.

If Canadian GAAP has not converged with IFRS at the transition date, Canadian companies might need to change their policy for accounting for jointly controlled entities. It will be important to obtain a good understanding of the structure of interests in joint venture since the accounting treatment will differ depending on whether they are jointly controlled entities, jointly controlled operations or jointly controlled assets.

Chapter 8
Investment Property

Standards Discussed in this Chapter

International

IAS 16 – Property, Plant and Equipment
IAS 17 – Leases
IAS 40 – Investment Property
SIC-15 – Operating Leases – Incentives
IFRS 5 – Non-current Assets held for Sale and Discontinued Operations

Canadian

CICA 3061 – Property, Plant and Equipment
CICA 3065 – Leases
CICA 3475 – Long-lived Assets and Discontinued Operations

INTRODUCTION

IAS 40 is a wide-ranging standard that covers investment property consisting of land or buildings used (whether by the owner or under a finance lease) to earn rental income, for capital appreciation or both. All entities holding such property could be affected by this standard, which:

- distinguishes between investment property and owner-occupied property by noting that the former generates cash flows largely independently of an enterprise's other assets;

- establishes rules for reporting investment property that differ from those applicable to other properties an entity might have (such as owner-occupied property);

- allows entities to choose to carry investment property at either: cost (net of depreciation and impairment, as required for owner-occupied property reported under IAS 16) or fair value (with changes in fair values recorded in the income statement, which differs from the revaluation model used under IAS 16 – see Chapter 12); and

- mandates that entities disclose additional information, including the fair value of investment property carried at cost and reconciliations of amounts of investment property reported on the balance sheet.

One of the objectives of IAS 40 was to address concerns about the pertinence of depreciating real estate properties held as investments.

Under Canadian GAAP, all real estate properties, whether held for investment or own use, have to be accounted for according to CICA 3061 requirements. The only exception is for investment companies as defined by AcG-18, *Investment Companies*, which must carry their real estate investment properties at fair value. All other companies are not allowed to measure these properties at fair value. Consequently, entities adopting IAS 40 will have to decide whether they want to measure their investment properties using the fair value model. Using this model might have a significant impact on their financial statements. In addition, irrespective of the valuation model chosen, the fair value of all investment properties has to be established since disclosure of that value is required when an entity opts for the cost model.

IAS 40 contains new concepts and requirements not addressed by Canadian GAAP. To help evaluate these concepts and requirements, this chapter discusses the following topics:

- key definitions;
- scope;
- initial recording and incurred costs:
  o recognition,
  o initial measurement,
  o subsequent expenditures;
- subsequent measurement:
  o principle,
  o fair value model,
  o cost model;
- special contexts and considerations:
  o investment property held under a lease,
  o investment property under construction or development,
  o ancillary services provided,
  o multipurpose property (part of the property is owner occupied),
  o property occupied by an associated company or joint venture;
- transfers (reclassifications):
  o accounting for transfers – general requirements,
  o transfers from owner-occupied property and self constructed property,
  o other change of use and redevelopment of investment property;
- disposals (derecognition).

IMPACT ON FINANCIAL STATEMENTS

The adoption of IAS 40 may have a major impact on financial statements of entities holding investment property as defined by that standard. Entities operating in the real estate industry (including listed and privately held corporations, investment funds, partnerships and trusts) should be the most concerned about the new requirements.

IAS 40 implementation should enhance the relevance of financial statements, particularly when investment property is measured at fair value, because:

- income statements would combine revenues and movements in the fair value of investment property, providing a comprehensive perspective of an entity's performance over the year;
- balance sheets would reflect current values instead of cost incurred years or decades ago, increasing gross assets and having the following consequences:
  o better reflection of an entity's actual financial strength,
  o decrease in the debt/equity ratio,
  o reduction in return on net assets, and
  o reduction in gains realized on property disposals.

ANALYSIS OF RELEVANT ISSUES

This section examines and illustrates some relevant issues related to IAS 40 requirements that are based on the presumption that the fair values of investment properties are relevant to users of financial statements.

To avoid unnecessary repetition when analyzing certain extracts, we will not refer to Canadian GAAP. The general comments below concerning IFRS/Canadian GAAP differences might apply to all of the extracts presented in this section:

Scope

- Contrary to Canadian GAAP (which do not contain any mention of investment property), IFRS have a specific standard on this asset category. Consequently, under Canadian GAAP, specifically CICA 3061, investment property is accounted for as property, plant and equipment unless it meets the criteria for classification as "held for sale" under CICA 3475.

- IAS 40 allows the classification of real estate property held by a lessee under an operating lease as investment property if certain criteria are met. Under Canadian GAAP, no operating lease can be recognized on the balance sheet.

Subsequent Measurement

- IAS 40 allows an entity to measure all of its investment property using either the fair value model (subject to limited exceptions) or the cost model. When the fair value model is chosen, any gains or losses resulting from the revaluation of investment property are recognized in income. CICA 3061 requires investment property to be measured according to the cost model.

- IAS 40 mandates the disclosure of the fair value of investment property when it is reported at cost. No such requirement exists under Canadian GAAP.

Special Contexts and Considerations

- Some properties comprise a portion that is held to earn rentals or for capital appreciation and another portion that is held for use in the production or supply of goods or services or for administrative purposes. If these portions could be sold separately (or leased out separately under a finance lease), an entity accounts for the portions separately. If the portions could not be sold separately, the property is investment property only if an insignificant portion is held for use in the production or supply of goods or services or for administrative purposes. Under Canadian GAAP, the entire dual-use property is classified as property, plant and equipment to be accounted for according to CICA 3061.

- Under IAS 40, a lessor classifies leaseholds for which it provides ancillary services as investment property when those services are a relatively insignificant component of the arrangement as a whole. Under Canadian GAAP, ancillary services provided by a lessor do not affect the treatment of the leasehold property.

Transfers

- Under IAS 40, transfers to or from investment property can be made only when there has been a change in the use of the property. The intention to sell an investment property without redevelopment does not justify reclassification from investment property into inventory. Under Canadian GAAP, investment property is accounted for as property, plant and equipment, so there are no provisions concerning transfers between an "investment property" category and property, plant and equipment (own-used category). Transfers from property, plant and equipment to inventory would presumably be done at carrying value, while transfers of property, plant and equipment to the "held for sale" category would result in gains or losses as required by CICA 3475.

Key Definitions

IAS 40 provides the following key definitions:

Investment property is property (land or a building – or part of a building – or both) held (by the owner or by the lessee under a finance lease) to earn rentals, or for capital appreciation, or both, rather than for:

(a) use in the production or supply of goods or services or for administrative purposes; or

(b) sale in the ordinary course of business.

Owner-occupied property is property held (by the owner or by the lessee under a finance lease) for use in the production or supply of goods or services or for administrative purposes.

A property interest held by a lessee under an operating lease may be classified and accounted for as investment property if, and only if, the property would otherwise meet the definition of an investment property and the lessee uses the fair value model for measuring the asset recognized. This classification alternative is available on a property-by-property basis. Once this classification alternative is selected for one such property interest held under an operating lease, all property classified as investment property must be accounted for using the fair value model.

These definitions have no relevance when reporting under Canadian GAAP since Canadian GAAP does not allow properties held by an entity for rental or capital appreciation to be accounted for differently than other properties and does not allow a lessee in an operating lease to account for the property leased at fair value. All properties are accounted for as any other property, plant and equipment (i.e., in accordance with CICA 3061) and all leases are accounted for under CICA 3065.

A property interest held by a lessee under an operating lease may be classified and accounted for as investment property provided that the:

* property meets the definition of investment property;
* operating lease is accounted as a finance lease in accordance with IAS 17; and
* lessee uses the IAS 40 fair value model for the asset recognized.

The classification alternative for leases is available on a property-by-property basis. But, because IAS 40 requires all investment property to be consistently accounted for by using the fair value or cost model, once this classification alternative is selected for one such property, all property classified as investment property has to be accounted for consistently on a fair value basis (see subsequent measurement discussion presented later in this chapter).

IAS 40 differentiates investment property (which generates cash flows largely independently of an enterprise's other assets) from an owner-occupied one (which earns revenues in combination with other assets normally in the production or supply process). IAS 40 describes the following as examples of investment property:

* land held for the purpose of selling it when the price is high (i.e., land is held for long-term capital appreciation rather than for short-term sale in the ordinary course of business);
* any building an entity owns or holds under a finance lease and then leases out under an operating lease;

- vacant buildings held to be leased under operating lease;
- land held for undecided future use (e.g., an entity has not determined that it will use the land as owner-occupied property or for short-term sale in the ordinary course of business); and
- property that is being constructed or developed for future use as investment property.

Note that judgement is needed to determine whether a property qualifies as investment property. An entity must develop criteria so that it can exercise that judgement consistently in accordance with the definition of investment property and with the related guidance contained in IAS 40. Entities must disclose these criteria when classification is difficult.

Scope

IAS 40 only covers investment property as defined, not all real estate properties that an entity might hold or lease for different purposes. The table below outlines the standards and a summary of measurement requirements that apply to real estate properties commonly reported in financial statements:

Categories of Real Estate Property	Applicable Standard	Measurement Model IFRS/Canadian GAAP
Owner-occupied property (held for use in the production of goods or services)	IAS 16	*Initial amount*: Cost *Subsequent amount*: Entity may use the cost model or the revaluation model (see Chapter 12) • Under the cost model, property is carried at cost less any accumulated depreciation and any accumulated impairment losses. • Under the revaluation model, property is carried at fair value at the date of the revaluation less any subsequent accumulated depreciation and subsequent accumulated impairment losses.
	CICA 3061	*Initial amount*: Basically same as IFRS. *Subsequent amount*: Only cost model is allowed.
Investment property (held to earn rentals or for capital appreciation)*	IAS 40	*Initial amount*: Cost. *Subsequent amount*: Entity may choose to use cost model or fair value model.
	CICA 3061	*Initial amount*: Basically same as IFRS. *Subsequent amount*: Only cost model is allowed.
Property under construction (Owner occupied)	IAS 16	*Initial amount*: Cost (could include finance cost as required by IAS 23, *Borrowing costs*). *Subsequent amount*: Entity may choose to use cost model or alternatively the revaluation model.
	CICA 3061	*Carrying amount*: Only cost model is allowed. Initial amount could be different since there are no specific requirements concerning finance cost capitalization.
Property under construction (Investment property)*	IAS 40	*Initial amount*: Cost (could include finance cost as required by IAS 23, *Borrowing costs*). *Subsequent amount*: Entity may choose to use cost model or alternatively fair value model (if fair value can be measured reliably).
	CICA 3061	*Carrying amount*: Only cost model is allowed. Initial amount could be different since there are no specific requirements concerning finance cost capitalization.
* See more detailed analysis provided later in this chapter.		

Categories of Real Estate Property	Applicable Standard	Measurement Model IFRS/Canadian GAAP
Property held under an operating lease classified as an investment property*	IAS 40	*Initial amount*: Leasehold interest accounted for as a finance lease under IAS 17 (lower of fair value and the present value of the minimum lease payments). (In practice, only the present value of the minimum lease payments would have to be calculated since fair value of the property held under an operating lease would normally be significantly higher than the discounted minimum lease payments). *Subsequent amount*: Leasehold interest measured at fair value.
	CICA 3065	Operating leases are off balance sheet items.
Property held under a finance lease*	IAS 17 IAS 16 or IAS 40	*Initial amount*: The lower of fair value and the present value of the minimum lease payments. *Subsequent amount*: Leasehold interest measured at fair value or cost (if investment property) or as required by IAS 16 (if owner-occupied).
	CICA 3065	Lease accounting should be used.
Property intended to be sold in the normal course of business (Inventories – see Chapter 11)	IAS 2 (Scoped out of IAS 40)	*Initial amount*: Cost incurred in bringing the inventory to its proper condition. *Subsequent amount*: The lower of cost and net realizable value (estimated selling price in the ordinary course of business less the estimated cost of completion and the estimated costs necessary to make the sale).
	CICA 3031	*Initial and subsequent amounts*: Same as IFRS.
Property held for sale (not in the normal course of business – see Chapter 12)	IFRS 5	*Carrying amount*: Lower of carrying amount and fair value less costs to sell.
	CICA 3475	*Carrying amount*: Same as IFRS.
Property part of a construction contract (Work in progress – see Chapter 11)	IAS 11	*Carrying amount*: Progress stage of contract completion or cost.
	CICA 3400	*Carrying amount*: Basically same as IFRS.
* See more detailed analysis provided later in this chapter.		

As the above table shows, several real estate properties are excluded from the scope of IAS 40. In addition to the exclusions indicated in the table, IAS 40 scopes out land containing biological assets, mineral rights, the exploration for and extraction of minerals, oil, natural gas and similar non-regenerative resources.

Illustrative Disclosures:

Extract 8(1) – Scope and valuation issues

Aviva plc (AR 2007), page 120
Accounting policies (in part)
(O) property and equipment (in part)

Owner-occupied properties are carried at their revalued amounts, which are supported by market evidence, and movements are taken to a separate reserve within equity. When such properties are sold, the accumulated revaluation surpluses are transferred from this reserve to retained earnings. These properties are depreciated down to their estimated residual values over their useful lives. All other items classed as property and equipment within the balance sheet are carried at historical cost less accumulated depreciation.

Investment properties under construction are included within property and equipment until completion, and are stated at cost less any provision for impairment in their values.

(P) Investment property

Investment property is held for long-term rental yields and is not occupied by the Group. Completed investment property is stated at its fair value, which is supported by market evidence, as assessed by qualified external valuers or by local qualified staff of the Group in overseas operations. Changes in fair values are recorded in the income statement in net investment income.

Commentary: In this extract, the company discloses its accounting policy for owner-occupied properties. Note that these properties are accounted for using the revaluation model and, as required by IAS 16, any movements in fair values (other than impairment and its reversal) are included in a separate section of equity (accumulated other comprehensive income).

All other items classified as property and equipment within the balance sheet are carried at historical cost less accumulated depreciation. Consequently, the company measures all fixed assets other than investment properties at cost.

Investment properties under construction are included within property and equipment until completion, and are stated at cost less any provision for impairment. This is in line with IFRS for periods that preceded January 1, 2009. The company could have early adopted IASB standard entitled *Improvements to International Financial Reporting Standards 2008*. This would have compelled it to measure property under construction at fair value (since company elected to carry all other investment properties using the fair value model as indicated in the above extract), presuming that the fair value of the property under construction can be measured reliably (see discussions on investment property under construction or development).

Note also that the company uses the services of qualified valuers to establish fair value of local properties only. The valuation of overseas properties is established internally, which might raise concerns over measurement uncertainties.

Extract 8(2) – Scope

A & J Mucklow Group plc (AR 2007), page 37 Consolidated Balance Sheet (in part)	Notes	2007 £000	2006 £000
Non-current assets			
Investment and development properties	10	**286,768**	257,406
Property, plant and equipment	11	**1,726**	1,602
Trade and other receivables	12	**370**	366
		288,864	259,374
Current assets			
Trading properties	13	**921**	1,282
Held for sale assets	14	**—**	—
Trade and other receivables	15	**4,306**	2,685
Cash and cash equivalents		**1,252**	11,065
		6,479	15,032
Total assets		**295,343**	274,406

A & J Mucklow Group plc (AR 2007), page 54 13 Trading properties	2007 £000	2006 £000
Land stock	**921**	1,282

14 Held for sale assets	2007 £000	2006 £000
Antiques	**—**	—

The held for sale assets represent antiques previously used as office furnishings in our Haden Cross offices. Following the relocation of the Group's head office in June 2006, a number of the antiques were put into storage for disposal at auction in the year ended 30 June 2007. A profit of £0.06m was made in the year.

The antiques had been written off in full in the accounts in prior years.

Commentary: In this extract, the company presents separately different categories of properties and other assets: investment properties (including those under development), own-use property (included with property, plant and equipment), trading properties (inventories) and held for sale assets (related to furnishings on properties).

Extract 8(3) – Scope

Skanska AB (AR 2007), page 82
Note 01 Consolidated accounting and valuation principles (in part)
IAS 40, "Investment Property"
Skanska reports no investment properties. Properties that are used in the Group's own operations are reported in compliance with IAS 16, "Property, Plant and Equipment." The Group's holdings of current-asset properties are covered by IAS 2, "Inventories" and thus fall outside the application of IAS 40, "Investment Property."

Commentary: In this extract, the company states that it does not hold investment property. Such a statement is not specifically required by IAS 40 and was only occasionally observed.

Extract 8(4) – Scope and valuation of various properties

A&J Mucklow Group plc (AR 2007), page 43
1 Accounting policies (in part)
Valuation of properties

Investment properties are valued at the balance sheet date at open market value. Where investment properties are being redeveloped the property continues to be treated as an investment property. Surpluses and deficits attributable to the Group arising from revaluation are recognised in the income statement. Valuation surpluses reflected in retained earnings are not distributable until realised on sale.

Properties under development, which were not previously classified as investment properties, are valued at open market value until practical completion, when they are transferred to investment properties. Valuation surpluses and deficits attributable to properties under development are taken to revaluation reserve until completion, when they are transferred to retained earnings. Where the valuation is below historic cost, the deficit is recognised in the income statement.

Owner-occupied properties are valued at the balance sheet date at open market value. Valuation changes in owner occupied property are taken to revaluation reserve.

Trading properties held for resale are stated at the lower of cost and net realisable value.

Commentary: Here, the company explains how it accounts for various properties, including investment properties, properties under development, owner-occupied properties and trading properties.

Extract 8(5) – Scope

UBS AG (AR 2007), page 32
17) Property and equipment (in part)
Classification for own-used property

Own-used property is defined as property held by the Group for use in the supply of services or for administrative purposes, whereas investment property is defined as property held to earn rental income and/or for capital appreciation. If a property of the Group includes a portion that is own-used and another portion that is held to earn rental income or for capital appreciation, the classification is based on whether or not these portions can be sold separately. If the portions of the property can be sold separately, they are separately accounted for as own-used property and investment property. If the portions cannot be sold separately, the whole property is classified as own-used property unless the portion used by the Group is minor. The classification of property is reviewed on a regular basis to account for major changes in its usage.

Property held for sale

Non-current property formerly own-used or leased to third parties under an operating lease and equipment the Group has decided to sell are classified as non-current assets held for sale and recorded in Other assets. Upon classification as held for sale, they are no longer depreciated and are carried at the lower of book value or fair value less costs to sell. Foreclosed properties and other properties classified as current assets are included in Properties held for sale and recorded in Other assets. They are carried at the lower of cost and net realizable value.

Investment property

Investment property is carried at fair value with changes in fair value recognized in the income statement in the period of change. UBS employs internal real estate experts to determine the fair value of investment property by applying recognized valuation techniques. In cases where prices of recent market transactions of comparable properties are available, fair value is determined by reference to these transactions.

page 110
Note 38 Swiss Banking Law Requirements (in part)
4. Investment property

Under IFRS, investment properties are carried at fair value, with fair value changes reflected in profit or loss.

Under Swiss law, investment properties are carried at amortized cost less impairment unless the investment properties are held for sale. Investment properties held for sale are recorded at the lower of cost or market value.

Commentary: The company describes the difference between own-used property and investment property. It also describes dual-use property (examined later in this chapter). Note that the company indicates that it reviews the classification of property on a regular basis to account for major changes in its usage.

The extract also describes the category of property held for sale (accounted according to IFRS 5) and other properties classified as current assets that are valued at the lower of cost and net realizable value.

Finally, the extract indicates that the company values investment property at fair value, which differs from the requirements under Swiss law that:

- investment properties be carried at amortized cost less impairment unless the investment properties are held for sale;
- investment properties held for sale be recorded at the lower of cost or market value.

These two requirements are in line with current Canadian GAAP.

Initial Recording and Incurred Costs

Recognition

According to IAS 40, an investment property is recognized as an asset when:

- it is probable that the future economic benefits associated with the investment property will flow to the entity; and
- the cost of the investment property can be measured reliably.

This principle of recognition meets the general requirement for the recording of any asset under both IFRS and Canadian GAAP.

Initial Measurement

An investment property is initially recorded at cost, which corresponds to the fair value of the consideration given at acquisition. The cost of an investment property is equal to:

- its purchase price plus any directly attributable expenditure, including professional fees for legal services, property transfer taxes and other transaction costs;
- its fair value at the date of acquisition if it is acquired at no cost or for a nominal amount; or
- lower of fair value and present value of minimum lease payments (as required by IAS 17 for a finance lease) if it is held under a lease classified as an investment property. (Leaseholds of investments property are covered later in this chapter);
- if payment for an investment property is deferred, its cost is the cash price equivalent. The difference between this amount and the total payments is recognized as interest expense over the period of credit.

The initial measurement at cost for an investment property (other than leaseholds) is generally in line with the one applied for property, plant and equipment acquisition prescribed by IAS 16 and CICA 3061.

There are restrictions for capitalizing certain costs on initial recognition of investment property:

- External transaction costs relating to the acquisition of an investment property are generally included in the carrying amount of the investment property while internal transaction costs are expensed as incurred.
- The cost of an investment property excludes start-up costs (unless they are necessary to bring the property to its working condition), initial operating losses incurred before the investment property achieves the planned level of occupancy

and abnormal amounts of wasted material, labour or other resources incurred in constructing or developing the property. Such costs must be expensed.

Subsequent Expenditures

Often, costs are incurred after a property's acquisition to add to, replace part of, or service the property. As required by IAS 40, such subsequent expenditures should be recognized in the carrying amount of the investment property if:

- they are expected to produce future economic benefits to the entity; and
- their costs can be reliably measured.

The costs of the regular servicing of the investment property (i.e., repairs and maintenance) are expensed as incurred. Entities holding investment property may pay surrender premiums or break-up costs to their tenants to remove them from the property before the expiry of their lease. If, subsequent to the removal of an old tenant, an investment property is either re-let or undergoes extensive redevelopment, the cost paid for surrender is expensed as incurred.

The capitalization criteria of subsequent expenditure on investment property are similar to those under IAS 16 and CICA 3061 (see Chapter 12).

Illustrative Disclosures:

Extract 8(6) – Initial measurement and subsequent expenditures

BOC Hong Kong Holdings Limited (AR 2007), pages 111 and 112
2. Summary of significant accounting policies (in part)
2.17 Investment properties (in part)
Investment properties are recognised initially at cost, including related transaction costs. ...
Subsequent expenditure is charged to the asset's carrying amount only when it is probable that future economic benefits associated with the item will flow to the Group and the cost of the item can be measured reliably. All other repairs and maintenance costs are expensed in the income statement during the financial period in which they are incurred.

Commentary: In this extract, the company provides some of the general criteria for recognition, initial measurement and subsequent treatment of repairs and maintenance costs.

Extract 8(7) – Initial measurement

A&J Mucklow Group plc (AR 2007), page 43
1 Accounting policies (in part)
Cost of properties
An amount equivalent to the total development outgoings, including interest, attributable to properties held for development is added to the cost of such properties. A property is regarded as being in the course of development until Practical Completion.

Interest associated with direct expenditure on investment properties, which are undergoing development or major refurbishment and development properties is capitalised. Direct expenditure includes the purchase cost of a site or property for development properties, but does not include the original book cost of investment property under development or refurbishment. Interest is capitalised gross from the start of the development work until the date of practical completion, but is suspended if there are prolonged periods when development activity is interrupted. The rate used is the rate on specific associated borrowings or, for that part of the development costs financed out of general funds, the average rate.

Commentary: In this extract, the company explains its capitalization of finance costs, which meets the requirements of IAS 23, *Borrowing costs.*

Subsequent Measurement

Principle

Accounting Choices

Subsequent to initial recognition, IAS 40 allows an entity to carry its investment property at fair value (with changes in fair value recognized in income) or at depreciated historical cost (less impairment losses).

More specifically, an entity may:

a) choose either the fair value model or the cost model for *all* of its investment properties backing liabilities that pay a return linked directly to the fair value of, or returns from, specified assets, including that investment property; and

b) choose either the fair value model or the cost model for all other investment properties, (regardless of the choice made in a).

IAS 40 requires an entity to disclose:

- whether it applied the fair value model or the cost model; and
- whether and under what circumstances it applied the fair value model (as required by IAS 40) to property interests held under operating leases.

When an entity chooses the cost model, it must disclose the fair values of its investment properties. Given this requirement, all entities will have to determine the fair value of their investment property irrespective of the measurement model they adopt.

Generally, entities will select the fair value model to provide relevant information on their performance. Using the cost model results in measuring an investment property in accordance with IAS 16 (at amounts that do not represent current values), unless the property meets the criteria to be classified as held for sale (in which case, it would be measured at fair value less costs to sell in accordance with IFRS 5).

The ability to choose the fair value model is the main significant difference between Canadian GAAP and IAS 40 in reporting investment property. Under Canadian GAAP, such property has to be measured at cost. In addition, there are no requirements under Canadian GAAP to disclose investment property fair values as this requirement applies only to financial assets and financial liabilities.

Consistency

IAS 40 requires an entity to consistently apply the valuation model it has selected. For example, if it chooses the fair value model, it will have to measure (with limited exception as described above for property backing liabilities) all of its investment property at fair value except where fair value cannot be measured reliably.

Under IFRS, there is a rebuttable presumption that an entity is able to determine the fair value of an investment property reliably on a continuing basis. If an entity determines (in exceptional cases) that it cannot reliably measure the fair value of a property, then it must continue to use cost until impairment or disposal (even if a reliable measure of fair value later becomes available).

A change from one model to another is allowed only if it results in the financial statements providing reliable and more relevant information about the effects of transactions, other events or conditions on the entity's financial position, financial performance or cash flows. Note that a change from fair value to historical cost is not likely to give a more relevant presentation.

An entity has to establish its choice when it first applies IAS 40 and then must use it consistently for all of its investment properties (with limited exception as described above for property backing liabilities). Any voluntary change in policy must comply with IAS 8, *Accounting Policies, Changes in Accounting Estimates and Errors* (i.e., a change may be made only where it results in more reliable and relevant information to users). Consequently, a change from fair value to cost is unlikely to be appropriate.

Fair Value Measurement

IAS 40 provides guidance for establishing the fair value of an investment property (under the fair value model) or for disclosures (under the cost model). Basically, fair value measurement of investment property under IAS 40 must take the following into consideration:

- Fair value has to be established from current prices for similar properties in an active market. If there is no such information, other information should be considered: current prices for different properties in an active market adjusted for differences in nature, condition or location, or if there is no active market, recent prices in less active market with adjustments to reflect changes in economic conditions.

- Discounted cash-flow techniques should be used only where there is no active market. Cash flows should be based on the property in its current condition, excluding future expenditure or associated inflows.

- The use of depreciated replacement cost is not an appropriate measurement method for establishing the fair value of investment property as rentals and capital appreciation are largely independent of asset cost.

- Reporting fair value means that measurement reflects market state and circumstances at the balance sheet date. Annual revaluation, although not mandated, is likely because market and circumstances are subject to changes in the current volatile markets.

- Entities assess the fair value on an individual basis without reflecting additional value derived from the creation of a portfolio of properties in different locations.

- Fair value determination by an independent valuer (who holds a recognized and relevant professional qualification and has recent experience in the location and category of the investment property being valued) is encouraged but not required.

- Transaction costs (for example, agent and legal fees on selling an investment property) should not be deducted from a property's estimated fair value.

Management could use the guidance provided by the International Valuation Standards (IVS) issued by the International Valuation Standards Committee. The valuation methods discussed by IVS include the sales comparison approach, the income capitalization approach and the cost approach.

It is generally accepted that a highest and best use valuation should be adopted, which means that fair value would consider any use that is financially feasible, justifiable and reasonably probable. Consequently, fair value might be determined on the basis of redevelopment of the site.

The transaction costs of a future sale should be considered only when a property is held for trading purposes (as inventory) under IAS 2 or is held for sale under IFRS 5. Under both IFRS and Canadian GAAP:

- An investment property in inventory is held "at the lower of cost and net realizable value."

- An investment property held for sale is measured at the lower of carrying amount and fair value less costs to sell.

Fair Value Disclosures

IAS 40 requires specific information on the fair value measurements of investment property, including:

- methods and significant assumptions used to determine the fair value, including a statement whether it was determined using market evidence or if it was more heavily based on other factors (to be disclosed) because of the nature of the property and lack of comparable market data;

- the extent to which the fair value is based on a valuation performed by an independent valuer who holds a recognized and relevant professional qualification and who has recent experience in the location and category of the investment property being valued. In absence of such an independent valuation, the entity must disclose that fact.

Other General Disclosures

IAS 40 requires the other disclosures for investment property outlined below, including (this is in addition to IAS 17 requirements, if applicable):

- whether the entity applied the fair value model or the cost model;

- if it applied the fair value model, whether, and in what circumstances, property interests held under operating leases are classified and accounted for as investment property;

- the criteria used for distinguishing investment property from other properties (such as owner-occupied and held for sale ones) when property classification into these categories is difficult to accomplish;

- the amounts recognized in profit or loss for:

    o rental income from investment property, and

    o direct operating expenses (including repairs and maintenance) arising from investment property that generated rental income during the period, as well as those arising from investment properties that did not generate rental income during the period;

- the existence and amounts of restrictions on the income realization of investment property, including the remittance of income and proceeds of disposal;

- contractual obligations to purchase, construct or develop investment property or for repairs, maintenance or enhancements.

Difficulties might arise in establishing whether a property (or a portion of it) is an investment property (to be accounted for according to IAS 40) or an owner-occupied property (to be accounted for according to IAS 16). Basically, as indicated in paragraph IAS 40.7, "an investment property generates cash flows largely independently of the other assets held by an entity," while owner-occupied property "generates cash flows that are attributable not only to property, but also to other assets used in the production or supply process." The application of that principle can present difficulties in certain circumstances, for example, when services are provided to occupants of a property and when a part of a property is owner occupied (see our analysis of particular considerations).

IAS 40 does not require fair values to be determined by an external independent valuer. Independent valuation, however, enhances the perceived reliability of the fair values reported. We have observed, in our analysis, that a majority of entities used independent valuers to establish the fair value of their investment property, especially when the fair value model is applied.

Fair Value Model

Requirements

Fair value is an optional measurement model that an entity may apply to measure all of its investment property. Under this model, gains or losses arising from a change in the fair value of the investment property are recognized in income in the period in which they arise.

In certain cases, IAS 40 requires an entity to use the fair value model. For example, when a leasehold interest held by a lessee under an operating lease is classified as an investment property, the fair value model must be applied (see the discussion related to leasehold property later in this chapter). Because of consistency requirements, this would compel the entity to value all other assets held as investment property (i.e., both leasehold and "freehold") at fair value.

Once an entity measures an investment property at fair value, it continues to do so even if market transactions become less frequent, market prices become less readily available or if the property is taken out of use and redeveloped as an investment property.

IAS 36, *Impairment* does not apply when investment property is accounted for using the fair value model.

Disclosures

In addition to the fair value and other general disclosures required for an investment property, an entity using the fair value model must present:

- A reconciliation between the carrying amounts of investment property at the beginning and the end of the period, showing the following:
  - additions, disclosing separately those additions resulting from acquisitions and those resulting from subsequent expenditure that were capitalized in the carrying amount of an asset,
  - additions resulting from acquisitions through business combinations,
  - assets classified as held for sale or included in a disposal group classified as held for sale in accordance with IFRS 5 and other disposals,
  - net gains or losses from fair value adjustments,
  - net exchange differences arising on the translation of the financial statements into a different presentation currency, and on translation of a foreign operation into the presentation currency of the reporting entity,
  - transfers to and from inventories and owner-occupied property, and
  - other changes.
- When a valuation obtained for an investment property is significantly adjusted for the financial statements, for example to avoid double-counting of assets or liabilities recognized as separate assets and liabilities, an entity must disclose a reconciliation between the valuation obtained and the adjusted valuation included in the financial statements, showing separately the aggregate amount of any recognized lease obligations that have been added back, and any other significant adjustments.
- In the exceptional circumstances where an entity measures investment property using the cost model described in IAS 16 because its fair value is not reliably determinable on a continuing basis, the reconciliation has to disclose amounts relating to that investment property separately from amounts relating to other investment property. In addition, the entity must disclose:
  - a description of the investment property,

- o   an explanation of why fair value cannot be determined reliably,
- o   if possible, the range of estimates within which fair value is highly likely to lie, and
- o   on disposal of investment property not carried at fair value:
  - the fact that the entity has disposed of investment property not carried at fair value,
  - carrying amount of that investment property at the time of sale, and
  - amount of gain or loss recognized.

Cost Model

Requirements

An entity choosing the cost model must use the cost model (not the revaluation model) described under IAS 16 (i.e., it must measure the investment property at cost less depreciation and impairment losses). Entities adopting the cost model are, however, required to determine the fair values of all their investment properties and disclose them in their financial statements.

Impairment

Investment property carried at cost, less any accumulated depreciation and any accumulated impairment, should be assessed for impairment in accordance with the provisions of IAS 36, *Impairment of Assets*. Properties carried at fair value are excluded from the scope of IAS 36.

Where an impairment of an investment property is identified, the carrying value should be written down to the recoverable amount. Often, this amount is the same as the investment property's fair value. There are, however, circumstances when this will not be the case because fair values are based on external market factors, whereas value in use also takes account of entity-specific factors such tax considerations.

Disclosures

In addition to fair value and other general disclosures required for investment property, an entity using the cost model must disclose:

- depreciation methods;
- useful lives or the depreciation rates;
- gross carrying amount and the accumulated depreciation (aggregated with accumulated impairment losses) at the beginning and end of the period;
- reconciliation of the carrying amount of investment property at the beginning and end of the period, showing the following:
  - o   additions, disclosing separately those additions resulting from acquisitions and those resulting from subsequent expenditure recognized as an asset,
  - o   additions resulting from acquisitions through business combinations,
  - o   assets classified as held for sale or included in a disposal group classified as held for sale in accordance with IFRS 5 and other disposals,
  - o   depreciation,
  - o   amount of impairment losses recognized, and the amount of impairment losses reversed, during the period in accordance with IAS 36,
  - o   net exchange differences arising on the translation of the financial statements into a different presentation currency, and on translation of a foreign operation into the presentation currency of the reporting entity,
  - o   transfers to and from inventories and owner-occupied property, and

o   other changes.

In the exceptional cases when an entity cannot determine the fair value of the invest-ment property reliably, it must describe the investment property, explain the reason why fair value cannot be reliably determined and, if possible, provide the ranges of estimates within which fair value is highly likely to lie.

Illustrative Disclosures:

Extract 8(8) – Valuer and fair value measurements

> **BAA Limited (AR 2007), page 28**
> **Significant accounting judgements and estimates (in part)**
> **Investment properties**
>
> Investment properties were valued at a fair value at 31 December 2007 by Drivers Jonas, Chartered Surveyors, Strutt and Parker, Chartered Surveyors, King Sturge, Valuers and Surveyors, and the Company's Head of BAA Professional Services, John Arbuckle BLE (Hons). These valuations were prepared in accordance with IFRS and the appraisal and valuation manual issued by the Royal Institution of Chartered Surveyors. Valuations were carried out having regard to comparable market evidence. In assessing fair value, current and potential future income (after deduction of nonrecoverable outgoings) has been capitalised using yields derived from market evidence.

Commentary: In this extract, the company indicates that it applied the fair value model and that it used both internal and external resources for fair value measurements. The company also discloses some elements related to these measurements.

Extract 8(9) – Measurement at cost and fair value measurements

> **Alma Media Corporation (AR 2007), page 54**
> **Accounting principles used in IFRS consolidated financial statements (in part)**
> **Investment properties**
>
> Investment properties are properties held by the Group for the purpose of obtaining rental income or capital appreciation. The Group applies the cost model in which investment pro-perties are valued at their acquisition cost less straightline depreciation and impairment losses. The fair values of the investment properties are shown in the notes to the financial statements. When estimating the fair value the company endeavours to use the most up-to-date market information possible. Measurements are made for the most part by the company itself.

Commentary: The company provides an IAS 40 definition of investment properties and indicates that it applied the cost model. As required by IAS 40, the company has disclosed fair value of investment properties in the notes to the financial statements (not presented in the extract above). The company specifies that it has generally established fair value using internal resources.

Extract 8(10) – Fair value measurement and IVS

> **BOC Hong Kong Holdings Limited (AR 2007), pages 111 and 112**
> **2. Summary of significant accounting policies (in part)**
> **2.17 *Investment properties* (in part)**
>
> ... After initial recognition, investment properties are measured at fair value assessed by professional valuers on the basis of open market value. If this information is not available, alternative valuation methods are used such as recent prices on less active markets or discounted cash flow projections. These valuations are performed in accordance with the guidance issued by the International Valuation Standards Committee. [...]
> Any changes in fair value are reported directly in the income statement.

Commentary: In this extract, the company specifies that it values its investment property on the basis of open market value. In the absence of this information, alternative valuation methods are used, such as recent prices on less active markets or discounted cash flow projections performed in accordance with IVS.

Extract 8(11) – Leases as investment property

BOC Hong Kong Holdings Limited (AR 2007), page 191

31. Investment properties (in part)

As at 31 December 2007, investment properties are included in the consolidated balance sheet at valuation carried out at 31 December 2007 on the basis of their fair value by an independent firm of chartered surveyors, Savills Valuation and Professional Services Limited.

The carrying value of investment properties is analysed based on the remaining terms of the leases as follows:

	2007 HK$'m	2006 HK$'m
Held in Hong Kong		
On long-term lease (over 50 years)	7,251	6,687
On medium-term lease (10 – 50 years)	528	545
On short-term lease (less than 10 years)	48	40
Held outside Hong Kong		
On long-term lease (over 50 years)	3	4
On medium-term lease (10 – 50 years)	224	201
On short-term lease (less than 10 years)	4	4
	8,058	7,481

Commentary: Here, the company discloses some details on the valuation of leaseholds held as investment property. It provides some information as required by IAS 17, as well as location of the property and the external valuer's name.

Extract 8(12) – Fair value estimates

Daejan Holdings PLC (Report & Financial Statements 2007), page 26

1. Significant accounting policies **(in part)**

(i) Investment property (in part)

… The valuations are prepared either by considering the aggregate of the net annual rent receivable from the properties using a yield which reflects the risks inherent in the net cash flow which is then applied to the net annual rents to arrive at the property valuation, or on a sales comparison basis. Any gains or losses arising from a change in fair value are recognised in the Income Statement.

Commentary: In this extract, the company discloses the two methods it uses for valuing its investment property.

Extract 8(13) – Valuation frequency

Port Otago Limited (AR 2007), page 23

Notes to the reconciliations (in part)

a. Investment property – valuation basis

Under previous NZ GAAP investment properties were revalued annually, at the end of each financial year, to open market value less costs of disposal that could reasonably be anticipated. Under NZ IFRS the Group measures investment property at fair value each six months, at 31 December and at 30 June. The fair value of each investment property reflects market conditions at the balance sheet date and is determined without any deduction for disposal costs.

Commentary: This extract shows that the company values its investment property every six months. Even though IAS 40 indicates that fair value needs to be evaluated once a year (at the end of the reporting period), the company performs such an evaluation more often. This might be necessary to ensure "fair presentation" (because properties fluctuate widely) as would be required by IAS 1, *Presentation of Financial Statements* or could be due to legal or contractual constraints.

Extract 8(14) – Use of external valuers

Quintain Estates and Development PLC (AR 2007), pages 90 and 91
NOTES TO THE ACCOUNTS (in part)
10 Investment and Development Properties (in part)

All of the Group's properties were externally valued as at 31 March 2007 on the basis of market value by professionally qualified valuers in accordance with the Appraisal and Valuation Standards of the Royal Institution of Chartered Surveyors.

The Group's landholding in Greenwich and the Wembley Complex have been valued by Savills Commercial Limited. The discount rates which have been applied in relation to these developments were 12% and 10% respectively. Other properties in the United Kingdom have been valued by Jones Lang LaSalle Limited and Christie + Co. Properties in the Channel Islands have been valued by Guy Gothard & Co.

A reconciliation of the valuations carried out by the external valuers to the carrying values shown in the Balance Sheet was as follows:

	2007 £000	2006 £000
Investment and development properties at market value as determined by valuers	**1,046,962**	878,295
Adjustment in respect of rent-free periods and other tenant incentives	**(466)**	(965)
Adjustment in respect of minimum payments under head leases separately included as a liability in the Balance Sheet	**11,747**	12,213
As shown in the Balance Sheet	**1,058,243**	889,543

The percentage of investment and development properties valued by each valuer was as follows:

	2007				2006
	Per valuers' reports £000	Adjustment for properties held in joint ventures and associates £000	Properties held as investment and development properties £000	Percentage value by each valuer %	Percentage value by each valuer %
Savills Commercial Limited	**766,650**	**(30,242)**	**736,408**	**70.3**	62.1
Jones Lang LaSalle Limited	**296,245**	**(1,600)**	**294,645**	**28.2**	36.7
Other valuers	**15,909**	**–**	**15,909**	**1.5**	1.2
	1,078,804	**(31,842)**	**1,046,962**	**100.0**	100.0

Copies of the valuation reports of Jones Lang LaSalle Limited and Savills Commercial Limited are included within the Annual Report on pages 62 and 63.

Commentary: This extract provides details about fair values established by different valuers. It also presents a reconciliation between amounts obtained from valuers and amounts reported in the financial statements.

Extract 8(15) – Fair value model, leaseholds and reconciliation schedule

Aviva plc (AR 2007), page 166

21 – Investment property (in part)

This note gives details of the properties we hold for long-term rental yields or capital appreciation.

	Freehold £m	Leasehold £m	Total £m
Carrying value			
At 1 January 2006	10,765	2,510	13,275
Additions	1,373	342	1,715
Capitalised expenditure on existing properties	125	48	173
Acquisitions of subsidiaries	35	–	35
Fair value gains	1,227	280	1,507
Disposals	(1,494)	(47)	(1,541)
Transfers from property and equipment	6	–	6
Foreign exchange rate movements	(41)	(6)	(47)
At 31 December 2006	11,996	3,127	15,123
Additions	1,413	109	1,522
Capitalised expenditure on existing properties	138	11	149
Acquisitions of subsidiaries	4	–	4
Disposals of subsidiaries	(3)	–	(3)
Fair value losses	(648)	(97)	(745)
Disposals	(831)	(432)	(1,263)
Transfers from property and equipment	10	31	41
Foreign exchange rate movements	210	39	249
At 31 December 2007	**12,289**	**2,788**	**15,077**

Investment properties are stated at their market values as assessed by qualified external valuers or by local qualified staff of the Group in overseas operations, all with recent relevant experience. Values are calculated using a discounted cash flow approach and are based on current rental income plus anticipated uplifts at the next rent review, assuming no future growth in rental income. This uplift and the discount rate are derived from rates implied by recent market transactions on similar properties.

The fair value of investment properties leased to third-parties under operating leases was as follows:

	2007 £m	2006 £m
Freeholds	11,925	10,423
Leaseholds	2,691	3,039
	14,616	**13,462**

Commentary: In this extract, the company presents a schedule of investment properties which shows leaseholds and freeholds separately. The company has capitalized certain subsequent expenditures and measures its investment properties at fair value. The basis for fair value measurement is presented. In addition, the company presents separately fair value of investment properties leased to third-parties under operating leases.

Extract 8(16) – Fair value model reconciliation

Daejan Holdings PLC (Report & Financial Statements 2007), page 33

8. Investment Properties

	Freehold £000	Long Leasehold £000	Short Leasehold £000	Total 2007 £000	Total 2006 £000
Professional Valuation at 1 April 2006	876,485	209,348	15,215	**1,101,048**	955,157
Disposals	(1,812)	(803)	–	**(2,615)**	(5,994)
New Acquisitions	834	407	23	**1,264**	1,597
Additions to existing properties	2,140	84	–	**2,224**	5,209
Revaluation	110,328	43,463	81	**153,872**	130,976
Foreign Exchange Movements	(18,142)	(3,766)	–	**(21,908)**	14,103
Professional Valuation at 31 March 2007	969,833	248,733	15,319	**1,233,885**	1,101,048

Professional valuations of all the Group's United Kingdom investment properties were carried out at 31 March 2007 by Colliers CRE, Chartered Surveyors. The revalued figures of £1,061,144,000 are based on open market values in accordance with the Practice Statements in the RICS Appraisal and Valuation Manual.

The Group's USA investment properties were also professionally valued at 31 March 2007 by KTR Newmark, Meredith & Grew, Joseph J Blake and Associates, Inc. and Metropolitan Valuation Services Inc., USA General Certified Appraisers. The revalued figures of £172,741,000 are based on open market values.

Commentary: This extract shows a reconciliation by category of investment property (freehold, long leasehold and short leasehold) as well as the names of professional valuers by country.

Extract 8(17) – Fair value model reconciliation and other disclosures

A&J Mucklow Group plc (AR 2007), pages 51 and 52

10 Investment and development properties

(a) Group

	Freehold £000	Leasehold £000	Total £000
At 1 July 2005	204,793	21,180	225,973
Acquisitions	7,859	—	7,859
Additions	3,814	1,105	4,919
Disposals	(3,150)	(7,790)	(10,940)
Transfer from owner-occupied property	1,980	—	1,980
Revaluation surplus	25,720	1,895	27,615
At 1 July 2006	241,016	16,390	257,406
Acquisitions	20,489	—	20,489
Additions	3,229	684	3,913
Capitalised interest	508	—	508
Disposals	(11,889)	—	(11,889)
Revaluation surplus	16,575	(234)	16,341
At 30 June 2007	269,928	16,840	286,768
Comprising:			
Investment properties	241,792	16,840	258,632
Properties for or under redevelopment	28,136	—	28,136
	269,928	16,840	286,768
Properties held at valuation:			
Cost	127,513	13,459	140,972
Valuation surplus	142,415	3,381	145,796
Valuation	269,928	16,840	286,768

A&J Mucklow Group plc (AR 2007) (continued)

Investment and development properties have been included at market value after having deducted an amount of £0.22m (2006: £0.22m) in respect of lease incentives and letting fees included in trade and other receivables.

The properties are stated at their 30 June 2007 market value and are valued by DTZ Debenham Tie Leung and CBRE, professionally qualified external valuers, in accordance with the RICS Appraisal and Valuation Standards published by the Royal Institution of Chartered Surveyors. DTZ Debenham Tie Leung and CBRE have recent experience in the relevant location and category of the properties being valued. A reconciliation to the amount included above is set out below.

	£000
DTZ and CBRE valuation as at 30 June 2007	288,266
Owner-occupied property included in property, plant and equipment	(1,407)
Lease inducements	(216)
Other adjustments	125
Investment and development properties as at 30 June 2007	286,768

Additions to freehold and leasehold properties include capitalised interest of £0.51m (2006: £nil). The capitalisation rate used was 6.1%. The total amount of interest capitalised included in freehold and leasehold properties is £2.85m (2006: £2.76m).

Properties valued at £87.9m (2006: £75.8m) were subject to a security interest.

(b) Company

	Freehold £000
At valuation 1 July 2006	2,052
Additions	54
Revaluation deficit	(56)
At valuation 30 June 2007	2,050

A&J Mucklow Group plc (AR 2007), page 61

27 Operating leases

The Group leases out all of its investment properties under operating leases.

Future aggregate minimum rentals receivable under non-cancellable operating leases are:

	2007 £000	2006 £000
Not later than one year	13,456	13,300
Later than one year but not later than five years	42,889	40,809
Later than five years	32,980	34,422
	89,325	88,531

Commentary: In this extract, the company provides a reconciliation by category of investment property (freehold and leasehold) as well as the names of the professional valuers. The company also provides two schedules: one adjusting amounts obtained from the valuers to obtain balance of investment property and the other giving the details concerning the operating leases.

Extract 8(18) – Cost model reconciliation

Tesco PLC (AR 2007), page 49
Note 1 Accounting policies (in part)
Investment property
Investment property is property held to earn rental income and/or for capital appreciation rather than for the purpose of Group operating activities. Investment property assets are carried at cost less accumulated depreciation and any recognised impairment in value. The depreciation policies for investment property are consistent with those described for owner-occupied property.

page 70
Note 12 Investment property

	2007 £m	2006 £m
Cost		
At beginning of year	785	595
Foreign currency translation	(32)	36
Additions	26	21
Acquisitions through business combinations	32	–
Transfers	101	194
Classified as held for sale	(4)	(58)
Disposals	(2)	(3)
At end of year	906	785
Accumulated depreciation and impairment losses		
At beginning of year	40	30
Foreign currency translation	(2)	2
Charge for the period	11	9
Classified as held for sale	–	(1)
Transfers	1	–
At end of year	50	40
Net carrying value	856	745

The net carrying value at 26 February 2005 was £565m.

The estimated fair value of the Group's investment property is £1,522m (2006 – £1,373m). This value has been determined by applying an appropriate rental yield to the rentals earned by the investment property. A valuation has not been performed by an independent valuer.

Commentary: In this extract, the company provides a reconciliation of investment property held at cost. As required by IAS 40, it presents the gross amounts and the accumulated depreciation and impairment losses separately. The company also discloses the fair value of the investment property and indicates that the valuation has not been performed by an independent valuer.

Extract 8(19) – Reconciliation - cost model

Kingfisher plc (AR 2007), page 59	
2 Significant accounting policies (in part)	
i. Investment property	
The Group's investment properties were restated at historical cost on transition to IFRS and are held in the balance sheet at cost less depreciation and provision for impairment.	
page 72	
15 Investment property	
£ millions	
Cost	
At 29 January 2005	19.2
Disposals	(0.9)
Transferred from property, plant and equipment	0.4
Exchange differences	3.8
At 28 January 2006	22.5
Additions	0.1
Disposals	(0.7)
Transferred from property, plant and equipment	15.6
Exchange differences	(0.8)
At 3 February 2007	36.7
Depreciation	
At 29 January 2005	0.5
Charge for the year	0.2
Impairment losses	5.8
Exchange differences	0.7
At 28 January 2006	7.2
Charge for the year	0.2
Transferred from property, plant and equipment	0.2
Exchange differences	(0.3)
At 3 February 2007	7.3
Net carrying amount	
At 3 February 2007	29.4
At 28 January 2006	15.3
The impairment loss in the prior year relates to the write-down of an asset from its carrying value to its recoverable amount.	
On transition to IFRS, investment properties were restated to historical cost. Their fair value as at 3 February 2007 is £38.7m (2006: £20.2m).	

Commentary: In this extract, the company provides a reconciliation of investment property held at cost. As required by IAS 40, it presents the gross amounts and the accumulated depreciation and impairment losses separately. The company also discloses the fair value of the investment property. In addition, the company indicates that it moved to the cost model on IFRS adoption. Such a change would not have been appropriate had it been undertaken after IFRS adoption.

Extract 8(20) – Investment income disclosure

Royal & Sun Alliance Insurance Group plc (AR 2007), page 86
2. Net investment return (in part)

A summary of the gross investment income, net realised and net unrealised gains/(losses) included in the income statement is given below.

	Investment income		Net realised gains/(losses)		Net unrealised gains/(losses)		Impairments		Total investment return	
	2007 £m	2006 £m	2007 £m	2006 £m	2007 £m	2006 £m	2007 £m	2006 £m	2007 £m	2006 £m
Investment property	19	13	12	12	(42)	42	–	–	(11)	67
Equity securities	48	56	185	52	(2)	–	(1)	(3)	230	105
Debt securities	391	372	(29)	(27)	–	–	(2)	–	360	345
Other investments:										
Loans secured by mortgages	1	1	1	–	–	–	–	–	2	1
Other loans	5	3	–	16	–	–	–	–	5	19
Other	31	8	(4)	7	(8)	–	–	–	19	15
Deposits, cash and cash equivalents	83	63	1	–	–	–	–	–	84	63
Derivatives	15	1	8	(14)	(3)	(2)	–	–	20	(15)
Net investment return	593	517	174	46	(55)	40	(3)	(3)	709	600

... Direct operating expenses (including repairs and maintenance) arising from investment properties were not material in 2007 and 2006.

Commentary: Here, the company provides details on its investment income that includes investment property and other financial assets. Direct expenses related to investment property were not material. This might confirm the proper classification of properties as investment property (see our subsequent discussion on ancillary services).

Extract 8(21) – Inability to measure fair value for certain properties

Skaninaviska Enskilda Banken AB (AR 2007), page 92
27 Tangible and intangible assets (in part)

	Group		Parent company	
	2007	2006	2007	2006
Office, IT and other tangible assets	1,398	1,411	278	202
Equipment leased to clients[1]			34,325	14,552
Properties for own operations	1,143	805	2	9
Properties taken over for protection of claims	23	86		
Property and equipment	**2,564**	**2,302**	**34,605**	**14,763**
Investment properties recognised at cost	201	629		
Investment properties recognised at fair value through profit and loss	5,038	4,411		
Investment properties	**5,239**	**5,040**		

Investment property

The fair value model is used for valuation of investment property held in the insurance business. The cost model is used for other investment properties. Investment property recognised at fair value through profit and loss is owned by SEB Pension in Denmark. The valuation of the portfolio is done by independent valuers with experience in the market. The investment property valued at costs is held in Germany and the Baltic countries. The valuation is done at costs due to uncertain market conditions. The best possible estimation is that the market value would be close to the book value. The depreciation is done by the straight line method and is ranging over 20 to 50 years depending on classification as building or improvements to the building. [...]

Skaninaviska Enskilda Banken AB (AR 2007), page 94
27 Tangible and intangible assets (in part)

Investment properties recognised at cost

Opening balance	871	1,206
Acquisitions during the year	2	2
Reclassifications	-4	-210
Sales during the year	-497	-89
Exchange rate differences	29	-38
Acquisition value	**401**	**871**
Opening balance	-242	-281
Current year's depreciations	-16	-28
Current year's impairments		-3
Reclassifications	1	29
Accumulated depreciations on current year's sales	67	31
Exchange rate differences	-10	10
Accumulated depreciations	**-200**	**-242**
Total	**201**	**629**

Investment properties recognised at fair value through profit and loss

Opening balance	4,411	4,046
Acquisitions during the year	354	428
Reclassifications	3	
Revaluation at fair value	97	222
Sales during the year	-36	-137
Exchange rate differences	209	-148
Total	**5,038**	**4,411**

Net operating earnings from investment properties

External income	317	287
Operating costs[1]	-97	-107
Total	**220**	**180**

1) Direct operating expenses arising from investment property that did not generate rental income amounts to SEK 5m (7).

Commentary: In this extract, the company uses the fair value model but it indicates that certain of the investment properties are valued at cost due to uncertain market conditions. It suggests that the best possible estimation is that the market value would be close to the book value.

Extract 8(22) – Capital commitments

Workspace Group PLC (AR 2007), page 62
27. Capital commitments

At the year-end the estimated amounts of contractual commitments for future capital expenditure not provided for were:

	2007 £m	2006 £m
Under contract:		
Purchases, construction or redevelopment of investment property	10.5	6.5
Repairs, maintenance or enhancement of investment property	0.1	0.2
	10.6	6.7
Authorised by directors but not contracted:		
Property, plant and equipment	0.5	0.2
Intangible assets	–	0.1
Purchases, construction or redevelopment of investment property	6.4	6.9
Repairs, maintenance or enhancement of investment property	7.5	8.5
	14.4	15.7

Commentary: In this extract, the company discloses its capital commitments for its investment properties (both contracted and only authorized).

Extract 8(23) – Adjustments to fair value valuation amounts

Workspace Group PLC (AR 2007), page 51
10. Investment properties (in part)
Valuation

The Group's investment properties were revalued at 31 March 2007 by CB Richard Ellis, Chartered Surveyors, a firm of independent qualified valuers. The valuations were undertaken in accordance with the Royal Institution of Chartered Surveyors Appraisal and Valuation Standards on the basis of market value. Market value is defined as the estimated amount for which a property should exchange on the date of valuation between a willing buyer and willing seller in an arm's length transaction.

The reconciliation of the valuation report total shown in the Consolidated Balance Sheet as non-current assets, investment properties, is as follows:

	2007 £m	2006 £m
Total per CB Richard Ellis valuation report	1,000.9	964.3
Owner occupied property	(2.5)	(2.4)
Property held for sale (shown as current assets)	–	(8.2)
Head leases treated as finance leases under IAS 17	3.6	0.7
Short leases valued as head leases	(0.4)	(0.4)
Total per balance sheet	1,001.6	954.0

Commentary: In this extract, the company presents a reconciliation of valuation amounts obtained from the external valuer and the amount reported on the balance sheet.

Extract 8(24) – Other disclosures

Aviva plc (AR 2007), page 222
55 – Risk management (in part)
Property price risk

The Group is subject to property price risk due to holdings of investment properties in a variety of locations worldwide. Investment in property is managed at business unit level, and will be subject to local regulations on asset admissibility, liquidity requirements and the expectations of policyholders as well as overall risk appetite. The Investment Committee also actively monitors property assets owned directly by the Group.

At 31 December 2007, no material derivative contracts had been entered into to mitigate the effects of changes in property prices.

A sensitivity to changes in property prices is given in section (g) below.

Commentary: In this extract, the company provides information on property price risk inherent in its holdings of investment properties. This information is required under IFRS 7, *Financial instruments: Disclosures*.

Special Contexts and Considerations

Investment Property Held under a Lease

General Requirements

IFRS require that leased investment properties are accounted as follows:

- All property interests held under a lease (both finance and operating leases) that are classified as investment property are recorded initially as a finance lease as prescribed by IAS 17, i.e., both an asset (at the lower of the fair value of the property and the present value of the minimum lease payments) and an equivalent amount of liability are recognized.

- If the leased property is classified as a finance lease and meets the definition of investment property, it *must* be accounted for in accordance with IAS 40. Accordingly, the investor/lessee has the choice of applying either the fair value model or the cost model. If a leased property is classified as an operating lease and meets the definition of investment property, the investor/lessee *may* account for the property in accordance with IAS 40. If the IAS 40 option is chosen, (1) the lease is accounted for as a finance lease and (2) the investor/ lessee must apply the fair value model.

- Note that:
    - o Fair value of leased assets classified as investment property relates to the fair value of the leasehold's not that of the underlying property.
    - o When a lease is signed, the leased interest is recorded at the lower of present value of minimum lease payments and the asset's fair value. A liability for the same amount is also recorded. Therefore the fair value of the net leasehold interest is nil.
    - o Subsequent to entering into effect, the fair value of the net leasehold interest is the amount the lessee would expect to receive (i.e., the premium) for this interest if the entity transfers the lease to another party. Premium obtained for the leasehold is calculated as the net expected cash flows (i.e., rentals to be received from tenants less the rentals payable to the owner/lessor) discounted at a market rate.
    - o Fair value of investment property held under a lease reflects expected cash flows (including contingent rent that is expected to become payable).
    - o If a valuation obtained for a property is net of all payments expected to be made, it will be necessary to add back any recognized lease liability, to arrive at the carrying amount of the investment property using the fair value model.

Lease Classification

According to the requirements described above, lease classification is a key consideration under IAS 40 as the investor/lessee must apply IAS 40 for a finance lease but can choose whether or not to do so for an operating lease. Below are some issues to consider when classifying a lease under IAS 17:

- The classification as an operating or finance lease should be made at the inception of the lease.
- When an entity acquires an interest in a leasehold property, it would be necessary to establish whether this is in substance a new lease. For this purpose, a sub-lease is regarded as a new lease.
- A legal assignment of a lease, resulting in an entity becoming party to its terms, may also represent a new lease in substance depending on the specific facts and circumstances.
- The acquisition of an entity with an existing leasehold property interest does not result in a new lease.

Premium Paid

Any premium paid to the lessor *or* to the previous lessee to enter into the lease is included in the minimum lease payments, both for determining the appropriate lease classification and for calculating the present value of the minimum lease payments.

Operating Lease

If IAS 40 is applied to a property held under an operating lease, the lease is accounted for as a finance lease. Consequently, the initial cost of the property and the corresponding lease liability are determined as the lower of its fair value or the minimum lease payments discounted at the interest rate implicit in the lease. In practice the discounted value of minimum lease payments will be lower than fair value of the property because operating lease term would be generally short or would not substantially transfer all risk and rewards to the lessee. Often, it is impractical to determine the interest rate implicit in the lease (particularly for operating leases). As required by IAS 17, the investor/lessee would then use the incremental borrowing rate.

As indicated previously, one of the significant consequences of reporting operating leases as investment property to be accounted for under IAS 40 is the obligation to apply the fair value model to all other investment property (including owned property). Note also, as observed previously, there is an exception to this rule: regardless of the measurement model selected for investment property, either the fair value or cost model may be applied to properties that back liabilities (i.e., liabilities that are linked to the fair value or returns from specified properties).

Land and Buildings

Under IAS 17, land and building elements are considered separately for the purposes of lease classification. Land is generally classified as an operating lease unless the lease transfers ownership to the lessee by the end of the lease term or contains a bargain purchase option.

A lease of both land and buildings is split into land and building elements. The land element is generally an operating lease. The building element is an operating or finance lease based on the criteria in IAS 17. Separate measurement of the land and buildings elements is not required if the lessee's interest in both land and buildings is classified as an investment property under IAS 40 and the fair value model is adopted. If the investor/lessee does not apply the fair value model to both the land and building elements, it must separate the lease unless the land element is immaterial.

Embedded Derivatives

An embedded derivative in a lease contract should be separated from its host contract and accounted for separately if:

- its economic characteristics and risks are not closely related to the lease contract's economic characteristics and risks; and
- a separate instrument with the same terms as the embedded derivative would meet the definition of a derivative within the scope of IAS 39 (see Chapter 9).

Property lease payments are often linked to:

- general country inflation indices, general country property indices and revenue generated by the lessee's business (all considered as closely related); or
- lessee's profitability or stock market price, or general country's stock exchange indices (all not closely related).

In some circumstances, foreign currency denominated lease payments/receipts may also represent a non-closely related embedded derivative.

Lease Incentives

IFRS mandate the disclosure of lease incentives since they allow users of financial statements to evaluate the results of the leasing strategy and the strength of the cash flows supporting the asset value. Note that lease incentives reduce the level of rental income and affect a property's valuation.

Many IAS 17 requirements also apply under CICA 3065. See Chapter 13 for details.

Investment Property under Construction or Development

An entity should measure investment property under construction at fair value if that is the entity's general accounting policy for investment property and the fair value of the property under construction can be measured reliably.

Valuing investment properties under construction at fair value could be difficult as:

- there are no active markets for investment property under construction;
- investment property under construction tends to be unique and so its fair value is not necessarily comparable to recent sales of other investment properties under construction.

In the exceptional cases when an entity is compelled to measure an investment property using the cost model in accordance with IAS 16, it measures at fair value all its other investment property, including investment property under construction. In these cases, although an entity may use the cost model for one investment property, the entity must continue to account for each of the remaining properties using the fair value model.

IAS 40 contains several requirements concerning exceptions to measurement of an investment property under construction at fair value (if that is the entity's general accounting policy for investment property):

- if an entity determines that the fair value of an investment property under construction is not reliably determinable but expects the fair value of the property to be reliably determinable when construction is complete, the investment property under construction is measured at cost until either its fair value becomes reliably determinable or construction is completed (whichever is earlier). Once construction of that property is complete, it is presumed that fair value can be measured reliably. If this is not the case, the property is accounted for using the cost model. In these exceptional cases, all other investment property is measured at fair value, including investment property under construction at fair value. In these cases, although an entity may use the cost model for one investment property, each of the remaining properties are accounted for using the fair value model;
- the presumption that the fair value of investment property under construction can be measured reliably can be rebutted only on initial recognition. An entity that has measured an item of investment property under construction at fair value may not conclude that the fair value of the completed investment property cannot be determined reliably.

Ancillary Services Provided

When an entity provides ancillary services to the occupants of one of its properties, the significance of those services is considered in determining the appropriate classification of the property (as a fixed asset or an investment property). The property would qualify as an investment property only if the ancillary services provided are insignificant when compared with the total revenue expected from the property.

Multipurpose Property (Part of the Property is Owner Occupied)

A property could be used for both investment purposes and administrative or productive purposes. Separate accounting can be applied (i.e., investment portion accounted for according to IAS 40 and owner-occupied portion accounted for according to IAS 16) only if it is possible for the portions to be sold separately or leased separately under a finance lease. The existence of a third party lessee indicates that a separate sale or finance lease is possible. If separate accounting cannot be applied, all of the property is accounted for according to IAS 16 requirements, unless only an insignificant portion is owner occupied.

Property Occupied by an Associated Company or Joint Venture

Property owned or held under a finance lease and occupied by a parent or a subsidiary cannot be accounted for as investment property in a group's consolidated financial statements. Such property is owner occupied from the perspective of the group as a whole. The property is classified as property, plant and equipment in the group financial statements but as investment property in the entity's own financial statements.

Properties occupied by an associated company or a joint venture accounted for using the equity method are accounted for as investment properties in the consolidated financial statements. Associates and joint ventures accounted for using the equity method are not considered part of the group for consolidation purposes and, therefore, from the group's perspective, the property is not owner occupied.

Property occupied by a joint venture accounted for using the proportionate consolidation method should be classified as property, plant and equipment in the consolidated financial statements. This requirement will not be an issue if proposals related to joint ventures are adopted (see Chapter 7).

Illustrative Disclosures:

Extract 8(25) – Internal leases and operating leases

BOC Hong Kong Holdings Limited (AR 2007), page 111
2. Summary of significant accounting policies (in part)
2.17 Investment properties (in part)

Properties that are held for long-term rental yields or for capital appreciation or both, and that are not occupied by the companies in the Group, are classified as investment properties. Properties leased out within group companies are classified as investment properties in individual companies' financial statements and as premises in consolidated financial statements. Land held under operating lease is classified and accounted for as investment property when the rest of the definition of investment property is met. The operating lease is accounted for as if it is a finance lease.

Commentary: This extract describes the accounting treatment of the company's leaseholds, both internal and external.

Extract 8(26) – Redevelopment, operating leases and dual purpose properties

Daejan Holdings PLC (Report & Financial Statements 2007), pages 26 and 27
1. Significant accounting policies (in part)
(i) Investment property (in part)

… When the Group begins to redevelop an existing investment property for continued future use as an investment property, the property remains an investment property, which is measured based on the fair value model.

A property interest under an operating lease is classified and accounted for as an investment property on a property-by-property basis when the Group holds it to earn rentals or for capital appreciation or both. Any such property interest under an operating lease classified as an investment property is carried at fair value.

When the Group uses only part of a property it owns and retains the remainder to generate rental income or capital appreciation the extent of the Group's utilisation is considered to determine the classification of the property. If the Group's utilisation is less than five per cent, this is regarded as immaterial such that the whole property is classified as an investment property and stated at fair value.

Commentary: This extract describes the accounting treatment of the company's operating leases. It also discloses how it classifies dual-use property.

Transfers (Reclassifications)

Transfers to, or from, investment property are recorded when there is a change in use, evidenced by the occurrence of specific events.

Transfers to, or from, investment property occur when:

- there is a change in use, which would be recorded at the:

  o commencement of owner-occupation (transfer from investment property to owner-occupied property),

  o end of owner-occupation (transfer from owner-occupied property to investment property), or

  o commencement of an operating lease to another party (transfer from inventories to investment property);

- investment property is developed with a view to sale (transfer from investment property to inventories);

Before discussing these various triggering events, it would be useful to examine the IAS 40 general accounting requirements that apply to all transfers, which will vary depending on the model used for measuring investment property.

Accounting for Transfers – General Requirements

Transfers Under the Cost Model

When an entity uses the cost model, all transfers between investment property, owner-occupied property and inventories are recorded at the carrying value (historical cost less depreciation and impairments) of the asset transferred. Consequently, transfers to and from investment property do not result in the recognition of any gain or loss in the financial statements. This treatment presents no particular difficulties.

Transfers Under the Fair Value Model

A transfer from investment property to owner-occupied property or inventories is accounted for at the fair value at the date of change in use, which then becomes the property's deemed cost for subsequent accounting under IAS 16 or IAS 2.

Transfers to investment property are accounted for as follows:

- If an owner-occupied property becomes an investment property, the entity must apply IAS 16 up to the date of change in use. The entity treats any difference at that date between the carrying amounts of the property and its fair value in the same way as a revaluation in accordance with IAS 16.

- If inventories become investment property, any difference between the fair value of the property at that date and its previous carrying amount is recognized in income.

Transfers from Owner-occupied Property

Owner-occupied property is accounted for according to IAS 16. Under IAS 16, two models can be used (cost or revaluation). Consequently, there are several accounting outcomes on transfers to investment property, which will depend on the accounting policy choice an entity has made. Basically, the outcomes could be summarized as follows:

- *IAS 16 cost model followed by IAS 40 cost model*: Investment property is valued at original cost.

- *IAS 16 cost model followed by IAS 40 fair value model*: Owner-occupied property would be valued at depreciated cost. Transfers to investment property are recorded at fair value and any resulting fair value gains or losses are recognized in the same way as a revaluation in accordance with IAS 16 (as specified immediately below).

- *IAS 16 revaluation model followed by IAS 40 fair value model*: Owner-occupied property is measured at fair value. Any losses resulting from the transfer are recognized in income unless there is a balance existing in the revaluation surplus in which case the decrease is recorded in other comprehensive income and reduces the revaluation surplus within equity. Any gains resulting from the transfer are recognized in other comprehensive income unless there is a previous impairment loss for that property, in which case the increase is recognized in profit or loss. Any remaining gains deferred in the revaluation surplus would be derecognized on disposal of the property and transferred to retained earnings. This treatment prevents cumulative net increases in fair value that arose before the current period from being reflected in the income statement.

Other Changes of Use and Redevelopment of Investment Property

Transfers from investment property should occur only where there is a change of use. This may happen when an owner decides to occupy a property that was previously used as an investment (as covered previously) or the owner may want to dispose of the property. Normally, in the latter case, an enterprise would continue to show the property as an investment property until it is sold. If, however, an entity intends to develop a property with a view to a sale before it is sold, it should be transferred to inventory.

Also note that:

- When an entity decides to dispose of an investment property without development, it continues to treat that property as an investment property until it is derecognized (eliminated from the balance sheet) and does not treat it as inventory.

- If an entity begins to redevelop an existing investment property for continued future use as investment property, the property remains an investment property and is not reclassified as owner-occupied property during the redevelopment.

As specified by IAS 40, a property could be transferred from inventory to investment property if that property were included in inventory (because it is available for sale) but was then leased out to a third party (as an operating lease). In this case, the transfer to investment property is recorded at fair value at the date of the transfer (see the discussion on leases). Gains or losses between fair value amounts and property carrying value immediately before the transfer are included in income of the period. This is consistent with the treatment of profits on the sale of inventories.

Finally, an investment property could be reclassified as a "non-current asset held for sale" under IFRS 5. To do so, it must be available for immediate sale in its present condition and sale must be highly probable (see Chapter 12). An investment property carried at fair value is not re-measured according to IFRS 5, whereas an investment property carried under the cost model that meets the criteria to be classified as held for sale is re-measured.

Illustrative Disclosures:
Extract 8(27) – Accounting for transfers

BOC Hong Kong Holdings Limited (AR 2007), page 112 **2. Summary of significant accounting policies (in part)** *2.17 Investment properties* **(in part)** If an investment property becomes owner-occupied, it is reclassified as premises, and its fair value at the date of reclassification becomes its cost for accounting purposes. If an item of premises becomes an investment property because its use has changed, any difference resulting between the carrying amount and the fair value of this item at the date of transfer is recognised in equity as a revaluation of premises [...]

Commentary: In this extract, the company explains how it accounts for transfers from and to investment property.

Extract 8(28) – Reconciliation including transfer to held for sale

Port Otago Limited (AR 2007), pages 31 and 32
12. Investment property

		Group	
	Notes	2007 $000	2006 $000
Balance at beginning of year		152,879	107,644
Property purchased		-	11,901
Property improvements during the period		1,984	3,506
Property sold		(105)	(5,550)
Unrealised change in the value of investment property		25,304	35,378
Transfer to property held for sale	13	(9,192)	-
Balance at end of year		**170,870**	**152,879**
Comprising:			
Property portfolio at cost		49,371	57,004
Revaluation		121,499	95,875
		170,870	152,879
Valuation analysis:			
Valued at 30 June balance date as determined by:			
Barlow Justice Limited		4,965	4,195
Colliers International		89,700	67,925
DTZ New Zealand Limited		23,960	20,125
Guy Stevenson & Petherbridge Limited		-	32,602
Seagar & Partners (Manukau) Limited		52,245	28,032
Property recorded at fair value		170,870	152,879

The Group's investment properties are valued annually at fair value effective 30 June. Fair value reflects, among other things, rental income from current leases and assumptions about rental income from future leases in light of the current market conditions.

All valuations were completed by independent valuers who conform with the New Zealand Property Institute Practice Standards. The valuers have extensive market knowledge in the types of investment properties owned by the Group.

All investment properties were valued based on open market evidence including market rentals, land sales and yield information available to the valuers.

Included within the gross values for investment properties are capitalised leasing costs. These costs represent expenditure incurred by the Group in relation to letting of property. These costs are initially recorded as an asset and amortised over the life of the lease they relate to.

Port Otago Limited (AR 2007), pages 31 and 32 (continued) 13. Property held for sale (in part)			
		Group	
	Notes	**2007 $000**	**2006 $000**
Balance at beginning of year		-	-
Transfer from investment property	12	9,192	-
Balance at end of year		9,192	-
Comprising:			
Property held for sale - at cost		6,372	-
Property held for sale - at valuation		2,820	-

Commentary: This extract shows a reconciliation of investment property accounted for under the fair value model, including information related to the external valuer. It also gives details on the transfer from investment property to "property held for sale."

Extract 8(29) – Transfers to investment property

Telent plc (AR 2007), page 52 18. Investment property (in part)
Subsequent to the disposal by the Group of the telecommunications equipment and international services businesses to Ericsson, two of the properties owned by the Group were reclassified to investment property, as the **telent** Group no longer occupies these sites. These properties in Germany and Italy have been leased to Ericsson for an agreed annual income. The directors consider that the fair value of these investment properties at 31 March 2007, using the Market Value basis, was £33 million (31 March 2006: £34 million). The Group disposed of the property in Germany in June 2007 (see note 40).

Commentary: In this extract, the company indicates that it reclassified two of the properties to investment property, as the company no longer occupies these sites.

Disposals (Derecognition)

An investment property is derecognized (eliminated from the balance sheet) on its disposal or when it is permanently withdrawn from use and no future economic benefit is expected. If the property is sold or let under a finance lease, gain or loss on disposal would be recorded. The following indicates the accounting of a disposal in particular circumstances:

- different rules apply for disposals under a sale and leaseback transaction (see Chapter 13);
- compensation from third parties for investment property that was impaired, lost or given up is recognized when it is receivable.

FUTURE DEVELOPMENTS

The IASB and the FASB are working on a joint long-term leasing project that is expected to fundamentally change accounting for leases. The project will cover all leases, including real estate properties. The boards have commenced discussions on the main components of an accounting model for lessees, with a view to publishing a Discussion Paper in 2009. The boards decided to defer consideration of lessor accounting until further progress has been made on a number of other projects (in particular, derecognition and revenue recognition). One of the reasons for the deferral of lessor accounting has to do with the boards views that there are significant economic differences between lessors of real estate and other lessors that will require detailed analysis.

The discussions held so far seem to point to a single approach for reporting all leases. Under this approach, leases would be accounted for using a rights (for the lessee the right of use and for the lessor the right to income) and obligations perspective. If this perspective is adopted, it will affect IAS 40 significantly (as investment properties are often held to earn rental income). These leasing arrangements for investment property are often classified as operating leases under IAS 17 (i.e., a contractual obligation off the balance sheet), which can create problems of substance when properties are leased over very long periods.

If adopted, the single approach would affect both lessors and lessees of investment properties.

Lessors: Currently, most lessors report operating leases in their financial statements because the risks and rewards of real estate ownership are rarely transferred to the lessee. Under the single approach, all leases would be recognized on the balance sheet, with a significant impact on the balance sheet and the income statement of lessors.

Lessees: Lessees might be affected depending on whether the properties held under an operating lease have been accounted for as a finance lease, as permitted by IAS 40 (as indicated previously, this option is available if the property meets the definition of an investment property and the entity has applied the fair value model). Entities using this option would not see significant changes under the right and obligation perspective. Other entities would, in fact, have to record both the right of use asset (measured at the present value of lease payments) and obligations in the lease (measured at the present value of the lease obligation).

IVS issues periodically guidance related to fair value measurement. One of the proposed guidance project deals with the valuation principles that should be adopted for investment property under construction. IVS expects to issue an Exposure Draft during the second quarter of 2009.

COMPREHENSIVE EXAMPLES

This section presents two comprehensive examples showing extensive disclosures for investment properties. We have selected relevant extracts of the notes to the financial statements that might provide good examples of disclosure under IAS 40.

Minerva plc – All extracts 8(A) were obtained from the annual report for the year ended June 30, 2007.

Extract 8(A1) – Minerva plc, Presentation of investment property on the balance sheet, page 55

As required by IAS 1, *Presentation of financial statements*, investment properties are presented on the face of the balance sheet.

Consolidated balance sheet (in part)			
As at 30 June 2007	Note	As at 30 June 2007 £000	As at 30 June 2006 £000
Assets			
Non-current assets			
Investment properties	11	**730,763**	580,150
Property, plant and equipment	12	**9,136**	9,108
Investment in joint ventures	14	**6,964**	3,923
Derivative financial instruments	20	**11,640**	3,887
Other financial assets	15	**276**	276
		758,779	597,344
Current assets			
Trading properties	16	**107,618**	26,933
Trade and other receivables	17	**7,117**	44,122
Cash and cash equivalents	18	**125,491**	161,640
		240,226	232,695
Total assets		**999,005**	830,039

Extract 8(A2) – Minerva plc, Measurement uncertainties and critical judgements, pages 60 and 61

In this extract, the company indicates that it has used outside valuers to assess the fair value of different elements reported in the financial statements, including investment property.

1. Accounting policies
Measurement convention (in part)
Areas requiring the use of estimates and critical judgement that may impact on the Group's earnings and financial position include:
– valuation of investment properties, where the Board has relied upon external valuations carried out by professionally qualified valuers in accordance with the Appraisal and Valuation Standards of the Royal Institution of Chartered Surveyors;
– valuation of derivative financial instruments, where the Board has relied upon the valuation carried out by JC Rathbone Associates Limited, finance risk consultants;
– recognition of a share-based payment charge, where the Board has relied upon actuarial estimates produced by Lane Clark & Peacock LLP;
– distinction between investment properties and owner occupied property, where the Board considers owner occupied property to be held for use in the supply of services and for administration purposes by the Group; and
– calculation of deferred tax, where indexation is used to reduce the provision for deferred tax on revaluation surpluses.
Other areas of judgement, risk and uncertainty, which are relevant to an understanding of the financial results and position of the Group, are referred to in the Business review.

Extract 8(A3) – Minerva plc, Accounting policies, page 61

Here, the company discloses its accounting policies under IFRS. Different categories of properties are described. Note that the company has selected the fair value model for subsequent measurement of investment property.

---

1. Accounting policies

Property expenses

Refurbishment expenditure in respect of major works is capitalised. Renovation and refurbishment expenditure of a revenue nature is charged to the income statement as incurred.

Costs directly attributable to the arrangement of a lease, which include letting and professional fees, are capitalised and amortised over the lease term.

Investment properties

Investment properties are measured initially at cost, including related transactions costs, and subsequently at fair value. Changes in the fair value of an investment property at the balance sheet date and its carrying amount prior to re-measurement, are recorded in the income statement.

Additions to properties in the course of development or refurbishment include the cost of finance and directly attributable internal and external costs incurred during the period of development until practical completion.

When the Group redevelops an existing investment property for continued use as an investment property, the property remains an investment property measured at fair value and is not reclassified.

Trading properties

Trading properties are included in the balance sheet at the lower of cost and net realisable value. Properties reclassified as trading properties are transferred at deemed cost, being the carrying amount at the date of reclassification.

Property transactions

Purchases and sales are recognised on exchange of contracts provided that, if the exchange is conditional, all material conditions have been satisfied.

Property, plant and equipment

This category comprises owner occupied property, motor vehicles and fixtures and fittings. These assets are stated at historical cost, or in the case of owner occupied property its carrying value at the date of transfer, less accumulated depreciation and any accumulated impairment. Owner occupied property is depreciated over 50 years and motor vehicles and fixtures and fittings are depreciated on a straight-line basis over their estimated useful lives of between three and five years.

Leases – the Group as a lessor

Properties leased out under operating leases are included in investment or trading properties, with lease income being recognised over the term of the lease on a straight-line basis.

Extract 8(A4) – Minerva plc, Investment property reconciliations, page 66

The company presents a reconciliation schedule of investment property, including acquisitions, additions, disposals, transfers and revaluations. The company also provides details about the fair value measurements established by the outside valuers.

11. Investment properties

Group	30 June 2007 £000	30 June 2006 £000
At 1 July: Net book value	580,150	804,099
Acquisitions	87,820	39,954
Additions	45,435	12,451
Disposals	–	(225,736)
Transfer to property, plant and equipment	–	(8,622)
Transfer to trading properties	–	(26,933)
Amounts receivable on surrender of lease	–	(26,133)
Revaluation movement	17,358	11,070
At 30 June: Net book value	730,763	580,150
Recognition of finance lease obligations	(2,134)	(2,136)
Amounts included within prepayments and accrued income	974	1,181
At 30 June: At valuation	729,603	579,195

The investment properties were valued on an open market value basis by CB Richard Ellis Limited, independent external valuers, as at the year-end in accordance with the current edition of the Appraisal and Valuation Standards issued by the Royal Institution of Chartered Surveyors. The total amount of interest capitalised as part of the cost of investment properties was £13,488,000 (2006: £6,911,000).

Investment properties include freehold properties with a net book value of £421,956,000 (2006: £279,483,000) and long leasehold properties with a net book value of £308,807,000 (2006: £300,667,000).

Extract 8(A5) – Minerva plc, Properties held by joint ventures, page 68

The company provides information on investment properties held by joint ventures. Note that the extract also present details on trading properties. These properties are valued at cost and include an amount of capitalized interest.

Notes to the financial statements
14. Investment in joint ventures continued (in part)

The Group's interests in joint ventures comprise a 25 per cent interest in the properties known as Skypark and Orchard Brae House, located in Glasgow and Edinburgh respectively. Both investment properties are held through joint venture vehicles which have as their main activity property investment or investment holding and operate and are registered in Great Britain. The investment properties were valued on an open market value basis by GVA Grimley LLP, independent external valuers, as at 30 June 2007 in accordance with the current edition of the Appraisal and Valuation Standards issued by the Royal Institution of Chartered Surveyors.

16. Trading properties

Group	30 June 2007 £000	30 June 2006 £000
At 1 July	26,933	–
Additions	80,685	26,933
At 30 June: Book value	107,618	26,933
At 30 June: Valuation	158,000	26,933

Trading properties comprise the Odeon Kensington and Lancaster Gate, which have been stated at cost in the consolidated balance sheet, but were valued at 30 June 2007 on an open market value basis by CB Richard Ellis Limited, independent external valuers. The total amount of interest capitalised as part of the cost of the properties was £3,895,000 (30 June 2006: £nil).

Both properties were acquired by the Group, in partnership with residential developer, Northacre Plc who will act as development manager. The Group holds a 95 per cent interest in both ventures, with Northacre also able to earn a range of returns, of up to 50 per cent in the case of Lancaster Gate and 60 per cent in the case of Odeon Kensington, on the incremental profits above pre-agreed thresholds.

Shaftesbury PLC – All extracts 8 (B) were obtained from the annual report for the year ended September 30, 2007.

Extract 8(B1) – Shaftesbury PLC, Presentation of investment property on the balance sheet and related revenues in the income statement, pages 63 and 64

The following extract presents an illustration of investment properties on the balance sheet and their related revenues in the income statement.

Group income statement for the year ended 30 September 2007 (in part)

	Note	2007 £'000	2006 £'000
Continuing operations			
Revenue from properties	3	62,423	58,792
Property charges	4	(12,843)	(11,809)
Net property income		49,580	46,983
Administration expenses	5	(5,628)	(5,320)
Charge in respect of equity settled remuneration	6	(1,140)	(2,101)
Total administration expenses		(6,768)	(7,421)
Operating profit before investment property disposals and valuation movements		42,812	39,562
Profit on disposal of investment properties	7	2,215	748
Investment property valuation movements	13	103,034	190,933
Operating Profit		148,061	231,243

Balance sheets as at 30 September 2007 (in part)

		Group		Company	
	Note	2007 £'000	2006 £'000	2007 £'000	2006 £'000
Non-current assets					
Investment properties	13	1,393,662	1,254,776	-	-
Office assets and vehicles	14	387	409	387	409
Investment in subsidiary undertakings	26	-	-	428,491	278,441
Investment in joint venture	27	-	-	78,958	78,958
Deferred tax assets	20	-	7,610	-	7,619
		1,394,049	1,262,795	507,836	365,427
Current Assets					
Trade and other receivables	15	24,622	15,058	506,513	589,899
Cash		336	9,090	-	8,898
Total assets		1,419,007	1,286,943	1,014,349	964,224

Extract 8(B2) – Shaftesbury PLC, Measurement uncertainties and critical judgements, page 66

In this extract, the company indicates that it has used outside valuers to assess the fair value of different elements reported in the financial statements, including investment property.

1. Basis of preparation
Accounting estimates and judgements (in part)
The measurement of fair value constitutes the principal area of judgement exercised by the Board in the preparation of these financial statements. The fair valuations of investment properties, financial derivatives and share based payments are carried out by external advisors who the Board considers to be suitably qualified to carry out such valuations.

Extract 8(B3) – Shaftesbury PLC, Accounting policies, page 66

Here, the company discloses its accounting policies under IFRS. It describes the accounting treatment of various costs (subsequent expenditure and finance costs). Note that the expensing of all finance costs might not be acceptable under revised IAS 23, *Borrowing costs*. Of particular interest is the accounting for dilapidations received from tenants and the effect of committed costs to be incurred on the valuation of refurbishment projects.

---

2. Accounting policies
Investment properties

Investment properties are properties owned or leased by the Group which are held for long term income and capital appreciation.

Investment properties are initially recognised on acquisition at cost and are revalued semi-annually to reflect fair value. Fair value is determined by either by external professional valuers on the basis of market value or by the Directors in the case of properties sold shortly after the year end.

In the case of investment properties which are leasehold interests, such leases are accounted for as finance leases and recognised as an asset and an obligation to pay future minimum lease payments. The investment property asset is held in the balance sheet at fair value, gross of the finance lease liability. Lease payments are allocated between the liability and finance charges so as to achieve a constant period rate of interest on the remaining balance of the liability.

Gains or losses arising on the revaluation of investment properties are included in the Income Statement in the accounting period in which they arise. Depreciation is not provided in respect of investment properties or any plant or equipment contained therein.

Additions to properties include costs of a capital nature only. Expenditure is classified as capital when it results in identifiable future economic benefits which are expected to accrue to the Group. All other property expenditure is written off in the Income Statement as incurred. Finance costs are not capitalised.

Where refurbishment projects are in progress at the balance sheet date, the contractually committed costs to be incurred in completing such projects are taken account of in the valuation.

Amounts received by way of dilapidations from tenants vacating properties are credited against the cost of reinstatement works. Where the Group has no intention of carrying out such works, the amounts received are credited to the Income Statement.

Extract 8(B4) – Shaftesbury PLC Investment property recognition, Accounting policies, page 67

This extract shows when the company recognizes an investment property.

---

2. Accounting policies
Purchases and sales of investment properties

Purchases and sales of investment properties are recognised in the financial statements on the date at which there is a legally binding and unconditional contract.

Extract 8(B5) – Shaftesbury PLC, Details related to revenues from properties, page 68

In this extract, the company provides certain elements of revenues and charges related to properties.

---

3. Revenue from properties	2007 £'000	2006 £'000
Rents due from tenants	55,348	51,535
Recognition of lease incentives	278	696
Rents receivable	55,626	52,231
Recoverable property expenses	6,797	6,561
	62,423	58,792

The Group's revenue is generated entirely from its principal activity of property investment located in London.

4. Property charges		
Property outgoings	6,046	5,248
Recoverable property expenses	6,797	6,561
	12,843	11,809

Extract 8(B6) – Shaftesbury PLC, Reconciliation of investment property held and valuation and commitments, page 72

The company provides a reconciliation schedule for the investment properties held, related capital commitments and the name of the valuers. Note that the report of the valuers was included outside the financial statements.

13. Investment properties

	Group 2007 £'000	Group 2006 £'000	Company 2007 £'000	Company 2006 £'000
At 1 October 2006 – book value	1,249,215	987,516	-	11,660
Acquisitions	32,101	107,667	-	-
Refurbishment and other capital expenditure	9,846	8,856	-	-
Disposals	(6,062)	(45,757)	-	(3,200)
Intra group disposals	-	-	-	(8,460)
Net surplus on revaluation	103,034	190,933	-	-
	1,388,134	1,249,215	-	-
Add: Head lease liabilities	5,528	5,561	-	-
Book value at 30 September 2007	1,393,662	1,254,776	-	-
Market value at 30 September 2007:				
Properties valued by DTZ Debenham Tie Leung Limited	1,312,295	1,184,255		
Properties valued by Knight Frank LLP	81,750	70,685		
	1,394,045	1,254,940		
Add: Head lease liabilities	5,528	5,561		
Less: Lease incentives recognised to date	(5,911)	(5,725)		
Book value at 30 September 2007	1,393,662	1,254,776		
Historic cost of properties at valuation	709,310	670,386		

Investment properties were subject to external valuation as at 30 September 2007 by qualified professional valuers, being members of the Royal Institution of Chartered Surveyors, either working for DTZ Debenham Tie Leung Limited, Chartered Surveyors (in respect of the Group's wholly owned portfolio) or Knight Frank LLP, Chartered Surveyors (in respect of properties owned by Longmartin Properties Limited), both firms acting in the capacity of External Valuers. All such properties were valued on the basis of Market Value in accordance with the RICS Appraisal and Valuation Standards.

A summary report by DTZ Debenham Tie Leung describing the basis of their valuation of the Group's wholly owned properties (which does not form part of these financial statements) is set out on pages 60 to 61.

Investment properties include freehold properties valued at £1,227.4 million (2006: £1,111.6 million), leasehold properties with an unexpired term of over 50 years valued at £88.9 million (2006: £77.3 million) and a notional apportionment of value in respect of part freehold/part leasehold properties, where the apportionment in respect of the leasehold element with over 50 years unexpired is £77.7 million (2006: £66.0 million).

Capital Commitments	Group 2007 £'000	Group 2006 £'000	Company 2007 £'000	Company 2006 £'000
Authorised and contracted	4,752	3,220	-	-
Authorised but not contracted	7,190	9,555	-	-

Extract 8(B6) – Shaftesbury PLC, Investment property held by joint ventures and valuation, pages 80 and 81

This extract provides information on investment property held by joint ventures.

27. Investment in Joint Venture	2007 £'000	2006 £'000
Shares at cost:		
At 1 October 2006	78,958	-
Acquired during the year:		
Shares acquired for cash	-	42,317
Shares acquired in consideration of assets contributed to joint venture	-	35,503
Incidental costs of acquisition	-	1,138
At 30 September 2007	78,958	78,958

The Company owns 7,782,100 Ordinary £1 shares in Longmartin Properties Limited, representing 50% of that company's issued share capital. The company is incorporated in Great Britain and registered in England and Wales and is engaged in property investment.

The Group's share of the results of Longmartin Properties Limited for the year ended 30 September 2007, and its assets and liabilities at that date, which have been consolidated in the Group's Income Statement and Balance Sheet, are as follows:

Income Statement	Year ended 30.9.2007 £'000	5.12.2006 to 30.9.2007 £'000
Rents receivable	2,841	2,485
Recoverable property expenses	176	272
	3,017	2,757
Property expenses	(619)	(275)
Recoverable property expenses	(176)	(272)
	(795)	(547)
Net property income	2,222	2,210
Administration expenses (2006 – restated to include administration fees payable to Shaftesbury PLC)	(382)	(349)
Operating profit before investment property disposals and revaluation	1,840	1,861
Profit on disposal of investment property	-	40
Investment property revaluation movements	9,217	8,479
Operating profit	11,057	10,380
Interest receivable	1,078	794
Interest payable	-	(208)
Profit before tax	12,135	10,966
Current tax	(875)	(746)
Deferred tax	(2,766)	(2,544)
Tax charge	(3,641)	(3,290)
Profit for the year	8,494	7,676
Dividends paid	(2,050)	(1,150)
Profit retained for the year	6,444	6,526

Balance Sheet	Year ended 30.9.2007 £'000	5.12.2006 to 30.9.2007 £'000
Non-current assets		
Investment properties at market value	81,750	70,685
Head lease liability grossed up	5,529	5,561
	87,279	76,246
Current assets		
Trade and other receivables	715	544
Amounts due from shareholders	18,800	19,875
Cash	335	193
Total assets	107,129	96,858

27. Investment in Joint Venture (continued)		
Current liabilities		
Trade and other payables	**2,389**	1,296
Non-current liabilities		
Deferred tax	**5,310**	2,544
Head lease liability	**5,529**	5,561
Total liabilities	**13,228**	9,401
Net assets attributable to the Shaftesbury Group	**93,901**	87,457

PLANNING FOR IMPLEMENTATION

Identifying and Reporting Investment Property

There is no specific Canadian standard dealing with accounting for investment property held by a reporting entity. Nor are there specific industry standards (as in the case of US GAAP) that apply to real estate investment entities.

Because of the absence of a specific standard in Canada, entities have not been particularly concerned about identifying investment properties other than those covered in AcG 18. This situation will change with IAS 40 implementation. Entities will have to establish whether they hold assets that meet the definition of investment property. Information systems must be modified to enable recognition and disclosure of items in accordance with IAS 40. For example, entities will have to gather data on:

- property classification (investment and others), including the basis for the assessment;

- property held under an operating lease that they choose to classify as investment property; and

- investment property held by an entity of a consolidated group but that is occupied by a related entity that must be accounted for in accordance with IAS 16 for consolidated financial statements.

IAS 40 notes that judgement is needed to determine whether a property qualifies as investment property and that entities should develop criteria so that they can exercise that judgement consistently in accordance with the definition of investment property. Specific questions related to this identification would include, for example, the following:

- Does the entity classify investment properties developed for sale as inventory?

- Is investment property to be occupied by the entity being correctly classified as property, plant and equipment?

Accounting Choices and Investment Property Valuation

IAS 40 gives entities the option to account for investment property using either the fair value model (with changes in fair value recognized in the income statement) or the depreciated historical cost (less impairment losses) model in accordance with IAS 16. The choice has to be made on first application and has to be applied consistently for all investment property.

An entity wishing to limit the impact of IAS 40 adoption might want to use the cost model, which would limit the recording of unrealized gains and losses in income. Consistent with this adoption, impairment should be accounted for in accordance with IAS 36. Doing so, all properties classified as owner-used and as investment property would be measured on the same basis in the financial statements.

The fair value model, on the other hand, provides more pertinent information. Under this model, a property held by a lessee under an operating lease may be classified as an investment property.

Fair value use or disclosure as required by IAS 40 could be a critical issue, particularly if a company's market capitalization is tied to an investment property. In this case, it will be essential to assess the adequacy and the impact of the model used to value the investment property. Use of an independent competent external valuer might be key in reducing the risks related to fair value measurements errors.

Informing Users of Financial Statements

It will be important to inform users that:

- Investment properties are initially recorded at cost.
- If fair value is chosen for use (which is expected for a majority of entities), that would increase the total value of the assets (when compared with current Canadian GAAP). This would affect an entity's financial ratios.
- Notes to financial statements contain valuable information about investment property, including reconciliation between the carrying amounts of investment property at the beginning and end of the period.

An interesting anomaly produced by IAS 40 and IAS 16 implementation is that a company may have two similar properties carried at their fair values. If one is an investment property and the other is owner-occupied, an increase in the value of the investment property would increase the company's reported income, but a similar increase in the owner-occupied property would be reported as a revaluation item, with no effect on income. This anomaly should be clearly explained to the investors.

Transitional Provisions

Transition provisions under IFRS 1 apply to various long-term assets, including property, plant and equipment, intangible assets and investment property. In case of investment property, when IAS 40 is first adopted, all adjustments to previous carrying amounts under the transitional provisions will be treated as an adjustment to the retained earnings of the period.

As discussed previously, an entity could choose to value its investment property at cost or at fair value and consequently transition provisions will be applied as follows:

If the entity selects the cost model to measure its investment property at the end of the period as permitted under IAS 40, it could measure it at the opening IFRS balance sheet either at (1) an amount as would have been established under IAS 40 assuming this Standard requirements have always been applied or (2) at fair value which would become its "deemed cost" under the IAS 40 cost model. Note that deemed cost is an amount used as a surrogate for cost or depreciated cost at a given date.

If the entity selects the fair value model to measure its investment property at the end of the period as permitted under IAS 40, it will record it at fair value in its opening IFRS balance sheet. It might be useful to note that an entity might change its accounting policies when presenting comparative statements. For example, an entity might use the cost model in 2014 and the fair value model in 2015. In this case, according to IAS 40, the entity would be encouraged to restate its comparative figures and adjust the opening balance of the retained earnings for the earliest presented period. This differs from rules in IAS 8 for dealing with changes in accounting polices.

Keep Posted

IAS 40 allows a lessee to treat a leasehold property held under an operating lease as a finance lease if that property meets the definition of an investment property and the fair value model is used. Applying this option means that assets and liabilities will be recognized and measured at fair value of the rights and obligation under the lease.

The IASB and FASB are reviewing the reporting of lease transactions as currently required under IFRS and US GAAP. This leasing project will involve the reconsideration of all aspects of lease accounting. Entities should monitor the evolution of this project given that it may lead to major changes in accounting and reporting methodologies of investment property, which might have a major impact on the real estate sector.

Chapter 9
Financial Instruments and Hedge Accounting

Standards Discussed in this Chapter

International

IAS 1 – Presentation of Financial Statements
IAS 32 – Financial Instruments: Presentation
IAS 39 – Financial Instruments: Recognition and Measurement
IFRS 4 – Insurance Contracts
IFRS 7 – Financial Instruments: Disclosures
IFRIC 9 – Reassessment of Embedded Derivatives
IFRIC 16 - Hedges of a Net Investment in a Foreign Operation

Canadian

CICA 3855 – Financial Instruments — Recognition and Measurement
CICA 3862 – Financial Instruments — Disclosures
CICA 3863 – Financial Instruments — Presentation
CICA 3865 – Hedges
AcG-12 – Transfers of receivables
EIC-88 – Debtor's accounting for a modification or exchange of debt instruments
EIC-122 – Balance sheet classification of callable debt obligations and debt obligations expected to be refinanced
EIC-149 – Accounting for retractable or mandatorily redeemable shares
EIC-164 – Convertible and other debt instruments with embedded derivatives
EIC-166 – Accounting policy choice for transaction costs on initial measurement
EIC-169 – Determining whether a contract is routinely denominated in a single currency

INTRODUCTION

Although Canadian standards for financial instruments are already generally harmonized with IFRS, some differences might have been created between Canadian GAAP and IFRS when the AcSB decided to:

- minimize conflicts with US GAAP (by allowing, for example, the use of short-cut methods for hedge accounting);

- limit modifications of Canadian accounting standards on issues currently being debated by the FASB and the IASB (by not adopting certain amendments to IAS 39); and

- address certain aspects of Canadian GAAP (for example the measurement of related party transactions).

Consequently, current Canadian accounting standards on financial instruments are a hybrid of US GAAP and IFRS. The following are the pertinent IFRS and Canadian standards concerning the recognition, the measurement and the presentation of financial instruments:

- IAS 32 and CICA 3863: classification as liabilities or as equity and criteria for offsetting financial assets and financial liabilities;

- IFRS 7 and CICA 3862: disclosures on (1) significance of financial instruments for an entity's financial position and performance and (2) nature and extent of risks arising from any financial instruments an entity is exposed to and how the entity manages those risks;

- IAS 39, CICA 3855 and AcG-12: recognition, measurement and derecognition of financial assets and financial liabilities and accounting for contracts to buy or sell non-financial items;

- IAS 39 and CICA 3865: qualification and hedge accounting models.

IAS 32 and, particularly, IAS 39 differ significantly from other IFRS because they are more rules based than principles based. They contain many definitions, rules and exceptions that must be continuously "improved." As indicated above, the AcSB decided not to adopt some of those "improvements," such as the February 26, 2008 amendment to IAS 32 and IAS 1, which requires the classification of financial instruments having specific characteristics as equity instead of as financial liabilities.

To reduce reliance on rules, the IASB launched several long-term projects that could modify significantly many aspects of financial instruments reporting. Even though these projects might lead to significant changes to current IFRS requirements, companies should start assessing the impact of adopting the current version of IAS 32 and IAS 39. To help in that assessment, this chapter discusses the following topics:

- key definitions;
- financial instruments classification;
- scope:
  - elements excluded,
  - entities exempted,
  - limited exclusions;
- initial recognition of financial instruments:
  - timing of recognition,
  - amount recognized,
  - transaction costs;
- financial assets and financial liabilities recognition and subsequent measurement:
  - primary financial assets and liabilities,
  - free-standing derivatives,
  - compound or hybrid instruments;
- presentation of financial instruments:
  - liability/equity classification,
  - compound or hybrid instruments,
  - offsetting,
  - classification of financial assets and financial liabilities as current, and non-current;
- impairment of financial assets:
  - impairment recognition,
  - grouping assets,
  - determining impairment loss and reversal,
  - particular considerations for loans and receivables,

- o requirements summary for recognition and reversals:
- derecognition:
  - o derecognition of financial assets,
  - o derecognition of financial liabilities;
- fair value:
  - o measurement,
  - o fair value option;
- hedge accounting:
  - o hedged item,
  - o hedging instruments,
  - o hedge accounting criteria,
  - o hedge accounting models,
  - o discontinuing hedge accounting;
- disclosures of financial instruments:
  - o information about the significance of financial instruments,
  - o nature and extent of exposure to risks arising from financial instruments;
- business combination.

IMPACT ON FINANCIAL STATEMENTS

The scope of the financial instruments standards is wide ranging. They apply to all entities and cover many elements reported in the financial statements. These standards are complex, and many of the concepts they raise are subject to interpretation.

Most companies preparing their financial statements according to Canadian GAAP implemented new Canadian financial instruments standards, in 2007. When changing to IFRS, those companies should refer to the IAS 39 interpretive materials and "improvements" that were not incorporated into the new Canadian standard. The absence of Canadian guidance in those areas could lead to diversity in practice and differences with IFRS, especially where companies refer to US guidance (instead of that provided under IFRS) to minimize Canadian/US differences. Such potential diversity in practice should be eliminated on IFRS adoption.

Although IAS 32, IAS 39 and IFRS 7 adoption should not have a significant impact on financial statements prepared according to Canadian GAAP, some potential differences could trigger unexpected earnings volatilities and higher debt equity ratios. Some of these differences will occur mainly because IAS 39:

1. restricts the use of fair value option while Canadian GAAP do not have such a restriction;
2. adopts a different derecognition model for financial assets than the one currently required under Canadian GAAP;
3. does not allow the use of "short cut" methods for hedge accounting, while CICA 3865 allows such use;
4. does not have particular measurement rules for related party transactions contained in Canadian GAAP;
5. requires the measurement at fair value of unquoted equity investments (unless it cannot be reliably estimated); this differs from CICA 3855, which prescribes that all unquoted equity investments be measured at cost;

6. uses different wordings for impairment of financial assets that might result in their earlier recognition than under CICA 3855;

7. requires impairment reversals for certain investments in debt securities that is prohibited under CICA 3855; and

8. requires identified embedded derivatives to be bifurcated in contracts that are still outstanding at the IFRS transition date and were entered into prior to the date the entity selected as the embedded derivatives transition date under CICA 3855.

In summary, changing to IFRS could result in presenting more liabilities on the balance sheet and making more measurements at fair value.

Additional fair value measurements might add to current controversies concerning the valuation of certain financial assets in current illiquid markets. Currently, fair value measurements have both a favourable and an unfavourable impact on financial analysis. On the positive side, financial statements reflect current market conditions and give greater insights into management views on the ultimate settlement amounts. On the negative side, financial statements are less reliable in absence of observable market data and report increased volatility in earnings, making it more difficult to predict future results.

ANALYSIS OF RELEVANT ISSUES

This section examines and illustrates some relevant issues related to IFRS requirements for financial instruments. Differences with corresponding Canadian GAAP are noted.

Key Definitions

Definitions

IAS 32 and IAS 39 provide the following definitions:

A *financial instrument* is any contract that gives rise to a financial asset of one entity and a financial liability or equity instrument of another entity.

A *financial asset* is any asset that is:

- cash;
- an equity instrument of another entity;
- a contractual right:
  o   to receive cash or another financial asset from another entity, or
  o   to exchange financial assets or financial liabilities with another entity under conditions that are potentially favourable to the entity; or
- a contract that will or may be settled in the entity's own equity instruments and is:
  o   a non-derivative for which the entity is or may be obliged to receive a variable number of its own equity instruments, or
  o   a derivative that will or may be settled other than by the exchange of a fixed amount of cash or another financial asset for a fixed number of the entity's own equity instruments. For this purpose, the entity's own equity instruments do not include instruments that are themselves contracts for the future receipt or delivery of its own equity instruments.

A *financial liability* is any liability that is:

- a contractual obligation:
  o   to deliver cash or another financial asset to another entity, or

- o to exchange financial assets or financial liabilities with another entity under conditions that are potentially unfavourable to the entity; or
- a contract that will or may be settled in the entity's own equity instruments and is:
  - o a non-derivative for which the entity is or may be obliged to deliver a variable number of its own equity instruments, or
  - o a derivative that will or may be settled other than by the exchange of a fixed amount of cash or another financial asset for a fixed number of the entity's own equity instruments. For this purpose, the entity's own equity instruments do not include instruments that are themselves contracts for the future receipt or delivery of its own equity instruments.

An *equity instrument* is any contract that evidences a residual interest in the assets of an entity after deducting all of its liabilities.

A *derivative* is a financial instrument or other contract with all three of the following characteristics:

- Its value changes in response to changes in a specified interest rate, financial instrument price, commodity price, foreign exchange rate, index of prices or rates, credit rating or credit index, or other variable. In the case of a non-financial variable, the variable cannot be specific to a party to the contract (sometimes called the "underlying").
- It requires no initial net investment or an initial net investment that is smaller than would be required for other types of contracts that would be expected to have a similar response to changes in market factors.
- It is settled at a future date.

These definitions are important because they affect the accounting for financial instruments. Generally, all definitions are identical to those provided by CICA 3855.

However, certain financial instruments may meet the definition of a derivative under IAS 39 but not under CICA 3855. For example, the lack of a notional amount would not exempt a contract from being treated as a derivative under IAS 39. This differs from CICA 3855, which states that a contract is not accounted for as a derivative if the notional amount is not specified or otherwise determinable.

Financial Instruments Classification

This section briefly reviews the classification of financial assets and financial liabilities established by the standards, along with the respective prescribed accounting treatment. The table below summarizes these requirements. Since IFRS and Canadian GAAP are generally harmonized, this high-level summary will apply to both IFRS and Canadian standards.

Category	Measurement after Initial Recognition (Generally Initial Recognition is Measured at Fair Value)	Recognition of Gains or Losses Related to Fair Value Changes
Loans and receivables	Amortized cost (using the effective interest method)	On derecognition, impairment and write-down
Held-to-maturity	Amortized cost (using the effective interest method)	On derecognition and write-down
Available-for-sale financial assets	Fair value	Recognized in other comprehensive income and recycled to net income on derecognition and impairment
Financial assets at fair value through profit or loss (both held-for-trading financial assets or designated as such)	Fair value	Recognized in net income

Category	Measurement after Initial Recognition (Generally Initial Recognition is Measured at Fair Value)	Recognition of Gains or Losses Related to Fair Value Changes
Financial liabilities at fair value through profit or loss (both held-for-trading financial liabilities or designated as such)	Fair value	Recognized in net income
Other liabilities	Amortized cost (using the effective interest method)	On derecognition

Below are some observations concerning the classification of financial assets and financial liabilities. Note that differences between IAS 39 and CICA 3855 requirements are identified.

Classification on Initial Recognition

Financial assets are classified on initial recognition into four categories: (1) loans and receivables, (2) held to maturity, (3) held for trading (fair value through profit or loss) or (4) available for sale. Financial liabilities are classified into two categories: (1) held for trading and (2) others.

Classification as "Loans and Receivables"

Loans and receivables are non-derivative financial assets with known payments that are not quoted in an active market, that do not qualify as trading assets, have not been designated as available for sale or as held for trading and for which the holder may recover substantially all of its initial investment, other than because of credit deterioration.

According to IAS 39, all loans and receivables quoted in an active market would be excluded from the loans and receivables category, while CICA 3855 excludes only "debt securities." This might lead to differences in accounting policies when entities apply CICA 3855. Some entities might focus on the word "debt" and, therefore, on the legal characteristics of the instrument, while others might focus on word "securities," which might refer to whether or not the instrument is "quoted in a market." One of the advantages of classifying financial assets as loans and receivables instead of held-to-maturity assets is the fact that the former category is not subject to the "tainting" provisions.

CICA 3855 specifically excludes loans and receivables from the held-for-trading category, while IAS 39 requires such classification if they meet the criteria for held-for-trading (for example when an entity intends to sell its loans in the near term). In addition, CICA 3855 does not have IAS 39 fair value option constraints and therefore an entity can elect to classify on initial recognition any loans or receivables in the held-for-trading category.

Classification as "Held for Trading" and "Financial Assets and Financial Liabilities Designated at Fair Value" or "Fair Value Option" Application

A financial asset or financial liability at fair value through profit or loss (designated as held for trading) is a financial asset or financial liability that is held for trading or a financial asset or financial liability that, on initial recognition, the entity has designated as at fair value through profit or loss (the fair value option).

IAS 39 divides the categories of financial assets and financial liabilities at fair value through profit or loss into two subcategories: those really held for trading (i.e., they will be traded in the very short term to realize gains or losses) and those merely designated as such. "Financial assets and financial liabilities designated at fair value" reflect the application of the "fair value option."

Under both IAS 39 and CICA 3855, any financial instrument (as defined by IAS 39 and CICA 3855) can be designated on initial recognition as held for trading. However, in June 2005 amendments to IAS 39 have introduced a number of restrictions on the use of the fair value option which do not exist in Canadian GAAP. The fair value option may be used only when it results in more relevant information, either because it eliminates or reduces a measurement or recognition inconsistency, or that a group of financial assets and/or liabilities are managed and evaluated on the fair value basis.

Since reclassification is restricted under both IAS 39 and CICA 3855, entities should evaluate the impact of making their designations on future periods.

Neither IAS 39 nor CICA 3855 permit the use of the fair value option for:

- lease receivables or payables, as they have been carved out of the standards;
- financial assets or liabilities whose fair value cannot be reliably measured; and
- financial assets and liabilities, after initial recognition.

Terminology Issues

The standards use several terms to designate financial assets and liabilities that are measured at fair value, including changes in fair values amounts in the income statement. Such measurements can be optional or required, depending on the standard.

Even though the term "held for trading" is widely accepted under both Canadian GAAP and IFRS, IASB and IFRS adopters often use the term "financial assets or financial liabilities at fair value through profit or loss" instead. The IASB is currently seeking clarification on the term to be used. It held discussions in March 2008, reaching a tentative decision for explaining the differences between "held primarily for the purpose of trading" under IAS 1 and "held for trading" under IAS 39.

Other wording might be used when measuring a financial asset or liability at fair value, such as "fair value option" and "designated as held for trading."

We use these various terms interchangeably throughout the text because wording in the extracts presented are not consistent and, until there is a consensus on the words to use, readers need to understand that they have the same meaning.

Classification as "Available for Sale"

Available-for-sale assets are non-derivative financial assets that are either designated as such or are a financial asset that cannot be categorized within one of the other three categories above.

If an entity intends to trade certain securities, those securities are not classified as available for sale.

Problems might arise for a portfolio of investments consisting of equity and debt securities that are traded according to an entity's established guidelines. Accordingly, it is possible that part of the investments could fall within the "available for sale" category and another part would be classified as "held for trading". In such situations, the label of "available for sale" or "held for trading" might not be appropriate for presenting the portfolio on the balance sheet. CICA 3855 explicitly permits an entity to use a different label from the one it uses to describe the different classes of its financial assets.

Classification as "Held to Maturity"

A *held-to-maturity investment* is a non-derivative financial asset with known payments and a fixed maturity date and the entity has the positive intention and ability to hold the asset to maturity other than those:

- the entity upon initial recognition designates as at fair value through profit or loss;
- the entity designates as available for sale; and
- that meet the definition of loans and receivables."

The classification "held to maturity" is used when an entity is virtually certain that an item will, indeed, be held to maturity. CICA 3855 allows the classification of "puttable" financial assets (where the holder has the right to require the issuer to repay or redeem the instrument before maturity) as held to maturity if the holder does intend to hold them until ultimate maturity. IAS 39 does not permit the classification of any puttable financial asset as held to maturity.

Consequently, it will be more difficult for companies to classify certain debt instruments as held to maturity under IFRS. This should not have a significant impact in practice as it is expected that most companies would not choose to include debt securities in this category because of the potential negative impact of "tainting rules" contained in both CICA 3855 and IAS 39. Under both IFRS and Canadian GAAP, all investments, except those classified as held to maturity, are measured at fair value. Because of this exception and because management intention to hold the investment to maturity could not be substantiated, standards setters introduced tainting provisions as a means to limit earnings management attempts. Basically, tainting provisions prevent an entity from classifying investments as held to maturity if during the current or preceding two financial years, it has sold or reclassified more than an insignificant amount of such investments before maturity, except in certain very narrowly defined circumstances. Both IAS 39 and CICA 3855 contain the tainting rule to ensure genuine intention and ability to hold a debt investment to maturity.

Financial Liabilities

Financial liabilities that are not classified as held for trading continue to be measured at amortized cost.

The held-for-trading liabilities category often comprises various unfavourable derivative contracts. Because IAS 39 and CICA 3855 contain different perspectives on notional amounts (see previous comment related to derivative definition), more liabilities might be classified as held for trading under IAS 39.

Reclassifications

Even though reclassification between main categories of financial assets is restricted, it is allowed or required in certain circumstances for available-for-sale and held-to-maturity investments.

Reclassification is required in certain circumstances, such as:

- in business combinations;
- on impairment (see impairment of loans and receivables under IAS 39, illustrated later in this chapter); or
- on "tainting" (see held-to-maturity debt investments analyzed later in this chapter).

The allowable reclassifications under both standards can have two significant effects:

- A held-to-maturity investment might be reclassified as available for sale if an entity no longer intends to, or is unable to, hold that investment to maturity (in which case, the investment is re-valued at fair value and the difference with the carrying value is included in other comprehensive income).

- An available-for-sale asset will be reclassified as held to maturity once the tainting period has passed (in which case, the amount recognized in other comprehensive income is amortized over the remaining life of the investment using the effective interest method).

Amendments to IAS 39 and IFRS 7 – Reclassification of Financial Assets

In October 2008, in response to exceptional circumstances of the current credit crisis, the IASB issued an amendment to IAS 39 and IFRS 7, *Reclassification of Financial Assets* that permits reclassification of certain non-derivative financial assets recognized in accordance with IAS 39. In the same month, the AcSB approved without exposure equivalent amendments to CICA 3855. The amendments are narrow in their scope and are unlikely to impact an entity's reporting under IAS 39 and CICA 3855 unless it has acquired assets for trading purposes or has classified loans and receivables as available-for-sale assets.

A financial asset within the scope of these amendments can only be reclassified out of the fair value through profit of loss (held-for-trading category) or available-for-sale classifications if very specific criteria are met. The criteria vary depending on whether the asset would have met the definition of 'loans and receivables' had it not been classified as held for trading or available for sale at initial recognition.

Below is a summary of the amendments that were introduced:

- reclassification out of Fair Value to Profit or Loss is:

  o permitted depending on whether or not the financial asset meets the definition of loans and receivables as follows:

    - non-derivative financial assets that would have met the definition of loans and receivables (i.e., if they had not been required to be classified as held for trading on initial recognition). For such assets, the entity must also have the intention and ability to hold the financial asset for the foreseeable future or until maturity,

      - other non-derivative financial assets: in *rare circumstances*[1];

  o recorded at the fair value of the financial asset on the date of reclassification which becomes the new cost or amortized cost, as applicable. Any gain or loss previously recognized in profit or loss is not reversed upon reclassification;

- reclassification out of the available-for-sale category is:

  o permitted only to financial asset that would have met the definition of loans and receivables (i.e., if they had not been designated as available for sale) if the entity has the intention and ability to hold the financial asset for the foreseeable future or until maturity,

  o recorded at its fair value on the date of reclassification and this fair value becomes its new cost or amortized cost, as applicable. Any gain or loss previously recognized in other comprehensive income is accounted for in accordance with IAS 39 paragraph 54 (if the financial asset has a fixed maturity, then

---

1   The amended standards do not define *rare circumstances* but the accompanying Basis for Conclusions specifies that "rare circumstances arise from a single event that is unusual and highly unlikely to recur in the near term." An accompanying IASB press release stated that "the deterioration of the world's financial markets that has occurred during the third quarter of this year is a possible example of rare circumstances cited in these IFRS amendments and therefore justifies its immediate publication."

any gain or loss is amortized to profit or loss over the remaining life of the held-to-maturity investment using the effective interest method);

- Effective Interest Rate Calculation: The amendment also addresses how to deal with increases in estimates of future cash receipts as a result of expected increased recoverability of those cash receipts subsequent to a financial asset being reclassified from either of the fair value through profit or loss or available-for-sale categories. The effect of such an increase is recognized as an adjustment to the effective interest rate from the date of the change in estimate rather than as an adjustment to the carrying amount of the asset at the date of change in estimate. As a result, the change in estimate is recognized in profit or loss as part of interest income over the remaining holding period of the asset, rather than being recognized immediately in profit or loss;

- disclosures related to reclassification: IFRS 7 is amended to require that the following be disclosed when a financial asset is reclassified in accordance with the amended requirements in IAS 39:

  o In the period in which a reclassification occurs;
    - the amount reclassified into and out of each category,
    - if reclassification is due to *rare circumstances*: facts and circumstances indicating that the situation was rare,
    - fair value gain or loss on the financial asset recognized in profit or loss or other comprehensive income in that reporting period and in the previous reporting period,
    - effective interest rate and estimated amounts of cash flows the entity expects to recover, as at the date of reclassification of the financial asset;

  o for the reporting period in which the financial asset was reclassified and each reporting period until the financial asset is derecognized: the fair value gain or loss that would have been recognized in profit or loss or other comprehensive income if the financial asset had not been reclassified, and the gain, loss, income and expense recognized in profit or loss,

  o For each reporting period until derecognition of the reclassified financial asset: the carrying amounts and fair values of all financial assets that have been reclassified in the current and previous reporting periods;

- effective Date and Transition: The transition requirements offer limited relief to treat a reclassification as if it had occurred at an earlier date. The effective date for the amendments is July 1, 2008. An entity can elect to make a reclassification and treat it as if it occurred on July 1, 2008. This relief is available only for reclassifications made prior to November 1, 2008; any reclassification of a financial asset made after that date takes effect from the date the reclassification is made. Reclassifications of a financial asset cannot be applied retrospectively prior to July 2008.

Illustrative Disclosures:

Extract 9(1) – Classification of financial assets and financial liabilities

---

Skandinaviska Enskilda Banken AB (AR 2007), pages 63 and 64
1 Accounting policies (in part)
Significant accounting policies for the Group
Financial assets
Classification

Financial assets are classified in the following four categories at initial recognition:
- Financial assets at fair value through profit or loss
- Loans and receivables
- Held-to-maturity investments
- Available-for-sale financial assets

Financial assets at fair value through profit or loss consist of financial assets classified as held for trading and financial assets which, upon initial recognition, have been designated at fair value through profit or loss (Fair Value Option). Financial assets are classified as held for trading if they are held with the intention to be sold in the short-term and for the purpose of generating profits. Derivatives are classified as held for trading unless designated as hedging instruments. The Fair Value Option can be applied to contracts including one or more embedded derivatives, investments that are managed and evaluated on a fair value basis and situations in which such designation reduces measurement inconsistencies.

The nature of the financial assets and financial liabilities which have been designated at fair value through profit or loss and the criteria for such designation are described in the relevant notes to the financial statements.

Loans and receivables are non-derivative financial assets with fixed or determinable payments that are not quoted in an active market.

Held-to-maturity investments are non-derivative financial assets designated with the intention and ability to hold until maturity. This category consists of financial assets with fixed or determinable payments and fixed maturity. Equity instruments cannot be classified as held to maturity as their life is indefinite.

Financial assets are designated in the available for sale category when intended to be held for an indefinite time and may be sold in response to specific needs for liquidity or anticipation of changes in equity price or those financial assets that have not been classified as financial assets measured at fair value through profit or loss, as loans and receivables or as investments held to maturity.

Financial liabilities
Classification

Financial liabilities are classified in two categories:
- Financial liabilities at fair value through profit or loss
- Financial liabilities.

Financial liabilities at fair value through profit or loss are either classified as held for trading or designated as fair value through profit or loss on initial recognition (Fair Value Option). The criteria for classification of financial liabilities under the Fair Value Option are the same as for financial assets.

Financial liabilities held for trading are primarily short positions in interest bearing securities and equities and negative replacement value of derivatives.

The category financial liabilities primarily include the Group's short-term and long-term borrowings.

Financial liabilities are derecognised when extinguished that is when the obligation is discharged, cancelled or expired.

Commentary: This extract provides an illustration of the financial assets and financial liabilities classification required under IAS 39. This accounting policy is in line with CICA 3855.

Extract 9(2) – Derivatives definition

Suez (Reference Document 2007), page 212
1.4.10 Financial instruments (in part)
1.4.10.3.1 Definition and scope of derivative financial instruments (in part)

Derivative financial instruments are contracts: (i) whose value changes in response to the change in one or more observable variables; (ii) that do not require any material initial net investment; and (iii) that are settled at a future date.

Derivative instruments therefore include swaps, options, futures and swaptions, as well as forward commitments to purchase or sell listed and unlisted securities, and firm commitments or options to purchase or sell non-financial assets that involve physical delivery of the underlying.

Commentary: This extract refers to the definition of derivatives provided in both IAS 39 and CICA 3855. The company lists certain derivatives meeting that definition, including contracts requiring physical delivery of the underlying and unlisted securities forwards (which might be difficult to value reliably). The company provides further details on contracts requiring physical delivery of the underlying (see extract 9 (3)). Under CICA 3855, unlisted securities forwards would be valued at cost.

Scope

IAS 32, IAS 39 and IFRS 7 and corresponding Canadian standards CICA 3855, CICA 3862 and CICA 3863 should be applied to all types of financial instruments and to all entities unless scoped out by these standards.

Elements Excluded from Canadian and International Financial Instruments Standards

The following elements are excluded from all standards on financial instruments:

- interests in subsidiaries, entities subject to significant influence and joint ventures;
- employers' rights and obligations arising from employee benefit plans;
- contracts for contingent consideration in a business combination (acquirer point of view);
- financial instruments, contracts and obligations under stock-based payment transactions; and
- pension obligations of defined benefit pension plans.

Some elements are excluded only from Canadian standards. For example, CICA 3855 scopes out contracts that require a payment based on specified volumes of sales or service revenues, while IAS 39 is silent on that issue. In addition, certain financial instruments are covered by a specific standard and scoped out from another one. For example, unrecognized financial instruments are within the scope of IFRS 7 (CICA 3862) but not within the scope of IAS 39 (CICA 3855). Similarly, rights and obligations under leases (with a few exceptions) are excluded from IAS 39 but included in IAS 32.

Entities Exempted from CICA 3855

CICA 3855 contains scope exceptions for the following industries:

- companies within the scope of AcG-18, *Investment companies*;
  Certain CICA 3855 requirements still apply to these companies, such as the accounting for transaction costs and the separation of embedded derivatives. Even though no equivalent scope exemptions exist under IAS 39, the availability of the fair value option should minimize reporting differences between Canadian and IFRS financial statements.

- insurance companies within the scope of CICA 4211, *Life Insurance Enterprises – Specific Items* and AcG-3, *Financial reporting by property and casualty insurance companies*;
Exemptions relate to insurance contracts only, which CICA 3855.09 defines (see limited exclusions below).

Insurance contracts (as defined in IFRS 4) are generally excluded from IAS 39 requirements. IAS 39 gives insurance companies the following accounting choice (which is not available under Canadian GAAP since there is no equivalent to IFRS 4):

- disclose information related to insurance contracts according to IFRS 7; or
- disclose information related to insurance contracts according to IFRS 4.

Limited Exclusions from IAS 39 Requirements and CICA 3855

As discussed below, depending on the circumstances, certain items might be excluded from IAS 39 requirements.

Leases

Rights and obligations under leases are accounted for according to IAS 17, *Leases* and CICA 3065, *Leases*. In certain circumstances, however, entities must refer to IAS 39 and CICA 3855 requirements, for example when:

- the lessor suffers impairments of receivable amounts;
- a capital lease requires derecognition of lessee liabilities; and
- derivatives are embedded in leases for both lessor and lessee.

As indicated previously, IAS 39 (CICA 3855) scope exemptions would have the following consequences:

- Leasing arrangements cannot be classified as assets held for trading or available for sale.
- Lease liabilities cannot be classified as held for trading.

Insurance Contracts

Both IFRS 4 and CICA 3855 define insurance contracts as contracts "under which one party (the insurer) accepts significant insurance risk from another party (the policyholder) by agreeing to compensate the policyholder if a specified uncertain future event (the insured event) adversely affects the policyholder." Though insurance contracts have the characteristics of derivatives, they differ in that they are not market driven but rather require a payment when an actual loss is incurred.

Insurance contracts (as defined) are generally excluded from the scope of IAS 39 and CICA 3855. Exceptions relate to embedded derivatives included in insurance contracts.

Certain insurance policies that require a payment based on climatic, geological or other physical variables (referred to as "weather derivatives") are covered under financial instruments standards when:

- they do not meet the definition of insurance contracts (IAS 39); or
- they are exchange traded (CICA 3855).

Commitments to Buy and Sell Non-financial Assets

Generally, commitments to buy and sell non-financial assets are excluded from IAS 39 and CICA 3855 because they do not meet the definition of financial instruments (they do not represent rights to receive or exchange a financial asset). When such commitments can be net settled in cash, however, and are not entered into and held for the purpose of the receipt/delivery of a non-financial item in accordance with the entity's expected purchase, sale or usage requirements, they would be within the scope of IAS 39 (CICA 3855).

According to both standards, net settlements can occur even if contract terms do not permit either counterparty to settle net, for example when:

- there is a past practice of net settling similar contracts;
- there is a past practice, for similar contracts, of taking delivery of the underlying asset and selling it within a short period after delivery to generate a profit from short-term fluctuations in price, or from a dealer's margin.

Commodity contracts cover non-financial items easily convertible to cash. Consequently, an entity holding commodity contracts must determine whether it has to account for them as derivatives or as regular commitments to buy and sell non-financial assets.

To treat commodity contracts as regular commitments (and, therefore, avoid their recognition and measurement as derivatives under CICA 3855), an entity must document its "own use" or "regular purchase, regular sales." Note that an entity could contravene the "own use" or "regular purchases, regular sales" rules when, in the past, it had settled similar contracts with a counterparty in cash (practice of net settlement) or bought the underlying commodity and then resold it to other parties within a short period (short-term trading). Such practices could raise questions such as:

- Would any net settlement practice compel an entity to account for all of its commodity contracts as derivatives?
- Does the closing out of normal sale or purchase commodity contracts for valid business reasons result in "tainting" in a similar manner as for held-to-maturity securities? (See discussion on debt investments later in this chapter.)

Guarantees

IAS 37, *Provisions, Contingent Liabilities and Contingent Assets* deals with non-financial guarantees (see Chapter 15). Financial guarantee contracts, which are covered by IAS 39 and CICA 3855, have various legal forms and include letters of credit and credit default contracts. IAS 39 clearly specifies the subsequent measurement requirements for financial guarantees.

IAS 39 provides three examples of financial guarantee contracts for which it prescribes different accounting treatment:

- A financial guarantee meeting the definition of insurance contract (i.e., risk transferred is significant): An entity could elect to apply either IAS 39 or IFRS 4. Under IAS 39, the issuer would initially recognize a financial guarantee contract at fair value. Subsequently, unless the financial guarantee contract was designated at inception to be at fair value through profit or loss, the issuer would measure it at the higher of:
  o the amount determined in accordance with IAS 37, and
  o the amount initially recognized less, where appropriate, cumulative amortization recognized in accordance with IAS 18, *Revenue*.

  This situation is covered by CICA 3855 and AcG-14, *Disclosure of guarantees*, both of which require that such a guarantee be measured at inception at fair value. Subsequent re-measurement is not specified under CICA 3855.

- Credit-related guarantees requiring payment for changes in the market and not subsequent to a loss related to the failure of the debtor to make payments when due (for example, guarantees based on changes in a specified credit rating or credit index): Such guarantees would constitute derivatives and be accounted for according to IAS 39.

CICA 3855 has the same requirement.

- Financial guarantees issued in connection with the sale of goods: The issuer would apply IAS 18 to establish when it recognizes the revenue from the guarantee and from the sale of goods.

  This corresponds to the situation of guarantees excluded from CICA 3855 and AcG-14, which are not recognized under CICA 3855.

Equity Instruments

An entity's equity instruments (including options, warrants and other instruments classified in equity) are exempted from IAS 39 and CICA 3855 requirements. To qualify for this exemption, the instrument must be presented in the equity section of the balance sheet according IAS 32 (CICA 3863) requirements.

Differences in requirements under IAS 32 and CICA 3863 will lead to IFRS/Canadian GAAP reporting differences. Note that the holders of equity investments recognize a financial asset according to IAS 39 (CICA 3855) requirements.

Loan Origination Commitments

Commitments to originate loans that cannot be net settled or for which an entity did not have a past practice of selling the loans shortly after origination are excluded from the scope of IAS 39 (CICA 3855).

Although an entity may choose to designate a loan commitment as held for trading, such an election is limited under IAS 39.

Illustrative Disclosures:

Extract 9(3) – Contracts to buy non-financial items

Suez (Reference Document 2007), page 212

1.4.10 Financial instruments (in part)

1.4.10.3.1 Definition and scope of derivative financial instruments (in part)

Electricity and natural gas purchase and sale contracts, in particular, are systematically analyzed to determined whether they represent purchases and sales arising in the ordinary course of business, in which case they do not fall within the scope of IAS 39. The first step of this analysis consists in demonstrating that the contract was entered into and continues to be held for the purpose of a purchase or sale with physical delivery of the underlying, in accordance with the Group's expected sale or usage requirements in the foreseeable future in the ordinary course of its operations. The second step is to demonstrate that:

- the Group has no practice of settling similar contracts on a net basis. In particular, forward purchases or sales with physical delivery of the underlying that are carried out with the sole purpose of balancing Group energy volumes are not considered by the Group as contracts that are settled net;
- the contract is not negotiated with the aim of realizing financial arbitration;
- the contract is not equivalent to a written option. In particular, in the case of electricity sales allowing the buyer a certain degree of flexibility concerning the volumes delivered, the Group distinguishes between contracts that are equivalent to capacity sales – considered as transactions falling within the scope of ordinary operations – and those that are equivalent to written financial options, which are accounted for as derivative financial instruments.

Only contracts that meet all of the above conditions are considered as falling outside the scope of IAS 39. Adequate specific documentation is compiled to support this analysis.

Commentary: This extract provides an analysis of contracts involving non-financial items that might be classified as derivatives or "regular" purchase commitments. The company describes elements that are taken into account for establishing "own use" or "regular purchase." The information presented in this extract goes beyond IAS 39 (CICA 3855) requirements and would be considered good disclosure under Canadian GAAP.

Extract 9(4) – Financial guarantee contracts

National Grid Electricity Transmission plc (AR 2007), page 44

1. Adoption of new accounting standards (in part)

New IFRS accounting standards and interpretations adopted in 2006/07 (in part)

Amendments to IAS 39 'Financial Instruments: Recognition and Measurement', and IFRS 4 'Insurance Contracts: Financial Guarantee Contracts' define a financial guarantee contract and specify which accounting standard will apply to such contracts. Generally, financial guarantee contracts are within the scope of IAS 39. However, where the issuer of a financial guarantee contract has previously asserted that it regards such contracts as insurance contracts, then they may elect to apply either IAS 39 or IFRS 4 to those contracts. The Company accounts for such contracts as insurance contracts.

Commentary: This extract provides an illustration of financial guarantee contracts previously described as insurance contracts. The company may, therefore, elect to apply either IAS 39 or IFRS 4 to those contracts as allowed by paragraph IAS 39.2e. No equivalent election exists in CICA 3855.

Extract 9(5) – Financial guarantee contracts

N M Rothschild & Sons Limited (AR 2007), page 44

1. Summary of Significant Accounting Policies (in part)

Financial assets and liabilities (in part)

Financial guarantee contracts

Financial guarantee contracts are contracts that require the issuer to make specified payments to reimburse the holder for a loss it incurs because a specified debtor fails to make payments when due, in accordance with the terms of a debt instrument. Financial guarantee liabilities are initially recognised at fair value, and the initial fair value is amortised over the life of the guarantee. The guarantee liability is subsequently carried at the higher of the amortised amount and the expected present value of any expected payment (when a payment under the guarantee has become probable).

Where one Group company enters into financial guarantee contracts to guarantee the indebtedness of other companies within the Group, that company considers these to be insurance arrangements and accounts for them as such. In this respect, the Group company treats the guarantee contract as a contingent liability until such time as it becomes probable that it will be required to make a payment under the guarantee.

Commentary: This extract provides an illustration of financial guarantee contracts considered to be insurance contracts. Accounting policy is in line with IFRS.

Initial Recognition of Financial Instruments

Timing of Recognition

According to IAS 39 and CICA 3855, an entity must recognize a financial asset or a financial liability on its balance sheet when, and only when, it becomes a party to the contractual provisions of the instrument. This is usually referred to as the trade date.

Not all financial instruments are recorded at their trade date. For example firm commitments for the sale or purchase of merchandise are not recorded. Rather, trade receivables (payables) are recognized when an entity delivers (receives) the ordered merchandise.

In addition, IAS 39 and CICA 3855 provide special rules for regular way purchases or sales of financial assets (i.e., for recording purchases or sales of securities on a stock exchange in the timeframe established by regulation or convention) by allowing an entity to select either the trade date or the settlement date as an accounting policy choice.

The recognition method used for regular way purchases or sales of financial assets should be applied consistently for "regular way" purchases and sales of financial assets belonging to a given category as defined in the standards (held for trading, designated as such, available for sale and held to maturity).

Amount Recognized

IAS 39 and CICA 3855 require that all financial assets and liabilities be measured initially at fair value. This is a significant change from previous requirements where many financial instruments were initially recorded at cost.

Generally, the fair value of a financial instrument at recognition will equal the transaction price (i.e., the fair value of the consideration given for an asset or received for a liability). In certain circumstances, valuation techniques might have to be used, for example, when consideration given or received relates to financial and non-financial elements. Such valuation would:

- separate the financial instrument component from the non-financial one, thus permitting reporting that reflects the substance of the transaction; and
- result in the recording of an immediate gain (Day 1 gain) or of other non-financial assets or liabilities.

In practice, it might be difficult to proceed with such a separation because the financial and non-financial components of an arrangement might be interlinked. Consequently, standards would not allow Day 1 gains to be recorded unless the fair value of that instrument is backed up by comparison to other observable current market transactions involving the same instrument (i.e., without modification or repackaging) or based on a valuation technique whose variables include only data from observable markets.

IAS 39 and CICA 3855 differ significantly in their requirements for the initial recognition measurement for financial instruments exchanged or issued in related party transactions. Such transactions have to be recorded in conformity with CICA 3840, *Related Party Transactions*, which has no counterpart in IFRS.

Transaction Costs

IAS 39 requires that transaction costs directly attributable to the acquisition or issue of a financial asset or liability be included in the initial carrying value of that asset or liability. These costs should, however, be expensed when the financial asset or liability is classified at fair value through profit or loss (held for trading).

Though CICA 3855 has the same requirement for financial assets and liabilities classified as held for trading, it allows an entity to make an accounting policy choice for other categories of financial assets and liabilities:

- recognize all transaction costs in net income (i.e., same treatment as held for trading, resulting in differences with IAS 39); or
- include transaction costs in the amount initially recognized for the financial assets and liabilities (same as IAS 39).

EIC-166 provides guidance on how this accounting choice should be applied by specifying that different accounting policy choices are permitted only for dissimilar financial assets and financial liabilities. The EIC provides guidance for determining whether or not financial assets and liabilities are similar for the purpose of this accounting policy choice.

CICA 3855 requirements for transaction costs do not agree with AcG-4, *Fees and costs associated with lending activities*, which indicates that lending fees be included as an adjustment to the yield of a loan (i.e., included in the amount of asset recorded).

Since IAS 39 does not provide an accounting choice for the treatment of transaction costs, this issue is not a concern under IFRS.

Illustrative Disclosures:

Extract 9(6) – Measurement of financial assets and financial liabilities

---

Skandinaviska Enskilda Banken AB (AR 2007), page 64

1 Accounting policies (in part)

Significant accounting policies for the Group (in part)

Financial assets (in part)

Measurement

Financial assets are recognised on the balance sheet when the Group becomes a party to the contractual provisions of the instrument and are measured at fair value on initial recognition. Transaction costs are included in the fair value on initial recognition except for financial assets designated at fair value through profit or loss where transaction costs are expensed in the profit and loss statement.

Financial assets are derecognised when the rights to receive cash flows have expired or the Group has transferred substantially all risks and rewards. Transfers of financial assets with retention of all or substantially all risks and rewards include for example repurchase transactions and securities lending transactions.

Trade date accounting is applied to financial assets classified in the categories, financial assets at fair value through profit or loss and available for sale financial assets. Settlement date accounting is applied to the other categories of financial assets.

The valuation of financial assets after initial recognition is governed by their classification. Financial assets at fair value through profit or loss are measured at fair value. Gains and losses arising from changes in fair value are reported in the income statement on an ongoing basis under the item Net income from financial transactions.

Loans and receivables and held-to-maturity investments are measured at amortised cost using the effective interest method.

Available for sale financial assets are measured at fair value. Gains and losses arising from changes in fair value are reported directly in the fair value revaluation reserve in equity until the financial asset with which they are associated is sold or impaired. In the case of sale or impairment of a financial asset, the accumulated gains and losses previously reported in equity are recognised in profit or loss. Interest on interest-bearing, available for sale financial assets is recognised in profit or loss, applying the effective interest method. Dividends on equity instruments, classified as available for sale, are also recognised in profit or loss.

Investments in equity instruments without a quoted market price in an active market are measured, if possible, at fair value on the basis of a recognised valuation method. Investments in equity instruments without a quoted market price in an active market and whose fair value cannot be reliably measured are measured at cost.

Financial liabilities (in part)

Measurement

Financial liabilities are measured at fair value on initial recognition. In the case of financial liabilities not included in the category financial liabilities measured at fair value through profit or loss, transaction costs directly attributable to the acquisition or the issuance of the financial liability are included in the calculation of fair value.

After initial recognition, financial liabilities measured at fair value through profit or loss, are measured and reported in a manner equivalent to the measurement and reporting of financial assets measured at fair value through profit or loss.

Financial liabilities are, after initial recognition, measured on an ongoing basis at amortised cost, using the effective interest method.

Commentary: This extract reflects accounting requirements under IAS 39. The company specifies that financial assets are:

- Recognized on the balance sheet when the company becomes a party to the contractual provisions of the instrument. This corresponds to requirements specified by CICA 3855.

- Measured at fair value on initial recognition, including transaction costs except for financial assets designated at fair value through profit or loss. Under CICA 3855, the company would also have an accounting policy choice to expense all transaction costs related to the acquisition of available-for-sale and held-to-maturity investments.

- Derecognized when the rights to receive cash flows have expired or the company has transferred substantially all risks and rewards. Note that, according to IAS 39, financial assets are not derecognized when they are transferred with retention of all or substantially all risks and rewards as in the case of repurchase transactions and securities lending transactions. This might differ under AcG-12. (See derecognition section discussed later in this chapter.)

- Recorded on the trade date for two categories of financial assets (those measured at fair value through profit or loss and those classified as available for sale). Settlement date accounting is applied to the other categories of financial assets. This corresponds to requirements specified in CICA 3855. Note that this election is available only for regular way purchases and sales.

- Accounted for subsequently as follows (all treatments correspond to CICA 3855 requirements except where otherwise noted):

  o Those at fair value through profit or loss are measured at fair value, with gains and losses arising from changes in fair value reported in the income statement on an ongoing basis. Note that the company discloses where such gains or losses are included in the income statement.

  o Loans and receivables and held-to-maturity investments are measured at amortized cost using the effective interest method.

  o Available-for-sale financial assets are measured at fair value, with gains and losses arising from changes in fair value reported directly in the fair value revaluation reserve in equity (other comprehensive income under CICA 3855 and amended IAS 1). As required under IAS 39 and CICA 3855, the amount of accumulated gains and losses previously reported in equity (accumulated other comprehensive income) are recycled to net income when the associated financial asset is sold or impaired.

  o Interest on interest-bearing, available-for-sale financial assets is recognized in profit or loss, applying the effective interest method. Dividends on equity instruments, classified as available for sale, are also recognized in profit or loss.

  o Investments in equity instruments without a quoted market price in an active market are measured, if possible, at fair value on the basis of a recognized valuation method. Investments in equity instruments without a quoted market price in an active market and whose fair value cannot be reliably measured are measured at cost. This differs from CICA 3855, which specifies that all investments in equity instruments without a quoted market rate be measured at cost.

For financial liabilities, the company specifies that (all treatments correspond to CICA 3855 requirements except where indicated otherwise):

- They are measured initially at fair value.

- Amounts initially recorded include transaction costs directly attributable to the issuance of a financial liability not included in the category of financial liabilities measured at fair value through profit or loss (note that, under CICA 3855, the company could have an accounting policy choice to expense all transaction costs related to debt issuance).

- After initial recognition, financial liabilities measured at fair value through profit or loss are measured and reported in the same way as measurement and reporting of financial assets measured at fair value through profit or loss.

- Financial liabilities are, after initial recognition, measured on an ongoing basis at amortized cost, using the effective interest method.

Extract 9(7) – Initial recognition of financial assets

Andritz AG (AR 2007), page 24
D. Accounting and Valuation Principles (in part)
m. Financial Instruments under IAS 39 and IFRS 7 (in part)
Financial assets (in part)

Financial instruments are recognized and derecognized on a trade. This is the day of purchase or sale of an investment on which the contract terms require delivery of the investment within the timeframe established by the market concerned, and financial instruments are initially measured at fair value plus transaction costs, except for those financial assets classified as at fair value through profit or loss, which are initially measured at fair value without transaction costs. ...

Commentary: In this extract, the company specifies that it uses the trade date for the recognition of regular way financial assets. This is one of the two dates possible for regular way trades of financial assets (the other being the settlement date).

The company includes (as required by IAS 39) transaction costs in the initial measurement of financial assets, except those classified as at fair value through profit or loss (or held for trading under CICA 3855). These accounting methods conform to CICA 3855 except that the latter allows, as an accounting choice, an entity to expense all transaction costs.

Extract 9(8) – Initial measurement at fair value

UBS AG (AR 2007), page 6
Critical accounting policies (in part)
Recognition of deferred day 1 profit or loss

A closely related issue to determining fair value of financial instruments is the recognition of deferred day 1 profit or loss. We have entered into transactions, some of which will mature in the long-term, where we determine fair value using valuation models for which not all material inputs are market observable prices or rates. We initially recognize such a financial instrument at the transaction price, which is the best indicator of fair value, although the value obtained from the relevant valuation model may differ. Such a difference between the transaction price and the model value is commonly referred to as "day 1 P / L". We do not immediately recognize that initial difference, usually a gain, in profit or loss because the applicable accounting literature prohibits immediate recognition of day 1 profit. The accounting literature does not, however, address its subsequent recognition prior to the time when fair value can be determined using market observable inputs or by reference to prices for similar instruments in active markets. It also does not address subsequent measurement of these instruments and recognition of subsequent fair value changes indicated by the model.

Our decisions regarding recognizing deferred day 1 profit are made after careful consideration of facts and circumstances to ensure we do not prematurely release a portion of the deferred profit to income. For each transaction, we determine, individually, the appropriate method of recognizing the day 1 profit amount in the income statement. It may be amortized over the life of the transaction, or deferred until fair value can be determined using market observable inputs, or realized through settlement. In all instances, any unrecognized day 1 profit is immediately released to income if fair value of the financial instrument in question can be determined either by using market observable model inputs or by reference to a quoted price for the same product in an active market.

Changes in fair value after day 1 resulting from changes in observable parameters or otherwise indicated by the model are recognized immediately in the income statement independently of the release of deferred day 1 profits. See Note 26e) to the Financial Statements for quantitative information on deferred day 1 profit or loss.

Note 1 Summary of Significant Accounting Policies (in part), page 26
5) Determination of fair value (in part)

... When entering into a transaction where model inputs are not market observable, the financial instrument is initially recognized at the transaction price, which is generally the best indicator of fair value. This may differ from the value obtained from the valuation model. The timing of the recognition in income of this initial difference in fair value ("Deferred day 1 profit or loss") depends on the individual facts and circumstances of each transaction but is never later than when the market data become observable. Refer to Note 26e) for details on deferred day 1 profit or loss.

UBS AG (AR 2007) (continued)

Note 26 Fair Value of Financial Instruments (in part), page 80

e) Deferred Day 1 Profit or Loss

The table reflects financial instruments for which fair value is determined using valuation models where not all inputs are market observable. Such financial instruments are initially recognized at their transaction price although the values obtained from the relevant valuation model on day 1 may differ. The table shows the aggregate difference yet to be recognized in profit or loss at the beginning and end of the period and a reconciliation of changes in the balance of this difference (movement of deferred day 1 profit or loss).

	For the year ended	
CHF million	31.12.07	31.12.06
Balance at the beginning of the year	951	1,343
Deferred profit/(loss) on new transactions	1,259	890
Recognized (profit) / loss in the income statement	(1,383)	(1,200)
Revision to fair value estimates	(224)	
Foreign currency translation	(53)	(82)
Balance at the end of the year	550	951

Commentary: This extract includes elements obtained from different portions of the annual report. It deals with fair measurement issues at initial recognition when the transaction price does not correspond to fair value resulting in the Day 1 gain. Note that such a gain could be recognized and included in income if fair value were evidenced by comparison to other observable current market transactions. The accounting method described is in accordance with IFRS and Canadian GAAP. Chapter 3 of this volume also discusses this issue (see Extract 3(7)).

There are many other instances where transaction price does not correspond to fair value, such as employee loans, private financing and government loans. These may constitute multi-element arrangements for which the isolation and measurement at fair value of financial component would better reflect the substance of the transaction.

Types of Financial Assets and Financial Liabilities

IAS 39 and CICA 3855 adopt a partial rather than a full fair value model. Consequently, financial assets and liabilities are measured at fair value or amortized cost depending on their type (debt, equity, derivative instrument or a combination of such instruments) and their classification as required by the standards.

Primary Financial Assets and Liabilities

Primary financial asset and liabilities consist of non-derivative or traditional financial instruments, including equity and debt investments, receivables and trade payables.

Equity Investments

Equity investments are categorized initially as either:

- financial assets at fair value through profit or loss (or held for trading), with any change in fair value being recognized in net income; or

- available-for-sale financial assets, with all changes in fair value (other than impairments) being recognized in other comprehensive income.

Note that equity investments cannot be classified as held to maturity as their life is indefinite.

All equity investments are carried at fair value at all times. There is an exception to this rule, which differs under IFRS and Canadian GAAP:

- IAS 39 requires that unlisted equity securities classified as available for sale be measured at fair value, with any changes in that value being recognized directly in other comprehensive income; when their fair value cannot be measured reliably, the securities are measured at cost.

- CICA 3855 requires all equity securities not traded on an active market to be measured at cost.

Both IFRS and Canadian GAAP require that dividends on equity investments classified as available for sale be recognized in income when an entity's right to receive payment is established.

Debt Investments

Debt investments include investments in debt securities quoted in an active market, investments in government debt, corporate bonds, commercial paper and securitized debt, as well as mandatory redeemable preferred shares.

Debt investments could be classified initially in one of the following three categories as defined in IAS 39 (CICA 3855):

1. Fair value through profit or loss (held for trading or designated as such): all changes in fair value would be recognized in income (same as for equity investments described above).

2. Available for sale (sometimes referred to as "fair value through other comprehensive income"): all changes in fair value (other than impairments) would be recognized in other comprehensive income (same as for equity investments described above).

   IFRS and Canadian GAAP prescribe different accounting treatments for foreign exchange gains or losses on debt investments classified as available for sale (see Chapter 10):

   - IAS 39 requires their inclusion in net income.
   - CICA 3855 requires that they be part of other comprehensive income.

3. Held to maturity: Fair value must be used in certain limited circumstances, for example, where an investment is carried at amortized cost (using the effective interest method) is "tainted". This will occur when an entity sells or reclassifies, during the current or preceding two financial years more than an insignificant amount of that investment, except in certain very narrowly defined circumstances. This is referred to as "tainting rule."

Both IAS 39 and CICA 3855 contain the tainting rule to ensure genuine intention and ability to hold a debt investment to maturity. In addition, hedge accounting cannot be used to cover interest rate risk associated with held-to-maturity debt investment (because an investor should be indifferent to interest rate risk when choosing to hold an investment to maturity). Note that IAS 39 permits hedging of such debt investments when there is a likelihood of exposure to foreign currency risk or credit risk. CICA 3865 allows prepayment risk to be hedged in addition to foreign currency and credit risk.

IAS 39 and CICA 3855 differ on the possible classification of puttable debt instruments:

- IAS 39 does not allow a puttable debt investment to be classified as held to maturity;
- CICA 3855 allows such a classification if the entity has the positive intent and ability to hold it to maturity.

Under both IFRS and Canadian GAAP:

- the effective interest method has to be used to calculate interest revenues for held-to-maturity and available-for-sale debt investments;
- foreign exchange gains or losses are included in income for held-to-maturity debt investments. Consequently, Canadian GAAP accounting treatment of foreign ex-

change gains or losses will depend on how a debt instrument is classified whereas treatment is consistent under IFRS.

Loans and Receivables

When an entity lends money, or provides goods or services directly to a debtor, loans and receivables are created. Under IAS 39 and CICA 3855, loans and receivables are measured at amortized cost, using the effective interest method.

Certain loans and receivables would be measured at fair value, for example, if they are designated as available for sale or as held for trading on initial recognition. In addition, IAS 39 requires quoted loans or loans that can be sold immediately or in the near future to be classified as held for trading, whereas they are measured at amortized cost under CICA 3855.

Financial Liabilities

IAS 39 and CICA 3855 classify financial liabilities into two categories:

- financial liability at fair value through profit or loss if it is either held for trading or designated as such on initial recognition;

- all other financial liabilities, which are measured at amortized cost.

The majority of financial liabilities will be measured at amortized cost. This will mean that the effective interest method will be used to calculate interest expense. There could, however, be a measurement mismatch when financial assets are measured at fair value, for example, in the case of financial institutions.

Illustrative Disclosures:

Extract 9(9) – Held for trading

ABB Grain Ltd. (Financial Report 2007), page 49

2. Significant accounting policies (in part)

(g) Financial assets (in part)

Financial assets at fair value through profit or loss

Financial assets are classified as financial assets at fair value through profit or loss where the financial asset:

(i)   has been acquired principally for the purpose of selling in the near future;

(ii) is a part of an identified portfolio of financial instruments that the Group manages together and has a recent actual pattern of short-term profit-taking; or

(iii) is a derivative that is not designated and effective as a hedging instrument.

Financial assets at fair value through profit or loss are stated at fair value, with any resultant gain or loss recognised in profit or loss. The net gain or loss recognised in profit or loss incorporates any dividend or interest earned on the financial asset. Fair value is determined in the manner described in note 32.

Commentary: This extract describes the method used for accounting for investments classified at fair value through profit or loss (held for trading). The accounting method described conforms to both IAS 39 and CICA 3855 requirements.

Extract 9(10) – Available-for-sale

BNP Paribas (Registration Document 2007), page 118

1.c.3 Securities (in part)

Categories of securities (in part)

Available-for-sale financial assets

Available-for-sale financial assets are fixed-income and variable-income securities other than those classified as "fair value through profit or loss" or "held-to-maturity".

Assets included in the available-for-sale category are initially recorded at fair value plus transaction costs where material. At the balance sheet date, they are remeasured to fair value, with changes in fair value (excluding accrued interest) shown on a separate line in shareholders' equity, "Unrealised or deferred gains or losses". On disposal, these unrealised gains and losses are transferred from shareholders' equity to the profit and loss account, where they are shown on the line "Net gain/loss on available-for-sale financial assets".

Income recognised using the effective interest method derived from fixed-income available-for-sale securities is recorded in "Interest income" in the profit and loss account. Dividend income from variable-income securities is recognised in "Net gain/loss on available-for-sale financial assets" when the Group's right to receive payment is established.

Commentary: Here, the company describes the method used for accounting for debt and equity investments classified as available for sale . It conforms to both IAS 39 and CICA 3855 requirements. Note that, under CICA 1530 (and amended IAS 1), the amount the company reports in shareholders' equity related to unrealized or deferred gains or losses would be part of other comprehensive income.

Extract 9(11) – Available-for-sale

Andritz AG (AR 2007), page 24

D. Accounting and Valuation Principles (in part)

m. Financial Instruments under IAS 39 and IFRS 7 (in part)

AFS financial assets

Available-for-sale financial assets are non-derivative financial assets that are designated as available for sale or are not classified as (a) loans and receivables, (b) held-to-maturity investments or (c) financial assets at fair value through profit or loss. Equity securities (e.g. shares), debt securities (e.g. bonds) and other investments (e.g. fund shares) held by the Andritz Group are designated as AFS financial assets.

AFS are stated at fair value. Resulting gains and losses arising from changes in fair value are recognized directly in equity in the investments revaluation reserve (IAS 39 reserve) with the exception of impairment losses, interest calculated using the effective interest method and foreign exchange gains and losses on monetary assets, which are recognized directly through profit or loss. Where the investment is disposed of or is determined to be impaired, the cumulative gain or loss previously recognized in the investments revaluation reserve is included in profit or loss for the period. Dividends on AFS equity instruments are recognized in profit or loss when the Group's right to receive payments is established.

The fair value of AFS monetary assets denominated in a foreign currency is determined in that foreign currency and translated at the spot rate at the balance sheet date. The change in fair value attributable to translation differences that result from a change in amortized cost of the asset is recognized in profit or loss, and other changes are recognized in equity.

Commentary: This extract describes the method used for accounting for debt and equity investment classified as available for sale (AFS). It conforms to both IAS 39 and CICA 3855 requirements, except that 3855 requires that:

- the fair value attributable to translation differences on monetary investments be recorded in other comprehensive income; and

- the amount the company reports in shareholders' equity related to unrealized or deferred gains or losses would be part of other comprehensive income. The adoption of amended IAS 1 has eliminated this difference.

Extract 9(12) – Held-to-maturity debt

Xstrata plc (AR 2007), page 152
6. Principal Accounting Policies (in part)
Held-to-maturity investments

Non-derivative financial assets with fixed or determinable payments and fixed maturity are classified as held-to-maturity when the Group has the positive intention and ability to hold to maturity. Investments intended to be held for an undefined period are not included in this classification. Other long term investments that are intended to be held-to-maturity, such as bonds, are subsequently measured at amortised cost. This cost is computed as the amount initially recognised minus principal repayments, plus or minus the cumulative amortisation using the effective interest method of any difference between the initially recognised amount and the maturity amount. This calculation includes all fees paid or received between parties to the contract that are an integral part of the effective interest rate, transaction costs and all other premiums and discounts. For investments carried at amortised cost, gains and losses are recognised in income when the investments are derecognised or impaired, as well as through the amortisation process.

Commentary: The company describes the method used for accounting for debt investment classified as held to maturity, as well as its calculation of the initial amount recognized. All accounting methods conform to both IAS 39 and CICA 3855 requirements except that the latter would permit the expensing of transaction costs.

Extract 9(13) – Loans and receivables

Albidon Limited (AR 2007), page 39
2. SUMMARY OF SIGNIFICANT ACCOUNTING POLICIES (in part)
n) Other financial assets (in part)
Loans and receivables

Loans and receivables are non derivative financial assets with fixed or determinable payments that are not quoted in an active market. They arise when the Group provides money, goods or services directly to a debtor with no intention of selling the receivable. They are included in current assets, except for those with maturities greater than 12 months after the balance sheet date which are classified as non-current assets. Loans and receivables are included in receivables in the balance sheet.

Commentary: This extract describes the method used for accounting for loans and receivables. It conforms to both IAS 39 and CICA 3855 requirements.

Extract 9(14) – Financial liabilities

Andritz AG (AR 2007), page 25
D. Accounting and Valuation Principles (in part)
m. Financial Instruments under IAS 39 and IFRS 7 (in part)
Financial liabilities

Financial liabilities can be classified either as financial liabilities at FVTPL or other financial liabilities.

Financial liabilities at FVTPL

The Andritz Group classifies financial liabilities at FVTPL if the financial liability is held for trading, which applies only to derivatives. The Group enters into a variety of derivative financial instruments to manage its exposure to changes in fair value, foreign exchange rate risk and commodity price risk, including foreign exchange forward contracts, interest rate swaps and commodity forwards. Financial liabilities at FVTPL are stated at fair value, with any resulting gain or loss recognized in profit or loss.

Other financial liabilities

Other financial liabilities, including borrowings, are initially measured at fair value, net of transaction costs. Subsequently they are measured at amortized costs using the effective interest method, with interest expense recognized on an effective yield basis.

Free Standing Derivatives

The lack of a notional amount would not exempt a contract from being treated as a derivative under IAS 39. This differs from CICA 3855, which states that a contract is not accounted for as a derivative if the notional amount is not specified or otherwise determinable. Certain financial instruments may meet the definition of a derivative under IAS 39 but not under CICA 3855.

IAS 39 and CICA 3855 require that all derivatives be considered as held for trading (measured at fair value through profit or loss).

There are exceptions to this general rule:

- derivatives still measured at fair value where certain amounts of gains or losses are excluded from net income because of special hedge accounting rules (see discussion below on cash flow hedge);
- derivatives measured at cost because:
  - o they are linked to unquoted equity instruments (CICA 3855),
  - o they are linked to unquoted equity instruments and their fair value cannot be measured reliably (IAS 39).

Consequently, derivatives linked to unquoted equity are automatically exempted from derivative accounting treatment under CICA 3855 and are measured at cost. To qualify for such an exemption under IAS 39, an entity would have to demonstrate that it would not be able to reliably measure such derivatives at fair value.

Illustrative Disclosure:

Extract 9(15) – Free standing derivatives

> **HSBC Holdings plc (Form 20-F 2006), page 405**
> **Derivatives and hedge accounting - IFRSs (in part)**
> - Derivatives are recognised initially, and are subsequently remeasured, at fair value. Fair values of exchange-traded derivatives are obtained from quoted market prices. Fair values of over-the-counter derivatives are obtained using valuation techniques, including discounted cash flow models and option pricing models.
> - In the normal course of business, the fair value of a derivative on initial recognition is considered to be the transaction price (that is the fair value of the consideration given or received). However, in certain circumstances the fair value of an instrument will be evidenced by comparison with other observable current market transactions in the same instrument (without modification or repackaging) or will be based on a valuation technique whose variables include only data from observable markets, including interest rate yield curves, option volatilities and currency rates.
>
> When such evidence exists, HSBC recognises a trading gain or loss on inception of the derivative. When unobservable market data have a significant impact on the valuation of derivatives, the entire initial difference in fair value indicated by the valuation model from the transaction price is not recognised immediately in the income statement but is recognised over the life of the transaction on an appropriate basis, or when the inputs become observable, or the transaction matures or is closed out.

Compound or Hybrid Instruments

Recognition of Embedded Derivatives

Terms and conditions of free-standing derivatives may be "embedded" within another financial instrument or non-financial contract (referred to as the "host" contract). The combination of host contract and embedded derivative is commonly referred to as "compound instrument" or "hybrid instrument."

From the issuer perspective, a compound instrument could combine both a liability host and an embedded equity derivative. The combination is sometimes referred to as a "hybrid instrument" (see analysis of hybrid instruments in the "Presentation of Financial Instruments" section).

It should be noted that a derivative that is attached to a financial instrument but is contractually transferable independently of that instrument would not be considered to be an embedded derivative, but rather a free-standing derivative.

An embedded derivative can originate from deliberate financial engineering, for example, when one tries to make a low interest-rate debt more attractive by including an equity-linked return. Embedded derivatives can also be created inadvertently through market practices and common contractual arrangements, such as leases, insurance contracts and purchase and sale contracts.

Many leases, insurance contracts and regular purchase or sale contracts are executory in nature and are usually not recognized in the financial statements. Standards still require an entity to bifurcate (separate) embedded derivatives when such features are not closely related to the host contract. This might lead to oversights when searching for embedded derivatives.

IAS 39 and CICA 3855 require an embedded derivative to be separated from its host contract and accounted for as a derivative when:

- the economic risks and characteristics of the embedded derivative are not closely related to those of the host contract;
- a separate instrument with the same terms as the embedded derivative would meet the definition of a derivative; and
- the entire instrument is not measured at fair value with changes in fair value recognized in the income statement.

These criteria are justified for financial reporting purposes. For example, it would be inappropriate to separate an embedded derivative from its hosts if the derivative displayed risks and economic characteristics closely related to its host contract. Such a separation could result in an unwarranted focus on the risks of the embedded derivative while ignoring similar risks in the host contract. If, however, the embedded derivative had economic characteristics and risks not closely related to those of the host contract, the separation would be required to better reflect the risk of the hybrid instrument.

Measurement of Embedded Derivatives

The accounting treatment for a separated embedded derivative is the same as for a standalone derivative. If an entity is unable to measure an embedded derivative that should be separated, both IAS 39 and CICA 3855 require that the entire combined contract be treated as a financial asset or financial liability that is held for trading (and, therefore, re-measured to fair value at each reporting date, with value changes in net income).

Embedded Foreign Currency Derivatives

IAS 39 and CICA 3855 state that an embedded foreign currency derivative does not have to be separated from its contract host if payments are denominated in one of the following currencies:

- the functional currency of any substantial party to that contract;

- the currency in which the price of the related good or service that is acquired or delivered is routinely denominated in commercial transactions around the world (such as the US dollar for crude oil transactions);

- a currency that is commonly used in contracts to purchase or sell non-financial items in the economic environment in which the transaction takes place (e.g., a relatively stable and liquid currency that is commonly used in local business). (This criterion can be used only under IFRS; CICA 3855 permits the use of this criterion only if an accounting policy election has been made).

EIC-169 expands on commodity contracts denominated in foreign currencies. No equivalent interpretations were included specifically in the IFRS.

Option or Automatic Provision to Extend the Remaining Term of a Debt

Embedded derivatives could be created by a renewal option or an automatic provision to extend the remaining term of a debt. Depending on the circumstances, this feature could be considered to constitute a contract combining a non-derivative host and an embedded derivative, which must be accounted for separately. IAS 39 and CICA 3855 specify that an option or automatic provision that can be executed at an amount close to a debt instrument's fair value does not constitute an embedded derivative that needs to be separated. This exemption from separation requirement is justified since:

- exercise of the option or automatic provision would not be triggered by a market factor but rather by particular factors related to the entity involved;

- an embedded option is not a derivative since its value is always zero (unlike a stand-alone option).

Multiple Embedded Derivatives

A single host contract can contain multiple embedded derivatives. IAS 39 requires that multiple embedded derivatives be accounted for as a single compound derivative, unless they relate to different risks and are readily separable and independent of each other. In that case, they are treated as separate derivatives. This differs from CICA 3855, which requires multiple embedded derivatives in a single instrument to be accounted for in aggregate as a single compound derivative. However, embedded derivatives that are classified as equity are accounted for separately from those classified as assets or liabilities.

Reassessment of Embedded Derivatives

IAS 39 and CICA 3855 require that embedded derivatives be examined for possible bifurcation at the date an entity first becomes a party to a contract. IFRIC 9 requires that a reassessment be performed only when a contract has been changed, significantly modifying the cash flows. Note, however, that following the issuance of Reclassification of Financial Assets (Amendments to IAS 39 and IFRS 7) in October 2008, the IASB published in December 2008, an Exposure Draft that proposes amendments to IFRIC 9 and IAS 39. It intends to clarify that the requirements to separate particular embedded derivatives from hybrid (combined) financial instruments cannot be circumvented as a result of the amendments to IAS 39 regarding the reclassification of financial assets (see Future Developments).

Illustrative Disclosures:

Extract 9(16) – Embedded derivatives

> **Suez (Reference Document 2007), page 212**
> **1.4.10 Financial instruments (in part)**
> **1.4.10.3 Derivatives and hedge accounting (in part)**
> **1.4.10.3.2 Embedded derivatives**
>
> An embedded derivative is a component of a hybrid (combined) instrument that also includes a non-derivative host contract – with the effect that some of the cash flows of the combined instrument vary in a way similar to a stand-alone derivative.
>
> The main Group contracts that may contain embedded derivatives are contracts with clauses or options affecting the contract price, volume or maturity. This is the case primarily of contracts for the purchase or sale of non-financial assets, whose price is revised based on an index, the exchange rate of a foreign currency or the price of an asset other than the contract's underlying.
>
> Embedded derivatives are separated from the host contract and accounted for as derivatives when:
>
> - the host contract is not a financial instrument measured at fair value through income;
> - if separated from the host contract, the embedded derivative fulfills the criteria for classification as a derivative instrument (existence of an underlying, no material initial net investment, settlement at a future date); and
> - its characteristics are not closely related to those of the host contract. The analysis of whether or not the characteristics of the derivative are "closely related" to the host contract is made when the contract is signed.
>
> Embedded derivatives that are separated from the host contract are recognized in the consolidated balance sheet at fair value, with changes in fair value recognized in income (except when the embedded derivative is part of a designated hedging relationship).

Commentary: This extract provides a definition for embedded derivatives, criteria for their separation and their subsequent accounting treatment. The company indicates that it analyzes whether or not the characteristics of a derivative are "closely related" to the host contract when the contract is concluded (signed), which reflects good internal procedures. Disclosures and accounting policy described are in conformity of both IAS 39 and CICA 3855.

Extract 9(17) – Issues related to derivatives accounting and presentation

> **HSBC Holdings plc (Form 20-F 2006), page 406**
> **Derivatives and hedge accounting - IFRSs (in part)**
>
> Derivatives may be embedded in other financial instruments; for example, a convertible bond has an embedded conversion option. An embedded derivative is treated as a separate derivative when its economic characteristics and risks are not clearly and closely related to those of the host contract, its terms are the same as those of a stand-alone derivative, and the combined contract is not held for trading or designated at fair value.
>
> These embedded derivatives are measured at fair value with changes in fair value recognised in the income statement. Derivatives are classified as assets when their fair value is positive, or as liabilities when their fair value is negative. Derivative assets and liabilities arising from different transactions are only netted if the transactions are with the same counterparty, a legal right of offset exists, and the cash flows are intended to be settled on a net basis.
>
> The method of recognising the resulting fair value gains or losses depends on whether the derivative is held for trading, or is designated as a hedging instrument and, if so, the nature of the risk being hedged. All gains and losses from changes in the fair value of derivatives held for trading are recognised in the income statement. When derivatives are designated as hedges, HSBC classifies them as either: (i) hedges of the change in fair value of recognised assets or liabilities or firm commitments ('fair value hedge'); (ii) hedges of the variability in highly probable future cash flows attributable to a recognised asset or liability, or a forecast transaction ('cash flow hedge'); or (iii) hedges of net investments in a foreign operation ('net investment hedge'). Hedge accounting is applied to derivatives designated as hedging instruments in a fair value, cash flow or net investment hedge provided certain criteria are met.

> *Commentary:* This extract, a follow-up of Extract 9 (15), describes:
> *   embedded derivative bifurcation and measurement requirements (under both IAS 39 and CICA 3855);
> *   offsetting of derivative assets and liabilities (under both IAS 32 and CICA 3863);
> *   treatment of fair values gains or losses (under IAS 39 and CICA 3855, as well as CICA 3865).

Presentation of Financial Instruments

Liability/Equity Classification

Both IAS 32 and CICA 3863 require that an entity classify a financial instrument as debt or equity based on the substance of the contractual arrangement. Consequently, a financial instrument is classified:

*   as a liability when the issuer is or can be required to deliver either cash or another financial asset to the holder ;
*   as an equity when it represents a residual interest in the net assets of the issuer.

Interest, dividends, gains and losses are presented in the:

*   income statement if the related instrument is classified as debt (for example, the dividends on preferred shares are reported as an expense if the latter are classified as liabilities);
*   statement of changes in equity if the related instrument is shown as equity (for example, the dividends on preferred shares are reported as a distribution if the shares are presented in equity).

IFRS raise a number of particular liability/equity classification issues, which are described below.

Puttable Financial Instruments

On February 14, 2008 the IASB amended IAS 32 and IAS 1 to address particular presentation difficulties inherent in deal puttable financial instruments. Consequently, IAS 32 contains new classification criteria for such instruments and IAS 1 requires additional disclosure of certain information relating to puttable instruments classified as equity. Amendments are effective for year ends commencing on or after January 1, 2009, with earlier adoption allowed.

Puttable financial instruments can:

*   provide the holder with an option to sell them back to the entity; or
*   have to be put back when an uncertain event, such as death or retirement, occurs.

Prior to the adoption of the amendment, instruments were classified as financial liabilities if an issuer had to pay cash or another financial asset in return for redeeming or repurchasing a financial instrument. This presentation applied even if the amount payable equalled the holder's interest in the net assets of the issuer, or if the amount was payable only upon certain liquidation (for example, if the liquidation date was fixed). This resulted in counter-intuitive presentation, for example:

*   recording an amount payable that exceeded the net assets of the entity; and
*   presenting as liabilities certain instruments that represented the last residual interest in the entity even when the instruments have characteristics similar to equity.

The objective of the IASB amendment introduced in February is to provide a "short-term, limited scope" change in the requirements permitting certain instruments to be classified as equity, as long as they meet the following criteria:

- They belong to the most subordinated class of instruments, and all instruments in that class have identical features. Because preference shares do not meet this requirement, they continue to be classified as liabilities. In the event of liquidation, the holder must receive a pro rata share of the entity's remaining assets once the liabilities have been repaid.
- They share in the performance of the entity, either with reference to its profits or losses, or its net assets.
- No other instruments share in the performance of the entity in a similar way, and the puttable instruments' return is not fixed or restricted by another instrument.

It is important to note that the amendments are mandatory, i.e., an instrument must be classified as equity if it meets the above criteria.

The amendments are most likely to affect some unit trusts and other limited-life entities, cooperative companies and certain partnerships. Careful analysis will still be required because, if these instruments are to be classified as equity, the criteria established by the amendment (as listed above) must all be met. In some cases, the clauses of a financial instrument contract will result in a financial liability classification. For example, a mandatory obligation to distribute profits can undermine the classification of an instrument as equity.

Canadian GAAP contains requirements equivalent to those introduced by amended IAS 32 and IAS 1 for retractable (i.e., capital stock redeemable at the option of the holder) and mandatorily redeemable shares. According to EIC-149, these instruments should be classified as a liability unless they meet all of the following conditions:

- They are the most subordinated of all equity securities issued by the enterprise (i.e., they represent the "residual equity interest" in the enterprise), and they participate on a pro rata basis in the residual equity of the enterprise.
- The redemption feature is extended to 100% of the common shares (and/or in-substance common shares), and the basis for determination of the redemption price is the same for all shares.
- The shares have no preferential rights over other classes of shares that have the same degree of subordination.

The redemption event should be the same for all the shares subject to the redemption feature.

Illustrative Disclosures:

Extract 9(18) – Loans and receivables

Andritz AG (AR 2007), page 25
D. Accounting and Valuation Principles (in part)
m. Financial Instruments under IAS 39 and IFRS 7 (in part)
Financial liabilities and equity instruments issued by the Group:
Classification as debt or equity
Debt and equity instruments are classified as either financial liabilities or as equity in accordance with the substance of the contractual arrangement.
Equity instruments
An equity instrument is any contract that evidences a residual interest in the assets of an entity after deducting all of its liabilities. Equity instruments are recorded at the proceeds received, net of direct issue costs.

Commentary: This extract provides a definition for equity instrument and its initial recognition. The description provided conforms to both IAS 32 and CICA 3863.

Extract 9(19) – Put options granted to minority stockholders

Groupe Danone (Form 20-F 2006), page F44			
NOTE 16 — Financial liabilities (in part)			
Classification by nature			
(In millions of euro)	2004	2005	2006
Convertible bonds	605	70	—
Equity-linked notes	130	—	—
Bank loans, other debt and employee profit-sharing debt	3,326	3,465	3,617
Financial liabilities linked to options granted to minority stockholders	2,440	2,626	2,504
Financial liabilities linked to securitized receivables	703	400	—
Total	7,204	6,561	6,121
—Including short-term portion	527	869	416
—Including long-term portion	6,677	5,692	5,705

page F45

NOTE 16 — Financial liabilities (in part)

Financial liabilities linked to options granted to minority stockholders

As indicated in Note 1.18, the exercise price of options granted to minority stockholders is reflected in financial liabilities in the consolidated balance sheet. As of December 31, 2006, financial liabilities relating to these options amounted to €2,504 million (€2,626 million as of December 31, 2005 and €2,440 million as of December 31, 2004). These liabilities do not bear interest.

The main commitment under these options relates to Danone Spain (€2,020 million). In addition, the majority of these options can be exercised at any time.

No significant investment due to the exercise of these options is currently considered as probable in the near future.

pages F20 and F21

NOTE 2 — Summary of differences between accounting principles followed by the Group and United States generally accepted accounting principles (in part)

b — Recognition and measurement differences

7. Put options granted to minority stockholders

As indicated in Notes 5 and 16 to the consolidated financial statements, the Group is committed to acquiring the minority shareholdings owned by third parties in some of the less than 100% owned subsidiaries, should these third parties wish to exercise their put options. IAS 32 — *Financial instruments: Disclosures and Presentation* requires that when minority stockholders hold a put option, a financial liability should be recognized for the present value of the consideration that the Group would have to pay if this option were exercised. Consequently, the share of these minority shareholders in the net assets of the subsidiary is eliminated from "Minority interests" in the consolidated balance sheet, and the difference between the amount of the eliminated minority interests and the amount of the financial liability recognized is recorded as goodwill.

Under U.S. GAAP, written puts on minority interests are treated as derivative instruments and measured at fair value. Accordingly, only the fair value of the put option granted to minority stockholders is recognized as a financial liability under U.S. GAAP as opposed to the present value of the full redemption price under IFRS. For put options having an exercise price that is equal to the fair value of the related minority interests at the closing date, the fair value of the derivative instruments is deemed to be equal to zero. As of December 31, 2006, 2005 and 2004, all put options granted to minority stockholders in consolidated subsidiaries had a redemption amount equal to the fair value of the related minority interests. Therefore, the fair value of the underlying put options was nil and consequently no liability was recorded under U.S. GAAP.

Accordingly, as of December 31, 2006, had U.S. GAAP been applied, financial liabilities would have been reduced by €2,504 million (€2,626 million as of December 31, 2005 and €2,440 million as of December 31, 2004), minority interests would have been increased by €420 million (€431 million as of December 31, 2005 and €422 million as of December 31, 2004), goodwill would have been decreased by €2,069 million (€2,179 million as of December 31, 2005 and €2,002 million as of December 31, 2004) and stockholders' equity attributable to the Group would have been increased by €16 million. This adjustment has no impact on net income.

> **Groupe Danone (Form F 20 - 2006) (continued)**
> As of December 31, 2006, the main put option related to Danone Espagne. The financial liability, minority interests that were reclassified to financial liabilities and goodwill relating to this option amounted to €2,020 million, €285 million and €1,720 million, respectively.

Commentary: In this extract, the company discloses details on the put options granted to minority stockholders, including the amounts involved. Differences between US and IFRS accounting principles are described. The required accounting treatment under Canadian GAAP is not established.

Compound or Hybrid Instruments

Compound instruments contain elements of both equity and liability in a single contract. Some designate such compound instruments, for example, convertible bonds, as hybrid instruments. According to IAS 32 and CICA 3863, compound instruments must be split into debt and equity components, each of which must be accounted for separately.

To establish the value of each component, IAS 32 requires an entity to determine the debt element first by fair valuing the cash flows, excluding any equity component, and then assigning the residual to equity. In addition, CICA 3863 also allows entities to value the liability and equity components separately and, to the extent necessary, adjust the amounts on a pro rata basis so that the sum of the components equals the amount of the instrument as a whole.

Illustrative Disclosures:

Extract 9(20) – Compound instruments

> **Alcatel-Lucent (AR 2007 on Form 20-F), page 161**
> **NOTE 1 SUMMARY OF ACCOUNTING POLICIES (in part)**
> **m/ Financial debt – compound financial instruments**
> Certain financial instruments contain both a liability and an equity component, including bonds that can be converted into or exchanged for new or existing shares and notes mandatorily redeemable for new or existing shares. The different components of compound financial instruments are accounted for in shareholders' equity and in bonds and notes issued according to their classification, as defined in IAS 32 "Financial Instruments: Disclosure and Presentation".
>
> For instruments issued by historical Alcatel, the financial liability component was valued on the issuance date at the present value (taking into account the credit risk at issuance date) of the future cash flows (including interest and repayment of the nominal value) of a bond with the same characteristics (maturity, cash flows) but without any equity component. The portion included in shareholders' equity is equal to the difference between the debt issue amount and the financial liability component.
>
> The financial liability component of Lucent's convertible bonds was computed at present value on the business combination closing date, using the method as described in the preceding paragraph, taking into account the contractual maturity dates. The difference between the fair value of the convertible bonds and the corresponding financial liability component was accounted for in shareholders' equity.
>
> In accordance with IAS 32 AG33 and AG34 requirements, the consideration paid in connection with an early redemption of a compound financial instrument is allocated at the date of redemption between the liability and the equity components with an allocation method consistent with the method used initially. The amount of gain or loss relating to the liability component is recognized in "other financial income (loss)" and the amount of consideration relating to the equity component is recognized in shareholders' equity.

Commentary: This extract describes various compound financial instruments. The company presents, with some detail, the method it uses for establishing the value of the two components (debt and equity) of the compound instrument. All disclosures and methods described are in line with both IAS 32 and CICA 3863, except that the latter allows the entity to value the liability and equity components separately and, to the extent necessary, adjust these amounts on a pro rata basis so that the sum of the components equals the amount of the instrument as a whole.

Offsetting

IAS 32 and CICA 3863 require a financial asset and a financial liability to be offset and the net amount presented in the balance sheet when an entity: (a) currently has a legally enforceable right to set off the recognized amounts; and (b) intends either to settle on a net basis, or to realize the asset and settle the liability simultaneously.

Illustrative Disclosure:

Extract 9(21) – Offsetting financial assets and financial liabilities

> **BNP Paribas (Registration Document 2007), page 123**
> **1.c FINANCIAL ASSETS AND FINANCIAL LIABILITIES (in part)**
> **1.c.14 Netting of financial assets and financial liabilities**
> A financial asset and a financial liability are offset and the net amount presented in the balance sheet if, and only if, the Group has a legally enforceable right to set off the recognised amounts, and intends either to settle on a net basis, or to realise the asset and settle the liability simultaneously.

Commentary: The company describes the conditions for offsetting a financial asset and a financial liability as required by IAS 32 and CICA 3863.

Classification of Financial Assets and Financial Liabilities as Current and Non-current

Classification of financial assets and financial liabilities as current and non-current are equivalent under IFRS and Canadian GAAP. There is, however, a difference for classifying financial liabilities to be refinanced.

IAS 1 requires an entity to classify its financial liabilities as current (i.e., due to be settled within 12 months after the balance sheet date) even if an agreement to refinance, or reschedule payments on a long-term basis is reached after the balance sheet date and before the financial statements are authorized for issue. According to IAS 1 such an agreement to refinance constitutes a non-adjusting event to be accounted for in accordance with IAS 10, *Events after the Reporting Period* (i.e., financial liabilities should still be classified as short term). This interpretation differs from the one under Canadian GAAP as EIC-122 specifically allows the classification of liabilities as non-current when an entity concludes an agreement to refinance, or to reschedule payments, on a long-term basis after the reporting period but before the financial statements are authorized for issue.

Illustrative Disclosure:

Extract 9(22) – Disclosures concerning current and non current amounts

Skanska AB (AR 2007), page 77
Note 01 Consolidated accounting and valuation principles (in part)
IAS 1, "Presentation of Financial Statements" (in part)
Liabilities (in part)

Liabilities are allocated between current liabilities and non-current liabilities. Recognized as current liabilities are liabilities that are either supposed to be paid within twelve months from the balance sheet date or, although only in the case of business-related liabilities, are expected to be paid within the operating cycle. Since the operating cycle is thus taken into account, no non-interest-bearing liabilities, for example trade accounts payable and accrued employee expenses, are recognized as non-current. Liabilities that are recognized as interest-bearing due to discount- ing are included among current liabilities, since they are paid within the operating cycle. ... Information on liabilities is provided in Notes 27, "Financial liabilities," and Note 30, "Trade and other payables."

In Note 32, "Expected recovery periods of assets and liabilities," liabilities are allocated between amounts for liabilities to be paid within twelve months of the balance sheet date and liabilities to be paid after twelve months from the balance sheet date. Note 31, "Specification of interest-bearing receivables per asset and liability," also provides information about the allocation between interest-bearing and non-interest-bearing liabilities.

page 116
Note 27 Financial liabilities

Financial liabilities are allocated between non-current and current liabilities. Normally, a maturity date within one year is required if a liability is to be treated as current. This does not apply to discounted operating liabilities, which are part of Skanska's operating cycle and are consequently recognized as current liabilities regardless of their maturity date. Regarding financial risks and financial policies, see Note 6, "Financial instruments."

Note 27 Financial liabilities

Financial non-current liabilities	2007	2006
Financial liabilities at fair value through profit or loss		
Derivatives		6
Other financial liabilities		
Bond loans		665
Liabilities to credit institutions	741	901
Other liabilities	214	467
Total	**955**	**2,039**
of which interest-bearing financial non-current liabilities	955	2,033
of which non-interest-bearing financial non-current liabilities	0	6
Financial current liabilities	**2007**	**2006**
Financial liabilities at fair value through profit or loss		
Derivatives	28	38
Derivatives to which hedge accounting is applied	61	22
Other financial liabilities		
Bond loans	678	275
Liabilities to credit institutions	425	313
Liabilities to joint ventures	3	10
Discounted liabilities [1]	1,468	694
Other liabilities	40	44
Total	**2,703**	**1,396**
of which interest-bearing financial current liabilities	2,614	1,336
of which non-interest-bearing financial current liabilities	89	60
Total carrying amount for financial liabilities	**3,658**	**3,435**

1   Of the total amount, SEK 1,468 M (694), SEK 439 M (0) consisted of discounted advance payments from customers, of which SEK 398 M was reclassified during the year from "Other operating liabilities." The amount also included SEK 596 M (292) in discounted liabilities in property operations consisting of discounted liabilities on purchases of current-asset properties. The remaining amount, SEK 433 M (402) consisted of discounted operating liabilities in the Czech Republic.

Skanska AB (AR 2007), page 121
Note 32 Expected recovery periods of assets and liabilities

	2007			2006		
Amounts expected to be recovered	Within 12 months	12 months or longer	Total	Within 12 months	12 months or longer	Total
ASSETS						
Non-current assets						
Property, plant and equipment [1]	1,180	4,793	5,973	1,070	4,387	5,457
Goodwill [1]		4,584	4,584		4,490	4,490
Other intangible assets [1]	107	551	658	97	643	740
Investments in joint ventures and associated companies [2]		1,945	1,945		1,894	1,894
Financial non-current assets		728	728		1,500	1,500
Deferred tax assets [3]		956	956		1,976	1,976
Total non-current assets	1,287	13,557	14,844	1,167	14,890	16,057
Current assets						
Current-asset properties [4]	7,100	6,098	13,198	6,050	5,777	11,827
Inventories	696	73	769	453	31	484
Financial current assets	4,686		4,686	2,763	391	3,154
Tax assets	411		411	330		330
Gross amount due from customers for contract work [5]	5,352	304	5,656	4,912	310	5,222
Trade and other receivables [5]	24,192	976	25,168	22,743	520	23,263
Cash and cash equivalents	521		521	2,131		2,131
Cash	13,688		13,688	8,839		8,839
Total current assets	56,646	7,451	64,097	48,221	7,029	55,250
TOTAL ASSETS	57,933	21,008	78,941	49,388	21,919	71,307
LIABILITIES						
Non-current liabilities						
Financial non-current liabilities		955	955	39	2,000	2,039
Pensions [6]	231	918	1,149	400	1,156	1,556
Deferred tax liabilities		2,069	2,069		2,892	2,892
Non-current provisions		96	96	4	115	119
Total non-current liabilities	231	4,038	4,269	443	6,163	6,606
Current liabilities						
Financial current liabilities	1,813	890	2,703	803	593	1,396
Tax liabilities	891		891	728		728
Current provisions	2,640	1,006	3,646	2,046	1,430	3,476
Gross amount due to customers for contract work	14,485	1,263	15,748	10,804	553	11,357
Trade and other payables	30,463	497	30,960	27,110	1,297	28,407
Total current liabilities	50,292	3,656	53,948	41,491	3,873	45,364
TOTAL LIABILITIES	50,523	7,694	58,217	41,934	10,036	51,970

1 In case of amounts expected to be recovered within twelve months, expected annual depreciation/ amortization has been recognized.

2 Allocation cannot be estimated.

3 Deferred tax assets are expected to be recovered in their entirety in more than twelve months.

4 Recovery within one year on current-asset properties is based on a historical assessment from the past three years.

5 Current receivables that fall due in more than twelve months are part of the operating cycle and are thus recognized as current.

6 "Within 12 months" refers to expected benefit payments.

Commentary: This extract includes the following:
- criteria the company used to classify current liabilities and non-current liabilities;
- a table with details on the financial liabilities classification;
- a table that provides expected recovery periods of assets and liabilities, allocating liabilities to those to be paid within 12 months of the balance sheet date and those to be paid after 12 months from the balance sheet date.

Impairment and Uncollectibility of Financial Assets

Impairment Recognition

IAS 39 and CICA 3855 require that an entity assesses, at each balance sheet date, whether there is objective evidence that its financial assets (except those measured at fair value through profit or loss) are impaired. Loans and receivables, held-to-maturity and available-for-sale assets, as well as finance lease receivables, are subject to impairment testing under IAS 39 and CICA 3855.

CICA 3855 requires that an entity recognize impairment when there is "objective evidence" of the impairment and the decline in fair value is "other than temporary." IAS 39 does not refer to the "other than temporary" notion. The difference in wording might lead to different interpretations, resulting in impairments being recorded in different accounting periods.

Both IAS 39 and CICA 3855 note that examples of objective evidence of loss events include:

- either issuer or obligor being in significant financial difficulty;
- a breach of contract (default or delinquency in interest or principal payments);
- lender granting the borrower a concession that the lender would not otherwise consider;
- it becoming probable that the borrower will enter bankruptcy or other financial reorganization; or
- disappearance of an active market for that financial asset because of financial difficulties.

Most of these loss events relate to the impairment of all categories of debt instruments (i.e., loans and receivables, held-to-maturity or available-for-sale instruments). IAS 39 and CICA 3855 note that examples of impairment indicators for equity securities are:

- a prolonged period where fair value remains substantially below cost;
- a significant decline in the fair value to below cost;
- significant adverse changes in the issuer's technological, market, economic or legal environment indicating that the cost of the investment in the equity instrument may not be recovered.

Grouping Assets

If there are any indicators of impairment, each individual asset of significant value must be tested for impairment. A group of similar assets (a portfolio) could be tested for impairment when it is not possible to establish impairment for an individual asset within the group.

An example of objective evidence of loss for a group of assets includes data indicating a measurable decrease in the estimated future cash flows for a group of assets (not necessarily related to a specific individual asset), including:

- adverse changes in the payment status of borrowers, such as increased number of delayed payments; or

- national or local economic conditions that correlate with defaults, such as an increasing unemployment rate or decreasing property prices. The holders of an equity instrument have only a residual interest in an entity's assets and rank after all other creditors. (Consequently, an equity security is likely to be impaired before a debt security.)

An individual asset already deemed to be impaired cannot subsequently be included in a group of assets that is tested for impairment on a portfolio basis.

Determining Impairment Loss and Reversal

The measurement of impairment loss and the accounting treatment of the subsequent reversal will vary according to the type of financial asset involved. Impairment loss and any reversal that is to be recognized are reported in net income. The reversal of any impairment cannot exceed the impairment originally recognized.

Particular Considerations for Loans and Receivables

IAS 39 requires that, if for some reason other than credit deterioration, an entity might not recover substantially all of its initial investment in certain loans and receivables, those loans and receivables should be classified as available for sale. CICA 3855 does not have such a requirement.

Requirements Summary for Recognition and Reversals

The table below provides a summary of both IFRS and Canadian GAAP requirements for impairment amounts and impairment reversals for various types of financial assets:

Financial Asset Type	Accounting for Impaired Loss under IFRS	Accounting for Impaired Loss under Canadian GAAP (comparison with IFRS)
Receivables and loans	**Impairment loss** = carrying amount *less* present value of estimated future cash flows (excluding future credit losses and using effective interest rate computed at initial recognition) **Reversal** of impairment loss is required.	**Same** for impaired loans per CICA 3025, *Impaired Loans*. **Different** for receivables for which discounting is not required (i.e., impairment continues to be established according to CICA 3020, *Accounts and Notes Receivable*). **Same** for reversal (reductions of valuation allowances related to receivables and loans are recognized in income).
Unquoted equity investment carried at cost	**Impairment loss** = carrying amount *less* fair value (present value of estimated future cash flows using current market rate for a similar financial asset). **Reversal** of impairment loss is prohibited.	Same for **both** impairment loss calculations and for reversal.

Financial Asset Type	Accounting for Impaired Loss under IFRS	Accounting for Impaired Loss under Canadian GAAP (comparison with IFRS)
Equity investment classified as available for sale	**Impairment loss** = amount of cumulative loss recognized in accumulated other comprehensive income, which is the difference between the acquisition cost (net of any principal repayment and amortisation) and current fair value, less any impairment loss on that financial asset previously recognized in profit or loss. **Reversal** of impairment losses is prohibited.	**Same** for both impairment loss calculations and for reversal.
Debt investment classified as held to maturity	**Impairment loss** = carrying amount less present value of estimated future cash flows (discounted at the asset's original effective interest rate). **Reversal** of impairment losses is required if (1), present value of the expected future cash flows increases and (2) it can be related objectively to an event occurring after the impairment was recognized (see note).	**Different** Impairment loss = carrying amount *less* fair value. **Reversal** of impairment losses is prohibited.
Debt investment classified as available for sale	**Impairment loss** = amount of cumulative loss recognized in accumulated other comprehensive income, which is the difference between the acquisition cost (net of any principal repayment and amortisation) and current fair value, less any impairment loss on that financial asset previously recognized in profit or loss. **Reversal** of impairment losses is required if (1) present value of the expected future cash flows increases and (2) it can be related objectively to an event occurring after the impairment was recognized (see note).	**Different** Impairment loss = carrying amount *less* fair value. **Reversal** of impairment losses is prohibited.

Note: The reversal of the impairment should not produce a carrying value for the financial asset that is greater than what the amortized cost would have been at the date the impairment was reversed.

Illustrative disclosures:
Extract 9(23) – Impairment of various financial assets

Alcatel-Lucent (AR 2007 on Form 20-F), page 160
NOTE 1 SUMMARY OF ACCOUNTING POLICIES (in part)
h/ Non-consolidated investments and other non-current financial assets

In accordance with IAS 39 "Financial Instruments: Recognition and Measurement", investments in non-consolidated companies are classified as available-for-sale and therefore measured at their fair value. The fair value for listed securities is their market price. If a reliable fair value cannot be established, securities are valued at cost. Fair value changes are accounted for directly in shareholders' equity. When objective evidence of impairment of a financial asset exists (for instance, a significant or prolonged decline in the value of an asset), an irreversible impairment loss is recorded. This loss can only be released upon the sale of the securities concerned.

Loans are measured at amortized cost and are subject to impairment losses if there is objective evidence of a loss in value. The impairment represented by the difference between net carrying amount and recoverable value is recognized in the income statement and can be reversed if recoverable value rises in the future.

The portfolio of non-consolidated securities and other financial assets is assessed at each quarter-end for objective evidence of impairment.

Page 166
NOTE 2 PRINCIPAL UNCERTAINTIES REGARDING THE USE OF ESTIMATES (in part)
b/ Impairment of customer receivables

An impairment loss is recorded for customer receivables if the present value of the future receipts is below the nominal value. The amount of the impairment loss reflects both the customers' ability to honor their debts and the age of the debts in question. A higher default rate than estimated or the deterioration of Alcatel-Lucent major customers' creditworthiness could have an adverse impact on Alcatel-Lucent future results. Accumulated impairment losses on customer receivables were €187 million at December 31, 2007 (€192 million at December 31, 2006 and €228 million at December 31, 2005). The impact of impairment losses on customer receivables on income (loss) before tax, related reduction of goodwill and discontinued operations, was a net charge of €3 million in 2007 (a net charge of €18 million in 2006 and a net gain of €19 million in 2005).

Commentary: In this extract, the company describes the accounting for impairment losses (performed as required by IAS 39 at the end of each quarter or at each balance sheet date of published financial statements) for the following investments categories:

- Equity securities in listed securities (valued at market price) and others for which reliable fair value cannot be established. For this category of investments, the company recognizes (when objective evidence of impairment exists) an irreversible impairment loss (i.e., loss can be recognized only on the sale of the securities concerned). Accounting method described is the same as the one required by CICA 3855 except that, under 3855, all unlisted equity securities have to be valued at cost.

- Loans (measured at amortized cost), where impairment losses are recorded if there is objective evidence of a loss in value. The impairment represented by the difference between net carrying amount and recoverable value is recognized in the income statement and can be reversed if the amount calculated is found to be recoverable in the future. The company also describes the meaning of recoverable amount for loans and receivables related to customers and specifies that impairment loss is recorded if the present value of the future receipts is below the nominal value. This differs from Canadian GAAP, which requires that impairment related to receivables and loans (other than those impaired under CICA 3025, *Impaired Loans*) be measured by comparing their nominal amounts with the undiscounted recoverable amounts. All other accounting methods are in line with Canadian GAAP.

- Other securities (which probably correspond to equity type securities in the available-for-sale category). For this category, securities are tested for impairment and, when required, an irreversible impairment loss is recorded which can be recognized only when the securities concerned are sold. The accounting method described is the same as the one required by CICA 3855.

Extract 9(24) – Impairment of various financial assets

Banesto Group (AR 2007), pages 107 and 108

2. Accounting policies and measurement bases applied (in part)

e) Impairment of financial assets

i. Definition

A financial asset is considered to be impaired –and, therefore, its carrying amount is adjusted to reflect the effect of impairment when there is objective evidence that events have occurred which:

- In the case of debt instruments (loans and debt securities), give rise to a negative impact on the future cash flows that were estimated at the transaction date.
- In the case of equity instruments, mean that their carrying amount cannot be fully recovered.

As a general rule, the carrying amount of impaired financial instruments is adjusted with a charge to the consolidated income statement for the year in which the impairment becomes evident. The reversal, if any, of previously recognised impairment losses is recognised in the consolidated income statement for the year in which the impairment ceases to exist or is reduced.

Balances are deemed to be impaired when there are reasonable doubts as to their full recovery and/or the collection of the related interest for the amounts and on the dates initially agreed upon, after taking into account the guarantees received by the consolidated entities to secure (fully or partially) collection of the related balances. Collections relating to impaired loans and advances are used to recognise the accrued interest and the remainder, if any, to reduce the principal amount outstanding. The amount of the financial assets that would be deemed to be impaired had the conditions thereof not been renegotiated is not material with respect to the Group's financial statements taken as a whole.

When the recovery of any recognised impairment is considered unlikely, the amount of the impairment is removed from the consolidated balance sheet, without prejudice to any actions that the consolidated entities may initiate to seek collection of the amount receivable until their contractual rights are extinguished definitively by expiry of the statute-of-limitations period, forgiveness or other cause.

ii. Debt instruments carried at amortised cost

The amount of an impairment loss incurred on a debt instrument measured at amortised cost is equal to the difference between its carrying amount and the present value of its estimated future cash flows, which is presented as a reduction of the balance of the asset adjusted.

Impairment losses on these assets are assessed as follows:

- Individually, for all significant debt instruments.
- Collectively: the Bank classifies transactions on the basis of the nature of the obligors, the conditions of the countries in which they reside, transaction status and type of collateral or guarantee, age of past-due amounts, etc. For each risk group, it establishes the impairment losses that are to be allocated to specific transactions.

The impairment losses recognised at any given time are the sum of the losses on specific transactions and the inherent impairment losses (losses incurred at the date of the financial statements, calculated using statistical methods). The Bank of Spain has established certain parameters for quantifying inherent impairment losses, based on its experience and on the information available to it on the Spanish banking industry.

Interest accrual is suspended for all debt instruments individually classified as impaired and for all the instruments for which impairment losses have been assessed collectively because they have payments more than three months past due.

iii. Debt or equity instruments classified as available for sale

Impairment losses on these instruments are the difference between the acquisition cost of the instruments (net of any principal repayment or amortisation, in the case of debt instruments) and their fair value less any impairment loss previously recognised in the consolidated income statement.

When there is objective evidence that the losses arising on measurement of these assets are due to impairment, they are no longer recognised in equity under "Valuation Adjustments - Available-for-Sale Financial Assets" and are recorded in the consolidated income statement. If all or part of the impairment losses are subsequently reversed, the reversed amount is recognised in the consolidated income statement for the year in which the reversal occurs (under "Valuation Adjustments - Available-for-Sale Financial Assets" in the consolidated balance sheet).

> **Banesto Group (AR 2007) (continued)**
>
> *iv. Equity instruments measured at cost*
>
> The impairment loss on equity instruments measured at cost is the difference between the carrying amount and the present value of the expected future cash flows discounted at the market rate of return for similar securities.
>
> Impairment losses are recognised in the consolidated income statement for the period in which they arise as a direct reduction of the cost of the instrument. These losses may only be reversed subsequently in the event of the sale of the assets.

Commentary: This extract describes the accounting for impairment losses (as required by IAS 39) of various financial assets, covering:

- timing of impairment;
- amount of impairment loss recorded;
- impairment reversal.

All disclosures and methods are in line with Canadian GAAP except for the reversal of impairment losses on debt instruments, which is prohibited by CICA 3855.

Extract 9(25) – Impairment of various financial assets

> **Xstrata plc (AR 2007), page 159**
>
> **6. Principal Accounting Policies (in part)**
>
> **Impairment of financial assets**
>
> The Group assesses at each balance sheet date whether a financial asset is impaired.
>
> **Financial assets carried at amortised cost**
>
> If there is objective evidence that an impairment loss on loans and receivables and held to maturity investments carried at amortised cost has been incurred, the amount of the loss is measured as the difference between the asset's carrying amount and the present value of estimated future cash flows (excluding future credit losses that have not been incurred) discounted at the financial asset's original effective interest rate (ie the effective interest rate computed at initial recognition). The carrying amount of the asset is reduced and the amount of the loss is recognised in the income statement.
>
> If, in a subsequent period, the amount of the impairment loss decreases and the decrease can be related objectively to an event occurring after the impairment was recognised, the previously recognised impairment loss is reversed. Any subsequent reversal of an impairment loss is recognised in the income statement, to the extent that the carrying value of the asset does not exceed its amortised cost at the reversal date.
>
> **Assets carried at cost**
>
> If there is objective evidence that an impairment loss on an unquoted equity instrument that is not carried at fair value (because its fair value cannot be reliably measured), the amount of the loss is measured as the difference between the asset's carrying amount and the present value of estimated future cash flows discounted at the current market rate of return for a similar financial asset.
>
> **Available-for-sale financial assets**
>
> If an available-for-sale financial asset is impaired, an amount comprising the difference between its cost (net of any principal payment and amortisation) and its current fair value, less any impairment loss previously recognised in profit or loss, is transferred from equity to the income statement. Reversals in respect of equity instruments classified as available-for-sale are not recognised in profit. Reversals of impairment losses on debt instruments are reversed through profit or loss, if the increase in fair value of the instrument can be objectively related to an event occurring after the impairment loss was recognised in profit or loss.

Commentary: As required by IAS 39, the company describes the accounting for impairment losses for the following investments categories:

- Financial assets carried at amortized cost (consisting of loans and receivables and held-to-maturity investments) that are considered impaired when there is objective evidence that an impairment loss has been incurred. The amount of the loss is measured as the difference between the asset's carrying amount and the present value of estimated future cash flows (excluding future credit losses that have not been incurred), discounted at the financial asset's original effective interest rate. The method of calculating impairment loss differs under Canadian GAAP: receivables impairment losses consist of a provision for the difference between the carrying amount and the amount that will be recovered without discounting. In practice, this difference would not be material as receivables are realized in the short term. The company's policy for subsequent reversal conforms to Canadian GAAP.
- Assets carried at cost, which would consist of unquoted equity instruments. According to IAS 39, such securities would be carried at cost because their fair value cannot be reliably measured. An impairment value would be measured as the difference between the assets' carrying amounts and the present value of estimated future cash flows, discounted at the current market rate of return for similar financial assets. This accounting policy would also conform to CICA 3855 except that all unquoted equity instruments would be carried at cost (not only those for which fair value cannot be reliably measured) and that impairment would be measured in relation to fair value methods, as described in the CICA 3855 hierarchy).
- Available-for-sale financial assets, for which reversal varies depending on whether they consist of debt or equity instruments. CICA 3855 prohibits all reversals for this category of assets.

Extract 9(26) – Impairment of various financial assets

<table>
<tr><td>

Skandinaviska Enskilda Banken AB (AR 2007), pages 65 and 66

1 Accounting policies (in part)

Significant accounting policies for the Group (in part)

Impairment of financial assets

All financial assets, except those classified at fair value through profit or loss, are tested for impairment.

On each balance sheet date the Group assesses whether there is objective evidence that a financial asset or group of financial assets is impaired. A financial asset or a group of financial assets is impaired and impairment losses are incurred if, and only if, there is objective evidence of impairment as a result of one or more events occurring after the initial recognition of the asset, and if that loss event will have an impact on the estimated future cash flows of the financial asset or group of financial assets that can be reliably measured.

Examples of objective evidence that one or more events have occurred which may affect estimated future cash flows include:

- significant financial difficulty pertaining the issuer or obligor,
- the borrower is granted a concession as a consequence of financial difficulty, the nature of which normally would not have been granted to the borrower,
- a breach of contract, such as a default or delinquency in the payment of interest or principal,
- it is probable that the borrower will go bankrupt or undergo some other kind of financial reconstruction,
- deterioration in the value of collateral and
- downgrading by official rating institute.

An impairment loss is reported as a write off, if it is deemed impossible to collect the contractual amounts due that have not been paid and/or are expected to remain unpaid, or if it is deemed impossible to recover the carrying amount by selling any collateral provided. In other cases, a specific provision is recorded in an allowance account. As soon as the non-collectible amount can be determined and the asset is written off, the amount reported in the allowance account is dissolved. Similarly, the provision in the allowance account is reversed if the estimated recovery value exceeds the carrying amount.

</td></tr>
</table>

Skandinaviska Enskilda Banken AB (AR 2007) (continued)

Financial assets measured at amortised cost

An impairment of a financial asset in the category loans and receivables or in the category held to maturity investments carried at amortised cost is calculated on the basis of the original effective interest rate of the financial instrument. The amount of the impairment is measured as the difference between the carrying amount of the asset and the present value of estimated future cash flows (recoverable amount). If the terms of an asset are renegotiated or otherwise modified due to financial difficulties on behalf of the borrower or issuer, impairment is measured using the original effective interest rate before modification of the terms and conditions. Cash flows relating to short-term receivables are not discounted if the effect of the discounting is immaterial. The entire, outstanding amount of each loan for which a specific provision has been established is included in impaired loans, i.e. including the portion covered by collateral.

In addition to an individual impairment test, a collective assessment is made of the value of receivables that have not been deemed to be impaired on an individual basis. Receivables with similar credit risk characteristics are grouped together and assessed collectively for impairment. The Group's internal risk classification system constitutes one of the components forming the basis for determining the total amount of the collective provision.

For certain homogeneous groups of individually insignificant credits (credit card claims, for example), provision models have been established on the basis of historical credit losses and the status of these claims. Collective impairment provisions are also established for credits to borrowers in countries with transfer obstacles, general problems in the banking system in question or similar circumstances.

Financial assets measured at acquisition cost

The impairment of unquoted equities, measured at acquisition cost, is calculated as the difference between the carrying amount and the present value of estimated future cash flows, discounted at the current market rate of return for similar equities.

Available for sale financial assets

If an impairment loss is recognised in an available for sale financial instrument, the accumulated loss that has been recognised directly in equity is reported in profit or loss. The amount of the accumulated loss that is transferred from equity and recognised in profit or loss is equal to the difference between the acquisition cost and the current fair value, with a deduction of any impairment losses on that financial asset which had been previously recognised in profit or loss.

Impairment losses on bonds or other interest-bearing instruments classified as available-for-sale are reversed via profit or loss if the increase in fair value can be objectively attributed to an event taking place subsequent to the write down. Impairment losses for equity instruments classified as available for sale are not reversed through profit or loss.

Renegotiated loans

Renegotiated loans are no longer considered to be past due unless further renegotiations.

Seized assets

Seized assets are seized as part of an impairment procedure to compensate for losses in an asset. Seized asset are valued at fair value at inception and the intention is to dispose of the asset at the earliest convenience.

Commentary: The company explains when financial assets are tested for impairment. It describes the accounting for impairment losses, as required by IAS 39, for the following investments categories:

- Financial assets measured at amortized cost, which include loans and receivables and held-to-maturity investments carried at amortized cost (calculated on the basis of the original effective interest rate of the financial instrument). Calculation of impairment losses is explained as follows:
  - o Amount of the impairment is calculated to be the difference between the asset's carrying amount and the present value of estimated future cash flows (recoverable amount).
  - o If the terms of an asset are renegotiated or modified because either the borrower or issuer are having financial difficulties, impairment is measured using the original effective interest rate before the modification of the terms and conditions. The entire outstanding amount of each loan for which a specific provision has been established is included in impaired loans, including the portion covered by collateral. (Note this corresponds to the requirements of CICA 3025, *Impaired loans*.)
  - o Cash flows relating to short-term receivables are not discounted if the effect of the discounting is immaterial.
  - o In addition to the individual impairment tests, a collective assessment is made of the value of receivables that have not been deemed to be impaired on an individual basis. Receivables with similar credit risk characteristics are grouped together and assessed collectively for impairment. (Note this corresponds to the requirements of CICA 3020.)
- Financial assets measured at acquisition cost. This refers to unquoted equities (for which, presumably fair value could not be reliably estimated) for which impairment is calculated as the difference between the carrying amount and the present value of estimated future cash flows, discounted at the current market rate of return for similar equities. (Note this corresponds to the requirements of CICA 3855.)
- Available-for-sale financial assets. When available-for-sale financial assets are impaired, the accumulated loss recognized directly in equity is reported in profit or loss. The amount of the accumulated loss transferred from equity and recognized in profit or loss is equal to the difference between the acquisition cost and the current fair value, with a deduction of any impairment losses for that financial asset previously recognized in profit or loss.
  - o Impairment losses on bonds or other interest-bearing instruments classified as available for sale are reversed via profit or loss if the increase in fair value can be objectively attributed to an event taking place subsequent to the write down. (Note this differs from CICA 3855 requirements, which prohibit impairment reversals.)
  - o Impairment losses for equity instruments classified as available for sale are not reversed through profit or loss. (Note this corresponds to the requirements of CICA 3855.)

Extract 9(27) – Reclassification of receivables due to impairment

Atos Origin (AR 2007), page 96

Note 2 Assets and liabilities held for sale (in part)

On 10 December 2007, the Group has signed an agreement to dispose of its activities in Italy to Engineering. This sale is subject to the approval of the Italian Anti-trust Authority. This activity made EUR 260.7 million revenue in 2007 for 2,572 people. The reclassification impact on the closing balance sheet is EUR 157.6 million on the asset side and EUR 129.0 million on the liabilities. These assets have been recognized at their fair value less cost to sell, which is lower than their carrying value. An impairment loss of EUR 9.9 million has consequently been recognized in other operating items, of which EUR 6 million have been allocated to non current assets and EUR 3.9 million to trade accounts and notes receivables.

Page 113

Note 17 Breakdown of assets by financial categories (in part)

As of 31 December 2007, the analysis was the following:

(In EUR million)	Loans, deposits, trade accounts and other receivables	Financial instrument – P&L measurement	Financial instrument – Equity measurement
Non-current financial assets	74.2	-	0.3
Trade accounts and notes receivables	1,683.2	-	-
Other current assets	202.2	-	-
Current financial instruments	-	1.1	-
Sub-total	1,959.6	1.1	0.3
Reclassified as held for sale	(254.0)	-	-
Total	1,705.6	1.1	0.3

Derecognition

Derecognition of Financial Assets

IAS 39 deals with derecognition of financial assets. There are no corresponding Canadian requirements in CICA 3855. Instead, AcG-12 and EIC-121, *Accounting for wash sales* – both of which were published before CICA 3855 – deal with this issue. EIC-121 actually expands the requirements of AcG-12.

Financial assets could be derecognized (i.e., removed from the balance sheet) when:

- they are disposed of in an outright sale;

- payment is received;

- they are renegotiated; or

- they are written off subsequent to counter-party default.

Establishing whether or not a financial asset should be derecognized is generally straight forward. It can, however, become a problem, for example, when an entity sells a portfolio of trade receivables in a securitization scheme while maintaining an involvement with the assets sold in the form of servicing, recourse, or retention of cash-flow rights. Standard setters have adopted two different approaches to address such derecognition problems:

- Risks and rewards approach (under IAS 39), where the characteristics of the transaction determine the accounting. If all or the majority of the risks and rewards of ownership are retained by the transferor, then the asset is not considered to have been sold and the transaction is viewed as a secured borrowing. If the majority of the risks and rewards of ownership have been transferred, the transaction is viewed as a sale and the entire asset is derecognized from the balance sheet. If the risks and rewards are neither transferred nor retained, IAS 39 defaults to a control approach.

- Control or financial components approach (under AcG-12), where financial assets can be disaggregated into components. Derecognition is appropriate to the extent the control of a component is surrendered.

Both approaches are difficult to apply.

The AcG-12 derecognition approach, which is based on US GAAP, differs from the one adopted by IAS 39. Under AcG-12, a financial asset is derecognized when the following conditions are met:

- The transferor can no longer have access to the transferred assets — they are presumptively beyond the reach of the transferor and its creditors, even in bankruptcy or other receivership.

- Transferee has the right to pledge or exchange the assets (or beneficial interests) received, without any constraints.

- Transferor does not maintain effective control over the transferred asset.

Generally, it would be more difficult to derecognize a financial asset under IFRS than under Canadian GAAP.

Below is a brief description of IAS 39 procedures for financial assets derecognition (which is examined by describing the specific steps that need to be completed):

- Step 1 – Ensure that all subsidiaries are consolidated: Many derecognition structures use entities (such as trusts or partnerships) specifically set up to acquire the transferred assets. Though such transfers usually qualify as a legal sale, the relationship between the transferor and the transferee suggests that the former controls the entity owning the transferred assets. IAS 39 requires that the transferor consolidate this entity before applying any derecognition principle. This will mean that the transferor first consolidates all subsidiaries and special purpose entities in accordance with IAS 27 and SIC-12 and then applies the derecognition principles to the resulting group. We cover such consolidation requirements in Chapter 6.

- Step 2 – Identify whole or parts of financial assets (of or group of similar financial assets) that should be tested for derecognition, including any of the following:
  - o an entire financial asset (for example, an unconditional sale of a financial asset) or group of similar financial assets,
  - o proportionate share of the cash flows related to a financial asset (for example, 10% of principal and interest cash flows),
  - o specifically identified cash flows related to a financial asset (for example, interest-only strip of a loan),
  - o proportionate share of specifically identified cash flows related to a financial asset (for example, 10% of an interest-only strip of a loan).

- Step 3 – Verify if contractual rights to the cash flows related to the financial asset (or part of the asset) have expired or were subject to forfeiture: This occurs when a debtor discharges its obligation by paying the holder of the financial asset or when the debtor's obligations to the holder have ceased (for example, when the rights under an option expire). The asset has no value and should be derecognized if cash flows no longer accrue to the entity.

- Step 4 – Examine if contractual rights were transferred to another party: If an entity has sold the financial asset and transferred all rights to an asset's cash flows, proceed to Step 5, which is to determine whether derecognition criteria have been met. In case of "pass through arrangements," where an entity transfers beneficial interests in some underlying financial assets to investors but continues to service those assets, additional requirements have to be fulfilled before proceeding to Step 5. These requirements are as follows (if any of those requirements are not met, then an entity cannot derecognize the assets included in the "pass through arrangements"):
  - o entity has no obligation to pay cash flows to the transferee unless it collects equivalent cash flows from the transferred asset,
  - o entity is prohibited from selling or pledging the original asset other than as security to the eventual recipients for the obligation to pass through cash flows, and
  - o entity is obliged to remit any cash flows without material delay and subject to certain investment restrictions.

- Step 5 – Evaluate whether an entity has transferred substantially all of an asset's risks and rewards of ownership, considering different scenarios:
  - o If an entity transfers substantially all of the risks and rewards of ownership of the financial asset, it should derecognize it and recognize separately as assets or liabilities any rights and obligations created or retained in the transfer.
  - o If the entity retains substantially all of the risks and rewards of ownership of the financial asset, it should continue to recognize the financial asset.
  - o If the entity neither transfers nor retains substantially of all the risks and rewards of ownership of the financial asset, it determines whether it has retained control of the financial asset and accounts for the transaction as follows:

- If the entity has not retained control, it derecognizes the financial asset and recognizes separately as assets or liabilities any rights and obligations created or retained in the transfer.

- If the entity has retained control, it continues to recognize the financial asset to the extent of its continuing involvement with that asset.

Illustrative Disclosures:

Extract 9(28) – Derecognition of financial assets

Alcatel-Lucent (AR 2007 on Form 20-F), page 164
NOTE 1 SUMMARY OF ACCOUNTING POLICIES (in part)
s/ Financial instruments and derecognition of financial assets (in part)
Derecognition of financial assets

A financial asset as defined under IAS 32 "Financial Instruments: Disclosure and Presentation" is either totally or partially derecognized (removed from the balance sheet) when the Group expects no further cash flow to be generated by it and retains no control of the asset or transfers substantially all risks and rewards attached to it.

In the case of trade receivables, a transfer without recourse in case of payment default by the debtor is regarded as a transfer of substantially all risks and rewards of ownership, thus making such receivables eligible for derecognition, on the basis that risk of late payment is considered marginal. A more restrictive interpretation of the concept of "substantial transfer of risks and rewards" could put into question the accounting treatment that has been adopted. The amount of receivables sold without recourse is given in note 18.

page 200
Note 18 Operating working capital (in part)
Receivables sold without recourse
Balances

(in millions of euros)	December 31, 2007	December 31, 2006	December 31, 2005
Outstanding amounts of receivables sold without recourse [1]	877	978	999

(1) Without recourse in case of payment default by the debtor. See accounting policies in note 1s.

Changes in receivables sold without recourse

	2007	2006	2005
Impact on cash flows from operating activities	(101)	(21)	158

Commentary: In this extract, the company describes the accounting for derecognition of a financial asset (totally or partially). Basically, the company refers to the five-step approach described by IAS 39. This differs significantly from AcG-12.

Extract 9(29) – Derecognition of financial assets

Lafarge (AR Document de référence 2007), page F17
Note 2 - Summary of significant accounting policies (in part)
(n) Derecognition of financial assets

Under IAS 39, "Financial Instruments: Recognition and Measurement", financial assets can only be derecognized when no further cash flow is expected to flow to the Group from the asset and if substantially all risks and rewards attached to the assets have been transferred.

For trade receivables, programs for selling receivables with recourse against the seller in case of recovery failure (either in the form of a subordinated retained interest or a direct recourse) do not qualify for derecognition.

Lafarge (AR Document de référence 2007) (continued)
page 42
Note 16 - Trade receivables (in part)
Securitization programs

In January 2000, the Group entered into a multi-year securitization agreement in France with respect to trade receivables. This program was renewed in 2005 for a 5-year period.

Under the program, the subsidiaries agree to sell on a revolving basis, some of their accounts receivables. Under the terms of the arrangement, the subsidiaries involved in these programs do not maintain control over the assets sold and there is neither entitlement nor obligation to repurchase the sold receivables. In these agreements, the purchaser of the receivables, in order to secure his risk, only finance a part of the acquired receivables as it is usually the case for similar commercial transactions. As risks and benefits cannot be considered as being all transferred, these programs do not qualify for derecognition of receivables, and are therefore accounted for as secured financing.

Trade receivables therefore include sold receivables totaling 265 million euros, 265 million euros and 265 million euros at December 31, 2007, 2006 and 2005, respectively.

The current portion of debt includes 230 million euros, 230 million euros and 230 million euros at December 31, 2007, 2006 and 2005, respectively, related to these programs.

The agreements are guaranteed by subordinated deposits totaling 35 million euros, 35 million euros and 35 million euros at December 31, 2007, 2006 and 2005, respectively.

The Group owns no equity share in the special purpose entities.

Commentary: The application of IAS 39 would prevent derecognition of receivables although the company does not maintain control over the assets sold and there is neither entitlement nor obligation to repurchase the sold receivables. Receivables could not be derecognized because risks and benefits could not be considered as sold to a special purpose vehicle. According to Canadian and US GAAP, such derecognition might have been possible.

Extract 9(30) – Derecognition of financial assets

Skandinaviska Enskilda Banken AB (AR 2007), page 65
1 Accounting policies (in part)
Significant accounting policies for the Group (in part)
Repurchase agreements

Repurchase agreements are generally treated as collateralised financing transactions. Market values of the securities received or delivered are monitored on a daily basis to require or deliver additional collateral. In repurchase transactions, the asset continues to be reported on the selling party's balance sheet and the payment received is reported as a deposit or borrowing. The sold instrument is reported as pledged assets. The buying party reports the payment as an outstanding loan to the selling party. The difference in amounts between the spot and the forward payments is allocated as interest over the life of the instrument.

Securities borrowing and lending

Securities borrowing and lending transactions are entered into on a collateralised basis. Fair values of securities received or delivered are monitored on a daily basis to require or provide additional collateral. Cash collateral delivered is derecognised with a corresponding receivable and cash collateral received is recognised with a corresponding obligation to return it. Securities lent remain on the balance sheet and are reported as pledged assets. Borrowed securities are not recognised as assets. When borrowed securities are sold (short position), an amount corresponding to the fair value of the securities is entered as a liability. Securities received in a borrowing or lending transaction are disclosed as off-balance sheet items.

Commentary: The application of IAS 39 would prevent derecognition of receivables related to repurchase agreements, securities borrowing and lending transactions. The same accounting treatment would also be required under Canadian GAAP.

Extract 9(31) – Derecognition of financial assets

Fiat S.p.A. (AR 2007), page 106
Significant accounting policies (in part)
Sales of receivables

The Group sells a significant part of its financial, trade and tax receivables through either securitisation programs or factoring transactions.

A securitisation transaction entails the sale of a portfolio of receivables to a securitisation vehicle.

This special purpose entity finances the purchase of the receivables by issuing asset-backed securities (i.e. securities whose repayment and interest flow depend upon the cash flow generated by the portfolio). Asset-backed securities are divided into classes according to their degree of seniority and rating: the most senior classes are placed with investors on the market; the junior class, whose repayment is subordinated to the senior classes, is normally subscribed for by the seller. The residual interest in the receivables retained by the seller is therefore limited to the junior securities it has subscribed for. In accordance with SIC 12 – Consolidation – Special Purpose Entities (SPE), all securitisation vehicles are included in the scope of consolidation, because the subscription of the junior asset-backed securities by the seller entails its control in substance over the SPE.

Furthermore, factoring transactions may be with or without recourse to the seller; certain factoring agreements without recourse include deferred purchase price clauses (i.e. the payment of a minority portion of the purchase price is conditional upon the full collection of the receivables), require a first loss guarantee of the seller up to a limited amount or imply a continuing significant exposure to the receivables cash flow. These kinds of transactions do not meet IAS 39 requirements for assets derecognition, since the risks and rewards have not been substantially transferred.

Consequently, all receivables sold through both securitisation and factoring transactions which do not meet IAS 39 derecognition requirements are recognised as such in the Group financial statements even though they have been legally sold; a corresponding financial liability is recorded in the consolidated balance sheet as "Asset-backed financing". Gains and losses relating to the sale of such assets are not recognised until the assets are removed from the Group balance sheet.

Commentary: The company does note that some receivables transferred through both securitization and factoring transactions might not be derecognized even though they were legally sold. The impact of non-derecognition is:

- a liability is presented on the consolidated balance sheet as "asset-backed financing";
- gains and losses related to the sale of the assets are not recognized until the assets are removed from the balance sheet.

According to Canadian GAAP, such derecognition might have been possible.

Derecognition of Financial Liabilities

Liabilities are derecognized under both IAS 39 and CICA 3855 by focusing more on the legal perspective than on the economic substance of a transaction. The two standards contain requirements for:

- The extinguishment of financial liabilities (i.e., obligation is discharged, cancelled or expires): The standards require derecognition and gains or losses to be recorded in case of extinguishment. They specify that a payment to a third party, including a trust (sometimes called "in substance or economic defeasance"), does not constitute an extinguishment and would not, in the absence of a legal release, result in derecognition.

- The substitution or modification of debt: The standards require that a substitution of debt through an exchange between existing borrower and lender be accounted as an extinguishment if the exchange results in "significantly different" terms. IAS 39 and Canadian standards (CICA 3855 and EIC-88), provide the following guidance for concluding that an existing debt is settled (i.e., rather than restructured):

  o net present value of cash flows under the new debt (including all fees), discounted at the original effective interest rate, differs by at least 10% from the present value of the remaining cash flow of the original debt, or o   the creditor changes and the original debt is legally discharged.

Note that if a substitution does not result in the extinguishment of an original debt, IAS 39 requires that fees related to be substitution or modification of debt be amortized over the remaining term of the modified liability. CICA 3855 and EIC-88 allow an accounting policy choice: capitalize (as required by IAS 39) or recognize these fees in income immediately.

Illustrative Disclosures:

Extract 9(32) – Derecognition of financial liabilities

> **BNP Paribas (Registration Document 2007), page 123**
> **1.c FINANCIAL ASSETS AND FINANCIAL LIABILITIES (in part)**
> **1.c.13 Derecognition of financial assets and financial liabilities (in part)**
> ... The Group derecognises all or part of a financial liability when the liability is extinguished in full or in part.

Commentary: In this extract, the company describes the conditions for financial liabilities derecognition as established in IAS 39 and CICA 3855.

Extract 9(33) – Derecognition

> **Xstrata plc (AR - 2007), page 153**
> **6. Principal Accounting Policies (in part)**
> **Financial liabilities**
> A financial liability is derecognised when the obligation under the liability is discharged or cancelled or expires.
>
> Gains on derecognition are recognised within finance income and losses within finance costs.
>
> Where an existing financial liability is replaced by another from the same lender on substantially different terms, or the terms of an existing liability are substantially modified, such an exchange or modification is treated as a derecognition of the original liability and the recognition of a new liability, and the difference in the respective carrying amounts is recognised in the income statement.

Commentary: The company describes the conditions for financial liabilities derecognition (including liabilities renegotiated with a lender) as established in IAS 39 and CICA 3855.

Fair Value

Measurement

Both IFRS and Canadian GAAP define fair value as "the amount for which an asset could be exchanged, or a liability settled, between knowledgeable, willing parties in an arm's length transaction." There is a general presumption, under IFRS, that fair value can be reliably measured for all financial instruments.

Published price quotations in an active market provide the best evidence of fair value. When a market does not exist or is inactive, fair value is determined by using a valuation technique that must maximize the use of observable market inputs. IAS 39 and CICA 3855 provide detailed guidance for measuring financial instruments at fair value. What follows is a discussion of some of the guidance provided under both standards, with comments on implementation issues (see also Chapter 3) and some of the recent publications related to fair value measurements in inactive markets that provide additional guidance under IAS 39:

- For fair value measurement purposes, financial instruments could basically be classified into two categories: those with quoted prices in an active market and all of the others.

This distinction into two categories is significant because:

CICA 3855 refers to this classification for subsequent measurement of equity investments (which are measured at cost if they do not have a quoted price in an active market). Note that, under IAS 39, equity investments are always measured at fair value (unless it cannot be measured reliably).

Both IAS 39 and CICA 3855 take this classification into account when initially establishing whether an immediate gain or loss can be recognized (note that the entire instrument does not have to be quoted in an active market as it would be acceptable to record an immediate gain if the instrument is valued using a valuation technique for which all inputs are observable).

- Quoted prices in an active market provide the best evidence of fair value.

    Measurement at current quoted prices is more appropriate than using a valuation technique even if that technique is considered best industry practice for establishing fair values.

- Unadjusted current quoted prices in an active market should be used.

    Prices should not be adjusted to take into consideration:

    - Any block discounts or control premiums. This is an IAS 39 requirement. CICA 3855 is silent on this issue possibly because, prior to the publication of FAS 157, *Fair Value* measurements, block discounts or control premiums were usually taken in consideration for establishing fair value. With the application of FAS 157, both IFRS and US GAAP requirements are converged.

    - Any amount related to transaction costs on disposal.

    Prices other than current ones could be used when:

    - If it can be demonstrated that the current quoted price is not based on fair value (for example, because it reflects the price of a distress sale), that price should be adjusted.

        Current prices are not available, in which case the entity would usually use the most recent price (with adjustments to subsequent changes in economics conditions). This is, in fact, one of the valuation technique to use when no current quoted price in an active market is available (see discussion below on Determining Fair Value in Inactive Markets).

Determining Fair Value in Inactive Markets

Several documents were prepared in 2008 that discussed fair measurement subsequent to credit crunch crisis. Below is a brief overview of three documents that might provide additional guidance for fair value measurement in inactive markets under IAS 39 (and CICA 3855).

The first two documents were posted on the IASB Website in October 2008. They include: (1) the IASB Expert Advisory Panel report *Measuring and disclosing the fair value of financial instruments in markets that are no longer active* (the Panel Report) and (2) the IASB Staff Summary entitled *Using judgement to measure the fair value of financial instruments when markets are no longer active* (the Staff Summary). Both documents are not intended to establish new IFRS requirements. Rather they aim to provide useful information and educational guidance related to fair value measurement of financial instruments in inactive markets.

Below are certain issues discussed in the two documents:

- Staff Summary includes following observations:

    o objective of fair value measurement is to arrive at the price at which an orderly transaction would take place between market participants at the measurement date,

- o judgement must be applied in determining whether a market is not active,
- o even in an inactive market, an entity considers transaction prices that do not represent distressed transactions, although they might require significant adjustment based on unobservable data,
- o regardless of the valuation technique used, an entity includes appropriate risk adjustments that market participants would make, such as for credit and liquidity risk,
- o a forced liquidation or distress sale (i.e., a forced transaction) is not an orderly transaction and is not determinative of fair value. Judgement must be applied in determining whether a particular transaction is forced,
- o when relevant observable market data does not exist, or when observable inputs require significant adjustment based on unobservable inputs, an entity determines fair values using a valuation technique based primarily on management's internal assumptions about future cash flows and appropriately risk-adjusted discount rates. Such a technique reflects appropriate risk adjustments that market participants would make for credit and liquidity risks,
- o an entity might use broker or pricing service quotes as inputs when measuring fair value, however, they are not necessarily determinative if an active market does not exist for the instrument. An entity places less reliance on quotes that do not reflect the result of market transactions; an entity also considers the nature of the quote (e.g., whether it is an indicative price or a binding offer) when weighting the available evidence;

- the Panel Report is divided in two parts:
  - o Part 1 – Measurement: this part deals with valuation considerations of financial instruments in inactive markets which include:
    - terms of the financial instrument (including those governing cash flows and credit protection),
    - market information (transaction prices for the same or similar financial instruments, appropriateness of specific index, how and whether prices from brokers or pricing services are consistent with the fair value measurement objective),
    - an entity's own credit risk (to be included as a variable when measuring fair value of an entity's financial liabilities),
    - timing of, and uncertainty about, the relevant cash flows (when using discounted cash flow methodologies),
    - calibration of a model (to test whether the model reflects current market conditions as models and assumptions may change over time because of changing market conditions or refinements in techniques),
    - measurement of the underlying components of an instrument (when modelling an instrument as a whole is difficult),
    - adjustments to fair value (when calculated using a model) for any factors that are not captured by the valuation model and that market participants would consider in determining fair value.
  - o Part 2 – Disclosure: this part discusses factors that would be helpful for an entity to consider when providing disclosures about financial instruments measured at fair value, including:
    - aggregation and granularity of disclosure,
    - frequency of disclosure,
    - disclosure of the control environment,

- disclosure of valuation techniques,
- disclosure of unobservable inputs, including the effect of using reasonably possible alternative unobservable inputs,
- disclosure of changes in own credit risk,
- disclosure within a fair value hierarchy,
- disclosure of a reconciliation of movements in the fair values of instruments measured using significant unobservable inputs.

The last two disclosures have been proposed in the Exposure Draft, *Improving Disclosures about Financial Instruments (Proposed amendments to IFRS 7: Disclosures)* discussed in the Future Development section of this chapter.

The Panel Report also includes a summary of the issues encountered in the credit crisis; IAS 39's requirements and guidance on those issues; and a summary of how to deal with the issues in practice (which focuses on processes and approaches used when there is no longer an active market). Examples are presented covering the following instruments and structures:

- commercial paper and auction rate securities,
- asset backed securities,
- loans in syndication,
- real estate loans, and
- structured derivatives.

The third document, issued in September 2008 was prepared by the SEC and the staff of the FASB. It provides guidance for determining fair value in inactive markets under SFAS 157, *Fair Value Measurements*: This additional guidance was prepared after extensive consultations with participants in the capital markets including support from the IASB Expert Advisory Panel and the FASB Valuation Resource Group. The IASB noted in its October 2008 that this document provides additional interpretative guidance on fair value measurement that is consistent with IAS 39.

Below are some issues discussed in SEC and FASB staff guidance:

- the use of management estimates, incorporating current market participant expectations of future cash flows and appropriate risk premiums, is acceptable;
- broker quotes may be an input when measuring fair value, but are not necessarily determinative if an active market does not exist for the security. In a liquid market, a broker quote should reflect market information from actual transactions. However, when markets are less active, brokers may rely more on models with inputs based on the information available only to the broker. In weighing a broker quote as an input to fair value, an entity should place less reliance on quotes that do not reflect the result of market transactions. Further, the nature of the quote (e.g. whether the quote is an indicative price or a binding offer) should be considered when weighing the available evidence;
- the results of disorderly transactions are not determinative when measuring fair value. The concept of a fair value measurement assumes an orderly transaction between market participants. An orderly transaction is one that involves market participants that are willing to transact and allows for adequate exposure to the market. Distressed or forced liquidation sales are not orderly transactions, and thus the fact that a transaction is distressed or forced should be considered when weighing the available evidence. Determining whether a particular transaction is forced or disorderly requires judgment.

- Transactions in inactive markets may be inputs when measuring fair value, but would likely not be determinative. A significant increase in the spread between the amount sellers are "asking" and the price that buyers are "bidding," or the presence of a relatively small number of "bidding" parties, are indicators that should be considered in determining whether a market is inactive. The determination of whether a market is active or not requires judgment.

When quoted prices in an active market are available, an entity should use the current bid price (offer price) for financial assets (held) and the current asking price (asking price) for financial liabilities (held) (note that for an asset to be acquired the asking price is used whereas for a liability to be issued it is usually the current bid price):

The previous practice of using mid-market prices is inappropriate except for assets and liabilities with offsetting risks.

- If prices are quoted in different markets, an entity should use the price quoted in the most advantageous active market accessible.

Prices in the more advantageous market (for example, the retail market rather than the wholesale market) should be adjusted to reflect any differences in counterparty credit risks.

- Valuation techniques include discounted cash flows, option pricing models and current quoted price of similar financial instruments.

Entities should use the valuation technique market participants most commonly use for valuing a particular financial instrument. It should incorporate all factors that market participants use for this purpose.

- Generally, the transaction price is the best evidence of fair value at initial recognition for an instrument that is not quoted on an active market. Exceptions to this general rule are in cases where fait value is:
  - evidenced by transactions in the same instrument on other observable current market transactions; or
  - based on a valuation technique incorporating only data from an observable market.

Recording amounts that differ from transaction prices might lead to "Day 1" profits.

- Fair value of a financial liability should be established by taking into consideration the credit quality of a financial instrument, which generally reflects own credit risk (note that the value of the instrument could be immune to changes in own credit quality, for example, when collateral is held to protect against declines in creditworthiness).

Reducing a financial liability because an entity's own credit risk has deteriorated might be counter intuitive. Consequently, IFRS and Canadian standards require disclosure of:
  - changes in reported financial liabilities carried at fair value that are not attributable to changes in a benchmark interest rate risk (which would be a proxy for changes in fair values related to credit risks);
  - differences between carrying values of the financial liabilities and the amount to be paid at maturity.

Illustrative Disclosures:

Extract 9(34) – Fair value measurement

> **Skandinaviska Enskilda Banken AB (AR 2007), page 64**
> **1 Accounting policies (in part)**
> **Significant accounting policies for the Group (in part)**
> **Fair value measurement**
>
> The fair value of financial instruments quoted in an active market, for example quoted derivatives, financial assets and financial liabilities held for trading, and available for sale financial assets, is based on quoted market prices. The current bid price is used for financial assets and the current offer price for financial liabilities considering offsetting positions.
>
> The fair value of financial instruments that are not quoted in an active market is determined by applying various valuation techniques with maximum use of observable market inputs. The valuation techniques used are discounted cash flows, option pricing models, valuations with reference to recent transactions in the same instrument and valuations with reference to other financial instruments that are substantially the same.
>
> The difference between the transaction price and the fair value calculated using a valuation technique, the so called Day 1 profit, is amortised over the life of the transaction, recognised when realised through settlement or released to income if variables used to calculate fair value is based on market observable prices or rates.

Commentary: In this extract, the company establishes fair value measurement procedures as follows:

- using quotes in an active market where current bid price is used for financial assets and the current offer price for financial liabilities;
- using various valuation techniques, with maximum use of observable market inputs (discounted cash flows, option pricing models, valuations with reference to recent transactions in the same instrument and valuations with reference to other financial instruments that are substantially the same).

It also discloses the subsequent accounting treatment resulting from the difference between the transaction price and the fair value calculated using a valuation technique (Day 1 profit) as follows:

- amortized over the life of the transaction;
- recognized when realized through settlement; or
- released to income if variables used to calculate fair value are based on market observable prices or rates.

All above policies are in line with IAS 39 and CICA 3855.

Fair Value Option

A company may choose to use the fair value option to:

- reduce the complexity of measurement of embedded derivatives in a hybrid instrument (the whole instrument is valued at fair value);
- reduce the volatility in net income when other instruments (such as derivatives) are valued at fair value; and
- permit the natural hedge of hedging items (derivatives) and hedged items and avoid the complexities of hedge accounting.

According to IAS 39 and CICA 3855, an entity can designate a financial asset or a financial liability to be held for trading at fair value through profit or loss. The designation is irrevocable (i.e., the asset or liability cannot subsequently be transferred to another category) and must be made when the standard is adopted or when the asset or liability is initially recognized. The option can only be applied to whole instruments. Note that the IASB has introduced amendments to IAS 39 in October 2008 that permit the reclassification of certain non-derivative financial assets (see previous discussion on reclassifications).

CICA 3855 allows almost all financial assets or financial liabilities within its scope to be designated as held for trading. The only two circumstances where the fair value option is not available are when:

- financial instruments are transferred in a related party transaction and were not classified as held for trading before the transaction; and

- when the fair value of a financial instrument is not reliably measurable (i.e., variability in the range of reasonable fair value estimate must not be significant to use the fair value option).

There are further restrictions under IAS 39, which requires one of the following criteria to be met if the fair value option is to be used:

- where the designation eliminates or significantly reduces an accounting mismatch;

- when a group of financial assets, financial liabilities, or both, are managed and their performance is evaluated on a fair value basis in accordance with a documented risk management or investment strategy and information about this group is provided to the entity's key management personnel;

- if a contract contains one or more embedded derivatives, an entity may designate the entire hybrid (combined) contract as a financial asset or financial liability at fair value through profit or loss unless:

  o the embedded derivative(s) does not significantly modify the cash flows that otherwise would be required by the contract; or

  o it is clear, with little or no analysis, when a similar hybrid (combined) instrument is first considered, that separation of the embedded derivative(s) is prohibited (for example, when a prepayment option is embedded in a loan that permits the holder to prepay the loan for approximately its amortized cost).

These additional requirements make it more difficult to use the fair value option under IAS 39 than under CICA 3855.

In June 2006, the Office of the Superintendent of Financial Institutions issued Guideline D10, *Accounting for Financial Instruments Designated as Fair Value Option*, which contains requirements and disclosures additional to the fair value option under CICA 3855. The additional requirements are derived from IAS 39.

Illustrative Disclosures:

Extract 9(35) – Fair value option

AstraZeneca PLC (AR & Form 20-F 2007), page 138

17 FINANCIAL INSTRUMENTS (in part)

Fair values of financial assets and financial liabilities

Set out below is a comparison by category of carrying values and fair values of all the Group's financial assets and financial liabilities as at 31 December 2007, 31 December 2006 and 31 December 2005. None of the financial assets or financial liabilities have been reclassified during the year.

	Designated at fair value $m	Derivatives and other items at fair value $m	Available for sale $m	Held for trading $m	Amortised cost $m	Total carrying value $m	Fair value $m
2007							
Cash and cash equivalents	-	-	-	-	5,867	5,867	5,867
Overdrafts	-	-	-	-	(140)	(140)	(140)
Loans due within one year	-	-	-	-	(4,140)	(4,140)	(4,140)
Loans due after more than one year	(1,090)	(1,544)	-	-	(8,242)	(10,876)	(11,235)
Derivative assets	67	19	-	-	-	86	86
Other investments	-	-	182	31	60	273	273
Other financial assets	-	-	-	-	5,973	5,973	5,973
Other financial liabilities	-	-	-	-	(8,070)	(8,070)	(8,070)

> *Commentary:* This extract presents part of the note and the table related to the fair value amounts of the company's financial assets and financial liabilities. The company indicates in the table that it designated loans due after more than one year at fair value. This disclosure and accounting policy is in line with CICA 3855.

Extract 9(36) – Fair value option (financial assets)

BNP Paribas (Registration Document 2007), page 122

1.c FINANCIAL ASSETS AND FINANCIAL LIABILITIES (in part)

1.c.10 Financial assets and liabilities designated at fair value through profit or loss (fair value option)

The amendment to IAS 39 relating to the "fair value option" was adopted by the European Union on 15 November 2005, with effect from 1 January 2005.

This option allows entities to designate any financial asset or financial liability on initial recognition as measured at fair value, with changes in fair value recognised in profit or loss, in the following cases:

- hybrid financial instruments containing one or more embedded derivatives which otherwise would have been extracted and accounted for separately;
- where using the option enables the entity to eliminate or significantly reduce a mismatch in the measurement and accounting treatment of assets and liabilities that would arise if they were to be classified in separate categories;
- where a group of financial assets and/or financial liabilities is managed and measured on the basis of fair value, under a properly documented management and investment strategy.

BNP Paribas applies this option primarily to financial assets related to unit-linked business (in order to achieve consistency of treatment with the related liabilities), and to structured issues containing significant embedded derivatives.

Page 129

2.c NET GAIN/LOSS ON FINANCIAL INSTRUMENTS AT FAIR VALUE THROUGH PROFIT OR LOSS

"Net gain/loss on financial instruments at fair value through profit or loss" includes all profit and loss items relating to financial instruments managed in the trading book and financial instruments (including dividends) that the Group has designated as at fair value through profit or loss under the fair value option, other than interest income and expense which are recognised in "Net interest income" (Note 2.a).

BNP Paribas (Registration Document 2007) (continued)

2.c NET GAIN/LOSS ON FINANCIAL INSTRUMENTS AT FAIR VALUE THROUGH PROFIT OR LOSS (continued)

In millions of euros	Year to 31 Dec. 2007			Year to 31 Dec. 2006		
	Trading book	Assets designated at fair value through profit or loss	Total	Trading book	Assets designated at fair value through profit or loss	Total
Fixed-income securities	(1,968)	758	(1,210)	266	273	539
Variable-income securities	7,737	643	8,380	9,888	276	10,164
Derivative instruments	51	-	51	(3,935)	-	(3,935)
Repurchase agreements	70	19	89	(20)	12	(8)
Loans	(118)	(120)	(238)	(3)	(133)	(136)
Borrowings	(36)	(12)	(48)	29	32	61
Remeasurement of interest-rate risk hedged portfolios	399	-	399	185	-	185
Remeasurement of currency positions	420	-	420	703	-	703
TOTAL	6,555	1,288	7,843	7,113	460	7,573

The net loss for the year on hedging instruments in fair value hedges amounted to EUR 314 million (net loss of EUR 428 million in 2006) and the net profit on the hedged components amounted to EUR 275 million (net profit of EUR 507 million in 2006).

In addition, net gains on the trading book included in 2007 and 2006 an immaterial amount related to the ineffective portion of cash flow hedges.

Pages 152 and 153

5.a FINANCIAL ASSETS, FINANCIAL LIABILITIES AND DERIVATIVES AT FAIR VALUE THROUGH PROFIT OR LOSS (in part)

Financial assets and financial liabilities at fair value through profit or loss consist of trading account transactions (including derivatives) and certain assets and liabilities designated by the Group as at fair value through profit or loss at the time of acquisition or issue.

Financial assets

Trading book assets include proprietary securities transactions, repurchase agreements, and derivative instruments contracted for position management purposes. Assets designated by the Group as at fair value through profit or loss include admissible investments related to unit linked insurance business, and to a lesser extent assets with embedded derivatives that have not been separated from the host contract.

In millions of euros	31 December 2007			31 December 2006		
	Trading book	Assets designated at fair value through profit or loss	TOTAL	Trading book	Assets designated at fair value through profit or loss	TOTAL
FINANCIAL ASSETS AT FAIR VALUE THROUGH PROFIT OR LOSS						
Negotiable certificates of deposit	82,476	554	83,030	48,633	174	48,807
Treasury bills and other bills eligible for central bank refinancing	65,077	12	65,089	34,680	9	34,689
Other negotiable certificates of deposit	17,399	542	17,941	13,953	165	14,118
Bonds	121,314	6,488	127,802	131,938	6,577	138,515
Government bonds	56,294	491	56,785	66,962	206	67,168
Other bonds	65,020	5,997	71,017	64,976	6,371	71,347
Equities and other variable-income securities	100,709	43,975	144,684	94,989	42,328	137,317
Repurchase agreements	334,033	95	334,128	254,967	103	255,070
Loans	2,791	2,351	5,142	231	3,451	3,682
to credit institutions	-	2,240	2,240	7	3,407	3,414
to corporate customers	2,781	111	2,892	214	44	258
to private individual customers	10	-	10	10	10	10
Trading book derivatives	236,920	-	236,920	161,467	-	161,467
Currency derivatives	23,627	-	23,627	17,799	-	17,799
Interest rate derivatives	99,308	-	99,308	78,707	-	78,707
Equity derivatives	75,243	-	75,243	51,661	-	51,661
Credit derivatives	30,342	-	30,342	9,487	-	9,487
Other derivatives	8,400	-	8,400	3,813	-	3,813
TOTAL FINANCIAL ASSETS AT FAIR VALUE THROUGH PROFIT OR LOSS	878,243	53,463	931,706	692,225	52,633	744,858

Commentary: Here, the company lists the conditions established by IAS 39 for making the fair value option designation. It indicates that it applied the fair value option to financial assets to achieve consistency of treatment with the related liabilities and to structured products containing significant embedded derivatives. The company also presents extensive disclosures, including tables (reproduced in part), detailing balance sheet amounts of financial assets valued at fair value and the related amounts of gains or losses. These disclosures and accounting policy are in line with CICA 3855 except that the latter does not contain any restrictions on the fair value option designation.

Extract 9(37) – Fair value option

Roche Holding Ltd (AR 2006), page 82

30. Debt (in part)

Fair Value Option

In 2005 the Group applied the Fair Value Option on three of its outstanding debt instruments on which the Group had been applying fair value hedge accounting in the past. These debt instruments are the 'European Medium Term Note programme' Euro bonds, the 'Chameleon' US dollar bonds and the 'Rodeo' Swiss franc bonds. The Fair Value Option treatment is based on the elimination of an accounting mismatch which had been recognised between the hedging swaps (reported at fair value) and the hedged bonds (reported at amortised cost). The difference between the carrying value and the principal amount for these debt instruments totals 14 million Swiss francs (2005: 68 million Swiss francs).

Commentary: This extract indicates that the company applied the fair value option to eliminate a mismatch between hedging swaps and the hedged bonds liabilities (reported at amortized cost). The fair value option allows the company to achieve results equalling the ones achieved through hedge accounting. This disclosure and accounting policy is in line with CICA 3855.

Extract 9(38) – Fair value option

Wolters Kluwer nv (AR 2007), page 98

BASIS OF CONSOLIDATION (in part)

Interest-bearing debt

Financial liabilities, such as bond loans and other loans from credit institutions are recognized initially at fair value less attributable transaction costs. Subsequent to initial recognition, interest-bearing debt is stated at amortized cost with any difference between cost and redemption value being recognized in the income statement over the period of the borrowings on an effective interest basis.

The Group opted to recognize the unsubordinated convertible bonds 2001-06 as a financial liability at fair value through profit or loss. Fair value changes during the year, which are derived from market quotations, are recognized in finance income or costs.

Commentary: In this extract, the company indicates that it applied the fair value option to unsubordinated convertible bonds (possibly a compound instrument). It indicates that the fair value (derived from market quotations) changes during the year and is recognized in finance income or costs.

The fair value option application appears to meet IAS 39 criteria. This disclosure and accounting policy is in line with CICA 3855.

Hedge Accounting

Hedge accounting modifies the normal basis for recognizing gains and losses on associated hedging instruments and hedged items so that both are recognized in earnings in the same accounting period.

Hedged Items[2]

Hedged items could be (same provisions under both IAS 39 and CICA 3865 unless specifically indicated):

- a recognized asset or a liability;

- a firm commitment (recognized and unrecognized) (note that, to qualify as a firm commitment under CICA 3865, a transaction must be with an unrelated party and contain a significant disincentive for non-performance.);

- a forecast transaction that has a high probability of occurring under IAS 39 (but needs to be only probable under CICA 3865);

- net investment in a foreign operation;

- a group of assets, liabilities, firm commitments or highly probable transactions (probable under CICA 3865) or forecast transactions or net investment in a foreign operation with similar risk characteristics.

In 2008, the IASB introduced amendments to IAS 39 concerning eligible hedged items. The amendments, which are effective July 1, 2009, provide clarification on two issues:

- *Identifying inflation as a hedged risk* – amendments specify that inflation could be designated as a hedged item only if changes in inflation are a contractually-specified portion of cash flows of a recognized financial instrument. For example, an entity that acquires or issues inflation linked debt could designate for hedge accounting purposes the portion of risk related to cash flow exposure to changes in future inflation. The amendments, therefore, do not permit an entity to designate an inflation component of issued or acquired fixed-rate debt in a fair value hedge as such a component is not separately identifiable and reliably measurable. The amendments also clarify that a risk-free or benchmark interest rate portion of the fair value of a fixed-rate financial instrument will normally be separately identifiable and reliably measurable and, therefore, may be hedged.

- *Hedging with options* – IAS 39 permits an entity to designate purchased (or net purchased) options as a hedging instrument in a hedge of a financial or non financial item. An entity may designate an option as a hedge of changes in the cash flows or fair value of a hedged item above or below a specified price or other variable (a one-sided risk). The amendments make clear that the intrinsic value, not the time value, of an option reflects a one-sided risk and therefore an option designated in its entirety cannot be perfectly effective. The time value of a purchased option is not a component of the forecast transaction that impacts profit or loss. Therefore, if an entity designates an option in its entirety as a hedge of a one-sided risk arising from a forecast transaction, hedge ineffectiveness will arise. Alternatively, an entity may choose to exclude time value as permitted by IAS 39 in order to improve hedge effectiveness. As a result of this designation, changes in the time value of the option will be recognized immediately in profit or loss.

If a non-financial asset or liability is hedged (such as inventory), entity can designate as the hedged risk either the foreign currency risk component, or the fair value risk of the entire item (because it is difficult to measure and isolate the other risks).

A held-to-maturity investment can be hedged only for foreign currency risk or credit risk but not interest rate risk because the entity holding such an investment would normally be indifferent to interest rate risk since it is committed to hold the investment to maturity.

---

2   In July 2008, the IASB has issued a revised IAS 39 dealing with eligible hedged. These amendments are not discussed in this section, but the changes that were proposed in the Exposure Draft are covered in the section "Clarification, improvements and Future Developments."

The overall fair value of a written repayment option in a held-to-maturity financial asset cannot be hedged under IAS 39. This differs from CICA 3865, which allows such a hedged item to be designated.

Even if other hedge criteria would otherwise be met, the following are examples of items or transactions (or related forecast transactions) that would not qualify as hedged items under either IAS 39 or CICA 3865:

- derivative instruments (except for purchased options in fair value hedges under IAS 39 only);
- equity method investments;
- future business combinations to which the entity is firmly committed (except for a hedge of foreign-currency risk);
- an entity's own equity instruments;
- interest rate risk or prepayment risk of held-to-maturity investments (however, a forecast purchase of a held-to-maturity investment may be designated as a hedged item);
- risk of a transaction not occurring;
- groups of assets or liabilities that do not have similar risk characteristics;
- transactions with shareholders, such as projected payments of dividends (except for declared and unpaid dividends in certain circumstances).

A hedge of overall net position is often referred to as a "macro-hedge." Neither IAS 39 and CICA 3855 permit macro-hedges because there is no way of determining when a net exposure has been settled. An exception is that IAS 39 permits macro-hedging of a position of a portfolio of assets and liabilities with common exposure to changes in interest rates. Note, however, that even though macro-hedging is not generally allowed, it could be done indirectly by designating an amount of assets or liabilities that corresponds to the net position.

Illustrative Disclosures:

Extract 9(39) – Hedged items

Atorka Group hf (AR 2007), page 121

2.10 Derivative financial instruments and hedging activities

Derivatives are initially recognised at fair value on the date a derivative contract is entered into and are subsequently remeasured at their fair value. The method of recognising the resulting gain or loss depends on whether the derivative is designated as a hedging instrument, and if so, the nature of the item being hedged. The Group designates certain derivatives as either:

(a) hedges of the fair value of recognised liabilities (fair value hedge);

(b) hedges of a particular risk associated with a recognised liability or a highly probable forecast transaction (cash flow hedge); or

(c) hedges of a net investment in a foreign operation (net investment hedge).

Fair value hedges

Changes in the fair value of derivatives that are designated and qualify as fair value hedges are recorded in the income statement, together with any changes in the fair value of the hedged asset or liability that are attributable to the hedged risk. The Group applies only fair value hedge accounting for hedging fixed interest risk on borrowings. The gain or loss relating to the effective portion of interest rate swaps hedging fixed rate borrowings is recognised in the income statement within finance costs. The gain or loss relating to the ineffective portion is recognised in the income statement within other gains/(losses) – net. Changes in the fair value of the hedge fixed rate borrowings attributable to interest rate risk are recognised in the income statement within finance costs.

Atorka Group hf (AR 2007) (continued)

Cash flow hedge

The effective portion of changes in the fair value of derivatives that are designated and qualify as cash flow hedges are recognised in equity. The gain or loss relating to the ineffective portion is recognised immediately in the income statement within other gains/(losses) – net.

Amounts accumulated in equity are recycled in the income statement in the periods when the hedged item affects profit or loss (for example, when the forecast sale that is hedged takes place). The gain or loss relating to the effective portion of interest rate swaps hedging variable rate borrowings is recognised in the income statement within finance costs. The gain or loss relating to the effective portion of forward foreign exchange contracts hedging export sales is recognised in the income statement within sales. However, when the forecast transaction that is hedged results in the recognition of a non-financial asset (for example, inventory or fixed assets), the gains and losses previously deferred in equity are transferred from equity and included in the initial measurement of the cost of the asset. The deferred amounts are ultimately recognised in cost of goods sold in case of inventory, or in depreciation in case of fixed assets.

When a hedging instrument expires or is sold, or when a hedge no longer meets the criteria for hedge accounting, any cumulative gain or loss existing in equity at that time remains in equity and is recognised when the forecast transaction is ultimately recognised in the income statement. When a forecast transaction is no longer expected to occur, the cumulative gain or loss that was reported in equity is immediately transferred to the income statement within other gains/(losses) – net.

Commentary: Here, the company indicates that hedged items consist of:

- recognized liabilities;
- a highly probable forecast transaction;
- net investment in a foreign operation.

Risks hedged include:

- interest rate risk on fixed and floating borrowings;
- foreign currency on export sales.

The extract also provides an example of disclosures related to different aspects of hedge accounting (both fair value and cash flow hedges). All disclosures are in line with CICA 3865 except that the amount the company reports in shareholders' equity related to unrealized or deferred gains or losses would be part of other comprehensive income. The adoption of amended IAS 1 has now eliminated this difference.

Hedging Instruments

Only derivatives can be designated as hedging instruments. Non-derivatives may be designated as hedging instruments only for hedges of a foreign currency risk.

Certain particular issues arise with designating derivatives as hedging instruments under IFRS:

- The *portion* of the time period during which a derivative remains outstanding can not be designated as the hedging instrument. CICA 3865 has similar provisions.

- The *combination* of non-derivatives and derivatives may be designated as the hedging instrument for hedges of foreign currency risk. CICA 3865 does not permit such a combination to be designated as the hedging instrument.

- Internal derivatives cannot be used as hedging instruments in the consolidated financial statements. CICA 3865 permits this use under certain limited conditions.

- Both IAS 39 and CICA 3865:

  o Do not allow a written option to be used as a hedging instrument (unless it offsets a purchased option).

  o Allow the separation of (1) intrinsic value and time value of an option contract, with only the intrinsic value being designated as the hedging instrument; and

(2) interest element and spot price of a forward contract, with the spot price being the designated hedging instrument.

o Permit the designation of (1) a single hedging instrument for more than one type of risk; and (2) two or more derivatives to be jointly designated as a hedging instrument if they do not include a written option or net written option.

Illustrative Disclosure:

Extract 9(40) – Hedging instruments

> **Air France-KLM S.A. (Reference Document 2006-07), page 96**
> **3.10. Financial instruments, valuation of financial assets and liabilities (in part)**
> **3.10.3. Derivative instruments (in part)**
> The group uses various derivative instruments to hedge its exposure to the risks of changes in interest rates, exchange rates or fuel prices. Forward currency contracts and options are used to cover exposure to exchange rates. For firm commitments, the unrealized gains and losses on these financial instruments are included in the carrying value of the hedged asset or liability.
> The Group also uses rate swaps to manage its exposure to the rate risk. Most of the swaps traded convert floating-rate debt to fixed-rate debt.
> Finally, exposure to the fuel risk is hedged by swaps or options on jet fuel, diesel or Brent.

Commentary: In this extract, hedging instruments include:
- forward currency contracts;
- options (on jet fuel, diesel or Brent);
- rate swaps (convert floating-rate debt to fixed-rate debt).

Hedged risks include changes in:
- interest rates;
- exchange rates;
- fuel prices.

All disclosures are in line with CICA 3865.

Hedge Accounting Criteria

To qualify for hedge accounting under IAS 39 and CICA 3865, a hedging relationship strategy must meet all the following conditions:

- the hedging relationship and the related risk management objective and hedging strategy are formally designated and documented at inception;
- the hedge is expected to be highly effective in achieving offsetting changes in fair value or cash flows attributable to the hedged risk, consistently with the originally documented risk management strategy for that particular hedging relationship;
- for cash flow hedges, a forecast transaction that is the subject of the hedge must be highly probable and must present an exposure to variations in cash flows that could ultimately affect profit or loss;
- the effectiveness of the hedge can be reliably measured, i.e., the fair value or cash flows of the hedged item that are attributable to the hedged risk and the fair value of the hedging instrument can be reliably measured;
- the hedge is assessed on an ongoing basis and determined actually to have been highly effective throughout the financial reporting periods for which the hedge was designated.

The formal documentation would normally include the following:

- entity's risk management objective and strategy for undertaking the hedge;
- type of hedging relationship (i.e., fair value hedge, cash flow hedge or net investment hedge - see discussion later). For a cash flow hedge, a company usually

would specify the method it uses for reclassifying into income amounts deferred in accumulated other comprehensive income (accounting policy choice between basis adjustment or deferral);

- the nature of the risk being hedged (for example interest rate, foreign currency or commodity);
- identification of the hedged item. With a forecast transaction, an entity must indicate the hedged amount, nature and expected price and timing of the transaction and how the entity determined that it is highly probable that the transaction will occur;
- identification of hedging instrument;
- effectiveness testing - description of the method and its application and
- frequency of testing (see *Note* below):
  - o prospective effectiveness testing,
  - o retrospective effectiveness testing.

Note: An entity must assess and track the hedging instrument's effectiveness at the beginning and on an ongoing basis. IAS 39 and CICA 3865 do not require a hedge to be perfectly effective, although it is expected to be "highly effective." A hedge is regarded as highly effective if both of the following conditions are met:

- At the inception of the hedge and in subsequent periods, the hedge is expected to be highly effective in achieving offsetting changes in fair value or cash flows attributable to the hedged risk during the period for which the hedge is designated.
- The actual results of the hedge are within a range of 80-125%.

CICA 3865 permits, if certain conditions are met, the use of the "critical terms match" approach and the "short-cut" method (which assumes no ineffectiveness) for assessing hedge effectiveness. This avoids the need for ongoing measurement of ineffectiveness. Although IAS 39 prohibits the use of this method, it does allow the use of the "critical terms match" approach for prospective assessments of hedge effectiveness.

Illustrative Disclosure:

Extract 9(41) – Hedge accounting criteria

Kingfisher plc (AR 2007), page 60
2 Significant accounting policies (in part)
q. Financial instruments (in part)
(v) Derivative financial instruments and hedge accounting (in part)

Where hedge accounting is not applied, changes in the fair value of derivatives transacted as hedges of financing items are recognised in net finance costs in the income statement as they arise.

Derivatives are initially accounted and measured at fair value on the date a derivative contract is entered into and subsequently measured at fair value with changes in fair value recognised in the income statement unless formally designated as a cash flow hedge or net investment hedge. The accounting treatment of derivatives classified as hedges depends on their designation, which occurs on the date that the derivative contract is committed to. ...

In order to qualify for hedge accounting, the Group documents in advance the relationship between the item being hedged and the hedging instrument. The Group also documents and demonstrates an assessment of the relationship between the hedged item and the hedging instrument, which shows that the hedge has been, and will be, highly effective on an ongoing basis. The effectiveness testing is re-performed at each period end to ensure that the hedge remains highly effective.

Commentary: In this extract, the company indicates that designation for hedge accounting treatment occurs on the date that the derivative contract is committed to, which increases the chances that it could be an effective hedge. The company specifies the conditions for hedge accounting:

- It documents in advance the relationship between the item being hedged and the hedging instrument.
- It documents and demonstrates an assessment of the relationship between the hedged item and the hedging instrument, which shows that the hedge has been, and will be, highly effective on an ongoing basis.
- It re-performs at each period end, effectiveness testing to ensure that the hedge remains highly effective.

All disclosures and policies adopted are in line with CICA 3865.

Hedge Accounting Types

According to IAS 39 and CICA 3865, hedge relationships must fall into one of the following three defined types:

- **Fair-value hedge**: This covers risks related to changes in the fair value of a recognized asset or liability or an unrecognized firm commitment to buy or sell an asset or liability at a fixed price. Such changes in fair value must be related to a specific risk that could affect net income.

  There are many factors that could affect the fair value of a hedged item. An entity could identify and document the specific risk that is being hedged or it could specify in its documentation that it hedges all risks. Covering specific risks could minimize the ineffectiveness caused by basis risks or other risks.

  If all hedging criteria are met, a fair value hedge is accounted for as follows:

  o The derivative hedging instrument is measured at fair value and the carrying value of the hedged item is adjusted for the hedged risk only (i.e., the hedged item is not adjusted to its full fair value).

  o All gains and losses are taken to the income statement, producing no net profit and loss effect other than any hedge ineffectiveness.

- **Cash flow hedge**: This covers exposure to variability in cash flows attributable to a particular risk associated with an asset or liability or a highly probable forecast transaction (probable transaction under CICA 3865) that could affect income. If all hedging criteria are met, a cash flow hedge is accounted for as follows:

  o The derivative hedging instrument is measured at fair value.

  o The portion of the gain or loss on the hedging instrument that is determined to be an effective hedge is recognized directly in other comprehensive income. The ineffective portion of the gain or loss on the hedging instrument is recognized in earnings.

  o The gain or loss deferred in other comprehensive income is recycled to the income statement when the hedged cash flows affect net income. If the hedged cash flows result in the recognition of a non-financial asset or liability on the balance sheet, the entity can choose to adjust the basis of the asset or liability by the amount deferred in accumulated other comprehensive income. This choice has to be applied consistently to all such hedges.

- **Hedge of a net investment in a foreign operation**: This type of hedge covers currency exposure in a net investment in foreign operations.

In addition to the general hedge accounting criteria, IFRIC 16, which is effective after October 1, 2008, specifies that:

- Presentation currency does not create an exposure to which an entity may apply hedge accounting. Consequently, a parent entity may designate as a hedged risk only the foreign exchange differences arising from a difference between its own functional currency and that of its foreign operation.

- Hedging instrument(s) may be held by any entity or entities within the group (other than the foreign operation that is itself being hedged).

Consequently, when hedging the foreign currency exposure of a net investment in a self sustaining foreign operation, hedge accounting may be applied only to the foreign exchange differences arising between the functional currency of the foreign operation and the functional currency of any parent entity (the immediate, intermediate or ultimate parent entity) of that foreign operation. The hedging instrument need not be held by the entity holding the net investment since effectiveness is assessed on a consolidated basis. Even though CICA 3865 specifies that hedge accounting may be applied only to the foreign exchange differences arising between the functional currency of the foreign operation and the functional currency of any parent entity, it requires that the parent entity that holds the net investment be party to the derivative hedging instrument, or that another member of the consolidated group that has the same functional currency as the parent entity be party to the derivative hedging instrument (provided there is no intervening subsidiary with a different functional currency).

When hedge accounting criteria are met, a net investment hedge is accounted for as follows:

- The hedging instrument (derivative or non-derivative) is accounted for similarly to a cash flow hedge.
- The gain or loss recognized in accumulated other comprehensive income is recycled to earnings on the foreign operation's disposal or partial disposal (IFRS only).

Illustrative Disclosures:

Extract 9(42) – Hedge accounting models

Air France-KLM S.A. (Reference Document 2006-07), page 157
Note 32 Financial instruments (in part)
32.1. Derivative instruments (in part)
Year ended March 31, 2007

	Book value			
	Assets		Liabilities	
	non-current	current	non-current	current
	(In euro millions)			
Currency exchange risk (operating and financial operations)				
Fair value hedge	5	2	96	50
Cash flow hedge	17	30	11	32
Interest rate risk (operating and financial operations)				
Cash flow hedge	61	1	23	2
Fair value hedge	27	16	90	34
Trading derivatives	50	-	9	1
Commodities risk				
Fair value hedge	-	-	-	-
Cash flow hedge	429	407	20	100

Commentary: The company uses a table to present the different risks it covers (currency, interest rate and commodity) and the types of hedge accounting it uses (fair value and cash flows) along with the values of hedging instruments recorded in the books. This presentation is in line with IFRS 7 and CICA 3865.

Extract 9(43) – Hedge accounting models

Kingfisher plc (AR 2007), page 60
2 Significant accounting policies (in part)
q. Financial instruments (in part)
(v) Derivative financial instruments and hedge accounting (in part)
The Group designates certain derivatives as:

- a hedge of a highly probable forecast transaction or firm commitment in a foreign currency ('cash flow hedge');
- a hedge of the fair value of an asset or liability or unrecognised firm commitment ('fair value hedge'); or
- a hedge of a net investment in a foreign currency ('net investment hedge').

Cash flow hedges

Changes in the effective portion of the fair value of derivative financial instruments that are designated as hedges of future cash flows are recognised directly in equity, and the ineffective portion is recognised immediately in the income statement where relevant. If the cash flow hedge of a firm commitment or forecast transaction results in the recognition of a nonfinancial asset or liability, then, at the time it is recognised, the associated gains or losses on the derivative that had previously been recognised in equity are included in the initial measurement. For hedges that result in the recognition of a financial asset or liability, amounts deferred in equity are recognised in the income statement in the same period in which the hedged item affects net profit or loss.

Fair value hedges

For an effective hedge of an exposure to changes in fair value, the hedged item is adjusted for changes in fair value attributable to the risk being hedged with the corresponding entry being recorded in the income statement. Gains or losses from remeasuring the corresponding hedging instrument are recognised in the same line of the income statement.

Net investment hedges

Where the Group hedges net investments in foreign entities through currency borrowings, the gains or losses on the retranslation of the borrowings are recognised in equity. If the Group uses derivatives as the hedging instrument, the effective portion of the hedge is recognised in equity, with any ineffective portion being recognised in the income statement. Gains and losses accumulated in equity are recycled through the income statement on disposal of the foreign entity.

Commentary: Here, the company uses the following types of hedging relationships to cover various hedged items:

- cash flow hedge for highly probable forecast transaction;
- cash flow hedge for firm commitment in a foreign currency;
- fair value hedge for asset or liability;
- fair value hedge for unrecognized firm commitment; and
- net investment hedge for a net investment in a foreign operation.

The company explains the accounting for the hedging relationships it uses for hedge accounting.

All disclosures and accounting policies are in line with CICA 3865. Note, however, that the forecast transaction has to be only probable to qualify for hedge accounting under 3865.

The company explains the accounting for the hedging relationships it uses for hedge accounting.

Extract 9(44) – Hedge accounting models

> **Alcatel-Lucent (AR 2007 on Form 20-F), page 157**
> **NOTE 1 SUMMARY OF ACCOUNTING POLICIES (in part)**
> **(e) Translation of foreign currency transactions (in part)**
>
> In order for a currency derivative to be eligible for hedge accounting treatment (cash flow hedge or fair value hedge), its hedging role must be defined and documented and it must be seen to be effective for the entirety of its period of use. Fair value hedges allow companies to protect themselves against exposure to changes in fair value of their assets, liabilities or firm commitments. Cash flow hedges allow companies to protect themselves against exposure to changes in future cash flows (for example, revenues generated by the company's assets).
>
> The value used for derivatives is their fair value. Changes in the fair value of derivatives are accounted for as follows:
>
> - For derivatives treated as cash flow hedges, changes in their fair value are accounted for in shareholders' equity and then reclassified to income (cost of sales) when the hedged reve- nue is accounted for. The ineffective portion is recorded in "other financial income (loss)";
> - For derivatives treated as fair value hedges, changes in their fair value are recorded in the income statement where they offset the changes in fair value of the hedged assets, liabili- ties and firm commitments.
>
> In addition to derivatives used to hedge firm commitments documented as fair value hedges, from April 1, 2005 onwards, Alcatel-Lucent designates and documents highly probable future streams of revenue with respect to which the Group has entered into hedge transactions. The corresponding derivatives are accounted for in accordance with the requirements governing cash flow hedge accounting.
>
> Certain foreign exchange derivatives are not considered eligible for hedge accounting treatment, as the derivatives are not designated as hedges for cost/ benefit reasons.
>
> Derivatives related to commercial bids are not considered eligible for hedge accounting treat- ment and are accounted for as trading financial instruments. Changes in fair values of such instruments are included in the income statement in cost of sales (in the business segment "other").
>
> Once a commercial contract is effective, the corresponding firm commitment is hedged with a derivative treated as a fair value hedge. Revenues made pursuant to such a contract are then accounted for, throughout the duration of the contract, using the spot rate prevailing on the date on which the contract was effective, insofar as the exchange rate hedging is effective.

Commentary: The company provides disclosures on various aspects of hedge accounting, including (which are in line with CICA 3865 unless otherwise noted):

- types of hedging relationships used for hedge accounting (cash flow hedge or fair value hedge);
- eligibility for hedge accounting treatment (hedging role defined and documented, must be seen to be effective for the entirety of its period of use);
- objectives of fair value hedges (protection against exposure to changes in fair value of assets, liabilities or firm commitments);
- objectives of cash flow hedges (protection against exposure to changes in future cash flows);
- details related to hedge accounting models;
- the fact that certain hedges (using foreign exchange derivatives) are not designated as hedges for cost/benefit reasons;
- the fact that derivatives related to commercial bids are not considered eligible for hedge accounting treatment and are accounted for as trading financial instruments.

Discontinuing Hedge Accounting

According to IAS 39 and CICA 3865, hedge accounting is discontinued prospectively if any of the following occurs:

- The hedge fails the effectiveness tests or any of the other criteria for hedge accounting.
- The hedging instrument is sold, terminated or exercised.
- The hedged item is settled.
- The entity decides to revoke the hedge relationship.

- For a cash flow hedge, the hedged forecast transaction is no longer expected to occur. Note that levels of probability differ under IFRS and Canadian GAAP (no longer highly probable per IAS 39 and no longer probable per CICA 3865).

Discontinuing hedge accounting can have a number of accounting consequences:

- When a non-derivative liability has been adjusted for changes in fair value under a hedging relationship, the adjusted carrying amount becomes amortized cost. Any adjustments are then amortized through the income statement over the remaining period to the liability's maturity.

- If a cash flow hedge relationship ceases, the related amounts in accumulated other comprehensive income will be maintained there until the hedged item affects earnings. If the hedge accounting is discontinued because the forecast transaction that was hedged is no longer expected to occur, amounts deferred in accumulated other comprehensive income are recognized in earnings. Similarly, any amounts accumulated in other comprehensive income while a hedge of net investment was effective remain in that account until the disposal of the related net investment.

- When hedge accounting is discontinued, IAS 39 will account for the cumulative gain or loss recognized in accumulated other comprehensive income depending on whether the hedged transaction is still expected to occur. Under both IAS 39 and 3865, when a forecast transaction is no longer probable (or highly probable) but is still expected to occur, hedge accounting is discontinued prospectively but amounts related to hedge accounting remain in accumulated other comprehensive income. If it is no longer highly probable that a transaction will occur, the amount recognized in accumulated other comprehensive income is recognized immediately in income for that portion of the hedged transaction that is not expected to occur; otherwise, the amount recognized in equity is not recorded in income until the forecast transaction has an impact on net income. Under CICA 3865, as long as it is probable that the entire forecast transaction will occur within two months of the original time frame, the entire cumulative gain or loss remains in other comprehensive income and is not recognized in income until the forecast transaction affects income; otherwise, the entire amount is recognized immediately in income.

Illustrative Disclosure:

Extract 9(45) – Hedge accounting discontinuance

Kingfisher plc (AR 2007), page 60
2 Significant accounting policies (in part)
q. Financial instruments (in part)
(v) Derivative financial instruments and hedge accounting (in part)
Net investment hedges
Hedge accounting is discontinued when the hedging instrument expires or is sold, terminated, or exercised, or no longer qualifies for hedge accounting. At that time, any cumulative gain or loss on the hedging instrument recognised in equity is retained in equity until the highly probably forecasted transaction occurs. If a hedged transaction is no longer expected to occur, the net cumulative gain or loss recognised in equity is transferred to the income statement for the period.

Commentary: The company presents circumstances of hedge accounting discontinuance as required by IAS 39 and CICA 3865. It explains the accounting subsequent to hedge accounting discontinuance, again as required by IAS 39 and CICA 3865.

Disclosure of Financial Instruments

IFRS 7, which contains all of the disclosure requirements for financial instruments, came into effect for fiscal years starting January 1, 2007, with earlier application encouraged. The disclosures are required in the annual financial statements and must also be provided for all comparative periods presented. CICA 3862 uses the same wording and paragraph numbers as IFRS 7 except that it provides some relief for comparative prior period disclosures.

IFRS 7 (CICA 3862) requires entities to disclose their use of financial instruments and their exposures to the risks they create. Risks disclosures include both qualitative and quantitative information.

Significant IFRS 7 requirements are listed in two sections: (1) information about the significance of financial instruments and (2) nature and extent of exposure to risks arising from financial instruments. Extracts illustrating disclosures related to each of the two sections are provided.

CICA 3862 and IFRS 7 have identical requirements except that the required hedge accounting disclosures are specified in CICA 3865.

Information about the Significance of Financial Instruments

Statement of Financial Position

The following information should be provided in the Statement of financial position or in the notes:

- The significance of financial instruments for an entity's financial position and performance by providing the carrying amounts for each of the following categories of financial instruments:
  - o financial assets measured at fair value through profit and loss, showing separately those held for trading and those designated at initial recognition,
  - o held-to-maturity investments,
  - o loans and receivables,
  - o available-for-sale assets,
  - o financial liabilities at fair value through profit and loss, showing separately those held for trading and those designated at initial recognition, and
  - o financial liabilities measured at amortized cost.
- Special disclosures about financial assets and financial liabilities designated to be measured at fair value through profit and loss, including disclosures about credit risk and market risk and changes in fair values.
- Reclassifications of financial instruments from fair value to amortized cost or vice versa. (see discussion of reclassification subsequent to IAS 39 amendment in October 2008 presented earlier in this chapter).
- Disclosures about derecognitions, including transfers of financial assets for which derecognition accounting is not permitted by IAS 39.
- Information about financial assets pledged as collateral and about financial or non-financial assets held as collateral.
- A reconciliation of changes in the allowance for credit losses for each class of financial asset.
- Information about compound financial instruments with multiple embedded derivatives.
- Breaches of terms of loan agreements.

Statement of Comprehensive Income

The following information should be provided in the statement of comprehensive income or in the notes:

- Items of income, expense, gains and losses, with separate disclosure of gains and losses from:
  - o financial assets measured at fair value through profit and loss, showing separately those held for trading and those designated at initial recognition,
  - o held-to-maturity investments,
  - o loans and receivables,
  - o available-for-sale financial assets, showing separately the amount of gain or loss recognized in other comprehensive income during the period and the amount reclassified from equity to income for the period,
  - o financial liabilities measured at fair value through profit and loss, showing separately those held for trading and those designated at initial recognition, and
  - o financial liabilities measured at amortized cost.

- Interest income and interest expense for those financial instruments that are not measured at fair value through profit and loss.

- Fee income and expense from financial assets or financial liabilities that are not at fair value through profit or loss and trust and other fiduciary activities.

- Separate identification of net gains or losses and the amount of any impairment loss for each category of financial assets.

- Interest income on impaired financial assets (see discussion of reclassification subsequent to IAS 39 amendment in October 2008 presented earlier in this chapter).

Other Disclosures

Entities would also have to provide information on:

- Accounting policies for financial instruments.

- Profit or loss arising on initial recognition of financial instruments (Day 1 profits or losses) that are not recognized in the financial statements, and a reconciliation of changes in this unrecognized balance during the period. The accounting policy applied determining when unrecognized amounts are recognized in profit or loss must also be disclosed.

- Information about hedge accounting, including:
  - o description of each hedge and hedging instrument, fair values of those instruments and the nature of risks being hedged,
  - o for cash flow hedges, the periods in which the cash flows are expected to occur, when they are expected to enter into the determination of profit or loss, and a description of any forecast transaction for which hedge accounting had previously been used but which is no longer expected to occur,
  - o the amount that was recognized in other comprehensive income during the period for cash flow hedges,
  - o if a gain or loss on a hedging instrument in a cash flow hedge has been recognized directly in equity, an entity should disclose the following:
- the amount recognized in equity during the period,
- the amount that was reclassified from equity to profit or loss for the period,
- the amount that was removed from equity during the period and included in the initial measurement of the acquisition cost or other carrying amount of a non-

financial asset or non-financial liability in a hedged highly probable forecast transaction,

  o for fair value hedges, information about the fair value changes of the hedging instrument and the hedged item,

  o hedge ineffectiveness recognized in profit and loss (separately for cash flow hedges and hedges of a net investment in a foreign operation).

- Information about the fair values of each class of financial asset and financial liability, along with:

  o comparable carrying amounts,

  o description of how fair value was determined, such as the methods and, when a valuation technique is used, the assumptions applied in determining fair values of each class of financial assets or financial liabilities and the basis of these assumptions.

  o the total amount of the change in fair value estimated using a valuation technique based on assumptions that are not supported by prices from observable current market transactions in the same instrument and not based on available observable market data that was recognized in profit or loss during the period,

  o detailed information if fair value cannot be reliably measured.

  Disclosure of fair values is not required when the carrying amount is a reasonable approximation of fair value, such as short-term trade receivables and payables, or for instruments whose fair value cannot be measured reliably. (See also proposals for additional disclosures in Future Developments discussed later in this chapter).

Illustrative Disclosures on Significance of Financial Instruments:

All extracts were obtained from the annual report of Siemens AG for the year ended September 30, 2007.

Extract 9(46) – Available-for-sale financial assets

Siemens AG (AR 2007), pages 238 and 239
10 Available-for-sale financial assets (in part)
The following tables summarize the current portion of the Company's investment in available-for-sale financial assets:

	September 30, 2007			
	Cost	Fair Value	Unrealized Gain	
Equity instruments	44	65	21	–
Debt instruments	94	94	–	–
Fund shares	34	34	–	–
	172	193	21	–

	September 30, 2006			
			Unrealized	
	Cost	Fair Value	Gain	Loss
Equity instruments	64	81	17	–
Debt instruments	498	492	–	6
Fund shares	23	23	–	–
	585	596	17	6

... Available-for-sale financial assets classified as non-current are included in *Other financial assets* (see also Note 19).

Commentary: this extract presents a table reporting investment amounts held by type of financial assets classified as available for sale as required by both IFRS 7 and CICA 3862.

Extract 9(47) – Trade and other receivables

Siemens AG (AR 2007), page 239
11 Trade and other receivables

	September 30,	
	2007	**2006**
Trade receivables from the sale of goods and services	12,864	13,620
Receivables from finance leases	1,658	1,482
Receivables from joint ventures and associated and related companies	98	46
	14,620	**15,148**

Related companies are those in which Siemens has an ownership interest of less than 20% and exercises no significant influence over their operating and financial policies.

The valuation allowance on the Company's current and long-term receivables (see Notes 12 and 19) changed as follows:

	Year ended September 30,	
	2007	**2006**
Valuation allowance as of beginning of fiscal year	956	1,199
Increase in valuation allowances recorded in the income statement in the current period	116	167
Write-offs charged against the allowance	(130)	(263)
Recoveries of amounts previously written-off	24	40
Foreign exchange translation differences	(30)	(22)
Reclassification to *Assets held for disposal*	(41)	(165)
Valuation allowance as of fiscal year-end	**895**	**956**

Receivables from finance leases are presented in the balance sheet as follows:

	September 30,	
	2007	**2006**
Receivables from finance leases, current	1,658	1,482
Receivables from finance leases, long-term portion	3,112	2,969
	4,770	**4,451**

Commentary: The company presents a table reporting trade and other receivable related amounts. The company also provides details on the valuation allowance and a classification of finance lease as short term and long term. Presentation is compatible with both IFRS and Canadian GAAP.

Extract 9(48) – Other financial assets and financial liabilities

Siemens AG (AR 2007), pages 241 and 248

12 Other current financial assets

	September 30,	
	2007	2006
Derivative financial instruments	758	424
Loans receivable	491	472
Receivables from joint ventures and associated and related companies	229	239
Other	1,454	1,235
	2,932	**2,370**

19 Other financial assets

	September 30,	
	2007	2006
Receivables from finance leases (see Note 11)	3,112	2,969
Available-for-sale financial assets	742	854
Loans receivable	596	452
Trade receivables from sale of goods and services	382	282
Derivative financial instruments	185	222
Other	544	263
	5,561	**5,042**

Available-for-sale financial assets include interests in other companies that are recorded at cost or at fair value if reliably measurable. *Derivative financial instruments* included in this item represent the non-current portion of derivatives designated as hedging instruments, for which hedge accounting is applied.

20 Other current financial liabilities

	September 30,	
	2007	2006
Derivative financial instruments	721	397
Liabilities to joint ventures and associated and related companies	315	318
Accrued interest expense	147	157
Other	1,370	1,057
	2,553	**1,929**

As of September 30, 2007, *Other* includes €201 related to the penalty imposed by German authorities in ending their investigation of past misconduct at the former Communications Group (Com). See Notes 6 and 29 for further information.

Commentary: This extract presents tables reporting various financial assets and liabilities. Presentation is compatible with both IFRS 7 and CICA 3862.

Extract 9(49) – Additional disclosures

Siemens AG (AR 2007), pages 286 to 289

30 Additional disclosures on financial instruments

This section gives a comprehensive overview of the significance of financial instruments for Siemens and provides additional information on balance sheet items that contain financial instruments.

The following table presents the carrying amounts of each category of financial assets and liabilities:

	September 30,	
	2007	2006
Financial assets		
Cash and cash equivalents	4,005	10,214
Available-for-sale financial assets	935	1,450
Loans and receivables	21,428	21,060
Financial assets held for trading	576	338
Derivatives with a hedging relationship	367	308
	27,311	**33,370**
Financial liabilities		
Financial liabilities measured at amortized cost	25,926	24,540
Financial liabilities held for trading	657	360
Derivatives with a hedging relationship	260	123
	26,843	**25,023**

The following table presents the fair values and carrying amounts of financial assets and liabilities measured at cost or amortized cost:

	September 30, 2007		September 30, 2006	
	Fair value	Carrying amount	Fair value	Carrying amount
Financial assets measured at cost or amortized cost				
Cash and cash equivalents	4,005	4,005	10,214	10,214
Available-for-sale financial assets*	–	655	–	710
Trade and other receivables	18,163	18,163	18,428	18,428
Other non-derivative financial assets	3,265	3,265	2,632	2,632
Financial liabilities measured at cost or amortized cost				
Trade payables	8,431	8,431	8,497	8,497
Notes and bonds	8,897	8,889	13,238	13,157
Loans from banks and other financial indebtedness	6,287	6,322	1,831	1,823
Obligations under finance leases	277	286	317	317
Other non-derivative financial liabilities	1,998	1,998	746	746

*   This caption consists of equity instruments classified as available-for-sale, for which a fair value could not be reliably measured and which are recognized at cost.

The fair values of cash and cash equivalents, current receivables, trade payables, other current financial liabilities and commercial paper and borrowings under revolving credit facilities approximate their carrying amount largely due to the short-term maturities of these instruments.

Long-term fixed-rate and variable-rate receivables, including receivables from finance leases, are evaluated by the Company based on parameters such as interest rates, specific country risk factors, individual creditworthiness of the customer and the risk characteristics of the financed project. Based on this evaluation, allowances are taken to account for the expected losses of these receivables. As of September 30, 2007 and 2006, the carrying amounts of such receivables, net of allowances, approximate their fair values.

The fair value of quoted notes and bonds is based on price quotations at the balance sheet date. The fair value of unquoted notes and bonds, loans from banks and other financial indebtedness, obligations under finance leases as well as other non-current financial liabilities is estimated by discounting future cash flows using rates currently available for debt of similar terms and remaining maturities.

Siemens AG (AR 2007) (continued)

Financial assets and liabilities measured at fair value are presented in the following table:

	September 30, 2007	2006
Financial assets measured at fair value		
Available-for-sale financial assets	280	740
Derivative financial instruments	943	646
Without hedging relationship	469	232
In connection with fair value hedges	176	236
In connection with cash flow hedges	191	72
Embedded derivatives	107	106
Financial liabilities measured at fair value		
Derivative financial instruments	917	483
Without hedging relationship	403	181
In connection with fair value hedges	103	5
In connection with cash flow hedges	157	118
Embedded derivatives	254	179

Fair values for available-for-sale financial assets are derived from quoted market prices in active markets, if available. In certain cases, fair values are estimated using a valuation technique.

The Company enters into derivative financial instruments with various counterparties, principally financial institutions with investment grade credit ratings. The calculation of fair values for derivative financial instruments depends on the type of instruments:

Derivative interest rate contracts – The fair values of derivative interest rate contracts (e.g. interest rate swap agreements) are estimated by discounting expected future cash flows using current market interest rates and yield curve over the remaining term of the instrument. Interest rate options are valued on the basis of quoted market prices or on estimates based on option pricing models.

Derivative currency contracts – The fair value of forward foreign exchange contracts is based on forward exchange rates. Currency options are valued on the basis of quoted market prices or on estimates based on option pricing models.

Credit default swaps – The fair value of credit default swaps is calculated by comparing discounted expected future cash flows using current bank conditions with discounted expected future cash flows using contracted conditions.

In determining the fair values of the derivative financial instruments, certain compensating effects from underlying transactions (e.g. firm commitments and anticipated transactions) are not taken into consideration.

30 Additional disclosures on financial instruments

Net gains (losses) of financial instruments are as follows:

	September 30, 2007	2006
Available-for-sale financial assets	(66)	69
Loans and receivables	(158)	(86)
Financial liabilities measured at amortized cost	57	7
Financial assets and financial liabilities held for trading	60	(43)

Net gains (losses) on available-for-sale financial assets include impairment losses, gains or losses on derecognition and the ineffective portion of fair value hedges. For the amount of unrealized gains or losses on available-for-sale financial assets recognized directly in equity during the fiscal year and the amount removed from equity and recognized in net income for the fiscal year see *Other components of equity* in Note 26.

Net losses on loans and receivables contain changes in valuation allowances, gains or losses on derecognition as well as recoveries of amounts previously written-off.

Net gains on financial liabilities measured at amortized cost are comprised of gains or losses from derecognition and the ineffective portion of fair value hedges.

Net gains (losses) on financial assets and financial liabilities held for trading consist of changes in the fair value of derivative financial instruments (including interest income and expense), for which hedge accounting is not applied.

Siemens AG (AR 2007) (continued)

31 Derivative financial instruments and hedging activities (in part)

As part of the Company's risk management program, a variety of derivative financial instruments are used to reduce risks resulting primarily from fluctuations in foreign currency exchange rates and interest rates, as well as to reduce credit risks. For additional information on the Company's risk management strategies, including the use of derivative financial instruments to mitigate or eliminate certain of these risks, see also Note 32.

The fair values of each type of derivative financial instruments are as follows:

	September 30, 2007		September 30, 2006	
	Asset	**Liability**	Asset	Liability
Foreign currency exchange contracts	602	420	171	242
Interest rate swaps and combined interest/currency swaps	175	239	298	59
Options	19	–	21	–
Embedded derivatives	107	254	106	179
Other	40	4	50	3
	943	**917**	**646**	**483**

Commentary: Here, the company presents various tables related to the significance of financial instruments and other additional information on balance sheet items that contain financial instruments. The presentation is a good example of the application of both IFRS 7 and the related Canadian standards (CICA 3862 and CICA 3865) for the disclosure of the significance of financial assets and liabilities and hedging activities.

Nature and Extent of Exposure to Risks Arising from Financial Instruments

Qualitative Disclosures

The following qualitative disclosures must be provided:

- risk exposures for each type of financial instrument;
- entity's objectives, policies and processes for managing and measuring its risks;
- changes from the prior period in these risk exposures and entity's policies and processes.

Quantitative Disclosures

The quantitative disclosures provide information about how much risk an entity is exposed to, based on information provided internally to the entity's key management personnel. These disclosures include:

- summary quantitative data about exposure to each risk at the reporting date;
- concentrations of risk;
- disclosures about specific financial risks:
  - o **Credit risk** – disclosures include:
    - maximum amount of exposure (before deducting the value of collateral),
    - information about credit quality of financial assets that are neither past due nor impaired, and information about credit quality of financial assets whose terms have been renegotiated,
    - for financial assets that are past due or impaired, analytical disclosures including a description of collateral held as security and the related fair value description of collateral,
    - information about collateral or other credit enhancements obtained or called;
  - o **Liquidity risk** – disclosures include:
    - a maturity analysis of financial liabilities, and
    - description of approach to risk management;

o **Market risk** (which reflects risk that the fair value or cash flows of a financial instrument will fluctuate due to changes in market prices and consequently includes interest rate risk, currency risk and other price risks) – disclosures include:

- a risk sensitivity analysis of each type of market risk an entity is exposed to, including the effect of a reasonably possible change in the risk variables, together with the methods and assumptions used in preparing the analysis (and any changes made to them from previous period with the reason for such changes).

Note that, if an entity prepares a sensitivity analysis for management purposes, determining, for example, the value at risk that reflects interdependencies of more than one component of market risk (for instance, interest risk and foreign currency risk), it may disclose that analysis in place of the analysis described above.

Illustrative Disclosures:

Extract 9(50) – Qualitative disclosures (foreign currency exchange risk management)

Siemens AG (AR 2007), pages 290 and 291
31 Derivative financial instruments and hedging activities
Foreign currency exchange risk management
As described in Note 32, the Company employs various derivative financial instruments in order to mitigate or eliminate certain foreign-currency exchange risks.
Derivative financial instruments not designated as hedges
The Company manages its risks associated with fluctuations in foreign-currency denominated receivables, payables, debt, firm commitments and anticipated transactions and to some extent planned transactions primarily through a Company-wide portfolio approach. This approach concentrates the associated Company-wide risks centrally, and various derivative financial instruments, primarily foreign exchange contracts and, to a lesser extent, interest rate and cross-currency interest rate swaps and options, are utilized to minimize such risks. Such a strategy does not qualify for hedge accounting treatment under IAS 39, all such derivative financial instruments are recorded at fair value on the Consolidated Balance Sheets, either as Other current financial assets or *Other current financial liabilities*, and changes in fair values are charged to net income (loss).
The Company also has foreign-currency derivative instruments, which are embedded in certain sale and purchase contracts denominated in a currency other than the functional currency of the significant parties to the contract, principally the U.S.$. Gains or losses relating to such embedded foreign-currency derivatives are reported in *Cost of goods sold and services rendered* in the Consolidated Statements of Income.
Hedging activities
The Company's operating units applied hedge accounting for certain significant anticipated transactions and firm commitments denominated in foreign currencies. Specifically, the Company entered into foreign exchange contracts to reduce the risk of variability of future cash flows resulting from forecasted sales and purchases and firm commitments resulting from its business units entering into long-term contracts (project business) and standard product business which are denominated primarily in U.S.$.
Cash flow hedges – Changes in fair value of forward exchange contracts that were designated as foreign-currency cash flow hedges are recorded in *Other components of equity*. During the years ended September 30, 2007 and 2006, net gains of €1 and € 3, respectively, were reclassified from *Other components of equity* into net income (loss) because the occurrence of the related hedged forecasted transaction was no longer probable.
It is expected that €119 of net deferred gains in *Other components of equity* will be reclassified into *Cost of goods sold and services rendered* during the year ended September 30, 2008, when the hedged forecasted foreign-currency denominated sales and purchases occur.
As of September 30, 2007, the maximum length of time over which the Company is hedging its future cash flows associated with foreign-currency forecasted transactions is 184 months.

> **Siemens AG (AR 2007) (continued)**
>
> **Fair value hedges** – As of September 30, 2007 and 2006, the Company hedged firm commitments using forward exchange contracts that were designated as foreign-currency fair value hedges of future sales related primarily to the Company's project business and, to a lesser extent, purchases. As of September 30, 2007 and 2006, the hedging transactions resulted in the recognition of financial assets of €2 and €6, respectively, and financial liabilities of €31 and €7, respectively, for the hedged firm commitments, whose changes in fair value were charged to *Cost of goods sold and services rendered*. Changes in fair value of the derivative contracts were also recorded in *Cost of goods sold and services rendered*.

Commentary: In this extract, the company presents information on how it uses derivatives to mitigate or eliminate certain foreign currency exchange risks. It describes:

- its macro-hedging policy, using derivatives that could not be designated as hedges;
- embedded derivatives in certain sale and purchase contracts denominated in a currency other than the functional currency of the significant parties to the contract, principally the US dollar; and
- hedging activities and different amounts related to the application of various hedge accounting models.

The presentation provides a good example of the application of both IFRS 7 and the related Canadian standards (CICA 3862 and CICA 3865) to the disclosure of foreign currency exchange risk management and hedge accounting.

Extract 9(51) – Qualitative disclosures (interest rate risk management)

> **Siemens AG (AR 2007), pages 291 and 292**
>
> **31 Derivative financial instruments and hedging activities**
>
> **Interest rate risk management**
>
> Interest rate risk arises from the sensitivity of financial assets and liabilities to changes in market rates of interest. The Company seeks to mitigate such risk by entering into interest rate derivative financial instruments such as interest rate swaps (see also Note 32), options and, to a lesser extent, cross-currency interest rate swaps and interest rate futures.
>
> **Derivative financial instruments not designated as hedges**
>
> The Company uses a portfolio-based approach to manage its interest rate risk associated with certain interest-bearing assets and liabilities, primarily interest bearing investments and debt obligations. This approach focuses on mismatches in the structure of the interest terms of these assets and liabilities without referring to specific assets or liabilities. Such a strategy does not qualify for hedge accounting treatment under IAS 39, *Financial Instruments: Recognition and Measurement*. Accordingly, all interest rate derivative instruments used in this strategy are recorded at fair value, either as *Other current financial assets* or *Other current financial liabilities*, and changes in the fair values are charged to *Financial income (expense), net*. Net cash receipts and payments relating to interest rate swaps used in offsetting relationships are also recorded in *Financial income (expense), net*.
>
> **Fair value hedges of fixed-rate debt obligations**
>
> Under the interest rate swap agreements outstanding during the year ended September 30, 2007, the Company agrees to pay a variable rate of interest multiplied by a notional principle amount, and receive in return an amount equal to a specified fixed rate of interest multiplied by the same notional principal amount. These interest rate swap agreements offset an impact of future changes in interest rates on the fair value of the underlying fixed-rate debt obligations. The interest rate swap contracts are reflected at fair value in the Company's Consolidated Balance Sheets and the related portion of fixed-rate debt being hedged is reflected at an amount equal to the sum of its carrying amount plus an adjustment representing the change in fair value of the debt obligations attributable to the interest rate risk being hedged. Changes in the fair value of interest rate swap contracts and the offsetting changes in the adjusted carrying amount of the related portion of fixed-rate debt being hedged, are recognized as adjustments to the line item *Financial income (expense), net* in the Consolidated Statements of Income. The net effect recognized in *Financial income (expense), net*, representing the ineffective portion of the hedging relationship, amounted to €7 in fiscal 2007. Net cash receipts and payments relating to such interest rate swap agreements are recorded as interest expense, which is part of *Financial income (expense), net*.

Siemens AG (AR 2007) (continued)

The Company had interest rate swap contracts to pay variable rates of interest (average rate of 5.2% and 5.0% as of September 30, 2007 and 2006, respectively) and received fixed rates of interest (average rate of 5.7% and 5.7% as of September 30, 2007 and 2006, respectively). The notional amount of indebtedness hedged as of September 30, 2007 and 2006 was €7,326 and €5,752, respectively. This resulted in 82% and 44% of the Company's underlying notes and bonds being subject to variable interest rates as of September 30, 2007 and 2006, respectively. The notional amounts of these contracts mature at varying dates based on the maturity of the underlying hedged items. The net fair value of interest rate swap contracts (excluding accrued interest) used to hedge indebtedness as of September 30, 2007 and 2006 was €20 and €207, respectively.

Fair value hedges of available-for-sale financial assets

During the year ended September 30, 2007, the Company applied fair value hedge accounting for certain fixed-rate available-for-sale financial assets. To offset the impact of future changes in interest rates on the fair value of the underlying fixed-rate available-for-sale financial assets, interest rate swap agreements were entered into. The interest rate swap contracts and the related portion of the available-for-sale financial assets are reflected at fair value in the Company's Consolidated Balance Sheets. Changes in the fair value of interest rate swap contracts and the offsetting changes in fair value of the available-for-sale financial assets being hedged attributable to the interest rate risk being hedged are recognized as adjustments to the line item *Financial income (expense), net* in the Consolidated Statements of Income. The net effect recognized in *Financial income (expense), net*, representing the ineffective portion of the hedging relationship, amounted to €9 in fiscal 2007.

Cash flow hedges of revolving term deposits

During the years ended September 30, 2007 and 2006, the Company applied cash flow hedge accounting for a revolving term deposit. Under the interest rate swap agreements entered into, the Company agrees to pay a variable rate of interest multiplied by a notional principle amount, and to receive in return an amount equal to a specified fixed rate of interest multiplied by the same notional principal amount. These interest rate swap agreements offset the effect of future changes in interest payments of the underlying variable-rate term deposit. The interest rate swap contracts are reflected at fair value and the effective portion of changes in fair value of the interest rate swap contracts that were designated as cash flow hedges are recorded in *Other components of equity*. Net cash receipts and payments relating to such interest rate swap agreements are recorded as interest income, which is part of *Financial income (expense), net*.

Commentary: The company presents information on how it uses derivatives to mitigate or eliminate certain interest rate risk. It describes:

- its macro-hedging policy, using derivatives that could not be designated as hedges; and
- its hedging activities and different amounts related to the application of various hedge accounting models.

The presentation provides a good example of the application of both IFRS 7 and the related Canadian standards (CICA 3862 and CICA 3865) to the disclosure of foreign currency exchange risk management and hedge accounting.

Extract 9(52) – Quantitative disclosures (market risks)

Siemens AG (AR 2007), page 293

32 Financial risk management

Market risks

Market fluctuations may result in significant cash-flow and profit volatility risk for Siemens. Its worldwide operating business as well as its investment and financing activities are affected by changes in foreign exchange rates, interest rates and equity prices. To optimize the allocation of the financial resources across the Groups, as well as to secure an optimal return for its shareholders, Siemens identifies, analyzes and proactively manages the associated financial market risks. The Company seeks to manage and control these risks primarily through its regular operating and financing activities, and uses derivative instruments when deemed appropriate.

Siemens AG (AR 2007) (continued)

Market risks

Management of financial market risk is a key priority for Siemens' Managing Board. As a member of this Board, the Chief Financial Officer covers the specific responsibility for this part of the overall risk management system. At the highest level, the Managing Board retains ultimate accountability. For practical business purposes, the Managing Board delegates responsibilities to central functions and to the Groups. SFS holds a minor trading portfolio which is subject to tight limits. As of September 30, 2007, it has a value-at-risk close to zero.

Within the various methodologies to analyze and manage risk, Siemens implemented a system based on "sensitivity analysis". This tool enables the risk managers to identify the risk position of the entities. Sensitivity analysis provides an approximate quantification of the exposure in the event that certain specified parameters were to be met under a specific set of assumptions. The risk estimates provided here assume:

- a 20% decrease in equity prices of all investments traded in an active market, which are classified as current available-for-sale financial assets;
- a simultaneous, parallel foreign exchange rates shift in which the Euro appreciates against all currencies by 10%;
- a parallel shift of 100-basis points of the interest rate yield curves in all currencies.

The potential economic impact, due to these assumptions, is based on the occurrence of adverse market conditions and reflects estimated changes resulting from the sensitivity analysis. Actual results that are included in the Consolidated Statements of Income may differ substantially from these estimates due to actual developments in the global financial market.

Any market sensitive instruments, including equity and interest bearing investments that our Company's pension plans hold are not included in the following quantitative and qualitative disclosure. For additional information see Note 23.

Commentary: Here, the company explains how it quantifies market fluctuations resulting from changes in foreign exchange rates, interest rates and equity prices. It describes its risk management tool, including the parameter for sensitivity analysis.

Again, the presentation provides a good example of the application of both IFRS 7 and CICA 3862 requirements to foreign currency exchange risk management.

Extract 9(53) – Quantitative disclosures (equity price risks)

Siemens AG (AR 2007), pages 294

32 Financial risk management

Equity price risk

Siemens' investment portfolio consists of direct and indirect investments in publicly traded companies held for purposes other than trading. These participations result from strategic partnerships, spin-offs, IPOs of strategic venture capital investments or compensation from M&A transactions.

The equity investments are monitored based on their current market value, affected by the fluctuations in the volatile stock markets worldwide. The market value of Siemens' portfolio as of September 30, 2007 was €197, a reduction of €19 compared to September 30, 2006.

An adverse move in equity prices of 20% as of September 30, 2007 would reduce the value of Siemens' equity investments by €39 compared to €43 the year before, meaning that the equity price risk has slighty decreased year-over-year.

Commentary: The company describes the management of its investment portfolio, which consists of direct and indirect investments in publicly traded companies.

The presentation provides a good example of the application of both IFRS 7 and CICA 3862 requirements to equity price risks management (though the latter standard would also require the disclosure of the impact on other comprehensive income).

Extract 9(54) – Quantitative disclosures (foreign currency exchange rate risk)

Siemens AG (AR 2007), pages 294 to 296

32 Financial risk management

Foreign currency exchange rate risk

Transaction risk and currency management

Siemens' international operations expose the Company to foreign-currency exchange risks in the ordinary course of business. The Company employs various strategies discussed below involving the use of derivative financial instruments to mitigate or eliminate certain of those exposures.

Foreign exchange rate fluctuations may create unwanted and unpredictable earnings and cash flow volatility. Each Siemens unit conducting business with international counterparties that leads to future cash flows denominated in a currency other than its functional currency is exposed to the risk from changes in foreign exchange rates. The risk is mitigated by closing all types of business transactions (sales and procurement of products and services as well as investment and financing activities) mainly in the functional currency. In addition, the foreign currency exposure is partly balanced by purchasing of goods, commodities and services in the respective currencies as well as production activities and other contributions along the value chain in the local markets.

Operating units are prohibited from borrowing or investing in foreign currencies on a speculative basis. Intercompany financing or investments of operating units are preferably done in their functional currency or on a hedged basis.

Siemens has established a foreign exchange risk management system that has an established track record for years. Each Siemens unit is responsible for recording, assessing, monitoring, reporting and hedging its foreign currency transaction exposure. The Group-wide binding guideline developed by the Corporate Finance department, provides the concept for the identification and determination of the single net currency position and commits the units to hedge it in a narrow band: at least 75% but no more than 100% of their net foreign currency exposure.

In addition, the Corporate Finance department provides a framework of the organizational structure necessary for foreign currency exchange management, proposes hedging strategies and defines the hedging instruments available to the entities: forward contracts, currency put and call options and stop-loss orders. The execution of the hedging transactions in the global financial markets is done by SFS as an exclusive service provider for all Siemens entities on behalf of Corporate Treasury. SFS executes hedging instruments used for hedge accounting relationships individually with external counterparts. For other hedging purposes Siemens has a Company-wide portfolio approach which generates a benefit from any potential off-set of divergent cash flows in the same currency, as well as optimized transaction costs. For additional information relating to the effect of this Company-wide portfolio approach on the Consolidated Financial Statements, as well as for a discussion of hedging activities employed to mitigate or eliminate foreign currency exchange risks, please refer to Note 31.

The foreign exchange rate sensitivity is calculated by aggregation of the net foreign exchange rate exposure of the Operations, Financing and Real Estate Groups and Corporate Treasury. The values and risks are the unhedged positions multiplied by an assumed 10% appreciation of the Euro against all other currencies. As of September 30, 2007, a parallel 10% negative shift of all foreign currencies would have resulted in a decline of €47 in future cash flows compared to a decline of €38 the year before. Such decline in Euro values of future cash flows might reduce the unhedged portion of revenues but would also decrease the unhedged portion of cost of materials. Since the Company's foreign currency inflows exceed the outflows, an appreciation of the Euro against foreign currencies would have a negative financial impact to the extent that future sales are not already hedged. Future changes in the foreign exchange rates can impact sales prices and may lead to margin changes, the extent of which is determined by the matching of foreign currency revenues and expenses.

Siemens defines foreign currency exposure generally as balance sheet items in addition to firm commitments which are denominated in foreign currencies, as well as foreign currency denominated cash inflows and cash outflows from anticipated transactions for the following three months. This foreign currency exposure is determined based on the respective functional currencies of the exposed Siemens' entities.

Siemens AG (AR 2007) (continued)

Foreign currency exchange rate risk

Transaction risk and currency management

The tables below show the net foreign exchange transaction exposure by major currencies as of September 30, 2007 and 2006. In some currencies Siemens has both substantial sales and costs, which have been off-set in the table:

	September 30, 2007*			
	USD	GBP	Other	Total
Gross balance sheet exposure	223	321	208	752
Thereof: Financial assets	7,858	3,642	4,769	16,269
Thereof: Financial liabilities	(7,635)	(3,321)	(4,561)	(15,517)
Gross exposure from firm commitments and anticipated transactions	3,730	392	1,193	5,315
Foreign exchange transaction exposure	3,952	713	1,398	6,063
Economically hedged exposure	(3,893)	(567)	(1,132)	(5,592)
Change in future cash flows after hedging activities resulting from a 10% appreciation of the Euro	(6)	(15)	(27)	(47)

	September 30, 2006*			
	USD	GBP	Other	Total
Gross balance sheet exposure	2,210	332	553	3,095
Thereof: Financial assets	13,778	3,483	5,522	22,783
Thereof: Financial liabilities	(11,568)	(3,151)	(4,969)	(19,688)
Gross exposure from firm commitments and anticipated transactions	5,344	(65)	279	5,558
Foreign exchange transaction exposure	7,554	267	832	8,653
Economically hedged exposure	(7,291)	(409)	(576)	(8,276)
Change in future cash flows after hedging activities resulting from a 10% appreciation of the Euro	(26)	14	(26)	(38)

* Including SV.

Effects of currency translation

Many Siemens subsidiaries are located outside the Euro zone. Since the financial reporting currency of Siemens is the Euro, the financial statements of these subsidiaries are translated into euros so that the financial results can be included in the Consolidated Financial Statements of Siemens. To consider the effects of foreign exchange translation risk within risk management, the assumption is that investments in foreign-based operations are permanent and that reinvestment is continuous. Whenever a divestment of a particular asset or entity is made, the value of this transaction risk is included in the sensitivity analyses. Effects from currency fluctuations on the translation of net asset amounts into Euro are reflected in the Company's consolidated equity position.

Commentary: This extract explains how the company manages foreign currency risks related to transactions and translation. It presents tables showing the net foreign exchange transaction exposure by major currencies at year end.

The presentation provides a good example of the application of both IFRS 7 and the related Canadian standards (CICA 3862 and CICA 3865) to foreign currency exchange risk management and hedge accounting.

Extract 9(55) – Quantitative disclosures (interest rate risk)

Siemens AG (AR 2007), page 297

32 Financial risk management

Interest rate risk

Siemens' interest rate risk exposure is mainly related to debt obligations like bonds, loans, commercial paper programs and interest-bearing deposits and investments. Siemens seeks to limit this risk through the use of derivative instruments which allow it to hedge fair value changes by swapping fixed rates of interest into variable rates of interest (for additional information see Note 31).

To optimize the Company's position with regard to interest income and interest expenses and to minimize the overall financial interest rate risk, Corporate Treasury performs corporate interest rate risk management together with SFS as operating service provider. Part of the interest rate risk management concept is a Corporate-wide interest rate overlay management to match interest periods of hedges with intended maturities of assets and liabilities. Where it is not contrary to country-specific regulations, all Groups and affiliated companies generally obtain any required financing through Corporate Treasury in the form of loans or inter-company clearing accounts. The same concept is adopted for deposits of cash generated by the units.

Interest rate risk is measured by using either fair value sensitivity or cash flow sensitivity depending on whether the instrument has a fixed or variable interest rate. The total fair value sensitivity as well as the total cash flow sensitivity is generated by aggregating the sensitivities of the various exposures denominated in different currencies. Depending on whether Siemens has a long or short interest rate position, interest rate risk can arise on increasing or decreasing market moves in the relevant yield curve.

The fair value sensitivity calculation for fixed interest rate instruments shows the change in fair value, defined as present value, caused by a hypothetical 100-basis point shift in the yield curve. The first step in this calculation is to use the yield curve to discount the gross cash flows, meaning the present value of future interest and principal payments of financial instruments with fixed interest rates. A second calculation discounts the gross cash flows using a 100-basis point shift of the yield curve. In all cases, Siemens uses the generally accepted and published yield curves on the relevant balance sheet date. The fair value interest rate risk results primarily from long-term fixed rate debt obligations and interest-bearing investments. Assuming a 100-basis point increase in interest rates, this risk was €40 as of September 30, 2007, increasing from the comparable value of €24 as of September 30, 2006, assuming a 100-basis point decrease.

For variable-rate instruments, the interest rate risk is monitored by using the cash flow sensitivity also assuming a 100-basis point shift of the yield curves. Such risk mainly results from hedges of fixed-rate debt obligations that swap fixed-rates of interest into variable-rates of interest. This exposure leads to a cash flow interest rate risk of €72 as of September 30, 2007, compared to €32 as of September 30, 2006, assuming a 100-basis point increase in interest rates.

Commentary: This extract shows the company's interest rate risk exposure, which is mainly related to debt obligations such as bonds, loans, commercial paper programs and interest-bearing deposits and investments. The company indicates that it seeks to limit this risk through the use of derivative instruments, which allow it to hedge fair value changes by swapping fixed rates of interest into variable rates of interest.

Again, the presentation provides a good example of the application of both IFRS 7 and CICA 3862 to interest risk exposure.

Extract 9(56) – Quantitative disclosures (liquidity)

Siemens AG (AR 2007), pages 298 and 299

32 Financial risk management

Liquidity risk

Liquidity risk results from the Company's potential inability to meet its financial liabilities, e.g. settlement of its financial debt, paying its suppliers and settling finance lease obligations. Beyond effective net working capital and cash management, Siemens mitigates liquidity risk by arranged borrowing facilities with highly rated financial institutions, via a medium-term note program and via its global multi-currency commercial paper program. For further information on sources of liquidity see Note 22.

In addition to the above mentioned sources of liquidity, Siemens constantly monitors funding options available in the capital markets, as well as trends in the availability and costs of such funding, with a view to maintaining financial flexibility and limiting repayment risks.

The following table reflects all contractually fixed pay-offs for settlement, repayments and interest resulting from recognized financial liabilities, including derivative financial instruments with a negative market value as of September 30, 2007. For derivative financial instruments the market value is presented, whereas for the other obligations the respective undiscounted cash flows for the respective upcoming fiscal years are presented. Cash outflows for financial liabilities without fixed amount or timing, including interest, are based on the conditions existing at September 30, 2007.

(€ in millions)	2008	2009	2010 to 2012	2013 and thereafter
Non-derivative financial liabilities				
Notes and bonds	1,161	992	4,068	6,707
Loans from banks	591	86	176	829
Other financial indebtedness	4,445	76	161	126
Obligations under finance leases	64	63	109	119
Trade payables	8,418	27	14	6
Other financial liabilities	1,405	86	22	93
Derivative financial liabilities	294	38	78	243

The risk implied from the values shown in the table above, reflects the one-sided scenario of cash outflows only. Leasing obligations, trade payables and other financial liabilities mainly originate from the financing of assets used in our ongoing operations such as property, plant, equipment and investments in working capital – e.g. inventories and trade receivables. These assets are considered in the Company's overall liquidity risk. To monitor existing financial assets and liabilities as well as to enable an effective controlling of future risks, Siemens has established a comprehensive risk reporting covering its worldwide business units.

The balanced view of liquidity and financial indebtedness is stated in the calculation of the net liquidity amount and is used for internal corporate finance management as well as external communication with investors, analysts and rating agencies. It results from the total amount of cash and cash equivalents as well as current available-for-sale financial assets, less the amount of commercial paper, medium-term notes, bonds, loans from banks and obligations under finance leases as stated on the balance sheet.

(€ in millions)	September 30, 2007	2006
Cash and cash equivalents	4,005	10,214
Current available-for-sale financial assets	193	596
Total liquidity	4,198	10,810
Short-term debt and current maturities of long-term debt	5,637	2,175
Long-term debt	9,860	13,122
Total debt	15,497	15,297
Net liquidity	(11,299)	(4,487)

The Company's capital resources are comprised of cash and cash equivalents, current available-for-sale financial assets and cash flow from operating activities. In contrast, capital requirements include scheduled debt service, regular capital spending and ongoing cash requirements from operating activities.

Commentary: This extract describes the company's liquidity risk resulting from its potential inability to meet its financial liabilities, e.g., the settlement of its financial debt, paying its suppliers and settling finance lease obligations. It describes the policies for mitigating that liquidity risk and provides tables reflecting its calculation of the "net liquidity amount."

The presentation provides a good example of the application of both IFRS 7 and CICA 3862 to liquidity risk exposure.

Extract 9(57) – Quantitative disclosures (credit risk)

Siemens AG (AR 2007), page 299 and 300

32 Financial risk management

Credit risk

The Company is exposed to credit risk in connection with its significant project business in the fields of public infrastructure and transport, healthcare, utilities and IT where direct or indirect financing in various forms may be provided to customers. In limited cases, the Company may also take an equity interest as part of the project financing.

The Company is also exposed to credit risk via its leasing activities, primarily related to medical engineering, data processing equipment and industrial and consumer products of third party manufacturers. Siemens' credit risk regarding such activities presents additional risks as the volume of such transactions is higher, customers tend to be smaller for which transparent credit histories are often not available.

Credit risk is defined as an unexpected loss in cash and earnings if the customer is unable to pay its obligations in due time, if the value of property that serves as collateral declines, or if the projects Siemens has invested in are not successful. The effective monitoring and controlling of credit risk is a core competency of our risk management system. Corporate Treasury has implemented a group-wide binding credit policy. Hence, credit evaluations and ratings are performed on all customers with an exposure or requiring credit beyond a centrally defined limit.

Customer ratings, analyzed and defined by a designated SFS department, and individual customer limits are based on generally accepted rating methodologies, the input from external rating agencies and Siemens default experiences. Such ratings are processed by internal risk assessment specialists. Ratings and credit limits are carefully considered in determining the conditions under which direct or indirect financing will be offered to customers by the operating units.

Credit risk is recorded and monitored on an ongoing basis applying different approaches dependent on the underlying product. Central systems are used for leasing business, factoring, monitoring of operating counterparty risk, real-time monitoring of treasury counterparty risk, as are a number of decentralized tools for management of individual credit risks within the operating units. A central IT application processes data from the operating units together with rating and default information and calculates an estimate which may be used as a basis for individual bad debt provisions. Apart from this automated process, individual management judgment is applied, in particular to incorporate the latest developments and qualitative information.

To mitigate credit risk, Corporate Treasury has developed a guideline under which operating units may sell portions of their receivable portfolio on a non-recourse basis, either directly to SFS or to external parties. Receivable sales to external parties are generally only performed for customers with a credit rating below investment grade or for long-term projects with a financing component. Beginning in fiscal 2008, Siemens will change its receivable management guidelines.

SFS uses credit default swaps, classified as derivatives, to protect from credit risks stemming from its receivables purchase business. In respect of financial assets that are not protected through the use of credit default swaps the maximum exposure to credit risk, without taking account of any collateral, is represented by their carrying amount. Credit risks arising from credit guarantees are described in Note 28. After consideration of credit default swap derivatives there were no significant concentrations of credit risk as of September 30, 2007.

Concerning trade receivables and other receivables, as well as other loans or receivables included in *Other financial assets* that are neither impaired nor past due, there were no indications as of September 30, 2007, that defaults in payment obligations will occur. For further information regarding the concept for the determination of allowances on receivables see Note 3.

Business Combinations

In January 2008, the IASB published revised versions of IFRS 3, *Business Combinations* and IAS 27, *Consolidated and Separate Financial Statements*. These standards require that, when a business combination takes place, the acquirer identify and measure at fair value the net assets acquired, including the financial assets and liabilities, which must be accounted for in accordance with IAS 39. For that purpose, the acquirer must base the accounting for any acquired financial instruments on the contractual terms, economic conditions and existing operating and accounting policies in place at the date of the acquisition.

Not all financial instruments have to be reassessed from the acquirer perspective. Revised IFRS 3 specifies exceptions for leases and insurance contracts, which are classified and designated based on their contractual terms and conditions at the date of the contract's inception.

Effectively, this will mean that the acquirer will need to address many issues, including answering each of the following questions:

- How should acquired financial instruments be classified?
- Do the hedging arrangements in place qualify for hedge accounting?
- Is it necessary to re-designate hedging arrangements?
- Should embedded derivatives be bifurcated?

While these issues have no impact on the values attached to the assets and liabilities acquired, they will have an impact on how the assets and liabilities are subsequently accounted for.

IASB and IFRIC meetings held at the end of 2007 and the beginning of 2008 clarified the new requirements that must be implemented for business combinations for annual periods beginning after July 1, 2009 (with early application permitted), which include the following:

- Financial instruments must be classified from the acquirer's perspective. This will not necessarily coincide with the classification adopted by the acquiree.
- Existing hedge accounting relationships of the acquiree do not automatically survive the business combination and the acquirer must re-designate (document) all hedge relationships it wishes to continue. Ineffectiveness might be introduced since derivatives would probably not have a zero fair value at the date of the business combination.
- The acquirer must reassess any embedded derivatives based on conditions and terms existing at the date of the business combination, which may result in the bifurcation of additional derivatives from host contracts.
- The acquiree's impairment allowances are eliminated since all financial assets would be measured at fair value, reflecting the possibility of default. Additional disclosures will be required.
- Pre-existing relationships between acquirer and acquiree consisting of:
  o Elements other than minority participation must be deemed settled at fair value. This difference with recorded amount will be included in income.

o Minority participation (in the context of a step acquisition) is measured at fair value and the difference between that amount and the one recorded is recognized in earnings. (Note that, if minority participation is classified as available for sale, the related accumulated other comprehensive income must be recognized in earnings).

- Any contingent consideration for a business combination is measured at fair value. If the contingent consideration is a financial instrument, it must be accounted for and presented according to IAS 32, IAS 39 and IFRS 7. Re-measurement of a contingent consideration presented as a liability is required, with changes in fair values included in income. No re-measurement of a contingent consideration is necessary if it is classified in equity.

- When an entity loses control over a subsidiary, any remaining interest must be valued at fair value, with difference between that amount and the previous carrying amount recognized in earnings. Amounts previously recorded in accumulated other comprehensive income (such as available-for-sale assets held by the subsidiary) are also reclassified in income as if the parent company had sold the assets.

FUTURE DEVELOPMENTS

This section provides an overview of recent IASB urgent actions related to financial instruments reporting in light of the current global economic crisis. In addition, the section covers long term IASB projects that could result in significant changes to IAS 39.

Exposure Draft – Investments in Debt Instruments Proposed Amendments to IFRS 7

In December 2008, the IASB published an Exposure Draft entitled *Investments in Debt Instruments Proposed amendments to IFRS 7* that proposes comprehensive disclosures in order to allow users of financial statements to compare investments in all debt instruments (other than those classified as at fair value through profit or loss). The enhanced disclosures aim to provide greater transparency and help to regain investors' confidence in the financial markets.

The Exposure Draft proposes additional disclosure requirements for all investments in debt instruments other than those classified as at fair value through profit or loss. Under the proposals, an entity would be required to disclose the following information in tabular format:

- pre-tax profit or loss as though the instruments had been:
  o classified as at fair value through profit or loss, and
  o accounted for at amortized cost;
- a summary of the different measurement bases of these instruments in a way that permits comparison of:
  o the carrying amount in the statement of financial position,
  o fair value, and
  o amortized cost.

Though the effective date of new IFRS and amendments to IFRS is usually 6–18 months from the date of issue, this Exposure Draft proposes an effective date for annual periods ending on or after December 15, 2008 because the urgent need for disclosures about investments in debt instruments demands earlier application.

Exposure Draft – Embedded Derivatives – Proposed Amendments to IFRIC 9, *Reassessment of Embedded Derivatives* and IAS 39

Following the issuance of *Reclassification of Financial Assets* (Amendments to IAS 39 and IFRS 7) in October 2008, the IASB published in December 2008, an Exposure Draft that proposes amendments to IFRIC 9 and IAS 39. These proposed amendments clarify that the requirements to separate particular embedded derivatives from hybrid (combined) financial instruments cannot be circumvented as a result of the amendments to IAS 39 regarding the reclassification of financial assets.

Consequently, this Exposure Draft proposes amendments that would require:

- an entity to assess whether an embedded derivative is required to be separated from a host contract when the entity reclassifies a hybrid (combined) financial asset out of the fair value through profit or loss category;

- the assessment to be made on the basis of the circumstances that existed when the entity first became a party to the contract; and

- that if the fair value of an embedded derivative that would have to be separated cannot be reliably measured, the entire hybrid financial instrument must remain in the fair value through profit or loss category.

Though the effective date of new IFRS and amendments to IFRS is usually 6–18 months from the date of issue, the urgent need to clarify some aspects of how to apply *Reclassification of Financial Assets* demands earlier application. Consequently, the IASB proposes an effective date for annual periods ending on or after December 15, 2008 which should ensure appropriate separation of embedded derivatives on reclassification of hybrid (combined) financial assets out of the fair value through profit or loss category.

Exposure Draft – Improving Disclosures about Financial Instruments – Proposed Amendments to IFRS 7

In December 2008, the IASB published an Exposure Draft entitled *Improving Disclosures about Financial Instruments - Proposed amendments to IFRS 7* proposing enhanced disclosures about fair value measurements and the liquidity risk of financial instruments. This Exposure Draft forms part of the IASB's response to the credit crisis and reflects discussions by the IASB's Expert Advisory Panel on measuring and disclosing fair values of financial instruments when markets are no longer active.

The proposed disclosure amendments contained in the Exposure Draft are based on a three-level hierarchy for the inputs used in valuation techniques to measure fair value (similar to that used in SFAS 157, *Fair Value Measurements*)[3]. They would require disclosures about:

- the level of the fair value hierarchy into which fair value measurements are categorized in their entirety. This requirement would apply both for fair values included in the statement of financial position and for other fair values that are disclosed but not included in that statement;

---

3   The three levels are as follows:
   - Level 1: fair values measured using quoted prices in an active market for identical assets or liabilities;
   - Level 2: fair values measured using valuation techniques for which all inputs significant to the measurement are based on observable market data;
   - Level 3: fair values measured using valuation techniques for which any input significant to the measurement is not based on observable market data.

- the fair value measurements resulting from the use of significant unobservable inputs to valuation techniques. For these measurements, the disclosures include a reconciliation from the beginning balances to the ending balances;

- the movements between different levels of the fair value hierarchy, and the reasons for those movements in the light of the present market conditions.

In addition, the Exposure Draft proposes amendments to IFRS 7 that would:

- clarify that liquidity risk disclosures are required only for financial liabilities that will result in the outflow of cash or another financial asset;

- require entities to provide quantitative disclosures based on how they manage liquidity risk for derivative financial liabilities;

- require entities to disclose the remaining expected maturities of non-derivative financial liabilities if they manage liquidity risk on the basis of expected maturities;

- strengthen the relationship between qualitative and quantitative disclosures about liquidity risk.

Though the effective date of new IFRS and amendments to IFRS is usually 6–18 months from the date of issue, the urgent need for enhanced disclosures about financial instruments demands earlier application. Consequently, the IASB aims to set an effective date of annual periods beginning on or after July 1, 2009.

Financial Instruments with Characteristics of Equity – IASB Discussion Paper (February 2008)

In February 2008, the IASB published a Discussion Paper that is the first stage of its project to improve and simplify the requirements set out in IAS 32. The project is a joint project with FASB, which led the research stage of this project and published its preliminary views (PV) document entitled *Financial Instruments with Characteristics of Equity* in November 2007.

The goal of the Discussion Paper is to solicit the views on whether the proposals in the FASB document should be a starting point for the IASB's deliberations.

The Invitation to Comment section of the Discussion Paper describes the following three approaches for distinguishing among instruments with the characteristics of liabilities and equity:

1. *Basic ownership*: Limits the instruments that can be classified as equity to the lowest residual interest in an entity. Holders of basic ownership instruments are considered to be the owners of the entity. All other instruments, including forward contracts, options and convertible debt, represent either financial liabilities or financial assets, recorded at fair value, with gains and losses reported in income.

   This approach allows only a limited range of instruments to be treated as equity and could result in greater income volatility.

2. *Ownership-settlement*: Instruments are classified based on the nature of their return and their settlement requirements. Instruments that have no stated settlement requirements are classified as equity. Basic ownership instruments (as defined above), other perpetual instruments and indirect ownership interests, such as forward contracts, written call options and the equity component of convertible debt, would be classified as equity (as long as they would be settled by delivering the basic ownership instrument from which they are derived).

   This approach is close to that used in IAS 32, but is not the same. It might trigger the same interpretation difficulties that currently arise under IAS 32.

3. *Reassessed expected outcome*: A model is used to predict the possible outcome, with subsequent reassessment at each reporting date. Similar to the ownership-settlement approach, classification is based on the nature of the instrument's return. Derivative financial instruments based on the price of an entity's basic ownership instruments (i.e., equity derivatives) would be classified as equity. Settlement does not affect the classification and, hence, cash settlement provisions would not preclude an instrument from equity classification. All changes are reported in earnings.

   This approach is complex and could create volatility of reported profit or loss.

In October 2008, the IASB and the FASB decided at a joint meeting to begin future deliberations using the principles underlying the perpetual and basic ownership approaches. Under the perpetual approach, an instrument would be classified as equity if it:

- lacks a settlement requirement; and
- entitles the holder to a share of the entity's net assets in liquidation.

Under the basic ownership approach, an instrument would be classified as equity if it:

- is the most subordinated claim; and
- entitles the holder to a share of the entity's net assets.

The IASB and the FASB acknowledged that they may decide to make exceptions to the basic principles as they continue to develop an approach to identify equity instruments.

Reducing Complexity in Reporting Financial Instruments – IASB Discussion Paper (March 2008)

In March 2008, the IASB issued a Discussion Paper that analyzes the main causes of complexity in reporting financial instruments and proposes possible intermediate approaches to dealing with some of them. Those approaches seek to improve and simplify measurement and hedge accounting by amending or replacing the existing requirements. The Discussion Paper also sets out the arguments for and against a possible long-term approach that would use one measurement method for all types of instruments in the scope of a financial instruments standard.

The Discussion Paper is the first stage in a project that aims to replace IAS 39 with a new standard for reporting financial instruments that is principles based and less complex. Basically, the Discussion Paper supports the view that fair value is the only measure appropriate for all types of financial instruments but acknowledges that it may not be feasible to require it for all types of financial instruments. The paper proposes, therefore, ways to improve and simplify existing measurement requirements for financial instruments in the interim. The following may be considered separately or in some combination:

- Amending the existing measurement requirements by eliminating perhaps two measurement categories under IAS 39: held to maturity or available for sale or both. Adopting these suggestions would require dealing with various presentation and disclosure issues and could increase volatility in profit or loss.

- Replacing the existing measurement requirements with a fair value measurement principle with some optional exceptions: a financial instrument could be measured using a cost-based method if it meets exception criteria that might depend on the variability of an instrument's cash flows. According to this view, instruments with highly variable future cash flows, such as derivative instruments and equity investments, would be measured at fair value. Instruments with fixed or slightly variable cash flows, such as market interest-bearing debt instruments, would be eligible for cost-based measurement.

- Simplifying hedge accounting requirements: two general approaches are proposed for hedge accounting:

  o Eliminate (or possibly replace) existing hedge accounting requirements, which would increase income volatility. The IASB is exploring some alternatives that might minimize this volatility, such as permitting recognition of gains and losses on financial instruments designated as hedging instruments outside income profit and even permitting recognition of gains and losses outside income on all financial instruments.

  o Maintain and simplify existing hedge accounting requirements.

COMPREHENSIVE EXAMPLE

This section presents a comprehensive example that illustrates the application of IAS 39 and IFRS 7 requirements.

Centrica plc – All extracts 9 (A) were obtained from the annual report for the year ended December 31, 2007. All disclosures and accounting policies are in line with Canadian GAAP unless otherwise indicated.

Extract 9(A1) – Centrica plc – Accounting for financial instruments, pages 65 and 66

In this extract (obtained from the note on summary of significant accounting policies), the company presents information related to different financial instruments. Similar notes are required under Canadian GAAP.

---

2. Summary of significant accounting policies

Financial instruments (in part)

Financial assets and financial liabilities are recognised in the Group Balance Sheet when the Group becomes a party to the contractual provisions of the instrument. Financial assets are de-recognised when the Group no longer has the rights to cash flows, the risks and rewards of ownership or control of the asset.

Financial liabilities are de-recognised when the obligation under the liability is discharged, cancelled or expires.

(a) Trade receivables

Trade receivables are recognised and carried at original invoice amount less an allowance for any uncollectible amounts.

Provision is made when there is objective evidence that the Group may not be able to collect the trade receivable. Balances are written off when recoverability is assessed as being remote.

(b) Share capital

Ordinary shares are classified as equity. Incremental costs directly attributable to the issue of new shares are shown in equity as a deduction from the proceeds received. Own equity instruments that are reacquired (treasury shares) are deducted from equity.

No gain or loss is recognised in the Income Statement on the purchase, sale, issue or cancellation of the Group's own equity instruments.

(c) Cash and cash equivalents

Cash and cash equivalents comprise cash in hand and current balances with banks and similar institutions, which are readily convertible to known amounts of cash and which are subject to insignificant risk of changes in value and have an original maturity of three months or less.

For the purpose of the consolidated Cash Flow Statement, cash and cash equivalents consist of cash and cash equivalents as defined above, net of outstanding bank overdrafts.

(d) Interest-bearing loans and other borrowings

All interest-bearing loans and other borrowings are initially recognised at fair value net of directly attributable transaction costs.

After initial recognition, interest-bearing loans and other borrowings are subsequently measured at amortised cost using the effective interest method, except when they are the hedged item in an effective fair value hedge relationship where the carrying value is also adjusted to reflect the fair value movements associated with the hedged risks. Such fair value movements are recognised in the Income Statement. Amortised cost is calculated by taking into account any issue costs, and any discount or premium.

(e) Units issued by The Consumers' Waterheater Income Fund

Prior to deconsolidation as explained in note 3, units issued by The Consumers' Waterheater Income Fund which contain redemption rights providing unit holders with the right to redeem units back to the Fund for cash or another financial asset are treated as a financial liability and recorded at the present value of the redemption amount. Gains and losses related to changes in the carrying value of the financial liability up to the date of deconsolidation are included in the Income Statement within discontinued operations.

(f) Other financial assets

Available-for-sale financial assets are those non-derivative financial assets that are designated as available-for-sale, which are initially recognised at fair value, and included within other financial assets within the Balance Sheet. Available-for-sale financial assets are subsequently recognised at fair value with gains and losses arising from changes in fair value recognised directly in equity and presented in the Statement of Recognised Income and Expense, until the asset is disposed of or is determined to be impaired, at which time the cumulative gain or loss previously recognised in equity is included in the Income Statement for the period. Accrued interest or dividends arising on available-for-sale financial assets are recognised in the Income Statement.

Impairment losses recognised in the Income Statement for equity investments classified as available-for-sale are not subsequently reversed through the Income Statement. Impairment losses recognised in the Income Statement for debt instruments classified as available-for-sale are subsequently reversed if an increase in the fair value of the instrument can be objectively related to an event occurring after the recognition of the impairment loss.

(g) Derivative financial instruments

The Group routinely enters into sale and purchase transactions for physical delivery of gas, power and oil. A portion of these transactions take the form of contracts that were entered into and continue to be held for the purpose of receipt or delivery of the physical commodity in accordance with the Group's expected sale, purchase or usage requirements, and are not within the scope of IAS 39.

Certain purchase and sales contracts for the physical delivery of gas, power and oil are within the scope of IAS 39 because they net settle or contain written options. Such contracts are accounted for as derivatives under IAS 39 and are recognised in the Balance Sheet at fair value. Gains and losses arising from changes in fair value on derivatives that do not qualify for hedge accounting are taken directly to the Income Statement for the year.

The Group uses a range of derivatives for both trading and to hedge exposures to financial risks, such as interest rate, foreign exchange and energy price risks, arising in the normal course of business. The use of derivative financial instruments is governed by the Group's policies approved by the Board of Directors.

Further detail on the Group's risk management policies is included within the Directors' Report – Governance on pages 39 to 40 and in note 4 to the Financial Statements.

The accounting treatment for derivatives is dependent on whether they are entered into for trading or hedging purposes. A derivative instrument is considered to be used for hedging purposes when it alters the risk profile of an underlying exposure of the Group in line with the Group's risk management policies and is in accordance with established guidelines, which require that the hedging relationship is documented at its inception, ensure that the derivative is highly effective in achieving its objective, and require that its effectiveness can be reliably measured. The Group also holds derivatives which are not designated as hedges and are held for trading.

All derivatives are recognised at fair value on the date on which the derivative is entered into and are re-measured to fair value at each reporting date. Derivatives are carried as assets when the fair value is positive and as liabilities when the fair value is negative. Derivative assets and derivative liabilities are offset and presented on a net basis only when both a legal right of set-off exists and the intention to net settle the derivative contracts is present.

The Group enters into certain energy derivative contracts covering periods for which observable market data does not exist. The fair value of such derivatives is estimated by reference in part to published price quotations from active markets, to the extent that such observable market data exists, and in part by using valuation techniques, whose inputs include data, which is not based on or derived from observable markets. Where the fair value at initial recognition for such contracts differs from the transaction price, a fair value gain or fair value loss will arise.

This is referred to as a day-one gain or day-one loss. Such gains and losses are deferred and amortised to the Income Statement based on volumes purchased or delivered over the contractual period until such time observable market data becomes available.

When observable market data becomes available, any remaining deferred day-one gains or losses are recognised within the Income Statement. Recognition of the gain or loss that results from changes in fair value depends on the purpose for issuing or holding the derivative. For derivatives that do not qualify for hedge accounting, any gains or losses arising from changes in fair value are taken directly to the Income Statement and are included within gross profit or interest income and interest expense.

Gains and losses arising on derivatives entered into for speculative energy trading purposes are presented on a net basis within revenue.

Embedded derivatives: Derivatives embedded in other financial instruments or other host contracts are treated as separate derivatives when their risks and characteristics are not closely related to those of the host contracts and the host contracts are not carried at fair value, with gains or losses reported in the Income Statement. The closely related nature of embedded derivatives is re-assessed when there is a change in the terms of the contract which significantly modifies the future cash flows under the contract. Where a contract contains one or more embedded derivatives and providing that the embedded derivative significantly modifies the cash flows under the contract, the option to fair value the entire contract may be taken and the contract will be recognised at fair value with changes in fair value recognised in the Income Statement.

Extract 9(A2) – Centrica plc – Hedge accounting models, pages 66 and 67

In this extract (obtained from the note on summary of significant accounting policies), the company presents information on its use of hedge accounting models. Similar notes are required under Canadian GAAP.

2. Summary of significant accounting policies
(h) Hedge accounting

For the purposes of hedge accounting, hedges are classified either as fair value hedges, cash flow hedges or hedges of net investments in foreign operations.

Fair value hedges: A derivative is classified as a fair value hedge when it hedges the exposure to changes in the fair value of a recognised asset or liability. Any gain or loss from re-measuring the hedging instrument at fair value is recognised immediately in the Income Statement. Any gain or loss on the hedged item attributable to the hedged risk is adjusted against the carrying amount of the hedged item and recognised in the Income Statement. The Group discontinues fair value hedge accounting if the hedging instrument expires or is sold, terminated or exercised, the hedge no longer qualifies for hedge accounting or the Group revokes the designation. Any adjustment to the carrying amount of a hedged financial instrument for which the effective interest method is used is amortised to the Income Statement. Amortisation may begin as soon as an adjustment exists and shall begin no later than when the hedged item ceases to be adjusted for changes in its fair value attributable to the risk being hedged.

Cash flow hedges: A derivative is classified as a cash flow hedge when it hedges exposure to variability in cash flows that is attributable to a particular risk either associated with a recognised asset, liability or a highly probable forecast transaction. The portion of the gain or loss on the hedging instrument which is effective is recognised directly in equity while any ineffectiveness is recognised in the Income Statement. The gains or losses that are recognised directly in equity are transferred to the Income.

Statement in the same period in which the highly probable forecast transaction affects income, for example when the future sale of physical gas or physical power actually occurs. Where the hedged item is the cost of a non-financial asset or liability, the amounts taken to equity are transferred to the initial carrying amount of the non-financial asset or liability on its recognition.

Hedge accounting is discontinued when the hedging instrument expires or is sold, terminated or exercised without replacement or rollover, no longer qualifies for hedge accounting or the Group revokes the designation.

At that point in time, any cumulative gain or loss on the hedging instrument recognised in equity remains in equity until the highly probable forecast transaction occurs. If the transaction is no longer expected to occur, the cumulative gain or loss recognised in equity is recognised in the Income Statement.

Net investment hedges: Hedges of net investments in foreign operations are accounted for similarly to cash flow hedges. Any gain or loss on the effective portion of the hedge is recognised in equity, any gain or loss on the ineffective portion of the hedge is recognised in the Income Statement. On disposal of the foreign operation, the cumulative value of any gains or losses recognised directly in equity is transferred to the Income Statement.

Extract 9(A3) – Centrica plc – Critical accounting judgements and measurement uncertainties, pages 67 and 68

This extract presents information on critical accounting judgments and uncertainties related to the derecognition of financial assets and the fair value measurement of its energy derivatives. Similar notes are required under Canadian GAAP except that asset derecognition might possibly be based on some other criteria.

3. Critical accounting judgements and key sources of estimation uncertainty

(a) Critical judgements in applying the Group's accounting policies

In the process of applying the Group's accounting policies as described in note 2, management has made the following judgements that have the most significant effect on the amounts recognised in the Financial Statements (apart from those involving estimations which are dealt with below).

The Consumers' Waterheater Income Fund

The Group has deconsolidated The Consumers' Waterheater Income Fund (the 'Fund') with effect from 1 December 2007, the date of an Internalisation Agreement entered into between Centrica and the Fund.

Centrica created the Fund in 2002 to refinance the water heater assets acquired with the Enbridge Services acquisition.

The Group consolidated the Fund in accordance with the requirements of SIC-12, Consolidation – Special Purpose Entities, as the substance of the agreements put in place by Centrica indicated that the Fund was created for and on behalf of the Group. These agreements both predetermined the Fund's activities and provided Centrica with operational control, via responsibilities for servicing the Fund's asset portfolio and administering the Fund's activities.

In October 2006 the Trustees of the Fund appointed an independent Chief Executive Officer. The activities undertaken by the Fund started to change following this appointment through the independent acquisition of an immaterial business in late 2006, and the independent acquisition of the Toronto Hydro water heater rental business in February 2007, which provided the Fund with a limited number of rental customers held outside of the original contractual arrangements entered into with Centrica. Almost all the significant parts of the relationship, however, remained predetermined or controlled by Centrica.

These changes in the conduct of the Fund were judged not to be sufficiently material to alter the Fund's status as a subsidiary in the 2006 Group accounts.

In 2007 the Trustees of the Fund have sought further changes in the conduct of the Fund. The Fund has recruited an independent Chief Financial Officer and has made further small acquisitions outside of the original contractual arrangements entered into with Centrica. On 1 December 2007, the existing Administration Agreement was replaced, at the instigation of the Fund, by a new Internalisation Agreement, which provides the Fund with access rights to key operational data and provides a basis for employees and business infrastructure to transfer to the Fund, such that it is capable of independent operation from Centrica. Subsequent to this Agreement the Fund has independently refinanced its activities. The Directors believe that the Internalisation Agreement represents a change to the original contractual arrangements with the Fund, and demonstrates that the Fund has both the desire and the ability to manage its own affairs. Accordingly, in 2007 the Directors judge that the Fund's activities are no longer predetermined such that its activities are being conducted on behalf of Centrica, and thus the Fund ceases to represent a subsidiary of the Centrica Group.

The Group has deconsolidated the Fund with effect from 1 December 2007, the date the Internalisation Agreement became effective and the date of the resultant loss of control, recognising an exceptional profit on disposal amounting to £227 million. The Fund's activities represented a separate major line of business of the Direct Energy segment, and contributed materially to Group borrowings. In order to provide a clear presentation of the impact of deconsolidating the Fund, the results in the current year and prior year have been presented as a discontinued operation distinct from continuing operations within the Group Income Statement. The details of the disposal and discontinued results are provided in note 35.

Determination of fair values – energy derivatives

Derivative contracts are carried in the Balance Sheet at fair value, with changes in fair value recorded in either the Income Statement or equity. Fair values of energy derivatives are estimated by reference in part to published price quotations in active markets and in part by using valuation techniques. More detail on the assumptions used in determining fair valuations is provided in notes 4 and 28.

Extract 9(A4) – Centrica plc – Risk management, pages 69 to 74

In this extract, the company presents information on its financial risks and describes how it manages them. Disclosures meet the requirements of both IFRS7 and CICA 3862.

4. Financial risk management

The Group's normal operating, investing and financing activities expose it to a variety of financial risks: market risk (including commodity price risk, currency risk, interest rate risk and equity price risk), credit risk and liquidity risk. The Group's overall risk management process is designed to identify, manage and mitigate business risk, which includes, among others, financial risk. Further detail on the Group's overall risk management process is included within the Directors' Report – Governance on pages 39 to 40.

Financial risk management is overseen by the Group Financial Risk Management Committee (FRMC) according to objectives, targets and policies set by the Board. Commodity price risk management, and the associated credit risk management, is carried out in accordance with individual business unit financial risk management policies, as approved by the FRMC and the Board. Treasury risk management, including management of currency risk, interest rate risk, equity price risk and liquidity risk, and the associated credit risk management, is carried out by a central Group Treasury function in accordance with the Group's financing and treasury policy, as approved by the Board. Downstream credit risk management is carried out in accordance with business unit credit policies.

(a) Market risk management

Market risk is the risk of loss that results from changes in market prices (commodity prices, foreign exchange rates, interest rates and equity prices). The level of market risk to which the Group is exposed at a point in time varies depending on market conditions, expectations of future price or market rate movements and the composition of the Group's physical asset and contract portfolios.

(i) Commodity price risk management

The Group is exposed to commodity price risk in its energy procurement, downstream and proprietary energy trading activities.

Energy procurement and downstream activities

The Group's energy procurement and downstream activities consist of downstream positions, equity gas and liquids production and power generation, strategic procurement and sales contracts, market-traded purchase and sales contracts and derivative positions taken on with the intent of securing gas and power for the Group's downstream customers in the UK, Europe and North America from a variety of sources at an optimal cost. The Group actively manages commodity price risk by optimising its asset and contract portfolios making use of volume flexibility.

The Group is exposed to commodity price risk in its energy procurement and downstream activities because the cost of procuring gas and electricity to serve its downstream customers varies with wholesale commodity prices. The risk is primarily that market prices for commodities will fluctuate between the time that sales prices are fixed or tariffs are set and the time at which the corresponding procurement cost is fixed, thereby potentially reducing expected margins or making sales unprofitable.

The Group uses specific volumetric limits to manage the exposure to market prices associated with the Group's energy procurement and downstream activities to an acceptable level. Volumetric limits are supported by a Profit at Risk (PaR) methodology in the UK and a Value at Risk (VaR) methodology in North America and Europe to measure the Group's exposure to commodity price risk. PaR measures the estimated potential loss in a position or portfolio of positions associated with the movement of a commodity price for a given confidence level, over the remaining term of the position or contract portfolio. VaR measures the estimated potential loss for a given confidence level, over a predetermined holding period. The standard confidence level used is 95%.

The Group measures and manages the commodity price risk associated with the Group's entire energy procurement and downstream portfolio. Only certain of the Group's energy procurement and downstream contracts constitute financial instruments under IAS 39 (note 2). As a result, while the Group manages the commodity price risk associated with both financial and non-financial energy procurement and downstream contracts, it is the notional value of energy contracts being carried at fair value that represents the exposure of the Group's energy procurement and downstream books to commodity price risk according to IFRS 7. This is because energy contracts that are financial instruments under IAS 39 are accounted for on a fair value basis and changes in fair value immediately impact profit or equity. Conversely, energy contracts that are not financial instruments under IAS 39 are accounted for as executory contracts and changes in fair value do not immediately impact profit or equity, and as such, are not exposed to commodity price risk as defined by IFRS 7. So while the PaR or the VaR associated with energy procurement and downstream contracts outside the scope of IAS 39 is monitored for internal risk management purposes, these measures are not required to comply with IFRS 7.

The carrying value of energy contracts used in energy procurement and downstream activities at 31 December 2007 is disclosed in note 21 and a sensitivity analysis that is intended to illustrate the sensitivity of the Group's financial position and performance to changes in the fair value or future cash flows of financial instruments associated with the Group's energy procurement and downstream activities as a result of changes in commodity prices is provided below in section (v).

Proprietary energy trading

The Group's proprietary energy trading activities consist of physical and financial commodity purchases and sales contracts taken on with the intent of benefiting in the short-term from changes in market prices or differences between buying and selling prices.

The Group conducts its trading activities over the counter and through exchanges in the UK, North America and parts of the rest of Europe. The Group is exposed to commodity price risk as a result of its proprietary energy trading activities because the value of its trading assets and liabilities will fluctuate with changes in market prices for commodities.

The Group sets volumetric and VaR limits to manage the commodity price risk exposure associated with the Group's proprietary energy trading activities. The VaR used measures the estimated potential loss for a 95% confidence level over a one-day holding period. The holding period used is based on market liquidity and the number of days the Group would expect it to take to close off a trading position.

As with any modelled risk measure, there are certain limitations that arise from the assumptions used in the VaR analysis. VaR assumes that the future will behave like the past and that the Group's trading positions can be unwound or hedged within the predetermined holding period. Furthermore the use of a 95% confidence level, by definition, does not take into account changes in value that might occur beyond this confidence level.

The VaR, before taxation, associated with the Group's proprietary energy trading activities at 31 December 2007 was £9 million (2006: £8 million). The carrying value of energy contracts used in proprietary energy trading activities at 31 December 2007 is disclosed in note 21.

(ii) Currency risk management

The Group is exposed to currency risk on foreign currency denominated forecast transactions, firm commitments, monetary assets and liabilities (transactional exposure) and on its net investments in foreign operations (translational exposure).

Transactional currency risk

The Group is exposed to transactional currency risk on transactions denominated in currencies other than the underlying functional currency of the commercial operation transacting. The Group's primary functional currencies are pounds sterling in the UK, Canadian dollars in Canada, US dollars in the US and euros in Europe. The risk is that the functional currency value of cash flows will vary as a result of movements in exchange rates. Transactional exposure arises from the Group's energy procurement activities in the UK and in Canada, where a proportion of transactions are denominated in euros or US dollars and on certain capital commitments denominated in foreign currencies. In addition, in order to optimise the cost of funding, the Group has, in certain cases, issued foreign currency denominated debt, primarily in US dollars, euros or Japanese yen.

It is the Group's policy to hedge all material transactional exposures using forward contracts to fix the functional currency value of non-functional currency cash flows. At 31 December 2007, there were no material unhedged non-functional currency monetary assets or liabilities, firm commitments or probable forecast transactions (2006: £nil).

Translational currency risk

The Group is exposed to translational currency risk as a result of its net investments in North America and Europe. The risk is that the pounds sterling value of the net assets of foreign operations will decrease with changes in foreign exchange rates. The Group's policy is to protect the pounds sterling book value of its net investments in foreign operations, subject to certain targets monitored by the FRMC, by holding foreign currency debt, entering into foreign currency derivatives or a mixture of both.

The Group measures and manages the currency risk associated with all transactional and translational exposures. In contrast, IFRS 7 requires disclosure of currency risk arising on financial instruments denominated in a currency other than the functional currency of the commercial operation transacting only. As a result, for the purposes of IFRS 7, currency risk excludes the Group's net investments in North America and Europe as well as foreign currency denominated forecast transactions and firm commitments. A sensitivity analysis that is intended to illustrate the sensitivity of the Group's financial position and performance to changes in the fair value or future cash flows of foreign currency denominated financial instruments as a result of changes in foreign exchange rates is provided below in section (v).

(iii) Interest rate risk management

In the normal course of business the Group borrows to finance its operations. The Group is exposed to interest rate risk because the fair value of fixed rate borrowings and the cash flows associated with floating rate borrowings will fluctuate with changes in interest rates. The Group's policy is to manage the interest rate risk on long-term recourse borrowings by ensuring that the exposure to floating interest rates remains within a 30% to 70% range, including the impact of interest rate derivatives. Note 25 details the interest rates on the Group's bank overdrafts, loans and other borrowings by the earlier of contractual re-pricing and maturity date and a sensitivity analysis that is intended to illustrate the sensitivity of the Group's financial position and performance to changes in interest rates is provided below in section (v).

(iv) Equity price risk management

The Group is exposed to equity price risk because certain available-for-sale financial assets, held by the Law Debenture Trust on behalf of the Company as security in respect of the Centrica Unapproved Pension Scheme, are linked to equity indices (note 34).

Investments in equity indices are inherently exposed to less risk than individual equity investments because they represent a naturally diverse portfolio. Note 34 details the Group's other retirement benefit assets and liabilities.

(v) Sensitivity analysis

A financial instrument is defined in IAS 32 as any contract that gives rise to a financial asset of one entity (effectively the contractual right to receive cash or another financial asset from another entity) and a financial liability (effectively the contractual obligation to deliver cash or another financial asset to another entity) or equity instrument (effectively a residual interest in the assets of an entity) of another. IFRS 7 requires disclosure of a sensitivity analysis that is intended to illustrate the sensitivity of the Group's financial position and performance to changes in market variables (commodity prices, foreign exchange rates, interest rates and equity prices) as a result of changes in the fair value or cash flows associated with the Group's financial instruments. The sensitivity analysis provided discloses the effect on profit or loss and equity at 31 December 2007 assuming that a reasonably possible change in the relevant risk variable had occurred at 31 December 2007 and been applied to the risk exposures in existence at that date to show the effects of reasonably possible changes in price on profit or loss and equity to the next annual reporting date. The reasonably possible changes in market variables used in the sensitivity analysis were determined based on implied volatilities where available or historical data.

The sensitivity analysis has been prepared based on 31 December 2007 balances and on the basis that the balances, the ratio of fixed to floating rates of debt and derivatives, the proportion of energy contracts that are financial instruments, the proportion of financial instruments in foreign currencies and the hedge designations in place at 31 December 2007 are all constant. Excluded from this analysis are all non-financial assets and liabilities and energy contracts that are not financial instruments under IAS 39. The sensitivity to foreign exchange rates relates only to monetary assets and liabilities denominated in a currency other than the functional currency of the commercial operation transacting, and excludes the translation of the net assets of foreign operations to pounds sterling, but not the corresponding impact of net investment hedges.

The sensitivity analysis provided is hypothetical only and should be used with caution as the impacts provided are not necessarily indicative of the actual impacts that would be experienced because the Group's actual exposure to market rates is constantly changing as the Group's portfolio of commodity, debt, foreign currency and equity contracts changes. Changes in fair values or cash flows based on a variation in a market variable cannot be extrapolated because the relationship between the change in market variable and the change in fair value or cash flows may not be linear. In addition, the effect of a change in a particular market variable on fair values or cash flows is calculated without considering interrelationships between the various market rates or mitigating actions that would be taken by the Group. The sensitivity analysis provided below excludes the impact of proprietary energy trading assets and liabilities because the VaR associated with the Group's proprietary energy trading activities has already been provided above in section (i).

The impacts of reasonably possible changes in commodity prices on profit and equity, both after taxation, based on the assumptions provided above are as follows:

		2007			2006	
Energy prices	Base price (i)	Reasonably possible increase in variable	Reasonably possible decrease in variable	Base price (i)	Reasonably possible increase in variable	Reasonably possible decrease in variable
UK gas (p/therm)	51	+12	-12	35	+6	-6
UK power (£/MWh)	52	+11	-11	35	+9	-9
UK coal (US$/tonne)	101	+15	-15	70	+10	-10
UK emissions (€/tonne)	24	+5	-5	7	+4	-4
UK oil (US$/bbl)	88	+14	-14	66	+7	-7
North American gas (p/therm)	38	+4	-4	36	+6	-6
North American power (£/MWh)	28	+5	-5	29	+5	-5

(i)   The base price represents the average forward market price over the duration of the active market curve used in the sensitivity analysis provided.

	2007		2006	
Incremental profit/(loss)	Impact on profit £m	Impact on equity £m	Impact on profit £m	Impact on equity £m
UK energy prices (combined) – increase	34	56	91	67
UK energy prices (combined) – decrease	(34)	(56)	(91)	(67)
North American energy prices (combined) – increase	103	54	78	95
North American energy prices (combined) – decrease	(103)	(54)	(78)	(95)

The impacts of reasonably possible changes in interest rates on profit and equity, both after taxation, based on the assumptions provided above are as follows:

	2007			2006		
Interest rates and incremental profit/(loss)	Reasonably possible change in variable %	Impact on profit £m	Impact on equity £m	Reasonably possible change in variable %	Impact on profit £m	Impact on equity £m
UK interest rates	+0.50	5	4	+0.50	1	–
	-0.50	(5)	(4)	-0.50	(1)	–
US interest rates	+0.50	–	2	+0.25	1	3
	-0.50	–	(2)	-0.25	(1)	(3)
Canadian interest rates	+0.50	(2)	–	+0.25	–	–
	-0.50	2	–	-0.25	–	–

The impacts of reasonably possible changes in foreign currency rates relative to pounds sterling on profit and equity, both after taxation, based on the assumptions provided above are as follows:

	2007			2006		
Foreign exchange rates and incremental profit/(loss)	Reasonably possible change in variable %	Impact on profit £m	Impact on equity £m	Reasonably possible change in variable %	Impact on profit £m	Impact on equity £m
US dollar	+10	(32)	14	+5	(1)	(1)
	-10	28	(12)	-5	1	1
Canadian dollar	+10	3	12	+5	(1)	5
	-10	1	(10)	-5	1	(5)
Euro	+10	(1)	18	+5	(1)	8
	-10	1	(17)	-5	1	(8)

The impacts of reasonably possible changes in equity prices on profit and equity, both after taxation, based on the assumptions provided above are as follows:

	2007			2006		
Equity prices and incremental profit/(loss)	Reasonably possible change in variable %	Impact on profit £m	Impact on equity £m	Reasonably possible change in variable %	Impact on profit £m	Impact on equity £m
FTSE 100	+5	–	1	+5	–	1
	-5	–	(1)	-5	–	(1)

(b) Credit risk management

Credit risk is the risk of loss associated with a counterparty's inability or failure to discharge its obligations under a contract. The Group is exposed to credit risk in its treasury, trading, energy procurement and downstream activities.

Treasury, trading and energy procurement activities

Counterparty credit exposures are monitored by individual counterparty and by category of credit rating, and are subject to approved limits. The majority of significant exposures are with A-rated counterparties or better. The Group uses master netting agreements to reduce credit risk and net settles payments with counterparties where net settlement provisions exist. In addition, the Group employs a variety of other methods to mitigate credit risk: margining, various forms of bank and parent company guarantees and letters of credit. 100% of the Group's credit risk associated with its treasury, trading and energy procurement activities is with counterparties in related energy industries or with financial institutions. The Group measures and manages the credit risk associated with the Group's entire treasury, trading and energy procurement portfolio. In contrast, IFRS 7 defines credit risk as the risk that one party to a financial instrument will cause a financial loss for the other party by failing to discharge an obligation and requires disclosure of information about the exposure to credit risk arising from financial instruments only. Only certain of the Group's energy procurement contracts constitute financial instruments under IAS 39 (note 2). As a result, while the Group manages the credit risk associated with both financial and non-financial energy procurement contracts, it is the carrying value of financial assets within the scope of IAS 39 (note 28) that represents the maximum exposure to credit risk in accordance with IFRS 7 because credit losses associated with contracts that are not recognised on the Balance Sheet will not be recognised as such in the Income Statement.

Downstream activities

In the case of business customers credit risk is managed by checking a company's credit-worthiness and financial strength both before commencing trade and during the business relationship. For residential customers, creditworthiness is ascertained normally before commencing trade by reviewing an appropriate mix of internal and external information to determine the payment mechanism required to reduce credit risk to an acceptable level. Certain customers will only be accepted on a prepayment basis.

In some cases, an ageing of receivables is monitored and used to manage the exposure to credit risk associated with both business and residential customers. In other cases, credit risk is monitored and managed by grouping customers according to method of payment or profile. Note 21 provides further detail of the Group's exposure to credit risk on derivative financial instruments, note 20 provides detail of the Group's exposure to credit risk on trade and other receivables, note 23 provides detail of the Group's exposure to credit risk on cash and cash equivalents and note 28 provides the carrying value of all financial assets representing the Group's maximum exposure to credit risk.

(c) Liquidity risk management

Liquidity risk is the risk that the Group will not have sufficient funds to meet it obligations as they come due. Cash forecasts identifying the Group's liquidity requirements are produced regularly and are stress-tested for different scenarios to ensure sufficient financial headroom exists for at least a 12-month period to safeguard the Group's ability to continue as a going concern.

In order to manage liquidity risk it is the Group's policy to maintain committed facilities of at least £1,000 million less available surplus cash resources, to raise at least 50% of its net debt (excluding non-recourse debt) over £200 million in the long-term debt market, to hold a maximum of £400 million of debt maturing in the same calendar year (excluding finance leases and non-recourse borrowings) and to maintain an average term to maturity in the recourse long-term debt portfolio greater than three years.

At 31 December 2007, the Group had undrawn committed bank borrowing facilities of £1,300 million (2006: £1,300 million), 321% (2006: 76%) of the Group's net debt over £200 million has been raised in the long-term debt market, the average term to maturity of the long-term debt portfolio was 7.1 years (2006: 7.3 years) and there is no calendar year where more than £400 million of debt (excluding finance leases and non-recourse borrowings) will be maturing (2006: same).

Extract 9(A5) – Centrica plc – Risk management, pages 96 to 98

This extract presents information about receivables, including their significance, as required under IFRS7. Similar notes are required by CICA 3862.

20. Trade and other receivables

	2007 Current £m	2007 Non-current £m	2006 Current £m	2006 Non-current £m
Financial assets:				
Trade receivables	1,405	22	1,491	13
Accrued energy income	1,678	–	1,730	–
Other receivables	553	11	382	3
	3,636	33	3,603	16
Less: Provision for credit losses	(431)	–	(319)	–
	3,205	33	3,284	16
Non-financial assets:				
Prepayments and other receivables	218	–	306	–
	3,423	33	3,590	16

Trade and other receivables include financial assets representing the contractual right to receive cash or other financial assets from residential customers, business customers and treasury, trading and energy procurement counterparties as follows:

	2007 Current £m	2007 Non-current £m	2006 Current £m	2006 Non-current £m
Financial assets by class:				
Residential customers	1,960	23	2,232	12
Business customers	802	9	681	4
Treasury, trading and energy procurement counterparties	874	1	690	–
	3,636	33	3,603	16
Less: Provision for credit losses	(431)	–	(319)	–
	3,205	33	3,284	16

Receivables from residential and business customers are generally considered to be fully performing until such time as the payment that is due remains outstanding past the contractual due date. Contractual due dates range from being due upon receipt to due in 30 days. An ageing of the carrying value of trade and other receivables that are past due but not considered to be individually impaired by class is as follows:

Days past due	2007 Residential customers £m	2007 Business customers £m	2006 Residential customers £m	2006 Business customers £m
Less than 30 days	276	55	281	68
30-89 days	174	41	103	28
Less than 90 days	450	96	384	96
90-182 days	91	47	72	34
183-365 days	98	37	62	21
Greater than 365 days	62	17	33	7
	701	197	551	158

At 31 December 2007 there were £87 million of receivables, net of provisions for credit losses, from residential customers (2006: £98 million) that were considered to be individually impaired. There were no individually impaired receivables, net of provisions for credit losses, from business customers or from treasury, trading and energy procurement counterparties. Receivables from residential customers are generally reviewed for impairment on an individual basis once a customer discontinues their relationship with the Group.

The provision for credit losses is based on an incurred loss model and is determined by application of expected default and loss factors, determined by historical loss experience and current sampling to the various balances receivable from residential and business customers on a portfolio basis, in addition to provisions taken against individual accounts. Balances are written off when recoverability is assessed as being remote. Movements in the provision for credit losses by class are as follows:

	Residential customers £m	Business customers £m	Total £m
1 January	(270)	(49)	(319)
Impairment of trade receivables	(132)	(52)	(184)
Receivables written off	55	20	75
Exchange adjustments	(3)	–	(3)
31 December	(350)	(81)	(431)

	Residential customers £m	Business customers £m	Total £m
1 January	(228)	(40)	(268)
Impairment of trade receivables	(143)	(36)	(179)
Receivables written off	102	27	129
Exchange adjustments	(1)	–	(1)
31 December	(270)	(49)	(319)

At 31 December 2007 the Group held £36 million (2006: £16 million) of customer deposits for the purposes of mitigating the credit risk associated with receivables from residential and business customers.

At 31 December 2007 there was no provision for credit losses associated with receivables from treasury, trading and energy procurement counterparties (2006: £nil) because all balances are considered to be fully recoverable. Exposure to credit risk associated with receivables from treasury, trading and energy procurement counterparties is monitored by counterparty credit rating as follows:

Receivables from treasury, trading and energy procurement counterparties by credit rating	Carrying value £m	AAA £m	AA £m	A £m	BBB £m	BB or lower £m	Unrated £m
2007	875	7	189	277	129	26	247
2006	690	4	116	252	125	46	147

The unrated counterparty receivables are comprised primarily of amounts due from subsidiaries of rated entities, exchanges or clearing houses. Receivables from treasury, trading and energy procurement counterparties are managed in accordance with the Group's credit risk management policies as described in note 4.

Extract 9(A6) – Centrica plc –Derivatives disclosures, pages 98 to 101

The company discloses information on its derivatives, as required by IFRS7. CICA 3862 calls for similar notes.

---

21. Derivative financial instruments

Derivative financial instruments are generally held for the purposes of proprietary energy trading, treasury management or energy procurement. Derivatives held for the purposes of proprietary energy trading are carried at fair value, with changes in fair value recognised in the Group's results for the year before exceptional items and certain re-measurements, with the exception of certain derivatives related to cross-border transportation and capacity contracts (note 2). Derivative financial instruments held for the purposes of treasury management or energy procurement are also carried at fair value, with changes in the fair value of derivatives relating to treasury management reflected in the results for the year before exceptional items and certain re-measurements, and those relating to energy procurement reflected in certain re-measurements. In cases where a derivative qualifies for hedge accounting, derivatives are classified as fair value hedges, cash flow hedges or hedges of a net investment in a foreign operation. Notes 2 and 22 provide further detail on the Group's hedge accounting.

Energy contracts designated at fair value through profit and loss include certain energy contracts that the Group has, at its option, designated at fair value through profit and loss under IAS 39 because the energy contract contains one or more embedded derivatives that significantly modify the cash flows under the contract (note 2).

The carrying values of derivative financial instruments by product type for accounting purposes are as follows:

	2007 £m	2006 £m
Derivative financial instruments – held for proprietary energy trading		
Derivative financial instruments – held for trading under IAS 39		
Energy derivatives – assets	44	225
Energy derivatives – liabilities	(52)	(199)
	(8)	26
Derivative financial instruments – held for the purposes of treasury management or energy procurement		
Derivative financial instruments – held for trading under IAS 39		
Energy derivatives – assets	789	503
Energy derivatives – liabilities	(1,100)	(1,143)
Interest rate derivatives – assets	2	2
Interest rate derivatives - liabilities	(5)	(4)
Foreign exchange derivatives – assets	19	17
Foreign exchange derivatives – liabilities	(80)	(4)
	(375)	(629)
Energy contracts designated at fair value through profit and loss		
Energy derivatives – assets	9	3
Energy derivatives – liabilities	(86)	(57)
	(77)	(54)
Derivative financial instruments in hedge accounting relationships		
Energy derivatives – assets	123	16
Energy derivatives – liabilities	(68)	(500)
Interest rate derivatives – liabilities	(7)	(40)
Foreign exchange derivatives – assets	–	11
Foreign exchange derivatives – liabilities	(17)	(10)
	31	(523)
Net total	(429)	(1,180)

The net total reconciles to the Balance Sheet as follows:

	2007 £m	2006 £m
Derivative financial instruments – non-current assets	72	17
Derivative financial instruments – current assets	914	760
Derivative financial instruments – current liabilities	986	777
	(1,404)	(1,737)
Derivative financial instruments – non-current liabilities	(11)	(220)
	(1,415)	(1,957)
Net total	(429)	(1,180)

The contracts included within energy derivatives are subject to a wide range of detailed specific terms but comprise the following general components:

	2007 £m	2006 £m
Short-term forward market purchases and sales of gas and electricity:		
UK and Europe	107	(260)
North America	(80)	(238)
Structured gas purchase contracts	250	(226)
Structured gas sales contracts	(553)	(390)
Other	(65)	(38)
Net total	(341)	(1,152)

	2007		2006	
Net gains/(losses) on derivative financial instruments due to re-measurement	Income Statement £m	Equity £m	Income Statement £m	Equity £m
Financial assets and liabilities measured at fair value through profit and loss:				
Derivative financial instruments – held for proprietary energy trading	(5)	–	8	–
Derivative financial instruments – held for trading under IAS 39	230	–	(840)	–
Energy contracts designated at fair value through profit and loss	(35)	–	(54)	–
Derivative financial instruments in hedge accounting relationships	3	535	(30)	(837)
	193	535	(916)	(837)

Derivative-related credit risk – assets

Credit risk from derivative transactions is generated by the potential for the counterparty to default on its contractual obligations.

Therefore, derivative-related credit risk is represented by the positive fair value of the instrument and is normally a small fraction of the contract's notional amount. Credit risk from derivatives is measured and managed by counterparty credit rating as follows:

Fair value of derivative financial instruments with a positive fair value by counterparty credit rating	Carrying value £m	AAA £m	AA £m	A £m	BBB £m	BB or lower £m	Unrated £m
2007	986	–	372	272	51	–	291
2006	777	–	236	322	111	53	55

To manage derivative-related counterparty credit exposure, the Group employs the use of margining and set-off rights in some agreements. Under margining agreements, the Group has the right to request that the counterparty pay down or collateralise the current fair value of its derivatives position when the position passes a specified threshold. At 31 December 2007 the Group was holding £93 million (2006: £33 million) of cash as collateral against counterparty balances, and had pledged £118 million (2006: £61 million) of cash as collateral, principally under margin calls to cover exposure to mark-to-market positions on derivative contracts.

Generally, cash paid or received as collateral is interest-bearing and is free from any restriction over its use.

Maturity profiles of derivative financial instruments – liabilities

IFRS 7 requires disclosure of a maturity analysis for financial liabilities that shows remaining contractual maturities on an undiscounted basis. The following maturity analysis shows the remaining contractual maturities on an undiscounted basis for the Group's derivative financial instruments that are in a loss position at the balance sheet date and will be settled on a net basis:

Energy derivatives that will be settled on a net basis	**2007 £m**	2006 £m
Less than one year	**(128)**	(296)
One to five years	**(53)**	(113)
More than five years	**(2)**	(15)
	(183)	(424)

Interest rate derivatives that will be settled on a net basis	**2007 £m**	2006 £m
Less than one year	**(9)**	(5)
One to five years	**(4)**	(25)
More than five years	**(1)**	(10)
	(14)	(40)

Certain of the Group's energy contracts that are accounted for as derivatives are for the physical purchase of energy. In these cases IFRS 7 requires disclosure of a maturity analysis that shows cash outflows on all purchase contracts on an undiscounted basis, including those derivative contracts in a gain position at the balance sheet date as follows:

Energy procurement contracts that are carried at fair value	**2007 £m**	2006 £m
Less than one year	**(12,076)**	(10,652)
One to five years	**(17,559)**	(16,175)
More than five years	**(6,719)**	(7,638)
	(36,354)	(34,465)

The Group's foreign exchange derivative contracts will be settled on a gross basis. In these cases IFRS 7 requires disclosure of a maturity analysis that shows cash outflows on all derivative contracts on an undiscounted basis, including those derivative contracts in a gain position at the balance sheet date. In addition to cash outflows on all foreign exchange derivative contracts that are gross settled on an undiscounted basis, the following analysis also provides disclosure of the related cash inflows as follows:

Foreign exchange derivatives that will be settled on a gross basis	**2007**		**2006**	
	Outflow £m	**Inflow £m**	Outflow £m	Inflow £m
Less than one year	**(1,898)**	**1,851**	(1,390)	1,404
One to five years	**(811)**	**785**	(436)	442
More than five years	**(130)**	**112**	(104)	81
	(2,839)	**2,748**	(1,930)	1,927

Extract 9(A7) – Centrica plc – Hedge accounting, pages 101 and 102

In this extract, the company discloses information related to hedge accounting as required by IFRS7. Similar notes are required by CICA 3865.

22. Hedge accounting

For the purposes of hedge accounting, hedges are classified either as fair value hedges, cash flow hedges or hedges of net investments in foreign operations. Note 2 details the Group's accounting policies in relation to derivatives qualifying for hedge accounting under IAS 39. The fair values of derivative and primary financial instruments in hedge accounting relationships at 31 December were as follows:

	2007 Assets £m	2007 Liabilities £m	2006 Assets £m	2006 Liabilities £m
Fair value hedges	–	9	–	12
Cash flow hedges	123	67	21	538
Net investment hedges:				
Primary financial instruments	–	74	–	117
Derivative financial instruments	–	16	6	–

Fair value hedges

The Group's fair value hedges consist of interest rate swaps, cross-currency interest rate swaps and forward rate agreements used to protect against changes in the fair value of fixed-rate long-term debt due to movements in market interest rates. For qualifying fair value hedges, all changes in the fair value of the hedging instrument and in the fair value of the hedged item in relation to the risk being hedged are recognised in income within net interest expense.

Gains or losses arising on fair value hedges at 31 December were as follows:

	2006 £m	2007 £m
On hedging instruments	5	(14)
On hedged items attributable to the hedged risk	(6)	16
	(1)	2

Cash flow hedges

The Group's cash flow hedges consist primarily of: (a), physical and financial gas and power purchase contracts used to protect against the variability in future cash flows associated with highly probable forecast purchases of gas and power due to movements in market commodity prices; (b) forward foreign exchange contracts used to protect against the variability of functional currency denominated cash flows associated with non-functional currency denominated highly probable forecast transactions; and (c) interest rate swaps, cross-currency interest rate swaps and forward rate agreements used to protect against the variability in cash flows associated with floating-rate borrowings due to movements in market interest rates.

Gains and losses are initially recognised in the cash flow hedging reserve in equity and are transferred to the Income Statement when the forecast cash flows affect the Income Statement. Note 30 details movements in the cash flow hedging reserve. The ineffective portion of gains and losses on cash flow hedging are recognised immediately in the Income Statement. During 2007 the Group recognised a gain of £nil (2006: loss of £9 million) due to cash flow hedge ineffectiveness.

Net investment hedges

The Group's net investment hedges consist of foreign currency debt issued in the same currency as the net investment, foreign exchange forwards and cross-currency interest rate swaps used to protect against the variability in the pounds sterling value of the Group's net investments in foreign operations due to movements in the relative strength of foreign currencies to pounds sterling.

Gains and losses on the effective portion of the hedge are recognised in equity and transferred to the Income Statement on disposal of the foreign operation. Gains and losses on the ineffective portion of the hedge are recognised immediately in the Income Statement.

During 2007 the Group did not recognise any gains or losses due to net investment hedge ineffectiveness (2006: £nil).

Extract 9(A8) – Centrica plc – Fair value disclosures, pages 109 to 111

This extract provides information on the fair values of financial instruments as required under IFRS7. CICA 3862 requires similar information.

28. Fair value of financial instruments

The fair value of a financial instrument is the amount at which the financial instrument could be exchanged in an arm's length transaction between knowledgeable and willing parties under no compulsion to act. The Group has documented internal policies for determining fair value, including methodologies used to establish valuation adjustments required for credit risk.

The fair values of the Group's financial instruments together with the carrying amounts included in the Balance Sheet are analysed as follows:

	2007		2006	
	Carrying value	Fair value	Carrying value	Fair value
Financial assets	£m	£m	£m	£m
Loans and receivables:				
Trade and other receivables, net of provisions				
Residential customers	1,633	1,633	1,974	1,974
Business customers	730	730	636	636
Treasury, trading and energy procurement counterparties	875	875	690	690
Cash and cash equivalents	1,130	1,130	640	640
	4,368	4,368	3,940	3,940
Financial assets measured at fair value through profit and loss:				
Derivative financial instruments – held for proprietary energy trading	44	44	225	225
Derivative financial instruments – held for trading under IAS 39	810	810	522	522
Energy contracts designated at fair value through profit and loss	9	9	3	3
Derivative financial instruments in hedge accounting relationships	123	123	27	27
	986	986	777	777
Available-for-sale financial assets:				
Debt	79	79	75	75
Equity	10	10	11	11
	89	89	86	86

	2007		2006	
	Carrying value	Fair value	Carrying value	Fair value
Financial liabilities	£m	£m	£m	£m
Financial liabilities measured at amortised cost:				
Trade and other payables	(3,107)	(3,107)	(2,989)	(2,989)
Bank overdrafts, loans and other borrowings				
Bank overdrafts and loans	(347)	(338)	(164)	(162)
Bonds	(1,250)	(1,246)	(1,181)	(1,176)
Commercial paper	–	–	(100)	(100)
Obligations under finance leases (including power station tolling arrangements)	(417)	(417)	(808)	(814)
Non-recourse Canadian dollar bonds	–	–	(218)	(227)
Non-recourse units of The Consumers' Waterheater Income Fund	–	–	(265)	(265)
Provisions	(169)	(169)	(259)	(259)
	(5,290)	(5,277)	(5,984)	(5,992)
Financial liabilities at fair value through profit and loss:				
Derivative financial instruments – held for proprietary energy trading	(52)	(52)	(199)	(199)
Derivative financial instruments – held for trading under IAS 39	(1,185)	(1,185)	(1,151)	(1,151)
Energy contracts designated at fair value through profit and loss	(86)	(86)	(57)	(57)
Derivative financial instruments in hedge accounting relationships	(92)	(92)	(550)	(550)
	(1,415)	(1,415)	(1,957)	(1,957)

Financial instruments valued at their carrying values

Due to their nature and/or short-term maturity, the fair values of trade and other receivables, cash and cash equivalents, trade and other payables and provisions are estimated to approximate their carrying values.

Available-for-sale financial assets

The fair values of available-for-sale financial assets are based on quoted market prices, when available. If quoted market prices are not available fair values are estimated using observable market data.

Bank overdrafts, loans and other borrowings

The fair values of bonds, Canadian dollar bonds and units of The Consumers' Waterheater Income Fund (prior to deconsolidation of the Fund as explained in note 3) are based on quoted market prices. The fair values of bank loans have been determined by discounting cash flows with reference to relevant market rates of interest. The fair values of overdrafts and commercial paper are assumed to equal their book values due to the short-term nature of these amounts. The fair values of obligations under finance leases have been determined by discounting contractual cash flows with reference to the Group's cost of borrowing.

Derivative financial instruments and energy contracts designated at fair value through profit and loss

The fair values of foreign exchange and interest rate derivatives are determined by reference to closing market rates at the balance sheet date. The fair values of energy derivatives are determined using valuation techniques based in part on observable market data and in part on internal estimates not currently supported by observable market data. The extent to which fair values of energy derivatives are based on observable market data is determined by the extent to which the market for the underlying commodity is judged to be active. The Group has judged each of the markets in which it operates as active, in both 2007 and 2006, for the purposes of accounting as follows:

Active period of markets	Gas	Power	Coal	Emissions	Oil
UK (years)	2	2	4	5	4
North America (years)	5	5	N/A	N/A	N/A

The fair values of energy contracts within the scope of IAS 39 that settle inside the active period of the market are based on quoted market prices and expected volumes, discounted at a rate of 6% (2006: 5%). The fair values of derivative financial instruments in North America and Europe are based primarily on quoted market prices. In the UK, however, certain energy contracts extend beyond the active period of the market. The fair values of energy contracts that extend beyond the active period of the market are determined by reference in part to published price quotations in active markets and in part by using valuation techniques based on commodity prices derived using assumptions that are based on internal market expectations and expected volumes, discounted using a discount rate of 5% (2006: 5%).

The net fair value of energy contracts recorded in the Financial Statements determined using valuation techniques based on nonobservable market variables at 31 December 2007 is a £322 million liability (2006: £262 million liability). The total change in fair value of energy contracts estimated using valuation techniques based on variables not supportable by market prices that was recognised in the Income Statement during the year ended 31 December 2007 amounted to a loss of £100 million (2006: loss of £117 million).

While internal market forecasts outside the active period of the market reasonably reflect all factors that market participants would consider in setting a price, these expectations are not currently supportable by active forward market quotes. The fair values of these contracts would change significantly if the assumptions in respect of gas, power, coal, emissions or oil prices were changed to reasonably possible alternatives. The impacts of reasonably possible changes to assumed gas, power, emissions, coal and oil prices on the net fair value of the Group's derivative financial instruments determined using valuation models based on non-observable market data are as follows:

| | 2007 | | 2006 | |
| | Reasonably possible increase in variable | Reasonably possible decrease in variable | Reasonably possible increase in variable | Reasonably possible decrease in variable |
Energy price				
UK gas (p/therm)	+12	-12	+6	-6
UK power (£/MWh)	+11	-11	+10	-10
UK coal (US$/tonne)	+15	-15	+10	-10
UK emissions (€/tonne)	+6	-6	+5	-5
UK oil (US$/bbl)	+14	-14	+7	-7

Increase/(decrease) in fair value	2007 £m	2006 £m
UK energy prices – increase	85	89
UK energy prices – decrease	(100)	(86)

The impacts disclosed above result from changing the assumptions used for fair valuing energy contracts in relation to gas, power, emissions, coal and oil prices to reasonably possible alternative assumptions at the balance sheet date. The fair value impacts only concern those contracts entered into which are within the scope of IAS 39 and are marked-to-market based on valuation models using assumptions that are not currently observable in an active market. The sensitivity analysis provided is hypothetical only and should be used with caution as the impacts provided are not necessarily indicative of the actual impacts that would be experienced because the Group's actual exposure to market rates is constantly changing as the Group's portfolio of energy contracts changes.

Changes in fair values based on a variation in a market variable cannot be extrapolated because the relationship between the change in market variable and the change in fair value may not be linear.

Where the fair value at initial recognition for such contracts differs from the transaction price a day-one gain or loss will arise. Such gains and losses are deferred and amortised to the Income Statement based on volumes purchased or delivered over the contractual period until such time as observable market data becomes available (see note 2 for further detail). The amount that has yet to be recognised in the Income Statement relating to the difference between the fair value at initial recognition (the transaction price) and the amount that would have arisen had valuation techniques used for subsequent measurement been applied at initial recognition, less subsequent releases, is as follows:

Net deferred (gains)/losses	2007 £m	2006 £m
At 1 January	(62)	13
Net losses deferred on new transactions	(103)	(9)
Recognised in the Income Statement during the period:		
Amortisation	3	–
Unobservable inputs becoming observable	(4)	(66)
At 31 December	(166)	(62)

PLANNING FOR IMPLEMENTATION
Generating New Data and Optimizing Information Systems

In 2007, all Canadian public companies had to adopt:

*   CICA 3855;
*   CICA 3861 *Financial Instruments — Disclosure and Presentation* (companies were permitted to adopt CICA 3862 and 3863 instead of CICA 3861); and
*   CICA 3865.

For fiscal years beginning October 1, 2007, companies had to adopt:

*   CICA 3855;
*   CICA 3862 (which requires more comprehensive disclosure than CICA 3861 and contains all the requirements of IFRS 7);
*   CICA 3863 (which has the same presentation requirements as CICA 3861); and
*   CICA 3865.

Companies that adopted CICA 3855, 3862, 3863 and 3865 would probably have modified their information systems to generate the new data required to comply with those standards. The new data requirements raise a number of issues, including some related to IFRS implementation:

Fair Value Measurement

If necessary, systems should be modified to allow an entity to:

*   identify and use the most appropriate fair value data;
*   track the changes in the fair value of financial instruments;
*   process the required accounting entries; and
*   generate the necessary information required for disclosure purposes.

As discussed in this chapter, investments are generally accounted for at fair value. Any change in fair value from one accounting period to another should be taken to either the income statement or to other comprehensive income (equity), depending on the classification of the investments.

IAS 39 requires more frequent measurements at fair value than CICA 3855 does (e.g., impairment reversals and valuation of unquoted equity securities). IAS 39 assumes that fair value can be determined in many cases. Although it may be difficult to determine fair value for some equity investments, management should not simply assume that it will be impossible to reliably estimate it. In limited circumstances (when the range of reasonable fair value estimates is significant or when it is not possible to make a reliable estimate), an entity is permitted to measure equity investments at cost. This is a last-resort measurement alternative.

The fact that unquoted investments may have to be measured at fair value would be a new requirement for companies using Canadian GAAP and contravenes the past practice of using cost. (CICA 3855 requires unquoted investments to be recorded at cost).

To allow systems to determine fair value for financial instruments, they must implement the following hierarchy set by IAS 39 (CICA 3855):

*   Published quotations from an active market (best evidence of fair value) should always be used when available.

- When there is no active market, companies are required to use well-established valuation techniques, which include:
  - o recent market transactions,
  - o reference to a transaction that is substantially the same, and
  - o discounted cash flows.

When fair values are established using a valuation technique, models must be reviewed to ensure:

- consistency with accepted economic methodologies used for pricing the specific financial asset or liability being measured; and

- inclusion of all factors that market participants would consider in setting a price.

Under both IAS 39 and CICA 3855, all exceptions to fair value accounting must be documented. Examples of such exceptions include:

- unquoted (or quoted) securities whose fair value cannot be reliably measured; and

- under CICA 3855 only, purchases and sales of non-financial items meeting the definition of a derivative that are used in normal operations and will be physically settled.

New Categorization of Financial Assets

An entity must establish procedures to:

- identify all contracts on a timely basis (i.e., when an entity enters into a contract);

- ensure that its risk management strategies and valuation policies are implemented. For example, systems must allow the entity to identify complex financial instruments so that they can receive prior approval and proper accounting treatment;

- document identification and classification of its financial assets and financial liabilities;

- ensure that the fair value option is implemented according to entity policies and IAS 39 (CICA 3855) requirements (note that the fair value option is restricted under IAS 39).

IAS 39 and CICA 3855 differ on available-for-sale debt securities denominated in foreign currencies. CICA 3855 requires all changes in carrying amounts to be included in other comprehensive income. Under IAS 39, systems must allow the separate calculations of any gains and losses in the foreign exchange rate for the purpose of including them in income.

Transaction Costs

CICA 3855 allows the expensing of all transaction costs or their capitalization for all financial assets and liabilities. An entity must expense these costs when its financial assets and liabilities are classified as held for trading. Consequently, the entity might decide to expense all transaction costs, thus eliminating all potential tracking problems.

Under IAS 39, transaction costs must be capitalized in the cost of financial assets or liabilities (except those in the held-for-trading category). This requirement means that companies have to track all transaction costs, including fees and commission paid to agents or employees acting as selling agents, advisers, brokers and dealers, levies by regulatory agencies and securities exchanges, and transfer taxes and duties. Transaction costs would exclude debt premiums or discounts, financing costs or internal administrative or holding costs.

Bifurcation of Embedded Derivatives

Systems must be designed to:

- generate data permitting the review of all outstanding contracts for possible embedded derivatives and determining whether those derivatives need to be accounted for separately;

- ensure that data is obtained to enable initial recognition of embedded derivatives and their subsequent measurement of at fair value; and

- document arguments on the separation (or non-separation) of embedded derivatives.

Systems must allow the bifurcation of embedded derivatives. Typical examples of contracts that might contain embedded derivatives requiring separation include:

- equity conversion option of a debt from the perspective of the holder;

- commodity indexed interest or principal payments in host debt contracts; and

- currency derivatives in purchase or sale contracts for non-financial items.

Effective Interest Method

Calculating the effective interest rate of a financial instrument might be challenging in practice because:

- It requires an estimate of cash flows considering all of a financial instrument's contractual terms, including prepayment, call and similar options. There is a presumption that the cash flows and the expected life of a group of similar financial instruments can be estimated reliably. When it is not possible to do that, the entity would base the calculation on the contractual cash flows over the full contractual term of the financial instrument (or group of financial instruments).

- Particular problems arise with floating rate financial assets and floating rate financial liabilities where periodic re-estimation of cash flows to reflect movements in market interest rates alters the effective interest rate.

Consequently, many features of debt instruments would require the compilation of new data to satisfy the requirements of IAS 39 (CICA 3855) for the establishment of an effective interest method.

Hedge Documentation and Ineffectiveness Measurement

An entity must decide whether or not to apply hedge accounting. If it decides to apply hedge accounting, it will have to:

- define hedge strategies;

- identify and document hedging relationships; and

- implement effectiveness testing.

Systems should be designed to meet all the criteria of hedge accounting by ensuring that:

- procedures are well established to ensure that hedge accounting documentation is prepared at the inception of a hedge;

- documented policies are reassessed periodically to determine that they are comprehensive and complete.

Note that the implementation of IAS 39 could require redesigns of hedging documentation (e.g., IAS 39 does not allow the use of the short-cut or critical terms match methods for measuring hedge ineffectiveness that is currently allowed by CICA

3855). This means that it will be more difficult to ignore hedge ineffectiveness resulting in greater fluctuations in income.

Measurement of Certain Items not Recorded Previously

Many items were ignored for accounting purposes before the introduction of IAS 39 (CICA 3855 and CICA 3865), such as hedged firm commitments, financial guarantees and loan commitments. Even existing IAS 39 requires firm commitments to be recognized only when at least one of the parties has performed under the agreement.

Consequently, an entity must design its systems to properly identify and account for items that should be recognized under IAS 39. Proper accounting treatment could mean:

- recognition of the item in the financial statements;
- its disclosure in the notes to the financial statements; or
- same treatment as before (i.e., they are ignored).

Derecognition of Financial Assets and Financial Liabilities

Even though derecognition rules for financial liabilities are the same under both IAS 39 and CICA 3855, they differ significantly for financial assets. Entities must, therefore, change their data gathering to determine if financial assets should be derecognized under IAS 39.

New Disclosures on Financial Risks

Systems must be designed to permit the identification and analysis of an entity's primary financial risks. Data must be collected to ensure that procedures exist for managing those risks.

In the current ever-changing environment and regulatory context, systems and data collected need to be reviewed continuously. Companies must implement systems that allow management to identify, analyze and manage any risks, both internal and external, that could reduce the likelihood of meeting their business objectives.

IFRS 7 (CICA 3862) requires entities to disclose:

- identification of risks on an ongoing basis;
- an analysis of risks (which involves assessing the likelihood of the risks occurring and their potential seriousness);
- their risk management procedures.

Assessing the Impact on Financial Statements

Generally, IAS 32 and IAS 39 adoption should not have much of an impact on financial statements that were prepared in accordance with Canadian GAAP. In addition, CICA 3862 has adopted IFRS 7 verbatim. There remain, however, many differences that could result in large adjustments in specific circumstances. This chapter has discussed these differences.

Differences between IFRS and Canadian GAAP could affect basic primary financial instruments. For example, under Canadian GAAP:

- receivables are recorded at estimated realizable value;
- unearned interest included in the nominal value of financial receivables is deferred to future periods when it is earned; and

- receivables sold to third parties with or without recourse (including those sold as part of securitization transactions) would be derecognized.

Under IAS 39:

- receivables are stated at amortized cost, less a provision for impairment, not estimated realizable value. The provision should reflect both the likelihood of being paid and the timing of the cash flows; and
- receivables sold with recourse would normally qualify for derecognition.

Initial Adoption of IFRS

Companies must prepare their opening IFRS balance sheet, which would:

- include all the assets and liabilities required under IFRS;
- exclude any assets and liabilities not permitted by IFRS;
- classify all assets, liabilities and equity in accordance with IFRS; and
- measure all items in accordance with IFRS.

IFRS 1, *First-time Adoption of International Financial Reporting Standards* contains optional exemptions or mandatory exceptions that do not require or permit recognition, classification and measurement in accordance with IFRS. Exceptions related financial instruments and hedge accounting are briefly described below.

Designation of Financial Assets and Financial Liabilities

IAS 39 allows a company to classify a financial instrument as a financial asset or financial liability at fair value through profit or loss or as available for sale only *at the inception* of the financial instrument . IFRS 1 contains an exemption that allows the classification to be made at the IFRS transition date.

Compound Financial Instruments

Compound financial instruments are analyzed into debt and equity components, based on the circumstances prevailing at the inception of the instrument. According to IFRS 1, companies do not have to identify separately the two elements of the equity component if the liability component is not outstanding at the IFRS transition date.

Derecognition of Financial Assets and Financial Liabilities

According to IAS 39, all financial assets and liabilities have to include all items as required by IFRS (i.e., January 1, 2004 for entities with December 31 year ends). IFRS 1 contains an option that allows an entity not to restate a previous derecognition.

All receivables that were derecognized from an entity's balance sheet under AcG-12 before January 1, 2004 (for entities with December 31 year ends) can remain derecognized in the IFRS financial statements. Receivables that were derecognized after January 1, 2004 do not qualify automatically for derecognition in the first IFRS financial statements. The IAS 39 criteria for derecognition need to be met.

The exemption from restating comparatives for IAS 32 and IAS 39 means, however, that AcG-12 rules for derecognition should be applied when presenting the comparatives. Consequently, a securitization that occurs, for example, on January 10, 2010 and meets the AcG-12 but not the IAS 39 derecognition criteria should be derecognized in the 2010 comparative balance sheet and should be re-recognized in the opening balance sheet as at January 1, 2011.

Hedge Accounting

Hedge accounting after the IFRS transition date may be applied only if all of the IAS 39 hedge accounting criteria have been met. CICA 3865 guidance should be followed for any period before the IFRS transition date. At that date, a company should consider whether its hedges under CICA 3865 qualify for hedge accounting under IFRS. If they do, it should follow the detailed guidance in IFRS 1 to recognize the hedging instrument and the hedging relationship.

Illustrative disclosure:

Extract 9(58) – Transition (optional choice not applied)

Benetton Group SpA (Form 20-F 2006, Part III, Financial Statements page Explanatory Notes, 30. Adoption of International Financial Reporting Standards (IFRS)) (in part), Transition to IFRS

> Derecognition of financial assets and liabilities.

IAS 39 requires recognition in the opening balance sheet at January 1, 2004 of financial assets and liabilities, other than derivatives, which were previously derecognized under the former accounting standards. However, IFRS 1 provides for an option to apply the principle of "derecognition" on an onward basis, meaning that it is applicable to financial assets and liabilities, other than derivatives, purchased after the transition date. The Benetton Group does not have any cases which would lead to adoption of the exemption in question.

Commentary: The company states that there are no reasons for adopting the exemption for derecognition allowed by IFRS 1. Listing all optional exemptions (even the ones that would not apply) could be useful.

Chapter 10
Foreign Currency Translation

Standards Discussed in this Chapter

International

IAS 21 – The Effects of Changes in Foreign Exchanges Rates
IAS 29 – Financial Reporting in Hyperinflationary Economies
SIC-7 – Introduction of the Euro

Canadian

CICA 1651 – Foreign Currency Translation
EIC-26 – Reductions in the net investment in self-sustaining foreign operations
EIC-130 – Translation method when the reporting currency differs from the measurement currency or there is a change in the reporting currency

INTRODUCTION

Many Canadian companies buy and sell products and services denominated in foreign currencies. Those companies may also hold interests in foreign operations that maintain their accounting records in local currencies. For financial reporting purposes, all these transactions and foreign operations have to be translated to the appropriate currency (which IFRS describe as the "functional currency" and Canadian GAAP as "currency of measurement"). Although CICA 1651 and IAS 21 establish the translation procedures under Canadian GAAP and IFRS, respectively, the two standards differ in several respects.

Not only do IAS 21 and CICA 1651 take different approaches to foreign currency translation, IAS 21 also contains specific guidance on certain issues not addressed by Canadian GAAP. To help readers evaluate the IFRS requirements, this chapter discusses the following topics:

- foreign currencies:
  - a new approach,
  - application of the new approach,
  - determination of the functional currency,
  - presentation currency,
  - changes in functional currency,
  - introduction of the euro;
- foreign currency transactions:
  - initial measurement,
  - subsequent measurement,

- foreign currency financial statements:
  - o translating financial statements into the presentation currency,
  - o particular issues related to consolidation,
  - o disposal of an interest in a foreign operation,
  - o highly inflationary economies;
- convenience translation.

IMPACT ON FINANCIAL STATEMENTS

Applying IAS 21 and CICA 1651 should generally result in similar financial statements except when a reporting entity consolidates interests held in hyperinflationary economies. In such circumstances, IAS 21 and IAS 29 require that financial statements be restated to remove the effects of price level changes before proceed- ing with the foreign currency translation. CICA 1651 does not require such a restatement. It is difficult to assess the impact of this difference on consolidated financial statements since it depends on many factors, including the significance of interests held and the level of inflation in the foreign economies.

ANALYSIS OF RELEVANT ISSUES

This section examines and illustrates some relevant foreign currency translation issues under IFRS, noting pertinent differences with Canadian GAAP.

Foreign Currencies

A New Approach

CICA 1651 uses the terms "reporting currency" and "unit of measure" in its foreign currency translation guidance. EIC-130 also uses the term "currency of measurement." IAS 21 adopts a new approach by:

- replacing the term "measurement currency" by the more commonly used "functional currency";
- breaking down the term "reporting currency" into two elements – "functional currency" (the currency of the primary economic environment in which an entity operates) and "presentation currency" (currency in which the financial statements are presented).

Even though Canadian standards have not specifically adopted the "functional currency" approach, the term is widely used in practice. We have observed that more than a quarter of the 200 Canadian companies surveyed in the CICA publication *Financial Reporting in Canada* (32nd edition) use the term "functional currency" even though their accounting policies do not appear to be completely in line with IAS 21 requirements.

Note that a previous version of IAS 21 adopted the "unit of measure" or "currency of measurement" approach for foreign currency translation as currently required under CICA 1651. IAS 21 was subsequently revised to adopt the "functional currency" approach, which is also required under US GAAP. Applying either of the two approaches (i.e., currency of measurement or functional currency) does not appear to result in significant differences in practice. The CICA study *Reported Canadian/US GAAP differences – Summary of survey of Canadian annual reports for years ending in 2006* found that, of 150 surveyed public Canadian companies presenting reconciliations to US GAAP, 22 identified differences related to foreign currency translation. These differences were broken down as follows:

- 15 concerned items affecting reported Canadian GAAP income by less than 5% though some have material balance sheet effects that the survey had not attempted to analyze;
- 6 concerned net investment in foreign operations and unexplained differences;
- one related to hedge accounting.

Based on the above observations, it seems that applying the functional currency approach instead of currency of measurement (as required by Canadian GAAP) might only occasion ally modify the results significantly.

Application of the New Approach

A prerequisite requirement of IAS 21 for translating foreign currency denominated amounts is to identify the reporting entity's functional currency and, when applicable, the functional currencies of its affiliates. Consequently, consolidated financial statements could include operations in different functional currencies.

Adoption of the functional currency approach as required under IAS 21, could affect foreign currency translation procedures. Under CICA 1651, an entity must only assess the unit of measure (functional currency) of its foreign operations or affiliates, not that of its *own* assets, liabilities, revenues and expenses. Even though not required to do so, many companies reporting under Canadian GAAP appear to establish the currency of measurement for their own Canadian operations. This is apparent from the fact that some Canadian companies present their current financial statements in US dollars. IAS 21 considers all elements not denominated in the functional currency to be expressed in foreign currencies that need to be translated. Note that one cannot assume that the functional currency is the currency of the country where an entity operates. For example, a company located in Canada could have the US dollar as its functional currency. If the company had a subsidiary in Japan, that subsidiary would not automatically have the Yen as its functional currency. If that subsidiary served as a direct extension of the Canadian parent company's operations, the US dollar might well be its functional currency.

The adoption of the functional currency approach could simplify foreign currency translation procedures. Only one translation method would be required. It would not be necessary to determine (as required by CICA 1651) whether a foreign operation is integrated into the reporting entity or is self-sustaining. This apparent major change in principles might, however, not have a great impact in practice.

Determination of the Functional Currency

An entity's functional currency is a matter of fact, not choice. Each individual entity included in a reporting entity's financial statements (parent, subsidiary, associate, joint venture or branch) must determine its own functional currency and measure its results and financial position in that currency. There is no "group" functional currency even though a parent company and corporate headquarters might have their own functional currencies.

IAS 21 gives specific guidance, which includes primary and secondary indicators, as well as additional factors that will help management determine an entity's functional currency. The table below summarizes this guidance.

Indicators	Evaluation	Example
Primary (IAS 21.9)	*Functional currency is:*	*Functional currency is the local currency.*
Sales and cash inflows	The currency in which sales prices for goods and services are denominated and settled.	Local sales market exists and products are priced and revenues are collected primarily in local currency.
	The currency of the country whose competitive forces and regulations mainly determine the sales prices of its goods and services.	Sales prices are determined locally rather than internationally.
Expenses and cash outflows	The currency that mainly influences labour, material and other costs of providing goods or services.	Labour, material and other operating costs are primarily sourced and incurred locally.
Secondary (IAS 21.10)	*Sometimes the functional currency is:*	*Functional currency is the local currency.*
Financing activities	The currency in which funds from financing activities are generated.	Financing is raised and servicing generated by the entity's local operation.
Retention of operating income	The currency in which receipts from operating activities are usually retained.	Excess working capital balance invested in local currency.
Others (IAS 21.11): considered only if not obvious	*Additional factors to be considered:*	*Functional currency is the local currency.*
Degree of autonomy	The degree of autonomy for carrying out activities (are activities an extension of the reporting entity's?).	Operations (cash collections and disbursements, borrowings) all substantially in local currency.
Frequency of transactions with reporting entity	Importance of inter-company transactions with the reporting entity.	Few inter-company transactions with the reporting entity.
Cash-flow impact on reporting entity	The relationship between the entity's cash flows and those of the reporting entity (are cash flows readily available for remittance to the reporting entity?).	Most cash flows are in local currency, with no direct impact on reporting entity's cash flows.
Financing	The reliance on the reporting entity for servicing existing and normally expected debt obligations.	Funding and servicing assured by funds generated by the entity's operation.

Generally, the primary indicators will serve to identify an entity's functional currency. When they do not, management has to also look at the secondary indicators and use its judgement to determine what the functional currency is (i.e., decide what currency most faithfully represents the economic effects of the underlying transactions, events and conditions). It is expected that most companies operating in Canada will use the Canadian or sometimes the US dollar as their functional currencies.

CICA 1651 does not provide a hierarchy of indicators for determining functional currencies. It merely lists certain factors for determining whether a foreign operation is integrated into the reporting entity or is a self-sustaining one. Since IAS 21 provides more detailed guidance than CICA 1651, its implementation should result in a more uniform application of foreign currency translation requirements.

Presentation Currency

Under IAS 21, an entity may choose a currency different from its functional currency (or currencies) for presenting its financial statements. Though the subject of presentation currency is not directly addressed, nothing in CICA 1651 prevents a company from choosing a particular currency to present its financial statements.

According to Canadian GAAP, an entity with operations in foreign countries may use different currencies for measuring its transactions. The approach under Canadian GAAP is similar to the one described in IAS 21:

- the currency of measurement for each of an entity's domestic and foreign operations (referred to as the operation's functional currency under IFRS) is not a matter of free choice;

- CICA 1651 and EIC-130 provide guidance on determining the currency of measurement of an operation, as well as the accounting required, when economic facts and circumstances change;

- while Canadian GAAP do not provide a free choice in the selection of the functional currency, they do not prohibit the selection of a reporting currency (referred as presentation currency under IAS 21) that differs from the functional currency. Consequently, an entity may choose any reporting currency that it deems "reasonable" (as noted in EIC-130) to its particular circumstances.

Companies will usually publish their financial reports using their functional currency because not doing so might result in misleading financial statements. Consequently, IAS 21 requires additional information if an entity decides to use a presentation currency that differs from its functional currency, including:

- the fact that the presentation currency is not the functional currency;

- disclosure of the functional currency; and

- the reason for using a different presentation currency.

Changes in Functional Currency

Functional currency reflects the economics underlying an entity's transactions, events and conditions. Consequently, any change in that currency should be rare and would occur only if there are significant changes in an entity's operations (e.g., a change in currency that mainly influences the sales prices of goods and services).

IAS 21 requires that any change in an entity's functional currency be accounted for prospectively. Any change in the functional currency of either the reporting entity or a significant foreign operation should be disclosed, including the reason for the change.

CICA 1651 has similar requirements. Changes of unit of measurement are accounted for prospectively to reflect new economic facts and circumstances affecting foreign operations.

Introduction of the Euro

SIC 7 deals with accounting for the euro introduction. Although this topic might be viewed as historical, it still applies when a reporting entity's affiliate is located in a country that joins the European Community in a current reporting period. Essentially, SIC 7 requires the application of IAS 21 when the changeover takes place.

Illustrative Disclosures:

Extract 10(1) – Functional currency approach

> **Océ N.V. (Financial Statements 2007), page 87**
> **Summary of Significant Accounting Policies (in part)**
> **Foreign currency translation (in part)**
> Items included in the financial statements of each of the Group's entities are measured using the currency of the primary economic environment in which the entity operates ['the functional currency'].

Commentary: This is a typical note that reflects the application of IAS 21 requirements: determining the functional currency of each entity of the consolidated group. Because CICA 1651 does not require functional currency identification, the above presentation would be new in principle.

Note, however, that some Canadian companies have adopted IAS 21 approach. As indicated previously, more than a quarter of the 200 Canadian companies surveyed in *Financial Reporting in Canada* (32nd Edition) use the term "functional currency." Below are two extracts obtained from financial statements of two Canadian companies included in that sample which specified the functional currencies used by *all* entities in a group (including the parent). All disclosures conform to IAS 21 requirements.

Inmet Mining Corporation (AR – 2006), page 91
Significant accounting polices (in part)
Basis of presentation and consolidation (in part)
The US dollar is the functional currency of Çayeli and Ok Tedi, and the euro is the functional currency of Pyhäsalmi and Las Cruces. The Canadian dollar is the functional currency of Troilus and Corporate.

Intrawest Corporation (AR – 2006), page 30
2. Significant accounting policies (in part)
(s) Foreign currency translation (in part):

These consolidated financial statements are presented in U.S. dollars. The majority of the Company's operations is located in the United States and are conducted in U.S. dollars. The Company's Canadian and European operations use the Canadian dollar and the Euro, respectively, as their functional currencies. In addition, the Company's subsidiary Abercrombie & Kent Group of Companies, S.A. operates in many countries and each branch operates in its own country's functional currency.

Extract 10(2) – Functional currency approach

> **Alcoa World Alumina and Chemicals (Form 20-F – 2006), page F-55**
> **A. Summary of Significant Accounting Policies (in part)**
> **Foreign Currency**
> The local currency is the functional currency for AWAC's significant operations outside the U.S., except in Brazil, Jamaica and Suriname, which use the U.S. dollar. The determination of the functional currency in these countries is made based on the appropriate economic and management indicators.

Commentary: In this extract, the company indicates that it has determined the functional currency outside the US (except in Brazil, Jamaica and Suriname, where the currency is the US dollar) to be the local currency. This means that CICA 1651 would consider these foreign operations (other than the ones located in Brazil, Jamaica and Suriname) to be "self-sustaining."

Under CICA 1651 operations located in Brazil, Jamaica and Suriname might either (1) be integrated into the parent or (2) be self-sustaining but using the US dollar as a functional currency. It is possible that US dollar could be the functional currency, since aluminium is traded on the markets in US dollars.

Note that under IAS 21 the company would not be able to justify the use of the US dollar by arguing that those three countries had a hyperinflation economy (if, indeed, any of the three countries had high inflation rates). (See our discussion on highly inflationary economies below).

Extract 10(3) – Presentation currency is not the functional currency

OAO Baltika Breweries (Financial statements 2007), pages 12 and 13

2 Basis of preparation (in part)

(c) Functional and presentation currency

The national currency of the Russian Federation is the Russian Rouble ("RUR"), which is the Company's functional currency and the functional currency of the majority of the Company's subsidiaries, because it reflects the economic substance of the underling events and circumstances of the Group.

These consolidated financial statements are presented in euro ("EURO") since management believes that this currency is more useful for the users of the consolidated financial statements. All financial information presented in EURO has been rounded to the nearest thousand, except where otherwise stated.

The RUR is not a readily convertible currency outside the Russian Federation and, accordingly, any conversion of RUR to EURO should not be construed as a representation that the RUR amounts have been, could be, or will be in the future, convertible into EURO at the exchange rate disclosed, or at any other exchange rate.

Commentary: This extract indicates that the company's presentation currency (euro) differs from its functional currency (RUR). The company could not have used the euro as a functional currency based on the fact that the RUR is not a readily convertible currency. The company did disclose the reason for using a different presentation currency (financial statements users' needs).

Extract 10(4) – Functional and presentation currencies change

Signet Group plc (AR 2007), page 37

Critical accounting policies (in part)

Foreign currency translation (in part)

The functional currency of the parent company moved to US dollars from 5 February 2007. At the same time the reporting currency of the Group changed to US dollars. The relative size of the Group's US and UK businesses means that the exposure of the Group's reported results to exchange rate fluctuations will be reduced.

Commentary: Here, the company indicates that it has modified the both the parent company's functional currency and the group's presentation currency (to US dollars). Justification of the changes is brief.

As indicated before, although CICA 1651 does not call for the functional currency approach, some companies have adopted it. One of the companies included in *Financial Reporting in Canada* (32nd Edition) changed its functional currency in 2006. An extract of its disclosure, which also complies with IAS 21, is presented below. Note that the company not only reported the change in functional currency, but also the reason for the change.

Silver Wheaton Corp. (AR – 2006), page 26

Change in functional and reporting currency

Effective September 1, 2004, the functional currency of the Company was changed from the Canadian to the United States dollar.

This resulted from a change in the nature of the business as all sales and the majority of expenses occur in United States dollars.

Concurrent with this change in functional currency, the Company adopted the United States dollar as its reporting currency. In accordance with Canadian GAAP, the change was effected by translating assets and liabilities, at the end of prior reporting periods, at the existing United States/Canadian dollar foreign exchange spot rate, while earnings, losses and shareholders' equity were translated at historic rates.

Extract 10(5) – Functional currency change

> **Holcim Ltd (AR 2006), page 102**
>
> **Accounting policies (in part)**
>
> **Foreign currency translation (in part)**
>
> As from January 1, 2005 a new functional currency was adopted for certain Group companies in order to reflect a change in the underlying economic conditions of the countries concerned (mainly Latin America). Consequently, the respective companies converted all balance sheet positions into the new functional currency on the basis of the exchange rate prevailing at the reference date of January 1, 2005. For non-monetary items, the resulting translated amounts represent their historical cost. The impact of changes in the functional currency has not been presented retrospectively.

Commentary: The company indicates that it has modified the functional currency for certain affiliates and explains how it has accounted for such changes. The justification for the change in functional currency is brief.

Foreign Currency Transactions

Initial Measurement

Foreign currency transactions are transactions expressed in a currency other than an entity's functional currency. According to both IAS 21 and CICA 1651, foreign currency transactions are recorded using the exchange rate (spot rate) at the date of the transaction. In certain cases, an approximation of the spot rate at time of transaction is used. For example, revenues and expenses denominated in foreign currencies are often translated using an average rate because the latter might approximate the actual exchange rate of the transaction.

The application of the above requirements may create a number of problems in practice, for example, when the transaction date cannot be clearly determined or when the average rate cannot be used as an approximate actual transaction rate. Neither IAS 21 nor CICA 1651 suggest guidance for such situations.

Subsequent Measurement

Foreign currency transactions may give rise to balances (assets and liabilities) expressed in a foreign currency at the reporting date. The procedure for translating such balances into an entity's functional currency will depend on whether they represent monetary or non-monetary items.

Monetary Items

Monetary assets and liabilities are: (a) units of currency held or (b) amounts receivable or payable in a number of units of currency that is fixed or determinable. Obvious examples of monetary items are financial assets, such as cash and receivables, and financial liabilities, such as debt and provisions, that are settled in cash. The standards also specify that "The essential feature of a monetary item is a right to receive (or an obligation to deliver) a fixed or determinable number of units of currency. Examples include: pensions and other employee benefits to be paid in cash; provisions that are to be settled in cash; and cash dividends that are recognized as a liability. Similarly, a contract to receive (or deliver) a variable number of the entity's own equity instruments or a variable amount of assets in which the fair value to be received (or delivered) equals a fixed or determinable number of units of currency is a monetary item."

In certain circumstances, it may not be readily apparent whether an item is monetary or non-monetary, for example:

*   Deferred taxes: Although IAS 21 does not specify whether this balance sheet element is a monetary or non-monetary item, CICA 1651 indicates that deferred (future) income taxes are monetary items.
*   Deposits or progress payments: neither IAS 21 nor CICA 1651 specify whether such amounts should be regarded as monetary or non-monetary items. A possible approach to deciding what they are is to examine the nature of the payments and the terms of the contract. If they are prepayments or progress payments, they would be considered to be non-monetary; if the payments are refundable, however, they could be possibly regarded as monetary.

According to IAS 21 and CICA 1651, monetary assets and liabilities denominated in a foreign currency should be translated into the entity's functional currency (measurement currency) using the closing rate at the balance-sheet date (spot rate).

Exchange differences resulting from the settlement of monetary items or from using subsequent translation rates that differ from those used at initial recording are recognized in income. There is an exception to this rule: with monetary items designated as effective hedging instruments in a cash flow or a net investment hedge, exchange differences could be recognized as a component of other comprehensive income.

Non-monetary Items

Non-monetary items are all items that are not monetary items. Their essential feature is the absence of a right to receive (or an obligation to deliver) a fixed or determinable number of units of currency.

Typical examples of non-monetary items include inventories, property, plant and equipment and intangible assets.

IAS 21 and CICA 1651 require the following measurements subsequent to original recognition of non-monetary items:

*   Non-monetary assets and liabilities accounted for at historical cost are translated at each balance-sheet date into the entity's functional currency (measurement currency) at historical rates. No retranslation is required.
*   IAS 21 requires that non-monetary assets measured at fair value be translated into the entity's functional currency at rates applicable when the fair values were determined. This differs from CICA 1651, which requires that translation should use the exchange rate in effect at the balance sheet date.

Measuring non-monetary assets at fair value might be required in three situations; when an entity:

*   Adjusts the carrying amounts of property, plant, equipment or inventories to reflect declines in the recoverable amount or net realizable value. Two values have to be calculated: (1) the net realizable value or recoverable amount translated at the closing rate at the date that the applicable values were determined (IAS 21) or balance sheet closing rate (CICA 1651) and (2) the cost or carrying amount translated at the exchange rate at the date the item was last measured on a historical cost basis. If value (1) is lower than (2), an impairment loss in the functional currency is recognized.
*   Selects the revaluation model permitted under IFRS to measure certain assets such as property, plant, or equipment at fair value.

- Uses fair value as an option for subsequent measurements of items such as investment properties.

Exchange differences resulting from non-monetary items disposal or from subsequent translation at rates different from those used at initial recording (arising from fair value re-measurement) are recognized in income. An exception to this rule concerns gains or losses on a non-monetary item recognized directly in equity (other comprehensive income). In this case, any exchange component of that gain or loss is recognized also directly in equity (other comprehensive income).

Financial Assets Classified as Available for Sale

"Available for sale" investments can consist of monetary or non-monetary assets expressed in foreign currencies. Under IAS 39, *Financial Instruments: Recognition and Measurement* and CICA 3855, *Financial Instruments — Recognition and Measurement*, foreign exchange gain or losses on such financial assets are accounted for differently depending on whether the financial assets are monetary or non-monetary. Under IAS 39, the foreign exchange gains or losses on monetary financial assets are recognized in the income statement even though *other* fair value gains and losses are included in other comprehensive income while under CICA 3855 all fair value gains or losses are included in other comprehensive income. For non-monetary financial assets, both IAS 39 and CICA 3855 require that *all* fair value gains or losses, including the foreign exchange portion, are recognized as a component of other comprehensive income.

Illustrative Disclosures:

Extract 10(6) – Foreign currency transactions

> **Alumina Limited (Form 20-F 2006), page F8**
> **D FOREIGN CURRENCY TRANSLATION (in part)**
> **Transactions and balances**
> Foreign currency transactions are initially translated into Australian currency using the exchange rates prevailing at the dates of the transactions.
> Foreign exchange gains and losses resulting from the settlement of such transactions and from the translation at year end exchange rates of monetary assets and liabilities denominated in foreign currencies are recognised in the income statement, except when deferred in equity as qualifying cash flow hedges and qualifying net investment hedges.

Commentary: In this extract, the company provides a brief description of translation procedures used for foreign currency transactions and monetary assets and liabilities denominated in foreign currencies held at the end of the year. It specifies the special hedge accounting rule for qualifying net investment hedges. This disclosure also conforms to Canadian GAAP.

Extract 10(7) – Foreign currency transactions and balances

> **BNP PARIBAS (Registration Document 2007), page 118**
> **1.c FINANCIAL ASSETS AND FINANCIAL LIABILITIES (in part)**
> **1.c.4 Foreign currency transactions**
> The methods used to account for assets and liabilities relating to foreign currency transactions entered into by the Group, and to measure the foreign exchange risk arising on such transactions, depends upon whether the asset or liability in question is classified as a monetary or a non-monetary item.
> **Monetary assets and liabilities (1) expressed in foreign currencies**
> Monetary assets and liabilities expressed in foreign currencies are translated into the functional currency of the relevant Group entity at the closing rate. Translation differences are recognised in the profit and loss account, except for those arising on financial instruments designated as a cash flow hedge or a net foreign investment hedge, which are recognised in shareholders' equity.

BNP PARIBAS (Registration Document 2007) (continued)

Non-monetary assets and liabilities expressed in foreign currencies

Non-monetary assets may be measured either at historical cost or at fair value. Non-monetary assets expressed in foreign currencies are translated using the exchange rate at the date of the transaction if they are measured at historical cost, and at the closing rate if they are measured at fair value.

Translation differences on non-monetary assets expressed in foreign currencies and measured at fair value (variable-income securities) are recognised in the profit and loss account if the asset is classified in "Financial assets at fair value through profit or loss", and in shareholders' equity if the asset is classified in "Available-for-sale financial assets", unless the financial asset in question is designated as an item hedged against foreign exchange risk in a fair value hedging relationship, in which case the translation difference is recognised in the profit and loss account.

Commentary: This extract provides detailed explanations of the translation procedures used for foreign currency transactions and for both monetary and non-monetary assets and liabilities denominated in foreign currencies at the balance sheet date. Foreign currency gains or losses on investments classified as "available-for-sale" are included in income if they are monetary (implied from the disclosure) and in equity (as a part of other comprehensive income as required by IAS 1 as subsequently amended) if they are non-monetary. This disclosure also conforms to Canadian GAAP.

Note, however that under Canadian GAAP all gains or losses on monetary securities classified as available for sale would be included in other comprehensive income.

Extract 10(8) – Foreign currency transactions and balances

Stora Enso Oyj (AR 2007), page 120

Note 1 Accounting Principles (in part)

Foreign Currency Transactions

Transactions in foreign currencies are recorded at the rate of exchange prevailing at the transaction date, but at the end of the month, foreign currency-denominated receivables and liabilities are translated using the month-end exchange rate.

Foreign exchange differences for operating items are recorded in the appropriate income statement account before operating profit, and, for financial assets and liabilities, are entered in the financial items of the Income Statement, except when deferred in equity as qualifying net investment hedges. Translation differences on non-monetary financial assets, such as equities classified as Available-for-Sale, are included in equity.

Commentary: Here we see explanations of the translation procedures related to foreign currency transactions and to foreign currency denominated receivables and liabilities expressed in foreign currencies. Foreign currency gains or losses presentation in the income statement is specified. This disclosure conforms to Canadian GAAP.

Extract 10(9) – Foreign currency transactions and balances

Transnet Ltd (AR 2007), page 154

ACCOUNTING POLICIES (in part)

FOREIGN CURRENCY (in part)

Foreign currency transactions

Transactions in currencies other than the entity's functional currency are defined as foreign currency transactions. Transactions in foreign currencies are translated at exchange rates ruling on transaction dates. Monetary assets and liabilities denominated in foreign currencies are translated into the functional currency at the rate of exchange ruling at the balance sheet date.

Non-monetary assets and liabilities that are measured in terms of historical cost in a foreign currency are translated at the exchange rates ruling at the original transaction date. Non-monetary assets and liabilities that are carried at fair value denominated in the foreign currency are translated into the functional currency at the exchange rate ruling when the fair value was determined.

All gains or losses arising on translation are recognised in the income statement and are classified as finance costs.

Commentary: The company provides explanations of the translation procedures related to (1) foreign currency transactions, (2) monetary assets and liabilities denominated in foreign currencies, (3) non-monetary assets and liabilities measured at historical cost in a foreign currency and (4) non-monetary assets and liabilities carried at fair value denominated in the foreign currency. Note that the exchange rate used is the exchange rate for translating item (4) at the date the fair value was determined (should be the balance sheet date according to CICA 1651). Besides differences in exchange rate used in (4), this disclosure also conforms to Canadian GAAP.

Foreign Currency Financial Statements

Translating Financial Statements into the Presentation Currency

Translated financial statements are frequently required for preparing consolidated statements or when applying the equity method. IAS 21 and CICA 1651 specify (a) the exchange rates to be used for such translation and (b) how a reporting entity should report any changes in exchange rates in its financial statements.

CICA 1651 identifies two types of foreign operations: integrated (which would have the same functional currency as the entity) and self-sustaining (which would have a functional currency different from the entity). Although IAS 21 does not provide such a classification, the relationship between an entity and its foreign operation is a factor in determining the functional currency of the foreign operation.

Both IAS 21 and CICA 1651 require that each entity in a group complete the following steps:

1. determine the functional currency of the foreign operation based on its own economic environment;

2. prepare financial statements in the functional currency; and

3. translate those financial statements into the group's presentation currency for consolidation purposes.

Completing Step 3, as required by IAS 21, will involve the following (depending on whether or not the functional currency is that of a hyperinflationary economy):

1. If the functional currency is not that of a hyperinflationary economy:

    a. translate assets and liabilities for each balance sheet at the closing rate for that balance sheet date;

    b. translate revenues and expenses for each income statement at the rates in place at the date of the transaction;

    c. translate cash flows in the cash flow statement at transaction rates; and

    d. translate resulting exchange differences recognized separately in other comprehensive income (equity).

2. If the functional currency is that of a hyperinflationary economy:

    a. all amounts (assets, liabilities, equity items, revenues and expenses) are translated at the closing rate at the date of the most recent balance sheet; except:

    b. when amounts are translated into the currency of a non-hyperinflationary economy, comparative amounts must be the current year amounts presented in the relevant prior year financial statements (i.e., figures are not adjusted for subsequent changes in the price level or subsequent changes in the exchange rates).

Note that the above translation procedures would also be applied under CICA 1651 since the individual entities would be self-sustaining (provided that functional currency is not that of a hyperinflationary economy).

Particular Issues Related to Consolidation

Goodwill and Fair Value Adjustments

These amounts are treated as assets and liabilities of the foreign operation. Consequently:

- they are expressed in the functional currency of the foreign operation; and
- translated at the closing rate.

Non-controlling Interests

A reporting entity may have a foreign operation that is not wholly owned. IAS 21 requires that a representative portion of the accumulated exchange differences resulting from translation of the financial statements of the foreign operation into the reporting entity's presentation currency be attributed to the non-controlling Interests and recognized as non-controlling interests in the consolidated balance sheet. Even though CICA 1651 does not address this issue, the same treatment would likely also be required under Canadian GAAP.

Intra-group Balances and Transactions

A reporting entity should apply normal consolidation procedures to incorporate the results and financial position of a foreign operation, including the elimination of intra-group balances and transactions. IAS 21 requires that exchange differences resulting from intra-group monetary items that are not part of the net investment in a foreign operation should be recognized in profit or loss. Even though CICA 1651 does not address this issue, the same treatment would also be required under Canadian GAAP.

Difference in the Reporting Dates

IAS 27, *Consolidated and Separate Financial Statements*, which requires the difference between the reporting date of the subsidiaries' financial statements and that of the consolidated group to be less than three months, applies. This would allow the reporting entity to use the exchange rate in place at the foreign operation's balance-sheet date to translate foreign operation's assets and liabilities. This exchange rate should be adjusted to take into account any significant changes in exchange rates up to the balance sheet date of the reporting entity. Even though CICA 1651 does not address this issue, the same treatment would also be required under Canadian GAAP.

Disposal of a Foreign Operation

Disposal (complete or partial) of a foreign operation could take the form of a sale, liquidation and abandonment. Under CICA 1651, any dividend paid by a foreign operation will be considered as a partial disposal. It appears that Canadian GAAP reflects various views on the treatment of dividend distributions. One point of view that might reflect the substance of such a distribution would be to presume dividends are not partial disposals if their amounts are lower than current net income. If dividends exceed the increase in the net investment realized through earnings, however, they would be considered to be a partial disposal. Particular problems might arise with quarterly reports.

Under both IAS 21 and CICA 1651, the cumulative amount of deferred exchange differences related to a foreign operation is transferred from accumulated other comprehensive income to the income statement when the gain or loss on disposal is recognized. Only a proportionate share of the related accumulated exchange differences is recognized for a partial disposal.

Highly Inflationary Economies

Accounting Requirements

An entity reporting in a hyperinflationary economy cannot adopt a hard currency as its functional currency just to avoid the use of IAS 29. It must use the domestic currency if the latter is its functional currency. If the functional currency is that of an hyper-inflationary economy, an entity – whether preparing consolidated, stand-alone financial statements or financial information for incorporation into another's financial statements – should restate its financial statements in terms of the measuring unit current at the balance sheet date. These financial statements are referred to as "purchasing power adjusted financial statements," which are then translated (as required) at the closing rate at the end of the current period.

Under CICA 1651 purchasing power adjustments are not permitted if the functional currency of a foreign operation is highly inflationary. The financial statements of a self-sustaining foreign operation in a highly inflationary economy are not adjusted, but instead are translated using the method applicable to integrated foreign operations (translation procedures corresponds to the ones used for foreign currency transactions).

General Characteristics of a Hyperinflationary Environment

CICA 1651 does not discuss that issue. IAS 29 identifies the general characteristics of a hyperinflationary environment as:

- people accumulate wealth in non-monetary assets or in a stable foreign currency;
- monetary amounts are expressed in terms of a relatively stable foreign currency;
- prices for credit sales and purchases are calculated to compensate for the expected loss of purchasing power during the credit period;
- interest rates, wages and prices are linked to a price index;
- the cumulative inflation rate over three years approaches, or exceeds, 100%.

IAS 29 indicates that an economy ceases to be hyperinflationary if the cumulative inflation rate drops below 100% in a three-year period. This quantitative measure would need to be evaluated in the context of overall economic developments and trends. Judgement is involved in determining when an economy is no longer hyper-inflationary. All entities in such an economic environment should cease to apply hyper-inflation reporting from the same date to ensure that financial statements are comparable from entity to entity.

Preparing Purchasing Power Adjusted Financial Statements

To prepare such statements, an entity has to:

- select a general price index;
- segregate financial statements elements into monetary and non-monetary items;
- restate non-monetary items;
- restate the income statement;
- calculate the monetary gain or loss;
- prepare the cash flow statement with recognition of inflationary effects; and
- restate of the corresponding figures.

Illustrative Disclosures:

Extract 10(10) – Foreign subsidiaries

Alumina Limited (AR 2006), page 08

D FOREIGN CURRENCY TRANSLATION (in part)

Controlled foreign entities

The results and financial position of all the Group entities that have a functional currency different from the presentation currency are translated into the presentation currency as follows:

- assets and liabilities for each balance sheet presented are translated at the closing rate at the date of that balance sheet;

- income and expenses for each income statement are translated at average rates (unless this is not a reasonable approximation of the cumulative effect of the rates prevailing on the transaction dates, in which case income and expenses are translated at the dates of the transactions); and

- all resulting exchange differences are recognised as a separate component of equity.

On consolidation, exchange differences arising from the translation of any net investment in foreign entities, and of borrowings and other currency instruments designated as hedges of such investments, are taken to the translation reserve in shareholders' equity. When a foreign operation is sold or borrowings are repaid, a proportionate share of such exchange differences are recognised in the income statement as part of the gain or loss on sale.

Goodwill and fair value adjustments arising on the acquisition of a foreign entity are treated as assets and liabilities of the foreign entity and translated at the closing rate.

Commentary: In this extract, the company describes the translation procedures for subsidiaries. Translation adjustments include exchange differences resulting from translation procedures and from gains or losses on borrowings used as hedging instruments of net investment. The company also describes the subsequent accounting resulting from the sale of net investment and repayment of borrowing. Note that the goodwill is translated at the closing rate as required by IAS 21. CICA 1651 does not specify the exchange rate to use for goodwill translation but, conceptually, the historical rate should be used since goodwill would be considered to be a non-monetary item. All other disclosures are in line with CICA 1651 since subsidiaries would be considered to be self-sustaining.

Extract 10(11) – Foreign subsidiaries

Stora Enso Oyj (AR 2007), page 120

Note 1 Accounting Principles (in part)

Foreign Currency Translations – Subsidiaries

The Income Statements of subsidiaries, whose functional and presentational currencies are not Euros, are translated into the Group reporting currency using the average exchange rates for the year, whereas the Balance Sheets of such subsidiaries are translated using the exchange rates at the reporting date.

Exchange differences arising from the retranslation of the net investments in foreign entities, being non-Euro area foreign subsidiary and associated undertakings, and of financial instruments which are designated as and are hedges of such investments, are recorded directly in shareholders' equity in the Cumulative Translation Adjustment ("CTA"), as shown in the Consolidated Statement of Recognised Income & Expense and Note 28. The cumulative translation differences of divestments and liquidations are combined with their gain or loss on disposal. CTA is also expensed on the repayment of share capital, return of investment and any partial disposal of a business unit.

Commentary: Here, the company describes the translation procedures for subsidiaries. Translation adjustments include exchange differences resulting from translation procedures and from gains or losses on hedging instruments of net investments. Subsequent accounting related to cumulative translation adjustments (CTA) are described and include divestments, liquidations, repayment of share capital, return of investment (through dividends probably) and any partial disposal of a business unit. All disclosures are in line with CICA 1651 since subsidiaries would be considered to be self-sustaining.

Extract 10(12) – Foreign operations

Vodafone Group Plc (Annual Report 2007), page 98
2. Significant accounting policies (in part)

For the purpose of presenting Consolidated Financial Statements, the assets and liabilities of entities with a functional currency other than sterling are expressed in sterling using exchange rates prevailing on the balance sheet date. Income and expense items and cash flows are translated at the average exchange rates for the period and exchange differences arising are recognised directly in equity. Such translation differences are recognised in the income statement in the period in which a foreign operation is disposed of.

Goodwill and fair value adjustments arising on the acquisition of a foreign operation are treated as assets and liabilities of the foreign operation and translated accordingly.

In respect of all foreign operations, any exchange differences that have arisen before 1 April 2004, the date of transition to IFRS, are deemed to be nil and will be excluded from the determination of any subsequent profit or loss on disposal.

Commentary: This extract describes the translation procedures used to prepare consolidated financial statements. The translation procedures are in line with CICA 1651 since subsidiaries would be considered to be self-sustaining.

Extract 10(13) – Foreign operations

DaimlerChrysler AG (IFRS Consolidated Financial Statements 2006), page 10
1. Summary of significant accounting policies (in part)
Foreign currency translation

Transactions in foreign currency are translated at the relevant foreign exchange rates prevailing at the transaction date. Subsequent gains and losses from the remeasurement of financial assets and liabilities denominated in foreign currency are recognized in profit and loss (except for available for sale equity instruments and financial liabilities designated as a hedge of a net investment in a foreign operation).

The assets and liabilities of foreign companies, where the functional currency is not the euro, are translated into euro using period end exchange rates. The resulting translation adjustments are recorded directly in equity. The consolidated statements of income and the consolidated statements of cash flows are translated into euro using average exchange rates during the respective periods.

The exchange rates of the US dollar, as the most significant foreign currency for DaimlerChrysler, were as follows:

	2006	2005
	€1 =	€1 =
Exchange rate at December 31	**1.3170**	1.1797
Average exchange rates		
First quarter	**1.2023**	1.3113
Second quarter	**1.2582**	1.2594
Third quarter	**1.2743**	1.2199
Fourth quarter	**1.2887**	1.1897

page 15
2. Explanation of transition to IFRS

Cumulative translation differences. Under IAS 21, "The Effects of Changes in Foreign Exchange Rates", differences arising from the translation of financial statements that are prepared using a currency other than the presentation currency of the consolidated financial statements are recognized as a separate component of equity. DaimlerChrysler made use of the exemption in IFRS 1 that such translation differences may be deemed zero at the date of transition.

Commentary: The company describes the translation procedures used to prepare consolidated financial statements. The translation procedures are in line with CICA 1651 since subsidiaries would be considered to be self-sustaining. In addition, the company provides a table detailing exchange rates used in the translation procedures. Note that the company has used an optional treatment allowed under IFRS 1 to bring previous cumulative adjustment to zero (see planning for implementation section).

Extract 10(14) – Foreign operations

Daimler AG (AR 2007), page 142

1. Summary of significant accounting policies (in part)

Foreign currency translation. Transactions in foreign currency are translated at the relevant foreign exchange rates prevailing at the transaction date. Subsequent gains and losses from the remeasurement of financial assets and liabilities denominated in foreign currency are recognized in profit and loss (except for available-for-sale equity instruments and financial liabilities designated as a hedge of a net investment in a foreign operation).

The assets and liabilities of foreign companies, where the functional currency is not the euro, are translated into euro using period end exchange rates. The translation adjustments generated after the transition to IFRS on January 1, 2005, are recorded directly in equity. The consolidated statements of income and cash flows are translated into euro using average exchange rates during the respective periods.

The exchange rates of the US dollar, as the most significant foreign currency for Daimler, were as follows:

		2007 €1 =	2006 €1 =	2005 €1 =
Exchange rate at December 31		**1.4721**	1.3170	1.1797
Average exchange rates	First quarter	**1.3106**	1.2023	1.3113
	Second quarter	**1.3481**	1.2582	1.2594
	Third quarter	**1.3738**	1.2743	1.2199
	Fourth quarter	**1.4487**	1.2887	1.1897

Commentary: This extract was obtained from the financial statements of the same company cited in the previous extract. It includes the disclosures for the same issues for the following year. Note that, in this extract, the company does not mention the optional treatment allowed under IFRS 1 as that was noted in 2006.

Extract 10(15) – Cumulative translation adjustments

Casino Guichard – Perrachon (AR 2006), page 103

NOTE 4.26.2 Other equity (in part)

Additional paid-in capital, treasury shares and reserves (in part)

(vii)*Translation reserve*

The translation reserve corresponds to cumulative exchange gains and losses on translating the equity of foreign subsidiaries and receivables and payables corresponding to the Group's net investment in these subsidiaries, at the closing rate.

Translation reserves by country

€millions	Attributable to equity holders of the parent			Attributable to minority interests			Total closing translation reserve
	At 1 January 2006	Exchange differences for the period	At 31 December 2006	At 1 January 2006	Exchange differences for the period	At 31 December 2006	
Brazil	246	(33)	214	0	0	0	213
Argentina	3	(13)	(10)	0		0	(10)
Colombia	46	(19)	27	0		0	27
Uruguay	27	(16)	11	0	0	0	11
Venezuela	(17)	(5)	(23)	(4)	(1)	(5)	(28)
United States	11	(18)	(7)	7	(12)	(4)	(11)
Taiwan	6	(3)	3	0		0	3
Thailand	9	9	18	2	5	8	26
Poland	152	(96)	57	0	0	0	57
Indian Ocean	(1)	(2)	(3)	0	(2)	(2)	(5)
Total	**482**	**(194)**	**288**	**6**	**(10)**	**(4)**	**284**

The decrease in 2006 concerned Poland and included €83 million reclassified to the income statement on disposal of the entities concerned.

Commentary: Here, we see detailed disclosures of translation adjustments by country and the amount allocated to minority interest. This presentation is in line with CICA 1651.

Extract 10(16) – Foreign operations

GlaxoSmithKline (AR 2007), page 95
2 Accounting policies (in part)
Foreign currency translation

Foreign currency transactions are booked in the functional currency of the Group company at the exchange rate ruling on the date of transaction. Foreign currency monetary assets and liabilities are retranslated into the functional currency at rates of exchange ruling at the balance sheet date. Exchange differences are included in the income statement.

On consolidation, assets and liabilities, including related goodwill, of overseas subsidiaries, associates and joint ventures, are translated into Sterling at rates of exchange ruling at the balance sheet date. The results and cash flows of overseas subsidiaries, associates and joint ventures are translated into Sterling using average rates of exchange.

Exchange adjustments arising when the opening net assets and the profits for the year retained by overseas subsidiaries, associates and joint ventures are translated into Sterling, less exchange differences arising on related foreign currency borrowings which hedge the Group's net investment in these operations, are taken to a separate component of equity.

When translating into Sterling the assets, liabilities, results and cash flows of overseas subsidiaries, associates and joint ventures which are reported in currencies of hyper-inflationary economies, adjustments are made to reflect current price levels. Any loss on net monetary assets is charged to the consolidated income statement.

Commentary: In this extract, the company describes the translation procedures for subsidiaries, associates and joint ventures. Translation adjustments include exchange differences resulting from translation procedures and from gains or losses on borrowings used as hedging instruments of the net investment. The company also provides a brief mention of the procedures used when subsidiaries, associates and joint ventures report financial statements expressed in currencies of hyperinflationary economies. All disclosures other than the one related to financial statements expressed in currencies of hyperinflationary economies are in line with CICA 1651 since subsidiaries would be considered to be self-sustaining.

Extract 10(17) – Companies operating in hyperinflationary economies

Benetton Group Spa (Form 20-F 2006)
Part III
Item 17: Financial Statements
Explanatory notes
7. Supplementary Information (in part)

Accounting treatment of companies operating in hyperinflationary economies.

The Group has not consolidated any subsidiaries in 2006 which operate in hyperinflationary economies. In 2005 the Turkish subsidiary's financial statements were expressed in New Turkish Lira (local currency and reporting currency) at historic cost, in the unit of measurement applicable on the closing date of the reference period. The values relevant to non-cash balance sheet items were revalued applying the variation of the general price index which has occurred between the capture date and the closing date of the reference period. The statements revalued in this way were then converted into the presentation currency of the consolidated income statement (Euro) using the method described in the paragraph "Consolidation methods" for companies using a reporting currency other than the Euro, with the exception of income statement items which were converted at the period-end exchange rate. The profit or loss on the cash position was attributed to the income statement, as financial income or a financial expense.

Commentary: The company indicates that it has not consolidated any subsidiaries operating in hyperinflationary economies in the current year. It does, though, describe the procedures used in the previous year (2005), which do not conform with CICA 1651 requirements because purchasing power adjustments are not permitted.

Convenience Translation

An entity may proceed with what is called "convenience translation" to display financial statements or other financial information in a currency that differs from either its functional or presentation currency. This is accomplished by simply translating all amounts at end-of-period exchange rates. Since the resulting financial information does not comply with IFRS, IAS 21 requires the following additional disclosures:

- clear indication that the information is supplementary and is distinct from the information that complies with IFRS;

- identification of the currency in which the supplementary information is displayed; and

- the entity's functional currency and the method of translation used to determine the supplementary information.

Though CICA 1651 does not address convenience translation issues, it is mentioned in EIC-130 (see commentary below).

Note that EIC-130 notes that convenience translation is supplementary information and provides the following guidance on how to present that information:

- Supplementary information should be presented only for the most recent fiscal year and any subsequent interim period.

- All items in the supplementary financial information (including income and cash flow amounts) should be translated using the exchange rate as of the most recent balance sheet included in the financial statements. If it is materially different, however, a more current exchange rate should be used.

- This information should be clearly identified as supplementary information.

- If a translation of convenience is used, the following disclosures should be made:
  o the method of translation used for presenting the supplementary information;
  o the exchange rate for translating the amounts; and
  o a caution as to the limited usefulness of the supplementary information.

The above requirements would be in line with those in IAS 21.

We examined whether the 200 Canadian companies sampled in *Financial Reporting in Canada* (32nd Edition) used convenience translation in their financial reports and observed that one company (NeuroChem) provided such information in its audited financial statements (see extract 10(20)).

Illustrative Disclosures:

Extract 10(18) – Limited convenience translation

TNT N.V. (AR 2006) Introduction and financial highlights, page X

We are domiciled in the Netherlands, which is one of the member states of the European Union (EU) that has adopted the euro as its currency. Accordingly, we have adopted the euro as our reporting currency. In this annual report the euro is also referred to as "€". For your convenience certain amounts in euro have been translated into United States dollars at an exchange rate of $1.3197 per €1.00. This is the noon buying rate in the City of New York on 29 December 2006 for cable transfers as certified by the Federal Reserve Bank of New York. References to "dollars", "US dollars" and "$" are references to United States dollars. The US dollar amounts presented are unaudited. Historical information on the dollar to euro exchange rate can be found in chapter 14, page 188. We do not represent that the US dollar amounts included in the US dollar convenience translations or any amounts translated from euro into any other currency could have been converted from euro at the rates indicated.

Commentary: The company indicates that it has presented some financial information (outside the financial statements) in a convenience currency (US dollars). It specifies clearly that these amounts are unaudited. The company did not report any convenience translated amounts in its financial statements, nor did it provide any convenience translated amounts in 2007.

Extract 10(19) – Convenience translation

Lafarge (AR on Form 20-F 2006)

Cover page

We publish our consolidated financial statements in euros. Solely for the convenience of the reader, this Annual Report contains translations into U.S. dollars of certain amounts in euros at the December 29, 2006 Noon Buying Rate of 1 euro = $1.3197.

Selected financial data: page 9

	AT OR FOR THE YEAR ENDED DECEMBER 31,			
	2006		2005	2004
(MILLION)	$**	€	€	€
BALANCE SHEETS				
ASSETS				
Non current assets	26,984	20,447	20,543	18,241
Current assets	12,362	9,367	7,352	6,259
Out of which assets held for sale	3,607	2,733		
TOTAL ASSETS	**39,346**	**29,814**	**27,895**	24,500
LIABILITIES				
Shareholder's equity – parent Company	13,729	10,403	9,758	7,782
Minority interests	1,836	1,391	2,571	2,119
Non current liabilities	15,650	11,859	9,707	9,867
Current liabilities	8,131	6,161	5,859	4,732
Out of which liabilities associated with assets held for sale	1,080	818		
TOTAL EQUITY AND LIABILITIES	**39,346**	**29,814**	**27,895**	24,500

** Amounts in U.S. dollars presented in the table have been translated solely for the convenience of the reader using the Noon Buying Rate on December 29, 2006 of €1= $1.3197.

Selected financial data: page 11

Dividends

			AT DECEMBER 31,			
	2006		2005	2004	2003	2002
	$ *	€	€	€	€	€
Total dividend paid (millions)	699 **	530 **	447	408	383	303
Basic dividend per share	3.96 **	3.00 **	2.55	2.40	2.30	2.30
Loyalty dividend per share ***	4.36 **	3.30 **	2.80	2.64	2.53	2.53

* Amounts in U.S. dollars presented in the table have been translated solely for the convenience of the reader using the Noon Buying Rate on December 29, 2006 of €1= $1.3197.

** Proposed dividend.

*** See Section 8.2 (Articles of Association (Status) – Rights, preferences and restrictions attached to shares) for an explanation of our "Loyalty dividend".

Financial statements page F 21

Note 2 – Summary of Significant Accounting Policies(in part)

(z) Convenience translation

The consolidated balance sheet and consolidated statements of income and cash flows include the presentation of amounts as of and for the year ended December 31, 2006 denominated in U.S. dollars ("$" or "U. S. dollar"). These amounts are presented for the convenience of the reader and have been prepared using an exchange rate of 1.00 euro to $1.3197 which was the Noon Buying Rate on December 29, 2006. Such translation should not be construed as representation that the Euro amount has been, could have been, or could in the future be, converted into U.S. dollars at that or any other exchange rate.

Lafarge (AR on Form 20-F 2006) continued
Financial statements page F 5
Consolidated statements of income (in part)

	NOTES	YEARS ENDED DECEMBER 31			
		2006	2006	2005 *	2004 *
		NOTE 2(Z)			
		(MILLION $, EXCEPT PER SHARE DATA)	*(MILLION EUROS, EXCEPT PER SHARE DATA)*		
REVENUE		**22,315**	**16,909**	14,490	12,976
Cost of sales		(16,345)	(12,385)	(10,585)	(9,425)
Selling and administrative expenses		(2,312)	(1,752)	(1,659)	(1,512)
Operating income before capital gains, impairment, restructuring and other		3,658	2,772	2,246	2,039
Gains on disposals, net	(5)	37	28	40	88
Other operating income (expenses)	(6)	(161)	(122)	(105)	(166)
OPERATING INCOME		**3,534**	**2,678**	**2,181**	**1,961**

Financial statements page F 6
Consolidated balance sheets (in part)

	NOTES	2006	2006	2005	2004
		NOTE 2(Z)		*(MILLION EUROS)*	
		(MILLION $)			
ASSETS					
NON CURRENT ASSETS		26,984	20,447	20,543	18,241
Goodwill	(10)	9,877	7,484	6,646	5,998
Intangible assets	(11)	562	426	355	308
Property, plant and equipment	(12)	14,758	11,183	12,171	10,587
Investments in associates	(13)	334	253	376	372
Other financial assets	(15)	1,096	830	626	696
Derivative instruments – assets	(27)	92	70	49	—
Deferred income tax assets	(23)	265	201	320	280

Financial statements page F 6
Consolidated statements of cash flows (in part)

	NOTES	YEARS ENDED DECEMBER 31,			
(MILLION EUROS)	NOTE 2(Z)	2006	2006	2005 *	2004 *
		(MILLION $)		*(MILLION EUROS)*	
NET CASH PROVIDED BY (USED IN) OPERATING ACTIVITIES					
NET INCOME		2,097	1,589	1,424	1,334
NET INCOME/(LOSS) FROM DISCONTINUED OPERATIONS		(5)	(4)	97	86
NET INCOME FROM CONTINUING OPERATIONS		2,102	1,593	1,327	1,248
Adjustments for income and expenses which are non cash or not related to operating activities, financial expenses or income taxes:					
Depreciation and amortization of assets	(4)	1,230	932	849	784

Commentary: In this extract, the company indicates that it has presented financial information (including amounts reported in financial statements) in a convenience currency (US dollars). The company applied the convenience translation requirements of IAS 21.

Extract 10(20) – Convenience translation

Neurochem Inc. (AR 2006), page 47

2. Significant accounting policies (in part)

k) Translation of convenience:

The Company's functional currency is the Canadian dollar. The Company also presents the consolidated financial statements as at and for the period ended December 31, 2006 in U.S. dollars, using the convenience translation method whereby all Canadian dollar amounts are converted into U.S. dollars at the noon exchange rate quoted by the Bank of Canada as at December 31, 2006, which was $0.8581 U.S. dollar per Canadian dollar. The information in U.S. dollars is presented only for the convenience of some readers and thus has limited usefulness. This translation should not be viewed as a representation that such Canadian dollar amounts actually represent such U.S. dollar amounts or could be or would have been converted into U.S. dollars at the rate indicated.

page 41

Consolidated Balance Sheets (in part)

December 31, 2006 and 2005 (in thousands of Canadian dollars, unless otherwise noted) (in accordance with Canadian GAAP)

	December 31, 2006	December 31, 2006	December 31, 2005
	(U.S.$ – note 2 (k))	(Cdn$)	(Cdn$)
Assets			
Current assets:			
Cash and cash equivalents	12,158	14,168	7,382
Marketable securities	36,600	42,653	63,709
Restricted cash (note 15(d))	6,000	6,992	6,995
Sales taxes and other receivables	1,043	1,216	728
Research tax credits receivable	928	1,082	2,404
Prepaid expenses	2,489	2,901	3,171
	59,218	69,012	84,389

page 42

Consolidated Statements of Operations (in part)

Years ended December 31, 2006, 2005 and 2004 and period from inception (June 17, 1993) to December 31, 2006 (in thousands of Canadian dollars, except per share data, unless otherwise noted) (in accordance with Canadian GAAP)

	Year ended December 31, 2006	Year ended December 31, 2006	Year ended December 31, 2005	2004	Cumulative since inception of operations
	(U.S.$ – note 2 (k))	(Cdn$)	(Cdn$)	(Cdn$)	(Cdn$)
Revenues:					
Collaboration agreement (note 4)	2,050	2,389	3,384	132	5,905
Reimbursable costs	693	808	1,057	195	2,060
Research contracts	–	–	–	–	9.216
License fees	–	–	–	–	1,106
	2,743	3,197	4,441	327	18,287

Neurochem Inc. (AR 2006) (continued)

Page 43

Consolidated Statements of Deficit

Years ended December 31, 2006, 2005 and 2004 and period from inception (June 17, 1993) to December 31, 2006 (in thousands of Canadian dollars, unless otherwise noted) (in accordance with Canadian GAAP)

	Year ended December 31, 2006 (U.S.$ – note 2 (k))	Year ended December 31, 2006 (Cdn$)	Year ended December 31, 2005 (Cdn$)	Year ended December 31, 2004 (Cdn$)	Cumulative since inception os operations (Cdn$)
Deficit, beginning of period:					
As previously reported	(189,424)	(220,748)	(140,926)	(86,365)	–
Adjustment to reflect change in accounting policy for stock options (note 3(a))	–	–		(2,162)	(2,162)
Adjustments to reflect change in accounting policy for long-term investment (note 3(b))	–	–	(2,501)	–	(2,501)
Deficit, beginning of period, as restated	(189,424)	(220,748)	(143,427)	(88,527)	(4,663)
Net loss	(64,690)	(75,387)	(72,366)	(52,399)	(274,990)
Share issue costs (notes 7 and 11)	(407)	(474)	(4,955)	–	(16,956)
Deficit, end of period	(254,521)	(296,609)	(220,748)	(140,926)	(296,609)

See accompanying notes to consolidated financial statements.

Neurochem Inc. (AR 2006) (continued)

Page 44

Consolidated Statements of Cash Flows (in part)

Years ended December 31, 2006, 2005 and 2004 and period from inception (June 17, 1993) to December 31, 2006 (in thousands of Canadian dollars, unless otherwise noted) (in accordance with Canadian GAAP)

	Year ended December 31, 2006	Year ended December 31, 2006	Year ended December 31, 2005	Year ended December 31, 2004	Cumulative since inception of operations
	(U.S.$ – note 2 (k))	(Cdn$)	(Cdn$)	(Cdn$)	(Cdn$)
Cash flows from operating activities:					
Net loss	**(64,690)**	**(75,387)**	(72,366)	(52,399)	(274,990)
Adjustments for:					
Depreciation, amortization and patent cost write-off	**1,513**	**1,764**	3,189	2,046	11,340
Unrealized foreign exchange loss	**1,347**	**1,570**	1,757	263	5,495
Stock-based compensation	**3,474**	**4,048**	4,795	4,038	12,881
Share of loss in a company subject to significant influence	**2,375**	**2,768**	3,124	–	5,892
Non-controlling interest	**(780)**	**(909)**	(930)	–	(1,839)
Amortization of deferred financing fees	**46**	**53**	–	–	53
Write-off of leasehold improvements and other property and equipment	**–**	**–**	–	1,189	1,189
Provision for lease exit obligations	**–**	**–**	–	487	487
Accretion expense	**544**	**634**	6	19	659
Amortization of gain on sale leaseback	**(1,223)**	**(1,425)**	(175)	–	(1,600)
Gain on technology transfer	**–**	**–**	–	–	(3,484)
Share issued for services	**–**	**–**	–	–	41
Change in operating assets and liabilities:					
Restricted cash	**–**	**–**	(7,898)	–	(7,898)
Amount receivable under collaboration agreement	**–**	**–**	14,443	(14,443)	–
Sales taxes and other receivables	**(418)**	**(488)**	54	(61)	(1,216)
Research tax credits receivable	**1,135**	**1,322**	(1,055)	762	(1,082)
Prepaid expenses	**232**	**270**	569	(2,165)	(3,222)
Long-term prepaid expenses	**374**	**436**	6	(1,135)	(693)
Deferred revenue	**(2,050)**	**(2,389)**	(3,384)	14,592	8,819
Accounts payable and accrued liabilities	**3,203**	**3,733**	2,613	3,771	16,155
	(54,918)	**(64,000)**	(55,252)	(43,036)	(233,013)

Commentary: The company (preparing financial statements according to Canadian GAAP) applied the convenience translation requirements of IAS 21 to present a set of complete primary financial statements expressed in US dollars.

FUTURE DEVELOPMENTS

There are no IASB or IFRIC projects on foreign currency translation underway at this time.

COMPREHENSIVE EXAMPLES

This section presents two comprehensive examples showing extensive disclosures related to foreign currency translation. We have selected relevant extracts of the notes that might provide good examples of disclosure under both IFRS and Canadian GAAP.

Thomson – All extracts 10 (A) were obtained from Form 20 F for the year ended December 31, 2007.

Extract 10(A1) – Thomson – Option under IFRS 1, page 190

In this extract, the company presents its application of the *First-time Adoption of International Financial Reporting Standards (IFRS)* voluntary option for the cumulative transition adjustment in its opening balance sheet.

Main accounting options selected by the Group for the preparation of the opening IFRS balance sheet at the transition date (January 1, 2004) (in part)

IFRS 1, First-time Adoption of IFRS sets out the rules to be followed by first-time adopters of IFRS when preparing their first IFRS financial statements. The Group has opted to apply the following main options and exemptions provided by IFRS 1:

- cumulative translation differences: the Group elected to recognize cumulative translation differences of the foreign subsidiaries into opening retained earnings as of January 1, 2004, after having accounted for the IFRS adjustments in the opening shareholders' equity. All cumulative translation differences for all foreign operations have therefore been deemed to be zero at the IFRS transition date. The gain or loss on a subsequent disposal of any foreign operation will exclude translation differences that arose before the IFRS transition date but will include later translation differences;

Extract 10(A2) – Thomson – Functional and presentation currency, page 190

In this extract, the company indicates that the euro is the presentation and functional currency, as required by IAS 21.

Functional and presentation currency

These consolidated financial statements are presented in euro, which is the functional currency of Thomson S.A. All financial information presented in euro has been rounded to the nearest million, unless otherwise stated.

Extract 10(A3) – Thomson – Translation procedures, page 192

In this extract, the company discloses its translation methods, including the exchange rates it used (as required by IAS 1, *Presentation of Financial Statements*). Note IAS 21 has no specific requirement to disclose accounting policies governing foreign currency transactions. IAS 1 does, however, require disclosure of significant policies that are relevant to an entity's financial statements.

Translation of foreign subsidiaries

For the financial statements of all the Group's entities for which the functional currency is different from that of the Group, the following methods are applied:

- the assets and liabilities are translated into euros at the rate effective at the end of the period;
- the revenues and costs are translated into euros at the average exchange rate of the period.

The translation adjustments arising are directly recorded in shareholders' equity.

Translation of foreign currency transactions

Transactions in foreign currency are translated at the exchange rate effective at the trade date. Monetary assets and liabilities in foreign currency are translated at the rate of exchange prevailing at the balance sheet date. The differences arising on the translation of foreign currency operations are recorded in the statement of operations as a profit or loss on exchange.

The non-monetary assets and liabilities are translated at the historical rate of exchange effective at the trade date. However, the recoverable value of depreciated tangible assets is determined by reference to the exchange rate at the balance sheet date.

The main exchange rates used for translation (one unit of each foreign currency converted to euros) are summarized in the following table:

	Closing Rate			Average Rate		
	2007	2006	2005	2007	2006	2005
US dollar (US$)	0.67983	0.75945	0.84331	0.72682	0.79180	0.80550
Pound sterling (GBP)	1.36103	1.48965	1.45590	1.45660	1.46462	1.46248
Canadian dollar	0.69367	0.65433	0.72546	0.68254	0.69940	0.66470
Hong Kong dollar	0.08719	0.09767	0.10877	0.09316	0.10191	0.10359
China Renminbi	0.09308	0.09728	0.10453	0.09585	0.09950	0.09844

The average rate is determined by taking the average of the month-end closing rates for the year period, unless such method results in a material distortion.

Extract 10(A4) – Thomson – Foreign gains or losses currency risk, page 218

As required by IAS 21, the company discloses the amount of foreign exchange gains or losses.

Note 9 **Net finance costs** *(in € millions)*	2007	2006	2005
Interest income	19	19	31
Interest expense [1]	(120)	(108)	(108)
Interest expense, net [2]	**(101)**	**(89)**	**(77)**
Financial component of pension plan expense	(22)	(33)	(28)
Other financial charges	(5)	(5)	(7)
Exchange profit (loss) [3]	8	7	(22)
Change in fair value on financial instrument (loss)	(16)	(11)	(8)
Change in fair value of the SLP convertible debt [4]	34	4	94
Other [5]	(3)	(75)	8
Other financial (expense) income, net	**(4)**	**(113)**	**37**
TOTAL FINANCE COSTS – NET	**(105)**	**(202)**	**(40)**

(1) From January 1, 2005 under IAS 32 the option components of our convertible bonds are split out and accounted for separately and the effective interest rate is used to calculate the interest expense. The IFRS impact for our convertible bonds compared to the accounting treatment under French GAAP (use of nominal rate) is an additional interest charge of €8 million, €9 million and €36 million for 2007, 2006 and 2005 respectively.

(2) Prepaid bank fees on debt issuances are included, according to IAS 32 and 39, in the effective interest rate on debt and classified in "Interest expense". There is no significant fee income and expense other than the amount included in determining the effective interest rate.

(3) Including a €3 million and €2 million exchange gain related to the embedded derivative of the SLP US$ convertible debt in 2007 and in 2006 respectively compared to a €11 million exchange loss in 2005.

(4) The SLP convertible bond contains an embedded derivative which is accounted for separately from the debt component of the bond. The change in fair value of the option is reflected in Finance costs – net for the amount mentioned under this caption. The option value was zero at December 31st, 2007; given the level of the Thomson share price and the potential short-term nature of the bond, changes in the variables affecting the option value would not be expected to have a significant impact.

(5) In 2006, it includes (70) million comprising the loss on disposal of a portion of the Group's shares in TCL Multimedia, the resulting mark-to-market of remaining shares classified as available-for-sale financial asset (see Note 16) and the charge accounted by the Group in counterpart of the release of the TCL Multimedia lock-up clause (see Note 14).

Extract 10(A5) – Thomson – Foreign currency risk, pages 244 to 246

In this extract, the company discloses information on its foreign exchange risks (as required by IFRS 7, *Financial Instruments: Disclosures*).

Financial instruments and market related exposures (in part)

26.1 Foreign exchange risk

(a) Translation risks

The assets, liabilities, revenues and expenses of the Group's operating entities are denominated in various currencies, the majority being in US dollars. The Group's consolidated financial statements are presented in euro. Thus, assets, liabilities, revenues and expenses denominated in currencies other than euro must be translated into euro at the applicable exchange rate to be included in the consolidated financial statements. This risk is measured by consolidating the Group's exposures and doing sensitivity analyses on the main exposures. It is the Group's general policy not to hedge this risk.

(b) Transaction risks

Thomson's foreign exchange risk exposure mainly arises on purchase and sale transactions by its subsidiaries in currencies other than their functional currencies. This risk is measured by consolidating the Group's exposures and doing sensitivity analyses on the main exposures. The general policy of the Group is for the subsidiaries to hedge with the corporate treasury department the full amount of the estimated exposure, with the objective of eliminating the currency risk for the period of the hedge. The corporate treasury hedges the net position in each currency with external banks using forward operations or occasionally options.

(c) Financial exposure

The Group's general policy is for subsidiaries to borrow and invest excess cash in the same currency as their functional currency thereby eliminating the exposure of its financial assets and liabilities to foreign exchange rate fluctuations.

(d) Foreign currency operations

In accordance with the Group's policies on financial risk management as described in Note 23, the Group enters into foreign currency operations to hedge its exposures as described above. The swap points on currency hedges that qualify as hedges under IAS 39 and the premiums paid on currency options are excluded from the hedging relationship and taken directly to financial result: these amounts totaled €(16) million in 2007, €(11) million in 2006 and €(8) million in 2005.

In order to match the currencies that Thomson's corporate treasury department borrows with the currencies that it lends, Thomson enters into currency swaps primarily (i) to convert euro borrowings into US dollars which are lent to the Group's US subsidiaries/associates and (ii) to convert U.S. dollars borrowed externally or from the Group's US subsidiaries/associates into euros. The forward points on these currency swaps are accounted for as interest and amounted to €5 million in interest income (netted against interest expense) in 2007, €(1) million in 2006 and €(6) million in 2005. At the December 31, 2007 exchange rate, there was a mark to market currency loss on these swaps of €(5) million. This amount is recognized in the Group's finance costs as an exchange loss and offsets the exchange gain on the revaluation in euro of intercompany loans and advances in foreign currency made by treasury. In the balance sheet the mark to market value of these swaps is recognized in Financial Derivatives and offsets the decrease in the euro value of the foreign currency intercompany loans and advances.

The future cashflows at the contracted rate of the Group's foreign currency operations are shown below. The cashflows shown for options are shown assuming the options were exercised.

Financial instruments and market related exposures (in part) (continued)

	2007	2006	2005
Forward exchange contracts (including currency swaps)			
Euro	475	486	1,229
Pound sterling	52	165	144
Hong Kong dollar	–	21	31
Canadian dollar	13	15	12
Singapore dollar	69	28	40
US dollar	760	652	599
Polish zloty	13	7	106
Other currencies	87	64	42
Total forward currency purchases	**1,469**	**1,438**	**2,203**
Forward metal purchases	**–**	**2**	**–**
Euro	(850)	(823)	(813)
Canadian dollar	(35)	(37)	(19)
Pound sterling	(57)	(125)	(58)
Japenese yen	(85)	(85)	(25)
US dollar	(401)	(311)	(1,099)
Polish zloty	(5)	(20)	(120)
Other currencies	(41)	(40)	(75)
Total forward currency sales	**(1,474)**	**(1,441)**	**(2,209)**
Forward metal sales	**(8)**	**(9)**	**(2,209)**
Currency options contracts purchased	**(8)**	**(9)**	**–**
Put US$/Call Euro	225	76	75
Call US$/Put Euro	172	91	–
Total	**397**	**167**	**75**
Deferred hedging gains (losses) related to forecast transactions	4	(2)	3

(e) Sensitivity to currency movements

Because of the Group's significant activities in the US and in other countries whose currencies are linked to the US dollar, the Group's main currency exposure is the fluctuation of the US$ against the euro. The Group believes a 10% fluctuation in the US$ versus the euro is reasonably possible in a given year and thus the tables below show the impact of a 10% increase in the US$ versus the euro on the Group's sales, on Profit from continuing operations before tax and net finance costs, on the currency translation adjustment component of equity and on net debt. A 10% decrease in the US$ versus the euro would have a symmetrical impact in the opposite amount.

2007 *(in € millions)*	Transaction	Translation	Total
Sales	29	270	299
Profit from continuing operations before tax and net finance costs	12	4	16
Equity Impact (Cumulative translation adjustment)	N/A	N/A	110
Impact on net debt	N/A	N/A	74

2006 *(in € millions)*	Transaction	Translation	Total
Sales	40	280	320
Profit from continuing operations before tax and net finance costs	20	20	40
Equity Impact (Cumulative translation adjustment)	N/A	N/A	120
Impact on net debt	N/A	N/A	76

Smith & Nephew plc – All extracts **10(B)** were obtained from Annual Report for the year ended December 31, 2007.

Extract 10(B1) – Smith & Nephew plc – Change in the presentation currency and IFRS 1 voluntary option, page 83

This extract shows that the company has modified the group's presentation and functional currency (to US dollars). In addition, the company presents its application of the IFRS 1 voluntary option for the cumulative transition adjustment in its opening balance sheet.

Presentation of financial information (in part)

The Group changed its presentational currency from Pounds Sterling to US Dollars with effect from 1 January 2006 as at that time the Group's principal assets and operations were in the US and the majority of its operations were conducted in US Dollars. Additionally, the Company redenominated its share capital into US Dollars on 23 January 2006 and will retain distributable reserves and declare dividends in US Dollars. Consequently its functional currency became the US Dollar. This lowers the Group's exposure to currency translation risk on its revenue, profits and equity. Financial information for prior periods was restated from Pounds Sterling into US Dollars in accordance with IAS 21.

The cumulative translation reserve was set to nil at 1 January 2003 (i.e. the transition date to IFRS). All subsequent movements comprising differences on the retranslation of the opening net assets of non US Dollar subsidiaries and hedging instruments have been charged to the cumulative translation reserve included in "Other Reserves". Share capital and share premium were translated at the rate of exchange on the date of redenomination.

As a result of the above, the presentational currency of the Group (i.e. US Dollars) for 2005 is different from the functional currency of the Company (i.e. Pounds Sterling).

Extract 10(B2) – Smith & Nephew plc – Translation procedures, page 85

Here, the company discloses its translation methods. Note that IAS 21 has no specific requirement to disclose accounting policies on foreign currency transactions. IAS 1 does, however, require disclosure of significant policies that are relevant to an entity's financial statements.

The company also provides additional explanations on its application of the IFRS 1 voluntary option for the cumulative transition adjustment in its opening balance sheet.

---

2 – Accounting Policies
Foreign Currencies (in part)

Balance sheet items of foreign operations and foreign currency borrowings are translated into US Dollars on consolidation at year end rates of exchange. Income statement items and the cash flows of overseas subsidiary undertakings and associated undertakings are translated at average rates as an approximation to actual transaction rates, with actual transaction rates used for large one off transactions.

Goodwill and fair value adjustments arising on the acquisition of a foreign entity are treated as assets and liabilities of the foreign entity and translated at the closing rate.

Transactions in foreign currencies are recorded at the exchange rate ruling at the date of the transaction. Monetary assets and liabilities denominated in foreign currencies are retranslated at the rate of exchange ruling at the balance sheet date.

The following are recorded as movements in Other reserves: exchange differences on the translation at closing rates of exchange of non-US Dollar opening net assets; the differences arising between the translation of profits into US Dollars at average and closing exchange rates; to the extent that the hedging relationship is effective, the difference on translation of foreign currency borrowings or swaps that are used to finance or hedge the Group's net investments in foreign operations; and the movement in the fair value of forward foreign exchange contracts used to hedge forecast foreign exchange cash flows. All other exchange differences are dealt with in arriving at profit before taxation. On disposal of a foreign operation, the deferred cumulative amount recognised in equity relating to that particular foreign operation, net of related movements on hedging instruments, would be recycled from equity into income.

Under IFRS 1, the Group was not required to record cumulative translation differences arising prior to the transition date. In utilising this exemption, all cumulative translation differences were deemed to be zero as at 1 January 2003 and subsequent foreign business disposals will exclude any translation differences arising prior to the date of transition. Full retrospective presentation of cumulative translation differences would either increase or decrease Other reserves depending on historic exchange rate fluctuations with the corresponding movement taken to "Accumulated profits". Gains or losses on the disposals of foreign operations in the future would be different as a result of the different amount of recycled cumulative translation differences.

Extract 10(B3) – Smith & Nephew plc – Exchange rates, page 120

This extract discloses the significant currency exchange rates for translation into US dollars.

---

31. Currency Translation

The exchange rates used for the translation of currencies into US Dollars that have the most significant impact on the Group results were:

	Average rates		
	2007	2006	2005
Sterling	2.00	1.86	1.81
Euro	1.37	1.27	1.24

	Year-end rates		
	2007	2006	2005
Sterling	1.99	1.96	1.72
Euro	1.46	1.32	1.18

PLANNING FOR IMPLEMENTATION

An entity can engage in foreign currency activities in two ways:

1. enter directly into transactions that are denominated in foreign currencies; or
2. participate in foreign operations.

Because only one translation method is applied under IFRS, the adoption of the IAS 21 functional currency approach will possibly result in simpler translation procedures and in more consistent reporting of the translation of foreign currency activities than is possible under current Canadian standards.

Generating New Data and Optimizing Information Systems

Determining functional currency is crucial to IAS 21 application. Unfortunately, this concept is difficult to apply in certain circumstances. Companies could have numerous foreign operations, each presenting their financial statements in a different functional currency. To prepare consolidated financial statements in the appropriate presentation currency, these companies will have to translate each of their foreign operation's results and financial position into that presentation currency.

Consequently, information systems should be designed to ensure that:

- all foreign operation included in a group's financial statements have appropriately determined their functional currency;
- each foreign operation clearly documents how it determined its functional currency and the factors it considered in making that determination, particularly where the functional currency is not obvious from the primary indicators;
- foreign operations located in hyperinflationary economies restate their financial statements expressed in local functional currencies according to IAS 29.

New Accounting Policies

Generally, financial statements prepared in accordance with Canadian GAAP would not be significantly affected by IAS 21 adoption. Certain companies might, however, experience a major impact when applying the IAS 21 functional currency approach. In addition, some companies might need to change their accounting methods for incorporating foreign subsidiaries operating in hyperinflationary economies in their financial statements. For example, changing to the functional currency approach can have a major impact on companies operating in sectors such as mining because they are likely to have operations in hyperinflationary economies.

Accounting Choices on Initial Adoption

Companies must apply the requirements of IAS 21 retrospectively. Companies could, however, use the IFRS 1, *First-time Adoption of International Financial Reporting Standards* voluntary exemption to consider cumulative translation differences carried in equity to be zero at the date of transition to IFRS. The corresponding adjustment is made to opening retained earnings.

Below is a typical extract that provides details of such an IFRS 1 voluntary exemption.

Extract 10(21) – Reversing accumulated foreign currency translation adjustments

Vivendi (AR 2006), page 189
1.3. Principles Governing the Preparation of the Consolidated Financial Statements
1.3.3. Foreign currency translation (in part)

... In accordance with the provisions of IFRS 1 "First time adoption of International Financial Reporting Standards", Vivendi decided to reverse the accumulated foreign currency translation differences against retained earnings as of January 1, 2004. These foreign currency translation differences resulted from the translation into euro of the financial statements of subsidiaries having foreign currencies as their functional currencies. Consequently, on the subsequent divestiture of the subsidiaries, joint ventures or other associated entities, whose functional currency is not the euro, as the case may be, these adjustments are not taken to earnings.

Commentary: In this extract, the company elected to reverse the accumulated foreign currency translation differences against retained earnings at the date of transition. This election will affect the amounts of gains and losses that would be realized on subsequent disposal of the subsidiaries, affiliates or joint ventures whose functional currency is not the euro.

Note that IFRS 1 does not allow other voluntary options and that the retrospective application of IAS 21 might present difficulties in certain situations. Consequently, IAS 21 provides some accounting choices. For example, goodwill and fair value adjustments are either already expressed in an entity's functional currency or are non-monetary foreign currency items, which are reported using the exchange rate at the date of the acquisition.

Extract 10(21) – Reversing accumulated foreign currency translation adjustments

Vivendi (AR 2005), page 183

1.3. Principles Governing the Preparation of the Consolidated Financial Statements

1.3.3. Foreign currency translation (in part)

In accordance with the provisions of IFRS 1 "First-time adoption of International Financial Reporting Standards", Vivendi decided to reverse the accumulated foreign currency translation differences against retained earnings as of January 1, 2004. Those foreign currency translation differences resulted from the translation into euro of the financial statements of subsidiaries having foreign currencies as their functional currencies. Consequently, on the subsequent divestiture of the subsidiaries, joint ventures or other associated entities, whose functional currency is not the euro, as the case may be, these adjustments are not taken to reamed.

Commentary – In this extract, the company elected to reverse the accumulated foreign currency translation differences against retained earnings at the date of transition. This election will affect the amounts of gains and losses that would be realized on subsequent disposal of the subsidiaries, affiliates or joint ventures whose functional currency is not the euro.

Note that IFRS 1 does not allow other voluntary options and that the retrospective application of IAS 21 might present difficulties in certain situations. Consequently, IAS 21 provides some accounting choices. For example, goodwill and fair value adjustments are either already expressed in an entity's functional currency or are non-monetary foreign currency items, which are reported using the exchange rate at the date of the acquisition.

Chapter 11
Revenues and Inventories

Standards Discussed in this Chapter

International

IAS 2 – Inventories
IAS 11 – Construction Contracts
IAS 18 – Revenue
IFRIC 12 – Service Concession Arrangements
IFRIC 13 – Customer Loyalty Programmes
IFRIC 15 - Agreements for the Construction of Real Estate
IFRIC 18 – Transfers of Assets from Customers [1]
SIC-29 – Service Concession Arrangements: Disclosures
SIC-31 – Revenue – Barter Transactions Involving Advertising Services

Canadian

CICA 3031 – Inventories
CICA 3400 – Revenue
AcG-2 – Franchise fee revenue
AcG-4 – Fees and costs associated with lending activities
EIC-18 – Accounting for the goods and services tax
EIC-78 – Construction contractors — revenue recognition when the percentage of completion method is applicable
EIC-84 – Revenue recognition on sales with a guaranteed minimum resale value
EIC-123 – Reporting revenue gross as a principal versus net as an agent
EIC-141 – Revenue recognition
EIC-142 – Revenue arrangements with multiple deliverables
EIC-143 – Accounting for separately priced extended warranty and product maintenance contracts
EIC-144 – Accounting by a customer (including a reseller) for certain consideration received from a vendor
EIC-156 – Accounting by a vendor for consideration given to a customer (including a reseller of the vendor's products)

INTRODUCTION

This chapter covers two topics: revenues and inventories. Since the Canadian standard (CICA 3031) and IFRS (IAS 2) requirements on the latter topic are essentially the same, we will focus the discussion in this chapter on issues related to revenue recognition.

Although revenue recognition standards under IFRS are sometimes more prescriptive than Canadian GAAP, there are also instances where IFRS are less prescriptive. In that case, management will need to exercise more judgment when dealing with revenue issues. The following is a brief overview of the more significant revenue reporting requirements under IFRS, contrasting them with the corresponding Canadian requirements:

---

1 Issued in January 2009 – see Future Developments section.

- Although both IFRS and Canadian GAAP contain requirements for disaggregating multiple element arrangements:

  o IAS 18 provides general principles for sales of goods and services while the corresponding EIC-142 is detailed. The appendix to IAS 18 provides some specific guidance by describing examples covering certain topics addressed by EIC-142.

  o IFRS offers guidance for service contracts (IAS 18), construction contracts (IAS 11), service concession arrangements (IFRIC 12) and customer loyalty programs (IFRIC 13). Corresponding Canadian guidance on these issues is limited.

- IAS 18 uses two different models for revenue recognition, both requiring the exercise of a good deal of judgment:

  o The first model, which applies to the sale of goods, is based on the general criterion of whether or not risks and rewards are transferred to the buyer. CICA 3400 has a similar model but its application is detailed in EIC-141, which contains many prescriptive rules.

  o The second model, which is applicable to services rendered, requires – subject to certain reliability considerations – the use of the stage-of-completion method, commonly referred to as the percentage-of-completion method (i.e., revenues are recognized as services are rendered). Canadian GAAP does mandate such a method for services revenue recognition but has specific standards for franchises (AcG-2), lending activities (AcG-4) and law firms (EIC-65, *Law firms – Revenue recognition*).

- IAS 11 covers the accounting and disclosures of construction contracts in some detail while CICA 3400 and EIC-78 provide limited guidance on such contracts. Though both IAS 11 and CICA 3400 require the percentage-of-completion method to be used for construction contracts, CICA 3400 permits the use of the completed-contract method, which is prohibited under IAS 11.

- IAS 18 requires that all revenue transactions, which do not exclude those with related parties, be initially recorded at fair value. CICA 3400 does not specifically address this issue; however, Canadian GAAP has special measurement rules that apply to related party transactions.

- IFRIC 12 and IFRIC 13 (both effective in 2008) introduce new guidance for service concessions and customer loyalty programs, respectively. IFRIC 15, which goes into effect in 2009, introduces new guidance for real estate construction agreements. All three standards require the application of significant judgment on certain issues not specifically addressed by Canadian standards.

- Both IFRS and Canadian GAAP contain only limited industry-specific revenue recognition guidance. In the absence of specific guidance, IFRS permit entities to consult the most recent pronouncements of other standard-setting bodies using a similar conceptual framework to develop accounting standards. For example, neither IFRS nor Canadian GAAP address software revenue recognition issues and, consequently, some companies might refer to the guidance in Statement of Position No. 97-2, *Software revenue recognition* issued by the American Institute of Certified Public Accountants. The reference to US guidance is found in some of the extracts presented in this chapter.

Currently, the IASB and the FASB are working on a joint project to develop revenue recognition concepts, which would be based on an assets and liabilities approach. This project aims to replace the existing standards on revenue recognition with a more general one that is consistent with the conceptual framework (which the boards are also currently revising). This is discussed in more detail in the section "Future Developments."

All the issues raised above can present difficulties when applying IFRS. To help readers evaluate those difficulties, this chapter discusses the following topics:

- sales transaction identification;
- scope;
- revenue definition;
- revenue measurement;
- sale of goods:
  - bill-and-hold arrangements,
  - layaway arrangements,
  - acceptance, installation and inspection,
  - recoverability,
  - reliable measurement of costs;
- rendering services:
  - revenue recognition method,
  - reliable revenue measurement,
  - stage-of-completion estimates,
  - consistency,
  - uncertainties;
- other revenues;
- revenue presentation and general disclosures;
- construction contracts:
  - key definition,
  - scope and guidance,
  - disclosures;
- service concession arrangements;
- customer loyalty programs;
- agreements for the construction of real estate;
- other issues related to revenue recognition and presentation:
  - up-front fees,
  - exchange or swap of goods or services,
  - consideration received from a vendor,
  - customers incentives,
  - guaranteed minimum resale value,
  - specific industries;
- inventories:
  - objective,
  - scope,
  - definitions,
  - initial measurement,
  - allocation of overhead,
  - costs excluded from inventories,

o   cost formulas (costs flows),

o   impairment,

o   impairment reversal,

o   presentation and disclosures.

IMPACT ON FINANCIAL STATEMENTS

The adoption of IFRS requirements for inventories will have no impact on financial statements prepared in accordance with Canadian GAAP as CICA 3031 requirements are essentially the same as those under IAS 2.

Revenue recognition principles under both IFRS and Canadian GAAP are similar, and their application often results in the same accounting treatment. In certain circumstances, however, differences in scope, guidance and wording could lead to differences in financial reporting. The adoption of IFRS will affect financial statements in several ways:

- Revenue on sale of goods and rendering of services could be recorded earlier than under Canadian GAAP because IAS 18:

  o   might allow an entity to identify and recognize revenue distinctly for a component of multi-element arrangements because the separation criteria under that standard are more general and less restrictive than those in EIC-142. For example, an entity might recognize separately the two components in a contract involving the sale and installation of a machine under IFRS, while it might account for the whole contract as one component (unit of accounting) under Canadian GAAP. Recognizing two components under IFRS would allow the entity to recognize a portion of the contract revenue at the time of machine delivery, whereas it might have to defer the whole revenue until the installation is completed if the separation criteria in EIC-142 are not met,

  o   mandates the stage-of-completion method for service contracts, while Canadian GAAP might allow or even require the use of the completed-contract method,

  o   provides examples of the recognition of revenue for only certain sales arrangements (such as customer acceptance, layaways and bill-and-hold sales), which suggest that revenue could be recognized before the restrictive conditions specified in EIC-141 are met.

- There could be differences in reported revenue (increases and decreases) for certain sales arrangements, including:

  o   *Construction contracts*: Even though the stage-of-completion method (percentage of completion) should generally be used under both IFRS and Canadian GAAP, CICA 3400 specifically allows the use of the completed-contract method, which is prohibited by IAS 11. Consequently, once IFRS is adopted, entities applying the completed-contract method will see a change in the pattern of revenues and expenses they report.

  o   *Loyalty programs*: The absence of specific guidance allows entities preparing their financial statements according to Canadian GAAP to record loyalty points as a marketing expense or a reduction of revenues. IFRIC 13 requires loyalty points to be accounted for as a separate identifiable component of a sales transaction, initially recorded as deferred revenue and measured at fair value. Consequently, Canadian entities currently recording loyalty points as a marketing expense (measured at cost) will see their revenues and income decrease when points are granted and the opposite when they are used. The net impact on revenue and income will be the same once the timing differences in the recognition of revenue are eliminated.

  o *Service concession arrangements*: These arrangements are often accounted for as joint ventures under Canadian GAAP (resulting in the reporting of an infrastructure as property, plant and equipment in entities' financial statements). IFRIC 12 prescribes a different approach that mandates the recording of a financial asset, or an intangible asset or a combination of both.

  o *"Off plan" sales agreements related to certain condominium building or houses*: these agreements might be accounted for under current Canadian GAAP as (1) construction contracts with revenue being recognized by reference to the stage of completion as construction progresses or (2) sales of goods with revenue being recorded when control and the risks and rewards of ownership had been transferred to the buyer (typically when the unit is ready for occupation and handed over to the buyer). Implementing IFRIC 15 results in revenue being deferred until the construction is completed.

- More consistent and comparable financial statements than under Canadian GAAP for some sales arrangements due to specific guidance for construction contracts (IAS 11), service concession arrangements (IFRIC 12), loyalty programs (IFRIC 13) and real estate sales (IFRIC 15).

- Increased transparency because disclosure requirements are more extensive under IFRS.

- Additional measurement uncertainties and earnings volatility since fair value is used as a measurement basis for all sources of revenues, including construction contracts and loyalty awards points.

ANALYSIS OF RELEVANT ISSUES

This section examines and illustrates some relevant issues related to revenues under IFRS. A comparison with Canadian GAAP is also provided.

Sales Transaction Identification

Before examining specific revenue recognition requirements, it might be useful to identify the sales transaction to be recorded. Generally, such identification is straightforward. However, when an entity bundles goods and/or services into a single contract (often referred to as a multi-element contract), it will be necessary to determine if that contract should be accounted for as a whole or, alternatively, if it must be disaggregated into individual sales transactions (which are referred to by various terms such as "deliverables," "units of accounting," "accounting units," "units of account," "components" or "elements").

Both IFRS and Canadian GAAP provide guidance for determining if a multi-element arrangement or contract should be disaggregated into accounting units:

- IAS 18 guidance requires that multi-elements be segregated unless the commercial effect cannot be understood without combining the elements into a single transaction.

- IAS 11, IFRIC 12 and IFRIC 13 provide specific guidance for separating construction contracts, service concession arrangements and customer loyalty programs, respectively.

- EIC-142 contains guidance for separating components of all multiple deliverable arrangements. The general guidance in EIC-142 is more detailed and criteria for segregation are more stringent than those found in IAS 18.

- EIC-143 provides guidance for separately priced extended warranty contracts. Even though IFRS do not cover this issue, the application of the general guidance under IAS 18 should yield similar results to those obtained under EIC-143.

Under IAS 18, the determination of whether multi-element arrangements should be segregated into their components requires considerable judgment as, in the absence of detailed guidance, the substance of the transaction must be evaluated.

Basically, EIC-142 provides guidance on two critical issues related to multi-elements arrangements: (1) determining whether separation is required and (2) allocation of consideration to the elements to be accounted for separately.

With respect to the first issue, EIC-142 requires the separation of an element only if all of the following criteria are met:

- The delivered item has value to the customer on a stand-alone basis (i.e., vendors sell it separately or the customer could resell the delivered item on a stand-alone basis).

- There is objective and reliable evidence of the fair value of the undelivered item (or items).

- If the arrangement includes a general right of return for the delivered item, delivery or performance of the undelivered item is considered probable and substantially in the control of the vendor.

IFRS do not contain such explicit criteria:

- IAS 18 states that, in certain circumstances, it is necessary to apply the revenue recognition criteria to the separately identifiable components of a single transaction in order to reflect its substance. Appendix to IAS 18 illustrates the general requirement in a situation where servicing fees were included in the price of the product sold.

- Even though IAS 18 provides only general guidance, certain IFRS standards cover specific sales transactions such as:

  o IAS 11 provides specific guidance for segmenting and combining construction contracts.

  o IFRIC 12 specifies that, where an operator performs more than one service under a single contract or arrangement, each component of the consideration must be separately recognized.

  o IFRIC 13 specifies that loyalty programs are multiple element arrangements in which a portion of the consideration received is allocated to award credits.

These types of sales transactions are discussed in detail later in this chapter.

For the second issue noted above, EIC-142 permits two allocation methods for the units of accounting: (1) the relative fair value method and (2) the residual method, which can be used only in cases where there is objective and reliable evidence of the fair value of the undelivered item(s) and no such evidence for the delivered item(s) (the reverse residual method is not allowed).

IAS 18 provides no specific guidance for allocating proceeds to the units of accounting. IFRS do, however, discuss the allocation of proceeds to units of account in three specific instances:

- The inclusion of servicing fees in the price of the product sold. The example in Appendix to IAS 18 suggests that the allocation should equal the expected cost of, plus a reasonable profit on, the undelivered item.

- Service concession arrangements. IFRIC 12 requires the relative fair value method.
- Customer loyalty programs. IFRIC 13 supports the use of the fair value of the undelivered item (residual value method).

In addition to the two issues described above, EIC-142 provides some answers to specific questions on the effect, if any, of:

- consideration that varies as a result of future customer actions on the measurement and/or allocation of arrangement consideration;
- a vendor's intent to not enforce its contractual rights in the event of customer cancellation on the measurement and/or allocation of arrangement consideration.

Illustrative Disclosures:

Extract 11(1) – Multiple deliverables arrangements (general policy)

Telstra Corporation Limited (AR 2007), page 128

2.17 Revenue recognition (in part)

Revenue arrangements with multiple deliverables

Where two or more revenue-generating activities or deliverables are sold under a single arrangement, each deliverable that is considered to be a separate unit of accounting is accounted for separately. When the deliverables in a multiple deliverable arrangement are not considered to be separate units of accounting, the arrangement is accounted for as a single unit.

We allocate the consideration from the revenue arrangement to its separate units based on the relative fair values of each unit. If the fair value of the delivered item is not available, then revenue is allocated based on the difference between the total arrangement consideration and the fair value of the undelivered item. The revenue allocated to each unit is then recognised in accordance with our revenue recognition policies described above.

Commentary: In the above extract the company states in general terms how it accounts for separate revenue-generating activities or deliverables it sells under a single arrangement. The company accounts for the arrangement as a single unit when it considers that units of accounting are not separate, which requires judgment. No specific criteria for separation are disclosed (as might be required under Canadian GAAP).

In addition, the company discloses how it allocates the consideration from the revenue arrangement to its separate units. The methods used seem consistent with Canadian GAAP.

Extract 11(2) – Combination of services (general)

Atos Origin (AR 2007), page 91

18.3.2 Basis of preparation and significant accounting policies (in part)

Revenue Recognition (in part)

The Group enters into multiple-element arrangements, which may include combinations of different services. Revenue is recognised for the separate elements when they have been subject to separate negotiation, the contractor and customer have been able to accept or reject that part of the contract relating to each component, and, each component's costs and revenues can be identified. A group of contracts is combined and treated as a single contract when that group of contracts is negotiated as a single package and the contracts are so closely interrelated that they are, in effect, part of a single project with an overall profit margin, and the contracts are performed concurrently or in a continuous sequence.

Commentary: Atos states that it enters into multiple element arrangements that include combinations of different services. It discloses its criteria for disaggregating into separate elements: (1) when the contractor and customer have been able to accept or reject that part of the contract relating to each component and (2) when each component's costs and revenues can be identified. These criteria are of a general nature and are based on certain considerations found in IAS 11 (see discussions on construction contracts).

Extract 11(3) – Collaboration agreement (general)

> **Bayer Aktiengesellschaft (AR 2007), page 109**
> **4. Basic principles, methods and critical accounting policies (in part)**
> **Net sales and other operating income (in part)**
>
> License or research and development collaboration agreements may consist of multiple elements and provide for varying consideration terms, such as upfront payments and milestone or similar payments. They therefore have to be assessed to determine whether separate delivery of the individual elements of such arrangements requires more than one unit of account. The delivered elements are separated if
> - they have value to the customer on a stand-alone basis,
> - there is objective and reliable evidence of the fair value of the undelivered element(s) and
> - the arrangement includes a general right of return relative to the delivered element(s) and delivery or performance of the as yet undelivered element(s) is probable and substantially within the control of the company.
>
> If all three criteria are fulfilled, the appropriate revenue recognition rule is then applied to each separate accounting unit.

Commentary: The company states it entered into collaboration agreements that were accounted for as separate agreements to reflect the economic substance of the transactions under IFRS. The company specifies the criteria it used to separate the units of account which are very similar to the ones specified in EIC 142. It is important to note that:
- EIC 142 revenue recognition requirements under Canadian GAAP are harmonized with US GAAP; and
- The company judged economic substance (which is the basis for separating unit of account under IAS 18) by considering existing guidance under US GAAP.

Extract 11(4) –Cooperation agreement (new technology)

> **SGL Carbon Aktiengesellschaft (Form 20-F 2006), page 57**
> **Significant Differences Between IFRS and U.S. GAAP (in part)**
> **Revenue Recognition**
>
> Audi and the SGL Group entered into a cooperation agreement in 2005, which targeted to develop SGL's existing carbon ceramic brakes technology for mass production. Under IFRS the components of these cooperation agreement were accounted for as separate agreements in order to reflect the economic substance of the transaction. Pursuant to paragraph 9 of EITF 00-21 "Revenue Arrangements with Multiple Deliverables", a delivered item is accounted for as a separate unit if 1) the delivered item has value on a standalone basis, 2) there is an objective and reliable evidence of the fair value of the undelivered items, and 3) when the customer has a general right of return relative to the delivered item, delivery or performance of the undelivered item is considered probable and substantially in the control of the vendor. After testing for these conditions, the two items were seen as one unit for revenue recognition purposes and a determinable period of performance existed from July 2005 to December 2006 and therefore revenue was recognized per "Proportional- Performance Method" (SAB 104) ratably over that period of performance. Accordingly the gross revenue related to the delivered component of the cooperation agreement was recognized immediately under IFRS but was deferred under U.S. GAAP as of December 31, 2005. As the performance period ended on December 31, 2006 the IFRS to U.S GAAP difference reversed in 2006 and there is no more difference as of December 31, 2006.

Commentary: In the above extract, the company states that it entered into a cooperation agreement that was accounted for as separate agreements to reflect the economic substance of the transaction under IFRS. The company notes that, when the criteria specified under EITF 00-21, *Revenue arrangements with multiple deliverables* (on which EIC-142 is based) are applied, only one unit would be allowed for revenue recognition purposes. Consequently, under Canadian GAAP (which also corresponds to related requirements under US GAAP), the "Proportional Performance Method" would be used. Accordingly, the gross revenue related to the delivered component of the cooperation agreement was recognized immediately under IFRS but would be deferred under Canadian GAAP. Note that the company stated that this difference was reversed in the subsequent year as the performance period ended, which resulted in its elimination.

Extract 11(5) – Extended warranty on sales of goods

Daimler AG (AR 2007), page 143
Accounting policies (in part)
Revenue recognition **(in part)**

The Group offers an extended, separately priced warranty for certain products. Revenue from these contracts is deferred and recognized into income over the contract period in proportion to the costs expected to be incurred based on historical information. In circumstances in which there is insufficient historical information, income from extended warranty contracts is recognized on a straight-line basis. A loss on these contracts is recognized in the current period, if the sum of the expected costs for services under the contract exceeds unearned revenue.

Commentary: In the above extract, the company specifies that extended warranty contracts are separately priced. This corresponds to EIC-143 requirements under Canadian GAAP. Note that the company also describes its accounting for these long-term service contracts, covered later in this chapter.

Extract 11(6) – Installation and training activities (sales of medical equipment)

Koninklijke Philips Electronics N.V. (AR 2007), page 206
Significant IFRS accounting policies (in part)
Revenue recognition (in part)

Revenues of transactions that have separately identifiable components are recognized based on their relative fair values. These transactions mainly occur in the Medical Systems segment for arrangements that require subsequent installation and training activities in order to become operable for the customer. However, since payment for the equipment is typically contingent upon the completion of the installation process, revenue recognition is deferred until the installation has been completed and the product is ready to be used by the customer in the way contractually agreed.

Commentary: The company specifies that revenue recognition is deferred until the installation has been completed and the product is ready to be used by the customer in the way contractually agreed on. Consequently, the whole contract is accounted for as a single unit of account as the installation is a significant part of the contract. The same would apply under Canadian GAAP.

Extract 11(7) – Contract products and prepaid products and services (telecommunication)

Vodacom Group Plc (AR 2007), page 101
I. REVENUE RECOGNITION (in part)
The main categories of revenue and bases of recognition for the Group are:

I.1 Contract products
Contract products that may include deliverables such as a handset and 24-month service are defined as arrangements with multiple deliverables. The arrangement consideration is allocated to each deliverable, based on the fair value of each deliverable on a stand alone basis as a percentage of the aggregated fair value of the individual deliverables. Revenue allocated to the identified deliverables in each revenue arrangement and the cost applicable to these identified deliverables are recognised based on the same recognition criteria of the individual deliverable at the time the product or service is delivered.

- Revenue from the handset is recognised when the product is delivered, limited to the amount of cash received.
- Monthly service revenue received from the customer is recognised in the period in which the service is delivered.
- Airtime revenue is recognised on the usage basis. The terms and conditions of the bundled airtime products, where applicable, allow the carry over of unused airtime. The unused airtime is deferred in full.

Vodacom Group Plc (AR 2007) (continued)

- Deferred revenue related to unused airtime is recognised when utilised by the customer. Upon termination of the customer contract, all deferred revenue for unused airtime is recognised in revenue.

I.2 Prepaid products

Prepaid products that may include deliverables such as a SIM-card and airtime are defined as arrangements with multiple deliverables. The arrangement consideration is allocated to each deliverable, based on the fair value of each deliverable on a stand alone basis as a percentage of the aggregated fair value of the individual deliverables. Revenue allocated to the identified deliverables in each revenue arrangement and the cost applicable to these identified deliverables are recognised based on the same recognition criteria of the individual deliverable at the time the product or service is delivered.

- Revenue from the SIM-card, representing activation fees, is recognised over the average useful life of a prepaid customer.
- Airtime revenue is recognised on the usage basis. Unused airtime is deferred in full.
- Deferred revenue related to unused airtime is recognised when utilised by the customer. Upon termination of the customer relationship, all deferred revenue for unused airtime is recognised in revenue.

Upon purchase of an airtime voucher the customer receives the right to make outgoing voice and data calls to the value of the airtime voucher. Revenue is recognised as the customer utilises the voucher.

Deferred revenue and costs related to unactivated starter packs which do not contain any expiry date, is recognised in the period when the probability of these starter packs being activated by a customer becomes remote. In this regard the Group applies a period of 36 months before these revenue and costs are released to the consolidated income statement.

I.3 Data revenue

Revenue net of discounts, from data services is recognised when the Group has performed the related service and depending on the nature of the service, is recognised either at the gross amount billed to the customer or the amount receivable by the Group as commission for facilitating the service.

I.4 Equipment sales

Equipment sales are recognised only when delivery and acceptance has taken place.

Equipment sales to third party service providers are recognised when delivery is accepted. No rights of return exist on sale to third party service providers.

page 180

45. US GAAP INFORMATION

(p) Revenue recognition

Under US GAAP, the Group applies Emerging Issues Task Force ("EITF") No. 00-21: Revenue Arrangements with Multiple Deliverables ("EITF 00-21"), to its revenue arrangements with multiple deliverables. This application has not resulted in a difference between the revenue recognised under US GAAP and IFRS.

Commentary: In this extract, the company provides details on two multi-elements arrangements, namely, contract products and prepaid products. It specifies that its accounting for these arrangements does not differ from that required under EITF 00-21 (on which EIC-142 is based). The extract also presents its accounting model for the sale of goods (equipment sales) and the rendering of services (data revenue) according to IAS 18. The accounting method the company uses is in line with Canadian GAAP (see our discussion later in this chapter).

Scope

The IASB has two standards on revenue recognition:

- IAS 18, which is a general standard that covers three significant types of revenue:
  - product sales,
  - service transactions, and
  - interest, royalties and dividends,

- IAS 11 covers many specific issues concerning construction contracts.

The IASB has also three standards addressing revenue recognition issues for:
- lessors in IAS 17, *Leases* (see Chapter 13);
- agriculture products in IAS 41, *Agriculture* (see Appendix A); and
- insurance industries in IFRS 4, *Insurance Contracts* (see Appendix A).

In addition, three IFRIC interpretations have been issued recently to provide specific guidance for:
- service concessions arrangements (IFRIC 12);
- customer loyalty programs (IFRIC 13); and
- agreements for the construction of real estate (IFRIC 15).

The following is noteworthy:
- Canadian GAAP includes CICA 3400, two AcGs and a number of EICs.
- The guidance provided in both CICA 3400 and IAS 18 is very limited.
- Coverage of certain issues dealt with in EIC-141 can be found in the appendix to IAS 18.
- IAS 18 prescribes different revenue recognition models for product sales (where seller's performance is immediate) and service rendering (where seller's performance often takes place over several reporting periods).
- Some industries and issues are not covered by any particular IFRS or Canadian standards. For example, neither address revenue issues related to the extraction of mineral ores and software products.

Illustrative Disclosures:

Extract 11(8) – Revenue recognition models (goods vs. services)

Wincanton plc (AR 2007), page 39

1 Accounting policies (in part)

Revenue recognition (in part)

Revenue from services rendered is recognised in the income statement on the delivery of those services based on the proportion of the total delivered at the balance sheet date. Revenue from the sale of goods is recognised in the income statement when the significant risks and rewards of ownership have been transferred to the buyer.

Commentary: Here, the company presents two of the revenue recognition models described under IAS 18: services rendered (revenue recognized on services delivery based on the proportion of the total delivered at the balance sheet date) and sale of goods (revenue recognized when the significant risks and rewards of ownership have been transferred to the buyer).

Extract 11(9) – Revenue recognition models (goods vs. services)

Corporate Express NV (AR 2007), page 79

2 Summary of accounting policies (in part)

Net sales (in part)

The criteria for recognition of sales of goods are:

- Significant risks and rewards of ownership have been transferred to the buyer. In most cases, the significant risks and rewards of ownership are transferred at the point of delivery or at the moment after installation (ready to operate), depending on shipping terms, contractual arrangements and performance obligations.
- Corporate Express retains neither continuing managerial involvement nor effective control over the goods sold.
- The amount of revenue can be measured reliably and collectibility is reasonably assured.
- The related cost (of sales) can be measured reliably.

Based on these criteria, sales of goods are in general recognised at the point of delivery, as Corporate Express has no future performance obligations.

The criteria for recognition of rendering services are:

- It is probable that the economic benefits associated with the transaction will flow to the entity.
- The stage of completion of the transaction at balance sheet date can be measured reliably.
- The amount of revenue can be measured reliably.
- The costs incurred for the transaction and the costs to complete the transaction can be measured reliably.

Based on these criteria, sales of machines in the Printing Systems business segment are recognised after installation while sales of supplies and spare parts are recognised at the point of delivery. Sales of services are recognised in the period in which the services are rendered.

The Company sells copiers and graphic machines together with subsequent servicing usually to third-party lease companies who enter into long-term lease contracts with our customers. The revenue from these contracts is allocated to the delivery of copiers and graphic machines and subsequent servicing in proportion to their fair value which means that any price discount given is allocated in proportion to their fair value.

The Company also rents copiers and graphic machines to customers of which the revenue is recognised on a linear basis over the contractual rental period.

Commentary: This extract presents two of the revenue recognition models described under IAS 18: sale of goods (revenue recognized at the point of delivery or upon installation) and services recognized when rendered. The company also explains how it accounts for its sales of goods together with subsequent servicing, usually to third-party lease companies (which are considered to be multi-element arrangements). Finally, the company records rental income according to IAS 17, *Leases*. All disclosures and accounting policies shown in this extract appear to be in line with Canadian GAAP.

Extract 11(10) – Revenue categories as scoped in by various IFRS standards

Telstra Corporation Limited (AR 2007), pages 127 and 128

2. Summary of accounting policies (in part)

2.17 Revenue recognition (in part)

Sales revenue

Our categories of sales revenue are recorded after deducting sales returns, trade allowances, discounts, sales incentives, duties and taxes.

(a) Rendering of services

Revenue from the provision of our telecommunications services includes telephone calls and other services and facilities provided, such as internet and data.

We record revenue earned from:

- telephone calls on completion of the call; and
- other services generally at completion, or on a straight line basis over the period of service provided, unless another method better represents the stage of completion.

Telstra Corporation Limited (AR 2007) (continued)

Installation and connection fee revenues are deferred and recognised over the average estimated customer life. Incremental costs directly related to these revenues are also deferred and amortised over the customer contract life in accordance with note 2.12(d).

In relation to basic access installation and connection revenue, we apply our management judgement to determine the estimated customer contract life. Based on our reviews of historical information and customer trends, we have determined that our average estimated customer life is 5 years (2006: 5 years).

(b) Sale of goods

Our revenue from the sale of goods includes revenue from the sale of customer equipment and similar goods. This revenue is recorded on delivery of the goods sold.

Generally we record the full gross amount of sales proceeds as revenue, however if we are acting as an agent under a sales arrangement, we record the revenue on a net basis, being the gross amount billed less the amount paid to the supplier. We review the facts and circumstances of each sales arrangement to determine if we are an agent or principal under the sale arrangement.

(c) Rent of network facilities

We earn rent mainly from access to retail and wholesale fixed and mobile networks and from the rent of dedicated lines, customer equipment, property, plant and equipment and other facilities. The revenue from providing access to the network is recorded on an accrual basis over the rental period.

(d) Construction contracts

We record construction revenue on a percentage of contract completion basis. The percentage of completion of contracts is calculated based on estimated costs to complete the contract.

Our construction contracts are classified according to their type. There are three types of construction contracts, these being material intensive, labour intensive and short duration. Revenue is recognised on a percentage of completion basis using the appropriate measures as follows:

- (actual costs / planned costs) x planned revenue - for material intensive projects;
- (actual labour hours / planned labour hours) x planned revenue - for labour intensive projects; and
- short duration projects are those that are expected to be completed within a month and revenues and costs are recognised on completion.

(e) Advertising and directory services

Classified advertisements and display advertisements are published on a daily, weekly and monthly basis for which revenues are recognised at the time the advertisement is published.

All of our Yellow Pages® and White Pages® directory revenues are recognised on delivery of the published directories using the delivery method. We consider our directories delivered when they have been published and delivered to customers' premises. Revenue from online directories is recognised over the life of service agreements, which is on average one year. Voice directory revenues are recognised at the time of providing the service to customers.

(f) Royalties

Royalty revenue is recognised on an accrual basis in accordance with the substance of the relevant agreements.

(g) Interest revenue

We record interest revenue on an accruals basis. For financial assets, interest revenue is determined by the effective yield on the instrument.

Commentary: The company describes various types of sales transaction that are recorded after deducting sales returns, trade allowances, discounts, sales incentives, duties and taxes. Each type of revenue is covered by specific accounting standards:

- rendering of services (IAS 18);
- sale of goods (IAS 18);
- rent of network facilities (IAS 17, *Leases*);
- construction contracts (IAS 11);
- advertising and directory services (IAS 18);
- royalties (IAS 18);
- interest revenue (IAS 18 and IAS 39, *Financial Instruments: Recognition and Measurement*).

The company states when revenue is recognized for each type of sales transaction. In addition, the company specifies its accounting policies for (see further details provided later in this chapter):

- Services: revenues recognized on installation or on a straight-line basis over the period the service is provided, unless another method better represents the stage of completion. Note that the company refers to completed-contract-method (prohibited under IAS 18). An explanation for using this method could be that it better represents the stage of completion (for example, customer approval is required) or that the service is rendered within one reporting period.
- Canadian GAAP allows for revenues to be recognized using the stage-of-completion method or the completed-contract method.
- Sale of goods: revenues recorded on delivery of the goods sold. This is the general requirement for sales of goods under both IAS 18 and Canadian GAAP.
- Presentation of revenues: the full gross amount of sales proceeds are recorded unless the company acts as an agent, in which case it records the gross amount billed less the amount paid to the supplier. This is also consistent with Canadian GAAP (see discussion on revenue definition later).
- Construction contracts: revenues are recognized according to the stage of completion. As required by IAS 11, the company provides further details on the methods it used for determining the stage of completion, which is specific to its operations. This accounting treatment is also consistent with Canadian GAAP, and details about the determination of the stage of completion illustrate the transparency of disclosures under IFRS (see our discussion on that topic later). Revenues for various advertising are recorded according to performance.

All disclosures and accounting policies discussed in this extract do not contradict current Canadian GAAP except for advertising and directory services would be usually deferred over the service period under Canadian GAAP.

Revenue Definition

IAS 18 defines revenue as the "gross inflow of economic benefits during the period arising from the course of the ordinary activities of the entity when those inflows result in an increase in equity, other than increases resulting from contributions by equity participants." CICA 3400 has a similar definition.

Under both IAS 18 and CICA 3400, the gross inflows must be generated for an entity's own account (as a principal). Amounts collected on behalf of third parties (as agents), such as sales taxes, are excluded. This is also consistent with EIC-18.

In certain circumstances, establishing whether an entity is acting on its own account as a principal or on behalf of a principal as an agent requires judgment. While EIC-123 provides guidance for making such judgments, IFRIC has not yet published an Interpretation on the issue (see commentary below).

EIC-123 suggests that an entity should decide whether to report gross revenue, with separate displays of costs of sales, or on a net basis by examining if it:

- acts as principal in the transaction (or as an agent or broker, including performing services, in substance, as an agent or broker, with compensation on a commission or fee basis);

- takes title to the products; or
- has the risks and rewards of ownership, such as the risk of loss for collection, delivery or returns (or performs as an agent or broker without assuming the risks and rewards).

Even though EIC-123 indicates that reporting at gross or net amounts is a matter of judgment that depends on the relevant facts and circumstances, it lists factors or indicators that should be considered in that evaluation. IASB has issued in August 2008 an Exposure Draft that proposes similar criteria to those described in EIC 123.

Illustrative Disclosures:

Extract 11(11) – Presentation net of taxes

Telstra Corporation Limited (AR 2007), page 129

2. Summary of accounting policies (in part)

(b) Goods and Services Tax (GST) (including other value added taxes)

We record our revenue, expenses and assets net of any applicable goods and services tax (GST), except where the amount of GST incurred is not recoverable from the Australian Taxation Office (ATO). In these circumstances the GST is recognised as part of the cost of acquisition of the asset or as part of the expense item.

Receivables and payables balances include GST where we have either included GST in our price charged to customers or a supplier has included GST in their price charged to us. The net amount of GST due, but not paid, to the ATO is included under payables.

Commentary: In the above extract, the company indicates that, as required by IAS 18, it has deducted GST from sales revenues. This is also the required presentation under EIC-18.

Extract 11(12) – Distribution agreements

Wincanton plc (AR 2007), page 39

1 Accounting policies (in part)

Revenue recognition (in part)

Certain distribution contracts oblige Wincanton to purchase goods from third parties and sell them on to the customer at cost. As Wincanton is rewarded for the physical distribution service provided acting only as an agent in these buy/sell transactions, and as the sale and purchase of the goods have no impact on the operating profit, the amounts invoiced to customers and charged by suppliers for the sale and purchase of these goods are excluded from revenue and cost of sales. Trade and other receivables and payables relating to such transactions are included in the balance sheet.

Commentary: Here, as required by IAS 18, the company explains the circumstances where it acts as an agent and the accounting treatment it has adopted. This is also in line with Canadian GAAP.

Extract 11(13) – Company acting as an agent (factors)

Atos Origin (AR 2007), page 91

18.3.2 Basis of preparation and significant accounting policies (in part)

Revenue Recognition (in part)

Revenue is reported net of supplier costs when the Group is acting as an agent between the client and the supplier. Factors generally considered to determine whether the Group is a principal or an agent, are most notably whether it is the primary obligor to the client, it assumes credit and delivery risks, or it adds meaningful value to the supplier's product or service.

Commentary: This extract specifies the factors the company used in determining whether it is acting as an agent between the client and the supplier. EIC-123 also requires that these factors be noted (even though the latter specifies additional factors) and, consequently, equivalent accounting treatment would result from its application.

Extract 11(14) – Shipping and handling, sales taxes and mining royalties

Rio Tinto Group (Full Financial Statements 2007), page 8
1 PRINCIPAL ACCOUNTING POLICIES (in part)
(c) Sales revenue (in part)

Sales revenue comprises sales to third parties at invoiced amounts, with most sales being priced ex works, free on board (f.o.b.) or cost, insurance and freight (c.i.f.). Amounts billed to customers in respect of shipping and handling are classed as sales revenue where the Group is responsible for carriage, insurance and freight. All shipping and handling costs incurred by the Group are recognised as operating costs. If the Group is acting solely as an agent, amounts billed to customers are offset against the relevant costs. Revenue from services is recognised as services are rendered and accepted by the customer.

Sales revenue excludes any applicable sales taxes. Mining royalties are presented as an operating cost or, where they are in substance a profit based tax, within taxes. Gross sales revenue disclosed as part of the income statement includes the Group's share of the sales revenue of equity accounted units. To avoid duplication, this excludes sales by jointly controlled entities to third parties of products purchased from the Group and excludes charges by jointly controlled entities to the Group. Co-product revenues are included in sales revenue.

Commentary: The company describes its accounting and presentation for various costs: shipping and handling, sales taxes and mining royalties. Accounting policies do not appear to contradict current Canadian GAAP (considering that equity-accounted units consist of joint ventures).

Extract 11(15) – Taxes and administrative fees

Vodacom Group Plc (AR 2007), page 100
I. REVENUE RECOGNITION (in part)

Revenue net of discounts, which excludes Value Added Taxation and sales between Group companies, represents the invoiced value of goods and services supplied by the Group.

The Group invoices its independent service providers for the revenue billed by them on behalf of the Group. The Group, within its contractual arrangements with its agents, pays them administrative fees. The Group receives in cash, the net amount equal to the gross revenue earned less the administrative fees payable to the agents.

Commentary: In this extract, the company indicates that, as required by IAS 18, it has:

- deducted GST from sales revenues; and
- recorded revenues on a gross basis, which corresponds to the customer billing less the administrative fee.

Its accounting policy seems in line with Canadian GAAP.

Extract 11(16) – Commissions and fees

Pearson plc (AR 2007), page 58
1. Accounting policies (in part)
q. Revenue recognition (in part)

On certain contracts, where the Group acts as agent, only commissions and fees receivable for services rendered are recognised as revenue. Any third party costs incurred on behalf of the principal that are rechargeable under the contractual arrangement are not included in revenue.

Commentary: This extract explains that only commissions and fees receivable for services rendered are recognized as revenue. This is in line with Canadian GAAP.

Extract 11(17) – Shipping and handling

Pearson plc (AR 2007), page 58
1. Accounting policies (in part)
q. Revenue recognition (in part)
Income from recharges of freight and other activities which are incidental to the normal revenue generating activities is included in other income.

Commentary: The company states that it accounts for income received from recharges of freight and other activities that are incidental to the normal revenue generating activities as other income. Even though no specific guidance is provided by IFRS and Canadian GAAP, this accounting policy choice would be allowed under both standards.

Extract 11(18) – Shipping and handling

Koninklijke Philips Electronics N.V. (AR 2007), page 206
Significant IFRS accounting policies (in part)
Revenue recognition (in part)
Shipping and handling costs billed to customers are recognized as revenues. Expenses incurred for shipping and handling costs of internal movements of goods are recorded as cost of sales. Shipping and handling costs related to sales to third parties are recorded as selling expenses and disclosed separately.

Commentary: In this extract, the company states that it accounts for shipping and handling costs billed to customers as revenue. It also discloses its accounting policy for shipping and handling expenses. Even though no specific guidance is provided by IFRS and Canadian GAAP, this accounting policy choice would be acceptable under both.

Extract 11(19) – Amounts included in revenue

Corporate Express NV (AR 2007), page 80
2 Summary of accounting policies (in part)
Net sales (in part)
Sales are recorded on a gross basis when Corporate Express acts as the primary obligor in a sales transaction and/or whether based on an assessment of certain indicators, such as general inventory risk and credit risks, Corporate Express bears the major part of the risks and rewards in a sales transaction. If the supplier acts as the primary obligor and/or bears the major part of the risks and rewards in a sales transaction, Corporate Express records the sales on a net basis (sales value less purchase value of goods or services).

In the Statements of Income, net sales represents the invoiced value, excluding sales tax, of trade goods sold and services rendered to third parties, less discounts, rebates to customers and less goods returned by the customers. Also included in net sales are shipping and other handling costs separately charged to the customers.

Commentary: This extract discusses many issues related to revenue amounts:
- Sales are recorded on a gross basis (the entity is the primary obligor in a sales transaction).
- Net sales represents the invoiced value, excluding sales taxes, of trade goods sold and services rendered to third parties less: discounts, rebates to customers and goods returned by the customers (see discussion on revenue measurement).
- Shipping and other handling costs charged separately to the customers are included in net sales (similar to Extract 11.19).

All accounting policies are in line with Canadian GAAP.

Revenue Measurement

IAS 18 requires that revenue be initially recorded at fair value. CICA 3400 does not contain such a general requirement.

The IAS 18 requirement on fair value dictates certain considerations:

- Revenue, the gross inflow of economic benefits, must take into account any reduction of proceeds, such as any trade discounts and volume rebates an entity might allow. Even though not specifically mentioned, IAS 18 implies that estimated returns should also be deducted from revenues to reflect the substance of the sales transaction. This is consistent with Canadian GAAP.

- Revenue must be measured at fair value of the consideration received or receivable, which means that:

  o cash sales are measured at the amount of cash received,

  o credit sales are measured at the fair value of the amount receivable (i.e., at the present value amount).

When determining the fair value of an amount receivable:

- Generally the effect of discounting can be ignored because it will not result in a material difference for short credit periods. Revenue and corresponding receivables should, however, be recorded at present value when credit terms extend over a longer period of time.

- The discount rate used should reflect the market borrowing rate reflecting the customer's credit risks.

- The difference between the fair value and the nominal amount of the consideration is deferred and is subsequently recognized as interest revenue using the effective interest method (as required by IAS 39, *Financial Instruments: Recognition and Measurement*).

Even though CICA 3400 does not specifically address discounting issues, receivables (which relate to revenues) are required to be initially measured at fair value under CICA 3855, *Financial Instruments — Recognition and Measurement*. Note, however, that IAS 18 requires all revenue transactions, including those with related parties, to be recorded at the fair value of the consideration received. Under Canadian GAAP, receivables (which relate to revenues) between related parties are initially measured at the carrying amount or exchange amount, according to CICA 3840, unless certain criteria are met.

Illustrative Disclosures:

Extract 11(20) – Loans to customers below the market

DAIMLER AG (AR 2007), page 143

Accounting policies (in part)

Revenue recognition (in part)

Revenue from receivables from financial services is recognized using the effective interest method. When loans are issued below market rates, related receivables are recognized at present value and revenue is reduced for the interest incentive granted.

Commentary: In the above extract, the company indicates that, as required by IAS 18, it discounted its loans on sales and reduced its revenue for the interest incentive granted. Note that market rates were used as basis for discounting. Canadian GAAP also requires loans to be discounted, using market rates, when those loans are issued below market rates.

Extract 11(21) – Measurement uncertainties (energy supply)

Centrica plc (AR 2007), page 68

3. Critical accounting judgements and key sources of estimation uncertainty (in part)

(b) Key sources of estimation uncertainty (in part)

The key assumptions concerning the future, and other key sources of estimation uncertainty at the balance sheet date, that have a significant risk of causing a material adjustment to the carrying amounts of assets and liabilities within the next financial year, are discussed below.

Revenue recognition – unread gas and electricity meters

Revenue for energy supply activities includes an assessment of energy supplied to customers between the date of the last meter reading and the year end (unread). Unread gas and electricity is estimated applying industry standards and using historical consumption patterns taking into account the industry reconciliation process for total gas and electricity usage by supplier. Management applies judgement to the measurement of the estimated energy supplied to customers and to the valuation of that energy consumption. An assessment is made of any factors that are likely to materially affect the ultimate economic benefits which will flow to the Group, including delays in processing, bill cancellation and re-bill rates and any customer or industry data quality issues. In the period subsequent to the implementation of the new billing system, operational exceptions have been running at a higher level and this has been taken account of in the judgements made. To the extent that the economic benefits are not expected to flow to the Group, the value of the revenue is not recognised. The judgements applied, and the assumptions underpinning these judgements, are considered to be appropriate. However, a change in these assumptions would have an impact on the amount of revenue recognised.

Commentary: Here, the company describes revenue measurement uncertainties in special circumstances. The disclosure of such uncertainties is in line with IAS 18 and Canadian GAAP.

Extract 11(22) – Sales discounts and other incentives

DAIMLER AG (AR 2007), page 143

Accounting policies (in part)

Revenue recognition (in part)

Revenue from sales of vehicles, service parts and other related products is recognized when the risks and rewards of ownership of the goods are transferred to the customer, the amount of revenue can be estimated reliably and collectibility is reasonably assured. Revenue is recognized net of discounts, cash sales incentives, customer bonuses and rebates granted.

Daimler uses price discounts in response to a number of market and product factors, including pricing actions and incentives offered by competitors, the amount of excess industry production capacity, the intensity of market competition, and consumer demand for the product. The Group may offer a variety of sales incentive programs at any point in time, including: cash offers to dealers and consumers, lease subsidies which reduce the consumers' monthly lease payment, or reduced financing rate programs offered to consumers.

Commentary: The company discloses the method it used to present discounts, cash sales incentives, customer bonuses and rebates granted, which is in line with IAS 18 and Canadian GAAP.

Extract 11(23) – Sales discounts, rebates and product returns

Bayer Aktiengesellschaft (AR 2007), pages 108 and 109

4. Basic principles, methods and critical accounting policies (in part)

Net sales and other operating income (in part)

Sales are stated net of sales taxes, other taxes and sales deductions. The latter are estimated amounts for cash discounts, rebates and product returns. They are deducted at the time the sales are recognized, and appropriate provisions are recorded. Sales deductions are estimated primarily on the basis of historical experience, specific contractual terms and future expectations of sales development in each business segment. It is unlikely that estimation parameters other than these could affect sales deductions in a way that would be material to the Bayer Group's business operations. The potential for variability in provisions for future sales deductions is not material in relation to the Group's reported operating results. Adjustments to provisions for rebates, cash discounts or returns for sales made in prior periods were not significant in relation to income before income taxes in the years under report.

Provisions for rebates in 2007 amounted to 1.4 percent of total net sales (2006: 1.6 percent). In addition to rebates, Group companies offer cash discounts for prompt payment in some countries. Provisions for cash discounts as of December 31, 2007 and December 31, 2006 were less than 0.1 percent of total net sales for the respective year.

Sales are reduced for expected returns of defective goods or in respect of contractual arrangements to return saleable products on the date of sale or at the time when the amount of future returns can be reasonably estimated. Provisions for product returns as of December 31, 2007 were 0.3 percent of total net sales for the year (December 31, 2006: 0.1 percent). If future product returns cannot be reasonably estimated and are significant to the sale transaction, the revenues and the related cost of sales are deferred until an estimate may reasonably be made or when the right to return the goods has expired.

Commentary: The company discloses the method it used to present cash discounts, rebates and product returns, which is in line with IAS 18 and Canadian GAAP. Note that the company provides quantitative information on these sales deductions. Such quantitative information would not normally be disclosed under Canadian GAAP.

Extract 11(24) – Cash discounts and extended payment term

Transnet Ltd (AR 2007), page 155

REVENUE (in part)

Transactions giving rise to adjustments to revenue/purchases

The Group accounts for cash discounts and rebates received (given) as follows:

- In the case of the Group as a purchaser, cash discounts and rebates received are estimated upfront and deducted from the cost of inventories purchased, and

- In the case of the Group as a seller, cash discounts and rebates given are estimated upfront and deducted from the amount of revenue recognised.

Where extended payment terms are granted by the Group, whether explicitly or implicitly, the effect of the time value of money is taken into account irrespective of other factors such as the cash selling prices of the goods.

Commentary: This extract provides details on revenue measurement:

- Cash discounts and rebates are estimated up front and deducted from the amount of revenue recognized.

- Extended payment terms are granted to customers and are taken into account irrespective of other factors such as the cash selling prices of the goods.

The measurement policy adopted is in line with IAS 18 and Canadian GAAP.

In addition, the company specifies how it accounts for rebates received from vendors (which are deducted from the cost of inventories purchased). Such treatment is in line with EIC-144. This issue is dealt with later in this chapter.

Sale of Goods

Under both IAS 18 and CICA 3400, revenue from the sale of goods is recognized when the following criteria are met:

1. The entity has transferred to the buyer the significant risks and rewards of ownership of the goods (CICA 3400 adds to this requirement by specifying that "all significant acts must be completed").

2. The entity has relinquished managerial involvement and effective control over the goods sold.

3. The amount of the revenue can be measured reliably (CICA 3400 uses different wording by requiring "reasonable assurance" regarding the measurement of the consideration to be derived from the sale of goods, and the extent to which goods may be returned).

4. It is probable that any economic benefits associated with the transaction will flow to the entity (CICA 3400 appears to require a higher level of probability as it specifies that ultimate collection of consideration should be reasonably assured).

5. The costs incurred or to be incurred by the transaction can be measured reliably.

EIC-141 contains detailed discussions on prerequisites for revenue recognition:

- *Persuasive evidence of an arrangement*. IAS 18 does not specifically address this issue, though it might be an element considered for Criterion 4 above (probability that economic benefits will flow to the entity). The absence of the specific requirement in IFRS might, however, affect the timing of revenue recognition when goods are delivered to a customer prior to the official approval of an agreement.

- *Fixed or determinable* sales price in the context of cancellable sales agreements, rights of return, price protections and refundable fees. IAS 18 indirectly addresses this issue in Criterion 3 (reliability of revenue measurement).

All five revenue recognition criteria are somewhat interrelated. A particular clause in a sales transaction can be examined from different perspectives for the purposes of revenue recognition. For example, the recognition of revenue from "initial fees" or "up-front payments" could be assessed from the risks and rewards transferred perspective (Criterion 1) and from probability that economic benefits will flow to the entity perspective (Criterion 4).

Although applying the above five revenue recognition criteria can be straightforward, difficulties might arise, for example, when risks and rewards of ownership are not transferred on the delivery of goods.

IAS 18 provides the following examples where delivery of goods would not result in revenue recognition:

- An entity retains an obligation for unsatisfactory performance not covered by normal warranty provisions.

- Receipt of the revenue from a particular sale is contingent on the derivation of revenue by the buyer from its sale of the goods.

- Goods are subject to installation and the installation is a significant part of the contract that the entity has not yet completed.

- The buyer has the right to rescind the purchase for a reason specified in the sales contract and the entity is uncertain about the probability of return.

Examples where, depending on the circumstances, revenue would be recognized include:

- The buyer requests that delivery be delayed but takes title and accepts billing.
- Goods are delivered but are subject to conditions such as:
  - o inspection,
  - o limited right of return.
- Goods are transferred to buyer but seller retains title for credit protection purposes.
- Goods are transferred to the buyer but seller has an option to repurchase goods at an amount below their fair value.

In dealing with revenue recognition issues in various circumstances, IAS 18 provides a number of illustrations while EIC-141 establishes prescriptive and detailed criteria.

Bill-and-hold Arrangements

The appendix to IAS 18 provides the following criteria for revenue recognition on bill-and-hold arrangements:

- Buyer takes title and has accepted billing.
- It is probable that delivery will be made.
- The item is on hand, identified and ready for delivery to the buyer at the time the sale is recognized.
- The buyer specifically acknowledges the deferred delivery instructions.
- The usual payment terms apply.

EIC-141 has similar criteria but they might be viewed as more restrictive than the ones in IAS 18. EIC-141 sets the following as prerequisites for revenue recognition on bill-and-hold arrangements:

- Risks of ownership have passed to buyer.
- Customer made a fixed commitment to purchase the goods, in written or in electronic form.
- The buyer, not the seller, requests the transaction be on a bill-and-hold basis and the buyer must have a substantial business purpose for ordering on this basis.
- Fixed schedule for delivery is specified and the date of delivery is reasonable and consistent in light of the business purpose of the transaction.
- The seller has not retained any specific performance obligations, therefore the earnings process is not complete.
- The ordered goods are segregated from the seller's inventory and may not be used to fill other orders.
- Product is complete and ready for shipment.

The criteria in EIC-141 appear to be more restrictive than those illustrated in the IAS 18 appendix. For example, EIC-141 requires not only that:

- Delivery be probable (as evidenced, for example, by the buyer making a partial payment) but also that the date of delivery be fixed, reasonable and consistent with buyer's business purpose.
- The item be identified but also that it is segregated in a way that it could not be used to fill other orders.
- The buyer initiates the arrangement and has valid justification for the arrangement.

Layaway Arrangements

The IAS 18 appendix illustrates the recognition of revenue on layaway arrangements when all of the following criteria are met:

* *A significant deposit is received.* The buyer in a layaway transaction has the right to stop making payments under the arrangement. Therefore, the buyer's risk of loss due to a decline in market value is limited to the deposit made. As a result, some of the risk of a market price decline remains with the seller and might only be partially covered by the forfeited payments. Therefore, the size of the initial deposit must be taken into consideration when assessing the transfer of the risk of loss to the buyer.

* *Experience indicates that most layaway transactions are eventually consummated.* Without historical evidence that most customers complete required payments and take delivery, it is difficult to conclude that a sale has occurred.

* *The goods are on hand, identified and ready for delivery to the buyer.*

Layaway sales are not recognized as revenue under EIC-141. Accordingly, payments received prior to delivery of goods to the customer are presented as a deposit liability, and the reserved inventory is not derecognized. The adoption of IAS 18 may, therefore, result in earlier revenue recognition than under Canadian GAAP.

Because forfeitures of initial payments on layaway sales do not arise from a revenue earnings event, under both IFRS and Canadian GAAP, it would be appropriate to account for forfeitures as gains to be classified below gross margins.

Acceptance, Installation and Inspection

Under both IFRS and Canadian GAAP, revenues on goods that are shipped subject to acceptance, installation and inspection are not recorded until these conditions are satisfied. The IAS 18 appendix illustrates that revenue can be recognized immediately on the buyer's acceptance of delivery when:

* The installation process is simple.

* The inspection is performed only for purposes of final determination of contract prices.

EIC-141 criteria concerning customer acceptance are more restrictive than the ones illustrated in the appendix to IAS 18. For example, EIC-141 requires that a buyer formally accept the goods unless it objectively demonstrates that the criteria in the contract have not been satisfied. In addition, EIC-141 provides more detailed guidance than the IAS 18 appendix by considering trial productions and right of return based on subjective matters.

Even though the principles underlying EIC-141 requirements are similar to those in IAS 18, the somewhat more restrictive and detailed requirements under the former standard might result in a deferral of revenue that would be recognized immediately under IFRS.

Recoverability

Gross revenue is recorded when it is probable that any economic benefits associated with a transaction will flow to the entity (IAS 18) or when collection is reasonably assured (CICA 3400). The provision for an uncollectible amount is recorded as an expense (with an offsetting reduction in the related receivable) rather than a reduction in revenue.

Reliable Measurement of Costs

To record revenues under IAS 18, companies must be able to reliably measure all costs related to a sale. The absence of reliable measurement could result in the deferral of revenue even if uncertain future costs were relatively small. This deferral is justified on the basis that it would be difficult to conclude that all of the seller's significant obligations had been fulfilled.

EIC-141 has no general requirement for reliable measurement of costs. The only reference to reliability relates to rebates and refunds, which are reductions of revenues, not costs (which were covered previously when dealing with revenue measurement).

Illustrative Disclosures:

Extract 11(25) – Customer's acceptance

> **Koninklijke Philips Electronics N.V. (AR 2007), page 206**
> **Significant IFRS accounting policies (in part)**
> **Revenue recognition (in part)**
> Transfer of risks and rewards varies depending on the individual terms of the contract of sale. For consumer-type products in the segments Lighting, DAP and Consumer Electronics, these criteria are generally met at the time the product is shipped and delivered to the customer and, depending on the delivery conditions, title and risk have passed to the customer and acceptance of the product, when contractually required, has been obtained, or, in cases where such acceptance is not contractually required, when management has established that all aforementioned conditions for revenue recognition have been met.
>
> Examples of the above-mentioned delivery conditions are 'Free on Board point of delivery' and 'Costs, Insurance Paid point of delivery', where the point of delivery may be the shipping warehouse or any other point of destination as agreed in the contract with the customer and where title and risk in the goods pass to the customer.

Commentary: This extract presents the company's revenue recognition policy for customer product acceptance. The company indicates that, in circumstances where customer acceptance is not contractually required, management would recognize revenue according to terms of delivery. This appears to be in line with IAS 18 and EIC-141.

Extract 11(26) – Right of return

> **Koninklijke Philips Electronics N.V. (AR 2007), page 206**
> **Significant IFRS accounting policies (in part)**
> **Revenue recognition (in part)**
> Revenues are recorded net of sales taxes, customer discounts, rebates and similar charges. For products for which a right of return exists during a defined period, revenue recognition is determined based on the historical pattern of actual returns, or in cases where such information is not available, revenue recognition is postponed until the return period has lapsed. Return policies are typically based on customary return arrangements in local markets.

Commentary: The company presents its revenue recognition policy when a right of return exists. The company does not record revenue in the absence of a historical pattern of actual returns. This appears to be in line with IAS 18 and EIC-141.

Extract 11(27) – Right of return

> **Pearson plc (AR 2007), page 58**
> **1. Accounting policies (in part)**
> **q. Revenue recognition (in part)**
> Revenue from the sale of books is recognised when title passes. A provision for anticipated returns is made based primarily on historical return rates. If these estimates do not reflect actual returns in future periods then revenues could be understated or overstated for a particular period.

Commentary: Besides providing its basis for estimating returns, the company discloses the uncertainties related to this estimate.

Extract 11(28) – Right of return

Vodafone Group Plc (AR 2007), page 97
2. Significant accounting policies (in part)
Revenue (in part)

For equipment sales made to intermediaries, revenue is recognised if the significant risks associated with the equipment are transferred to the intermediary and the intermediary has no general right of return. If the significant risks are not transferred, revenue recognition is deferred until sale of the handset to an end customer by the intermediary or the expiry of the right of return.

Commentary: The company specifies that it defers the recognition of revenue on equipment transferred to certain intermediaries. This appears to be in line with IFRS and Canadian GAAP.

Extract 11(29) – Warranty contracts

Koninklijke Philips Electronics N.V. (AR 2007), page 206
Significant IFRS accounting policies
Revenue recognition (in part)

A provision for product warranty is made at the time of revenue recognition and reflects the estimated costs of replacement and free-of-charge services that will be incurred by the Company with respect to the products. The customer has the option to purchase such an extension, which is subsequently billed to the customer. Revenue recognition occurs on a straight-line basis over the contract period.

Commentary: The company presents its accounting for warranties. A separate unit of accounting is recorded when a customer purchases an extended warranty (see our discussion on identifying sales transaction). This is in line with IFRS and Canadian GAAP.

Extract 11(30) – Warranty (costs)

Metso Corporation (AR 2007), page 66
3 Critical accounting estimates and judgements (in part)
Reserve for warranty costs
The warranty reserve is based on the history of past warranty costs and claims for machines and equipment under warranty. The typical warranty period is 12 months from the date of customer acceptance of the delivered equipment. For larger projects, the average warranty period is two years. For sales involving new technology and long-term delivery contracts, additional warranty reserves can be established on a case by case basis to take into account the potentially increased risk.
page 94
24 Provisions
Warranty and guarantee provisions
The provisions for warranty and guarantee liabilities have changed as follows during the financial year 2007:

EUR million	Balance at beginning of year	Impact of exchange rates	Increase for current year's deliveries	Increase for previous years' deliveries	Increase from business acquisitions	Deductions	Balance at end of year
Warranty and guarantee provisions	194	(3)	76	28	0	(102)	193

Metso issues various types of contractual product warranties under which it generally guarantees the performance levels agreed in the sales contract, the performance of products delivered during the agreed warranty period and services rendered for a certain period or term. The warranty liability is based on historical realized warranty costs for deliveries of standard products and services. The usual warranty is 12 months from the date of customer acceptance of the delivered equipment. For larger projects, the average warranty period is two years. For more complex contracts, including long-term projects sold by Metso Paper and Metso Minerals, the warranty reserve is calculated contract by contract and updated regularly to take into consideration any changes in the potential warranty liability.

Commentary: This extract discloses warranty costs related to various sales of equipment. Detailed disclosures are provided, as required by both IAS 18 and IAS 37, *Provisions* (which we covered in Chapter 15). This level of detailed disclosures is not generally required by Canadian GAAP.

Rendering Services

An entity renders services when it performs an agreed-on task for a customer, such as maintenance, membership services, professional services and the development or customization of a product. Services are also rendered in the context of a construction contract, which is covered by IAS 11.

Service contracts could include one type of service or consist of multiple-element arrangements providing for several services or a combination of both goods and services (see previous discussion on sales transaction identification).

A service may be linked to a discrete event or service that occurs in the short term, or may involve rendering a service over a period longer than a particular reporting period. The latter is referred to as "long-term contract" and prompts special accounting considerations.

The main accounting issue relating to long-term service contracts (IAS 18) and construction contracts (IAS 11) is the determination of what revenues and costs to recognize at various points throughout the term of the construction work performed or services provided using the percentage-of-completion method.

We discuss below some of the specific IAS 18 requirements for long-term contracts as they present particular difficulties for revenue recognition and measurement purposes.

Revenue Recognition Method

IAS 18 requires that revenues from services rendered be recognized by reference to the stage (or percentage) of completion of the transaction (i.e., when services are rendered) when the following criteria are met:

- The amount of revenue can be measured reliably.
- The flow of economic benefits to the entity is probable.
- The stage of completion at the period end can be measured reliably.
- The costs incurred to date and the costs to completion can be measured reliably.

Long-term service contracts (IAS 18) are accounted for similarly to construction contracts (IAS 11). Canadian GAAP has similar requirements for all long-term contracts although, unlike IFRS, methods other than percentage of completion could be used, including the completed-contract method (which is specifically prohibited under IFRS).

Note that the stage-of-completion method is not always required for recognizing service revenues. IAS 18 specifies that:

- For practical reasons, a straight-line basis of revenue recognition is permitted when services are performed by an indeterminate number of acts over a specified time period and when no other method provides a better measure of the stage of completion.
- When a specific act is much more significant than any other ones, the recognition of revenue is postponed until the significant act is executed.
- Progress payments and advances received from customers often do not reflect the services performed.

Reliable Revenue Measurement

IAS 18 provides specific guidance for assessing revenue measurement reliability when using the percentage-of-completion method. Before it can apply that method, an entity must have agreed to the following with the other parties to the transaction:

- each party's enforceable rights regarding the service to be provided and received;
- the consideration to be exchanged; and
- the manner and terms of settlement.

IAS 18 refers to certain elements that must be in place to ensure revenue measurement reliability, such as:

- an adequate information system, which includes an effective budgeting and reporting system;
- a review and adjustment, when necessary, of estimates as services are performed (note that the need to revise estimates is not necessarily indicative that the outcome of the transaction cannot be estimated reliably).

Stage-of-completion Estimates

The method used to determine the stage of completion depends on the nature of the contract involved. Entities must use the method that measures reliably the services performed.

IAS 18 lists the following methods of determining the stage of completion:

- surveys of work performed;
- services performed to date as a percentage of total services to be performed; or
- the proportion of costs incurred to the estimated total costs of the transaction (which includes only costs reflecting services performed to date or to be performed).

Consistency

As generally required by IFRS, a consistent approach should be use for recognizing revenues of similar contracts.

Uncertainties

When the outcome of a contract cannot be estimated reliably, but the contract overall is expected to be profitable, IAS 18 requires that revenue be recognized to the extent that expenses recognized are recoverable. This is described as the "zero profit method." If it is not probable that the costs incurred will be recovered, revenue is not recognized and the costs incurred are recognized as an expense. Entities reporting under Canadian GAAP generally apply the completed-contract method when an outcome cannot be measured reliably. In any case, costs exceeding the anticipated revenues are recognized as a loss.

Entities should resume using the stage-of-completion method to determine the amount of revenue to recognize when the uncertainties that prevented the outcome of the contract from being estimated reliably no longer exist.

Canadian GAAP and IFRS might generate differences in the accounting for long-term service contracts because of the following:

- Canadian GAAP provides little guidance. Even though the requirements in CICA 3400, EIC-65 and EIC-78 are in line with those of IAS 18, they are limited in scope.
- CICA 3400 requires the use of completed-contract method when an entity cannot reasonably estimate the extent of progress toward completion. This differs from IAS 11 and IAS 18, which require the use of the cost-recovery method in these circumstances. The completed-contract method differs from the cost-recovery method in that:
  - o under the completed-contract method, neither revenue nor cost is recognized until performance is complete or substantially complete,
  - o under the cost-recovery method, costs are expensed as incurred and revenue is recognized only to the extent that it is probable that any contract costs incurred will be recoverable.
- When a service contract includes a specific act that is much more significant than any other, IAS 18 requires that recognition of revenue be postponed until the significant act is executed. Since no equivalent requirement exists under Canadian GAAP, it is possible that entities facing these circumstances would use another revenue recognition method.
- Many entities reporting under Canadian GAAP will recognize revenues on long-term service contracts on a straight-line basis over the term of the contract, even if the performance pattern is other than straight line since it is easier to apply. In contrast, IAS 18 allows the use of the straight-line method only when the service is provided by an indeterminate number of acts over a specified time period and when no other method provides a better measure of the stage of completion.

Illustrative Disclosures:

Extract 11(31) – Information technology and business process outsourcing

Atos Origin (AR 2007), page 91

18.3.2 Basis of preparation and significant accounting policies (in part)

Revenue Recognition (in part)

The Group provides information technology (IT) and business process outsourcing (BPO) services. Depending on the structure of the contract, revenue is recognised accordingly to the following principles:

Revenue based on variable IT work units is recognised as the services are rendered.

Where the outcome of fixed price contracts such as Consulting and Systems Integration contracts can be estimated reliably, revenue is recognised using the percentage-of-completion (POC) method. Under the POC method, revenue is recognised based on the costs incurred to date as a percentage of the total estimated costs to fulfil the contract. Revenue relating to these contracts is recorded in the Consolidated Balance Sheet under "Trade accounts and notes receivable" for services rendered in excess of billing, while billing exceeding services rendered is recorded as deferred income under "other current liabilities". Where the outcome of a fixed price contract cannot be estimated reliably, contract revenue is recognised to the extent of contracts costs incurred that are likely to be recoverable.

Revenue for long-term fixed price Managed Operations services is recognised when services are rendered.

If circumstances arise, that change the original estimates of revenues, costs, or extent of progress toward completion, then revisions to the estimates are made. The Group performs on-going profitability analyses of its services contracts in order to determine whether the latest estimates of revenue, costs and profits, require updating. If, at any time, these estimates indicate that the contract will be unprofitable, the entire estimated loss for the remainder of the contract is recorded immediately through a provision for estimated losses on completion.

Commentary: In the above extract, the company discloses that it has two types of contracts:

- Revenue based on variable IT work units, which is recognized as the services are rendered using the percentage-of-completion method. Where the outcome of a fixed-price contract cannot be estimated reliably, the cost-recovery method is used (contract revenue is recognized to the extent that contracts costs incurred are likely to be recovered). This is also consistent with IAS 11. The same accounting policy would apply under Canadian GAAP except that the completed-contract method would normally be used instead of the cost-recovery method.

- Revenue for long-term, fixed-price Managed Operations services is recognized when services are rendered. Revisions to estimates are made in instances that change the original estimates of revenues, costs or extent of progress toward completion. In addition, the company recognizes the entire estimated loss for the remainder of a contract when it becomes unprofitable. This is also consistent with IAS 11. The same accounting policy would apply under Canadian GAAP.

Extract 11(32) – Conference related activities

Informa plc (AR - 2007), page 75

3 Accounting policies (in part)

Revenue (in part)

Subscription income is deferred and recognised over the term of the subscription. Conference income is deferred and recognised when the conference is held. Income from managed events represents fees earned and is recognised when the event is held. Consulting and training revenues are recognised as services are delivered. Where consultancy services are provided over a period of time, revenue is recognised using the stage of completion method when the outcome of the contract can be measured reliably. The stage to completion is determined with regard to key milestones in the contract being attained and the percentage of services performed under the contract as a percentage of the total services to be performed. Royalty revenue is recognised as the franchisee recognises their revenue.

Commentary: The company describes the various revenue recognition methods for service rendering:

- straight line for subscriptions;
- significant event for conferences and managed events;
- short-term consulting and training revenues, which are recognized as the services are delivered;
- stage of completion for long-term consulting and training revenues where stage to completion is determined with regard to key milestones and the percentage of services performed.

All methods described are in line with both IAS 18 and Canadian GAAP.

Extract 11(33) – Hotel operations

InterContinental Hotels Group PLC (AR 2007), page 55

Summary of significant accounting policies (in part)

Revenue recognition (in part)

Owned and leased – primarily derived from hotel operations, including the rental of rooms and food and beverage sales from owned and leased hotels operated under the Group's brand names. Revenue is recognised when rooms are occupied and food and beverages are sold.

Management fees – earned from hotels managed by the Group, usually under long-term contracts with the hotel owner. Management fees include a base fee, which is generally a percentage of hotel revenue, and an incentive fee, which is generally based on the hotel's profitability or cash flows. Revenue is recognised when earned and realised or realisable under the terms of the contract.

Franchise fees – received in connection with the license of the Group's brand names, usually under long-term contracts with the hotel owner. The Group charges franchise royalty fees as a percentage of room revenue. Revenue is recognised when earned and realised or realisable under the terms of the agreement.

Where, in addition to licensing the use of a Group brand, a Group company manages the hotel for third party owners. The Group derives revenues from base and incentive management fees and provides the system infrastructure necessary for the hotel to operate. Management contract fees are generally a percentage of hotel revenue and may have an additional incentive fee linked to profitability or cash flow. The terms of these agreements vary, but are often long term (for example, 10 years or more). The Group's responsibilities under the management agreement typically include hiring, training and supervising the managers and employees that operate the hotels under the relevant brand standards. In order to gain access to central reservation systems, global and regional brand marketing and brand standards and procedures, owners are typically required to make a further contribution.

page 57

2 SEGMENTAL INFORMATION (in part)

Owned and leased

Where a Group company both owns (or leases) and operates the hotel and, in the case of ownership, takes all the benefits and risks associated with ownership.

Franchised

Where Group companies neither own nor manage the hotel, but license the use of a Group brand and provide access to reservation systems, loyalty schemes and know-how. The Group derives revenues from a brand royalty or licensing fee, based on a percentage of room revenue.

Commentary: The company describes three sources of revenues for service rendered:

- services related to owned and leased property, which are recognized when significant events occur;
- management fees (consisting of long-term contracts), which are recognized when earned and realized or realizable under the terms of the contract (terms that are used under US GAAP); and
- franchise fees, which are recognized when earned and realized or realizable under the terms of the agreement.

These methods are in line with both IAS 18 and Canadian GAAP.

Extract 11(34) – Advertising

WPP Group PLC (AR 2007), pages 156 and 157

Accounting policies (in part)

Advertising and Media Investment Management

Revenue is typically derived from commissions on media placements and fees for advertising services. Revenue may consist of various arrangements involving commissions, fees, incentive-based revenue or a combination of the three, as agreed upon with each client.

Revenue is recognised when the service is performed, in accordance with the terms of the contractual arrangement. Incentive-based revenue typically comprises both quantitative and qualitative elements; on the element related to quantitative targets, revenue is recognised when the quantitative targets have been achieved; on the element related to qualitative targets, revenue is recognised when the incentive is received or receivable.

Information, Insight & Consultancy

Revenue recognised in proportion to the level of service performed for market research contracts is based on proportional performance. In assessing contract performance, both input and output criteria are reviewed. Costs incurred are used as an objective input measure of performance. The primary input of all work performed under these arrangements is labour. As a result of the relationship between labour and cost, there is normally a direct relationship between costs incurred and the proportion of the contract performed to date. Costs incurred as a proportion of expected total costs is used as an initial proportional performance measure. This indicative proportional performance measure is subsequently validated against other more subjective criteria (i.e. relevant output measures) such as the percentage of interviews completed, percentage of reports delivered to a client and the achievement of any project milestones stipulated in the contract. In the event of divergence between the objective and more subjective measures, the more subjective measures take precedence since these are output measures.

While most of the studies provided in connection with the Group's market research contracts are undertaken in response to an individual client's or group of clients' specifications, in certain instances a study may be developed as an off-the-shelf product offering sold to a broad client base. For these transactions, revenue is recognised when the product is delivered. Where the terms of transaction provide for licensing the product on a subscription basis, revenue is recognised over the subscription period on a straight-line basis or, if applicable, based on usage.

Substantially all services are provided on a fixed price basis. Pricing may also include a provision for a surcharge where the actual labour hours incurred in completing a project are significantly above the labour hours quoted in the project proposal. In instances where this occurs, the surcharge will be included in the total revenue base on which to measure proportional performance when the actual threshold is reached provided that collectibility is reasonably assured.

Public Relations & Public Affairs and Branding & Identity, Healthcare and Specialist Communications

Revenue is typically derived from retainer fees and services to be performed subject to specific agreement. Revenue is recognised when the service is performed, in accordance with the terms of the contractual arrangement. Revenue is recognised on long-term contracts, if the final outcome can be assessed with reasonable certainty, by including in the income statement revenue and related costs as contract activity progresses.

Commentary: In the above extract, the company presents in detail the way it accounts for various service rendering arrangements:

- Commissions on media placements and fees for advertising services: Revenue is recognized when the service is performed.
- Incentive-based revenue: Revenue is recognized when quantitative targets have been achieved or when an incentive is received or receivable for qualitative targets.
- Off-the-shelf product offerings sold to a broad client base: Revenues are recognized when the product is delivered.
- Licensing of products on a subscription basis: Revenues are recognized over the subscription period on a straight-line basis or, if applicable, based on usage.
- Surcharges: Revenues are recognized when the actual threshold is reached provided that collectibility is reasonably assured.
- Information, insight and consultancy: Revenue is recognized in proportion to the level of service performed for market research contracts. The company provides extensive details on the measurement of stage of completion.
- Public relations and public affairs and branding and identity, healthcare and specialist communications: Revenue is recognized when the service is performed.

This extract provides a good example of transparent disclosure for the provision of advertising services. Accounting policies are in line with both IAS 18 and Canadian GAAP.

Extract 11(35) – Installation and maintenance contracts

Oxford Instruments plc (AR 2007), page 43

Accounting Policies (in part)

(p) Revenue (in part)

(i) Goods sold and services rendered

Revenue is recognised in the income statement when the significant risks and rewards of ownership have been transferred to the buyer.

Revenue, which excludes value added tax and similar sales based taxes, represents sales to external customers of products and services and is stated before commissions payable to agents. Revenue is recognised on shipment, except for installation, service contracts and long term contracts. Revenue from installation is separately recognised on completion of the installation. Revenue from contracts for maintenance and support is recognised on a pro-rata basis over the contract period.

(ii) Long term contracts

Contracts which take more than six months to complete and are significant in size are included in the financial statements to reflect progress towards completion. Revenue includes the value of work carried out during the year in respect of these long term contracts including amounts not invoiced to customers. Profit recognition reflects the stage reached, the estimated costs to complete and the degree of risk remaining on each long term contract.

Commentary: The company presents its accounting policies for:

- revenue recognition (IAS 18 general criteria for sales of goods is stated);
- revenue measurement (which excludes value-added tax and other similar sales, as well as commissions payable to agents);
- sale of goods for which revenue is recognized on shipment unless they include installation;
- multi-element contracts where revenue from installation is separately recognized on completion of the installation (i.e., revenue is recognized on the occurrence of significant events);
- maintenance and support service for which revenue is recognized on a pro-rata basis over the contract period;
- long-term contracts, as defined for the entity's particular circumstances (taking into account possibly materiality considerations) for which revenue is recognized using the stage of completion.

All disclosures and accounting policies described in this extract appear to be consistent with both IAS 18 and Canadian GAAP.

Extract 11(36) – Telecommunication

BT Group PLC (AR & Form 20-F 2007), pages 78 and 79
Accounting policies (in part)
(III) REVENUE (in part)

Revenue arising from separable installation and connection services is recognised when it is earned, upon activation. Revenue from the rental of analogue and digital lines and private circuits is recognised evenly over the period to which the charges relate. Revenue from calls is recognised at the time the call is made over the group's network.

Subscription fees, consisting primarily of monthly charges for access to broadband and other internet access or voice services, are recognised as revenue as the service is provided. Revenue arising from the interconnection of voice and data traffic between other telecommunications operators is recognised at the time of transit across the group's network.

Revenue from the sale of peripheral and other equipment is recognised when all the significant risks and rewards of ownership are transferred to the buyer, which is normally the date the equipment is delivered and accepted by the customer.

Revenue from long term contractual arrangements is recognised based on the percentage of completion method. The stage of completion is estimated using an appropriate measure according to the nature of the contract. For long term services contracts revenue is recognised on a straight line basis over the term of the contract. However, if the performance pattern is other than straight line, revenue is recognised as services are provided, usually on an output or consumption basis. For fixed price contracts, including contracts to design and build software solutions, revenue is recognised by reference to the stage of completion, as determined by the proportion of costs incurred relative to the estimated total contract costs, or other measures of completion such as contract milestone customer acceptance. In the case of time and materials contracts, revenue is recognised as the service is rendered.

Costs related to delivering services under long term contractual arrangements are expensed as incurred. An element of costs incurred in the initial set up, transition or transformation phase of the contract are deferred and recorded within non current assets. These costs are then recognised in the income statement on a straight line basis over the remaining contractual term, unless the pattern of service delivery indicates a different profile is appropriate. These costs are directly attributable to specific contracts, relate to future activity, will generate future economic benefits and are assessed for recoverability on a regular basis.

The percentage of completion method relies on estimates of total expected contract revenues and costs, as well as reliable measurement of the progress made towards completion. Unless the financial outcome of a contract can be estimated with reasonable certainty, no attributable profit is recognised. In such circumstances, revenue is recognised equal to the costs incurred to date, to the extent that such revenue is expected to be recoverable. Recognised revenue and profits are subject to revisions during the contract if the assumptions regarding the overall contract outcome are changed. The cumulative impact of a revision in estimates is recorded in the period in which such revisions become likely and can be estimated. Where the actual and estimated costs to completion exceed the estimated revenue for a contract, the full contract life loss is immediately recognised.

Where a contractual arrangement consists of two or more separate elements that have value to a customer on a standalone basis, revenue is recognised for each element as if it were an individual contract. The total contract consideration is allocated between the separate elements on the basis of relative fair value and the appropriate revenue recognition criteria applied to each element as described above.

Commentary: In the above extract, the company describes the various revenue recognition methods applied to communication services and equipment sales:

- separation of contractual multi elements (in conformity with IAS 18 but not necessarily with EIC-142);
- separable installation and connection services, for which revenue is recognized as a single element on activation (in conformity with IAS 18 and, possibly, EIC-141 and EIC-142);
- rental of analogue and digital lines and private circuits, for which revenue is recognized using the straight-line method (in accordance with IAS 18 and CICA 3400);
- calls, for which revenue is recognized at the time of significant events, such as when the call is made over the group's network (in accordance with IAS 18 and CICA 3400);
- interconnection of voice and data traffic between other telecommunications operators, for which revenue is recognized at the time of transit across the group's network (in accordance with IAS 18 and CICA 3400);
- subscription fees, for which revenue is recognized as the service is provided (in accordance with IAS 18 and CICA 3400);
- sale of peripheral and other equipment, for which revenue is normally recognized on the date the equipment is delivered and accepted by the customer (in accordance with IAS 18 and CICA 3400);
- long-term service contracts, for which revenue is recognized on a straight-line basis over the term of the contract unless the performance pattern is other than straight line, in which case revenue is recognized as services are provided, usually on an output or consumption basis (in accordance with IAS 18 and CICA 3400, though the latter does not specifically require the use of a method other than straight line);
- fixed-price contracts to design and build software solutions, for which revenue is recognized by reference to the stage of completion (determined by the proportion of costs incurred relative to the estimated total contract costs, or other measures of completion such as contract milestone customer acceptance) (in line with both IAS 18 and EIC-78);
- time and materials contracts, for which revenue is recognized as the service is rendered (in accordance with IAS 18 and CICA 3400).

In addition, the extract presents:

- the policies for the recognition of various costs related to services and long-term contracts in expenses;
- uncertainties that might lead to using the zero-profit method;
- the impact of changes in estimates.

All accounting treatments of the above three issues described in the extract conform with IFRS and Canadian GAAP except that the completed-contract method would normally be used instead of the zero-profit method.

Extract 11(37) – Edition and publication

Pearson plc (AR 2007), page 58

1. Accounting policies (in part)

q. Revenue recognition (in part)

Circulation and advertising revenue is recognised when the newspaper or other publication is published. Subscription revenue is recognised on a straight-line basis over the life of the subscription.

Where a contractual arrangement consists of two or more separate elements that can be provided to customers either on a stand-alone basis or as an optional extra, such as the provision of supplementary materials with textbooks, revenue is recognised for each element as if it were an individual contractual arrangement.

Revenue from multi-year contractual arrangements, such as contracts to process qualifying tests for individual professions and government departments, is recognised as performance occurs. The assumptions, risks, and uncertainties inherent in long-term contract accounting can affect the amounts and timing of revenue and related expenses reported. Certain of these arrangements, either as a result of a single service spanning more than one reporting period or where the contract requires the provision of a number of services that together constitute a single project, are treated as long-term contracts with revenue recognised on a percentage of completion basis. Losses on contracts are recognised in the period in which the loss first becomes foreseeable. Contract losses are determined to be the amount by which estimated total costs of the contract exceed the estimated total revenues that will be generated by the contract.

Commentary: This extract covers many issues related to revenue recognition, including:

- circulation and advertising (revenue is recognized when the newspaper or other publication is published);
- subscription (revenue is recognized on a straight-line basis over the life of the subscription);
- optional supplementary materials (revenue is recognized for each element as if it were an individual contractual arrangement);
- long-term contract for:
  - single service (revenue recognized when performance occurs), and
  - number of services that together constitute a single project (revenue recognized on a percentage-of-completion basis).

All disclosures and accounting policies provided in this extract appear to be in line with Canadian GAAP.

Extract 11(38) – Long term service contracts

Detica Group plc (AR 2007), page 46

1. Accounting policies (in part)

Revenue

Revenue derived from professional fees billed to clients on a time and materials or fixed-price basis represents the value of work completed, including attributable profit, based on the stage of completion achieved on each project. For time and materials projects, revenue is recognised as services are performed. For fixed-price projects, revenue is recognised according to the stage of completion which is determined using the percentage-of-completion method based on the Directors' assessment of progress against key project milestones and risks, and the ratio of costs incurred to total estimated project costs.

Revenue from support contracts is spread evenly over the period of the support contract.

Revenue from the sale of products is recognised on delivery of the product to the client.

Revenue from recharging to clients the cost of specialist managed subcontractors and the purchase of software or hardware for client assignments, together with associated mark-up, is recognised as these costs are incurred. Where the Group acts as agent in the transaction, only the mark up is recognised as Group revenue. No revenue or expense is recognised in respect of travel and subsistence expenses recharged to clients.

Income is accrued where these revenue recognition policies result in the recognition of revenue before invoices are sent to clients. The cumulative impact of any revisions to the estimate of percentage-of-completion of any fixed price contracts is reflected in the period in which such impact becomes known.

Commentary: In the above extract, the company describes various issues related to long-term contracts, including the accounting for:

- time and materials and fixed-price basis type contracts;
- support contracts, recognized on a straight-line basis;
- sale of products, recognized on delivery;
- recharging to clients, at a markup, the cost of subcontractors and the purchase of software or hardware;
- travel and subsistence expenses recharged to clients (which are netted);
- cumulative impact of any revisions to the estimate of percentage-of-completion of any fixed price contracts.

The above accounting for long-term contracts does not contradict Canadian GAAP.

Extract 11(39) – Airline

Transnet Ltd (AR 2007), page 164

ACCOUNTING POLICIES RELATING TO DISCONTINUED OPERATIONS (in part)

Air traffic liability and revenue recognition

The air traffic liability balance represents the proceeds from tickets and airway bills sold but not yet utilised. The balance includes the value of coupons sold by South African Airways (Pty) Ltd (SAA), which will be flown and claimed in future periods by code-share and inter-line partners. The liability is of a short-term nature and is reflected as a current liability.

Due to system limitations affecting SAA's ability to accurately compute the forward sales liability on a ticket for ticket basis, management had in the past applied a conservative approach in accounting for tickets sold but not yet flown. Industry norms indicate a non-utilisation rate of between 0% and 3%. Management's estimates made around the expected percentage of tickets sold that will not be flown was 2% for passenger tickets and 4% for industry.

Management has revised its assumptions and judgement regarding the period over which the unlisted air tickets and airway bills are released to income from a three-year rolling period to eighteen months. In making its judgement, management has considered the following:

- The successful implementation of a new sales-based revenue accounting system that makes it possible to accurately determine what part of this liability could be taken to revenue each financial year.
- The terms and conditions of the air tickets as stipulated in the International Air Transport Association (IATA) air tickets rules. In terms of the rules, an air ticket is valid for a period of 12 months from the date of purchase. If it is not utilised within this period it expires.
- Interline settlement and rejections can, however, take longer than 12 months to be processed.

Commentary: The company provides details about service rendered in the specific context of airline transportation. The accounting policy does not appear to contradict Canadian GAAP.

Extract 11(40) – Long term contracts uncertainties

Detica Group plc (AR 2007), page 42

1. Accounting policies (in part)

Critical accounting estimates and judgements (in part)

In preparing the consolidated financial statements, management has to make judgements, estimates and assumptions that affect the reported amounts of assets and liabilities, income and expenses. The critical judgements and key sources of estimation uncertainty that have been made in preparing the consolidated financial statements are detailed below. These judgements involve assumptions or estimates in respect of future events which can vary from what is anticipated.

Revenue and profit recognition

Fixed price contracts are accounted for in accordance with IAS 11 "Construction Contracts". Revenue and profits are recognised on a percentage-of-completion basis, when the outcome of a contract can be estimated reliably. Determining whether a contract's outcome can be estimated reliably, requires management to exercise judgement, whilst the calculation of the contract's profit requires estimates of the total contract costs to completion. Cost estimates and judgements are continually reviewed and updated as determined by events or circumstances.

Commentary: This extract describes the company's uncertainties about using the stage-of-completion method. The disclosure is in line with both IFRS and Canadian GAAP (except that the latter would possibly refer to EIC-78 instead of IAS 11).

Other Revenues

IAS 18 covers interest, royalties and dividends revenues, which are recognized as follows:

- Interest is recognized using the effective interest method (see IAS 39).
- Royalties are recognized on an accrual basis in accordance with the substance of the relevant agreement.
- Dividends are recognized when the shareholder's right to receive payment is established.

IAS 18 requires the following probability and reliability criteria to be met to recognize other revenue:

- It is probable that the economic benefits associated with the transaction will flow to the entity.
- The amount of the revenue can be reliably measured.

IAS 18 (including the appendix) covers specific issues such as:

- When unpaid interest has accrued before the acquisition of an interest-bearing investment, the subsequent receipt of interest is allocated between pre-acquisition and post-acquisition periods; only the post-acquisition portion is recognized as revenue.
- Royalty revenue is recognized on an accrual basis in accordance with the substance of the agreement.

Note that royalties:

- are earned over the course of the contract as the customer accesses the benefits of the asset;
- are recorded typically on a straight-line basis over the life of the agreement;
- that are conditional on a future event can be recognized if it is probable that revenue will be received (which is normally when the event occurs).

If an entity gives a customer an indefinite right to use an intangible asset but provides only negligible post-sales support, it could recognize revenue immediately (i.e., the transaction would be accounted for as a sale of goods).

Even though Canadian standards do not address most of the specific issues raised by IAS 18 for interest, royalties and dividends revenue, all requirements discussed above are consistent with Canadian GAAP.

Illustrative Disclosures:

Extract 11(41) – Other revenues

> **Vodacom Group Plc (AR 2007), page 101**
> **I. REVENUE RECOGNITION (in part)**
> **I.5 Other revenue and income**
> • INTERCONNECT AND INTERNATIONAL REVENUE
> Interconnect and international revenue is recognised on the usage basis.
> • DIVIDENDS
> Dividends from investments or subsidiaries are recognised when the right to receive payment has been established.
> • INTEREST
> Interest is recognised on a time proportion basis with reference to the principal amount receivable and the effective interest rate applicable.

Commentary: In this extract, the company discloses its accounting for the following revenue sources:

- interconnect and international revenue, which was presented similarly to royalties, as covered by IAS 18;
- interest, which is recognized as required by IAS 18 and IAS 39;
- dividend income, which is recognized as required by IAS 18.

All of the above accounting methods are consistent with Canadian GAAP.

Extract 11(42) – Other revenues

> **Steinoff International Holdings Limited (AR 2007), page 114**
>
> **Revenue recognition (in part)**
>
> *Insurance premiums*
>
> Insurance premiums are stated before deducting reinsurances and commissions, and are accounted for at the commencement of the risk.
>
> *Interest*
>
> Interest is recognised on the time proportion basis, taking account of the principal debt outstanding and the effective rate over the period to maturity.
>
> *Rental income*
>
> Rental income is recognised in the income statement on a straight-line basis over the term of the lease.
>
> *Dividend income*
>
> Dividend income from investments is recognised when the right to receive payment has been established.
>
> *Government grants*
>
> Government grants are recognised in the balance sheet initially as deferred income when there is reasonable assurance that it will be received and that the group will comply with the conditions attached to it. Grants that compensate the group for expenses incurred are recognised as other operating income in the income statement on a systematic basis in the same periods in which the expenses are incurred. Grants that compensate the group for the cost of an asset are deducted from the carrying amount of the asset.
>
> *Royalty Income*
>
> Royalty income is recognised on an accrual basis in accordance with the substance of the relevant agreement.

Commentary: The company discloses its accounting for the following revenue sources:

- insurance premiums, which is covered by IFRS 4 (see Chapter 20);
- interest, which is recognized as required by IAS 18 and IAS 39;
- rental income, which is covered by IAS 17 (see Chapter 13) and is recognized in the income statement on a straight-line basis over the term of the lease;
- dividend income, which is recognized as required by IAS 18;
- government grants, which are covered by IAS 20;
- royalty income, which is recognized as required by IAS 18.

All of the above accounting methods are consistent with Canadian GAAP.

Revenue Presentation and General Disclosures

IAS 1, *Financial statements presentation* requires revenues to be reported as a separate item in the income statement. In addition, details of revenue amounts must be disclosed in an appendix or in the notes to the financial statements. More specifically, IAS 18 requires the disclosure of the amount of each significant category of revenue recognized during the period, including revenue arising from:

- sale of goods;
- rendering of services;
- interest;
- royalties;
- dividends; and
- the amount of revenue arising from exchanges of goods or services included in each significant category of revenue.

IAS 18 also requires that entities disclose their accounting policies for revenue recognition, including the methods adopted to determine the stage-of-completion of transactions involving the rendering of services. The nature and extent of the disclosure appropriate in the circumstances will depend on whether the policy used is specific to the industry in which the entity operates, or whether the policy or the method of its application is unusual or significant.

Illustrative Disclosures:

Extract 11(43) – Revenue amounts by sources in the notes

Telstra Corporation Limited (AR 2007), page 143
6.Income (in part)

	Note	Telstra Group Year ended 30 June 2007 $m	2006 $m	Telstra Entity Year ended 30 June 2007 $m	2006 $m
Sales revenue					
Rendering of services		12,541	12,402	10,225	10,402
Sale of goods		1,134	808	820	536
Rent of network facilities		8,069	7,641	8,075	7,643
Construction contracts		94	150	129	173
Advertising and directory services		1,835	1,711	549	464
Procurement (a)		-	-	642	647
		23,673	22,712	20,440	19,865
Other revenue (excluding finance income)					
Dividend revenue from controlled entities	33	-	-	186	560
Rent from property		36	22	36	22
		36	22	222	582
Total revenue (excluding finance income)		23,709	22,734	20,662	20,447

Commentary: The company discloses revenue amounts by source, as required by IAS 18. Even though such details are not required under Canadian GAAP, they do provide a good example of transparent disclosures.

Extract 11(44) – Revenue amounts by sources in an appendix

Vodacom Group Plc (AR 2007), page 109
1. REVENUE

	2005 Rm	2006 Rm	2007 Rm
Airtime and access	16,190.8	20,085.8	23,707.5
Data revenue	1,340.5	2,037.6	3,341.7
Interconnect revenue	5,923.6	6,696.8	7,835.6
Equipment sales	2,687.3	3,985.6	4,699.1
International airtime	886.8	971.2	1,305.8
Other	286.3	265.5	256.7
	27,315.3	34,042.5	41,146.4

Commentary: In the above extract the company discloses revenue amounts by source as required by IAS 18. The company provides these details, as well as details related to other elements presented in the income statement (not reproduced in the extract) in a table incorporated in the notes. Even though such an appendix is not required under Canadian GAAP, it does provide a good example of transparent disclosures.

Extract 11(45) – Revenue amounts by sources in an appendix

Fiat S.p.A. (AR 2007), page 118
Composition and principal changes (in part)
Income Statement (in part)
1. Net revenues

Net revenues can be analysed as follows:

(in millions of euros)	2007	2006
Sales of goods	53,742	46,105
Rendering of services	2,512	2,827
Contract revenues	669	917
Rents on operating leases	120	519
Rents on assets sold with a buy-back commitment	314	311
Interest income from customers and other financial income of financial services companies	979	1,077
Other	193	76
Total Net revenues	**58,529**	**51,832**

page 119
5. Other income (expenses) (in part)

This item consists of income arising from trading operations which is not attributable to the sale of goods and services (such as royalties and other income from licences and know-how), net of miscellaneous operating costs which cannot be allocated to specific functional areas, such as indirect taxes and duties, and accruals for various provisions not attributable to other items of Cost of sales or Selling, general and administrative costs.

The detail of Other income (expenses) is as follows:

(in millions of euros)	2007	2006
Gains on disposal of Property, plant and equipment	183	95
Royalties and other income from licences and know-how	17	20
Rental income	31	42
Recovery of expenses and compensation for damages	24	64
Release of excess provisions	94	130
Prior period income	152	272
Other income	197	362
Total Other income	698	985
Indirect taxes	142	112
Losses on disposal of Property, plant and equipment	54	32
Impairment of assets	14	7
Charges for other provisions	161	282
Prior period expenses	100	184
Other expenses	139	263
Total Other expenses	610	880
Other income (expenses)	88	105

pages 120 and 121
9. Financial income (expenses) (in part)

In addition to the items included in the specific lines of the income statement, Net financial income (expenses) in 2007 also includes the income from financial services companies included in Net revenues for 979 million euros (1,077 million euros in 2006) and the costs incurred by financial services companies included in Interest cost and other financial charges from financial services companies included in Cost of sales for 756 million euros (897 million euros in 2006).

Fiat Group (AR 2007) (continued)		
Reconciliation to the income statement is provided at the foot of the following table.		
(in millions of euros)	**2007**	2006
Financial income		
Interest earned and other financial income	**322**	295
Interest income from customers and other financial income of financial services companies	**979**	1,077
Gains on disposal of securities	**13**	7
Total Financial income	**1,314**	1,379
of which:		
Financial income, excluding financial services companies	**335**	302
Interest and other financial expenses		
Interest expense and other financial expenses	**1,496**	1,616
Write-downs of financial assets	**84**	115
Losses on disposal of securities	**3**	2
Interest costs on employee benefits	**155**	166
Total Interest and other financial expenses	**1,738**	1,899
Net income (expenses) from derivative financial instruments and exchange differences	**83**	124
of which:		
Interest and other financial expenses, effects resulting from derivative financial instruments and exchange differences, excluding financial services companies	**899**	878
Net financial income (expenses) excluding financial services companies	**(564)**	(576)
...		
Interest earned and other financial income may be analysed as follows:		
(in millions of euros)	**2007**	2006
Interest income from banks	**195**	106
Interest income from securities	**11**	17
Commission income	**1**	2
Other interest earned and financial income	**115**	170
Total Interest earned and other financial income	**322**	295

Commentary: In this extract, the company discloses revenue amounts by source, as required by IAS 18. The details provided cover different revenue categories including "other income," again as required by IAS 18.

The company provides details about financial income, as well as details related to other elements presented in the income statement (not reproduced in the extract) in a table incorporated in the notes.

Extract 11(46) – Accounting policy disclosure (mining)

Rio Tinto Group (Full Financial Statements 2007), page 9
1 PRINCIPAL ACCOUNTING POLICIES (in part)
(c) Sales revenue (in part)
A large proportion of Group production is sold under medium to long term contracts, but sales revenue is only recognised on individual sales when persuasive evidence exists that all of the following criteria are met:
- the significant risks and rewards of ownership of the product have been transferred to the buyer;
- neither continuing managerial involvement to the degree usually associated with ownership, nor effective control over the goods sold, has been retained;
- the amount of revenue can be measured reliably;
- it is probable that the economic benefits associated with the sale will flow to the Group; and
- the costs incurred or to be incurred in respect of the sale can be measured reliably.

These conditions are generally satisfied when title passes to the customer. In most instances sales revenue is recognised when the product is delivered to the destination specified by the customer, which is typically the vessel on which it will be shipped, the destination port or the customer's premises.

Sales revenue is commonly subject to adjustment based on an inspection of the product by the customer. In such cases, sales revenue is initially recognised on a provisional basis using the Group's best estimate of contained metal, and adjusted subsequently.

Certain products are 'provisionally priced', ie the selling price is subject to final adjustment at the end of a period normally ranging from 30 to 180 days after delivery to the customer, based on the market price at the relevant quotation point stipulated in the contract.

Revenue on provisionally priced sales is recognised based on estimates of the fair value of the consideration receivable based on forward market prices. At each reporting date provisionally priced metal is marked to market based on the forward selling price for the quotational period stipulated in the contract. For this purpose, the selling price can be measured reliably for those products, such as copper, for which there exists an active and freely traded commodity market such as the London Metals Exchange and the value of product sold by the Group is directly linked to the form in which it is traded on that market.

The marking to market of provisionally priced sales contracts is recorded as an adjustment to sales revenue.

Commentary: The company presents its accounting policy for:
- revenue recognition concerning the sale of goods. It specifies that its sales agreements consist of medium-to-long-term production contracts and that revenue is recognized when the product is delivered to the destination specified by the customer, which is typically the vessel on which it will be shipped, the destination port or the customer's premises.
- revenue on sales is initially measured using the company's best estimate of the contained metal, and adjusted subsequently after a customer inspection of the product. Revenue on provisionally priced sales is initially measured using estimates of the fair value of the consideration receivable based on forward market prices, and is adjusted subsequently based on the market price at the relevant quotation point stipulated in the contract.

This extract provides a good example of transparent disclosure specific to mining. All disclosures and accounting policies as provided in this extract appear to be in line with both IAS 18 and Canadian GAAP.

Extract 11(47) – Accounting policy disclosure and uncertainties

ClinPhone plc (AR 2007), pages 33 and 34

1. Accounting policies (in part)

Revenue recognition

Revenue comprises the fair value of the sale of services and products to external customers, net of value added tax, rebates, and discounts. Revenue is recognised as follows:

- Revenue in respect of design and modification of services or products to meet customer requirements are recognised by reference to the percentage of completion of the work from the commencement of work to customer acceptance;

- Revenue in respect of the provision and processing of data in providing services is recognised in the period in which the service is provided;

- Revenue from maintenance and support agreements are recognised rateably over the term of the maintenance and support period;

- Revenue from licensed products is recognised upon delivery where there are no remaining obligations.

Where invoicing milestones on service arrangements are such that the proportion of work performed (calculated on the cost basis described above) is greater than the proportion of the total contract value which has been invoiced, the Group evaluates whether it has obtained, through its performance to date, the right to the uninvoiced consideration and therefore whether revenue should be recognised. In particular it considers:

- Whether there is sufficient certainty that the invoice will be raised in the expected time-frame, particularly where the invoicing milestone is dependent on customer activity;

- Whether it has sufficient evidence that the customer considers that the Group's contractual obligations have been, or will be, fulfilled;

- Whether there is sufficient certainty that only those costs budgeted to be incurred will be incurred before the customer will accept that a future invoice may be raised; and

- The extent to which previous experience with similar product groups and similar customers support the conclusions reached.

Where the Group considers there to be sufficient evidence that it has the right to consideration, taking into account this criteria, revenue is recognised and included in amounts recoverable on contracts until invoiced.

Where the Group considers that there is insufficient evidence that it has the right to consideration, taking into account these criteria, revenue is not recognised until there is sufficient evidence that the Group has obtained the right to consideration for its performance under such arrangements.

Where agreements involve multiple elements, the entire fee from such arrangements has been allocated to each of the individual elements based on each element's fair value. Evidence of fair value is determined by reference to agreements with other customers where elements are sold separately.

The Group makes significant estimates in applying its revenue recognition policies. In particular, as discussed in detail above, estimates are made in relation to the use of the percentage-of-completion accounting method, which requires that the extent of progress toward completion of contracts may be anticipated with reasonable certainty. The use of the percentage-of-completion method is itself based on the assumption that, at the outset of agreements there is customer acceptance. In addition, when allocating revenue to individual elements of multiple element arrangements, it is assumed that the fair value of each element is reflected by its price when sold separately. The complexity of the estimation process and issues related to the assumptions, risks and uncertainties inherent with the application of the revenue recognition policies affect the amounts reported in the financial statements. If different assumptions were used, it is possible that different amounts would be reported in the financial statements.

Commentary: In the above extract, the company presents its accounting policy for:

- Revenue recognition for the sale of various services and products. The disclosure also describes how the company decides whether to recognize service arrangement revenues on un-invoiced milestones.
- Revenue measurement including:
  - o The allocation of fees from multiple element arrangements to each of the individual elements is based on the fair value of each element, assuming that the fair value of each element is reflected by its price when sold separately.
  - o The estimates are made based on the percentage-of-completion accounting method.

The accounting policies described in this extract do not appear to contradict Canadian GAAP.

Construction Contracts

Key Definition

IAS 11 defines a *construction contract* as one specifically negotiated for the construction of an asset or a combination of assets that are closely interrelated or interdependent in terms of their design, technology and function, or their ultimate purpose and use. Construction contracts include contracts for rendering services directly related to the construction of a particular asset, for the destruction or restoration of assets and restoration of the environment following the demolition of assets. Canadian GAAP does not provide specific guidance for construction contracts; these contracts are accounted for in a manner similar to that for other long-term contracts.

Scope and Guidance

IAS 11 guidance reflects many of IAS 18 requirements for long-term service contracts, including the use of stage of completion for revenue recognition. In addition, IAS 11 covers many specific construction contract issues, including:

- *The segmenting of separately identifiable components of a single contract*: If a contract covers two or more assets, the construction of each asset is accounted for as a separate contract if (a) separate proposals were submitted for each asset, (b) the terms in the contract that relate to each asset were negotiated and accepted separately and (c) the costs and revenues of each asset can be measured.

- *The grouping of contracts*: Two or more contracts are accounted for as a single contract if they are negotiated together, the work is interrelated and the contracts are performed concurrently or in a continuous sequence.

- *The construction of an additional asset*: The construction of each additional asset is accounted for as a separate contract if (a) the additional asset differs significantly from the original one or (b) the price of the additional asset is separately negotiated.

- *The contract price*: Total revenue of a contract (or asset) consists of the initial amount agreed on in the contract, as well as any variations in contract work, claims and incentives payments (to the extent that they are probable and can be reliably measured). Revenue is measured at the fair value of the consideration received or receivable; it could increase or decrease from one period to the next as a result of revisions triggered by variations or claims, cost escalation clauses, penalties and production incentives.

- *The contract costs*: These include:
  - o direct costs relating to a specific contract;
  - o costs that are attributable to contract activity in general and can be allocated to the contract (i.e., overheads); and
  - o other costs that are specifically chargeable to the customer under the terms of the contract.

The following is noteworthy:

- IAS 11 excludes costs that cannot be attributed to contracts (e.g., general administration and research and development costs that are not specified in a contract).

- Segregation into elements is prescriptive in IAS 11. This differs from the IAS 18 approach for separating multi-elements contracts into components. Therefore, entities reporting construction contracts (as defined by IAS 11) must refer to this standard's specific requirements (and not to the general ones in IAS 18) for segregating or grouping the assets included in contracts.

- Revenue recognized includes claims to the extent that it is probable that they will be agreed on and they can be reliably measured. Note that IAS 37, *Provisions* prohibits the reimbursement for contingent asset (and its related revenue) from being recognized until there is virtually certainty of recovery. For example, a bonus for early completion of a contract is recognized only when the contract has been completed within the timescale set. As required by IAS 37, a contingent asset (and its related revenue) should be disclosed where receipt is probable (see Chapter 15).

No specific standard on construction contracts exists under Canadian GAAP. This might lead to differences in practice. For example:

- There is no specific guidance on combining and segmenting long-term contracts and, consequently, a construction contract including more than one asset that is segregated under IAS 11 might not be segregated under Canadian GAAP.

- Canadian standards do not address amendments or penalties related to contracts and, consequently, such amounts could be recorded in different periods under Canadian GAAP.

Disclosures

IAS 11 prescribes some very specific disclosures:

- the amount of contract revenue recognized as revenue in the period;

- methods used to determine contract revenue;

- methods used to determine stage of completion of contracts in progress;

- for contracts in progress at the balance sheet date:

  o aggregate costs incurred and recognized profits (less recognized losses) to date,

  o amount of advances received,

  o amount of retentions;

- the gross amount due from customers for contracts as an asset (calculated as costs incurred plus recognized profits less the sum of recognized losses and progress billings for all contracts in progress for which costs incurred plus recognized profits (less recognized losses) exceeds progress billings); and

- the gross amount due to customers for contract work as a liability (calculated as costs incurred plus recognized profits less the sum of recognized losses and progress billings for all contracts in progress for which progress billings exceed costs incurred plus recognized profits (less recognized losses)).

Illustrative Disclosures:

Extract 11(48) – Revenue recognition and costs capitalized

Sasol Limited (Annual Financial Statements 2007), pages 60 and 61
Principal accounting policies (in part)
Construction contracts

When the outcome of a construction contract can be estimated reliably, contract revenue and contract costs associated with that construction contract are recognised as revenue and expenses respectively by reference to the stage of completion of the contract activity at the balance sheet date. The stage of completion is generally based on physical progress, man-hours or costs incurred, based on the appropriate method for the type of contract.

To the extent that the outcome of a construction contract cannot be reliably measured, revenue is recognised only to the extent that contract costs incurred are likely to be recovered.

Any expected loss on a construction contract is charged immediately to the income statement.

Contract costs relating to future activity on a contract are recognised as an asset provided it is likely that they will be recovered.

Commentary: In the above extract, the company provides disclosures on construction contracts, specifically with on the recognition of revenue and expenses when the outcome:
- can be reliably estimated (the stage-of-completion method is used, based on physical progress, man-hours or costs incurred, depending on type of contract;
- cannot be reliably measured (revenue is recognized only to the extent that contract costs incurred are likely to be recovered).

All disclosures and accounting policies provided in this extract appear to be in line with IAS 11 and Canadian GAAP.

Extract 11(49) – Revenue recognition, valuation and presentation

Telstra Corporation Limited (AR 2007), pages 121 and 122
2.7 Construction contracts (in part)
(a) Valuation

We record construction contracts in progress at cost (including any profits recognised) less progress billings and any provision for foreseeable losses.

Cost includes:
- both variable and fixed costs directly related to specific contracts;
- amounts which can be allocated to contract activity in general and which can be allocated to specific contracts on a reasonable basis; and
- costs expected to be incurred under penalty clauses, warranty provisions and other variances.

Where a significant loss is estimated to be made on completion, a provision for foreseeable losses is brought to account and recorded against the gross amount of construction work in progress.

(b) Recognition of profit

Profit is recognised on an individual project basis using the percentage of completion method. The percentage of completion is calculated based on estimated costs of completion, refer to note 2.17(d) for further details.

Profits are recognised when:
- the stage of contract completion can be reliably determined;
- costs to date can be clearly identified; and
- total contract revenues to be received and costs to complete can be reliably estimated.

(c) Disclosure

The construction work in progress balance is recorded in current inventories after deducting progress billings. Where progress billings exceed the balance of construction work in progress, the net amount is shown as a current liability within trade and other payables.

> *Commentary:* In this extract, the company provides details on construction contracts, including:
> - costs attributable to the contracts;
> - revenue recognition methods; and
> - amounts shown on the balance sheet.
>
> All disclosures and accounting policies provided in this extract appear to be in line with IAS 11 and Canadian GAAP.

Extract 11(50) – Revenue recognition, capitalized costs and uncertainties

Aker Kvaerner ASA (AR 2007), page 43

Note 2: Accounting principles (in part)

Revenue recognition (in part)

Construction contracts

Engineering and construction contract revenues are recognised using the percentage of completion method, based primarily on contract cost incurred to date compared to estimated total contract costs. When the final outcome of a contract cannot be reliably estimated, contract revenue is recognised only to the extent of costs incurred that are expected to be recoverable. Losses on contracts are fully recognised when identified.

Contract revenues include variation orders and incentive bonuses when it is probable that they will result in revenue and the amount can be measured reliably. Disputed amounts are recognised when their realisation is reasonably certain and can be measured reliably. Contract costs include costs that relate directly to the specific contract and costs that are attributable to contract activity in general and can be allocated to the contract. Costs that cannot be attributed to contract activity are expensed. Bidding costs are capitalised when it is probable that the company will be the preferred bidder. All other bidding costs are expensed as incurred.

Construction work in progress

Construction work in progress represents the value of construction work performed less payments by customers. The value of construction work performed is measured at revenue recognised to date. Payments by customers are deducted from the value of the same contract or, to the extent they exceed this value, disclosed as advances from customers (see revenue recognition).

page 46

Note 3: Accounting estimates and judgements (in part)

Revenue recognition

As described in the accounting principles the percentage-of-completion method is used to account for construction contracts. Use of this method requires estimates of the final outcome (revenue and costs) of the contract as well as measurement of progress achieved to date as a proportion of the total work to be performed.

The main uncertainty of contract revenue is related to recoverable amounts from variation orders, claims and incentive payments which are recognised to the extent that it is probable that they will result in revenue, and they are capable of being reliably measured. In many projects there are frequent changes of scope of work resulting in a number of variation orders. Normally the contracts with customers include procedures for presentation of and agreement of variation orders. At any point in time, there will be such variation orders and claims not being finally decided upon. Even though management has extensive experience in assessing the outcome of such negotiations there will always be uncertainties.

Cost to complete depends on productivity factors as well as the cost level for the input factors. In an environment with high capacity utilisation in the industry there is an increasing uncertainty in the cost estimates. Experience, systematic use of the project execution model and focus on core competencies reduces this risk.

Progress measurement based on costs has an inherent risk related to the cost estimate as described above. In situations where cost is not seen to properly reflect actual progress, alternative measures such as hours or plan progress are used to achieve more precise revenue recognition. The estimation uncertainty during the early stages of a contract is mitigated by a policy of normally not recognising revenue in excess of costs on a large project before the contract reaches 20 percent completion.

Commentary: Here, the company provides details on its construction contracts, including:

- revenue recognition method (percentage-of-completion method or revenue recognized to the extent of costs incurred that are expected to be recoverable);
- policy for recognizing revenue for variation orders, incentive bonuses, disputed amounts;
- contract costs (costs that pertain directly to a specific contract and costs that are attributable to contract activity in general and can be allocated to the contract);
- bidding costs (capitalized only when it is probable that the company will be the preferred bidder);
- method by which construction work in progress is derived;
- measurement uncertainties related to contracts;

The above extract reflects IAS 11 requirements and is an illustration of transparent disclosures.

Extract 11(51) – Construction contracts disclosures

Transnet Ltd. (AR 2007), page 195

COMPANY				GROUP	
2006 Restated R million	2007 R million			2007 R million	2006 Restated R million
		28.	**CONSTRUCTION CONTRACTS**		
			Contracts in progress at the balance sheet date:		
			Construction costs incurred plus recognised profits less		
44	122		losses to date	122	44
(10)	(7)		*Less*: Probable losses due to onerous contract*	(7)	(10)
34	115			115	34
			Recognised and included in the financial statements:		
			Income statement		
188	538		Contract revenue	538	188
			Balance sheet		
162	199		Amounts due from customers under construction contracts	199	162
12	1		Advances received	1	12
9	20		Retention debtors	20	9
11	13		Retention creditors	13	11
			Contract revenue for coaches is recognised when the completed stage has been signed off as proof of quality satisfaction by the external debtor.		

* Relates to the contract for the upgrade and general overhaul of Class 9E electric locomotives between Alstom and Transwerk.

Commentary: The company provides certain IAS 11 disclosures. These disclosures are beyond what is normally provided under Canadian GAAP.

Service Concession Arrangements

Service concession arrangements are those whereby a government or other body grants contracts for the supply of public services – such as roads, energy distribution, prisons or hospitals – to private operators.

The objective of IFRIC 12 is to clarify how to account for service concession arrangements (which are sometimes referred as public private partnerships). It is effective for annual periods beginning on or after January 1, 2008, with earlier application permitted.

Depending on circumstances, IFRIC 12 recognizes two types of rights related to service concession arrangements:

- *Right to receive a financial asset*: The operator receives an unconditional contractual right to receive cash or another financial asset from the government in return for constructing or upgrading the public sector asset. The financial asset is recorded at fair value. The operator has an unconditional right to receive cash if the government contractually guarantees to pay a specified or determinable amount or the shortfall, if any, from amounts received from users of the public service and specified or determinable amounts.

- *Right to charge for the usage of an asset*: The operator receives an intangible asset for its right to charge for use of the public sector asset that it constructs or up-grades. That intangible asset is recorded at fair value.

Under both models, the operator of a service concession arrangement recognizes and measures revenue in accordance with IAS 11 for construction or upgrade service contracts and with IAS 18 for the operation services it performs.

In certain circumstances, both models would apply. For example a government can give an unconditional guarantee of payment for the construction of a public sector asset (i.e., the operator has a financial asset) and the right to charge the public for the use of services (i.e., the operator has an intangible asset).

The financial asset created when a government pays for the shortfall between amounts received from users of the public service and specified or determinable amounts would be recorded even if payment is contingent on the operator ensuring that the infrastructure meets specified quality or efficiency requirements.

Disclosure requirements for service concession arrangements are established by SIC 29. According to this interpretation, all aspects of a service concession arrangement should be considered for disclosures purposes, including:

- a description of the arrangement;
- significant terms of the arrangement (including period of the concession, re-pricing dates and the basis on which re-pricing or re-negotiation is determined);
- the nature and extent (e.g., quantity, time period or amount as appropriate) of:
  - o rights to use specified assets,
  - o obligations to provide or rights to expect provision of services,
  - o obligations to acquire or build items of property, plant and equipment,
  - o obligations to deliver or rights to receive specified assets at the end of the concession period,
  - o renewal and termination options, and
  - o other rights and obligations (e.g., major overhauls);
- changes in the arrangement occurring during the period;
- classification of service arrangement; and
- the amount of revenue and profits or losses recognized in the period on exchanging construction services for a financial asset or an intangible asset.

SIC 29 specifies that disclosure requirements apply individually for each service concession arrangement or in aggregate for each class of service concession arrangements. It defines a class as a grouping of service concession arrangements involving services of a similar nature (such as toll collections, telecommunications and water treatment services).

Illustrative Disclosure:

Extract 11(52) – IFRIC 12 and SIC 29

SUEZ (Reference Document 2007), pages 208 and 209

1.4 Significant accounting policies (in part)

1.4.6 Concessions

SIC 29, Disclosure – Service Concession Arrangements was published in May 2001 and prescribes the information that should be disclosed in the notes to the financial statements of a concession grantor and a concession operator.

On November 30, 2006 the IFRIC published IFRIC 12 – Service Concession Arrangements, which deals with the accounting treatment to be applied by the concession operator in respect of certain concession arrangements. SUEZ has chosen to early adopt the provisions of this interpretation, which comes into force in 2008.

These interpretations set out the common features of concession arrangements:

- concession arrangements involve the provision of a public service and the management of associated infrastructure, together with specific capital renewal and replacement obligations;
- the grantor is contractually obliged to offer these services to the public (this criteria must be met for the arrangement to qualify as a concession);
- the operator is responsible for at least some of the management of the infrastructure and does not merely act as an agent on behalf of the grantor;
- the contract sets the initial prices to be levied by the operator and regulates price revisions over the concession period.

For a concession arrangement to fall within the scope of IFRIC 12, usage of the infrastructure must be controlled by the concession grantor. This requirement is met when:

- the grantor controls or regulates what services the operator must provide with the infrastructure, to whom it must provide them, and at what price;
- the grantor controls the infrastructure, i.e., retains the right to take back the infrastructure at the end of the concession.

In view of the above, concession infrastructure that does not meet the requirements of IFRIC 12 is still presented as property, plant and equipment.

Under IFRIC 12, the operator's rights over infrastructure operated under concession arrangements should be accounted for based on the party primarily responsible for payment:

- the "intangible asset model" is applied when users have primary responsibility to pay for the concession services;
- and the "financial asset model" is applied when the grantor has the primary responsibility to pay the operator for the concession services.

"Primary responsibility" signifies that while the identity of the payer of the services is not an essential criterion, the person ultimately responsible for payment should be identified.

In cases where the local authority pays the Group but merely acts as an intermediary fee collector and does not guarantee the amounts receivable ("pass through arrangement"), the intangible asset model should be used to account for the concession since the users are, in substance, primarily responsible for payment.

However, where the users pay the Group, but the local authority guarantees the amounts that will be paid over the term of the contract (e.g., via a guaranteed internal rate of return), the financial asset model should be used to account for the concession infrastructure, since the local authority is, in substance, primarily responsible for payment. In practice, the financial asset model is used to account for BOT (Build, Operate and Transfer) contracts entered into with local authorities for public services such as waste treatment and household waste incineration.

Pursuant to these principles:

- infrastructure to which the operator is given access by the grantor of the concession at no consideration is not recognized in the consolidated balance sheet;
- start-up capital expenditure is recognized as follows:

SUEZ (Reference Document 2007) (continued)

- under the intangible asset model, the fair value of construction and other work on the infrastructure represents the cost of the intangible asset and should be recognized when the infrastructure is built provided that this work is expected to generate future economic benefits (e.g., the case of work carried out to extend the network). Where no such economic benefits are expected, the present value of commitments in respect of construction and other work on the infrastructure is recognized from the outset, with a corresponding adjustment to concession liabilities,

- under the financial asset model, the amount receivable from the grantor is recognized at the time the infrastructure is built, at the fair value of the construction and other work carried out,

- when the grantor has a payment obligation for only part of the investment, the cost is recognized in receivables for the amount guaranteed by the grantor, with the balance included in intangible assets.

Renewal costs consist of obligations under concession arrangements with potentially different terms and conditions (obligation to restore the site, renewal plan, tracking account, etc.).

Renewal costs are recognized as either (i) intangible or financial assets depending on the applicable model when the costs are expected to generate future economic benefits (i.e., they bring about an improvement); or (ii) expenses, where no such benefits are expected to be generated (i.e., the infrastructure is restored to its original condition).

Costs incurred to restore the asset to its original condition are recognized as a renewal asset or liability when there is a timing difference between the contractual obligation calculated on a time proportion basis, and its realization.

The costs are calculated on a case-by-case basis based on the obligations associated with each arrangement.

page 244

10.1 Movements in the carrying amount of intangible assets (in part)

10.1.1 Intangible rights arising on concession contracts

The Group manages a large number of concessions as defined by SIC 29 covering drinking water distribution, water treatment, waste collection and treatment, and electricity distribution. The rights granted to concession operators are accounted for as intangibles (see Note 24).

page 254

14.2 Financial liabilities (in part)

14.2.3 Trade and other payables

In millions of euros	Dec. 31, 2007	Dec. 31, 2006	Dec. 31, 2005
Trade payables	8,305.7	7,470.0	8,277.6
Advances and down-payments received	644.5	601.0	524.3
Payable on fixed assets	374.4	304.3	423.1
Concession liabilities	21.4	133.6	141.3
Capital renewal and replacement liabilities	692.1	700.4	712.5
TOTAL	**10,038.1**	**9,209.4**	**10,078.8**

The carrying amount of trade and other payables represents a reasonable estimate of fair value.

page 293

NOTE 24 CONCESSION CONTRACTS

SUEZ manages a large number of concession contracts as defined by SIC 29, covering drinking water distribution, water treatment, waste collection and treatment, and electricity distribution.

The terms of the concessions vary between 10 and 65 years, depending mainly on the level of investments to be made by the concession operator.

The concession contracts specify a number of rights and obligations with regard to the infrastructure to be built, as well as rights and obligations relating to the public service concerned.

Contracts provide for a general obligation allowing users access to the public service, and in certain cases according to a specified timeframe.

SUEZ (Reference Document 2007) (continued)

A general obligation also exists to return the concession infrastructure in good working condition at the end of the concession. Where appropriate, this obligation leads to the recognition of a capital renewal and replacement liability (see Note 14.2.3). By exception, water distribution concessions in the United States do not provide for the return of the infrastructure to the grantor of the concession at the end of the contract. The infrastructure will remain the property of SUEZ and is therefore accounted for using the tangible asset model (see Note 1.4.6).

Certain contracts provide for an additional obligation to extend the service to new users or improve the existing service. Where necessary, these obligations lead to the recognition of an intangible asset and a related liability (see Note 1.4.6).

As consideration for these obligations, SUEZ is entitled to bill either the local authority granting the concession (mainly incineration activities and BOT water treatment contracts) or the users (distribution of drinking water or electricity) for the services provided. The rights to bill for expenses incurred in extending or improving the concession infrastructure give rise to a receivable or an intangible asset, depending on the party primarily responsible for payment (see Note 1.4.6).

Services are generally billed at a fixed price which is linked to a particular index over the term of the contract. However, contracts may contain clauses providing for price adjustments (usually at the end of a five-year period) if there is a change in the economic conditions forecasted at the inception of the contracts. By exception, contracts exist in certain countries (e.g., the United States and Spain), under which the price is fixed on a yearly basis according to the costs incurred in connection with the concession, which is therefore recognized in assets (see Note 1.4.6).

Commentary: In the above extract, the company notes that it has adopted IFRIC 12 early, using the two models under this standard to recognize start-up capital expenditures:

- It uses the financial asset model where the amount receivable from the grantor is recognized at the time the infrastructure is built, at the fair value of the construction and other work carried out.

- It uses the intangible asset model, where the fair value of construction and other work on the infrastructure represents the cost of the intangible asset, which is recognized when the infrastructure is built provided that this work is expected to generate future economic benefits (e.g., work carried out to extend the network). Where no such economic benefits are expected, the present value of commitments for construction and other work on the infrastructure is recognized from the outset, with a corresponding adjustment to concession liabilities.

SUEZ uses a combination of the two models to recognize start-up capital expenditures when the grantor has a payment obligation for only part of the investment. The cost is recognized in receivables for the amount guaranteed by the grantor, with the balance included in intangible assets.

The extract also explains that renewal costs are recognized as either:

- intangible or financial assets depending on the applicable model when the costs are expected to generate future economic benefits (i.e., they bring about an improvement); or

- expenses where no such benefits are expected to be generated (i.e., the infrastructure is restored to its original condition).

The company manages a large number of concession contracts in exchange for rights accounted for as intangibles. In the United States, water distribution concessions are not within the scope of IFRIC 12 since they do not provide for the return of the infrastructure to the grantor of the concession at the end of the contract. Consequently, the infrastructure associated with water distribution concessions is accounted for as property, plant and equipment.

Note that the extract provides the disclosures required by SIC 29, including the detail of concession liabilities.

Customer Loyalty Programs

Many companies, including retailers, airlines, hotels, telecommunications operators, offer customer loyalty programs as incentives to their customers. Some companies treat these incentives as a marketing expense. Others account for them as reduction of revenue, using various methods (including fair value and marginal costs) for measuring the obligation of supplying the free or discounted product or service. IFRIC 13 should eliminate the inconsistencies. It is effective for annual periods beginning on or after July 1, 2008, with earlier application permitted. No equivalent Canadian guidance exists.

According to IFRIC 13, customers implicitly pay for award points when the products or services are purchased and, therefore, some revenue should be allocated to the points. Consequently, loyalty programs should be accounted for as multiple-element arrangements, in which the consideration received for the sale of goods or services (from which awards credits are earned) is allocated to:

- goods or service delivered; and
- award credits that will be redeemed in the future.

The amount allocated to the award credits is:

- Based on the fair value of the credits. Note that this value should reflect fair value to the holder, not the cost of redemption to the issuer.

- Presented as "deferred revenue" in the balance sheet. The entity derecognizes the deferred revenue as revenue when it has fulfilled its obligation or when it engages and pays a third party to do so. If at any time the expected costs exceed the amount of deferred revenue, the entity would record an onerous contract to be accounted for according to IAS 37 (see Chapter 15).

Even though IFRIC 13 emphasizes that the methodology used to measure a program operator's obligation should be standardized with the measurement techniques for other customer obligations, it does not mandate a specific approach for such measurement.

The fair value of an individual award credit takes into consideration:

- the value of goods award credits can buy (or value for which the award credits could have been sold separately); and
- proportion of incentives expected to be redeemed.

Illustrative Disclosures:

Extract 11(53) – IFRIC 13 adoption (expected impact not material)

> **Westpac Banking Corporation (AR 2007), page 119**
> **Note 1. Summary of significant accounting policies (in part)**
> **k. Future accounting developments (in part)**
> Interpretation 13: Customer Loyalty Programmes was released by the Australian Accounting Standards Board Interpretations Committee on 1 July 2007. Interpretation 13 will apply to Westpac's 30 September 2009 financial report. The guidance will result in the re-measurement and reclassification of the existing credit card loyalty provision to deferred income. Deferred income will be recognised as revenue when the expense of providing the rewards is incurred. It is expected that there will be some delay in the timing of recognition of revenue from the credit card loyalty program going forward. The guidance is not expected to have a material impact for the Westpac Group.

Commentary: The company states that IFRIC 13 is not expected to have a material impact on its financial statements. No corresponding Canadian standard exists for loyalty programs.

Extract 11(54) – IFRIC 13 adoption (expected impact being assessed)

Deutsche Telekom AG (AR 2007), page 109

Standards, interpretations and amendments issued, but not yet adopted. (in part)

In June 2007, the IFRIC issued IFRIC 13 "Customer Loyalty Programmes." The European Union has not yet endorsed IFRIC 13. The interpretation addresses the accounting of customer loyalty programs that grant customers points (credits) that allow them to acquire free or discounted goods or services from the seller or a third party. The question to be clarified was whether the award credits are a liability in the context of a completed sale or an advance payment for a future sales transaction. The interpretation now issued requires the proceeds of the sale to be divided into two components. One component is attributable to the transaction which resulted in the credit awards. The other component is allocable to the future sales transaction resulting from the credit awards to be redeemed. The portion of the proceeds allocated to the goods or service already delivered is recognized as revenue. The portion of the proceeds allocated to the award credits is deferred as an advance payment until the customer redeems the credit award, or the obligation in respect of the credit award is fulfilled. Since the guidance under IFRIC 13 deviates from Deutsche Telekom's current accounting policy, the accounting method will have to be adjusted. The interpretation shall be applied for financial years beginning on or after July 1, 2008. Deutsche Telekom is currently analyzing the impact of applying IFRIC 13 on the presentation of Deutsche Telekom's results of operations, financial position or cash flows.

Commentary: The company briefly discloses the requirements set out in IFRIC 13. It states that it is analyzing the impact of applying IFRIC 13 on the presentation of its results of operations, financial position or cash flows. No corresponding Canadian standard exists for loyalty programs.

Extract 11(55) – IFRIC 13 early adoption

Qantas Airways Limited (AR 2007), page 83

1. Statement of Significant Accounting Policies (in part)

(T) Frequent Flyer (in part)

On 28 June 2007, the International Financial Reporting Interpretations Committee (IFRIC) released IFRIC Interpretation 13 – Customer Loyalty Programmes (IFRIC 13). IFRIC 13 was adopted by the Australian Accounting Standards Board on 2 August 2007 and is effective from 1 July 2008. It requires comparatives to be restated.

IFRIC 13 fundamentally changes the way that Qantas is required to account for the Frequent Flyer Program. On adoption of IFRIC 13, revenue received in relation to a flight eligible to earn points will be split, based on fair value, between the flight and the value of the points awarded. The value attributable to the eligible flight will be recognised on passenger uplift whilst the value attributed to the awarded points will be deferred as a liability until the points are ultimately utilised.

Qantas has early adopted IFRIC 13 from 1 July 2007 with initial adoption on 1 July 2006 resulting in a reduction in opening retained earnings of approximately $297 million assuming the following:

- revenue associated with breakage is recognised when the points are awarded;
- the fair value of points awarded is the weighted average value of points sold to third parties; and
- the liability for awarded points is not discounted.

Commentary: This extract shows the impact of adopting IFRIC 13. No corresponding Canadian standard exists for loyalty programs.

Extract 11(56) – Loyalty program (IFRIC 13 not adopted early)

InterContinental Hotels Group PLC (AR 2007), page 54

Summary of significant accounting policies (in part)

Loyalty programme

The hotel loyalty programme, Priority Club Rewards, enables members to earn points, funded through hotel assessments, during each stay at an IHG hotel and redeem the points at a later date for free accommodation or other benefits. The future redemption liability is included in trade and other payables and is estimated using eventual redemption rates determined by actuarial methods and points values.

The Group pays interest to the loyalty programme on the accumulated cash received in advance of redemption of the points awarded.

page 56

Use of accounting estimates and judgements (in part)

Loyalty programme – the future redemption liability included in trade and other payables is estimated using actuarial methods based on statistical formulae that project the timing of future point redemptions based on historical levels to give eventual redemption rates and points values.

page 72

19 TRADE AND OTHER PAYABLES

	2007 £m	2006 £m
Current		
Trade payables	49	47
Other tax and social security payable	19	26
Other payables	172	190
Accruals	148	139
Derivatives	2	–
	390	402
Non-current		
Other payables	139	109

Trade payables are non-interest bearing and are normally settled within 45 days.

Other payables include £212m (2006 £180m) relating to the future redemption liability of the Group's loyalty programme, of which £84m (2006 £83m) is classified as current and £128m (2006 £97m) as non-current.

Commentary: The company indicates that it established a future redemption liability (which is included in trade and other payables and is estimated using eventual redemption rates determined by actuarial methods and point values). In addition, the company presents the amount of the liability in the notes to the financial statements. The company has stated in those notes that it did not adopt IFRIC 13 early. No corresponding Canadian requirements exist for loyalty programs.

Extract 11(57) – Loyalty program as a cost (IFRIC 13 not adopted early)

Air France-KLM S.A. (Reference Document 2006-2007), page 95
Note 3 Accounting policies (in part)
3.7. Loyalty programs

Until June 1, 2005, each of the two sub-groups (Air France and KLM) comprising the Group had its own frequent flyer program: "Fréquence Plus" and "Flying Dutchman". Each program allowed members to acquire "miles" as they flew on Air France, KLM or with other partner companies. These miles entitled members to a variety of benefits such as free flights with the two companies.

Subsequent to the acquisition of KLM, a joint frequent flyer program "Flying Blue" was launched in June 2005 combining the miles accumulated from the two previous programs.

The probability of air miles being converted into award tickets is estimated using a statistical method.

The value of air miles is estimated based on the specific terms and conditions for the use of free tickets. This estimate takes into consideration the discounted marginal cost of the passenger carried (e.g. catering, ticket issue costs, etc.) and discounted cost of the miles used on participating partner companies.

The estimated value of air miles is recorded as a deduction from revenues and recorded under the caption "Deferred revenue on ticket sales" as debt on the balance sheet at the same time the qualifying flight for which air miles are awarded is recognized.

The Group also sells miles to partner companies participating in current loyalty programs, such as credit card companies, hotel chains and car rental firms. The Group defers a portion of the miles sold representing the value of the subsequent travel award to be provided, in a manner consistent with the determination of the liability for earned flight awards discussed above. The remainder is recognized as revenue immediately.

Commentary: Here, the company explains that it combined two programs and explains how it estimates the value of air miles. Even though the company has recorded a reduction of revenue and not an expense (in accordance with IFRIC 13), it specifies that the estimate of the value of the air miles is based on the marginal cost of the passenger concerned and discounted cost of the miles used on participating partner companies (and not fair value which is not in accordance with IFRIC 13). The company will probably change this valuation when adopting IFRIC 13. No corresponding Canadian requirements exist for loyalty programs.

Agreements for the Construction of Real Estate

IFRIC 15 clarifies when agreements for the construction of real estate should be accounted for as:

- a construction contract in accordance with the requirements under IAS 11; and/or

- an agreement for the rendering of services or sale of goods in accordance with the requirements under IAS 18.

Some entities that undertake the construction of residential real estate may start to market individual condominium or housing units "off plan", which typically results in these units being sold before the completion of the condominium or housing project.

Currently Canadian GAAP might allow an entity to consider an off-plan sale agreement as a (1) construction contract with revenue being recognized by reference to the stage of completion as construction progressed or (2) sale of goods with revenue being recorded when control and the risks and rewards of ownership have been transferred to the buyer (typically when the unit is ready for occupation and handed over to the buyer).

IFRIC 15 is based on the assumption that the entity has previously analyzed the agreement for the construction of real estate and any related agreements and concluded that all other requirements for the recognition of revenue have been satisfied. In particular, the entity must not retain continuing managerial involvement to the degree usually associated with ownership, and it must not retain effective control over the constructed real estate to an extent that would preclude recognition of some or all of the consideration as revenue. If recognition of some of the consideration as revenue is precluded, the detailed guidance in IFRIC 15 applies only to the part of the agreement for which revenue will be recognized.

IFRIC 15 which is effective for annual periods beginning on or after 1 January 2009 (with earlier application permitted), addresses the following issues:

- Determining whether the agreement is within the scope of IAS 11 or IAS 18, which depends on the terms of the agreement and all the surrounding facts and circumstances:

    o When IAS 11 applies, the construction contract also includes any contracts or components for the rendering of services that are directly related to the construction of the real estate. An agreement meets the definition of a construction contract and is to be accounted for in accordance with IAS 11 when the buyer is able to specify:

      • the major structural elements of the design of the real estate before construction begins, and/or

      • the major structural changes once construction is in progress:

    o An agreement is considered to be for the sale of goods and/or the rendering of services within the scope of IAS 18 when the buyer only has limited influence over the design of the real estate (e.g. to select a design from a range of options specified by the entity, or to specify only minor variations to the basic design). The applicable requirements of IAS 18 will be determined by the nature of the agreement (i.e., whether it is for the rendering of services or for the sale of goods).

Note that in some circumstances, a single agreement may need to be split into separately identifiable components, with each such component being accounted for separately. When an agreement is split into separately identifiable components, including one for the construction of real estate, the fair value of the total consideration received or receivable for the agreement is allocated to each component. The entity then applies the requirements of IFRIC 15 to the component for the construction of real estate in order to determine whether that component is within the scope of IAS 11 or IAS 18.

- Accounting for revenue from construction of real estate:

    o *Construction contracts (within the scope of IAS 11)*: if their outcome can be estimated reliably, revenue is recognized by reference to the stage of completion of the contract activity.

    o *Agreements for the rendering of services (in accordance with IAS 18)*: where the entity is not required to acquire and supply construction materials (i.e., in arrangements where the customer acts in essence as its own general contractor and enters into agreements with individual suppliers for specific goods and services). Under these circumstances, the agreement may only be for the rendering of services, and revenue is recognized by reference to the stage of completion of the transaction using the percentage of completion method. The requirements of IAS 11 are generally applicable to the recognition of revenue and the associated expenses for such a transaction.

    o *Agreements for the sale of goods (in accordance with IAS 18)*: where the entity is required to provide services together with construction materials. For such contracts, the applicable recognition criteria are those set out in IAS 18 which permit the recognition of revenue only when the entity has transferred to the buyer control and the significant risks and rewards of ownership of the goods. IFRIC 15 notes that this transfer may occur:

- at a single point in time; or

- continuously as work progresses. An important indicator of a 'continuous transfer' is when the buyer retains the work in progress and the entity has the right to be paid for the work performed to date if the agreement were to be terminated before construction is completed. In this case, all of the criteria set out in IAS 18 are met continuously as construction progresses, and revenue is recognized by reference to the stage of completion using the percentage of completion method. The requirements of IAS 11 are generally applicable to the recognition of revenue and expenses for such a transaction. Additional disclosures are required when an entity recognizes revenue continuously as construction progresses using the percentage of completion method.

Other Issues Related to Revenue Recognition and Presentation

Various other issues related to revenue recognition on the sale of goods, rendering of services and other revenues warrant discussion.

Up-front Fees

Some sales arrangements call for customers to make non-refundable initial payments (up-front fees or initial fees). These arrangements can be for the sale of goods, rendering of services, royalties or a combination of such transactions. Both IAS 18 and EIC-141 cover these up-front fees:

- The appendix to IAS 18 provides examples where up-front fees are recognized on a basis that reflects the timing, nature and value of the benefits provided.

- EIC-141 examines up-front payment issues in detail and requires that such payment be deferred and recognized systematically as revenue over the periods that they are earned (unless the up-front payment represent the culmination of the earnings process).

- Up-front license fees can be recognized when:

    o the product has been physically delivered,

    o the license period has started, or

    o there is no remaining continuing involvement required of the licensor.

Illustrative Disclosures:

Extract 11(58) – Licensing agreement and up-front fees

> **Bayer Aktiengesellschaft (AR 2007), page 109**
> **4. Basic principles, methods and critical accounting policies (in part)**
> **Net sales and other operating income (in part)**
> Some of the Bayer Group's revenues are generated on the basis of licensing agreements under which third parties are granted rights to its products and technologies. Payments relating to the sale or outlicensing of technologies or technological expertise – once the respective agreements have become effective – are immediately recognized in income if all rights relating to the technologies and all obligations resulting from them have been relinquished under the contract terms and Bayer has no continuing obligation to perform under the agreement. However, if rights to the technologies continue to exist or obligations resulting from them have yet to be fulfilled, the payments received are recorded in line with the actual circumstances. Upfront payments and similar non-refundable payments received under these agreements are recorded as other liabilities and recognized in income over the estimated performance period stipulated in the agreement. Revenues such as license fees or rentals are recognized according to the same principles.

Commentary: This extract presents the company's policy on up-front payments received, which are recognized in income over the estimated performance period in the agreement. This policy is in line with both IAS 18 and EIC-141.

Extract 11(59) – Collaborative agreements including up-front (success milestone) fees

> **Acambis plc (AR 2007), page 61**
>
> **1 Accounting policies (in part)**
>
> **Collaboration agreements**
>
> The Group's collaboration agreements may include up-front and success-based milestone receipts and/or reimbursement for development and other expenditure incurred by the Group (typically including a mark-up on a cost-plus basis), as well as royalties for future sales of the product.
>
> Up-front milestone receipts are typically considered to represent consideration for services performed over the entire collaboration arrangement. Where these services are performed by an indeterminate number of acts over the period of the arrangement, revenue is recognised on a straight-line basis over that period, unless there is evidence that some other method better represents the stage of completion. Where elements of the arrangement are separately identifiable and the fair values are readily available, the recognition criteria are applied to the separately identifiable components of the arrangement.
>
> Success-based milestone receipts are recognised when they are achieved.
>
> Revenues arising from the reimbursement of development and other expenditure are recognised on an accruals basis, when the related expenditure has been incurred.

Commentary: The company presents its revenue recognition policy for collaboration agreements (which may include amounts received up front and for success-based milestone and/or reimbursement for development and other expenditures it incurs).

Exchange or Swap of Goods or Services

According to IAS 18, when goods or services are exchanged or swapped for other ones that are similar in nature and value, the exchange is not regarded as a sale. When such exchanges are for dissimilar goods or services, they are accounted for as revenue and measured at the fair value of goods or services received, adjusted for any cash or cash equivalents transferred. When the fair value of goods or services received cannot be measured reliably, revenue is measured at the fair value of goods or services given up, adjusted for any cash or cash equivalents transferred.

SIC 31 specifically addresses barter transactions involving advertising. This standard presumes that such exchanges cannot be measured reliably at the fair value of advertising services received. A seller can, however, overcome this presumption when it can reliably measure revenue at the fair value of the advertising services it provides in the exchange by referring to non-barter transactions that:

- involve advertising similar to the advertising in the barter transaction;
- occur frequently;
- represent a predominant number of transactions and amounts when compared to all transactions where advertising is provided that is similar to the advertising in the barter transaction;
- involve cash and/or another form of consideration that has a reliably measurable fair value; and
- do not involve the same counterparty as in the barter transaction.

SIC 31 notes that:

- A swap of cash for equal or substantially equal amounts between the same entities that provide and receive advertising services does not provide reliable evidence of fair value.

- The fair value of advertising services is reliably measurable when independent non-barter transactions involving similar advertising services provide reliable evidence to substantiate the fair value of the barter exchange. Additional factors that could be taken in consideration include the nature of the services and the number of market transactions.

CICA 3400 does not specifically address revenue from barter transactions involving advertising services. Entities typically refer to the general guidance in CICA 3831 because Canadian GAAP does not specifically address these types of transactions. Under CICA 3831, an asset that is acquired is measured at the fair value of the asset given up, or the fair value of the asset received, whichever is more reliably measurable, unless certain criteria are met, in which case, the asset acquired would be measured at the carrying amount of the asset given up. Depending on the circumstances, the measurement of revenue from barter transactions involving advertising services under CICA 3831 may differ from the measurement under SIC 31.

Illustrative disclosure:

Extract 11(60) – Exchanges of goods or services

Land of Leather Holdings plc (AR 2007), page 42 **3 Revenue**	52 weeks trading to 30.7.06 £000	17 weeks trading to 29.7.07 £000	Proforma Unaudited 52 weeks trading to 30.7.06 £000
Revenue in the income statement is analysed as follows:			
Sale of goods	239,980	69,831	205,642
Rental income	5,766	1,643	4,074
Revenue	245,746	71,474	209,716
Finance revenue	920	206	363
Total revenue	246,666	71,680	210,079
No revenue was derived from exchange of goods or services for non-monetary consideration for the periods under review.			

Commentary: There are very few situations that involve exchange of goods and services. This extract specifically indicates that no revenue was recorded subsequent to exchanges of goods.

Consideration Received from a Vendor

Rebates and allowances received from a vendor can take various forms, including volume rebates, advertising contributions and promotional discounts. EIC-144 contains detailed guidance on such rebates or allowances. It presumes that the consideration an entity received from its supplier is a reduction of costs and the related inventory. To overcome this presumption, the vendor's payment must:

- specifically relate to assets or services delivered, in which case it is recognized as revenue; or

- represent a reimbursement of costs incurred by the retailer to sell the supplier's product, in which case it is recognized as a reduction of such costs.

IFRS do not have specific guidance concerning vendor's rebates or allowances.

Illustrative Disclosures:

Extract 11(61) – Vendors contribution as revenue

Corporate Express NV (AR 2007), page 80
2 Summary of accounting policies (in part)
Net sales (in part)

Corporate Express receives contributions from vendors for inclusion of their products in Corporate Express' catalogues which have no relationship with purchased volumes. Catalogue contributions are in principle recognised as income on a linear basis over the period the catalogue is generating sales and included in net sales. Catalogue contributions received for promoting and advertising are recognised in income when the catalogue is released.

Commentary: This extract discusses contributions received from vendors for the inclusion of their products in the company's catalogues. The company states that the contributions have no relationship with purchased volumes. The contributions are accounted for as revenue using a linear basis over the period the catalogue is generating sales and included in net sales. This accounting treatment does not contradict EIC-144 if appropriate criteria are met.

Extract 11(62) – Vendor allowances as reduction of costs of sales, inventory and expenses

Delhaize Group SA (AR 2007), page 70
2. Summary of Significant Accounting Policies (in part)
Supplier Allowances

Delhaize Group receives allowances and credits from suppliers primarily for instore promotions, co-operative advertising, new product introduction and volume incentives. These allowances are included in the cost of inventory and recognized when the product is sold unless they represent reimbursement of a specific, identifiable cost incurred by the Group to sell the vendor's product in which case they are recorded as a reduction in selling, general and administrative expenses. Income from new product introduction consists of allowances received to compensate for costs incurred for product handling and is recognized over the product introductory period in cost of sales.

page 100
30. Cost of Sales

(in millions of EUR)	2007	2006	2005
Product cost, net of vendor allowances and cash discounts	13,630.1	13,844.9	13,212.7
Purchasing, distribution and transportation costs	531.8	527.3	497.4
Total	**14,161.9**	**14,372.2**	**13,710.1**

Delhaize Group receives allowances and credits from suppliers primarily for instore promotions, co-operative advertising, new product introduction and volume incentives. These allowances are included in the cost of inventory and recognized as a reduction to cost of sales when the product is sold, unless they represent the reimbursement of a specific and identifiable cost incurred by the Group to sell the vendor's product in which case they are recorded as a reduction in selling, general and administrative expenses. Supplier allowances that represented a reimbursement of advertising costs incurred by the Group were recognized as a reduction of advertising costs in selling, general and administrative expenses of EUR 4.3 million, EUR 4.8 million and EUR 4.3 million in 2007, 2006 and 2005, respectively.

Commentary: The company presents its accounting policy for various vendor allowances and also discloses the amounts received. The presentation and accounting policy are in line with IFRS and EIC-144 requirements.

Customer Incentives

Customer incentives take various forms, including cash discounts, rebates, promotions and cooperative advertising. We covered cash discounts and rebates (which are treated as a reduction in revenue by the vendor) under the section on revenue measurement. Conceptually, the accounting of other expenditures, such as promotions and cooperative advertising, should reflect their substance, which results in the vendor recording them as:

- cost of sales;
- reduction in revenue;
- marketing and selling expense; or
- general and administrative expense.

IFRS provide no guidance to vendors on accounting for non-cash incentives, such as certain promotions and cooperative advertising, they might offer to customers. On the other hand, EIC-156 requires that such non-cash incentives be recognized as an expense, which is generally recorded at the later of the date of recognizing revenue and the date that the incentive is offered. In addition, EIC-156 specifies that classification as an expense should be presented as part of cost of sales when the incentive is delivered at the same time as the product/service and that the liability must be recognized for the maximum potential obligation to the customer if a reasonable estimate cannot be made.

Illustrative Disclosures:

Extract 11(63) – Non cash incentives recorded as reduction of revenue

> **Delhaize Group SA (AR 2007), page 70**
> **2. Summary of Significant Accounting Policies (in part)**
> **Revenue Recognition (in part)**
>
> Discounts and incentives, including discounts from regular retail prices for specific items and "buy one, get one free" incentives, are offered to retail customers through certain loyalty card programs and are recognized as a reduction in sales as the products are sold. Loyalty programs also exist whereby customers earn points for future purchases. Sales are reduced when the points are awarded and a liability is recognized for expected redemption of points.

Commentary: The company specifies that discounts and incentives offered to retail customers through certain loyalty card programs are recognized as a reduction in sales as the products are sold. This accounting treatment appears to be in line with IFRIC 13 (assuming that the points are valued at fair value). Under Canadian GAAP, various accounting treatments would be allowed.

Extract 11(64) – Incentives payments as expense

> **Vodacom Group Plc (AR 2007), page 107**
> **ACCOUNTING POLICIES (in part)**
> **R. INCENTIVES**
>
> Incentives paid to service providers and dealers for products delivered to the customer are expensed as incurred. Incentives paid to service providers and dealers for services delivered are expensed over the period that the related revenue is recognised.
>
> Distribution incentives paid to service providers and dealers for exclusivity are deferred and expensed over the contractual relationship period.

Commentary: This extract specifies that incentives paid to service providers and dealers for products delivered to the customer are expensed as incurred. This accounting treatment is in line with IFRS but may be inconsistent with EIC-156, which might require that such incentive be treated as a reduction in sales revenue.

Extract 11(65) – Incentives as reduction of revenue

> **Vodafone Group Plc (AR 2007), page 97**
> **2. Significant accounting policies (in part)**
> **Revenue (in part)**
>
> Incentives are provided to customers in various forms and are usually offered on signing a new contract or as part of a promotional offering. Where such incentives are provided on connection of a new customer or the upgrade of an existing customer, revenue representing the fair value of the incentive, relative to other deliverables provided to the customer as part of the same arrangement, is deferred and recognised in line with the Group's performance of its obligations relating to the incentive.

Commentary: The company specifies that it provides incentives on signing a new contract with new customers or as part of a promotional offering to existing customers. Incentives are identified as separate elements of a multi-element arrangement and are accounted for as reductions of revenue. This accounting treatment does not contradict IFRS.

It is possible to account for the contract as a multi-element arrangement and, consequently, the above accounting policy would be acceptable under Canadian GAAP.

Guaranteed Minimum Resale Value

An entity may sell equipment and contractually guarantee its resale value to the purchaser. In this case, EIC-84 requires that the entity accounts for the transaction as a lease according to CICA 3065. Since there is no specific requirement under IFRS, the guaranteed minimum resale value could be accounted as follows, depending on circumstances:

- an embedded derivative; or
- a lease (same as EIC-84).

Illustrative Disclosures:

Extract 11(66) – Guaranteed residual value

> **Koninklijke Philips Electronics N.V. (AR 2007), page 206**
> **Significant IFRS accounting policies (in part)**
> **Revenue recognition (in part)**
>
> For products for which a residual value guarantee has been granted or a buy-back arrangement has been concluded, revenue recognition takes place in accordance with the requirements for lease accounting of IAS 17 *Leases.* ... Service revenue related to repair and maintenance activities for goods sold is recognized ratably over the service period or as services are rendered.

Commentary: The company accounts for sales of products for which a residual value guarantee has been granted or a buy-back arrangement has been concluded as a lease. This is in line with EIC-84.

Extract 11(67) – Buy-back commitment

Fiat S.p.A. (AR 2007), page 108

Significant accounting policies (in part)

Revenue recognition (in part)

Revenue is recognised if it is probable that the economic benefits associated with the transaction will flow to the Group and the revenue can be measured reliably.

Revenues from the sale of products are recognised when the risks and rewards of ownership of the goods are transferred to the customer, the sales price is agreed or determinable and receipt of payment can be assumed: this corresponds generally to the date when the vehicles are made available to non-group dealers, or the delivery date in the case of direct sales. New vehicle sales with a buy-back commitment are not recognised at the time of delivery but are accounted for as operating leases when it is probable that the vehicle will be bought back. More specifically, vehicles sold with a buy-back commitment are accounted for as assets in Inventory if the sale originates from the Fiat Group Automobiles business (agreements with normally a short-term buy-back commitment); and are accounted for in Property, plant and equipment, if the sale originates from the Commercial Vehicles business (agreements with normally a long-term buy-back commitment). The difference between the carrying value (corresponding to the manufacturing cost) and the estimated resale value (net of refurbishing costs) at the end of the buy-back period is depreciated on a straight-line basis over the same period. The initial sale price received is recognised as an advance payment (liability). The difference between the initial sale price and the buy-back price is recognised as rental revenue on a straightline basis over the term of the operating lease.

Commentary: The company accounts for new vehicle sales with a buy-back commitment as operating leases when it is probable that the vehicles will be bought back. This is in line with EIC-84.

Extract 11(68) – Minimum resale value

Daimler AG (AR 2007), page 143

Accounting policies (in part)

Revenue recognition (in part)

Sales under which the Group guarantees the minimum resale value of the product, such as in sales to certain rental car company customers, are accounted for similar to an operating lease. The guarantee of the resale value may take the form of an obligation by Daimler to pay any deficiency between the proceeds the customer receives upon resale in an auction and the guaranteed amount, or an obligation to reacquire the vehicle after a certain period of time at a set price. Gains or losses from the resale of these vehicles are included in gross profit.

Revenue from operating leases is recognized on a straight-line basis over the lease term.

Commentary: Daimler accounts for sales under which the company guarantees the minimum resale value of the product in a manner that is similar to an operating lease. This is in line with EIC-84.

Specific Industries

IFRS and Canadian GAAP contain little industry-specific revenue recognition guidance. This differs from US GAAP, which contains numerous standards covering specific industries. Both Canadian GAAP and IFRS allow (with some restrictions) an entity to use US GAAP guidance. This was observed in some extracts presented previously and will be seen in the comprehensive examples presented later in this chapter.

IFRIC had on its agenda a project on initial fees received by fund managers. Even though this project was removed from the IFRIC's active agenda in January 2007 (because of lack of consensus), the following considerations were raised in committee discussions:

• The following services might be provided to a customer before an initial investment is made:

- o investment advice in preparation for investing in a particular fun,
- o creation of units or accounts in the fund and/or brokerage services,
- o payment of a sales commission,
- o ongoing fund management.
- IFRIC concluded that:
  - o If a customer was rendered identifiable services, either before or at inception of a fund management relationship, the criteria for revenue recognition under IAS 18 would be met. Any portion of the fee related to future services to be provided by the fund manager should, however, be deferred.
  - o Revenue deferred would be recognized as revenue on a "systematic basis" that reflects how the service is provided to the investor:
  - o Allocation between services provided at inception and those to be provided in the future must be based on a "systematic approach" that reflects the fair value of the services provided to the customer.

Inventories

Inventories are assets held for sale in the ordinary course of business, in the process of production for sale, or in the form of materials or supplies to be consumed in production or in rendering services.

The scope and requirements of IAS 2 and CICA 3031 are essentially the same. Both:

- provide extensive guidance on the determination of cost, including the allocation of overhead;
- limit the choice of cost formulas permitted;
- require impairment testing; and
- have disclosure requirements aiming to increase transparency.

CICA 3031, which is effective for years starting January 1, 2008 (with earlier application encouraged), converged Canadian GAAP on inventories with IFRS. Except for minor differences (some of which are mentioned below), CICA 3031 is essentially a reproduction of the requirements under IAS 2.

Objective

The objective of IAS 2 is to prescribe the accounting treatment for inventories including their initial measurement as an asset and subsequent recognition as an expense. It also provides guidance on the cost formulas that can be used to assign costs to inventories.

Scope

IAS 2 applies to:

- assets held for sale in the ordinary course of business (finished goods),
- assets in the production process for sale in the ordinary course of business (work in process), and
- materials and supplies that are consumed in production (raw materials and supplies).

Examples of inventories include:

- harvested agricultural produce from biological assets (both IAS 2 and CICA 3031 scope out these products to the extent that they are measured at net realizable value in accordance with well-established practices in those industries. Note that IAS 41, *Agriculture* specifically deals with agricultural and forest products, agricultural produce after harvest);

- minerals and mineral products (both IAS 2 and CICA 3031 scope out these products to the extent that they are measured at net realizable value);

- commodities (both IAS 2 and CICA 3031 scope out these products when held by commodity broker-traders who measure their inventories at fair value less costs to sell);

- cost of services rendered when revenue is not recognized;

- construction in progress when revenue is recognized at the completion of the contract (this only applies to Canadian GAAP as IAS 11 specifically prohibits the use of completed contract method); and

- spare parts and servicing equipment which are usually carried as inventory and recognized in net income as consumed(this is specifically addressed in IAS 16, *Property, Plant and Equipment* which also identifies circumstances in which such items should be accounted for as property, plant and equipment. CICA 3031 also indicates that major spare parts and stand-by equipment may qualify as property, plant and equipment).

To avoid inappropriate applications, IAS 2 and CICA 3031 have been specifically scoped out financial assets.

Definitions

- Inventories are assets:
  - o held for sale in the ordinary course of business,
  - o in the process of production for such sale, or
  - o in the form of materials or supplies to be consumed in the production process or in the rendering of services.

- *Net realisable value* is the estimated selling price in the ordinary course of business less the estimated costs of completion and the estimated costs necessary to make the sale.

Initial Measurement

Inventories are initially recorded as follows:

- for materials to be used in production and finished goods acquired for resale: all direct costs including those necessary to bring these inventories to their existing condition and location (such as transportation, import duties, insurance and handling);

- note that trade discounts, rebates and other similar items are deducted from purchase costs;

- for work in progress and finished goods produced: all costs of converting materials into finished goods (see allocation of overhead below).

Standard cost and retail methods may be used provided that they approximate actual cost.

Allocation of Overhead

Entities engaged in manufacturing goods must include all conversion and other costs incurred in the production of finished goods. Under both IAS 2 and CICA 3031 an entity cannot use the direct costing method, where all production overheads are expensed. Such costs must be allocated to inventory, whether or not the entity classifies them internally as production overhead.

IAS 2 and CICA 3031 require that:

- variable production overhead costs be included in each unit produced on the basis of actual production;
- fixed production overheads be allocated to inventories based on normal capacity (i.e., the level of production that an entity expects to achieve on average over a number of periods);
- all unallocated fixed production overheads, such as idle capacity variances, be included in the cost of sales in the current period.

Costs Excluded from Inventories

The following costs must be excluded from inventories:

- administrative overheads not related to production;
- selling costs;
- foreign exchange differences arising directly on the recent acquisition of inventories invoiced in a foreign currency;
- interest cost when inventories are purchased with deferred settlement terms.

Storage costs are also generally expensed. They are only included in the cost of inventories if storage is necessary in the production process prior to a further production stage or to make the product saleable.

Cost Formulas (Costs Flows)

The cost of inventories is determined based on specific identification for goods not ordinarily interchangeable or those segregated for specific projects. When inventories consist of homogeneous products (such as raw materials to be used in production and spare parts) and are purchased at different prices, an entity may use either the weighted average or the first-in, first-out (FIFO) cost formula.

An entity must use the same cost formula for all inventories of a similar nature and use to the entity. For inventories with a different nature or use, different cost formulas may be justified. Whichever application method an entity chooses, it should apply that method consistently.

Impairment

Subsequent to initial recognition, entities must measure inventories at the lower of cost and net realizable value (NRV). This results in impairment losses being recognized as they occur. Write-downs to NRV may be triggered when:

- products are damaged;
- quantities held are obsolete;
- selling prices decline;
- costs of completion increase;
- direct selling costs increase.

Impairment is determined on an item-by-item basis and when appropriate, for a group of similar or related items. Items are considered similar or related if they:

- are from the same product line;
- have similar purposes or end uses;

- are produced and marketed in the same geographical segment; and
- cannot be practicably evaluated separately from other items in that product line.

Note that:

- write-down to NRV might be difficult to establish for certain work-in progress inventories as it would require (1) determining the expected sales price and (2) estimating the completion and disposal costs which would arise in future stages of production;
- IAS 2 and CICA 3031 establish impairment based on NRV, not replacement cost. For example if market prices for materials and supplies held for use in manufacturing fall below cost, this would not necessarily lead to an impairment unless the related finished products are expected to be sold below their costs;
- NRV is determined based on the conditions that existed at the balance sheet date. Events after the balance sheet date are only taken into consideration if they confirm conditions existing at or before the balance sheet date.

Impairment Reversal

Both IAS 2 and CICA 3031 require that a write-down to NRV taken in a prior period be reinstated when the conditions causing the write-down cease to exist.

Presentation and Disclosures

IAS 1 requires that inventories be presented as a current asset on a distinct line on the face of the statement of financial position.

IAS 2 and CICA 3031 require that categories of inventories be disclosed in the statement of financial position or in the notes (most commonly presented as supplies, raw materials, work-in-progress and finished goods) and applied consistently.

The following disclosures are required by IAS 2 (which correspond basically to the ones required under CICA 3031):

- accounting policies adopted including cost formula used;
- carrying amount of inventories and carrying amount in classifications appropriate to the entity;
- carrying amount of inventories carried at fair value less costs to sell;
- the amount of inventories recognized as an expense during the period;
- the amount of any write-down of inventories;
- the amount of any reversal of a previous write-down that is recognized as income in the period;
- the circumstances that led to the reversal of a previous write-down; and
- the carrying amount of inventories pledged as security for liabilities.

Illustrative Disclosures:
Extract 11(69) - Inventories

> **Bayer Aktiengesellschaft (AR 2007) , page 113 and 152**
> **4. Basic principles, methods and critical accounting policies (in part)**
> **Inventories**
> In accordance with IAS 2 (Inventories), inventories encompass assets (finished goods and goods purchased for resale) held for sale in the ordinary course of business, in the process of production for such sale (work in process) or in the form of materials or supplies to be consumed in the production process or in the rendering of services (raw materials and supplies). Inventories are recognized at the lower of acquisition or production cost – calculated by the weighted-average method – and net realizable value which is the realizable sale proceeds under normal business conditions less estimated cost to complete and selling expenses.

Bayer Aktiengesellschaft (AR 2007) , page 152

22. Inventories

Inventories comprised:

€million	Dec. 31, 2006	Dec. 31, 2007
Raw materials and supplies	1,004	1,012
Work in process, finished goods and goods purchased for resale	5,145	5,197
Advance payments	4	8
Total	6,153	6,217

Of the inventories totaling €6,217 million as of December 31, 2007 (2006: €6,153 million), €691 million (2006: €910 million) were carried at fair value less costs to sell.

The changes in the inventory reserve, which are reflected in the cost of goods sold, were as follows:

€million	2006	2007
January 1	(340)	(311)
Changes in the scope of consolidation	-	(3)
Additions expensed	(180)	(149)
Deductions due to reversal or utilization	151	130
Reclassifications to current assets	46	-
Exchange differences	12	15
December 31	(311)	(318)

Commentary: In the above extract the company disclosed the following information:
- a description of different classes of inventories and the measurement basis;
- classes of inventories held and their related carrying amounts; and
- the carrying amount of inventories carried at fair value less cost to sell.

This extract conforms with IAS 2 and CICA 3031 requirements. The company also provided a reconciliation of impairment reserves which is not specifically required under IAS 2.

Extract 11(70) – Inventories

Diageo plc (AR 2007), pages 82 and 102

Accounting policies of the group (in part)

Inventories

Inventories are stated at the lower of cost and net realisable value. Cost includes raw materials, direct labour and expenses, an appropriate proportion of production and other overheads, but not borrowing costs. Cost is calculated on an actual usage basis for maturing inventories and on a first in, first out basis for other inventories.

page 102

13 Biological assets

	Grape vines £ million
Fair value	
At 30 June 2005	14
Exchange differences	(1)
Harvested grapes transferred to inventories	(19)
Changes in fair value	19
At 30 June 2006	13
Exchange differences	(1)
Harvested grapes transferred to inventories	(19)
Changes in fair value	19
At 30 June 2007	12

(a) Biological assets comprise grape vines and grapes on the vine. At 30 June 2007, grape vines comprise approximately 1,910 hectares (2006 – 1,769 hectares) of vineyards, ranging from newly established vineyards to vineyards that are 88 years old.

(b) There are no outstanding commitments for the acquisition or development of vineyards.

Diageo plc (AR 2007), page 105

17 Inventories

	2007 £ million	2006 £ million
Raw materials and consumables	239	236
Work in progress	14	17
Maturing inventories	1,745	1,644
Finished goods and goods for resale	467	489
	2,465	2,386

Inventories are disclosed net of provisions for obsolescence, an analysis of which is as follows:

	2007 £ million	2006 £ million	2005 £ million
Balance at beginning of the year	44	45	49
Exchange differences	(2)	–	(1)
Income statement charge	9	2	5
Written off	(8)	(3)	(8)
	43	44	45

Commentary: In the above extract the company disclosed the following information:
- a description of the measurement basis of inventories;
- transfers from biological assets to inventories (the former are scoped out of IAS 2);
- the amount of write-downs of inventories; and
- classes of inventories held and their related carrying amounts.

This extract conforms with IAS 2 and CICA 3031 requirements. Note that maturing inventories correspond to goods probably held for a period in excess of one year and relate to spirits such as vodka and whisky.

The company also provided a reconciliation of inventory obsolescence which is not specifically required under IAS 2.

Extract 11(71) – Inventories

Rio Tinto Group (Full Financial Statements 2007), page 12 and 22

1 PRINCIPAL ACCOUNTING POLICIES (in part)

(l) Inventories

Inventories are valued at the lower of cost and net realisable value, primarily on a weighted average cost basis. Average costs are calculated by reference to the cost levels experienced in the current month together with those in opening inventory. Cost for raw materials and stores is purchase price and for partly processed and saleable products is generally the cost of production. For this purpose the costs of production include:

- labour costs, materials and contractor expenses which are directly attributable to the extraction and processing of ore;
- the depreciation of mining properties and leases and of property, plant and equipment used in the extraction and processing of ore; and
- production overheads.

Stockpiles represent ore that has been extracted and is available for further processing. If there is significant uncertainty as to when the stockpiled ore will be processed it is expensed as incurred. Where the future processing of this ore can be predicted with confidence, eg because it exceeds the mine's cut off grade, it is valued at the lower of cost and net realisable value. If the ore will not be processed within the 12 months after the balance sheet date it is included within non current assets. Work in progress inventory includes ore stockpiles and other partly processed material. Quantities are assessed primarily through surveys and assays.

Rio Tinto Group (Full Financial Statements 2007), page 22
16 INVENTORIES

	2007 US$m	2006 US$m
Raw materials and purchased components	1,078	448
Consumable stores	1,054	581
Work in progress	1,727	459
Finished goods and goods for resale	1,701	1,151
	5,560	2,639
Comprising:		
Expected to be used within one year	5,382	2,540
Expected to be used after more than one year	178	99
	5,560	2,639

Commentary: In the above extract the company disclosed the following information:

- details on how its inventories are valued which consist of minerals (not solely valued at net realizable value and consequently within the scope of IAS 2); and
- classes of inventories held and their related carrying amounts.

This extract conforms with IAS 2 and CICA 3031 requirements.

Although not specifically required under IAS 2, the company separately discloses the carrying amount of inventories that are expected to be used within one year and inventories that are expected to be used after more than one year. The disclosure of this information is encouraged under IAS 1.65.

FUTURE DEVELOPMENTS

Revenue recognition is widely addressed in accounting literature. The IASB is working on a long-term project that contemplates major changes to revenue recognition practice. Currently, the IASB and IFRIC have Exposure Drafts outstanding that propose changes on some revenue recognition issues over the short term. A discussion of these issues follows.

IASB Annual Improvements Exposure Draft

In August 2008 the IASB issued an Exposure Draft that contains amendments to the Appendix of IAS 18.

Currently IAS 18 does not provide guidance on how to determine whether an entity is acting as a principal or as an agent. The amendments propose to specify that an entity is acting as a principal when it has exposure to the significant risks and rewards associated with the sale of goods or the rendering of services.

The Exposure Draft proposes a similar guidance to that in EIC-123 which was harmonized with US GAAP. More specifically, it proposes features that, individually or in combination, indicate that an entity is acting as a principal, which include situations where the entity:

- has the primary responsibility for providing the goods or services to the customer or for fulfilling the order, for example by being responsible for the acceptability of the products or services ordered or purchased by the customer;
- has inventory risk before or after the customer order, during shipping or on return;
- has discretion in establishing prices, either directly or indirectly, for example by providing additional goods or services;
- bears the customer's credit risk.

One feature indicating that an entity is acting as an agent is that the amount the entity earns is predetermined, being either a fixed fee per transaction or a stated percentage of the amount billed to the customer.

IFRIC Interpretation 18 – Transfers of Assets from Customers (issued in January 2009)

An interpretation on transfers of assets from customers was issued in January 2009 because the accounting for transfers of items of property, plant and equipment by entities that receive such transfers from their customers differed in practice, specifically with regards to determining whether:

- the transferred item gives rise to an asset;
- the initial measurement should be at fair value or at cost, if an asset is recognized; and
- the resulting credit should be recognized as revenue immediately or deferred and amortized over the period of the ongoing service, if initial measurement is at fair value.

When a transferred item qualifies for recognition as an asset, the interpretation requires the transferred item to be recognized as property, plant and equipment and measured on initial recognition at its fair value. Such a transfer is effectively an exchange for dissimilar goods or services; therefore, revenue should be recognized in accordance with IAS 18, since it considers such an exchange to be a transaction that generates revenue.

If an entity provides only one service in exchange for a transferred item, revenue is recognized when the service is performed.

If an entity provides more than one service in exchange for a transferred item, the fair value of the total consideration received or receivable for the agreement is allocated to each service. The recognition criteria are then applied to each service.

If an entity provides an ongoing service in exchange for a transferred item, revenue is recognized over a period that is generally determined by the terms of the agreement with the customer. If the agreement does not specify a term, the revenue is recognized over a period that is no longer than the useful life of the transferred asset used to provide the ongoing service.

IFRIC 18 requires entities to apply the Interpretation prospectively to transfers of assets from customers received on or after July 1, 2009. Earlier application is permitted provided the valuations and other information needed to apply to the Interpretation to past transfers were obtained at the time those transfers were made.

Long-term Impact: Revenue Recognition Project

The IASB is undertaking a joint project with the FASB to develop concepts and a general standard for revenue recognition, which would replace the existing IAS 11 and IAS 18.

In December 2008, the IASB issued a Discussion Paper on its preliminary views on revenue recognition in contracts with customers, which will be open for comment until June 19, 2009. The IASB expects to publish an Exposure Draft on revenue recognition in 2010 and the final standard in 2011.

The Discussion Paper presents a single, *contract-based revenue recognition model*, which is being developed to improve financial reporting by providing clearer guidance on when an entity should recognize revenue. As a result, the IASB expects that entities will recognize revenue more consistently for similar contracts regardless of the industry in which it operates. That consistency should improve the comparability and understandability of revenue for users of financial statements.

For many contracts (particularly for commonplace retail transactions), the proposed revenue recognition model would cause little change.

Recognition

When an entity becomes a party to a contract with a customer, the combination of the rights and the obligations in that contract gives rise to a net contract position. Under the contract-based revenue recognition model, revenue should be recognized on the basis of increases in the entity's net position in a contract with a customer (i.e., when a contract asset increases or a contract liability decreases).

An entity's performance obligation is a promise in a contract with a customer to transfer an asset (such as a good or a service) to that customer. Performance obligations are accounted for separately if the promised assets are transferred to the customer at different times.

An entity has satisfied a performance obligation when it transfers a promised asset to the customer (i.e., when the customer obtains control of the asset). Consequently, activities that an entity undertakes in fulfilling a contract would result in the recognition of revenue only if they simultaneously transfer assets to the customer.

Measurement

The IASB currently does not have a preliminary view on how an entity should measure its rights in a contract.

The *original transaction price approach* should be used to measure performance obligations at contract inception; therefore, performance obligations should be initially measured at the transaction price (i.e., the customer's promised consideration). If a contract comprises more than one performance obligation, an entity should allocate the transaction price to the performance obligations on the basis of the relative stand-alone selling prices of the goods and services underlying those performance obligations.

Subsequent measurement of the performance obligations should depict the decrease in the entity's obligation to transfer goods and services to the customer. When a performance obligation is satisfied, the amount of revenue recognized is the amount of the transaction price that was allocated to the satisfied performance obligation at contract inception. Consequently, the total amount of revenue that an entity recognizes over the life of the contract is equal to the transaction price.

After contract inception, the measurement of a performance obligation should not be updated unless that performance obligation is deemed onerous (i.e., when an entity's expected cost of satisfying the performance obligation exceeds the carrying amount of that performance obligation). In that case, the performance obligation is remeasured to the entity's expected cost of satisfying the performance obligation and the entity would recognise a contract loss.

COMPREHENSIVE EXAMPLES

This section presents two comprehensive examples showing extensive disclosures related to revenue and inventories. All disclosures and accounting policies provided in both examples appear to be in line with Canadian GAAP.

Comprehensive examples were selected from annual reports of companies that are SEC registrants as disclosures might be more transparent and reflect the possible application of IFRS within a Canadian context. It is important to note that the companies have applied IAS 18 requirements by considering existing guidance under the US GAAP. Many of the Canadian guidance on revenue recognition have been harmonized with the US.

Deutsche Telekom AG – All extracts 11(A) were obtained from the annual report for year ended December 31, 2007. Extracts 11(A1) to 11(A5) and Extracts 11(A6) to 11(A8) relate to revenue and inventories disclosures respectively.

Extract 11(A1) – Deutsche Telekom AG, pages 108 and 109

In this extract the company describes IFRIC 12 and IFRIC 13, which were issued but not yet adopted. The company specifies that:

- The adoption of IFRIC 12 is not expected to have a material impact on the presentation of its results of operations, financial position or cash flows.
- It is currently analyzing the impact of applying IFRIC 13 on the presentation of its results of operations, financial position or cash flows.

In November 2006, the IFRIC issued IFRIC 12 "Service Concession Rights." The European Union has not yet endorsed IFRIC 12. Service concessions are arrangements whereby a government or other public sector entity as the grantor grants contracts for the supply of public services – such as roads, airports, prisons and energy and water supply and distribution facilities – to private sector entities as operators. IFRIC 12 addresses how service concession operators should apply existing IFRS to account for the obligations they undertake and rights they receive in service concession arrangements. Depending on the consideration the operator receives from the grantor, the operator recognizes a financial or an intangible asset. A financial asset is recognized if the operator has an unconditional contractual right to receive cash or another financial asset from the grantor. If the consideration the operator receives from the grantor is a right to charge users, an intangible asset is recognized. Depending on the contractual arrangements, recognition of both a financial asset and an intangible asset is possible as well. The provisions of IFRIC 12 are effective for financial years beginning on or after January 1, 2008. The adoption of IFRIC 12 is not expected to have a material impact on the presentation of Deutsche Telekom's results of operations, financial position or cash flows.

In June 2007, the IFRIC issued IFRIC 13 "Customer Loyalty Programmes." The European Union has not yet endorsed IFRIC 13. The interpretation addresses the accounting of customer loyalty programs that grant customers points (credits) that allow them to acquire free or discounted goods or services from the seller or a third party. The question to be clarified was whether the award credits are a liability in the context of a completed sale or an advance payment for a future sales transaction. The interpretation now issued requires the proceeds of the sale to be divided into two components. One component is attributable to the transaction which resulted in the credit awards. The other component is allocable to the future sales transaction resulting from the credit awards to be redeemed. The portion of the proceeds allocated to the goods or service already delivered is recognized as revenue. The portion of the proceeds allocated to the award credits is deferred as an advance payment until the customer redeems the credit award, or the obligation in respect of the credit award is fulfilled. Since the guidance under IFRIC 13 deviates from Deutsche Telekom's current accounting policy, the accounting method will have to be adjusted. The interpretation shall be applied for financial years beginning on or after July 1, 2008. Deutsche Telekom is currently analyzing the impact of applying IFRIC 13 on the presentation of Deutsche Telekom's results of operations, financial position or cash flows.

Extract 11(A2) – Deutsche Telekom AG, pages 127

In this extract, the company describes its accounting policies for revenue measurement and recognition in relation to:

- customer activation fees;
- multiple-element arrangements (where US GAAP guidance is used in its entirety as it does not contradict IFRS);
- payments to customers;
- systems integration contracts;

- segmentation and grouping of contracts.

Revenues include all revenues from the ordinary business activities of Deutsche Telekom. Revenues are recorded net of value-added tax and other taxes collected from customers that are remitted to governmental authorities. They are recognized in the accounting period in which they are earned in accordance with the realization principle. Customer activation fees are deferred and amortized over the estimated average period of customer retention, unless they are part of a multiple-element arrangement, in which case they are a component of the arrangement consideration to be paid by the customer. Activation costs and costs of acquiring customers are deferred, up to the amount of deferred customer activation fees, and recognized over the average customer retention period.

For **multiple-element arrangements**, revenue recognition for each of the elements identified must be determined separately. The framework of the Emerging Issues Task Force Issue No. 00-21 "Accounting for Revenue Arrangements with Multiple Deliverables" (EITF 00-21) was applied to account for multiple-element revenue agreements entered into after January 1, 2003, as permitted by IAS 8.12. EITF 00-21 requires in principle that arrangements involving the delivery of bundled products or services be separated into individual units of accounting, each with its own separate earnings process. Total arrangement consideration relating to the bundled contract is allocated among the different units based on their relative fair values (i.e., the relative fair value of each of the accounting units to the aggregated fair value of the bundled deliverables). If the fair value of the delivered elements cannot be determined reliably but the fair value of the undelivered elements can be determined reliably, the residual value method is used to allocate the arrangement consideration.

Payments to customers, including payments to dealers and agents (discounts, provisions) are generally recognized as a decrease in revenue. If the consideration provides a benefit in its own right and can be reliably measured, the payments are recognized as expenses.

Revenue from systems integration contracts requiring the delivery of customized products is recognized by reference to the stage of completion, as determined by the ratio of project costs incurred to date to estimated total contract costs, with estimates regularly revised during the life of the contract. A group of contracts, whether with a single customer or with several customers, is treated as a single contract when the group of contracts is negotiated as a single package, the contracts are closely interrelated and the contracts are performed concurrently or in a continuous sequence. When a contract covers a number of assets, the construction of each asset is treated separately when separate proposals have been submitted for each asset, each asset has been negotiated separately and can be accepted or rejected by the customer separately, and the costs and revenues of each asset can be identified. Receivables from these contracts are classified in the balance sheet item "trade and other receivables." Receivables from these contracts are calculated as the balance of the costs incurred and the profits recognized, less any discounts and recognized losses on the contract; if the balance for a contract is negative, this amount is reported in liabilities. If the total actual and estimated expenses exceed revenues for a particular contract, the loss is immediately recognized.

Extract 11(A3) – Deutsche Telekom AG, pages 128 and 129

In this extract, the company describes its revenue by operating segment. It describes in detail the revenue measurement and recognition for each of the identified segments.

Revenue recognition in Deutsche Telekom's operating segments is as follows:

Mobile Communications Europe and Mobile Communications USA. Revenue generated by the operating segments Mobile Communications Europe and Mobile Communications USA include revenues from the provision of mobile services, customer activation fees, and sales of mobile handsets and accessories. Mobile services revenues include monthly service charges, charges for special features, call charges, and roaming charges billed to T-Mobile-customers, as well as other mobile operators. Mobile services revenues are recognized based upon minutes of use and contracted fees less credits and adjustments for discounts. The revenue and related expenses associated with the sale of mobile phones, wireless data devices, and accessories are recognized when the products are delivered and accepted by the customer.

Broadband/Fixed Network.

The Broadband/Fixed Network operating segment provides its customers with narrow and broadband access to the fixed network as well as Internet access. It also sells, leases, and services telecommunications equipment for its customers and provides additional telecommunications services. The Broadband/Fixed Network operating segment also conducts business with national and international network operators and with resellers (wholesale including resale). Service revenues are recognized when the services are provided in accordance with contractual terms and conditions. Revenue and expenses associated with the sale of telecommunications equipment and accessories are recognized when the products are delivered, provided there are no unfulfilled company obligations that affect the customer's final acceptance of the arrangement. Revenue from rentals and operating leases is recognized monthly as the entitlement to the fees accrues. Revenues from customer activation fees are deferred over the average customer retention period. Revenues also result from charges for advertising and e-commerce. Advertising revenues are recognized in the period that the advertisements are exhibited. Transaction revenues are recognized upon notification from the customer that qualifying transactions have occurred and collection of the resulting receivable is reasonably assured.

Business Customers.

Business Services. Telecommunication Services include Network Services, Hosting & ASP Services, and Broadcast Services. Contracts for network services, which consist of the installation and operation of communication networks for customers, have an average duration of approximately three years. Customer activation fees and related costs are deferred and amortized over the estimated average period of customer retention. Revenues for voice and data services are recognized under such contracts when used by the customer. When an arrangement contains a lease, the lease is accounted for separately in accordance with IFRIC 4 and IAS 17. Revenues from Hosting & ASP Services and Broadcast Services are recognized as the services are provided.

Enterprise Services. Enterprise Services derives revenues from Computing & Desktop Services, Systems Integration and Telecommunication Services. Revenue is recognized when persuasive evidence of a sales arrangement exists, products are delivered or services are rendered, the sales price or fee is fixed or determinable and collectibility is reasonably assured.

The terms of contracts awarded by Enterprise Services generally range from less than one year to ten years.

Revenue from Computing & Desktop Services is recognized as the services are provided using a proportional performance model. Revenue is recognized ratably over the contractual service period for fixed-price contracts and on an output or consumption basis for all other service contracts. Revenue from service contracts billed on the basis of time and material used is recognized at the contractual hourly rates as labor hours are delivered and direct expenses are incurred.

Revenue from hardware sales or sales-type leases is recognized when the product is shipped to the customer, provided there are no unfulfilled company obligations that affect the customer's final acceptance of the arrangement. Any costs of these obligations are recognized when the corresponding revenue is recognized.

Revenue from rentals and leases is recognized on a straight-line basis over the rental period.

Revenue from systems integration contracts requiring the delivery of customized products is generally recognized by reference to the stage of completion, as determined by the ratio of project costs incurred to date to estimated total contract costs, with estimates regularly revised during the life of the contract. For contracts including milestones, revenues are recognized only when the services for a given milestone are provided and accepted by the customer, and the billable amounts are not contingent upon providing remaining services.

Revenue for Telecommunication Services rendered by Enterprise Services is recognized in accordance with the methods described under Business Services.

When an arrangement contains a lease, the lease is accounted for separately in accordance with IFRIC 4 and IAS 17.

Extract 11(A4) – Deutsche Telekom AG, page 132

The company describes various measurement uncertainties caused by the use of estimates to recognize revenues.

Revenue recognition.

Customer activation fees. The operating segments Mobile Communications Europe, Mobile Communications USA and Broadband/Fixed Network receive installation and activation fees from new customers. These fees (and related directly attributable external costs) are deferred and amortized over the expected duration of the customer relationship. The estimation of the expected average duration of the relationship is based on historical customer turnover. If management's estimates are revised, material differences may result in the amount and timing of revenue for any period.

Service contracts. T-Systems conducts a portion of its business under long-term contracts with customers. Under these contracts, revenue is recognized as performance progresses. Contract progress is estimated. Depending on the methodology used to determine contract progress, these estimates may include total contract costs, remaining costs to completion, total contract revenues, contract risks and other judgments. All estimates involved in such long-term contracts are subject to regular reviews and adjusted as necessary.

Multiple-element arrangements. The framework of the Emerging Issues Task Force Issue No. 00-21 was adopted to account for multiple-element arrangements in accordance with IAS 8.12. EITF 00-21 requires that arrangements involving the delivery of bundled products or services be separated into individual units of accounting, each with its own separate earnings process. Total arrangement consideration relating to the bundled contract is allocated among the different units based on their relative fair values (i.e., the relative fair value of each of the accounting units to the aggregated fair value of the bundled deliverables). The determination of fair values is complex, because some of the elements are price sensitive and, thus, volatile in a competitive marketplace. Revisions to the estimates of these relative fair values may significantly affect the allocation of total arrangement consideration among the different accounting units, affecting future operating results.

Extract 11(A5) – Deutsche Telekom AG, page 133

This extract presents a table detailing the different sources of the company's revenue.

1 Net revenue.

Net revenue breaks down into the following revenue categories:

millions of €	2007	2006	2005
Revenue from the rendering of services	59,125	57,730	55,942
Revenue from the sale of goods and merchandise	3,174	3,240	3,345
Revenue from the use of entity assets by others	217	377	317
	62,516	61,347	59,604

Net revenue increased by EUR 1.2 billion to EUR 62.5 billion in the 2007 financial year, mainly as a result of changes in the composition of the Group. Customer growth in the mobile communications business also contributed to the increase in revenue. The increase was partly offset by exchange rate effects that resulted primarily from the translation of U.S. dollars (USD).

Extract 11(A6) – Deutsche Telekom AG, page 109

In this extract, the company specifies that IAS 23, *Borrowing Costs* would not require the capitalization of borrowing costs related to inventories that are manufactured or produced in large quantities on a repetitive basis.

Standards, interpretations and amendments issued, but not yet adopted. (in part)

In March 2007, the IASB issued an amendment to IAS 23 "Borrowing Costs." The European Union has not yet endorsed the amendment to IAS 23. The amendment to the standard mainly relates to the elimination of the option of immediately recognizing borrowing costs directly attributable to the acquisition, construction or production of a qualifying asset as an expense. Currently, Deutsche Telekom recognizes these costs directly as an expense. A qualifying asset in this context is an asset that takes a substantial period of time to get ready for its intended use or sale. In future, an entity is therefore required to capitalize borrowing costs as part of the cost of the qualifying assets. The revised standard does not require the capitalization of borrowing costs relating to assets measured at fair value, and inventories that are manufactured or produced in large quantities on a repetitive basis, even if they take a substantial period of time to get ready for use or sale. The standard applies to borrowing costs relating to qualifying assets for which the commencement date for capitalization is on or after January 1, 2009. Deutsche Telekom is currently analyzing the date of adoption of the amendment to IAS 23 and the resulting effects on the presentation of Deutsche Telekom's results of operations, financial position or cash flows.

Extract 11(A7) – Deutsche Telekom AG, page 122

In this extract, the company describes its accounting policy related to inventories valuation. It describes elements included in the costs of inventories and explains why handsets are not reduced to net realizable value (estimated selling price in the ordinary course of business less the estimated costs of completion and the estimated costs necessary to make the sale) under certain circumstances.

Accounting policies. (in part)

Inventories are carried at the lower of net realizable value or cost. Cost comprises all costs of purchase, costs of conversion and other costs incurred in bringing the inventories to their present location and condition. Borrowing costs are not capitalized. Cost is measured using the weighted average cost method. Net realizable value is the estimated selling price in the ordinary course of business less the estimated costs of completion and the estimated costs necessary to make the sale. Deutsche Telekom sells handsets separately and in connection with service contracts. As part of the strategy to acquire new customers, it sometimes sells handsets, in connection with a service contract, at below its acquisition cost. Because the handset subsidy is part of the Company's strategy for acquiring new customers the loss on the sale of handset is recognized at the time of the sale.

Extract 11(A8) – Deutsche Telekom AG, page 144

In this note, the company provides a breakdown of the inventories it holds. It also discloses following amounts as required by IAS 2 and CICA 3031:

- inventories recognized at their net realizable value;
- write-downs recognized in profit or loss; and
- carrying amount of inventories recognized as expense.

19 Inventories.		
millions of €	Dec. 31, 2007	Dec. 31, 2006
Raw materials and supplies	138	106
Work in process	66	79
Finished goods and merchandise	1,255	937
Advance payments	4	7
	1,463	1,129

Of the inventories reported as of December 31, 2007, EUR 640 million (December 31, 2006: EUR 383 million) were recognized at their net realizable value. Write-downs of EUR 55 million (2006: EUR 93 million; 2005: EUR 199 million) on the net realizable value were recognized in profit or loss.

The carrying amount of inventories recognized as expense amounted to EUR 5,713 million (2006: EUR 5,667 million).

Alcatel-Lucent – All extracts 11(B) were obtained from AR 2007 on Form 20-F for the year ended December 31, 2007. Extracts 11(B1) to 11(B3) and Extracts 11(B4) to 11(B7) relate to revenues and inventories disclosures respectively.

Extract 11(B1) – Alcatel-Lucent, pages 162 and 163

In the following extract, the company specifies that judgment is required to account for its arrangements. In addition, the company describes its accounting policies for:

- sales of goods (where many of the criteria described correspond to those in EIC-141, which was converged with US GAAP);
- multiple-element arrangements (where many of the criteria described correspond to those in EIC-142, which was converged with US GAAP);
- construction contracts;
- software revenue recognition (where of the many criteria described correspond to those in US GAAP);
- sale of services;
- product sales made through retailers and distributors;
- product rebates (promotional activities giving rise to free products are deducted from revenues, which is not consistent with the treatment under EIC-156);
- measurement of revenue;
- recoverability of amounts receivable.

---

o/ Revenues

Revenues include net sales and service revenues from the Group's principal business activities, net of value added taxes (VAT) and income due from licensing fees and from income grants, net of VAT.

Most of the Group's sales are generated from complex contractual arrangements that require significant revenue recognition judgments, particularly in the areas of the sale of goods and equipment with related services constituting multiple-element arrangements, construction contracts and contracts including software. Judgment is also needed in assessing the collectibility of corresponding receivables.

Revenues from the sale of goods and equipment are recognized when persuasive evidence of an arrangement with the customer exists, delivery has occurred, the significant risks and rewards of ownership of a product have been transferred to the customer, the amount of revenue can be measured reliably and it is probable that the economic benefits associated with the transaction will flow to the Group. For arrangements in which the customer specifies formal acceptance of the goods, equipment, services or software, revenue is generally deferred until all the acceptance criteria have been met.

Revenues from contracts with multiple-element arrangements, such as those including products with installation and integration services, are recognized as the revenue for each unit of accounting is earned based on the relative fair value of each unit of accounting as determined by internal or third-party analyses of market-based prices. A delivered element is considered a separate unit of accounting if it has value to the customer on a standalone basis, there is objective and reliable evidence of the fair value of the undelivered elements in the arrangement, and delivery or performance of the undelivered elements is considered probable and substantially under the Group's control. If these criteria are not met, revenue for the arrangement as a whole is accounted for as a single unit of accounting in accordance with the criteria described in the preceding paragraph.

Under IAS 11, construction contracts are defined as contracts specifically negotiated for the construction of an asset or a combination of assets that are closely interrelated or interdependent in terms of their design, technology and function or their ultimate purpose of use (primarily those related to customized network solutions and network build-outs with a duration of more than two quarters). For revenues generated from construction contracts, the Group applies the percentage of completion method of accounting in application of the above principles, provided certain specified conditions are met, based either on the achievement of contractually defined milestones or on costs incurred compared with total estimated costs. Any probable construction contract losses are recognized immediately in cost of sales. If uncertainty exists regarding customer acceptance, or the contract's duration is relatively short, revenues are recognized only to the extent of costs incurred that are recoverable, or on completion of the contract. Construction contract costs are recognized as incurred when the outcome of a construction contract cannot be estimated reliably. In this situation, revenues are recognized only to the extent of the costs incurred that are probable of recovery. Work in progress on construction contracts is stated at production cost, excluding administrative and selling expenses. Changes in provisions for penalties for delayed delivery or poor contract execution are reported in revenues and not in cost of sales.

Advance payments received on construction contracts, before corresponding work has been carried out, are recorded in customers' deposits and advances. Costs incurred to date plus recognized profits less the sum of recognized losses (in the case of provisions for contract losses) and progress billings, are determined on a contract-by-contract basis. If the amount is positive, it is included as an asset under "amount due from customers on construction contracts". If the amount is negative, it is included as a liability under "amount due to customers on construction contracts".

In the absence of a specific guidance in IAS 18 "Revenue", software revenue recognition rules, as prescribed by the AICPA's SOP 97-2, are applied for revenues generated from licensing, selling or otherwise marketing software solutions when the software is sold on a standalone basis. When the software is embedded with the Group's hardware and the software is considered more than incidental, guidance given in AICPA'S SOP 97-2 is generally applied with limited exceptions, such as determining fair value using methods other than vendor-specific objective evidence (VSOE) of fair value, if deferring revenue related to the delivered elements due to the impossibility of determining VSOE of an undelivered element is not considered as IFRS compliant (e.g. IFRS does not require VSOE of fair value). If VSOE of fair value or fair value of an undelivered element cannot be determined or any undelivered element is essential to the functionality of the delivered element, revenue is deferred until either such criteria are met or the last element is delivered, or revenue is deferred and recognized ratably over the service period if the last undelivered element is a service.

For arrangements to sell services only, revenue from training or consulting services is recognized when the services are performed. Maintenance service revenue, including post-contract customer support, is deferred and recognized ratably over the contracted service period. Revenue from other services is generally recognized at the time of performance.

For product sales made through retailers and distributors, assuming all other revenue recognition criteria have been met, revenue is recognized upon shipment to the distribution channel, if such sales are not contingent on the distributor selling the product to third parties and the distribution contracts contain no right of return. Otherwise, revenue is recognized when the reseller or distributor sells the product to the end user.

page 163

Product rebates or quantity discounts are deducted from revenues, even in the case of promotional activities giving rise to free products.

Revenue in general is measured at the fair value of the consideration received or to be received. Where a deferred payment has a significant impact on the calculation of fair value, it is accounted for by discounting future payments.

The assessment of collectibility is critical in determining whether revenue or expense should be recognized. As part of the revenue recognition process, the Group assesses whether it is probable that economic benefits associated with the transaction will flow to the Group. If the Group is uncertain as to whether economic benefits will flow to the Group, revenue is deferred and recognized on a cash basis. However, if uncertainty arises about the collectibility of an amount already included in revenue, the amount in respect of which recovery has ceased to be probable is recognized as an expense in "cost of sales".

Extract 11(B2) – Alcatel-Lucent, pages 169 and 170

In the following extract, the company identifies sources of uncertainty:

- outcome of construction contracts, accounted for using the percentage-of-completion method (particularly in early stages of the contract);

- separation of components in arrangements where incidental software is sold along with other products and/or services;

- product returns on product sales through distributors;

- recoverability of receivables.

h/ Revenue recognition

As indicated in note 1o, revenue is measured at the fair value of the consideration received or to be received when the company has transferred the significant risks and rewards of ownership of a product to the buyer.

For revenues and expenses generated from construction contracts, the Group applies the percentage of completion method of accounting, provided certain specified conditions are met, based either on the achievement of contractually defined milestones or on costs incurred compared with total estimated costs. The determination of the stage of completion and the revenues to be recognized rely on numerous estimations based on costs incurred and acquired experience. Adjustments of initial estimates can, however, occur throughout the life of the contract, which can have significant impacts on future net income (loss).

Although estimates inherent in construction contracts are subject to uncertainty, certain situations exist whereby management is unable to reliably estimate the outcome of a construction contract. These situations can occur during the early stages of a contract due to a lack of historical experience or throughout the contract as significant uncertainties develop related to additional costs, claims and performance obligations, particularly with new technologies. During the fourth quarter of 2007, it was determined that the final outcome related to a large W-CDMA construction contract could not be estimated with reliability due to reasons indicated above. As a result, all the contract costs incurred have been expensed, but revenues have been recognized only to the extent that the contract costs incurred were recoverable. Consequently, revenues of €72 million and cost of sales of €298 million were recognized in 2007 in connection with this construction contract. The negative impact on income (loss) before tax, related reduction of goodwill and discontinued operations of changing from the percentage of completion method to this basis of accounting was €98 million. If and when reliable estimates become available, revenue and costs associated with the construction contract will then be recognized respectively by reference to the stage of completion of the contract activity at the balance sheet date. Future results of operations may therefore be impacted.

page 170

For arrangements to sell software licenses with services, software license revenue is recognized separately from the related service revenue, provided the transaction adheres to certain criteria (as prescribed by the Statement of Position SOP 97-2 of the American Institute of Certified Accountants, or the AICPA), such as the existence of sufficient vendor-specific objective evidence ("VSOE") to determine the fair value of the various elements of the arrangement.

Some of the Group's products include software that is embedded in the hardware at delivery. In those cases, where indications are that software is more than incidental, such as where the transaction includes software upgrades or enhancements, more prescriptive software revenue recognition rules are applied to determine the amount and timing of revenue recognition. As products with embedded software are continually evolving, as well as the features and functionality of the product driven by software components that are becoming more critical to their operation and success in the market, the Group is continually assessing the applicability of some of the guidance of SOP 97-2 including whether software is more than incidental. Several factors are considered in making this determination including (i) whether the software is a significant focus of the marketing effort or is sold separately, (ii) whether updates, upgrades and other support services are provided on the software component and (iii) whether the cost to develop the software component of the product is significant in relation to the costs to develop the product as a whole. The determination of whether the evolution of our products and marketing efforts should result in the application of some of SOP 97-2 guidance requires the use of significant professional judgment. Further, the Group believes that reasonable people evaluating similar facts and circumstances may come to different conclusions regarding the most appropriate accounting model to apply in this environment. Our future results of operations may be significantly impacted, particularly due to the timing of revenue recognition, if we change our assessment as to whether software is incidental, particularly if VSOE or similar fair value cannot be obtained with respect to one or more of the undelivered elements.

For product sales made through distributors, product returns that are estimated according to contractual obligations and past sales statistics are recognized as a reduction of sales. Again, if the actual product returns were considerably different from those estimated, the resulting impact on the net income (loss) could be significant.

It can be difficult to evaluate the Group's capacity to recover receivables. Such evaluation is based on the customers' creditworthiness and on the Group's capacity to sell such receivables without recourse. If, subsequent to revenue recognition, the recoverability of a receivable that had been initially considered as likely becomes doubtful, a provision for an impairment loss is then recorded (see note 2b above).

Extract 11(B3) – Alcatel-Lucent, page 179

The following extract presents a table showing the different sources of revenue, as required by IAS 18.

NOTE 6 REVENUES *(in millions of euros)*	2007	2006	2005
Construction contracts revenues	2,493	1,566	1,620
Other product sales	12,101	9,247	8,436
Other service revenues	2,949	1,352	1,062
License revenues	139	40	36
Rental income and other revenues	110	77	65
TOTAL	17,792	12,282	11,219

Extract 11(B4) – Alcatel-Lucent, page 160

In this note, the company briefly describes its accounting policy related to inventories valuation.

NOTE 1 SUMMARY OF ACCOUNTING POLICIES (in part)

l/ Inventories and work in progress

Inventories and work in progress are valued at the lower of cost (including indirect production costs where applicable) or net realizable value.

Net realizable value is the estimated sales revenue for a normal period of activity less expected selling costs.

Extract 11(B5) – Alcatel-Lucent, pages 163 and 200

In this note, the company specifies that most of its activities have long-term operating cycles and as a result, its balance sheet presents current asset balances (i.e., inventories, trade receivables and related accounts) comprised of amounts due within one year and amounts due after one year. The extract also presents details related to working capital, which include inventories.

NOTE 1 SUMMARY OF ACCOUNTING POLICIES (in part)

r/ Structure of consolidated balance sheet

Most of the Group's activities in the various business segments have long-term operating cycles. As a result, the consolidated balance sheet combines current assets (including other inventories and work in progress and trade receivables and related accounts) and current liabilities (including other provisions, customers' deposits and advances, trade payables and related accounts) without distinction between the amounts due within one year and those due after one year.

NOTE 18 OPERATING WORKING CAPITAL (in part)

(In millions of euros)	December 31, 2007	December 31, 2006	December 31, 2005
Inventories and work in progress, net	2,235	2,259	1,438
Trade receivables and related accounts, net	4,163	3,877	3,420
Advances and progress payments	110	87	124
Customers' deposits and advances	(847)	(778)	(1,144)
Trade payables and related accounts	(4,514)	(4,027)	(3,755)
Amounts due from customers on construction contracts	704	615	917
Amounts due to customers on construction contracts	(407)	(273)	(138)
OPERATING WORKING CAPITAL, NET	**1,444**	**1,760**	**862**

Analysis of amounts due from/to customers on construction contracts

(in millions of euros)	December 31, 2007	December 31, 2006	December 31, 2005
Amounts due from customers on construction contracts	704	615	917
Amounts due to customers on construction contracts	(407)	(273)	(138)
TOTAL	**297**	**342**	**779**
Work in progress on construction contracts, gross	272	347	281
Work in progress on construction contracts, depreciation	(42)	(23)	(29)
Customer receivables on construction contracts	438	299	700
Advance payments received on construction contracts	(224)	(211)	-
Product sales reserves – construction contracts	(147)	(70)	(173)
TOTAL	**297**	**342**	**779**

NOTE 18 OPERATING WORKING CAPITAL (in part) (continued)

(In millions of euros)	December 31, 2006	Cash flow	Change in consolidated companies	Translation adjustments and other	December 31, 2007
Inventories and work in progress[(1) & (2)]	2,961	311	110	(403)	2,979
Trade receivables and related accounts[(1)]	4,367	685	55	(319)	4,788
Advances and progress payments	87	29	1	(7)	110
Customers' deposits and advances[(1)]	(988)	(164)	(8)	89	(1,071)
Trade payables and related accounts	(4,027)	(627)	(139)	279	(4,514)
Operating working capital, gross	2,400	234	19	(361)	2,292
Product sales reserves – construction contracts[(1)]	(70)	-	-	(77)	(147)
Cumulated valuation allowances	(570)	-	-	(131)	(701)
OPERATING WORKING CAPITAL, NET	**1,760**	**234**	**19**	**(569)**	**1,444**

(1) Including amounts relating to construction contracts presented in the balance sheet caption "amounts due from/to customers on construction contracts".

(2) Of which €(247) million in the column "translation adjustments and other" related to the step-up of inventories accounted for in the purchase accounting of the Lucent business combination as described in note 3.

Extract 11(B6) – Alcatel-Lucent, page 166

In this note, the company describes the basis on which valuation allowances for inventories and work in progress are calculated, and provides amounts related to:

- accumulated valuation allowances, and
- write-downs recognized in income (loss).

NOTE 2 PRINCIPAL UNCERTAINTIES REGARDING THE USE OF ESTIMATES (in part)

a/ Valuation allowance for inventories and work in progress

Inventories and work in progress are measured at the lower of cost or net realizable value. Valuation allowances for inventories and work in progress are calculated based on an analysis of foreseeable changes in demand, technology or the market, in order to determine obsolete or excess inventories and work in progress.

The valuation allowances are accounted for in cost of sales or in restructuring costs depending on the nature of the amounts concerned. Accumulated valuation allowances on inventories and work in progress were €514 million at December 31, 2007 (€378 million at December 31, 2006 and €423 million at December 31, 2005).

The impact of inventory and work in progress write-downs on income (loss) before tax, related reduction of goodwill and discontinued operations was a net charge of €186 million in 2007 (a net charge of €77 million in 2006 and a net charge of €18 million in 2005).

Extract 11(B7) – Alcatel-Lucent, page 201

In this note, the company discloses the classes of inventories held and their related carrying amounts. The company also provides a reconciliation of the accumulated valuation allowance, which is not specifically required under IAS 2.

NOTE 19 INVENTORIES AND WORK IN PROGRESS

a/ Analysis of net value

(In millions of euros)	2007	2006	2005
Raw materials and goods	564	542	467
Work in progress excluding construction contracts	958	752	712
Finished products	1,185	1,320	653
Gross value (excluding construction contracts)	**2,707**	**2,614**	**1,832**
Valuation allowance	(472)	(355)	(394)
NET VALUE (EXCLUDING CONSTRUCTION CONTRACTS)	**2,235**	**2,259**	**1,438**
Work in progress on construction contracts, gross[1]	272	347	281
Valuation allowance[1]	(42)	(23)	(29)
WORK IN PROGRESS ON CONSTRUCTION CONTRACTS, NET	**230**	**324**	**252**
TOTAL, NET	**2,465**	**2,583**	**1,690**

(1) Included in the amounts due from/to customers on construction contracts.

b/ Change in valuation allowance

(In millions of euros)	2007	2006	2005
At January 1	(378)	(423)	(495)
(Additions) / reversals	(186)	(77)	(18)
Utilization	38	54	131
Changes in consolidation group	-	54	11
Net effect of exchange rate changes and other changes	12	14	(52)
AT DECEMBER 31	**(514)**	**(378)**	**(423)**

Extract 11(B8) – Alcatel-Lucent, page 242

In this note, the company discloses the inventory amounts given as guarantees.

NOTE 31 CONTRACTUAL OBLIGATIONS AND DISCLOSURES RELATED TO OFF BALANCE SHEET COMMITMENTS (in part)

b/ Off balance sheet commitments (in part)

Guarantees granted on debt, advance payments received, contingencies and security interests granted at December 31, 2007

(In millions of euros)	Less than one year	1 to 3 years	4 to 5 years	After 5 years	Total	Total of the balance sheet caption	% of the balance sheet caption
Guarantees on borrowings and advance payments received							
Security interests granted	-	-	-	4	4		
Other guarantees given	2	4	6	9	21		
TOTAL	**2**	**4**	**6**	**13**	**25**		
Net book value of assets given in guarantee:							
- intangible assets	-	-	-	-	-	4,230	-
- tangible assets	-	-	-	-	-	1,428	-
- financial assets	-	-	-	4	4	704	0.57%
- inventories and work in progress	-	-	-	-	-	2,235	-
TOTAL	**-**	**-**	**-**	**4**	**4**	**8,597**	**0.05%**

PLANNING FOR IMPLEMENTATION
Adapting Information Systems

Depending on their circumstances and operations, certain entities might have to make significant changes to their information systems so that they collect the new data required to comply with revenue guidance under IFRS. All entities should examine their sales arrangements so that they can assess their new information needs.

IFRS guidance on revenue recognition and measurement is more prescriptive than Canadian GAAP in some instances (such as for service rendering and construction contracts); however, there are also instances where IFRS is less prescriptive than Canadian GAAP. In such instances (for example, for the segmenting of multiple arrangements and revenue recognition for the sale of goods), management may need to exercise more judgment. In general, the adoption of IFRS will require more judgment from management.

Information systems should be modified during the implementation phase to accommodate the need for more judgment from management, who will require reliable and timely data for preparing estimates for the purpose of recognizing revenues, costs and expenses in accordance with IFRS. The criteria used to arrive at these decisions must also be clearly documented so users of financial statements, which include external auditors, can assess the reasonableness of the conclusions made by management.

It is important to emphasize that:

- Sales transactions have to be recorded according to their substance. This is essentially a matter of judgement in absence of specific IFRS standards. In instances where IFRS do not provide sufficiently clear guidance, certain companies might choose to refer to existing US standards. If that is their choice, they must adopt all the requirements of the particular US standard selected, but this could prove to be onerous for some companies.

- The substance of a sales transaction could be modified by minor changes to a contract. For example, a contract for the sale of goods that provides extended rights of return might be considered to be a sale on consignment (i.e., the risks and rewards of ownership were not transferred to the buyer) and, consequently, no revenue would be recorded. To prevent such unwanted consequences, it is essential for companies to have strong controls in place over the process of negotiating and signing contracts with customers.

Information systems will have to permit the collection of additional data (not currently required under Canadian GAAP) to ensure compliance with additional disclosures and other specific IFRS requirements. To illustrate the extent of some of the new requirements, we examine below certain elements related to IAS 11, IAS 18 and IFRIC 13.

IAS 11

Current Canadian GAAP does not contain specific guidance on construction contracts. Some companies refer to AICPA, *Audit and Accounting Guide* on *Construction Contractors,* which includes Statement of position 81-1, *Accounting for Performance of Construction-type and certain Production-type Contracts* (SOP 81-1), for guidance. Even though many of the requirements in IAS 11 are consistent with SOP 81-1, there are important differences.

The adoption of IAS 11 means that information systems and procedures will have to be tailored to allow for the gathering of various data to meet the requirements in the standard, including:

- Scrutinizing each significant contract to ensure that it is within the scope of the IAS 11 (i.e., it meets the definition in IAS 11). For example, a contract held by a real estate developer to build a house, where the contract terms state that the buyer has only limited ability to influence the design of the real estate, would be scoped out of IAS 11. Such a contract is considered a sale of goods and would be accounted for in accordance with IAS 18.
- Ensuring that consistent methods are applied throughout an entity (including affiliated entities) for:
  - grouping contracts and/or segregating assets of individual contracts according to the nature of the asset constructed and the price negotiations,
  - treating as a separate contract any changes including the construction of an additional asset, if the asset differs from the one previously built or if the price is negotiated without regard to the original contract price (determining that the asset is different is a matter of judgment and would take into consideration its design, technology and function),
  - determining the fair value of the consideration received and receivable of all contracts, which would require the discounting of any deferred payments,
  - allocating certain costs to the contracts such as design, technical assistance and certain overhead costs, such as insurance attributable to contract activity and depreciation of equipment used in a particular contract, and
  - recognizing revenues and expenses using the stage of completion method unless specific criteria are not met.
- Controlling application, which may require a cost tracking system for:
  - budgets,
  - incurred costs,
  - cost to be incurred,
  - stage of completion at the balance sheet date, and
  - various pricing elements, such as performance bonuses, penalties and retentions.

Accounting for construction contracts (and other long-term contracts) can present difficulties as IAS 11 requires that:

- revenues be measured at the fair value of the consideration received or receivable, which would include:
  - initial agreed upon price specified in the contract, and
  - any variation in receipts and disbursements relating to:
    - claims (amounts that the entity is seeking to collect for costs not included in the contract price),
    - incentives (additional amounts paid to the entity if the specified performance standards are met or exceeded), or
    - other changes (to the extent that the customer will probably approve them and the amount of revenue can be reliably measured).
- New disclosures necessitating additional data collection. For example, "retentions" (defined by IAS 11 as progress billings that are not paid until the satisfaction of conditions specified in the contract for the payment of such amounts or until defects have been rectified at the balance sheet date) have to be disclosed (this is not a requirement under Canadian GAAP) and, consequently, classification issues have to be addressed (retentions might be excluded from current assets in certain circumstances).

IAS 18

IAS 18 contains specific requirements for services rendering that may necessitate the collection of data similar to that needed under IAS 11. Information systems should be adapted to ensure compliance with new measurement, presentation and additional descriptive and quantitative disclosures. For example, all sales transactions (including those with related parties) have to be measured initially at fair value of the consideration received or receivable. This would mean taking into account:

- amount of trade discounts;
- volume rebates allowed by the entity;
- interest-free credit granted as part of sale of goods; and
- all commercial discounts and rebates.

IFRIC 13

As discussed previously, IFRIC 13 requires that all reward points issued to customers through loyalty programs be measured at their fair value and accounted for as deferred revenues (i.e., discounts on sales). This means that total revenues will decrease for the current period, when awards are granted, but will increase subsequently when awards are redeemed.

The adoption of IFRIC 13 necessitates that information systems be adapted to ensure that reliable and timely data is collected and that reward schemes are integrated with revenue reporting. Historical information will often provide the best estimate of the rate of redemption and, where records are electronically stored, there should be sufficient data to make an assessment. The assumptions used in certain complex arrangements may, however, need to be discussed with an expert in statistical analysis.

In certain cases, estimating the fair value of the points might be difficult in the following circumstances:

- *Informal loyalty programs*: Some "fidelity" programs are informal. For example, a customer might receive a free cup of coffee after purchasing a number of cups of coffee that are stamped on a card. IFRIC 13 does not consider informal reward schemes and the method for collecting data required to support the fair values for accounting entries.
- *Industry specific reward programs*: Many industries have complex reward schemes. For example, airline companies grant reward points based on distance travelled. The fair value of the points granted is difficult to measure because the price of airline tickets fluctuates constantly (i.e., due to the time of booking, route, time of the flight, flexibility in cancelling the ticket).

Ensuring the Input from Personnel Outside the Accounting Department

The application of revenue recognition standards under IFRS requires the input of personnel, including those working outside of the accounting department. For example, the recognition of revenue on construction contracts requires input from project engineers and the foreman at the construction site to:

- determine whether the design, technology and function of assets under construction are similar or dissimilar for segmentation purposes; and
- monitor the stage of completion and identify costs attributable to the contracts.

Legal, customer care and sales personnel will also contribute to the revenue recognition process by providing contract terms, extra billing details and settlement terms negotiated with client.

Informing Users of Financial Statements

Revenue and income reported under IFRS will most likely be more volatile than under Canadian GAAP due to increased reliance on estimates and fair value measurements, which require management to exercise more judgment. In addition, certain IFRS standards introduce new approaches and concepts, which will need to be clearly communicated to users. For example, the adoption of IFRIC 13 will result in the deferral of revenue at fair value instead of an accrual of expense at cost. It will be important to disclose this difference to users of the financial statements.

In certain circumstances, the change in accounting policy will be significant. For example, a construction company currently using the completed-contract method will have to use the stage-of-completion method, which will affect the timing of the recognition of revenues. These changes must also be communicated to the users of the financial statements.

Transitional Provisions

IFRS 1 might require the retroactive application of certain revenue recognition standards. For example, if an entity recorded an outstanding long-term contract using the completed-contract method in the prior year, the opening balance sheet and comparative results would have to be adjusted to reflect the use of the stage-of-completion method (assuming IAS 11 or IAS 18 criteria are met). To further illustrate, comparative loyalty program liability balances will most likely have to be restated when IFRS are implemented, unless IFRIC 13 is adopted (as a secondary source of Canadian GAAP), prior to the transition to IFRS.

IFRS 1 does provide some exemptions and exceptions to retroactive adjustments. One such exception relates to the use of estimates. For example, an entity cannot benefit from hindsight to revise estimates for the provision of doubtful accounts in the previously reported opening balance sheet unless there was an error.

Keep Posted

IASB and FASB are currently reviewing the revenue recognition standards. A Discussion Paper is expected to be published during the fourth quarter of 2008. In the meantime, the IFRIC has issued three interpretations and one Exposure Draft in response to the need for guidance on revenues.

Chapter 12
Property, Plant and Equipment and Discontinued Operations

Standards Discussed in this Chapter

International

IAS 16 – Property, Plant and Equipment
IFRS 5 – Non-current Assets held for Sale and Discontinued Operations

Canadian

CICA 3061 – Property, Plant and Equipment
CICA 3475 – Disposal of Long-lived Assets and Discontinued Operations
EIC-27 – Revenues and expenditures during the pre-operating period

INTRODUCTION

IAS 16, which provides guidance on property, plant and equipment (PPE), contains the same basic principles as Canadian GAAP: items are recognized at cost and depreciated over their useful economic lives. The adoption of IAS 16 might not impact significantly financial statement of Canadian companies. Differences might arise from:

- the fact that certain properties (held by an entity for rental or capital appreciations) are accounted for separately from PPE because they are covered specifically by a distinct standard IAS 40, *Investment*. No such distinct standard exists under Canadian GAAP;

- the use of option available under IAS 16 permitting an entity to record PPE at a revalued (fair value) amount, a measurement model that is generally prohibited under Canadian GAAP. This use of this option might impact significantly both the balance sheet and net income of future periods;

- the more explicit requirements of component accounting under IAS 16 than under CICA 3061. Note that even though component accounting is required under CICA 3061, it is not typically applied in practice;

- IAS 16 and CICA 3061 are not aligned concerning expenditures to be included or excluded from the historical cost.

To provide a better understanding of the issues related to PPE, this chapter discusses the following topics:

- recognition and initial measurement:
  - o component accounting,
  - o deferred payment,

o   incidental income,

o   non-monetary transactions;

- subsequent measurement:

o   cost model and revaluation model;

- depreciation;

- derecognition; and

- general disclosures.

IAS 16 does not apply to assets held for sale, which are dealt in IFRS 5. This topic and discontinued operations, are discussed at the end of this chapter.

IMPACT ON FINANCIAL STATEMENTS

The impact of adopting IFRS requirements to PPE on the financial statements will essentially depend on the entity's accounting policy choice, the nature of PPE it holds and expenditures it makes. The following observations are noteworthy:

- An entity selecting the revaluation model (as allowed under IAS 16) might report higher assets volatility because of fair value changes and lower net income because of higher depreciation expense. Note that under this model net revaluation increases do not have an impact on net income as they are recognized other comprehensive income.

- Component accounting required by IAS 16 might result in a higher depreciation expense since components with shorter useful life would have to be depreciated separately instead of being included in the asset as a whole for depreciation purposes.

- Constructed and internally developed PPE might include amounts of borrowing costs that have to be capitalized according to IAS 23, *Borrowing Costs.* Under Canadian GAAP an entity could choose to either capitalize or expense interest costs. (Refer to Chapter 19, which covers borrowing costs in more detail).

- Certain qualifying real estate properties could be carried at fair value, with changes in fair value included in net income under IFRS (refer to Chapter 8 on IAS 40, *Investment Property* for more details). This option does not generally exist under Canadian GAAP.

ANALYSIS OF RELEVANT ISSUES

Scope

IAS 16 applies to property, plant and equipment (PPE) unless they are covered by another standard. More specifically, IAS 16 does not apply to: biological assets related to agricultural activity (IAS 41, *Agriculture*); recognition and measurement of exploration and evaluation assets (IFRS 6, *Exploration for and Evaluation of Mineral Resources*) and mineral rights and reserves. It does, however, apply to PPE used to develop or maintain those assets. Note also that IAS 16 does not apply to assets classified as held for sale (IFRS 5).

Recognition and Initial Measurement

CICA 3061 and IAS 16 are generally converged on PPE recognition and initial measurement. A PPE item is to be recognized as an asset if it has probable future economic benefits and the cost of the item can be measured reliably. IAS 16(10) states that: "An entity evaluates under the general recognition principle all property, plant and equipment costs at the time they are incurred. Those costs include costs incurred initially to acquire or construct an item of property, plant and equipment and costs incurred subsequently to add to, replace part of, or service an item."

Under both Canadian GAAP and IFRS, cost includes all expenditures directly attributable to acquiring an asset, transporting it to the location where it will be used and ensuring it is in working condition for its intended purpose. The cost comprises:

- the purchase price, including import duties and non-refundable purchase taxes, after deducting trade discounts and rebates;
- costs directly attributable to bringing the asset to the location where it will be used and making it ready to operate in the manner intended by management;
- the initial estimate of the costs of dismantling and removing the item and restoring the site where it is located to its original condition. An entity will incur that obligation either at acquisition or after having used the item during a particular period for purposes other than to produce inventories. This obligation could arise from a legal obligation (Canadian GAAP) and both a legal or a constructive obligation (IFRS). Changes to an existing decommissioning or restoration obligation generally are added to, or deducted from, the cost of the related asset and depreciated prospectively over the asset's remaining useful life. (Decommissioning liabilities are covered in Chapter 15, "Provisions, Contingent Liabilities and Contingent Assets.")

Examples of directly attributable costs are:

- costs of employee benefits arising directly from the construction or acquisition of the PPE item;
- costs of site preparation;
- initial delivery and handling costs;
- installation and assembly costs;
- costs of testing whether the asset is functioning properly, after deducting the net proceeds from selling any items produced while bringing the asset to that location and condition (such as samples produced when testing equipment); and
- professional fees.

Administration and general overhead costs are not, however, considered direct costs and are expensed as incurred.

Spare parts and servicing equipment are usually carried as inventory and recognized in profit or loss as consumed. Major spare parts and stand-by equipment do, however, qualify as PPE when an entity expects to use them during more than one period or if they can only be used with one item of PPE.

Illustrative Disclosures:

Extract 12(1) – Disclosure – Elements included in the cost of PPE

United Utilities PLC (AR 2007), page 75

Accounting policies (in part)

e) property, plant and equipment

Property, plant and equipment comprises infrastructure assets (mains, sewers, impounding and pumped raw water storage reservoirs, dams, sludge pipelines and sea outfalls) and other assets (including properties, overground plant and equipment and electricity operational assets).

Water and wastewater infrastructure assets

Infrastructure assets comprise a network of water and wastewater systems. Expenditure on the infrastructure assets relating to increases in capacity or enhancements of the network are treated as additions. Amounts incurred in maintaining the operating capability of the network in accordance with defined standards of service are expensed in the year in which the expenditure is incurred. Infrastructure assets are depreciated by writing off their deemed cost, less the estimated residual value, evenly over their useful lives, which range from 15 to 300 years.

Employee costs incurred in implementing the capital schemes of the group are capitalised within infrastructure assets.

Other assets

All other property, plant and equipment is stated at historical cost less accumulated depreciation.

Historical cost includes expenditure that is directly attributable to the acquisition of the items. Subsequent costs are included in the asset's carrying amount or recognised as a separate asset, as appropriate, only when it is probable that future economic benefits associated with the item will flow to the group and the cost of the item can be measured reliably. All other repairs and maintenance are charged to the income statement during the financial period in which they are incurred.

Freehold land and assets in the course of construction are not depreciated. Other assets are depreciated by writing off their cost less their estimated residual value evenly over their estimated useful lives, based on management's judgement and experience, which are principally as follows:

Buildings 30-60 years

Operational assets 5-80 years

Fixtures, fittings, tools and equipment 3-40 years

Depreciation methods, residual values and useful lives are reassessed annually and, if necessary, changes are accounted for prospectively.

The gain or loss arising on the disposal or retirement of an asset is determined as the difference between the sales proceeds and the carrying amount of the asset and is recognised in income.

Commentary: This extract shows detailed disclosures of how PPE costs were determined at initial and subsequent recognition.

Extract 12(2) – Disclosure – Elements included in the cost of PPE

Akzo Nobel N.V. (AR 2007), page 109

Note 1 Summary of significant accounting policies (in part)

Principles of valuation of assets and liabilities (in part)

Property, plant, and equipment (in part)

Property, plant, and equipment are valued at cost less accumulated depreciation and impairment charges. Costs include expenditures that are directly attributable to the acquisition of the asset, including financing expenses of capital investment projects under construction. Government grants to compensate for the cost of an asset are deducted from the cost of the related asset.

Commentary: This extract indicates that "costs include expenditures that are directly attributable to the acquisition of the asset" without giving the detail of such costs, except for "financing expenses of capital investment projects under construction."

Component Accounting

IAS 16 requires the application of component accounting, that is, separate accounting for an asset's significant components. The component accounting in IAS 16 was developed in response to entities accruing expenses for pending major overhauls and inspections. Such provisions did not meet the definition of a liability. The main objective of the component accounting is to ensure that the costs of an asset's significant components are depreciated over their appropriate useful lives rather than the useful life of the asset taken as a whole.

CICA 3061 also requires that the cost of a PPE item made up of significant separable components be allocated to those components when practicable and when it is possible to make reliable estimates of their lives. IAS 16 does not provide an exemption on the basis of practicality. As the practicability exemption may have been widely used in Canada, corporations with significant investments in PPE may now have to make an extra effort to ensure the component allocations are done. IAS 16 also puts more emphasis on component accounting than CICA 3061 does, by providing guidance on allocating the cost or replacement of a component and on the level at which component accounting is required.

Costs incurred subsequently to add to, replace part of or service an item are capitalized if they meet the recognition criteria. The standard provides some guidance on those types of costs, which are discussed in the section "Costs Incurred After Initial Recognition." The standard also requires an entity to derecognize the carrying amount of a part of a PPE item if that part has been replaced. This applies whether or not the replaced item had been separately identified and depreciated since acquisition. If the carrying amount of the replaced part cannot be identified, the cost of the replacement can be used to estimate the carrying value of the part that is being replaced and derecognized.

IAS 16 requires that each part of a PPE item costing a significant amount in relation to the item's total cost be depreciated separately. When, however, significant parts of a PPE item have the same useful lives and depreciation method, they may be grouped together for depreciation purposes.

Note that a separate component can be either physical (e.g. a motor on an aircraft) or non physical (e.g. major overhaul). Consequently, scheduled maintenance overhaul must be treated as a separate component of PPE under IAS 16. Such separate component would be amortized over the period between scheduled maintenance overhauls.

Illustrative Disclosure:

Extract 12(3) – Disclosure – Component

> **Akzo Nobel N.V. (AR 2007), page 109**
> **Note 1 Summary of significant accounting policies (in part)**
> **Principles of valuation of assets and liabilities (in part)**
> **Property, plant, and equipment (in part)**
> Parts of property, plant, and equipment that have different useful lives are accounted for as separate items of property, plant, and equipment. Cost of major maintenance activities is capitalized as a separate component of property, plant, and equipment, and depreciated over the estimated useful life. Maintenance costs which cannot be separately defined as a component of property, plant, and equipment are expensed in the period in which they occur.

Commentary: This extract mentions that parts of PPE that have different useful lives are accounted for as separate items of PPE, without giving more detail. It also describes the accounting treatment for maintenance costs, which is discussed below in the "Subsequent Measurement" section.

Deferred Payment and Borrowing Costs

If payment for a PPE item is deferred beyond normal credit terms, the difference between the cash price equivalent and the total payment is recognized as interest expense at a market rate over the credit term, unless the interest is capitalized in accordance with IAS 23, *Borrowing Costs*. Starting 2009, however, capitalization as part of the costs of the asset will be mandatory. Although CICA 3061 does not deal with the deferred payment for an asset, the concept of discounting is discussed in different sections of the *Handbook*.

Under CICA 3061 costs directly attributable to the acquisition, construction, or development activity over time are included in the initial cost. Consequently interest costs may be included in cost when the entities accounting policy is to capitalize interest costs, IAS 23, *Borrowing Costs* does not allow a choice. An entity must capitalize interest for certain qualifying assets. For more details refer to Chapter 19.

Incidental Income and Initial Operating Losses

Incidental income derived from operating property, plant and equipment prior to its substantial completion and readiness for use is recognized as part of the cost of the asset provided that it is necessary to bring the asset to its intended use. However, income and related expenses of incidental operations that are not necessary to bring an asset to the condition and location for its intended use – for example, using a construction site as a car park until construction begins – or that are incurred after the asset is already in the location and condition necessary for operating as intended are recognized in profit and loss. IAS 16 does not permit including in the cost of PPE any initial operating losses, such as those incurred while demand for the item's output builds up. Under Canadian GAAP (CICA 3061), net revenue or expense derived from PPE prior to substantial completion and readiness for use may be included in the cost. EIC-27, *Revenues and expenditures during the pre-operating period* specifies that incidental revenue and expenditures incurred during the pre-operating period that would not normally qualify for capitalization may be eligible for deferral.

Non-monetary Transactions

Under both IAS 16 and CICA 3831, *Non-monetary transactions,* an entity generally measures an item of PPE acquired in exchange for a non-monetary asset or assets, or a combination of monetary and non-monetary assets, at fair value unless the exchange transaction lacks commercial substance or the fair value of neither the asset received nor the asset given up is reliably measurable.

Subsequent Measurement

Cost Model and Revaluation Model

Under Canadian GAAP (CICA 3061), PPE is recorded using the cost model. Appraisal increases to PPE were proscribed after December 1, 1990. IAS 16 permits a choice of using either the cost model or the revaluation model, whereby fair value increases to PPE are recognized in other comprehensive income. Fair value must be measured reliably, otherwise the cost model should be chosen. Although the revaluation model may be applied to one or more asset classes, it has to be applied to entire classes of assets. Revaluations must be made with sufficient regularity to ensure that the carrying amount does not differ materially from what would be determined using fair value at the balance sheet date.

If an asset's carrying amount increases as a result of a revaluation, the increase is to be credited to comprehensive income and accumulated in equity under the heading of revaluation surplus. The increase has to be recognized in profit or loss to the extent that it reverses a revaluation decrease of the same asset previously recognized in profit or loss. If an asset's carrying amount decreases as a result of a revaluation, the decrease must be recognized in profit or loss. The decrease is to be recognized in comprehensive income under the heading of revaluation surplus to the extent that any credit balance exists in the revaluation surplus for that asset. It is not permitted to carry a negative revaluation reserve for any asset.

IAS 16 defines fair value as "the amount for which an asset could be exchanged between knowledgeable, willing parties in an arm's length transaction." It also mentions that, if there is no market-based evidence of fair value because of the specialized nature of a particular PPE item and the item is rarely sold (except as part of a continuing business), an entity may need to estimate fair value using an income or a depreciated replacement cost approach.

If fair value can be measured reliably, an entity may carry all items of a PPE class at a revalued amount, which is the fair value of the items at the date of the revaluation less any subsequent accumulated depreciation and accumulated impairment losses. When a PPE item is revalued, any accumulated depreciation at the date of the revaluation is treated in one of two ways:

- it is restated proportionately with the change in the gross carrying amount of the asset so that the carrying amount of the asset after revaluation equals its revalued amount. This method is often used when an asset is revalued by applying an index to determine its depreciated replacement cost;

- it is eliminated against the gross carrying amount of the asset and the net amount is restated to the asset's revalued amount. This method is often used for buildings.

These two methods will result in the same net balance sheet amount for PPE although the gross amounts reported in the notes to the financial statements (i.e., cost and accumulated depreciation) will be different. The effect on the income statement will also be the same.

Costs Incurred after Initial Recognition

Under both IFRS and Canadian GAAP, subsequent expenditure on an asset is capitalized only when it is probable that it will create future economic benefits. CICA 3061 defines betterment as the cost incurred to enhance the service potential of a PPE item. "Service potential may be enhanced when there is an increase in the previously assessed physical output or service capacity, associated operating costs are lowered, the life or useful life is extended, or the quality of output is improved." The concept of betterment does not exist in IAS 16; to capitalize a cost, it must meet the criteria for initial recognition of an asset.

Day-to-day servicing costs, such as repairs and maintenance costs, are expensed.

Major Inspections and Overhauls

Under IAS 16, , when an entity acquires an item of PPE, it might have to account distinctly major inspections and expenditures component and amortize such component over the period between scheduled maintenance overhauls. Separating scheduled maintenance overhaul might pose certain difficulties as this component would not form a part of acquired PPE and might not be readily obtainable from the PPE seller. Consequently, the entity will have to estimate the maintenance overhaul component of PPE which would reflect current market price not the estimated price when the maintenance will be performed. Once the scheduled maintenance overhaul has taken place any remaining carrying amount (i.e., the unamortized portion) must be derecognized and a new maintenance overhaul capitalized. If the carrying value of the replaced part cannot be directly determined, the cost of the replacement part, depreciated to the extent of the asset of which it is a part, would be used to measure the cost. CICA 3061 is silent on the accounting treatment of replacements. Also see component accounting discussed previously.

Illustrative Disclosures:

Extract 12(4) – Cost and revaluation models

The Go-ahead Group Plc (AR 2007), page 37

2 Summary of significant accounting policies (in part)

Property, plant and equipment

Plant and equipment is stated at cost less accumulated depreciation and any impairment in value. Land and buildings are recognised initially at cost and thereafter measured at fair value less depreciation on buildings and impairment subsequent to the date of valuation. Freehold land is not depreciated.

Valuations of land and buildings are performed by either the directors or by a qualified valuer, frequently enough to ensure that the fair value of a revalued asset does not differ materially from its carrying amount. The assets' residual values and useful lives are reviewed and adjusted on a prospective basis if appropriate at each financial year end.

Assets held under finance leases are depreciated over the shorter of their expected useful lives and the lease terms.

Depreciation is charged to the income statement based on cost or fair value, less estimated residual value of each asset evenly over its expected useful life as follows:

Short leasehold land and buildings	The life of the lease
Freehold buildings and long leasehold land and buildings	over 10 to 100 years
Rolling stock	over 8 to 15 years
Plant and equipment	over 3 to 15 years

The carrying values of items of property, plant and equipment are reviewed for impairment when events or changes in circumstances indicate the carrying value may not be recoverable. If any such indication exists the assets are written down to their recoverable amount.

Any revaluation surplus is credited to the revaluation reserve except where it reverses a decrease in the carrying value of the same asset previously recognised in the income statement, in which case the increase is recognised in the income statement. A revaluation deficit is recognised in the income statement except to the extent of any existing surplus in respect of that asset in the revaluation reserve. An annual transfer is made from the revaluation reserve to revenue reserves for the depreciation relating to the revaluation surplus. Upon disposal any revaluation reserve relating to the particular asset being sold is transferred to retained earnings.

---

12 Property, plant and equipment, page 48

	Freehold land and buildings £m	Leasehold properties £m	Rolling stock £m	Plant and equipment £m	Total £m
Cost:					
At 2 July 2005	139.1	13.3	263.4	134.6	550.4
Additions	7.1	2.0	50.2	11.6	70.9
Acquisitions	2.3	–	5.8	0.3	8.4
Disposals	–	–	(13.1)	(8.2)	(21.3)
Acquired on franchise handover	–	–	–	25.4	25.4
Revaluations	12.2	0.2	–	–	12.4
At 1 July 2006	160.7	15.5	306.3	163.7	646.2
Reclassification	(2.1)	7.9	–	(5.8)	–
Additions	1.6	2.1	28.8	25.1	57.6
Acquisitions	1.6	–	10.0	0.8	12.4
Disposals	(1.7)	(8.0)	(9.3)	(3.8)	(22.8)
Revaluations	11.9	(0.3)	–	–	11.6
Transfer to assets held for resale	(0.9)	–	–	–	(0.9)
At 30 June 2007	**171.1**	**17.2**	**335.8**	**180.0**	**704.1**
Depreciation and impairment:					
At 2 July 2005	5.0	3.3	109.6	82.4	200.3
Charge for the year	0.6	1.7	21.4	14.3	38.0
Acquisitions	–	–	2.3	0.1	2.4
Disposals	–	–	(13.0)	(6.7)	(19.7)
At 1 July 2006	5.6	5.0	120.3	90.1	221.0
Charge for the year	0.6	0.7	24.7	18.6	44.6
Reclassification	–	(0.3)	–	0.3	–
Acquisitions	–	–	3.4	0.5	3.9
Disposals	(0.3)	(2.3)	(7.4)	(2.7)	(12.7)
At 30 June 2007	**5.9**	**3.1**	**141.0**	**106.8**	**256.8**
Net book value					
At 30 June 2007	**165.2**	**14.1**	**194.8**	**73.2**	**447.3**
At 1 July 2006	155.1	10.5	186.0	73.6	425.2
At 2 July 2005	134.1	10.0	153.8	52.2	350.1

The net book value of leased assets and assets acquired under hire purchase contracts is:

	2007 £m	2006 £m
Rolling stock	166.0	129.3
Plant and equipment	4.8	7.7
	170.8	137.0

Additions during the year included £14.5m (2006 – £15.4m) of rolling stock and £nil (2006 – £0.3m) of plant and equipment held under finance leases and hire purchase contract.

The freehold and leasehold properties occupied by the group were valued by Doherty Baines as external valuers, as at 1 July 2006, in accordance with the Appraisal and Valuation Manual of The Royal Institution of Chartered Surveyors. Properties have been revalued under a director's valuation on a market value basis as at 30 June 2007.

If the properties had not been revalued the historic cost and accumulated depreciation would have been:

	2007 £m	2006 £m
Historic cost		
Freehold land and buildings	145.6	147.1
Leasehold property	17.3	15.3
	162.9	162.4
Accumulated depreciation		
Freehold land and buildings	4.5	4.2
Leasehold property	3.1	5.0
	7.6	9.2

Commentary: This extract presents an example of notes reflecting the option to fair value a class of PPE. In the summary of significant accounting policies, we can observe that land and buildings are measured at fair value, while plant and equipment are stated at cost. Therefore, the measurement model is applied to entire classes of PPE. While the note does not precisely state the frequency of the revaluation, it mentions that it is done "frequently enough to ensure that the fair value of a revalued asset does not differ materially from its carrying amount."

The last paragraph of this first extract describes how revaluation adjustments are treated: any revaluation surplus is credited to equity except where it reverses a decrease in the carrying value of the same asset previously recognized in the income statement; a revaluation deficit is recognized in the income statement except to the extent that a surplus exists for that asset. Note it also mentions that, on disposal, any revaluation reserve relating to a particular asset being sold is transferred to retained earnings.

Note that as of January 1, 2009, revaluation adjustments are accounted for as part of comprehensive income and accumulated in equity as part of the revaluation surplus.

The last part of the second note provides information on what would have been the historic cost and accumulated depreciation if the properties had not been revalued.

Depreciation

In both IFRS and Canadian GAAP the requirements for charging depreciation on PPE are similar, though differences exist in relation to how the depreciation charge is determined. The following present an analysis of elements that would impact depreciation amounts.

Depreciation – Cost Model

The initial cost basis is reduced by depreciation and impairment losses under both IFRS and Canadian GAAP.

Depreciation – Revaluation Method

If the revaluation model is chosen for an asset class, the value of that class is also reduced by depreciation and impairment. A portion of the revaluation surplus related to the asset depreciated may be realized as the asset is used by transferring from the revaluation surplus to retained earnings an amount equivalent to the difference between the depreciation calculated on the asset's revalued carrying amount and the one on its original cost. Alternatively, the whole of the surplus can be transferred to retained earnings when the asset is retired or disposed of.

Component Accounting

As discussed before, IAS 16 requires that each part of a PPE item having a significant cost in relation to the item's total cost, and for which different depreciation methods or rates are appropriate, be depreciated separately. In describing how it came to that conclusion, the IASB notes that: "Of particular concern to the Board were situations in which the unit of measure is the 'item as a whole' even though that item may be composed of significant parts with individually varying useful lives or consumption patterns. The Board did not believe that, in these situations, an entity's use of approximation techniques, such as a weighted average useful life for the item as a whole, resulted in depreciation that faithfully represents an entity's varying expectations for the significant parts." Each significant part of an asset should, therefore, be depreciated separately unless it has the same depreciation method and useful life as other parts. In that case, they may be grouped for depreciation purposes. Since significant parts of an asset are identified in relation to their significant cost rather than their depreciation methods or rates, it may be necessary to use approximation techniques to calculate the proper depreciation on the remainder of the asset, that is, the parts that are individually not significant and have not been identified separately.

Calculation of Depreciation

Under both IFRS and Canadian GAAP, depreciation of a PPE item begins when it is available for use and ceases at the earlier of when the asset is classified as held for sale (or included in a disposal group that is classified as held for sale) or when it is derecognized.

However differences in depreciation amounts might arise because:

1. Basis of depreciation differences

    IFRS, require that the annual charge to income for depreciation be based on an allocation of the cost of an asset less its residual value over its useful life, including any idle period.

    Canadian GAAP specify that the depreciation is based on the greater of:

    -   an allocation of the cost of an asset less its residual value over its useful life; and
    -   an allocation of the cost less salvage value over the life of the asset.

2. Frequency of reviews

    IFRS requires that estimates of useful life and residual value, and the method of depreciation, be reviewed at least at each annual reporting date.

    Canadian GAAP require that the useful life and method of depreciation be reviewed periodically, but residual value is reviewed only when events or changes in circumstances indicate that the current estimates may no longer be appropriate.

3. Depreciation method

    IAS 16 specifies that depreciation method must closely reflects the pattern in which the asset's future economic benefits are expected to be consumed by the entity over its estimated useful life.

    Canadian GAAP is less explicit as it only requires that objective of the depreciation method is to provide a rational and systematic basis for allocating the amortizable amount of an item of PPE over its estimated life.

    In addition IFRS are more explicit that Canadian GAAP as they specify that:

    -   estimated residual value should reflect the amount an entity would receive currently for the asset if it were already of the age and in the condition expected at the end of its useful life. It is not increased for changes in prices (future inflation). CICA 3061 defines residual value, but does not contain guidance on dealing with the effect of changes in prices.
    -   PPE item is depreciated even if it is idle (unless it is held for sale). CICA 3061 does not mention whether an entity must record depreciation on an idle item of PPE.

Changes in Depreciation Method

Under IAS 8, *Accounting Policies, Changes in Accounting Estimates and Errors*, a change in depreciation method is accounted for prospectively as a change in an accounting estimate. CICA 1506, *Accounting Changes* is converged with IAS 8 in requiring that a change in depreciation method be accounted for prospectively.

Impairment

An impairment loss is the amount by which the carrying amount of an asset exceeds its recoverable amount. IAS 16 defines recoverable amount as the higher of an asset's fair value less costs to sell and its value in use. To determine whether a PPE item is impaired, an entity has to apply IAS 36, *Impairment of Assets*, which differs significantly from CICA 3063. See Chapter 4, "Impairment of Assets," for more details.

Under IFRS, an increase in the recoverable amount of an asset can be recognized. For assets carried at cost, the amount of the recovery is limited to the carrying value of the asset prior to impairment less the appropriate depreciation charge that would have been recognized in the interim. Canadian GAAP does not permit the reversal of impairment charges for PPE.

Illustrative Disclosures:

Extract 12(5) – Depreciation by components

Gecina (AR 2006), page 152
3 VALUATION METHODS (in part)
3.1 Fixed assets (in part)
3.1.1 GROSS VALUE OF FIXED ASSETS AND DEPRECIATION (in part)
The following table presents:
- A breakdown of the value of buildings between their four main components:
  - Large-scale work
  - Roofing, façade
  - Technical equipment
  - Fittings
- The depreciation schedules for each component

| | **Component share** | | **Amortization period (years)** | |
Gross value of fixed assets and depreciation	Residential	Commercial	Residential	Commercial
Large-scale work	60%	50%	80	60
Roofing, facade	20%	20%	40	30
Equipment, technical facilities	15%	25%	25	20
Fittings	5%	5%	15	10

Commentary: This extract shows that the value of buildings is separated into four main components, each of the components having different amortization periods.

Derecognition of PPE

The carrying amount of an item of PPE is to be derecognized:
- on disposal; or
- when no future economic benefits are expected from its use or disposal.

The disposal date is the date the criteria for the sale of goods in IAS 18, *Revenue* would be met.

An entity is required to derecognize the carrying amount of a part of a PPE item if that part has been replaced and the entity has included the cost of the replacement in the carrying amount of the item.

Under IAS 16, when a PPE item is disposed of, the gain or loss on disposal is included in the income statement. The gain or loss is determined as the difference between the net disposal proceeds, if any, and the carrying amount of the asset. The gain or loss arising from the derecognition of a PPE item is not to be classified as revenue. Canadian GAAP contains similar requirements.

However, an entity that, in the course of its ordinary activities, routinely sells PPE items that it has held for rental to others should transfer such assets to inventories at their carrying amount when they cease to be rented and become held for sale. The proceeds from the sale of such assets should be recognized as revenue.

PPE that is not held for sale or derecognized is subject to depreciation.

General Disclosures Related to PPE

IAS 16 requires more extensive disclosures than CICA 3061 for each class of PPE. In addition to the basic disclosures about depreciation methods, useful lives or depreciation rates, gross carrying amounts and accumulated depreciation, it requires the following elements:

- the measurement bases used for determining the gross carrying amount;
- a reconciliation of the carrying amount at the beginning and end of the period showing:
  - o additions,
  - o disposals,
  - o assets classified as held for sale or included in a disposal group classified as held for sale in accordance with IFRS 5, *Non-current Assets Held for Sale and Discontinued Operations* and other disposals,
  - o acquisitions through business combinations,
  - o increases or decreases resulting from revaluations (IAS 16) and from impairment losses recognized or reversed in other comprehensive income (IAS 36),
  - o impairment losses recognized in profit or loss in accordance with IAS 36,
  - o impairment losses reversed in profit or loss in accordance with IAS 36,
  - o depreciation,
  - o the net exchange differences arising on the translation of the financial statements from the functional currency into a different presentation currency, including the translation of a foreign operation into the presentation currency of the reporting entity, and
  - o other changes;
- the existence and amounts of restrictions on title, and property, plant and equipment pledged as security for liabilities;
- the amount of expenditures recognized in the carrying amount of an item of property, plant and equipment in the course of its construction;
- if not disclosed separately on the face of the income statement, the amount of compensation from third parties for items of PPE that were impaired, lost or given up that is included in profit or loss; and
- the amount of contractual commitments for the acquisition of PPE; only certain types of commitments are required to be disclosed under CICA 3280, *Contractual Obligations*.

As in Canadian GAAP, an entity must disclose the nature and effect of any change in a PPE accounting estimate that has an effect in the current period or is expected to have an effect in subsequent periods (see IAS 8, *Accounting Policies, Changes in Accounting Estimates and Errors*).

The changes in estimate could be related to:

- residual values;
- the estimated costs of dismantling, removing and restoring items of property, plant or equipment;
- useful lives; and
- depreciation methods.

If items of PPE are stated at revalued amounts, the following must be disclosed:

- the effective date of the revaluation;
- whether an independent valuer was involved;
- the methods and significant assumptions applied in estimating the items' fair values;
- the extent to which the items' fair values were determined directly by reference to observable prices in an active market or recent market transactions on arm's length terms or were estimated using other valuation techniques;
- for each revalued PPE class, the carrying amount that would have been recognized had the assets been carried under the cost model; and
- the revaluation surplus, indicating the change for the period and any restrictions on the distribution of the balance to shareholders.

Any impacts on income taxes resulting from the revaluation of property, plant and equipment are recognized and disclosed in accordance with IAS 12, *Income Taxes*.

IAS 36, *Impairment of Assets* says an entity must disclose information on impaired PPE. CICA 3063 calls for similar information.

Additional disclosures are encouraged but not required for: temporarily idle PPE, fully depreciated PPE still in use, PPE retired from active use but not classified as held for sale, and fair value of PPE recorded under the cost model when materially different from carrying amount.

Illustrative Disclosures:

Extract 12(6) – Disclosure of amount of contractual commitments for the acquisition of PPE

Alcatel-Lucent (AR 2007 on Form 20-F), page 240
NOTE 31 CONTRACTUAL OBLIGATIONS AND DISCLOSURES RELATED TO OFF BALANCE SHEET COMMITMENTS (in part)

a/ Contractual obligations

The following table presents minimum payments that the Group will have to make in the future under contracts and firm commitments as of December 31, 2007. Amounts related to financial debt and finance lease obligations are fully reflected in the consolidated balance sheet.

(In millions of euros) Contractual cash obligations	Less than one year	2009-2010	2011-2012	Maturity date 2013 and after	Total
Financial debt (excluding finance leases)	483	1,134	959	2,472	5,048
Finance lease obligations	–	–	–	–	–
Equity component of convertible bonds	–	205	81	385	671
Sub-total – included in balance sheet	**483**	**1,339**	**1,040**	**2,857**	**5,719**
Finance costs on financial debt[(1)]	231	481	353	1,500	2,565
Operating leases	242	361	331	374	1,308
Commitments to purchase fixed assets	63	–	–	–	63
Unconditional purchase obligations[(2)]	398	110	2	–	510
Sub total – Commitments	**934**	**952**	**686**	**1,874**	**4,446**
TOTAL – CONTRACTUAL OBLIGATIONS	**1,417**	**2,291**	**1,726**	**4,731**	**10,165**

(1) To compute finance costs on financial debt, all put dates have been considered as redemption dates. For debentures with calls but no puts, call dates have not been considered as redemption dates. Further details on put and call dates are given in note 24. If all outstanding debentures at December 31, 2007 were not redeemed at their respective put dates, an additional finance cost of approximately €397 million (of which €29 million would be incurred in 2010-2011 and the remaining part in 2012 or later) would be incurred until redemption at their respective contractual maturities.

(2) Other unconditional purchase obligations result mainly from obligations under multi-year supply contracts linked to the sale of businesses to third parties.

Commentary: This extract illustrates the disclosure required for contractual commitments for PPE. The commitments to purchase PPE are split among different maturity dates although this additional information is not required by IAS 16.

Non-current Assets Held for Sale

Scope

Long-term assets held for sale, which are outside the scope of IAS 16, are covered by IFRS 5. According to this standard, when an asset's carrying amount is expected to be recovered principally through a sale rather than through continuing use, it should be classified as held for sale, within current assets. CICA 3475, *Disposal of Long-lived Assets and Discontinued Operations* is generally converged with IFRS 5, except that it deals with non-monetary, long-lived assets rather than non-current assets.

Criteria for Classification as "Held for Sale"

Both under IFRS 5 and CICA 3475, to be classified as "held for sale," an asset must be available for immediate sale in its present condition and the sale must be highly probable within 12 months. This requires management to commit to a plan to sell the asset that is unlikely to change and to actively market the asset at a reasonable price.

Furthermore, all the assets and liabilities of a subsidiary should be classified as held for sale when an entity is committed to a sale plan involving the loss of control of that subsidiary and the abovementioned criteria are met. These assets and liabilities are classified as held for sale regardless of whether the entity will retain a non-controlling interest in its former subsidiary after the sale.

Both IFRS and Canadian GAAP also permit assets that are to be exchanged to be classified as held for sale when the exchange has commercial substance.

As well, under both IFRS and Canadian GAAP, an entity may not classify as held for sale a non-current asset or disposal group (that is, a group of assets to be disposed of, by sale or otherwise, together as a group in a single transaction, and liabilities directly associated with those assets that will be transferred in the transaction) that is to be abandoned because their carrying amount will be recovered principally through continuing use.

Measurement of Assets Held for Sale

Both CICA 3475 and IFRS 5 require that assets held for sale be (1) measured at the lower of fair value less costs to sell and carrying amount and (2) be no longer depreciated.

Presentation of Assets Held for Sale

Both non-current asset classified as held for sale and the assets of a disposal group classified as held for sale meeting the criteria in IFRS 5 are presented in current assets separately from other assets in the balance sheet.

The liabilities of a disposal group classified as held for sale must also be presented separately from other liabilities in the balance sheet. Assets and liabilities classified as held for sale cannot be offset and presented as a single amount. The major classes of assets and liabilities classified as held for sale must be separately disclosed, either on the face of the balance sheet or in the notes, except where the disposal group is a newly acquired subsidiary that meets the criteria of being classified as held for sale on acquisition.

Under CICA 3475, the classification in current assets is allowed only when an enterprise has sold the assets prior to the date of completion of the financial statements and the proceeds of the sale will be realized within a year of the date of the balance sheet.

Disclosures

Disclosure consists of the following:

- gain or loss recognized on measurement to fair value, less costs to sell;
- description of asset, and facts and circumstances leading to disposal; and
- segment in which the asset is reported in accordance with IFRS 8, *Operating Segments*.

Assets that Cease to be Classified as Held for Sale

Where a non-current asset or disposal group is remeasured because it has ceased to be classified as held for sale after no longer meeting the relevant criteria, the adjustment to the carrying amount of the asset should:

- be treated as a revaluation increase or decrease if the asset is PPE that had been revalued in accordance with IAS 16 before classification as held for sale; and

- be included in profit or loss from continuing operations in the period in which the criteria are no longer met if it had not been revalued in accordance with IAS 16 before classification as held for sale.

When an entity decides to change the plan to sell a non-current asset (or disposal group), it has to disclose a description of the facts and circumstances leading to that decision and the effect of the decision on the results of operations for the period and any prior periods presented.

Illustrative Disclosures:

Extract 12(7) – Assets held for sale

FLSmidth & Co. A/S (AR 2007), pages 66 and 67 Consolidated balance sheet Assets DKKm		2007	2006
Notes			
	Completed development projects	26	29
	Patents and rights acquired	1,091	6
	Goodwill	3,191	131
	Customer relations	914	–
	Other intangible assets	203	143
16	**Intangible assets**	**5,425**	**309**
	Land and buildings	760	605
	Plant and machinery	477	395
	Operating equipment, fixtures and fittings	200	114
	Tangible assets in course of construction	109	105
17	**Tangible assets**	**1,546**	**1,219**
18	Investments in associated undertakings	4	7
18	Other securities and investments	58	47
18	Other financial assets	8	9
27	Pension assets	6	2
19	Deferred tax assets	752	762
	Financial assets	**828**	**827**
	Total long-term assets	**7,799**	**2,355**
20	**Stocks**	**1,463**	**832**
22	Trade debtors	4,939	3,087
21	Work-in-progress for third parties	3,072	2,338
	Amounts owed by associated undertakings	0	3
22	Other debtors	1,070	338
	Prepayments	120	34
	Debtors	**9,201**	**5,800**
	Securities	**244**	**366**
22	**Cash funds**	**957**	**2,766**
23	**Assets held for sale**	**8**	**132**
	Total current assets	**11,873**	**9,896**
	TOTAL ASSETS	**19,672**	**12,251**

FLSmidth & Co. A/S (AR 2007) (continued) Consolidated balance sheet Equity and liabilities DKKm	2007	2006
Notes		
Share capital	1,064	1,064
Exchange rate adjustments regarding translation of investments	(24)	(85)
Exchange rate adjustments regarding hedging transactions	14	(2)
Retained earnings	2,778	1,839
Proposed dividend	372	372
FLSmidth & Co. A/S shareholders' share of shareholders' equity	**4,204**	**3,188**
Minority interests' share of shareholders' equity	**10**	**4**
Total equity	**4,214**	**3,192**
19 Deferred tax liabilities	688	28
27 Pension liabilities	126	97
24 Other provisions	1.077	808
25 Mortgage debt	386	149
25 Bank loans	1,829	0
25 Financial lease commitment	10	12
25 Prepayments from customers	681	616
Long-term liabilities	**4,797**	**1,710**
Mortgage debt	7	50
Bank loans	481	79
Financial lease commitment	3	3
Prepayments from customers	3,178	2,194
21 Work-in-progress for third parties	2,206	1,586
Trade creditors	2,464	1,859
Corporation tax payable	299	129
26 Other liabilities	1,288	676
24 Other provisions	699	656
Deferred income	36	112
	10,661	7,344
23 Liabilities regarding assets held for sale	0	5
Current liabilities	**10,661**	**7,349**
Total liabilities	**15,458**	**9,059**
TOTAL EQUITY AND LIABILITIES	**19,672**	**12,251**

FLSmidth & Co. A/S (AR 2007), page 62

Accounting policies (in part)

Assets held for sale

Assets held for sale consist of assets and disposal groups that are held for sale. Disposal groups are a group of assets that are to be disposed of by sale or otherwise, together in a single transaction, and associated liabilities that are transferred through the transaction. Assets are classified as 'held for sale' if their carrying value will primarily be recovered by sale within 12 months in accordance with a formal plan rather than by continued use.

Assets or disposal groups held for sale are measured at the lower of the carrying value and the fair value less selling costs. Assets are not depreciated from the time when they are classified as 'held for sale'.

Impairment losses arising from the initial classification as 'held for sale' and gains or losses from subsequent measurement at the lower of carrying value and fair value less selling costs are recognised in the profit and loss account among the items to which they belong. Gains and losses are disclosed in the notes.

FLSmidth & Co. A/S (AR 2007) (continued)

Presentation of assets held for sale and discontinuing activities

Assets held for sale and Discontinuing activities consist of activities or companies for which it has been announced that the activities or companies have been discontinued or are discontinuing in the Group or closure has been initiated.

Earnings and value adjustments after tax of assets held for sale and discontinuing activities are presented on a separate line in the profit and loss account and with comparative figures. In the notes, turnover, costs and tax of the discontinuing activities are disclosed.

Assets held for sale are presented on a separate line in the balance sheet as short term assets. Liabilities directly associated to the assets concerned are presented as short term liabilities in the balance sheet.

Cash flow from operating, investing and financing activities for assets held for sale and discontinuing activities appear from note 1.

FLSmidth & Co. A/S (AR 2007), page 83

23. Assets held for sale and liabilities regarding same

DKKm	2007	2006
Tangible assets	8	108
Stocks	0	5
Debtors and work-in-progress	0	19
Assets held for sale	**8**	**132**
Provisions regarding assets held for sale	0	(5)
Net assets held for sale	**8**	**127**

2007

Properties

Properties held for sale represent a book value of DKK 8m. The properties are expected to be sold during 2008 at least at book value.

2006

Maag Gear – turbo and marine gear activities

Net assets held for sale regarding the turbo and marine gear activities in Maag Gear represent a book value of DKK 87m and mainly consist of tangible assets in the form of production plant plus stocks and work-in-progress and provisions for losses on the latter. In continuation of the sales preparations that took place in 2006, on 23 January 2007 an agreement was signed to transfer most of these activities to Renk – presumably with effect from 30 April 2007. The expected sales price does not require writing down of the book value of the net assets.

The sales transaction took place in 2007 as expected.

Properties

Properties held for sale represent a book value of DKK 40m. The properties are expected to be sold during 2007 at least at book value, so no write-down of the book values has been made.

The sales transaction took place in 2007 as expected.

Air France-KLM S.A. (Reference Document 2006-07), page 100
Note 3 Accounting policies (in part)
3.22. Non-current assets held for sale and discontinued operations

Non-current assets or groups of assets intended for sale meet the criteria of such a classification if their carrying amount will be recovered principally through a sale rather than through their continuing use. This condition is considered to be met when the sale is highly probable and the asset (or the group of assets intended for sale) is available for immediate sale in its present condition. Management must be committed to a plan to sell, with the expectation that the sale will be realized within a period of twelve months from the date on which the asset or group of assets was classified as a non-current asset held for sale.

The Group determines on each closing date whether any assets or group of assets meet the above criteria and presents such assets, if any, as "non-current assets held for sale".

Any liabilities related to non-current assets to be sold are also presented on a separate line in liabilities on the balance sheet.

Non-current assets and groups of assets held for sale are valued at the lower of their book value or their fair value minus exit costs. As of the date of such a classification, the asset is no longer depreciated.

The results from discontinued operations are presented separately from the results from continuing operations in the income statement.

Commentary: Extract (12-7) shows the balance sheet presentation of assets held for sale and related provision, the accounting policies for those assets and the specific note providing details of those assets.

The final extract in the series above describes the accounting policy for assets held for sale. This note states the criteria of IFRS 5:

- "their carrying amount will be recovered principally through a sale rather than through their continuing use";
- "the sale is highly probable";
- "the asset is available for immediate sale in its present condition";
- "management must be committed to a plan to sale"; and
- "with the expectation that the sale will be realized within a period of twelve months from the date on which the asset or group of asset was classified as a non-current asset held for sale."

It also states that liabilities must be presented separately, that assets are valued at the lower of their book value or the fair value minus exit costs and that the company ceased to depreciate this asset.

Discontinued Operations

IFRS 5 also deals with discontinued operations, which it describes as components of an entity that either have been disposed of, or are classified as held for sale, and

- represent a separate major line of business or geographical area of operations;
- are part of a single coordinated plan to dispose of a separate major line of business or geographical area of operations; or
- are subsidiaries acquired exclusively with a view to resale.

IFRS 5 contains a more restrictive definition of discontinued operations than does CICA 3475, which also includes a reportable segment, an operating segment, a reporting unit, a subsidiary, an asset group or an operation without long-lived or other assets.

Under Canadian GAAP, an entity's components comprise operations and cash flows that can be clearly distinguished – operationally and for financial reporting purposes – from the rest of the entity.

Disclosures and Presentation

IFRS 5 requires that discontinued operations be presented separately in the income statement and the cash flow statement, while CICA 3475 requires separate presentation only in the income statement. Note that CICA 3475 requires presentation of pre-tax profits on the face of the income statement, which is not required by IFRS 5 (although it is not precluded).

Under IFRS 5, an entity (including one that is committed to a sale plan involving loss of control of a subsidiary when it is a disposal group that meets the definition of a discontinued operation) must disclose a single amount on the face of the income statement comprising the total of:

- the post-tax profit or loss of discontinued operations; and
- the post-tax gain or loss recognized on the measurement to fair value less costs to sell, or on the disposal of the assets or disposal group(s) constituting the discontinued operations.

Note that the entity has to allocate the single amount disclosed to the following categories:

- the revenue, expenses and pre-tax profit or loss of discontinued operations;
- the related income tax expense;
- the gain or loss recognized on the measurement to fair value less costs to sell, or on the disposal of the assets or disposal group(s) constituting the discontinued operation; and
- the related income tax expense.

This analysis may be presented in the notes or on the face of the income statement. If it is presented on the face of the income statement, it must be identified as part of discontinued operations, i.e., separately from continuing operations.

The net cash flows attributable to the operating, investing and financing activities of discontinued operations also have to be presented either in the notes or on the face of the financial statements.

The analysis of the single amount in the income statement and the presentation of the net cash flows are not required for disposal groups that are newly acquired subsidiaries meeting the criteria to be classified as held for sale on acquisition.

Both IFRS 5 and CICA 3475 require the results of the income statement for prior periods to be restated to segregate continuing and discontinuing assets and liabilities.

Illustrative disclosure:

Extract 12(8) – Discontinued operations

Akzo Nobel N.V. (AR 2007), pages 102, 104, 107, 117, 118
Consolidated statement of income
for the year ended December 31

Millions of euros	Note	2007	2006[1]
Continuing operations			
Revenue		10,217	10,023
Cost of sales		(6,252)	(6,224)
Gross profit		3,965	3,799
Selling expenses		(2,230)	(2,203)
Research and development expenses		(282)	(280)
General and administrative expenses		(654)	(636)
Other operating income/(expenses)	4	(52)	179
		(3,218)	(2,940)
Operating income		747	859
Financing income	5	157	123
Financing expenses	5	(277)	(229)
Operating income less financing income and expenses		627	753
Results from associates and joint ventures	6	(20)	87
Profit before tax		607	840
Income tax	7	(166)	(96)
Profit for the period from continuing operations		441	744
Discontinued operations			
Profit for the period from discontinued operations (Organon BioSciences)	8	8,920	438
PROFIT FOR THE PERIOD		9,361	1,182
Attributable to:			
– Equity holders of the company		9,330	1,153
– Minority interests		31	29
PROFIT FOR THE PERIOD		9,361	1,182
Earnings per share, in euros	10		
Continuing operations:			
– Basic		1.49	2.49
– Diluted		1.47	2.48
Discontinued operations:			
– Basic		32.33	1.53
– Diluted		32.08	.52
Total operations:			
– Basic		33.82	4.02
– Diluted		33.55	4.00

1   Reclassified to present Organon BioSciences as a discontinued operation.

Akzo Nobel N.V. (AR 2007) (continued)
Consolidated statement of cash flows
for the year ended December 31

Millions of euros	2007	2006[1]
Profit for the period	9,361	1,182
Income from discontinued operations	(8,920)	(438)
Adjustments to reconcile earnings to cash generated from operating activities		
Depreciation and amortization	355	371
Impairment losses	11	29
Financing income and expenses	120	106
Results from associates and joint ventures	(27)	(77)
Income tax	166	96
Operating profit before changes in working capital and provisions	1,066	1,269
Changes in working capital[2]	73	185
Changes in provisions	(256)	(202)
Other	13	18
	(170)	1
Cash generated from operating activities	896	1,270
Interest paid	(212)	(205)
Income tax paid	(111)	(285)
Pre-tax loss/(gain) on divestments	70	(206)
	(253)	(696)
Net cash from operating activities	643	574
Capital expenditures	(359)	(371)
Interest received	119	109
Repayments and dividends from associates and joint ventures	26	36
Acquisition of consolidated companies[3]	(159)	(318)
Currency swap for investing purposes	(349)	–
Proceeds from sale of interests[3]	171	360
Other changes in non-current assets	(292)	43
Net cash from investing activities	(843)	(141)
Changes in borrowings	422	(17)
Termination of currency swap	68	21
Issue of shares for stock option plan	73	40
Buyback of shares	(1,600)	–
Dividends	(398)	(369)
Net cash from financing activities	(1,435)	(325)
NET CASH USED FOR CONTINUING OPERATIONS	(1,635)	108
Net cash from operating activities	437	533
Net cash from investing activities	10,678	(167)
Net cash from financing activities	(32)	(10)
CASH FLOWS FROM DISCONTINUED OPERATIONS	11,083	356
NET CHANGE IN CASH AND CASH EQUIVALENTS	9,448	464
Cash and cash equivalents at January[1]	1,631	1,188
Effect of exchange rate changes on cash and cash equivalents	(12)	(21)
CASH AND CASH EQUIVALENTS	11,067	1,631

1 Reclassified to present Organon BioSciences as a discontinued operation and to include debt to credit institutions in the statement of cash flows.
2 Comprises an increase of EUR 62 million in trade and other receivables (2006: EUR 17 million), an increase of EUR 16 million in inventories (2006: EUR 31 million), and an increase of EUR 151 million in trade and other payables (2006: EUR 233 million).
3 Net of cash acquired or disposed of.

Akzo Nobel N.V. (AR 2007) (continued)

Note 1 Summary of significant accounting policies (in part)

Discontinued operations

A discontinued operation is a component of the company's business that represents a separate major line of business or geographical area of operations that has been disposed of or is held for sale, or is a subsidiary acquired exclusively with a view to resale. Classification as a discontinued operation occurs upon disposal or when the operation meets the criteria to be classified as held for sale, if earlier. When an operation is classified as a discontinued operation, the comparative statement of income and the statement of cash flows are reclassified as if the operation had been discontinued from the start of the comparative period. In 2007, Organon BioSciences was classified as discontinued operation and the statements of income and cash flows have been reclassified accordingly.

Note 8 Statement of income of discontinued operations

On November 19, 2007, Akzo Nobel sold Organon BioSciences to Schering-Plough for an amount of EUR 11 billion. During 2007, Organon BioSciences was presented as a discontinued operation. The statements of income and cash flows for 2006 were reclassified to present comparative figures for Akzo Nobel's continuing operations. For the purpose of comparison, an additional pro forma column for the balance sheet at December 31, 2006, is provided as if Organon BioSciences qualified as a discontinued operation at that date.

Akzo Nobel and Organon BioSciences will have continuing relationships for a limited period, mainly to complete the divestment and facilitate the transition. Further, Akzo Nobel has provided several guarantees and indemnities, that are disclosed in note 27.

RESULTS FROM DISCONTINUED OPERATIONS

MILLIONS OF EUROS	2007	2006
Revenue	3,285	3,714
Expenses	(2,656)	(3,114)
Results from operating activities	**629**	**600**
Income tax	(169)	(162)
Results from operating activities, net of income tax	**460**	**438**
Gain on the sale of Organon BioSciences	8,486	-
Income tax on the sale	(26)	-
PROFIT FOR THE PERIOD	**8,920**	**438**

BALANCE AT DIVESTMENT DATE

MILLIONS OF EUROS	2007
Property, plant, and equipment	1,153
Intangible assets	158
Financial non-current assets	349
Inventories	876
Receivables	869
Non-current liabilities and provisions	(342)
Current liabilities	(983)
Net assets and liabilities	**2,080**
Consideration received, satisfied in cash	10,971
Cash disposed of	(274)
NET CASH INFLOW	**10,697**

DEAL RESULT

MILLIONS OF EUROS	2007
Net cash inflow	10,697
Net assets and liabilities	(2,080)
Liabilities assumed and cost allocated to the deal	(107)
Realization cumulative translation reserves	(24)
DEAL RESULT BEFORE TAX	**8,486**

Commentary: This extract presents information on the impact of discontinued operations on net income and cash flows. We can note the breakdown of the discontinued operations amount in revenue, expenses and pre-tax profit, as well as the related income tax expense.

Air France-KLM S.A. (Reference Document 2006-07), page 122

Note 13 Discontinued operations

During the years ended March 31, 2007 and March 31, 2006, the Group initiated no disposal process which could be considered as a "discontinued operation".

As of December 30, 2004 the Group sold its shares in Amadeus France SNC to Amadeus GTD. This company's activity was to distribute the Amadeus booking system in France. The conditions allowing its classification as a "discontinued activity" occurred as of April 1, 2004. Amadeus France SNC was therefore reclassified from April 1, 2004 until December 30, 2004. Previously, Amadeus France SNC's activity was disclosed in the "Passenger" segment.

13.1. Net income from discontinued operations

Information regarding discontinued operations:

Year ended March 31 (In euro millions)	2007	2006	2005
Sales	–	–	71
Expenses	–	–	(65)
Gain on disposal	–	–	66
Income before tax	–	–	72
Income taxes	–	–	(13)
Net income from discontinued operations	–	–	**59**

For the year ended March 31 2005, the gain on the disposal of subsidiaries and affiliates (€66 million) is mainly due to the sale of Amadeus France SNC to Amadeus GTD at December 30, 2004. This company was previously fully consolidated in the Air France-KLM consolidated financial statements. Between April 1, 2004 and December 30, 2004, the disposal date, operations of Amadeus France SNC have been classified as discontinued operations.

13.2. Impact on the cash flow statement of discontinued operations

Amadeus France's contribution to the cash flows statement of the Group is as follows:

Year ended March 31 (In euro millions)	2007	2006	2005
Cash flows from operating activities	–	–	6
Cash flows from investing activities	–	–	66
Cash flows from financing activities	–	–	(4)

Commentary: This extract presents information on the impact of discontinued operations on net income and cash flows. It also describes the breakdown of the discontinued operations amount in revenue, expenses and pre-tax profit, as well as the related income tax expense. Also, note 13.2 describes the impact on the cash-flow statements of discontinued operations, as required by IFRS 5.

FUTURE DEVELOPMENTS

The IASB issued an Exposure Draft on amendments to IFRS 5 in September 2008, which was open for public comment until January 23, 2009.

The Exposure Draft proposes that:

- the definition of a discontinued operation should be changed to a component of an entity that:
  - o is an operating segment (as that term is defined in IFRS 8) and either has been disposed of or is classified as held for sale, or
  - o is a business (as that term is defined in IFRS 3, *Business Combinations*) that meets the criteria to be classified as held for sale on acquisition;
- an entity should determine whether the component of an entity meets the definition of an operating segment regardless of whether it is required to apply IFRS 8;

- the amounts presented for discontinued operations should be based on the amounts presented in the income statement (other comprehensive income statement), even if segment information disclosed to comply with IFRS 8 includes different amounts that are reported to the chief operating decision maker;

- disclosures should be provided for all components of an entity that have been disposed of or are classified as held for sale, except for businesses that meet the criteria to be classified as held for sale on acquisition.

COMPREHENSIVE EXAMPLES

The comprehensive example below shows the sections of an annual report that deal with PPE.

Air France-KLM S.A. – All extracts were obtained from the Reference Document of 2006-07.

Extract 12(A1) – Air France-KLM S.A., page 86

This extract shows the presentation of PPE on the consolidated balance sheets. Note the separate presentation of two classes of PPE: Flight equipment and Other property, plant and equipment.

Consolidated balance sheets (in part)				
Assets *(In euro millions)*	**Notes**	**March 31, 2007**	**March 31, 2006**	**March 31, 2005**
Goodwill	15	204	208	205
Intangible assets	16	424	428	437
Flight equipment	18	11,551	11,017	10,394
Other property, plant and equipment	18	2,007	1,955	1,895
Investments in equity associates	20	228	204	577
Pension assets	21	2,097	1,903	1,767
Other financial assets (which includes €835 million of deposits related to financial leases as of March 31, 2007, €895 million as of March 31, 2006 and €875 million as of March 31, 2005)	22	1,095	1,182	1,113
Deferred tax assets	12.5	26	7	140
Other non-current assets	25	604	1,082	336
Total non-current assets		**18,236**	**17,986**	**16,864**

Extract 12(A2) – Air France-KLM S.A., page 97

This extract shows the accounting policy note describing the specific IFRS transition rule used for valuing certain elements of PPE at the opening balance sheet.

Note 3 Accounting policies (in part)
3.13. Property, plant and equipment (in part)
3.13.1. Specific rule applicable to the IFRS transition opening balance sheet
In accordance with IFRS 1, the Group has elected to value certain of its aircraft at the date of transition to IFRS (April 1, 2004) at their fair value and to use this fair value as deemed cost.
This treatment thus allows the Group to have a portion of its fleet recorded at fair value (fair value was used when accounting for KLM's business combination at May 1, 2004).
The fair value exercise was based on independent valuation by third parties.

Extract 12(A3) – Air France-KLM S.A., page 97

This extract presents the accounting policy note on the cost of PPE at initial recognition and afterwards, with specific description of the treatment of maintenance costs and interests on assets under construction.

> **Note 3 Accounting policies (in part)**
> **3.13. Property, plant and equipment (in part)**
> *3.13.2. Principles applicable since April 1, 2004*
> Property, plant and equipment are recorded at the historical acquisition or manufacturing cost, less accumulated depreciation and any accumulated impairment losses.
>
> The financial interest attributed to progress payments made on account of aircraft and other significant assets under construction is capitalized and added to the cost of the asset concerned. Insofar as investment installments are not financed by specific loans, the Group uses the average interest rate on the current unallocated loans of the period.
>
> Maintenance costs are recorded as expenses during the period when incurred, with the exception of programs that extend the useful life of the asset or increase its value, which are then capitalized (e.g. maintenance on airframes and engines, excluding parts with limited useful lives).

Extract 12(A4) – Air France-KLM S.A., page 98

These extracts (notes 3.13.3 and 3.13.4) describe the accounting policy related to flight equipment, notably the component accounting used for aircrafts, depreciation methods and useful lives of PPE.

> **Note 3 Accounting policies (in part)**
> **3.13. Property, plant and equipment (in part)**
> *3.13.3. Flight equipment*
> The purchase price of aircraft equipment is denominated in foreign currencies. It is translated at the exchange rate at the date of the transaction or, if applicable, at the hedging price assigned to it. Manufacturers' discounts, if any, are deducted from the value of the related asset.
>
> Aircraft are depreciated using the straight-line method over their average estimated useful life of 20 years, assuming no residual value. IFRS requires an annual review of the residual value and the amortization schedule. During the operating cycle, in developing fleet replacement plans, the Group reviews whether the amortizable base or the useful life should be adjusted and, if necessary, determines whether a residual value should be recognized.
>
> Any major airframes and engines (excluding parts with limited useful lives) are treated as a separate asset component with the cost capitalized and depreciated over the period between the date of acquisition and the next major overhaul.
>
> Aircraft components are recorded in the consolidated balance sheet as fixed assets. The useful lives vary from 3 to 20 years depending on the technical properties of each item.
>
> *3.13.4. Other property, plant and equipment*
> Other property, plant and equipment are depreciated using the straight line method over their useful life. Such useful lives are as follows:
>
> | | |
> |---|---|
> | Buildings | 20 to 40 years |
> | Fixtures and fittings | 8 to 15 years |
> | Flight simulators | 10 to 20 years |
> | Equipment and tooling | 5 to 15 years |

Extract 12(A5) – Air France-KLM S.A., page 98

This extract (Note 3.14) describes the accounting method used for impairment of assets, including PPE.

Note 3 Accounting policies (in part)

3.14. Impairment

In accordance with IAS 36, "Impairment of Assets", the Group reviews at each balance sheet date whether there is any indication of impairment of tangible and intangible assets. If such an indication exists, the recoverable value of the assets is estimated in order to determine the amount, if any, of the impairment. The recoverable value is the higher of the following values: the fair value reduced by selling costs and its value in use. The value in use is determined using discounted cash flow assumptions established by management.

When it is not possible to estimate the recoverable value for an individual asset, this asset is grouped together with other assets which form a cash generating unit (CGU).

Therefore, the Group has determined that the lowest level at which assets shall be tested are CGU, which correspond to group's operating segments (see segment information).

When the recoverable value of a CGU is lower than its carrying value, an impairment charge is recognized. When applicable, this impairment loss is allocated first to the goodwill, the remainder is allocated to the other assets of the CGU pro rata on the basis of the carrying amount of each asset in the unit.

The recoverable value of the CGUs is their value in use determined, notably, by the use of a discount rate corresponding to the Group's weighted average cost of capital and a growth rate reflecting the market assumptions specific to the activities.

Extract 12(A6) – Air France-KLM S.A., page 114

This extract presents the amortization and depreciation expense for PPE. Note that provisions for PPE are not generally recognized under IFRS unless they relate to asset retirement obligations or specific obligations.

Note 8 Amortization, depreciation and provisions

Year ended March 31

(In euro millions)	2007	2006	2005
Amortization and depreciation			
Intangible assets	42	39	30
Flight equipment	1,488	1,371	1,280
Other property, plant and equipment	252	246	251
Total	*1,782*	*1,656*	*1,561*
Provisions			
Fixed assets	–	–	34
Inventories	–	1	–
Trade receivables	5	12	7
Risks and contingencies	3	59	(13)
Total	*8*	*72*	*28*
Total	1,790	1,728	1,589

A description of changes in amortization and impairment is included in notes 16 and 18.
The detail of changes in inventory impairment is included in notes 23, 24 and 25.
The movements in provisions for risks and charges are detailed in note 29.

Extract 12(A7) – Air France-KLM S.A., pages 128 – 130

This extract shows the reconciliation of opening and closing amounts of PPE.

Note 18 Tangible assets

(In euro millions)	Flight equipment					Other tangible assets					Total
	Owned aircraft	Leased aircraft	Assets in progress	Other	Total	Land and buildings	Equipment and machinery	Assets in progress	Other	Total	
Gross value											
Amount as of April 1, 2004	*4,343*	*1,452*	*624*	*1,155*	*7,574*	*1,234*	*594*	*73*	*683*	*2,584*	*10,158*
Additions	439	174	261	914	1,788	100	80	79	91	350	2,138
Disposals	(512)	(108)	–	(326)	(946)	(52)	(32)	–	(32)	(116)	(1,062)
KLM acquisition	1,026	1,997	235	291	3,549	553	144	80	28	805	4,354
Transfer	328	203	(69)	(299)	163	77	7	(69)	(4)	11	174
Currency translation adjustment	(28)	211	(20)	(1)	162	–	–	–	(1)	(1)	161
Amounts as of March 31, 2005	*5,596*	*3,929*	*1,031*	*1,734*	*12,290*	*1,912*	*793*	*163*	*765*	*3,633*	*15,923*
Additions	613	62	1,030	511	2,216	49	62	169	52	332	2,548
Disposals	(227)	(101)	(52)	(302)	(682)	(19)	(37)	(7)	(21)	(84)	(766)
Changes in consolidation scope	–	–	(32)	–	(32)	–	7	–	2	9	(23)
Transfer	231	310	(853)	324	12	139	26	(199)	(23)	(57)	(45)
Currency translation adjustment	11	–	14	–	25	–	(2)	–	–	(2)	23
Amounts as of March 31, 2006	*6,224*	*4,200*	*1,138*	*2,267*	*13,829*	*2,081*	*849*	*126*	*775*	*3,831*	*17,660*
Additions	662	397	547	431	2,037	116	100	56	75	347	2,384
Disposals	(259)	(31)	(30)	(335)	(655)	(59)	(22)	–	(16)	(97)	(752)
Changes in consolidation scope	–	(5)	–	(11)	(16)	–	(2)	–	–	(2)	(18)
Fair value hedge	–	–	111	–	111	–	–	–	–	–	111
Transfer	1,352	(131)	(597)	(636)	(12)	34	9	(37)	(3)	3	(9)
Currency translation adjustment	(7)	5	1	–	(1)	–	(1)	–	–	(1)	(2)
Amounts as of March 31, 2007	*7,972*	*4,435*	*1,170*	*1,716*	*15,293*	*2,172*	*933*	*145*	*831*	*4,081*	*19,374*

Note 18 Tangible assets (continued)

(In euro millions)	Flight equipment					Other tangible assets					Total
	Owned aircraft	Leased aircraft	Assets in progress	Other	Total	Land and buildings	Equipment and machinery	Assets in progress	Other	Total	Total
Depreciation and impairment											
Amounts as of April 1, 2004	(528)	(103)	–	(436)	(1,067)	(640)	(436)	–	(485)	(1,561)	(2,628)
Charge to depreciation	(508)	(444)	–	(362)	(1,314)	(106)	(69)	–	(76)	(251)	(1,565)
Realeses on disposal	282	25	–	300	607	25	21	–	24	70	677
Changes in consolidation scope	–	–	–	–	–	2	–	–	22	24	24
Transfer	(90)	83	–	(143)	(150)	–	(1)	–	(23)	(24)	(174)
Currency translation adjustment	26	4	–	(2)	28	(2)	5	–	1	4	32
Amounts as of March 31, 2005	(818)	(435)	–	(643)	(1,896)	(721)	(480)	–	(537)	(1,738)	(3,634)
Charge to depreciation	(591)	(294)	–	(485)	(1,370)	(110)	(73)	–	(64)	(247)	(1,617)
Realeses on disposal	171	39	–	245	455	14	33	–	17	64	519
Transfer	(32)	32	–	–	–	1	7	–	37	45	45
Currency translation adjustment	3	(1)	–	(3)	(1)	–	–	–	–	–	(1)
Amounts as of March 31, 2006	(1,267)	(659)	–	(886)	(2,812)	(816)	(513)	–	(547)	(1,876)	(4,688)
Charge to depreciation	(716)	(311)	–	(461)	(1,488)	(115)	(72)	–	(65)	(252)	(1,740)
Loss for future disposal	(20)	–	–	–	(20)	–	–	–	–	–	(20)
Realeses on disposal	209	25	–	329	563	24	19	–	14	57	620
Changes in consolidation scope	–	5	–	4	9	–	1	–	–	1	10
Transfer	(300)	36	–	271	7	(2)	(7)	–	5	(4)	3
Currency translation adjustment	3	(4)	–	–	(1)	–	–	–	–	–	(1)
Amounts as of March 31, 2007	(2,091)	(908)	–	(743)	(3,742)	(909)	(572)	–	(593)	(2,074)	(5,816)
Net value											
As of April 1, 2004	3,815	1,349	624	719	**6,507**	594	158	73	198	1,023	7,530
As of March 31, 2005	4,778	3,494	1,031	1,091	**10,394**	1,191	313	163	228	1,895	12,289
As of March 31, 2006	4,957	3,541	1,138	1,381	**11,017**	1,265	336	126	228	1,955	12,972
As of March 31, 2007	5,881	3,527	1,170	973	**11,551**	1,263	361	145	238	2,007	13,558

Note 35 details the amount of pledged tangible assets.

Commitments to property purchases are detailed in notes 34 and 35.

The net value of tangible assets financed under capital lease amounts to €3,811 million as of March 31, 2007 against €3,912 million as of March 31, 2006 and €3,710 million as of March 31, 2005.

Extract 12(A8) – Air France-KLM S.A., page 130

This extract discloses the detail of investments in PPE included in the cash-flow statements.

Note 19 Capital expenditure

The detail of investments in property, plant and equipment and intangible assets presented in the consolidated cash flow statements is as follows:

Year ended March 31 (In euro millions)	2007	2006	2005
Acquisition of tangible assets	2,384	2,548	2,138
Acquisition of intangible assets	38	30	23
Accounts payable on acquisitions and capitalized interests	(44)	(34)	(30)
Total	**2,378**	**2,544**	**2,131**

Extract 12(A9) – Air France-KLM S.A., page 169

This extract discloses the commitments for flight equipment orders.

Note 34 Flight equipment orders

Due dates for commitments in respect of flight equipment orders are as follows:

Year ended March 31 (In euro millions)	2007	2006	2005
N+1	870	989	1,157
N+2	571	951	608
N+3	688	731	422
N+4	416	545	537
N+5	287	137	121
> 5 years	–	135	117
Total	**2,832**	**3,488**	**2,962**

These commitments relate to amounts in US dollars, converted into euros at the closing date exchange rate.

The number of aircraft on firm order as of March 31, 2007 fell by one unit compared with March 31, 2006 to 47 units. The number of options decreased by one unit over the same period to reach 34 aircraft. These movements can be explained by:

- the delivery of seventeen aircraft over the period;
- new orders: eleven firm orders and twelve options;
- the conversion of eleven options into firm orders, and the cancellation of two options;
- the change in the financing of the Embraer order involving a six unit reduction in the backlog.

Furthermore, in early October, Airbus signalled a significant change in the scheduled A380-800 deliveries to the Group, the first deliveries being postponed from summer 2008 to summer 2009.

Long-haul fleet

Passenger

The Group took delivery of three Airbus A330s and seven Boeing B777. As far as the Boeing B777s are concerned, it also confirmed two options and took out a further two options.

As of March 31, 2007, the Group's backlog for the long-haul fleet comprised firm orders for ten Airbus A380s and eleven Boeing B777s, as well as options on four Airbus A380s and eight Boeing B777s.

Cargo

The Group has an outstanding order with Boeing for eight B777F (five firm orders and three options), the new cargo unit based on the B777.200LR and the B777-300ER. The first deliveries will begin during the winter of 2008-09.

Medium-haul fleet

The Group took delivery of six Airbus A318s, and one Boeing B737. As far as the Boeing B737 is concerned, it placed a new firm order for nine aircraft and confirmed two options. Additionally, two options were cancelled: one for an Airbus A318 and one for an Airbus A320.

As of March 31, 2007, the Group's backlog comprised ten Boeing B737 under firm order as well as eight Boeing B737 and three Airbus A318 under option.

Regional fleet

The Group placed an order with Canadair for three CRJ700 and 16 CRJ1000 (eight firm orders and eight options). The order for six Embraer ERJ 190 does not appear because of the change in the financing terms for these aircraft.

PLANNING FOR IMPLEMENTATION
Selecting Accounting Policies

Canadian companies adopting IFRS will have to choose between keeping the cost method or migrating to the revaluation model for some or all PPE classes. This decision should be made carefully as it can have significant implications for the financial statements and accounting work required.

Although the revaluation model may result in presenting a higher amount in the balance sheet, this higher amount will generate a higher depreciation charge. In addition, if the fair value of the PPE fluctuates, so will the amounts presented in the balance sheet, but without necessarily affecting net income since the adjustments might be carried in other comprehensive income. More specifically, if an asset's carrying amount increases as a result of a revaluation, the increase is credited to other comprehensive income except when it reverses a revaluation decrease of the same asset previously recognized in profit or loss (as per IAS 16(39)), in which case it is recognized in profit or loss. IAS 16(40) mentions that, if an asset's carrying amount decreases as a result of a revaluation, the decrease must be recognized in profit or loss, except when there is a balance for that asset in the revaluation surplus. In that case, the decrease is applied to that surplus first.

Entities choosing the revaluation model will also have to revalue those assets on a regular basis. As well, IFRS require the amounts that would otherwise be calculated under the cost model to also be presented in the notes. That means that both schedules would have to be produced going forward. Considering the additional work, the revaluation model seems more pertinent for entities holding significant buildings and land which do not qualify as investment property.

IAS 16 allows an entity to choose between cost and revaluation models for subsequent measurement. This choice will be made independently of the choices made under IFRS 1, i.e., an entity can choose to fair value assets at the date of the transition to IFRS and use the cost model thereafter. The entity may make this choice independently for different classes of PPE but must apply it to all assets in a class.

The choice of the accounting policy – cost or fair value – needs to be made carefully because, once adopted, the revaluation model cannot easily be abandoned. To change an accounting policy, IAS 8 requires a demonstration that the new accounting policy is more reliable and relevant, and that may be difficult to do.

Obviously, choosing the cost model will minimize the IFRS conversion work. Adopting the revaluation model (fair value) will require more effort, not only in the implementation phase, but also in the future. It will be important to consider, however, the extent of impairment under IFRS that would not have been recognized under Canadian GAAP. Further, any impairments previously recognized will have to be re-examined for potential recoveries in fair value less costs to sell or value in use.

Initial Adoption of IAS 16

IFRS 1, *First-time Adoption of International Financial Reporting Standards* requires full retrospective application. Considering that it would be extremely difficult to achieve this for both the cost and the fair value models, IASB permits the use of "deemed cost" in place of actual cost in the opening IFRS balance sheet. Under IFRS 1, deemed cost can be one of the following:

* fair value at date of transition;

- revaluation under previous GAAP at or before transition if broadly comparable to:
  - o fair value, or
  - o cost (or depreciated cost) adjusted using a price index;
- deemed cost under previous GAAP established as fair value at an event date, such as a privatization or IPO;
- carrying amount immediately after acquisition in a business combination.

An entity can use any of these methods to determine the deemed cost of an individual asset regardless of the class to which it belongs or the measurement basis to be used after transition.

If an entity uses fair value in its opening IFRS statement of financial position as deemed cost for a PPE item, the entity's first IFRS financial statements must disclose, for each line item in the opening IFRS statement of financial position:

- the aggregate of those fair values; and
- the aggregate adjustment to the carrying amounts reported under previous GAAP.

Since IFRS require the component approach in both models, preparers will have to identify significant parts of assets at transition and make sure that they have been depreciated on an appropriate basis. This break-down of PPE will have an impact on the rate of future depreciation charges which, in turn, will have an impact on net income.

The exemption in IFRS 1 concerning the application of IFRIC 1, *Changes in Existing Decommissioning, Restoration and Similar Liabilities* permits entities to estimate liabilities associated with decommissioning costs at the transition date in accordance with IAS 37. The special transition rules concerning the decommissioning liabilities included in the cost of PPE are discussed in "Initial Adoption of IFRS" in Chapter 15, "Provisions."

Identifying Missing Data

Applying IAS 16 will require that Canadian financial statement preparers review the items included in their PPE to determine whether they need to use the component approach. They will need to analyze their significant assets to determine if they include significant components that should be depreciated separately because they have different useful lives. If it does not already exist, this data might need to be identified and reflected in the schedules and the systems. Management systems should also provide proper information for the derecognition and recognition of the replacement parts.

If entities opt for the revaluation method, they will have to determine the fair value amounts of their PPE assets not only at the transition date but also on a timely basis going forward. Fair value might be difficult to measure for some PPE items. If fair values are available, the amounts presented in the financial statements need to approximate the current fair values, requiring periodic revaluation. Since the information obtained under the cost model needs to be presented anyway, management systems will need to calculate and maintain both schedules.

Chapter 13
Leases

Standards Discussed in this Chapter

International

IAS 17 – Leases
IFRIC 4 – Determining whether an Arrangement Contains a Lease
SIC-15 – Operating Leases – Incentives
SIC-27 – Evaluating the Substance of Transactions in the Legal Form of a Lease

Canadian

CICA 3065 – Leases
EIC-19 - Minimum lease payments and contingent rentals
EIC-21 – Accounting for lease inducements by the lessee
EIC-25 – Accounting for sales with leasebacks
EIC-150 – Determining whether an arrangement contains a lease

INTRODUCTION

IAS 17 and CICA 3065, both devoted to the subject of leases, contain the same basic principles: the classification of leases is based on the extent to which the risks and rewards incidental to the ownership of a leased asset lie with the lessor or the lessee. More specifically, under both standards:

- A lease is classified as a finance (capital) lease if it transfers substantially all of the risks and rewards incidental to ownership to the lessee. Under IFRS, the lessor does not sub-classify leases into sales-type leases and direct financing leases as it would under Canadian GAAP. IAS 17 does, however, deal with similar issues for finance leases offered by manufacturer and dealer lessors.

- A lease is classified as an operating lease if it does not transfer substantially all of the risks and rewards incidental to ownership.

Canadian GAAP provides more detailed guidance for determining the classification of a lease. Notably, quantitative thresholds are provided for determining if a lease transfers substantially all of the economic benefits and risks of ownership to the lessee. For its part, IAS 17 covers leased intangible assets, which CICA 3065 does not address.

This chapter discusses the following topics:

- for lessees:
  - o operating leases,
  - o finance leases;
- for lessors:
  - o operating leases,
  - o finance leases;
- leases involving land and buildings;

- sale and leaseback transactions;
- determining whether an arrangement contains a lease;
- transactions involving the legal form of a lease;
- embedded derivatives;
- general disclosures related to leases.

IMPACT ON FINANCIAL STATEMENTS

Both IFRS and Canadian GAAP use the same underlying approach for recognizing a capital lease, i.e., determining whether substantially all of the risks and rewards incidental to ownership of a leased asset have been transferred from the lessor to the lessee. Although Canadian GAAP specifies quantitative guidelines for making the determination, IFRS does not. Instead, IFRS takes a substance over form approach, stating that the classification of a lease depends on the substance of the transaction rather than on the form of the contract. This should not generate a significant difference in the application of the principles involved. An entity would, however, need to reconsider the classification of any leases designated as operating leases under GAAP because they did not meet the quantitative guidelines for capital leases, and determine whether the substance of those lease transactions basically transfers all of the risks and rewards incidental to the assets' ownership from the lessor to the lessee.

ANALYSIS OF RELEVANT ISSUES

Scope

IAS 17 must be applied in accounting for all leases except for the following:

- lease agreements for exploring or using minerals, oil, natural gas and similar non-regenerative resources; and
- licensing agreements for items such as motion picture films, video recordings, plays, manuscripts, patents and copyrights.

Furthermore, IAS 17 should not be applied as the basis of measurement for:

- property held by lessees that is accounted for as investment property;
- investment property provided by lessors under operating leases; in these cases, IAS 40, *Investment Property* applies (discussed in Chapter 8);
- biological assets held by lessees under finance leases; or
- biological assets provided by lessors under operating leases; in these cases, IAS 41, *Agriculture* applies.

Lease Definition

IAS 17 defines a lease as "an agreement whereby the lessor conveys to the lessee in return for a payment or series of payments the right to use an asset for an agreed period of time." The standard applies to agreements that transfer the right to use assets even though those agreements may well ask the lessor to provide substantial services related to the operation or maintenance of the assets involved. On the other hand, it does not apply to contracts for services that do not transfer the right to use assets from one contracting party to the other.

Classification of a Lease

Both IFRS and Canadian GAAP classify leases as either a finance lease[1] or an operating lease. Leases are classified at their inception depending on whether substantially all of the risks and rewards incidental to ownership of a leased asset have been transferred from the lessor to the lessee.

Risks include:

- the possibility of losses from idle capacity or technological obsolescence; and
- variations in return because of changing economic conditions.

Rewards are:

- the expectations of profitable operation over the asset's economic life; and
- gain from appreciation in value or realization of a residual value.

Although both standards describe several indicators to help classify leases, entities often use the quantitative thresholds set out in Canadian GAAP as bright lines to make the determination.

In contrast, IAS 17 takes a more principles-based substance over form approach, stating that the classification of a lease depends on the substance of the transaction rather than on the form of the contract. Although IAS 17 does not provide any quantitative guidelines, it lists a number of situations that individually or in combination would normally lead to classifying a lease as a finance lease:

- the lease transfers ownership of the asset to the lessee by the end of the lease term;
- the lease contains an option to purchase the asset at a price expected to be sufficiently lower than the asset's fair value at the option's exercise date so that it will be reasonably certain that, at the inception of the lease, the option will be exercized;
- the lease term is for the major part of the asset's economic life even if title is not transferred (note: "major part" is unquantified under IFRS while Canadian GAAP specifies that it is usually "75% or more");
- at the inception of the lease, the present value of the minimum lease payments amounts to at least substantially all of the fair value of the leased asset (note: "substantially all" is unquantified under IFRSs while Canadian GAAP specifies that it is usually "90% or more");
- the leased assets are of such a specialized nature that only the lessee can use them without major modifications;
- if the lessee is entitled to cancel the lease, it will recompense the lessor for any losses associated with a cancellation;
- gains or losses from the fluctuation in the fair value of the residual accrue to the lessee (e.g., in the form of a rent rebate equalling most of the sales proceeds at the end of the lease);
- the lessee has the option of continuing the lease for a secondary period at a rent that is substantially lower than market rent.

CICA 3065 covers some of the latter situations described above but notes that they are insufficient by themselves to conclude that substantially all the benefits and risks of ownership have been transferred to the lessee. Also, CICA 3065 specifies more criteria for the lessors: the credit risk associated with the lease needs to match that associated with collecting similar receivables, and it must be possible to reasonably estimate any unreimbursable costs the lessor is likely to incur under the lease.

---

1   CICA 3065 refers to a "finance lease" as a "capital lease" for lessees and as a "direct-financing" or "sales-type" lease for lessors.

All of these are indicators that the lessor will look to the lessee to obtain a return from the leasing transaction, so it can be presumed that the lessee will, in fact, pay for the asset.

Under IAS 17, these principles will have to be applied to all leases, including those that might not have been capitalized under Canadian GAAP because they did not meet the quantitative criteria. Using IFRS may, therefore, result in more leases being accounted for as capital leases. It will not be possible to avoid using the principle-based approach by having a lease term a little shorter than the 75% Canadian guideline or by lowering the minimum lease payments to just below the 90% Canadian guideline.

As indicated in IAS 17, the examples and indicators noted above are not always conclusive. If other lease features clearly indicate that the lease does not transfer substantially all of the risks and rewards incidental to ownership, it should be classified as an operating lease. For example, this may be the case if ownership of an asset is transferred at the end of the lease for a variable payment equal to its then fair value, or if there are contingent rents. In such circumstances, the lessee would not receive substantially all the risks and rewards.

Lease classification determined at the inception of the lease is not subsequently revisited. Changes in estimates (e.g., of the economic life or of the residual value of the leased property), or changes in circumstances (e.g., default by the lessee), do not require a new classification of a lease for accounting purposes. However, lease changes such as renewal extension may result in a new lease classification as under CICA 3065.

Lessee Accounting

Operating Leases

Both IAS 17 and CICA 3065 require the recognition of lease payments for an operating lease as an expense on a straight-line basis over the lease term unless another systematic basis is more representative of the time pattern of the user's benefit, even if the payments are not on that basis. For example, the lease expense might be reflected more accurately if it were calculated based on a unit of use or unit of production rather than the lease term.

The recognition of the lease expense on a straight-line basis does not require the anticipation of contingent rental increases, such as those resulting from periodic repricing to market rates or based on some other index. Nevertheless, some features of the lease, such as lease incentives or fixed increments intended to compensate for inflation, must be taken into consideration in the calculation of the expense. In addition, SIC-15 and EIC-21 require that incentives be recognized as a reduction of rental expense over the lease term by using generally a straight-line basis.

Under IFRS, a lessee may classify a property interest held under an operating lease as an investment property. In that case, the lessee would account for that lease as if it were a finance lease and measure the investment property using the fair value model (Chapter 8 discusses accounting for investment properties). Unlike IFRS, there is no concept of "investment property" under Canadian GAAP, and the usual lease classification requirements apply.

If a lease contract is onerous, the present obligation under the contract must be recognized and measured as a provision in accordance with IAS 37, *Provisions, Contingent Liabilities and Contingent Assets*. An onerous lease is defined as one in which the unavoidable costs of meeting the obligations under the contract exceed the economic benefits expected to be received. The unavoidable costs under a lease reflect the least net cost of exiting from the lease, which is the lower of the cost of fulfilling it and any compensation or penalties arising from failure to fulfil it. Chapter 15 on provisions discusses this in more detail.

Finance Leases

Both IFRS and Canadian GAAP require that lessees recognize finance leases, at the beginning of their term, as assets and liabilities at amounts equal to the lower of:

- the fair value of the leased property; and
- the present value of the minimum lease payments.

IAS 17 and CICA 3065 state that minimum lease payments exclude service charges, taxes and reimbursements of expenses paid by the lessor on behalf of the lessee.

Initial direct costs identified as directly attributable to activities the lessee performs for a finance lease are added to the amount recognized as an asset. Initial direct costs are often incurred, for example, when negotiating and securing leasing arrangements. CICA 3065 does not provide explicit guidance on the accounting for initial direct costs from the lessee's perspective.

The discount rate to be used in calculating the present value of the minimum lease payments under IFRS is:

- the interest rate implicit in the lease, if this is practicable to determine;
- if not, the lessee's incremental borrowing rate is to be used.

Under Canadian GAAP, the lower of those two rates is used if it is practicable to determine the interest rate implicit in the lease.

Both IAS 17 and CICA 3065 require that lease payments be apportioned between a reduction in the lease liability and interest expense. The finance charge is to be allocated to each period during the lease term in a way that produces a constant periodic rate of interest on the remaining balance of the liability.

Both standards call for contingent rents to be charged as expenses in the periods they are incurred. Contingent rent is the portion of the lease payments that is not fixed but is, instead, based on some future amount that changes other than with the passage of time (e.g., percentage of future sales, amount of future use, future price indices, future market rates of interest). In establishing minimum lease payments, IFRS might differ from Canadian GAAP. Under the latter, EIC-19 specifies that lease payments that depend on factors that are measurable at the inception of the lease, such as the consumer price index or the prime interest rate, are not, in substance, contingent rentals in their entirety and should be included in minimum lease payments based on the index or rate existing at the inception of the lease. No equivalent guidance exists under IFRS and consequently practice might differ.

If, for presentation on the balance sheet, a distinction is made between current and non-current liabilities, the same distinction has to be made for lease liabilities.

The leased assets must be amortized and are subject to the same depreciation policy used for all other assets an entity owns. The depreciation recognized is to be calculated in accordance with IAS 16, *Property, Plant and Equipment* and IAS 38, *Intangible Assets*. Both IFRS and Canadian GAAP state that, if there is no reasonable certainty that the lessee will own the asset by the end of the lease term, the asset must be fully depreciated over the shorter of the lease term and its useful life.

Illustrative disclosure:

Extract 13(1) – Lessees

BNP Paribas (Registration Document 2007), page 125

1. SUMMARY OF SIGNIFICANT ACCOUNTING POLICIES APPLIED BY THE BNP PARIBAS GROUP (in part)

1.f.2 LESSEE ACCOUNTING

Leases contracted by the Group as lessee are categorised as either finance leases or operating leases.

Finance leases

A finance lease is treated as an acquisition of an asset by the lessee, financed by a loan. The leased asset is recognised in the balance sheet of the lessee at the lower of its fair value or the present value of the minimum lease payments calculated at the interest rate implicit in the lease. A matching liability, equal to the fair value of the leased asset or the present value of the minimum lease payment, is also recognised in the balance sheet of the lessee. The asset is depreciated using the same method as that applied to owned assets, after deducting the residual value from the amount initially recognised, over the useful life of the asset. The lease obligation is accounted for at amortised cost.

Operating leases

The asset is not recognised in the balance sheet of the lessee. Lease payments made under operating leases are taken to the profit and loss account of the lessee on a straight-line basis over the lease term.

Commentary: This extract presents the accounting policy note describing the accounting treatment for finance and operating leases for the lessee.

Lessor Accounting

Operating Leases

Both IAS 17 and CICA 3065 require lessors to recognize rental revenue from an operating lease as income over the lease term. The leased asset remains on the balance sheet of the lessor.

Lease income from operating leases is to be recognized in income on a straight-line basis over the lease term, unless another systematic basis is more representative of the time pattern of the user's benefit.

Lessors must present assets subject to operating leases on their balance sheets according to the nature of those assets. The depreciation policy for depreciable leased assets has to be consistent with the lessor's normal depreciation policy for similar assets, and depreciation will be calculated in accordance with IAS 16, *Property, Plant and Equipment* and IAS 38, *Intangible Assets*.

The initial direct costs incurred by lessors in negotiating and arranging an operating lease must be added to the carrying amount of the leased asset and recognized as an expense over the lease term on the same basis as the lease income.

SIC-15 requires that lessors recognize the aggregate cost of incentives as a reduction of rental income, over the lease term, usually on a straight-line basis. EIC-21 does not cover recognition of the lessor's incentives.

Finance Leases

IAS 17 and CICA 3065 require lessors to recognize assets held under a finance lease in their balance sheets and present them as a receivable at an amount equal to the net investment in the lease. The lessor has to allocate receipts to both a reduction in the receivable and interest income. The recognition of finance income is to be based on a pattern reflecting a constant periodic rate of return on the lessor's net investment in the finance lease.

Under Canadian GAAP, finance leases are sub-categorized as either sales-type leases or direct financing leases. There is no such clear classification under IFRS. IAS 17 does, however, require manufacturer or dealer lessors to recognize selling profit or loss in the period of the "sale" in accordance with the policy followed for outright sales. The normal selling prices should be used, reflecting any applicable volume or trade discounts. The cost of sale is the cost, or the lessor's carrying amount if different, of the leased property less the present value of the unguaranteed residual value. If artificially low rates of interest were quoted, the selling profit has to be restricted to that which would apply if a market rate of interest had been charged.

So, in fact, IAS 17 conditions are similar to those set out in CICA 3065. Under IAS 17, sales revenue is the lower of the fair value of the asset and the present value of the minimum lease payments accruing to the lessor, computed at a market rate of interest. Under CICA 3065, sales revenue is the present value of the minimum lease payments, computed at the interest rate implicit in the lease. The cost of sale is the lessor's carrying amount of the asset prior to the lease transaction, reduced by the present value of the unguaranteed residual value to the lessor, computed at the interest rate implicit in the lease. Since the market interest rate and the interest rate implicit in the lease should be similar, they both should result in similar sale revenue.

Both IFRS and Canadian GAAP require costs incurred by manufacturer or dealer lessors in connection with negotiating and arranging a lease to be recognized as an expense when the selling profit is recognized.

Under IFRS, for finance leases other than those involving manufacturer or dealer lessors, initial direct costs must be included in the initial measurement of the finance lease receivable. Under CICA 3065, however, initial direct costs should be expensed as incurred, and a portion of unearned income equal to the initial direct costs should be recognized in income in the same period. The remaining income should be deferred and taken into income over the lease term to produce a constant rate of return on the investment in the lease.

Illustrative Disclosures:

Extract 13(2) – Lessors

Barclays Bank PLC (AR 2007), page 23
Significant Accounting Policies (in part)
20. Leases (in part)
Lessor

Assets leased to customers under agreements, which transfer substantially all the risks and rewards of ownership, with or without ultimate legal title, are classified as finance leases. When assets are held subject to a finance lease, the present value of the lease payments, discounted at the rate of interest implicit in the lease, is recognised as a receivable. The difference between the total payments receivable under the lease and the present value of the receivable is recognised as unearned finance income, which is allocated to accounting periods under the pre-tax net investment method to reflect a constant periodic rate of return.

Assets leased to customers under agreements which do not transfer substantially all the risks and rewards of ownership are classified as operating leases. The leased assets are included within property, plant and equipment on the Group's balance sheet and depreciation is provided on the depreciable amount of these assets on a systematic basis over their estimated useful lives. Lease income is recognised on a straight-line basis over the period of the lease unless another systematic basis is more appropriate.

Barclays Bank PLC (AR 2007), page 49
23 Property, plant and equipment

2007	The Group				The Bank			
	Property £m	Equipment £m	Operating leased assets £m	Total £m	Property £m	Equipment £m	Operating leased assets £m	Total £m
Cost								
At 1st January 2007	2,154	2,429	365	4,948	1,731	1,383	–	3,114
Acquisitions and disposals	5	13	–	18	3	1	–	4
Additions	506	638	105	1,249	321	281	–	602
Disposals	(241)	(112)	(57)	(410)	(194)	(37)	–	(231)
Fully depreciated assets written off	(1)	(8)	–	(9)	(1)	–	–	(1)
Exchange and other adjustments	28	35	–	63	9	8	–	17
At 31st December 2007	2,451	2,995	413	5,859	1,869	1,636	–	3,505
Accumulated depreciation and impairment								
At 1st January 2007	(993)	(1,454)	(9)	(2,456)	(890)	(866)	–	(1,756)
Acquisitions and disposals	(1)	(7)	–	(8)	–	–	–	–
Depreciation charge	(91)	(370)	(6)	(467)	(66)	(191)	–	(257)
Impairment	(2)	–	–	(2)	(2)	–	–	(2)
Disposals	58	37	–	95	48	18	–	66
Fully depreciated assets written off	1	8	–	9	1	1	–	2
Exchange and other adjustments	(16)	(18)	–	(34)	(6)	(3)	–	(9)
At 31st December 2007	(1,044)	(1,804)	(15)	(2,863)	(915)	(1,041)	–	(1,956)
Net book value	1,407	1,191	398	2,996	954	595	–	1,549

2006	The Group				The Bank			
	Property £m	Equipment £m	Operating leased assets £m	Total £m	Property £m	Equipment £m	Operating leased assets £m	Total £m
Cost								
At 1st January 2006	2,450	2,541	365	5,356	1,972	1,580	–	3,552
Acquisitions and disposals	–	–	–	–	–	–	–	–
Additions	180	475	–	655	130	270	–	400
Disposals	(422)	(382)	–	(804)	(368)	(362)	–	(730)
Fully depreciated assets written off	(1)	(89)	–	(90)	–	(89)	–	(89)
Exchange and other adjustments	(53)	(116)	–	(169)	(3)	(16)	–	(19)
At 31st December 2006	2,154	2,429	365	4,948	1,731	1,383	–	3,114
Accumulated depreciation and impairment								
At 1st January 2006	(1,022)	(1,575)	(5)	(2,602)	(914)	(1,121)	–	(2,035)
Acquisitions and disposals	–	–	–	–	–	–	–	–
Depreciation charge for year	(118)	(335)	(2)	(455)	(96)	(171)	–	(267)
Impairment	(14)	–	–	(14)	(14)	–	–	(14)
Disposals	148	341	–	489	137	333	–	470
Fully depreciated assets written off	1	89	–	90	–	89	–	89
Exchange and other adjustments	12	26	(2)	36	(3)	4	–	1
At 31st December 2006	(993)	(1,454)	(9)	(2,456)	(890)	(866)	–	(1,756)
Net book value	1,161	975	356	2,492	841	517	–	1,358

Operating leased assets represent assets such as plant and equipment leased to customers under operating leases.

Barclays Bank PLC (AR 2007) (continued)

Certain of the Group's equipment is held on finance leases. See Note 38.

In 2007 the value of an existing office building in the UK property portfolio was impaired by £2m reflecting local market conditions that had prevented its disposal in the year. In 2008 the freehold of the building will be disposed of by a short- or long-term leaseback. Consequently the value has been written down to fair value, less cost of sale.

page 77

38 Leasing

The Group and the Bank are both lessor and lessee under finance and operating leases, providing asset financing for their customers and leasing assets for their own use. In addition, assets leased by the Group and the Bank may be sublet to other parties. An analysis of the impact of these transactions on the Group and the Bank balance sheet and income statement is as follows:

(a) As Lessor

Finance lease receivables

The Group and the Bank specialise in asset-based lending and work with a broad range of international technology, industrial equipment and commercial companies to provide customised finance programmes to assist manufacturers, dealers and distributors of assets.

Finance lease receivables are included within loans and advances to customers.

The Group and the Bank's net investment in finance lease receivables was as follows:

	The Group							
	2007				2006			
	Gross investment in finance lease receivables £m	Future finance income £m	Present value of minimum lease payments receivable £m	Unguaranteed residual values £m	Gross investment in finance lease receivables £m	Future finance income £m	Present value of minimum lease payments receivable £m	Unguaranteed residual values £m
Not more than one year	3,657	(780)	2,877	213	3,650	(734)	2,916	166
Over one year but not more than five years	7,385	(1,613)	5,772	374	5,824	(1,490)	4,334	334
More than five years	3,476	(935)	2,541	14	3,790	(898)	2,892	15
Total	14,518	(3,328)	11,190	601	13,264	(3,122)	10,142	515

	The Bank							
	2007				2006			
	Gross investment in finance lease receivables £m	Future finance income £m	Present value of minimum lease payments receivable £m	Unguaranteed residual values £m	Gross investment in finance lease receivables £m	Future finance income £m	Present value of minimum lease payments receivable £m	Unguaranteed residual values £m
Not more than one year	7	(1)	6	–	7	(1)	6	–
Over one year but not more than five years	91	(2)	89	–	48	(2)	46	–
More than five years	67	(3)	64	–	29	(2)	27	–
Total	165	(6)	159	–	84	(5)	79	–

The allowance for uncollectible finance lease receivables included in the allowance for impairment for the Group amounted to £113m at 31st December 2007 (2006: £99m).

Barclays Bank PLC (AR 2007) (continued)

Operating lease receivables

The Group and the Bank acts as lessor, whereby items of plant and equipment are purchased and then leased to third parties under arrangements qualifying as operating leases. The items purchased to satisfy these leases are treated as plant and equipment in the Group and the Bank's financial statements and are generally disposed of at the end of the lease term (see Note 23).

The future minimum lease payments expected to be received under non-cancellable operating leases at 31st December 2007 were as follows:

	The Group		The Bank	
	2007	2006	2007	2006
	Plant and equipment £m	Plant and equipment £m	Plant and equipment £m	Plant and equipment £m
Not more than one year	29	18	–	–
Over one year but not more than two years	24	5	–	–
Over two years but not more than three years	22	3	–	–
Over three years but not more than four years	20	3	–	–
Over four years but not more than five years	11	3	–	–
Over five years	10	7	–	–
Total	116	39	–	–

Commentary: The first extract describes the significant accounting policies related to the lessor accounting for finance and operating leases. The second extract shows that the property, plant and equipment leased by the lessor under operating leases are presented separately from other property, plant and equipment. The last extract presents the finance lease receivables and the operating lease receivables.

Leases Involving Land and Buildings

Both IAS 17 and CICA 3065 treat a lease of land and buildings as two separate leases, a lease of land and a lease of the buildings, unless the land element would be immaterial or minor. The two leases may be classified differently. Note that because IAS 17 refers to "immaterial" while CICA 3065 refers to "minor," the application of the guidance could potentially lead to different conclusions as to whether the land component needs to be treated separately from the building component. The allocation between the lease of land and the lease of the buildings might be different under IAS 17 and CICA 3065. Under IAS 17, the allocation is based on relative fair value of the leasehold interests in the land and building elements while under CICA 3065 the allocation is based on fair value of the land and buildings. IAS 17 has an exception from separation of land and building if allocation cannot be made reliably.

Generally, a lease of land is classified as an operating lease since land normally has an indefinite economic life; if, however, title transfers to the lessee by the end of the lease term, the lease would be classified as a capital lease. The building element is classified as a finance or operating lease, depending on whether the lessee receives substantially all the risks and rewards of ownership.

Sale and Leaseback Transactions

Sale-leaseback describes a transaction where the owner of property (the seller-lessee) sells the property and then immediately leases all or part of it back from the new owner (the buyer-lessor). The lease payment and the sale price are usually interdependent because they are negotiated as a package. The accounting treatment of a sale and leaseback transaction depends on the type of lease involved.

Under IAS 17 and CICA 3065, if a sale and leaseback transaction results in a finance lease, any excess of sales proceeds over the carrying amount will be deferred and amortized over the lease term.

If a sale and leaseback transaction results in an operating lease, IAS 17 requires immediate recognition of losses and gains on such transactions unless:

- the sale price is below fair value and a loss is compensated for by future lease payments below market price, in which case the loss is deferred and amortized over the expected useful life of the asset in proportion to the lease payments; or
- the sale price is above fair value, in which case the excess is deferred and amortized over the expected useful life of the asset.

CICA 3065 requires deferral and amortization of all losses and gains on such transactions, except that, consistent with IAS 17, a loss must be recognized immediately if the fair value of the leased asset is less than its carrying amount. EIC-25 however, permits immediate recognition of a gain when the seller leases back only a minor portion of the property sold and the lease is classified as an operating lease. When the seller leases back more than a minor portion but less than substantially all of the property sold, the gain deferred and amortized is the amount allocable to the portion of the property covered by the leaseback agreement.

So, under IFRS, gains resulting from a sale and leaseback transaction resulting in an operating lease might now be recognized at the transaction date, which is possible under Canadian GAAP only when the seller leases back a minor portion of the property sold.

Illustrative Disclosure:
Extract 13(3) – Sale and leaseback note

Koninklijke Ahold N.V. (AR 2007), page 44
3 Significant accounting policies (in part)
Sale and leaseback
The gain or loss on sale and operating leaseback transactions is recognized in the consolidated statements of operations immediately if (i) Ahold does not maintain or maintains only minor continuing involvement in these properties, other than the required lease payments and (ii) these transactions are established at fair value. Any gain or loss on sale and finance leaseback transactions is deferred and amortized over the term of the lease. In classifying the leaseback in a sale and leaseback transaction, similar judgments have to be made as described above under "Leases".

In some sale and leaseback arrangements, Ahold sells a property and only leases back a portion of that property. These properties generally involve shopping centers, which contain an Ahold store as well as other stores leased to third-party retailers. Ahold recognizes a sale and the profit thereon on the portion of the shopping center that is not leased back to the extent that (i) the property is sold for fair value and (ii) the risks and rewards of owning stores, which are not leased back to Ahold, have been fully transferred to the buyer. The leaseback of the Ahold store and any gain on the sale of the Ahold store is accounted for under the sale and leaseback criteria described above.

In some sale and leaseback arrangements, Ahold subleases the property to third parties (including franchisees) or maintains a form of continuing involvement in the property sold, such as earn-out provisions or obligations or options to repurchase the property. In such situations, the transaction generally does not qualify for sale-leaseback accounting, but rather is accounted for as a financing transaction ("financing"). The carrying amount of the asset remains on the balance sheet and the sale proceeds are recorded as a financing obligation. The financing obligation is amortized over the lease term, using either the effective interest rate or Ahold's cost of debt rate, whichever is higher. Once Ahold's continuing involvement ends, the sale is accounted for under the sale and leaseback criteria described above.

Commentary: This extract describes different types of sale and leaseback transactions, as well as the accounting treatment adopted, notably for the gain or loss on the sale of the asset.

Determining Whether an Arrangement Contains a Lease

Determining the Substance of the Arrangement

Recent years have seen the development of new types of arrangements that do not take the legal form of leases. They take many forms, but essentially combine rights to use assets and, possibly, provide services or outputs, for agreed periods of time in return for a payment or series of payments. For example:

- outsourcing arrangements, such as outsourcing an entity's data processing functions;

- arrangements in the telecommunications industry, where suppliers of network capacity enter into contracts to provide purchasers with rights to capacity; and

- take-or-pay and similar contracts, in which purchasers must make specified payments regardless of whether they take delivery of the contracted products or services (e.g., where purchasers are committed to acquiring substantially all of the output of a supplier's power generator).

IFRIC 4 provides guidance for determining whether certain arrangements that do not take the legal form of a lease but convey the right to use an asset in return for a payment, or series of payments, are, or contain, leases.

Determining whether an arrangement is, or contains, a lease should be based on the substance of the arrangement rather than their legal form and requires an assessment of whether:

- fulfilment of the arrangement depends on the use of a specific asset or assets; and
- the arrangement conveys a right to use the asset.

A use of an asset is implicitly specified if, for example, its supplier owns or leases only one asset that can fulfil the obligation and it is not economically feasible or practicable to perform the obligation with alternative assets.

Although a specific asset may be explicitly identified in an arrangement, it is not the subject of a lease if fulfilment of the arrangement does not depend on the use of the specified asset. For example, if the supplier is obliged to deliver a specified quantity of goods or services and has the right and ability to provide those goods or services using other assets not specified in the arrangement, fulfilment of the arrangement does not depend on the specified asset and the arrangement does not contain a lease. A warranty obligation that permits or requires the substitution of the same or similar assets when a specified asset does not operate as intended does not preclude lease treatment. In addition, a contractual provision (contingent or otherwise), permitting or requiring the supplier to substitute other assets for any reason on or after a specified date does not preclude lease treatment before the date of substitution.

EIC-150 is converged with IFRIC 4 except that, under Canadian GAAP, it applies only if the asset is a tangible asset such as property, plant and equipment.

Reassessing Whether an Arrangement Contains a Lease

IFRIC 4 requires reassessment of whether an arrangement contains a lease after the inception of the arrangement in the following circumstances:

- there is a change in the contractual terms, unless the change only renews or extends the arrangement;

- a renewal option is exercised or the parties agree to an extension of the arrangement, unless the term of the renewal or extension had initially been included in the lease term;
- there is a change in the determination as to whether or not fulfillment depends on specified assets;
- the asset is substantially changed, for example a substantial physical change has been made to property, plant or equipment.

EIC-150 contains similar requirements except that they apply only to tangible assets.

Accounting for the Lease Element

If an arrangement contains a lease, payments and other consideration required by the arrangement should be separated at the inception of the arrangement or upon a reassessment of the arrangement into those for the lease and those for other elements on the basis of their relative fair values, unless it is impracticable to separate the payments reliably.

When a purchasing entity concludes that it is impracticable to separate the payments reliably, it should:

- in the case of a finance lease, recognize an asset and a liability at an amount equal to the fair value of the underlying asset that is the subject of the lease, and subsequently reduce the liability as payments are made; and then recognize a finance charge on the liability using the purchaser's incremental borrowing rate of interest;
- in the case of an operating lease, treat all payments under the arrangement as lease payments to comply with the disclosure requirements of IAS 17, but disclose those payments separately from the minimum lease payments of other arrangements that do not include payments for non-lease payments, and state that the disclosed payments also include payments for non-lease elements in the arrangement.

Like IFRIC 4, EIC-150 mentions that payments and other consideration called for by an arrangement containing a lease should be separated at the inception of the arrangement, or when an arrangement has been reassessed, into payments pertaining to the lease (including the related executory costs and profits thereon) and those for other services, on a relative fair value basis. EIC-150 is less specific, however, on the treatment of the other services. It mentions that other elements of the arrangement not within the scope of CICA 3065 should be accounted for in accordance with other applicable generally accepted accounting principles.

Any arrangement that has been determined to involve a lease will fall within the scope of IAS 17, and will be subject to the presentation and disclosure requirements of that standard.

Illustrative Disclosure:
Extract 13(4) – IFRIC 4

Electricité de France S.A. (Financial Report 2007), pages 22, 48 and 62

Note 2 Summary of the principal accounting and valuation methods (in part)

2.13 Leases (in part)

2.13.3 Arrangements containing a lease

In compliance with interpretation IFRIC 4, the Group identifies agreements that convey the right to use an asset or group of specific assets to the purchaser although they do not have the legal form of a lease contract, as the purchaser in the arrangement benefits from a substantial share of the asset's production and payment is not dependent on production or market price.

Such arrangements are treated as leases, and analyzed with reference to IAS 17 for classification as either finance or operating leases.

page 48

Note 11 Contractual obligations and commitments (in part)

11.4 Operating lease commitments

The Group is a party to agreements classified as operating leases under IFRIC 4, which account for most of its operating lease commitments as lessor. These agreements concern the Asian IPPs. The decrease in this item compared to December 31, 2006 essentially results from the sale of the Mexican power plants.

page 62

Note 22 Property, plant and equipment used in generation and other tangible assets owned by the Group (in part)

22.3 Finance lease obligations

The Group is a party to agreements classified as finance leases under IFRIC 4, which account for almost all of its finance lease commitments as lessor. These agreements mainly concern EDF Energy.

The Group is also bound by irrevocable finance-lease contracts for premises, equipment and vehicles used in the course of its business. The corresponding payments are subject to renegotiation at intervals defined in the contracts. The main companies concerned are Tiru and Sofilo.

Commentary: These extracts illustrate the impact of IFRIC 4 on the EDF Group. In this case, some agreements that have the substance, but not the legal form, of a lease are accounted for as leases.

Transactions Involving the Legal Form of a Lease

Not all transactions involving the legal form of a lease will fall within the definition of a lease for the purposes of IAS 17. For example, some transactions may be designed to achieve a particular tax effect, which is shared between the parties involved, rather than conveying the right to use an asset. SIC 27 addresses issues that may arise when an entity enters into a transaction, or a series of structured transactions, with an unrelated party or parties that involves the legal form of a lease.

SIC 27 requires a series of transactions involving the legal form of a lease to be accounted for as one transaction when the overall economic effect cannot be understood without reference to the series as a whole. This is the case, for example, when the transactions are closely related, negotiated as a single transaction and take place concurrently or in a continuous sequence.

Such arrangements might not be treated as a lease under IAS 17. According to SIC-27, any of the following situations indicate that an arrangement may not, in substance, involve a lease under IAS 17:

- an entity retains all the risks and rewards of ownership of an asset and enjoys substantially the same rights to its use as before the arrangement;
- the primary reason for the arrangement is to achieve a particular tax result;
- an option is included on terms that make its exercise almost certain.

SIC-27 notes that the form of each arrangement and its terms and conditions can vary significantly. The consensus is that the accounting should reflect the substance of an arrangement, and that all aspects and implications of the arrangement should be evaluated to determine that substance, giving particular weight to the aspects and implications that have an economic effect. All aspects of an arrangement involving the legal form of a lease that does not, in substance, involve a lease under IAS 17 (as determined using the principles set out in SIC-27) have to be considered in determining the appropriate disclosures necessary for understanding the arrangement and the accounting treatment adopted.

An entity must disclose the following in each period of an arrangement that takes the legal form of a lease but does not, in substance, involve a lease under IAS 17 (as determined using the principles set out in SIC-27):

- a description of the arrangement, including:
  - o the underlying asset and any restrictions on its use,
  - o the life and other significant terms of the arrangement, and
  - o the transactions that are linked together, including any options; and
- the accounting treatment applied to any fee received, the amount recognized as income in the period and the line item of the income statement in which it is included.

The disclosures required in accordance with SIC-27 should be provided individually for each arrangement or in aggregate for each class of arrangement. A class is a grouping of arrangements with underlying assets of a similar nature (e.g., power plants).

Any fee an entity (as a lessor) might receive from an investor (which may be a mechanism the investor uses to share a tax advantage with the entity) has to be presented in the income statement based on its economic substance and nature.

Unlike IFRS, Canadian GAAP does not provide specific guidance on the accounting for a series of linked transactions in the legal form of a lease.

Illustrative Disclosure:
Extract 13(5) – SIC-27

Swisscom AG (AR 2006), pages 116 and 117
25 Financial liabilities (in part)
Financial liabilities from cross-border tax lease arrangements
Between 1996 and 2002, Swisscom entered into cross-border tax lease arrangements, under the terms of which parts of its fixed and mobile networks were to be sold or leased long-term to US Trusts and leased back with terms of up to 30 years. Swisscom has an early buyout option on these assets after a contractually agreed period. The financial liabilities are based on lease and leaseback transactions from the years 1999, 2000, and 2002. The sale and leaseback from the years 1996 and 1997 are presented as finance lease obligations. The finance lease obligations from the year 1996 were repaid in 2005.

Swisscom AG (AR 2006) (continued)

Swisscom defeased a major part of the lease obligations through highly rated financial assets and payment undertaking agreements. The financial assets were irrevocably placed with trusts. The payment undertaking agreements were signed with financial institutions with minimal credit risk. In accordance with Interpretation SIC-27 "Evaluating the substance of transactions involving the legal form of a lease", these financial assets or payment undertaking agreements and the liabilities in the same amount are offset in the balance sheet because the criteria for offsetting assets and liabilities are met. One of the transactions entered into in 2000 does not meet the conditions of SIC-27 and is consequently reported in the balance sheet as a long-term financial asset and a corresponding long-term financial liability.

As of December 31, 2006, the assets and liabilities resulting from these transactions totalled USD 4,092 million (CHF 5,055 million) and USD 3,823 million (CHF 4,721 million), respectively. Of this amount USD 2,947 million (CHF 3,596 million) are not reported in the balance sheet in accordance with SIC-27. Of the liabilities reported in the amount of CHF 1,459 million (previous year CHF 1,474 million), CHF 1,125 million (previous year CHF 1,125 million) are covered by financial assets.

The gains from the transactions were recorded as financial income in the period the transactions were closed.

In the transaction concluded in 2002, Swisscom entered into a contingent liability in favor of the investors. The "Standby-Letter-of-Credit" issued serves as a security for any financial claim that the investors may assert in the event of the transaction being terminated prematurely due to the fault of Swisscom. A provision has been created for future costs in 2002. Swisscom is obliged to issue further Standby-Letters-of-Credit if the Swiss Confederation gives up its majority shareholding in Swisscom.

In connection with these lease transactions, Swisscom committed to meet minimum credit ratings. Shortly before the end of 2004, the credit rating of some financial assets was reduced by the rating agencies such that they had dropped below the minimum rating agreed in the contracts. Swisscom estimated it would cost CHF 34 million to restore the minimum rating required. As a result, in 2004 a provision was recorded as financial expense. In the third quarter of 2005, the minimum credit ratings could be finally restored at the expense of CHF 10 million. The unused provision of CHF 24 million was therefore reversed.

Financial liabilities from cross-border tax lease arrangements

Future minimum payments resulting from cross-border tax lease arrangements are due as follows:

CHF in millions	31.12.2006	31.12.2005
Within 1 year	303	77
Within 1 to 2 years	116	261
Within 2 to 3 years	18	124
Within 3 to 4 years	129	19
Within 4 to 5 years	117	138
After 5 years	2,920	3,247
Total future minimum lease payments	**3,603**	**3,866**
Less future interest charges	(2,234)	(2,396)
Total present value of financial liability from cross-border tax lease arrangements	**1,369**	**1,470**
Fair value adjustments	2	4
Accrued interest	88	–
Long-term financial liability from cross-border tax lease arrangements	**1,459**	**1,474**

Commentary: This extract illustrates transactions that have the legal form of a lease but are not leases in substance since they don't meet the criteria stated in SIC 27. Relevant disclosures are provided in accordance with SIC 27.

Embedded Derivatives in Leases

Embedded derivatives may be present in a lease host contract. IAS 39, *Financial Instruments: Recognition and Measurement* defines an embedded derivative (refer to Chapter 9 for details).

IAS 39 requires an embedded derivative to be split from the host contract and accounted for separately only if it is not closely related to the economic characteristics and risks of the host contract. Some examples of leases that may contain embedded derivatives are:

- the lease payments are linked to an underlying variable such as an interest rate, index or other price that is not closely related to the lease contract;
- there are terms or conditions in the lease agreement that change the economic characteristics of the lease.

CICA 3855 requires a similar analysis for defining embedded derivatives.

General Disclosures Related to Leases

For Lessees

In addition to meeting the requirements of IFRS 7, *Financial Instruments: Disclosures*, lessees have to make the following disclosures for operating leases:

- the total of future minimum lease payments under non-cancellable operating leases for each of the following periods:
  - o   not later than one year,
  - o   later than one year and not later than five years, or
  - o   later than five years (more detailed than CICA 3065);
- the total of future minimum sublease payments expected to be received under non-cancellable subleases at the balance sheet date (might be required under CICA 3065 depending on the circumstances);
- lease and sublease payments recognized as an expense for the period, with separate amounts for minimum lease payments, contingent rents and sublease payments (desirable under CICA 3065); and
- a general description of the lessee's significant leasing arrangements including, but not limited to, the following:
  - o   the basis for determining contingent rent payable,
  - o   the existence and terms of renewal or purchase options and escalation clauses; and
- restrictions imposed by lease arrangements, such as those concerning dividends, additional debt and further leasing (desirable under CICA 3065).

In addition to meeting the requirements of IFRS 7, *Financial Instruments: Disclosures*, lessees need to make the following disclosures for finance leases:

- for each class of asset, the net carrying amount at the balance sheet date (required under CICA 3065);
- a reconciliation between the total of future minimum lease payments at the balance sheet date and their present value (required under CICA 3065);
- the total of future minimum lease payments at the balance sheet date, and their present value, for each of the following periods:
  - o   not later than one year,

- o later than one year and not later than five years,
- o later than five years (more detailed than CICA 3065);
- contingent rents recognized as an expense for the period (desirable under CICA 3065);
- the total of future minimum sublease payments expected to be received under non-cancellable subleases at the balance sheet date (desirable under CICA 3065); and
- a general description of the lessee's material leasing arrangements including, but not limited to, the following:
  - o the basis on which contingent rent payable is determined,
  - o the existence and terms of renewal or purchase options and escalation clauses; and
- restrictions imposed by lease arrangements, such as those concerning dividends, additional debt and further leasing (desirable under CICA 3065).

The requirements for disclosure under IAS 16, *Property, Plant and Equipment*, IAS 36, *Impairment of Assets*, IAS 38, *Intangible Assets*, IAS 40, *Investment Property* and IAS 41, *Agriculture* also apply to lessees for leased assets under finance leases.

For Lessors

Lessors must present assets subject to operating leases in their balance sheets according to the nature of those assets.

In addition to meeting the requirements of IFRS 7, *Financial Instruments: Disclosures*, lessors have to disclose the following for operating leases:

- the future minimum lease payments under non-cancellable operating leases in aggregate (desirable disclosure under CICA 3065);
- the future minimum lease payments under non-cancellable operating leases for each of the following periods:
  - o not later than one year,
  - o later than one year and not later than five years,
  - o later than five years (more detailed than the desirable disclosure under CICA 3065);
- total contingent rents recognized as income in the period (desirable under CICA 3065); and
- a general description of the lessor's leasing arrangements (desirable under CICA 3065).

As well, the requirements for disclosure under IAS 16, *Property, Plant and Equipment*, IAS 36, *Impairment of Assets*, IAS 38, *Intangible Assets*, IAS 40, *Investment Property* and IAS 41, *Agriculture* apply to lessors for assets provided under operating leases.

In addition to meeting the requirements of IFRS 7, *Financial Instruments: Disclosures*, lessors must disclose the following for finance leases:

- a reconciliation between the gross investment in the lease at the balance sheet date and the present value of minimum lease payments receivable at the balance sheet date (desirable under CICA 3065);
- the gross investment in the lease and the present value of minimum lease payments receivable at the balance sheet date, for each of the following periods:
  - o not later than one year,

- o later than one year and not later than five years,
- o later than five years (more detailed than the desirable disclosure under CICA 3065);
- unearned finance income (not required under CICA 3065);
- the unguaranteed residual values accruing to the benefit of the lessor (desirable under CICA 3065);
- the accumulated allowance for uncollectible minimum lease payments receivable (not required under CICA 3065);
- contingent rents recognized as income in the period (desirable under CICA 3065); and
- a general description of the lessor's material leasing arrangements (desirable under CICA 3065).

The disclosure requirements for lessees and lessors set out above apply equally to sale and leaseback arrangements.

IAS 17 requires more extensive disclosures than CICA 3065:

- a lessor's gross investment and unearned income in finance leases;
- a lessor's operating lease assets by class, when significant; and
- for lessees, the renewal of purchase options, contingent rentals and other contingencies.

Many of the disclosures desirable under CICA 3065 are now required under IAS 17.

FUTURE DEVELOPMENTS

The IASB is working on a joint project with the FASB to develop new standards for lease accounting, with a Discussion Paper expected at the end of the first quarter of 2009. The IASB is also analyzing other potential accounting models for leases, notably the right-of-use model. Under this model, a lessee should initially measure both its right-of-use asset and its lease obligation at the present value of the expected lease payments and that a lessee should discount the lease payments using the lessee's incremental borrowing rate for secured borrowings. The IASB and FASB have decided to defer the development of a new accounting model for lessors and decided instead to include in the proposed Discussion Paper a high-level discussion of lessor accounting issues. The Boards also decided on an overall approach that would apply the existing finance lease model, adapted where necessary, to all leases.

COMPREHENSIVE EXAMPLES

This section presents two comprehensive extracts showing various lease disclosures, the first for a lessee and the second for a lessor.

Extracts A: Lessee Presentation

Extract 13(A1) – Air France-KLM S.A. (Reference Document 2006-07), pages 98 and 99, Accounting policies

This extract describes the accounting policies for the various aspects of leases, covering:

- classification of leases, with description of accounting treatments;
- provisions for restitution of aircraft under operating leases; note that the group accrues for restitution costs as soon as an asset does not meet the return condition criteria.

Note 3 Accounting policies (in part)

3.13. Property, plant and equipment (in part)

3.13.5. Leases

In accordance with IAS 17 "Leases", leases are classified as finance leases when the lease arrangement transfers substantially all the risks and rewards of ownership to the lessee. All other leases are classified as operating leases.

The assets held under a finance lease are recognized as assets at the lower of the following two values: the present value of the minimum lease payments under the lease arrangement or their fair value determined at inception of the lease. The corresponding obligation to the lessor is accounted for as long term debt.

These assets are depreciated over the shorter of the useful life of the assets and the lease term when there is no reasonable certainty that the lessee will obtain ownership by the end of the lease term.

In the context of sale and operating leaseback transactions, the related profit or losses are accounted for as follows:

- they are recognized immediately when it is clear that the transaction is established at fair value;
- if the sale price is below fair value, any profit or loss is recognized immediately except that, if the loss is compensated for by future lease payments at below market price, it is deferred and amortized in proportion to the lease payments over the period for which the asset is expected to be used; and
- if the sale price is above fair value, the excess over fair value is deferred and amortized over the period for which the asset is expected to be used.

In the context of sale and finance leaseback transactions, any gain on the sale is deferred and recognized as finance income over the lease term. No loss is recognized unless the asset is impaired.

3.18. Provisions for restitution of aircraft under operating leases

For certain operating leases, the Group is contractually committed to restitute aircraft to a defined level of potential. The Group accrues for restitution costs related to aircraft under operating leases as soon as the asset does not meet the return condition criteria.

The restitution costs for airframes and engines relating to operating lease contracts are provisioned.

When the condition of aircraft exceeds the return condition as set per the lease arrangement, the Group capitalizes the related amount in excess. Such amount is subsequently amortized on a straight line basis over the period during which the potential exceeds the restitution condition. Any remaining capitalized excess potential upon termination of a lease is reimbursable by the lessor.

Extract 13(A2) – Air France-KLM S.A. (Reference Document 2006-07), page 116, Disclosure of the lease interests

In this note, under "Net cost of financial debt," Air France KLM presents the lease interests separately from other costs of financial debt.

Note 11 Net cost of financial debt and other financial income and expenses			
Year ended March 31 *(In euro millions)*	**2007**	**2006**	**2005**
Income from cash and cash equivalents			
Income from marketable securities	71	52	36
Other financial income	196	116	89
	267	168	125
Cost of financial debt			
Loan interests	(200)	(205)	(284)
Lease interests	(241)	(220)	(83)
Capitalized interests	38	40	25
Other financial expenses	(4)	(7)	(5)
	(407)	(392)	(347)
Net cost of financial debt	*(140)*	*(224)*	*(222)*
Other financial income and expenses			
Foreign exchange gains (losses), net	(3)	(13)	(2)
Change in fair value of financial assets and liabilities	43	6	–
Net (charge) release to provisions	(10)	(24)	(6)
Other	(6)	–	–
	25	(31)	(8)
Total	**(115)**	**(255)**	**(230)**

The interest rate used in the calculation of capitalized interest is 4.60% for the year ended March 31, 2007, 3.76% for the year ended March 31, 2006 and 3.80% for the year ended March 31, 2005.

Net foreign exchange results for the period include an unrealized net gain/(loss) of €5 million, €(8) million for the year ended March 31, 2006 and €(4) million for the year ended March 31, 2005. The impact related to currency derivatives amounted to €(13) million for the year ended March 31, 2007 and €(4) million for the year ended March 31, 2006.

Net charge to provisions includes an unrealized loss on shares of Alitalia for an amount of €9 million, as a result of the stock price decreasing significantly during the year ended March 31, 2007.

Net charge to provisions includes an unrealized loss on shares of Alitalia for an amount of €9 million, as a result of the stock price decreasing significantly during the year ended March 31, 2006.

Extract 13(A3) – Air France-KLM S.A. (Reference Document 2006-07), pages 128, 129 and 130, Disclosure of lease assets

This note presents the leased assets separately from other tangible assets owned by Air France KLM, as required.

Note 18 Tangible assets
(In euro millions)

	Flight equipment					Other tangible assets					Total
	Owned aircraft	Leased aircraft	Assets in progress	other	Total	Land and buildings	Equip-ment and machinery	Assets in progress	Other	Total	Total
Gross value											
Amount as of April 1, 2004	*4,343*	*1,452*	*624*	*1,155*	*7,574*	*1,234*	*594*	*73*	*683*	*2,584*	**10,158**
Additions	439	174	261	914	1,788	100	80	79	91	350	**2,138**
Disposals	(512)	(108)	-	(326)	(946)	(52)	(32)	-	(32)	(116)	**(1,062)**
KLM acquisition	1,026	1,997	235	291	3,549	553	144	80	28	805	**4,354**
Transfer	328	203	(69)	(299)	163	77	7	(69)	(4)	11	**174**
Currency translation adjustment	(28)	211	(20)	(1)	162	-	-	-	(1)	(1)	**161**
Amounts as of March 31, 2005	*5,596*	*3,929*	*1,031*	*1,734*	*12,290*	*1,912*	*793*	*163*	*765*	*3,633*	**15,923**
Additions	613	62	1,030	511	2,216	49	62	169	52	332	**2,548**
Disposals	(227)	(101)	(52)	(302)	(682)	(19)	(37)	(7)	(21)	(84)	**(766)**
Changes in consolidation scope	-	-	(32)	-	(32)		7		2	9	**(23)**
Transfer	231	310	(853)	324	12	139	26	(199)	(23)	(57)	**(45)**
Currency translation adjustment	11	-	14	-	25		(2)			(2)	**23**
Amounts as of March 31, 2006	*6,224*	*4,200*	*1,138*	*2,267*	*13,829*	*2,081*	*849*	*126*	*775*	*3,831*	**17,660**
Additions	662	397	547	431	2,037	116	100	56	75	347	**2,384**
Disposals	(259)	(31)	(30)	(335)	(655)	(59)	(22)	-	(16)	(97)	**(752)**
Changes in consolidation scope	-	(5)	-	(11)	(16)	-	(2)	-	-	(2)	**(18)**
Fair value hedge	-	-	111	-	111	-	-	-	-	-	**111**
Transfer	1,352	(131)	(597)	(636)	(12)	34	9	(37)	(3)	3	**(9)**
Currency translation adjustment	(7)	5	1	-	(1)	-	(1)	-	-	(1)	**(2)**
Amounts as of March 31, 2007	*7,972*	*4,435*	*1,170*	*1,716*	*15,293*	*2,172*	*933*	*145*	*831*	*4,081*	**19,374**
Depreciation and impairment											
Amounts as of April 1, 2004	*(528)*	*(103)*	-	*(436)*	*(1,067)*	*(640)*	*(436)*	-	*(485)*	*(1,561)*	**(2,628)**
Charge to depreciation	(508)	(444)	-	(362)	(1,314)	(106)	(69)	-	(76)	(251)	**(1,565)**
Realeases on disposal	282	25	-	300	607	25	21	-	24	70	**677**
Changes in consolidation scope	-	-	-	-	-	2	-	-	22	24	**24**
Transfer	(90)	83	-	(143)	(150)	-	(1)	-	(23)	(24)	**(174)**
Currency translation adjustment	26	4	-	(2)	28	(2)	5	-	1	4	**32**
Amounts as of March 31, 2005	*(818)*	*(435)*	-	*(643)*	*(1,896)*	*(721)*	*(480)*	-	*(537)*	*(1,738)*	**(3,634)**
Charge to depreciation	(591)	(294)	-	(485)	(1,370)	(110)	(73)	-	(64)	(247)	**(1,617)**
Realeases on disposal	171	39	-	245	455	14	33	-	17	64	**519**
Transfer	(32)	32	-	-	-	1	7	-	37	45	**45**
Currency translation adjustment	3	(1)	-	(3)	(1)	-	-	-	-	-	**(1)**
Amounts as of March 31, 2006	*(1,267)*	*(659)*	-	*(886)*	*(2,812)*	*(816)*	*(513)*	-	*(547)*	*(1,876)*	**(4,688)**

Note 18 Tangible assets
(In euro millions)

| | Flight equipment | | | | | Other tangible assets | | | | | |
	Owned aircraft	Leased aircraft	Assets in progress	other	Total	Land and buildings	Equip-ment and machinery	Assets in progress	Other	Total	Total
Charge to depreciation	(716)	(311)	–	(461)	(1,488)	(115)	(72)	–	(65)	(252)	(1,740)
Loss for future disposal	(20)	–	–	–	(20)	–	–	–	–	–	(20)
Realases on disposal	209	25	–	329	563	24	19	–	14	57	620
Changes in consolidation scope	–	5	–	4	9	–	1	–	–	1	110
Transfer	(300)	36	–	271	7	(2)	(7)	–	5	(4)	3
Currency translation adjustment	3	(4)	–	–	(1)	–	–	–	–	–	(1)
Amounts as of March 31, 2007	**(2,091)**	**(908)**	**–**	**(743)**	**(3,742)**	**(909)**	**(572)**	**–**	**(593)**	**(2,074)**	**(5,816)**
Net value											
As of April 1, 2004	3,815	1,349	624	719	6,507	594	158	73	198	1,023	7,530
As of March 31, 2005	4,778	3,494	1,031	1,091	10,394	1,191	313	163	228	1,895	12,289
As of March 31, 2006	4,957	3,541	1,138	1,381	11,017	1,265	336	126	228	1,955	12,972
As of March 31, 2007	**5,881**	**3,527**	**1,170**	**973**	**11,551**	**1,263**	**361**	**145**	**238**	**2,007**	**13,558**

Note 35 details the amount of pledged tangible assets.

Commitments to property purchases are detailed in notes 34 and 35.

The net value of tangible assets financed under capital lease amounts to €3,811 million as of March 31, 2007 against €3,912 million as of March 31, 2006 and €3,710 million as of March 31, 2005.

Extract 13(A4) – Air France-KLM S.A. (Reference Document 2006-07), page 152, Disclosure of capital lease obligations

In this note, the capital lease obligation and its current portion are presented separately from other debt. Information on capital lease commitments for future years is also provided.

Note 30 Financial debt (in part)			
Year ended March 31 *(In euro millions)*	**2007**	**2006**	**2005**
Non-current financial debt			
Perpetual subordinated loan stock in Yen	204	226	225
Perpetual subordinated loan stock in Swiss francs	258	265	270
Repackaged perpetual loans	–	122	152
OCEANE (convertible bonds)	386	382	–
Bonds	550	–	–
Capital lease obligations	3,917	4,668	5,008
Other long-term debt	2,104	2,163	2,234
Total	**7,419**	**7,826**	**7,889**
Current financial debt			
Perpetual subordinated loan stock	122	25	23
Capital lease obligations (current portion)	657	763	444
Accrued interest	95	107	79
Other	224	365	498
Total	**1,098**	**1,260**	**1,044**

Air France-KLM S.A. (Reference Document 2006-07), page 154

30.5. Capital lease commitments

The breakdown of total future minimum lease payments related to capital leases is as follows:

As of March 31 (In euro millions)	2007	2006	2005
Aircraft			
Future minimum lease payments – due dates			
N+1	813	979	671
N+2	624	974	974
N+3	603	632	946
N+4	610	682	581
N+5	535	648	495
Over 5 years	1,968	2,381	2,227
Total	**5,153**	**6,296**	**5,894**
Including interest	*873*	*1,224*	*713*
Principal	*4,280*	*5,072*	*5,181*
Buildings			
Future minimum lease payments – due dates			
N+1	42	45	35
N+2	42	44	35
N+3	41	44	34
N+4	41	42	33
N+5	41	41	32
Over 5 years	215	273	211
Total	**422**	**489**	**380**
Including interest	*131*	*133*	*112*
Principal	*291*	*356*	*268*
Other property, plant and equipment	***3***	***3***	***3***

The lease expenses over the period do not include contingent leases. Deposits made on purchase options are presented in note 22.

Extract 13(A5) – Air France-KLM S.A. (Reference Document 2006-07), pages 168 and 169, Disclosure of lease commitments

This note discloses the minimum future payments for operating leases.

Note 33 Lease commitments

33.1. Capital leases

The debt related to capital leases is detailed in note 30.

33.2. Operating leases

The minimum future payments on operating leases are as follows:

Year ended March 31 (In euro millions)	Minimum lease payments		
	2007	2006	2005
Flight equipment			
Due dates			
N + 1	637	645	631
N + 2	555	580	531
N + 3	427	457	438
N + 4	369	354	345
N + 5	282	298	256
Over 5 years	516	613	573
Total	**2,786**	**2,947**	**2,774**

33.2. Operating leases (continued)

Year ended March 31	Minimum lease payments		
(In euro millions)	2007	2006	2005
Buildings			
Due dates			
N + 1	146	106	144
N + 2	130	102	119
N + 3	118	90	107
N + 4	102	79	88
N + 5	95	67	73
Over 5 years	654	592	633
Total	**1,245**	**1,036**	**1,164**

The expense relating to operating leases for flight equipment amounted to €600 million for the year ended March 31, 2007, to €637 million for the year ended March 31 2006 and to €595 million for the Year ended March 31 2005.

The Group may sub-lease flight equipment and buildings. The revenue generated by this activity is not significant for the Group.

Extracts B: Lessor Presentation

Extract 13(B1) – ABN AMRO Holding N.V. (AR 2007), page 110, Accounting policies

In this extract, the accounting policy describes the criteria for the classification of leases (transfers substantially all the risks and rewards...). Also, it specifies where each component is presented in the financial statements.

Accounting policies (in part)

Property and equipment (in part)

Leasing

As *lessee*: most of the leases that the Group has entered into are classified as operating leases (including property rental). The total payments made under operating leases are charged to the income statement on a straight-line basis over the period of the lease. Lease incentives received are recognised in the income statement as an integral part of the total lease expense. When it is decided that an operating lease will be terminated or vacated before the lease period has expired, the lesser of any penalty payments required and the remaining payments due once vacated (less sub-leasing income) is recognised as an expense.

As *lessor*: assets subject to operational leases are included in property and equipment. The asset is depreciated on a straight-line basis over its useful life to its estimated residual value. Leases where the Group transfers substantially all the risks and rewards resulting from ownership of an asset to the lessee are classified as finance leases. A receivable at an amount equal to the present value of the lease payments, using the implicit interest rate, including any guaranteed residual value, is recognised. Finance lease receivables are included in loans and receivables to customers.

Extract 13(B2) – ABN AMRO Holding N.V. (AR 2007), pages 146-147, Disclosure of lease assets

The property and equipment leased under operating leases are included in the section "other," rather than being presented separately. This follows the IFRS requirement that lessors must present assets subject to operating leases in their balance sheets according to the nature of those assets. At the end of the extract, the future minimum lease payments under non-cancellable operating leases are presented, as required.

20 Property and equipment

The book value of property and equipment in 2007 and 2006 changed as follows:

	Property			
	Used in operations	Other	Equipment	Total
Balance at 1 January 2007	4,263	247	1,760	6,270
Reclassification related to businesses held for sale/discontinued operations	(2,421)	(195)	(862)	(3,478)
	1,842	52	898	2,792
Movements:				
Acquired in business combinations	25	4	7	36
Additions	162	71	458	691
Disposals	(87)	(52)	(43)	(182)
Impairment losses	(2)	–	(36)	(38)
Depreciation	(154)	(3)	(388)	(545)
Currency translation differences	14	3	–	17
Other	2	(7)	(19)	(24)
Balance at 31 December 2007	1,802	68	877	2,747
Representing:				
Cost	3,007	83	2,520	5,610
Cumulative impairment	(20)	(12)	(3)	(35)
Cumulative depreciation	(1,185)	(3)	(1,640)	(2,828)

	Property			
	Used in operations	Other	Equipment	Total
Balance at 1 January 2006	3,340	2,979	1,791	8,110
Movements:				
Acquired in business combinations	1,010	98	215	1,323
Divestment of business	(269)	(2,846)	(171)	(3,286)
Additions	450	783	688	1,921
Disposals	(108)	(767)	(148)	(1,023)
Impairment losses	(17)	–	–	(17)
Depreciation	(161)	(4)	(436)	(601)
Depreciation discontinued operations	(42)	–	(115)	(157)
Currency translation differences	(93)	(7)	(43)	(143)
Other	153	11	(21)	143
Balance at 31 December 2006	4,263	247	1,760	6,270
Representing:				
Cost	5,881	276	4,448	10,605
Cumulative impairment	(44)	(17)	(4)	(65)
Cumulative depreciation	(1,574)	(12)	(2,684)	(4,270)

Divestment of businesses in 2006 mainly relates to development property of Bouwfonds. For discontinued operations refer to note 45.

20 Property and equipment (continued)

As lessee

The Group leases equipment under a number of finance lease agreements. At 31 December 2007 the net carrying amount of leased equipment included in property and equipment was EUR 7 million (2006: EUR 8 million).

As lessor

The Group also leases out various assets, included in 'Other', under operating leases. Non-cancellable operating lease rentals are as follows:

	2007	2006
Less than one year	48	56
Between one and five years	175	140
More than five years	95	49
Total	**318**	245

During the year ended 31 December 2007, EUR 80 million (2006: EUR 59 million) was recognised as rental income in the income statement and EUR 63 million (2006: EUR 48 million) in respect of directly related expenses.

PLANNING FOR IMPLEMENTATION

This chapter explains certain IAS 17 requirements and notes differences with corresponding Canadian GAAP. This section discusses certain implementation measures of IAS 17 and related IFRICs.

The accounting for lease transactions involves a number of complexities originating partly from the range of alternative structures that are available to the parties. Leases can transfer some or all of the risks normally associated with ownership. The financial reporting challenge under IFRS is to establish the economic substance of the transaction in absence of "bright lines" for guidance as is currently available under Canadian GAAP.

Assessing the Impact on Financial Statements

Since IFRS and Canadian GAAP requirements for dealing with leases are quite similar, adopting IFRS might not have much of an impact. If some leases accounted for as operating leases under Canadian GAAP need to be reclassified as capital leases, an additional asset will have to be recognized, along with the related debt. As for the statement of earnings, lease costs will be replaced by depreciation and interest expense.

Initial Adoption of IFRS

Canadian companies applying IAS 17 will need to review the way they classify leases into either operating or finance leases, to be sure they respect the less specific guidelines prescribed by IAS 17. This could result in more leases having to be classified as finance leases. Moreover, some arrangements not recognized as leases under Canadian GAAP may need to be reclassified as leases under IFRS. All leases must be reviewed and, to determine if a change in classification is required, it is necessary to go back to the inception of the lease. This analysis could result in some re-classification of arrangements into either finance or operating leases (and, possibly, recognition of some arrangements as leases for the first time).

Given the practical difficulties in going back many years to determine whether an arrangement contains a lease, IFRIC 4 includes transitional provisions that would limit the analysis to the facts and circumstances existing at the date of implementing IFRIC 4. IFRS 1 includes a specific exemption from retrospective restatement of IFRIC 4, however there may still be an impact on transition for Canadian companies because of the effective date of EIC-150. Although IFRIC 4 is essentially converged with EIC-150, Canadian entities may need to review arrangements that are still effective as of the transition date that have been grandfathered under EIC-150, which required application to new or modified arrangements after the beginning of an entity's next reporting period beginning after December 2004 (see developments under the 'Keep Posted' section below or further details regarding additional proposed relief on this exemption).

If a Canadian entity has to capitalize some leases that were previously accounted for as operating leases, the opening balance sheet figures for finance leases will have to be calculated as if the new rules had been in place all along. IAS 17 does, however, address the possible impracticality of the retrospective examination of property leases in view of separating land and building, which requires estimating the fair values of the two elements.

Keep Posted

In September 2008, the IASB issued an Exposure Draft for additional exemptions offered to first-time adopters for comments to be received by January 23, 2009. The Exposure Draft proposes to offer first-time adopters additional relief from having to reassess whether an arrangement contains a lease when the first-time adopter made the same determination under previous GAAP as that required by IFRIC 4 but at a date other than that required by the transitional provisions of that standard. In these cases, the first-time adopter would not be required to reassess that determination upon transition to IFRS.

Chapter 14
Intangible Assets

Standards Discussed in this Chapter[1]

International

IAS 38 – Intangible Assets
IFRS 3 – Business Combinations
SIC-32 – Intangible Assets – Web Site Costs
IFRIC 3 - Emission Rights (withdrawn)

Canadian

CICA 3064 – Goodwill and Intangible Assets
CICA 1581 – Business Combinations
CICA 3831 – Non-Monetary Transactions
CICA 3475 – Disposal of Long-Lived Assets and Discontinued Operations
EIC-137 – Recognition of customer relationship intangible assets acquired in a business combination

INTRODUCTION

Entities reporting intangible assets in their financial statements, whether acquired externally or generated internally, must apply IAS 38 and CICA 3064. In addition, such entities must apply IFRS 3 and CICA 1581 when the acquisition is part of a business combination.

CICA 3064, which is effective for annual periods beginning on or after October 1, 2008 is based on IAS 38. CICA 3064 replaced CICA 3062, *Goodwill and Other Intangible Assets* and CICA 3450, *Research and Development Costs*.

Both IAS 38 and CICA 3064:

• reinforce the principles-based approach to the recognition of an asset;

• clarify the application of the matching principle to eliminate the practice of recognizing amounts on the statement of financial position that do not meet the definition of an asset;

• provide guidance for the recognition of internally generated intangible assets, including those resulting from research and development activities.

Even though IAS 38 and CICA 3064 requirements are converged, differences in the reporting of intangible assets under Canadian GAAP and IFRS arise because:

• IAS 38 requires more extensive disclosure than CICA 3064; and

• IAS 38 and other IFRS measurement requirements (for example under IAS 36, *Impairment of* Assets) diverge from corresponding ones under Canadian GAAP.

---

1 IAS 38 was amended in May 2008 as part of the annual improvements to IFRSs. IFRS 3, *Business Combinations* was also revised in 2008, and the new version was used in this chapter's discussion.

Entities with significant intangible assets must carefully examine IFRS requirements. To help in that examination, this chapter discusses the following topics:

- scope;
- key definitions;
- recognition:
  - general considerations,
  - intangible assets acquired in a business combination,
  - internally generated intangible assets,
  - subsequent expenditures related to intangible assets,
  - expenditures prohibited from being recognized as intangible assets;
- initial measurement:
  - separately acquired intangible assets,
  - intangible assets acquired as part of a business combination,
  - intangible assets acquired by way of a government grant,
  - intangible assets acquired by way of an exchange,
  - internally generated intangible assets;
- subsequent measurement:
  - cost model,
  - revaluation model;
- amortization:
  - useful life,
  - finite life,
  - indefinite life,
  - residual value;
- impairment;
- retirements and disposals;
- disclosures.

IMPACT ON FINANCIAL STATEMENTS

Although applying IFRS and Canadian GAAP requirements to intangible assets should result in the recognition of similar intangible assets, the amount reported in financial statements would not be the same as:

- IAS 38 allows entities to measure certain intangible assets using the revaluation model. An entity holding such intangible assets and electing to use this model would report increased volatility in other comprehensive income (and, possibly, earnings) and in its assets. Note, however, that the revaluation model is not expected to be used frequently by Canadian entities adopting IFRS as IAS 38 restricts its application to intangible assets that are exchanged on an active market.

- Canadian entities adopting IFRS will have to use different rules when measuring intangible assets. These rules include those concerning impairment of intangible assets and goodwill (IAS 36 and CICA 3064 – see Chapter 4) and capitalization of borrowing costs (there is no Canadian equivalent to IAS 23, *Borrowing Costs* – see Chapter 19).

ANALYSIS OF RELEVANT ISSUES
Scope
The objective of IAS 38 is to prescribe the accounting treatment for intangible assets that are not dealt with specifically in another Standard. IAS 38 scopes out the following assets:

- financial assets within the scope of IAS 32, *Financial Instruments: Presentation*. The recognition and measurement of some financial assets are covered by IAS 27, *Consolidated and Separate Financial Statements*, IAS 28, *Investments in Associates* and IAS 31, *Interests in Joint Ventures*;

- exploration and evaluation assets (see IFRS 6, *Exploration for and Evaluation of Mineral Resources*);

- expenditures on the development and extraction of, minerals, oil, natural gas and similar non-regenerative resources;

- intangible assets held for sale in the ordinary course of business within the scope of inventories (IAS 2, *Inventories*) and construction contracts (IAS 11, *Construction Contracts*);

- deferred tax assets (IAS 12, *Income Taxes*);

- leases that are within the scope of IAS 17, *Leases*;

- assets arising from employee benefits (IAS 19, *Employee Benefits*);

- goodwill acquired in a business combination (IFRS 3, *Business Combinations*);

- deferred acquisition costs and intangible assets arising from an insurer's contractual rights under insurance contracts within the scope of IFRS 4, *Insurance Contracts*. IFRS 4 sets out specific disclosure requirements for those deferred acquisition costs but not for those intangible assets. Therefore, the disclosure requirements in this standard apply to those intangible assets;

- non-current intangible assets classified as held for sale (or included in a disposal group that is classified as held for sale) in accordance with IFRS 5, *Non-current Assets Held for Sale and Discontinued Operations.*

Under Canadian GAAP:

- CICA 3063 applies to impairment of non-monetary long-lived assets, including intangible assets with finite useful lives.

- CICA 3064 prescribes standards for impairment of goodwill and indefinite life intangible assets.

- CICA 1581 applies to the accounting for business combinations, including the initial recognition of goodwill.

The table below presents some observations related to the scope of IFRS and Canadian GAAP in particular circumstances involving intangible assets:

Particular Circumstances involving Intangible Assets	Observations Related to Scope
Goodwill	IAS 38 specifically excludes from its scope goodwill acquired in a business combination whereas CICA 3064 specifies that it applies to goodwill subsequent to initial recognition. A major difference exists in the fact that CICA 3064 discusses the accounting for impairments related to goodwill and intangible assets whereas, under IFRS, impairments are dealt with in IAS 36 – and the requirements differ significantly (see Chapter 4).
Intangible assets contained in: • an asset with physical substance such as a disk (computer software) • a legal document (licence or patent) • a film (movie)	To determine whether an asset that incorporates both intangible and tangible elements should be accounted for under IAS 16, *Property, Plant and Equipment* or as an intangible asset under IAS 38, judgment is required to assess which element is more significant. Below are common examples of circumstances where such judgement is required: • computer software for a computer-controlled machine tool that cannot operate without that specific software would be an integral part of property, plant and equipment, • software (e.g. operating system of a computer) is treated as an intangible asset (is not an integral part of the related hardware), • knowledge embodied in asset with physical substance (e.g., a prototype), the physical element of the asset is secondary to its intangible component.
Research and development activities resulting in an asset with physical substance (e.g. a prototype)	Development of knowledge is an intangible asset covered by IAS 38 even though it may result the physical element of an asset which would be considered secondary to its intangible component.
Finance lease	Underlying asset of a finance lease may be either tangible or intangible. After initial recognition, a lessee accounts for an intangible asset held under a finance lease in accordance with IAS 38. Rights under licensing agreements for items such as motion picture films, video recordings, plays, manuscripts, patents and copyrights are excluded from the scope of IAS 17 and are, instead, within the scope of IAS 38.
Specialized industry expenditures (exploration for, or development and extraction of, oil, gas and mineral deposits, insurance contracts)	IAS 38 does not apply to expenditures on such activities and contracts but would apply to other intangible assets used (such as computer software) and other expenditure incurred (such as start-up costs) in extractive industries or by insurers.

Illustrative Disclosure:

Extract 14(1) – Scoping application related to intangible and tangible assets

Vodafone Group Plc (AR 2007), page 96 **2. Significant accounting policies (in part)** **Intangible assets (in part)** **Computer software (in part)** Software integral to a related item of hardware equipment is accounted for as property, plant and equipment.

Commentary: This extract illustrates the company's policy for accounting for software as part of property, plant and equipment under IAS 16 and not as intangible assets under IAS 38 because this intangible component is integral to the hardware.

Key Definitions

The table below presents key concepts and definitions when examining requirements related to intangible assets:

Term	Definition
Intangible asset	An identifiable non-monetary asset without physical substance. Encompasses the following characteristics: identifiability and control over future economic benefits.
Class of intangible assets	A grouping of assets of a similar nature and use in an entity's operations. Examples include: brand names; mastheads and publishing titles; computer software; licences and franchises; copyrights, patents and other industrial property rights, service and operating rights; recipes, formulae, models, designs and prototypes; and intangible assets under development.
Identifiability	Exists when an intangible asset: • is separable: is capable of being separated or divided from the entity and sold, transferred, licensed, rented or exchanged either individually or together with a related contract, asset or liability; or • arises from contractual or other legal rights.
Control over a resource (control over future economic benefits)	An entity controls an asset if the entity has the power to obtain the future economic benefits flowing from the underlying resource and to restrict the access of others to those benefits.
Future economic benefits	The future economic benefits flowing from an intangible asset may include revenue from the sale of products or services, cost savings, or other benefits resulting from the use of the asset by the entity.
Cost	The amount of cash or cash equivalents paid or the fair value of other consideration given to acquire an asset at the time of its acquisition or construction, or, when applicable, the amount attributed to that asset when initially recognised in accordance with the specific requirements of other IFRSs.
Active market	A market in which all of the following conditions exist: • the items traded in the market are homogeneous; • willing buyers and sellers can normally be found at any time and prices are available to the public.
Research	Original and planned investigation undertaken with the prospect of gaining new scientific or technical knowledge and understanding.
Development	The application of research findings or other knowledge to a plan or design for the production of new or substantially improved materials, devices, products, processes, systems or services before the start of commercial production or use.
Probable	More likely than not.

Recognition

General Considerations

IAS 38 (CICA 3064) requires an entity to recognize an intangible asset if, and <u>only if</u>:

• it is probable that the expected future economic benefits that are attributable to the asset will flow to the entity; and

• the cost of the asset can be measured reliably.

This requirement applies whether an intangible asset is acquired externally, or generated internally.

IAS 38 includes additional guidance for internally generated intangible assets by requiring the expensing of expenditures (when incurred) that do not meet both the definition and the recognition criteria, for the recognition of an intangible asset. In case of business acquisition, such expenditures would often form part of the amount attributed to goodwill.

The table below presents certain general factors or considerations that are taken into account when establishing whether an intangible asset should be recognized:

Factor or Considerations	Observation
Identifiability	This is a significant factor for distinguishing an intangible asset from goodwill.
Control	This is most easily demonstrated when an entity possesses legal rights that are enforceable in a court of law. For example, a company owning a trademark to sell products using a recognizable brand name can easily demonstrate that, as the owner of the trademark, it has the legal right to use the brand name in the sale of its products. In contrast, intangible assets arising from technical knowledge of staff, customer loyalty, long-term training benefits, etc., will have difficulty demonstrating the presence of control in spite of expected future economic benefits to be derived from them or to demonstrate that the entity can prevent others from obtaining access to the future economic benefits expected to be generated by these assets since for example, trained employees could leave their current employment and move on to other employers at any time.
Probable future economic benefits	The term "probable" is not defined in IAS 38. In some cases, it is easy to meet this criteria, such as when intangible assets are separately acquired or acquired as part of a business combination. In these cases, the price paid or fair value reflects market expectations about the probability that the future economic benefits associated with the intangible asset will flow to the acquirer. Therefore, the probability recognition criterion is always considered to be satisfied for separately acquired intangible assets, and those acquired as part of a business combination.
Reliable measurement of cost	This can be demonstrated when an entity purchases a particular intangible asset for a consideration in the form of cash or other monetary assets. Fair values of identifiable intangible assets acquired in a business combination can normally be measured with sufficient reliability for those assets to be recognized separately from goodwill. The effects of uncertainty resulting from a range of possible outcomes with different probabilities are reflected in the measurement of the asset's fair value. The IASB concluded that the existence of such a range does not demonstrate an inability to measure fair value reliably.

Illustrative Disclosure:

Extract 14(2) – Intangible assets that do not meet the definition of an intangible asset

> **Xstrata Plc (AR 2007), page 163**
> **7. Acquisitions (in part)**
> Included in this goodwill are certain intangible assets that cannot be individually separated or reliably measured from the acquisition due to their nature. These items include the expected value of synergies and an assembled workforce.

Commentary: This extract shows the accounting for typical intangible assets that do not meet the definition of intangible assets and, therefore, cannot be recognized separately from goodwill, such as the value of operational synergies and an assembled workforce.

Intangible Assets Acquired in a Business Combination

Much like Canadian GAAP, IAS 38 and IFRS 3 require an acquirer to recognize, at the acquisition date, separately from goodwill, an intangible asset of the acquiree, irrespective of whether the acquiree recognized the asset before the business combination. For example, an acquirer would recognize as an asset, separately from goodwill, an acquiree's in-process research and development project if that project meets the definition of an intangible asset. An acquiree's in-process research and development project meets the definition of an intangible asset when it:

- meets the definition of an asset; and
- is identifiable, i.e., is separable or arises from contractual or other legal rights.

Therefore, although intangible assets must be recognized separately if they meet the criteria above, in practice, the greatest difficulties arise in first detecting them and then, once they have been detected, in determining how to measure their value.

A thorough review of the acquiree's business is the most important step in detecting intangible assets in a business combination. Understanding the business rationale for the combination, the acquiree's business resources and how the acquired business generates revenues provides very useful insights into what its intangible assets might be. It should be possible to explain the acquired business in terms of the resources it uses to generate profits and how these are reflected in the acquiree's assets and liabilities. Some of the procedures that are relevant for identifying intangible asset would include:

- an examination of acquisition project related documentation including purchase agreement, due diligence reports and other current information, both public (such as press releases and websites), and internal (such as legal documents, minutes of board meetings);
- an analysis of possible revisions to business model and purchase agreement to identify intangible assets specifically mentioned, such as a non-compete agreement or use of a brand name or trademark;
- a review of acquiree's official documents and contractual arrangements to identify economic resources such as patents, trademarks and similar rights of use, access or protection.

Illustrative Disclosure:

Extract 14(3) – Significant accounting policy note on the recognition of intangible assets acquired as part of a business combination

---

WPP Group PLC (AR 2007), page 154

Accounting policies (in part)

Goodwill and other intangible assets (in part)

Corporate brand names acquired as part of acquisitions of businesses are capitalised separately from goodwill as intangible assets if their value can be measured reliably on initial recognition and it is probable that the expected future economic benefits that are attributable to the asset will flow to the Group.

Commentary: This extract illustrates the application of the recognition criteria to intangible assets acquired in a business combination. Often, corporate brand names are intangible assets not previously recognized in the books of the acquiree (since they are often internally generated intangible assets specifically prohibited from recognition) and, therefore, need to be detected for the purposes of the purchase price allocation.

Sometimes, detection difficulties arise because an intangible asset acquired in a business combination might be determined to be separable, but only together with a related tangible or intangible asset. For example, it may not be possible to sell a magazine's publishing title separately from a related subscriber database, or a trademark for natural spring water might be tied to a particular spring and cannot be sold separately from that spring. If the individual fair values of the assets in a group are not reliably measurable, IAS 38 specifies that the acquirer must recognize the group of assets as a single asset separately from goodwill. If the individual fair values of the complementary assets are reliably measurable, the acquirer may recognize them as a single asset provided the individual assets have similar useful lives. Although this guidance is not included in CICA 3064, the same guidance exists in the Appendix to CICA 1581.

Although IFRS refer to combining intangible assets in only limited circumstances (as described above), judgment is required to determine the appropriate level of aggregation. This is sometimes referred to as the "unit of account" issue. As no specific guidance exists on determining a unit of account, it is logical to extend the approach set out for brands to other groups of similar assets.

The concept of materiality will often justify treating large groups of similar assets like customer relationships, on a portfolio basis. To determine whether separate identifiable intangible assets may be similar enough to be measured on a combined basis, however, one should consider several factors, such as: the general characteristics of the intangible assets, any related services and product functionality and/or design and other shared features of the intangible assets, similar legal or regulatory conditions that affect the intangible assets, geographical regions or markets and the economic lives of the assets. The consideration of these factors may result in reporting different intangible assets on a combined basis (or even combinations of intangible and tangible assets). It is important to note, however, that identifiable intangible assets should not be combined with goodwill for financial reporting purposes. If similar intangible assets are combined for measurement purposes, they should continue to be amortized and accounted for in the future on the same combined basis.

Illustrative Disclosures:

Extract 14(4) – Detection of intangible assets in a business combination

Xstrata Plc (AR 2007), page 163

7. Acquisitions (in part)

(a) The fair values of identified assets and liabilities acquired have been finalised in 2007. This has resulted in updates to a number of fair values reflected at 31 December 2006.

The main adjustments relate to:

• Intangibles increased after a review to identify such assets was undertaken, and includes long-term feed contracts and rights to a hydroelectricity development project.

Commentary: This extract illustrates the detection of intangible assets subsequent to the initial purchase price allocation in a business combination when a specific review was undertaken to identify such assets.

Extract 14(5) – Intangible assets in a business combination

Stora Enso Oyj (AR 2007), page 122

Note 1 Accounting Principles (in part)

Intangible Assets (in part)

Intangible assets recognised separately from goodwill in acquisitions consist of marketing and customer related or contract and technology-based intangible assets. Typical marketing and customer related assets are trademarks, trade names, service marks, collective marks, certification marks, customer lists, order or production backlogs, customer contracts and the related customer relationships. The contract and technology-based intangible assets are normally licensing and royalty agreements or patented technology and trade secrets such as confidential formulas, processes or recipes. The fair value determination of customer contracts and related relationships is derived from expected retention rates and cash flow over the customers' remaining estimated life time. The value of trademarks is derived from discounted cash flow analysis using the relief from royalty method.

Commentary: This extract illustrates the various types of intangible assets that are often recognized separately from goodwill in a business combination.

Internally Generated Intangible Assets

Internally generated intangible assets refer to expenditures an entity makes in hopes of reaping some future economic benefits. These benefits can include in-process research and development activities or new technical knowledge, or items that can be proven to be useful by adding value to the entity by allowing it to function more efficiently or effectively. For example, the building of an internal distribution mapping system would allow a company to more efficiently plan and deliver products to its customers.

However, it is more difficult to assess whether these criteria are met when applying them to internally generated intangible assets because of problems in:

• establishing whether and when there is an identifiable asset that will generate expected future economic benefits; and

• determining the cost of the asset reliably. In some cases, the cost of generating an intangible asset internally cannot be distinguished from the cost of maintaining or enhancing an entity's internally generated goodwill or of running day-to-day operations.

Canadian companies that invest significantly in the research and/or development of assets, or have large deferred charges capitalized as assets, will find the guidance on internally generated intangible assets to be very relevant. The changes recently introduced by CICA 3064 to harmonize with IAS 38 may have significant impacts on their financial reporting.

IAS 38 specifies an approach to determining whether such costs can qualify for asset recognition. The first step is to classify the expenditures into one of two phases: a research phase or a development phase.

Research activities are not eligible for asset recognition and are expensed as incurred.

Examples of research activities are:

- activities aimed at obtaining new knowledge;
- the search for, evaluation and final selection of, applications of research findings or other knowledge;
- the search for alternatives for materials, devices, products, processes, systems or services; and
- the formulation, design, evaluation and final selection of possible alternatives for new or improved materials, devices, products, processes, systems or services.

Development activities that can be specifically attributed to a product or project in its development phase can qualify for recognition as an asset. An entity may incur costs to develop new products that have not hit the market yet, such as a new model of a product the entity currently sells but with innovative features not yet available in the marketplace. It may also develop products for its own use to enable it to operate more efficiently or in a more productive capacity. For example, it might enhance the design and construction of its own technology to increase production capacity in its warehouse, or increase sales by offering internet sales or customer service options from its website for which it had to incur costs of modifying or building its website.

IAS 38 specifies that expenditures incurred during development (or from the development phase of an internal project) are recognized as an asset only if, an entity can demonstrate all of the following:

1. the technical feasibility of completing the intangible asset so that it will be available for use or sale;
2. its intention to complete the intangible asset and use or sell it;
3. its ability to use or sell the intangible asset;
4. how the intangible asset will generate probable future economic benefits. Among other things, the entity can demonstrate the existence of a market for the output of the intangible asset or the intangible asset itself or, if it is to be used internally, the usefulness of the intangible asset;
5. the availability of adequate technical, financial and other resources to complete the development and to use or sell the intangible asset;
6. its ability to measure reliably the expenditure attributable to the intangible asset during its development.

It is often difficult to demonstrate how an intangible asset will generate probable future economic benefits (the forth criterion above). To do this, IAS 38 requires an entity to assess the future economic benefits to be received from the asset using the principles in IAS 36, *Impairment of Assets*. In defining the recognition criteria of an intangible asset, IAS 38 mentions that an entity would assess the probability of expected future economic benefits using reasonable and supportable assumptions that represent management's best estimate of the set of economic conditions that will exist over the useful life of the asset. IAS 36 further clarifies that, in measuring "value in use" for the purposes of measuring the recoverable amount, an entity:

- bases cash flow projections on reasonable and supportable assumptions that represent management's best estimate of the range of economic conditions that will exist over the remaining useful life of the asset. Greater weight shall be given to external evidence;

- bases cash-flow projections on the most recent financial budgets/forecasts approved by management, but excludes any estimated future cash inflows or outflows expected to arise from future restructurings or from improving or enhancing the asset's performance. Projections based on these budgets/forecasts should cover a maximum period of five years, unless a longer period can be justified;

- estimates cash-flow projections beyond the period covered by the most recent budgets/forecasts by extrapolating the projections based on the budgets/forecasts using a steady or declining growth rate for subsequent years, unless an increasing rate can be justified. This growth rate should not exceed the long-term average growth rate for the products, industries, or country or countries in which the entity operates, or for the market in which the asset is used, unless a higher rate can be justified.

This differs from CICA 3064 where it refers to CICA 3063, *Impairment of Long-Lived Assets* for guidance on determining the future economic benefits to be received from the asset. The guidance for determining recoverability differs from the above where it states that: "Estimates of future cash flows used to test the recoverability of a long-lived asset should include only the future cash flows (cash inflows less associated cash outflows) that are directly associated with, and that are expected to arise as a direct result of, its use and eventual disposition. These cash flows include the principal amount of any liabilities included in the asset group, but not interest that will be recognized as an expense when incurred."

Therefore, depending on the situation, this difference in measurement approach will likely lead to different amounts being computed to substantiate the presence of future economic benefits which, when compared to the carrying amount of the project, can affect the conclusion on whether this criteria is satisfied.

If an asset will generate economic benefits only in combination with other assets, the entity would apply the concept of cash-generating units in IAS 36 (discussed in more detail in Chapter 4).

Availability of resources to complete, use and obtain the benefits from an intangible asset (the fifth criterion above) can be demonstrated by, for example, a business plan showing the technical, financial and other resources needed and the entity's ability to secure those resources. In some cases, an entity demonstrates the availability of external finance by obtaining a lender's indication of its willingness to fund the plan.

An entity's costing systems can often measure reliably the cost of generating an intangible asset internally, such as salaries and other expenditures incurred in securing copyrights or licences or developing computer software (for the purposes of demonstrating criterion 6 above).

Examples of development activities are:

- the design, construction and testing of pre-production or pre-use prototypes and models;

- the design of tools, jigs, moulds and dies involving new technology;

- the design, construction and operation of a pilot plant that is not of a scale economically feasible for commercial production; and
- the design, construction and testing of a chosen alternative for new or improved materials, devices, products, processes, systems or services.

It is important to note that it will be difficult to assess at which point in a development project an entity meets the criteria above to be able to begin capitalizing the costs incurred as an intangible asset. It is important for management to continuously assess the project in accordance with these criteria, as well as to clearly define the indicators that will demonstrate that those criteria have been met. This timing is especially important as capitalization of costs can only begin once <u>all</u> of the recognition criteria are met. It is more likely that, in practice, certain recognition criteria will be met at different phases of a development project and it will become increasingly important for management to recognize the point in the development phase when each of the recognition criteria will be determined to be met.

IAS 38 clarifies how to account for payments to a supplier to construct goods in accordance with a supply contract that gives an entity the right to access those goods. This guidance is not specifically included in CICA 3064. It specifies that, when an entity has received goods or services, it ceases to have the right to receive them. Because the entity no longer has an asset that it can recognize, it recognizes an expense.

IAS 38 and CICA 3064 agree that prepayments for goods or services can be recognized as assets when payments for goods or services are made in advance of receiving those goods or services.

Lastly, under IFRS, SIC 32 provides specific guidance on the accounting for internal expenditures on the development and operation of an entity's own web site for internal or external access, addressing issues such as:

- whether the web site is an internally generated intangible asset subject to the requirements of IAS 38; and
- the appropriate accounting treatment of such expenditures.

It is important to note that SIC 32 does not apply to expenditures on purchasing, developing and operating a website's hardware (e.g., web servers, staging servers, production servers and internet connections). Such expenditures are accounted for under IAS 16. Additionally, when an entity pays an internet service provider for hosting its web site, the expenditure is recognized as an expense under IAS 1.88 and the Framework when the services are received. Lastly, SIC 32 does not apply to expenditures on the development or operation of a web site (or web site software) for sale to another entity. When a web site is leased under an operating lease, the lessor applies the guidance provided by SIC 32. When a web site is leased under a finance lease, the lessee applies SIC 32 after initial recognition of the leased asset. Canadian GAAP provides no specific guidance on accounting for web site development costs following the elimination of EIC-118, *Accounting for costs incurred to develop a web site*[2].

---

2   In addition to EIC-118, the EIC decided in 2008 to withdraw the following two abstracts because it was concerned that they may not be fully consistent with CICA 3064:
   - EIC-33, *Distribution costs of mutual funds paid by special purpose entities*;
   - EIC-86, *Accounting for the costs of a business process re-engineering project*.

Illustrative Disclosure:

Extract 14(6) – Application of IAS 38 to software development costs

Nationwide Building Society (AR 2008), page 55

1 Statement of Accounting Policies (in part)

Intangible assets (in part)

(b) Software

IAS 38 'Intangible Assets' requires the capitalisation of certain expenditure relating to software development costs. Software development costs are capitalised if it is probable that the asset created will generate future economic benefits. Costs incurred to establish technological feasibility or to maintain existing levels of performance are recognised as an expense.

Web costs are capitalised where the expenditure is incurred on developing an income generating website.

Where software costs are capitalised, they are amortised using the straight line method over their estimated useful lives (3 to 5 years). The amortisation periods used are reviewed annually.

Computer application software licences are recognised as intangible fixed assets and amortised using the straight line method over their useful lives.

Commentary: This extract illustrates the application of the principles prescribed by IAS 38, which is consistent with the principles prescribed by SIC 32.

Subsequent Expenditures Related to Intangible Assets

IAS 38 requires that expenditure on an intangible asset, after its purchase, or completion, should be recorded as an expense, when it is incurred, unless:

- these costs will enable the asset to generate future benefits, in excess of its anticipated standard of performance; and

- the expenditure can be measured, and attributed, to the asset.

If these conditions apply, the subsequent expenditure must be added to the cost of the intangible asset.

If expenditure on an intangible item was initially recorded as an expense, in previous interim, or annual financial statements, IAS 38 prohibits the undertaking from recording this expenditure as part of the cost of an asset at a later date.

Note that most subsequent expenditures are likely to maintain the expected future economic benefits embodied in an existing intangible asset rather than meet the definition of a new intangible asset. In addition, it is often difficult to attribute subsequent expenditures directly to a particular intangible asset rather than to the business as a whole. Therefore, only rarely will expenditures incurred after the initial recognition of an acquired intangible asset, or after completion of an internally generated intangible asset, be recognized in the carrying amount of that asset.

Illustrative Disclosure:

Extract 14(7) – Significant accounting policy note on additions to intangible assets

Transnet Ltd (AR 2007), page 158

ACCOUNTING POLICIES (in part)

INTANGIBLE ASSETS AND GOODWILL (in part)

Subsequent expenditure

Subsequent expenditure on capitalised intangible assets is capitalised only when it increases the future economic benefits embodied in the specific asset to which it relates. All other expenditure is expensed as incurred.

Commentary: This extract illustrates the company's policy for capitalizing additions to intangible assets, which is consistent with the requirements of IAS 38.

Expenditures Prohibited from being Recognized as Intangible Assets

IAS 38 and CICA 3064 require that all costs of research to be recorded as an expense, when they are incurred. The table below provides examples of other costs that must be recorded as an expense (when they are incurred) under both standards:

Categories of Expenditures	Accounting Treatment Details
Certain internally generated intangible assets	The following internally generated intangible assets must be expensed: • brands; • mastheads; • publishing titles; • customer lists; • intangible assets arising from research; • selling, administrative and other general overhead expenditure unless this expenditure can be directly attributed to preparing the asset for use; • identified inefficiencies and initial operating losses incurred before the asset achieves planned performance; and • expenditure on training staff to operate the asset.
Internally generated goodwill	Internally generated goodwill must be expensed since it: • does not meet the definition of an identifiable resource controlled by the entity that can be measured reliably at cost, • is not separable nor does it arise from contractual or other legal rights.
Costs not included in the carrying amount of an intangible asset	The following costs incurred in using or redeploying an intangible asset are not included in the carrying amount of that asset (must be expensed): • costs of introducing a new product or service (including costs of advertising and promotional activities); • costs of conducting business in a new location or with a new class of customer (including costs of staff training); • administration and other general overhead costs; • costs incurred while an asset capable of operating in the manner intended by management has yet to be brought into use; • initial operating losses, such as those incurred while demand for the asset's output builds up.
Various (specifically identified)	Even though expenditures below might provide future economic benefits, they do not result in intangible assets (i.e., they are expensed): • start-up costs such as legal and secretarial costs incurred in establishing a legal entity, pre-opening costs, pre-operating costs, unless included in an item of property, plant and equipment in accordance with IAS 16; • expenditures on training activities; • expenditures on advertising and promotional activities (including mail order catalogues); • expenditures on relocating or reorganizing part or all of an entity.

Initial Measurement

An intangible asset is measured initially at cost which is determined differently depending on how it is acquired or derived. The table below summarizes the measurement at initial recognition.

Type of Acquisition	Initial Measurement
Separately acquired intangible assets	At cost, which comprises: (a) its purchase price, including import duties and non-refundable purchase taxes, after deducting trade discounts and rebates; and (b) any directly attributable cost of preparing the asset for its intended use. Examples of directly attributable costs include: (a) costs of employee benefits arising directly from bringing the asset to its working condition; (b) professional fees arising directly from bringing the asset to its working condition; and (c) costs of testing whether the asset is functioning properly.
Intangible assets acquired as part of a business combination	At fair value at the acquisition date in accordance with IFRS 3.
Intangible assets acquired free of charge, or for nominal consideration, by way of a government grant	At fair value or nominal amount plus any expenditure that is directly attributable to preparing the asset for its intended use (in accordance with IAS 20, *Accounting for Government Grants and Disclosure of Government Assistance*). Examples: landing rights, licenses to operate radio or television stations.
Intangible asset acquired in exchange for nonmonetary asset(s)	At fair value. The carrying value of the asset given up is used if the exchange lacks commercial substance or the fair value of neither the asset received nor the asset given up is reliably measurable.
Internally generated intangible asset that qualify for recognition	At cost determined as the sum of expenditure incurred from the date when the intangible asset first meets the recognition criteria. Comprises all directly attributable costs necessary to create, produce, and prepare the asset to be capable of operating in the manner intended by management. Examples of directly attributable costs are: (a) costs of materials and services used or consumed in generating the intangible asset; (b) costs of employee benefits arising from the generation of the intangible asset; (c) fees to register a legal right; (d) amortization of patents and licences that are used to generate the intangible asset; and (e) borrowing costs to the extent eligible in accordance with IAS 23, *Borrowing Costs*.

The following paragraphs analyze further the initial measurement considerations requirements as they relate to different types of acquisitions.

Separately Acquired Intangible Assets

Capitalizing costs in the carrying amount of an intangible asset ceases when the asset is in the condition necessary for it to be capable of operating in the manner intended by management. This represents a bit of a grey area for Canadian preparers as IAS 38 provides guidance on how to account for expenditures on operations required to develop an intangible asset but are not essential for bringing the asset to the condition necessary for it to be capable of operating in the manner intended by management. CICA 3064 does not deal with this issue. The incidental operations re-ferred to may occur before or during the development activities. Because incidental operations are not necessary to bring an asset to the condition necessary for it to be capable of operating in the manner intended by management, the income and re-lated expenses of incidental operations are recognized immediately in profit or loss and are included in their respective classifications of income and expense. IFRS pro-hibit the capitalization of incidental revenue earned during the development period of any capital asset whereas CICA 3061, *Property, Plant and Equipment* requires it. The AcSB decided that this issue is not germane to the recognition of intangible as-sets. Including this provision from IAS 38 in CICA 3064 would have created an incon-sistency with CICA 3061 for the treatment of tangible capital assets. Because the AcSB did not intend to change Canadian practice for measuring tangible capital as-sets in its revision of CICA 3064, it chose not to include this provision in that section. This issue, therefore, represents a difference between Canadian GAAP and IFRS.

Illustrative Disclosure:

Extract 14(8) – Significant accounting policy note on the recognition and measurement of separately acquired intangible assets

> **SAP AG (IFRS Financial Reports 2007), page 87**
> **(3) Summary of Significant Accounting Policies (in part)**
> **Other Intangible Assets**
>
> Purchased intangible assets with finite useful lives are recorded at acquisition cost, amortized on a straight-line basis over their estimated useful life of two to 12 years, and reviewed for impairment when significant events occur or changes in circumstances indicate that the carrying amount of the asset or asset group may not be recoverable. All of our intangible assets, with the exception of goodwill, have estimable useful lives and are therefore subject to amortization.
>
> We capitalize the fair value of acquired identifiable in-process research and development ("in-process R&D"), which represents acquired research and development efforts that have not reached technological feasibility. Amortization for these intangible assets starts when the projects are complete and are taken to the market.

Commentary: This extract illustrates the application of the recognition criteria to separately acquired intangible assets, including in-process R&D. This is an interesting example since it mentions that purchased in-process R&D is capitalized even though it has not reached techno-logical feasibility, which is a requirement for the expenditure to be eligible for capitalization under the criteria of internally generated intangible assets (see discussion below).

Intangible Assets Acquired as Part of a Business Combination

IAS 38 specifies that, when estimates are used to measure an intangible asset's fair value in a business combination, the effect of uncertainty is reflected in the fair value of the intangible asset (using probabilities to measure the uncertainty). CICA 3064 does not have this requirement and, although similar guidance is found in the appen-dix to CICA 1581, that guidance is not as explicit as that found in IFRS. This may repre-sent a difference for Canadian preparers in their initial measurement of intangible assets acquired in a business combination.

IAS 38 includes specific guidance on the determination of fair value which is tailored specifically to the measurement of intangible assets acquired as part of a business combination. CICA 3064 does not provide equivalent guidance. The appendix of CICA 1581 provides guidance on estimating fair value in the general context of valuing a business for the purposes of the accounting for a business combination. Its provisions do not substantially differ from those of IAS 38 although the latter more specifically applies this guidance to intangible assets as set out in the following paragraphs.

IAS 38 provides the following guidance for measuring the fair value of an intangible asset acquired in a business combination:

- Quoted market prices in an active market provide the most reliable estimate of the fair value of an intangible asset. The appropriate market price is usually the current bid price.

- If current bid prices are unavailable, the price of the most recent similar transaction may provide a basis for estimating fair value, provided that there has not been a significant change in economic circumstances between the transaction date and the date at which the asset's fair value is estimated.

- If no active market exists for an intangible asset, its fair value is the amount that an entity would have paid for the asset at the acquisition date in an arm's length transaction between knowledgeable and willing parties, on the basis of the best information available. In determining this amount, an entity considers the outcome of recent transactions for similar assets.

Entities that are regularly involved in the purchase and sale of unique intangible assets may have developed techniques for estimating their fair values indirectly. These techniques may be used for initial measurement of an intangible asset acquired in a business combination if their objective is to estimate fair value and if they reflect current transactions and practices in the industry to which the asset belongs. These techniques include, when appropriate:

- applying multiples reflecting current market transactions to indicators that drive the profitability of the asset (such as revenue, market shares and operating profit) or to the royalty stream that could be obtained from licensing the intangible asset to another party in an arm's length transaction (as in the "relief from royalty" approach); or

- discounting the asset's estimated future net cash flows.

In practice, specific valuation models and techniques have emerged for estimating fair values, or for providing inputs into such estimates. These models and techniques can be grouped into three broad approaches: the market approach, the cost approach and the income approach. The selection of the appropriate approach, technique or combination of techniques depends both on the nature of the asset in question and the availability and reliability of the information available to apply the technique. Three methods of approaching fair value have been most commonly used under IFRS and two of them – the market approach and the income approach – are also commonly used under Canadian GAAP. Therefore, depending on the circumstances and the practical application of these approaches, measurement differences might arise for some intangible assets acquired as part of a business combination on transition to IFRS. See Chapter 5, "Business Combinations," for further discussion and examples on this topic.

Intangible Assets Acquired by Way of a Government Grant

In certain circumstances, entities could obtain intangible assets by way of a form of a government grant. An example of such circumstances concerns schemes introduced by governments (mostly European) subsequent to the signing of Kyoto Protocol in 1997 (which established legally binding targets aimed to reduce emissions of the six main greenhouse gases by at least 5% below 1990 levels over the period 2008-2012)[3].

---

3   The European Emission Trading Scheme, which started in January 2005, is one of the largest company-level, multi-sector cap and trade emissions trading scheme in the world.

In order to achieve Kyoto Protocol target, certain governments introduced the following "cap and trade" scheme:

- overall cap on the amount of emissions that can be released in a specified compliance period is established;

- cap is then allocated to entities by distributing free "allowances to emit" consisting of a right to emit one tonne of CO_2 (or other greenhouse gas);

- allowances can be traded (entities holding allowances in excess of its actual or anticipated emissions could sell them to another entity that requires allowances because of growth in emissions or an inability to make cost-effective reductions in emissions).

Guidance related to emission right raises several issues and consequently IFRIC 3, *Emission Rights* issued in December 2004 required that:

- allowances are an intangible asset;

- the issue of allowances free of charge by government is a government grant; accordingly, the allowances are initially recognized as an intangible asset at fair value and the corresponding entry is a deferred credit;

- during the year, as the entity emits CO_2, a liability is recognized for the obligation to deliver allowances at the end of the year to cover those emissions. This liability is measured at the end of each reporting period by reference to the current market value of the allowances;

- during the year, the entity amortizes the government grant (deferred credit) to profit or loss;

- allowances are derecognised on their sale (if sold into the market) or on their delivery to the government in settlement of the entity's obligation to deliver allowances to cover emissions. If the allowances are traded in an active market they are not amortized.

During 2005, the IASB decided to withdraw IFRIC 3 to undertake a larger project (see future developments and Chapter 15). Canadian GAAP do not contain any guidance that cover specifically intangible asset acquired by way of a government grant.

Illustrative Disclosure:

Extract 14(9) – Significant accounting policy note for intangible assets (emission allowances) acquired by way of a government grant

> **Norsk Hydro ASA (AR 2007), page F10**
>
> **Note 1 Significant accounting policies and reporting entity (in part)**
>
> **Intangible assets (in part)**
>
> **Emission rights** Hydro accounts for government granted and purchased CO_2 emission allowances at nominal value (cost) as an intangible asset. The emission rights are not amortized as they are either settled on an annual basis before year-end (matched specifically against actual CO_2 emissions) or rolled over to cover the next year's emissions; impairment testing is done on an annual basis. Actual CO_2 emissions over the level granted by the government are recognized as a liability at the point in time when emissions exceed the level granted. Any sale of government granted CO_2 emission rights is recognized at the time of sale at the transaction price.

Commentary: This extract illustrates the company's accounting policy choice for the government grant received for its emission allowances, which the company measures at a nominal value as permitted by IAS 20, *Accounting for Government Grants and Disclosure of Government Assistance*. Note that the company has not adopted the now withdrawn IFRIC 3.

Extract 14(10) – IFRS accounting policies and critical accounting estimates note related to intangible assets including emission rights

> **Norsk Hydro ASA (Conversion to International Financial Reporting Standards 2006), page 17 and 18**
>
> **IFRS accounting policies and critical accounting estimates (in part)**
>
> **Intangible assets**
>
> Intangible assets acquired individually or as a group are recorded at fair value when acquired. Intangible assets acquired in a business combination are recognized at fair value separately from goodwill when they arise from contractual or legal rights or can be separated from the acquired entity and sold or transferred. Intangible assets with finite useful lives are amortized on a straight-line basis over their benefit period. Intangible assets determined to have an indefinite useful life are not amortized but are subject to impairment testing on an annual basis.
>
> **Emission rights** Hydro accounts for Norwegian and EU government granted and purchased CO_2 emission allowances at nominal value (cost) as an intangible asset. The emission rights are not amortized as they are either settled on an annual basis before year-end (matched specifically against actual CO_2 emissions) or rolled over to cover the next year's emissions; impairment testing is done on an annual basis. Actual CO_2 emissions over the 95 percent level granted by the government are recognized as a liability at the point in time when emissions exceed the 95 percent level. Any sale of government granted CO2 emission rights is recognized at the time of sale at the transaction price.
>
> **Research and development**
>
> All expenditures on research are expensed as incurred. Development costs are capitalized as an intangible asset at cost when all of the recognition criteria in IAS 38 *Intangible Assets* (IAS 38) are met, it is probable that Hydro will receive a future economic benefit that is attributable to the asset, and the cost can be measured reliably.

Commentary: This extract was obtained from a document prepared by the company aimed to provide a basis for understanding the company's IFRS financial reporting going forward. As the company has adopted IFRS in January 1, 2007, it states that this document should be referred to for additional information in connection with their 2007 quarterly financial reports.

The particular extract above illustrates the company's accounting policy choice for its emission rights received for the government, which the company measures at a nominal value as permitted by IAS 20, *Accounting for Government Grants and Disclosure of Government Assistance*. Note that the company has not adopted all the requirements of the now withdrawn IFRIC 3. Other disclosures included in the extract concern a general note on intangible assets and capitalization of development costs.

Extract 14(11) – Significant accounting policy note for intangible assets including emission allowances and certificates

---

Vattenfall AB (AR 2007), page 87

Note 2 Accounting principles (in part)

Intangible assets: current

Emission allowances

As of 2005, a trading system applies in the EU with the purpose of reducing emissions of the greenhouse gas carbon dioxide. Within the framework of this system, concerned plants have received, without payment or for prices below fair value, so-called emission allowances from the authorities in each country. Sales and purchases of emission allowances are accomplished at applicable exchanges.

Purchased emission allowances are reported as intangible assets under current assets at cost less accumulated impairment losses, while emission allowances that have been received free of charge from the respective countries' authorities are stated at a value of SEK nil. As carbon dioxide is emitted, an obligation arises to deliver emission allowances to the authorities in the respective countries. An expense and a liability are booked only in cases where the emission allowances that were received free of charge do not cover this obligation. This liability is valued in the amount at which it is expected to be settled.

Certificates

With the aim to increase renewable energy sources for electricity generation, Sweden and Poland have so-called certificate systems. Plants included in a system receive, earned free of charge, certificates from the authorities in Sweden and Poland, respectively, in pace with their generation of electricity qualifying for certificates.

Accumulated certificates, earned free of charge, are reported as an intangible asset under current assets at fair value when obtained, whereas purchased certificates are reported at cost less accumulated impairment losses.

When electricity is sold, an obligation arises to deliver certificates to the authorities in the respective countries. This obligation is reported as an expense and as a liability. The liability is valued at the amount at which it is expected to be settled.

Commentary: This extract illustrates the company's accounting policy choice for the government grant received for its emission allowances, which the company measures at a nominal value as permitted by IAS 20, *Accounting for Government Grants and Disclosure of Government Assistance*. As for certificates earned free of charge from government by company's plants, they are reported as an intangible asset under current assets at fair value when obtained. Note the company has adopted some aspects of the now withdrawn IFRIC 3.

Intangible Asset Acquired by Way of an Exchange

IAS 38 includes guidance on the accounting for intangible assets that may be acquired in exchange for non-monetary assets, or a combination of monetary and non-monetary assets. CICA 3064 does not offer similar guidance but Canadian GAAP does address the issue in the general provisions of CICA 3831, *Non-Monetary Transactions*, which do not substantially differ from the guidance in IAS 38.

IAS 38 specifies that, when intangible assets are acquired and the consideration paid is in the form of a non-monetary asset or a combination of monetary and non-monetary assets, the cost of such an intangible asset is measured at fair value unless (a) the exchange transaction lacks commercial substance or (b) the fair value of neither the asset received nor the asset given up is reliably measurable. The acquired asset is measured this way even if an entity cannot immediately derecognize the asset given up. If the acquired asset is not measured at fair value, its cost is measured at the carrying amount of the asset given up.

CICA 3831 specifies that an entity should measure an asset exchanged or transferred in a non-monetary transaction at the more reliably measurable fair value of the asset given up and the fair value of the asset received, unless:

a) the transaction lacks commercial substance;

b) the transaction is an exchange of a product or property held for sale in the ordinary course of business for a product or property to be sold in the same line of business to facilitate sales to customers other than the parties to the exchange;

c) neither the fair value of the asset received nor the fair value of the asset given up is reliably measurable; or

d) the transaction is a non-monetary, non-reciprocal transfer to owners that represents a spin-off or other form of restructuring or liquidation at the carrying amount of the non-monetary assets or liabilities transferred.

If the asset is not measured at fair value due to the criteria above, it should be measured at the carrying amount (after reduction, when appropriate, for impairment) of the asset given up, adjusted by the fair value of any monetary consideration received or given.

The slight difference in CICA 3831 (par. b) above) does not conflict with general IFRS standards because IAS 18, *Revenue* (par. 12) specifies the same accounting treatment for such exchanges. The other difference in CICA 3831 (par. d) above results from the fact that, at present, IFRS do not currently address how an entity should measure distributions to owners acting in their capacity as owners. Because of the significant diversity in practice in how entities measure distributions of non-cash assets, on November 27, 2008, IFRIC 17, *Distribution of Non-Cash Assets to Owners* was issued. The IFRIC, which is effective for annual periods beginning on or after 1 July 2009, clarifies the following:

- a dividend payable should be recognized when the dividend is appropriately authorized and is no longer at the discretion of the entity;

- an entity should measure the dividend payable at the fair value of the net assets to be distributed;

- an entity should recognize the difference between the dividend paid and the carrying amount of the net assets distributed in profit or loss.

IAS 38 specifies that a condition for recognizing an intangible asset is the ability to reliably measure the cost of the asset, which may sometimes be difficult to adhere to when intangible assets are acquired through an exchange of assets having no comparable market transactions. IAS 38 provides guidance on how to meet this condition, which does not differ from the requirements in CICA 3831. It explains that such transactions can be considered "reliably measurable" if (a) the variability in the range of reasonable fair value estimates is not significant for that asset or (b) the probabilities of the various estimates within the range can be reasonably assessed and used in estimating fair value. IAS 38 further clarifies, that when an entity is able to reliably determine the fair value of either the asset received or the asset given up, the fair value of the asset given up is used to measure cost unless the fair value of the asset received is more clearly evident.

Illustrative Disclosure:

Extract 14(12) – Significant accounting policy note on accounting for intangible assets acquired by way of an exchange of assets

> **Norsk Hydro ASA (AR 2007), page F10**
> **Note 1 Significant accounting policies and reporting entity (in part)**
> **Exchanges of nonmonetary assets**
> Nonmonetary transactions that have commercial substance are accounted for at fair value and any resulting gain or loss on the exchange is recognized in the income statement. A nonmonetary exchange has commercial substance if Hydro's future cash flows are expected to change significantly as a result of the exchange. Hydro accounts for certain nonmonetary exchanges of oil and gas related assets at fair value and accounts for certain other nonmonetary exchanges of oil and gas producing assets where Hydro has substantial continuing involvement without recognizing a gain or loss on the exchange.

Commentary: This extract illustrates the accounting policy adopted by the company for exchanges of non-monetary assets, which is consistent with the guidance provided by IAS 38 for the accounting of intangible assets acquired in this way.

Internally Generated Intangible Assets

All qualifying expenditures incurred subsequent to the point in time at which the initial recognition criteria are met must be capitalized. Any costs incurred prior to this point must be expensed as incurred and are not eligible for capitalization at a later date.

Note that costs could include amounts capitalized according to IAS 23, *Borrowing Costs*. Thus the amount initially recognized as intangible assets might differ from the one recorded under Canadian GAAP as the latter do not have equivalent guidance that require capitalization of borrowing costs under certain circumstances as covered by IAS 23. Consequently, depending on an entity's accounting policy under Canadian GAAP, the way such costs are accounted might have to be changed on transition to IFRS (see Chapter 19).

Illustrative Disclosures:

Extracts 14(13)-14(14) – Significant accounting policy for the recognition and measurement of internally generated intangible assets

> **SAP AG (IFRS Financial Reports 2007), page 83**
> **(3) Summary of Significant Accounting Policies (in part)**
> **Research and Development**
> All research and development costs are expensed as incurred. Development is the application of research findings or other knowledge to a plan or design for the production of new or substantially improved products before the start of commercial production or use. Development expenditures are capitalized only if all of the following criteria are met:
> 1. Development cost can be measured reliably,
> 2. The product is technically and commercially feasible,
> 3. Future economic benefits are probable, and
> 4. We intend to complete development and market the product.
>
> We have determined that technological feasibility for our software products is reached shortly before the products are available for sale. Costs incurred after technological feasibility is established are generally not material.

Commentary: This extract illustrates the application of the recognition criteria to internally generated intangible assets and explains at which point in the phase of development the company considers the criteria to be met and the fact that costs are not capitalized after this point since they are not material.

Norsk Hydro ASA (AR 2007), page F10
Note 1 Significant accounting policies and reporting entity (in part)
Intangible assets (in part)

Research and development All expenditures on research are expensed as incurred. Development costs are capitalized as an intangible asset at cost when all of the recognition criteria in IAS 38 *Intangible Assets* (IAS 38) are met. These criteria are when it is probable that Hydro will receive a future economic benefit that is attributable to the asset and when the cost can be measured reliably.

Commentary: This extract illustrates the company's policy for capitalizing costs associated with development costs.

Extract 14(15) – Significant accounting policy application of the measurement principles for internally generated intangible assets

TeliaSonera AB (AR 2007), page 47
Note 4 (Consolidated) Significant Accounting Policies (in part)
Intangible assets, and property, plant and equipment (in part)
***Measurement bases* (in part)**

Other intangible assets are measured at cost, including directly attributable borrowing costs, less accumulated amortization and any impairment losses. Direct external and internal development expenses for new or substantially improved products and processes are capitalized, provided that future economic benefits are probable, costs can be measured reliably and the product and process is technically and commercially feasible. Activities in projects at the feasibility study stage as well as maintenance and training activities are expensed as incurred. Mobile and fixed telecommunication licenses are regarded as integral to the network and the amortization of a license does not commence until the related net- work is ready for use. Intangible assets acquired in a business combination are identified and recognized separately from goodwill where they satisfy the definition of an intangible asset and their fair values can be measured reliably. The cost of such intangible assets is their fair value at the acquisition date. Subsequent to initial recognition, intangible assets acquired in a business combination are measured on the same basis as intangible assets acquired separately.

Commentary: This extract illustrates the application of the measurement principles for internally generated intangible assets. It describes the costs that are capitalized and for which types of products (note that it refers only to products and processes that would meet the recognition principles). It further illustrates the technique of identifying the stages of a project and determining whether the recognition criteria would be met at the various stages. It also describes the point at which amortization begins, which is in line with the requirements of IAS 38 (which are further discussed below).

Extract 14(16) – Application of the recognition and measurement principles to intangible assets that are separately acquired, acquired as part of a business combination and internally generated

---

Unilever (AR on Form 20F 2006), page 132

1 Accounting information and policies (in part)

Intangible assets

On acquisition of group companies, Unilever recognises any specifically identifiable intangible assets separately from goodwill, initially measuring the intangible assets at fair value. Separately purchased intangible assets are initially measured at cost. Finite-lived intangible assets mainly comprise patented and non-patented technology, know-how and software. These assets are capitalised and amortised on a straight-line basis in the income statement over the period of their expected useful lives, or the period of legal rights if shorter, none of which exceeds ten years. Periods in excess of five years are used only where the Directors are satisfied that the life of these assets will clearly exceed that period.

Indefinite-lived intangibles are not amortised, but are subject to review for impairment.

Unilever monitors the level of product development costs against all the criteria set out in IAS 38. These include the requirement to establish that a flow of economic benefits is probable before costs are capitalised. For Unilever this is evident only shortly before a product is launched into the market. The level of costs incurred after these criteria have been met is currently insignificant.

Commentary: This extract illustrates the application of the recognition and measurement principles of intangible assets. It further identifies, for internally generated development costs, the stage at which the costs qualify for recognition and notes that they were not recognized since they were assessed to be insignificant.

Extract 14(17) – Significant accounting policy note regarding acquired intangible assets and internally generated goodwill

---

Xstrata plc (AR 2007), page 150

6. Principal Accounting Policies (in part)

Intangible assets

Purchased intangible assets are recorded at the cost of acquisition including expenses incidental to the acquisition, less accumulated amortisation and any impairment in value. Intangible assets acquired as part of an acquisition of a business are capitalised separately from goodwill if the asset is separable or arises from contractual or legal rights and the fair value can be measured reliably on initial recognition.

Internally generated goodwill is not recognised.

Commentary: This extract illustrates the company's accounting policies for the recognition and measurement of separately acquired intangible assets, those acquired as part of a business combination, as well as their policy for not recognizing internally generated goodwill. All conform to IAS 38.

Subsequent Measurement

Unlike Canadian GAAP, IAS 38 permits an entity to make a choice between the cost model and the revaluation model in accounting for its intangible assets subsequent to initial recognition and measurement.

Cost Model

An intangible asset accounted for using the cost model is carried at its cost less any accumulated amortization and any accumulated impairment losses. This is not substantially different from the cost method currently used by Canadian preparers.

Revaluation Model

An intangible asset accounted for using the revaluation model is carried at a revalued amount, being its fair value at the date of the revaluation less any subsequent accumulated amortization and any subsequent accumulated impairment losses.

The revaluation model may, however, be adopted only if the intangible assets are traded in an active market – which is rare for many intangible assets. Examples of intangible assets that may have an active market are taxi licenses, fishing licenses or production quotas. An active market cannot exist for brands, newspaper mastheads, music and film publishing rights, patents or trademarks, however, because each such asset is unique. Also, although intangible assets are bought and sold, contracts are negotiated between individual buyers and sellers, and transactions are relatively infrequent. For these reasons, the price paid for one asset may not provide sufficient evidence of the fair value of another. Moreover, prices are often not available to the public. Therefore, most intangible assets would not qualify as having an active market.

When a company chooses to use the revaluation model for assets that do have an active market, it also has to account for all of the assets in the intangible asset class using the revaluation model, unless there is no active market for those assets. Where there is no active market for an individual intangible asset within that class, that asset must be carried at cost less accumulated amortization and impairment losses (i.e., the cost model). When the fair value of a revalued intangible asset can no longer be determined by reference to an active market, the carrying amount of the asset becomes the amount of its last revaluation (by reference to its active market at that time) less any subsequent accumulated amortization and any subsequent impairment losses. It is important to note, however, that where a revalued intangible asset no longer has an active market, this change in circumstances may be an indicator that the intangible asset is impaired.

IAS 38 specifies that the revaluation model applies to an intangible asset only after its initial recognition and measurement at cost. The only exception to this rule is where only part of an asset has been recognized because the asset did not meet the recognition criteria until part of the way through the process of developing or acquiring it (similar to a development project where the recognition criterion is only met at a certain phase of development in the middle or at a later stage in the project, when many or most costs have been expensed). Although IAS 38 is clear that any costs expensed up to this point cannot be re-capitalized as assets later on, it does allow the whole asset to be revalued in accordance with the revaluation model and not just the part of the asset represented by the capitalized costs. This means that an element of the revalued amount relates to the costs that have been written off.

The revaluation model may also be applied to an asset acquired by way of government grant and measured on initial recognition at a nominal amount. Revaluations have to be made with sufficient frequency that the carrying amount of the asset does not differ materially from its fair value at the reporting date. Therefore, the frequency of revaluations will really depend on the nature of the assets and the volatility of the markets to which they are referenced. It is important to note that all of the items within a class of intangible assets are revalued simultaneously to avoid selective revaluation of assets and the reporting of amounts in the financial statements representing a mixture of costs and values at different dates.

The revaluation model, as it applies to intangible assets, is not frequently used in practice for many reasons. First, as previously mentioned, many intangible assets do not have an active market. Second, even when an intangible asset happens to have an active market, using the revaluation model requires much more tracking of adjustments, which many find cumbersome and not worthwhile. When an intangible asset is revalued, for example, it still needs to be amortized and any accumulated amortization at the date of the revaluation is either:

- restated proportionately with the change in the gross carrying amount of the asset so that the carrying amount of the asset after revaluation equals its revalued amount and the amount of the adjustment to accumulated amortization forms part of the gain or loss on revaluation; or

- eliminated against the gross carrying amount of the asset and the net amount restated to the revalued amount of the asset.

When an intangible asset's carrying amount increases as a result of a revaluation, the increase is not recognized in profit or loss but is, instead, recognized in other comprehensive income and accumulated in equity under the heading of revaluation surplus. The only time that a revaluation increase is recognized in profit or loss is when it reverses an asset's revaluation decrease previously recognized in profit or loss.

When an intangible asset's carrying amount is decreased as a result of a revaluation, the decrease is recognized in other comprehensive income to the extent of any credit balance in that asset's revaluation surplus. If the decrease exceeds the credit balance in the revaluation surplus, the excess is recognized as an expense in profit or loss.

The cumulative revaluation surplus included in equity may be transferred directly to retained earnings when the surplus is realized when the asset is sold, disposed of, or otherwise retired. Some of the surplus may, however, be realized as an entity uses the asset; in such a case, the amount of the surplus realized is the difference between amortization based on the revalued carrying amount of the asset and amortization that would have been recognized based on the asset's historical cost. The transfer from revaluation surplus to retained earnings is not made through profit or loss but by a reserve transfer.

When selecting the most appropriate model for the subsequent measurement of an intangible asset, it is important to realize that the revaluation model is more onerous than the cost model as it requires regular revaluations, as well as more record keeping to track the revaluation adjustments.

Illustrative Disclosure:

Extract 14(18) – Revaluation method

The Institute of Chartered Accountants in England and Wales (ICAEW) prepared the report *EU Implementation of IFRS and the Fair Value Directive* at the request of, and with funding from, the European Commission (EC). The report's objective is to provide the European Commission with a general analysis of the first year of application of IFRS in the EU so that the DG Internal Market has the necessary information to carry out an evaluation. That evaluation looks at the functioning of the IAS regulation. Another objective of the report is to provide input into discussions of the Accounting Regulatory Committee on how the IAS regulation has worked in practice. Yet another objective is to provide information on the application of the modernized Accounting Directives, especially provisions for fair value accounting in the Fourth Company Law Directive 78/660/EEC as amended by the Fair Value Directive so that the DG Internal Market has the necessary information to carry out a review of these provisions.

Note: The DG Internal Market is The Internal Market and Services Directorate General (DG MARKT). It is one of the Directorate's general and specialized services that make up the European Commission. Its main role is to coordinate the commission's policy on the European Single Market and to seek the removal of unjustified obstacles to trade, in particular in the field of services and financial markets.

EU Implementation of IFRS and the Fair Value Directive Report, page 123

14.5 Intangible assets (in part)

Sample 1 results

No companies use the revaluation model for intangible assets.

EU Implementation of IFRS and the Fair Value Directive Report, page 9

1.4 Approach to the study (in part)

We performed a technical analysis of the IFRS consolidated financial statements of a sample (referred to as Sample 1) of 200 publicly traded companies established across the 25 countries that were EU member states in 2005. The financial statements related to the first financial year starting on or after 1 January 2005. The objectives of our analysis were to:

- assess compliance with IFRS requirements;
- assess whether IFRS were applied consistently across industries, EU markets and member states;
- determine whether there are common application or enforcement issues that need to be addressed in order to achieve more consistent application of IFRS;
- determine whether there are significant issues which require changes to IFRS; and
- carry out technical analysis of selected issues.

Commentary: These extracts illustrate that the application of the revaluation method for intangible assets is extremely rare and no disclosure examples were found to illustrate the application of this method.

Amortization

Amortization is the systematic allocation of the cost (or revalued amount) of an asset, less any residual value, to reflect the consumption over time of the future economic benefits embodied in that asset. Amortization begins when the asset is available for use, i.e., when it is in the location and condition necessary for it to be capable of operating in the manner intended by management; whether it is actually used or not is not relevant. Amortization ceases at the earlier of the date the asset is classified as held for sale (or included in a disposal group that is classified as held for sale) in accordance with IFRS 5 and the date that the asset is derecognized.

The amortization method reflects the pattern in which an entity expects to consume an asset's future economic benefits. If that pattern cannot be determined reliably, the straight-line method is used. The amortization charge for each period is recognized in profit or loss. When an asset's future economic benefits are absorbed in producing other assets the amortization charge constitutes part of the cost of the other asset and is included in its carrying amount, for example, when the amortization of intangible assets used in a production process is included in the carrying amount of inventories (see IAS 2, *Inventories*).

The method of amortization selected should be based on the nature of the asset and its use by the entity. There are three most commonly used methods of amortization:

- the straight-line method;
- the diminishing balance method; and
- the units of production method.

The straight-line method is the most common, not only because it reflects usage based on the time pattern of benefits consumed, which is often most appropriate given the nature of the assets such as licenses and patents, but it is also the default method where the pattern of consumption cannot be reliably determined. The unit of production method is likely to be the most appropriate amortization method for intangible assets associated with depleting resources, for example, a license to extract minerals in the mining industry.

The amortization period and method has to be reviewed at least annually. If an asset's expected useful life is different from previous estimates, the amortization period needs to be changed accordingly. If there has been a change in the expected pattern of consumption of the future economic benefits embodied in the asset, the amortization method should be changed to reflect the changed pattern. Such changes are accounted for as changes in accounting estimates in accordance with IAS 8, *Accounting Policies, Changes in Accounting Estimates and Errors.*

Illustrative Disclosures:

Extracts 14(19)-14 (20) – Application of guidance regarding amortization methods

---

Xstrata plc (AR 2007), page 150

6. Principal Accounting Policies (in part)

Coal export rights

Coal export rights are carried at cost and amortised using a units-of-production method based on the reserves that exist in the location that has access to such rights.

Xstrata plc (AR 2007), pages 150 and 151

6. Principal Accounting Policies (in part)

Software and technology patents

Software and technology patents are carried at cost and amortised over a period of 3 years and 20 years respectively.

Hydroelectricity rights

Hydroelectricity rights acquired in connection with the acquisition of the Falconbridge Group (refer to note 7) have been recorded at fair value at the date of acquisition and will be amortised over the expected life of the operation following the completion of construction.

Long-term feed contract

A long-term feed contract acquired in connection with the acquisition of the Falconbridge Group (refer to note 7) has been recorded at fair value at the date of the acquisition and is being amortised over the remaining contract term.

Commentary: These extracts illustrate the bases the company felt were the most appropriate for reflecting the consumption over time of the future economic benefits embodied in the assets. Also, the policy for the hydroelectricity rights illustrates the application of the guidance that amortization will begin only when an asset is available for use, in this case, when the construction is complete.

Extracts 14(21) – Change in useful life and amortization rate

Xstrata plc (AR 2007), page 197

14. Intangible Assets (in part)

The Group has a 20.91% interest in the service organisation, Richards Bay Coal Terminal Company Limited, acquired in a business combination, through which the shareholders gain access to export markets enabling them to realise higher coal sales prices than in the domestic market. Previously, the directors regarded the right to export coal afforded by the interest in the terminal to have an indefinite life, as the operations utilising the terminal had appropriate reserves (including undeveloped reserves) to allow the use of the terminal for an indefinite period. Further, the land on which the terminal operates is leased on a long-term basis and there has been a history of lease extensions. As outlined in the 2006 financial statements, the directors reassessed whether it was appropriate to treat the export rights as an indefinite life intangible asset in light of the approval of the Goedgevonden Project and determined that it would be appropriate to begin amortisation in 2007 based on a units-of-production method.

Commentary: This extract illustrates the change in the useful life and amortization method of an intangible asset, as well as the factors that led to the determination that a change was necessary.

Useful Life

The useful life is the period that an asset is used by a particular entity. IAS 38 provides much more detailed guidance on determining the useful life of an intangible asset than does CICA 3064. Determining the useful life of an asset establishes the period over which an entity expects the asset to be available for use, or the number of production or similar units the entity can expect to obtain from the asset, which is a key factor in adequately reflecting amortization in profit or loss.

An asset's useful life is not necessarily the same as its economic life. The economic life of an intangible asset is the period during which the asset produces economic benefits, no matter who is using it at the time.

IAS 38 provides examples of the many factors that should be considered in determining the useful life of an intangible asset, which are substantially the same in principle as the factors listed in CICA 3064:

- the entity's expected usage of the asset and whether the asset could be managed efficiently by another management team;
- typical product life cycles for the asset and public information on estimates of useful lives of similar assets that are used in a similar way;
- technical, technological, commercial or other types of obsolescence;
- the stability of the industry in which the asset operates and changes in the market demand for the products or services output from the asset;
- expected actions by competitors or potential competitors;
- the level of maintenance expenditure required to obtain the expected future economic benefits from the asset and the entity's ability and intention to reach such a level;
- the period of control over the asset and legal or similar limits on the use of the asset, such as the expiry dates of related leases; and
- whether the useful life of the asset depends on the useful life of other entity assets.

An intangible asset's useful life should generally not exceed the period of the contractual or other legal rights, but may be shorter depending on how long an entity expects to use the asset. When the terms of the contractual or other legal rights can be renewed, however, the useful life includes the renewal period(s) only if there is evidence to support renewal by the entity without significant cost. This can be demonstrated when:

- there is evidence, possibly based on experience, that the contractual or other legal rights will be renewed. If renewal is contingent on the consent of a third party, this includes evidence that the third party will give its consent;
- there is evidence that any conditions necessary to obtain renewal will be satisfied;
- the entity's renewal cost is not significant when compared with the future economic benefits expected to flow to the entity from renewal.

If the cost of renewal is significant when compared with the future economic benefits expected to flow to the entity from renewal, the renewal cost represents, in substance, the cost to acquire a new intangible asset at the renewal date.

Illustrative Disclosure:

Extract 14(22) – Application of guidance on useful lives and amortization methods

> **Vodafone Group Plc (AR 2007) page 96**
> **2. Significant accounting policies (in part)**
> **Intangible assets (in part)**
> **Licence and spectrum fees**
> Licence and spectrum fees are stated at cost less accumulated amortisation. The amortisation periods range from 3 to 25 years and are determined primarily by reference to the unexpired licence period, the conditions for licence renewal and whether licences are dependent on specific technologies. Amortisation is charged to the income statement on a straight-line basis over the estimated useful lives from the commencement of service of the network.

Commentary: This extract illustrates the consideration of renewals in the determination of the useful lives of the license and spectrum fees. It also illustrates the selection of the straight-line method as an appropriate method given the nature of the intangible assets and how the company expects to consume their future economic benefits.

IAS 38 explains in greater detail than does CICA 3064 the approach to take when dealing with useful asset life and amortization. It specifies that, in establishing the useful life of an intangible asset, the first step is to determine whether the intangible asset has a finite or indefinite life.

Finite-life intangible assets are amortized while indefinite-life intangible assets are not amortized.

Finite Life

When the useful life is determined to be finite, the length of, or number of production or similar units constituting that useful life is assessed. The depreciable amount of an intangible asset with a finite life is amortized on a systematic basis over its useful life.

Indefinite Life

A useful life is determined to be indefinite when, based on an analysis of all of the relevant factors, there is no foreseeable limit to the period over which the asset is expected to generate net cash inflows for the entity. An indefinite useful life does not mean that an asset is expected to generate net cash inflows forever but, rather, for an as yet undetermined amount of time. The useful life of an intangible asset reflects only that level of future maintenance expenditure required to maintain the asset at its standard of performance assessed at the time of estimating the asset's useful life, and the entity's ability and intention to reach such a level. A conclusion that the useful life of an intangible asset is indefinite should not depend on planned future expenditure in excess of that required to maintain the asset at that standard of performance. Normally, only mature products and brand names would be considered to have an indefinite life. While an intangible asset may not currently have an indefinite life, the passage of time and more evidence could lead to a reassessment of the useful life and result in a conclusion that the life has changed to indefinite. For example, an acquired brand name that has been in the market for only a few years would not likely have an indefinite life but, after a longer history of stable cash flows, the brand name may be determined to have an indefinite life. On such a determination, the unamortized carrying amount of the asset, if any, would cease to be amortized.

Illustrative Disclosures:
Extracts 14(23) – Determination of useful lives

Unilever (AR on Form 20-F 2006), page 153
9 Goodwill and intangible assets (in part)

Indefinite-lived intangible assets principally comprise those trademarks for which there is no foreseeable limit to the period over which they are expected to generate net cash inflows. These are considered to have an indefinite life, given the strength and durability of our brands and the level of marketing support. Brands that are classified as indefinite have been in the market for many years, and the nature of the industry we operate in is such that brand obsolescence is not common, if appropriately supported by advertising and marketing spend. Finite-lived intangible assets, which primarily comprise patented and non-patented technology, know-how, and software, are capitalised and amortised in operating profit on a straight-line basis over the period of their expected useful lives, none of which exceeds ten years. The level of amortisation for finite-lived intangible assets is not expected to change materially over the next five years.

Commentary: This extract illustrates why the company determined the trademarks and brands to have indefinite useful lives after considering the strength and durability of the brands and the level of marketing support, as well as their histories and the nature of the industry. It further describes the useful lives of the finite-life intangible assets, explaining how they were determined to be such, and states that finite-life intangible assets are capitalized and amortized on a straight-line basis in the income statement over the period of their expected useful lives, or the period of legal rights if shorter, none of which exceeds 10 years. Periods in excess of five years are used only where the directors are satisfied that the life of these assets will clearly exceed that period. This illustrates the factors that management considered in the determination of useful lives.

Extract 14(24) – Indefinite lived intangible assets

WPP Group PLC (AR 2007), page 154
Accounting policies (in part)
Goodwill and other intangible assets (in part)

Certain corporate brands of the Group are considered to have an indefinite economic life because of the institutional nature of the corporate brand names, their proven ability to maintain market leadership and profitable operations over long periods of time and the Group's commitment to develop and enhance their value. The carrying value of these intangible assets is reviewed at least annually for impairment and adjusted to the recoverable amount if required.

Commentary: This extract explains why the company determined the corporate brands to have indefinite useful lives, which included considering the maturity of the brands over the company's long history of profitability. It indicated that these assets are expected to generate net cash inflows for an as yet undetermined period of time.

Residual Value

The residual value amount plays a significant role in determining the ultimate annual charge for amortization that will go through profit or loss. This amount is, therefore, at risk of manipulation for the purposes of earnings management. The IASB has clearly stated that the residual value of an intangible asset with a finite useful life is assumed to be zero unless the following criteria are met:

*   a third party has made a commitment to purchase the asset at the end of its useful life; or

*   there is an active market for the asset and:

    o   residual value can be determined by reference to that market, and

    o   it is probable that such a market will exist at the end of the asset's useful life.

A residual value other than zero implies that an entity expects to dispose of the intangible asset before the end of its economic life. IAS 38 includes the requirement for assuming that the residual value of an intangible asset is zero unless the above criteria are met as a means of preventing entities from circumventing the requirement to amortize all intangible assets by claiming that the residual value of such assets was equal to or greater than their carrying amount. Using that strategy, an entity could avoid amortizing such assets, even though their useful lives are finite. This issue will likely be addressed as part of a forthcoming project on intangible assets.

An estimate of an asset's residual value is based on the amount recoverable from disposal using prices prevailing at the date of the estimate for the sale of a similar asset that has reached the end of its useful life and has operated under conditions similar to those in which the asset will be used.

The residual value is reviewed at least at each financial year end. This requirement is not specified in CICA 3064 and, in practice, this amount is rarely reviewed annually. Depending on the significance of the amount, this change in practice may increase earnings volatility for Canadian preparers who are not used to reassessing this amount so frequently and, therefore, might experience changes in estimates that may provoke more frequent impairment testing.

A change in an asset's residual value is accounted for as a change in an accounting estimate in accordance with IAS 8, *Accounting Policies, Changes in Accounting Estimates and Errors*.

Impairment

The most significant difference between CICA 3064 and IAS 38 lies in the fact that CICA 3064 prescribes guidance for the recognition and measurement of impairment losses on intangible assets and goodwill, whereas IAS 38 refers to IAS 36 for guidance on the impairment of these assets. The IFRS approach to impairment is significantly different than the Canadian GAAP approach; impairments are likely to be experienced more frequently under IFRS than under Canadian GAAP. The details of these differences are further discussed in Chapter 4 and readers should refer to this chapter for additional discussion on this topic and how it relates to intangible assets.

Retirements and Disposals

IAS 38 provides guidance on the accounting for the retirement and/or disposal of intangible assets; CICA 3064 does not offer equivalent guidance. CICA 3475, *Disposal of Long-Lived Assets and Discontinued Operations* does, however, address similar issues.

IAS 38, consistent with IAS 16, requires the derecognition of an intangible asset:

- on disposal; or
- when no future economic benefits are expected from its use or disposal.

CICA 3475 specifies that long-lived assets (which include intangible assets) to be disposed of other than by sale should continue to be classified as held and used until disposed of. A long-lived asset to be abandoned is considered to be disposed of when it ceases to be used. A long-lived asset to be distributed to owners in a spin-off is considered to be disposed of when it is distributed. Assets to be disposed of by sale should be classified as held for sale when specified criteria are met. Therefore, although CICA 3064 does not specifically address the topic of retirements and disposal as IAS 38 does, Canadian GAAP has similar provisions in CICA 3475 and, in practice, asset retirement and disposals should not lead to significant accounting differences upon changeover to IFRS.

The gain or loss arising from the derecognition of an intangible asset in accordance with IAS 38 should be determined as the difference between the net disposal proceeds, if any, and the carrying amount of the asset. Although CICA 3064 does not offer similar guidance, in practice, the treatment under Canadian GAAP would likely be the same.

IAS 38 further specifies that, when an intangible asset is derecognized, the resulting gain or loss is recognized in profit or loss (unless IAS 17 requires otherwise on a sale and leaseback). Gains are not permitted to be classified as revenue. Canadian GAAP does not contradict this guidance.

Unlike Canadian GAAP, IAS 38 also specifically addresses accounting for replacement parts. It states that an entity is not only required to recognize, in the carrying amount of an asset, the cost of a replacement for part of an intangible asset, it also has to derecognize the carrying amount of the replaced part. IAS 38 also says that, when it is not practicable for an entity to determine the carrying amount of the replaced part, it may use the cost of the replacement as an indication of what the cost of the replaced part was at the time it was acquired or internally generated.

IAS 38 continues to provide more detailed guidance than Canadian GAAP, stating that the consideration receivable on disposal of an intangible asset is recognized initially at its fair value. If payment for the intangible asset is deferred, the consideration received is recognized initially at the cash price equivalent. The difference between the nominal amount of the consideration and the cash price equivalent is recognized as interest revenue in accordance with IAS 18, *Revenue*, reflecting the effective yield on the receivable. Similar results would be obtained under Canadian GAAP by applying the requirements of CICA 3855, *Financial Instruments — Recognition and Measurement*.

Amortization of an intangible asset with a finite useful life does not cease when the intangible asset is no longer used, unless the asset has been fully depreciated or is classified as held for sale (or included in a disposal group that is classified as held for sale) in accordance with IFRS 5. This is consistent with the provisions of CICA 3475 but is not specifically stated in CICA 3064.

Disclosures

As the table below shows, IAS 38 requires more extensive disclosures for each class of intangible assets, distinguishing between internally generated intangible assets and other intangible assets (Canadian GAAP does not always require this distinction between internally generated intangible assets and other intangible assets; where this distinction is required, it is specifically stated below):

IAS 38	Canadian GAAP
Whether the useful lives are indefinite or finite and, if finite, the useful lives or the amortization rates used.	This requirement is the same under Canadian GAAP, although it is not specifically stated in CICA 3064 in the same way.
The amortization methods used for intangible assets with finite useful lives.	This requirement is the same.
The gross carrying amount and any accumulated amortization (aggregated with accumulated impairment losses) at the beginning and end of the period.	This requirement is the same.
The line item(s) of the statement of comprehensive income in which any amortization of intangible assets is included.	This requirement does not exist.
A reconciliation of the carrying amount at the beginning and end of the period showing: (i) additions, indicating separately those from internal development, those acquired separately and those acquired through business combinations;	(i) This disclosure requirement is less specific since CICA 3064 requires disclosure of the aggregate amount of intangible assets that were acquired and, separately, those that were developed during the period (business combinations are not mentioned, also a beginning and end of period reconciliation is not specified).
(ii) assets classified as held for sale, or included in a disposal group classified as held for sale, in accordance with IFRS 5 and other disposals;	(ii) Similar disclosure is required by CICA 3475.
(iii) increases or decreases during the period resulting from revaluations (adjustments made under paragraphs 75, 85 and 86 of IAS 38) and from impairment losses recognized or reversed in other comprehensive income in accordance with IAS 36 (if any);	(iii) Since the revaluation model is not recognized, this requirement does not exist.
(iv) impairment losses recognized in profit or loss during the period in accordance with IAS 36 (if any);	(iv) Similar disclosure is required by CICA 3064.
(v) impairment losses reversed in profit or loss during the period in accordance with IAS 36 (if any);	(v) Since reversals of impairment losses are not recognized, this requirement does not exist.
(vi) any amortization recognized during the period;	(vi) This requirement is the same.
(vii) net exchange differences arising on the translation of the financial statements into the presentation currency, and on the translation of a foreign operation into the presentation currency of the entity; and	(vii) This requirement does not exist.
(viii) other changes in the carrying amount during the period.	(viii) This requirement does not exist.
The carrying amount of an intangible asset assessed as having an indefinite useful life and the reasons supporting the assessment of an indefinite useful life. In giving these reasons, an entity must describe the factor(s) that played a significant role in determining that the asset has an indefinite useful life.	Although the carrying amount has to be disclosed, the reasons supporting the assessment of an indefinite useful life are not required disclosure.
A description, the carrying amount and remaining amortization period of any individual intangible asset that is material to an entity's financial statements.	This is not specifically required by CICA 3064.

IAS 38	Canadian GAAP
For intangible assets acquired by way of a government grant and initially recognized at fair value: (i) the fair value initially recognized for these assets; (ii) their carrying amount; and (iii) whether they are measured after recognition under the cost model or the revaluation model.	This is not discussed in CICA 3064.
The existence and carrying amounts of intangible assets whose title is restricted and the carrying amounts of intangible assets pledged as security for liabilities.	This is not specifically discussed in CICA 3064.
The amount of contractual commitments for the acquisition of intangible assets.	This is not specifically discussed in CICA 3064 but is required under CICA 3280, *Contractual Obligations*.
If intangible assets are accounted for at revalued amounts, an entity is required to disclose the following:	
By class of intangible assets: (i) the effective date of the revaluation; (ii) the carrying amount of revalued intangible assets; and (iii) the carrying amount that would have been recognized had the revalued class of intangible assets been measured after recognition using the cost.	
The amount of the revaluation surplus that relates to intangible assets at the beginning and end of the period, indicating the changes during the period and any restrictions on the distribution of the balance to shareholders.	Since the revaluation model is not recognized, this requirement does not exist.
The methods and significant assumptions applied in estimating the assets' fair values.	
For research and development expenditures, the following additional disclosure is required:	
The aggregate amount of research and development expenditure recognized as an expense during the period.	This is not specifically required by CICA 3064.

Illustrative Disclosures:

Extract 14(25) – Application of the disclosure requirements

> **SAP AG (IFRS Financial Reports 2007), page 87**
> **(3) Summary of Significant Accounting Policies (in part)**
> **Other Intangible Assets**
>
> Purchased intangible assets with finite useful lives are recorded at acquisition cost, amortized on a straight-line basis over their estimated useful life of two to 12 years, and reviewed for impairment when significant events occur or changes in circumstances indicate that the carrying amount of the asset or asset group may not be recoverable. All of our intangible assets, with the exception of goodwill, have estimable useful lives and are therefore subject to amortization.
>
> We capitalize the fair value of acquired identifiable inprocess research and development ("in-process R&D"), which represents acquired research and development efforts that have not reached technological feasibility. Amortization for these intangible assets starts when the projects are complete and are taken to the market.

SAP AG (IFRS Financial Reports 2007), pages 106-107

(16) Goodwill/Intangible Assets (in part)

€ millions	Goodwill	Software and database licenses	Acquired technology	Other intangibles	Total
Purchase cost					
1/1/2007	1,091	202	215	38	1,546
Exchange rate differences	- 80	- 1	- 12	- 5	- 98
Additions from business combination	517	0	83	90	690
Other additions	0	65	0	0	65
Retirements/disposals	0	- 2	0	- 2	- 4
Reclassifications to Assets held for sale	- 7	0	0	0	- 7
12/31/2007	1,521	264	286	121	2,192
Accumulated amortization					
1/1/2007	97	128	52	11	288
Exchange rate differences	- 2	- 1	- 1	0	- 4
Additions	0	26	45	10	81
Retirements/disposals	0	- 2	0	- 2	- 4
Reclassifications to Assets held for sale	0	0	0	0	0
12/31/2007	95	151	96	19	361
Carrying value 12/31/2007	**1,426**	**113**	**190**	**102**	**1,831**
Weighted average amortization period in years	N/A	3	5.2	7	5.3
Purchase cost					
1/1/2006	740	160	194	25	1,119
Exchange rate differences	- 50	- 1	- 13	- 3	- 67
Additions from business combination	401	1	120	16	538
Other additions	0	52	0	0	52
Retirements/disposals	0	- 11	- 85	- 1	- 97
Reclassifications	0	1	0	0	1
12/31/2006	1,091	202	216	37	1,546
Accumulated amortization					
1/1/2006	100	124	109	7	340
Exchange rate differences	- 3	- 1	- 8	- 1	- 13
Additions	0	16	36	6	58
Retirements/disposals	0	- 11	- 85	- 1	- 97
Reclassifications	0	0	0	0	0
12/31/2006	97	128	52	11	288
Carrying value 12/31/2006	**994**	**74**	**164**	**26**	**1,258**

All intangible assets except for goodwill have finite useful lives and are therefore subject to amortization. Intangible assets consist of three major asset classes: Software and database licenses, Acquired technology and Other intangibles.

Software and database licenses consist primarily of technology for internal use whereas Acquired technology consists primarily of purchased software to be incorporated into our product offerings and in-process research and development which are amortized over their useful lives. The additions to Software and database licenses in 2007 were individually acquired from third parties, whereas the additions to Acquired technology and Other intangibles primarily result from our business combinations discussed in Note 4.

Other intangibles consist primarily of acquired trademark licenses and customer contracts.

SAP AG (IFRS Financial Reports 2007) (continue)	
The estimated aggregate amortization expense for our intangible assets as at December 31, 2007, for each of the five succeeding years ending December 31, is as follows:	
€ millions	
2008	96
2009	96
2010	71
2011	49
2012	36
thereafter	55
Amortization expenses of intangible assets are included based on usage in Cost of software and software-related services, Cost of professional services and other services, Research and development, Sales and marketing as well as General and administration.	

Commentary: These extracts illustrate the application of the disclosure requirements as follows: intangible assets (other than goodwill) have finite useful lives; those useful lives range from two to 12 years and are amortized using the straight-line method.

The table illustrates the gross carrying amount and any accumulated amortization at the beginning and end of the year. The table also illustrates the reconciliation of the carrying amount at the beginning and end of the year showing:

- additions, indicating separately those acquired separately, and those acquired through business combinations;
- assets classified as held for sale and other disposals;
- amortization expense recognized during the year; and
- net exchange differences.

The disclosure includes a description, the carrying amount and remaining amortization period of intangible assets that are material to the company's financial statements.

FUTURE DEVELOPMENTS

The IASB has a number of projects that relate to intangible assets, some of which has limited scope. We describe these projects below:

Research Work on Intangible Assets

The IASB is still contemplating undertaking an active project on identifiable intangible assets (excluding goodwill) jointly with the FASB but, as of yet, the topic has not been added to the IASB's active agenda. Acknowledging the importance of addressing the accounting issues related to intangible assets, the IASB has decided to continue the research work begun as part of the development of the original agenda proposal until it can once again consider the subject for addition to the active agenda. Although it is now considering determining the scope and a process for continuing this research work, the timing of the completion of the project is still uncertain. Companies with significant internally generated intangible assets should pay particular attention to the progress of this agenda proposal.

Annual Improvement Project

In August 2008, the IASB issued an Exposure Draft proposing additional minor amendments to IAS 38 to further clarify the effect of its decisions in IFRS 3 on the accounting for intangible assets acquired in a business combination. If adopted, these amendments would apply on a prospective basis to annual periods beginning on or after July 1, 2009. It also proposes to clarify the description of valuation techniques entities commonly use when measuring the fair value of intangible assets acquired in a business combination that are not traded in active markets. These amendments would apply on a prospective basis to annual periods beginning on or after January 1, 2010 because retrospective application might require some entities to remeasure fair values associated with previous transactions. This is not appropriate because remeasurement might involve the use of hindsight.

Accounting for Emissions Trading Schemes

As indicated previously, the IASB decided to withdraw IFRIC 3 in 2005. Currently the IASB has a project outstanding on its agenda aimed to develop comprehensive guidance on the reporting of schemes designed to achieve reduction of greenhouse gases through the use of tradable permits.

In 2008 the IASB tentatively decided to address the accounting of all tradable emissions rights and obligations arising under emissions trading schemes. In addition, it will address the accounting of activities that an entity undertakes in contemplation of receiving tradable rights in future periods, e.g. certified emissions reductions (CERs). The Board confirmed that in addressing the accounting issues the staff should not be constrained by existing IFRSs, but the Framework would still be relevant. The IASB noted that there was a risk of diverse accounting practices for such schemes following the withdrawal of IFRIC 3. *Emission Rights* and that this would impair the comparability and usefulness of financial statement information. Though the IASB staff plans to prepare a comprehensive package of alternative accounting models in the first quarter of 2009, the date of issuance of an initial due process document is yet to be determined.

Customer-related Intangible Assets

IFRS 3 requires an acquirer to recognize the identifiable intangible assets of the acquiree (which might include customer-related intangible assets) separately from goodwill. Customer-related intangible assets are identifiable if they meet either the contractual-legal criterion or the separable criterion in IAS 38.

Customer-related intangible assets may be either contractual or non-contractual. Contractual customer relationships are always recognized separately from goodwill as they meet contractual-legal criterion under IFRS 3. However, non-contractual customer relationships are recognized separately from goodwill only if they meet the separable criterion. Consequently, determining whether a relationship is contractual is critical to identifying and measuring both separately recognized customer relationship intangible assets and goodwill, and different conclusions could result in substantially different accounting outcomes.

The issue will therefore be added to the IFRIC agenda however, the IFRIC decided that developing an Interpretation reflecting its conclusion is not possible. Noting widespread confusion in practice on this issue, the IFRIC decided that it could be best resolved by referring it to the IASB and the FASB with a recommendation to review and amend IFRS 3. Therefore, companies investing in significant customer-related intangible assets should ensure to keep up to date on the status of this issue.

Measurement of Certain Intangible Assets in Business Combination

In December 2008, the Board has tentatively decided to confirm its decision in IFRS 3 Business Combinations (as revised in 2008) that an acquirer should, in a business combination, recognize defensive intangible assets and measure them at fair value. Defensive intangible assets are assets that the acquirer does not intend to use directly or does not intend to use in the same way as other market participants.

The Board has also tentatively decided:

* not to provide explicit guidance on measuring the fair value of such intangible assets. The Exposure Draft will describe how these intangible assets are identified and the implications of the notions of highest and best use, valuation premise and market participant;
* not to address subsequent accounting for these intangible assets;
* not to require additional disclosures about these intangible assets.

COMPREHENSIVE EXAMPLES

This section presents two comprehensive disclosure examples. We have selected relevant extracts related to intangible assets.

BASF Aktienge Sellschaft – All extracts 14A were obtained from the annual report for the year ended December 31, 2007.

Extract 14(A1) – BASF Aktienge Sellschaft – Balance sheet, page 139

In this extract, intangible assets are shown distinctly on the balance sheet, as required by paragraph IAS 1.54.

Consolidated balance sheet Assets (million €)	Explanations in Note	2007	2006
Long-term assets			
Intangible assets	(11)	**9,559.5**	8,921.6
Property, plant and equipment	(12)	**14,215.1**	14,901.5
Investments accounted for using the equity method	(13)	**834.6**	650.5
Other financial assets	(13)	**1,951.7**	1,190.3
Deferred taxes	(8)	**678.8**	622.4
Other receivables and miscellaneous long-term assets	(15)	**654.7**	612.2
		27,894.4	26,898.5
Short-term assets			
Inventories	(14)	**6,577.9**	6,672.4
Accounts receivable, trade	(15)	**8,561.2**	8,222.8
Other receivables and miscellaneous short-term assets	(15)	**2,337.1**	2,607.3
Marketable securities	(16)	**50.7**	55.8
Cash and cash equivalents	(16)	**766.6**	834.2
Assets of disposal groups	(2)	**614.2**	-
		18,907.7	18,392.5
Total assets		**46,802.1**	45,291.0

Extract 14(A2) – BASF Aktienge Sellschaft – Significant accounting policies note, page 147

This extract shows the significant accounting policies related to intangible assets presented, as required by IAS 1.

1 — Summary of accounting policies (in part)
C — Accounting policies (in part)
Acquired intangible assets – excluding goodwill and intangible assets with indefinite useful lives are valued at cost less scheduled straight-line amortization. The useful life is determined based on the period of the underlying contract and the period of time over which the intangible asset is expected to be used.
Impairment losses are recognized if the recoverable amount of the asset is lower than the carrying amount. The recoverable amount is the higher of net sales price and the value-in-use. Reversals of impairment losses are recorded if the reasons for the previous years' impairment losses no longer exist.
Depending on the type of intangible asset, the amortization expense is recorded as cost of sales, selling expense, research and development expense or other operating expense.
Intangible assets with indefinite useful lives: Intangible assets with indefinite useful lives are trade names and trademarks that have been acquired as part of the 2006 acquisitions. They are tested for impairment annually.
Internally generated intangible assets are primarily comprised of internally developed software. Such software, as well as other internally generated assets for internal use, are valued at cost and amortized over their useful lives. Impairments are recorded if the carrying amount of an asset exceeds the recoverable amount.
Development costs also include, in addition to those costs directly attributable to the development of the asset, an appropriate allocation of overhead cost. Borrowing costs are capitalized to the extent that they are material and related to the period over which the asset is generated.
The average amortization period for intangible assets with definite useful lives, provided not a part of the amortization on the basis on produced and distributed volumes, was 10 years in both 2007 and 2006 based on the following expected useful lives:

Amortization periods in years	
Distribution, supply and similar rights	2–20
Product rights, licenses and trademarks	2–30
Know-how, patents and production technologies	3–25
Internally generated intangible assets	3–5
Other rights and values	2–20

Extract 14(A3) – BASF Aktienge Sellschaft – Intangible assets note, page 168

This extract shows the general disclosure note related to intangible assets, as required by paragraphs IAS.38.118 through IAS.38.123.

11 — Intangible assets Development 2007 (million €)

	Distribution, supply and similar rights	Product rights, licenses and trademarks	Know-how, patents and production technology	Goodwill	Internally generated intangible assets	Other rights and values*	Total
Acquisition costs							
Balance as of January 1, 2007	1,835.0	1,211.6	1,683.8	4,713.2	215.5	964.4	**10,623.5**
Changes in scope of consolidation	5.8	–	1.7	6.4	–	1.7	**15.6**
Additions	1,773.5	5.8	6.1	11.3	19.7	44.9	**1,861.3**
Disposals	(9.6)	(2.1)	(28.5)	(91.3)	(94.6)	(68.0)	**(294.1)**
Transfers	1.1	(24.4)	34.2	30.9	0.2	(108.3)	**(66.3)**
Exchange differences	(134.1)	(25.3)	(46.5)	(365.8)	(5.2)	(45.5)	**(622.4)**
Balance as of December 31, 2007	3,471.7	1,165.6	1,650.8	4,304.7	135.6	789.2	**11,517.6**
Amortization							
Balance as of January 1, 2007	297.3	377.0	427.4	–	149.5	450.7	**1,701.9**
Changes in scope of consolidation	(0.2)	(0.1)	1.1	–	–	0.7	**1.5**
Additions	177.8	82.8	143.5	65.0	26.0	120.0	**615.1**
Disposals	(6.5)	(1.9)	(28.4)	(65.0)	(93.6)	(62.1)	**(257.5)**
Transfers	6.7	(28.1)	7.1	–	–	(30.8)	**(45.1)**
Exchange differences	(16.0)	(12.3)	(5.7)	–	(2.4)	(21.4)	**(57.8)**
Balance as of December 31, 2007	459.1	417.4	545.0	–	79.5	457.1	**1,958.1**
Net carrying amount as of December 31, 2007	3,012.6	748.2	1,105.8	4,304.7	56.1	332.1	**9,559.5**

* Including licenses on such rights and values

Intangible assets Development 2006 (million €)

	Distribution, supply and similar rights	Product rights, licenses and trademarks	Know-how, patents and production technology	Goodwill	Internally generated intangible assets	Other rights and values*	Total
Acquisition costs							
Balance as of January 1, 2006	548.3	723.3	995.7	2,138.5	272.6	807.3	**5,485.7**
Changes in scope of consolidation	–	3.0	–	6.1	1.4	22.6	**33.1**
Additions	1,411.5	522.2	1,069.3	2,775.1	24.7	167.7	**5,970.5**
Disposals	(84.8)	(16.7)	(357.4)	(47.2)	(76.7)	(57.9)	**(640.7)**
Transfers	4.7	0.1	(0.5)	–	–	68.4	**72.7**
Exchange differences	(44.7)	(20.3)	(23.3)	(159.3)	(6.5)	(43.7)	**(297.8)**
Balance as of December 31, 2006	1,835.0	1,211.6	1,683.8	4,713.2	215.5	964.4	**10,623.5**
Amortization							
Balance as of January 1, 2006	260.4	322.7	652.2	–	179.0	351.8	**1,766.1**
Changes in scope of consolidation	–	–	–	–	–	22.5	**22.5**
Additions	122.7	80.6	111.3	–	50.1	126.7	**491.4**
Disposals	(84.1)	(15.5)	(330.6)	–	(76.4)	(29.3)	**(535.9)**
Transfers	2.7	–	0.4	–	–	0.2	**3.3**
Exchange differences	(4.4)	(10.8)	(5.9)	–	(3.2)	(21.2)	**(45.5)**
Balance as of December 31, 2006	297.3	377.0	427.4	–	149.5	450.7	**1,701.9**
Net carrying amount as of December 31, 2006	1,537.7	834.6	1,256.4	4,713.2	66.0	513.7	**8,921.6**

* Including licenses on such rights and values

As part of the asset swap with Gazprom, there was an addition to intangible assets from a marketing contract for the natural gas from the Yuzhno Russkoye gas field.

Disposals from goodwill in 2007 related in particular to impairment losses of €65.0 million in the North American coatings business of the Performance Products segment. Further impairment losses of €18.7 million were recognized on a variety of intangible assets. Impairment losses are recorded under 'other operating expenses'.

Concessions for oil and gas production with a net carrying amount of €61.6 million in 2007 and €59.0 million in 2006 convey the right to produce oil and gas at certain sites. To a limited extent, these rights entail obligations to deliver a portion of the produced amount to local companies. At the end of the term of a concession, the rights are returned.

The amounts recorded under transfers resulted primarily from the reclassification of intangible assets as assets held for sale. Further information on disposal groups can be found in Note 2.

The valuation adjustments of emission rights as of the balance sheet date are included in the line item transfers in the column 'Other rights and values'.

There were no material write-ups in 2007.

Additions in 2006 related in particular to the acquisition of Engelhard Corp., the construction chemicals business of Degussa AG and Johnson Polymer.

In 2006, impairment losses of 9.5 million related primarily to know-how and patents. These were reported under other operating expenses. There were no material write-ups.

Extract 14(A4) – BASF Aktienge Sellschaft – Acquisitions/divestitures note, page 155

This extract explains the details of an acquired intangible asset through an asset swap that also included an amount paid in cash.

2 — Acquisitions/Divestitures (in part)

BASF cooperates with Gazprom in gas exploration and production in Siberia. Production started at the Yuzhno Russkoye field in the fourth quarter of 2007. At the end of 2007, Wintershall acquired a stake of 25% less one share in OAO Severneftegazprom (SNG), through an asset swap with Gazprom. SNG holds the production license to the Yuzhno Russkoye natural gas field in Western Siberia. By means of an additional preference share, Wintershall holds a 35% share in the economic rewards of this field. SNG is accounted for using the equity method as an associated company in the BASF Group Consolidated Financial Statements.

In return, Gazprom received a 49% interest in a German company that holds onshore exploration and production rights in Libya. In addition, Gazprom's stake in our natural gas trading company, WINGAS GmbH, Kassel, was increased from 35% to 50% minus one share. Both the Libyan activities and WINGAS GmbH continue to be included in the BASF Group Consolidated Financial Statements.

A cash payment of €598 million was made by BASF to compensate for the assets swapped with Gazprom.

The marketing of BASF's share of the gas produced will be carried out through a project company. By means of a non-voting preference share, BASF is entitled to 100% of the earnings of the project company. As BASF bears all the economic risks and rewards of the project company, it is consolidated.

Gazprom's additional shares have led to an increase in minority interests of €216 million in the balance sheet. The measurement of the swapped assets at fair value of €850 million resulted in an excess of €634 million which was recognized in retained earnings.

Effects on the balance sheet of the asset swap with Gazprom

(million €)

Fair value of the assets given up	849.9
Compensation payment	598.1
Fair value of the assets received	**1,448.0**
Balance sheet items affected	
Long-term assets	**1,871.5**
Thereof intangible assets	1,761.5
Thereof financial assets	110.0
Deferred tax liabilities from the measurement at fair value	423.5

Swisscom Ltd. – All extracts 14B were obtained from the annual report for year ended December 31, 2007.

Extract 14(B1) – Swisscom Ltd. – Significant accounting policies note, pages 75-76

This extract shows the significant accounting policies related to intangible assets presented, as required by IAS 1.

2.10 Intangible assets

Goodwill

Goodwill is the excess of the cost of the business combination over the fair value of Swisscom's share in the net assets acquired on the acquisition date. Goodwill acquired in connection with a business combination is presented under intangible assets. Goodwill is tested for impairment, at a minimum, annually and recorded at cost less any recognized impairment losses. The reversal of any recorded impairment is not allowed. Where a company is disposed of, the carrying amount of the goodwill is removed from equity and presented as a component of the gain or loss on disposal. For the purposes of the impairment test, goodwill is allocated to cash generating units. More specifically goodwill is allocated to those cash generating units that are expected to gain an economic advantage from the business combination that generated the goodwill.

Research and development costs

Research costs are expensed as incurred. Development costs are capitalized under intangible assets if they can be identified as an intangible asset that is expected to generate probable future economic benefit and the costs of this asset can be reliably calculated. The capitalized development costs are amortized using the straight-line method over their estimated useful life. The estimated useful lives are reviewed at least annually and, if necessary, adjusted. Development costs that do not fulfill the requirements for capitalization are expensed as incurred.

Software development costs

Development costs of identifiable software under Swisscom's control are recorded as intangible assets, if they will generate probable future economic benefits, and amortized using the straight-line method over their estimated useful life of three to five years. Expenditure which enhances or extends the performance of computer software programs beyond their original specifications are capitalized and added to the original cost of the software. The estimated useful lives and residual values are reviewed at least annually and, if necessary, adjusted.

Other intangible assets

Other intangible assets comprise primarily mobile license fees and purchased software as well as trademarks and customer relationships acquired in a business combination. Mobile license fees and purchased software are capitalized at cost and amortized using the straight-line method over the shorter of their legal or their estimated useful life. Amortization begins when the associated asset is put into operation.

Scheduled depreciation of mobile license fees is based on the term of the contract and begins as soon as the network is ready for operation, unless for any reason a different useful life applies. The estimated useful lives are reviewed at least once annually and, if necessary, adjusted.

Depreciation is computed using the straight-line method based on the following estimated useful lives:

	Years
Software	3 to 7
UMTS licenses	12
GSM Licenses	7
Customer relationships	7 to 11
Trademark	5 to 10

Extract 14(B2) – Swisscom Ltd. – Note 23 Goodwill and other intangible assets (in part) pages 114 and 115

This extract displays reconciliation of the carrying amount at the beginning and end of the period showing for intangible assets, distinguishing between internally generated intangible assets and other intangible assets:

- additions, indicating separately those from internal development, those acquired separately, and those acquired through business combinations;
- impairment losses recognised in profit or loss during the period in accordance with IAS 36;
- any amortisation recognised during the period;
- net exchange differences arising on the translation of the financial statements into the presentation currency, and on the translation of a foreign operation into the presentation currency of the entity; and
- other changes in the carrying amount during the period.

23 Goodwill and other intangible assets

CHF in millions	Goodwill	Internally generated software	Customer relation-ships	Trade-mark	Other intangible assets	Total
At cost						
Balance at December 31, 2005	315	277	38	–	532	1,162
Additions	–	13	–	–	220	233
Disposals	–	(9)	–	–	(15)	(24)
Purchase price adjustments	(10)	–	–	–	–	(10)
Reclassifications	–	24	–	–	(25)	(1)
Acquisition of subsidiaries	165	1	24	6	40	236
Acquisition of minority interests	3,693	–	–	–	–	3,693
Currency translation adjustments	6	–	1	–	2	9
Balance at December 31, 2006	4,169	306	63	6	754	5,298
Additions	–	41	–	–	344	385
Disposals	–	(5)	–	–	(6)	(11)
Purchase price adjustments	(3)	–	–	–	–	(3)
Reclassifications	(6)	44	–	–	(33)	5
Acquisition of subsidiaries	2,961	20	1,408	364	254	5,007
Disposal of subsidiaries	(162)	–	(41)	–	(36)	(239)
Currency translation adjustments	2	–	–	–	–	2
Balance at December 31, 2007	6,961	406	1,430	370	1,277	10,444
Accumulated amortization and impairment						
Balance at December 31, 2005	–	230	1	–	209	440
Amortization	–	29	8	1	117	155
Disposals	–	(9)	–	–	(15)	(24)
Currency translation adjustments	–	–	–	–	1	1
Balance at December 31, 2006	–	250	9	1	312	572
Amortization	–	51	106	24	230	411
Impairment	49	–	3	–	21	73
Disposals	–	(5)	–	–	(5)	(10)
Disposal of subsidiaries	(8)	–	(10)	–	(19)	(37)
Currency translation adjustments	–	–	–	–	–	–
Balance at December 31, 2007	41	296	108	25	539	1,009
Net book value						
At December 31, 2007	6,920	110	1,322	345	738	9,435
At December 31, 2006	4,169	56	54	5	442	4,726
At December 31, 2005	315	47	37	–	323	722

The sale of the card business of Accarda led to an impairment of goodwill in 2007 of CHF 8 million. See Note 4.

Business activities for the interactive TV remote control Betty were discontinued at the end of 2007. The intangible assets were then tested for impairment. As a result of this test, impairments of CHF 12 million were recorded on goodwill and CHF 17 million were recorded on other intangible assets.

The goodwill from the acquisition of minority interests in the previous year is attributable to the repurchase of the 25% share in Swisscom Mobile. See Note 31.

As of December 31, 2007 other intangible assets include prepayments of CHF 171 million (previous year 145 CHF million).

Impairment test of goodwill

Goodwill is allocated to the cash generating units according to their business activities. Goodwill acquired in a business combination is allocated to the cash generating units that are expected to benefit from the synergies of the combination.

The allocation of goodwill to the cash generating units is as follows:

CHF in millions	31.12.2007	31.12.2006
Swisscom Mobile	3,693	3,693
Fastweb	2,957	–
Antenna Hungária	–	134
Swisscom IT Services	156	156
Minick	7	42
Other cash generating units	107	144
Total Goodwill	**6,920**	**4,169**

Apart from goodwill, there are no intangible assets with indefinite useful lives.

The value of goodwill was tested in the fourth quarter after business planning had been completed. The recoverable amount of a cash generating unit was determined based on its value in use, using the discounted cash flow (DCF) method. These discounted cash flow calculations use cash flow projections that are based on the business plan approved by management covering a three-year period. Cash flows beyond the detailed period are extrapolated using appropriate growth rates. The growth rates applied are the growth rates normally assumed for the country or market.

The key assumptions used for value in use calculation are as follows:

Information in %	WACC pre-tax	WACC post-tax	Long-term growth rate
Mobile	9.20	7.30	0.5
Fastweb	10.97	8.52	1.5
Swisscom IT Services	8.01	6.27	1.0
Minick	12.76	10.43	1.5
Other cash generating units	9.40–12.07	7.48–10.27	1.0–1.5

The application of pre- or post-tax discount rates (WACC pre-tax and WACC post-tax) both result in the same value in use. The discount rates used take into consideration the specific risks relating to the cash generating unit in question.

The cash flow projections and management assumptions are supported by external sources of information.

As of December 31, 2007 the impairment test led to an impairment of goodwill in the cash generating unit Minick of CHF 29 million. The underlying principles and assumptions for Minick and the other significant cash generating units Swisscom Mobile and Fastweb are presented below.

Extract 14(B3) – Swisscom Ltd. – Future commitments note, page 141

This extract displays the commitments for the intangible assets presented, as required by IAS 1.114.

---

35 Future Commitments (in part)

Contractual commitments for future capital expenditure

Contractual commitments for future capital expenditure and other intangible assets at December 31, 2007 amounted to CHF 429 million (previous year CHF 364 million).

Extract 14(B4) – Swisscom Ltd. – Research and development note, page 141

This extract displays the aggregate amount of research and development expenditure recognized as an expense during the period, as required by IAS 38.126.

---

36 Research and development

The research and development costs in 2007 amounted to CHF 34 million (previous year CHF 34 million) and are recorded as an expense.

PLANNING FOR IMPLEMENTATION

This chapter has covered most of the IAS 38 requirements and noted differences with corresponding Canadian GAAP. This section discusses suggestions for implementing IAS 38 and its related SIC.

Assessing the Impact on Financial Statements

As previously mentioned, the application of IAS 38 will not have a significant impact for Canadian financial statement preparers on the initial recognition and measurement of most intangible assets. The one exception might be that intangible assets initially recognized as part of a business combination may be measured differently depending on the approach used to estimate the fair values of their intangible assets at their acquisition date. Canadian preparers will feel a major impact when they consider using the revaluation model for measuring their intangible assets subsequent to initial recognition. Most significantly, they will likely realize an increase in impairments, specifically for finite-life intangible assets, where IFRS measurement criteria differ significantly from those under Canadian GAAP. As a result of these and other differences discussed above, Canadian preparers will likely experience more volatility in their intangible asset balances, resulting in offsetting volatility in profit or loss and, sometimes, in comprehensive income.

Initial Adoption of IFRS

When a company decides to transition to IFRS, it must apply all IFRS in existence at the time of transition retrospectively as if it had always applied them. This implies that entities will have to recognize all intangible assets that meet the criteria in IAS 38 as well as derecognize intangible assets that do not meet those criteria. IFRS 1 does, however, include an election that allows companies either to record intangible assets at the date of transition to IFRSs at their fair values or to use a previous GAAP revaluation as their deemed cost at that date. If a first-time adopter elects to use a previous GAAP revaluation for its intangible asset's deemed cost at the date of transition to IFRS, it must ensure that the revaluation was, at the date of the revaluation, broadly comparable to:

- fair value; or

- cost or depreciated cost under IFRSs, adjusted to reflect, for example, changes in a general or specific price index.

It is important to note, however, that the election above is only available for intangible assets that meet the recognition criteria of IAS 38 and have an active market.

For intangible assets acquired as part of business combinations, the exemption in IFRS 1 requires that they be measured, immediately after the business combination, at their carrying amount under previous GAAP assumed in that business combination, and that would represent their deemed cost under IFRSs at that date, unless such assets would qualify for recognition under IFRSs in the separate statement of financial position of the acquiree. Therefore, when intangible assets are recognized for the first time goodwill is adjusted accordingly. When an intangible asset was recognized separately as a result of a business combination that does not meet the criteria of IAS 38, this item (and any related deferred tax and non-controlling interest) should be reclassified and recognized as part of goodwill.

From a recognition perspective, transitioning to IFRS should not represent a problem for Canadian adopters since CICA 3064 has been substantially converged with IAS 38. As previously mentioned, the impact of transition will be felt in a measurement capacity. First time adopters may consider using the IFRS 1 election noted above to increase intangible assets to their fair values if their key performance indicators are asset based. Increasing the intangible assets' balances may attract investors and more faithfully represent a company's earnings potential. On the other hand, if the fair values of a company's intangible assets have decreased, using this option or applying IAS 36 for the first time will likely result in the same adjustments on first-time adoption of IFRS, which will bypass the income statement and be reflected immediately in retained earnings.

Selecting Accounting Policies

Since IAS 38 allows entities to choose between the cost model and the revaluation model to measure intangible assets after their initial measurement, corporate managers will need to evaluate whether they qualify for the revaluation option (i.e., whether an active market exist for their intangible assets) and whether the use of this model will result in more relevant and reliable financial statements. Since the presence of an active market for intangible assets is rare, this option is not frequently used in practice.

Obtaining Inputs from Personnel

Companies that invest large amounts in research and development need to identify performance indicators or milestones in a project's development at the start of a project so that they can determine at which point their costs qualify for recognition in accordance with the criteria discussed above. Information should be communicated clearly and efficiently, since costs can only begin to be capitalized once they meet the criteria and any costs that had previously been expensed are not allowed to be re-capitalized later. It is critical, therefore, that management be aware of what stage of completion each project is at to begin capitalizing costs at the earliest possible point, which is when all the recognition criteria are satisfied.

Generating New Data and Optimizing Information Systems

As mentioned above, companies that invest large amounts in internally generated intangible assets, such as development projects, and companies that are eligible to choose the revaluation model, must track their data for these purposes. The tracking requirements to properly apply the revaluation method dictate that information systems be adapted to ensure that revaluations and accumulated amortization balances are being adjusted accordingly. Similarly, companies that invest in development projects will need to keep track of the costs and the various stages of project development to efficiently determine when costs should begin to be capitalized. These changes will require companies to invest in training their staff and likely modifying their information technology systems. Where these changes are significant, their costs should be factored into planning budgets and cash-flow projections.

Keep Posted

The IASB is currently reviewing IAS 38 and some minor changes may be introduced for application to periods beginning on or after July 1, 2009 and January 1, 2010. No active project other than the one dealing with the accounting for emissions trading schemes has been added to the IASB's agenda. Companies investing in significant customer-related intangible assets should ensure to keep up to date on the status of the issue addressed by the IFRIC regarding the circumstances in which a non-contractual customer relationship arises in a business combination.

Chapter 15
Provisions, Contingent Liabilities and Contingent Assets

Standards Discussed in this Chapter

International

IAS 37 – Provisions, Contingent Liabilities and Contingent Assets
IFRIC 1 – Changes in Existing Decommissioning, Restoration and Similar Liabilities
IFRIC 5 – Rights to Interests Arising from Decommissioning, Restoration and Environmental Rehabilitation Funds
IFRIC 6 – Liabilities Arising from Participating in a Specific Market – Waste Electrical and Electronic Equipment
ED – IAS 37 – Amendments to IAS 37, Provisions, Contingent Liabilities and Contingent Assets, and IAS 19, Employee Benefits

Canadian

CICA 3110 – Asset Retirement Obligations
CICA 3290 – Contingencies
CICA 3461 – Employee Future Benefits
EIC-134 – Accounting for severance and termination benefits
EIC-135 – Accounting for costs associated with exit and disposal activities (including costs incurred in a restructuring)
EIC-159 – Conditional asset retirement obligation

INTRODUCTION

When reporting various liabilities of uncertain amounts or timing, Canadian financial statement preparers adopting IFRS will have to refer to a single general standard, IAS 37, and sometimes to IFRIC implementation guidance. Currently, preparers of Canadian financial statements have to meet various requirements scattered throughout the *CICA Handbook*, including CICA 3290, CICA 3110, EIC-159, EIC-135, and EIC-134.

IAS 37 is a broad standard that covers many issues related to legal and constructive obligations. Canadian companies applying IAS 37 will be affected differently depending on their business practices and activities. At a minimum, IAS 37 adoption will result in greater earnings volatility and more extensive disclosures than under current Canadian GAAP.

The International Accounting Standards Board is currently reviewing IAS 37 and expects to introduce some changes before 2011. A final standard will likely be issued in the first half of 2009. It is possible that a modified version of existing IAS 37 will result in greater measurement difficulties.

Meanwhile, even though the changes proposed in ED 37 are significant, companies should have a close look at the impact of the current IAS 37 requirements on their financial statements. To help in that review, this chapter discusses the following topics:

- recognition of provisions;
- recognition of recoveries;
- derecognition of provisions;
- measurement of provisions;
- categories of provisions:
  - o warranties,
  - o customers' refunds,
  - o onerous contracts,
  - o restructuring costs,
  - o decommissioning liabilities (asset retirement obligations),
  - o tax uncertainties;
- general disclosures related to provisions;
- contingent liabilities;
- contingent assets; and
- exceptions to recognition or disclosure.

IMPACT ON FINANCIAL STATEMENTS

Although applying IFRS and Canadian GAAP requirements to provisions and contingencies will often result in similar financial information, there may also be significant differences. Under IAS 37:

- companies will have to present provision amounts on the face of their balance sheet. Currently, such amounts are often grouped with other liabilities;
- companies may recognize provisions or contingencies earlier than currently because IAS 37 has set a lower probability recognition threshold than CICA 3290;
- because of this lower probability threshold, companies may have to recognize more uncertain amounts as liabilities. The uncertainties become even more significant when these amounts reflect the time value of money as required by IAS 37 (note that such discounting is generally not allowed under Canadian GAAP unless cash flows are fixed and determinable);
- consequently, reported earnings may be (1) more volatile because of the frequent adjustments of recorded provisions and (2) more difficult to audit because recorded provisions will depend more on management estimates and assumptions;
- companies will have to make more extensive disclosures, including new information on provision categories and their reconciliation.

ANALYSIS OF RELEVANT ISSUES
Recognition of Provisions
Scope

IAS 37 identifies provisions as a subset of liabilities – defining them as liabilities of uncertain timing or amounts – that should be disclosed separately on the balance sheet. It covers the recognition, measurement and disclosure of provisions. IAS 37 notes that they are more uncertain than trade payables (invoiced amounts) and accruals (unpaid amounts for goods and services received but not invoiced), which the standard does not cover. Note that, because it might be difficult to distinguish between provisions and accruals, reclassifications of amounts between these two categories of liabilities might be arbitrary.

The term "provision" used in IAS 37 refers to a recognized liability, not to a contra-asset account such as a provision for doubtful receivables or other provisions that reduce the carrying amount of impaired assets. Since, according to IAS 37, provisions must be presented separately in the financial statements, it might be preferable to use a different term to denote a contra-asset. For example, it might be more appropriate to describe it as an "allowance for doubtful receivables" instead of a "provision for doubtful receivables."

Executory contracts fall outside the scope of IAS 37 unless they are considered onerous, in which case they should be recorded as a provision. In addition, IAS 37 does not deal with certain other provisions and contingencies because they are covered by other standards. For example, IFRS 3 deals with contingent liabilities arising from business combinations.

IAS 37 also covers the measurement of certain financial guarantee contracts, for example, when disbursements are made after a debtor fails to make a payment that has come due. IAS 39, *Financial Instruments* provides specific guidance that might require measuring such a financial guarantee according to IAS 37, as the following two extracts illustrate.

Illustrative Disclosures:

Extract 15(1) – Financial guarantees

Nokia Corporation (Form 20-F 2006), page F10
1. Accounting principles (in part)
Basis of presentation (in part)
The Group adopted Amendments to IAS 39 and IFRS 4, Financial Guarantee Contracts, in which all financial guarantee contracts are initially recognized at fair value and subsequently measured at the higher of either the amount determined in accordance with IAS 37 or the amount initially recognized less any cumulative amortization.

Extract 15(2) – Financial guarantees

BP p.l.c. (AR 2006), page 107
1 Significant accounting policies (in part)
Impact of new International Financial Reporting (in part)
Standards Adopted for2006 (in part)
In August 2005, the IASB issued amendments to IAS 39 and IFRS 4 'Insurance Contracts' regarding financial guarantee contracts. These amendments require the issuer of financial guarantee contracts to account for them under IAS 39 as opposed to IFRS 4 unless an issuer has previously asserted explicitly that it regards such contracts as insurance contracts and has used accounting applicable to insurance contracts. In these instances the issuer may elect to apply either IAS 39 or IFRS 4. Under the amended IAS 39, a financial guarantee contract is initially recognized at fair value and is subsequently measured at the higher of (a) the amount determined in accordance with IAS 37 'Provisions, Contingent Liabilities and Contingent Assets' and (b) the amount initially recognized, less, when appropriate, cumulative amortization recognized in accordance with IAS 18 'Revenue'. This standard impacts guarantees given by group companies in respect of equity-accounted entities as well as in respect of other third parties; these are recorded in the group's financial statements at initial fair value less cumulative amortization. The effect on the group's reported income and net assets as a result of adoption of this amendment was not material.

> *Commentary:* Both extracts deal with financial guarantees covered by amended IAS 39, *Financial Instruments* and IFRS 4, *Insurance Contracts*. Financial guarantees are recorded initially at fair value. Subsequently, according to amended IAS 39, an entity would measure the financial guarantee at the higher of (1) an amount of provision established according to IAS 37 and (2) an amount of deferred revenue calculated according to IAS 18. This requirement is consistent with CICA 3855, *Financial Instruments — Recognition and Measurement*.

Recognition Criteria

According to IAS 37, provisions are recorded when they meet the following three criteria:

1. they originate from a legal or constructive obligation as a result of a past event;
2. their settlement requires a "probable" outflow of resources; and
3. their amount can be estimated reliably.

The term "probable" used in the second criteria above means "more-likely than not."

In CICA 3290, "contingent liability" refers to both recognized and unrecognized uncertain obligations. No distinct term is used to describe contingent liabilities that meet the recognition criteria versus those that do not. Under CICA 3290, contingencies are recorded as liabilities when it is "likely" that an event will confirm that a liability existed and that a reasonable estimate of the amount can be made. These requirements are similar to the provisions criteria set by IAS 37. The only difference lies in the required level of probability that an event might occur that would trigger the recognition of a liability. Under CICA 3290, the term "likely" refers to "high chances of occurrence," which is a higher threshold than "more-likely than not" established by IAS 37.

In addition to the differences in the recognition probability thresholds in IAS 37 and CICA 3290, there are other significant differences in the accounting for specific provisions in Canadian standards and IAS 37 (refer to the section dealing with categories of provisions).

Illustrative Disclosures:

Extract 15(3) – General recognition criteria

> **Swisscom AG (AR 2006), page 77**
> **2 Summary of significant accounting policies (in part)**
> **2.15 Provisions (in part)**
> Provisions are recorded when a present legal or constructive obligation results from past events, it is probable that an outflow of resources will be required to settle the obligation and when a reliable estimate of the amount of the obligation can be made.

Extract 15(4) – General recognition criteria

> **Kingfisher plc (AR 2007), page 60**
> **2 Significant accounting policies (in part)**
> **p. Provisions (in part)**
> Provisions are recognised when:
> - the Group has a present legal or constructive obligation as a result of past events;
> - it is more likely than not that an outflow of resources will be required to settle the obligation; and
> - the amount can be reliably estimated.
> Provisions are not recognised for future operating losses...

Extract 15(5) – General recognition criteria

Heidelberger Druckmaschinen Aktiengesellschaft (AR 2007), page 27
6 General accounting and valuation policies (in part)
Other provisions (in part)

Other provisions are recognized to the extent that a past event gives rise to a current obligation, that the amount of the charge is more probable than improbable, and that the amount can be reliably estimated (IAS 37). This means that there must be a probability greater than 50 percent that the liability will be realized.

Commentary: All the above three extracts were obtained from accounting policies notes. Extract 15(3) reflects IAS 37 provision recognition criteria in general terms. Extract 15(4) refers to the specific probability threshold defined in IAS 37, which could help alleviate some confusion for first time readers of IFRS financial statements. Note also that Extract 15(4) specifies that provisions exclude future operating losses, a precision that might also be pertinent to these readers. In Extract 15(5), the company explains the meaning of the term "probable" as defined by IAS 37.

Even though the majority of companies in our sample disclosed their accounting policies for provisions using a formulation similar to the one in Extract 15(3), the use of the more precise probability terms reflected in Extract 15(4) and Extract 15(5) would be more informative.

Recognition of Recoveries

Provisions can relate to events and transactions that trigger claims being made against third parties, such as an insurance company. These claims can result in recoveries of certain costs included in provisions.

The accounting treatments under IAS 37 and CICA 3290 could create timing differences in the recording of recoveries. IAS 37 requires that a reimbursement right be recorded as a separate asset when recovery is virtually certain, while CICA 3290 would allow recording such amounts when recovery is likely (refer also to our discussion on contingent assets below).

Presentation requirements of provisions and recoveries are similar under both Canadian GAAP (CICA 3290 and EIC-91) and IAS 37. Provisions are to be reported at the gross amount on the balance sheet, with the related insurance recoveries recognized as a separate asset and not offset against the provision.

IAS 37 contains two other pieces of pertinent guidance on recoveries:

- amounts of recognized reimbursements cannot exceed corresponding provisions and;

- expenses related to provisions can be netted of the amount of recognized reimbursements on the income statement. This netting is also acceptable under Canadian GAAP.

Illustrative Disclosures:

Extract 15(6) – Recoveries (environmental costs)

Lafarge (AR on Form 20-F 2006), page F-19
Note 2 Summary of Significant Accounting Policies (in part)
(t) Provisions (in part)
3) Environmental Costs (in part)

Costs incurred that result in future economic benefits, such as extending useful lives, increased capacity or safety, and those costs incurred to mitigate or prevent future environmental contamination are capitalized. When the Group determines that it is probable that a liability for environmental costs exists and that its resolution will result in an outflow of resources, an estimate of the future remediation is recorded as a provision without the offset of contingent insurance recoveries (only virtually certain insurance recoveries are recorded as an asset in the balance sheet).

Extract 15(7) – Recoveries (environmental costs)

Novartis AG (AR 2006), page 165
1. Accounting policies (in part)
Environmental liabilities

Novartis is exposed to environmental liabilities relating to its past operations, principally in respect to remediation costs. Provisions for non-recurring remediation costs are made when expenditure on remedial work is probable and the cost can be reliably estimated. Cost of future expenditures do not usually reflect any insurance or other claims or recoveries, as Novartis only recognizes insurance or other recoveries at such time the amount is reasonably estimable and collection is virtually certain. Recurring remediation costs are provided under non-current liabilities and are estimated by calculating the discounted amounts of such annual costs for the next 30 years.

Commentary: Both extracts indicate that provisions are recorded gross, i.e., without deducting the amount of contingent insurance recoveries. The latter amounts are recorded only when a company is virtually certain that it will recover its insurance claims. Extract 15(6), provides also the general recognition criteria for provisions and the capitalization policy of environmental costs. Extract 15(7), provides a precision concerning the length of time used for discounting.

Derecognition of Provisions

Under IAS 37, companies record provisions to cover specific expenditures. Such provisions are reversed when companies determine they are no longer required because the particular expenditures will not be incurred or the obligation provided for has been met. Companies cannot hold provisions as a general reserve to be applied against some other unrelated expenditure. Even though fewer provisions are recorded under Canadian GAAP, companies should apply the same derecognition principles required by IAS 37.

Illustrative Disclosures:

Extract 15(8) – Derecognition of financial guarantees

Nokia Corporation (Form 20-F 2006), page F52
31. Commitments and contingencies (in part)

Guarantees for loans and other financial commitments on behalf of other companies of EUR 23 million in 2006 (EUR 0 million in 2005) represent guarantees relating to payment by a certain Networks' customer and other third parties under specified loan facilities between such a customer and other third parties and their creditors. Nokia's obligations under such guarantees are released upon the earlier of expiration of the guarantee or payment by the customer.

Commentary: The information in this extract concerns the derecognition of financial guarantees. Extract 15(1), presented previously, dealt with the accounting policies for the measurement of these guarantees. The accounting policy for the derecognition of provisions satisfies the general requirements of liabilities derecognition (including IAS 37) and the specific requirements of both IAS 39 and CICA 3855.

Measurement of Provisions

IAS 37 requires that the amount recognized as a provision should be the best estimate of the expenditures required to settle a present obligation at the balance sheet date. Under CICA 3290, the amount recognized corresponds to a reasonable estimate of the amount to be paid. Under IAS 37, the best estimate is "the amount that an entity would rationally pay to settle the obligation at the balance sheet date or to transfer it to a third party at that time."

Several general measurement scenarios could be contemplated when measuring "best estimate" under IAS 37, including the following:

IAS 37	Canadian GAAP
Fair value	
Fair value not used unless it is observable in the market. Best estimate of the expenditure to be incurred should be used.	Fair value has to be estimated and recorded for certain types of provisions, such as asset retirement obligations, as required by CICA 3110.
Single obligation	
Best estimate is the individual most likely outcome. Other possible outcomes should be considered if they are either mostly higher or mostly lower than this most likely outcome. In these situations, best estimate should be adjusted to a higher or a lower amount.	Generally, most likely outcome (other outcomes distribution does not have to be considered).
A large population of outcomes	
Best estimate is the expected value (all possible outcomes should be weighted by their associated probabilities).	Although not addressed specifically in Canadian primary sources of GAAP, expected value could be used in practice because it better reflects the fair value of a liability to be recorded when there is a large homogeneous population of outcomes. CICA 3110 requires expected value referred to as "expected cash flow approach" for measuring asset retirement obligations.)
Each point of a range of possible outcomes is equally likely	
Best estimate is the midpoint (for large population of equally possible outcomes).	Amount to be accrued corresponds to the lowest value in the range (not limited to large populations).
Effect of the time value of money is material	
Best estimate should reflect the present value of the obligation. The appropriate discount rate is the pre-tax rate that reflects current market assessments of the time value of money and those risks specific to the liability, except where future cash flows have already been adjusted for risk. Note: Under both IAS 37 and Canadian GAAP, the unwinding of discount rate is presented as interest expense except for provisions accounted for under CICA 3110, where such unwinding is shown as an operating expense.	No requirements to discount to present value in order to measure provisions unless the timing of cash flows is fixed or reliably determinable. CICA 3110 does, however, require discounting to present value when recording asset retirement obligations.

Illustrative Disclosures:

Extract 15(9) – Settlement amount and expected value

Heidelberger Druckmaschinen Aktiengesellschaft (AR 2007), page 27

Other provisions (in part)

Measurement is based on either the settlement amount that is most likely to be incurred or, in the case of a uniform distribution of the probabilities of occurrence, on the expected value.

7 Estimates and judgements (in part), page 30

The amount and probability of utilization are estimated in the recognition and measurement of other provisions. Measurement is based on the settlement value that has the greatest probability of occurrence, or if the probability of occurrence is equally distributed, on the expected value of the settlement values. The amount of the actual utilization could deviate from the estimates.

Commentary: As can be observed, the company measures its provisions using two different measurement methods: (1) the settlement amount (most likely to be incurred or with the greatest probability of occurrence); and (2) the expected value (weighting all possible outcomes by their associated probabilities). Depending on the circumstances and taking into consideration the probability thresholds set out in CICA 3290, these two methods could also be used to record liabilities under Canadian GAAP.

Extract 15(10) – Population of similar obligations

Alumina Limited (Form 20-F 2006), page F13

1. SUMMARY OF SIGNIFICANT ACCOUNTING POLICIES (in part)

U PROVISIONS (in part)

Where there are a number of similar obligations, the likelihood that an outflow will be required in settlement is determined by considering the class of obligations as a whole. A provision is recognised even if the likelihood of an outflow with respect to any one item included in the same class of obligations may be small.

Commentary: Provision amounts for a large number of similar obligations can be grouped for establishing a provision. This grouping of similar obligations would also be acceptable for Canadian GAAP purposes. The company does not specify if it uses for each grouping the expected value (which could be the required method in this case under IAS 37) or the most likely outcome (which is generally the method used under Canadian GAAP).

Extract 15(11) – Rate used for discounting

Douglas Holding AG (AR 2007), page 110

5. ACCOUNTING AND VALUATION PRINCIPLES (in part)

PROVISIONS (in part)

The carrying amount of the provision is given – for individual risks – as the most probable amount for fulfillment taking into account all recognizable risks, or – for a large number of risks – the amount computed according to the expected value method. Non current provisions are discounted and carried on the balance sheet at their present value.

As of September 30, 2007, long-term provisions were discounted using an interest rate of 5.25 percent (previous year: 4.5 percent).

Commentary: The company measures its provisions using the most likely outcome method and the expected value method (weighting all possible outcomes by their associated probabilities). It also discloses the discount rates it has applied for present value calculations. Such a disclosure is not common. Generally, Canadian GAAP does not permit discounting.

Extract 15(12) – No discounting (effect not material)

> **Nestlé Group (AR 2006), page 63**
> **23. Provisions (in part)**
> **Restructuring**
> Restructuring provisions arise from a number of projects across the Group. These include plans to optimise industrial manufacturing capacities by closing inefficient production facilities and reorganising others, mainly in Europe. Restructuring provisions are expected to result in future cash outflows when implementing the plans (usually over the following two to three years) and are consequently not discounted.

Commentary: As IAS 37 requires, the time value of money is taken in consideration if its effect is material. Here, the materiality threshold is not attained and, consequently, the company did not discount its restructuring provisions.

Categories of Provisions

Provisions arise from a number of different types of events. Consequently, IAS 37 requires that provisions be described and reported according to their nature. In addition to the general recognition and measurement requirements, IAS 37 and IFRIC 5 and 6 contain requirements for specific types of situations, such as restructuring, onerous contracts and future operating losses. They also contain a number of examples illustrating the application of those requirements. Below are some examples of these specific provisions and of others described most commonly in the financial statements of the sampled corporations.

Warranties

Manufactured products are often covered by warranty plans. Manufacturers must record warranty provisions at the time of sale although they are sometimes difficult to measure. For example, companies that continuously introduce new products incorporating complex technology will find it difficult to calculate warranty provisions.

Illustrative Disclosures:

Extract 15(13) – Best estimate (product warranties)

> **Nokia Corporation (Form 20-F 2006), page F20**
> **1. Accounting principles (in part)**
> *Warranty provisions*
> The Group provides for the estimated cost of product warranties at the time revenue is recognized. The Group's warranty provision is established based upon best estimates of the amounts necessary to settle future and existing claims on products sold as of each balance sheet date. As new products incorporating complex technologies are continuously introduced, and as local laws, regulations and practices may change, changes in these estimates could result in additional allowances or changes to recorded allowances being required in future periods.

Commentary: This is an illustration of uncertainties related to warranty provision measurements. It is consistent with current Canadian GAAP.

Extract 15(14) – Expected value (product warranties)

> **Reunert Limited (AR 2007), page 49**
> **PROVISIONS (in part)**
> **Product warranties**
> Provision is made for the group's estimated liability on all products still under warranty at the balance sheet date. The provision is based on historical warranty data and returns and a weighting of possible outcomes against their associated probabilities.

Commentary: The company has based its warranty provision calculations on the expected value method. Even though this measurement would be in line with Canadian practices, it is not a requirement under Canadian standards.

Extract 15(15) – Volatility (product warranties)

HEAD N.V. (Form 20-F 2006), page F19
Note 4 - Critical Accounting Estimates and Judgments (in part)
Provision for Product Warranties

The Company provides for the estimated cost of product warranties and product returns at the time revenue is recognized. The warranty provision amounting to EUR 2.1 million is established based on the Company's best estimates of the amounts necessary to settle future and existing claims on products sold as of the balance sheet date. Product return provisions are based on historical experiences. While the Company believes that its warranty and product return provisions are adequate and that the judgment applied is appropriate, such amounts estimated to be due and payable could differ materially from what will actually transpire in the future. The Company updates these estimated charges periodically. The actual product performance and/or field expense profiles may differ, and in those cases the Company adjusts its warranty reserves accordingly. Future warranty expenses may exceed the Company's estimates, which could lead to an increase in cost of sales. Significant differences from estimates did not occur in the past.

If revenues and claims were to increase by 10%, the Company would have to recognise an additional provision of EUR 0.2 million.

Commentary: This extract reports the volatility of warranty estimates by including sensitivity of reported earnings. Even though this information is not required under IAS 37, nor under CICA 3290, it provides useful information.

Customers' Refunds

Customers claim refunds for a variety of reasons: sales rebates; contracts not fulfilled as specified; goods damaged in transit; and merchandise returns. Because provisions recorded are usually settled in the short term, usually no discounting is required.

Illustrative Disclosures:

Extract 15(16) – Uncertainties (sales rebates)

Novo Nordisk A/S (AR 2007), page 61
3 Critical accounting estimates and judgements (in part)
Sales rebate accruals and provisions (in part)

Sales rebate accruals and provisions are established in the same period as the related sales. The sales rebate accruals and provisions are recorded as a reduction in sales and are included in Other provisions and Other liabilities.

The accruals and provisions are based upon historical rebate payments. They are calculated based upon a percentage of sales for each product as defined by the contracts with the various customer groups.

Factors that complicate the rebate calculations are:
- Identification of the products which have been sold subject to a rebate.
- The customer or government price terms apply.
- The estimated time lag between sale and payment of a rebate.

Commentary: Here, the company has based its provisions calculations (which are probably established according to best estimates) on many factors. Because of important time lags in certain circumstances, the time value of money also appears to have been taken into consideration. This would not be in line with Canadian GAAP.

Extract 15(17) – Non-performance refunds

Nokia Corporation (Form 20-F 2006), pages F51 and F52

31. Commitments and contingencies (in part)

Other guarantees include guarantees of Nokia's performance of EUR 316 million in 2006 (EUR 234 million in 2005). EUR 259 million (EUR 182 million in 2005) of these guarantees are provided to certain Networks' customers in the form of bank guarantees, standby letters of credit and other similar instruments. These instruments entitle the customer to claim payment as compensation for non-performance by Nokia of its obligations under network infrastructure supply agreements. Depending on the nature of the instrument, compensation is payable either immediately upon request, or subject to independent verification of non-performance by Nokia.

Commentary: This extract illustrates the financial guarantee disclosures related to performance obligations. These disclosures are also in line with CICA 3290.

Extract 15(18) – Rebates, discounts and free products

Alcatel-Lucent (AR 2006 on Form 20-F), page F19

Note 1 - Summary of accounting policies (in part)

(o) Revenues (in part)

Product rebates or quantity discounts are deducted from revenues with the exception of promotional activities giving rise to free products, which are accounted for in cost of sales and provided for in accordance with IAS 37 "Provisions, Contingent Liabilities and Contingent Assets", or IAS 11 "Construction Contracts". The accounting treatment of free products could be amended in the future depending upon the final IFRIC determination related to customer loyalty programmes.

Commentary: This extract covers various refunds to customers. It also refers to the accounting for free products covered by the newly issued IFRIC 13, *Customer Loyalty Programmes*, which is effective for annual periods beginning on or after July 1, 2008, with earlier application permitted. Note that this IFRIC specifies that such programs could result in "onerous contracts."

Onerous Contracts

Onerous contracts can arise from different arrangements including leases, construction contracts, supply agreements, unconditional loan commitments and loyalty programs.[1] Paragraph IAS 37.66 requires recognition of a provision for all onerous contracts where "unavoidable costs of meeting the obligations under the contract exceed the economic benefits expected to be received under it."[2] Unavoidable costs are set to be the lower of (1) the cost of exiting the contract and (2) continuing to fulfil it. Expected benefits are not defined.[3]

Canadian GAAP has no requirements for recording provisions related to onerous contracts. Canadian GAAP does allow the recognition of expected losses in specific circumstances, for example, long-term construction contracts and leases in the context of a restructuring.

Note that EIC-135, which covers restructuring, takes a legal perspective to allow the recognition of a provision for contract termination. Under this perspective, a provision could be recorded only when the contract is terminated according to its terms or when an entity has ceased to use the rights conveyed by a contract.

---

1   Based on our observations, the most common onerous contracts seem to concern leases.

2   Note that IAS 37 specifies that operating losses other than those related directly to onerous contracts should not be recognized in the recorded provision.

3   IAS 37 does not address the presentation of gross versus net when recoveries are expected. It could be assumed that a net amount would be preferable since it would reflect the onerous part of the contract for which a provision needs to be accounted for.

Illustrative Disclosures:

Extract 15(19) – Unfavourable leases and supply agreements

> **Nestlé Group (AR 2006), page 63**
> **23. Provisions (in part)**
> **Other**
>
> Other provisions are mainly constituted by onerous contracts for CHF 91 million (2005: CHF 149 million) resulting from unfavourable leases or supply agreements above world market prices in which the unavoidable costs of meeting the obligations under the contract exceed the economic benefits expected to be received or for which no benefits are received. These agreements have been entered into as a result of selling and closing inefficient facilities. The duration of those contracts is an average of three years.

Extract 15(20) – Uneconomic lease agreements

> **NH Hoteles, S.A. (Consolidated Financial Statements 2006), pages 26 and 27**
> **4 ACCOUNTING POLICIES (in part)**
> **4.14 Onerous contracts**
>
> The NH Hoteles Group classifies as onerous contracts those agreements in which the unavoidable costs of performing the obligations stipulated therein exceed the economic benefits it expects to receive under the contracts.
>
> The NH Hoteles Group policy is to record a provision for the present value of the aforesaid difference between the costs and benefits of a contract.
>
> The pre-tax discount rates used reflect the present value of the money in the market, and the specific risks of these contracts; specifically, rates between 7.7% and 9% have been used.
>
> **20 PROVISIONS FOR LIABILITIES AND CHARGES (in part), page 48**
> **Onerous contracts**
>
> The NH Hoteles Group has classified as onerous a series of contracts of hotels operated under leases scheduled to expire between 2007 and 2028. The management of these hotels if being positive at gross operating profit (G.O.P.) is loss-making at net operating profit (ebitda) and cancellation of these contracts would imply full payment of the rent for the years pending under the lease.

Commentary: IAS 37 does not explain on what basis a contract is considered to be onerous when examining expected benefits (which are not defined). As a comparison of the two extracts shows, this could lead to diversity in practice.

Even though Extract 15(19) specifies the average duration of onerous contracts, it does not provide any detail on the calculations of the net benefits. We observed that most companies included in our sample provided few details on these calculations. This extract represented typical disclosures of companies examined in our sample.

In Extract 15(20), the company failed to specify the duration of contracts. It did, however, present several additional disclosures, including the discount rates and the method it used to establish net benefit or loss (which was based on EBITDA rather than gross operating profit). Equivalent detailed disclosures appear to be rare as we could not identify another equivalent example.

Restructuring Costs

Differences between IFRS and Canadian GAAP might create difference in the timing of recognizing provisions for restructuring costs. According to IAS 37, companies must recognize obligations arising from restructuring plans when they have detailed formal plans in place and there is a valid expectation that those plans will be carried out by either starting to implement them or announcing their main features. According to EIC-135, a company has to be "committed" to an exit or disposal plan. A formal plan by itself does not create a present obligation.

Some of the restructuring costs are related to onerous contracts, where the timing of provisions recognition will also be different under Canadian GAAP and IFRS. For example, according to IAS 37, provisions related to leases are recognized as soon as it is determined that the costs will exceed the expected economic benefits. Under EIC-135, a liability for a cost to terminate a contract before the end of its term is recognized at fair value at the cease-use date.

Illustrative Disclosure:

Extract 15(21) – Restructuring costs

Pernod Ricard (Financial Report 2007), page 186

19. Provisions (in part)

19.2 Provisions for restructuring

The cost of restructuring is fully provided for in the financial year, and is recognised in profit and loss within "other operating income and expenses", when it is material and results from a Group obligation to third parties arising from a decision taken by the appropriate board that has been announced to the third parties in question before the balance sheet date. These costs mainly involve redundancy payments, early-retirement payments, costs of notice periods not served, training costs of departing individuals and costs of site closure. Scrapping of property, plant and equipment, impairment of inventories and other assets, as well as other costs (moving costs, training of transferred individuals, etc.) directly related to the restructuring measures are also recognised in restructuring costs. The amounts provided for correspond to forecasted future payments to be made in connection with restructuring plans, discounted to present value when the timetable for payment is such that the effect of the time value of money is significant.

Commentary: As required by IAS 37, restructuring costs are recognized at the time of decision and announcement, which might create timing differences with Canadian GAAP. Furthermore, even though described expenditures appear to have been incurred as a direct consequence of the restructuring (as required by IAS 37), the classification of certain costs as restructuring costs (such as training of transferred individuals) might not be acceptable under either IAS 37 or Canadian GAAP.

Decommissioning Liabilities (Asset Retirement Obligations)

Decommissioning costs or asset retirement obligations cover a number of expenditures incurred to deal with environmental issues. All IFRIC interpretations referenced in this chapter cover particular aspects of environmentally related expenditures.

Accounting for decommissioning or asset retirement obligations under IAS 37 (and related IFRIC 1) and CICA 3110 (and related EIC-159) differ. The table below shows the main differences:

IFRS	Canadian GAAP
Measurement	
Provisions for these expenditures should be measured based on management's assumptions and estimates.	Provisions should be measured at fair value, incorporating market assumptions.
Discount rate	
Use of a discount rate that reflects the risks specific to the provision.	Use of credit-adjusted risk-free rate (interest rate on monetary assets that are essentially free of default risk, adjusted for the effect of an entity's credit standing).
Adjustments to provisions	
Provisions should be adjusted at each period for changes in the timing or amount of cash flows, changes in the discount rate and the unwinding of the discount.	Even though changes in timing or amount and unwinding of discount should be recorded, changes in discount rate alone are not reflected in the provision balance. Consequently, increases in the provision balances are calculated using the current discount rate (as in IAS 37) and decreases in the provision using the initial recognition rate.
Presentation of unwinding of provisions	
Any increase in the carrying amount of the liability due to the passage of time results in a financing expense (interest expense).	CICA 3110 does not allow such classification and requires that these amounts be presented as an operating item in the income statement.
Legal and constructive obligations	
Provisions are recorded on the basis of a legal or a constructive obligation for these expenditures.	Recognition of the provisions based solely on "legal" related considerations.
Presentation of adjustments	
The corresponding adjustments of decommissioning provision should be included in the cost of the related asset except when the obligation arises from the use of the asset to produce inventories.	Such adjustments should always be included in the cost of the related asset (refer to Extract 15(25)).

In addition to addressing decommissioning liabilities in general, the IASB has issued a number of IFRICs providing implementation guidance for specific contexts. Below are these contexts, for which there are no equivalent Canadian standard:

• Obligations and rights related to emissions: IFRIC 3, *Emission Rights* was issued in 2004 but was withdrawn in 2005 for a wider assessment. Consequently, companies have used different accounting policies (including the one required by IFRIC 3) to account for emission rights they receive and trade, as well as for obligations related to emissions.

• Waste Electrical and Electronic Equipment (WEEE) liabilities: IFRIC 6 provides guidance for the recognition of these special liabilities that might be incurred under the *European Unions Directive on Waste Electrical and Electronic Equipment*.

• Participation in a decommissioning fund: IFRIC 5 provides guidance on how to account in a contributor's financial statements for interests arising from decommissioning funds in which the assets are administered separately and the contributor's right to access the assets is restricted. The Interpretation clarifies that parties contributing to such funds should recognize their obligation to pay decommissioning costs as a liability and recognize their interest in the fund separately.

Illustrative Disclosures:

Extract 15(22) – Decommissioning and environmental obligations

Northam Platinum Limited (AR 2007), page P63

10 Provisions (in part)

10.1 Environmental rehabilitation provisions (in part)

10.1.1 Decommissioning provision

Provision is made for the present value of the estimated future decommissioning costs at the end of the mine's life. When this provision gives rise to future economic benefits, a decommissioning asset is recognised, otherwise the costs are charged to the income statement.

The estimates are discounted at a pre-tax discount rate that reflects current market assessments of the time value of money.

The increase in the decommissioning provision due to the passage of time is recognised as a borrowing cost in the income statement. Other changes in the carrying value of the provision subsequent to initial recognition are included in the determination of the carrying value of the decommissioning asset.

10.1.2 Environmental restoration provision

Provision is made for the estimated cost to be incurred on long-term environmental obligations, comprising expenditure on pollution control and closure over the estimated life of the mine.

The estimates are discounted at a pre-tax discount rate that reflects current market assessments of the time value of money.

The increase in the restoration provision due to the passage of time is recognised as a borrowing cost in the income statement.

In assessing the future liability, no account is taken of the potential proceeds from the sale of assets and metals from the plant clean-up. The future liability is reviewed regularly and adjusted as appropriate for new facts and changes in legislation.

The cost of ongoing programmes to prevent and control pollution and rehabilitate the environment is recognised as an expense when incurred.

Commentary: This extract reflects the accounting for decommissioning and environmental obligations as required by IAS 37. All the accounting treatments described are in line with CICA 3110 requirements, except for the discount rate used and the classification of the unwinding of provisions as interest.

Extract 15(23) – Decommissioning, environmental remediation and litigation

BP p.l.c. (AR 2006), page 152

40 Provisions (in part)

The group makes full provision for the future cost of decommissioning oil and natural gas production facilities and related pipelines on a discounted basis on the installation of those facilities. The provision for the costs of decommissioning these production facilities and pipelines at the end of their economic lives has been estimated using existing technology, at current prices and discounted using a real discount rate of 2.0% (2005 2.0%). These costs are expected to be incurred over the next 30 years. While the provision is based on the best estimate of future costs and the economic lives of the facilities and pipelines, there is uncertainty regarding both the amount and timing of incurring these costs.

Provisions for environmental remediation are made when a clean-up is probable and the amount reasonably determinable. Generally, this coincides with commitment to a formal plan of action or, if earlier, on divestment or closure of inactive sites. The provision for environmental liabilities has been estimated using existing technology, at current prices and discounted using a real discount rate of 2.0% (2005 2.0%). The majority of these costs are expected to be incurred over the next 10 years. The extent and cost of future remediation programmes are inherently difficult to estimate. They depend on the scale of any possible contamination, the timing and extent of corrective actions, and also the group's share of liability.

BP p.l.c. (AR 2006), page 152 (continued)

The group also holds provisions for litigation, expected rental shortfalls on surplus properties, and sundry other liabilities. Included within the new or increased provisions made for 2006 is an amount of $925 million (2005 $700 million) in respect of the Texas City incident of which a total of $1,355 million has been disbursed to claimants ($863 million in 2006 and $492 million in 2005).

To the extent that these liabilities are not expected to be settled within the next three years, the provisions are discounted using either a nominal discount rate of 4.5% (2005 4.5%) or a real discount rate of 2.0% (2005 2.0%), as appropriate.

Commentary: This extract illustrates the disclosures related to decommissioning, environmental remediation and litigation. It describes the provisions recognition criteria and measurement considerations used (including the method for establishing the amounts of expenditures, the discount rate and the period in which the expenditures will be incurred). Generally, the elements described would be compatible with Canadian GAAP not taking into consideration the probability threshold for recognition and the discount rate.

Extract 15(24) – Environmental, remediation and maintenance

AstraZeneca PLC (AR & Form 20-F 2006), page 136
26 COMMITMENTS AND CONTINGENT LIABILITIES (in part)

AstraZeneca has made provisions for the estimated costs of future environmental investigation, remediation and operation and maintenance activity beyond normal ongoing expenditure for maintaining the Group's R&D and manufacturing capacity and product ranges where a present obligation exists, it is probable that such costs will be incurred, and they can be estimated reliably. With respect to such estimated future costs, there were provisions at 31 December 2006 in the aggregate of approximately $107m, of which approximately $96m relates to the US. These provisions do not include possible additional costs that are not currently probable. Where we are jointly (but not jointly and severally) liable with third parties we reflect only our share of the obligation. Where the liability is insured in part or in whole by insurance or other arrangements for reimbursement, an asset is recognised to the extent that this recovery is virtually certain.

Commentary: This extract provides information on expenditures beyond normal expenditures for maintaining R&D and manufacturing capacity and product ranges that represents a present obligation under IAS 37. It is possible that these provisions would not be allowed under Canadian GAAP.

Note that the company provides additional important information by stating that provision amounts (1) exclude "possible additional costs that are not currently probable," (2) include a large proportion that relates to the US and (3) include only its share of the obligation. Note also that the company states its accounting policy related to recoveries from insurance companies.

Extract 15(25) – Reported differences

BP p.l.c. (AR 2006), pages 181 and 182
53 US GAAP reconciliation (in part)
(b) Provisions (in part)

Under IFRS, provisions for decommissioning and environmental liabilities are measured on a discounted basis if the effect of the time value of money is material. In accordance with IAS 37 'Provisions, Contingent Liabilities and Contingent Assets', the provisions for decommissioning and environmental liabilities are estimated using costs based on current prices and discounted using rates that take into consideration the time value of money and risk inherent in the liability. The periodic unwinding of the discount is included in other finance expense. Similarly, the effect of a change in the discount rate is included in other finance expense in connection with all provisions other than decommissioning liabilities.

BP p.l.c. (AR 2006) (continued)

(b) Provisions (in part)

Upon initial recognition of a decommissioning provision, a corresponding amount is also recognized as an item of property, plant and equipment and is subsequently depreciated as part of the capital cost of the facilities. Adjustments to the decommissioning liabilities, associated with changes to the future cash flow assumptions or changes in the discount rate, are reflected as increases or decreases to the corresponding item of property, plant and equipment and depreciated prospectively over the asset's remaining economic useful life.

Under US GAAP, decommissioning liabilities are recognized in accordance with SFAS No. 143 'Accounting for Asset Retirement Obligations'. SFAS 143 is similar to IAS 37 and requires that when an asset retirement liability is recognized, a corresponding amount is capitalized and depreciated as an additional cost of the related asset. The liability is measured based on the risk-adjusted future cash outflows discounted using a credit-adjusted risk-free rate. The unwinding of the discount is included in operating profit for the period. Unlike IFRS, subsequent changes to the discount rate do not impact the carrying value of the asset or liability. Subsequent changes to the estimates of the timing or amount of future cash flows, resulting in an increase to the asset and liability, are remeasured using updated assumptions related to the credit-adjusted risk-free rate.

In addition, the use of different oil and natural gas reserves volumes between US GAAP and IFRS until 1 October 2006 (see note (c) Oil and natural gas reserves differences) resulted in different field lives and hence differences in the manner in which the subsequent unwinding of the discount and the depreciation of the corresponding assets associated with decommissioning provisions were recognized.

Under US GAAP, environmental liabilities are discounted only where the timing and amounts of payments are fixed and reliably determinable.

Under IFRS, an expected loss is recognized immediately as a provision for an executory contract if the unavoidable costs of meeting the obligations under the contract exceed the economic benefits expected to be received under it. Under US GAAP, an expected loss can only be recognized if the contract is within the scope of authoritative literature that specifically provides for such accruals. The group has recognized losses under IFRS on certain sales contracts with fixed-price ceilings which do not meet loss recognition criteria under US GAAP.

Commentary: This is an extract of a note pertaining to the reconciliation of IFRS income with US GAAP. It provides a summary of some measurement differences related to decommissioning and environmental liabilities recognized and measured according to IAS 37 and Canadian GAAP since CICA 3110 is harmonized with SFAS 143. The differences reported include discounting issues, onerous contracts and corresponding adjustments for provision changes.

Extract 15(26) – WEEE liabilities

Vivendi (AR 2006), page 186

Note 1 Accounting Policies and Valuation Methods (in part)

1.1. Compliance with Accounting Standards (in part)

Vivendi applied IFRIC Interpretation 6 "Liabilities arising from Participating in a Specific Market – Waste Electrical and Electronic Equipment".... to each of its activities in the jurisdictions concerned. The first application of IFRIC 6 did not have any significant impact on the Consolidated Financial Statements for the Year Ended December 31, 2006.

Extract 15(27) – WEEE liabilities

Thomson (Form 20-F 2006), page F-14

IFRIC 6, Liabilities arising from participating in a specific market – Waste Electrical and Electronic Equipment (WEEE). This interpretation establishes the recognition date for liabilities arising from the European Directive relating to the disposal of WEEE. The Group took the directive into account as soon as the directive came into effect at the end of 2005. A provision was recognized as of December 31, 2005 and updated as of December 2006. This provision amounts to less than 1 million as of December 31, 2006.

Commentary: Information about WEEE liabilities is rare. Often, companies inform readers that such provisions do not apply to their operations or do not have a significant impact on financial statements. Extract 15(26), provides an illustration of a disclosure when the impact is not significant. Extract 15(27) is an extract that discloses the amount related to the provision on WEEE.

Extract 15(28) – Accounting for CO_2 emission rights

Solvay S.A. (AR 2006), page 69

17. Accounting for CO_2 emission rights

CO_2 emission rights are accounted for based on IAS 38 (intangible assets), IAS 37 (provisions) and IAS 20 (government grants).

Emission rights which have been granted free of charge are accounted for as intangible assets at a symbolic EUR 1 to the extent that they are 100 % subsidized, with a balancing entry in other current liabilities in the same amount.

To the extent that the rights granted to the Group for 2005-2007 exceed the expected actual emission, no obligation exists at balance sheet date, and no provision needs to be recorded.

Market sales of emission rights acquired free of charge generate a profit that is immediately recognized in income.

Extract 15(29) – Accounting for CO_2 emission rights

CRH public limited company (Form 20-F 2006), page F-21

STATEMENT OF SIGNIFICANT ACCOUNTING POLICIES (in part)

Emission rights

Emission rights are accounted for such that a liability is recognized only in circumstances where emission rights have been exceeded from the perspective of the Group as a whole and the differential between actual and permitted emissions will have to be remedied through the purchase of the required additional rights at fair value; assets and liabilities arising in respect of under and over-utilization of emission credits respectively are accordingly netted against one another in the preparation of the consolidated financial statements.

Commentary: Information about emission rights is rare. Both extracts describe certain accounting aspects related to CO_2 emission rights and obligations. The two companies deal with different aspects of emission rights and obligations. The only aspect that is common to both is the offset of the rights assets and actual emission liability. Note that, in the second extract, the company specifies that it presents the offset on a consolidated basis, which might be questionable under Canadian GAAP and IFRS.

Extract 15(30) – Environmental rehabilitation fund

Northam Platinum Limited (AR 2007), pages P63 and P64

10 Provisions (in part)

10.1.3 Environmental rehabilitation fund (in part)

The group makes annual contributions to a dedicated trust fund, the Northam Platinum Restoration Trust Fund ("the Fund"), to fund the expenditure on future decommissioning and restoration. Income earned by the fund is credited to the group's income statement in the period to which it relates.

In terms of IFRIC 5 – Rights to Interests arising from Decommissioning, Restoration and Environmental Rehabilitation Funds, the Fund is consolidated. The assets of the Fund are separately administered and the group's right of access to these funds is restricted.

Commentary: Information about environmental rehabilitation fund is rare. Note that the fund is consolidated (meaning that the company has effective control) even though the assets held by the fund are separately administered and the company's right of access to these funds is restricted. This treatment appears to be in accordance with IFRIC 5 if the funds are effectively controlled by the company even though the company's access is restricted.

Tax Uncertainties

Although IAS 37 covers all contingencies, including contingent tax liabilities and assets, it does not provide any specific guidance on how to establish provisions for taxes payable when a company files an aggressive tax return. A company could adopt (1) an uncertain liability perspective (i.e., it sets up a liability when disbursement is more likely than not); or (2) an uncertain asset perspective (i.e., it recognizes a reimbursement only when it is virtually certain). Canadian GAAP is also silent on the issue of uncertain tax positions.

Recently, the FASB adopted Financial Interpretation FIN 48, *Accounting for Uncertainty in Income Taxes — An Interpretation of FASB Statement No. 109*, which requires the use of the uncertain asset perspective. This perspective seems to differ from current reporting practices under IFRS and Canadian GAAP, which appear to be more in line with the uncertain liability perspective. Consequently, according to IAS 37, a contingent tax liability has to be recorded if it meets the criteria of a provision. Otherwise, it would only be disclosed in the notes unless the contingent liability is remote. When a provision is recorded, IAS 37 requires the use of expected amount, which differs from FIN 48 requirements. As for contingent tax assets, they are disclosed if it is more likely than not that they will materialize.

Illustrative Disclosures:

Extract 15(31) – Uncertain tax position

Koninklijke Ahold N.V. (AR 2007), page 43

3 Significant accounting policies (in part)

Income taxes (in part)

The ultimate tax effects of certain transactions can be uncertain for a considerable period of time, requiring management to estimate the related current and deferred tax positions. The Company recognizes liabilities for uncertain tax positions when it is more likely than not that additional taxes will be due.

Commentary: The extract reflects the uncertainties related to taxes in general terms and shows that the company has adopted an uncertain liability perspective.

Extract 15(32) – Uncertain tax position

AstraZeneca PLC (AR & Form 20-F 2006), page 102

BASIS OF ACCOUNTING AND PREPARATION OF FINANCIAL INFORMATION (in part)

Taxation (in part)

Accruals for tax contingencies require management to make judgments and estimates of ultimate exposures in relation to tax audit issues. Tax benefits are not recognized unless the tax positions will probably be sustained. Once considered to be probable, management reviews each material tax benefit to assess whether a provision should be taken against full recognition of that benefit on the basis of potential settlement through negotiation and/or litigation. All provisions are included in creditors due within one year. Any recorded exposure to interest on tax liabilities is provided for in the tax charge.

26 COMMITMENTS AND CONTINGENT LIABILITIES (in part), page 145

Taxation

Where tax exposures can be quantified, a provision is made based on best estimates and management's judgement. Details of the movements in relation to material tax exposures are discussed below.

AstraZeneca PLC (AR & Form 20-F 2006) (continued)

AstraZeneca faces a number of transfer pricing audits in jurisdictions around the world. The issues under audit are often complex and can require many years to resolve. Accruals for tax contingencies require management to make estimates and judgements with respect to the ultimate outcome of a tax audit, and actual results could vary from these estimates. The total net accrual included in the Financial Statements to cover the worldwide exposure to transfer pricing audits is $995m, an increase of $452m due to a number of new audits, revisions of estimates relating to existing audits, offset by a number of negotiated settlements. For certain of the audits, AstraZeneca estimates the potential for additional losses above and beyond the amount provided to be up to $445m; however, management believes that it is unlikely that these additional losses will arise. Of the remaining tax exposures, the Company does not expect material additional losses. It is not possible to estimate the timing of tax cash flows in relation to each outcome. Included in the provision is an amount of interest of $265m. Interest is accrued as a tax expense.

ADDITIONAL INFORMATION FOR US INVESTORS (in part), page 150

New accounting standards adopted (in part)

In June 2006, the FASB issued FASB Interpretation No. 48 'Accounting for Uncertainty in Income Taxes – an interpretation of FASB Statement No. 109' (FIN 48). The Interpretation establishes a two-step approach for recognising and measuring tax benefits, with tax positions only to be recognised when considered to be more likely than not sustained upon examination by the taxing authority. Explicit disclosures are required at the end of each reporting period about uncertainties in the entity's tax position. The Company is currently in the process of quantifying the effect of adoption of FIN 48 on the results and net assets of AstraZeneca.

ACCOUNTING POLICIES (in part), page 159

Taxation (in part)

Accruals for tax contingencies require management to make judgements and estimates in relation to tax audit issues. Tax benefits are not recognised unless the tax positions will probably be sustained. Once considered to be probable, management reviews each material tax benefit to assess whether a provision should be taken against full recognition of that benefit on the basis of potential settlement through negotiation and/or litigation. Any recorded exposure to interest on tax liabilities is provided for in the tax charge. All provisions are included in creditors due within one year.

Commentary: The above extract includes four sections related to taxes. Extract sections taken from pages 102 and 150 set out the accounting policy related to uncertain tax positions; the first relates to the provisions, the second to the assets. This policy appears to be partially in line with FIN 48 requirements as it seems that the company has adopted the uncertain asset perspective. In the extract sections taken from pages 145 and 159, the company presents the amounts it has recorded and the sources of uncertainties. The detailed information presented in this extract might reflect the company's decision to comply with certain FIN 48 disclosure requirements.

Extract 15(33) – Uncertain tax position

Xstrata plc (AR 2006), page 196

11. Income Taxes (in part)

Tax audits

The company periodically assesses its liabilities and contingencies for all tax years open to audit based upon the latest information available. For those matters where it is probable that an adjustment will be made, the company recorded its best estimate of the tax liability, including related interest charges, in the current tax liability. Inherent uncertainties exist in estimates of tax contingencies due to changes in tax laws. Whilst management believes they have adequately provided for the probable outcome of these matters, future results may include favourable or unfavourable adjustments to these estimated tax liabilities in the period the assessments are made, or resolved, or when the status of limitation lapses. The final outcome of tax examinations may result in a materially different outcome than assumed in the tax liabilities.

Commentary: This extract reflects the accounting policies related to tax provisions and uncertainties in general terms. The company has adopted an uncertain liability perspective, and the disclosures it provides are more detailed than what is reported in Extract 15(31) but far less detailed than what is shown in Extract 15(32). Since Canadian GAAP is silent on this issue, companies should weigh the cost and benefits of additional transparency, an important qualitative characteristic of IFRS financial statements.

General Disclosures Related to Provisions

IAS 37 requires extensive disclosures for each class of provisions that includes:

- descriptive information of the nature of the obligation and the expected timing of any resulting outflows of economic benefits;
- a reconciliation of beginning and ending balances in a schedule showing (comparative information is not required):
    - carrying amount at the beginning and end of the period,
    - additional provisions recognized during the period, including any increase to existing provisions,
    - amounts used (i.e., incurred and charged against the provision during the reporting period, such as reductions resulting from payments or other sacrifices or the re-measurement of estimated future sacrifices of economic benefits or from settlement of the provision without cost to the entity),
    - unused amounts reversed during the reporting period, and
    - increase during the period in the discounted amount arising from the passage of time and the effect of any change in the discount rate;
- information on any uncertainties relating to the amount or timing of any outflow;
- the amount of any expected reimbursement, stating the amount of any asset that has been recognized for that expected reimbursement.

Illustrative Disclosures:

Extract 15(34) – Provisions – descriptive information and reconciliation schedule

Roche Holding Ltd (AR 2006), page 79
28. Provisions and contingent liabilities
Provisions: movements in recognised liabilities *in millions of CHF*

	Environmental and legal provisions	Restructuring provisions	Other provisions	Total
Year ended 31 December 2005				
At 1 January 2005	1,198	348	360	1,906
Major legal cases[7]				
- additional provisions created	356	–	–	356
- utilised during the year	(180)	–	–	(180)
Other provisions				
- additional provisions created	39	51	404	494
- unused amounts reversed	(34)	(12)	(27)	(73)
- utilised during the year	(16)	(119)	(294)	(429)
Unwinding of discount[8]	73	4	1	78
Currency translation effects	142	6	80	228
At 31 December 2005	1,578	278	524	2,380
Of which				
- current portion	418	126	289	833
- non-current portion	1,160	152	235	1,547
Total provisions	1,578	278	524	2,380
Year ended 31 December 2006				
At 1 January 2006	1,578	278	524	2,380
Major legal cases[7]				
- additional provisions created	–	–	–	–
- utilised during the year	(31)	–	–	(31)
Other provisions				
- additional provisions created	35	54	588	677
- unused amounts reversed	(29)	(62)	(95)	(186)
- utilised during the year	(13)	(98)	(331)	(442)
Unwinding of discount[8]	66	2	6	74
Currency translation effects	(100)	–	(23)	(123)
At 31 December 2006	1,506	174	669	2,349
Of which				
- current portion	388	79	289	756
- non-current portion	1,118	95	380	1,593
Total provisions	1,506	174	669	2,349
Expected outflow of resources				
- within one year	388	79	289	756
- between one to two years	929	35	135	1,099
- between two to three years	67	20	74	161
- more than three years	122	40	171	333
Total provisions	1,506	174	669	2,349

Roche Holding Ltd (AR 2006), page 80

Environmental and legal provisions

These provisions include 186 million Swiss francs (2005: 212 million Swiss francs) for environmental matters and 1,320 million Swiss francs (2005: 1,366 million Swiss francs) for litigation, including major legal cases and the vitamin case.

Provisions for environmental matters include various separate environmental issues in a number of countries. Approximately half of these were pre-existing in companies acquired by the Group. By their nature the amounts and timing of any outflows are difficult to predict. The Group estimates that approximately half of the amount provided for may result in cash outflows over the next five years. Significant provisions are discounted by between 5% and 6%.

Legal provisions consist mainly of the major legal cases as described in Note 7. The amounts, timing and uncertainties of any outflows are discussed in those notes, as are the discount rates used. The remaining legal provisions, which account for less than 5% of the balance, consist of a number of other separate legal matters in various Group companies. The majority of any cash outflows are expected to occur within the next one to three years, although these are dependent on the development of the various litigations. These provisions are not discounted as the time value of money is not material in these matters.

Restructuring provisions

These arise from planned programmes that materially change the scope of business undertaken by the Group or the manner in which business is conducted. Such provisions include only the costs necessarily entailed by the restructuring which are not associated with the recurring activities of the Group. The remaining amounts are mostly in respect of obligations towards former employees arising from the Pharmaceuticals Division restructuring and other previous restructuring plans. The timings of these cash outflows are reasonably certain on a global basis and are shown in the table above. Significant provisions are discounted by 3%.

Other provisions

Other provisions consist mostly of claims arising from trade, sales returns, certain employee benefit obligations and various other provisions from Group companies that do not fit into the above categories. The timings of cash outflows are by their nature uncertain and the best estimates are shown in the table above. Significant provisions are discounted by between 4% and 6%.

Contingent liabilities

The operations and earnings of the Group continue, from time to time and in varying degrees, to be affected by political, legislative, fiscal and regulatory developments, including those relating to environmental protection, in the countries in which it operates. The industries in which the Group operates are also subject to other risks of various kinds. The nature and frequency of these developments and events, not all of which are covered by insurance, as well as their effect on future operations and earnings, are not predictable. See also Note 7 in respect of major legal cases.

The Group has entered into strategic alliances with various companies in order to gain access to potential new products or to utilise other companies to help develop the Group's own potential new products. Potential future payments may become due to certain collaboration partners achieving certain milestones as defined in the collaboration agreements. The Group's best estimate of future commitments for such payments is 334 million Swiss francs in 2007, 160 million Swiss francs in 2008 and 121 million Swiss francs in 2009.

Commentary: This extract illustrates the significant additional disclosures required when applying IAS 37 to provisions.

In this extract, the company describes the composition of the three categories of provisions it has identified (environmental and legal provisions, restructuring provisions and others). It also discloses details on certain amounts and discount rates used in the measurement of each provision category are.

The company provides a detailed reconciliation schedule for its provisions, including comparative information (which is not required by IAS 37). The company distinguishes short-term and long-term portions of provisions and presents information on the expected timing of outflows.

Note that, in this extract, the company delineates between provisions and contingencies. For example, in its reference to collaboration agreements, the company has applied requirements of paragraph IAS 37.29. Hence, a provision should be recognized for its part of the obligation for which an outflow of resources embodying economic benefits is probable. It seems, however, that the provision has not been recorded in this case because it is not a liability at the balance sheet date, but rather a constructive obligation or a commitment to pay when its partners achieve certain milestones.

Contingent Liabilities

IAS 37 distinguishes between contingent liabilities and provisions by specifying that the former are not recognized as liabilities because:

- they represent possible obligations, not current ones;

- it is not probable that an outflow of resources embodying economic benefits will be required to settle the obligation;

- it is not possible to make a sufficiently reliable estimate of the amount of the obligation.

Under CICA 3290, the term "contingent liabilities" refers to both recognized and unrecognized uncertain obligations. Disclosures related to contingent liabilities are similar under IAS 37 and CICA 3290. Unless the contingent liabilities are remote, the disclosures include:

- an estimate of their financial effect;

- an indication of the uncertainties relating to the amount or timing of any outflow; and

- the possibility of any reimbursement.

Illustrative Disclosures:

Extract 15(35) – Factors hindering provisions recognition

> **AstraZeneca PLC (AR & Form 20-F 2006), page 136**
> **26 COMMITMENTS AND CONTINGENT LIABILITIES (in part)**
> It is possible that the Company, or its affiliates, could incur future environmental costs beyond the extent of our current provisions. The extent of such possible, additional costs is inherently difficult to estimate due to a number of factors, including, but not limited to: (1) the nature and extent of claims that may be asserted in the future; (2) whether the Company or any of its affiliates has or will have any legal obligation with respect to asserted or unasserted claims; (3) the type of remedial action, if any, that may be selected at sites where the remedy is presently not known; (4) the potential for recoveries from or allocation of liability to third parties; and (5) the length of time that the environmental investigation, remediation and liability allocation process can take. Notwithstanding and subject to the foregoing, it is estimated that potential additional loss for future environmental investigation, remediation and remedial operation and maintenance activity above and beyond our provisions could be, in the aggregate, in the order of $15-30 million.

AstraZeneca PLC (AR & Form 20-F 2006) (continued)
Legal proceedings

AstraZeneca is involved in various legal proceedings considered typical to its businesses, including litigation relating to employment, product liability, commercial disputes, infringement of intellectual property rights, the validity of certain patents, antitrust and securities law. The more significant matters are discussed below. No provisions have been established for any of the claims discussed below (other than the European Union fine which has been paid).

Commentary: This extract provides a good disclosure of the reasons why certain amounts are not recognized as provisions as required by IAS 37. Note that, under Canadian GAAP, corporations do not distinguish between recognized and unrecognized uncertain obligations. Also note that the company has disclosed certain maximum amounts related to contingencies.

Contingent Assets

Contingent assets are not recognized on the balance sheet unless the inflow of benefits is virtually certain. These requirements differ from Canadian GAAP since, under CICA 3290, contingent assets are not recognized until realized.

IAS 37 contains some specific recognition and presentation requirements for reimbursements by another party. These requirements are consistent with those for other contingent assets, as paragraph IAS 37.53 indicates that such reimbursements should not be recognized unless they are virtually certain (refer to our discussion on recognition of recoveries).

Disclosures

Where it is likely to have an inflow of economic benefits, an entity should disclose a brief description of the nature of the contingent assets at the balance sheet date and, where practicable, an estimate of their financial effect, except in the extremely rare cases where such information can seriously prejudice the entity's position in a dispute with other parties over the provision, contingent liability or contingent asset. In such cases, the entity would disclose the general nature of the dispute, together with the fact that, and reason why, the information has not been disclosed. This exception to disclosure of contingency assets does not exist in Canadian GAAP.

Illustrative Disclosures:

Extract 15(36) – Contingent assets and liabilities (exposures)

Nestlé Group (AR 2006), page 70
35. Contingent assets and liabilities

The Group is exposed to contingent liabilities amounting to CHF 957 million (2005: CHF 870 million) representing various potential litigations for CHF 905 million (2005: CHF 784 million) and other items for CHF 52 million (2005: CHF 86 million).

Contingent assets for litigation claims in favour of the Group amount to CHF 267 million (2005: CHF 258 million).

Commentary: This extract provides disclosures of exposures related to contingent liabilities and amounts of claims related to contingent assets. None of the amounts reported was recorded as a liability. Even though we rarely observed such quantification of contingencies that do not qualify as provisions, it reflects a concern for increased transparency.

Extract 15(37) – Recoveries and other contingent assets

BP p.l.c. (AR 2006), page 105

1 Significant accounting policies (in part)

Provisions and contingencies

Provisions are recognized when the group has a present obligation (legal or constructive) as a result of a past event, it is probable that an outflow of resources embodying economic benefits will be required to settle the obligation and a reliable estimate can be made of the amount of the obligation. Where the group expects some or all of a provision to be reimbursed, for example, under an insurance contract, the reimbursement is recognized as a separate asset, but only when the reimbursement is virtually certain. The expense relating to any provision is presented in the income statement net of any reimbursement. If the effect of the time value of money is material, provisions are determined by discounting the expected future cash flows at a pre-tax rate that reflects current market assessments of the time value of money and, where appropriate, the risks specific to the liability. Where discounting is used, the increase in the provision due to the passage of time is recognized as other finance expense. Any change in the amount recognized for environmental and litigation and other provisions arising through changes in discount rates is included within other finance expense.

A contingent liability is disclosed where the existence of an obligation will only be confirmed by future events or where the amount of the obligation cannot be measured with reasonable reliability. Contingent assets are not recognized, but are disclosed where an inflow of economic benefits is probable.

Commentary: This disclosure reflects an accounting policy related to contingent assets and recoveries related to recorded provisions. The accounting policy conforms to Canadian GAAP. Even though it is only briefly mentioned in the note, it should be noted that the recording of insurance reimbursement (recovery) is based on a lower probability threshold under Canadian GAAP than under IFRS.

Extract 15(38) – Disclosures related to contingent assets

British Sky Broadcasting Group plc (AR 2007), page 78

26. Contracted commitments, contingencies and guarantees (in part)

b) Contingent assets

The Group has served a claim for a material amount against EDS (an information and technology solutions provider) which provided services to the Group as part of the Group's investment in customer management systems software and infrastructure. The amount which may be recovered by the Group will not be finally determined until resolution of the claim.

Commentary: This extract provides IFRS disclosures for contingent assets that are not recorded. Such disclosure is in line with Canadian GAAP.

Exceptions to Recognition or Disclosure

IAS 37 provides for very limited exceptions for not measuring or disclosing amounts of provisions. There are no corresponding exceptions under Canadian GAAP.

Below are the two "extremely rare" circumstances where IAS 37 might tolerate exceptions:

- non-recognition of a provision: the entity is unable to determine a range of possible outcomes (paragraph IAS 37.25);

- the nature and amounts of any provisions are not disclosed: the entity establishes that such disclosure can prejudice seriously its interest, in which case it will have to "disclose the general nature of the dispute, together with the fact that, and reason why, the information has not been disclosed" (paragraph IAS 37.92).

Illustrative Disclosures:

Extract 15(39) – Non disclosure of recognized provisions

> **Nestlé Group (AR 2006), page 63**
>
> **23. Provisions (in part)**
>
> **Litigation**
>
> Litigation provisions have been set up to cover legal and administrative proceedings that arise in the ordinary course of business. These provisions concern numerous cases that are not of public knowledge and whose detailed disclosure could seriously prejudice the interests of the Group. Reversal of such provisions refer to cases resolved in favour of the Group.

Commentary: This extract illustrates the omission to disclose the nature and amounts of particular provisions. Such an exception is not allowed under Canadian GAAP. We believe that this extract did not adequately provide all the additional disclosures required under these circumstances by paragraph IAS 37.92.

Extract 15(40) – Non disclosure of recognized provisions

> **Innogenetics NV (Annual Brochure 2006), page 99**
>
> **Note 19 – Contingencies (in part)**
>
> In the opinion of the Management, resolution of the matters described above is not expected to have a materially adverse effect on the consolidated financial position of Innogenetics. However, depending on the amount and timing of such resolution, an unfavourable resolution of some or all of these matters could materially affect the Company's future results of operations or cash flows in a particular quarter. The Company believes it has adequately accrued for these matters until December 31, 2006, and continues to periodically review the accrual. Legal fees related to such matters are expensed as incurred. The information usually required by IAS 37 is not disclosed on the grounds that it can be expected to prejudice seriously the outcome of the litigation.

Commentary: This extract illustrates the omission to disclose the nature and amounts of particular provisions. Such an exception is not allowed under Canadian GAAP. We believe that the additional disclosure under these circumstances, as required by paragraph IAS 37.92, has been adequately provided.

FUTURE DEVELOPMENTS

The IASB has an Exposure Draft outstanding entitled "Amendments to IAS 37, *Provisions, Contingent Liabilities and Contingent Assets,* and IAS 19, *Employee Benefits*" (ED 37).

The main objectives of the amendments proposed by ED 37 are to:

* align application guidance for costs associated with restructuring in IAS 37 (and termination benefits in IAS 19, *Employee Benefits*) with the more recent and conceptually superior requirements in SFAS 146, *Accounting for Costs Associated with Exit or Disposal Activities*;

* re-analyze contingent assets and contingent liabilities in terms of assets and liabilities as defined in the IASB Framework.

Adoption of ED 37 would result in the recognition of all items that meet the definition of a liability (unless they cannot be measured reliably). Uncertainty about the amount or timing of the economic benefits required to settle a liability would be reflected in the measurement of that liability. Below are some of the specific proposals contained in ED 37:

* The term "provision" as a defined term in IAS 37 will be eliminated. Rather than using the term "non-financial liability," as proposed in ED 37, the IASB decided to use the term "liability" in both the title and the text of the standard.

- The notion of "stand ready obligation," which concerns the amount required to settle a liability that is contingent (or conditional) on the occurrence or non-occurrence of one or more uncertain future events, will be discussed further to address the non-contractual context.

- The boundary between a constructive obligation that constitutes a liability and a business risk that does not constitute a liability will be examined. The IASB confirmed that a management decision or an intention to incur a future outflow of economic benefits by itself is not sufficient to justify recognizing a liability.

- Only present obligations (not possible obligations) give rise to liabilities. Once a liability has been identified, the probability recognition criterion in IAS 37 would, in almost all cases, not be a determinant for recognition, because some outflow of resources would be probable.

- IASB confirmed that the current definition of a "contingent liability" is confusing because it is used to describe two distinct notions: an unrecognized present obligation (a liability to be recorded) and a possible obligation (not a liability). Consequently, the IASB proposes eliminating the term contingent liability and plans to consider special disclosures about items that do not satisfy the definition of a liability.

- Liabilities will be measured at "the amount an entity would rationally pay to settle an obligation on the balance sheet date" a current settlement notion. An entity may settle a liability on the balance sheet date in one of two ways: paying the counter-party to release the entity from its obligation or paying a third party to assume its obligation. An entity should give precedence to market information when available. In the absence of market information, entity-specific information is consistent with the measurement principle provided there is no indication it is inconsistent with information the market would use.

Application of the above proposals will present challenges in practice. Note, however, that some of the changes proposed to termination benefits and restructuring costs would align IAS 37 requirements with those under US GAAP and, consequently, with Canadian GAAP (which are harmonized with US GAAP).

COMPREHENSIVE EXAMPLES

We present in this section two comprehensive disclosure examples. We have selected relevant extracts related to provisions, putting emphasis on potential differences between IFRS and Canadian GAAP.

Vodafone Group Plc – All extracts 15A were obtained from the Annual Report for the year ended March 31, 2007.

Extract 15(A1) – Vodafone Group Plc – Balance sheet, page 93

In this extract, provisions (short term and long term) are shown distinctly on the balance sheet, as required by paragraph IAS 1.68 (k).

Consolidated Balance Sheet at 31 March (in part)	Note	2007 $m	2007 £m	2006 £m
Non-current liabilities				
Long term borrowings	24	35,035	17,798	16,750
Deferred tax liabilities	6	9,106	4,626	5,670
Post employment benefits	25	242	123	120
Provisions	26	583	296	265
Trade and other payables	27	1,053	535	566
		46,019	23,378	23,371
Current liabilities				
Short term borrowings:				
Third parties	24	7,825	3,975	3,070
Related parties	24, 36	1,657	842	378
Current taxation liabilities		10,016	5,088	4,448
Trade and other payables	27	17,272	8,774	7,477
Provisions	26	525	267	139
		37,295	18,946	15,512

Extract 15(A2) – Vodafone Group Plc, page 99

This extract shows the significant accounting policies related to provisions presented, as required by IAS 8.

2. Significant accounting policies (in part)

Provisions

Provisions are recognised when the Group has a present obligation as a result of a past event and it is probable that the Group will be required to settle that obligation. Provisions are measured at the directors' best estimate of the expenditure required to settle the obligation at the balance sheet date and are discounted to present value where the effect is material.

Extract 15(A3) – Vodafone Group Plc, page 129

This extract shows the general disclosure note related to categories of provisions (page 129), as required by paragraphs IAS.37.84 and IAS.37.85.

26. Provisions

	Asset retirement obligations £m	Legal £m	Other provisions £m	Total £m
1 April 2005	135	188	199	522
Exchange movements	4	3	3	10
Amounts capitalised in the year	14	–	–	14
Amounts charged to the income statement	–	1	38	39
Utilised in the year – payments	(3)	(74)	(77)	(154)
Amounts released to the income statement	(2)	(19)	(6)	(27)
31 March 2006	**148**	**99**	**157**	**404**
Exchange movements	**(4)**	**(2)**	**(6)**	**(12)**
Amounts capitalised in the year	**17**	**–**	**–**	**17**
Amounts charged to the income statement	**–**	**34**	**186**	**220**
Utilised in the year – payments	**(2)**	**(11)**	**(45)**	**(58)**
Amounts released to the income statement	**–**	**(4)**	**(4)**	**(8)**
31 March 2007	**159**	**116**	**288**	**563**

Provisions have been analysed between current and non-current as follows:	2007 £m	2006 £m
Current liabilities	267	139
Non-current liabilities	296	265
	563	404

Asset retirement obligations

In the course of the Group's activities, a number of sites and other assets are utilised which are expected to have costs associated with exiting and ceasing their use. The associated cash outflows are generally expected to occur at the dates of exit of the assets to which they relate, which are long term in nature.

Legal

The Group is involved in a number of legal and other disputes, including notification of possible claims. The directors of the Company, after taking legal advice, have established provisions after taking into account the facts of each case. The timing of cash outflows associated with legal claims cannot be reasonably determined. For a discussion of certain legal issues potentially affecting the Group, refer to note 31 "Contingent liabilities".

Other provisions

Included within other provisions are amounts provided for property and restructuring costs. The associated cash outflows for restructuring costs are substantially short term in nature. The timing of the cash flows associated with property is dependent upon the remaining term of the associated lease.

Siemens AG – All extracts 15B were obtained from the annual report for year ended September 30, 2007.

Extract 15(B1) – Siemens AG, Balance sheet, page 202

This extracts distinctly shows provisions (short term and long term) on the balance sheet, as required by IAS 1.68 (k).

As of September 30, 2007 and 2006 (in millions of €) (in part)	Note	Siemens 9/30/07	9/30/06
Liabilities and equity			
Current liabilities			
Short-term debt and current maturities of long-term debt	22	5,637	2,175
Trade payables		8,382	8,443
Other current financial liabilities	20	2,553	1,929
Intragroup liabilities		–	–
Current provisions	24	3,581	3,859
Income tax payables		2,141	1,582
Other current liabilities	21	17,058	15,591
Liabilities associated with assets classified as held for disposal		4,542	5,385
Total current liabilities		43,894	38,964
Long-term debt	22	9,860	13,122
Pension plans and similar commitments	23	2,780	5,083
Deferred tax liabilities	9	580	184
Provisions	24	2,103	1,858
Other financial liabilities		411	248
Other liabilities	25	2,300	2,174
Intragroup liabilities		–	–
Total liabilities		61,928	61,633

Extracts 15(B2) – Siemens AG, pages 217 and 220

The first note shows the significant accounting policies related to onerous contracts presented according to IAS 8. The second note illustrates the disclosure of significant accounting policies related to provisions in general.

---

2. Summary of significant accounting policies (in part)

Product-related expenses and losses from onerous contracts – Provisions for estimated costs related to product warranties are recorded in *Cost of goods sold and services rendered* at the time the related sale is recognized, and are established on an individual basis, except for consumer products. The estimates reflect historic trends of warranty costs, as well as information regarding product failure experienced during construction, installation or testing of products. In the case of new products, expert opinions and industry data are also taken into consideration in estimating product warranty provisions. Expected losses from onerous contracts are recognized in the period when the current estimate of total contract costs exceeds contract revenue.

page 220

Provisions – A provision is recognized in the balance sheet when the Company has a present legal or constructive obligation as a result of a past event, it is probable that an outflow of economic benefits will be required to settle the obligation and a reliable estimate can be made of the amount of the obligation. If the effect is material, provisions are recognized at present value by discounting the expected future cash flows at a pre-tax rate that reflects current market assessments of the time value of money. Provisions for onerous contracts are measured at the lower of the expected cost of fulfilling the contract and the expected cost of terminating the contract. Additions to provisions are generally recognized in the income statement.

The present value of legal obligations associated with the retirement of property, plant and equipment (asset retirement obligations) that result from the acquisition, construction, development or normal use of an asset is added to the carrying amount of the associated asset. The additional carrying amount is depreciated over the life of the asset. If the asset retirement obligation is settled for other than the carrying amount of the liability, the Company recognizes a gain or loss on settlement.

Extracts 15(B3) – Siemens AG, page 225

This extract illustrates the disclosure of management estimates and judgments related to provisions in accordance with IAS 1.

---

3. Management estimates and judgments (in part)

Provisions – Significant estimates are involved in the determination of provisions related to onerous contracts, warranty costs and legal proceedings. A significant portion of the business of certain of the operating Groups is performed pursuant to long-term contracts, often for large projects, in Germany and abroad, awarded on a competitive bidding basis. Siemens records a provision for onerous sales contracts when current estimates of total contract costs exceed expected contract revenue. Such estimates are subject to change based on new information as projects progress toward completion. Onerous sales contracts are identified by monitoring the progress of the project and updating the estimate of total contract costs which also requires significant judgment relating to achieving certain performance standards, for example in the IT service business, and estimates involving warranty costs.

Siemens is subject to legal and regulatory proceedings and government investigations in various jurisdictions. These proceedings are, amongst others, related to the area of competition law and to possible breaches of anticorruption legislation in Germany, the Foreign Corrupt Practices Act in the United States and similar legislation in other countries. Such proceedings may result in criminal or civil sanctions, penalties or disgorgements against the Company. If it is more likely than not that an obligation of the Company exists and will result in an outflow of resources, a provision is recorded if the amount of the obligation can be reliably estimated. Regulatory and legal proceedings as well as government investigations often involve complex legal issues and are subject to substantial uncertainties. Accordingly, management exercises considerable judgment in determining whether it is more likely than not that such a proceeding will result in an outflow of resources and whether the amount of the obligation can be reliably estimated. The Company periodically reviews the status of these proceedings with both inside and outside counsel. These judgments are subject to change as new information becomes available. The required amount of a provision may change in the future due to new developments in the particular matter. Revisions to estimates may significantly affect results of future operations. Upon resolution of any legal or regulatory proceeding or government investigation, Siemens may incur charges in excess of the recorded provisions for such matters. It can not be excluded that the financial condition or results of operations of Siemens will be materially affected by an unfavorable outcome of legal or regulatory proceedings or government investigations. Refer to Note 29, "Legal Proceedings", for additional information.

Extract 15(B4) – Siemens AG, pages 267 to 269

This extract shows the general disclosures note for categories of provisions (pages 267 to 269), as required by paragraphs IAS.37.84 and IAS.37.85.

---

24 Provisions
Provisions changed during fiscal 2007 as follows:

	Warranties	Order related losses and risks	Asset retirement obligations	Other	Total
Balance as of beginning of fiscal year	2,628	1,338	704	1,047	5,717
Additions	1,470	1,002	15	962	3,449
Usage	(888)	(710)	(23)	(436)	(2,057)
Reversals	(642)	(355)	(7)	(322)	(1,326)
Translation differences	(56)	(20)	(2)	(4)	(82)
Accretion expense and effect of changes in discount rates	3	3	(52)	1	(45)
Other changes*	(75)	38	–	65	28
Balance as of fiscal year-end	2,440	1,296	635	1,313	5,684

* In fiscal 2007, *Other changes* includes €330 reclassified to *Liabilities associated with assets classified as held for disposal* (see Note 4 for further information).

Except for asset retirement obligations (see discussion below), the majority of the Company's provisions are generally expected to result in cash outflows during the next 1 to 15 years.

Warranties

Warranties mainly relate to products sold. Refer to Note 2 for further information concerning our policy for estimating warranty provisions. Additions to provisions already existing at the beginning of the period amounted to €446 in fiscal 2007.

Order related losses and risks

Provisions for order related losses and risks are recognized for anticipated losses and risks on uncompleted construction, sales and leasing contracts.

Asset retirement obligations

The Company is subject to asset retirement obligations related to certain items of property, plant and equipment. Such asset retirement obligations are primarily attributable to environmental clean-up costs which amounted to €597, and €658, respectively, as of September 30, 2007 and 2006 (thereof non-current portion of €575 and €635, respectively) and to costs primarily associated with the removal of leasehold improvements at the end of the lease term amounting to €38, and €46, respectively as of September 30, 2007 and 2006 (thereof non-current portion of €27 and €31, respectively).

Environmental clean-up costs are mainly related to remediation and environmental protection liabilities which have been accrued for the estimated costs of decommissioning facilities for the production of uranium and mixed-oxide fuel elements in Hanau, Germany (Hanau facilities), as well as in Karlstein, Germany (Karlstein facilities). According to the German Atomic Energy Act, when such a facility is closed, the resulting radioactive waste must be collected and delivered to a government-developed final storage facility. In this regard, the Company has developed a plan to decommission the Hanau and Karlstein facilities in the following steps: clean-out, decontamination and disassembly of equipment and installations, decontamination of the facilities and buildings, sorting of radioactive materials, and intermediate and final storage of the radioactive waste. This process will be supported by continuing engineering studies and radioactive sampling under the supervision of German federal and state authorities. The decontamination, disassembly and sorting activities are planned to continue until 2011; thereafter, the Company is responsible for intermediate storage of the radioactive materials until a final storage facility is available. The final location for all kinds of radioactive waste is not expected to be available before approximately 2030. With respect to the Hanau facility, the process of setting up inter-mediate storage for radioactive waste has neared completion; on September 21, 2006, the Company received official notification from the competent authorities that the Hanau facility has been released from the scope of application of the German Atomic Energy Act and that its further use is unrestricted. The ultimate costs of the remediation are contingent on the decision of the federal government on the location of the final storage facility and the date of its availability. Consequently, the provision is based on a number of significant estimates and assumptions. The Company does not expect any recoveries from third parties and did not reduce the provisions for such recoveries. The Company believes that it has adequately provided for this exposure.

As of September 30, 2007 and 2006, the provision totals €597 and €658, respectively, and is recorded net of a present value discount of €1,353, and €1,300, respectively. The total expected payments for each of the next five fiscal years and the total thereafter are €22, €38, €17, €6, €1, and €1,866 (includes €1,811 for the estimated costs associated with final storage in 2033).

The Company recognizes the accretion of the provision for asset retirement obligations using the effective interest method applying current interest rates prevailing at the balance sheet date. During the year ended September 30, 2007 the Company recognized €31 in accretion expense in *Financial income (expense) net*. Changes in discount rates decreased the carrying amount of provisions by €83 as of September 30, 2007. Refer to Note 4 for further information on provisions reclassified to *Liabilities associated with assets classified as held for disposal*.

Extract 15(B5) – Siemens AG, page 277

This extract illustrates the portion of the note on commitments and contingencies related to guarantees and other commitments.

---

28. Commitments and contingencies (in part)

Guarantees and other commitments (in part)

Credit guarantees cover the financial obligations of third parties in cases where Siemens is the vendor and/or contractual partner. These guarantees generally provide that in the event of default or non-payment by the primary debtor, Siemens will be required to settle such financial obligations. In addition, Siemens provides credit guarantees generally as credit-line guarantees with variable utilization to joint ventures and associated and related companies. The maximum amount of these guarantees is subject to the outstanding balance of the credit or, in case where a credit line is subject to variable utilization, the nominal amount of the credit line. These guarantees usually have terms of between one and five years.

Except for statutory recourse provisions against the primary debtor, credit guarantees are generally not subject to additional contractual recourse provisions. As of September 30, 2007 and 2006, the Company has accrued €13 and €24, respectively, relating to credit guarantees.

Furthermore, Siemens issues *Guarantees of third-party performance*, which include performance bonds and guarantees of advanced payments in cases where Siemens is the general or subsidiary partner in a consortium. In the event of nonfulfillment of contractual obligations by the consortium partner(s), Siemens will be required to pay up to an agreed-upon maximum amount. These agreements span the term of the contract, typically ranging from three months to seven years.

Generally, consortium agreements provide for fallback guarantees as a recourse provision among the consortium partners. No significant liability has been recognized in connection with these guarantees.

PLANNING FOR IMPLEMENTATION

We have covered in this chapter most of the IAS 37 requirements and noted significant differences with corresponding Canadian GAAP. This section discusses suggested measures when implementing IAS 37 and its related IFRIC.

Assessing the Impact on Financial Statements

As noted at the beginning of this chapter, IAS 37 is a broad standard that covers many issues related to legal and constructive obligations. Canadian companies applying IAS 37 will be affected differently depending on their business practices and activities. At a minimum, IAS 37 adoption will result in greater earnings volatility and more extensive disclosures than under current Canadian GAAP. In most circumstances, it will also result in additional liabilities on the balance sheet originating from the recognition of provisions related to:

- constructive obligations pertaining to events and management decisions not previously recognized under Canadian GAAP;
- contingent losses not recorded under Canadian GAAP because of the insufficient probability threshold level; and
- onerous contracts related to sales, leases and supply agreements.

The additional liabilities and the inherent uncertainties in the amounts of provisions reported might compel companies to renegotiate certain financing covenants.

Initial Adoption of IFRS

On the opening IFRS balance sheet, companies will have to apply IAS 37, including:

- recording liabilities not previously recognized under Canadian GAAP. For example, the provision on the opening balance sheet for an onerous rental contract in a foreign operation should be calculated using rental rates, interest rates and exchange rates current at the date of transition;

- revising amounts of liabilities recorded under Canadian GAAP. For example, a liability that was not discounted under Canadian GAAP should be restated to its net present value.

Note that special transition rules apply to decommissioning liabilities included in the cost of property, plant and equipment. According to IFRIC 1, any changes in a decommissioning liability, for which an asset is recognized, are added to, or deducted from, the cost of that asset. Such changes could be modifications of the discount rate used or in the cash flows estimates. Adjusted asset value is depreciated over the remaining useful life of the asset in accordance with IAS 16, *Property, Plant and Equipment*.

Retrospective application of IFRIC 1 would require identification of all the revisions to the discount rate and estimated cash flows that would have been recognized since the inception of the decommissioning obligation. IFRS 1 provides an exemption from full retrospective application of IFRIC 1. This exemption allows a company to elect, on transition to IFRS, to not apply retrospectively the provisions of IFRIC 1.

A company making such an election calculates the present value of the decommissioning liability at the date that the obligation first arose, but using the cash flow assumptions at transition date and the best estimate of historical discount rates. The value of the asset tied to the decommissioning obligation increases by the value of the decommissioning liability at the date the obligation first arose, less depreciation from that date to transition date. The corresponding adjustment is to opening retained earnings at the transition date.

Selecting Accounting Policies

Even though IAS 37 and the related IFRIC contain specific requirements for provisions, they leave some issues open to certain accounting choices. In selecting its accounting policy, a company has to refer to IAS 8, *Operating Segments*, which requires that management use its judgment in developing and applying an accounting policy that results in information that is both relevant and reliable.

Below are examples of circumstances where management has to select an accounting policy under IAS 37:

- *Onerous contract*: establish and select benchmarks to measure economic benefits in order to determine if a provision must be recognized.
- *Uncertain tax positions*: establish the approach to be adopted (contingent asset or contingent liability).
- *Emission rights and obligations*: since the withdrawal of IFRIC 3, companies have used different accounting methods. Consequently, companies receiving or trading such rights or incurring such obligations will have to address the following specific questions:
  - Should initial grant allowance be measured at cost or at fair value?
  - Should the allowance be measured subsequently at amortized cost or at fair value?
  - How should the obligations related to emissions be measured?
  - How should the sales of allowances be reported?
  - How should fair value be established?

Obtaining Inputs from Personnel

Accounting for provisions will require the input of many technical personnel and specialists involved in company operations. Fundamental to the recognition of provisions is the identification of past events that give rise to present obligations.

According to IAS 37, provisions are recorded at a probability threshold of more that 50% likelihood, which is a lower threshold level than under current Canadian GAAP. This probability threshold creates significant difficulties in many situations presenting complex fact patterns where assessments of likelihood are judgemental and not susceptible to precise determination.

Adapting Performance Measures

The recording of provisions under IAS 37 might also create difficulties in internal performance assessments. For example the recording of onerous contracts, which were previously ignored, might be contested by persons whose performance is based on financial reports. Implementing the requirements of IAS 37 will require not only an assessment of differences between IAS 37 and the corresponding CICA standard, but also an examination of context surrounding a company and its peers operating in a particular industry.

Generating New Data and Optimizing Information Systems

Canadian GAAP already requires important data for certain provisions reporting, as in the case of restructuring costs and asset retirement obligations. Converging to IFRS will require additional data on other contractual obligations.

In addition, data on some constructive obligations, such as onerous contracts, will have to be generated internally. Consequently, all significant agreements have to be identified and monitored, which will require a company obtaining information on any projected payments it has to make and the value of the related rights, taking full account of changing business circumstances. Amounts of provision recorded will have to rely on data presenting the range of possible outcomes to ensure that the payments the company has to make are covered by the economic benefits expected to be realized. Should the monitoring reveal that these payments exceed the economic benefits expected to be realized, systems have to allow the recognition of a provision for an onerous contract. In some cases, sensitivity analysis will have to be performed to verify the volatility of recognized provisions.

Information systems have to be adapted to collect the new data and information that will be essential to the management assumptions and calculations required in the recognition and measurement of different categories of provisions. Since the information systems will be examined and challenged by auditors, companies will have to ensure that proper internal controls are maintained.

Keep Posted

IAS 37 is currently under review and expected changes might be introduced prior to 2011. A final standard is expected to be issued in the first half of 2009. It is possible that a modified version of existing IAS 37 will result in greater measurement difficulties.

Even though the changes proposed in ED 37 are significant, companies should examine closely the impact of present requirements of IAS 37 on their financial statements. Many of the requirements are significantly different from current Canadian GAAP and will not change with the adoption of ED 37 proposals, for example the requirements for the measurement and disclosures of uncertain liabilities (provisions).

Chapter 16
Employee Benefits and Share-based Payment

Standards Discussed in this Chapter

International

IFRS 2 – Share-based Payment
IAS 19 – Employee Benefits
IFRIC 8 – Scope of IFRS 2
IFRIC 11 – IFRS 2 – Group and Treasury Share Transactions
IFRIC 14 – IAS 19 – The Limit on a Defined Benefit Asset, Minimum Funding Requirements and their Interaction

Canadian

CICA 3461 – Employee Future Benefits
CICA 3870 – Stock-based Compensation and Other Stock-based Payments
EIC-134 – Accounting for severance and termination Benefits

INTRODUCTION

Employee remuneration and benefits are a large portion of any company's expenses and, although accounting for them can be simple, complexities do arise when entitlement is uncertain and settlement is in the distant future.

Canadian financial statement preparers currently turn to CICA 3461 and CICA 3870 for guidance on accounting for employee benefits and share-based payment transactions. Once they adopt IFRS, they will refer instead to IAS 19 and IFRS 2.

Although CICA 3461 and CICA 3870 share many of the same fundamental principles with IAS 19 and IFRS 2, significant differences do exist. These may affect the recognition, measurement and disclosure of employee benefits and share-based payment transactions. To help companies understand the differences when they adopt IAS 19 and IFRS 2, this chapter covers the following topics:

- short-term employee benefits:
  o compensated absences,
  o profit-sharing and bonus plans;
- long-term employee benefits (other than post-employment benefits);
- termination benefits;
- classification of post-employment benefit plans;
- defined contribution plans;
- defined benefit plans:
  o asset ceiling,

o   minimum funding requirements,

o   present value of defined benefit obligations, current service cost and interest cost,

o   insured benefits,

o   plan assets,

o   reimbursement rights,

o   expected return on plan assets and reimbursement rights,

o   past service cost,

o   actuarial gains and losses,

o   curtailments and settlements,

o   business combinations,

o   multi-employer plans,

o   state plans,

o   group administration plans,

o   group plans;

- equity-settled share-based payment transactions:

  o   fair value of equity instruments granted,

  o   equity-settled share appreciation rights,

  o   treasury share transactions,

  o   reload features,

  o   modifications, repurchases, cancellations and settlements,

  o   when fair value cannot be estimated reliably;

- cash-settled share-based payment transactions;

- share-based payment transactions with settlement alternatives:

  o   choice of settlement with the counterparty,

  o   choice of settlement with the entity;

- group share-based payment transactions.

IMPACT ON FINANCIAL STATEMENTS

Although CICA 3461 and CICA 3870 are generally converged with their IFRS counterparts IAS 19 and IFRS 2, significant differences do exist:

- IAS 19 applies to the accounting for employee benefits, including those provided through informal practices that give rise to a constructive obligation. CICA 3461, on the other hand, applies to the accounting for employee benefits, including those provided through informal practices that give rise to a substantive commitment. A *constructive obligation* may be broader than a *substantive commitment* because it includes informal practices (such as increasing benefits to keep pace with inflation) that give rise to an obligation where an entity has no realistic alternative but to pay those employee benefits (i.e., because a change in those informal practices would greatly damage its relationship with employees).

- IAS 19 requires the present value of a defined benefit obligation and the fair value of plan assets to be determined at the balance sheet date. CICA 3461 permits such items to be measured as of a date not more than three months before the balance sheet date, provided that this practice is consistent from year to year.

- IAS 19 requires the present value of defined benefit obligations to be determined by attributing benefit to periods of service based on a plan's benefit formula. CICA 3461 requires that the obligation for benefits (in defined benefit plans other than pension plans) be attributed on a straight-line basis to each year of service in the attribution period.

- IAS 19 requires past service cost (related to a post-employment benefit plan classified as a defined benefit plan) to be recognized on a straight-line basis over the average period until the benefits become vested. CICA 3461 provides several different options for recognizing past service cost.

- IAS 19 permits actuarial gains and losses (related to a post-employment benefit plan classified as a defined benefit plan) to be recognized in full immediately in other comprehensive income. CICA 3461 does not provide for such an option as it requires actuarial gains and losses to be recognized in the income statement.

- IFRS 2 requires an amount for the goods or services received (in an equity-settled share-based payment transaction) during the vesting period to be recognized based on the best available estimate of the number of equity instruments expected to vest (without taking market conditions into account) when a grant of equity instruments does not vest immediately. The estimate is revised if subsequent information indicates that the number of equity instruments expected to vest differs from previous estimates. CICA 3870 provides for the option to recognize forfeitures by individual employees only as they occur.

- IFRS 2 requires that in accounting for awards that vest in installments, each installment should be treated as a separate arrangement. The standard does not permit such awards to be accounted for as a single award in which related compensation cost is recognized on a straight-line basis. CICA 3870 requires the use of this alternative under certain conditions.

- IFRS 2 requires goods or services received (in an equity-settled share-based payment transaction with a non-employee) to be measured directly at their fair value. CICA 3870 requires such goods or services to be measured based on the fair value of the consideration received, or the fair value of the equity instruments, whichever is more reliably measurable.

- IFRS 2 requires that cash-settled awards are measured initially at fair value and must be remeasured until the date of settlement. When services are received from an employee, CICA 3870 requires such awards to be initially measured at intrinsic value and remeasured until the date of settlement.

- IFRS 2 requires a transaction in which the terms of the arrangement allow the counterparty to choose the method of settlement to be accounted for as a compound financial instrument. CICA 3870 requires such a transaction to be accounted for as cash-settled.

The impact that these differences will have on the financial statements of Canadian companies will depend on the individual facts and circumstances for a given company. The adoption of IAS 19 and IFRS 2 may, for example, result in:

- the accrual of more obligations because the accounting for employee benefits includes those provided through informal practices that give rise to a constructive obligation, which may be broader than a substantive commitment;

- increased volatility in the income statement because:

  o in accounting for awards that vest in installments, each installment should be treated as a separate arrangement. Compensation cost for such awards cannot be recognized on a straight-line basis,

o cash-settled awards are measured at fair value instead of intrinsic value. Fair values are higher than intrinsic values because the former includes both intrinsic and time values components;

• reduced volatility in the income statement (in exchange for increased volatility in equity) because actuarial gains and losses cannot be recycled through the income statement in a subsequent period once recognized in other comprehensive income.

ANALYSIS OF RELEVANT ISSUES

Employee Benefits

Objective
The objective of IAS 19 is to ensure that an expense is recognized for the cost of employee benefits when an entity consumes the economic benefits arising from the services provided by an employee in exchange for employee benefits.

Scope
IAS 19 applies to the accounting for all employee benefits, which represent all forms of consideration provided to employees (or their dependents) in exchange for services they render, and includes benefits provided through:

• formal plans or other formal agreements;

• under legislative requirements, or through industry arrangements; and

• informal practices that trigger a constructive obligation.

Employee benefits may be settled by direct payments (or the provision of goods or services) made either to the employees, their spouses, children or other dependants, or to others, such as insurance companies.

IAS 19 does not apply to employee benefits provided through shared-based payment transactions, which are covered under IFRS 2, nor does it deal with reporting by employee benefit plans, which is covered under IAS 26, *Accounting and Reporting by Retirement Benefit Plans*[1].

Short-term Employee Benefits
Short-term employee benefits are payable within 12 months of the end of the period in which an employee rendered services, and consist of:

• wages, salaries, and social security contributions;

• short-term compensated absences, such as paid annual leave and paid sick leave;

• profit-sharing and bonuses; and

• non-monetary benefits for current employees, such as medical care, housing, cars and free or subsidized goods or services.

CICA 3461 differs from IAS 19 because short-term employee benefits are excluded from its scope. In practice, short-term employee benefits are generally accrued, which is consistent with IAS 19.

---

1   The AcSB decided that on adoption of IFRS, financial statements for pension plans should continue to be prepared in accordance with CICA 4100, *Pension Plans*, rather than IAS 26. The AcSB is reviewing CICA 4100 to determine whether any modifications will be required as a result of adopting IFRS.

General Recognition and Measurement

In general, a liability and an expense (unless capitalization is required or permitted by another IFRS, such as IAS 2, *Inventories* or IAS 16, *Property, Plant and Equipment*) are recognized for short-term employee benefits when an employee renders services.

The liability and expense are measured at the undiscounted amount of short-term employee benefits expected to be paid in exchange for the services.

Illustrative Disclosures:

Extract 16(1) – Accounting policy for short-term employee benefits

> **Telkom SA Limited (Form 20-F 2008), page F-20**
> **2 Significant accounting policies (in part)**
> **Employee benefits (in part)**
> **Short-term employee benefits**
> The cost of all short-term employee benefits is recognised during the year the employees render services, unless the Group uses the services of employees in the construction of an asset and the benefits received meet the recognition criteria of an asset, at which stage it is included as part of the related property, plant and equipment or intangible asset item.

Extract 16(2) – Accounting policy for short-term employee benefits

> **Roche Holding Ltd (AR 2007), page 33**
> **1. Summary of significant accounting policies (in part)**
> **Employee benefits**
> Wages, salaries, social security contributions, paid annual leave and sick leave, bonuses, and non-monetary benefits are accrued in the year in which the associated services are rendered by employees of the Group.

Short-term Compensated Absences

A liability and an expense are recognized for the expected cost of non-accumulating compensated absences when the absences actually occur. Examples of non-accumulating compensated absences include sick pay, maternity or paternity leave and compensated absences for jury service or military service.

Non-accumulating compensated absences lapse when the current period's entitlement is not used in full and do not entitle employees to a cash payment for any unused entitlements should they leave the company.

A liability and an expense are recognized for the expected cost of accumulating compensated absences when an employee renders services. The expected cost is measured as the additional amount expected to be paid as a result of the unused entitlement that has accumulated at the balance sheet date.

When a current period's entitlement is not used in full, accumulating compensated absences can be carried forward and used in future periods. Accumulated compensated absences may be vesting or non-vesting. When compensated absences are non-vesting, the measurement of the related liability should reflect the possibility that employees may leave before utilizing their entitlement.

Illustrative Disclosure:

Extract 16(3) – Accounting policy for short-term compensated absences

> **Barloworld Limited (AR 2007), page 158**
> **Accounting policies (in part)**
> **Financial statement items (in part)**
> **Income statement (in part)**
> **30. Employee benefit costs (in part)**
> The cost of providing employee benefits is accounted for in the period in which the benefits are earned by employees.
> The cost of short-term employee benefits is recognised in the period in which the service is rendered and is not discounted. The expected cost of short-term accumulating compensated absences is recognised as an expense as the employees render service that increases their entitlement or, in the case of non-accumulating absences, when the absences occur.

Profit-sharing and Bonus Plans

A liability and an expense are recognized for the expected cost of profit-sharing and bonus payments when:

- an entity has a present legal or constructive obligation to make such payments as a result of past events (i.e., there is no realistic alternative but to make the payments); and
- a reliable estimate of the liability can be made, which is only when:
    o the formal terms of the plan contain a formula for determining the amount payable,
    o the amount payable is determined before the financial statements are authorized for issue, or
    o past practice gives clear evidence of the amount payable.

When the terms of a profit-sharing plan or bonus plan stipulate that an employee must remain with the company for a specified period before receiving a particular benefit, the measurement of the liability should reflect the possibility that some employees may leave without receiving such profit-sharing payments or bonus payments.

Illustrative Disclosure:

Extract 16(4) – Accounting policy for profit-sharing and bonuses

> **Akzo Nobel N.V. (AR 2007), page 112**
> **Note 1 Summary of significant accounting policies (in part)**
> **Principles of valuation of assets and liabilities (in part)**
> **Short-term employee benefits**
> Short-term employee benefits are measured on an undiscounted basis and are expensed as the related service is provided.
> A provision is recognized for the amounts expected to be paid under short-term bonus or profit sharing plans if a present legal or constructive obligation as a result of past services provided exists, and the obligation can be estimated reliably.

Disclosure

IAS 19 does not require specific disclosures about short-term employee benefits.

Illustrative Disclosures:

Extract 16(5) – Expenses related to short-term employee benefits

Carl Zeiss AG (AR 2007), page 133 **10 Personnel Expenses**	2006/07 **EUR thou**	2005/06 EUR thou
Wages and salaries	682,013	637,992
Social security costs	113,563	121,835
Pension costs	32,054	34,346
Other benefits	976	285
	828,606	**794,458**

Commentary: In the above extract, the company discloses expenses related to short-term employee benefits separately, namely wages, salaries and social security costs.

Extract 16(6) – Liabilities related to short-term employee benefits

Carl Zeiss AG (AR 2007), page 161 **31 Other Liabilities (in part)**	Sept. 30, 2007 EUR thou	of which due in one year or less EUR thou	Sept. 30, 2006 EUR thou	of which due in one year or less EUR thou
Accrued personnel liabilities	74,473	74,473	61,782	61,782
Accruals in sales	143,551	143,551	126,181	126,181
Other accruals	7,613	7,613	8,087	8,087
Liabilities to subsidiaries	11,961	11,961	17,161	17,161
Liabilities to associated and related companies	2,394	2,394	3,005	3,005
Advance payments received on orders	200,224	186,317	136,651	123,304
Tax liabilities (non-income)	11,892	11,892	12,321	11,898
Wage tax withheld	10,134	10,134	15,550	15,548
Liabilities for social security	4,984	4,984	3,386	3,386
Deferred income	31,252	28,014	32,611	27,447
Other non-financial liabilities	17,572	17,336	38,652	38,434
	516,050	**498,669**	**455,387**	**436,233**

The accrued personnel liabilities mainly relate to vacation pay and salary entitlements and to accrued special payments.

Commentary: Here, the company discloses current liabilities related to short-term employee benefits separately, namely vacation pay, salary entitlements, special payments, wage tax withheld and liabilities for social security.

Long-term Employee Benefits (Other than Post-employment Benefits)

Long-term employee benefits (other than post-employment benefits) are very similar in nature to short-term employee benefits, except that they are payable more than 12 months after of the end of the period in which an employee rendered the related service. Long-term employee benefits include:

- long-term compensated absences, such as long-services or sabbatical leave;
- jubilee or other long-service benefits;
- long-term disability benefits;

- profit-sharing and bonuses payable; and
- deferred compensation.

Liability Components

The accounting for long-term employee benefits is very similar to that for post-employment benefit plans classified as defined benefit plans. As such, the liability (or asset, if negative) in the balance sheet for long-term employee benefits is calculated as the net total of:

- the present value of the defined benefit obligation at the balance sheet date;
- minus the fair value of plan assets (if any) at the balance sheet date.

In general, the recognition and measurement of these items are the same as for post-employment benefit plans classified as defined benefit plans, which are covered later in the discussion on defined benefit plans; however, when the level of a long-term employee benefit (other than post-employment benefits) is the same for any employee, regardless of years of service, the expected cost of those benefits is recognized when the event that obligates the entity occurs.

Illustrative Disclosure:

Extract 16(7) – Liability components for long-term employee benefits

Swiss Post Group (AR 2007), page 151
27 Provisions (in part)
Other long-term benefits due to employees
Other long-term employee benefits primarily include anniversary bonuses for long years of service to the company and staff vouchers (mainly for retirees). The trend is set out in the following tables.

Trend in "Other long-term benefits due to employees"

	Loyalty bonuses		Staff vouchers	
CHF m	2007	2006	2007	2006
As at 1.1.	232	234	107	102
Accrued benefit claims	13	13	3	2
Benefits paid	-18	-18	-5	-4
Interest on employee benefit obligations	5	5	3	3
Income from plan amendment	-12	–	-3	–
Annual (gains)/losses	-7	-2	2	4
As at 31.12.	213	232	107	107

Cost Components

The expense (income) recognized in the income statement is the net total of the following:

- current service cost;
- interest cost;
- the expected return on any plan assets and on any reimbursement rights;
- actuarial gains and losses;
- past service cost; and
- the effect of any curtailments or settlements.

The recognition and measurement of these items are the same as for post-employment benefit plans classified as defined benefit plans, which are covered later in the discussion on defined benefit plans. The only difference is that actuarial gains and losses, and past service cost related to long-term employee benefits (other than post-employment benefits) must be recognized in full immediately in the income statement.

Illustrative Disclosures:
Extract 16(8) – Cost components for long-term employee benefits

Swiss Post Group (AR 2007), page 151
27 Provisions (in part)
Other long-term benefits due to employees
Other long-term employee benefits primarily include anniversary bonuses for long years of service to the company and staff vouchers (mainly for retirees). The trend is set out in the following tables.
Expenses booked under staff costs

CHF m	Loyalty bonuses		Staff vouchers	
	2007	2006	2007	2006
Accrued benefit claims	13	13	3	2
Interest cost	5	5	3	3
Recognition of (gains)/losses	–19	–2	–2	4
Total expenses for other long-term employee benefits	–1	16	4	9

Extract 16(9) – Accounting policy for long-term employee benefits

Koninklijke Ahold N.V. (AR 2007), pages 46 and 47
3 Significant accounting policies (in part)
Pension and other post-employment benefits (in part)

The net assets and net liabilities recognized in the consolidated balance sheets for defined benefit plans represent the present value of the defined benefit obligations, less the fair value of plan assets, adjusted for unrecognized actuarial gains or losses and unamortized past service costs. Any net asset resulting from this calculation is limited to unrecognized actuarial losses and past service cost, plus the present value of available refunds and reductions in future contributions to the plan.

Defined benefit obligations are actuarially calculated at least annually on the balance sheet date using the projected unit credit method. The present value of the defined benefit obligations is determined by discounting the estimated future cash outflows using interest rates of high-quality corporate bonds denominated in the currency in which the benefits will be paid, and that have an average duration similar to the expected duration of the related pension liabilities. Actuarial gains and losses are recognized using the corridor approach. Under this approach, if, for a specific plan, the net unrecognized actuarial gains and losses at the balance sheet date exceed the greater of 10% of the fair value of the plan assets and 10% of the defined benefit obligation, the excess is taken into account in determining net periodic expense for the subsequent period. The amount then recognized in the subsequent period is the excess divided by the expected remaining average working lives of employees covered by that plan at the balance sheet date. Past service costs are recognized immediately to the extent that the associated benefits are already vested, and are otherwise amortized on a straight-line basis over the average period until the associated benefits become vested. Results from curtailments or settlements, including the related portion of net unrecognized actuarial gains and losses, are recognized immediately.

For other long-term employee benefits, such as long-service awards, provisions are recognized on the basis of discount rates and other estimates that are consistent with the estimates used for the defined benefit obligations. For these provisions the corridor approach is not applied and all actuarial gains and losses are recognized in the consolidated statements of operations immediately.

Commentary: The above extract discloses the company's accounting policy for defined benefit plans and long-term employee benefits (other than post-employment benefits). Provisions for long-term employee benefits are recognized on the basis of discount rates and other estimates that are consistent with the estimates used for the defined benefit obligations. For these provisions, all actuarial gains and losses are recognized in the income statement immediately.

CICA 3461 differs from IAS 19 because long-term employee benefits (other than post-employment benefits), with the exception of compensated absences, are excluded from its scope. In practice, these benefits are typically accrued at their expected cost, which is inconsistent with IAS 19.

CICA 3461 and IAS 19 differ in their accounting for compensated absences in much the same way as they do in accounting for post-employment benefit plans classified as defined benefit plans, which are covered later in the discussion on defined benefit plans. There are, however, a few specific differences in how the two standards deal with compensated absences.

For compensated absences (that vest or accumulate), CICA 3461 differs from IAS 19 because the former requires:

- The obligation for benefits to be attributed on a straight-line basis to each year of service in the attribution period except when the plan formula attributes a significantly higher level of benefits to early years of service. In that case, the obligation should be attributed based on the plan's benefit formula.

- Actuarial gains and losses to be recognized:
  o in accordance with the corridor approach, in the income statement,
  o by adopting any systematic method that results in faster recognition, in the income statement, or
  o in full immediately in the income statement.

- Past service cost to be recognized:
  o by assigning an equal amount to each remaining service period up to the full eligibility date of each employee working at the date of the plan initiation or amendment who was not fully eligible for benefits at that date, or
  o by using an alternative approach that amortizes past service costs more rapidly (e.g., on a straight-line basis over the average remaining service period of active employees expected to receive benefits under the plan up to the full eligibility date).

When all, or almost all, of the employees are retired, however, the past service cost for compensated absences (that vest or accumulate) is recognized on a straight-line basis over the average remaining life expectancy of the former employees.

For compensated absences (that do not vest or accumulate), CICA 3461 differs from IAS 19 because the former requires:

- actuarial gains and losses to be recognized:
  o over a period linked to the type of benefit, or
  o in full immediately in the income statement;

- past service cost to be recognized:
  o over a period linked to the type of benefit, or
  o immediately in the income statement.

Disclosure

IAS 19 does not require specific disclosures about long-term employee benefits (other than post-employment benefits).

Illustrative Disclosure:

Extract 16(10) – Liabilities related to long-term employee benefits

Swiss Post Group (AR 2007), page 150
27 Provisions (in part)

CHF m	Other long-term benefits due to employees	Restructuring	Incurred claims	Litigation risks	Other	Total
As at 1.1.2007	**341**	**135**	**46**	**33**	**31**	**586**
Increase	16	9	15	16	21	77
Present value adjustment	8	5	–	–	1	14
Utilized	–23	–21	–11	–19	–20	–94
Released	–22	–7	–5	–3	–2	–39
As at 31.12.2007	**320**	**121**	**45**	**27**	**31**	**544**
of which current	–23	111	9	1	22	166

Commentary: In the above extract, the company discloses the current portion of, total of and changes in the provisions related to other long-term employee benefits separately. The disclosure of this information is required under IAS 1, *Presentation of Financial Statements* and IAS 37, *Provisions, Contingent Liabilities and Contingent Assets.*

Termination Benefits

Termination benefits result from:

- an entity's decision to terminate an employee's employment before the normal retirement date; or
- an employee's decision to accept voluntary redundancy in exchange for those benefits.

Recognition

A liability and an expense for termination benefits are recognized when an entity is demonstrably committed to:

- terminate the employment of an employee or group of employees before the normal retirement date; or
- provide termination benefits as a result of an offer made to encourage voluntary redundancy.

An entity is demonstrably committed to a termination when there is no realistic possibility that it will rescind it and it has a formal plan for carrying out the termination, which details:

- the location, function and approximate number of employees whose services are to be terminated;
- the termination benefits for each job classification or function; and
- the schedule for the implementation of the plan, which should begin as soon as possible. The period of time for completing the termination plan should make it clear that material changes to it are unlikely.

The timing of the recognition of the cost for termination benefits under CICA 3461 may differ from IAS 19 because the former has distinct recognition requirements for:

- severance benefits (that do not accumulate or vest), which are payable when an event that obligates the entity occurs;

- severance benefits (that accumulate or vest), which accrue as employees render the service that gives rise to such benefits;

- contractual termination benefits, which are recognized as a liability and an expense when it is probable that employees will be entitled to benefits and the amount of the benefits can be reasonably estimated;

- special termination benefits (for voluntary terminations), which are recognized as a liability and an expense when employees accept the offer and the amount can be reasonably estimated; and

- special termination benefits (for involuntary terminations), which are recognized as a liability and an expense when:

  o management at the appropriate level of authority approves and commits an entity to a plan of termination and establishes the benefits that employees will receive when their employment is terminated,

  o the benefit arrangement is communicated to employees in sufficient detail to enable them to determine the type and amount of benefits they will receive when their employment is terminated,

  o the plan of termination specifically identifies the target level of reduction in the number of employees, the job classifications or functions and their locations, and

  o the period of time for completing the termination plan indicates that significant changes to the plan are not likely.

Measurement

Termination benefits are discounted when payable more than 12 months after the balance sheet date. The discount rate is determined by reference to market yields at the balance sheet date on high-quality corporate bonds of the same currency and term as the termination benefits obligation.

If an offer is made to encourage voluntary redundancy, the measurement of termination benefits must be based on the number of employees expected to accept the offer.

Disclosure

IAS 19 does not require specific disclosures about termination benefits.

Canadian GAAP differs from IAS 19 because EIC-134, *Accounting for severance and termination benefits* provides specific disclosure requirements for severance and termination benefits.

Illustrative Disclosures:

Extract 16(11) – Expenses related to termination benefits

PSA Peugeot Citroën (2007 Registration Document), page 184
Note 9 – Non-recurring operating income and (expenses) (in part)
9.4. Restructuring costs (in part)
A. Analysis by type

(in millions of euros)	2007	2006	2005
Early-termination plan costs[1]	1	(5)	4
Workforce reductions	(379)	(347)	(152)
Discontinued production operations	(2)	(77)	(12)
Total	**(380)**	**(429)**	**(160)**

(1)   Early-termination plans relate to the agreements signed in 1999 for the Automobile Division and in 2001 for the Automotive Equipment Division. At the 2007 year-end, 4,428 employees were concerned by the plans, including 200 Faurecia group employees.

Commentary: In the above extract, the company discloses expenses for early-termination plan costs and workforce reductions separately. An analysis by business segment and the estimated number of employees affected are discussed in the next two extracts.

Extract 16(12) – Expenses related to termination benefits by business segment

PSA Peugeot Citroën (2007 Registration Document), pages 184 and 185
Note 9 – Non-recurring operating income and (expenses) (in part)
9.4. Restructuring costs (in part)
B. Analysis by business segment

(in millions of euros)	2007	2006	2005
Automobile Division	(229)	(245)	(21)
Automotive Equipment Division	(105)	(169)	(137)
Transportation and Logistics Division	(42)	(6)	-
Finance companies	-	-	-
Other businesses	(4)	(9)	(2)
Total	**(380)**	**(429)**	**(160)**

Automobile Division

On May 9, 2007, Management in France presented its workforce streamlining plan to Peugeot Citroën Automobiles' Central Works Committee. This plan, which was designed to adapt the Group to its changing economic environment, offers voluntary departure incentives over the period June 1, 2007 to December 13, 2007.

The Group estimates the net cost of the plan, which concerns 6,217 employees, at €211 million. This amount was recognized in full in the 2007 financial statements.

The estimated net cost corresponds to termination payments amounting to €263 million as well as €14 million in regulatory expenses and €5 million in career consultancy services, and takes account of an €71 million fall in the provision for pension obligations.

The cost of workforce reduction measures in other European countries amounts to €15 million.

In 2006, restructuring costs included €237 million in connection with the discontinuation of production at the PSA Peugeot Citroën site at Ryton, UK. In 2005, this item included the costs of phasing out the third team at the Ryton plant, in an amount of €26 million.

Automotive Equipment Division (Faurecia Group)

Restructuring costs attributable to the Faurecia Group amount to €105 million in 2007, and concern 1,728 employees.

Restructuring costs attributable to the Faurecia Group amounted to €169 million in 2006 and €137 million in 2005.

Transportation and Logistics Division

Restructuring costs attributable to Gefco in Germany amount to €40 million in 2007, and concern 430 employees.

Commentary: In the above extract, the company also discloses the estimated termination costs, expected number of employees affected by business segment and period over which voluntary departure incentives were offered.

Extract 16(13) – Expected number of employees affected by workforce reduction plans by country

PSA Peugeot Citroën (2007 Registration Document), page 185
Note 9 – Non-recurring operating income and (expenses) (in part)
9.4. Restructuring costs (in part)
C. Employees affected

(number of employees)	2007	2006	2005
France	6,812	1,820	1,111
United Kingdom	101	2,266	932
Germany	853	617	689
Rest of Europe	1,130	363	498
Rest of world (excluding Europe)	422	88	258
Total	**9,318**	**5,154**	**3,488**

Extract 16(14) – Liabilities related to termination benefits

Qantas Airways Limited (AR 2007), pages 84 and 99
1. Statement of Significant Accounting Policies (in part)
(U) Employee Benefits (in part)
Employee Termination Benefits
Provisions for termination benefits are only recognised when there is a detailed formal plan for the termination and where there is no realistic possibility of withdrawal.
16. Provisions (in part)

	Qantas Group		Qantas	
Current	**2007 $M**	2006 $M	**2007 $M**	2006 $M
Dividends	**2.2**	2.1	**2.2**	2.1
Employee benefits				
– annual leave	**322.9**	325.5	**268.9**	281.2
– long service leave	**37.6**	40.7	**28.9**	30.9
– staff redundancy	**51.0**	21.2	**51.0**	21.2
Frequent Flyer	**33.7**	28.4	**33.7**	28.4
Onerous contracts	**9.3**	27.2	**8.7**	26.6
Insurance, legal and other	**77.7**	23.9	**76.6**	19.6
	534.4	469.0	**470.0**	410.0

Commentary: In the above extract, the company discloses provisions for staff redundancy separately.

Post-employment Benefits

Post-employment benefits are payable when an employee leaves a company, either to retire or to take another job elsewhere. They include pensions and other post-employment benefits such as post-employment life insurance and medical care.

Classification of Post-employment Benefit Plans

Post-employment benefit plans are classified as defined contribution plans or defined benefit plans based on an evaluation of the legal and constructive obligations that an entity assumes.

Defined contribution plans specify how an entity's contributions to the plan are determined. Under such plans, the entity's legal or constructive obligation is limited to the amount that it agrees to pay into the fund.

Defined benefit plans specify the benefits to be received by current and former employees. Under such plans, an entity assumes actuarial and investment risks because it is obligated to provide the agreed benefits to current and former employees.

Defined Contribution Plans

Recognition and Measurement

A liability and an expense (unless capitalization is required or permitted by another IFRS, such as IAS 2, *Inventories*, or IAS 16, *Property, Plant and Equipment*), in the amount of the contribution payable to a defined contribution plan, are recognized when an employee renders services.

Contributions to a defined contribution plan are discounted when payable more than 12 months after the end of the period in which an employee rendered the services. The discount rate is determined by reference to market yields at the balance sheet date on high-quality corporate bonds of the same currency and term as the defined contribution plan obligation.

Disclosure

For defined contribution plans, IAS 19 requires the disclosure of the amount recognized as an expense.

CICA 3461 differs from IAS 19 because the former also requires the disclosure of:

- a description of the nature and effect of each significant change during the period affecting the comparability of the expenses for the current and prior periods; and
- the total cash amount initially recognized in the period as paid or payable for that period for employee future benefits.

Illustrative Disclosure:

Extract 16(15) – Expenses related to defined contribution plans

> Solvay S.A. (AR 2007), page 92
> (28) Provisions (in part)
> – Defined contribution plans
> Defined contribution plans are those for which the company pays fixed contributions into a separate entity or fund in accordance with the provisions of the plan. Once these contributions have been paid, the company has no further obligation. EUR 32 million of contributions to these plans were charged to income in 2007 (EUR 28 million in 2006). This increase is mainly due to the law change on TFR (Trattamento Fine Rapporto) in Italy.

Insured Benefits

A post-employment benefit plan funded through an insurance policy is accounted for as a defined contribution plan.

A post-employment benefit plan funded through an insurance policy is, however, accounted for as a defined benefit plan when an entity retains (either directly or indirectly through the plan) a legal or constructive obligation to either:

- pay the employee benefits directly when they fall due; or
- pay further amounts if the insurer does not pay all future employee benefits related to employee service in the current and prior periods.

The accounting treatment for defined benefit plans is covered later in the discussion on defined benefit plans.

Past Service Cost

IAS 19 does not provide guidance on accounting for a past service cost related to defined contribution plans.

CICA 3461 differs from IAS 19 because the former requires a past service cost to be recognized in a rational and systematic manner over the period during which an entity expects to realize economic benefits from a plan initiation or amendment. This period may be the average remaining service period of active employees expected to receive benefits under the plan. In some circumstances, however, a shorter period may be appropriate.

Defined Benefit Plans

Liability Components

The defined benefit liability (or asset, if negative) in the balance sheet is calculated as the net total of:

- the present value of the defined benefit obligation at the balance sheet date;
- minus the fair value of plan assets (if any) at the balance sheet date;
- plus any actuarial gains (less any actuarial losses) not recognized;
- minus any past service cost not yet recognized.

The present value of the defined benefit obligation and the fair value of plan assets must be determined at the balance sheet date.

CICA 3461 differs from IAS 19 because the former permits the defined benefit obligation and the plan assets to be measured as of a date not more than three months before the balance sheet date, provided that this practice is consistent from year to year.

Asset Ceiling

When the net total results in a defined benefit asset (i.e., the net total is negative), IAS 19 restricts the amount recognized to prevent it from exceeding the asset's recoverable amount. Therefore, the defined benefit asset is subject to an *asset ceiling* test, which results in it being measured at the lower of:

- the amount of the defined benefit asset as previously determined; and
- the asset ceiling, which is the total of:
  - o any cumulative unrecognized net actuarial losses and past service cost, and
  - o the present value of any economic benefits available in the form of refunds from the plan or reductions in future contributions to the plan.

The application of the asset ceiling must not result in:

- a gain being recognized solely as a result of an actuarial loss or the past service cost in the current period; or
- a loss being recognized solely as a result of an actuarial gain in the current period.

Therefore, when the application of the asset ceiling results in a defined benefit asset that is equal to the asset ceiling, IAS 19 requires the immediate recognition of either:

- The net actuarial losses of the current period and past service cost of the current period to the extent that they exceed any reduction in the present value of the economic benefits available in the form of refunds from the plan or reductions in future contributions to the plan. If the present value of the economic benefits remains the same or increases, the entire net actuarial losses of the current period and past service cost of the current period must be recognized immediately.

- The net actuarial gains of the current period after the deduction of past service cost of the current period to the extent that they exceed any increase in the present value of the economic benefits available in the form of refunds from the plan or reductions in future contributions to the plan. If the present value of the economic benefits remains the same or decreases, the entire net actuarial gains of the current period after the deduction of past service cost of the current period must be recognized immediately.

Any adjustments that result from the application of the asset ceiling must be recognized in the income statement. If, however, an entity adopts a policy of recognizing actuarial gains and losses in full immediately in other comprehensive income, the adjustments must instead be recognized in other comprehensive income.

CICA 3461 differs from IAS 19 because:

- The asset ceiling test also takes into account:
  - o any unamortized transitional obligations and assets, and
  - o surplus amounts for which there is a legally enforceable right to withdraw.
- The application of the asset ceiling may result in:
  - o a gain being recognized solely as a result of an actuarial loss or the past service cost in the current period, or
  - o a loss being recognized solely as a result of an actuarial gain in the current period.
- Any adjustments that result from the application of the asset ceiling must be accounted for in the income statement (there is no option to account for this item in other comprehensive income).

Illustrative Disclosures:

Extract 16(16) – Recognition of pension assets and the effect of the asset ceiling

> **Roche Holding Ltd (AR 2007), page 33**
> **1. Summary of significant accounting policies (in part)**
> **Pensions and other post-employment benefits (in part)**
> The recognition of pension assets is limited to the total of the present value of any future refunds from the plans or reductions in future contributions to the plans and any cumulative unrecognised past service costs. Adjustments arising from the limit on the recognition of assets for defined benefit plans are recorded directly in equity.

Extract 16(17) – Defined benefit plan liability components, including the impact of the asset ceiling

Solvay S.A. (AR 2007), page 93 (28) Provisions (in part) – Defined benefit plans (in part) The amounts recorded in the balance sheet in respect of defined benefit plans are:		
EUR Million	2006	2007
Defined benefit obligations - funded plans	1 663	1 580
Fair value of plan assets at end of period	-1 298	-1 342
Deficit for funded plans	365	238
Defined benefit obligations - unfunded plans	828	775
Funded status	1 193	1 013
Unrecognized actuarial gains / losses (-)	-282	-150
Unrecognized past service cost	6	5
Amounts not recognized as asset due to asset ceiling	15	15
Net liability (asset) in balance sheet	932	883
Liability recognized in the balance sheet	988	956
Asset recognized in the balance sheet	-56	-73

Minimum Funding Requirements

IFRIC 14 addresses the following issues that arise when the asset ceiling is applied:

- when refunds or reductions in future contributions should be regarded as available;
- how a minimum funding requirement might affect the availability of reductions in future contributions; and
- when a minimum funding requirement might give rise to a liability.

The existence of a minimum funding requirement may restrict the availability of refunds or reductions in future contributions, and may even trigger a liability if the required contributions will not be available to an entity once they have been paid.

Availability of a Refund or Reduction in Future Contributions

An economic benefit, in the form of a refund or a reduction in future contributions, is available if it can be realized at some point during the life of a plan or when the plan liabilities are settled, even if it is not realizable immediately at the balance sheet date.

A refund is considered to be available only if there is an unconditional right to that refund:

- during the life of the plan, without assuming that the plan liabilities must be settled to obtain the refund;
- assuming the gradual settlement of the plan liabilities over time until all members have left the plan; or
- assuming the full settlement of the plan liabilities in a single event.

Therefore, an asset cannot be recognized where there is no unconditional right (i.e., when the right to a refund of a surplus depends on the occurrence or non-occurrence of one or more uncertain future events that are not wholly within an entity's control).

The determination of whether or not an unconditional right exists may be difficult. There is no unconditional right to a refund when, for example, its payment requires the approval of another party. If, however, there is substantive evidence to support that approval will be received, an unconditional right probably exists. Management will need to carefully review the terms and conditions of a plan, and perhaps even seek legal advice, to determine whether an unconditional right exists.

The economic benefit available as a refund is measured as:

- the surplus at the balance sheet date (i.e., the fair value of the plan assets less the present value of the defined benefit obligation) for which there is a right to receive as a refund;
- less any associated costs, including those to wind up the plan.

A refund is not discounted when it is not a fixed amount (i.e., the amount of the refund is determined as the full amount or a proportion of the surplus), even if the refund is realizable only at a future date.

When there is no minimum funding requirement, the economic benefit available as a reduction in future contributions is calculated as the lower of:

- the surplus in the plan; and
- the future service cost to the entity for each year, discounted over the shorter of the expected life of the plan and the expected life of the entity, assuming that:
  o there will be no change to the benefits to be provided in the future until the plan is amended, and
  o the workforce remains stable in the future, unless there is a demonstrable commitment at the balance sheet date to reduce the number of employees covered by the plan.

The Effect of a Minimum Funding Requirement on the Economic Benefit Available as a Reduction in Future Contributions

Contributions may be required at a given date to cover minimum funding requirements for:

- any existing shortfall for past service on the minimum funding basis; and
- the future accrual of benefits.

When there is a minimum funding requirement for contributions for the future accrual of benefits, the economic benefit available as a reduction in future contributions is determined as the present value of:

- the estimated future service cost in each year;
- less the estimated minimum funding contributions required for the future accrual of benefits in that year.

When the future minimum funding contribution required for the future accrual of benefits exceeds the future service cost in any given year, the present value of that excess reduces the amount of the asset available as a reduction in future contributions at the end of the reporting period. The amount of the asset available as a reduction in future contributions can, however, never be less than zero.

CICA 3461 differs from IAS 19 because the former does not address the effect of a minimum funding requirement on the measurement of the defined benefit liability (or asset).

When a Minimum Funding Requirement May Give Rise to a Liability

A liability is recognized when there is an obligation under a minimum funding requirement to pay contributions to cover an existing shortfall in the minimum funding basis for services already received. The liability is recognized to the extent that those contributions will not be available as a refund or reduction in future contributions after they are paid into the plan. The liability reduces the defined benefit asset or increases the defined benefit liability so that, when the contributions are paid, no gain or loss is expected to result from the application of the asset ceiling.

This liability and any subsequent remeasurement are recognized immediately in accordance with the policy for recognizing actuarial gains and losses (i.e., in the income statement or in other comprehensive income).

Illustrative Disclosures:

Extract 16(18) – Adopting IFRIC 14 in 2008 (currently assessing the impact)

UBS AG (AR 2007), page 40

Note 1 Summary of Significant Accounting Policies (in part)

c) International Financial Reporting Standards and Interpretations to be adopted in 2008 and later (in part)

IFRIC 14 The Limit on a Defined Benefit Asset Minimum

Funding Requirements and their Interaction – IAS 19 IFRIC 14 was issued on 5 July 2007 and is effective for annual periods beginning on or after 1 January 2008. IFRIC 14 provides guidance regarding the circumstances under which refunds and future reductions in contributions from a defined benefit plan can be regarded as available to an entity for the purpose recognizing a net defined benefit asset. Additionally, in jurisdictions where there is both a minimum funding requirement and restrictions over the amounts that companies can recover from the plan, either as refunds or reductions in contributions, additional liabilities may need to be recognized. UBS is currently assessing the impact of this interpretation on its Financial Statements.

Extract 16(19) – Adopting IFRIC 14 in 2008 (no significant impact expected)

AB Volvo (AR 2007), page 87

Note 1 Accounting principles (in part)

Changes of accounting principles (in part)

New accounting principles 2008 and 2009 (in part)

IFRIC 14 IAS 19 The limit on a defined benefit asset, minimum funding requirements and their interaction.

The interpretation becomes effective on January 1, 2008 and applies to fiscal years beginning after that date. The interpretation discusses funding of defined benefit pension plans and minimum funding requirements in connection to IAS 19 and the limit on the measurement for a defined benefit asset. The Group will apply IFRIC 14 as of January 1, 2008, but this is not expected to have a significant impact on the Group's financial statements.

Extract 16(20) – Adopting IFRIC 14 in 2008 (quantified impact for 2007)

Koninklijke Philips Electronics N.V. (AR 2007), page 210

Significant IFRS accounting policies (in part)

IFRS accounting standards effective as from 2008 (in part)

IFRIC Interpretation 14 'The Limit on a Defined Benefit Asset, Minimum Funding Requirements and their Interaction'

This interpretation becomes effective for annual reports beginning on or after January 1, 2008. IFRIC 14 addresses (1) when refunds or reductions in future contributions should be regarded as 'available' in the context of paragraph 58 of IAS 19 Employee Benefits ; (2) how a minimum funding requirement might affect the availability of reductions in future contributions; and (3) when a minimum funding requirement might give rise to a liability. The Company has assessed that application of this interpretation would result in recognition of additional prepaid assets of EUR 2,504 million and a simultaneous increase in equity of EUR 1,866 million (net of tax).

Commentary: In the above extract, the company discloses that the early adoption of this interpretation would have resulted in the recognition of additional prepaid assets and a related increase in equity in the current fiscal year.

The company plans to adopt this interpretation in the next fiscal year.

Extract 16(21) – Early adoption of IFRIC 14 (quantified impact)

InterContinental Hotels Group PLC (AR 2007), page 52
Summary of significant accounting policies (in part)
Statement of compliance

The Group has early adopted International Financial Reporting Interpretations Committee 14 'IAS 19 – The Limit on a Defined Benefit Asset, Minimum Funding Requirements and their Interaction' (IFRIC 14). IFRIC 14 provides guidance on assessing the limit in International Accounting Standard 19 'Employee Benefits' (IAS 19) on the amount of the surplus that can be recognised as an asset. It also explains how the pension asset or liability may be affected by a statutory or contractual minimum funding requirement. Under IFRIC 14, the Group has recognised retirement benefit assets of £32m on the balance sheet at 31 December 2007.

Commentary: Here, the company discloses that it has recognized retirement benefit assets on the balance sheet as a result of adopting this interpretation early.

Extract 16(22) – Early adoption of IFRIC 14 (impact not quantified)

Cadbury Schweppes plc (Annual Report & Accounts 2007), page 137
40. Changes and proposed changes to generally accepted accounting principles (in part)

IFRIC 14, "IAS 19 – The limit on a defined benefit asset, minimum funding requirements and their interaction" provides guidance on assessing the limit in IAS 19, "Employee benefits" on the amount of the surplus that can be recognised as an asset. It also explains how the pension asset or liability may be affected by a statutory or contractual minimum funding requirement. IFRIC 14 is effective for annual periods beginning on or after 1 January 2008. This interpretation has not yet been endorsed by the EU. The Group has considered IFRIC 14 when applying the current IAS 19 standard in its 2007 Report and Accounts.

Present Value of Defined Benefit Obligations, Current Service Cost and Interest Cost

The *present value* of a defined benefit obligation reflects the present value of expected future payments (without deducting any plan assets) required to settle the obligation resulting from employee service in the current and prior periods; it comprises not only the legal obligations under the formal terms of a defined benefit plan, but also any constructive obligations arising from an entity's informal practices.

Current service cost represents the increase in the present value of the defined benefit obligation resulting from employee service in the current period.

Interest cost represents the increase during the period in the present value of a defined benefit obligation that arises because the benefits are one period closer to settlement. Interest cost is computed by multiplying the discount rate determined at the start of the period by the present value of the defined benefit obligation throughout that period, taking account of any material changes in the obligation.

Measurement

The present value of the defined benefit obligations and the related current service cost are measured by:

- applying an actuarial valuation method (i.e., the projected unit credit method);
- attributing the benefit to periods of employee service; and
- making actuarial assumptions.

CICA 3461 requires the use of the projected benefit method prorated on services or the accumulated benefit method, both of which are similar to the projected unit credit method required by IAS 19.

Attribution of Benefit to Periods of Employee Service

The present value of defined benefit obligations and the related current service cost (and, where applicable, past service cost) are determined by attributing the benefit to periods of service based on a plan's benefit formula.

When a plan's formula attributes a materially higher level of benefit to later years of service, however, the benefit is attributed on a straight-line basis from:

- the date when an employee's services first earn benefits under the plan (whether or not the benefits are conditional on further service); until
- the date when further employee services earn no further material benefits under the plan, other than salary increases.

Management judgment will be required to determine what is considered a materially higher level of benefit.

Employee services give rise to an obligation under a defined benefit plan even if the benefits are not vested. When benefits are not vested, the measurement of the defined benefit obligation takes into account the probability that some employees may not satisfy any vesting requirements.

Similarly, an obligation is created when an employee renders services that will entitle that employee to receive post-employment benefits only if a specified event occurs after the employee is no longer employed (for example, the employee becomes ill). Thus, the measurement of the defined benefit obligation takes into account the probability that the specified event will occur.

IAS 19 is silent on the accounting for post-employment benefits (that do not vest or accumulate). In practice, a liability is recognized when the event that obligates the entity to provide the benefit occurs.

CICA 3461 differs from IAS 19 because the former:

- specifically addresses the accounting for post-employment benefits (that do not vest or accumulate), which is the same as in practice under IFRS; and
- requires for defined benefit plans other than pension plans that the obligation for benefits be attributed on a straight-line basis to each year of service in the attribution period except when the plan formula attributes a significantly higher level of benefits to early years of service. In that case, the obligation should be attributed based on the plan's benefit formula.

Actuarial Assumptions

Actuarial assumptions represent an entity's best estimate of the variables that will determine the ultimate cost of providing post-employment benefits. They comprise:

- demographic assumptions about the future characteristics of current and former employees (and their dependants) eligible for benefits. Demographic assumptions deal with matters such as:
  - o mortality, both during and after employment,
  - o rates of employee turnover, disability and early retirement,
  - o the proportion of plan members with dependants who will be eligible for benefits, and

o   claim rates under medical plans; and

• financial assumptions determined in nominal terms and, based on market expectations at the balance sheet date, for the period over which the obligation will be settled. Financial assumptions deal with matters such as:

o   the discount rate,

o   future salary and benefit levels,

o   future medical costs, including material costs of administering claims and benefit payments, and

o   the expected rate of return on plan assets.

Discount Rate

The discount rate is determined by reference to market yields at the balance sheet date on high-quality corporate bonds, consistent with the currency and estimated term of the benefit obligations. Management judgment will be required to determine what is considered a high-quality corporate bond.

In some cases, there may not be a deep market in bonds with a sufficiently long maturity to match the estimated maturity of all the benefit payments. In such cases, the discount rate for longer maturities is extrapolated from the current market rates for shorter-term payments.

CICA 3461 differs from IAS 19 because, when immediate settlement of the plan is possible, CICA 3461 allows the discount rate to be determined by reference to rates in available annuity contracts.

Salary and Benefit Levels

Financial assumptions about future salary and benefit levels must reflect:

• estimated future salary increases;

• the benefits set out in the terms of the plan or resulting from any constructive obligation beyond those terms, at the balance sheet date; and

• estimated future changes in state benefits (e.g., governmental programs) that affect the defined benefit payable, only when those changes were enacted before the balance sheet date, or past history or other reliable evidence indicates that those state benefits will change in some predictable manner.

CICA 3461 differs from IAS 19 because the former permits future changes in state benefits that affect the defined benefit payable to be reflected only after they are enacted.

Illustrative Disclosure:

Extract 16(23) – Measurement uncertainty resulting from actuarial assumptions

---

AB Volvo (AR 2007), page 93

Note 2 Key sources of estimation uncertainty (in part)

Pensions and other post-employment benefits (in part)

Provisions and costs for post-employment benefits, i.e. mainly pensions and health-care benefits, are dependent on assumptions used by actuaries in calculating such amounts. The appropriate assumptions and actuarial calculations are made separately for each population in the respective countries of Volvo's operations. The assumptions include discount rates, health care cost trends rates, inflation, salary growth, long-term return on plan assets, retirement rates, mortality rates and other factors. Discount rate assumptions are based on long-term high quality corporate bond and government bond yields available at year-end. Health care cost trend assumptions are developed based on historical cost data, the near-term outlook, and an assessment of likely long-term trends. Inflation assumptions are based on an evaluation of external market indicators. The salary growth assumptions reflect the long-term actual experience, the near-term outlook and assumed inflation. Retirement and mortality rates are based primarily on officially available mortality statistics. The actuarial assumptions are reviewed on an annual basis and modifications are made to them when it is deemed appropriate to do so. Actual results that differ from management's assumptions are accumulated and amortized over future periods and, therefore, generally affect the recognized expense and recorded provisions in such future periods.

Insured Benefits

As previously mentioned, a post-employment benefit plan funded through an insurance policy is accounted for as a defined benefit plan when an entity retains (either directly or indirectly through the plan) a legal or constructive obligation to either:

- pay the employee benefits directly when they fall due; or
- pay further amounts if the insurer does not pay all future employee benefits related to employee service in the current and prior periods.

Therefore, an entity:

- accounts for a qualifying insurance policy as a plan asset; and
- recognizes a non-qualifying insurance policy as a reimbursement right if certain criteria are satisfied.

A qualifying insurance policy is a policy issued by an insurer that is not a related party of the reporting entity, where the proceeds:

- can be used only to pay or fund employee benefits under a defined benefit plan; and
- are not available to the reporting entity's own creditors (even in bankruptcy) and cannot be paid to the reporting entity unless either:
  - o the proceeds represent surplus assets that are not needed for the policy to meet all the related employee benefit obligations, or
  - o the proceeds are returned to the reporting entity to reimburse it for employee benefits already paid.

CICA 3461 differs from IAS 19 because an insurance contract refers exclusively to arrangements where an insurance enterprise assumes an unconditional legal obligation to provide specified benefits to specified individuals. A post-employment benefit plan funded through an insurance contract would be accounted for as a defined contribution plan, in accordance with CICA 3461. This treatment would also be required under IAS 19.

When an arrangement does not meet the definition of an insurance contract, CICA 3461 differs from IAS 19 because the former:

- requires the arrangement to be accounted for as a plan asset, irrespective of whether the arrangement is qualifying or non-qualifying; and

- does not require the arrangement to be issued by an insurer that is not a related party of the reporting entity.

Plan Assets

Plan assets are assets held by a long-term employee benefit fund and qualifying insurance policies but exclude:

- unpaid contributions due from the reporting entity to the fund; and

- any non-transferable financial instruments issued by the entity and held by the fund.

Plan assets are reduced by any liabilities of the fund that are not directly related to the payment of employee benefits, such as trade and other payables and liabilities resulting from derivative financial instruments.

Assets held by a long-term employee benefit fund are assets, excluding non-transferable financial instruments issued by the reporting entity, that:

- are held by an entity (a fund) that is legally separate from the reporting entity and exist solely to pay or fund employee benefits; and

- are available to be used only to pay or fund employee benefits, are not available to the reporting entity's own creditors (even in bankruptcy) and cannot be returned to the reporting entity, unless either:
  - o the remaining assets of the fund are sufficient to meet all the related employee benefit obligations of the plan or the reporting entity, or
  - o the assets are returned to the reporting entity to reimburse it for employee benefits already paid.

Measurement

Plan assets must be measured at fair value at the balance sheet date. When no market price is available, the fair value of plan assets should be estimated, for example, by using discounted cash flows.

IAS 19 does not provide specific guidance on how fair value should be determined, except for qualifying insurance policies that exactly match the amount and timing of some or all of the benefits payable under the plan. The fair value of such qualifying insurance policies is deemed to be the present value of the related obligations, subject to any reduction required if the amounts receivable under the insurance policies are not recoverable in full.

Reimbursement Rights

Recognition

A reimbursement right is recognized as a separate asset when it is virtually certain that another party will reimburse some or all of the expenditure required to settle a defined benefit obligation.

In all other respects, this separate asset is treated in the same way as a plan asset. In particular, the expense related to a defined benefit plan may be presented net of the amount recognized for a reimbursement in the statement of comprehensive income.

Illustrative Disclosure:

Extract 16(24) – Recognition of reimbursement rights in the balance sheet

SUEZ (2007 Reference Document), page 271
NOTE 17 OTHER ASSETS

In millions of euros	Dec. 31, 2007			Dec. 31, 2006			Dec. 31, 2005		
	Non-current	Current	Total	Non-current	Current	Total	Non-current	Current	Total
Reimbursement rights	449.2	39.7	488.9	523.7	40.8	564.5	1,393.6	267.3	1,660.9
Tax receivables		1,229.8	1,229.8		923.1	923.1		726.3	726.3
Other receivables	281.3	1,287.0	1,568.3	255.1	1,372.7	1,627.8	292.9	1,699.5	1,992.4
TOTAL	**730.5**	**2,556.5**	**3,287.0**	**778.8**	**2,336.6**	**3,115.4**	**1,686.5**	**2,693.1**	**4,379.6**

Reimbursement rights at December 31, 2007 include:

- Electrabel's reimbursement rights relating to pension obligations for employees of the distribution business of Walloon mixed intermunicipal companies (€309.5 million, including a current portion of €39.7 million). Reimbursement rights arise because Electrabel makes its personnel available to the inter-municipal companies for the day-to-day operation of the networks. All related personnel costs (including pension costs) are billed by Electrabel to the intermunicipal companies based on actual costs. Electrabel's pension obligations regarding these employees are now included within liabilities under provisions for pensions and other employee benefit obligations. The matching entry is a reimbursement right in respect of the inter-municipal companies for a similar amount;

- insurance policies taken out with Contassur, a related party, in order to finance certain Group pension obligations, representing €179.3 million;

Changes in reimbursement rights between 2006 and 2005 are mainly attributable to the sale of Electrabel Netten Vlaanderen and to the creation of Brussels Network Operations (see Note 2.2.2).

Commentary: In the above extract, the company recognizes reimbursement rights in other assets, which relate to pension obligations for employees of the distribution business of Walloon mixed inter-municipal companies, and insurance policies taken out with a related party to finance certain pension obligations.

Measurement

Reimbursement rights must be measured at fair value at the balance sheet date.

IAS 19 does not provide specific guidance on how fair value should be determined, except for reimbursement rights arising under insurance policies that exactly match the amount and timing of some or all of the benefits payable under a defined benefit plan. The fair value of such reimbursement rights is deemed to be the present value of the related obligation, subject to any reduction required if the reimbursement is not recoverable in full.

Illustrative Disclosure:

Extract 16(25) – Recognition and measurement of reimbursement rights

Akzo Nobel N.V. (AR 2007), page 128
Note 22 Provisions (in part)
Provisions for pensions and other post-retirement benefits (in part)
This reimbursement right has been recognized as an asset under other financial non-current assets, measured at fair value. At December 31, 2007, this value was EUR 35 million (December 31, 2006: EUR 46 million).

Cost Components

The expense (income) recognized in the income statement comprises the net total of the following:

- current service cost;

- interest cost;
- the expected return on any plan assets and on any reimbursement rights;
- actuarial gains and losses (unless recognized in full immediately in other comprehensive income);
- past service cost;
- the effect of any curtailments or settlements; and
- the effect of the asset ceiling test (unless recognized in other comprehensive income).

CICA 3461 differs from IAS 19 because the former requires actuarial gains and losses that are recognized in full immediately, and any adjustments that result from the application of the asset ceiling, to be accounted for in the income statement (there is no option to account for these items in other comprehensive income).

Illustrative Disclosure:

Extract 16(26) – Defined benefit plan expense components

Carl Zeiss AG (AR 2007), page 154 **27 Pension Provisions (in part)** The consolidated income statement contains the following:	2006/07 EUR thou	2005/06 EUR thou
Current service cost	30,375	29,917
Interest cost	60,371	56,221
Expected return on plan assets	–23,348	–7,236
Past service cost	615	692
Amortization of actuarial gains / losses	–2,189	2,659
Other	132	232
Net expenses for the fiscal year	65,956	82,485

Expected Return on Plan Assets and Reimbursement Rights

The *return on plan assets* is interest, dividends and other revenue derived from the plan assets, together with realized and unrealized gains or losses on the plan assets, less any costs of administering the plan (other than those included in the actuarial assumptions used to measure the defined benefit obligation) and less any tax payable by the plan itself.

The *expected return on plan assets* is based on market expectations, at the beginning of the period, for returns over the entire life of the related obligation. The expected return on plan assets reflects changes in the fair value of plan assets held during the period as a result of actual contributions paid into the fund and benefits paid out of the fund. In determining the expected return on plan assets, expected administration costs (other than those included in the actuarial assumptions used to measure the obligation) are deducted.

The expected return on plan assets is recognized as an expense in the income statement. The difference between the expected return on plan assets and the actual return on plan assets is an actuarial gain or loss.

CICA 3461 differs from IAS 19 because the former requires that the expected return on plan assets be based on:

- the expected long-term rate of return of plan assets; and

* the fair value or a market-related value of plan assets.

A market-related value is a calculated amount that incorporates changes in the fair value of plan assets in a systematic and rational manner over a period not exceeding five years.

Past Service Cost

Past service cost is the change in the present value of the defined benefit obligation for employee service in prior periods. It arises in the current period from the introduction of, or changes to, post-employment benefits or other long-term employee benefits.

Recognition

Past service cost is recognized on a straight-line basis over the average period until the benefits become vested. If any benefits are already vested, past service cost is recognized immediately.

When benefits payable under an existing defined benefit plan are reduced, the resulting reduction in the defined benefit liability (i.e., *negative* past service cost) is recognized over the average period until the reduced portion of benefits becomes vested.

CICA 3461 differs from IAS 19 because the former:

* does not have separate requirements for past service cost for which benefits are vested and unvested;

* requires negative past service cost to be applied first to reduce any existing unamortized past service cost and then to reduce any existing unamortized transitional obligation;

* requires any past service cost related to post-employment benefits (that do not vest or accumulate) to be recognized:

   o over a period linked to the type of benefit, or

   o immediately in the income statement;

* requires past service cost related to pension benefits, other retirement benefits or post-employment benefits (that vest or accumulate) to be recognized:

   o by assigning an equal amount to each remaining service period up to the full eligibility date of each employee active at the date of the plan initiation or amendment who was not yet fully eligible for benefits at that date, or

   o by using an alternative approach that amortizes past service cost more rapidly (e.g., on a straight-line basis over the average remaining service period of active employees expected to receive benefits under the plan up to the full eligibility date).

When all or almost all of the employees are no longer actively working, however, the past service cost related to pension benefits, other retirement benefits or post-employment benefits (that vest or accumulate) is recognized on a straight-line basis over the average remaining life expectancy of the former employees.

Actuarial Gains and Losses

Actuarial gains and losses may result from increases or decreases in either the present value of a defined benefit obligation or the fair value of any related plan assets. They comprise experience adjustments and the effects of changes in actuarial assumptions.

Recognition

Actuarial gains and losses may be recognized:

- in accordance with the corridor approach, in the income statement;

- by adopting any systematic method that results in faster recognition (provided that the same basis is applied to both gains and losses consistently from period to period), in the income statement; or

- in full immediately (provided that the same basis is applied to both gains and losses consistently from period to period), in the income statement or in other comprehensive income (as long as this is done for all defined benefit plans and all actuarial gains and losses).

When a policy is adopted of recognizing actuarial gains and losses in full immediately in other comprehensive income, any adjustments arising from the asset ceiling test must also be recognized in other comprehensive income.

Actuarial gains and losses and adjustments arising from the asset ceiling test that have been recognized directly in other comprehensive income are recognized immediately in retained earnings and cannot be recycled through the income statement in a subsequent period.

CICA 3461 differs from IAS 19 because the former requires actuarial gains and losses that:

- relate to pension benefits, other retirement benefits or post-employment benefits (that vest or accumulate) to be recognized:
  - o   in accordance with the corridor approach, in the income statement,
  - o   by adopting any systematic method that results in faster recognition, in the income statement, or
  - o   in full immediately in the income statement (there is no option to account for this item in other comprehensive income);

- relate to post-employment benefits (that do not vest or accumulate) to be recognized:
  - o   over a period linked to the type of benefit, or
  - o   in full immediately in the income statement (there is no option to account for this item in other comprehensive income).

Corridor Approach

When an entity decides to use the corridor approach, the *corridor limit* (which must be calculated and applied separately for each defined benefit plan) is determined as 10% of the greater of:

- the present value of the defined benefit obligation (before deducting plan assets) at the end of the previous reporting period; and

- the fair value of any plan assets at the end of the previous reporting period.

Then it can calculate the excess of the net cumulative unrecognized actuarial gains and losses at the end of the previous reporting period over the corridor limit.

Finally, it will recognize an amount equal to that excess divided by the expected average remaining working lives of the employees participating in that plan.

CICA 3461 differs from IAS 19 because the former:

- provides the option to use the market-related value of plan assets instead of fair value in determining the corridor limit; and

- requires the amount of actuarial gains and losses recognized to be calculated as the excess (i.e., the net cumulative unrecognized actuarial gains and losses at the end of the previous reporting period over the corridor limit) divided by the average remaining service period of active employees expected to receive benefits under the plan.

When all or almost all of the employees are no longer actively working, however, the amount of actuarial gains and losses recognized is calculated as the excess (i.e., the net cumulative unrecognized actuarial gains and losses at the end of the previous reporting period over the corridor limit) divided by the average remaining life expectancy of the former employees.

Illustrative Disclosure:

Extract 16(27) – Change in accounting policy for the recognition of actuarial gains and losses

---

Alcatel-Lucent (AR 2007on Form 20-F), page 176

NOTE 4 CHANGE IN ACCOUNTING POLICY AND PRESENTATION (in part)

a/ Change in accounting policy

On January 1, 2007, Alcatel-Lucent adopted (with retrospective effect as of January 1, 2005) the option offered by Amendment to IAS 19 "Employee benefits – Actuarial gains and losses, Group plans and Disclosures", to immediately recognize all actuarial gains and losses and any adjustment arising from an asset ceiling, net of deferred tax effects, in the period in which they occur outside the income statement in the Statement Of Recognized Income and Expense (SORIE). Management believes that the change will more fairly present the fair value of assets and liabilities related to retiree benefits in the company's balance sheet and eliminate significant volatility in its results of operations for certain plans, the participants of which are all, or almost all, fully eligible to receive benefits.

Previously, Alcatel-Lucent applied the corridor method, under which actuarial gains and losses exceeding 10% of the greater of (i) the benefit obligation or (ii) the fair value of plan assets were recognized in the income statement over the expected remaining working lives of the employees participating in the plans. The impact of the limitation in the value of plan assets to the lower of: (i) the value resulting from applying IAS 19 "Employee Benefits" prior to the Group's adoption of the option provided by the amendment to IAS 19, and (ii) the net total present value of any available refund from the plan or reduction in future contributions to the plan (arising from asset ceilings) was accounted for in the income statement.

The impact of this change in accounting policies on the balance sheet in the prior periods is as follows:

(in millions of euros)	December 31, 2006	December 31, 2005
Prepaid pension costs	701	231
Assets held for sale	10	-
Deferred tax assets (liabilities)	(291)	(80)
Pensions, retirement indemnities and other post-retirement benefits	(36)	(277)
Shareholders' equity attributable to equity holders of the parent	387	(126)
Minority interests	(3)	(2)

The impact on the income statements in the prior periods is as follows:

(in millions of euros)	Year ended December 31, 2006	Year ended December 31, 2005
Income (loss) from operating activities	(7)	(5)
Other financial income (loss)	78	(1)
Income tax (expense) income	-	-
Income (loss) from discontinued operations	(1)	(2)
NET RESULT	**70**	**(8)**
Basic earnings per share	0.05	(0.01)
Diluted earnings per share	0.05	(0.01)

Commentary: In the above extract, the company discloses that it has changed its accounting policy for recognizing actuarial gains and losses from the corridor approach to recognition in full immediately outside profit or loss in the statement of recognized income and expense (SORIE). As a result, adjustments arising from the asset ceiling test are recognized outside profit or loss in the SORIE. The company also discloses the impact of this change on the balance sheet and income statement in the prior periods.

Note that companies with a policy of recognizing actuarial gains and losses in full immediately and adjustments arising from the asset ceiling test outside profit or loss in the SORIE will, instead, recognize these items in other comprehensive income, displayed in the statement of comprehensive income, for annual periods beginning on or after January 1, 2009.

Curtailments and Settlements

Curtailments and settlements are events not covered by normal actuarial assumptions that materially change the obligations of defined benefit plans.

The defined benefit obligation and any related plan assets must be remeasured using current actuarial assumptions (including current market interest rates and other current market prices) before assessing the impact of a curtailment or settlement.

Recognition

Gains or losses on the curtailment or settlement of a defined benefit plan are recognized when the curtailment or settlement occurs.

A curtailment occurs when an entity:

- can demonstrate it is committed to make a significant reduction in the number of employees covered by a plan; or
- amends the terms of a defined benefit plan so that a significant element of future service by current employees will no longer qualify for benefits, or will qualify only for reduced benefits.

A settlement occurs when an entity enters into a transaction that eliminates all further legal or constructive obligations for part or all of the benefits provided under a defined benefit plan.

The acquisition of an insurance policy to fund some or all of the employee benefits related to employee service in the current and prior periods is not a settlement if the entity retains a legal or constructive obligation to pay further amounts should the insurer not pay the employee benefits specified in the insurance policy.

CICA 3461 differs from IAS 19 because the former:

- further specifies that a *settlement* is a transaction that is *irrevocable* and *eliminates the significant risks* associated with a defined benefit obligation and the assets used to effect the settlement;
- requires any gain on the settlement of a defined benefit plan other than a pension plan to be applied to reduce any unamortized transitional obligation at the date of settlement; and
- requires the recognition of:
  - o a loss on curtailment when it is probable that a curtailment will occur and the net effects are reasonably estimable, and
  - o a gain on curtailment when an event giving rise to a curtailment has occurred.

Measurement

A gain or loss on a curtailment or settlement of a defined benefit plan comprises:

- any resulting change in the present value of the defined benefit obligation;

- any resulting change in the fair value of the plan assets;
- any related actuarial gains and losses and past service cost that had not previously been recognized; and
- any related part of unrecognized transitional liability.

Where a curtailment relates to only some of the employees covered by a plan, or where only part of an obligation is settled, the gain or loss includes a proportionate share of the previously unrecognized past service cost and actuarial gains and losses (and of transitional amounts remaining unrecognized). The proportionate share is determined on the basis of the present value of the obligations before and after the curtailment or settlement, unless another basis is more rational in the circumstances.

CICA 3461 differs from IAS 19 because:

- The gain or loss on the settlement of a defined benefit plan includes any unamortized transitional asset at the date of settlement, but excludes any unamortized past service cost and any unamortized transitional obligation at the date of settlement.

- The gain or loss on the curtailment of a defined benefit plan:

  o includes the change resulting from the remeasurement of the defined benefit obligation due to the curtailment, to the extent that this change does not represent the reversal of an unamortized actuarial gain or loss (for the purposes of calculating a curtailment gain or loss, any unamortized transitional asset is treated as an unamortized actuarial gain and is combined with the unamortized actuarial gain or loss arising subsequent to the date as of which the transitional asset was determined), but

  o excludes any resulting change in the fair value of the plan assets.

Business Combinations

In a business combination, an entity recognizes assets and liabilities arising from post-employment benefits at the present value of the obligation less the fair value of any plan assets. The present value of the obligation includes all of the following, even if the acquiree has not yet recognized them at the acquisition date:

- actuarial gains and losses that arose before the acquisition date (whether or not they fell inside the 10% corridor);
- past service cost that arose from benefit changes, or the introduction of a plan, before the acquisition date; and
- transitional amounts that the acquiree has not recognized.

Presentation

Offset

In instances where an entity operates more than one plan, an asset of one plan is offset against a liability of another plan only when the entity:

- has a legally enforceable right to use a surplus in one plan to settle obligations under the other plan; and
- intends either to settle the obligations on a net basis or to realize the surplus in one plan and settle its obligation under the other plan simultaneously.

In practice, the offset of an asset of one plan against a liability of another plan is not likely to be possible due to the abovementioned restrictions.

CICA 3461 differs from IAS 19 because the former allows an entity to offset an accrued benefit asset of one defined benefit plan against an accrued benefit liability of another defined benefit plan when the entity:

- has the right to use the assets of one plan to pay for the benefits to be provided by the other plan; and
- intends to exercise that right.

Current Versus Non-current Distinction

IAS 19 does not specify whether an entity should distinguish current and non-current portions of assets and liabilities arising from post-employment benefits.

In practice, the consensus is that the current and non-current portions of assets and liabilities arising from post-employment benefits should be segregated if they can be reasonably determined. Most entities, however, have classified assets and liabilities arising from post-employment benefits as non-current.

Cost Components

IAS 19 does not specify whether an entity should present current service cost, interest cost and the expected return on plan assets as components of a single item in the statement of comprehensive income.

Disclosure

Information that helps users of financial statements evaluate the nature of defined benefit plans and the financial impact of changes in those plans during the period must be disclosed. At minimum, the following information about defined benefit plans must be disclosed:

- the accounting policy for recognizing actuarial gains and losses;
- a general description of the type of plan;
- a reconciliation of the opening and closing balances of the present value of the defined benefit obligation showing separately, if applicable, the effects during the period attributable to each of the following:
  - o current service cost,
  - o interest cost,
  - o contributions by plan participants,
  - o actuarial gains and losses,
  - o foreign currency exchange rate changes on plans measured in a currency different from the entity's presentation currency,
  - o benefits paid,
  - o past service cost,
  - o business combinations,
  - o curtailments, and
  - o settlements;
- an analysis of the defined benefit obligation into amounts arising from plans that are wholly unfunded and amounts arising from plans that are wholly or partly funded;
- a reconciliation of the opening and closing balances of the fair value of plan assets and of the opening and closing balances of any reimbursement right recognized as an asset, showing separately, if applicable, the effects during the period attributable to each of the following:

- o   expected return on plan assets,
- o   actuarial gains and losses,
- o   foreign currency exchange rate changes on plans measured in a currency different from the entity's presentation currency,
- o   contributions by the employer,
- o   contributions by plan participants,
- o   benefits paid,
- o   business combinations, and
- o   settlements;
- a reconciliation of the present value of the defined benefit obligation and the fair value of the plan assets to the assets and liabilities recognized on the balance sheet, showing at least:
  - o   the net actuarial gains or losses not recognized on the balance sheet,
  - o   the past service cost not recognized on the balance sheet,
  - o   any amount not recognized as an asset because of the asset ceiling test,
  - o   the fair value at the balance sheet date of any reimbursement right recognized as an asset (with a brief description of the link between the reimbursement right and the related obligation), and
  - o   the other amounts recognized on the balance sheet;
- the total expense recognized in the income statement for each of the following, and the line item(s) in which they are included:
  - o   current service cost,
  - o   interest cost,
  - o   expected return on plan assets,
  - o   expected return on any reimbursement right recognized as an asset,
  - o   actuarial gains and losses,
  - o   past service cost,
  - o   the effect of any curtailment or settlement, and
  - o   the effect of the asset ceiling test;
- the total amount recognized in other comprehensive income for each of the following:
  - o   actuarial gains and losses, and
  - o   the effect of the asset ceiling test;
- the cumulative amount of actuarial gains and losses recognized in other comprehensive income (this is required only for entities that recognize actuarial gains and losses in other comprehensive income);
- the percentage or amount of the fair value of the total plan assets represented by each major category of plan assets, which must include, but is not limited to, equity instruments, debt instruments, property and all other assets;
- the amounts included in the fair value of plan assets for:
  - o   each category of the entity's own financial instruments, and
  - o   any property occupied by, or other assets used by, the entity;
- a narrative description of the basis used to determine the overall expected rate of return on assets, including the effect of the major categories of plan assets;

- the actual return on plan assets, as well as the actual return on any reimbursement right recognized as an asset;
- the principal actuarial assumptions (in absolute terms) used as at the balance sheet date, including, when applicable:
  o the discount rates,
  o the expected rates of return on any plan assets for the periods presented in the financial statements,
  o the expected rates of return on any reimbursement right recognized as an asset for the periods presented in the financial statements,
  o the expected rates of salary increases (and of changes in an index or other variables specified in the formal or constructive terms of a plan as the basis for future benefit increases),
  o medical cost trend rates, and
  o any other material actuarial assumptions used;
- the effect of an increase of one percentage point and the effect of a decrease of one percentage point in the assumed medical cost trend rates (assuming that all other assumptions are held constant) on:
  o the aggregate of the current service cost and interest cost components of net periodic post-employment medical costs, and
  o the accumulated post-employment benefit obligation for medical costs;
- the amounts for the current fiscal year and previous four fiscal years of:
  o the present value of the defined benefit obligation,
  o the fair value of the plan assets,
  o the surplus or deficit in the plan, and
  o the experience adjustments arising on:
    - the plan liabilities at the balance sheet date expressed either as:
      - an amount, or
      - a percentage of the plan liabilities, and
    - the plan assets at the balance sheet date expressed either as:
      - an amount, or
      - a percentage of the plan assets;
- the employer's best estimate (as soon as it can reasonably be determined) of contributions expected to be paid to the plan during fiscal year beginning after the balance sheet date.

The requirement to disclose a general description of the type of plan should be distinguished by plan risks (e.g., flat salary pension plans, final salary pension plans and post-employment medical plans). The description of the plan must include informal practices that give rise to constructive obligations included in the measurement of the defined benefit obligation. Further detail is not required.

Illustrative Disclosures:

Extract 16(28) – General description of the type of plan

Roche Holdings Ltd (AR 2007), page 60

10. Pensions and other post-employment benefits (in part)

Defined benefit plans

The Group's major defined benefit plans are located in Switzerland, the United States, Germany, the United Kingdom and Japan. Plans are usually established as trusts independent of the Group and are funded by payments from the Group and by employees. In some cases, notably for the major defined benefit plans in Germany, the plan is unfunded and the Group pays pensions to retired employees directly from its own financial resources.

Commentary: The company discloses the location of its major defined benefit plans and whether they are funded or unfunded.

Extract 16(29) – Reconciliation of opening and closing balances of the present value of the defined benefit obligation, and analysis of amounts that are funded and unfunded

Roche Holdings Ltd (AR 2007), page 62

10. Pensions and other post-employment benefits (in part)

Defined benefit plans: defined benefit obligation in millions of CHF

	2007			2006		
	Pension plans	Other post-employment benefit plans	Total	Pension plans	Other post-employment benefit plans	Total
At 1 January	13,572	1,026	14,598	13,540	1,066	14,606
Current service cost	361	22	383	334	18	352
Interest cost	556	56	612	522	49	571
Employee contributions	45	–	45	42	–	42
Actuarial (gains) losses	(718)	35	(683)	(159)	24	(135)
Currency translation effects and other	(235)	(79)	(314)	(158)	(76)	(234)
Benefits paid – funded plans	(448)	(46)	(494)	(427)	(53)	(480)
Benefits paid – unfunded plans	(134)	(12)	(146)	(109)	(2)	(111)
Past service cost	1	–	1	2	–	2
Business combinations	–	–	–	–	–	–
Curtailments	(11)	–	(11)	–	–	–
Settlements	(1)	–	(1)	(15)	–	(15)
At 31 December	12,988	1,002	13,990	13,572	1,026	14,598
Of which						
– Funded plans	9,904	742	10,646	10,258	744	11,002
– Unfunded plans	3,084	260	3,344	3,314	282	3,596

Commentary: The company discloses a reconciliation of opening and closing balances of the present value of the defined benefit obligation for pension plans and other post-employment benefit plans. The company also discloses a breakdown of the defined benefit obligation for pension plans and other post-employment benefit plans into funded and unfunded portions.

Extract 16(30) – Reconciliation of opening and closing balances of the fair value of plan assets and reimbursement rights

Roche Holdings Ltd (AR 2007), page 61
10. Pensions and other post-employment benefits (in part)
Defined benefit plans: fair value of plan assets and reimbursement rights in millions of CHF

	2007			2006		
	Fair value of plan assets	Reimburse-ment rights	Total	Fair value of plan assets	Reimburse-ment rights	Total
At 1 January	11,632	116	11,748	10,858	122	10,980
Expected return on plan assets	663	7	670	631	5	636
Actuarial gains (losses)	491	4	495	626	–	626
Currency translation effects and other	(373)	(10)	(383)	(246)	(8)	(254)
Employer contributions	207	(1)	206	215	(3)	212
Employee contributions	45	–	45	42	–	42
Benefits paid – funded plans	(494)	–	(494)	(480)	–	(480)
Past service cost	–	–	–	–	–	–
Business combinations	–	–	–	–	–	–
Curtailments	–	–	–	–	–	–
Settlements	(1)	–	(1)	(14)	–	(14)
At 31 December	12,170	116	12,286	11,632	116	11,748

Commentary: The company discloses a reconciliation of opening and closing balances of the fair value of plan assets and reimbursement rights.

Extract 16(31) – Reconciliation of the present value of the defined benefit obligation and the fair value of the plan assets to the assets and liabilities on the balance sheet

Roche Holdings Ltd (AR 2007), page 61
10. Pensions and other post-employment benefits (in part)
Defined benefit plans: funding status at 31 December in millions of CHF

	2007			2006		
	Funded plans	Unfunded plans	Total	Funded plans	Unfunded plans	Total
Fair value of plan assets	12,170	–	12,170	11,632	–	11,632
Defined benefit obligation	(10,646)	(3,344)	(13,990)	(11,002)	(3,596)	(14,598)
Over (under) funding	1,524	(3,344)	(1,820)	630	(3,596)	(2,966)
Unrecognised past service costs	(23)	(1)	(24)	(28)	–	(28)
Limit on asset recognition	(818)	–	(818)	(396)	–	(396)
Reimbursement rights	99	17	116	95	21	116
Net recognised asset (liability)	782	(3,328)	(2,546)	301	(3,575)	(3,274)
Reported as						
– Defined benefit plans	1,034	–	1,034	831	–	831
– Reimbursement rights	99	17	116	95	21	116
Post-employment benefit assets	1,133	17	1,150	926	21	947
Post-employment benefit liabilities	(351)	(3,345)	(3,696)	(625)	(3,596)	(4,221)
Net recognised asset (liability)	782	(3,328)	(2,546)	301	(3,575)	(3,274)

Commentary: The company discloses a reconciliation of the present value of the defined benefit obligation and the fair value of the plan assets to the assets and liabilities on the balance sheet.

Extract 16(32) – Accounting policy for recognizing actuarial gains and losses, and the total expense in the income statement

Roche Holdings Ltd (AR 2007), page 60

10. Pensions and other post-employment benefits (in part)

Defined benefit plans

Current and past service costs are charged to the appropriate income statement heading within the operating results. Pension plan administration and funding is overseen at a corporate level, and any settlement gains and losses resulting from changes in funding arrangements are reported as general and administration expenses within the Corporate segment. The expected returns on plan assets and interest costs are charged to financial income and financing costs, respectively. Actuarial gains and losses are recorded directly in equity. The recognition of pension assets is limited to the total of the present value of any future refunds from the plans or reductions in future contributions to the plans and any cumulative unrecognised past service costs. Adjustments arising from the limit on the recognition of assets for defined benefit plans are recorded directly in equity.

Defined benefit plans: expenses in millions of CHF

	Pension plans	Other post-employment benefit plans	Total	Pension plans	Other post-employment benefit plans	Total
	2007					**2006**
Current service cost	361	22	383	334	18	352
Past service cost	(2)	–	(2)	(3)	–	(3)
(Gain) loss on curtailment	(11)	–	(11)	–	–	–
(Gain) loss on settlement	–	–	–	(1)	–	(1)
Total operating expenses	348	22	370	330	18	348
Expected return on plan assets	(630)	(40)	(670)	(606)	(30)	(636)
Interest cost	556	56x	556	522	49	571
Total financial (income) expense	(74)	16	(58)	(84)	19	(65)
Total expense recognised in income statement	274	38	312	246	37	283

Commentary: The company discloses the total expense recognized in the income statement and the financial statement line items in which each cost is included. The company also discloses that actuarial gains and losses, as well as adjustments arising from the asset ceiling test, are recognized directly in equity.

Note that companies with a policy of recognizing actuarial gains and losses in full immediately and adjustments arising from the asset ceiling test outside profit or loss in the SORIE will instead recognize these items in other comprehensive income, displayed in the statement of comprehensive income, for annual periods beginning on or after January 1, 2009.

Extract 16(33) – Total amounts recognized directly in equity in the current period and amount of cumulative actuarial gains recognized directly in equity

Roche Holdings Ltd (AR 2007), page 64

10. Pensions and other post-employment benefits (in part)

Amounts recorded in equity

The actuarial gains and losses recognised in the statement of recognised income and expense were gains of 1,178 million Swiss francs (2006: gains of 761 million Swiss francs). The total amount at 31 December 2007 was accumulated gains of 1,387 million Swiss francs (2006: gains of 209 million Swiss francs).

In addition the recognition of pension assets is limited to the total of the present value of any future refunds from the plans or reductions in future contributions to the plans and the cumulative unrecognised past service costs. Adjustments arising from this limit on asset recognition are recorded directly in equity. In 2007 this adjustment was 422 million Swiss francs (2006: 396 million Swiss francs).

Commentary: The company discloses the amount of actuarial gains and the amount of the adjustment resulting from the asset ceiling test recognized in equity. The company also discloses the amount of cumulative actuarial gains recognized in equity.

Note that companies with a policy of recognizing actuarial gains and losses in full immediately and adjustments arising from the asset ceiling test outside profit or loss in the SORIE will instead recognize these items in other comprehensive income, displayed in the statement of comprehensive income, for annual periods beginning on or after January 1, 2009.

Extract 16(34) – Major categories of plan assets

Roche Holdings Ltd (AR 2007), page 61

10. Pensions and other post-employment benefits (in part)

Defined benefit plans: fair value of plan assets and reimbursement rights in millions of CHF (in part)

	2007	2006
Invested as		
– Shares and other equity instruments	6,055	5,819
– Bonds, debentures and other debt instruments	4,343	4,405
– Property	337	478
– Other assets	1,551	1,046
Total	12,286	11,748

Commentary: The company discloses what amount each major category of plan assets constitutes of the fair value of total plan assets.

Extract 16(35) – Amounts included in the fair value of plan assets for each category of the entity's own financial instruments

Roche Holdings Ltd (AR 2007), page 61

10. Pensions and other post-employment benefits (in part)

Defined benefit plans: fair value of plan assets and reimbursement rights in millions of CHF (in part)

Included within the fair value of plan assets are 340 thousand of the Group's non-voting equity securities with a fair value of 66 million Swiss francs (2006: 311 thousand non-voting equity securities with a total fair value of 68 million Swiss francs).

Extract 16(36) – Description of the basis used to determine the overall expected rate of return on assets and actual return on plan assets

Roche Holdings Ltd (AR 2007), page 63

10. Pensions and other post-employment benefits (in part)

Defined benefit plans: financial actuarial assumptions (in part)

Expected returns on plan assets are based on market expectations of expected returns on the assets in funded plans over the duration of the related obligation. This takes into account the split of the plan assets between equities, bonds, property and other investments. The calculation includes assumptions concerning expected dividend and interest income, realised and unrealised gains on plan assets and taxes and administration costs borne by the plan. These are based on long-term market expectations and the actual performance is continually monitored by corporate management. Due to the long-term nature of the obligations, the assumptions used for matters such as returns on investments may not necessarily be consistent with recent historical patterns. The expected return on plan assets included in the income statement is calculated by multiplying the expected rate of return by the fair value of plan assets. The difference between the expected return and the actual return in any twelve month period is an actuarial gain/loss and is recorded directly to equity. The actual return on plan assets was 703 million Swiss francs (2006: 1,262 million Swiss francs).

Extract 16(37) – Principal actuarial assumptions

Roche Holdings Ltd (AR 2007), pages 62 and 63

10. Pensions and other post-employment benefits (in part)

Actuarial assumptions

Actuarial assumptions are unbiased and mutually compatible estimates of variables that determine the ultimate cost of providing post-employment benefits. They are set on an annual basis by local management and actuaries and are subject to approval by corporate management and the Group's actuaries. Actuarial assumptions consist of demographic assumptions on matters such as mortality and employee turnover, and financial assumptions on matters such as salary and benefit levels, interest rates, return on investments and costs of medical benefits. The Group operates defined benefit plans in many countries and the actuarial assumptions vary based upon local economic and social conditions.

Demographic assumptions: The most significant demographic assumptions relate to mortality rates. The Group's actuaries use mortality tables which take into account historic patterns and expected changes, such as further increases in longevity. The mortality tables used for the major schemes are:

- Germany: Heubeck tables 2005G.
- Japan: National Census (No. 19 Life Table).
- Switzerland: BVG 2005.
- United Kingdom: non-pensioners – PA92C25 rated down one year.
- United Kingdom: pensioners – PA92C10 rated down one year.
- United States: RP2000 projected to 2010.

Rates of employee turnover, disability and early retirement are based on historical behaviour within Group companies.

Financial assumptions: These are based on market expectations for the period over which the obligations are to be settled. The ranges of assumptions used in the actuarial valuations of the most significant plans, which are in countries with stable currencies and interest rates, are shown below.

Defined benefit plans: financial actuarial assumptions (in part)

	2007		2006	
	Weighted average	Range	Weighted average	Range
Discount rates	4.96%	2%–8%	4.30%	2%–9%
Expected rates of return on plan assets	5.83%	1%–10%	5.82%	1%–9%
Expected rates of salary increases	3.59%	0%–7%	3.60%	2%–6%
Medical cost trend rate	9.39%	8%–10%	8.16%	7%–9%

Discount rates, which are used to calculate the discounted present value of the defined benefit obligation, are determined with reference to market yields on high quality corporate bonds, or government bonds in countries where there is not a deep market in corporate bonds. The currency and term of the bonds is consistent with the obligation being discounted. The interest cost included in the income statement is calculated by multiplying the discount rate by the defined benefit obligation.

Expected rates of salary increases, which are used to calculate the defined benefit obligation and the current service cost included in the income statement, are based on the latest expectation and historical behaviour within Group companies.

Medical cost trend rates are used to calculate the defined benefit obligation and the current service cost included in the income statement of post-employment medical plans. These take into account the benefits set out in the plan terms and expected future changes in medical costs. Since the Group's major post-employment medical plans are for US employees, these rates are driven by developments in the United States. The effect of one percentage point increase or decrease in the medical cost trend rate is shown below.

Commentary: The company discloses the principal actuarial assumptions as well as additional information about the basis for determining financial actuarial assumptions (such as discount rates, expected rates of salary increases and medical cost trend rates).

Extract 16(38) – Sensitivity of medical cost trend rates

Roche Holdings Ltd (AR 2007), page 63
10. Pensions and other post-employment benefits (in part)
Defined benefit plans: sensitivity of medical cost trend rate in millions of CHF

	2007		2006	
	+1%	–1%	+1%	–1%
Current service cost and interest cost	10	(9)	10	(7)
Defined benefit obligation	60	(151)	125	(99)

Commentary: The company discloses the impact of an increase or a decrease of one percentage point in the assumed medical cost trend rates on current service cost and interest cost, and the defined benefit obligation.

Extract 16(39) – Summary of funding status over the last five years

Roche Holdings Ltd (AR 2007), pages 63 and 64
10. Pensions and other post-employment benefits (in part)
Funding summary
A five-year summary of the funding status of the Group's defined benefit plans is shown in the table below.
Defined benefit plans: summary of funding status in millions of CHF

	2007	2006	2005	2004	2003
Funded plans					
– Fair value of plan assets	12,170	11,632	10,858	9,922	9,490
– Defined benefit obligation	(10,646)	(11,002)	(10,976)	(10,233)	(9,785)
– Over (under) funding	1,524	630	(118)	(311)	(295)
Unfunded plans					
– Defined benefit obligation	(3,344)	(3,596)	(3,630)	(2,731)	(2,626)
Increase (decrease) in funding status arising from experience adjustments					
– Fair value of plan assets	40	626	547	13	472
– Defined benefit obligation	(235)	(249)	49	77	(46)
Increase (decrease) in funding status arising from changes in actuarial assumptions					
– Fair value of plan assets	–	–	–	–	–
– Defined benefit obligation	1,295	384	(1,148)	(636)	(603)

Commentary: The company discloses its funding status and experience adjustments over the last five years.

Extract 16(40) – Estimate of contributions expected to be paid in the upcoming fiscal year

Roche Holdings Ltd (AR 2007), page 64
10. Pensions and other post-employment benefits (in part)
Cash flows
The Group incurred cash flows from its defined benefit plans as shown in the table below.
Defined benefit plans: cash flows in millions of CHF

	2007	2006
Employer contributions – funded plans	(206)	(212)
Benefits paid – unfunded plans	(146)	(111)
Total cash inflow (outflow)	(352)	(323)

Based on the most recent actuarial valuations, the Group expects that employer contributions for funded plans in 2008 will be approximately 190 million Swiss francs and benefits paid for unfunded plans will be approximately 142 million Swiss francs.

Commentary: The company discloses its estimate of contributions expected to be paid in the upcoming fiscal year as well as additional information about cash outflows resulting from defined benefit plan transactions.

When an entity has more than one defined benefit plan, disclosures may be made:

- in total;
- separately for each plan; or
- in groupings (that are considered to be the most useful), such as the following:
  o the geographical location of the plans, or
  o whether plans are subject to materially different risks.

When an entity provides disclosures in total for a group of plans, such disclosures are provided in the form of weighted averages or of relatively narrow ranges.

CICA 3461 differs from IAS 19 because the former's disclosure requirements are less extensive.

Illustrative Disclosure:

Extract 16(41) – Information about defined benefit plans by geographic region

AB Volvo (AR 2007), pages 110 and 112 Note 24 Provisions for post-employment benefits (in part) Assumptions applied for actuarial calculations, %	December 31 2006	December 31 2007
Sweden		
Discount rate	4.00	4.50
Expected return on plan assets[1]	6.00	6.00
Expected salary increases	3.20	3.20
Inflation	1.50	2.00
United States		
Discount rate	5.50	5.75–6.25
Expected return on plan assets[1]	7.65	7.65
Expected salary increases	3.50	3.50
Inflation	2.50	2.50
France		
Discount rate	4.25	5.25
Expected salary increases	3.00	3.00
Inflation	2.00	2.00
Great Britain		
Discount rate	5.00	5.75
Expected return on plan assets[1]	5.00–5.80	5.30–6.10
Expected salary increases	4.00–4.60	4.20–4.90
Inflation	3.00	3.40

AB Volvo (AR 2007) (continued)

Obligations in defined benefit plans	Sweden Pensions	United States Pensions	France Pensions	Great Britain Pensions	US Other benefits	Other plans	Total
Acquisitions, divestments and other changes	57	688	(8)	–	216	1,949	**2,902**
Current year service costs	259	267	47	90	89	211	**963**
Interest costs	295	653	60	251	311	115	**1,685**
Past service costs							
– Unvested	–	2	457	–	–	(10)	**449**
– Vested	–	7	–	–	–	26	**33**
Termination benefits	165	–	–	–	–	36	**201**
Curtailments and settlements	7	(1)	(1)	–	–	(34)	**(29)**
Employee contributions	–	–	–	33	–	–	**33**
Actuarial (gains) and losses	822	(923)	(143)	(402)	(308)	(156)	**(1,110)**
Exchange rate translation	–	(706)	76	(206)	(354)	131	**(1,059)**
Benefits paid	(296)	(797)	(259)	(145)	(571)	(756)	**(2,824)**
Obligations at December 31, 2007	**8,451**	**11,207**	**1,800**	**4,608**	**5,582**	**4,336**	**35,984**
of which							
Funded defined benefit plans	7,847	10,928	–	4,050	3,617	1,884	**28,326**

Commentary: The company discloses its actuarial assumptions and obligations in defined benefit plans by geographic region. The company also discloses the fair value of plan assets in funded plans, and net provisions for post-employment benefits by geographic region, which were not included in this extract.

Multi-employer Plans

Multi-employer plans pool assets contributed by various entities that are not under common control. The pooled assets are used to provide benefits to employees of several entities, with contribution and benefit levels being determined without considering who employs the employees involved.

Multi-employer plans are classified as defined contribution plans or a defined benefit plans under the terms of the plans, which include constructive obligations beyond the formal terms.

Illustrative Disclosure:

Extract 16(42) –Accounting policies for and description of multi-employer plans

SUEZ (Reference Document 2007), page 281
NOTE 20 PENSIONS AND OTHER EMPLOYEE BENEFIT OBLIGATIONS (in part)
20.1 Description of the main pension plans and related benefits (in part)
20.1.4 Multi-employer plans

Employees of some Group companies are affiliated to multi-employer pension plans, covering pension, death and disability benefits legally paid in the form of annuities. Multi-employer plans are particularly common in the Netherlands, where electricity and gas sector employees are normally required to participate in a compulsory industry-wide scheme.

Multi-employer plans can be classified as either defined contribution or defined benefit plans, depending on the terms and conditions applicable to the plan (and any constructive obligation beyond the formal terms and conditions of the plan). In the absence of any regulations governing the calculation of the share of the underlying financial position and the performance attributable to each participating employer, and in the absence of any surplus or shortfall that could affect future levels of contributions, these multi-employer plans are treated as defined contribution plans in accordance with IAS 19.

SUEZ (Reference Document 2007) (continued)

This concerns mainly subsidiaries of SUEZ Energy Services (SES) based in the Netherlands (mainly GTI Nederland and Axima Services B.V.), together with Electrabel Nederland and SITA Nederland, which participate in three multi-employer plans: Pensioenfonds Metaal en Techniek (PMT), Stichting Bedrijfstakpensioenfonds voor het beroepsvervoer over de weg (BPF Vervoer) and Algemeen Burgerlijk Pensioenfonds (ABP).

GTI Nederland and Axima Services are affiliated to PMT. This multiemployer fund has one million members originating from 31,000 different employers. Based on the market value of its plan assets, PMT was 138%-funded at December 31, 2006.

Since January 1, 2006, the retirement annuity payable has been set at 2.236% of the portion of the retiree's salary below the grensbedrag (€70,108 in 2007) and at 1.75% of the portion of the salary in excess of this limit. The salary used to calculate annuities is the employee's annual remuneration, less a deductible of €14,224 for 2007. Indexation of retirement annuities is not guaranteed, but is decided by PMT's Management Committee based on the financial position of the fund.

PMT provides retirement and death benefits for its members. The cost of these benefits equals 26% of the portion of salary between the deductible and the grensbedrag and 17% of the portion of salary in excess of the grensbedrag limit, and are shared equally between employer and employee.

Most SITA Nederland employees are affiliated to the industry-wide pension fund BPF Vervoer. This fund has 550,000 members originating from 8,600 different employers in the freight and passenger transport industries. BPF Vervoer manages assets worth €5.4 billion.

The fund grants annuities to affiliated employees upon retirement. Since 2006, annuities accrued each year equal 2.05% of the employee's annual salary less a deductible of €9,819 in 2007. Rights which vested before 2006 are calculated in accordance with the fund's previous regulations. Retirement annuities may be indexed on an annual basis, at the discretion of the fund's Board of Directors, but the indexation rate may not exceed the salary increase rate for the sector.

Contributions paid into this fund represent 28.2% of the employee's annual salary less the deductible, and 9.6% of the contributions are paid by the employee.

Electrabel Nederland's employees are affiliated to the ABP by law. ABP is one of the largest multi-employer funds in the Netherlands, with 2.6 million members originating from 4,000 employers. ABP manages assets worth €200 billion.

ABP's regulations provide for the payment of retirement annuities. For years of service after 2006, these annuities are equal to 2.05% of the employee's salary less a deductible of €9,600 in 2007. For years of service prior to 2006, the fund's previous regulations apply. Retirement annuities paid are indexed to the fund's financial position.

In 2006, employee and employer contributions were respectively calculated as 5.82% and 13.58% of the portion of the employee's annual salary in excess of the deductible, and therefore represented 19.40% of the total benchmark salary.

An entity that participates in a multi-employer plan with defined benefit plan characteristics must use defined benefit plan accounting to account for and disclose information on its proportionate share of the defined benefit obligation, plan assets and costs.

When an entity cannot obtain enough information to use defined benefit plan accounting, it must account for its participation in a plan using defined contribution plan accounting and disclose:

• the fact that the plan is a defined benefit plan; and

• why it could not obtain sufficient information to use defined benefit accounting.

To the extent that a surplus or deficit in the plan may affect the amount of contributions, the entity must also disclose:

• any available information about that surplus or deficit;

• the basis used to determine that surplus or deficit; and

- the implications, if any, for the entity.

When there is a contractual agreement between a multi-employer plan and its participants that determines how a surplus in the plan will be distributed to the participants (or a deficit funded), an entity that accounts for its participation in the plan using defined contribution plan accounting must recognize the asset or liability arising from the contractual agreement and the resulting income or expense in the income statement.

CICA 3461 differs from IAS 19 because the former does not require an entity that accounts for its participation in a multi-employer plan (which has a contractual agreement that specifies how a surplus will be distributed or a deficit funded) using defined contribution plan accounting to recognize the asset or liability arising from the contractual agreement and the resulting income or expense in the income statement.

Illustrative Disclosure:

Extract 16(43) – Multi-employer plans with defined benefit characteristics (insufficient information available)

Koninklijke Ahold N.V. (AR 2007) page 61
21 Pensions and other post-employment benefits (in part)
Defined contribution plans

In the United States, there are defined contribution plans principally in the form of savings, incentive compensation and bonus plans. Additionally, certain union employees in the United States are covered by multi-employer plans, which can be defined benefit plans on the basis of the terms of the benefits provided, but that are accounted for as defined contribution plans if sufficient information is not available to account for these plans as defined benefit plans. These plans are generally flat salary plans. Ahold is only one of several employers participating in each of these plans and the financial information that is provided by the third party managers of the plans on the basis of the contractual agreements is usually insufficient to reliably measure Ahold's proportionate share in the plan assets and liabilities on defined benefit accounting principles. Furthermore, the financial statements of the multi-employer plans are drawn up on the basis of other accounting policies than those applied by Ahold. Consequently, these multi-employer plans are not included in Ahold's balance sheets.

On the basis of the financial statements of the plans in which the Company participates in the United States, the total unfunded liability of the plans with a deficit amounts to EUR 3,997 as of January 1, 2006 (the latest date as of which reliable information is available). During 2006, these plans received approximately EUR 919 in total contributions, of which approximately EUR 44 was for current or former employees of Ahold. Based upon the relative amount of contributions for current active Ahold employees entitled to benefits provided by these plans in relation to the total amount of contributions for all active employees entitled to such benefits, the proportionate share of the total unfunded liability of these plans relevant to Ahold would be EUR 458. The unfunded liabilities of these plans may result in increased future payments by the Company and the other participating employers. Ahold's risk of such increased contributions may be greater if any of the participating employers in an underfunded multi-employer plan withdraws from the plan due to insolvency and is not able to contribute an amount sufficient to fund the unfunded liabilities associated with its participants of the plan.

During 2007 and 2006, the Company contributed EUR 292 and EUR 334, respectively, to multi-employer plans as well as other defined contribution plans which is recognized as an expense in the consolidated statements of operations, of which EUR 40 and EUR 71, respectively, related to discontinued operations.

Commentary: Here, the company discloses that it participates in US multi-employer plans with defined benefit characteristics; however, these multi-employer plans are accounted for using defined contribution accounting because the financial information provided by the third party managers of the plans in accordance with the contractual agreements is usually insufficient to reliably measure the company's proportionate share in the plan assets and liabilities. Furthermore, the financial statements of these multi-employer plans are drawn up on the basis of other accounting policies than those applied by the company. Consequently, these multi-employer plans are not included in the company's balance sheet.

The company also discloses the total unfunded liability of the plans, which is a deficit, and estimates its proportionate share of the total unfunded liability of the plans.

State Plans

A state plan is accounted for in the same way as a multi-employer plan. Most state plans are defined contribution plans because they typically require entities to pay contributions only as they fall due.

CICA 3461 differs from IAS 19 because the former is silent on the accounting for state plans. In practice, state plans are accounted for using defined contribution plan accounting, which is consistent with IAS 19.

Illustrative Disclosure:

Extract 16(44) – State plans with defined benefit characteristics (sufficient information available)

Aker Kvaerner ASA (AR 2007), page 61
Note 20: Employee benefits – pension cost and liabilities (in part)
The Norwegian group companies are obliged by law to have a pension plan for their employees. The companies have, through Aker Pension Fund, a pension plan according to the law. About 11 000 Aker Kvaerner employees are covered by the Aker Pension Fund which also covers employees from some Aker companies. Aker Kvaerner participates together with the Norwegian state and other employers in a multi-employer plan called AFP. The participating employers pay a contribution to the plan independent of the company's use of it. The employers also pay 25 percent of the pension paid to own pensioneers. The Norwegian state pays a contribution of 40 percent of paid pensions. The figures regarding defined benefit below include Aker Kvaerner's cost and liability related to the AFP-plan.

Commentary: In the above extract, the company discloses that it participates in a state plan with defined benefit characteristics, which is accounted for using defined benefit plan accounting.

Group Administration Plans

A group administration plan (i.e., a multiple-employer plan) is merely an aggregation of single employer plans combined to allow participating employers to pool their assets for investment purposes and reduce investment management and administration costs. In a group administration plan, separate accounts are maintained for each participating entity so that the contributions provided benefit only the employees of the contributing entity; therefore, such plans do not expose the participating entities to actuarial risks associated with the current and former employees of other entities.

Each individual employer plan within a group administration plan is classified as a defined contribution plan or a defined benefit plan in accordance with the terms of the plan, including any constructive obligation beyond the formal terms.

Group Plans

Group plans are defined benefit plans that share risks between various entities under common control, for example, a parent and its subsidiaries. Group plans are not multi-employer plans.

An entity participating in a group plan has to obtain information about the plan as a whole, measured in accordance with IAS 19 on the basis of assumptions that apply to the plan as a whole.

If there is a contractual agreement or stated policy for charging the net defined benefit cost for the plan as a whole, measured in accordance with IAS 19, to individual group entities, each group entity is required to recognize its share of the net defined benefit cost in its separate or individual financial statements.

If there is no such agreement or policy, the group entity that is legally the sponsoring employer for the plan is required to recognize the net defined benefit cost in its separate or individual financial statements. The other group entities are only required to recognize a cost equal to their contribution payable for the period in their separate or individual financial statements.

An entity that participates in a group plan has to make the following disclosures in its separate or individual financial statements:

- the contractual agreement or stated policy for charging the net defined benefit cost or the fact that there is no such policy;
- the policy for determining its contribution and:
  - o all defined benefit plan disclosures for the plan as whole, if each entity accounts for an allocation of the net defined cost, or
  - o selected defined benefit plan disclosures for the plan as a whole, if each entity accounts only for its contribution payable for the period.

CICA 3461 differs from IAS 19 because the former only provides guidance on group plans in which individual entities within a related group are not able to identify their share of the underlying assets and liabilities. In such circumstances, the group plan is accounted for using:

- defined contribution plan accounting in the individual financial statements of the parent company and its subsidiaries, along with additional disclosures to indicate that defined contribution plan accounting has been used; and
- defined benefit plan accounting in the consolidated financial statements.

Share-based Payment

Objective

The objective of IFRS 2 is to specify the financial reporting of share-based payment transactions to ensure they are reflected in the balance sheet and income statement.

Scope

IFRS 2 applies to the accounting for all share-based payment transactions.

Share-based payment transactions may:

- involve employees and non-employees; and
- take the form of:
  - o an equity-settled share-based payment transaction, in which the entity receives (identifiable and unidentifiable) goods or services as consideration for equity instruments of the entity (including shares or share options),
  - o a cash-settled share-based payment transaction, in which the entity acquires (identifiable and unidentifiable) goods or services by incurring a liability to transfer cash or other assets to the supplier of those goods or services for

Chapter 16

amounts that are based on the price (or value) of the entity's shares or other equity instruments of the entity, or

o a transaction in which the entity receives or acquires (identifiable and unidentifiable) goods or services and the terms of the arrangement allow either the entity or the counterparty to choose the method of settlement.

IFRS 2 also specifically applies to:

- transfers of an entity's equity instruments by its shareholders, equity instruments of the entity's parent or equity instruments of another entity in the same group as the entity, to parties that have supplied goods or services to the entity (including employees);

- equity instruments granted to employees of an acquiree in their capacity as employees (e.g., in return for continued service after a business combination); and

- the cancellation, replacement or other modification of share-based payment arrangements resulting from a business combination or other equity restructuring.

IFRS 2 does not apply to:

- transfers of an entity's equity instruments by its shareholders, equity instruments of the entity's parent or equity instruments of another entity in the same group as the entity, to parties that have supplied goods or services to the entity (including employees), which are clearly for a purpose other than payment for goods or services supplied to the entity;

- transactions with employees or non-employees in their capacity as holders of equity instruments of the entity;

- transactions in which an entity acquires goods as part of the net assets acquired in a business combination to which IFRS 3, *Business Combinations* applies; and

- transactions in which an entity receives or acquires goods or services under a contract within the scope of IAS 32, *Financial Instruments: Presentation* or IAS 39, *Financial Instruments: Recognition and Measurement.*

CICA 3870 differs from IFRS 2 because the former:

- does not apply to related party transactions (other than stock-based compensation plans with a principal shareholder); and

- has an exception for the recognition of an expense when an employee share purchase plan provides a discount to employees that does not exceed the per share amount of share issuance costs that would have been incurred to raise a significant amount of capital by a public offering and is not extended to other holders of the same class of shares.

Equity-settled Share-based Payment Transactions

Recognition

Goods or services received in an equity-settled share-based payment transaction are recognized as an expense or an asset when received, with a corresponding increase in equity.

Vesting Conditions

A grant of equity instruments might be conditional on satisfying specified vesting conditions. Vesting conditions determine whether an entity has received the services that entitle a counterparty to receive the entity's equity instruments under an equity-settled share-based payment arrangement. Vesting conditions are either:

- service conditions, which require the counterparty to complete a specified period of service; or
- performance conditions, which require the counterparty to complete a specified period of service and specified performance targets to be met.

A performance condition might include a market condition, which is a condition (on which the exercise price, vesting or exercisability of an equity instrument depends) that is related to the market price of an entity's equity instruments.

When a grant of equity instruments vests immediately, an entity presumes that services rendered by the counterparty as consideration for the equity instruments have been received (unless there is evidence to the contrary); therefore, the services received are recognized in full on the grant date.

When the equity instruments do not vest immediately, an amount for the goods or services received during the vesting period is recognized based on the best available estimate of the number of equity instruments expected to vest (without taking market conditions into account). The estimate is revised if subsequent information indicates that the number of equity instruments expected to vest differs from previous estimates. On the vesting date, the estimate is revised to equal the number of equity instruments that ultimately vest (irrespective of whether any market conditions is satisfied).

The grant date is the date when an entity and a counterparty agree to a share-based payment arrangement, which is when they have a shared understanding of the terms and conditions of the arrangement. If that agreement is subject to an approval process, the grant date is the date when that approval is obtained.

In some cases, the grant date might occur after the employees receiving the equity instruments have begun rendering services. The employer should then estimate the grant date fair value of the equity instruments for the purpose of recognizing the services received during the period between the service commencement date and grant date. Once the date of grant has been established, the entity should revise the earlier estimate so that the amounts recognized for services received for the grant are ultimately based on the grant date fair value of the equity instruments.

Once the goods or services received (and the corresponding increase in equity) have been recognized, adjustments to total equity are not permitted after the vesting date.

CICA 3870 differs from IFRS 2 because:

- it allows forfeitures by individual employees to be either:
  - o estimated at the grant date and subsequently revised, or
  - o recognized only as they occur;
- expense recognition can never occur before the grant date.

Graded Vesting

When share options or other equity instruments granted vest in installments over the vesting period, each installment should be treated as a separate share option grant.

CICA 3870 differs from IFRS 2 because the former requires awards granted with a graded vesting schedule to be accounted for:

- using the *graded approach* (i.e., as several separate awards, each with a different vesting date) when the fair value of the award is determined based on different expected lives for the options that vest each year; or

- using the *straight-line approach* (i.e., as a single award in which related compensation cost is recognized on a straight-line basis) when the expected life or lives of the award is determined in another manner.

Measurement

Transactions with Non-employees

There is a general presumption that, for transactions with non-employees, the fair value of goods or services received can be reliably estimated. Therefore, these goods or services received (and the corresponding increase in equity) are measured directly at their fair value at the date an entity obtains the goods or the counterparty renders service.

In the rare cases where this presumption does not hold true, the goods or services received (and the corresponding increase in equity) are measured indirectly by reference to the fair value of the equity instruments granted at the measurement date.

In some cases, it might be difficult to demonstrate that goods or services have been (or will be) received. In the absence of specifically identifiable goods or services, other circumstances may indicate that goods or services have been (or will be) received. In particular, if the identifiable goods or services received (if any) appear to be worth less than the fair value of the equity instruments granted, this typically indicates that unidentifiable goods or services have been (or will be) received.

These unidentifiable goods or services received (or to be received) are measured, at the grant date, as the difference between the fair value of the share-based payment and the fair value of any identifiable goods or services received (or to be received).

CICA 3870 differs from IFRS 2 because the former requires goods or services received (and the corresponding increase in equity) to be measured based on the fair value of the consideration received, or the fair value of the equity instruments, whichever is more reliably measurable.

Transactions with Employees

Shares or share options are often granted to employees as part of their remuneration package and sometimes as part of a bonus arrangement. When an entity grants shares or share options to employees, it is paying additional remuneration to obtain additional benefits. Estimating the fair value of those additional benefits is likely to be difficult because:

- it is usually not possible to directly measure the services received for particular components of an employee's remuneration package; and

- it might not be possible to measure the fair value of the total remuneration package independently, without directly measuring the fair value of the equity instruments granted.

Therefore, services received from employees are measured indirectly by reference to the fair value of the equity instruments granted at the measurement date.

Fair Value of Equity Instruments Granted

For transactions measured by reference to the fair value of equity instruments granted, an entity is required to measure the fair value of those equity instruments at the measurement date, based on market prices (if available), taking into account the terms and conditions upon which those equity instruments were granted.

If market prices are not available, the fair value of the equity instruments granted is determined using a valuation technique to estimate what their price would have been on the measurement date in an arm's length transaction between knowledgeable, willing parties. The valuation technique must be consistent with generally accepted valuation methodologies for pricing financial instruments, and must incorporate all factors and assumptions that knowledgeable, willing market participants would consider in setting the price.

Market conditions and all non-vesting conditions must be taken into account when estimating the fair value of the equity instruments granted.

The measurement date is:

- for transactions with non-employees, the date the entity obtains the goods or the counterparty renders service;
- for transactions with employees, the grant date.

CICA 3870 differs from IFRS 2 because the measurement date for transactions with non-employees is the earliest of the following:

- the date at which the non-employee's performance is complete;
- the date at which a performance commitment by a non-employee has been reached; or
- the grant date of the equity instruments if they are fully vested and non-forfeitable at that date.

Equity-settled Share Appreciation Rights

Equity-settled share appreciation rights are accounted for in the same manner as any other equity-settled share-based payment transaction.

CICA 3870 differs from IFRS 2 because the former requires share appreciation rights that call for settlement by the issuance of equity instruments to be presented as equity and measured using the guidance for:

- equity instruments awarded to employees; or
- awards calling for settlement in cash or other assets.

Treasury Share Transactions

IFRIC 11 addresses arrangements where an entity grants rights to its own equity instruments to employees and either chooses or is required to buy equity instruments (i.e., treasury shares) from another party to settle its obligations to its employees. Although the entity disburses cash to buy the equity instruments, these (rather than a liability to transfer cash or other assets) represent the consideration for the services received from employees. Therefore, such arrangements must be accounted for as equity-settled.

CICA 3870 differs from IFRS 2 because the former is silent on the accounting treatment of equity-settled share-based payment transactions where an entity chooses or is required to buy equity instruments from another party to satisfy its obligations to its employees. In practice, the accounting treatment for such transactions is determined by analogy to the repurchase of equity instruments awarded to employees. For these types of transactions, CICA 3870 requires the accounting treatment to be as a liability when:

- the repurchase price differs from the fair value of the stock at the date of the repurchase; and
- the enterprise:
  - o has equity securities traded in a public market,
  - o makes a filing with a regulatory agency in preparation for the sale of any class of equity securities in a public market, or
  - o is controlled by an enterprise that meets either one of the abovementioned criteria.

Reload Features

Some share options contain a reload feature, which provides for an automatic grant of additional share options whenever the option holder exercises previously granted options using the entity's shares, rather than cash, to satisfy the exercise price. A reload feature is not taken into account when estimating the fair value of options granted at the measurement date.

A reload option is a new share option that is granted when a share is used to satisfy the exercise price of a previous share option. A reload option is accounted for as a new option grant, if and when a reload option is subsequently granted.

Modifications, Repurchases, Cancellations and Settlements

The requirements discussed below also apply to share-based payment transactions with non-employees that are measured by reference to the fair value of the equity instruments granted.

Modifications

When an entity modifies the terms and conditions on which equity instruments were granted in a share-based payment transaction with employees, it must:

- recognize, as a minimum, the services received measured at the fair value of the equity instruments granted at the measurement date, unless those equity instruments do not vest because of failure to satisfy a vesting condition (other than a market condition) that was specified at the measurement date; and
- recognize the effects of modifications that increase the total fair value of the share-based payment arrangement or are otherwise beneficial to the employee.

Repurchases of Vested Equity Instruments

A payment made to an employee to repurchase vested equity instruments must be accounted for as a deduction from equity, except to the extent that the payment exceeds the fair value of the equity instrument repurchased, measured at the repurchase date. Any such excess is recognized as an expense.

Cancellations and Settlements

The cancellation or settlement of a grant of equity instruments during the vesting period (other than a grant cancelled by forfeiture when the vesting conditions are not satisfied) is accounted for as an acceleration of vesting, which results in the immediate recognition of the amount that otherwise would have been recognized for services received over the remainder of the vesting period.

Any payment made to an employee on the cancellation or settlement of the grant is accounted for as a repurchase of an equity interest, except to the extent that the payment exceeds the fair value of the equity instruments granted, measured at the repurchase date. Any such excess is recognized as an expense.

When, however, a share-based payment arrangement includes liability components, the fair value of the liability is remeasured at the date of cancellation or settlement. Any payment made to settle the liability component is accounted for as an extinguishment of the liability.

If an entity or counterparty can choose whether to meet a non-vesting condition, either party's failure to meet that non-vesting condition during the vesting period is accounted for as a cancellation.

New equity instruments granted to an employee as a result of a cancellation are accounted for:

- as a modification of the original grant of equity instruments when identified on the date granted as replacements for the cancelled equity instruments; or
- as a new grant of equity instruments when not identified on the date granted as replacements for the cancelled equity instruments.

When Fair Value Cannot be Estimated Reliably

Measurement

An entity required to measure a share-based payment transaction by reference to the fair value of the equity instruments granted may be (in rare cases) unable to estimate that fair value reliably at the measurement date. When this occurs, the entity is instead required to:

- Measure the equity instruments granted at their intrinsic value initially at the date the entity obtains the goods or the counterparty renders service, then subsequently at each reporting date and at the date of final settlement. Any change in intrinsic value is recognized in the income statement. For a grant of share options, the share-based payment arrangement is finally settled when the options are exercised, forfeited or lapse.
- Recognize the goods or services received based on the number of equity instruments that ultimately vest or (where applicable) are ultimately exercised.

The intrinsic value represents the difference between:

- the fair value of the shares to which the counterparty has:
  o the (conditional or unconditional) right to subscribe, or
  o the right to receive, and
- the price (if any) the counterparty is (or will be) required to pay for those shares.

CICA 3870 differs from IFRS 2 because the former requires the final measure of compensation cost to be the fair value based on the stock price and other pertinent factors (i.e., compensation cost is no longer measured at intrinsic value) at the first date at which it is possible to reasonably estimate that value.

Settlements

The settlement of the grant of equity instruments during the vesting period is accounted for as an acceleration of vesting, which results in the immediate recognition of the amount that would otherwise have been recognized for services received over the remainder of the vesting period.

Any payment made on settlement is accounted for as a repurchase of equity instruments, except to the extent that the payment exceeds the intrinsic value of the equity instruments, measured at the repurchase date. Any such excess is recognized as an expense.

Cash-settled Share-based Payment Transactions

Recognition

Goods or services received in a cash-settled share-based payment transaction are recognized as an expense or an asset when received, with a corresponding increase in liabilities.

Measurement

The goods or services received (and the liability incurred) are measured at the fair value of the liability. The fair value of the liability is remeasured at the end of each reporting period and at the date of settlement, with any changes in fair value recognized in the income statement.

In some cases, it might be difficult to demonstrate that goods or services have been (or will be) received. In the absence of specifically identifiable goods or services, other circumstances may indicate that goods or services have been (or will be) received. In particular, if the value of the identifiable goods or services received (if any) appears to be less than the fair value of the liability incurred, this typically indicates that unidentifiable goods or services have been (or will be) received.

These unidentifiable goods or services received (or to be received) are measured, at the grant date, as the difference between the fair value of the share-based payment and the fair value of any identifiable goods or services received (or to be received). The liability incurred is remeasured at the end of each reporting period until it is settled.

CICA 3870 differs from IFRS 2 because the former requires goods or services received (and the liability incurred) from:

- non-employees to be measured based on the fair value of the consideration received, or liabilities incurred, whichever is more reliably measurable;

- employees to be measured at the intrinsic value of the share-based award (i.e., the amount by which the quoted market value of the shares covered by the grant exceeds the option price or value specified, by reference to a market price or otherwise, subject to any appreciation limits under the plan).

Transactions with Settlement Alternatives

When the terms of an arrangement for a share-based payment transaction allow either the entity or the counterparty to choose the method of settlement, that transaction (or the components of that transaction) is accounted for:

- as a cash-settled share-based payment transaction if, and to the extent that, a liability has been incurred to settle in cash or other assets; or

- as an equity-settled share-based payment transaction if, and to the extent that, no such liability has been incurred.

Choice of Settlement with the Counterparty

If an entity has granted a counterparty the right to choose whether a share-based payment transaction is to be settled in cash or by issuing equity instruments, the entity is considered to have granted a compound financial instrument, which consists of:

- a debt component (i.e., the right to demand payment in cash); and
- an equity component (i.e., the right to demand settlement in equity instruments by giving up the right to demand payment in cash).

For transactions with:

- non-employees, in which the fair value of goods or services received is measured:
  - o directly, the equity component of the compound financial instrument is measured as the difference between the fair value of the goods or services received and the fair value of the debt component, at the date when the goods or services are received, or
  - o indirectly by reference to the fair value of the equity instruments granted, the fair value of the compound financial instrument is measured at the measurement date, taking into account the terms and conditions on which the rights to cash or equity instruments were granted (i.e., the counterparty must forfeit the right to receive cash in order to receive the equity instrument). This is accomplished by measuring:
    - the fair value of the debt component, and then
    - the fair value of the equity component;
- employees, the fair value of the compound financial instrument is measured at the measurement date, taking into account the terms and conditions on which the rights to cash or equity instruments were granted (i.e., the counterparty must forfeit the right to receive cash in order to receive the equity instrument). This is accomplished by measuring:
  - o the fair value of the debt component, and then
  - o the fair value of the equity component.

At the date of settlement, the liability is remeasured to its fair value.

On settlement, if the entity issues:

- equity instruments rather than a payment in cash, the liability is transferred directly to equity, as consideration for the equity instruments issued; and
- a payment in cash rather than issuing equity instruments, that payment is applied to settle the liability in full. Any equity component previously recognized remains within equity; however, an entity may still recognize a transfer from one component of equity to another.

CICA 3870 differs from IFRS 2 because the former requires a transaction where the terms of the arrangement allow the counterparty to choose the method of settlement to be accounted for as a cash-settled share-based payment transaction.

Choice of Settlement with the Entity

When an entity can choose the method of settlement, it must determine whether it has a present obligation to settle in cash. The entity has such an obligation if:

- the choice of settlement in equity instruments has no commercial substance;
- the entity has a past practice or a stated policy of settling in cash; or
- the entity generally settles in cash whenever requested by the counterparty.

If the obligation to settle in cash:

- exists, the transaction is accounted for as a cash-settled share-based payment transaction; or

- does not exist, the transaction is accounted for as an equity-settled share-based payment transaction. On settlement, if an entity elects to settle:

  o in cash, the cash payment is accounted for as a deduction from equity. When this election is the settlement alternative with the higher fair value at the date of settlement, an additional expense is recognized for the excess value given, which represents the difference between the cash paid and the fair value of the equity instruments that would otherwise have been issued, or

  o by issuing equity instruments, a transfer is made from one component of equity to another, if necessary. When this election is the settlement alternative with the higher fair value as at the date of settlement, an additional expense is recognized for the excess value given, which represents the difference between the fair value of the equity instruments issued and the amount of cash that would otherwise have been paid.

Disclosure

Nature and Extent of Share-based Payment Arrangements

Information that enables users of financial statements to understand the nature and extent of share-based payment arrangements that existed during the period must be disclosed. At minimum, the following information must be disclosed:

- A description of each type of share-based payment arrangement that existed at any time during the period, including the general terms and conditions of each arrangement, such as vesting requirements, the maximum term of options granted and the method of settlement. An entity with substantially similar types of share-based payment arrangements may aggregate this information, unless separate disclosure of each arrangement is considered necessary.

- The number and weighted average exercise prices of share options for each of the following groups of options:

  o outstanding at the beginning of the period,

  o granted during the period,

  o forfeited during the period,

  o exercised during the period,

  o expired during the period,

  o outstanding at the end of the period, and

  o exercisable at the end of the period.

- The weighted average share price at the date share options were exercised during the period. The weighted average share price during the period may be disclosed instead if options were exercised on a regular basis throughout the period.

- The range of exercise prices and weighted average remaining contractual life of share options outstanding at the end of the period. If there is a wide range of exercise prices, the outstanding options are divided into ranges that are meaningful for assessing the number and timing of additional shares that may be issued and the cash that may be received when those options are exercised.

Illustrative Disclosures:

Extract 16(45) – Description of each type of share-based payment arrangement (cash-settled)

Barloworld Limited (AR 2007), page 241

35. Share incentive schemes and share-based payments (in part)

35.2 Cash-settled share appreciation rights scheme (in part)

During the year the group introduced the Barloworld Cash-settled Share Appreciation Right Scheme 2007.

The scheme allows executive directors and certain senior employees to earn a long-term incentive amount calculated based on the increase in the Barloworld Limited share price between the grant date and the vesting and exercise of such rights.

No shares are issued in terms of this scheme and all amounts payable will be settled in cash. The objective of the scheme is to recognise the contributions of senior staff to the group's financial position and performance and to retain key employees.

The vesting of the rights are subject to specific performance conditions, based on group headline earnings per share. Rights are granted for a period of six years and vest one-third after three years from grant date, a further one-third after four years and the final third after five years.

The grant price of these appreciation rights equals the volume weighted average market price of the underlying shares on the three trading days immediately preceding grant date.

On resignation, share appreciation rights which have not yet vested are forfeited. On death or retirement the Barloworld remuneration committee may permit a portion of unvested rights to be exercised within one year (or such extended periods as the committee may decide) of the date of cessation of employment.

It is group policy that employees should not deal in Barloworld Limited shares (and this is extended to the share appreciation rights and share options schemes) for the periods from 1 April for half-year and 1 October for year-end until 24 hours after publication of the results and at any other time during which they have access to price-sensitive information.

Commentary: In the above extract, the company discloses a description of the cash-settled share appreciation rights scheme, including the general terms and conditions, such as the vesting period and the maximum term.

Extract 16(46) – Description of each type of share-based payment arrangement (equity-settled)

Barloworld Limited (AR 2007), page 241

35. Share option incentive scheme and share-based payments (in part)

35.3 Equity-settled share option scheme (in part)

Equity-settled share options were granted to executive directors and senior employees in terms of the Barloworld Share Option Scheme 1985.

The objectives of the scheme are similar to that of the share appreciation rights scheme.

The options have a total contractual life of 10 years, with the exception of the May 2004 grant which has a six-year contractual life.

The options vest one-third after three years from grant date, a further one-third after four years and the final third after five years.

Commentary: The company describes the equity-settled share option scheme, including the general terms and conditions, such as the vesting period and the maximum term.

Extract 16(47) – Share options (movement, exercised and outstanding)

Nobel Biocare Holding AG (AR 2007), page 119

18 Share-based payment transactions (in part)

The movements of options outstanding and their weighted average exercise price are as follows:

Number of options	2007 Weighted average exercise price (CHF)	2007 Number of options	2006 Weighted average exercise price (CHF)	2006 Number of options
Options outstanding at 1 Jan	256.89	792,355	180.96	805,613
Options granted	423.50	417,450	298.30	358,150
Options exercised	208.12	−258,257	122.12	−344,342
Options forfeited	319.98	−35,852	259.36	−27,066
Options outstanding at 31 Dec	**343.52**	**915,696**	**256.89**	**792,355**
Options exercisable at 31 Dec	**252.40**	**204,746**	**159.80**	**133,405**

The weighted average remaining contractual life of the options outstanding at 31 December 2007 is 1.72 years (1.77 years). The weighted average share price at the date of the exercise of the options was CHF 404.76 (CHF 304.61).

Commentary: In the above extract, the company discloses:
- the number and weighted average exercise prices of share options;
- the weighted average share price at the date of the exercise of share options; and
- the weighted average remaining contractual life of the share options outstanding at the end of the period.

Extract 16(48) – Share options (outstanding)

Pearson plc (AR 2007), page 85

25. Share-based payments (in part)

The options outstanding at the end of the year have weighted average remaining contractual lives and exercise prices as follows:

Range of exercise prices £	2007 Number of share options 000s	2007 Weighted average contractual life Years	2006 Number of share options 000s	2006 Weighted average contractual life Years
0 – 5	930	1.56	1,649	1.94
5 – 10	4,909	3.22	5,254	3.85
10 – 15	7,257	2.62	7,638	3.63
15 – 20	980	1.85	1,050	2.88
20 – 25	400	2.19	424	3.19
>25	2,305	2.19	2,846	3.22
	16,781	2.62	18,861	3.42

Commentary: The company discloses the range of exercise prices and weighted average remaining contractual life of share options outstanding.

Fair Value of Goods/Services Received or Equity Instruments Granted

Information that enables users of the financial statements to understand how, during the period, the fair value of the goods or services received, or the fair value of the equity instruments granted, was determined must be disclosed.

Measured Indirectly

At minimum, the following information must be disclosed when the fair value of goods or services received as consideration for equity instruments of the entity is measured indirectly by reference to the fair value of the equity instruments granted:

- for share options granted during the period:
  - o the weighted average fair value of those options at the measurement date, and
  - o information on how that fair value was measured, including:
    - the option pricing model used and the inputs to that model, including:
      - the weighted average share price,
      - exercise price,
      - expected volatility,
      - option life,
      - expected dividends,
      - the risk-free interest rate, and
      - any other inputs to the model, including the method used and the assumptions made to incorporate the effects of expected early exercise;
    - how expected volatility was determined, including an explanation of the extent to which expected volatility was based on historical volatility, and
    - whether and how any other features of the option grant were incorporated into the measurement of fair value, such as a market condition;
- for other equity instruments granted during the period (i.e., other than share options):
  - o the number and weighted average fair value of those equity instruments at the measurement date, and
  - o information on how that fair value was measured, including:
    - how fair value was determined if it was not measured on the basis of an observable market price,
    - whether and how expected dividends were incorporated into the measurement of fair value, and
    - whether and how any other features of the equity instruments granted were incorporated into the measurement of fair value;
- for share-based payment arrangements that were modified during the period:
  - o an explanation of those modifications,
  - o the incremental fair value granted (as a result of those modifications), and
  - o information on how the incremental fair value granted was measured.

Illustrative Disclosures:

Extract 16(49) – Weighted average fair value of share options granted at the measurement date

Nobel Biocare Holding AG (AR 2007), page 119		
18 Share-based payment transactions (in part)		
The fair value of services received in return for options granted are measured by reference to the fair value of options granted. The fair value of the options is measured based on the Black-Scholes option pricing model.		
in CHF	**2007**	**2006**
Fair value of options granted at measurement date	71.34	50.25
Assumptions		
Share price	423.50	298.30
Exercise price	423.50	298.30
Expected volatility (%)	25	25
Option life (months)	34	34
Expected dividends (yield)	1.3	1.3
Risk-free interest rate	**2.00**	**2.00**
The expected volatility is based on the historic volatility (calculated based on the weighted average remaining life of the share options), adjusted for any expected changes to future volatility due to publicly available information. The share options are granted under a service condition. Service conditions are not taken into account in the grant date fair value measurement of the services received.		

Commentary: The above extract discloses the weighted average fair value of share options granted at the measurement date, and the option pricing model used to determine that fair value, along with the inputs to that model, and how the expected volatility was determined.

Extract 16(50) – Number and weighted average fair value of share awards at the measurement date (observable market price)

Qantas Airways Limited (AR 2007), page 113				
24. Key Management Personnel and Executive Equity Benefits (in part)				
Share-based payment (in part)				
Performance Share Plan				
The PSP delivers deferred shares to employees upon the achievement of a Balanced Scorecard relating to Customer, Operational, People and Financial performance. The actual incentive earned is based on a combination of Qantas' results and individual performance. Performance of the Qantas Group against the Balanced Scorecard determines the amount (if any) of the pool of shares available for payment.				
Deferred shares awarded under this Plan are purchased on-market or issued and are held subject to a holding lock for 10 years. Participants may call for the deferred shares prior to the expiration of the holding lock, but not before the end of one year from the completion of the performance period for up to half of the deferred shares and the end of two years in relation to the remaining deferred shares. Generally, any shares held subject to the holding lock are forfeited on cessation of employment.				
		2007		2006
Shares Granted	Number of Shares	Weighted Average Fair Value $	Number of Shares	Weighted Average Fair Value $
Performance shares granted – 22 August 2006	2,984,116	3.30	–	–
Performance shares granted – 17 August 2005	–	–	3,055,257	3.29
Shares are valued based on the volume weighted average price of Qantas shares as traded on the ASX for the seven calendar days up to and including the date of allocation. Expected dividends are not taken into account when calculating the fair value.				

Commentary: This extract discloses the number and weighted average fair value of share awards granted during the period at the measurement date, which was calculated without taking expected dividends into account.

Extract 16(51) – Number and weighted average fair value of share awards at the measurement date (observable market price and other than observable market price)

Koninklijke Ahold N.V. (AR 2007), pages 74 and 75

32 Share-based compensation (in part)

Conditional share grant program (GRO) (in part)

Main characteristics **(in part)**

Under the GRO program, introduced in 2006, Ahold shares are granted through a mid-term (three-year) and a long-term (five-year) program. The number of conditional shares to be granted depends on the at-target value, the annual incentive multiplier of the preceding year and the average share price for six months preceding the date of the grant. The conditional shares granted under the mid-term component vest after three years of continued employment. The Corporate Executive Board members are not allowed to sell these shares within a period of five years from the grant date, except to finance tax due at the date of vesting. The conditional shares granted through the long-term component vest after a performance period of five years. During this five-year period, performance will be measured using the Total Shareholder Return ("TSR", share price growth and dividends) of the peer group (refer to "Remuneration" section of this annual report for the composition of the peer group).

For participants in the program other than the Corporate Executive Board members, the mid-term component of the program contains a matching feature. For every five shares a participant holds for an additional two years after the vesting date, the participant will receive one additional share.

Upon termination of employment due to retirement, disability or death the same vesting conditions as described above apply. Upon termination of employment without cause (e.g., restructuring or divestiture), a pro rata part of the granted shares will vest on the date of termination of employment.

The following table summarizes the status of the GRO program during 2007 for the individual Corporate Executive Board members and for all other employees in the aggregate:

	Non vested at the beginning of 2007	Granted	Vested	Forfeited	Non vested at the end of 2007
J.F. Rishton					
Three-year 2006 grant	34,924	–	–	–	34,924
Five-year 2006 grant	34,924	–	–	–	34,924
Three-year 2007 grant	–	35,268	–	–	35,268
Five-year 2007 grant	–	35,268	–	–	35,268
P.N. Wakkie					
Three-year 2006 grant	29,987	–	–	–	29,987
Five-year 2006 grant	29,987	–	–	–	29,987
Three-year 2007 grant	–	24,226	–	–	24,226
Five-year 2007 grant	–	24,226	–	–	24,226
A.D. Boer					
Three-year 2006 grant	28,963	–	–	–	28,963
Five-year 2006 grant	28,963	–	–	–	28,963
Three-year 2007 grant	–	39,779	–	–	39,779
Five-year 2007 grant	–	39,779	–	–	39,779
A.C. Moberg					
Three-year 2006 grant	32,516	–	13,469	19,047	–
Five-year 2006 grant	32,516	–	2,021	30,495	–
Three-year 2007 grant	–	–	–	–	–
Five-year 2007 grant	–	–	–	–	–
Other employees					
Three-year	4,814,621	2,011,505	755,163	1,652,313	4,418,650
Five-year	4,814,621	2,011,505	277,781	2,129,695	4,418,650
Total number of shares	**9,882,022**	**4,221,556**	**1,048,434**	**3,831,550**	**9,223,594**

Koninklijke Ahold N.V. (AR 2007) (continued)

Valuation model and input variables

The weighted average fair value of the conditional shares granted in 2007 amounted to EUR 9.28 and EUR 9.05 per share for the three-year and five-year component, respectively (2006: EUR 6.35 and EUR 6.39, respectively). These fair values are based on the share price on the measurement date (three-year component) and a Monte Carlo simulation model (five-year component). The most important assumptions used in the valuation were as follows:

Weighted average assumptions	2007	2006
Risk-free interest rate	4.2%	3.8%
Volatility	32.4%	37.0%
Assumed annual forfeitures	6.0%	6.0%
Assumed dividend yield	**1.3%**	**0.6%**

Expected volatility has been determined as the average of the implied volatility and the historical volatility, whereby the extraordinarily volatile month after February 24, 2003 has been excluded.

Commentary: This extract shows the number and weighted average fair values of share awards granted during the period at the measurement date. The weighted average fair values were based on the share price on the measurement date (three-year component) and a Monte Carlo simulation model (five-year component).

Extract 16(52) – Modified share-based payment arrangements

Barloworld Limited (AR 2007), page 242

35. Share option incentive scheme and share-based payments (in part)

35.4 Modification for cement unbundling (in part)

The existing equity-settled share options were modified in line with shareholder approval granted as a result of the unbundling of cement effective 16 July 2007. Cash settled share appreciation rights awarded on 15 November 2006 were modified in terms of the rules of the scheme.

The modification did not result in any incremental fair value being granted to option or right holders, as the objective was to maintain intrinsic value at the same level before and after unbundling.

The modification entailed a downward repricing of exercise prices combined with additional entitlements to compensate for the impact of a lower Barloworld share price after un-bundling. The cement unbundling resulted in an estimated 41.7% reduction in the Barloworld share price, based on the pre- and post-unbundling share price of R214.50 and R125 respectively. Corresponding fair values were demonstrated before and after unbundling based on a binomial option pricing model, as were intrinsic values.

The modified option entitlement ratio was as follows:

Entitlement before unbundling	Entitlement after unbundling
[1 Barloworld option]	[1 Barloworld option + 0.866 new Barloworld options] or
	[1 Barloworld option + 1.8555 PPC subdivided options]

Commentary: Here, the company discloses the modifications made to existing equity-settled share options, which did not result in any incremental fair value being granted to option or right holders.

Measured Directly

When the fair value of goods or services received during the period is measured directly, the method of determining that fair value must be disclosed.

When the presumption that the fair value of the goods or services can be estimated reliably has been rebutted, that fact and an explanation of why the presumption was rebutted must be disclosed.

Effect of Share-based Payment Transactions

Information that enables users of the financial statements to understand the effect of share-based payment transactions on the income statement and the balance sheet must be disclosed. At minimum, the following information must be disclosed:

- the total expense recognized for the period arising from share-based payment transactions, including separate disclosure of that portion of the total expense that arises from transactions accounted for as equity-settled share-based payment transactions;

- for liabilities arising from share-based payment transactions:
  - o the total carrying amount at the end of the period, and
  - o the total intrinsic value at the end of the period of liabilities for which the coun-ter- party's right to cash or other assets has vested by the end of the period.

CICA 3870 differs from IFRS 2 because the former's disclosure requirements are less extensive.

Illustrative Disclosure:

Extract 16(53) – Effect of share-based payment transactions on the income statement and balance sheet

Barloworld Limited (AR 2007) page 240
35. Share incentive schemes and share-based payments (in part)
35.1 Financial effect of share-based payment transactions

	2007 Rm	2006 Rm	2005 Rm
Income statement effect			
Expense arising from share-based payment transactions	5		15
Compensation expense arising from equity-settled share option incentive plan	16	20	23
Compensation expense arising from cash-settled share appreciation rights incentive plan	20		
Share-based payment expense included in operating profit	41	20	38
Taxation benefit on cash-settled share appreciation rights	(6)		
Net share-based payment expense after taxation	35	20	38
Balance sheet effect			
Non-current liability raised for cash-settled share appreciation rights granted (to be incurred within 2 – 5 years)	(20)		
Deferred taxation asset raised on share appreciation rights liability	6		
Net reduction in shareholders' interest as a result of share-based payment transactions	(14)		

Commentary: In the above extract, the company discloses the total expense arising from share-based payment transactions, as well as the portion for equity-settled share-based payment transactions. The company also discloses the total carrying amount of liabilities arising from share-based payment transactions.

Group Transactions

The requirements discussed below also apply to similar share-based payment trans-actions with non-employees.

IFRIC 11 addresses the accounting for share-based payment arrangements that in-volve two or more entities within the same group, where:

- a parent grants rights to its equity instruments directly to employees of its subsidiary; and
- a subsidiary grants rights to equity instruments of its parent to its employees.

A Parent Grants Rights to its Equity Instruments to the Employees of its Subsidiary

Provided that the share-based arrangement is accounted for as equity-settled in the consolidated financial statements of the parent, the subsidiary is required to measure the services received from its employees in accordance with the requirements applicable to equity-settled share-based payment transactions, with a corresponding increase recognized in equity as a contribution from the parent.

Transfers of Employees between Group Entities

A parent may grant rights to its equity instruments to the employees of its subsidiaries, conditional upon the completion of continuing service with the group for a specified period. Under such conditions, when an employee transfers from one subsidiary to another subsidiary during the specified vesting period without affecting the employee's rights to equity instruments of the parent under the original share-based payment arrangement, each subsidiary must measure the services received from the employee by reference to the fair value of the equity instruments at the date those rights were originally granted by the parent, and the proportion of the vesting period served by the employee with each subsidiary.

Such an employee, after transferring between group entities, may fail to satisfy a vesting condition other than a market condition. In this case, the rights to the equity instruments granted by the parent are forfeited and each subsidiary must adjust the amount previously recognized for services received from the employee.

A Subsidiary Grants Rights to Equity Instruments of its Parent to its Employees

When a subsidiary grants rights to equity instruments of its parent to its employees, the subsidiary is required to account for the transaction as cash-settled.

FUTURE DEVELOPMENTS

Employee Benefits

In July 2006, the IASB decided to undertake a project on post-employment benefits, which involves a fundamental review of all aspects of post-employment benefit accounting.

The objective of this project is to issue an interim standard that would significantly improve pension accounting, specifically:

- presentation and disclosure;
- definition of defined benefit and defined contribution arrangements and accounting for cash balance plans;
- smoothing and deferral mechanisms; and
- treatment of settlements and curtailments.

The IASB issued a Discussion Paper on the amendments to IAS 19 in March 2008, which was open for public comment until September 26, 2008.

The Discussion Paper proposed three significant improvements:

- require all changes in the value of plan assets and in the post-employment benefit obligation to be recognized in the period in which they occur;

- define a new category of promises (i.e., contribution-based promises), which would be measured at fair value (assuming the terms of the benefit promise do not change) in an attempt to overcome the lack of faithful representation in the measurement of the liability for some benefit promises that are based on contributions and a promised return on assets; and

- require the separate recognition and measurement at fair value (assuming the terms of the benefit promise do not change) of any option to receive the higher of a defined benefit or contribution-based promise, in an attempt to prevent the underestimation of the liability for such promises.

The IASB expects to issue an Exposure Draft at the end of the third quarter of 2009, and hopes to issue the final standard at the end of the second quarter of 2011 (with an effective date from January 1, 2013).

Share-based Payment

The IASB has also proposed amendments to IFRS 2 and IFRIC 11. The proposed amendment to IFRS 2 clarifies that, when an entity receives goods or services from a supplier, it must apply IFRS 2 even if it has no obligation to make the required share-based cash payments. The proposed amendment to IFRIC 11 specifies that, when an entity receives goods or services from a supplier, but has no obligation to make the required share-based cash payments, these goods or services should be measured in accordance with the requirements applicable to cash-settled share-based payment transactions in IFRS 2.

The IASB issued an Exposure Draft in December 2007, which was open for public comments until March 17, 2008. The majority of the comments agreed with the proposed amendments.

The IASB expects to publish the amendments in the first quarter of 2009.

COMPREHENSIVE EXAMPLES

This section presents two comprehensive examples: one provides extensive disclosures for employee benefits, while the other provides extensive disclosures for share-based payment transactions under IFRS.

Heidelberger Druckmaschinen Aktiengesellschaft – All extracts **16(A)** were obtained from the Annual Report for the year ended March 31, 2008.

Extract 16(A1) – Heidelberger Druckmaschinen Aktiengesellschaft, page 7
In this extract, the company discloses the amount of actuarial gains and losses, and the amount of the adjustment resulting from the asset ceiling test recognized in equity.

Note that companies with a policy of recognizing actuarial gains and losses in full immediately and adjustments arising from the asset ceiling test outside profit or loss in the SORIE will instead recognize these items in other comprehensive income, displayed in the statement of comprehensive income, for annual periods beginning on or after January 1, 2009.

STATEMENT OF RECOGNIZED INCOME AND EXPENSE 2007/2008

	Figures in € thousands	
	1-Apr-2006 to 31-Mar-2007	1-Apr-2007 to 31-Mar-2008
Consolidated net profit	**262,929**	141,543
Pension obligations[1]	**44,919**	82,155
Currency translation	**– 53,260**	– 81,530
Financial assets		
Market valuation of financial assets	**– 602**	– 378
Cash flow hedges		
Fair value of cash flow hedges in equity	**29,177**	77,988
Cash flow hedges recognized in income	**– 11,234**	– 49,058
Deferred income taxes	**– 24,361**	– 42,975
Total income and expense recognized in equity	**– 15,361**	– 13,798
Total recognized income and expense	**247,568**	127,745
– of which: Heidelberg Group	**247,450**	128,023
– of which: minority interests	**118**	– 278

1) Changes in actuarial gains and losses and in adjustment amount due to IAS 19.58b)

Extract 16(A2) – Heidelberger Druckmaschinen Aktiengesellschaft, page 30

In this extract, the company discloses its accounting policy for recognizing actuarial gains and losses, which is to recognize them directly in equity. The company discloses that it has adopted the following general accounting policies to account for defined benefit plans:

- the projected unit credit method is used to calculate pension obligations, commissioned to actuaries annually;

- the current Heubeck mortality tables (2005G) or comparable foreign mortality tables are used to calculate mortality;

- plan assets are carried at fair value and are offset against defined benefit obligations;

- service cost is reported under staff costs, and interest cost is reported under net financial income;

- the return on plan assets is offset from staff costs at the level of the individual company up to the amount of expenses for pension claims. Any excess amounts are reported in the net financial income.

The company also discloses its accounting policy to account for defined contribution plans.

Note that companies with a policy of recognizing actuarial gains and losses in full immediately and adjustments arising from the asset ceiling test outside profit or loss in the SORIE will instead recognize these items in other comprehensive income, displayed in the statement of comprehensive income, for annual periods beginning on or after January 1, 2009.

> **Provisions for pensions and similar obligations**
>
> The provisions for pensions and similar obligations comprise the obligations of the Group to establish provisions under both defined benefit plans as well as defined contribution plans. In the case of defined benefit plans the pension obligations are calculated using the projected unit credit method (IAS 19). Under this method, expert actuarial reports are commissioned each year. Mortality is calculated on the basis of the current Heubeck mortality tables (2005G) or comparable foreign mortality tables. Plan assets carried at fair value are offset against defined benefit obligations. The service cost is reported under staff costs and the interest portion of the additions to provisions under net financial income. The return on plan assets is offset from staff costs at the level of the individual company up to the amount of expenses for pension claims. Any excess amount is reported in net financial income.
>
> Actuarial gains and losses are entirely offset in equity. Gains and losses recognized in shareholders' equity are shown separately in the statement of recognized income and expense together with the related deferred taxes.
>
> In the case of defined contribution plans (e.g., direct insurance policies), compulsory contributions are offset directly as an expense. No provisions for pension obligations are recognized, as in these cases the Company does not have any obligation beyond that to pay premiums.

Extract 16(A3) – Heidelberger Druckmaschinen Aktiengesellschaft, pages 32 and 33

In this extract, the company identifies the recognition and the measurement of provisions for pensions and similar obligations as being vulnerable to measurement uncertainties resulting from assumptions and estimates.

The company also discloses the impact of an increase or a decrease of one quarter of a percentage point in the interest rate on the calculation of the provisions for pensions and similar obligations.

> When preparing consolidated financial statements, certain assumptions and estimates are made that have an effect on the amount and reporting of assets and liabilities, information on contingent assets and liabilities on the balance sheet date and on income and expense reported in the period under review. The preparer of consolidated financial statements has a degree of discretion here.
>
> The following are the key issues affected by assumptions and estimates:
> > the recognition and the measurement of provisions for pensions and similar obligations.
>
> The calculation of the provisions for pensions and similar obligations is based on the parameters listed in note 26. Increasing or reducing the interest rate used in calculations by one quarter of a percentage point to 6.25 percent or 5.75 percent respectively would result in a €19,207 thousand reduction in pension claims or a €20,433 thousand increase respectively. After income taxes, the gains offset in equity would be increased by €13,802 thousand or reduced by €14,683 thousand respectively.

Extract 16(A4) – Heidelberger Druckmaschinen Aktiengesellschaft, page 35

In this extract, the company discloses its expenses for employee benefits and the financial statement line items in which each cost related to retirement benefits is included.

	2006/2007	2007/2008
Wages and salaries	978,323	994,426
Retirement benefit expenses[1]	44,862	38,310
Return on plan assets	– 30,703	– 24,425
Other social security contributions and expenses	170,851	171,370
	1,163,333	1,179,681

The interest component of the pension claims is shown under net financial income. The return on plan assets is offset against staff costs at the level of the individual company up to the amount of retirement benefit expenses. Any excess amount is shown in net financial income.

Extract 16(A5) – Heidelberger Druckmaschinen Aktiengesellschaft, page 35

In this extract, the company discloses the number of employees by geographic region.

The number of employees was:	2006/2007	Average 2007/2008	31-Mar-2007	As of 31-Mar-2008
Europe, Middle East and Africa	13,686	14,182	14,016	14,324
Eastern Europe	695	712	697	779
North America	1,358	1,357	1,374	1,341
Latin America	407	405	402	408
Asia/Pacific	2,003	2,061	2,031	2,087
	18,149	18,717	18,520	18,939
Trainees	712	729	651	657
	18,861	19,446	19,171	19,596

Extract 16(A6) – Heidelberger Druckmaschinen Aktiengesellschaft, page 42

Here, the company discloses that non-current other assets include plan assets.

	31-Mar-2007			31-Mar-2008		
	Current	Non-current	Total	Current	Non-current	Total
Receivables from sales financing	111,523	319,880	431,403	128,205	194,839	323,044
Trade receivables	704,538	–	704,538	596,473	–	596,473
Other receivables and other assets						
Other tax refund claims	21,717	1,430	23,147	19,113	–	19,113
Loans	248	6,008	6,256	549	8,785	9,334
Derivative financial instruments	23,018	6,462	29,480	67,722	39,208	106,930
Deferred interest	1,795	–	1,795	242	–	242
Prepaid expenses	12,389	1,054	13,443	16,063	–	16,063
Other assets	62,929	73,098	136,027	67,464	130,853	198,317
	122,096	88,052	210,148	171,153	178,846	349,999

Non-current other assets include plan assets of € 94,136 thousand (previous year: € 32,639 thousand) (see note 26).

Extract 16(A7) – Heidelberger Druckmaschinen Aktiengesellschaft, page 54

In this extract, the company discloses:

- a general description of the types of defined benefit plans;

- the amount of expenses relating to defined contribution plans;

- its accounting policy for recognizing actuarial gains and losses and the adjustment resulting from the asset ceiling test, which is to recognize both in equity; and

- the establishment of the Heidelberg Pension-Trust e.V to finance all pension obligations.

Note that companies with a policy of recognizing actuarial gains and losses in full immediately and adjustments arising from the asset ceiling test outside profit or loss in the SORIE will instead recognize these items in other comprehensive income, displayed in the statement of comprehensive income, for annual periods beginning on or after January 1, 2009.

The Heidelberg Group operates pension schemes – either directly or through premium payments to schemes financed by private institutions – for the majority of employees for the time after their retirement. The amount of benefit payments depends on the conditions in particular countries. The amounts are generally based on the term of employment and the salary of the employees. Liabilities include both those arising from current pensions as well as vested pension rights for pensions payable in the future. The pension payments expected following the start of benefit payments are distributed over the employee's full period of employment. The group of beneficiaries participating in the defined benefit plans financed by funds at Heidelberger Druckmaschinen Aktiengesellschaft and Heidelberger Druckmaschinen Vertrieb Deutschland GmbH has been closed.

The expenses for defined contribution plans amounted to € 80,918 thousand (previous year: €71,189 thousand) in the reporting year and essentially includes contributions to the statutory pension insurance.

A so-called third option was exercised in line with IAS 19. In line with this, actuarial gains and losses and the restrictions of IAS 19.58b) are offset in equity.

As part of a contractual trust arrangement (CTA) of Heidelberger Druckmaschinen Aktiengesellschaft and Heidelberger Druckmaschinen Vertrieb Deutschland GmbH set up in March 2006, assets were transferred to a trustee, Heidelberg Pension-Trust e.V., Heidelberg. The purpose of the CTA is to finance all pension obligations.

Extract 16(A8) – Heidelberger Druckmaschinen Aktiengesellschaft, page 55

In this extract, the company discloses the principal actuarial assumptions used at the end of the reporting period.

The calculation of the pension provisions is based on the following assumptions:

| | Figures shown in percent | | | |
| | 2006/2007 | | 2007/2008 | |
	Germany	Abroad	Germany	Abroad
Discount rate	4.75	4.48	6.00	5.34
Expected return on plan assets	6.50	5.40	6.50	5.40
Expected future salary increases	2.75	2.97	3.00	2.98
Expected future pension increases	1.75	2.49	1.75	2.05

Extract 16(A9) – Heidelberger Druckmaschinen Aktiengesellschaft, page 55

The company describes the basis used to determine the overall expected rate of return on assets.

To determine the expected return on plan assets, we use amounts generated in the past experience and forecasts concerning the expected development of plan assets. The forecasts are prepared by experienced portfolio managers and investment and real estate sector experts.

Extract 16(A10) – Heidelberger Druckmaschinen Aktiengesellschaft, pages 55 and 56

In this extract, the company discloses the amount of the provisions for pensions and similar obligations, as well as the amount of the plan assets on the balance sheet. The company also discloses a reconciliation of the opening and closing balances of the net carrying amounts.

The information on pensions is structured as follows:
1) Composition and development of the net carrying amounts.
2) Reconciliation of the defined benefit obligation and the fair value of plan assets to the provisions for pensions.
3) Development of the defined benefit obligation.
4) Development of the fair value of plan assets.
5) Composition of plan assets.
6) Breakdown of retirement benefit expenses.
7) Three-year comparison: total defined benefit obligation and experience adjustments.

1) The net carrying amounts break down as follows:	31-Mar-2007	31-Mar-2008
Provisions for pensions and similar obligations	132,940	115,969
Reported assets	32,639	94,136
Net carrying amounts at the end of the financial year	100,301	21,833
The net carrying amounts developed as follows:		
	2006/2007	2007/2008
Net carrying amounts at the start of the financial year	206,797	100,301
Expenses for pension obligations	66,968	58,792
Pension payments	– 7,721	– 2,218
Funding of pensions/contributions	– 71,115	– 6,753
Change in actuarial gains (–) / losses (+)	– 45,249	– 83,485
Expected return on plan assets	– 49,733	– 51,432
Change in adjustment amount due to IAS 19.58b)	668	1,571
Change in the scope of the consolidation, currency adjustments, other changes	– 314	5,057
Net carrying amounts at the end of the financial year	100,301	21,833

Extract 16(A11) – Heidelberger Druckmaschinen Aktiengesellschaft, page 56

The company discloses a reconciliation of the present value of the defined benefit obligation and the fair value of plan assets to the assets and liabilities on the balance sheet.

2) The provisions for pensions and similar obligations are derived from the defined benefit obligation and the fair value of plan assets as follows:	31-Mar-2007	31-Mar-2008
Present value of defined benefit obligation (funded)	946,726	810,564
Less fair value of plan assets	– 875,990	– 817,618
	70,736	– 7,054
Present value of defined benefit obligation (unfunded)	23,450	21,201
Adjustment amount due to IAS 19.58b)	6,115	7,686
Net carrying amount	100,301	21,833
Reported assets included therein	32,639	94,136
Provisions for pensions and similar obligations	132,940	115,969

Extract 16(A12) – Heidelberger Druckmaschinen Aktiengesellschaft, page 57

In this extract, the company discloses a reconciliation of opening and closing balances of the present value of the defined benefit obligation for pension plans, and a breakdown of the defined benefit obligation for pension plans into funded and unfunded portions.

3) The defined benefit obligation developed as follows:	2006/2007	2007/2008
Defined benefit obligation at the start of the financial year	986,671	970,176
Current service cost	25,136	23,257
Interest expense	41,832	44,004
Pension payments	– 31,720	– 36,650
Change in actuarial gains (–)/ losses (+)	– 53,211	– 140,556
Past service cost	–	– 8,469
Change in the scope of the consolidation, currency adjustments, other changes	1,468	– 19,997
Defined benefit obligation at the end of the financial year	970,176	831,765
– of which: funded	946,726	810,564
– of which: unfunded	23,450	21,201
The past service cost is based on the adjustment of the pension age due to the German Pension Age Adjustment Act.		

Extract 16(A13) – Heidelberger Druckmaschinen Aktiengesellschaft, page 57

In this extract, the company discloses a reconciliation of the opening and closing balances of the fair value of plan assets.

4) The fair value of plan assets developed as follows:	2006/2007	2007/2008
Fair value of plan assets at the start of the financial year	785,321	875,990
Expected return on plan assets	49,733	51,432
Funding of pensions/contributions	71,115	6,753
Pension payments from funds	– 23,999	– 34,432
Change in actuarial gains (–)/ losses (+)	– 7,962	– 57,071
Change in the scope of the consolidation, currency adjustments, other changes	1,782	– 25,054
Fair value of plan assets at the end of the financial year	875,990	817,618

Extract 16(A14) – Heidelberger Druckmaschinen Aktiengesellschaft, page 57

In this extract, the company discloses the actual return on plan assets.

The actual return on plan assets is € –5,639 thousand (previous year: € 41,771 thousand).

Extract 16(A15) – Heidelberger Druckmaschinen Aktiengesellschaft, page 58

Here, the company discloses the amount that each major category of plan assets constitutes of the fair value of total plan assets.

5) Plan assets break down as follows:	31-Mar-2007	31-Mar-2008
Fixed-income securities	425,280	461,044
Shares	322,896	258,669
Real estate	28,199	31,233
Qualifying insurance policy	27,799	28,086
Cash and cash equivalents	59,830	26,846
Other	11,986	11,740
	875,990	817,618

Extract 16(A16) – Heidelberger Druckmaschinen Aktiengesellschaft, page 58

The company discloses the total expense recognized in the income statement and the financial statement line items in which each cost is included.

6) Retirement benefit expenses break down as follows:	2006/2007	2007/2008
Current service cost[1]	25,136	23,257
Interest expense	41,832	44,004
Past service cost[1]	–	– 8,469
Expenses for pension obligations	66,968	58,792
Expected return on plan assets	– 49,733	– 51,432
Expenses for other pension plans[1]	19,726	23,522
	36,961	30,882

[1] Retirement benefit expenses reported under staff costs before netting against the return on plan assets amount to € 38,310 thousand (previous year: € 44,862 thousand)

The return on plan assets on an individual entity level is included in staff costs up to the amount of the corresponding expense for pension claims; any excess is shown together with interest expenses in net financial income.

Extract 16(A17) – Heidelberger Druckmaschinen Aktiengesellschaft, page 58

The company discloses that it was not possible to reliably estimate contributions expected to be paid in the upcoming fiscal year.

> It was not possible to reliably estimate expected future contributions to the employee pension funds as of the balance sheet date.

Extract 16(A18) – Heidelberger Druckmaschinen Aktiengesellschaft, page 58

In this extract, the company discloses the amount of cumulative actuarial gains, and the amount of cumulative adjustments resulting from the asset ceiling test recognized in equity.

Note that companies with a policy of recognizing actuarial gains and losses in full immediately and adjustments arising from the asset ceiling test outside profit or loss in the SORIE will instead recognize these items in other comprehensive income, displayed in the statement of comprehensive income, for annual periods beginning on or after January 1, 2009.

> The cumulative actuarial gains and the cumulative adjustment amount in accordance with IAS 19.58b) is € 19,845 thousand as of the balance sheet date (previous year: € 62,712 thousand).

Extract 16(A19) – Heidelberger Druckmaschinen Aktiengesellschaft, page 59

In this extract, the company discloses its funding status and experience adjustments over the last three years. Although IAS 19 requires disclosures for the past five year, IFRS 1, *First-time Adoption of International Financial Reporting Standards* permits first-time adopters to comply with this particular disclosure requirement as the amounts are determined for each accounting period prospectively from the date of transition to IFRS. As a result, the company has disclosed this information since its adoption of IFRS, which was three years ago.

7) Three-year comparison: total defined benefit obligation and experience adjustments

The defined benefit obligations, the fair values of plan assets, the funding status at the end of reporting periods and experience adjustments to liabilities and plan assets are shown in the following tables:

	31-Mar-2006	31-Mar-2007	31-Mar-2008
Present value of defined benefit obligation (funded)	841,874	946,726	810,564
Less fair value of plan assets	− 785,321	− 875,990	− 817,618
	56,553	70,736	− 7,054
Present value of defined benefit obligation (unfunded)	144,797	23,450	21,201

	2005/2006	2006/2007	2007/2008
Experience adjustments to liabilities	3,926	2,318	− 1,699
Experience adjustments to assets	27,825	− 7,962	− 57,071

Extract 16(A20) – Heidelberger Druckmaschinen Aktiengesellschaft, pages 59 and 60

In this extract, the company discloses the current and non-current portions of staff obligations, as well as the changes in the balance throughout the year.

	31-Mar-2007			31-Mar-2008		
	Current	Non-current	Total	Current	Non-current	Total
Tax provisions	19,444	250,450	269,894	37,705	257,271	294,976
Other provisions						
Staff obligations[1]	92,700	53,286	145,986	91,365	51,747	143,112
Sales obligations	161,879	30,567	192,446	180,104	11,735	191,839
Other[1]	54,645	39,732	94,377	69,212	39,621	108,833
	309,224	123,585	432,809	340,681	103,103	443,784
	328,668	374,035	702,703	378,386	360,374	738,760

	As of 31-Mar-2007	Changes in the scope of consolidation, currency adjustments, reclassification	Utilization	Release	Addition	As of 31-Mar-2008
Tax provisions	269,894	– 5,543	16,982	1,681	49,288	294,976
Other provisions						
Staff obligations[1]	145,986	– 3,750	77,271	8,483	86,630	143,112
Sales obligations	192,446	– 8,455	73,549	42,901	124,298	191,839
Other[1]	94,377	– 6,946	23,041	14,388	58,831	108,833
	432,809	– 19,151	173,861	65,772	269,759	443,784
	702,703	– 24,694	190,843	67,453	319,047	738,760

Additions include interest of € 7,102 thousand. € 2,406 thousand of this relates to staff obligations, € 436 thousand to sales obligations and € 4,260 thousand to miscellaneous other provisions.

Staff provisions essentially relate to bonuses (€ 44,191 thousand, previous year: € 49,199 thousand), expenses for early retirement payments and for the partial retirement program (€ 28,474 thousand; previous year: € 21,924 thousand), anniversary expenses (€ 16,506 thousand; previous year: € 17,399 thousand) and provisions for the stock option program and the long-term incentive plan (€ 582 thousand; previous year: € 971 thousand).

Extract 16(A21) – Heidelberger Druckmaschinen Aktiengesellschaft, page 64

In this extract, the company discloses the current and non-current portions of deferred staff liabilities and social security payable.

	31-Mar-2007			31-Mar-2008		
	Current	Non-current	Total	Current	Non-current	Total
Deferred staff liabilities[1]	81,760	–	81,760	84,307	–	84,307
Advance payments on orders	79,653	–	79,653	81,912	–	81,912
From derivative financial instruments	6,505	861	7,366	24,175	2,600	26,775
From other taxes	39,592	–	39,592	54,630	–	54,630
Relating to social security	9,254	–	9,254	6,041	2,704	8,745
Deferred income	34,561	35,587	70,148	49,381	35,116	84,497
Other	54,036	72,922	126,958	57,447	73,970	131,417
	305,361	109,370	414,731	357,893	114,390	472,283

Roche Holding Ltd – All extracts **16(B)** were obtained from the Annual Report for the year ended December 31, 2007.

Extract 16(B1) – Roche Holding Ltd, page 33

In this extract, the company discloses its accounting policy to account for equity compensation plans.

Equity compensation plans

Certain employees of the Group participate in equity compensation plans, including separate plans at Genentech and Chugai. The fair value of all equity compensation awards granted to employees is estimated at the grant date and recorded as an expense over the vesting period. The expense is charged to the appropriate income statement heading within the operating results. For equity-settled plans, an increase in equity is recorded and any subsequent cash flows from exercises of vested awards are recorded as an increase in equity. For cash-settled plans, a liability is recorded, which is measured at fair value at each balance sheet date with any movements in fair value being recorded to the appropriate income statement heading within the operating results. Any subsequent cash flows from exercise of vested awards are recorded as a reduction of the liability.

Extract 16(B2) – Roche Holding Ltd, pages 64 and 65

The company discloses the total expense arising from share-based payment transactions, as well as the portion for equity-settled share-based payment transactions.

The Group operates several equity compensation plans, including separate plans at Genentech and Chugai. Effective 1 January 2005 the Group adopted IFRS 2: 'Share-based Payment'. Amongst other matters, the standard requires that the fair value of all equity compensation plan awards granted to employees be estimated at grant date and recorded as an expense over the vesting period. The expense is charged against the appropriate income statement heading.

Expenses for equity compensation plans *in millions of CHF*

	2007	2006
Cost of sales	90	118
Marketing and distribution	132	149
Research and development	206	229
General and administration	180	194
Total operating expense	608	690
Share option plans		
Roche Option Plan	6	7
Genentech Stock Option Plan	433	468
Chugai Stock Acquisition Rights	3	1
Total share option plans	442	476
Other equity compensation plans		
Roche Connect	13	11
Genentech Employee Stock Purchase Program	32	42
Roche Stock-settled Stock Appreciation Rights	100	76
Roche Performance Share Plan	16	15
Roche Stock Appreciation Rights	5	70
Total other equity compensation plans	166	214
Total operating expense	608	690
Of which		
– equity-settled	603	620
– cash-settled	5	70

Extract 16(B3) – Roche Holding Ltd, page 65

This extract discloses the cash inflow and outflow arising from share-based payment transactions, and the portion related to equity-settled share-based payment transactions.

Cash inflow (outflow) from equity compensation plans *in millions of CHF*	2007	2006
Share option plans		
Roche Option Plan	(19)	55
Genentech Stock Option Plan	408	361
Chugai Stock Acquisition Rights	1	1
Total share option plans	390	417
Other equity compensation plans		
Roche Connect	(13)	(11)
Genentech Employee Stock Purchase Program	134	121
Roche Stock-settled Stock Appreciation Rights	(61)	(47)
Roche Performance Share Plan	–	–
Roche Stock Appreciation Rights	(97)	(107)
Total other equity compensation plans	(37)	(44)
Total cash inflow (outflow)	353	373
Of which		
– equity-settled	450	480
– cash-settled	(97)	(107)

Roche Long-Term: During 2005 the Group implemented a new global long-term incentive programme which is available to certain directors, management and employees selected at the discretion of the Group. The programme consists of Stock-settled Stock Appreciation Rights (S-SARs), with the Group having the alternative of granting awards under the existing Roche Option Plan.

Extract 16(B4) – Roche Holding Ltd, page 66

The company describes its equity-settled share option plan (i.e., Roche Option Plan), including the general terms and conditions, such as the vesting period and the maximum term.

Share option plans

Roche Option Plan: Awards under this plan give employees the right to purchase non-voting equity securities at an exercise price specified at the grant date. The options, which are non-tradable equity-settled awards, have a seven-year duration and vest on a phased basis over three years, subject to continued employment. The Group covers such obligations by purchasing non-voting equity securities or derivatives thereon (see Note 28). With the introduction of Roche Long-Term in 2005, the number of options granted under the Roche Option Plan was significantly reduced, as most eligible employees now receive Roche Stock-settled Stock Appreciation Rights instead.

Extract 16(B5) – Roche Holding Ltd, page 66

In this extract, the company discloses the number and weighted average exercise prices of share options.

Share option plans Roche Option Plan – movement in number of options outstanding	2007		2006	
	Number of options (thousands)	Weighted average exercise price (CHF)	Number of options (thousands)	Weighted average exercise price (CHF)
Outstanding at 1 January	1,416	117.83	1,854	105.85
Granted	194	229.68	141	195.14
Forfeited	(10)	163.98	(15)	123.52
Exercised	(397)	105.64	(564)	97.73
Expired	–	–	–	–
Outstanding at 31 December	1,203	139.50	1,416	117.83
– of which exercisable	875	115.71	894	103.00

Extract 16(B6) – Roche Holding Ltd, page 66

This extract discloses the weighted average remaining contractual life of all share options outstanding and of exercisable share options outstanding.

Share option plans Roche Option Plan – terms of options outstanding as at 31 December 2007			Options outstanding		Options exercisable
Year of grant	Number outstanding (thousands)	Weighted average years remaining contractual life	Weighted average exercise price (CHF)	Number exercisable (thousands)	Weighted average exercise price (CHF)
2002	75	1.19	115.19	75	115.19
2003	261	2.17	78.44	261	78.44
2004	416	3.17	129.49	416	129.49
2005	136	4.17	123.13	81	123.00
2006	124	5.17	195.17	39	195.17
2007	191	6.18	229.68	3	229.60
Total	1,203	2.64	139.50	875	115.71

Extract 16(B7) – Roche Holding Ltd, page 66

In this extract, the company discloses a description of an equity-settled stock option plan (i.e., Genentech Stock Option Plan), including the general terms and conditions, such as the vesting period and the maximum term.

> **Share option plans**
>
> *Genentech Stock Option Plan*: The Genentech Stock Option Plan was adopted in 1999 and amended thereafter. In April 2004 Genentech's shareholders approved an equity incentive plan. The plans allow for the granting of various stock options, incentive stock options and stock purchase rights to employees, directors and consultants of Genentech. No incentive stock options and stock purchase rights have been granted under this plan to date. The options granted, which are non-tradable equity-settled awards, have a ten-year duration and vest on a phased basis over four years, subject to continued employment.

Extract 16(B8) – Roche Holding Ltd, page 66

In this extract, the company discloses the number and weighted average exercise prices of stock options.

Share option plans
Genentech Stock Option Plan – movement in number of options outstanding

| | 2007 | | 2006 | |
	Number of options (millions)	Weighted average exercise price (USD)	Number of options (millions)	Weighted average exercise price (USD)
Outstanding at 1 January	88	54.53	83	46.64
Granted	18	79.40	17	79.85
Forfeited	(4)	76.45	(3)	62.09
Exercised	(10)	32.76	(9)	30.42
Expired	–	–	–	–
Outstanding at 31 December	92	60.94	88	54.53
– of which exercisable	54	48.46	47	38.48

Extract 16(B9) – Roche Holding Ltd, page 67

The company discloses the range of exercise prices and the weighted average remaining contractual life of stock options outstanding and of exercisable stock options outstanding.

Share option plans
Genentech Stock Option Plan – terms of options outstanding at 31 December 2007

Range of exercise prices (USD)	Number outstanding (millions)	Weighted average years remaining contractual life	Options outstanding Weighted average exercise price (USD)	Number exercisable (millions)	Options exercisable Weighted average exercise price (USD)
6.27–8.89	0.3	4.64	7.41	0.3	7.41
10.00–14.35	8.2	3.86	13.68	8.2	13.68
15.04–22.39	6.1	3.33	20.87	6.1	20.87
22.88–33.00	0.2	3.46	26.33	0.2	26.33
35.63–53.23	26.6	5.73	47.05	23.6	46.31
53.95–75.90	1.7	7.90	64.79	0.8	59.09
78.99–98.80	49.0	8.66	81.78	14.5	83.79
Total	92.1	6.99	60.94	53.7	48.46

Extract 16(B10) – Roche Holding Ltd, page 67

This extract describes equity-settled stock acquisition rights, including the general terms and conditions, such as the vesting period and the maximum term.

Share option plans
Chugai Stock Acquisition Rights: During 2003 Chugai adopted a Stock Acquisition Rights programme. The programme allows for the granting of rights to employees and directors of Chugai. Each right entitles the holder to purchase 100 Chugai shares at a specified exercise price. The options, which are non-tradable equity-settled awards, have a ten-year duration and vest after two years.

Extract 16(B11) – Roche Holding Ltd, page 67

The company discloses the number and weighted average exercise prices of stock acquisition rights.

Share option plans				
Chugai Stock Acquisition Rights – movement in number of rights outstanding				
		2007		2006
	Number of options	Weighted average exercise price (JPY)	Number of options	Weighted average exercise price (JPY)
Outstanding at 1 January	**9,886**	**182,925**	6,800	160,166
Granted	**3,550**	**303,900**	3,440	224,500
Forfeited	**–**	**–**	–	–
Exercised	**(434)**	**148,965**	(354)	149,770
Expired	**–**	**–**	–	–
Outstanding at 31 December	**13,002**	**217,089**	9,886	182,925
– of which exercisable	**6,012**	**161,587**	3,926	158,066

Extract 16(B12) – Roche Holding Ltd, page 67

This extract discloses the weighted average remaining contractual life of stock acquisition rights outstanding and of exercisable stock acquisition rights outstanding.

Share option plans					
Chugai Stock Acquisition Rights – terms of rights outstanding at 31 December 2007					
			Rights outstanding		Rights exercisable
Year of grant	Number outstanding	Weighted average years remaining contractual life	Weighted average exercise price (JPY)	Number exercisable	Weighted average exercise price (JPY)
2003	1,312	5.50	145,400	1,312	145,400
2004	2,180	6.25	167,500	2,180	167,500
2005	2,520	7.25	164,900	2,520	164,900
2006	3,440	8.25	224,500	–	224,500
2007	3,550	9.25	303,900	–	303,900
Total	13,002	7.72	217,089	6,012	161,587

Extract 16(B13) – Roche Holding Ltd, pages 67 and 68

This extract discloses the weighted average fair value of share options granted at the measurement date, and the option pricing model used to determine that fair value, along with the inputs to that model and how the expected volatility was determined.

Share option plans

Issues of share options in 2007: Issues for share options in 2007, including the methodology used to calculate fair value and the main inputs to the valuation models, are described below.

Issues of share option plans in 2007

	Roche Option Plan	Genentech Stock Option Plan	Chugai Stock Acquisition Rights
Number of options granted	194 thousand	18 million	3,550
Underlying equity	Roche non-voting	Genentech common	Chugai shares in equity securities stock blocks of 100
Currency	Swiss francs	US dollars	Japanese yen
Vesting period	Progressively over 3 years	Progressively over 4 years	After 2 years
Contractual life	7 years	10 years	10 years
Weighted average fair value of options issued	37.96	23.63	1,051.01
Option pricing model used	Binomial	Binomial	Binomial
Inputs to option pricing model			
– share price at grant date	229.68	79.40	289,500
– exercise price	229.68	79.40	303,900
– expected volatility	25.30%	25.1%	33.03%
– expected dividend yield	4.52%	0%	1.04%
– early exercise factor	1.705	1.482	n/a
– expected exit rate	12.82%	8.59%	0%

Volatility for Roche and Chugai options was determined primarily by reference to historically observed prices of the underlying equity. Volatility for Genentech options was determined primarily by reference to the implied volatility of Genentech's traded options. Risk-free interest rates are derived from zero coupon swap rates at the grant date taken from Datastream. The early exercise factor describes the ratio between the expected market price at the exercise date and the exercise price at which early exercises can be expected, based on historically observed behaviour. For the Chugai grants in 2007 it was assumed that all awards would be held for the full term length, since there was insufficient historically observed early exercise behaviour.

Extract 16(B14) – Roche Holding Ltd, page 68

In this extract, the company describes other equity compensation plans and their related cost in the current year.

Other equity compensation plans

Roche Connect: This programme enables all employees worldwide, except for those in the United States and certain other countries, to make regular deductions from their salaries to purchase non-voting equity securities. It is administered by independent third parties. The Group contributes to the programme, which allows the employees to purchase non-voting equity securities at a discount (usually 20%). The administrator purchases the necessary non-voting equity securities directly from the market. At 31 December 2007 the administrator held 1,104 thousand non-voting equity securities (2006: 911 thousand). The programme has been operational since 1 October 2002. During the year the cost of the plan was 13 million Swiss francs (2006: 11 million Swiss francs), which was reported within the relevant expenditure line by function.

Genentech Employee Stock Purchase Program (ESPP): Genentech has an employee stock purchase programme that allows employees to purchase Genentech's common stock at 85% of the lower of market value at the grant date or purchase date. In 2007 a total of 1.7 million shares of Genentech common stock were purchased (2006: 1.9 million shares) resulting in a cash inflow of 134 million Swiss francs (2006: 121 million Swiss francs). During the year the cost of the plan was 32 million Swiss francs (2006: 42 million Swiss francs), which was reported within the relevant expenditure line by function.

Extract 16(B15) – Roche Holding Ltd, page 68

This extract describes stock-settled stock appreciation rights, including the general terms and conditions, such as the vesting period and the maximum term.

Other equity compensation plans

Roche Stock-settled Stock Appreciation Rights: With the introduction of Roche Long-Term in 2005, the Group offers Stock-settled Stock Appreciation Rights (S-SARs) to certain directors, management and employees selected at the discretion of the Group. The S-SARs give employees the right to receive non-voting equity securities reflecting the value of any appreciation in the market price of the non-voting equity securities between the grant date and the exercise date. The options, which are non-tradable equity-settled awards, have a seven-year duration and vest on a phased basis over three years, subject to continued employment. The Group covers such obligations by purchasing non-voting equity securities, or derivatives thereon.

Extract 16(B16) – Roche Holding Ltd, page 69

In this extract, the company discloses the number and weighted average exercise prices of stock-settled stock appreciation rights.

Other equity compensation plans
Roche S-SARs – movement in number of rights outstanding

	2007 Number of rights (thousands)	2007 Weighted average exercise price (CHF)	2006 Number of rights (thousands)	2006 Weighted average exercise price (CHF)
Outstanding at 1 January	5,883	156.07	3,868	123.34
Granted	3,025	229.37	2,762	195.13
Forfeited	(189)	180.91	(151)	149.44
Exercised	(937)	142.36	(596)	126.35
Expired	–	–	–	–
Outstanding at 31 December	7,782	185.60	5,88	156.07
– of which exercisable	2,101	149.17	900	126.49

Extract 16(B17) – Roche Holding Ltd, page 69

In this extract, the company discloses the weighted average remaining contractual life of stock-settled stock appreciation rights outstanding and of exercisable stock-settled stock appreciation rights outstanding. The company discloses the weighted average fair value of stock-settled stock appreciation rights granted at the measurement date, and the option pricing model used to determine that fair value, along with the inputs to that model and how the expected volatility was determined.

Other equity compensation plans

Roche S-SARs – terms of rights outstanding at 31 December 2007

Year of grant	Number outstanding (thousands)	Weighted average years remaining contractual life	Rights outstanding Weighted average exercise price (CHF)	Number exercisable (thousands)	Rights exercisable Weighted average exercise price (CHF)
2005	2,452	4.17	123.33	1,361	123.37
2006	2,356	5.17	195.16	709	195.17
2007	2,974	6.17	229.37	31	229.60
Total	**7,782**	**5.24**	**185.60**	**2,101**	**149.17**

The weighted average fair value of the options granted in 2007 was calculated using a binomial model. The inputs to the model were consistent with those used for the Roche Option Plan 2007 awards given previously. The resulting weighted average fair value per right is CHF 37.97, giving a total fair value of 115 million Swiss francs which is charged over the vesting period of three years.

Extract 16(B18) – Roche Holding Ltd, page 69

This extract describes the equity-settled performance share plan, including the general terms and conditions, such as the vesting period. The company also discloses the number and weighted average fair value of awards granted during the period at the measurement date. The weighted average fair value was based on a Monte Carlo simulation model.

Other equity compensation plans

Roche Performance Share Plan: The Group offers future non-voting equity security awards (or, at the discretion of the Board of Directors, their cash equivalent) to certain directors and key senior managers. The programme was established at the beginning of 2002 and was in effect for three years. During 2004 the Board of Directors approved a new three-year cycle of the Roche Performance Share Plan (PSP) to operate during 2005–2007. The amount of non-voting equity securities allocated will depend upon the individual's salary level, the achievement of performance targets linked to the Group's Total Shareholder Return (shares and non-voting equity securities combined) relative to the Group's peers during the three-year period from the date of the grant, and the discretion of the Board of Directors. These are non-tradable equity-settled awards. Each award will result in between zero and two non-voting equity securities, depending upon the achievement of the performance targets. Additional cycles of the PSP with similar conditions were approved to operate during 2006–2008 and 2007–2009. The terms of these awards are set out in the table below.

Roche Performance Share Plan – terms of awards

	2005–2007	2006–2008	2007–2009
Number of awards (thousands)	240	55	78
Vesting period	3 years	3 years	3 years
Allocated to recipients in	Feb. 2008	Feb. 2009	Feb. 2010
Fair value per unit (CHF)	145.39	210.06	239.49
Total fair value (CHF millions)	35	12	19

The weighted average fair value of the awards granted in 2007 was calculated using a Monte Carlo simulation. The input parameters to the model were the covariance matrix between Roche and the other individual companies of the peer group based on a three-year history and a risk-free rate of 2.671%. The valuation also takes into account the defined rank and performance structure which determines the payout of the PSP.

Extract 16(B19) – Roche Holding Ltd, page 70

In this extract, the company discloses a description of cash-settled stock appreciation rights, including the general terms and conditions, such as the vesting period.

Other equity compensation plans

Roche Stock Appreciation Rights: Some employees of certain North American subsidiaries of the Group receive Stock Appreciation Rights (SARs) as part of their compensation. The SARs, which are non-tradable cash-settled awards, may be exercised after a vesting period of between one and three years for a cash payment, based upon the amount by which the market price of the Group's American Depositary Receipts (ADRs) at the point of exercise exceeds the strike price (grant price at issuance). Following the implementation of Roche Long-Term (see above), the Group does not plan to award any further cash-settled SARs and no awards have been made since 2004.

Extract 16(B20) – Roche Holding Ltd, page 70

The company discloses the total carrying amount and the total intrinsic value of liabilities arising from share-based payment transactions.

Other equity compensation plans
Roche Stock Appreciation Rights *in millions of CHF*

	2007	2006
Liability at 31 December	97	199
Intrinsic value of vested rights at 31 December	97	198

Extract 16(B21) – Roche Holding Ltd, page 70

This extract discloses the number and weighted average exercise prices of stock appreciation rights outstanding and exercisable. It also discloses that the fair value was calculated using a binomial model.

Other equity compensation plans
Roche Stock Appreciation Rights – terms of rights outstanding at 31 December 2007

Year of grant	Number outstanding and exercisable (thousands)	Expiry	Rights outstanding and exercisable Weighted average exercise price (USD)
2001	70	Jul. 2008	36.30
2002	282	Dec. 2008	34.68
2003	560	Feb. 2010	28.83
2004	1,092	Feb. 2011	52.08
Total	2,004		42.58

The fair value at 31 December 2007 was calculated using a binomial model. The inputs to the model were the ADR price at 31 December 2007 (USD 85.40), the exercise prices given in the above table, and other inputs consistent with those used for the Roche Option Plan 2007 awards given previously.

PLANNING FOR IMPLEMENTATION

Assessing the Impact on Financial Statements

Although CICA 3461 and CICA 3870 are generally converged with IAS 19 and IFRS 2, significant differences do exist. These differences may affect the recognition, measurement and disclosure of employee benefits and share-based payment transactions. The most significant of these differences and an assessment of their impact on the financial statements are discussed below.

Employee Benefits
Post-employment Benefit Plan Classified as a Defined Benefit Plan
Measurement date

IAS 19 requires the present value of the defined benefit obligation and the fair value of plan assets to be determined at the balance sheet date.

CICA 3461 permits the defined benefit obligation and the plan assets to be measured as of a date not more than three months before the balance sheet date, provided that this practice is consistent from year to year.

Once IFRS is adopted, Canadian companies using a measurement date before the balance sheet date will have to change to the balance sheet date instead.

Attribution of Benefit

IAS 19 requires the present value of defined benefit obligations to be determined by attributing benefit to periods of service based on a plan's benefit formula. When a plan's formula attributes a materially higher level of benefit to later years of service, however, the benefit is attributed on a straight-line basis from:

- the date when employee services first earn benefits under the plan; until
- the date when further employee services will earn no further material benefits under the plan.

Under CICA 3461, the obligation for benefits for defined benefit plans other than pension plans must be attributed on a straight-line basis to each year of service in the attribution period. The exception is when the plan formula attributes a significantly higher level of benefits to early years of service, in which case, the obligation should be attributed based on the plan's benefit formula.

Canadian companies adopting IFRS will be required to attribute benefits differently.

Expected Return on Plan Assets

IAS 19 requires that the expected return on plan assets be based on market expectations, at the beginning of the period, for returns over the life of the related obligation. The expected return on plan assets reflects changes in the fair value of plan assets held during the period as a result of actual contributions paid into the fund and benefits paid out of the fund.

CICA 3461 requires that the expected return on plan assets be based on:

- the expected long-term rate of return on plan assets; and
- the fair value or a market-related value of plan assets.

When IFRS is adopted, Canadian companies currently using a market-related value of plan assets to determine the expected return on plan assets will be required to use the fair value of plan assets instead.

Past Service Cost

IAS 19 requires past service cost to be recognized on a straight-line basis over the average period until benefits become vested. To the extent that benefits are already vested, past service cost is recognized immediately.

CICA 3461 does not have separate requirements for past service cost for which benefits are vested and unvested. Furthermore, CICA 3461 requires that a past service cost:

- for post-employment benefits (that do not vest or accumulate) be recognized:
    o over a period linked to the type of benefit, or
    o immediately in the income statement;
- for pension benefits, other retirement benefits or post-employment benefits (that vest or accumulate) be recognized:
    o by assigning an equal amount to each remaining service period up to the full eligibility date of each employee active at the date of the plan initiation or amendment who was not yet fully eligible for benefits at that date, or
    o by using an alternative approach that amortizes past service costs more rapidly.

Canadian companies will be required to amortize past service cost differently once they adopt IFRS.

Actuarial Gains and Losses

IAS 19 requires actuarial gains and losses to be recognized:

- in accordance with the corridor approach, in the income statement;
- by adopting any systematic method that results in faster recognition, in the income statement; or
- in full immediately in the income statement or in other comprehensive income.

CICA 3461 requires actuarial gains and losses that:

- relate to pension benefits, other retirement benefits or post-employment benefits (that vest or accumulate) to be recognized:
    o in accordance with the corridor approach, in the income statement,
    o by adopting any systematic method that results in faster recognition, in the income statement, or
    o in full immediately in the income statement (there is no option to account for this item in other comprehensive income);
- relate to post-employment benefits (that do not vest or accumulate) to be recognized:
    o over a period linked to the type of benefit, or
    o in full immediately in the income statement (there is no option to account for this item in other comprehensive income).

Canadian companies that implement a policy of recognizing actuarial gains and losses in full immediately in other comprehensive income when they adopt IFRS will report less volatility in their income statements because the actuarial gains and losses recognized in other comprehensive income cannot be recycled through the income statement in a subsequent period.

Share-based Payment

Scope

IFRS 2 applies to the accounting for all share-based payment transactions, except for:

- transfers of an entity's equity instruments by its shareholders, equity instruments of the entity's parent or equity instruments of another entity in the same group as the entity, to parties that have supplied goods or services to the entity (including employees), which are clearly for a purpose other than payment for goods or services supplied to the entity;
- transactions with employees or non-employees in their capacity as holders of equity instruments of the entity;
- transactions in which the entity acquires goods as part of the net assets acquired in a business combination to which IFRS 3, *Business Combinations* applies; and
- transactions in which the entity receives or acquires goods or services under a contract within the scope of IAS 32, *Financial Instruments: Presentation* or IAS 39, *Financial Instruments: Recognition and Measurement*.

The scope of CICA 3870 is similar, except that the standard:

- does not apply to related party transactions (other than stock-based compensation plans with a principal shareholder); and
- has an exception for the recognition of an expense when an employee share purchase plan provides a discount to employees that does not exceed the per share amount of share issuance costs that would have been incurred to raise a significant amount of capital by a public offering and is not extended to other holders of the same class of shares.

This difference may result in more transactions being accounted for as share-based payment transactions on the adoption of IFRS.

Equity-settled Share-based Payment Transactions
Vesting Conditions

IFRS 2 requires an amount for the goods or services received during the vesting period to be recognized based on the best available estimate of the number of equity instruments expected to vest (without taking market conditions into account) when a grant of equity instruments does not vest immediately. The estimate is revised if subsequent information indicates that the number of equity instruments expected to vest differs from previous estimates.

CICA 3870 allows forfeitures by individual employees to be either:

- estimated at the grant date and subsequently revised; or
- recognized only as they occur.

When IFRS is adopted, Canadian companies that currently recognize forfeitures by individual employees only as they occur will be instead required to estimate forfeitures by individual employees at the grant date (which will be revised for subsequent information).

Measurement of Transactions with Non-employees

IFRS 2 requires goods or services received to be measured directly at their fair value at the date an entity obtains the goods or a counterparty renders service. When this is not possible, the goods or services received are measured indirectly by reference to the fair value of equity instruments granted at the measurement date.

CICA 3870 requires goods or services received to be measured based on the fair value of the consideration received, or the fair value of equity instruments, whichever is more reliably measurable.

Canadian companies adopting IFRS will be required to measure goods or services received differently.

Measurement Date for Transactions with Non-employees

IFRS 2 defines the measurement date as the date that an entity obtains goods or a counterparty renders service.

CICA 3870 defines the measurement date as the earliest of the following:

- the date at which the non-employee's performance is complete;
- the date at which a performance commitment by the non-employee has been reached; or
- the grant date of the equity instruments if they are fully vested and non-forfeitable at that date.

On adoption of IFRS, this difference may result in a later measurement date.

Cash-settled Share-based Payment Transactions

IFRS 2 requires that goods or services received be measured at the fair value of the liability.

CICA 3870 requires that goods or services received from:

- non-employees be measured based on the fair value of the consideration received, or liabilities incurred, whichever is more reliably measurable; and
- employees be measured at the intrinsic value of the share-based award.

On adoption of IFRS, this difference results in more complex measurements for cash-settled share-based payment transactions with employees and in more volatility in the income statements of Canadian companies.

Transactions with Settlement Alternatives

IFRS 2 requires a transaction in which the terms of the arrangement allow the counterparty to choose the method of settlement to be accounted for as a compound financial instrument.

CICA 3870 requires such a transaction to be accounted for as a cash-settled share-based payment transaction.

On adoption of IFRS, this difference results in more complex measurements for transactions in which the terms of the arrangement allow the counterparty to choose the method of settlement and in more volatility in the income statements of Canadian companies.

Initial Adoption of IFRS

Employee Benefits

Actuarial Gains and Losses

IFRS 1, *First-time Adoption of International Financial Reporting Standards* requires a first-time adopter to apply retrospectively the current version of IAS 19 in its entirety. The retrospective application of IAS 19 may, however, prove to be cumbersome for an entity that has elected to use the corridor approach to recognize actuarial gains and losses arising from a defined benefit plan. The retrospective application of this approach would require a first-time adopter to recalculate the cumulative unrecognized actuarial gains and losses from the inception of the plan until the date of transition to IFRS in accordance with IAS 19. As a result, a first-time adopter may elect to recognize all cumulative actuarial gains and losses at the date of transition to IFRS, even if the corridor approach is used after the adoption of IFRS to recognize actuarial gains and losses. A first-time adopter using this election must apply it to all plans.

Disclosure

IAS 19 requires the disclosure of the following amounts relating to defined benefit plans, for the current fiscal year and previous four fiscal years:

- the present value of the defined benefit obligation;
- the fair value of the plan assets;
- the surplus or deficit in the plans; and
- the experience adjustments arising on:
  - o the plan liabilities at the balance sheet date expressed either as:
    - an amount, or
    - a percentage of the plan liabilities, and
  - o the plan assets at the balance sheet date expressed either as:
    - an amount; or
    - a percentage of the plan assets.

The disclosure of this historical information may also prove to be cumbersome for a first-time adopter. Therefore, IFRS 1 permits a first-time adopter to comply with this particular disclosure requirement as the amounts are determined for each accounting period prospectively from the date of transition to IFRS.

Share-based Payment

Equity-settled Transactions

Mandatory Application

A first-time adopter is required to apply IFRS 2 to equity instruments that were granted after November 7, 2002, but have not vested as of the date of transition to IFRS.

Voluntary Application

A first-time adopter is encouraged, but not required, to apply IFRS 2 to equity instruments that were granted:

- on or before November 7, 2002; and
- after November 7, 2002 and vested before the date of transition to IFRS, if the fair value of those equity instruments (determined at the measurement date) was previously disclosed publicly.

If a first-time adopter modifies the terms or conditions of a grant of equity instruments to which IFRS 2 has not been applied, there is no need to apply the IFRS 2 requirements for modifications, cancellations and settlements made before the date of transition to IFRS.

Disclosure

For all grants of equity instruments to which IFRS 2 has not been applied, IFRS 1 still requires the disclosure of the following information:

- a description of each type of share-based payment arrangement that existed at any time during the period;

- the number and weighted average exercise prices of share options for each of the following groups of options:
    - o   outstanding at the beginning of the period,
    - o   granted during the period,
    - o   forfeited during the period,
    - o   exercised during the period,
    - o   expired during the period,
    - o   outstanding at the end of the period, and
    - o   exercisable at the end of the period;
- the weighted average share price at the exercise date of share options exercised during the period;
- the range of exercise prices and weighted average remaining contractual life of share options outstanding at the end of the period.

IFRS 1 does not provide any guidance on accounting for grants of equity instruments to which IFRS 2 has not been applied. It appears, therefore, that expenses relating to equity-settled share-based payment transactions previously recognized in accordance with CICA 3870 should be reversed and disclosed only as required by IFRS 1.

Cash-settled Transactions
Mandatory Application
A first-time adopter is required to apply IFRS 2 to liabilities arising from share-based payment transactions outstanding at the date of transition to IFRS, and to restate comparative information unless this information relates to a period or date earlier than November 7, 2002.

Voluntary Application
A first-time adopter is encouraged, but not required, to apply IFRS 2 to liabilities arising from share-based payment transactions settled before the date of transition to IFRS.

Adapting Performance Measures
Differences in the timing of recognition and the measurement of plan assets, obligations and expenses arising from the adoption of IAS 19 and IFRS 2 will affect the analysis, interpretation and comparability of a significant number of financial ratios, such as the debt-to-equity ratio, which were calculated previously using financial information in accordance with CICA 3461 and CICA 3870.

As a result, Canadian public companies will need to evaluate the strategic impact of IFRS and adapt existing performance measurement systems to this new environment. This entails working closely with finance, operations and human resources to perform a comprehensive review of employee remuneration and benefit packages to ensure that they continue to be consistent with current business strategies. As well, actuaries and other external advisers who are well versed in IFRS and best practices in an IFRS environment can help senior management obtain an in-depth understanding of the potential accounting and business impacts of alternative employee remuneration and benefit packages.

A review of the current processes and systems for entering into, drafting, approving and monitoring employment compensation contracts will also be necessary to ensure that future compensation packages are consistent with business strategies.

Legal Implications

A constructive obligation under IFRS may be broader than a substantive commitment under Canadian GAAP because it includes informal practices that give rise to an obligation where an entity has no realistic alternative but to pay employee benefits (i.e., where a change in the entity's informal practices would greatly harm its relationship with employees). Therefore, to identify potential constructive obligations and assess their impact on financial statements, accounting and operational personnel will need to seek the advice of legal counsel in interpreting contractual terms and conditions in accordance with IFRS.

Generating New Data and Optimizing Information Systems

The information required to account for and disclose employee benefits and share-based payment transactions under Canadian GAAP is very similar to that required under IFRS. Thus, the adoption of IAS 19 and IFRS 2 will most likely not result in a significant overhaul of reporting and consolidation systems. Modifications may be required, however, to ensure that consistent methods are applied throughout an entity (including affiliated entities) to account for all defined benefit plans and to gather the additional disclosure information required by IFRS.

Keep Posted

Employee Benefits

As noted earlier, the IASB issued a Discussion Paper on the amendments to IAS 19 in March 2008, which proposes significant improvements to:

- the recognition and presentation of defined benefit liabilities;
- the accounting for benefits that are based on a promised return; and
- the accounting for benefit promises with a "higher of" option.

Canadian public companies transitioning to IFRS should be aware of the changes that the IASB expects to issue in an Exposure Draft to be released at the end of the third quarter of 2009. A final standard is expected at the end of the second quarter of 2011 (with an effective date from January 1, 2013).

Share-based Payments

The IASB also proposed amendments to IFRS 2 and IFRIC 11 that would clarify that an entity must apply IFRS 2 even if it has no obligation to make the required share-based cash payments. The proposed amendment to IFRIC 11 specifies that, when an entity has no obligation to make the required share-based cash payments, the goods or services received should be measured in accordance with the IFRS 2 requirements applicable to cash-settled share-based payment transactions. The majority of the comments on the Exposure Draft issued in December 2007 agreed with the proposed amendments, which are expected to be published in the first quarter of 2009.

Chapter 17

Income Taxes

Standards Discussed in this Chapter

International

IAS 12 – Income Taxes
SIC 21 – Income Taxes – Recovery of Revalued Non-Depreciable Assets
SIC 25 – Income Taxes – Changes in the Tax Status of an Entity or its Shareholders

Canadian

CICA 3465 – Income Taxes
CICA 3805 – Investment Tax Credits
EIC-111 – Determination of substantively enacted tax rates under CICA 3465

INTRODUCTION

Income taxes are considered to be a business expense, which needs to be allocated among accounting periods.

Over the years, two approaches have evolved to account for income taxes:

- the *timing difference approach*, which focuses on the differences in the timing of the recognition of income and expenses for financial reporting purposes and for tax purposes; and

- the *temporary difference approach* (developed by FASB), which focuses on differences between the carrying amount of assets and liabilities on the balance sheet and their tax base.

Canadian financial statement preparers currently turn to CICA 3465 for guidance on accounting for income taxes, which follows the temporary difference approach. Once they adopt IFRS, they will likely have to refer to a new IFRS on accounting for income taxes, which is currently being developed by the IASB and expected to be issued in 2010.

Although IAS 12 will be replaced by a new IFRS on accounting for income taxes, entities that are planning to early adopt IFRS should refer to the existing IAS 12 requirements. As a result, this chapter covers the following topics that these entities should consider when adopting IAS 12:

- current taxes:
  - o current tax liabilities,
  - o current tax assets;
- deferred taxes:
  - o tax base,
  - o taxable and deductible temporary differences,
  - o deferred tax liabilities,

o deferred tax assets,
o specific exceptions:
   • initial recognition of an asset or liability,
   • goodwill,
o specific applications:
   • business combinations,
   • intragroup transfers,
   • investments in subsidiaries, branches and associates, and interests in joint ventures,
   • foreign currency translations,
   • compound financial instruments,
   • assets carried at fair value,
   • share-based payment transactions;
• changes in tax status;
• uncertain tax positions;
• investment tax credits.

IMPACT ON FINANCIAL STATEMENTS

CICA 3465 and IAS 12 are both based on the *balance sheet liability approach*, which focuses on temporary differences between the carrying amounts of assets and liabilities on the balance sheet and their tax base. Differences arise, however, because both standards have numerous exceptions to this basic principle. The most significant of these differences are as follows:

• IAS 12 requires a deferred tax expense or benefit to be recognized outside profit or loss (i.e., in other comprehensive income or directly in equity) if it relates to items that are recognized outside profit or loss in the same or a different period. CICA 3465 prohibits *backwards tracing* (i.e., tracking changes in recognized deferred tax liabilities and assets back to components of comprehensive income and equity in which the tax was originally recognized). Therefore, the adoption of IAS 12 may result in reduced volatility in the income statement (in exchange for increased volatility in equity).

• IAS 12 prohibits the recognition of a deferred tax liability or asset when it arises from the initial recognition of an asset or liability in a transaction that is not a business combination, and affects neither accounting profit nor taxable profit (tax loss) at the time of the transaction. For an asset acquired outside of a business combination, CICA 3465 requires a deferred tax liability or a deferred tax asset to be recognized and the carrying amount of the asset to be adjusted.

• IAS 12 requires a deferred tax liability or asset to be recognized for temporary differences that arise from the elimination of profits and losses resulting from intragroup transactions that are recognized in assets (i.e., inventory and fixed assets). CICA 3465 prohibits the recognition of a deferred tax liability or asset when such temporary differences arise.

• IAS 12 requires entities to recognize a deferred tax liability or asset for temporary differences that arise on the translation of non-monetary assets and liabilities that are remeasured from the local currency to the functional currency using historical rates and result from changes in exchange rates and indexing for tax purposes.

CICA 3465 prohibits the recognition of a deferred tax liability or asset when such temporary differences arise.

- IAS 1, *Presentation of Financial Statements* prohibits entities from presenting deferred tax assets and liabilities as current when a classified balance sheet is presented. CICA 3465 requires entities to present the current and non-current portions of deferred tax liabilities and assets when a classified balance sheet is presented.

ANALYSIS OF RELEVANT ISSUES

Objective

The objective of IAS 12 is to prescribe the accounting, presentation and disclosure of income taxes resulting from current and future tax consequences arising from:

- current period transactions and other events; and
- the future recovery (settlement) of the carrying amount of assets (liabilities).

Scope

IAS 12 applies to accounting for:

- income taxes, which include:
  - o all domestic and foreign taxes based on taxable profits, and
  - o taxes payable by a subsidiary, associate or joint venture on distributions to the reporting entity (e.g., withholding taxes);
- deferred tax assets arising from unused tax losses or unused tax credits; and
- temporary differences arising from government grants or investment tax credits.

IAS 12 does not deal with accounting for investment tax credits or government grants, which are accounted for under IAS 20, *Accounting for Government Grants and Disclosure of Government Assistance*.

Taxes outside the scope of IAS 12, should be accounted for in accordance with IAS 37, *Provisions, Contingent Liabilities and Contingent Assets*.

CICA 3465 differs from IAS 12 because the former also addresses accounting for some specific aspects of the Canadian tax system, such as alternative minimum income taxes. This results in the recognition of the minimum tax recoverable as an asset when it is more likely than not that future income tax liabilities will be sufficient to recover the minimum tax.

Current Tax Liabilities

Recognition

A current tax liability is recognized to the extent that taxes for current and prior periods have not been paid.

The corresponding current tax expense is accounted for in the same way as the items to which it relates. In general, current tax expense is accounted for in the income statement. It is, however, accounted for in other comprehensive income when it is related to items that are recognized in other comprehensive income in the same period. It is accounted for directly in equity when it is related to items that are recognized directly in equity in the same period.

In exceptional circumstances, it may be difficult to determine what amount of current tax expense relates to items recognized either in other comprehensive income or directly in equity. In such cases, the current tax expense for those items is based on a reasonable pro rata allocation or another method that achieves a more appropriate allocation.

Measurement

The current tax liability is measured at the amount expected to be paid to the taxation authorities, based on enacted or substantively enacted tax rates (and tax laws) at the balance sheet date.

Substantive Enactment

IAS 12 does not provide guidance on determining when substantive enactment is considered to have occurred during the enactment process.

Canadian GAAP differs from IAS 12 because EIC-111, *Determination of substantively enacted tax rates under CICA 3465* does provide guidance on determining when substantive enactment is considered to have occurred during the enactment process in the context of Canadian federal and provincial income tax legislation.

Tax Rates Applicable when Net Profit or Retained Earnings are Distributed

When part or all of the net profit or retained earnings is paid out as a dividend to shareholders, some jurisdictions may:

- require income taxes to be paid at a higher rate;
- require income taxes to be paid at a lower rate;
- require additional income taxes to be paid; or
- refund income taxes already paid.

In these circumstances, current and deferred tax assets and liabilities are measured at the tax rate applicable to undistributed profits.

Entities recognize a current tax liability or asset for the income tax consequences of dividends when they recognize a liability to pay the dividends. The corresponding current tax expense or benefit is accounted for in the same manner as a current tax expense, which was previously covered in the discussion on recognition.

CICA 3465 differs from IAS 12 because the former requires:

- taxes for distributions or future distributions to be given the same accounting treatment as the distributions themselves;
- refundable taxes to be charged:
  - o to the income statement, or
  - o to retained earnings when they are:
    - in the nature of advance distributions related to a component of an instrument classified as equity, and
    - more likely than not to be recovered in the foreseeable future;
- the refundable amount of income taxes previously paid to be recognized as a deferred tax asset when a payment related to a component of an instrument classified as a liability will trigger a refund.

Current Tax Assets

A current tax asset is recognized for:

- the excess of amounts already paid for current and prior periods over the amount due for those periods; and

- the benefit inherent in a tax loss that can be carried back to recover current tax of a previous period.

The current tax asset is measured in the same way as a current liability and the corresponding current tax benefit is accounted for in the same way as a current tax expense. These issues were previously covered in the discussion on current tax liabilities.

Deferred Tax Concepts

Deferred tax is accounted for using the balance sheet liability method, which is based on the fundamental principle that:

- an asset will be recovered for at least its carrying amount in the form of future economic benefits; and

- a liability will be settled for its carrying amount through a future outflow of resources embodying economic benefits.

Carrying Amount

The *carrying amount* represents the balance of an asset or liability reported on the balance sheet.

Tax Base

The *tax base* of an asset or liability represents the amount attributed to that asset or liability for tax purposes.

The tax base of an asset is the amount that will be deductible for tax purposes against any taxable economic benefits that will flow to an entity when it recovers the carrying amount of the asset. If those economic benefits will not be taxable, the tax base of the asset is equal to its carrying amount.

The tax base of a liability is its carrying amount, less any amount that will be deductible for tax purposes for that liability in future periods. When revenue is received in advance, the tax base of the resulting liability is its carrying amount, less any amount of the revenue that will not be taxable in future periods.

Taxable and Deductible Temporary Differences

Temporary differences are differences between the carrying amount of an asset or liability on the balance sheet and its tax base. Temporary differences may be either:

- *taxable temporary differences*, which are temporary differences that will result in taxable amounts in determining taxable profit (tax loss) of future periods when the carrying amount of the asset or liability is recovered or settled; or

- *deductible temporary differences*, which are temporary differences that will result in amounts that are deductible in determining taxable profit (tax loss) of future periods when the carrying amount of the asset or liability is recovered or settled.

Deferred Tax Liabilities

Deferred tax liabilities refer to income taxes payable in future periods for taxable temporary differences.

Recognition

A deferred tax liability is recognized for all taxable temporary differences except for those arising from:

- the initial recognition of goodwill; or
- the initial recognition of an asset or liability in a transaction which:
  - o is not a business combination, and
  - o at the time of the transaction, affects neither accounting profit nor taxable profit (tax loss).

The corresponding deferred tax expense is accounted for in the same way as the items to which it relates. In general, deferred tax expense is accounted for in the income statement. It is, however, accounted for in other comprehensive income when it is for items recognized in other comprehensive income in the same or a different period. It is accounted for directly in equity when it pertains to items recognized directly in equity in the same or a different period.

In exceptional circumstances, it may be difficult to determine the amount of deferred tax expense for items recognized either in other comprehensive income or directly in equity. In such cases, the deferred tax expense is based on a reasonable pro rata allocation or another method that achieves a more appropriate allocation.

CICA 3465 differs from IAS 12 because, as noted earlier, the former prohibits backwards tracing.

Measurement

A deferred tax liability is measured:

- without being discounted;
- at the tax rates expected to apply to the period when the asset is realized or the liability is settled, based on enacted or substantively enacted tax rates (and tax laws) at the balance sheet date; and
- by reference to the tax consequences flowing from the way in which the carrying amount of assets and liabilities are expected, at the balance sheet date, to be recovered or settled.

Substantive Enactment

The determination of when substantive enactment is considered to have occurred during the enactment process was previously covered in the discussion on current tax liabilities.

Tax Rates Applicable to Taxable Profit (Tax Loss)

When tax rates are graduated, deferred tax assets and liabilities are measured using the average rates expected to apply to the taxable profit (tax loss) of the periods in which the temporary differences are expected to reverse.

Tax Rates Applicable when Net Profit or Retained Earnings are Distributed

The tax rates applicable when net profit or retained earnings are distributed were previously covered in the discussion on current tax liabilities.

Expected Manner of Recovery of Assets or Settlement of Liabilities

In some jurisdictions, the method of recovering (settling) the carrying amount of an asset (liability) may affect either or both of:

- the tax rate applicable when the carrying amount of the asset (liability) is recovered (settled); and
- the tax base of the asset (liability).

In such cases, a deferred tax liability is measured using the tax rate and tax base that are consistent with the expected manner of recovery or settlement.

Assets that have different tax treatments depending on how they are recovered (i.e., through use or sale) are commonly referred to as *dual-based assets*.

Depreciable Dual-based Assets

The tax consequences of a depreciable dual-based asset should reflect a dual manner of recovery, for example, when management intends to use the asset for a number of years and then sell it. SIC 21 supports the view that depreciable dual-based assets have a dual manner of recovery because the recognition of depreciation implies that the carrying amount of a depreciable asset is expected to be recovered through use to the extent of its depreciable amount and through sale at its residual value.

CICA 3465 differs from IAS 12. The former requires that, when the tax amount of an asset that will be deductible in determining future taxable income depends on whether the asset is utilized or sold, the tax base of that asset is the greater of:

- the amount deductible if the asset is utilized; and
- the amount deductible if the asset is sold.

Non-depreciable Dual-based Assets

The tax consequences of a non-depreciable dual-based asset should reflect the presumption that such assets will be recovered solely through sale. SIC 21 supports the view that non-depreciable dual-based assets will be recovered only through sale because the assets are not depreciated, thus no part of their carrying amount is expected to be recovered (i.e., consumed) through use.

Change in Expected Manner of Recovery

IAS 12 is silent on the accounting for any changes in the way management intends to recover an asset or settle a liability. In practice, the deferred tax liability previously recognized for that asset or liability is remeasured in the period in which management changes its mind.

Deferred Tax Assets

Deferred tax assets are the amounts of income taxes recoverable in future periods for:

- deductible temporary differences;
- the carryforward of unused tax losses; and
- the carryforward of unused tax credits.

Recognition
Deductible Temporary Differences

A deferred tax asset is recognized for all deductible temporary differences (to the extent that it is probable that a deductible temporary difference can be offset against taxable profit), except for deductible temporary differences arising from the initial recognition of an asset or liability in a transaction that:

- is not a business combination; and

- at the time of the transaction, affects neither accounting profit nor taxable profit (tax loss).

It is probable that taxable profit will be available against which a deductible temporary difference can be utilized when there are sufficient taxable temporary differences related to the same taxation authority and the same taxable entity that are expected to reverse:

- in the same period as the expected reversal of the deductible temporary difference; or
- in periods into which a tax loss arising from the deferred tax asset can be carried back or forward.

IAS 12 does not provide guidance on the meaning of probable. In practice, probable is interpreted as meaning *more likely than not*, which is based on:

- the interpretation of probable in IAS 37, *Provisions, Contingent Liabilities and Contingent Assets*; or
- the definition of probable in Appendix A to IFRS 5, *Non-current Assets Held for Sale and Discontinued Operations*.

When there are not enough taxable temporary differences related to the same taxation authority and the same taxable entity, the deferred tax asset is recognized to the extent that:

- it is probable that the entity will have sufficient taxable profit (ignoring taxable amounts arising from deductible temporary differences expected to originate in future periods) relating to the same taxation authority and the same taxable entity in the same period as the reversal of the deductible temporary difference (or in the periods into which a tax loss arising from the deferred tax asset can be carried back or forward); or
- the entity can take advantage of tax planning opportunities that will create taxable profit in appropriate periods.

Tax planning opportunities are actions undertaken to create or increase taxable income in a particular period before the expiry of a tax loss or tax credit carryforward. Where tax planning opportunities advance taxable profit from a later period to an earlier period, the utilization of a tax loss or tax credit carryforward still depends on the existence of future taxable profit from sources other than future originating temporary differences.

When a deferred tax asset is recognized, the corresponding deferred tax benefit is accounted for in the same manner as deferred tax expense, which was previously covered in the discussion on deferred tax liabilities.

CICA 3465 differs from IAS 12 because the former clearly specifies that the amount of a deferred tax asset recognized should be limited to the amount that is more likely than not to be realized.

Unused Tax Losses and Unused Tax Credits

The existence of unused tax losses is strong evidence that there may be no future taxable profit. Therefore, when an entity has a history of recent losses, it recognizes a deferred tax asset arising from unused tax losses or tax credits only to the extent that:

- it has sufficient taxable temporary differences; or

- there is convincing other evidence that sufficient taxable profit will be available against which the unused tax losses or unused tax credits can be utilized.

An entity considers the following criteria for assessing the probability that taxable profit will be available for using any unused tax losses or credits:

- whether the entity has sufficient taxable temporary differences related to the same taxation authority and the same taxable entity, which will result in taxable amounts against which the unused tax losses or credits can be used before they expire;
- whether it is probable that the entity will have taxable profits before the unused tax losses or credits expire;
- whether the unused tax losses result from identifiable causes that are unlikely to recur; and
- whether tax planning opportunities are available to create taxable profit in the period in which the unused tax losses or credits can be utilized.

Reassessment of Unrecognized Deferred Tax Assets

Unrecognized deferred tax assets are reassessed at each balance sheet date. A previously unrecognized deferred tax asset is recognized to the extent that it has become probable that future taxable profit will allow the deferred tax asset to be recovered.

Subsequent Review of Deferred Tax Assets

The carrying amount of a deferred tax asset is reviewed at each balance sheet date and written down to the extent that it is no longer probable that sufficient taxable profit will be available to allow using the benefit.

A write-down is reversed to the extent that it becomes probable that sufficient taxable profit will be available.

Measurement

The deferred tax asset is measured in the same manner as a deferred tax liability, which was previously covered in the discussion on deferred tax liabilities.

Specific Exceptions

Initial Recognition of an Asset or Liability

As previously mentioned, a deferred tax liability or asset is not recognized when it arises from the initial recognition of an asset or liability in a transaction that:

- is not a business combination; and
- at the time of the transaction, affects neither accounting profit nor taxable profit (tax loss).

Furthermore, subsequent changes in the unrecognized deferred tax liability or asset are not recognized as an asset is depreciated.

CICA 3465 differs from IAS 12 because the former requires a deferred tax liability or asset for an asset acquired outside of a business combination to be recognized and calculated as follows:

$$\frac{([\text{cost} - \text{tax basis}] \times \text{tax rate})}{(1 - \text{tax rate})}$$

A deferred tax liability is recognized and the carrying amount of the acquired asset is increased when its cost is greater than its tax base.

A deferred tax asset is recognized and the carrying amount of the acquired asset is decreased when its cost is less than its tax base.

Goodwill

As previously mentioned, a deferred tax liability is not recognized when it arises from the initial recognition of goodwill.

Furthermore, subsequent reductions in the unrecognized deferred tax liability are not recognized.

Deferred tax liabilities for taxable temporary differences related to goodwill are, however, recognized to the extent they do not arise from the initial recognition of goodwill.

Note that a deferred tax asset is recognized for deductible temporary differences arising from the initial recognition of goodwill.

Specific Applications

Business Combinations

The accounting for business combinations is addressed by IFRS 3, *Business Combinations*, which is discussed in further detail in Chapter 5.

Identifiable Assets and Liabilities Acquired

In a business combination, the identifiable assets acquired and liabilities assumed are typically recognized at their fair values at the acquisition date. The tax bases of the identifiable assets acquired and liabilities assumed may not, however, be affected by the business combination or may be affected differently.

When temporary differences arise from identifiable assets acquired and liabilities assumed, the resulting deferred tax liability or asset affects the measurement of goodwill.

Unrecognized Deferred Tax Assets Acquired

An acquired deferred tax asset might not satisfy the criteria for separate recognition when a business combination is initially accounted for but might be realized subsequently. When an acquired deferred tax asset is realized after a business combination, the corresponding deferred tax benefit is accounted as follows:

- Acquired deferred tax benefits recognized within the measurement period that results from new information about facts and circumstances that existed at the acquisition date are applied to first reduce the carrying amount of any goodwill related to that acquisition to zero. Any remaining deferred tax benefits are recognized in the income statement.

- All other acquired deferred tax benefits recognized are accounted for in the same way as deferred tax expense, which was previously covered in the discussion on deferred tax liabilities.

CICA 3465 differs from IAS 12. The former requires that, when an acquirer does not recognize a deferred tax asset acquired in a business combination at the date of the acquisition, but does so at a later date, the benefit should be applied:

- first to reduce to zero any unamortized goodwill related to the acquisition;

- then to reduce to zero any unamortized intangible assets related to the acquisition; and
- then to reduce income tax expense.

Unrecognized Pre-acquisition Deferred Tax Assets of an Acquiring Entity

As a result of a business combination, an acquirer may consider it probable that it will recover a deferred tax asset of its own that was not previously recognized. In such case, that deferred tax asset would be recognized separately in the period of the business combination and the corresponding deferred tax benefit would be accounted for in the income statement.

CICA 3465 differs from IAS 12. If, at the time of a business combination, the acquirer considers it more likely than not that it will realize a deferred tax asset of its own that was previously unrecognized, CICA 3465 requires it to include a deferred tax asset as an identifiable asset when allocating the cost of the purchase.

Intragroup Transfers

IAS 27, *Consolidated and Separate Financial Statements* requires profits and losses resulting from intragroup transactions that are recognized in assets (i.e., inventory and fixed assets) to be eliminated in full.

A deferred tax liability or asset may result from temporary differences that arise from the elimination of profits and losses resulting from intratroup transactions.

IAS 12 does not specifically address the measurement of such items. It does, however, require the measurement of deferred tax liabilities and deferred tax assets to be consistent with the expected manner of recovery. Therefore, such items should be measured using the tax rate applicable to the buyer rather than the seller, since the buyer will be taxed when the assets are sold to a third party.

Again, CICA 3465 differs from IAS 12. The former requires that, when an asset is transferred between enterprises within a consolidated group:

- a deferred tax liability or asset should not be recognized in the consolidated financial statements for a temporary difference arising between the tax base of the asset in the buyer's tax jurisdiction and its cost as reported in the consolidated financial statements; and
- any taxes paid or recovered by the transferor as a result of the transfer should be recorded as an asset or liability in the consolidated financial statements until the gain or loss is recognized by the consolidated entity.

Investments in Subsidiaries, Branches and Associates, and Interests in Joint Ventures

A deferred tax liability is recognized for all taxable temporary differences associated with investments in subsidiaries, branches and associates, and interests in joint ventures, except to the extent that both of the following conditions are satisfied:

- the parent, investor or venturer is able to control the timing of the reversal of temporary differences; and
- it is probable that the temporary difference will not reverse in the foreseeable future.

A deferred tax asset is recognized for all deductible temporary differences arising from investments in subsidiaries, branches and associates, and interests in joint ventures, to the extent that it is probable that:

- the temporary difference will reverse in the foreseeable future; and
- taxable profit will be available against which the temporary difference can be utilized.

Foreign Currency Translations

A deferred tax liability or asset is recognized for temporary differences that arise on the translation of non-monetary assets and liabilities that are remeasured from the local currency to the functional currency using historical rates and result from changes in exchange rates and indexing for tax purposes. The corresponding deferred tax expense or benefit is accounted for in the income statement.

CICA 3465 differs from IAS 12 because the former does not permit a deferred tax asset or liability to be recognized for a temporary difference arising from the difference between the historical exchange rate and the current exchange rate translations of the cost of non-monetary assets or liabilities of integrated foreign operations.

Compound Financial Instruments

IAS 32, *Financial Instruments: Presentation* requires a compound financial instrument to be accounted for using *split accounting* (i.e., separate accounting for the liability and equity components of a compound financial instrument).

In some jurisdictions, the tax base of the liability component on initial recognition is equal to the face value of the compound financial instrument. Therefore, a deferred tax liability is recognized for the taxable temporary difference that arises from the initial recognition of the equity component as a result of split accounting. The corresponding deferred tax expense is charged directly to the carrying amount of the equity component.

Subsequent changes in the deferred tax liability are recognized as a deferred tax expense or benefit in the income statement.

CICA 3465 differs from IAS 12 because the former considers the tax base of the liability to be the same as its carrying amount (i.e., there is no temporary difference) when the enterprise is able to settle a compound financial instrument without the incidence of tax.

Assets Carried at Fair Value

IFRS permits or requires certain assets to be carried at fair value or to be revalued.

In some jurisdictions, the revaluation or other restatement of an asset to fair value affects the taxable profit (tax loss) for the current period. As a result, the tax base of the asset is adjusted and no temporary difference arises.

In other jurisdictions, the revaluation or restatement of an asset does not affect taxable profit in the period of the revaluation or the restatement, hence the tax base of the asset is not adjusted. The difference between the carrying amount of a revalued asset and its tax base is a temporary difference and gives rise to a deferred tax liability or asset. This is true even if:

- an entity does not intend to dispose of the asset. In such cases, the revalued carrying amount of the asset will be recovered through use and this will generate taxable income that exceeds the depreciation that will be allowable for tax purposes in future periods; or

- tax on capital gains is deferred if the proceeds of the disposal of the asset are invested in similar assets. In such cases, the tax will ultimately become payable on sale or use of the similar assets.

CICA 3465 differs from IAS 12 because the former does not address temporary differences between the carrying amount of a revalued asset and its tax base, since Canadian GAAP does not allow revaluations.

Expected Manner of Recovery of the Revaluation of Non-depreciated Dual-based Assets

The deferred tax liability or asset that arises from the revaluation of a non-depreciable dual-based asset must be measured on the basis of the tax consequences that would follow from recovery of the carrying amount of that asset through sale, regardless of the basis of measuring the carrying amount of that asset.

Share-based Payment Transactions

In some tax jurisdictions, an entity receives a tax deduction for remuneration paid in its shares, share options or other equity instruments.

IFRS 2, *Share-based Payment* requires the goods or services received or acquired in a share-based payment transaction to be recognized as expenses when they do not qualify for recognition as assets. For the purposes of IAS 12, goods or services received or acquired that have been expensed are considered to be assets with a carrying amount of nil on the balance sheet.

Therefore, the difference between the tax base of employee services received to date (i.e., the amount the taxation authorities will permit as a deduction in future periods) and the carrying amount of nil is a deductible temporary difference that results in a deferred tax asset. If the amount the taxation authorities will permit as a deduction in future periods is not known at the balance sheet date, it is estimated, based on information available at the balance sheet date.

When the amount of the tax deduction (or estimated future tax deduction) exceeds the amount of the related cumulative remuneration expense, the excess of the associated current or deferred tax should be recognized directly equity.

CICA 3465 differs from IAS 12 because the former does not address the treatment of deductible share-based payment transactions.

Changes in Tax Status

Although the current and deferred consequences of a change in tax status are generally recognized in the income statement, they are instead recognized in other comprehensive income when they pertain to items recognized in other comprehensive income in the same or a different period. They are recognized directly in equity when related to items recognized directly in equity in the same or a different period.

CICA 3465 differs from IAS 21 because the former requires:

- changes in deferred income tax assets and liabilities to be recorded as capital transactions when directly related to a shareholders' action or to the injection of new equity; and
- the effects of changes in tax status to be included in the income statement when related to the enterprise's actions or decisions.

Uncertain Tax Positions

An *uncertain tax position* describes a situation where an entity claims a tax benefit on a tax return but the complexity and varying interpretations of the tax law create uncertainty about whether the entity will actually realize that tax benefit. In other words, the tax authorities may audit and subsequently reject an uncertain tax position, which would result in additional taxes, penalties or interest due for the current or prior years or affect the amount of existing future income tax assets or liabilities.

IAS 12 is silent on the accounting for uncertain tax positions. As a result, considerable diversity has developed in practice.

Unit of Accounting

In practice, an entity may adopt an accounting policy that accounts for uncertain tax positions at a unit of accounting that is at the level of:

- an individual uncertainty;
- a group of related uncertainties; or
- the total tax liability to each tax authority.

Recognition and Measurement

Once the unit of accounting has been established, an entity adopts an accounting policy to recognize and measure uncertain tax positions. Some of the practices commonly found include the adoption of:

- a best estimates approach; or
- an expected outcomes approach.

Best Estimates Approach

A *best estimates approach* is a combined recognition and measurement approach in which current and deferred taxes are initially recorded based on *as-filed* or *to-be-filed* positions taken or to be taken on an income tax return. Afterwards, additional income tax expense is recorded for the effect of uncertain tax items based on the single best estimate of the additional tax amount expected to be paid.

Expected Outcomes Approach

An *expected outcomes approach* is a combined recognition and measurement approach in which current and deferred taxes are initially recorded based on *as-filed* or *to-be-filed* positions taken or to be taken on an income tax return. Afterwards, additional income tax expense is recorded for the effect of uncertain tax items using a probability weighted average of all possible outcomes.

CICA 3465 is also silent on the accounting for uncertain tax positions. As a result, considerable diversity has developed in practice, which includes the adoption of:

- a best estimates approach;
- an expected outcomes approach; or
- FIN 48, *Accounting for Uncertainty in Income Taxes – an interpretation of FASB Statement No. 109*.

Illustrative Disclosures:

Extract 17(1) – Accounting policy: uncertain tax positions (liability for tax exposure)

> **Koninklijke Ahold N.V. (AR 2007), page 43**
>
> **3 Significant accounting policies (in part)**
>
> **Income taxes**
>
> The ultimate tax effects of certain transactions can be uncertain for a considerable period of time, requiring management to estimate the related current and deferred tax positions. The Company recognizes liabilities for uncertain tax positions when it is more likely than not that additional taxes will be due. These liabilities are presented as current income taxes payable, except in jurisdictions where prior tax losses are being carried forward to be used to offset future taxes that will be due; in these instances the liabilities are presented as a reduction to deferred tax assets.

Extract 17(2) – Accounting policy: uncertain tax positions (recognition of an uncertain tax position and liability for tax exposure)

> **Diageo plc (AR 2007), page 83**
>
> **Accounting policies of the group (in part)**
>
> **Taxation (in part)**
>
> Tax benefits are not recognised unless it is probable that the tax positions are sustainable. Once considered to be probable, management reviews each material tax benefit to assess whether a provision should be taken against full recognition of the benefit on the basis of potential settlement through negotiation and/or litigation. Any interest and penalties on tax liabilities are provided for in the tax charge.

Commentary: In the above extract, the company discloses its accounting policy for uncertain tax positions. The company accounts for uncertain tax positions at the level of each individual uncertainty, recognizes an uncertain tax position when it is probable that the tax position is sustainable and then assesses whether a liability for tax exposure is required.

Presentation

Tax Expense

Profit or Loss from Ordinary Activities

The tax expense (benefit) related to profit or loss from ordinary activities must be presented in the statement of comprehensive income.

When an entity presents the components of profit or loss in a separate income statement, it presents the tax expense (benefit) related to profit or loss from ordinary activities in that separate statement.

Exchange Differences

IAS 21, *The Effects of Changes in Foreign Exchange Rates* requires certain exchange differences to be recognized as income or expense but does not specify where such differences should be presented in the statement of comprehensive income. Accordingly, where exchange differences on deferred foreign tax liabilities or assets are recognized in the statement of comprehensive income, such differences may be classified as deferred tax expense (benefit) if that presentation is considered to be the most useful to financial statement users.

Tax Assets and Liabilities

IAS 1, *Presentation of Financial Statements* requires current and deferred tax assets and liabilities to be presented as line items on the face of the balance sheet.

Current Versus Non-current Distinction

IAS 1 prohibits an entity from presenting deferred tax assets and liabilities as current when it presents a classified balance sheet.

IAS 1 does, however, require an entity to disclose the non-current amount for each asset and liability for which current and non-current amounts were presented on a combined basis on the face of the balance sheet.

CICA 3465 differs from IAS 1 because the former requires an entity to present the current and non-current portions of deferred tax liabilities and assets when it presents a classified balance sheet.

Offsetting

Current tax assets and liabilities are offset only when an entity:

* has a legally enforceable right to set off the recognized amounts; and
* intends either:
  o to settle on a net basis, or
  o to realize the asset and settle the liability simultaneously.

An entity will normally have a legally enforceable right to set off a current tax asset against a current tax liability when they are related to income taxes levied by the same taxation authority and that authority permits the entity to make or receive a single net payment.

In consolidated financial statements, a current tax asset of one entity in a group is offset against a current tax liability of another entity in the group only when:

* the entities concerned have a legally enforceable right to make or receive a single net payment; and
* the entities intend:
  o to make or receive such a net payment, or
  o to recover the asset and settle the liability simultaneously.

Deferred tax assets and deferred tax liabilities are offset only when:

* an entity has a legally enforceable right to set off current tax assets against current tax liabilities; and
* the deferred tax assets and liabilities are related to income taxes levied by the same taxation authority on either:
  o the same taxable entity, or
  o different taxable entities that intend either to settle current tax liabilities and assets on a net basis, or to realize the assets and settle the liabilities simultaneously, in each future period in which significant amounts of deferred tax liabilities or assets are expected to be settled or recovered.

In rare circumstances, an entity may have a legally enforceable right of set-off, and an intention to settle net, for some periods but not for others. In those circumstances, detailed scheduling may be required to establish reliably whether the deferred tax liability of one taxable entity will result in increased tax payments in the same period in which a deferred tax asset of another taxable entity will result in decreased payments for that second taxable entity.

CICA 3465 differs from IAS 12 because the former requires that:

- Current tax liabilities and assets should be offset if they are related to the same taxable entity and the same taxation authority.
- Although deferred tax liabilities and assets should be offset if they are related to the same taxable entity and the same taxation authority:
  - o the current portion of deferred tax balances should not offset any deferred tax balances classified as non-current when an enterprise classifies assets and liabilities as current and non-current, and
  - o when enterprises in a group are taxed separately by the same taxation authority, a deferred tax asset recognized by one enterprise in the group should not be offset against a deferred tax liability of another enterprise in the group unless tax planning strategies could be implemented to satisfy all the requirements for offsetting when the deferred tax liability becomes payable.

Disclosure

Major Components of Tax Expense (Benefit)

The major components of tax expense (benefit) must be disclosed separately. These may include:

- with respect to current taxes:
  - o current tax expense (benefit),
  - o any adjustments recognized in the period for current tax of prior periods,
  - o the amount of the benefit arising from a previously unrecognized tax loss, tax credit or temporary difference of a prior period that is used to reduce current tax expense, and
  - o the amount of current tax expense (benefit) for any changes in accounting policies and errors that are included in the income statement in accordance with IAS 8, *Accounting Policies, Changes in Accounting Estimates and Errors* because they cannot be accounted for retrospectively;
- with respect to deferred taxes:
  - o the amount of deferred tax expense (benefit) for the origination and reversal of temporary differences,
  - o the amount of deferred tax expense (benefit) related to changes in tax rates or the imposition of new taxes,
  - o the amount of the benefit arising from a previously unrecognized tax loss, tax credit or temporary difference of a prior period that is used to reduce deferred tax expense,
  - o deferred tax expense arising from the write-down, or reversal of a previous write-down, of a deferred tax asset, and
  - o the amount of deferred tax expense (benefit) related to those changes in accounting policies and errors that are included in the income statement in accordance with IAS 8 because they cannot be accounted for retrospectively.

Illustrated Disclosures:

Extract 17(3) – Major components of tax expense

ABN AMRO Holding N.V. (AR 2007), page 135			
11 Income tax expense			
Recognised in the income statement:			
	2007	**2006**	**2005**
Current tax expense			
Current year	1,306	1,453	1,106
Under/(over) provided in prior years	97	(96)	(87)
Subtotal	1,403	1,357	1,019
Deferred tax (benefit)/expense			
Origination and reversal of timing differences	(930)	(331)	257
Reduction in tax rate	55	3	(35)
Subtotal	(875)	(328)	222
Total	**528**	**1,029**	**1,241**
Continuing operations	(48)	366	735
Discontinued operations	574	674	506
Taxation on disposal	2	(11)	–
Total	**528**	**1,029**	**1,241**

Commentary: The above extract discloses current tax expense, adjustments recognized for current tax of prior periods, the amount of deferred tax income related to the origination and reversal of timing differences and the amount of deferred tax expense related to changes in tax rates. The company also discloses the tax expense for discontinued operations and tax expense on disposal.

Extract 17(4) – Benefit from a previously unrecognized tax loss

ABN AMRO Holding N.V. (AR 2007), page 136			
11 Income tax expense			
Total tax charge continuing operations			
The effective tax rate on the Group's profit before tax differs from the theoretical amount that would arise using the basic tax rate of the Netherlands. This difference can be explained as follows:			
	2007	**2006**	**2005**
Dutch tax rate	25.5%	29.6%	31.5%
Current tax charge at current rate on ordinary activities	446	909	1,277
Tax exempt income relating to private equity	(87)	10	–
Tax exempt profit on sales	(58)	(46)	–
Other tax exempt income	(182)	(72)	(68)
Total tax exempt income effect	(327)	(108)	(68)
Tax related to adjustments to prior years' tax calculations	97	(96)	(23)
Effect of adjustment to valuation allowance	46	10	39
Effect of changes in tax legislation	26	(97)	5
Effect of changes in tax rates	55	3	(2)
Amount of benefit from a previously unrecognized tax loss, tax credit or temporary difference of a prior period used to reduce current tax expense	(66)	–	–
Amount of benefit from a previously unrecognised tax loss, tax credit or temporary difference of a prior period used to reduce deferred tax expense	(95)	(1)	–
Other movements	(230)	(254)	(493)
Total	**(48)**	**366**	**735**
Other movements in 2007 includes changes in local tax rates of EUR 106 million.			

Commentary: In the above extract, the company discloses a numerical reconciliation of tax expense and the product of accounting profit multiplied by the applicable tax rate, which includes reconciling items for:

- the amount of benefit arising from a previously unrecognized tax loss, tax credit or temporary difference of a prior period that is used to reduce current tax expense; and
- the amount of benefit arising from a previously unrecognized tax loss, tax credit or temporary difference of a prior period that is used to reduce deferred tax expense.

Extract 17(5) – Change in applicable tax rate

Heidelberger Druckmaschinen Aktiengesellschaft (AR 2008), page 38
17 Taxes on income (in part)
As a result of the 2008 business tax reform in Germany, the tax expense has been reduced considerably. The nominal tax rate has dropped from 37.37 percent to 28.14 percent. The adjustment of deferred taxes in Germany to the new tax rate resulted in deferred tax income of € 11,678 thousand.

Extract 17(6) – Reduction of current tax expense as a result of previously unrecognized tax losses

Heidelberger Druckmaschinen Aktiengesellschaft (AR 2008), page 38
17 Taxes on income (in part)
Current taxes were reduced in the reporting year by € 10,273 thousand (previous year: € 18,116 thousand) as a result of deferred tax assets for tax loss carryforwards that had not previously been taken into account.

Extract 17(7) – Write-down of deferred tax assets

Heidelberger Druckmaschinen Aktiengesellschaft (AR 2008), page 38
17 Taxes on income (in part)
There were no write-downs of deferred tax assets for loss carryforwards recognized in previous years in the year under review (previous year: € 72 thousand).

Other Disclosures

Breakdown of Deferred Taxes

The following must be disclosed separately for each type of temporary difference and for each type of unused tax losses and credits:

- the amount of the deferred tax assets and liabilities recognized in the balance sheet for each period presented; and
- the amount of the deferred tax benefit or expense recognized in the income statement, if this is not apparent from the changes in the amounts recognized in the balance sheet.

Illustrated Disclosures:

Extract 17(8) – Breakdown of deferred tax liabilities (assets)

Corus Group plc (AR 2006), page 117

27. Deferred tax (in part)

The following are the major deferred tax assets and liabilities recognised by the Group, and the movements thereon, during the current and prior reporting periods.

2006	Accelerated tax depreciation £m	Losses £m	Pension £m	Other £m	Total £m
At beginning of period	(231)	314	(13)	(24)	46
Credited/(charged) to profit and loss	122	(72)	(71)	(18)	**(39)**
Exchange rate movements	1	(2)	–	2	1
Credited to equity	–	–	10	11	21
Disposal of group undertakings (Note 40)	31	(28)	(7)	30	26
At end of period	(77)	212	(81)	1	55

2005	Accelerated tax depreciation £m	Losses £m	Pension £m	Other £m	Total £m
At beginning of period	(209)	259	(14)	1	37
(Charged)/credited to profit and loss	(24)	55	(20)	(8)	3
Exchange rate movements	2	–	1	1	4
Credited/(charged) to equity	–	–	20	(13)	7
Reclassifications	–	–	–	(5)	(5)
At end of period	(231)	314	(13)	(24)	46

Commentary: Here, the company discloses the amount of the deferred tax assets and liabilities recognized in the balance sheet for each type of temporary difference and for each type of unused tax losses.

Extract 17(9) – Breakdown of deferred tax liabilities (assets), and deferred tax expense

ABN AMRO Holding N.V. (AR 2007), page 159

29 Deferred tax assets and liabilities (in part)

Recognised deferred tax assets and liabilities (in part)

Deferred tax assets and liabilities are attributable to the following items:

	Assets		Liabilities		Recognised in income		Recognised in equity	
	2007	2006	2007	2006	2007	2006	2007	2006
Property and equipment	43	9	122	160	187	(15)	–	2
Intangible assets including goodwill	236	613	–	457	(23)	61	–	5
Derivatives	29	68	73	128	(8)	232	33	(243)
Investment securities	190	170	58	170	87	9	66	300
Employee benefits	316	288	104	–	5	38	–	(2)
Servicing rights	1	1	–	521	–	29	–	–
Allowances for loan losses	831	978	39	–	103	372	6	105
Leasing	2	–	212	399	(42)	(10)	(1)	4
Tax credits	18	13	–	–	3	29	–	
Other	721	389	62	61	258	(408)	45	(509)
Tax value of carryforward losses recognised	1,009	950	452	567	304	(9)	1	233
Total	3,396	3,479	1,122	2,463	874	328	150	(105)

Commentary: In the above extract, the company discloses:

- the amount of the deferred tax assets and liabilities recognized in the balance sheet for each type of temporary difference and for each type of unused tax losses and credits; and

- the amount of deferred tax expense recognized in the income statement and directly in equity for each type of temporary difference and for each type of unused tax losses and credits.

Recognition of Deferred Tax Assets

The amount of a deferred tax asset and the nature of the evidence supporting its recognition are disclosed when:

- the utilization of the deferred tax asset depends on future taxable profits in excess of the profits arising from the reversal of existing taxable temporary differences; and

- the entity has suffered a loss in either the current or preceding period in the tax jurisdiction to which the deferred tax asset relates.

CICA 3465 differs from IAS 12 because the former does not require such disclosure.

Illustrated Disclosure:

Extract 17(10) – Recovery of deferred tax assets

Givaudan SA (Annual and Financial Report 2007) page 33
12. Income taxes (in part)

Deferred income tax assets are recognised for tax loss carry forwards only to the extent that realisation of the related tax benefit is probable. Deferred tax assets of CHF 11 million have been recognised in 2007 in loss making entities. To the extent that the utilisation of these deferred tax assets is dependent on future taxable profits in excess of the reversal of existing temporary differences, management considers it is probable that these tax losses can be used against additional future taxable profits based on its business projections for these entities. The Group has no material unrecognised tax losses.

Commentary: The company discloses the amount of deferred tax assets recognized for tax loss carryforwards and the nature of the evidence supporting their recognition.

Unrecognized Deferred Tax Assets

The amount (and expiry date, if any) of deductible temporary differences, unused tax losses and unused tax credits for which no deferred tax asset is recognized in the balance sheet must be disclosed separately.

Illustrated Disclosures:

Extract 17(11) – Unrecognized deferred tax asset on unused tax losses and unused tax credits (narrative)

Heidelberger Druckmaschinen Aktiengesellschaft (AR 2008), page 38
17 Taxes on income (in part)

Total tax loss carryforwards not yet utilized of € 340,578 thousand (previous year: € 330,982 thousand) are attributable to foreign subsidiaries in particular. Total tax loss carryforwards for which no deferred tax assets were recognized amount to € 330,876 thousand (previous year: € 325,986 thousand). Of this figure, € 2,963 thousand can be used until 2011 (previous year: € 929 thousand until 2010), none can be used until 2012 (previous year: € 5,492 thousand until 2011) and € 327,913 thousand can be used until 2014 and later (previous year: € 319,565 thousand until 2013 and later).

The as yet unutilized tax credit for which no deferred tax assets have been recognized on the balance sheet to date amounts to € 3,873 thousand (previous year: € 925 thousand) and expires no later than March 31, 2025.

Extract 17(12) – Unrecognized deferred tax asset on unused tax losses (table)

Akzo Nobel N.V. (AR 2007), page 123

Note 13 Deferred tax assets and liabilities (in part)

Loss carryforwards with unrecognized deferred tax assets

At December 31, 2007, the gross amounts of the net operating loss carryforwards for which no deferred tax assets have been recognized in the balance sheet, with a total of EUR 80 million, expire as follows:

Millions of euros	2008	2009	2010	2011	2012	later	unlimited
	3	6	5	6	7	23	30

Direct Recognition in Equity

The following must be disclosed separately:

- the aggregate current and deferred tax related to items charged or credited directly to equity; and

- the amount of income tax related to each component of other comprehensive income.

Illustrated Disclosures:

Extract 17(13) – Aggregate current and deferred tax charged or credited directly to equity

TeliaSonera AB (AR 2007), page 59

Note 14 (Consolidated) Income Taxes (in part)

Income tax expense (in part)

In 2007 and 2006, pre-tax income was SEK 25,251 million and SEK 25,226 million, respectively. Income tax expense was distributed as follows.

	January–December	
SEK in millions	2007	2006
Tax expense brought to income		
Current taxes	5,781	4,901
Deferred taxes	-828	1,042
Total tax expense brought to income	**4,953**	**5,943**
Tax expense recognized directly in shareholders' equity		
Current taxes	-44	–
Deferred taxes	14	-37
Total tax expense recognized directly in shareholders' equity	**30**	**-37**

Extract 17(14) – Aggregate tax charged or credited directly to equity

ABN AMRO Holding N.V. (AR 2007), page 136

11 Income tax expense (in part)

Recognised directly in equity

(Benefits)/charges	2007	2006	2005
Relating to currency translation	(81)	114	(198)
Relating to cash flow hedges	(158)	(223)	(235)
Relating to available-for-sale assets	389	190	169
Total	**150**	**81**	**(264)**

Commentary: The above extract discloses the aggregate tax for items charged or credited directly to equity by type of temporary difference.

Relationship Between Tax Expense (Benefit) and Accounting Profit

An explanation of the relationship between tax expense (benefit) and accounting profit must be disclosed separately, in either or both of the following forms:

- a numerical reconciliation of the tax expense (benefit) and the product of accounting profit multiplied by the applicable tax rate(s); or

- a numerical reconciliation of the average effective tax rate (i.e., the tax expense (benefit) divided by the accounting profit) and the applicable tax rate.

The following must also be disclosed:

- the basis on which the applicable tax rate(s) is (are) computed; and

- an explanation of changes in the applicable tax rate(s) compared to the previous accounting period.

Illustrated Disclosures:

Extract 17(15) – Reconciliation of tax expense and the product of accounting profit multiplied by the applicable tax rate

Heidelberger Druckmaschinen Aktiengesellschaft (AR 2008), page 39		
17 Taxes on income (in part)		
Taxes on income can be derived from earnings before taxes as follows:		
	2006/2007	**2007/2008**
Earnings before taxes	299,632	198,955
Theoretical tax rate in percent[1]	37.37	28.14
Theoretical tax expense	111,972	55,986
Change in theoretical tax income due to:		
– corporate income tax credit from previous years due to a change in the German Corporation Tax Act	– 73,375	– 8,856
– corporate income tax reduction plus solidarity surcharge for dividend	– 7,556	–
– differing tax rate	– 12,487	– 14,985[2]
– tax loss carryforwards[3]	– 17,468	– 5,620
– reduction due to tax-free income	– 25,167	– 7,920
– tax increase due to non-deductible expenses	17,147	16,925
– change in tax provisions/taxes attributable to previous years	50,634	22,650
– other	– 6,997	– 768
Taxes on income	36,703	57,412
Tax rate in percent	12.25	28.86
1) The reduction in the theoretical tax rate results from the 2008 business tax reform in Germany		
2) Including € 11,678 thousand of deferred tax income due to the 2008 business tax reform in Germany		
3) Amortization of loss carryforwards, utilization of non-recognized loss carryforwards and non-recognition of current losses		

Commentary: The company discloses a numerical reconciliation of tax expense and the product of accounting profit multiplied by the applicable tax rate. It also explains the reduction in the theoretical tax rate compared to the previous year.

Extract 17(16) – Reconciliation of the average effective tax rate and the applicable tax rate

TeliaSonera AB (AR 2007), page 59

Note 14 (Consolidated) Income Taxes (in part)

Income tax expense (in part)

The difference between the nominal Swedish income tax rate and the effective tax rate comprises the following components.

	January–December	
Percent	**2007**	**2006**
Swedish income tax rate	28.0	28.0
Effect of higher or lower tax rates in subsidiaries	-2.6	-2.3
Withholding tax on dividends from subsidiaries, associate companies and joint ventures	3.1	2.3
Underprovided or overprovided taxes in prior years	0.6	0.5
Recognition of previously unrecognized tax losses	-3.4	0.3
Effect of changes in tax rates	0.4	0.3
Income from associated companies and joint ventures	-8.5	-6.2
Current year losses for which no deferred tax asset was recognized	2.2	0.9
Non-deductible expenses	0.1	0.2
Tax-exempt income	-0.3	-0.4
Tax rate as per the income statement	19.6	23.6
Tax recognized directly in shareholders' equity	-0.1	-0.1
Effective tax rate	19.5	23.5

Commentary: This extract discloses a numerical reconciliation of the average effective tax rate and the applicable tax rate.

Business Combinations

The following must be disclosed separately:

- if a business combination in which an entity is the acquirer changes the amount recognized for its pre-acquisition deferred tax asset, the amount of that change; and

- if the deferred tax benefits acquired in a business combination are recognized after the acquisition date, a description of the event or change in circumstances that cause the deferred tax benefits to be recognized.

The new disclosure requirements for business combinations are effective for annual periods beginning on or after July 1, 2009. None of the companies surveyed have adopted these requirements early.

CICA 3465 differs from IAS 12 because the former does not require such disclosure.

Investments in Subsidiaries, Branches and Associates, and Interests in Joint Ventures

The aggregate amount of temporary differences associated with investments in subsidiaries, branches and associates, and interests in joint ventures for which deferred tax liabilities have not been recognized must be disclosed separately.

Where practicable, entities are encouraged to disclose the amounts of the unrecognized deferred tax liabilities.

CICA 3465 differs from IAS 12 because the former only mentions that it is desirable to disclose the amount of temporary differences related to investments in subsidiaries and interests in joint ventures for which deferred tax liabilities have not been recognized.

Illustrated Disclosure:

Extract 17(17) – Temporary differences associated with investments

> **Corus Group plc (AR 2006), page 117**
> **27. Deferred tax (in part)**
> At the balance sheet date, the aggregate amount of temporary differences associated with undistributed earnings of subsidiaries, joint ventures and associates for which deferred tax liabilities have not been recognised is £1,737m (2005: £1,397m). No liability has been recognised in respect of these differences because the Group is in a position to control the timing of the reversal of the temporary differences and it is probable that such differences will not reverse in the foreseeable future.

Dividends

The following must be disclosed:

- the income tax consequences of dividends to shareholders that were proposed or declared before the financial statements were authorized for issue but were not recognized as a liability in the financial statements; and

- for jurisdictions where the payment of dividends to shareholders would trigger income tax consequences:

  o the nature of those potential income tax consequences,

  o the amounts of the potential tax consequences practicably determinable,

  o whether any potential income tax consequences are not practicably determinable, and

  o the important features of the income tax systems and the factors that will affect the amount of the potential income tax consequences of dividends.

CICA 3465 differs from IAS 12 because the former does not require such disclosure.

Discontinued Operations

For discontinued operations, an entity must disclose separately the tax expense for:

- the gain or loss on discontinuance; and

- the profit or loss from the ordinary activities of the discontinued operation for the period, together with the corresponding amounts for each prior period presented.

CICA 3465 differs from IAS 12 because the former does not require such disclosure.

Illustrative Disclosure:

Extract 17(18) – Tax expense for discontinued operations

Corporate Express NV (AR 2007), page 96

6 Divestments, discontinued operations (in part)

As of 12 November 2007, Corporate Express sold ASAP Software to Dell Computers for a total consideration of US$353 million. After considering the impact of the related transaction expenses and the taxation, the transaction resulted in a net gain of €97 million. In these financial statements, the net result of ASAP Software has been reported retrospectively as the line item Net result from discontinued operations. Likewise, ASAP Software's cash flows has been reported retrospectively as the line items Net cash from operating / investing / financing activities discontinued operations. Until disposal ASAP Software was our fifth business segment and reported likewise.

Results from discontinued operations

	2007[1]	2006	2005
Net sales	**602**	809	772
Purchase value trade goods sold	**[542]**	[727]	[693]
Depreciation and amortisation	**[3]**	[3]	[3]
Operating result	**15**	29	33
Result before taxes	**15**	28	33
Taxes	**[6]**	[11]	[13]
Net result	**9**	18	20
Gain before tax on sale ASAP Software	**142**	–	–
Tax on sales ASAP Software	**[45]**	–	–
Gain after tax on sale ASAP Software	**97**	–	–
Net cash provided by operating activities	**[5]**	45	15
Capital expenditure	**[4]**	[5]	[5]
Number of employees at year-end	**–**	603	544

1   Results ASAP Software for the period 1 January-11 November 2007.

Commentary: The company discloses the tax expense for:

- the profit or loss from the ordinary activities of the discontinued operation; and
- the gain on discontinuance.

Contingencies

The following must be disclosed:

- any tax-related contingent liabilities and contingent assets in accordance with IAS 37, *Provisions, Contingent Liabilities and Contingent Assets*; and

- when new tax rates or tax laws are enacted or announced after the reporting period, any significant effect of the changes on current and deferred tax assets and liabilities, in accordance with IAS 10, *Events after the Reporting Period*.

Illustrative Disclosures:

Extract 17(19) – Contingent liability for unresolved dispute with taxation authorities

---

Vodafone Group Plc (AR 2007), page 134

31. Contingent liabilities (in part)

Legal proceedings (in part)

A subsidiary of the Company, Vodafone 2, is responding to an enquiry ("the Vodafone 2 enquiry") by Her Majesty's Revenue and Customs ("HMRC") with regard to the UK tax treatment of its Luxembourg holding company, Vodafone Investments Luxembourg SARL ("VIL"), under the Controlled Foreign Companies section of the UK's Income and Corporation Taxes Act 1988 ("the CFC Regime") relating to the tax treatment of profits earned by the holding company for the accounting period ended 31 March 2001. Vodafone 2's position is that it is not liable for corporation tax in the UK under the CFC Regime in respect of VIL. Vodafone 2 asserts, inter alia, that the CFC Regime is contrary to EU law and has made an application to the Special Commissioners of HMRC for closure of the Vodafone 2 enquiry. In May 2005, the Special Commissioners referred certain questions relating to the compatibility of the CFC Regime with EU law to the European Court of Justice (the "ECJ") for determination ("the Vodafone 2 reference"). HMRC subsequently appealed against the decision of the Special Commissioners to make the Vodafone 2 reference but its appeal was rejected by both the High Court and Court of Appeal. The Vodafone 2 reference has still to be heard by the ECJ. Vodafone 2's application for closure was stayed pending delivery of the ECJ's judgment.

In September 2006, the ECJ determined in the Cadbury Schweppes case ©-196/04) (the "Cadbury Schweppes Judgment") that the CFC Regime is incompatible with EU law unless it applies to wholly artificial arrangements intended to escape national tax normally payable. The correct application of the Cadbury Schweppes Judgment to Vodafone 2's case is a matter for the Special Commissioners to determine.

At a hearing in March 2007, the Special Commissioners heard submissions from both parties as to whether the Vodafone 2 reference should be maintained or withdrawn by the Special Commissioners in light of the Cadbury Schweppes Judgement. The Special Commissioners are expected to rule on this question in the coming months.

In addition to the Vodafone 2 enquiry, on 31 October 2005, HMRC commenced an enquiry into the residence of Vodafone Investments Luxembourg Sarl (the "VIL enquiry"). VIL's position is that it is resident for tax purposes solely in Luxembourg and therefore it is not liable for corporation tax in the UK. On 8 December 2006, HMRC confirmed that it had closed the VIL enquiry.

The Company has taken provisions, which at 31 March 2007 amounted to approximately £2.1 billion, for the potential UK corporation tax liability and related interest expense that may arise in connection with the Vodafone 2 enquiry. The provisions relate to the accounting period which is the subject of the proceedings described above as well as to accounting periods after 31 March 2001 to date. The provisions at 31 March 2007 reflect the developments during the year, in particular the Cadburys Schweppes Judgment.

Commentary: In the above extract, the company discloses a contingent liability stemming from an unresolved dispute with taxation authorities.

Extract 17(20) – Events after the reporting period

Detica Group plc (AR 2007), page 54

7. Tax (in part)

Deferred tax (in part)

The Government has recently announced that the UK rate of corporation tax is to reduce from 30% to 28% for periods commencing 1 April 2008. As this was not enacted or substantively enacted at the balance sheet date, the UK deferred tax asset is based on a corporation tax rate of 30%. If a rate of 28% had been applied from1 April 2008, this would have decreased the deferred tax asset from £5,418,000 to £5,137,000 and decreased the deferred tax liability from £1,321,000 to £1,256,000.

Commentary: The above extract discloses the effect of the reduction in the UK corporate tax rate from 30% to 28%, which had not been enacted nor substantively enacted at the balance sheet date.

Income Taxed Directly to Owners

CICA 3465 differs from IAS 12 by requiring:

- an enterprise that is not subject to income taxes because its income is taxed directly to its owners to disclose that fact; and

- a public enterprise, life insurance enterprise, deposit taking institution or co-operative business enterprise that is not subject to income taxes because its income is taxed directly to its owners to disclose the net difference between the tax bases and the reported amounts of the enterprise's assets and liabilities.

Consolidated Income Tax Returns

CICA 3465 differs from IAS 12 because the former requires that, when an enterprise is a member of a group that files a consolidated income tax return, that enterprise should disclose in its separately issued financial statements:

- the aggregate amount of current and future income tax expense for the period and the amount of any tax-related balances due to or from affiliates as of the balance sheet date; and

- the principal provisions of the methods by which the consolidated amount of current and future income tax expense is allocated to members of the group and the nature and effect of any changes in that method (and in determining related balances to or from affiliates) during the periods for which the abovementioned disclosures are presented.

Investment Tax Credits

IAS 12 and IAS 20, *Accounting for Government Grants and Disclosure of Government Assistance* do not deal with accounting for investment tax credits. In practice, however, investment tax credits are accounted for by analogy to either of these standards.

Investment tax credits that are in the nature of tax allowances are typically accounted for by analogy to IAS 12. Therefore, investment tax credits are recognized as a current asset (with a corresponding reduction to current tax expense) to the extent that they can be claimed in the current reporting period. Any unused investment tax credits are recognized as a deferred tax asset to the extent that it is probable that future taxable profit will be available for using up those credits.

Investment tax credits that are in the nature of government grants are typically accounted for by analogy to IAS 20. Therefore, investment tax credits are either:

- deducted from the carrying amount of the related asset acquired with any amortization calculated on the net amount; or

- deferred and amortized on the same basis as the related asset acquired.

Canadian GAAP differs from IFRS because it does specifically deal with investment tax credits. CICA 3805 requires investment tax credits to be accrued when an enterprise has made the qualifying expenditures (provided there is reasonable assurance that the credits will be realized) and accounted for using the cost reduction approach, which requires investment tax credits that are:

- related to the acquisition of assets to be either:

  o deducted from the related assets with any amortization calculated on the net amount, or

  o deferred and amortized to income on the same basis as the related assets;

- related to current expenses to be included in the determination of net income for the period.

FUTURE DEVELOPMENTS

In September 2002, the IASB launched a project on income taxes, which is part of the IASB and FASB's short-term convergence project on eliminating differences between IFRS and US GAAP.

The objective of this project is to reduce the differences between IAS 12 and FAS 109, *Accounting for Income Taxes* by eliminating the numerous exceptions to the basic principle (i.e., the balance sheet liability approach) on which both these standards are based.

The IASB expects to finally issue an Exposure Draft in early 2009 and has tentatively decided that it should take the form of a draft IFRS instead of amendments to IAS 12. The final standard is expected to be issued in 2010.

To date, the IASB has made a number of tentative decisions on the following:

- definition of a tax base;
- other definitions;
- exceptions from the temporary difference approach;
- measurement of deferred tax assets and liabilities;
- recognition of deferred tax assets;
- backwards tracing;
- balance sheet classification;
- adoption of additional guidance from SFAS 109;
- uncertain tax positions;
- disclosures; and
- transitional arrangements.

The most significant of these tentative decisions are discussed below in further detail.

Definition of a Tax Base

The IASB began by amending the definition of *tax base*. Thus, a *tax base* is a measurement attribute under existing tax law applicable to a present asset or liability recognized for tax purposes as a result of one or more past events. That asset or liability may or may not be recognized for financial reporting purposes.

The tax base of an asset or liability is not affected by the manner in which the carrying amount of that asset or liability is expected to be recovered or settled. Instead, the tax base is determined by the deductions that will be available on the sale of the asset or settlement of the liability.

The manner in which the carrying amount of an asset or liability is expected to be recovered or settled does, however, affect:

- whether any difference between the carrying amount and the tax base is a temporary difference; and
- the rate used to measure any temporary differences.

Exceptions from the Temporary Difference Approach

Initial Recognition Exception

The initial recognition exception has been tentatively eliminated, but new requirements are being proposed in its place. Therefore, when a temporary difference arises on the initial recognition of an asset or liability, an entity should:

- separate that asset or liability into two items:
  - o an asset or liability (with a tax base available to market participants in a transaction for the individual asset or liability in that tax jurisdiction), and
  - o a tax advantage or disadvantage arising from any difference between:
    - the tax base available to market participants in a transaction for the individual asset or liability in that tax jurisdiction, and
    - the tax base available to the entity;
- measure the asset or liability (with a tax base available to market participants in a transaction for the individual asset or liability in that tax jurisdiction) in accordance with the IFRS applicable to that asset or liability, excluding any entity-specific tax effects;
- recognize a deferred tax asset or liability for the temporary difference between:
  - o the carrying amount of the asset or liability, and
  - o the tax base available to the entity;
- recognize a premium or allowance as part of the deferred tax asset or liability when the transaction does not affect comprehensive income, equity or taxable profit at the time of the transaction and is not a business combination.

Investments in Subsidiaries, Branches and Associates, and Interests in Joint Ventures

The IASB has tentatively decided that entities should not recognize a deferred tax asset or liability for temporary differences arising on investments in foreign subsidiaries and joint ventures to the extent that the investment is permanent in duration.

Measurement of Deferred Tax Assets and Liabilities

Substantively Enacted Rate

The IASB has tentatively decided that tax rates should be regarded as substantively enacted when future events required by the enactment process historically have not affected the outcome and are unlikely to do so.

Distributed or Undistributed Rate

When measuring current and deferred tax assets and liabilities, an entity should:

- use the rate(s) it expects will apply to the item being measured, incorporating the entity's past practices and future expectations of distributions in jurisdictions that have a different tax rate depending on whether taxable earnings are distributed to owners; and
- include assumptions about future deductions, incorporating the entity's past practices and future expectations of distributions in jurisdictions that offer deductions from taxable earnings for amounts distributed to owners.

When determining future expectations of distributions, an entity must have the intention and ability to make distributions for the foreseeable future.

Recognition of Deferred Tax Assets

The IASB has tentatively decided that *probable* should be defined as meaning *more likely than not*.

Backwards Tracing

The IASB would like to include a general prohibition on tracking changes in recognized tax assets and liabilities back to the components of comprehensive income and equity in which the tax was originally recognized.

Current Versus Non-current Distinction

Deferred tax assets and liabilities should be allocated to current and non-current categories on the balance sheet based on the classification of the related non-tax asset or liability.

Uncertain Tax Positions

The IASB tentatively decided to adopt an *expected outcomes approach* to account for uncertain tax positions; therefore, an entity has a *stand-ready liability* to pay additional taxes, which should be recognized and measured using a probability weighted average of all possible outcomes. No probability threshold should be applied to the recognition of the stand-ready liability.

The effects of changes in uncertain tax positions should be recognized in the income statement, even if the related tax assets and liabilities were originally recognized in other comprehensive income or directly in equity.

Disclosures

Intragroup Transfers of Inventory

The IASB tentatively decided to require the disclosure of:

- the component of deferred tax assets and liabilities that represents the effect of an intragroup transfer of an asset between tax jurisdictions with different effective tax rates;
- any such effect recognized as part of income tax expense (benefit) in the income statement for interim or annual periods; and
- the tax effects of any modifications, including unwinding (reversal), of terms of such transfers.

Recognition of Deferred Tax Assets

The IASB tentatively decided to no longer require the disclosure of the amount of a deferred tax asset and the nature of the evidence supporting its recognition when:

- the utilization of the deferred tax asset depends on future taxable profits in excess of the profits arising from the reversal of existing taxable temporary differences; and
- the entity has suffered a loss in either the current or preceding period in the tax jurisdiction to which the deferred tax asset relates.

Income Taxed Directly to Owners

The IASB proposes requiring entities not subject to income taxes because their income is taxed directly to their owners to disclose that fact and the net difference between tax bases and carrying amounts.

Relationship Between Tax Expense (Benefit) and Accounting Profit

The IASB decided that the reconciliation of tax expense and accounting profit must be prepared using the statutory rate applicable to the parent company.

Consolidated Income Tax Returns

The IASB tentatively decided to require an entity that is a member of a group filing a consolidated tax return to disclose in its separately issued financial statements:

- the aggregate amount of current and deferred tax expense for each income statement presented and the amount of any tax-related balances due to or from affiliates as of the date of each balance sheet presented; and

- the principal provisions of the method by which the consolidated amount of current and deferred tax expense is allocated to members of the group and the nature and effect of any changes in that method (and in determining related balances to or from affiliates) during the years for which the abovementioned disclosures are presented.

Transitional Arrangements

AcSB staff discussed transitional requirements with IASB staff, and it is expected that these requirements will allow Canadian entities to adopt the new requirements to account for income taxes in 2011 and to apply them to comparative information.

COMPREHENSIVE EXAMPLES

This section presents two comprehensive disclosure examples. We have selected relevant extracts to illustrate the disclosure of income taxes in accordance with IFRS.

Xstrata plc – All extracts **17(A)** were obtained from the Annual Report for the year ended December 31, 2007.

Extract 17(A1) – Xstrata plc, page 156

In this extract, the company discloses its accounting policy for current tax.

6. Principal Accounting Policies (in part) **Taxation** **Current tax** Current tax for each taxable entity in the Group is based on the local taxable income at the local statutory tax rate enacted or substantively enacted at the balance sheet date and includes adjustments to tax payable or recoverable in respect of previous periods.

Extract 17(A2) – Xstrata plc, pages 156 and 157

Here, the company discloses its accounting policy for deferred tax.

> **6. Principal Accounting Policies (in part)**
>
> **Taxation**
>
> **Deferred tax**
>
> Deferred tax is recognised using the balance sheet method in respect of all temporary differences between the tax bases of assets and liabilities, and their carrying amounts for financial reporting purposes, except as indicated below:
>
> Deferred income tax liabilities are recognised for all taxable temporary differences, except:
>
> - where the deferred income tax liability arises from the initial recognition of goodwill, or the initial recognition of an asset or liability in a transaction that is not a business combination and, at the time of the transaction, affects neither the accounting profit nor taxable profit or loss; and
>
> - in respect of taxable temporary differences associated with investments in subsidiaries, associates and interests in joint ventures, where the timing of the reversal of the temporary differences can be controlled and it is probable that the temporary differences will not reverse in the foreseeable future.
>
> Deferred income tax assets are recognised for all deductible temporary differences, carry-forward of unused tax assets and unused tax losses, to the extent that it is probable that taxable profit will be available against which the deductible temporary differences, and the carry-forward of unused tax assets and unused tax losses can be utilised, except:
>
> - where the deferred income tax asset relating to the deductible temporary difference arises from the initial recognition of an asset or liability in a transaction that is not a business combination and, at the time of the transaction, affects neither the accounting profit nor taxable profit or loss; and
>
> - in respect of deductible temporary differences associated with investments in subsidiaries, associates and interests in joint ventures, deferred tax assets are recognised only to the extent that it is probable that the temporary differences will reverse in the foreseeable future and taxable profit will be available against which the temporary differences can be utilised.
>
> The carrying amount of deferred income tax assets is reviewed at each balance sheet date and reduced to the extent that it is no longer probable that sufficient taxable profit will be available to allow all or part of the deferred income tax asset to be utilised. To the extent that an asset not previously recognised fulfils the criteria for recognition, a deferred income tax asset is recorded.
>
> Deferred tax is measured on an undiscounted basis at the tax rates that are expected to apply in the periods in which the asset is realised or the liability is settled, based on tax rates and tax laws enacted or substantively enacted at the balance sheet date. Current and deferred tax relating to items recognised directly in equity are recognised in equity and not in the income statement. Mining taxes and royalties are treated and disclosed as current and deferred taxes if they have the characteristics of an income tax.

Extract 17(A3) – Xstrata plc, page 168

This extract discloses the tax expense related to the gain on discontinuance and the tax expense related to the profit or loss from the ordinary activities of the discontinued operation for the period.

8. Discontinued operations and disposals (in part)		
Disposals		
Aluminium		

The Aluminium business was sold on 18 May 2007 to Apollo Management LP. The disposal proceeds amounted to US$1,150 million before disposal costs of US$24 million, resulting in the Group realising a gain of US$1 million after tax of US$12 million. The results of the aluminium business for the periods ended are presented below:

US$m	01.01.07 to 18.05.07	15.08.06 to 31.12.06
Revenue	542	530
Cost of sales (before depreciation and amortisation)	(406)	(396)
Distribution costs	(9)	(11)
Administrative expenses	(7)	–
Profit before interest, taxation, depreciation and amortisation	120	123
Depreciation and amortisation – cost of sales	(31)	(25)
Profit before interest and taxation	89	98
Finance income	2	2
Finance costs	(2)	(7)
Profit before taxation	89	93
Income tax expense	(37)	(29)
Profit for the period from discontinued operation	52	64
Gain on disposal of the discontinued operation	1	–
Profit after tax for the period from discontinued operations	53	64

Extract 17(A4) – Xstrata plc, page 192

The company discloses the major components of tax expense (income) and the aggregate deferred tax charged (credited) directly to equity.

11. Income Taxes (in part)		
Income tax charge (in part)		
Significant components of income tax expense for the years ended:		
US$m	**2007**	**2006**
Consolidated income statement		
Current tax:		
Based on taxable income of the current year	**2,183**	1,386
Prior year over provision	**(14)**	–
Total current taxation charge for the year	**2,169**	1,386
Deferred taxation:		
Origination and reversal of temporary differences	**276**	144
Change in tax rates	**(91)**	(6)
Benefit from previously unrecognised tax losses, tax credits or temporary differences of a prior year that are used to reduce deferred tax expense	**–**	(4)
Prior year under provision	**6**	43
Total deferred taxation charge for the year	**191**	177
Total taxation charge	**2,360**	1,563
Total taxation charge reported in consolidated income statement	**2,311**	1,534
Income tax attributable to discontinued operations	**49**	29
Total taxation charge	**2,360**	1,563
UK taxation included above:		
Current tax	**10**	2
Deferred tax	**4**	(4)
Total taxation charge/(credit)	**14**	(2)
Recognised directly in equity		
Deferred tax:		
Available-for-sale financial assets	**16**	(75)
Cash flow hedges	**(15)**	16
Other equity classified items	**6**	44
Total taxation charge/(credit) reported in equity	**7**	(15)
The amounts above include the tax charge attributable to exceptional items.		

Extract 17(A5) – Xstrata plc, page 193

In this extract, the company discloses the numerical reconciliation of the tax expense and the product of accounting profit multiplied by the weighted average statutory income tax rate. The company also discloses the basis for computing the weighted average statutory income tax rate, and explains changes in the rate compared to the previous accounting period.

---

11. Income Taxes (in part)

Income tax charge (in part)

A reconciliation of income tax expense applicable to accounting profit before income tax at the weighted average statutory income tax rate to income tax expense at the Group average effective income tax rate for the years ended is as follows:

US$m	2007	2006
Profit before taxation from continuing operations	8,127	3,376
Profit before taxation from discontinued operations	102	93
Profit before taxation	8,229	3,469
At average statutory income tax rate 25.2% (2006 23.2%)	2,075	803
Goodwill impairment	–	602
Additional mining and other taxes	239	72
Foreign currency gains and losses	156	67
Non-deductible expenses	81	30
Non-taxable capital gains	(53)	–
Rebatable dividends received	(3)	(8)
Research and development allowances	(9)	(17)
Resource and other allowances	(25)	(22)
Change in tax rates	(91)	(6)
Prior year under/(over) provision	(8)	43
Other	(2)	(1)
At average effective income tax rate	2,360	1,563
Total taxation charge reported in consolidated income statement	2,311	1,534
Income tax attributable to discontinued operations	49	29
At average effective income tax rate	2,360	1,563

The above reconciling items are disclosed at the tax rates that apply in the country where they have arisen.

The average statutory income tax rate is the average of the standard income tax rates applicable in the countries in which the Group operates, weighted by the profit/(loss) before tax of the subsidiaries in the respective countries as included in the consolidated accounts. The change in the average statutory income tax rate is due to the variation in the weight of subsidiaries' profits, by various changes in the enacted standard income tax rates and due to the acquisition of subsidiaries in countries with different tax rates.

Extract 17(A6) – Xstrata plc, page 193

The company discloses its accounting policy for the recognition of deferred tax assets for unused tax losses and unused tax credits.

---

11. Income Taxes (in part)

Deferred income taxes (in part)

Deferred tax assets are recognised for the carry-forward of unused tax losses and unused tax credits to the extent that it is probable that taxable profits will be available against which the unused tax losses/credits can be utilised.

Extract 17(A7) – Xstrata plc, page 193

This extract discloses the amount of unused tax losses for which no deferred tax asset is recognized.

---

11. Income Taxes (in part)

Unrecognised tax losses

The Group has unrecognised deferred tax assets in relation to tax losses that are available indefinitely of US$9 million (2006 US$8 million) to carry forward against future taxable income of the companies in which the losses arose. Deferred tax assets have not been recognised in respect of these losses as they may not be used to offset taxable profits elsewhere in the Group and they have arisen in subsidiaries that have been loss-making for some time. There are no other deductible temporary differences that have not been not recognised at balance sheet date.

Extract 17(A8) – Xstrata plc, pages 193 and 194

The company discloses the aggregate amount of temporary differences associated with investments in subsidiaries, associates, and interests in joint ventures for which deferred tax liabilities have not been recognized.

---

11. Income Taxes (in part)

Temporary differences associated with Group investments (in part)

At 31 December 2007, there was US$nil recognised deferred tax liability (2006 US$nil) for taxes that would be payable on the un-remitted earnings of certain of the Group's subsidiaries, associates or joint ventures as:

- the Group has determined that undistributed profits of its subsidiaries will not be distributed in the foreseeable future;
- the profits of the associates will not be distributed until they obtain the consent of the Group; and
- the investments are not held for resale and are expected to be recouped by continued use of these operations by the subsidiaries.

The temporary differences associated with investments in subsidiaries, associates and joint ventures, for which deferred tax liabilities have not been recognised amount to US$2,218 million (2006 US$2,608 million).

Extract 17(A9) – Xstrata plc, page 194

The company discloses that there are no tax consequences for the payment of dividends to shareholders.

---

11. Income Taxes (in part)

There are no income tax consequences for the Group attaching to the payment of dividends by the Company to its shareholders.

Extract 17(A10) – Xstrata plc, page 194

In this extract, the company discloses for each type of temporary difference and for each type of unused tax losses and unused tax credits:

- the amount of the deferred tax liabilities (assets) recognized; and
- the amount of the deferred tax expense (income) recognized in the income statement.

11. Income Taxes (in part)

The deferred tax assets/(liabilities) included in the balance sheet are as follows:

US$m	2007	2006
Tax losses	244	78
Derivative financial instruments	45	35
Employee provisions	75	65
Other provisions	244	235
Rehabilitation and closure	157	120
Accelerated depreciation	(5,826)	(5,110)
Coal export rights	(260)	(253)
Other intangibles	(411)	(364)
Government grants	(14)	(13)
Deferred stripping	(83)	(49)
Available-for-sale financial assets	(20)	(7)
Other equity-related items	(36)	(3)
Other	(164)	(175)
	(6,049)	**(5,441)**
Represented on the face of the balance sheet as:		
Deferred tax assets	7	22
Deferred tax liabilities	**(6,056)**	(5,463)
	(6,049)	**(5,441)**

The deferred tax included in the Group income statement are as follows:

US$m	2007	2006
Tax losses	(185)	112
Accelerated depreciation	360	96
Deferred stripping	27	17
Rehabilitation and closure	(16)	(29)
Other provisions	(17)	(2)
Other	12	(28)
From continuing operations	181	166
From discontinued operations	10	11
	191	177

Extract 17(A11) – Xstrata plc, page 194

The company discloses that it estimates and accrues a tax liability when it is probable that an adjustment would be made on a tax filing open to audit.

11. Income Taxes (in part)

Tax audits

The Company periodically assesses its liabilities and contingencies for all tax years open to audit based upon the latest information available. For those matters where it is probable that an adjustment will be made, the Company recorded its best estimate of the tax liability, including related interest charges, in the current tax liability. Inherent uncertainties exist in estimates of tax contingencies due to changes in tax laws. Whilst management believes they have adequately provided for the probable outcome of these matters, future results may include favourable or unfavourable adjustments to these estimated tax liabilities in the period the assessments are made, or resolved, or when the status of limitation lapses. The final outcome of tax examinations may result in a materially different outcome than assumed in the tax liabilities.

Stagecoach Group plc – All extracts **17(B)** were obtained from the Annual Report for the year ended April 30, 2007.

Extract 17(B1) – Stagecoach Group plc, page 46

In this extract, the company discloses that the measurement of tax liabilities and assets requires an assessment of the potential tax consequences of certain items that will be resolved when the tax authorities agree.

Note 1 IFRS accounting policies (in part)

Use of estimates

The preparation of financial statements in conformity with generally accepted accounting principles requires the use of estimates and assumptions that affect the reported amounts of assets and liabilities at the date of the financial statements and the reported amounts of revenues and expenses for the period. Although these estimates and assumptions are based on management's best knowledge, actual results may ultimately differ from those estimates and assumptions used.

The key sources of estimation uncertainty that have a significant risk of causing material adjustments to the carrying amounts of assets and liabilities within the next financial year are the measurement of tax assets and liabilities, the measurement of retirement benefit obligations, the measurement and impairment of goodwill and the measurement of insurance provisions. The measurement of tax assets and liabilities requires an assessment to be made of the potential tax consequence of certain items that will only be resolved when agreed by the relevant tax authorities. The measurement of retirement benefit obligations requires the estimation of future changes in salaries, inflation, the expected return on scheme assets and the selection of a suitable discount rate (see note 27). The Group determines whether goodwill arising on business combinations is impaired on an annual basis and this requires the estimation of value in use of the cash generating units to which the goodwill is allocated. This requires estimation of future cash flows and the selection of a suitable discount rate (see note 11). The estimation of the insurance provisions is based on an assessment of the expected settlement on known claims together with an estimate of settlements that will be made in respect of incidents occurring prior to the balance sheet date but for which claims have not been reported to the Group.

Those accounting policies that the Directors believe require the greatest exercise of judgement are described on page 14.

Extract 17(B2) – Stagecoach Group plc, page 47

This extract discloses the accounting policy for current and deferred taxes. The company also discloses that tax is calculated using tax rates and laws enacted or substantively enacted at the balance sheet date.

Note 1 IFRS accounting policies (in part)

Taxation

Tax, current and deferred, is calculated using tax rates and laws enacted or substantively enacted at the balance sheet date.

Corporation tax is provided on taxable profits at the current rate applicable. Tax charges and credits are accounted for through the same primary statement as the related pre-tax item.

Deferred income tax is provided in full, using the liability method, on temporary differences arising between the tax bases of assets and liabilities and their carrying amounts in the financial statements. Deferred income tax is measured at tax rates that are expected to apply in periods in which the temporary differences reverse based on tax rates and law enacted or substantively enacted at the balance sheet date.

Deferred tax assets are recognised to the extent that it is probable that future taxable profit will be available against which the temporary differences can be utilised.

Deferred income tax is provided on temporary differences arising on investments in subsidiaries, associates and joint ventures, except where the timing of the reversal of the temporary difference can be controlled and it is probable that the temporary difference will not reverse in the foreseeable future.

Extract 17(B3) – Stagecoach Group plc, page 60

In this extract, the company discloses the major components of tax expense (income). The company also discloses the amount of tax expense for discontinued operations.

Note 8 Taxation (in part)
(a) Analysis of charge in the year

	2007			2006		
	Performance pre intangibles and exceptional items £m	Intangibles and exceptional items £m	Results for the year £m	Performance pre intangibles and exceptional items £m	Intangibles and exceptional items £m	Results for the year £m
Current tax:						
UK corporation tax at 30% (2006: 30%)	21.2	(0.6)	20.6	13.9	Nil	13.9
Prior year (over)/under provision for corporation tax	(0.9)	Nil	(0.9)	1.4	Nil	1.4
Foreign tax (current year)	1.2	Nil	1.2	Nil	Nil	Nil
Foreign tax (adjustments in respect of prior years)	(0.6)	Nil	(0.6)	2.4	Nil	2.4
Total current tax	20.9	(0.6)	20.3	17.7	Nil	17.7
Deferred tax:						
Origination and reversal of timing differences	17.0	6.4	23.4	7.8	(5.0)	2.8
Adjustments in respect of prior years	(0.1)	Nil	(0.1)	(0.2)	Nil	(0.2)
Total deferred tax	16.9	6.4	23.3	7.6	(5.0)	2.6
Tax on profit on ordinary activities from continuing operations	37.8	5.8	43.6	25.3	(5.0)	20.3

In addition to the above tax charge for continuing businesses, £1.8m (2006: £7.4m) of tax charges were recognised in relation to our disposed London bus and New Zealand businesses.

Extract 17(B4) – Stagecoach Group plc, page 60

The company discloses the numerical reconciliation of the tax expense and the product of accounting profit multiplied by the standard rate of corporation tax in the UK.

(b) Factors affecting tax charge for the year

	2007 £m	2006 £m
Profit before taxation	184.1	91.5
Profit multiplied by standard rate of corporation tax in the UK of 30% (2006: 30%)	55.2	27.4
Effects of:		
Intangible asset allowances/deductions	2.8	3.9
Non-deductible expenditure	7.0	6.9
Utilisation of tax losses not previously recognised as deferred tax assets	(14.6)	(19.2)
Foreign taxes differences	0.7	(0.6)
Adjustments to tax charge in respect of prior years	(1.6)	3.6
Tax effect of share of results of joint ventures	(5.9)	(1.7)
Total taxation (note 8a)	43.6	20.3

Extract 17(B5) – Stagecoach Group plc, page 60

In this extract, the company discloses that:

- there are no temporary differences associated with investments in overseas subsidiaries for which deferred tax liabilities have not been recognized; and

- the amount of deductible temporary differences for which no deferred tax assets are recognized.

Note 8 Taxation (in part)

(c) Factors that may affect future tax charges (in part)

There are no temporary differences associated with investments in overseas subsidiaries for which deferred tax liabilities have not been recognised.

Gross deductible temporary differences of £244.0m (2006: £306.0m) have not been recognised due to restrictions in the availability of their use.

Extract 17(B6) – Stagecoach Group plc, page 60

In this extract, the company discloses that it has not recognized temporary differences for the revaluation of land and buildings, and rolled over capital gains due to the existence of capital losses. In effect, the company has offset the deferred tax liability for taxable temporary differences arising from these items against the deferred tax asset arising from capital losses.

Note 8 Taxation (in part)

(c) Factors that may affect future tax charges (in part)

Temporary differences have not been recognised in respect of the revaluation of land and buildings (see Note 13) due to the availability of capital losses.

Temporary differences have also not been recognised in respect of rolled over capital gains due to the existence of capital losses.

Extract 17(B7) – Stagecoach Group plc, page 60

This extract discloses the effect of the reduction in the UK rate of corporation tax from 30% to 28%, and the abolishment of the Industrial Buildings Allowances in the UK, which had not been enacted nor substantively enacted at the balance sheet date.

Note 8 Taxation (in part)

(c) Factors that may affect future tax charges (in part)

In the 2007 budget the UK government announced its intention to propose Parliament to reduce the UK Corporate Income tax rate from 30% to 28%. As of 30 April 2007, the tax change was not substantively enacted. Had the change of rate been substantively enacted as of the balance sheet date the estimated impact on the balance sheet would be a reduction in the deferred tax liability of £2.9m.

In the 2007 budget the UK government also announced its intention to propose Parliament to abolish Industrial Buildings Allowances ("IBAs"). As of 30 April 2007, this change was not substantively enacted. Had the change been substantively enacted as of the balance sheet date the estimated impact on the balance sheet would be an increase in the deferred tax liability of £10.0m.

Extract 17(B8) – Stagecoach Group plc, page 61

In this extract, the company discloses the aggregate tax charged (credited) directly to equity.

Note 8 Taxation (in part) (d) Tax on items charged/(credited) to equity	2007 £m	2006 £m
Tax on foreign exchange differences on translation of foreign operations	0.3	0.2
Tax effect of actuarial gains on Group defined benefit pensions schemes	20.3	4.2
Tax effect of share of actuarial gains on joint ventures' defined benefit pension schemes	1.5	1.5
Tax effect of share based payments	(3.8)	(2.9)
Total tax on items charged to equity	18.3	3.0
Tax recognised on the adoption of IAS 39	n/a	(0.5)

Extract 17(B9) – Stagecoach Group plc, page 69

The company discloses the tax expense for discontinued operations. No tax arose as a result of the gain on disposition.

Note 18 Disposals (in part)

The Group disposed of its London bus business during the year ended 30 April 2007. The business was disposed of on 30 August 2006 to Macquarie Bank Limited. The Group also disposed of its New Zealand operations on 29 November 2005 to Infratil Limited and therefore the year ended 30 April 2006 comparatives include the results of the New Zealand business as discontinued, in addition to the London bus business.

The results of the discontinued London bus and New Zealand operations, which have been included in the consolidated income statement, were as follows:

	2007			2006		
	London bus £m	New Zealand £m	Total £m	London bus £m	New Zealand £m	Total £m
Revenue	76.1	Nil	76.1	224.6	37.4	262.0
Operating costs	(72.0)	Nil	(72.0)	(205.0)	(33.1)	(238.1)
Other operating income	1.1	Nil	1.1	4.0	1.2	5.2
Operating profit	5.2	Nil	5.2	23.6	5.5	29.1
Finance income/(costs) (net)	0.6	Nil	0.6	(0.1)	0.1	Nil
Taxation	(1.8)	Nil	(1.8)	(6.1)	(1.3)	(7.4)
Profit for the year before gain on disposal	4.0	Nil	4.0	17.4	4.3	21.7
Gain on disposal	132.2	0.6	132.8	Nil	22.5	22.5
Profit for the year from discontinued operations	136.2	0.6	136.8	17.4	26.8	44.2

A gain of £132.2m arose on the disposal of the London bus operations, being the net proceeds from disposal less the carrying amount of the disposed business' net assets at the date of disposal. No tax arose as a result of this gain.

The gain of £0.6m relating to New Zealand for the year ended 30 April 2007 arises from the release of a liability that was previously recorded for amounts potentially owing to the disposed business, which is now no longer payable.

Extract 17(B10) – Stagecoach Group plc, page 75

In this extract, the company discloses for each type of temporary difference:

- the amount of the deferred tax liabilities (assets) recognized; and
- the amount of the deferred tax expense (income) recognized in the income statement.

The company also discloses the following:

- significant changes in deferred tax liabilities (assets) throughout the year in order to reconcile the opening balances to the closing balances;
- the current and non-current portions of deferred tax asset; and
- when the deferred tax asset for tax losses is expected to be utilized.

Note 25 Deferred tax

The Group movement in deferred tax during the year was as follows:

	Deferred tax liabilities	Deferred tax asset	Net
	£m	£m	£m
Beginning of year	(5.2)	8.4	3.2
Provided during year:			
Charge to income statement	(22.2)	(1.1)	(23.3)
Sale/closure of subsidiary undertakings and other businesses	1.3	Nil	1.3
Charge to equity	(17.7)	Nil	(17.7)
Foreign exchange	(0.3)	(0.5)	(0.8)
End of year	(44.1)	6.8	(37.3)

The deferred tax liabilities after more than one year are £44.1m (2006: £5.2m). The deferred tax asset due after more than one year is £2.2m (2006: £3.0m). The deferred tax asset of £6.8m (2006: £8.4m) has been recognised in respect of tax losses. Based on tax workings scheduling the reversal of the asset, it is expected to be utilised over the next three years (2006: three years).

Deferred taxation is calculated as follows:

	2007	2006
	£m	£m
Accelerated capital allowances	(75.4)	(90.4)
Pension temporary differences	10.9	64.3
Short-term temporary differences	27.2	29.3
	(37.3)	3.2

The amount of deferred tax recognised in the income statement by type of temporary difference is as follows:

	2007	2006
	£m	£m
Accelerated capital allowances	4.3	(4.3)
Pension temporary differences	17.5	(2.0)
Short-term temporary differences	1.5	3.5
	23.3	(2.8)

PLANNING FOR IMPLEMENTATION

Assessing the Impact on Financial Statements

CICA 3465 and IAS 12 are both based on the balance sheet liability approach, which focuses on temporary differences between the carrying amounts of assets and liabilities on the balance sheet and their tax base. Differences arise, however, because both standards have numerous exceptions to this basic principle.

Backwards Tracing

When an entity recognizes a deferred tax liability or asset, IAS 12 requires it to account for the corresponding deferred tax expense or benefit in the same way as the items to which it relates. In general, a deferred tax expense or benefit is accounted for in the income statement. It is, however, accounted for in other comprehensive income when it is related to items recognized in other comprehensive income in the same or a different period. It is accounted for directly in equity when related to items recognized directly in equity in the same or a different period.

CICA 3465 prohibits backwards tracing.

Expected Manner of Recovery of Assets or Settlement of Liabilities

In some jurisdictions, the method for recovering (settling) the carrying amount of an asset (liability) may affect either or both of:

- the tax rate applicable when the carrying amount of the asset (liability) is recovered (settled); and
- the tax base of the asset (liability).

In such cases, IAS 12 requires a deferred tax liability or asset to be measured using the tax rate and tax base that are consistent with the expected manner of recovery or settlement.

CICA 3465 requires:

- the rate used to measure deferred tax assets and liabilities to reflect the expected manner of recovery of the asset; and
- the tax base of the asset to be the greater of:
  - o the amount deductible if the asset is utilized, and
  - o the amount deductible if the asset is sold.

Initial Recognition of an Asset or Liability

IAS 12 prohibits the recognition of a deferred tax liability or asset when it arises from the initial recognition of an asset or liability in a transaction that:

- is not a business combination; and
- at the time of the transaction, affects neither accounting profit nor taxable profit (tax loss).

For an asset acquired outside of a business combination, CICA 3465 requires that:

- a deferred tax liability is recognized and the carrying amount of the asset acquired is increased when its cost is greater than its tax base; and
- a deferred tax asset is recognized and the carrying amount of the asset acquired is decreased when its cost is less than its tax base.

Intragroup Transfers

IAS 27, *Consolidated and Separate Financial Statements* requires profits and losses resulting from intragroup transactions that are recognized in assets (i.e., inventory and fixed assets) to be eliminated in full.

IAS 12 requires a deferred tax liability or asset to be recognized for temporary differences that arise from the elimination of profits and losses resulting from intragroup transactions.

When an asset is transferred between enterprises within a consolidated group, CICA 3465 prohibits the recognition of a deferred tax liability or asset in the consolidated financial statements for a temporary difference arising between the tax base of the asset in the buyer's tax jurisdiction and its cost as reported in the consolidated financial statements.

Foreign Currency Translations

IAS 12 requires a deferred tax liability or asset to be recognized for temporary differences that arise on the translation of non-monetary assets and liabilities that are remeasured from the local currency to the functional currency using historical rates and result from changes in exchange rates and indexing for tax purposes.

CICA 3465 prohibits the recognition of a deferred tax liability or asset when such temporary differences arise.

Current Versus Non-current Distinction

IAS 1, *Presentation of Financial Statements* prohibits an entity from presenting deferred tax assets and liabilities as current when a classified balance sheet is presented.

CICA 3465 requires the current and non-current portions of deferred tax liabilities and deferred tax assets to be segregated when a classified balance sheet is presented.

Initial Adoption of IFRS

IFRS 1, *First-time Adoption of International Financial Reporting Standards* provides no exemptions from, or exceptions to, the retrospective application of IAS 12 to first-time adopters. IAS 12 is, therefore, applied to temporary differences between the carrying amount of the assets and liabilities in the opening IFRS balance sheet and their tax bases.

Thus, the deferred tax liability (asset) on the opening IFRS balance sheet is calculated only after having made all the necessary adjustments and revaluations to the carrying amount of assets and liabilities in accordance with IFRS 1. This calculation should not benefit from hindsight. It should solely be based on the facts, circumstances and probabilities that existed at the time a deferred tax liability (asset) was measured under Canadian GAAP. The guidance for implementing IFRS 1 notes that enacted or substantively enacted tax rates and tax laws at the balance sheet date should be reflected in the measurement of current and deferred tax, as required by IAS 12.

Obtaining Inputs from Personnel

The information required to account for and disclose income taxes under Canadian GAAP is similar to that required under IFRS. Thus, the adoption of IAS 12 may result in only minor adjustments to current processes for gathering the additional information required. Accounting personnel should continue to work closely with the tax department to:

- monitor and calculate the tax bases of assets and liabilities;
- monitor tax losses and tax credits;
- monitor changes in tax rates;
- assess the recoverability of deferred tax assets;
- assess the likelihood of uncertain tax positions being accepted by the CRA;
- identify opportunities to offset deferred tax liabilities against deferred tax assets; and
- prepare disclosures.

Generating New Data and Optimizing Information Systems

The adoption of IAS 12 will most likely not result in a significant overhaul of accounting and management reporting systems, which should continue to:

- monitor the carrying amount and tax base of assets and liabilities; and
- evaluate the tax effects of options selected and tax treatments over time.

Modifications will most likely be required to gather the additional disclosure information required by IAS 12 and to account for deferred tax liabilities (assets) that arise from temporary differences from:

- the translation of non-monetary assets and liabilities remeasured from the local currency to the functional currency using historical rates and result from changes in exchange rates and indexing for tax purposes; and
- an intragroup asset transfer.

The retrospective application of the new IFRS on accounting for income taxes will likely require Canadian first-time adopters to gather information even before the final standard is issued. Although the new IFRS on accounting for income taxes is expected to reduce several of the differences that currently exist between CICA 3465 and IAS 12, some new differences are also expected to arise. These new differences may require the collection of additional information, for example, to:

- recognize deferred tax liabilities or assets for all temporary differences associated with investments in subsidiaries and interests in joint ventures, except for temporary differences arising from investments in foreign subsidiaries and interests in foreign joint ventures that are essentially permanent in duration;
- assess probability weighted amounts for uncertain tax positions.

Keep Posted

In September 2002, the IASB launched a project on income taxes, which is part of the IASB and FASB's short-term convergence project aimed at eliminating differences between IFRS and US GAAP. The IASB expects to finally issue an Exposure Draft in early 2009 and has tentatively decided that it should take the form of a draft IFRS instead of amendments to IAS 12. The final standard is expected to be issued in 2010.

Chapter 18
Related Parties

Standards Discussed in this Chapter

International
IAS 24 – Related Party Disclosures

Canadian
CICA 3840 – Related Party Transactions
EIC-79 – Gain recognition in arm's-length and related party transactions when the consideration received includes a claim on the assets sold
EIC-83 – Identification of related party transactions in the normal course of operations

INTRODUCTION

Canadian financial statement preparers adopting IFRS should refer to IAS 24 when drafting related party disclosures. IAS 24 does not address the recognition and measurement of related party transactions. Its objective is to make users aware of the influences related parties might have had on an entity's operations, financial position and profit or loss. To that end, the entity needs to disclose the nature of any relationships, transactions and outstanding balances between related parties. Canadian companies transitioning to IFRS may, therefore, find the IAS 24 disclosure requirements to be much more extensive than those of its Canadian counterpart, CICA 3840, particularly in the compensation of key management personnel.

This chapter discusses the following topics:

* identification of related parties;
* recognition and measurement of related party transactions;
* general disclosures of related party relationships, and transactions; and
* disclosure of key management personnel compensation.

IMPACT ON FINANCIAL STATEMENTS

The adoption of IAS 24 will have an impact on the financial statements of Canadian companies due to:

* potential differences in the recognition and measurement of related party transactions, because there are no specific requirements for these transactions under IFRS. Instead, related party transactions are recognized and measured in accordance with the requirements of relevant IFRSs. For example, the measurement of related party transactions without commercial substance may differ because, under CICA 3840, these transactions are measured at their carrying amount;
* additional disclosures in the notes to the financial statements, which are not required under CICA 3840, such as:

   o disclosures of relationships, transactions and outstanding balances with post-employment benefit plans, which are included in the definition of a "related party",

   o disclosures of relationships between parents and subsidiaries, which are required even if there have been no transactions between them,

   o disclosures of the name of an entity's parent and its ultimate controlling entity/individual,

   o disclosures of the compensation of key management personnel, and

   o separate disclosures for each category of related party.

ANALYSIS OF RELEVANT ISSUES

Identification of Related Parties

Scope

IAS 24 establishes the framework for the identification and disclosure of related party relationships, transactions and balances in the financial statements, including the separate financial statements of a parent, venture or investor presented in accordance with IAS 27.

Definition of a "Related Party"

IAS 24, defines a *related party transaction* as a transfer of resources, services or obligations between related parties, regardless of whether any consideration is exchanged. The standard also prescribes criteria for identifying related parties, and deems certain parties to be related parties.

Under IAS 24, a related party is defined as:

- a party that directly or indirectly, through one or more intermediaries:

  - o controls, is controlled by, or is under common control with an entity (this includes parents, subsidiaries and fellow subsidiaries),

  - o has an interest in an entity that gives it significant influence over the entity, or

  - o has joint control over an entity;

- an entity that is controlled, jointly controlled or significantly influenced by, or in which significant voting power resides with, directly or indirectly:

  - o a member of key management of an entity or its parent,

  - o a close family member of any member of key management of an entity or its parent, or

  - o a close family member of any individual that controls, has joint control or significant influence over an entity.

In addition to the above criteria, IAS 24 deems the following to be related parties:

- associates (as defined in IAS 28);

- joint ventures (as defined in IAS 31);

- members of key management personnel of an entity or its parent;

- close family members of key management personnel of an entity or its parent, or of any individual who exercises control, joint control or significant influence over the entity; and

- post-employment benefit plans for the benefit of employees of an entity, or of any entity that is a related party of the entity.

The definition of a related party makes reference to certain terms, which are defined as follows:

- *key management personnel*: are individuals who have the authority and responsibility for planning, directing and controlling an entity's activities directly or indirectly;

- *close family members:* are relatives of a person who can influence, or be influenced by, that person in their dealings with an entity, and include:

  o that person's domestic partner and children,

  o children of that person's domestic partner, and

  o dependants of that person or that person's domestic partner.

Although IAS 24 is prescriptive, it requires that the identification of related party relationships be based on the substance of a relationship and not its legal form. Furthermore, an entity's economic dependence on another business does not in itself create a related party relationship.

The definitions under CICA 3840 are similar, except that post-employment benefit plans are not included in the definition of a related party.

An IASB Exposure Draft issued in 2007 proposes some amendments to the definition of a related party that are meant to clarify its meaning and to remove the inconsistencies that arise in some situations. These amendments are discussed in the "Future Developments" section of this chapter.

Illustrative Disclosures:

Extract 18(1) – Related party (an individual)

Altana Aktiengesellschaft (AR 2007), pages 166 and 167

28. Related Party Transactions

Susanne Klatten is considered a related party, as she owns indirectly via SKion GmbH 50.1 % of the shares of ALTANA AG. She is deputy chairwoman of the Supervisory Board. During the years reported there were no transactions between her and the Company except for dividends distributed and the regular compensation for her function on the Supervisory Board. Mrs. Klatten is also chairwoman of the board of counselors of the Herbert Quandt Foundation and she has an interest of 50 % in the ALTANA Kulturstiftung gemeinnützige GmbH (ALTANA Cultural Foundation). In 2006, assets relating to the cultural activities of ALTANA AG were transferred to that entity. Property, cash and art works were donated as a one-time charitable contribution amounting to €13 million.

Additionally, Susanne Klatten is shareholder and member of the Supervisory Board of Bayerische Motoren Werke AG (BMW AG). In the years reported the Company purchased or leased company cars from the BMW group. These lease and purchase contracts are not disclosed separately as they were insignificant to the Company's financial statements and were carried out at normal third party terms.

Joint ventures and associated companies that are not included in the consolidated financial statements are considered related parties. Balances due to and due from related parties are recorded in other assets, other liabilities and debt, as they are not material.

Except for the assets and liabilities reported as of December 31, 2006 the disclosures below include the related party transactions of the discontinued operations.

Altana Aktiengesellschaft (AR 2007) (continued)

	Dec. 31, 2007	Dec. 31, 2006
Balances due from related parties	181	345
Balances due to related parties	282	2,012
Deposit from Herbert Quandt Foundation	0	35,447
	2007	**2006**
Related party transactions		
Sales	393	1,739
Services and goods acquired	0	56,967
Interest income	16	3
Interest expense	526	1,812

Regarding the terms and conditions relating to the deposits from the Herbert Quandt Foundation see note 17.

In 2006, the amounts in the line items "services and goods acquired" were mainly related to the toll manufacturing of Bracco ALTANA Pharma GmbH. The terms and conditions of those agreements were based on normal third party terms and were part of discontinued operations.

Commentary: Altana identifies Susanne Klatten as a related party and discloses related party transactions with her because she indirectly controls the company. Furthermore, the company discloses that she is a member of key management personnel.

Note that the company also discloses related party transactions with other entities controlled or significantly influenced by Susanne Klatten, as well as the existence of related party relationships with joint ventures and associated companies.

Extract 18(2) – Related party (post-employment benefit plans)

BNP Paribas (Registration Document 2007), page 211
8.d RELATED PARTIES (in part)
8.d.2 Entities managing post-employment benefit plans offered to Group employees

The main post-employment benefits of the BNP Paribas Group are retirement bonus plans, and top-up defined-benefit and defined contribution pension plans.

In France, some of these benefits are paid by the BNP and Paribas pension funds (*Caisses de retraite*) and the BNP welfare benefit fund (*Caisse de Prévoyance*). As from 1 January 2006, the obligations concerning pension benefits paid by the BNP pension fund have been assumed in full by BNP Paribas SA. The BNP pension fund was liquidated in the first half of 2007. Furthermore, over the six months to 30 June 2007, all of the pension benefits provided by the Paribas pension fund as well as the provisions for retirement bonuses existing within the BNP welfare benefit fund were transferred to an external insurance company.

In other countries, post-employment benefit plans are generally managed by independent fund managers or independent insurance companies, and occasionally by Group companies (in particular BNP Paribas Asset Management, BNP Paribas Assurance, Bank of the West and First Hawaiian Bank). In Switzerland, a dedicated foundation manages benefit plans for BNP Paribas Switzerland's employees.

At 31 December 2006, the value of plan assets managed by Group companies was EUR 991 million (EUR 1,174 million at 31 December 2006). Amounts received relating to services provided by Group companies in the year to 31 December 2007 totalled EUR 1.1 million, and mainly comprised management and custody fees (2006: EUR 1.4 million).

At 31 December 2007, the BNP and Paribas pension funds and the BNP welfare benefit fund showed a credit balance of EUR 44,040 in the Group's accounting books (compared with a credit balance of EUR 216,767 at 31 December 2006).

Commentary: In this extract, BNP Paribas identifies post-employment benefit plans as related parties, and discloses the nature of these relationships in accordance with IAS 24. Post-employment benefit plans are not considered related parties under CICA 3840.

Recognition and Measurement of Related Party Transactions

IAS 24 does not specify requirements for the recognition and measurement of related party transactions in the financial statements. Instead, related party transactions are recognized and measured in accordance with the requirements of relevant IFRS.

For example, IAS 39 requires financial assets and liabilities, including those resulting from related party transactions, to be initially measured using fair values. Its Canadian counterpart, CICA 3855, requires financial assets and financial liabilities resulting from related party transactions to be initially measured using a two-step process. First, financial assets and financial liabilities resulting from related party transactions are measured at their carrying amount or exchange amount, determined in accordance with CICA 3840. Second, financial assets and financial liabilities resulting from related party transactions are then measured based on their classification on initial recognition.

Thus, financial assets and financial liabilities classified on initial recognition as held for trading or available for sale are measured at fair value. Any gain or loss arising as a result of a difference between fair value and the carrying amount or exchange amount, determined in accordance with CICA 3840 is recognized in net income, except when the recipient of a financial asset classifies it as available for sale. In that case, the gain or loss is recognized in other comprehensive income until the financial asset is derecognized.

Financial assets and financial liabilities classified on initial recognition as a held-to-maturity investment, a loan or receivable, or a financial liability other than one held for trading will continue to be measured at their carrying amount or exchange amount, determined in accordance with CICA 3840, which forms the basis for subsequent measurement at amortized cost.

Measurement differences may arise in instances where financial assets and financial liabilities result from related party transactions without commercial substance but classified as a held-to-maturity investment, a loan or receivable, or a financial liability other than one held for trading. Under these circumstances, financial assets and financial liabilities are measured at their carrying amount in accordance with CICA 3840, but are measured at fair value under IAS 39. For example, receivables resulting from related party transactions without commercial substance and classified as a loan or receivable are measured at their carrying amount in accordance with CICA 3840, but are measured at fair value under IAS 39.

General Disclosures of Related Party Relationships and Transactions

IAS 24 requires the disclosure of the following information about related parties in the financial statements:

- relationships between parents and subsidiaries, irrespective of whether there have been transactions between them. This requirement is in addition to the disclosure requirements in IAS 27, IAS 28 and IAS 31, which require an appropriate listing and description of significant investment in subsidiaries, associates and jointly controlled entities;
- the name of an entity's parent and its ultimate controlling entity/individual;
- details of related party transactions, and balances outstanding at the balance sheet date, which at a minimum consist of:
  - o the amount of the transactions,

o the amount of outstanding balances, including their terms and conditions,

o provisions for doubtful debts relating to outstanding balances, and

o the expense recognized as a result of bad debts or provisions for doubtful debts on amounts due from related parties.

Furthermore, these disclosures should be made separately for each of the following:

* the parent;
* entities that have joint control or significant influence over the entity;
* subsidiaries;
* associates;
* joint ventures;
* key management personnel of the entity or of its parent; and
* other related parties.

For example, the following types of related party transactions are to be disclosed under IAS 24:

* rendering or receiving of services;
* leases;
* transfers of research and development;
* transfers under licence agreements;
* provision of guarantees or collateral; and
* settlement of liabilities on behalf of an entity or by the entity on behalf of another party.

Participation by a parent or subsidiary in a defined benefit plan that shares risks between group entities is also considered to be a transaction between related parties.

IAS 24 prescribes that related party transactions should be disclosed as being at arm's length only when such terms can be substantiated.

Clearly, IAS 24 requirements can result in lengthy related party disclosures. To provide some relief, the standard permits the aggregation of transactions and balances for items of a similar nature, except when separate disclosure would provide a better understanding of the effects related party transactions have had on the financial statements.

The disclosure requirements under CICA 3840 are generally converged with IAS 24, except that CICA 3840 does not require:

* the disclosure of relationships between parents and subsidiaries when there have been no transactions between them;
* the disclosure of the name of an entity's parent and its ultimate controlling entity/individual; and
* separate disclosures for each category of related party.

Illustrative Disclosures:

Extract 18(3) – Parent of an entity and ultimate controlling entity

CEVA Group Plc (AR 2007), page 51

General Information and Description of our Business (in part)

On 9 August 2006, CEVA Group Plc was incorporated in England and Wales as a public company with limited liability (registered number 5900853). The ultimate controlling party of CEVA Group Plc is Apollo Management VI, L.P. The immediate parent of CEVA Group Plc is CEVA Investments Ltd, a company incorporated in the Cayman Islands.

Commentary: In this extract, the company discloses its immediate parent and ultimate controlling entity.

Extract 18(4) – Related party transactions (arm's length)

Aker Kvaerner ASA (AR 2007), page 48

Note 5: Related parties

The group has several related party relationships between parents and subsidiaries (see note 28 Group companies as at 31 December 2007), associates (see note 21 Investments accounted for in accordance with the equity method), joint ventures (see note 22 Investments in Joint Ventures) and with its directors and executive officers (see note 18 Salaries, wages and social security costs).

The largest shareholder Aker Holding AS is controlled by Aker ASA which is controlled by Kjell Inge Røkke through TRG Holding AS. All entities which Kjell Inge Røkke controls or has significant influence over are considered related parties to the Aker Kvaerner group.

In accordance with recommended accounting practice, information regarding significant related party transactions, benefits and agreements should be disclosed where such information may assist users of the financial statements in their understanding of the activities of the group. All transactions have been based on arm's length terms. The transactions below are considered to be significant related party transactions not disclosed in the notes listed above.

Aker Drilling ASA

In 2005, Aker Drilling ASA and Aker Kvaerner entered into a contract for the turn-key delivery of two sixth-generation deepwater drilling semisubmersibles. The contract value including mooring systems was originally approximately NOK 7.8 billion. The two drilling rigs are scheduled for delivery in July and December 2008.

Aker Floating Production ASA

A contract with Aker Floating Production ASA to deliver a complete subsea production system for a Reliance Industries Ltd in India was signed in 2007. Aker Kvaerner will also deliver the marine installation of the floating production storage and offloading (FPSO) vessel to be leased out by Aker Floating Production. There is a separate contract with Aker Floating Production ASA to deliver process technology to the FPSO. The total value of Aker Kvaerner's contracts is approximately USD 250 million and NOK 610 million.

Aker Oilfield Services

Aker Kvaerner has invested NOK 72.3 million in Aker Oilfield Services and owns 19.1 percent of the shares, see note 26 Subsequent events. Aker Kvaerner has signed a letter of intent with Aker Oilfield Services and is set to expand its subsea service offering by providing equipment and personnel to the world's first deepwater Subsea Equipment Support Vessel (SESV). The contract, to commence latest 2010, is worth approximately USD 60 million over an initial five year period.

Aker Clean Carbon AS

Aker Kvaerner has agreed to transfer its Just Catch technology for CO_2 capture to the company Aker Clean Carbon AS, which will develop CO_2 capture projects. The transaction to take place I 2008 will give Aker Kvaerner 30 percent of the shares in Aker Clean Carbon AS, while Aker ASA will own 70 percent. The ownership ratio has been determined following valuations and negotiations that have also recognised the value of Aker Kvaerner's exclusive rights to participate in building future carbon capture facilities in co-operation with Aker Clean Carbon.

Aker Kvaerner ASA (AR 2007) (continued)

Intellectual Property Holding AS

Aker Kværner ASA has an agreement with Intellectual Property Holdings AS (IPH) that holds all rights, titles and interests in and to registered trademarks and domain names containing "Aker" and "Kværner". IPH will act as a joint branding tool where the companies in the Aker group join forces in selected initiatives. The annual royalty cost for Aker Kvaerner is approximately NOK 10 million.

Aker Insurance AS

After Aker ASA had received an accumulated dividend of NOK 80 million, Aker Kvaerner acquired in 2007 the 9.9 percent of the shares controlled by Aker ASA for NOK 10 million. After the transaction, Aker Kvaerner owns 100 percent of the shares in Aker Insurance AS.

Shared Resources

Aker Kvaerner Business Partner and Aker Kvaerner's corporate functions are offering services to other Aker companies on arm's length terms.

Commentary: Aker Kvaerner discloses that related party transactions were carried out on an arm's length basis. This statement should be made only when such terms can be substantiated.

Note that the company identifies and discloses the nature of related party relationships with subsidiaries, associates, joint ventures, directors and executive officers.

Extract 18(5) – Related party transactions (non-arm's length)

China Telecom Corporation Limited (AR 2007), page 179

34. RELATED PARTY TRANSACTIONS (in part)

(a) Transactions with China Telecom Group (in part)

The Group is a part of a large group of companies under China Telecom, a company owned by the PRC government, and has significant transactions and relationships with members of China Telecom. Because of these relationships, it is possible that the terms of these transactions are not the same as those that would result from transactions among unrelated parties.

Commentary: China Telecom Corporation Limited discloses that related party transactions with China Telecom Group may not be at arm's length. This statement warns users of the influences related parties may have had on the financial position, and profit or loss.

Disclosure of Key Management Personnel Compensation

In addition to the general disclosures discussed above, IAS 24 specifically requires the disclosure of key management personnel compensation, which includes all employee benefits (as defined in IAS 19, *Employee Benefits*), including those to which IFRS 2, *Share-based Payment* applies. Employee benefits comprise all forms of compensation paid, payable or provided by an entity, or on its behalf, in return for services rendered to the entity, and any compensation paid on behalf the entity's parent in respect of the entity.

This disclosure should be presented in aggregate and for each of the following categories:

- short-term employee benefits, such as wages, salaries and social security contributions, vacation pay and sick pay, profit-sharing and bonuses and non-monetary benefits for current employees;

- post-employment benefits, such as pensions, other retirement rights, post-employment life insurance and post-employment medical care;

- other long-term benefits, such as long-service or sabbatical leave, long-term disability benefits, and profit-sharing, bonuses and deferred compensation not payable within 12 months of the end of the period;

- termination benefits; and
- share-based payment, such as share options.

CICA 3840 does not require the disclosure of key management personnel compensation; however, National Instrument 51-102 requires Canadian publicly traded companies to disclose executive compensation in an *Information Circular*.

Illustrative Disclosures:

Extracts 18(6) – Disclosure of key management compensation

Roche Holding Ltd (AR 2007), page 100

33. Related parties (in part)

Key management personnel

Members of the Board of Directors of Roche Holding Ltd receive an annual remuneration and payment for their time and expenses related to their membership of Board committees. Total remuneration of the Board of Directors in 2007 totalled 5 million Swiss francs (2006: 4 million Swiss francs).

Members of the Corporate Executive Committee of Roche Holding Ltd receive remuneration, which consists of an annual salary, bonus and an expense allowance. The Group pays social insurance contributions in respect of the above remuneration and pays contributions to pension and other post-employment benefit plans for members of the Corporate Executive Committee. Members of the Corporate Executive Committee also participate in certain equity compensation plans as described below. The terms, vesting conditions and fair value of these awards are disclosed in Note 11.

Remuneration of members of the Corporate Executive Committee *in millions of CHF*

	2007	2006
Salaries, including bonuses and expenses	23	18
Social security costs	2	1
Pensions and other post-employment benefits	6	6
Equity compensation plans	22	18
Other employee benefits	–	–
Total	53	43

Commentary: This extract illustrates the disclosure of key management personnel compensation, including the disclosure of total key management personnel compensation and separate disclosures for short-term employee benefits, post-employment benefits, other long-term benefits, termination benefits and share-based payment.

Extracts 18(7) – Disclosure of key management compensation

Qantas Airways Limited (AR 2007), pages 107 and 111

24. Key Management Personnel and Executive Equity Benefits (in part)

Key Management Personnel remuneration

The aggregate remuneration of the KMP of the Qantas Group and Qantas is set out below:

	Qantas Group		Qantas	
	2007 $	2006 $	2007 $	2006 $
Short-term employee benefits	18,886,101	13,051,473	17,226,863	12,163,132
Post employment benefits	1,455,156	3,360,335	1,147,071	3,147,708
Other long-term benefits	402,984	716,324	344,916	690,605
Termination benefits	–	1,358,024	–	1,358,024
Share-based payment	5,678,628	3,655,992	5,040,057	3,359,149
	26,422,869	22,142,148	23,758,907	20,718,618

Qantas Airways Limited (AR 2007) (continued)

Loans and other transactions with Key Management Personnel

Loans

No KMP or their related parties held any loans from the Qantas Group during or at the end of the year.

Other transactions with the Qantas Group

Related party disclosures

Roger Donazzan, a related party to Ms Jackson, is Chairman of Harmony Resorts Niseko Pty Ltd (HRN). During the year, no sponsorship was provided to Hanazano (2006: $6,400) or Mt Hotham which are related entities of HRN.

Paul Meadows, a related party to Mrs Cross, is a Partner of Allens Arthur Robinson. Mr Meadows performs no work for Qantas. Total legal fees paid to the Allens Arthur Robinson Group during the year were $5,141,000 (2006: nil). During the year, the Allens Arthur Robinson Group purchased air travel of $2,189,000 (2006: $1,621,000) from the Qantas Group. All transactions between the Qantas Group and the Allens Arthur Robinson Group are conducted on normal commercial arms length terms.

Toolangi Vineyards is a related entity to Mr Hounsell. During the year, the Qantas Group purchased wine totalling $106,000 (2006: nil) from Toolangi Vineyards, for use on Qantas International Business Class services. All transactions were conducted on normal commercial arms length terms.

Publishing and Broadcasting Limited (PBL) and its controlled entities, including Consolidated Press Holdings Limited, Nine Network, ACP Magazines, Crown Casino, Burswood Casino, Ticketek, Hoyts and Premier Media Group, is a related entity to Mr Packer. During the year, PBL purchased air travel of $15,226,000 (2006: $13,500,000) from the Qantas Group. The Qantas Group purchased directly or indirectly advertising services from PBL of $4,047,000 (2006: $2,500,000) during the year. In addition, Qantas and PBL have various contra arrangements in place for advertising and sponsorship. The value of these contra arrangements with Qantas was $139,000 (2006: $63,000) and nil (2006: $210,000) for other entities within the Qantas Group. During the year, Qantas spent $297,000 (2006: $1,000,000) with Crown Limited and $1,487,000 (2006: $1,600,000) with ACP Publishing Pty Ltd. All transactions were conducted on normal commercial arms length terms.

General Cosgrove became a Director of the Australian Rugby Union (ARU), which as such is a related entity to General Cosgrove, on 28 April 2007. During the year, Qantas purchased sponsorship and advertising rights of $226,000 from the ARU and the ARU purchased air travel of $1,111,000 from the Qantas Group. In addition, Qantas and the ARU have contra arrangements in place for sponsorship and advertising rights in return for air travel. The value of these contra arrangements with Qantas during the year was $3,164,000. All transactions were conducted on normal commercial arms length terms.

Commentary: This extract illustrates the disclosure of key management personnel compensation, including the disclosure of total key management personnel compensation, and separate disclosures for short-term employee benefits, post-employment benefits, other long-term benefits, termination benefits and share-based payment.

This extract also illustrates the general disclosures of related party relationships and transactions between the company and key management personnel by indicating that there are no outstanding balances, and the amount of the transactions.

Extracts 18(8) – Disclosure of key management compensation

Koninklijke Ahold N.V. (AR 2007), pages 72-74

31 Related party transactions)

Compensation of key management personnel

Key management personnel are those persons having authority and responsibility for planning, directing and controlling the activities of the Company as a whole. The Company determined that key management personnel consists of members of the Supervisory Board, members and acting members of the Corporate Executive Board, the continental Chief Operating Officers and Senior Vice Presidents reporting directly to a Corporate Executive Board member, acting in that capacity.

Koninklijke Ahold N.V. (AR 2007) (continued)
Employment contracts with individual Corporate Executive Board members
Amounts in the discussion below are in thousands of EUR, unless otherwise indicated.

John Rishton

The Company's revised employment agreement with John Rishton to account for his appointment as CEO of the Company, dated November 20, 2007, provides for a base salary of EUR 945 per year retroactively as of July 1, 2007. It also provides for participation in the annual cash incentive plan, as well as participation in the Company's equity based long-term incentive program (GRO) (see Note 32). The at-target payout under the annual cash incentive plan is 100 percent of the base salary and is capped at 125 percent in case of extraordinary performance. On the starting date of his employment, John Rishton was granted 100,000 Ahold common shares to compensate the loss of long-term perquisites from his previous employer. The vesting of these shares is conditional upon three years employment. Unless John Rishton's employment agreement is otherwise terminated, he will be eligible for reappointment in 2010. In the event the Company terminates John Rishton's employment agreement for reasons other than cause or because he is not reappointed, John Rishton is entitled to a severance payment equal to one year's base salary. John Rishton's employment agreement may be terminated by the Company with a notice period of 12 months and by John Rishton with a notice period of six months. John Rishton is offered the same pension plan available to all members of the Corporate Executive Board.

Peter Wakkie

The Company's employment agreement with Peter Wakkie, dated October 9, 2003, provides for a base salary currently set at EUR 600 per year, participation in the annual cash incentive plan, as well as participation in the Company's equity based long-term incentive program (GRO) (see Note 32). The at-target payout under the annual cash incentive plan is 100 percent of the base salary and is capped at 125 percent in case of extraordinary performance. Unless Peter Wakkie's employment agreement is otherwise terminated, he will be eligible for reappointment in 2008. Peter Wakkie's employment agreement does not include any severance arrangement and the agreement may be terminated with a notice period of three months by either Peter Wakkie or the Company. Peter Wakkie is offered the same pension plan available to all other Dutch employees in the Netherlands born before 1950.

Dick Boer

The Company's employment agreement with Dick Boer, dated March 29, 2007, provides for a base salary of EUR 625 per year, participation in the annual cash incentive plan, as well as participation in the Company's equity based long-term incentive plan (GRO) (see Note 32). The at-target payout under the annual cash incentive plan is 100 percent of base salary and is capped at 125 percent in case of extraordinary performance. Unless Dick Boer's employment agreement is otherwise terminated, he will be eligible for reappointment in 2011. In the event the Company terminates Dick Boer's employment agreement for reasons other than cause or because he is not reappointed, Dick Boer is entitled to a severance payment equal to one year's base salary. Dick Boer's employment agreement may be terminated by the Company with a notice period of 12 months and by Dick Boer with a notice period of six months. Dick Boer is offered the same pension plan available to all members of the Corporate Executive Board.

Koninklijke Ahold N.V. (AR 2007) (continued)

Remuneration of the individual Corporate Executive Board members

Remuneration of the individual Corporate Executive Board members, which is disclosed as of the year the General Meeting of Shareholders approved the appointment of a member, can be specified as follows:

Euros in thousands		Base salary	Bonuses[1]	Share-based compensation[2]	Pensions[3]	Termination benefits	Other[4]	Total
J.F. Rishton	2007	835	1,044	224	177	–	149	2,429
	2006	725	573	704	201	–	133	2,336
P.N. Wakkie	2007	600	1,050	231	165	–	13	2,059
	2006	600	474	338	315	–	15	1,742
A.D. Boer	2007	625	781	908	239	–	10	2,563
	2006	–						–
A.C. Moberg	2007	750	2,556	457	–	3,379	111	7,253
(resigned from the Board effective July 1, 2007)[5]	2006	1,500	1,689	437	–	–	122	3,748
Total	2007	2,810	5,431	1,820	581	3,379	283	14,304
	2006	2,825	2,736	1,479	516		270	7,826

1 Bonuses represent accrued bonuses to be paid in the following year, except as disclosed in footnote 5 below. Peter Wakkie's 2007 bonus includes EUR 300 as a reward for the successful completion of the divestment program.

2 The amounts included in the table for share-based compensation represent the share-based compensation expense calculated under IFRS 2 related to the grants to Corporate Executive Board members. The fair value of share-based compensation grants is expensed on a straight-line basis over the vesting period of the grants. For Dick Boer, the amount includes a pro rated part of the fair value of 190,333 conditional shares granted to him in January 2006, which vest after two years continued employment. For more information on share-based compensation programs, see Note 32.

3 Pension costs are the total net periodic pension costs.

4 "Other" mainly includes representation allowances, employer's contributions to social security plans, relocation expenses, allowances for private medical insurance and benefits in kind such as tax advice and medical expenses. Anders Moberg received a contractually agreed allowance of EUR 52 and EUR 83 in 2007 and 2006, respectively, for pensions in lieu of participation in a pension plan.

5 Anders Moberg's 2007 bonus, which includes EUR 1,500 on account of his major contributions to the value added to U.S. Foodservice, was fully paid in 2007. His termination benefit includes one year base salary, one year bonus (based on the 2006 amount) and his base salary for the period between resignation from the Corporate Executive Board and the end-date of his employment contract (July 1, 2007 until August 15, 2007). The termination benefit is payable in three installments: EUR 1,379 was paid in 2007 and the remaining EUR 2,000 is payable in equal installments at January 1, 2008 and January 1, 2009. The termination benefit is also in consideration that Anders Moberg, at the request of the Company, agreed a non-compete clause for a period of two years for retail activities in any of the markets that Ahold serves.

Remuneration of the Supervisory Board members

Euros in thousands	2007	2006
R. Dahan (appointed in 2004)	71	73
T. de Swaan (appointed in 2007)	75	–
K.M.A. de Segundo (appointed in 2004)	75	72
D.C. Doijer (appointed in 2005)	75	66
S.M. Shern (appointed in 2005)	86	83
J. Sprieser (appointed in 2006)	79	68
M. Hart (resigned in 2007)	50	64
J. Hommen (resigned in 2007)	26	83
Total	**537**	**509**

Koninklijke Ahold N.V. (AR 2007) (continued)

Shares and other interests in Ahold

As of December 30, 2007, Corporate Executive Board members held the following shares and other interests in Ahold:

	Common shares
J.F. Rishton	–
P.N. Wakkie	6,000
A.D. Boer	33,818
Total	**39,818**

On January 1, 2006, the starting date of his employment, John Rishton was conditionally granted 100,000 Ahold common shares. He will receive these shares after three years employment per January 1, 2009. Dick Boer was granted 190,333 conditional shares in January 2006, which vest after two years of continued employment.

As of December 30, 2007, René Dahan held 112,000 Ahold common shares. None of the other Supervisory Board members held Ahold shares.

Other key management personnel

The Company recognized remuneration expenses of EUR 28 (2006: EUR 8) for consideration paid, payable or provided to other key management personnel (i.e., not members of the Corporate Executive Board or Supervisory Board). This consisted of short-term employee benefits of EUR 23 (2006: EUR 7), which in 2007 included amounts paid in connection with the successful completion of the divestment program, post-employment benefits of EUR 1 (2006: nil) and share-based compensation of EUR 4 (2006: EUR 1).

Trading transactions

Ahold has entered into arrangements with a number of its subsidiaries and affiliated companies in the course of its business. These arrangements relate to service transactions and financing agreements. Transactions were conducted at market prices, adjusted to reflect the volume of transactions and the relationship between the parties.

During 2007 and 2006, the Company entered into the following transactions with unconsolidated related parties:

For the year ended December 30, 2007	Sales to related parties	Purchases from related parties	Amounts owed by related parties	Amounts owed to related parties
ICA	7	1	3	5
JMR	5	–	1	2
Stationsdrogisterijen	14	–	–	2
Real estate joint ventures	2	–	9	–
Accounting Plaza B.V.	1	22	–	–
Kobalt Media Services B.V.	1	63	–	–
Loyalty Management Nederland B.V.	13	1	6	8
A.M.S. Coffee Trading	–	41	–	2
Related parties of Schuitema	1	11	2	1
Ahold Dutch managers and employees	–	–	27	–
Total	**44**	**139**	**48**	**20**

Koninklijke Ahold N.V. (AR 2007) (continued)				
For the year ended December 31, 2006	Sales to related parties	Purchases from related parties	Amounts owed by related parties	Amounts owed to related parties
ICA	1	6	6	7
JMR	4	–	4	2
Stationsdrogisterijen	12	–	–	2
Real estate joint ventures	3	–	6	–
Accounting Plaza B.V.	–	23	–	3
Kobalt Media Services B.V.	–	50	2	6
Loyalty Management Nederland B.V.	–	19	2	11
A.M.S. Coffee Trading	–	35	–	–
Related parties of Schuitema	–	13	6	2
Ahold Dutch managers and employees	–	–	28	–
Total	**20**	**146**	**54**	**33**

These unconsolidated related parties consist of:

- ICA, a joint venture of Ahold in the retail business.
- JMR, a joint venture of Ahold in the retail business.
- Stationsdrogisterijen, a joint venture of Ahold in the retail business.
- Real estate joint ventures, in which Ahold has an interest, holding properties operated by Ahold or its subsidiaries.
- Accounting Plaza B.V., an associate of Ahold that renders accounting and administrative services to certain Ahold subsidiaries in the Netherlands.
- Kobalt Media Services B.V., a former associate of Ahold that renders promotional and advertising services to certain Ahold subsidiaries in the Netherlands. Ahold sold its stake in Kobalt Media Services B.V. in December 2007.
- Loyalty Management Nederland B.V., an associate of Ahold that renders services relating to the management of customer loyalty programs to certain Ahold subsidiaries in the Netherlands.
- A.M.S. Coffee Trading, an associate of Ahold that generates sales transactions with Ahold Coffee Company.
- Several related parties of Schuitema render services in support of certain projects of franchisees and associated food retailers serviced by Schuitema.

Ahold Dutch managers and employees

In January 1994, a group of Ahold's Dutch managers and employees acquired a EUR 15 capital investment in the Dutch Customer Fund, an independent investment fund that primarily invested all of its assets in Ahold's shares and debt. The capital investment had previously been held by Het Weerpad B.V., an investment company of the Heijn family, founders of Ahold.

Ahold made loans to this group of managers and employees to assist them with their investment in the Dutch Customer Fund. In July 1996 and April 1998, additional loans were granted to Ahold's Dutch managers and employees to purchase additional investments in the Dutch Customer Fund. For more information on these loans, see Note 18.

BNP Paribas (Registration Document 2007), pages 211-217

8.d RELATED PARTIES (in part)

8.d.3 Relations with key management personnel

Remuneration and benefits awarded to the Group's corporate officers

Remuneration and benefits policy relating to the Group's corporate officers

Remuneration paid to the Group's corporate officers

- The remuneration paid to the Group's corporate officers is determined by the method recommended by the Compensation Committee and approved by the Board of Directors.
- This remuneration comprises both a fixed and a variable component, the levels of which are determined using market benchmarks established by firms specialised in surveys of executive remuneration in the European banking sector.
- The variable component is determined by reference to a basic bonus which is calculated as a proportion of the officer's fixed remuneration and varies in line with Group performance criteria as well as the attainment of personal objectives.
- Group performance criteria account for 70% of the basic bonus and comprise parameters including earnings per share, core business pre-tax net income, and the fulfilment of gross operating income targets at consolidated and core business level.
- Personnel objective-based criteria concern managerial performance as assessed by the Board of Directors. The Board's assessment is made in view of the foresight, decision-making and leadership skills shown by the officer in implementing the Group's strategy and preparing its future. These criteria are clearly defined and account for 30% of the basic bonus.
- The variable component of corporate officers' remuneration is capped at a level set in proportion to the basic remuneration, and since 2005 has been paid in full during the following year.
- The Chairman of the Board of Directors, the Chief Executive Officer and the Chief Operating Officers do not receive any remuneration from Group companies except BNP Paribas SA.

Post-employment benefits

Compensation on termination of office

Corporate officers are not entitled to any contractual compensation on termination of office.

Retirement bonuses

Michel Pébereau is not entitled to a retirement bonus. Baudouin Prot (Chief Executive Officer), Georges Chodron de Courcel and Jean Clamon (Chief Operating Officers) are entitled under their employment contracts to the standard retirement bonus benefits awarded to all BNP Paribas employees. Under this standard scheme, employees receive a bonus on retirement from the Group of up to 11.66 months' basic salary, depending on their initial contractual position and length of service at their retirement date.

Pension plans

- The defined benefit plans previously granted to executive managers of the Group who were formerly employed by BNP, Paribas or Compagnie Bancaire have all been converted into top-up type plans. The amounts allocated to the beneficiaries were fixed when the previous schemes were closed to new entrants.
- A similar procedure was applied to Michel Pébereau (Chairman of the Board of Directors), Baudouin Prot (Chief Executive Officer), and to Georges Chodron de Courcel and Jean Clamon (Chief Operating Officers). Pursuant to articles L. 137.11 and R. 137.16 of the French Social Security Code, these four corporate officers now belong to a contingent collective top-up pension plan. Under this plan, their pensions will be calculated (subject to their still being part of the Group on retirement) on the basis of the fixed and variable remuneration received in 1999 and 2000, with no possibility of acquiring any subsequent rights.
- The amount of retirement benefits, including the pensions paid out by the general French Social Security scheme and the ARRCO and AGIRC top-up schemes, plus any additional banking industry pension arising from the industry-wide agreement that took effect on 1 January 1994 and pension rights acquired as a result of payments by the employer into top-up funded schemes, is capped at 50% of the above-mentioned remuneration amounts.

BNP Paribas (Registration Document 2007) (continued)

- These retirement benefits will be revalued from 1 January 2002 until their actual payment date, based on the average annual rate of increase in pension benefits paid by the French Social Security, ARRCO and AGIRC schemes. On payment of the benefits, the top-up pensions will be equal to the differential between these revalued amounts and the pension benefits provided by the above-mentioned general and top-up schemes. Once the amount of these top-up benefits has been finally determined, the benefit will then be indexed to the growth rate in the benefit value per point under the AGIRC scheme.

- These obligations were covered by provisions recorded by BNP or Paribas as appropriate. The amount of these provisions was adjusted when the legacy plans were closed and the obligations transferred to an external insurance company.

- The Chairman of the Board of Directors, the Chief Executive Officer and the Chief Operating Officers belong to the defined-contribution pension plan set up for all BNP Paribas SA employees, in accordance with article 83 of the French General Tax Code.

Welfare benefit plans

- The Chairman of the Board of Directors, the Chief Executive Officer and the Chief Operating Officers are entitled to the same flexible welfare benefits (death and disability cover) as all BNP Paribas SA employees.

- They are also entitled to the same benefits under the Garantie Vie Professionnelle Accidents death/disability cover plan as all BNP Paribas SA employees, and to the supplementary plan set up for members of the Group Executive Committee, which pays out additional capital of EUR 1.08 million in the event of work-related death or total and permanent disability.

- If Baudouin Prot, Georges Chodron de Courcel or Jean Clamon die before the age of 60, their heirs will receive compensation under an insurance policy. The premium applicable under this policy is paid by the Group and treated in accordance with the social security rules applicable to employers' contributions to top-up welfare schemes in France.

Amount of remuneration and benefits awarded to the Group's corporate officers.

BNP Paribas (Registration Document 2007) (continued)

REMUNERATION PAYABLE TO THE GROUP'S CORPORATE OFFICERS FOR 2007

The tables below show (i) gross remuneration payable to the Group's corporate officers for the year to 31 December 2007, including benefits in kind and directors' fees; and (ii) gross remuneration paid in 2007, including benefits in kind and directors' fees.

Remuneration payable for 2007 In euros	Remuneration				
	Fixed[1]	Variable [2]	Directors' fees[3]	Benefits in kind[4]	TOTAL Remuneration
Michel Pébereau					
Chairman of the Board of Directors					
2007	700,000	875,000	29,728	2,490	1,607,218
(2006)	(700,000)	(1,051,070)	(29,728)	(4,609)	(1,785,407)
Baudouin Prot					
Chief Executive Officer					
2007	900,000	2,272,608	142,278	5,362	3,320,248
(2006)	(883,333)	(2,324,348)	(129,551)	(5,227)	(3,342,459)
Georges Chodron de Courcel					
Chief Operating Officer					
2007	545,833	1,772,120	147,977	4,271	2,470,201
(2006)	(500,000)	(1,631,593)	(125,189)	(4,274)	(2,261,056)
Jean Clamon					
Chief Operating Officer					
2007	460,000	702,255	139,690	4,703	1,306,648
(2006)	(460,000)	(796,130)	(130,637)	(4,703)	(1,391,470)
Total remuneration payable to the Group's corporate officers for 2007					8,704,315
(for 2006)					(8,780,392)

(1) Remuneration actually paid in 2007.

(2) Variable remuneration payable for 2006 and 2007, paid the following year. The amount due to Michel Pébereau in respect of 2007 has been capped in accordance with the provisions on restrictions placed on the variable remuneration payable to corporate officers.

(3) The Chairman of the Board of Directors and the Chief Executive Officer do not receive directors' fees from any Group companies other than from BNP Paribas SA, and from Erbé and BNL in the case of the Chief Executive Officer. Directors' fees received in 2007 by the Chief Executive Officer from Erbé and BNL will be deducted from the variable remuneration paid to him in 2008.

Georges Chodron de Courcel receives fees in his capacity as a director of BNP Paribas Suisse, BNL and Erbé. Jean Clamon receives fees in his capacity as a director of Cetelem, BNP Paribas Lease Group, Paribas International, Erbé, CNP and BNL. The fees received by Georges Chodron de Courcel and Jean Clamon in their capacity as directors of these companies will be deducted from the variable remuneration paid to them in 2008.

(4) The Chairman of the Board of Directors, the Chief Executive Officer and the Chief Operating Officers each have a company car and a mobile telephone.

BNP Paribas (Registration Document 2007) (continued)

REMUNERATION PAID TO THE GROUP'S CORPORATE OFFICERS IN 2007

Remuneration payable for 2007 In euros	Remuneration			Directors' fees	Benefits in kind	TOTAL Remuneration[5]
	Fixed	Variable	Deferred[1]			
Michel Pébereau						
Chairman of the Board of Directors						
2007	700,000	1,051,070	247,940	29,728	2,490	2,031,228
(2006)	(700,000)	(1,081,601)	(385,414)	(29,728)	(4,609)	(2,201,352)
Baudouin Prot						
Chief Executive Officer						
2007 [2]	900,000	2,233,999	277,830	143,418	5,362	3,560,609
(2006)	(883,333)	(1,817,599)	(325,940)	(120,078)	(5,227)	(3,152,177)
Georges Chodron de Courcel						
Chief Operating Officer						
2007[3]	545,833	1,519,045	249,030	149,117	4,271	2,467,296
(2006)	(500,000)	(1,316,247)	(323,920)	(112,548)	(4,274)	(2,256,989)
Jean Clamon						
Chief Operating Officer						
2007 [4]	460,000	704,122	89,030	172,393	4,703	1,430,248
(2006)	(460,000)	(567,370)	(120,130)	(92,008)	(4,703)	(1,244,211)
Total remuneration payable to the Group's corporate officers for 2007						9,489,381
(for 2006)						(8,854,729)

(1) Corresponding to the transfer of the final third of the deferred bonus awarded in 2003 in the form of BNP Paribas shares and to the second third of the 2004 deferred bonus in cash.

(2) Baudoin Prot's variable remuneration in respect of 2006 paid in 2007 was reduced by EUR 90,349, corresponding to directors' fees received in 2006.

(3) Georges Chodron de Courcel's variable remuneration in respect of 2006 paid in 2007, was reduced by EUR 112,548 corresponding to directors' fees received in 2006.

(4) Jean Clamon's variable remuneration in respect of 2006 paid in 2007, was reduced by EUR 92,008, corresponding to directors' fees received in 2006.

(5) The average payroll tax rate on this remuneration was 31.6% in 2007 (30.7% in 2006).

BENEFITS AWARDED TO THE GROUP'S CORPORATE OFFICERS

Benefits awarded to the Group's corporate officers	2007	2006
Post-employment benefits		
Retirement bonuses		
Present value of the benefit obligation	524,901	499,556
Contingent collective defined-benefit top-up pension plan		
Total present value of the benefit obligation	30,5 M	30,9 M
Defined contribution pension plan		
Contributions paid by the company during the year	1,416	1,367
Welfare benefits		
Flexible personal risk plan		
Premiums paid by the company during the year	10,312	9,954
Garantie Vie Professionnelle Accidents death/disability cover plan		
Premiums paid by the company during the year	9,365	9,366
Supplementary personal risk plan		
Premiums paid by the company during the year	229,924	224,219

BNP Paribas (Registration Document 2007) (continued)
Stock subscription option plans

Under the authorisation granted by the Extraordinary General Meeting of 18 May 2005, BNP Paribas set up a Global Share-based Incentive Plan, which combines stock options with share awards. The provisions of this plan were approved by the Board of Directors and apply in full to the corporate officers.

In principle, the Board of Directors grants stock options to the Group's corporate officers on an annual basis. The options do not carry a discount. The plans are subject to vesting conditions under which a portion of the options granted is conditional upon the performance of the BNP Paribas share relative to the Euro Stoxx Bank index. This relative performance is measured at the end of the second, third and fourth years of the compulsory holding period. Depending on the results of this measurement, the exercise price of the portion of the options subject to this performance-related condition may be increased or their exercise may be deemed null and void.

Stock options are granted to corporate officers as a long-term incentive, in accordance with shareholders' interests. The number of options granted to corporate officers is determined by the Board of Directors using market benchmarks established by firms specialised in surveys of executive remuneration in the European banking sector.

Corporate officers are not entitled to share awards.

The table below shows the number and the valuation of stock subscription options granted to and/or exercised by the Group's corporate officers in 2007.

Stock subscription options granted to and/or exercised by the Group's corporate officers	Number of options granted/ exercised	Exercise price (in euros)	Grant date	Plan expiry date	Individual allocation valuation		
					in euros[1]	as a % of the recognised expense[2]	as a % of share capital
OPTIONS GRANTED IN 2007							
Michel Pébereau	50,000	82.70	03/08/2007	03/06/2015	703,450	0.600%	0.005%
Baudouin Prot	170,000	82.70	03/08/2007	03/06/2015	2,403,420	2.100%	0.018%
Georges Chodron de Courcel	90,000	82.70	03/08/2007	03/06/2015	1,266,210	1.100%	0.010%
Jean Clamon	65,000	82.70	03/08/2007	03/06/2015	914,485	0.800%	0.007%
Aggregate					5,287,565	4.600%	0.040%
OPTIONS EXERCISED IN 2007							
Michel Pébereau	60,000	36.95	05/13/1998	05/13/2008			
Baudouin Prot	40,000	36.95	05/13/1998	05/13/2008			
Baudouin Prot	36,000	18.29	05/22/1997	05/22/2007			
Baudouin Prot	14,438	18.29	05/22/1997	05/22/2007			
Georges Chodron de Courcel	56,000	36.78	03/21/2003	03/20/2013			
Georges Chodron de Courcel	8,069	38.62	03/21/2003	03/20/2013			
Georges Chodron de Courcel	8,069	38.62	03/21/2003	03/20/2013			
Jean Clamon	1,266	48.57	05/15/2001	05/14/2011			
Jean Clamon	15,000	48.57	05/15/2001	05/14/2011			
OPTIONS GRANTED IN 2006							
Michel Pébereau	100,000	75.25	04/05/2006	04/04/2014	1,496,100	1.600%	0.011%
Baudouin Prot	180,000	75.25	04/05/2006	04/04/2014	2,692,980	2.800%	0.019%
Georges Chodron de Courcel	90,000	75.25	04/05/2006	04/04/2014	1,346,490	1.400%	0.010%
Jean Clamon	65,000	75.25	04/05/2006	04/04/2014	972,465	1.000%	0.007%
Aggregate					6,508,035	6.800%	0.047%
OPTIONS EXERCISED IN 2006							
Michel Pébereau	20,000	18.45	05/22/1997	05/22/2007			
Michel Pébereau	30,263	18.29	05/22/1997	05/22/2007			
Georges Chodron de Courcel	5,000	37.64	05/03/1999	05/03/2009			
Georges Chodron de Courcel	80,710	48.57	05/15/2001	05/14/2011			
Jean Clamon	60,523	44.77	12/22/1999	12/22/2009			
Jean Clamon	70,623	20.23	11/17/1998	11/17/2006			

(1) The stock options granted in 2007 which were not subject to performance conditions have been valued for accounting purposes at EUR 14.57 each (EUR 15.36 in 2006).

The stock options granted in 2007 which were subject to performance conditions have been valued for accounting purposes at EUR 12.90 each (EUR 14.03 in 2006).

(2) % of the expense recognised for the Global Share-based Incentive Plan, which combines stock options with share awards.

BNP Paribas (Registration Document 2007) (continued)

The table below shows the number of outstanding options held by the Group's corporate officers at 31 December 2007.

Originating company	BNP	BNP	BNP Paribas	BNP Paribas	BNP Paribas	BNP Paribas	BNP Paribas
Date of grant	05/13/1998	12/22/1999	05/15/2001	03/21/2003	03/25/2005	04/05/2006	03/08/2007
Number of options outstanding at end-2007	91,698	353,050	407,454	492,738	353,081	435,000	375,000

Compulsory share ownership – Holding period for shares received on exercise of stock options

As from 1 January 2007, the Group's corporate officers are required to own a minimum number of shares for the duration of their term of office, calculated based on both the opening BNP Paribas share price and their fixed remuneration at 2 January 2007. The number of shares must correspond to seven years' fixed remuneration for Michel Pébereau (58,700 shares) and Baudouin Prot (75,500 shares) and five years' fixed remuneration for Georges Chodron de Courcel (30,000 shares) and Jean Clamon (27,600 shares). This obligation must be complied with by 13 February 2010 at the latest.

The Chairman of the Board of Directors, Chief Executive Officer and Chief Operating Officers are also required to hold a quantity of shares issued following the exercise of stock options for the duration of their term of office. This holding requirement represents 50% of the net gain realised on the purchase of shares under options granted as from 1 January 2007, and will be considered as satisfied once the threshold defined for compulsory share ownership has been reached based on shares resulting from the exercise of options as of said date.

Remuneration and benefits awarded to employee elected directors

Total remuneration paid in 2007 to employee-elected directors – calculated based on their actual attendance – amounted to EUR 81,045 in 2007 (EUR 89,942 in 2006), excluding directors' fees. The total amount of directors' fees paid in 2007 to employee-elected directors was EUR 69,103 (EUR 76,551 in 2006). These sums were paid directly to the trade union bodies of the directors concerned.

Employee-elected directors are entitled to the same death/disability cover and the same Garantie Vie Professionnelle Accidents benefits as all BNP Paribas SA employees. The total amount of premiums paid into these schemes by BNP Paribas in 2007 on behalf of the employee-elected directors was EUR 1,026 (EUR 989 in 2006).

The employee-elected directors belong to the defined-contribution plan set up for all BNP Paribas SA employees, in accordance with article 83 of the French General Tax Code. The total amount of contributions paid into this plan by BNP Paribas in 2007 on behalf of the employee-elected directors was EUR 649 (EUR 639 in 2006). Employee-elected directors are also entitled to top-up banking industry pensions under the industrywide agreement that took effect on 1 January 1994.

Loans, advances and guarantees granted to the Group's corporate officers

At 31 December 2007, total outstanding loans granted directly or indirectly to the Group's corporate officers amounted to EUR 6,340,882 (EUR 4,095,895 at 31 December 2006).

Commentary: These two extracts illustrate the disclosure of key management personnel compensation, which includes the disclosure of total key management personnel compensation and separate disclosures for short-term employee benefits, post-employment benefits, other long-term benefits, termination benefits and share-based payment. In addition to this information, both extracts provide information about relationships with key management personnel that goes beyond the minimum disclosure requirements by divulging details of the compensation awarded to individual members of key management personnel, and the terms and conditions of their compensation.

In the first extract, Ahold defines "key management" in accordance with IAS 24 and identifies the members of the Supervisory Board, members of the Corporate Executive Board, the continental Chief Operating Officers and Senior Vice Presidents as key management.

The company names the members of the Corporate Executive Board, discloses details of their employment contracts, and presents details of their remuneration for the current year, which consisted of a base salary, bonuses, share-based compensation, pensions, termination benefits and other compensation.

Ahold also discloses the remuneration awarded to members of the Supervisory Board, and other key management personnel.

In the second extract, BNP Paribas identifies its corporate officers and employee-elected directors as key management.

The company lists the names of its corporate officers and discloses the nature of their compensation, which consists of remuneration, post-employment benefits and stock options. The company presents details on the fixed remuneration, variable remuneration, deferred remuneration, directors' fees, benefits in kind, post-employment benefits, welfare benefits and stock options awarded to its corporate officers in the current fiscal year.

BNP Paribas also discloses the remuneration awarded to employee-elected directors.

FUTURE DEVELOPMENTS

The IASB has issued the following Exposure Drafts:

- *Proposed amendments to IAS 24, Related Party Disclosures – State-controlled Entities and the Definition of a Related Party*, on February 22, 2007, which was open for comment until May 25, 2007; and

- *Relationships with the State – Proposed amendments to IAS 24*, on December 11, 2008, which will be open for comment until March 13, 2009.

The changes proposed in the Exposure Drafts would amend the definition of a related party and exempt some state-controlled entities from related party disclosures. The proposed changes to the definition of a related party are described in further detail in the following paragraphs.

An Associate of the Subsidiary's Controlling Investor

IAS 24 requires disclosure of transactions between an associate and a subsidiary of an investor in the individual or separate financial statements of the associate, but not in the individual or separate financial statements of the subsidiary. The proposed changes to the definition of a related party will ensure that an entity's associate and subsidiary are deemed to be related parties for their individual or separate financial statements. Similarly, if the investor is a person who significantly influences one entity and controls another entity, those entities will be considered to be related parties.

Two Associates of a Person

IAS 24 does not consider associates to be related to each other if the investor is an entity. If a person significantly influences one entity, however, and a close member of that person's family significantly influences another, those entities are currently considered to be related to each other. The amendment to the definition of a related party will exclude such entities, thereby ensuring consistent treatment of all associates.

Investments of Members of Key Management Personnel

Although IAS 24 treats some investees of the key management personnel of a reporting entity as related to that entity, IAS 24 does not include the reciprocal of this (i.e., the reporting entity is not considered to be a related party in the financial statements of the investee). The proposed amendment will include these entities in the definition of a related party in both sets of financial statements.

Two Entities of a Person with Joint Control

The proposed changes to the definition of a related party will treat two entities as related to each other whenever a person or a third entity has joint control over one entity and that person (or a close member of that person's family) or the third entity has joint control or significant influence over the other entity or has significant voting power in it.

The IASB expects to publish the amendments in the second half of 2009.

COMPREHENSIVE EXAMPLES

This section presents two comprehensive disclosure examples. We have selected relevant extracts to illustrate the disclosure of related party relationships, transactions and balances in accordance with IFRS.

Ansell Limited – All extracts 18(A) were obtained from the 2007 financial report.

Extract 18(A1) – Ansell Limited, page 66

This extract discloses related party information by reference to other notes.

---

30. Related Party Disclosures

(a) Subsidiaries

Ansell Limited is the parent entity of all entities detailed in Note 32 and from time to time has dealings on normal commercial terms and conditions with those entities, the effects of which are eliminated in the consolidated financial statements.

Refer to the following Notes for additional information:

Note 2 Total Revenue - Dividends and interest received or receivable from subsidiaries

Note 10 Trade and Other Receivables - Amounts owing by subsidiaries

Note 13 Other Financial Assets - Investments in subsidiaries

Note 17 Trade and Other Payables - Amounts owing to subsidiaries

(b) Key management personnel

Disclosures relating to key management personnel are set out in Note 26.

(c) Other Related Company

Effective 25 January 2006, the Group disposed of its interest in South Pacific Tyres N.Z. Ltd. Up until the date of disposal, the Group received royalties from South Pacific Tyres N.Z. Ltd. as detailed below:

	Consolidated		The Company	
$ in millions	2007	2006	2007	2006
Royalty revenue				
South Pacific Tyres N.Z. Ltd.	-	0.4	-	-

(d) Partnership

Effective 28 January 2006, the Group disposed of its share of the South Pacific Tyres partnership. Up until the date of disposal the Group conducted financial transactions with South Pacific Tyres on normal commercial terms and conditions being:

	Consolidated		The Company	
$ in millions	2007	2006	2007	2006
Other revenue				
South Pacific Tyres	-	2.4	-	-

Extract 18(A2) – Ansell Limited, pages 67-69

This extract lists the names of subsidiaries under the control of Ansell Ltd.

32. Particulars Relating to Subsidiaries

	Country of Incorporation	Beneficial Interest	
		2007 %	2006 %
Ansell Limited	Australia		
Ansell Healthcare Japan Co. Ltd.	*Japan	100	100
Ansell Japan Limited	*Japan	100	-
Ativ Pac Pty. Ltd.	Australia	100	100
BNG Battery Technologies Pty. Ltd.	Australia	100	100
Cliburn Investments Pty. Ltd.	Australia	100	100
Dexboy International Pty. Ltd.	Australia	100	100
Corrvas Insurance Pty. Ltd.	Australia	100	100
Dunlop Olympic Manufacturing Pty. Ltd.	Australia	100	100
FGDP Pty. Ltd.	Australia	100	100
H.C. Sleigh Services Pty. Ltd.	Australia	100	100
N Harvesters Pty. Ltd.	Australia	100	100
PSL Industries Pty. Ltd.	Australia	100	100
International Better Brands Pty Ltd	Australia	100	100
Licknib Pty. Ltd.	Australia	100	100
Nucleus Ltd.	Australia	100	100
Lifetec Project Pty. Ltd.	Australia	100	100
Medical TPLC Pty. Ltd.	Australia	100	100
N&T Pty. Ltd.	Australia	100	100
Nucleus Trading Pte. Ltd.	*Singapore	100	100
THLD Ltd.	Australia	100	100
TNC Holdings Pte. Ltd.	*Singapore	100	100
TPLC Pty. Ltd.	Australia	100	100
Societe de Management Financier S.A.	*France	100	100
Olympic General Products Pty. Ltd.	Australia	100	100
Foamlite (Australia), pty. Ltd.	Australia	100	100

32. Particulars Relating to Subsidiaries (continued)

	Country of Incorporation	Beneficial Interest 2007 %	Beneficial Interest 2006 %
Pacific Distribution Properties Pty. Ltd.	Australia	100	100
Pacific Dunlop Finance Pty. Ltd.	Australia	100	100
Pacific Dunlop Holdings (China) Co. Ltd.	*China	100	100
Ansell (Shanghai) Commercial and Trading Co. Ltd.	*China	100	100
Pacific Dunlop Linings Pty. Ltd.	Australia	100	100
P.D. Holdings Pty. Ltd.	Australia	100	100
P.D. International Pty. Ltd.	Australia	100	100
Ansell Canada Inc.	*Canada	100	100
Ansell Lanka (Pvt.) Ltd.	*Sri Lanka	100	100
Ansell Participacoes Ltda.	*Brazil	100	-
Fabrica de Artefatos de Latex Blowtex Ltda.	*Brazil	100	-
Ansell Services (Asia) Sdn. Bhd.	*Malaysia	100	100
Ansell Ambi Sdn. Bhd.	*Malaysia	100	100
Ansell (Kedah) Sdn. Bhd.	*Malaysia	100	100
Ansell (Kulim) Sdn. Bhd.	*Malaysia	100	100
Ansell Malaysia Sdn. Bhd.	*Malaysia	75	75
Ansell Medical Sdn. Bhd.	*Malaysia	75	75
Ansell N.P. Sdn. Bhd.	*Malaysia	75	75
Ansell Shah Alam Sdn. Bhd.	*Malaysia	100	100
Ansell (Thailand) Ltd.	*Thailand	100	100
CE Gloves (India) Limited	*India	(a) 100	100
Corrvas Insurance (Singapore), pte. Ltd.	*Singapore	100	100
Llesna Healthcare Pty. Ltd.	Australia	100	100
Medical Telectronics N.V.	*Netherlands Ant.	100	100
Mt Waverley Estates Pty. Ltd.	Australia	100	100
Pacific Dunlop Holdings (Europe) Ltd.	*U.K.	100	100
Ansell Healthcare Europe N.V.	*Belgium	100	100
Ansell GmbH	*Germany	100	100
Ansell Italy Srl	* Italy	100	100
Ansell S.A.	*France	100	100
Ansell Spain SL (Sociedad de Responsabilidad Limitada)	*Spain	100	100
Medical Telectronics Holding & Finance (Holland) B.V.	*Netherlands	100	100
Unimil SA	*Poland	100	-
Condomi Erfurt Produktions GmbH	*Germany	76	-
Mpt Med Production and Trading GmbH	*Germany	100	-
Condomi France SAS	*France	100	-
Condomi Health International GmbH	*Germany	100	-
Ansell UK Limited	*U.K.	100	100
Pacific Dunlop Holdings (Singapore), pte. Ltd.	*Singapore	100	100
JK Ansell Ltd.	*India	(b) 50	(b) 50
Pacific Dunlop (Hong Kong) Limited.	*Hong Kong	100	100
Pacific Dunlop Investments (USA) Inc.	*USA	100	100
Ansell Brazil LTDA	*Brazil	100	100

32. Particulars Relating to Subsidiaries (continued)

	Country of Incorporation	Beneficial Interest 2007 %	2006 %
Ansell Edmont Industrial de Mexico S.A. de C.V.	*Mexico	100	100
Ansell Perry de Mexico S.A. de C.V.	*Mexico	100	100
Commercializadora GNK S.A de C.V.	*Mexico	100	100
Golden Needles de Mexico S.A de C.V.	*Mexico	100	100
Pacific Dunlop Holdings (USA) Inc.	*USA	100	100
Ansell Healthcare Products LLC.	*USA	100	100
Ansell Protective Products Inc.	*USA	100	100
Pacific Chloride Inc.	*USA	100	100
Pacific Dunlop Holdings Inc.	*USA	100	100
Pacific Dunlop USA Inc.	*USA	100	100
TPLC Holdings Inc.	*USA	100	100
Accufix Research Institute Inc.	*USA	100	100
TPLC S.A.	*France	100	100
Cotac Corporation	*USA	100	100
Pacific Dunlop Finance Company Inc.	*USA	100	100
PDOCB Pty. Ltd.	Australia	100	100
Ansell Medical Products Pvt. Ltd.	*India	100	100
Suretex Ltd.	*Thailand	100	100
Latex Investments Ltd.	Mauritius	100	100
Suretex Prophylactics (India) Ltd.	*India	100	100
STX Prophylactics S.A .(Pty.) Ltd.	*Sth Africa	100	100
Wuhan Jissbon Sanitary Products Company Ltd.	*China	(c) 75	(c) 75
Dongguan Junwen Trading Co. Ltd.	*China	(d) 90	(d) 90
Guangzhou Kangwei Trading Co. Ltd.	*China	(d) 90	(d) 90
PD Licensing Pty. Ltd.	Australia	100	100
PD Shared Services Pty. Ltd.	Australia	100	100
PD Shared Services Holdings Pty. Ltd.	Australia	100	100
Siteprints Pty. Ltd.	Australia	100	100
S.T.P. (Hong Kong) Ltd.	*Hong Kong	100	100
Pacific Dunlop Holdings N.V.	*Netherlands Ant.	100	100
Pacific Dunlop (Netherlands) B.V.	*Netherlands	100	100
Textile Industrial Design & Engineering Pty. Ltd.	Australia	100	100
The Distribution Group Holdings Pty. Ltd.	Australia	100	100
The Distribution Group Pty. Ltd.	Australia	(e) 100	(e) 100
Nwodhsa Enterprises (Wholesale), pty. Ltd.	Australia	100	100
TDG Warehousing Pty. Ltd.	Australia	100	100
The Distribution Trust	Australia	100	100
Union Knitting Mills Pty. Ltd.	Australia	100	100
Xelo Pty. Ltd.	Australia	100	100
Xelo Sacof Pty. Ltd.	Australia	100	100

Subsidiary Liquidated during the year

TPLC Medizinprodukte GmbH.	*Germany	-	100

* Subsidiaries incorporated outside Australia carry on business in those countries.

(a) Owned 74.9% by P.D. International Pty. Ltd. and 25.1% by Suretex Prophylactics (India) Ltd.

(b) Ansell Healthcare has day-to-day management control of this entity.

(c) Owned 34.2% by P.D. International Pty. Ltd. and 40.8% by Pacific Dunlop Holdings (China) Co. Ltd.

(d) Owned 90% by Wuhan Jissbon Sanitary Products Company Ltd.

(e) The trustee of The Distribution Trust is The Distribution Group Pty. Ltd. The beneficiary of the trust is Ansell Limited.

Extract 18(A3) – Ansell Limited, page 41

This extract separately discloses amounts receivable from subsidiaries.

10. Trade and Other Receivables	Consolidated		The Company	
$ in millions	2007	2006	2007	2006
Current				
Trade debtors	223.5	227.5	19.6	19.9
Less provision for impairment	9.3	7.3	0.3	0.5
Less provision for rebates and allowances	24.3	23.5	4.1	3.9
	189.9	196.7	15.2	15.5
Amounts owing by subsidiaries	-	-	943.9	831.5
Less provision for impairment	-	-	699.8	699.8
Other amounts receivable	17.9	24.8	1.8	4.7
Total Current	**207.8**	**221.5**	**261.1**	**151.9**
Non-Current				
Other amounts receivable	18.1	19.8	-	1.2
Total Non-Current	**18.1**	**19.8**	**-**	**1.2**
Total Receivables	**225.9**	**241.3**	**261.1**	**153.1**

The reconciliations of provision for impairment - trade debtors are presented below:

$ in millions	Consolidated		The Company	
	2007	2006	2007	2006
Balance at the beginning of the financial year	7.3	5.8	0.5	0.6
Amounts charged/(credited) to the income statement	(0.5)	0.9	(0.2)	-
Amounts utilised for intended purposes	(0.4)	(0.1)	-	(0.1)
Acquired entities	3.6	0.3	-	-
Net exchange differences on translation of foreign operations	(0.7)	0.4	-	-
Balance at the end of the financial year	**9.3**	**7.3**	**0.3**	**0.5**

Extract 18(A4) – Ansell Limited, page 42

This extract presents investments in the subsidiaries, which only need be disclosed in the separate financial statements.

13. Other Financial Assets (Investments)	Consolidated		The Company	
$ in millions	2007	2006	2007	2006
Shares in Subsidiaries				
Subsidiaries				
Not quoted on a prescribed stock exchange:				
At cost	-	-	2,161.8	2,161.8
Less Provision for impairment	-	-	698.5	698.5
Total Other Financial Assets	**-**	**-**	**1,463.3**	**1,463.3**

Extract 18(A5) – Ansell Limited, page 46

This extract separately discloses amounts payable to subsidiaries.

17. Trade and Other Payables	Consolidated		The Company	
$ in millions	2007	2006	2007	2006
Current				
Amounts owing to subsidiaries	-	-	878.9	609.9
Trade creditors	122.2	126.1	5.4	5.1
Other creditors	31.9	16.0	4.7	6.1
Total Current	**154.1**	**142.1**	**889.0**	**621.1**
Non-Current				
Other creditors	0.5	0.7	-	-
Total Non-Current	**0.5**	**0.7**	**-**	**-**
Total Payables	**154.6**	**142.8**	**889.0**	**621.1**

Extract 18(A6) – Ansell Limited, pages 57-62

This extract lists the names and roles of key management personnel, and discloses key management personnel compensation in accordance with IAS 24.

---

26. Key Management Personnel Disclosures

This note is to be read in conjunction with the Remuneration Report.

Key Management Personnel

The following were key management personnel of the Group during the financial year:

Non-Executive Directors

Peter L Barnes	Chairman
Glenn L L Barnes	
Ronald J S Bell	
L Dale Crandall	
Herbert J Elliott (retired 18 October 2006)	
Marissa T Peterson (appointed 22 August 2006)	

Mr W Peter Day was appointed a non-executive director on 20 August 2007.

Executive Director

Douglas D Tough	Managing Director and Chief Executive Officer

Other Key Management Personnel

Phil W Corke	Senior Vice President, Human Resources and Communications
Scott R Corriveau[1]	Chief Strategy and Global Marketing Officer (appointed 1 July 2006)
Werner J Heintz	Senior Vice President and Regional Director, Europe, Middle East and Africa
Rustom F Jilla	Senior Vice President and Chief Financial Officer
Neil R O'Donnell	Senior Vice President and Regional Director, Asia Pacific (retired 31 December 2006)
Scott Papier	Regional Director, Professional/Consumer, Americas (appointed 1 July 2006)
William J Reed	Senior Vice President and Regional Director, Occupational, Americas
William G Reilly Jnr	Senior Vice President and Legal Counsel

(1) Mr Corriveau's role of Head of Business Development was expanded on 1 July 2006 to include responsibility for Occupational new product development and in March 2007 was further expanded to encompass responsibility for Global Marketing across the three businesses.

Key Management Personnel Remuneration in whole $	Consolidated		The Company	
	2007	2006	2007	2006
Short-term benefits	8,199,680	6,691,726	817,513	969,266
Post-employment benefits	863,707	813,580	49,455	86,534
Termination benefits	97,113	-	97,113	-
Share-based payments	4,426,934	2,061,613	49,639	126,855
	13,587,434	9,566,919	1,013,720	1,182,655

Details of remuneration
Directors of Ansell Limited

Details of the remuneration of all directors of Ansell Limited is set out in the following tables:

2007	Short-term Benefits			Post Employment Benefits	Termination Benefits	Share-based Payments	
	Cash salary and fees	Cash bonus	Non-monetary benefits	Superannuation Contributions		Options, Performance Share Rights and Performance Rights	Total
	$	$		$	$	$	$
Non-executive							
P L Barnes	216,562	-	-	19,490	-	-	236,052
G L L Barnes	105,200	-	-	-	-	-	105,200
R J S Bell	95,242	-	-	3,675	-	-	98,917
L D Crandall	103,455	-	-	4,455	-	-	107,910
H J Elliott	29,632	-	-	8,029	-	-	37,661
M T Peterson	80,260	-	-	3,456	-	-	83,716
Executive							
D D Tough (CEO and Managing Director)	914,738	1,109,838	195,551	252,738	-	1,390,762	3,863,627
Total	1,545,089	1,109,838	195,551	291,843	-	1,390,762	4,533,083

2006	Short-term Benefits			Post Employment Benefits	Termination Benefits	Share-based Payments	
	Cash salary and fees	Cash bonus	Non-monetary benefits	Superannuation Contributions		Options, Performance Share Rights and Performance Rights	Total
	$	$	$	$	$	$	$
Non-executive							
P L Barnes	206,879	-	-	18,707	-	-	225,586
G L L Barnes	77,715	-	-	-	-	-	77,715
R J S Bell	85,736	-	-	2,928	-	-	88,664
L D Crandall	98,145	-	-	8,833	-	-	106,978
H J Elliott	97,538	-	11,774	8,778	-	-	118,090
M J McConnell	32,827	-	-	2,954	-	-	35,781
E D Tweddell	21,484	-	-	1,934	-	-	23,418
Executive							
D D Tough (CEO and Managing Director)	984,164	1,059,949	189,936	229,062	-	637,804	3,100,915
Total	1,604,488	1,059,949	201,710	273,196	-	637,804	3,777,147

Other Key Management Personnel

Details of the remuneration of each of the Other Key Management Personnel of the Group are set out in the following tables:

2007	Short-term Benefits			Post Employment Benefits	Termination Benefits	Share-based Payments	Total
	Cash salary and fees	Cash bonus	Non-monetary benefits	Superannuation Contributions		Options, Performance Share Rights and Performance Rights	
	$	$	$	$	$	$	$
P W Corke	308,878	249,834	51,870	65,598	-	389,470	1,065,650
S R Corriveau	284,641	230,616	190,245	28,800		274,555	1,008,857
W Heintz	510,440	447,400	57,310	145,134		268,015	1,428,299
R F Jilla	454,992	465,807	46,073	110,590	-	819,485	1,896,947
N R O'Donnell	115,000	54,683	17,479	10,350	97,113	49,639	344,264
S Papier	296,621	147,270	38,152	53,267		377,671	912,981
W Reed	336,265	291,028	77,843	78,418		420,684	1,204,238
W G Reilly	355,859	288,269	32,627	79,707	-	436,653	1,193,115
Total	2,662,696	2,174,907	511,599	571,864	97,113	3,036,172	9,054,351

2006	Short-term Benefits			Post Employment Benefits	Termination Benefits	Share-based Payments	Total
	Cash salary and fees	Cash bonus	Non-monetary benefits	Superannuation Contributions		Options, Performance Share Rights and Performance Rights	
	$	$	$	$	$	$	$
P W Corke	332,906	214,854	58,925	71,861	-	199,427	877,973
W Heintz	532,222	233,649	61,092	150,718	-	219,561	1,197,242
R F Jilla	489,971	316,266	50,305	107,635	-	462,249	1,426,426
N R O'Donnell	212,000	91,201	33,967	42,400	-	126,855	506,423
W Reed	366,167	75,074	139,087	92,115	-	216,290	888,733
W G Reilly	352,688	227,746	37,459	75,655	-	199,427	892,975
Total	2,285,954	1,158,790	380,835	540,384	-	1,423,809	5,789,772

Equity Instruments

Options, Performance Share Rights (PSRs) and Performance Rights (PRs) granted as compensation

Equity grants made to Key Management Personnel

The number of options, PSRs and PRs granted to key management personnel as compensation is set out in the tables below. No grants of PSRs were made in the current year.

2007	Number of Options granted during the year	Number of PRs granted during the year	Future financial years that grant may vest	Maximum total value of grant ($ per tranche)[1]
Director				
D D Tough	207,883	207,883	2009	971,345
			2010	1,410,445
Other Key Management Personnel				
P W Corke	56,156	56,156	2009	262,391
			2010	380,478
S R Corriveau	45,400	45,400	2009	212,133
			2010	307,602
W Heintz	33,174	33,174	2009	115,528
			2010	167,521
R F Jilla	115,810	115,810	2009	541,126
			2010	784,657
S Papier	53,996	53,996	2009	252,298
			2010	365,844
W Reed	61,124	61,124	2009	285,604
			2010	414,138
W G Reilly	64,794	64,794	2009	302,752
			2010	439,004

(1) The values per option was calculated at $2.61. The values per PR were calculated as $11.11 and $10.89 for the tranches that may vest in financial years 2009 and 2010 respectively.

2006	Number of PSRs granted during the year	Future financial years that grant may vest	Maximum total value of grant ($ per tranche)[2]
Other Key Management Personnel			
P W Corke	25,000	2007	81,913
		2008	80,330
		2009	78,757
W Heintz	25,000	2007	81,913
		2008	80,330
		2009	78,757
R F Jilla	55,000	2007	180,213
		2008	176,730
		2009	173,256
N R O'Donnell	15,000	2007	49,150
		2008	48,200
		2009	47,250
W Reed	25,000	2007	81,913
		2008	80,330
		2009	78,757
W G Reilly	25,000	2007	81,913
		2008	80,330
		2009	78,757

(2) The values per PSR were calculated as $9.83, $9.64 and $9.45 for the tranches that may vest in financial years 2007, 2008 and 2009 respectively.

Movement in Options, PSRs and PRs on issue

The movement in the number of options, PSRs and PRs over ordinary shares of Ansell Limited held, directly, indirectly or beneficially, by each key management person, including their related parties, is as follows:

2007

| | Held at 1 July 2006 | Granted during the year | Options exercised/ PSRs/PRs vested during the year | Options lapsed/ forfeited | Other changes | Held at 30 June 2007 | Vested at the date of this report | |
							Options vested and exercisable/ PSRs/PRs vested(1)	Options not yet exercisable
Options								
Director								
D D Tough	472,358	207,883	-	45,167	-	635,074	252,191	154,583
Other Key Management Personnel								
P W Corke	-	56,156	-	-	-	56,156		
S R Corriveau	-	45,400	-	-	-	45,400		
W Heintz	-	33,174	-	-	-	33,174		
R F Jilla	240,000	115,810	-	-	-	355,810	240,000	-
S Papier	-	53,996	-	-	-	53,996		
W Reed	-	61,124	-	-	-	61,124		
W G Reilly	-	64,794	-	-	-	64,794		
PSRs & PRs								
Director								
D D Tough	115,041	207,883	40,491	-	-	282,433	60,124	
Other Key Management Personnel								
P W Corke	43,334	56,156	20,000	-	-	79,490	15,000	
S R Corriveau	-	45,400	5,000	-	10,000	50,400	2,500	
W Heintz	51,667	33,174	26,666	-	-	58,175	16,667	
R F Jilla	105,001	115,810	51,667	-	-	169,144	35,000	
N R O'Donnell	29,667	-	15,667	-	(14,000)	-	9,000	
S Papier	-	53,996	23,334	-	46,668	77,330	15,000	
W Reed	50,001	61,124	25,000	-	-	86,125	16,667	
W G Reilly	43,334	64,794	20,000	-	-	88,128	15,000	

2006

| | Held at 1 July 2005 | Granted during the year | Options exercised/ PSRs vested during the year | Options lapsed/forf eited | Other changes | Held at 30 June 2006 | Vested at the date of the 2006 financial report | |
							Options vested and exercisable/ PSRs vested(1)	Options not yet exercisable
Options								
Director								
D D Tough	525,000	-	-	52,642	-	472,358	122,358	129,833
Other Key Management Personnel								
R F Jilla	300,000	-	60,000	-	-	240,000	240,000	-
PSRs								
Director								
D D Tough	150,000	-	34,959	-	-	115,041	40,491	
Other Key Management Personnel								
P W Corke	38,334	25,000	20,000	-	-	43,334	20,000	
W Heintz	53,334	25,000	26,667	-	-	51,667	26,666	
R F Jilla	83,334	55,000	33,333	-	-	105,001	51,667	
N R O'Donnell	30,334	15,000	15,667	-	-	29,667	15,667	
W Reed	51,667	25,000	26,666	-	-	50,001	25,000	
W G Reilly	38,334	25,000	20,000	-	-	43,334	20,000	

(1) PSRs that vest after 30 June result in the allocation of one fully paid ordinary share to the holder of each PSR that has vested. The date of testing of the performance condition and vesting of the PSRs for each of the years above was 23 August 2007 and 22 August 2006.

Movements in shares

The movement in the number of ordinary shares of Ansell Limited held directly, indirectly or beneficially, by each of the Key Management Personnel, including their personally-related entities during the 2007 financial year is as follows:

	Held at 1 July 2006	Purchases[(a)]	Received on vesting of PSRs	Sales	Other changes	Held at 30 June 2007
Directors						
P L Barnes	14,545	1,902	-	-	-	16,447
G L L Barnes	5,658	3,793	-	-	-	9,451
R J S Bell	746	793	-	-	-	1,539
L D Crandall	9,862	864	-	-	-	10,726
H J Elliott	10,730	244			(10,974)	
M T Peterson	-	5,655	-	-	-	5,655
D D Tough	43,318	-	40,491	18,828	-	64,981
Other Key Management Personnel						
P W Corke	22,105	-	20,000	12,660	-	29,445
S R Corriveau	-	-	5,000	1,665	-	3,335
W Heintz	13,334	-	26,666	26,668	-	13,332
R F Jilla	55,999	-	51,667	41,666	-	66,000
N R O'Donnell	7,833	-	15,667	15,667	(7,833)	-
S Papier	-	-	23,334	17,770	23,333	28,897
W Reed	43,148	-	25,000	33,705	-	34,443
W G Reilly	34,913	-	20,000	6,660	-	48,253

The movement in the number of ordinary shares of Ansell Limited held directly, indirectly or beneficially, by each of the Key Management Personnel, including their personally-related entities during the 2006 financial year is as follows:

	Held at 1 July 2005	Purchases[(a)]	Received on vesting of PSRs	Sales	Other changes	Held at 30 June 2006
Directors						
P L Barnes	12,639	1,906	-	-	-	14,545
G L L Barnes	-	5,658	-	-	-	5,658
R J S Bell	-	746	-	-	-	746
L D Crandall	8,963	899	-	-	-	9,862
H J Elliott	9,831	899	-	-	-	10,730
M J McConnell	5,354	960	-	6,314	-	-
D D Tough	20,000	-	34,959	11,641		43,318
E D Tweddell	16,664	-	-	16,664	-	-
Other Key Management Personnel						
P W Corke	16,105	-	20,000	14,000	-	22,105
W Heintz	26,666	-	26,667	39,999	-	13,334
R F Jilla	22,666	60,000	33,333	60,000	-	55,999
N R O'Donnell	5,833	-	15,667	13,667	-	7,833
W Reed	16,482	-	26,666	-	-	43,148
W G Reilly	14,913	-	20,000	-	-	34,913

(a) Includes shares purchased on market pursuant to the Non-executive Directors' Share Plan.

Service Agreements

The Company has no service agreements with the Non-executive Directors. Refer to Section 2D of the Remuneration Report for details of service agreements with the Managing Director and other Key Management Personnel.

Other Transactions with specified directors and specified executives

From time to time, Key Management Personnel of the Company or its subsidiaries, or their personally-related entities, may purchase goods from the Group. These purchases are on terms and conditions no more favourable than those entered into by unrelated customers and are trivial or domestic in nature.

Australian Worldwide Exploration Limited – All extracts 18(B) were obtained from the 2007 annual report.

Extracts 18(B1) – Australian Worldwide Exploration Limited, pages 84-91

This extract lists the names and roles of key management personnel, and discloses key management personnel compensation in accordance with IAS 24.

At the end of the extract, the company discloses related party relationships, transactions and balances with its controlled entities and joint ventures by reference to other notes.

The company also states that the related party transactions it engaged in with its controlled entities were in the ordinary course of business, generally on normal terms and conditions. Under IAS 24, related party transactions should be disclosed as being at "arm's length" only when such terms can be substantiated.

---

33. Related party disclosures

Key management personnel disclosures

The following were key management personnel of the Company and of the consolidated entity at any time during the reporting period and unless otherwise indicated were key management personnel for the entire period.

(a) Key management personnel

Directors

The names of each person holding the position of director of the Company during the financial year are:

B. G. McKay	Chairman (non-executive)
B. J. Phillips	Managing Director
B. J. W. Wood	Director (executive, appointed 11 April 2007)
C. C. Green	Director (non-executive)
E. S. Smith	Director (non-executive)
D. I. McEvoy	Director (non-executive)
R. Dumbrell	Director (non-executive, retired 23 November 2006)
R. M. Griffin AM	Director (non-executive, retired 23 November 2006)
J. C. M. A. M. Deuss	Director (non-executive, retired 8 September 2006)
T. W. Ulrich	Alternate Director (non-executive, retired 8 September 2006)

Executives

The names and position of each of the group executives of the consolidated entity are:

L. J. Brooks	Manager, Australian and International Exploration
R. D. Frith	Manager, Australian and International Development and Production
N. F. Kelly	Chief Financial Officer/Company Secretary

(b) Key management personnel compensation

Remuneration levels for directors and senior executives of the Company are competitively set to attract, retain and motivate appropriately qualified and experienced directors and senior executives. The Remuneration Committee evaluates the appropriateness of remuneration packages given trends in comparable companies, the need to drive a performance based culture, and the objectives of the Company's remuneration strategy.

The remuneration structures explained below are designed to attract suitably qualified candidates, reward the achievement of strategic objectives, and achieve the broader outcome of sufficiently motivating senior executives to create value for shareholders. The remuneration structures take into account:

- the capability and experience of the directors and senior executives;
- the ability of directors and senior executives to control the performance of the relevant area of responsibility;
- the performance of consolidated entity including:
  - the success of exploration and production activities;
  - compliance with regulatory regimes;
  - adherence to health, environment and safety policies;
  - the consolidated entity's earnings;
  - the growth in share price and returns to shareholders;
- the level of performance benefits within each executive's remuneration package; and
- the relative value of each component of the remuneration package.

Remuneration packages consist of fixed remuneration in the form of base salary and superannuation, short-term performance benefits in the form of cash bonuses and long-term performance benefits in the form of share options.

Fixed remuneration consists of base remuneration (which is calculated on a total cost basis and includes any FBT charges related to employee benefits), as well as employer contributions to superannuation.

Variable remuneration is designed to reward the Managing Director and senior executives for meeting or exceeding their respective financial, operational and individual objectives. Those benefits are an "at risk" bonus provided in the form of cash and/or options over ordinary shares in the Company.

Short-term benefits are awarded in the form of cash bonuses paid on an annual basis for performance during a given financial year. The award of short-term bonuses is based on both consolidated entity and individual performance.

Long-term performance benefits are in the form of share options awarded annually on a three year rolling basis and are able to be exercised if individual performance measures are met.

Long-term benefits are only awarded if the Company achieves relative and absolute targeted total shareholder returns (TSR). These measures ensure that professional investors and retail shareholders are adequately compensated for their investment before executives are awarded any options.

Relative performance of the Company is measured by comparing AWE's TSR over a rolling three-year period against a comparator group comprised of any combination of the ASX All Ordinaries, ASX 200, ASX Energy Index and comparable international energy companies and indices. Depending on the market circumstances, the Board may wish to nominate any one of the above indices or a combination to apply as the benchmark in any given year.

The key management personnel compensation included in Note 20 are as follows:

	Consolidated		The Company	
	2007 $'000	2006 $'000	2007 $'000	2006 $'000
Salaries and wages	2,144	1,739	394	285
Share based payments	569	538	569	538
Other associated personnel costs	106	90	–	–
	2,819	2,367	963	823

(c) Key management personnel compensation disclosures

Information regarding individual directors and executives compensation is also provided in the Remuneration Report section of the Directors' Report.

		Short-term				Post employ-ment	Other long-term	Share-based payments			
		Salary package and fees[a] $	Cash bonus[b] $	Non-monetary benefits $	Total $	Super-annuation benefits[c] $	(d) $	Value of options[e] $	Total $	Perfor-mance related %	Value of options %
Directors											
Company and Consolidated entity											
B. G. McKay	2007	117,023	–	–	117,023	10,532	–	–	127,555	–	–
	2006	100,000	–	–	100,000	9,000	–	–	109,000	–	–
B. J. Phillips	2007	550,000	200,000	8,003	758,003	49,500	4,270	106,566	918,339	33%	12%
	2006	430,000	150,000	7,767	587,767	38,700	32,473	249,917	908,857	44%	27%
B. J. W. Wood	2007	93,750	–	–	93,750	8,438	2,913	–	105,101	–	–
	2006	–	–	–	–	–	–	–	–	–	–
C. C. Green	2007	73,015	–	–	73,015	6,571	–	–	79,586	–	–
	2006	50,000	–	–	50,000	4,500	–	–	54,500	–	–
E. S. Smith	2007	61,793	–	–	61,793	5,561	–	–	67,354	–	–
	2006	50,000	–	–	50,000	4,500	–	–	54,500	–	–
D. McEvoy	2007	58,966	–	–	58,966	5,308	–	–	64,274	–	–
	2006	–	–	–	–	–	–	–	–	–	–
R. Dumbrell	2007	27,798	–	24,772	52,570	–	–	–	52,570	–	–
	2006	54,500	–	–	54,500	–	–	–	54,500	–	–
R. M. Griffin	2007	27,028	–	13,210	40,238	–	–	–	40,238	–	–
	2006	53,375	–	–	53,375	1,125	–	–	54,500	–	–
Total*	2007	1,009,373	200,000	45,985	1,255,358	85,910	7,183	106,566	1,455,017	21%	7%
	2006	737,875	150,000	7,767	895,642	57,825	32,473	249,917	1,235,857	32%	20%
Executives											
Consolidated entity											
L. J. Brooks	2007	230,000	40,000	8,003	278,003	20,700	10,714	155,038	464,455	42%	33%
	2006	220,000	60,000	7,767	287,767	19,800	9,092	79,737	396,396	35%	20%
R. D. Frith	2007	230,000	50,000	8,003	288,003	20,700	10,714	155,038	474,455	43%	33%
	2006	220,000	40,000	7,767	267,767	19,800	7,248	79,737	374,552	32%	21%
N. F. Kelly	2007	200,000	40,000	8,003	248,003	18,000	7,764	151,823	425,590	45%	36%
	2006	170,000	30,000	7,767	207,767	15,300	8,713	128,437	360,217	44%	36%
Total	2007	660,000	130,000	24,009	814,009	59,400	29,192	461,899	1,364,500	43%	34%
	2006	610,000	130,000	23,301	763,301	54,900	25,053	287,911	1,131,165	37%	25%

* Mr J. C. M. A. M. Deuss and Mr T. W. Ulrich who retired as directors of the Company on 8 September 2006 did not receive remuneration as directors of the Company. Mr R. Dumbrell and Mr R. M. Griffin AM retired as directors on 23 November 2006. Mr B. J. W. Wood was appointed as a director of the Company on 11 April 2007.

Notes in relation to table of directors' and executives' remuneration:

a) Salary package and fees includes amounts salary sacrificed.

b) The 2007 primary cash bonus is for performance during the 30 June 2007 financial year. The amount was finally determined in July 2007 after performance reviews were completed and approved by the remuneration committee.

c) Superannuation benefits include the amount required to be contributed by the consolidated entity by law and does not include amounts salary sacrificed.

d) Other long-term benefits comprise the amount of long service leave accrued in the period.

e) The fair value of the options is calculated at the award date using a modified binomial option-pricing model and allocated to each reporting period evenly over the period from award date to vesting date. The value disclosed is the portion of the fair value of the options allocated to this reporting period. In valuing the options, market conditions have been taken into account.

The fair value of options can only be derived in cash by the employee if on exercise of these options the Company's share price exceeds the exercise price by the amount shown as "Fair value per option awarded" in the table in Section 6 of the Remuneration Report. Option-pricing models for valuing options are an accounting guideline only. The reported fair values do not reflect the taxable benefit to the executive.

The following factors and assumptions were used in determining the fair value of options on award date:

Grant Date	Weighted average share price	Exercise price	Expected volatility	Option life	Expected dividends	Risk-free rate
2007						
21 July 2006	$3.27	$3.27	25.0%	5 years	0% to 3%	6.18%
2006						
26 September 2005	$2.10	$2.10	22.3%	5 years	0% to 3%	5.67%
24 November 2005	$2.10	$2.10	22.3%	5 years	0% to 3%	5.64%
24 November 2005	$2.10	$2.21	22.3%	5 years	0% to 3%	5.64%
24 November 2005	$2.10	$2.31	22.3%	5 years	0% to 3%	5.64%
20 March 2006	$2.46	$2.59	22.3%	5 years	0% to 3%	5.67%
20 March 2006	$2.46	$2.71	22.3%	5 years	0% to 3%	5.67%

f) Amounts disclosed for remuneration exclude insurance premiums paid by the consolidated entity in respect of directors' and officers' liability insurance contracts. The premium paid has not been allocated to the individuals covered by the insurance policy as, based on all available information, the directors believe that no reasonable basis for such allocation exists.

(d) Options over equity instruments

Details of vesting profile of the options awarded as remuneration to each of the key management personnel are detailed below.

	Number (a)	Award date	Vested %	Financial years in which award vests	Fair value per option awarded $ (b)
2007					
Executives					
L. J. Brooks	150,000	21 July 2006	–	30 June 2010**	0.65
R. D. Frith	150,000	21 July 2006	–	30 June 2010**	0.65
N. F. Kelly	130,000	21 July 2006	–	30 June 2010**	0.65
2006					
Directors					
B. J. Phillips	300,000	24 November 2005	100%	30 June 2006*	0.47
	300,000	24 November 2005	100%	30 June 2007*	0.41
	300,000	24 November 2005	–	30 June 2008*	0.38
Executives					
L. J. Brooks	100,000	26 September 2005	100%	30 June 2006	0.49
	300,000	20 March 2006	–	30 June 2008**	0.35
	450,000	20 March 2006	–	30 June 2009**	0.32
R. D. Frith	100,000	26 September 2005	100%	30 June 2006	0.49
	300,000	20 March 2006	–	30 June 2008**	0.35
	450,000	20 March 2006	–	30 June 2009**	0.32
N. F. Kelly	200,000	26 September 2005	100%	30 June 2006	0.49
	300,000	20 March 2006	–	30 June 2008**	0.35
	450,000	20 March 2006	–	30 June 2009**	0.32

* Approved by shareholders at the 2005 Annual General Meeting of the Company.

** The exercise of these options are conditional upon satisfaction of individual key performance indicators as determined by the Remuneration Committee for the financial year prior to the financial year in which the option vests.

a) The number of options issued during the 2006 financial year are as a consequence of the implementation of a rolling three year vesting period.

b) The fair value per option awarded represents the modified binomial option-pricing model valuation for options awarded during the year.

c) No terms of options awarded as remuneration have been altered or modified during the reporting period or the prior period.

The movement during the financial year in the number of options in the Company held, directly, indirectly or beneficially, by each key management person, including their related parties is as follows:

	Opening balance	Granted as remuneration	Exercised	Net change other	Closing balance
2007*					
Directors					
B. J. Phillips	2,900,000	–	(1,000,000)	–	1,900,000
Executives					
L. J. Brooks	1,850,000	150,000	(500,000)	–	1,500,000
R. D. Frith	1,850,000	150,000	–	–	2,000,000
N. F. Kelly	1,450,000	130,000	(300,000)	–	1,280,000
2006					
Directors					
B. J. Phillips	2,000,000	900,000	–	–	2,900,000
Executives					
L. J. Brooks	1,000,000	850,000	–	–	1,850,000
R. D. Frith	1,000,000	850,000	–	–	1,850,000
N. F. Kelly	550,000	950,000	(50,000)	–	1,450,000

* In addition it was agreed in the 2007 financial year that 500,000 options would be issued to Mr B. J. W. Wood at an exercise price of $2.77 and with an expiry date of 10 April 2012. The issue of these options is subject to shareholder approval at the 2007 Annual General Meeting of the Company and exercise is conditional upon satisfaction of Key Performance Indicators (KPI's) in July 2008 and July 2009.

During the financial year, the following shares were issued on the exercise of options previously granted as remuneration:

	Number of shares No.	Amount paid per share $/share	Market value of shares at exercise date $/share
2007			
Directors			
B. J. Phillips	1,000,000	0.76	3.06
Executives			
L. J. Brooks	500,000	0.76	3.40
N. F. Kelly	300,000	0.76	3.40
2006			
Executives			
N. F. Kelly	50,000	0.57	2.21

There are no amounts unpaid on the shares issued as a result of the exercise of the options.

(e) Movements in shares

The movement during the financial year in the number of ordinary shares in the Company held, directly, indirectly or beneficially, by each key management person, including their related parties is as follows:

	Opening balance	Granted as remuneration	Received on exercise of options	Net change other	Closing balance
2007					
Directors					
B. G. McKay	321,213	-	-	-	321,213
B. J. Phillips	3,743,913	-	1,000,000	(1,000,000)	3,743,913
B. J. W. Wood	-	-	-	50,050	50,050
C. C. Green	43,293	-	-	-	43,293
E. S. Smith	12,019,239	-	-	-	12,019,239
R. Dumbrell	43,293	-	-	(43,293)	-
R. M. Griffin	33,805	-	-	(33,805)	-
D. I. McEvoy	-	-	-	30,000	30,000
J.C.M.A.M Deuss	48,660,000	-	-	(48,660,000)	-
T. W. Ulrich	-	-	-	-	-
Executives					
L. J. Brooks	621,147	-	500,000	(144,237)	976,910
R. D. Frith	-	-	-	-	-
N. F. Kelly	25,476	-	300,000	(300,000)	25,476
2006					
Directors					
B. G. McKay	316,213	-	-	5,000	321,213
B. J. Phillips	3,741,413	-	-	2,500	3,743,913
R. Dumbrell	40,793	-	-	2,500	43,293
C. C. Green	40,793	-	-	2,500	43,293
E. S. Smith	12,016,739	-	-	2,500	12,019,239
R. M. Griffin	31,305	-	-	2,500	33,805
D. I. McEvoy	-	-	-	-	-
J.C.M.A.M Deuss	-	-	-	48,660,000	48,660,000
T. W. Ulrich	-	-	-	-	-
Executives					
L. J. Brooks	622,647	-	-	(1,500)	621,147
R. D. Frith	465,000	-	-	(465,000)	-
N. F. Kelly	22,976	-	50,000	(47,500)	25,476

No shares were granted to key management personnel during the financial year as compensation.

The disclosures above may not be consistent with the disclosure in the Directors' Report as the basis of calculation differs due to the differing requirements of the Corporations Act 2001 and the Accounting Standards.

(f) Key management personnel transactions with the Company or its controlled entities

No loans have been made to key management personnel.

The Company has entered into Indemnity Deeds to indemnify executives of the Company against certain liabilities incurred in the course of performing their duties.

Non-key management personnel disclosures

The consolidated entity has a related party relationship with its controlled entities (Note 29), joint ventures (Note 26) and with its key management personnel.

The Company and its controlled entities engage in a variety of related party transactions in the ordinary course of business.

These transactions are generally conducted on normal terms and conditions.

Details of related party transactions and amounts with controlled entities are set out in:

Note 6 – Interest income from controlled entities

Note 12 – Amounts receivable from controlled entities

Note 18 – Amounts owing to controlled entities

Extracts 18(B2) – Australian Worldwide Exploration Limited, page 79

This extract lists the names of entities under the control of Australian Worldwide Exploration Limited.

29. Controlled entities				
Name	**Note**	**Country of incorporation**	**2007 %**	**2006 %**
Parent entity				
Australian Worldwide Exploration Limited				
Controlled entities				
AWE Administration Pty Limited	(a)	Australia	**100**	100
AWE Finance Pty Limited		Australia	**100**	100
AWE Overseas Pty Limited	(a)	Australia	**100**	100
AWE Offshore Pty Limited	(a)	Australia	**100**	100
AWE Argentina Pty Limited	(a),(b)	Australia	**100**	100
AWE New Zealand Pty Limited	(a),(b)	Australia	**100**	100
AWE Australia Pty Limited		Australia	**100**	100
AWE Satria (NZ) Ltd	(b)	New Zealand	**100**	–
AWE Singapore Pte. Ltd	(b)	Singapore	**100**	100
AWE Holdings NZ Limited	(b)	New Zealand	**100**	100
New Zealand Overseas Petroleum Limited	(b)	New Zealand	**100**	100
Omega Oil Pty Ltd	(a)	Australia	**100**	100
Greenslopes Limited	(b)	Papua New Guinea	**100**	100
Wells Fargo Resources Pty Ltd	(a)	Australia	**100**	100
AWE Petroleum Pty Ltd		Australia	**100**	100
Peedamullah Petroleum Pty Ltd		Australia	**100**	100
AWE Timor Sea Pty Ltd	(a)	Australia	**100**	100
AWE Resources (Western Australia), pty Ltd		Australia	**100**	100
AWE Oil (Western Australia), pty Ltd		Australia	**100**	100
Perthshire Petroleum Pty Ltd	(a)	Australia	**100**	100
Tepstew Pty Ltd	(a)	Australia	**100**	100
Western Petroleum Management Pty Ltd	(a)	Australia	**100**	100
AWE (NSW), pty Ltd	(a)	Australia	**100**	100
AWE (Australia) Energy Pty Ltd	(a)	Australia	**100**	100
AWE Energy (Australasia), pty Ltd	(a)	Australia	**100**	100
(a) These controlled entities are small proprietary companies as defined by the Corporations Act 2001 and are not required to prepare and lodge financial reports and directors' reports.				
(b) These controlled entities are required to lodge audited individual entity financial statements with the appropriate overseas authority.				

Extracts 18(B3) – Australian Worldwide Exploration Limited, pages 75-76

This extract lists the names of Australian Worldwide Exploration Limited's joint venture interests.

---

26. Interests in joint ventures

(a) At the end of the financial year the consolidated entity held the following interests in oil and gas production, exploration and appraisal joint ventures:

Joint venture	Country	Beneficial Interest 2007 Consolidated %	Beneficial Interest 2006 Consolidated %	Beneficial Interest 2007 The Company %	Beneficial Interest 2006 The Company %
TP/15	Australia	25.00	25.00	–	–
WA 31 L	Australia	27.50	27.50	–	–
WA 286 P	Australia	27.50	27.50	–	–
T/L1	Australia	30.00	30.00	–	–
T/RL1	Australia	30.00	30.00	–	–
T/18P	Australia	30.00	22.60	–	–
PPL 62	Australia	–	24.29	–	–
PPL 168	Australia	–	24.29	–	–
PPL 202	Australia	–	24.29	–	–
PRL 2	Australia	–	24.29	–	–
VIC/L 24	Australia	25.00	25.00	–	–
VIC/P 44	Australia	25.00	25.00	–	–
PMP 38158	New Zealand	42.50	42.50	–	–
PEP 38259	New Zealand	25.00	25.00	–	–
PEP 38401	New Zealand	50.00	–	–	–
PEP 38481	New Zealand	40.00	40.00	–	–
PEP 38482	New Zealand	40.00	40.00	–	–
PEP 38483	New Zealand	44.32	44.32	–	–
PEP 38499	New Zealand	42.50	–	–	–
PEP 381202	New Zealand	100.00	–	–	–
Hector South Sub-block	New Zealand	42.50	42.50	–	–
Bulu Production Sharing Contract (PSC)	Indonesia	42.50	–	–	–
Las Bases Exploitation Concession	Argentina	15.00	15.00	–	–

(b) Included in the assets and liabilities of the Company and the consolidated entity are the following items which represent the Company's and the consolidated entity's interest in the assets and liabilities employed in the joint ventures.

	Consolidated 2007 $'000	Consolidated 2006 $'000	The Company 2007 $'000	The Company 2006 $'000
Current assets				
Cash and cash equivalents	18,402	69,666	–	–
Trade and other receivables	3,947	4,544	–	–
	22,349	74,210	–	–
Non-current assets				
Exploration and evaluation assets	22,315	9,897	–	–
Oil and gas assets	586,469	532,966	–	–
	608,784	542,863	–	–
Total assets	631,133	617,073	–	–
Current liabilities				
Trade and other payables	30,954	61,410	–	–
Total liabilities	30,954	61,410	–	–

Refer to Notes 27 and 28 for details of commitments and contingent liabilities.

Extracts 18(B4) – Australian Worldwide Exploration Limited, page 62

This extract separately discloses interest income from controlled entities.

6. Net financing (expenses)/income	Consolidated		The Company	
	2007 $'000	2006 $'000	2007 $'000	2006 $'000
Interest income:				
Other parties	6,274	8,561	378	1,447
Controlled entities	–	–	–	316
Financial income	6,274	8,561	378	1,763
Interest expense	(8,272)	(8,890)		
Other borrowing costs	(4,493)	(619)	–	–
Unwinding of discount – restoration provisions	(932)	(585)	–	–
	(13,697)	(10,094)	–	–
Less: Borrowing costs capitalised	2,448	8,293	–	–
Financial expenses	(11,249)	(1,801)	–	–
Net financing (expenses)/ income	(4,975)	6,760	378	1,763

Extracts 18(B5) – Australian Worldwide Exploration Limited, page 65

This extract separately discloses amounts receivable from controlled entities and joint ventures.

12. Trade and other receivables	Consolidated		The Company	
	2007 $'000	2006 $'000	2007 $'000	2006 $'000
Current				
Trade receivables	16,008	10,016	–	–
Interest receivable	77	289	23	43
Amounts receivable from controlled entities	–	–	15,163	543
Joint venture receivables	3,947	4,544	–	–
Prepayments	1,971	418	955	118
Other	424	153	–	–
	22,427	15,420	16,141	704

PLANNING FOR IMPLEMENTATION

The adoption of IAS 24 will have an impact on the preparation of Canadian financial statements because it does not address the recognition and measurement of related party transactions. In addition, the more extensive disclosures required by IAS 24 will likely entail some additional work for Canadian corporations.

IFRS 1 requires the retrospective application of IFRS effective at the reporting date for the first financial statements prepared in accordance with IFRS unless there is a specific exemption. It is silent on the treatment of related party transactions, which is not surprising given that there are no specific international financial reporting standards dealing with recognition and measurement for these transactions. In an attempt to determine to what extent Canadian companies adopting IFRS might have to restate related party transactions previously accounted for in accordance with CICA 3840, the AcSB IFRS Advisory Committee (IAC) developed two viewpoints on this issue:

1. The recognition and measurement of related party transactions under Canadian GAAP do not currently contravene the requirements of a specific standard under

IFRS because no such standard exists; therefore, no change in accounting policy would be required on adoption of IFRS.

2. Related party transactions are recognized and measured in accordance with the requirements of relevant IFRS in the absence of specific guidance; therefore, a change in accounting policy may be required if the existing one under Canadian GAAP for related party transactions conflicts with the relevant requirements under IFRS.[1]

A Canadian company adopting the first viewpoint would generally continue to use its existing accounting policies for the recognition and measurement of related party transactions, but disclose both those accounting policies and the information required by IAS 24. The entity might make the case that it recognizes related party transactions in accordance with the IASB's "Framework for the Preparation and Presentation of Financial Statements," since it recorded its related party transactions in accordance with a consistent accounting policy. In such circumstances, however, the entity would need to carry forward that accounting policy, or make a retrospective change in accordance with IAS 8, *Accounting Policies, changes in accounting estimates and errors*.

Most Canadian entities adopting the second viewpoint would not be affected by the measurement issues since transactions with commercial substance that have been recorded at the "exchange amount," as defined in Section 3840, would not change because "initial cost," in accordance with the measurement guidance in many IFRSs, equals the exchange amount. The exception is financial instruments for which IAS 39, *Financial Instruments: Recognition and Measurement* requires the use of fair value on initial recognition. This is in contrast to the requirements of Section 3855, *Financial Instruments — Recognition and Measurement*, which includes specific guidance for related parties to use cost or amortized cost based on the carrying or exchange amount in specific circumstances. Moreover, an adjustment might be necessary in instances where related party transactions without commercial substance were measured at the carrying amount, in accordance with CICA 3840.

Because the disclosure requirements under IAS 24 are more extensive than those under CICA 3840, particularly for the disclosure of key management personnel compensation (which consists of all employee benefits and share-based payments), adopters of IFRS should ask management, directors and staff to gather sufficient information to identify and disclose related party relationships, transactions and balances. Significant new data will need to be obtained and processed on a continuous basis and will likely require changes to entity information systems.

Keep Posted

The IASB is currently reviewing IAS 24, and expects to publish amendments to the standard in the second half of 2009. The proposed amendments primarily revise the definition of a related party.

---

1   See notes of the April 10, 2008 meeting of the AcSB IFRS Advisory Committee.

Chapter 19
Other Specific Topics

Standards Discussed in this Chapter

International

IAS 20 – Accounting for Government Grants and Disclosure of Government Assistance
IAS 23 – Borrowing Costs
IAS 41 – Agriculture
SIC-10 – Government Assistance – No Specific Relation to Operating Activities

Canadian

CICA 3800 – Government Assistance
CICA 3805 – Investment Tax Credits
CICA 3850 – Interest Capitalized – Disclosure Considerations

INTRODUCTION

This chapter examines two IFRS that might not be particularly important for most enterprises: IAS 20 on government grants and assistance and IAS 23 on borrowing costs. They could, however, be significant for entities receiving particular types of government grants and for entities expensing all borrowing costs. The accounting required by these two standards does not contradict Canadian GAAP but lack of specific Canadian guidelines could lead to differences in practice.

IAS 20 establishes requirements aimed at giving readers of financial statements information on government assistance an entity may have received during a reporting period. Requirements cover the accounting treatment of various forms of government grants and the disclosures to be provided on the details of government assistance in general.

With respect to the accounting treatment, IAS 20 specifies that government grants are:

- recognized only when there is a reasonable assurance that both (1) an entity will comply with their conditions and (2) they will be received;

- measured at their fair value and any related contingent liability or contingent asset accounted for in accordance with IAS 37, *Provisions, Contingent Liabilities and Contingent Assets*;

- either included as profit and loss (1) on a systematic basis over the periods when costs related to the grants are recorded or (2) in the period in which they become receivable if they relate to expenses or losses already incurred, or provide immediate financial support to an entity, with no future related costs expected to be incurred.

IAS 20 has also accounting requirements for other particular issues, including nonmonetary grants and forgivable loans. In addition, IAS 41 covers recognition of government grants related to biological assets measured at fair value. That standard's criteria differ from those set by IAS 20 by requiring that grants for biological assets be recognized as profit and loss when they are unconditionally receivable.

CICA 3800 requirements are very similar to IAS 20 although there are some differences in the accounting of forgivable loans and non-monetary government grants. In addition, CICA 3800 has more prescriptive disclosure requirements.

IAS 23 requires that borrowing costs be expensed as they are incurred unless they relate to "qualifying" assets (as defined by the standard), in which case they must be capitalized if certain conditions are met. When interest is capitalized, IAS 23 requires the following steps:

- begin capitalization when borrowing costs are incurred and expenditures and activities to develop a qualifying asset are in progress;
- suspend capitalization when development is interrupted for extended periods; and
- cease capitalization when a qualifying asset is ready for its intended use or sale.

Canadian GAAP does not provide general guidance for interest capitalization. The only discussion on that matter is in CICA 3061, *Property, Plant and Equipment*, which permits but does not require an entity to capitalize interest costs directly attributable to property, plant and equipment when its accounting policy is to capitalize interest costs.

To illustrate various issues covered by IAS 20 and IAS 23, this chapter analyzes the following:

- government grants and assistance:
    o scope,
    o definitions,
    o grants,
    o assistance,
    o disclosures;
- special issues involving government grants:
    o agriculture,
    o emission rights;
- borrowing costs:
    o scope,
    o key terms,
    o capitalization.

IMPACT ON FINANCIAL STATEMENTS

IFRS and Canadian GAAP require borrowing costs and government grants to be generally accounted for and presented similarly. Consequently, in many instances the adoption of IAS 20 and IAS 23 would not have a significant impact on the financial statements of Canadian companies.

In certain circumstances, however, the impact of IAS 23 adoption might indeed be significant. For example, a Canadian entity could see its reported assets and income increase if it expensed, as permitted by Canadian GAAP, significant amounts of borrowing costs that are required to be capitalized under IAS 23. It is significant to note that, even if a Canadian entity capitalized interest costs directly attributable to assets, as permitted by CICA 3061, the amount capitalized might differ from the amount determined under IAS 23. Such a difference arises from the fact that Canadian GAAP does not contain any guidance on what amounts are eligible for capitalization.

ANALYSIS OF RELEVANT ISSUES

This section analyzes and illustrates the reporting of:

- government grants and assistance as required by IAS 20;
- special issues involving government grants, including IAS 41 requirement and emission rights; and
- borrowing costs as required by IAS 23.

This section identifies some significant differences between IFRS and Canadian GAAP in the areas of recognition and measurement of government grants and capitalization of borrowing costs.

Government Grants and Assistance

Scope

Government grants or other types of government assistance are intended to encourage entities to undertake activities that might not be otherwise economically viable. IAS 20 distinguishes between government grants and government assistance. It deals with the accounting treatment and disclosure requirements of both types of government aid.

IAS 20 provides four exclusions from its scope:

1. problems arising in accounting for government grants in financial statements reflecting the effects of changing prices or similar supplementary information;

2. government assistance provided in the form of tax benefits (including income tax holidays, investment tax credits, accelerated depreciation allowances and reduced income tax rates);

3. government participation in the ownership of an entity;

4. government grants covered by IAS 41.

SIC 10 clarifies that government assistance aimed at encouraging or supporting business activities in certain regions or industry sectors (which may not specifically relate to an entity's operating activities) are within the scope of IAS 20. Examples of such assistance are government grants to operate in an economically depressed area or in an agriculture-based industry with low profitability, such as fishery.

Definitions

The table below provides definitions of key terms used in IAS 20. All definitions correspond to the meanings of terms used by CICA 3800, except that the latter does not specifically differentiate between government assistance and government grants.[1]

Term	IAS 20 Definition
Forgivable loans	Loans where the lender waives repayment as long as certain prescribed conditions are met.
Government	Government, government agencies and similar bodies, whether local, national or international.
Government assistance	Action by government designed to provide an economic benefit specific to an entity or range of entities qualifying under certain criteria. Note that government assistance: • includes government grants and other kinds of non-monetary government assistance, such as providing, at no cost, legal advice to an entrepreneur for setting up a business in a free-trade zone; and • excludes benefits provided only indirectly through actions affecting general trading conditions, such as the provision of infrastructure in development areas (for example, constructing roads that connect the industrial area in which an entity operates to the nearest city) or imposing trade constraints on foreign companies to protect domestic entrepreneurs in general.
Government grant	Assistance by government in the form of transfers of resources to an entity in return for past or future compliance with certain conditions relating to the operating activities of the entity. Government grants exclude forms of government assistance that cannot reasonably have a value placed on them and transactions with government that cannot be distinguished from an entity's normal trading transactions.
Grants related to assets	Government grants whose primary condition is that an entity qualifying for them should purchase, construct or otherwise acquire long-term assets. Subsidiary conditions may also be attached restricting the type or location of the assets or the periods during which they are to be acquired or held.
Grants related to income	Government grants other than those related to assets.

---

1 Under IAS 20, government assistance refers to a general term that comprises grants (which entails the transfer of resources), forgivable loans and indirect or non-monetary forms of assistance, such as technical advice.

Grants[2]

The table below describes the main IAS 20 accounting and presentation requirements for government grants. None contradict Canadian GAAP unless noted otherwise.

Issue	IAS 20 Requirement
Recognition criteria	Grants are not recognized until there is *reasonable assurance* that both of the following criteria are met: • the entity will comply with the conditions attached to the grant; and • the grant(s) will be received.
Recognition in profit and loss	Government grants are generally not gratuitous. Receipt of a grant does not of itself provide conclusive evidence that the conditions attached to the grant have been, or will be, fulfilled. An entity earns grants by complying with their conditions and meeting the envisaged obligations. Consequently, the grants should be recognized as profit and loss and matched with the costs which the grant is intended to cover. Hence, a grant is recognized in profit and loss: • over the same period as the relevant expense if it relates to specific costs; • over the periods and in the proportions of depreciation if it relates to depreciable assets; • over periods that bear the cost of meeting the grant obligations if it relates to non-depreciable assets (for example, a grant of land may be conditional upon the erection of a building on the site and it may be appropriate to recognize it as profit and loss over the life of the building); • in the period in which it becomes receivable if it relates to expenses or losses already incurred or is obtained for giving immediate financial support to an entity with no future related costs expected to be incurred (examples of such grants include those awarded to revive an insolvent commercial business or to compensate an entity for losses incurred in the past for operating in an area that has been hit recently by, say, flooding).
Measurement	Measured at their fair value and any related contingent liability or contingent asset would be accounted for in accordance with IAS 37, *Provisions, Contingent Liabilities and Contingent Assets.*
Grant in the form of a reduction of a liability to the government	Accounted for in the same manner as if received in cash.
Grant in the form of a transfer of a non-monetary asset Example: piece of land or a building obtained from government in a remote area (Note 1)	Accounting choice: • assess the fair value of the non-monetary asset and account for both grant and asset at that fair value; or • record both asset and grant at a nominal amount.
Forgivable loan (Note 2)	Treated as a government grant when there is reasonable assurance that the entity will meet the terms for forgiveness of the loan.

---

2   Government grants are sometimes called by other names, such as subsidies, subventions or premiums.

Issue	IAS 20 Requirement
Government loan with a below-market rate of interest	IAS 20 was amended by *Improvements to IFRSs* in May 2008 to require that loans received from a government that have a below-market rate of interest should be recognized and measured in accordance with IAS 39, *Financial Instruments: Recognition and Measurement*. The benefit of the government loan is measured at the inception of the loan as the difference between the cash received and the amount at which the loan is initially recognized in the statement of financial position. This benefit is accounted for in accordance with IAS 20. Entities must apply the amendments prospectively to government loans received in periods beginning on or after January 1, 2009. Earlier application is permitted. If an entity applies the amendments for an earlier period, it must disclose that fact.
Grants received as part of a package of financial or fiscal aids	Identify the conditions giving rise to costs and expenses that determine the periods over which the grant will be earned. It may be appropriate to allocate part of a grant on one basis and part on another.
Repayment of government grant related to income (consists of a change in accounting estimate) (Note 3)	Apply first against any unamortized deferred credit recognized in respect of the grant. If the repayment exceeds the deferred credit, or where no deferred credit exists, recognize repayment immediately in profit or loss.
Repayment of government grant related to an asset (consists of a change in accounting estimate) (Note 3)	Increase the carrying amount of the asset or reduce the deferred income balance by the amount repayable. Cumulative additional depreciation that would have been recognized in profit or loss to date in the absence of the grant is recognized immediately in profit or loss. Note: Consider whether new carrying amount of the asset is impaired.
Presentation of grants related to assets, including non-monetary grants at fair value	Present in the statement of financial position either: • by setting up the grant as deferred income; or • by deducting the grant in arriving at the carrying amount of the asset. When grants related to assets are received in cash, two elements are shown under the investing activities section of the cash-flow statement: • cash inflows from the grant; and • cash outflows resulting from the purchase of the asset. An entity presents both these movements separately (i.e., they should not be netted) regardless of whether the grant is deducted from the related asset in the statement of financial position or not.
Presentation of grants related to income	Free choice between two presentations is allowed: • Option 1: present the grant as a credit in the statement of comprehensive income, either separately or under a general heading of other income. • Option 2: deduct the grant from the related expense presented in the statement of comprehensive income. Since two options are allowed, IAS 20 specifies that disclosure of the effect of the grants on any item of income or expense may be appropriate.

Note 1: Since CICA 3800 has no specific requirements for grants taking the form of a transfer of a non-monetary asset, entities might refer to CICA 3831, *Non-monetary Transactions* for guidance, which might result in their measuring the grant at fair value.

Note 2: CICA 3800 requires that a forgivable government loan be recorded as a grant when an entity is entitled to receive it (this date might not correspond to the one at which the entity is reasonably assured of meeting the terms for forgiveness set by IAS 20).

Note 3: CICA 3800 specifies that, when repayment of government assistance will be required, it is accounted for prospectively.

Assistance

Government assistance comprises government grants and other forms of government assistance (i.e., those that do not involve transfer of resources). IAS 20 excludes from its government grants' definition certain forms of government benefits that cannot:

- reasonably have a value placed on them, such as free technical or other professional advice, and
- be distinguished from an entity's normal trading transactions.

Note, however, that these forms of government benefits may be so significant that disclosure of their nature, extent and duration is necessary to ensure that the financial statements are not misleading.

Disclosures

IAS 20 prescribes the following three disclosures:

- the accounting policy adopted for government grants, including the methods of presentation adopted in the financial statements;
- the nature and extent of government grants recognized in the financial statements and an indication of other forms of government assistance from which an entity has directly benefitted; and
- unfulfilled conditions and other contingencies attached to government assistance that has been recognized.

Illustrative Disclosures:

The illustrative disclosures presented below are in line with Canadian GAAP unless stated otherwise.

Extract 19(1) – Government grant accounting

Aker Kvaerner ASA (AR 2007), page 43
Note 2: Accounting principles (in part)
Revenue recognition (in part)
Government grants
Government grants are recognised in the balance sheet initially as deferred income when there is reasonable assurance that they will be received and that the group will comply with applicable conditions. Grants that compensate the group for expenses incurred are recognised as revenue in the income statement on a systematic basis in the same periods in which the expenses are incurred. Grants that compensate the group for the cost of an asset are deducted from acquisition cost.

Commentary: This specifies IAS 20 criteria for government grant recognition and the policy for realization into profit or loss.

Extract 19(2) – Government grants related to assets

Stora Enso Oyj (AR 2007), page 123
Note 1 Accounting Principles (in part)
Government Grants

Government grants relating to the purchase of property, plant and equipment are deducted from the carrying value of the asset, the net cost being capitalised. Other government grants are recognised as income on a systematic basis over the periods necessary to match them with the related costs which they were intended to compensate.

Commentary: This extract specifies that the company has deducted government grants related to assets from their carrying amount.

Extract 19(3) – Government grants related to assets

Bayer Aktiengesellschaft (AR 2007), page 119
4. Basic principles, methods and critical accounting policies (in part)
Other receivables and liabilities

Accrued items, advance payments and non-financial assets and liabilities are carried at amortized cost. They are amortized to income by the straight-line method or according to performance of the underlying transaction.

In accordance with IAS 20 (Accounting for Government Grants and Disclosure of Government Assistance), grants and subsidies that serve to promote investment are reflected in the balance sheet under other liabilities and amortized to income over the useful lives of the respective assets.

Commentary: In this extract, the company specifies that it has presented government grants related to assets as a deferred liability that is amortized to income over the useful lives of the respective assets.

Extract 19(4) – Government assistance – Export credit guarantees

Deutsche Bank Aktiengesellschaft (Annual Review 2007), page 218
[37] RISK DISCLOSURES (in part)
GOVERNMENT ASSISTANCE

In the course of the Group's business we regularly apply for and receive government support by means of Export Credit Agency ("ECA") guarantees covering transfer and default risks for the financing of exports and investments into Emerging Markets and to a lesser extent developed markets for Structured Trade & Export Finance business. Almost all export-oriented states have established such ECAs to support its domestic exporters. The ECAs act in the name and on behalf of the government of their respective country but are either constituted directly as governmental departments or organized as private companies vested with the official mandate of the government to act on its behalf. Terms and conditions of such ECA guarantees granted for mid-term and long-term financings are quite comparable due to the fact that most of the ECAs act within the scope of the Organisation for Economic Co-operation and Development ("OECD") consensus rules. The OECD consensus rules, an intergovernmental Agreement of the OECD member states defines benchmarks to ensure that a fair competition between the different exporting nations will take place. The majority of such ECA guarantees we have received were issued by the Euler-Hermes Kreditversicherungs AG acting on behalf of the Federal Republic of Germany. The Group also receives as collateral, in certain financings, government guarantees from national and international governmental institutions to support financings in the interest of the respective governments.

Commentary: This extract shows the disclosures of government assistance that took the form of guarantees covering transfer and default risks for the financing of exports and investments into emerging markets and, to a lesser extent, developed markets. Terms and conditions are described.

Extract 19(5) – Government grants related to assets

Beaconsfield Gold NL (Annual Financial Report 2007), page 47

2. SUMMARY OF SIGNIFICANT ACCOUNTING POLICIES (in part)

(ac) Government grants

Government grants are recognized when there is reasonable assurance that the grant will be received and all attaching conditions will be complied with.

When the grant relates to an expense item, it is recognized as income over the periods necessary to match the grant on a systematic basis to the costs that it is intended to compensate. They are not credited directly to shareholders equity.

When the grant relates to an asset, the fair value is credited to a deferred income account and is released to the income statement over the life of the related asset (being the decline development asset) on a unit-of-production basis.

Commentary: This extract shows an accounting policy disclosure of grant recognition criteria and how grants are recognized, including the depreciation method of the deferred income account.

Extract 19(6) – Government grants – Change in presentation and R&D related amounts

Ricardo plc (AR 2007), page 69

1 Accounting policies (in part)

(h) Government grants

The Group receives income-related grants from various national and supranational government agencies, principally as part funding of research and development projects. A grant is not recognised in the income statement until there is reasonable assurance that the Group will comply with its conditions and that the grant will be received. Grants are presented in the income statement as a deduction from the related expenses.

In the previous year's financial statements income from government grants was included within revenue. This has been changed in order to more clearly recognise grants differently to revenue from work carried out on normal commercial terms. This has resulted in £1.2m being reclassified from revenue to cost of sales in the year ended 30 June 2006.

Grants are not normally received until after qualification conditions have been met and the related expenditure has been incurred. Where this is not the case, they are recorded within trade and other payables as a payment in advance.

Page 74

5 Profit before tax (in part)

	2007 £m	2006 £m
The following items have been charged/(credited) in arriving at operating profit:		
Amortisation of intangible assets recognised as expense in cost of sales	0.6	0.6
Depreciation of property, plant and equipment:		
– recognised as an expense in cost of sales	6.3	6.5
– recognised as an expense in administration expenses	1.9	1.9
Inventories		
– consumed and recognised as expense in cost of sales	28.5	26.5
Other operating lease rentals payable		
– plant and machinery	0.8	0.6
– property	3.0	3.2
Repairs and maintenance on property, plant and equipment	2.6	2.1
Trade receivables impairment	0.2	0.1
Exchange differences on foreign currency borrowings	–	0.1
Pensions credit	–	(3.7)

Ricardo plc (AR 2007), page 74

	2007 £m	2006 £m
With respect to the Group research and development activities (other than normal client projects) the following items have been charged/(credited) in arriving at operating profit:		
Research and development expenditure in the period	8.9	8.7
Government grant income received in respect of part of this expenditure	(1.1)	(1.2)
	7.8	7.5

Commentary: This extract provides an illustration of a change in accounting policy related to the presentation of income from a government grant (reclassification from revenue to cost of sales). In addition, the company details the gross amounts of R&D activities and the related government grant.

Extract 19(7) – Government grant policy and disclosures of amounts

Svenska Cellulosa Aktiebolaget SCA (AR 2007), page 72

Note 1 Accounting Principles (in part)

Government Grants

Government grants are recognized at fair value when there is reasonable assurance the grants will be received and that the Group will comply with the conditions attached to them. Government grants related to acquisition of assets are recognized in the balance sheet by the grant reducing the carrying amount of the asset. Government grants received as compensation for costs are accrued and recognized in the income statement during the same period as the costs. If the government grant or assistance is neither related to the acquisition of assets nor to compensation for costs, the grant is recognized as other income.

Page 79

Note 5 Other Income

Other income comprises income derived from activities outside the normal operations. The income may be recurrent such as sale of energy, royalties and rental income or income of a more temporary nature such as gains from the sale of non-current assets and government grants. In 2007 sales of energy amounted to SEK 546m, income from royalties to SEK 153m, rental income to SEK 46m and gains from the sale of non-current assets to SEK 75m.

Page 84

Note 8 Other Expenses (in part)

Other expenses include R&D costs amounting to SEK 595m (562; 545) in the Group.

Consolidated operating profit includes a net result from exchange differences of SEK –6m (12; 27). Hedging positions had an impact on operating profit of SEK –5m (146; –237). Government grants received reduced other expenses with SEK 38m (68; 38). Energy and transport expenses amounted to SEK 6,579m (7,389) and SEK 7,337m (7,528), respectively.

Other expenses also include marketing, sales, rent for premises, other consultant fees, administrative expenses, and other similar expenses.

Page 87

Note 13 Property, Plant and Equipment (in part)

Government grants reduced investments for the year in buildings by SEK 1m (–; –), machinery and equipment by SEK 86m (22; 13) and construction in progress by SEK –m (3; –). In total, government grants reduced accumulated costs for buildings by SEK 10m (9; 5), land by SEK 1m (1; 1), machinery and equipment by SEK 367m (270; 268) and construction in progress by SEK –m (3; –).

Commentary: In this extract, the company provides the following:
- its accounting policy for government grants;
- details of other income comprising government grants;
- details of other expenses, which include government grants received; and
- amounts of government grants related to property, plant and equipment.

Extract 19(8) – Government grants – Presentation and reconciliation

NIREUS AQUACULTURE S.A. (AR 2007), page 49

Balance Sheet (in part)

	Note	GROUP		COMPANY	
		31/12/2007	31/12/2006	31/12/2007	31/12/2006
Non-current liabilities					
Long-term borrowings	7.18	129.357.321	83.219.532	74.325.478	51.829.195
Deferred income tax liabilities	7.19	8.190.054	4.981.033	6.342.620	4.333.010
Retirement benefit obligations	7.20	2.655.038	2.155.854	1.990.487	1.876.440
Government grants	7.21	6.666.581	6.057.942	4.812.059	5.039.770
Other non-current liabilities	7.22	4.676.605	5.297.740	-	308.471
Total non-current liabilities		151.545.599	101.712.101	87.470.644	63.386.886

Cash Flow Statement (in part) page 52

	GROUP		COMPANY	
	31/12/2007	31/12/2006	31/12/2007	31/12/2006
Cash flows from operating activities				
Profit before taxes	20.351.818	14.539.051	13.710.804	12.432.733
Plus/less adjustments for:				
Depreciation charge	7.798.207	7.108.782	5.180.747	4.713.072
Provisions	-	60.886	-	-
Government Grants	(1.534.449)	(1.932.520)	(1.335.380)	(1.368.154)
Cash flows from investing activities				
Acquisition of subsidiaries, associates, joint-ventures and other investments	(57.939.388)	(864.779)	(58.912.425)	(6.394.887)
Proceeds from sale of subsidiaries, associates, joint-ventures and other investments	8.076.123	5.067.048	7.600.000	2.208.381
Purchases of property, plant and equipment (PPE) and of intangible assets	(15.577.195)	(9.078.454)	(10.755.457)	(6.325.215)
Proceeds from sale of PPE and intangible assets	1.920.467	1.005.635	1.529.696	378.036
Proceeds from Government grants	1.607.630	1.515.139	1.607.630	1.167.617
Interest received	821.166	121.016	764.420	117.026
Dividends received	8.840	33	50.033	51.230

Page 71

3. Summary of Significant accounting policies (in part)

3.16 Government grants

The Group recognizes the government grants, which satisfy the following criteria: a) There is reasonable assurance that the enterprise will comply with all attached conditions and b) the grants will be received. Grants are recognised at fair value and recognised on a systematic basis in income, based on the correlation principle of the grants with the respective cost, which will be granted.

Government grants related to assets are included in the long-term liabilities as deferred income and are recognised on a systematic basis and correctly in income over the useful lives of the asset.

Page 105

7. Notes to the Financial Statements (in part)

7.21 Government Grants

The analysis of Grants of the Group and the Company, is as follows:

Amounts in Euro	GROUP	COMPANY
Balance at 1 January 2006	5.806.629	4.654.290
Balance at date of acquisition of new companies	668.694	586.017
Proceeds received over the year	1.515.139	1.167.617
Recognised in the income statement	(1.932.520)	(1.368.154)
Balance at 31 December 2006	**6.057.942**	**5.039.770**
Balance at date of acquisition of new companies	1.035.418	
Balance of spin-off sector	(499.960)	(499.960)
Proceeds received over the year	1.607.630	1.607.630
Recognised in the income statement	(1.534.449)	(1.335.380)
Balance at 31 December 2007	**6.666.581**	**4.812.059**

Commentary: This extract provides an illustration of government grant presentation on the statement of financial position (deferred liability) and on the statement of cash flows (receipts of government grant shown separately in investment activities).

In addition, the extract presents IAS 20 criteria for the recognition of government grants and specifies that the grants are measured at fair value and included in profit and loss on a systematic basis in income, based on the principle of correlating the grants with their respective cost. The company has opted to show government grants related to assets as deferred income instead of deducting them from the assets' costs.

Finally, the extract presents an illustration of a schedule detailing changes in amounts of deferred income liability.

Extract 19(9) – Government grants – Presentation and disclosures

Italtel Group S.p.A. (AR 2007), page 53
Summary of significant accounting principles adopted (in part)
L - Government grants

Grants, together with relating expenses, are recorded in the period when the contract is signed with the agency providing the grant, following a formal grant allocation resolution, and at any rate when there is reasonable certainty that they will be cashed.

Grants on fixed asset investments related to building, plant and equipment are recorded in the balance sheet as a deferred revenue within "Other non-current liabilities" for the long-term portion, and within "Other liabilities" for the short-term portion. The deferred revenue is recognized in the income statement, within "Other income", on a straight-line basis over the useful economic life of the asset to which the grant refers.

Grants related to income are recognized in the income statement within "Other income".

Page 65
Note 17 Other current assets
The item "Other current assets" may be broken down as follows:

	12/31/2007	12/31/2006
Receivables due from employees	2,943	3,298
Receivables due from social entities	237	460
Pre-paid expenses	3,323	4,049
Other tax receivables	5,559	5,826
Government grant receivables	4,673	2,041
Other receivables	2,314	8,044
Allowance for doubtful other current receivables	(1,595)	(738)
Total	**17,454**	**22,980**

The carrying value of Other current assets is believed to approximate their fair value.

Page 78
Note 34 Other Income (in part)
The item "Other income" is made up as follows:

	2007	2006
Government grants	7,007	6,332
Provision releases	5,189	3,380
Gains on disposals of property, plant and equipment	1,735	1,903
Other	13,930	28,011
Total	**27,861**	**39,626**

Commentary: This extract shows government grant disclosures, including:

- accounting policy note (criteria for recognition, presentation as deferred revenue of grants received and receivable and line item where amounts related to government grants are presented);
- details of other current assets (including grants receivable) and other income (including government grants recognized in profit and loss).

Extract 19(10) – Government grants and low-interest government loans

---

Acta S.p.A (AR 2007), page 35

1 Significant Accounting policies (in part)

p. Government grants (IAS 20)

A government grant is not recognised until there is reasonable certainty that the Group will comply with the conditions attaching to it, and that the grant will be received. Receipt of a grant does not of itself provide conclusive evidence that the conditions attaching to the grant have been or will be fulfilled.

The interest costs of government grants received in the form of a repayable, low-interest loan are recalculated at market rates and recognised as a financial cost at market rates in the period. Any difference between the market rate cost and the actual interest cost incurred in the period is recognised as grant income. The grants recognised in the period are registered within other operating costs.

Page 39

5 Other operating expenses (in part)

	31 December 2007 €000	31 December 2006 €000
Research expenses	674	342
Credit for government grants utilised in the period	(365)	(47)
Commercial and operations expenses	320	202
Finance, management and administration expenses	1,410	1,092
Foreign exchange losses	28	3
Other operating costs	30	33
	2,097	1,625

Research expenses relate to external costs incurred by the research and development department, which increased during the year primarily due to costs incurred in relation to the FIT grant project. This does not include external patent costs of €146,000 (2006: €102,000) which were capitalised.

Credit for government grants utilised in the period refers to grant income recognised by Idea Lab on the FIT project (€194,000; 2006: Nil) and FISR project (€171,000; 2006: €47,000). During the year, Idea Lab undertook work on both the FISR project (development of inorganic and hybrid catalysts for fuel cells) and the FIT project (development of a prototype direct ethanol fuel cell stack). Grant income is recognised over the duration of each project, in accordance with the stage payments received or approved following the achievement of each project milestone. Project costs are expensed as incurred.

During the year the Group also received €291,000 as a low-interest, ten-year repayable loan in relation to the FIT project. The cost of this loan has been recognised at market rates in financial costs, and the difference between market rates and the effective interest paid has been recognised as grant income in the year (€6,000; 2006: Nil).

Commercial and operations expenses refer to costs of attendance at trade fairs and commercial travel. These increased due to the higher level of commercial activity undertaken during the year.

Commentary: In this extract, the company specifies the criteria for government grant recognition and its accounting for government grants received in the form of a repayable, low-interest loan. The company applies IAS 20 as amended in 2008.

In addition, the company provides details on its research expenses and the related credit for government grants. Grant income is recognized over the duration of each project, in accordance with the stage payments received or approved following the achievement of each project milestone. Details related to low-interest loan from the government are also provided.

Extract 19(11) – Government grants – Accounting policy

Fugro N.V. (AR 2007), page 85
5.21 _Revenue_ (in part)
5.21.4 Government grants

An unconditional government grant is recognised in the balance sheet when the grant becomes receivable. Any other government grant is initially recognised as deferred income when there is reasonable assurance that it will be received and that the Group will comply with the conditions attached to it. Grants that compensate the Group (partly) for expenses incurred are recognised in the income statement on a systematic basis in the same periods in which the expenses are incurred. Grants that (partly) compensate the Group for the cost of an asset are recognised in the income statement on a systematic basis over the useful life of the asset.

Commentary: This extract describes the company's accounting policy under IAS 20. Note that the company refers to notion of "unconditional government grant" used under IAS 41.

Extract 19(12) – Government grants – Various aspects

AMG Advanced Metallurgical Group N.V. (AR 2007), page 49
Consolidated Balance Sheet (in part)
As at 31 December 2007

In thousands of US Dollars	Note	2007	2006
Liabilities			
Loans and borrowings	21	**115,726**	185,386
Related party debt	22	**–**	721
Employee benefits	24	**102,809**	94,245
Provisions	26	**12,011**	9,988
Government grants	27	**8,585**	–
Other liabilities	28	**9,087**	5,426
Derivative financial instruments	31	**77**	–
Deferred tax liabilities	10	**32,112**	12,989
Total non-current liabilities		**280,407**	308,755

Page 54
2. Basis of preparation (in part)
(c) Use of estimates and judgements (in part)

The preparation of financial statements requires management to make judgements, estimates and assumptions that affect the application of accounting policies and the reported amounts of assets, liabilities, income and expenses. Actual results may differ from these estimates.

Estimates and underlying assumptions are reviewed on an ongoing basis. Revisions to accounting estimates are recognized in the period in which the estimate is revised and in any future periods affected.

In particular, information about significant areas of estimation uncertainty and critical judgements in applying accounting policies that have the most significant effect on the amount recognized in the financial statements are described in the following notes:

- Note 6 – furnace construction contract revenue
- Note 10 – utilisation of tax losses
- Note 12 – measurement of the recoverable amounts of cash-generating units
- Note 24 – measurement of defined benefit obligations
- Note 25 – measurement of share-based payments
- Note 26 – provisions
- Note 27 – government grants
- Note 31 – valuation of financial instruments

AMG Advanced Metallurgical Group N.V. (AR 2007), page 62

3. Significant accounting policies (in part)

(q) Government grants

Certain subsidiaries receive government grants related to early retirement provisions and workforce creation. Government grants are recognized when there is reasonable assurance that the grant will be received and all attaching conditions will be complied with. Since the grants relate to expense items, they are recognized as income over the period necessary to match the grant on a systematic basis to the costs for which they are intended to compensate.

Pages 66-67

5. Acquisitions of associates (in part)

Purchase of land in Berlin by ALD (in part)

... This acquisition does not qualify for purchase accounting since operational assets were acquired rather than an existing business. Therefore, this purchase is being accounted for using government grant accounting to allocate the income of the government grant over the term of the expected personnel expenses that will be incurred. As of 31 December 2007, 84 permanent jobs have been created at the site and ALD IMP has recognised $649 of government grant income. The land purchase created a release of $5,100 that was recognised in connection with this acquisition (note 7). See note 27 for further disclosure of government grants.

Page 97

27. Government grants

	Government Grants
Balance at 1 January 2007	–
Provisions made during the period	15,503
Provisions used during the period	–
Currency and reversals	1,009
Balance at 31 December 2007	16,512
Non-current	8,585
Current	7,927
Balance at 31 December 2007	16,512

As discussed in note 5, ALD has an obligation for personnel expenses relating to its investment in Berlin. Under the government grant accounting being used, ALD established a provision for the personnel expenses which will be reduced by the income from the government grant over the expected term that these expenses will be incurred. As of 31 December 2007, the current and non-current portions of this provision were $7,927 and $8,585 respectively.

Commentary: In the above extract, the company discloses different elements of its accounting and presentation of government grants, including:

- government grant liability in the statement of financial position;
- use of estimates and judgments;
- accounting policy;
- business acquisition; and
- reconciliation of amounts presented on statement of financial position.

Special Government Grant Issues

Agriculture

IAS 41 contains specific requirements for grants given for agricultural activities. Canadian GAAP does not have distinct rules for government assistance on biological assets. IAS 41 includes the following requirements:

- An unconditional government grant related to a biological asset measured at its fair value, less costs to sell, must be recognized as profit or loss when, and only when, the government grant becomes receivable. If the government grant is for a biological asset measured at its cost, less any accumulated depreciation and any accumulated impairment losses, IAS 20 applies.

- A conditional government grant related to a biological asset (including a biological asset that forbids an entity from engaging in a specified agricultural activity) measured at its fair value, less costs to sell, is recognized in profit and loss when, and only when, the conditions attached to the government grant are met.

  o IAS 41 provides an example to illustrate the accounting requirement for conditional government grants. Consider a grant that requires an entity to farm in a particular location for five years. If it farms in that location for less than five years, it has to return the entire amount received. In this case, the grant is not recognized in profit or loss until the five years are up. If, however, the terms of the grant allow the entity to retain a part of the amount, based on the proportion of time that has elapsed, the entity would recognize that part in profit or loss.

IAS 41 does not deal with government grants for agricultural produce. These grants or subsidies are normally payable when the produce is sold and would be recognized as income on the sale.

Emission Rights[3]

IFRIC 3, *Emission Rights* was issued in 2004 but was withdrawn in 2005 for further review. Following the withdrawal of IFRIC 3, the IASB concluded that emission rights are a form of government grant. Accordingly, its intention at that time was to consider emission rights as part of the project to replace IAS 20. To date, there has been no publicly reported progress on issues of government grants, or on the narrow matter of emission rights.

Consequently, companies can use different accounting policies for reporting any emission rights they receive and trade, as well as for reporting any emission obligations. From the perspective of IAS 20, an entity could apply two accounting policies when a government has granted it emission allowances:

1. recognize an intangible asset initially at fair value, together with the government grant (i.e., the government grant is initially recorded at fair value);

2. no recognition of an asset or deferred income (i.e., government grant is initially recorded at nominal amount which is zero). According to our limited analysis, this option appears to be more widely adopted.

Illustrative Disclosures:

None of the disclosures below contradict Canadian GAAP as there are no specific Canadian standards on this issue. Entities could, perhaps, refer to CICA 3831, *Non-monetary Transactions*, which might prompt them to select a different accounting policy.

Extract 19(13) – Government grants – Emission rights

> Österreichische Elektrizitätswirtschafts-Aktiengesellschaft (AR 2007), page 80
> ACCOUNTING POLICIES (in part)
> CONTRIBUTIONS TO BUILDING COSTS AND GOVERNMENT GRANTS
> Contributions to building costs and government grants received are recognized as deferred income under liabilities and are reversed over the useful lives of the assets. Notes to the recognition of grants in connection with emission rights can be found under "Emission rights".

---

3   See also Chapter 15, which addresses emissions rights from the perspective of provisions.

Österreichische Elektrizitätswirtschafts-Aktiengesellschaft (AR 2007), page 77
ACCOUNTING POLICIES (in part)
EMISSION RIGHTS

Emission rights that are held for consumption to the extent of CO_2 emissions at thermal power plants are accounted for on the basis of the provisions of IAS 38, IAS 20 and IAS 37. The rights are recognized as assets at their fair value or at cost on the day of allocation or acquisition. If the rights are freely allocated, deferred income is set up for the grant in the amount of the right's fair value, which is reversed as the rights are consumed, amortized or sold. Those rights that are held for trading purposes are measured, according to IAS 2, at their net realizable value, with the measurement effects being recognized in the income statement.

Commentary: In the above extract, the company provides a specific note on emission rights that are held for consumption, specifically dealing with CO_2 emissions at its thermal power plants, which are accounted at fair value or at cost on the day of allocation or acquisition, respectively.

Extract 19(14) – Government grants – Emission rights

Akzo Nobel N.V. (AR 2007), page 113
Note 1 Summary of significant accounting policies (in part)
Principles of determination of income (in part)
Government grants

Government grants related to cost are recognized in the statement of income in the same periods as the related cost to be compensated and are deducted from the relevant cost. Emission rights granted by the government are recognized at cost, which is generally nil. A provision is recorded if the actual emission is higher than the emission rights granted. For government grants related to assets, see the accounting policy for property, plant, and equipment.

Commentary: Here, the company specifies that emission rights granted by the government are recognized at cost (which is generally nil) and that a provision is recorded if the actual emission is greater than the emission rights granted.

Extract 19(15) – Government grants – Emission rights

Borealis AG (AR 2007), page 64
Balance sheet (in part)
Intangible fixed assets (in part)

Emission rights are reported as intangible fixed assets. They are measured at cost. A liability to return emission rights for actual emissions made, is recognised as well.

Page 65
Balance sheet (in part)
Government grants

Government grants include grants for research and development as well as investment grants. Research and development grants are recognised in the income statement on a systematic basis to offset the related cost, or offset against capitalised development costs. Investment grants are recognised in the balance sheet as deferred income and recognised as income over the useful life of the asset.

Page 79
13. Government grants

Borealis was allowed government grants for the investment in new production plants, CO_2 emission allowances and research and development of EUR 9 million (EUR 11 million), which was recognised in the income statement.

Commentary: This extract provides details on various government grants, including CO_2 emission allowances and research and development. Emission rights are reported as intangible fixed assets measured at cost. CO_2 emission allowances are recognized in the balance sheet as deferred income and are recognized as income over the useful life of the asset.

Borrowing Costs

Scope

IAS 23 must be applied in accounting for borrowing costs. Although these costs are generally expensed, IAS 23 requires their capitalization in certain circumstances.

IAS 23 does not deal with the imputed or actual cost of equity, including preferred capital not classified as liability. It applies only to borrowing costs owed to external creditors.

In addition, IAS 23 does not require (but allows) that borrowing costs be capitalized for:

- assets measured at fair value (such as biological assets accounted for under IAS 41) as it might not be useful in light of the subsequent adjustment to fair value;

- inventories, manufactured or otherwise produced in large quantities on a repetitive basis, even if it takes a long time to get them ready for sale (e.g., maturing whisky); the costs involved in allocating borrowing costs to such inventories and monitoring them until they are sold would most likely exceed any potential benefits.

Key Terms

IAS 23 refers to two key terms: qualifying asset and borrowing costs.

Qualifying assets: are those that require a substantial period of time to get ready for their intended use or sale. They may include inventories, manufacturing plants, intangible assets and investment properties. Excluded from qualifying assets are financial assets, manufactured inventories produced over a short period of time and acquired assets that are ready for their intended use or sale.

Borrowing costs: include more than just interest costs incurred on borrowings. They may include:

- interest expense calculated using the effective interest method as described in IAS 39, *Financial Instruments: Recognition and Measurement*;

- finance charges for finance leases recognized in accordance with IAS 17, *Leases*; and

- exchange differences arising from foreign currency borrowings to the extent that they are regarded as an adjustment to interest costs.

Capitalization

The table below provides a summary of specific IAS 23 guidance on the capitalization of borrowing costs. Canadian GAAP does not contain equivalent guidance.

Issues	IAS 23 Requirements (Note)
Commencement of capitalization	Capitalization should commence when: • expenditure on a qualifying asset is incurred; • borrowing costs are incurred; and • activities necessary to prepare an asset for its intended use or sale have been undertaken (i.e., the asset is being prepared for use). IAS 23 provides additional guidance by specifying that: • expenditures on a qualifying asset include only those expenditures that have resulted in payments of cash, transfers of other assets or the assumption of interest-bearing liabilities; • expenditures are reduced by any progress payments received and government grants received for an asset; • the average carrying amount of an asset during a particular period, including borrowing costs previously capitalized, is normally a reasonable approximation of the expenditures to which the capitalization rate is applied in that period; • activities necessary to prepare an asset for its intended use or sale encompass more than the physical construction of the asset; they also include technical and administrative work prior to the commencement of physical construction, such as the activities associated with obtaining permits prior to the commencement of the physical construction. Such activities, however, exclude holding an asset when no production or development that changes the asset's condition is taking place. For example, borrowing costs incurred while land acquired for building purposes is held without any development work being carried out are expensed, as they do not qualify for capitalization based on criteria set above.

Borrowings eligible for capitalization	Depends on source of funding:
	• If specific to obtaining a qualifying asset: actual borrowing costs incurred on that borrowing during the period, less any investment income on the temporary investment of those borrowings.
	• If general or organized centrally (e.g., within a group of companies): the weighted-average capitalization rate is applied to the expenditures on the qualifying asset. More specifically:
	  o Weighted average of the borrowing costs is calculated based on the borrowings of the entity that are outstanding during the period. Specific funds borrowed to acquire another qualifying asset are excluded from the calculation of the weighted average capitalization rate.
	  o Borrowing costs capitalized in a period cannot exceed the amount of borrowing costs incurred by the entity during that period.
	  o Depending on the circumstances, it may be appropriate to include all borrowings of a parent and its subsidiaries when computing a weighted average of the borrowing costs; in other circumstances, it is appropriate for each subsidiary to use a weighted average of the borrowing costs applicable to its own borrowings.

Issues	IAS 23 Requirements (Note)
Suspension of capitalization	Capitalization is suspended during extended periods in which an entity suspends active development of a qualifying asset. Note, however, that an entity does not normally suspend capitalizing borrowing costs: • during a period when it carries out substantial technical and administrative work; and • when a temporary delay is a necessary part of the process of getting an asset ready for its intended use or sale.
Cessation of capitalization	Capitalization of borrowing costs ceases when substantially all the activities necessary to prepare an asset for its intended use or sale are complete. This will be the case, for instance, where minor modifications are required, such as decorating a property to a purchaser's specification, or where only routine administrative work is required for completion. If an asset is developed in stages, and each stage can be independently used or sold, capitalization of borrowing costs ceases for each stage as it is completed. An example of this is developing a business park, where each unit can be used or sold independently.
Excess of the carrying amount of the qualifying asset over recoverable amount	When the carrying amount or the expected ultimate cost of a qualifying asset exceeds its recoverable amount or net realizable value, the carrying amount is to be written down or written off in accordance with the requirements of other standards, such as IAS 36, *Impairment of Assets.*

Note: The previous version of IAS 23 permitted two accounting treatments for borrowing costs: include these costs as a period expense when incurred or add borrowing costs to the carrying value of the qualifying assets. The revised IAS 23 requires interest to be capitalized in certain circumstances. It is mandatory for annual periods beginning on or after 1 January 2009. Early application is permitted. If an entity previously had an accounting policy of expensing borrowing costs that should be capitalized according to revised IAS 23, the change of accounting policy may be applied prospectively. The requirement to capitalize borrowing costs applies to qualifying assets acquired after the date of adoption of the revised standard. There is no requirement to restate existing assets (although an earlier date from which borrowing costs are capitalized can be designated if an entity wishes to do so).

Disclosures

The following items must be disclosed:

• the amount of borrowing costs capitalized during the period; and
• the capitalization rate used to determine the amount of borrowing costs eligible for capitalization.

Illustrative Disclosures:

The disclosures below do not contradict Canadian GAAP.

Extract 19(16) – Borrowing costs – Impact of amended IAS 23

Deutsche Telekom AG (AR 2007), page 109

Standards, interpretations and amendments issued, but not yet adopted (in part)

In March 2007, the IASB issued an amendment to IAS 23 "Borrowing Costs." The European Union has not yet endorsed the amendment to IAS 23. The amendment to the standard mainly relates to the elimination of the option of immediately recognizing borrowing costs directly attributable to the acquisition, construction or production of a qualifying asset as an expense. Currently, Deutsche Telekom recognizes these costs directly as an expense. A qualifying asset in this context is an asset that takes a substantial period of time to get ready for its intended use or sale. In future, an entity is therefore required to capitalize borrowing costs as part of the cost of the qualifying assets. The revised standard does not require the capitalization of borrowing costs relating to assets measured at fair value, and inventories that are manufactured or produced in large quantities on a repetitive basis, even if they take a substantial period of time to get ready for use or sale. The standard applies to borrowing costs relating to qualifying assets for which the commencement date for capitalization is on or after January 1, 2009. Deutsche Telekom is currently analyzing the date of adoption of the amendment to IAS 23 and the resulting effects on the presentation of Deutsche Telekom's results of operations, financial position or cash flows.

Commentary: This extract illustrates an accounting policy for the application of current IAS 23. The company specifies that it is assessing the impact of the amendment to the standard on its financial statements.

Extract 19(17) – Borrowing costs – Impact of amended IAS 23

Gold Fields Limited (AR 2008), page 121

1. BASIS OF PREPARATION (in part)

Standards, interpretations and amendments to published standards effective in fiscal 2008 (in part)

IAS 23 Borrowing Costs (revised) requires an entity to capitalise borrowing costs directly attributable to the acquisition, construction or production of a qualifying asset as part of the cost of that asset. The option of immediately expensing those borrowing costs has been removed. This standard does not have any impact on the Group's financial statements as Gold Fields had already adopted in its accounting policies the allowed alternative of the previous statement which allowed capitalisation of borrowing costs.

Commentary: This extract shows an accounting policy for the application of current IAS 23. The company specifies that amendment would not have an impact on its financial statements.

Extract 19(18) – Borrowing costs – Impact of amended IAS 23

Aker Kvaerner ASA (AR 2007), page 42

Note 2: Accounting principles (in part)

New standards effective in 2007 (in part)

Except for the standard on borrowing costs, it is assumed that the new standards will have only insignificant effect on reported results or balance sheet items. The main effects will relate to presentation formats for financial statements and for the note disclosures.

The standard on borrowing costs requires that interest be included as part of the cost of qualifying assets which includes property plant and equipment and construction contracts. Today, borrowing costs are expensed as incurred. Although the company does not believe the new standard will have a significant impact on its financial statements in the aggregate, there could be some effects within segment reporting.

Commentary: This extract shows an accounting policy for the application of current IAS 23. The company specifies that amendment will not have a significant impact on its financial statements.

Extract 19(19) – Borrowing costs – Early adoption of amended IAS 23

Acc-Ross Holdings Limited (AR 2007), page 29

1. ADOPTION OF NEW AND REVISED STANDARDS (in part)

IAS 23 Borrowing costs

The option of immediately recognising as an expense borrowing costs that relate to assets that take a substantial period of time to get ready for use or sale, has been removed. An entity is therefore required to capitalise borrowing costs as part of the cost of such assets. The only exceptions are the capitalisation of borrowing costs relating to assets measured at fair value, and inventories that are manufactured or produced in large quantities on a repetitive basis, even if they take a substantial period of time to get ready for use or sale.

The revised Standard applies to borrowing costs relating to qualifying assets for which the commencement date for capitalisation is on or after 1 January 2009. However, early adoption is permitted and encouraged. In light of these changes the Group decided to adopt the revised standard in 2007 which resulted in a restatement of results retrospectively.

Page 33

2. SIGNIFICANT ACCOUNTING POLICIES (in part)

Borrowing costs

Borrowing costs directly attributable to the acquisition, construction or production of qualifying assets, which are assets that necessarily take a substantial period of time to get ready for their intended use or sale, are added to the cost of those assets, until such time as the assets are substantially ready for their intended use or sale. Investment income earned on the temporary investment of specific borrowings pending their expenditure on qualifying assets is deducted from the borrowing costs eligible for capitalisation.

All other borrowing costs are recognised in profit of loss in the period in which they are incurred.

Page 48

19. FINANCE COSTS

	28/02/07	Restated 28/02/06
	R	R
Interest on bank balances	21 746	38 417
Interest on other loans and payables	26 896 365	20 739 768
Interest on obligations under finance leases	74 253	20 356
Dividends on cumulative redeemable preference shares classified as financial liabilities	7 281 109	5 236 520
Total interest expense	34 273 473	26 035 061
Less: amounts included in the cost of qualifying assets	(20 428 017)	(16 272 832)
	13 845 456	**9 762 229**

The amounts included in the cost of qualifying assets related to finance costs directly attributed to the project or development. A weighted average capitalisation rate on funds borrowed is not used.

Commentary: This extract provides an illustration of an accounting policy showing the application of current IAS 23 retrospectively. The company discloses details of borrowing costs, including amounts capitalized.

Extract 19(20) – Borrowing costs – Presentation and disclosures

Dimension Data Holdings plc (AR 2007), page 58

2. SIGNIFICANT ACCOUNTING POLICIES (in part)

Borrowing costs

Borrowing costs directly attributable to the acquisition, construction or production of qualifying assets, which are assets that necessarily take a substantial period of time to get ready for their intended use or sale, are added to the cost of those assets, until such time as the assets are substantially ready for their intended use or sale. Investment income earned on the temporary investment in specific borrowings pending their expenditure on qualifying assets is deducted from the borrowing costs eligible for capitalisation.

All other borrowing costs are recognised in the income statement in the period in which they are incurred.

Page 68

10. FINANCE COSTS

Interest on bank overdrafts and loans	**(6,630)**	(5,596)
Interest on convertible loan notes	**–**	(1,722)
Interest on obligations under finance leases	**(23,413)**	(23,944)
Total borrowing costs	**(30,043)**	(31,262)
Less: amounts included in the cost of qualifying assets	**–**	177
	(30,043)	(31,085)
Other	**(272)**	(972)
	(30,315)	(32,057)

Commentary: This extract shows an accounting policy for the application of current IAS 23. The extracts include disclosures and presentation of accounting policy and details of finance costs, including amounts capitalized.

Extract 19(21) – Borrowing costs – Presentation and disclosures

Transnet Limited (AR 2008), page 147

Accounting policies (in part)

Change in accounting policy (in part)

IAS 23: Borrowing Costs

The Group has elected to early adopt the amendments to IAS 23 revised. All borrowing costs incurred on qualifying assets are capitalised to the cost of property, plant and equipment. This amendment has been applied to all qualifying assets that commenced construction on or after 1 April 2006. The financial effect of this change in accounting policy has resulted in a reduction of finance costs by R52 million before taxation in the March 2007 financial year.

Page 150

Accounting policies (in part)

Borrowing costs

The Group capitalises borrowing costs that are directly attributable to the acquisition, construction or production of a qualifying asset, as part of the cost of that asset, until such time that the asset is substantially ready for its intended use. The Group identifies a qualifying asset as one that necessarily takes six months or more to get ready for its intended use.

To the extent that funds are borrowed specifically for the purpose of obtaining a qualifying asset, the Group capitalises the actual borrowing costs incurred on that borrowing during the period less any investment income on the temporary investment of these borrowings.

To the extent that a qualifying asset is funded via general borrowings, the Group determines borrowing costs eligible for capitalisation by applying the weighted average cost of borrowings for the period, to the expenditures on that asset.

All other borrowing costs are recognised in profit or loss in the period in which they are incurred.

Transnet Limited (AR 2008) (continued)

Net financing costs

Net financing costs comprise interest payable on borrowings calculated using the effective interest rate method, dividends on redeemable preference shares, amortisation of discounts on bonds and foreign exchange gains and losses, less amounts capitalised to qualifying assets.

Page 163

Cash flow statements (in part)

COMPANY				GROUP	
2007 Restated* R million	2008 R million		Notes	2008 R million	2007 Restated* R million
7 893	10 459	Cash flows from operating activities		10 858	8 903
11 703	12 533	Cash generated from operations	35.1	13 143	13 540
412	771	Changes in working capital	35.2	860	133
12 115	13 304	Cash generated from operations after working capital changes		14 003	13 673
(2 077)	(2 497)	Finance costs	35.3	(2 782)	(2 791)
225	730	Finance income		768	304
(1 901)	(915)	Taxation paid	35.4	(928)	(1 961)
(421)	(223)	Settlement of post-retirement benefit obligations		(227)	(453)
(48)	60	Derivatives raised and settled		24	139
–	–	Dividends paid to minorities	35.5	–	(8)
(7 957)	(13 554)	**Cash flows from investing activities**		(8 234)	(10 307)
(4 780)	(6 720)	Investment to maintain operations		(1 183)	(6 809)
(7 907)	(8 531)	Replacements to property, plant and equipment		(8 729)	(8 176)
(6)	(34)	Additions to intangible assets		(34)	(108)
(52)	(287)	Borrowing costs capitalised		(287)	(52)
(1)	–	Intercompany transfers of intangible assets		–	–
220	468	Proceeds on the disposal of property, plant and equipment		519	315
2	11	Proceeds on the disposal of intangible assets		11	3
–	990	Net proceeds on the disposal of subsidiaries/division	35.6	878	(1 922)
–	–	C-class preference share redeemed		5 622	–
1 854	47	Proceeds on the disposal of associates		47	1 854
–	–	Minorities acquired		(150)	–
47	111	Dividend income		9	36
59	–	Acquisition of subsidiary/division	35.7	–	–
(4)	(1)	Acquisition of associates		(1)	(4)
117	(440)	Net loans to subsidiaries and associates		(69)	4
525	1 291	Net receipts of long-term loans and advances		1 291	522
366	(345)	(Increase)/decrease in investments		(290)	719
(3 177)	(6 834)	*Investment to expand operations*		(7 051)	(3 498)
(3 177)	(6 834)	Expansions – property, plant and equipment		(7 051)	(3 498)
2 599	5 743	**Cash flows from financing activities**		9	3 669
6 172	12 044	Borrowings raised		8 952	6 465
(3 573)	(6 301)	Borrowings repaid		(8 943)	(2 796)
2 535	2 648	Net increase in cash and cash equivalents		2 633	2 265
1 082	3 617	Cash and cash equivalents at the beginning of the year		3 956	1 691
3 617	6 265	**Total cash and cash equivalents at the end of the year**	19	6 589	3 956

Transnet Limited (AR 2008) (continued)
Page 170

COMPANY			GROUP	
2007 Restated* R million	2008 R million		2008 R million	2007 Restated* R million
		6. Finance costs		
32	10	Net foreign exchange losses/(gains) on translation	15	(32)
303	242	Discounts on bonds amortised	242	303
30	14	Finance lease obligation	21	40
2 047	2 483	Interest cost – Financial liabilities at amortised cost	2 761	2 751
2 412	2 749		3 039	3 062
(52)	(287)	Borrowing costs capitalised	(287)	(52)
2 360	2 462		2 752	3 010
–	–	Discontinued operations	(44)	(500)
2 360	2 462	Continuing operations	2 708	2 510

Commentary: This extract provides an illustration of an accounting policy for the application of current IAS 23. Extracts include the following disclosures and presentation:

- accounting policy;
- extract of the cash-flow statement showing borrowing costs capitalized in investing activities;
- details of finance costs, including amounts capitalized.

Extract 19(22) – Borrowing costs – Policy for capitalization

Lihir Gold Limited (AR 2007), page 52
NOTE 1: STATEMENT OF SIGNIFICANT ACCOUNTING POLICIES (in part)
(vii) Capitalisation of interest and financing costs

Interest and other financing costs that are directly attributable to the acquisition, construction or production of a qualifying asset are capitalised as part of the cost of that asset. To the extent that funds are borrowed specifically for the purpose of obtaining a qualifying asset, the amount of borrowing costs eligible for capitalisation on that asset is determined as the actual borrowing costs incurred on that borrowing during the period. Capitalisation of borrowing costs ceases when all the activities necessary to prepare the qualifying asset for its intended use or sale are substantially complete. Interest earned on the temporary investment of borrowed funds is deducted from interest paid on the borrowed funds in arriving at the amounts so capitalised. These costs are amortised on the same basis as the qualifying asset.

To the extent that funds are borrowed generally and used for the purpose of obtaining a qualifying asset, the amount of borrowing costs eligible for capitalisation shall be determined by applying a capitalisation rate to the expenditures on that asset. The capitalisation rate is the weighted average of the borrowing costs applicable to the borrowings of the entity that are outstanding during the period, other than borrowings made specifically for the purpose of obtaining a qualifying asset.

Lihir Gold Limited (AR 2007) (continued)

Page 54

(xiii) Leases

Leases are classified as finance leases whenever the terms of the lease transfer substantially all the risks and rewards of ownership to the lessee. All other leases are classified as operating leases.

Finance leases are capitalised, recording an asset equal to the fair value of the leased asset or, if lower, the present value of the minimum lease payments, including any guaranteed residual values. The corresponding liability, net of finance charges, is included in other short-term and long term payables in the Statement of Financial Position. Finance charges are charged directly to profit or loss, unless they are directly attributable to qualifying assets, in which case they are capitalised in accordance with the Consolidated Entity's general policy on borrowing costs. Assets acquired under finance leases are amortised over the shorter of their estimated useful lives or the lease term. Lease payments are allocated between the reduction of the lease liability and the lease interest expense for the period.

Lease payments for operating leases (net of any incentives received from the lessor), are charged to the Statement of Comprehensive Income in the periods in which they are incurred.

Penalties paid for early settlement of leases are expensed.

Commentary: This extract shows how the company applied IAS 23 in its capitalization of borrowing costs, including imputed interest on leases.

Extract 19(23) – Borrowing costs – Amount capitalized and rate used

Luminar plc (AR 2007), page 56

3 NET FINANCE COSTS

Net finance costs relating to continuing operations are as follows:

	Year ended 1 March 2007 £m	Year ended 2 March 2006 £m
Interest payable on bank borrowings	(7.6)	(10.1)
Interest payable on obligations under finance leases	(0.4)	(0.3)
Amortisation of issue costs of bank loan (note 18)	(0.2)	(0.1)
Other interest payable	(0.1)	(0.3)
Total borrowing costs	(8.3)	(10.8)
Less amounts capitalised in the cost of qualifying assets	—	0.2
Losses arising on derivatives	—	(0.5)
FINANCE COSTS	(8.3)	(11.1)
Income on bank deposits	1.4	1.8
Interest on loan to associate	0.2	—
Other interest receivable	—	0.8
INTEREST RECEIVABLE	1.6	2.6
FINANCE COSTS — NET	(6.7)	(8.5)

Finance costs relating to discontinued operations, being interest payable on obligations under finance leases, total £0.1m (2006: £0.1m).

Interest capitalised in the cost of qualifying assets is calculated using the borrowing rate obtainable by the Group under its current facility at the start of each financial year. Interest is calculated from the date capital expenditure commences until the opening of the relevant unit.

Commentary: This extract presents an illustration of finance costs details, including amounts capitalized. Note that the company uses the rate at the group level for borrowing cost capitalization.

Extract 19(24) – Borrowing costs – Capitalization rate

Sasol Limited (Annual Financial Statements 2007), page 61

Principal accounting policies (in part)

Borrowing costs

Borrowing costs are capitalised against qualifying assets as part of property, plant and equipment.

Such borrowing costs are capitalised over the period during which the asset is being acquired or constructed and borrowings have been incurred. Capitalisation ceases when construction is interrupted for an extended period or when the asset is substantially complete. Further borrowing costs are charged to the income statement.

Where funds are borrowed specifically for the purpose of acquiring or constructing a qualifying asset, the amount of borrowing costs eligible for capitalisation on that asset is the actual borrowing costs incurred on the borrowing during the period less any investment income on the temporary investment of those borrowings.

Where funds are made available from general borrowings and used for the purpose of acquiring or constructing qualifying assets, the amount of borrowing costs eligible for capitalisation is determined by applying a capitalisation rate to the expenditures on these assets. The capitalisation rate is the weighted average of the interest rates applicable to the borrowings of the group that are outstanding during the period, other than borrowings made specifically for the purpose of obtaining qualifying assets. The amount of borrowing costs capitalised will not exceed the amount of borrowing costs incurred.

Commentary: This extract discloses the rates used for capitalization of borrowing cost, as required by IAS 23.

Extract 19(25) – Borrowing costs – Accounting policy

Steinoff International Holdings Limited (AR 2007), pages 114 and 115

Summary of accounting policies for the year ended 30 June 2007 (in part)

Borrowing costs

Borrowing costs are recognised as an expense in the period in which they are incurred, except to the extent that it is directly attributable to the acquisition, construction or production of assets that necessarily take a substantial period to prepare for their intended use or sale. Borrowing costs directly attributable to these qualifying assets are capitalised as part of the costs of those assets.

To the extent that funds are borrowed specifically for the purpose of obtaining a qualifying asset, the amount of borrowing costs capitalised are the actual borrowing costs incurred on that borrowing during the period less any investment income on the temporary investment of those borrowings. To the extent that funds are borrowed generally and used for the purposes of obtaining a qualifying asset, the amount of borrowing costs capitalised are determined by applying a capitalisation rate to the expenditures on that asset. The capitalisation rate applied is the weighted average of the borrowing costs applicable to the borrowings of the group that are outstanding during the period, other than borrowings made specifically for the purpose of obtaining a qualifying asset.

Capitalisation of borrowing costs is suspended during extended periods in which active development is interrupted.

Capitalisation of borrowing costs ceases when the assets are substantially ready for their intended use or sale.

Commentary: This extract provides an illustration of accounting policy disclosure under IAS 23.

FUTURE DEVELOPMENTS

The IASB has two government grant projects on its agenda:

- amendments to IAS 20; and
- emission trading schemes (ETS).

Note that the second project deals with different ETS issues, including emission rights obtained from a government, which are a form of government grant. There is no outstanding project on changes to IAS 23.

Amendments to IAS 20

This project has been deferred since 2006 and the IASB is monitoring progress in other related projects, including the one on ETS and revenue recognition, to determine appropriate timing for launching this project.

The IASB has many reservations about IAS 20 requirements:

- it is inconsistent with the IASB Framework;
- it might be preferable to use the guidelines in IAS 41, *Agriculture* to distinguish unconditional from conditional grants;
- it contains many options that could affect financial statement comparability.

Emission Trading Schemes (ETS)

The IASB and the FASB are conducting a joint project to develop comprehensive guidance on accounting for emission trading schemes. Such schemes are designed to achieve a reduction of greenhouse gases through the use of tradable emission permits.

The IASB has noted the increasing international use of emissions trading schemes and the considerable diversity in practice that appears to have arisen in the absence of authoritative guidance. It has, therefore, decided to limit the scope of the project to accounting for ETS, rather than broadly addressing the accounting for all government grants (which would have involved activating the IAS 20 project). Finally, it has tentatively decided to address the accounting of all tradable emissions rights and obligations arising under ETS, as well as activities that entities undertake when they expect to receive tradable rights in future periods, e.g., certified emissions reductions (CERs).

COMPREHENSIVE EXAMPLE

This chapter does not contain a comprehensive example because it covers two distinct standards that have been illustrated in the other extracts above.

PLANNING FOR IMPLEMENTATION

The standards covered in this chapter have limited impact on IFRS implementation. In particular circumstances, the adoption of IAS 23 requirements for the capitalization of borrowing costs might have an impact on information systems. Entities must ensure that their systems can record capital expenditures, borrowing costs and construction activities in sufficient detail to enable them to comply with revised IAS 23.

There are no specific provisions in IFRS 1, *First-time Adoption of International Financial Reporting Standards* related to government grants. Consequently, an entity will have to apply requirements IAS 20 retroactively. As for borrowing costs, an entity implementing IFRS may apply the transitional provisions set out in IAS 23 as revised in 2007, i.e., effective date shall be interpreted as 1 January 2009 or the date of transition to IFRS, whichever is later.

Current IFRS allow an entity to use various acceptable accounting treatments for emission rights. Consequently, financial statements might be affected differently depending on an entity's accounting choices. When emission rights are significant, companies will have to explain their accounting policies for those rights to ensure that financial statement users can understand the impact of that accounting on their financial performance.

Chapter 20
First-time Adoption of IFRS[1]

Standard Discussed in this Chapter
IFRS 1 – First-time Adoption of International Financial Reporting Standards

INTRODUCTION

IFRS 1 is not a static standard and consequently entities have to refer to the most recent version published by the IASB. This Standard establishes the procedures to follow when IFRS standards are initially adopted. Under the Canadian AcSB plan to transition to IFRS, a publicly accountable is required to apply IFRS 1 to its first IFRS financial statements (i.e., for the year ended December 31, 2011) as well as to each interim financial report presented in the period covered by those first IFRS statements (i.e., each quarter in 2011). IFRS 1 does not apply to changes in accounting policies made by an entity that is already using IFRS.

IFRS 1 requires companies to prepare their first IFRS financial statements, as well as all comparative periods covered in those statements, in accordance with IFRS standards in effect as of December 31, 2011 or for which early adoption is allowed). As a starting point, they must prepare and present an opening statement of financial position at the date of transition to IFRS (i.e., January 1, 2010), which reflects the retrospective application of IFRS standards, unless mandatory or optional exemption is applied. All adjustments to the opening statement of financial position must generally be recorded in retained earnings or another category of equity, as appropriate.

IFRS 1 also requires that the first IFRS financial statements disclose the reconciliations of certain items previously reported under Canadian GAAP, which were restated to comply with IFRS.

This chapter discusses some of the decisions Canadian entities will have to make when they apply IFRS 1 as a result of adopting IFRS for the first time. It covers the following topics:

- overview;
- scope;
- definitions;
- preparing the opening IFRS statement of financial position:
    - o general requirements,
    - o procedures,
    - o optional exemptions,

---

1 Unless otherwise indicated, all discussions in this chapter assume a Canadian company with a calendar year end that has to present only one year of comparative financial statements.

o   mandatory exceptions;

- financial reports prior to IFRS adoption;
- first interim IFRS reports;
- first annual IFRS reports;
- disclosures in periods subsequent to IFRS adoption.

IMPACT ON FINANCIAL STATEMENTS

The first IFRS financial statements start with an opening IFRS statement of financial position at the transition date (i.e., January 1, 2010) which:

- includes all assets and liabilities that IFRS require;
- excludes any assets and liabilities that IFRS do not permit;
- classifies all assets, liabilities and equity in accordance with IFRS; and
- measures all items in accordance with IFRS.

The application of these principles will result in adjustments to the opening statement of financial position for differences among specific Canadian and IFRS standards (see discussions in the specific chapters) and exemptions elected under IFRS 1. For example, adjustments to the opening statement of financial position may be required as a result of:

- the recognition of liabilities for contingent losses due to the lower recognition threshold under IAS 37, *Provisions, Contingent Liabilities and Contingent Assets* than under Canadian GAAP;
- the measurement of impairment of property, plant and equipment, which differs under IFRS and Canadian GAAP.

In addition to all of the disclosures required by IFRS, the first IFRS financial statements will also, in accordance with IFRS 1, include the disclosure of information to help users understand the effect the transition from Canadian GAAP to IFRS had on the financial statements.

ANALYSIS OF RELEVANT ISSUES

This section discusses the key considerations to keep in mind when adopting IFRS for the first time, along with its requirements and optional exemptions. Extracts of disclosures in the financial reports of entities at various stages of the transition to IFRS are also provided for illustrative purposes.

Overview

The adoption of IFRS results in the full retrospective application of all IFRS standards in effect as of the closing statement of financial position date (i.e., December 31, 2011). Since the retrospective application of IFRS may not always be practical, IFRS 1 was issued to provide some relief.

More specifically, the objective of IFRS 1 is to ensure that an entity's first IFRS financial statements, and its interim financial reports for part of the period that those financial statements cover, contain high-quality information that:

- is transparent for users and comparable over all periods presented;
- provides a suitable starting point for accounting in accordance IFRS; and
- can be generated at a cost that does not exceed the benefits to users.

IFRS 1 contains optional exemptions that provide practical accommodations to help make first-time adoption less onerous. In addition, IFRS 1 provides mandatory exceptions to prevent the use of hindsight and the application of successive versions of the same standards.

Scope

IFRS 1 applies when an entity prepares its first IFRS financial statements, which contain an explicit and unreserved statement of compliance with IFRS. Such an entity is a "first-time adopter."

Although, in general, all Canadian entities moving to IFRS are considered to be first-time adopters, some may have to take a deeper look at the applicability of IFRS 1 to their particular circumstances. For example, a Canadian subsidiary might prepare, at the request of its parent, IFRS consolidation packages. Since these packages are used internally, they might not be corrected for any inconsistencies with IFRS (because of materiality considerations). Consequently, the consolidation packages would not normally be subject to an explicit and unreserved statement of compliance with IFRS.

When an entity's prior-year financial statements contained such an explicit and unreserved statement of compliance with IFRS, but did not, in fact, fully comply with all aspects of IFRS, it is not considered a first-time adopter. The disclosed or undisclosed departures from IFRS in those financial statements are errors, which require correction in accordance with IAS 8, *Accounting Policies Changes in Accounting Estimates and Errors*.

Definitions

The table below presents definitions of certain key terms and some related observations that might be helpful when analyzing IFRS 1 requirements.

Term	Date	IFRS 1 Definition	Observations
Opening IFRS statement of financial position	January 1, 2010 (i.e., December 31, 2009 year end)	An entity's statement of financial position at the date of transition to IFRS.	This statement is the starting point for all subsequent accounting under IFRS. It must be presented in the first IFRS financial statements because, when a policy is applied retrospectively, IAS 1, *Presentation of Financial Statements* requires a company to present a statement of financial position as of the beginning of the earliest comparative period.
Date of transition to IFRS	January 1, 2010	The beginning of the earliest period for which an entity presents full comparative information under IFRS in its first IFRS financial statements.	The date of transition to IFRS depends on: • the date of adoption of IFRS; and • the number of years of comparative information that an entity is required to present along with the financial information of the year of adoption. In general, Canadian companies are to present one year of comparative financial statements.
Date of adoption	January 1, 2011	The date of adoption is not defined in IFRS 1, but is commonly understood.	The date of adoption is the beginning of the fiscal year for which IFRS financial statements are first prepared.

Term	Date	IFRS 1 Definition	Observations
First IFRS financial statements	December 31, 2011	The first annual financial statements in which an entity adopts IFRS, by an explicit and unreserved statement of compliance with IFRS.	See the above discussion on the scope of IFRS 1.
Deemed cost		An amount used as a surrogate for cost or depreciated cost at a given date. Subsequent depreciation or amortization assumes that the entity had initially recognized the asset or liability at the given date and that its cost was equal to the deemed cost.	
First IFRS reporting period	December 31, 2011 year end	The latest reporting period covered by an entity's first IFRS financial statements.	
First-time adopter		An entity that presents its first IFRS financial statements.	

Preparing Opening IFRS Statement of Financial Position

General Requirements

The opening IFRS statement of financial position (as at January 1, 2010) serves as the starting point for financial reporting under IFRS. To prepare its opening statement of financial position, an entity:

- recognizes all assets and liabilities whose recognition is required by IFRS;

- derecognizes assets or liabilities if IFRS do not permit such recognition;

- reclassifies items that it recognized under Canadian GAAP as one type of asset, liability or component of equity, but are a different type of asset, liability or component of equity under IFRS; and

- measures all recognized assets and liabilities in accordance with IFRS.

IFRS 1 requires that an opening IFRS statement of financial position be based on accounting policies that comply with the *current* version of IFRS. This means that the opening statement of financial position will reflect balances as if an entity had *always applied IFRS*. This relieves the entity from having to apply different versions of IFRS promulgated at earlier dates.

Consequently, all statements of financial position, including the opening statement of financial position at January 1, 2010, have to be prepared in accordance with IFRS standards that are effective as at December 31, 2011. In general, IFRS 1 prohibits an entity from applying the transitional provisions contained in other IFRS standards (as these transitional provisions typically apply to entities that have already adopted IFRS rather than first-time adopters).

When preparing its opening statement of financial position, an entity has to apply IFRS requirements retrospectively, unless IFRS 1:

- grants optional exemptions because the cost of retroactive application would be likely to exceed the benefits obtained from it;
- prohibits retrospective application of IFRS because that requires management to make judgments about past conditions after the outcome of a particular transaction is already known.

Procedures

An entity would adjust its last statement of financial position, prepared in accordance with Canadian GAAP (as at December 31, 2009) by sequentially completing the following steps:

- recognize assets and liabilities as required by IFRS;
- derecognize assets and liabilities whose recognition is not permitted under IFRS;
- adjust values of recognized assets and liabilities as required by IFRS;
- recognize and measure deferred taxes in accordance with IFRS;
- recognize and measure non-controlling interest in accordance with IFRS;
- adjust goodwill balances and test for impairment by comparing the carrying amount of cash generating units (CGU) to which goodwill has been allocated to the recoverable amount of the CGU.

Optional Exemptions

IFRS 1 provides optional exemptions in the following areas:

- business combinations;
- fair value or revaluation as deemed cost;
- employee benefits;
- cumulative translation differences;
- compound financial instruments;
- assets and liabilities of subsidiaries, associates and joint ventures;
- designation of previously recognized financial instruments;
- share-based payment transactions;
- insurance contracts;
- decommissioning liabilities included in the cost of property, plant and equipment;
- leases;
- fair value measurement of financial assets or financial liabilities at initial recognition;
- a financial asset or an intangible asset accounted for in accordance with IFRIC 12, *Service Concession Arrangements*;
- borrowing costs; and
- investments in subsidiaries, jointly controlled entities and associates.

An entity:

- may take advantage of all, some or none of these exemptions;
- cannot apply any of these exemptions by analogy to other items; and

- should be aware that the use of these exemptions has no impact on the ongoing accounting policy choices it can make under IFRS.

The impact of optional exemptions to retrospective application was discussed in detail in previous chapters, which cover specific standards. The election to use an optional exemption affects both the opening IFRS statement of financial position and subsequent results. The table below summarizes the effect of optional exemptions that are of relevance to Canadian entities.

Areas	Choices (see note)	Comments
Business combinations (exemption is also available for past acquisitions of investments in associates and interests in joint ventures)	An entity can select one of the following: - restate retrospectively *all* business combinations after a particular date in accordance with IFRS 3; or - not restate *any* business combinations retrospectively (i.e., apply IFRS 3 prospectively).	- An entity choosing to apply this exemption is not required to restate business combinations to comply with IFRS 3, *Business Combinations* where control was obtained before the transition date. - As the exemption can be applied to all transactions that meet the definition of a business combination under IFRS 3, the prior Canadian GAAP classification is not relevant for determining whether the exemption can be applied. - The exemption also applies to acquisitions of investments in associates and joint ventures, which means that entities taking advantage of the exemption will not have to recalculate the goodwill related to these acquisitions in accordance with IFRS. - IFRS 1 contains supplementary guidance for an entity that elects to use this optional exemption (see the "Implementation" section in Chapter 5 for more details). - Goodwill must be tested for impairment at the date of transition to IFRS, using the method required under IAS 36 (which differs from the one used under Canadian GAAP), regardless of whether this exemption is used. - Note that CICA 1582, *Business Combinations* is substantially converged with IFRS 3 and will be effective at the changeover date, with early adoption permitted. CICA 1582 does not require retrospective application, which is consistent with the optional exemption under IFRS 1. (See Chapters 5 and 7 for further details.)

Areas	Choices (see note)	Comments

Fair value as deemed cost	In general, a Canadian entity could use one of the following as deemed cost for an item of property, plant and equipment:
	• fair value at the date of transition;
	• a revaluation under previous GAAP (e.g., impairment value); or
	• a previous GAAP event-driven fair value measurement (e.g., initial public offering).
	Note that the "fair value as deemed cost" exemption may be applied on an asset-by-asset basis.
		• An entity that decides not to use this optional exemption will have to account for property, plant and equipment as if the requirements of IAS 16, *Property, Plant and Equipment* had always been applied. While the requirements under Canadian GAAP do not differ significantly from IFRS, the adoption of IAS 16 may result in adjustments for:
		  o depreciation because IAS 16 requires depreciation to be calculated for each significant component of an item of property, plant and equipment (while this approach is allowed under Canadian GAAP, it is not frequently applied in practice), and
		  o any previous overhauls that were expensed must be capitalized and depreciated on the expected time to the next overhaul.
		• An entity may also apply this exemption to investment property if it elects to use the cost model in IAS 40, *Investment Property* or to intangible assets that meet both the recognition and revaluation criteria in IAS 38, *Intangible Assets* (including reliable measurement of original cost and the existence of an active market). An entity may not use these elections for other assets or for liabilities.
		• An entity that applies the fair value as deemed cost exemption at the IFRS transition date is not required to revalue these assets in subsequent periods.
		• An entity that elects to use an impairment value established previously (i.e., in accordance with CICA 3063, *Impairment of Long-lived Assets*) as deemed cost, may do so only if it is broadly comparable to fair value in accordance with IFRS.
		• When the exemption is applied, deemed cost is the basis for subsequent depreciation and impairment tests.
		(See Chapter 12 for more details.)

Areas	Choices (see note)	Comments
Employee benefits	An entity can elect to recognize all cumulative actuarial gains and losses for all defined benefit plans. If the entity uses this election, it must apply it to all defined benefit plans. IFRS 1 also provides an optional exemption for certain disclosure requirements under IAS 19, *Employee Benefits*.	• Even though Canadian GAAP also allows an entity to use the corridor approach, the amounts calculated may differ from those calculated under IAS 19. • Without this exemption, if an entity chose to use the corridor approach allowed by IAS 19, it would have to recalculate actuarial gains and losses from the date of inception of its defined benefit plan in order to determine the cumulative amounts at the date of transition. • An entity can use this election even if it intends to select a different accounting treatment for such gains and losses going forward (for example, the corridor approach). • Despite this exemption, an entity may need to obtain new actuarial valuations for its defined benefit plans on adoption of IFRS because of potential differences between Canadian GAAP and IFRS. For example, differences may arise from the actuarial method used (IAS 19 requires the use of the projected unit credit method), the accounting treatment of vested past service costs (IAS 19 requires immediate recognition) and different amortization periods for unrealized gains and losses and past service costs. Therefore, an entity should ensure that its actuary is capable of performing valuations in accordance with IAS 19 (which may differ from those performed in accordance Canadian GAAP). • By applying this exemption, an entity recognizes in opening retained earnings all previously unrecognized actuarial gains and losses from inception of the plans. Such actuarial gains and losses are not subsequently recycled through profit and loss. (See Chapter 16 for more details.)
Cumulative translation differences	A Canadian entity can elect to reset to zero all cumulative translation differences arising on monetary items that form part of an entity's net investment in a foreign operation.	An entity that elects to use this optional exemption would reset to zero all cumulative translation gains and losses at the transition date through an adjustment to opening retained earnings. Such an adjustment is permanent, and gains or losses on subsequent disposals of foreign operations will exclude translation differences that arose before the transition date. Translation differences arising after the transition date are recorded in other comprehensive income. (See Chapter 10 for more details.)

Areas	Choices (see note)	Comments
Compound financial instruments	An entity need not apply split accounting (i.e., allocate debt and equity components) to a compound instrument if the liability component of that instrument is no longer outstanding at the transition date.	This exemption may not seem relevant in a Canadian context; however, the method in which the debt and equity components of a compound financial instrument are allocated under Canadian GAAP differs from the one used under IFRS. Broadly, under Canadian GAAP, there are two methods of allocating the proceeds: (1) the relative fair value method, where the fair value of each component is determined and the proceeds are allocated on a pro-rata basis, or (2) the residual method, where an entity determines the fair value of the component, which is easier to determine, and then allocates the residual proceeds to the other component. Under IFRS, the liability component is always calculated first and the equity component is allocated to the residual amount. (See Chapter 9 for more details.)
Assets and liabilities of subsidiaries, associates and joint ventures	A Canadian subsidiary converting to IFRS at a later date than its parent may elect to measure its assets and liabilities either: • in accordance with IFRS 1 as applied at the subsidiary level; or • at the amounts at which they are included in the parent's financial statements. A similar choice may be made by associates or joint ventures that adopt IFRS later than the entity that exercises significant influence or joint control over them. A Canadian parent adopting IFRS later than its subsidiaries, associates or joint ventures must measure the assets and liabilities of the subsidiaries, associates or joint ventures in its consolidated financial statements at the same carrying amounts as reported in the IFRS-based standalone financial statements of the subsidiary, associate or joint venture.	• Canadian entities with global operations may be affected by this exemption. For example, if a foreign subsidiary, associate, or joint venture has already adopted IFRS in its standalone financial statements, a Canadian parent cannot revise the amounts reported at the subsidiary, associate, or joint venture levels. Since the subsidiary, associate or joint venture has already converted to IFRS, it cannot convert to IFRS a second time. Instead, the parent continues to report the balances already being reported in the standalone financials of the subsidiary, associate or joint venture. Therefore, Canadian parent companies with subsidiaries that have already adopted IFRS will need to live with the exemption decisions made at the subsidiary level. • Parent companies may elect different IFRS accounting policies than their subsidiaries, but they would need to align those policies when preparing consolidated IFRS financial statements. (See Chapter 7 for more details.)

Areas	Choices (see note)	Comments
Designation of previously recognized financial instruments	An entity has the choice to make an available-for-sale designation and to designate any financial asset or financial liability as at "fair value through profit or loss" provided the asset or liability meets certain criteria.	CICA 3855, *Financial Instruments — Recognition and Measurement* and IAS 39, *Financial Instruments: Recognition and Measurement* are similar but IAS 39 has more restrictions on the use of the fair value option. (See Chapter 9 for more details.)
Share-based payment transactions	An entity has the choice of whether or not to apply the fair value method in accounting for share-based payment arrangements to equity instruments that vested before the transition date (i.e., January 1, 2010). It will only have to apply the fair value method to account for equity instruments that remain unvested as at the transition date (January 1, 2010).	Given that Canadian companies were required to adopt a fair value method to account for share-based payment trans-actions in 2004, it is unlikely that they will have any unvested equity instruments that are not already being accounted for via a fair value approach. Note that IFRS 1 provides companies with the option of applying the requirements of IFRS 2 to liabilities arising from cash-settled share-based payment transactions that were settled prior to the transition date. (See Chapter 16 for more details.)
Insurance contracts	An entity may elect to use the transitional provisions provided in IFRS 4, *Insurance Contracts*.	IFRS 4 restricts the changes in accounting policies for insurance contracts, which means that Canadian entities can continue to use their current accounting policies subject to certain modifications.
Decommissioning liabilities included in the cost of property, plant and equipment	A Canadian entity may elect not to apply the requirements of IFRIC 1, *Changes in Existing Decommissioning, Restoration and Similar Liabilities* fully retrospectively in determining the IFRS carrying amount of the assets to which the decommissioning liabilities relate.	Differences exist between Canadian GAAP and IFRS including the fact that decommissioning liabilities are recognized solely when the entity has a legal obligation where-as they might also be recorded earlier under the latter when a constructive obligation is incurred. Adopting this option would provide relief because an entity will not have to attempt to determine when and how the changes in estimates arose. Instead, it will have to re-calculate the liability in accordance with IFRS and then adjust the cost of the asset and accumulated depreciation. (See Chapters 12 and 15 for more details.)
Leases	An entity may elect to apply the transitional provisions in IFRIC 4, *Determining Whether an Arrangement Contains a Lease*.	IFRIC 4 is very similar to EIC-150, *Determining whether an arrangement contains a lease*. (See Chapter 13 for more details.)
Fair value measurement of financial assets or financial liabilities at initial recognition	An entity may elect to apply the IFRS valuation techniques prospectively to transactions entered into after January 1, 2004.	This optional exemption does not apply to Canadian companies.

Areas	Choices (see note)	Comments
A financial asset or an intangible asset accounted for in accordance with IFRIC 12, *Service Concession Arrangements*	An entity may elect to apply the transitional provisions in IFRIC 12.	IFRIC 12 applies to contractual arrangements in which a private sector operator participates in the development, financing, operation and maintenance of infrastructure for public sector services. When it is impractical (as defined in IAS 8, *Accounting Policies, Changes in Accounting Estimates and Errors*) to apply IFRIC 12 retrospectively to the start of the earliest period presented, the IFRIC 12 transition provisions allow a company to: • recognize financial and intangible assets that existed at the start of the earliest period presented; • use the previous carrying amounts as the carrying amount at that date (no matter how they were previously classified); and • test the financial and intangible assets recognized at that date for impairment.
Borrowing costs	A Canadian entity may elect to apply the transitional provisions of IAS 23, *Borrowing Costs*.	The IAS 23 transitional provisions permit a company to apply IAS 23 to borrowing costs related to qualifying assets capitalized on or after the date of transition to IFRS if the accounting treatment for capitalized interest required by IAS 23 is different from the company's previous accounting policy. Where an entity does not elect to use deemed cost for property, plant and equipment and elects to apply capitalization of borrowing costs from a date prior to the date of transition to IFRS, the capitalization of borrowing costs in the cost of property, plant and equipment should be in accordance with IAS 23. This may require a change in the actual cost of the property, plant and equipment from that recorded previously under Canadian GAAP.

Investments in subsidiaries, jointly controlled entities and associates	In the opening IFRS statement of financial position of its separate financial statements, an entity can measure its investment in one of the following manners:
	• at cost, determined in accordance with IAS 27;
	• at deemed cost, which is defined as:
	  o fair value (determined in accordance with IAS 39) at the company's IFRS transition date, or
	  o previous GAAP carrying amount at the IFRS transition date.
		IAS 27 requires a company to account for its investment in subsidiaries, jointly controlled entities and associates either at cost or at fair value in accordance with IAS 39 in its separate financial statements (in the stand-alone, unconsolidated parent-company-only financial statements).
		Because Canadian companies generally are not required to prepare such separate financial statements, it is unlikely that many Canadian companies would use this exemption.

Note: It is important to note that IFRS 1 does not provide a hierarchy to any of the voluntary exemptions; therefore, when a first-time adopter deals with an item covered by more than one exemption, it has free choice in determining the order in which to apply the exemptions.

Mandatory Exceptions

While IFRS 1 allows for voluntary exemptions from restatement on the initial adoption of IFRS, it also specifically prohibits restatement for certain amounts as retrospective application in those areas would require management to make judgments about past conditions after they have occurred. The following four mandatory exceptions to retrospective application are relevant to Canadian first-time adopters:

- derecognition of financial assets and financial liabilities;
- hedge accounting;
- estimates; and
- non-controlling interests.

IFRS 1 mandatory exceptions provide some relief, but may also create difficulties such as in case of estimates. Note that the mandatory exceptions do not relieve an entity from having to apply IFRS prospectively. The table below presents mandatory exceptions and summarizes some of the issues.

Areas (see note)	Comments and Issues
Derecognition of financial assets and financial liabilities	If an entity derecognized a financial asset or a financial liability under Canadian GAAP before January 1, 2004, it is not required to reconsider the accounting of the transaction. For example, It does not have to reconsider the accounting treatment, in accordance with IAS 39, of a securitization agreement that was entered into in 2003 and accounted for as a sale in accordance with AcG-12, *Transfers of receivables*.
Hedge accounting	This exception under IFRS 1 will require a Canadian entity to first determine if its hedges under CICA 3865, *Hedges* qualify for hedge accounting under IAS 39: • If they qualify, the entity must follow the detailed guidance in IFRS 1 to recognize the hedging instrument and the hedging relationship in the opening IFRS statement of financial position. o Hedge accounting after the transition date may be applied only if all of the IAS 39 hedge accounting criteria are met. If the criteria are not met, the entity must apply IAS 39 guidance for discontinuing hedge accounting until the criteria are met. • If the hedges do not qualify for hedge accounting under IAS 39, the hedging relationship must not be reflected in the opening IFRS statement of financial position. Instead, the related derivatives must be recognized at fair value with a corresponding adjustment to retained earnings. Even though the hedge accounting guidance under IAS 39 and CICA 3865 is similar, some differences do exist. For example, CICA 3865 allows an entity to use the shortcut method, whereas IAS 39 does not permit use of this method. Therefore, Canadian entities that currently use the shortcut method should assess their hedging instruments and strategies using IAS 39 criteria sufficiently in advance of their conversion to IFRS. By ensuring that the necessary designations and documentation are prepared contemporaneously – even prior to adoption of IFRS – an entity can mitigate the risk that the hedge accounting treatment will need to be discontinued under IAS 39 during first-time adoption of IFRS.

Areas (see note)	Comments and Issues
Estimates	IFRS 1 prohibits the use of hindsight to adjust previous estimates unless there is objective evidence of an error. Estimated amounts established under Canadian GAAP must be adjusted only when the basis of calculation does not comply with IFRS. Consequently, IFRS 1 requires: • estimates made at the same date under Canadian GAAP (December 31, 2009) to be used for the opening IFRS statement of financial position (at January 1, 2010), unless there is objective evidence of an error; • estimates made under Canadian GAAP to be revised if necessary to comply with IFRS, but they should reflect conditions present at the date of transition; • an entity may need to make estimates under IFRS at the date of transition to IFRS that were not required at that date under Canadian GAAP. To achieve consistency with IAS 10, *Events after the Reporting Period*, the IFRS estimates must reflect conditions that existed at the date of transition to IFRS. Note that it is likely that most entities will have better information on estimates established in prior periods as of the first IFRS reporting date. As indicated above, however, IFRS 1 prohibits an entity from adjusting previously reported estimates (at both the transition date and during the comparative periods presented) based on additional information available at the time of conversion to IFRS. This means that any subsequent adjustments to estimates must be recognized in the appropriate period's income statement.
Accounting for non-controlling interests	IAS 27, *Consolidated and Separate Financial Statements* (as amended in 2008) requires certain amounts to be allocated between owners and non-controlling interests. This exception mandates a prospective application for the following requirements: • attribution of comprehensive income to the owners of the parent and to the non-controlling interests; • changes in the parent's ownership interest in a subsidiary that do not result in a loss of control; and • accounting for a loss of control over a subsidiary, and classifying all the assets and liabilities of a subsidiary as held for sale when an entity is committed to a sale plan involving loss of control of that subsidiary (and certain other criteria are met). This exception provides relief from requiring companies to gather information and calculate allocations between owners and non-controlling interests under IFRS for transactions in periods prior to the transition date. If a first-time adopter elects to apply the business combination standard retrospectively to past business combinations (see optional exemptions on business combination above), it must also apply the IAS 27 requirements from that date forward.

Note: IFRS 1 has a mandatory exception for assets classified as held for sale and discontinued operations that applies only to entities with IFRS adoptions dates before January 1, 2006. This exception is unlikely to apply to most Canadian entities. Therefore, Canadian entities will need to retrospectively apply IFRS 5, *Non-Current Assets Held for Sale and Discontinued Operations* at the transition date.

Financial Reports Prior to IFRS Adoption

CICA 1506, *Accounting Changes* requires entities to disclose known or reasonably estimable information relevant to assessing the possible impact that the application of a new primary source of GAAP would have on their financial statements in the period of initial application. Hence, in the context of IFRS adoption, Canadian public companies would have to disclose the nature of the impending changes in accounting policy and the impact that the initial application of IFRS is expected to have on their financial statements.

The omnibus Exposure Draft *Adopting IFRSs in Canada*, issued in April 2008, includes a proposal to amend the scope of CICA 1506. With this amendment, the AcSB aims to clarify that CICA 1506 is concerned with changes in individual accounting standards, and not with the wholesale replacement of GAAP, as in the case of IFRS adoption.

The Canadian Securities Administrators (CSA) have recognized that changing from Canadian GAAP to IFRS is a significant undertaking that may materially affect an issuer's reported financial position and results of operations. Consequently, the CSA believes that the MD&A should provide investors and other market participants with timely and meaningful information about these matters during the reporting periods leading up to an issuer's changeover to IFRS.

In May 2008, the CSA published CSA Staff Notice 52-320, *Disclosure of Expected Changes in Accounting Policies Relating to Changeover to International Financial Reporting Standards*, which provides the following guidance on MD&A disclosures for reporting periods leading up to the adoption of IFRS:

- Interim and annual MD&A for the financial year ending December 31, 2008:
  - o If an entity has developed an IFRS changeover plan, it should discuss the key elements and timing of its plan in its interim MD&A and certainly no later than its annual MD&A for the 2008 year end.
  - o Key elements of an entity's plan may address the impact of IFRS on:
    - accounting policies, including choices among policies permitted under IFRS, and implementation decisions such as whether certain changes will be applied on a retrospective or a prospective basis,
    - information technology and data systems,
    - internal control over financial reporting,
    - disclosure controls and procedures, including investor relations and external communications plans,
    - financial reporting expertise, including training requirements, and
    - business activities, such as foreign currency and hedging activities, as well as matters that may be influenced by GAAP measures such as debt covenants, capital requirements and compensation arrangements.
  - o If an entity is well advanced in its IFRS changeover project, it should discuss the impact of the changeover on its financial reporting.
- Interim MD&A for the financial year ending December 31, 2009:
  - o An entity should provide an update of progress on its IFRS changeover plan and any changes in its plan.
- Annual MD&A for the financial year ending December 31, 2009:
  - o An entity should provide relevant details of its preparations for changeover to IFRS, which include an update of progress on its IFRS changeover plan and any changes in its plan, and a description of the major identified differences between the entity's current accounting policies and those it is required or expects to apply in preparing IFRS financial statements. The information should enable investors to understand which key elements of the financial statements will be affected by the changeover to IFRS.
- Annual and interim MD&A for the financial year ending December 31, 2010:

o An entity should provide relevant details of its preparations for changeover to IFRS, which include an update of progress on its IFRS changeover plan and any changes in its plan, and an updated description of the major identified differences between the entity's current accounting policies and those it is required or expects to apply in preparing IFRS financial statements. The entity should be able to discuss in more detail the key decisions and changes it has made, or will have to make, in the changeover to IFRS. The entity's discussion of changes in accounting policies should include decisions about accounting policy choices available under IFRS 1.

o If an entity has quantified information about the impact of IFRS on the key line items in its financial statements when it prepares its interim and annual MD&A for the financial year ending December 31, 2010, it should include this information in its MD&A.

In October 2008, the CICA's Canadian Performance Reporting Board issued *Pre-2011 Communications About IFRS Conversion*, which elaborates on CSA Staff Notice 52-320 by discussing all aspects of conversion and advocating a proactive and transparent communication strategy to serve both preparers', investors' and analysts' needs through the period leading up to the changeover.

Illustrative Disclosures:

Extract 20(1) – Interim MD&A of an early adopter two years before changeover to IFRS

Brookfield Asset Management Inc. (Interim Report Q3 2008), pages 47-49

PART 5 – Supplemental information

This section contains information required by applicable continuous disclosure guidelines and to facilitate additional analysis.

Future Changes In Accounting Policies

International Financial Reporting Standards

The Accounting Standards Board ("AcSB") confirmed in February 2008 that International Financial Reporting Standards ("IFRS") will replace Canadian GAAP for publicly accountable enterprises for financial periods beginning on and after January 1, 2011. Brookfield applied to the Canadian Securities Administrators ("CSA") and was granted exemptive relief to prepare its financial statements in accordance with IFRS earlier and intends to do so for periods beginning January 1, 2010 and prepare its first financial statements in accordance with IFRS for the three month period ended March 31, 2010. As part of Brookfield's conversion plan, it intends to provide condensed IFRS financial statements for periods beginning January 1, 2009.

Impact of Adoption of IFRS

IFRS are premised on a conceptual framework similar to Canadian GAAP, however, significant differences exist in certain matters of recognition, measurement and disclosure. The following paragraphs outline the significant accounting policies which are required or are currently expected to be applied by the Corporation on its adoption of IFRS that will be significantly different than its Canadian GAAP accounting policies. As the Corporation continues to evaluate the impact of adoption on its processes and accounting policies it will provide updated disclosure where appropriate. While the adoption of IFRS will not have a material impact on the reported cash flows of the Corporation, it will have a material impact on the Corporation's consolidated balance sheet and statement of income.

Basis of Consolidation

Under Canadian GAAP Brookfield determines whether it should consolidate an entity using two different frameworks: the variable interest entity ("VIE") and voting control models. Under IFRS Brookfield will consolidate an entity if it is determined to be controlled by the Corporation. Control is defined as the power to govern the financial and operating policies of an entity to obtain a benefit from its activities. Control is presumed to exist when the parent owns, directly or indirectly through subsidiaries, more than one half of an entity's voting power, but also exists when the parent owns half or less of the voting power but has legal or contractual rights to control, or de facto control. This change in policy will result in certain entities to be consolidated by Brookfield that were not consolidated under Canadian GAAP and will also result in certain entities that are currently consolidated by Brookfield under the VIE model to be deconsolidated.

Brookfield Asset Management Inc. (Interim Report Q3 2008) (continued)

Property, Plant and Equipment

Consistent with Canadian GAAP, under IFRS, separable components of property, plant and equipment are recognized initially at cost. Under IAS 16 Property, Plant and Equipment an entity is required to choose, for each class of property, plant and equipment, to account for each class using either the cost model or the revaluation model. The cost model is generally consistent with Canadian GAAP where an item of property, plant and equipment is carried at its cost less any accumulated depreciation and any accumulated impairment losses. Under the revaluation model an item of property, plant and equipment is carried at its revalued amount, being its fair value at the date of the revaluation less any accumulated depreciation and accumulated impairment losses. Increases in fair value are recorded in a revaluation surplus account in equity while decreases in fair value serve to reduce the revaluation surplus account, related to the asset, with any excess recognized in income.

Investment Property

Investment property includes land and buildings held to earn rentals or for capital apprecia-tion or both, rather than for use in the production or supply of goods or services or administrative purposes or for sale in the ordinary course of business. Generally, all of the Corporation's commercial properties will be considered investment property under IFRS. Like Canadian GAAP, investment property is initially measured at cost under IAS 40 Investment Property ("IAS 40"). However, subsequent to initial recognition, IAS 40 requires that an entity choose either the cost or fair value model to account for its investment property. The fair value model which requires the Corporation to record a gain or loss in income arising from a change in the fair value of investment property in the period of change. The cost model is generally consistent with Canadian GAAP. The determination of fair value model is based upon, among other things, rental income from current leases and reasonable and supportable assumptions that represent what knowledgeable, willing parties would assume about rental income from future leases in the light of current conditions less future cash outflows in respect of leases and the investment property. No depreciation related to investment property is recognized under the fair value model.

Biological Assets

Under IFRS the Corporation's timberlands are considered biological assets and accounted for under IAS 41 Agriculture ("IAS 41"). Currently under Canadian GAAP Brookfield's timberland assets are recorded at cost, less accumulated depletion which is based upon harvested amounts. Depleted amounts are recorded in cost of goods sold at the time of sale. Under IAS 41 the Corporation's timberland assets will be measured on initial recognition at cost and at the end of each reporting period at fair value, less estimated point-of-sale costs. Fair value is determined as the market price for similar species and age of timberlands at the measurement date. Changes in fair value or point of sale costs after initial recognition are recognized in income in the period in which the change arises. At the point of harvest, timberland assets are recorded in inventory at fair value less their point-of-sale costs under IAS 2, Inventories which is substantially the same as CICA Handbook section 3031 Inventories.

Impairments

Under Canadian GAAP for assets other than financial assets, a write-down to estimated fair value is recognized if the estimated undiscounted future cash flows from an asset or group of assets is less than their carried value. Under IFRS, IAS 36 Impairment of Assets ("IAS 36") requires a write-down to be recognized if the recoverable amount, determined as the higher of the estimated fair value less costs to sell or value in use is less than carried value. Consistent with Canadian GAAP, impairments are measured at the amount by which carried value exceeds fair value less costs to sell.

Share-based Payment

The Corporation issues stock-based awards in the form of stock options that vest evenly over a five year period. Under Canadian GAAP Brookfield recognizes the fair value of the award, determined at the time of the grant, on a straight-line basis over the five year vesting period. Under IFRS the fair value of each tranche of the award is considered a separate grant based on the vesting period with the fair value of each tranche determined separately and recognized as compensation expense over the term of its respective vesting period. Accordingly, this will result in a higher amount of each grant being recognized in income at a faster rate than under Canadian GAAP.

Brookfield Asset Management Inc. (Interim Report Q3 2008) (continued)

Joint Ventures

The IASB is currently considering Exposure Draft 9 Joint Arrangements ("ED 9") which is intended to modify IAS 31 Interests in Joint Ventures ("IAS 31"). The IASB has indicated that it expects to issue a new standard to replace IAS 31 in early 2009. Currently, under Canadian GAAP the Corporation proportionately accounts for interests in joint ventures. ED 9 proposes to eliminate the option to proportionately consolidate such interests and require an entity to recognize its interest in a joint venture, using the equity method.

Business Combinations

IFRS 3 Business Combinations as revised in 2008 ("IFRS 3R") sets out requirements for accounting for business combinations. Both IFRS and Canadian GAAP require the acquisition method of accounting for all business combinations, however significant differences exist between the two frameworks in other areas. The most significant differences from the Corporation's current Canadian GAAP policy are that under IFRS 3R transaction costs are expensed immediately whereas under Canadian GAAP such amounts are capitalized; contingent consideration under IFRS 3R is recognized at fair value on the date of acquisition, with subsequent changes recognized in income, whereas under Canadian GAAP such amounts are only recognized initially to the extent probable; and under IFRS 3R the acquirer can elect to measure any non-controlling interests at fair value at the date of acquisition or at its proportionate interest in the fair value of the identifiable assets and liabilities of the acquiree and can make this election on a transaction-by-transaction basis.

First-time Adoption of International Financial Reporting Standards

Brookfield's adoption of IFRS will require the application of IFRS 1 First-time Adoption of International Financial Reporting Standards ("IFRS 1"), which provides guidance for an entity's initial adoption of IFRS. IFRS 1 generally requires that an entity apply all IFRS effective at the end of its first IFRS reporting period retrospectively. However, IFRS 1 does require certain mandatory exceptions and limited optional exemptions in specified areas of certain standards from this general requirement. The following are the optional exemptions available under IFRS 1 significant to Brookfield that the Corporation expects to apply in preparing its first financial statements under IFRS.

Business combinations

IFRS 1 allows for IFRS 3R to be applied either retrospectively or prospectively. Retrospective application would require that Brookfield restate all business combinations occurring before the date of its transition to IFRS. Brookfield will adopt IFRS 3R prospectively.

Fair value of revaluation as deemed cost

IFRS 1 allows an entity to initially measure an item of property, plant and equipment upon transition to IFRS at fair value or under certain circumstances using a previous GAAP revaluation, as opposed to recreating depreciated cost under IFRS. The Corporation will, for items of property, plant and equipment where it is impracticable to recreate depreciated cost under IFRS, use either fair value or a previous GAAP revaluation as deemed cost. Brookfield expects to use a measure of deemed cost for a significant portion of its fixed assets, the cumulative effect of which will generally result in carrying values under IFRS in excess of those under Canadian GAAP. This increase in carrying value is the result of the accounting depreciation taken under Canadian GAAP no longer attributed to the assets at transition, in addition to the value appreciation of such assets in aggregate since acquisition.

Cumulative translation differences

IAS 21 The Effects of Changes in Foreign Exchange Rates requires a company to determine the translation differences in accordance with IFRS from the date on which a subsidiary was formed or acquired. IFRS allows cumulative translation differences for all foreign operations to be deemed zero at the date of transition to IFRS, with future gains or losses on subsequent disposal of any foreign operations to exclude translation differences arising from prior to the date of transition to IFRS. Brookfield expects to reset all cumulative translation differences to zero on transition to IFRS.

Brookfield Asset Management Inc. (Interim Report Q3 2008) (continued)

Share-based payments

On adoption of IFRS, an entity is not required under IFRS 2 Share-based Payment ("IFRS 2") to recognize share-based payments settled before the entity's IFRS transition date. IFRS 1 encourages, but does not require, application of its provisions to equity instruments granted on or before November 7, 2002. Brookfield will recognize under IFRS 2 the share-based awards that were recognized under Canadian GAAP.

IFRS 1 allows for certain other optional exemptions; however, the Corporation does not expect such exemptions to be significant to the Corporation's adoption of IFRS.

Q2/2008 Interim Report page 44

PART 4 – Supplemental information

This section contains information required by applicable continuous disclosure guidelines and to facilitate additional analysis.

Changes in Accounting Policies (in part)

Future Changes in Accounting Policies

The Accounting Standards Board confirmed in February 2008 that International Financial Reporting Standards ("IFRS") will replace Canadian GAAP for publicly accountable enterprises for financial periods beginning on and after January 1, 2011. The Canadian Securities Administrators ("CSA") in Staff Notice 52-321 – *Early adoption of International Financial Reporting Standards, use of US GAP and reference to IFRS-IASB* also indicated that it would be prepared to provide exemptive relief to a Canadian reporting issuer permitting it to prepare its financial statements in accordance with IFRS for financial periods beginning before January 1, 2011. Brookfield is giving consideration to preparing its financial statements in accordance with IFRS for periods beginning on and after January 1, 2009 subject to regulatory and other approvals.

The Corporation's IFRS conversion plan is comprehensive and addresses matters including changes in accounting policy, the restatement of comparative periods, organizational and internal control, the modification of existing systems and the training and awareness of staff, in addition to other related business matters. Each of the Corporation's operating platforms has also established implementation teams comprised of members of senior management to facilitate Brookfield's conversion to IFRS. Overall responsibility for the implementation and success of the Corporation's conversion plan rests with Brookfield's senior financial management who report to and are overseen by the Corporation's Audit Committee.

IFRS are premised on a conceptual framework similar to Canadian GAAP, however, significant differences exist in certain matters of recognition, measurement and disclosure. While the adoption of IFRS will not change the actual cash flows generated by the Corporation, the adoption of IFRS will result in changes to the reported financial position and results of operations of the Corporation, the effects of which management expect to be material. A detailed analysis of the differences between IFRS and Brookfield's current accounting policies under Canadian GAAP is currently in process. Management expects the most significant effects of adopting IFRS to be to the carrying values of real estate, power generation, infrastructure, and certain other property, plant and equipment along with the corresponding impact on reported earnings, the recognition of performance fee income and carried interests earned, the Corporation's accounting for joint ventures, deferred taxes, financial instruments, the determination of whether to consolidate certain entities and the accounting for business combinations.

Q1/2008 Interim Report

No information provided.

Commentary: This extract is from one of the two Canadian companies that intend to adopt IFRS early, in 2010. It illustrates disclosures in the MD&A for consecutive quarters, starting with the most recent as follows:

- Q3 /2008 deals with conversion to IFRS in details, including fact that the CSA granted Brookfield early adoption permission and that, consequently, it will prepare its first financial statements in accordance with IFRS for the three-month period ended March 31, 2010. Brookfield indicates that it intends to provide condensed IFRS financial statements for periods beginning January 1, 2009. Note that this report contains (1) a detailed disclosure of the impact of IFRS adoption by explaining the impact of the differences between Canadian GAAP and IFRS and (2) an explanation of the application of IFRS 1 and optional exemptions the company expects to apply in preparing its opening IFRS statement of financial position.

- Q2 /2008 presents an overview of IFRS conversion, including the fact Brookfield is considering early adoption. It presents elements of its conversion plan by disclosing:

  o the matters addressed (i.e., changes in accounting policy, restatement of comparative periods, organizational and internal control, modification of existing systems and the training and awareness of staff, in addition to other related business matters),

  o the formation of the implementation teams (i.e., members of senior management),

  o the individuals charged with the overall responsibility for the implementation and success of conversion plan (i.e., senior financial management who report to and are overseen by the audit committee).

First Interim IFRS Financial Report

A Canadian issuer's first interim IFRS financial report will be for the first quarter ended March 31, 2011 (Q1 2011). This quarterly report must include:

- comparative information for Q1 2010, restated in accordance with IFRS;

- opening statement of financial position (as at January 1, 2010), prepared in accordance with IFRS 1;

- reconciliations for the following comparative information, restated in accordance with IFRS:

  o equity at January 1, 2010,

  o equity and comprehensive income for Q1 2010,

  o equity and comprehensive income for the year ended December 31, 2010.

The reconciliations must provide sufficient detail to explain material adjustments to the statements of financial position and statements of comprehensive income. Any corrections of errors made under Canadian GAAP identified during the conversion process should be distinguished from adjustments arising from changes in accounting policies.

In addition, if a company recognized or reversed any impairment losses in preparing its opening IFRS statement of financial position, it will have to include the disclosures required by IAS 36, *Impairment of Assets*.

As indicated previously, IFRS 1 requires the preparation of all financial reports presented in Q1 2011 using the same accounting policies. Those accounting policies must comply with all IFRS standards effective at the end of the first IFRS reporting period (i.e., December 31, 2011), except for the IFRS 1 requirements and optional exemptions reflected in the opening IFRS statement of financial position.

In addition, entities must include, in their Q1 2011 reports, disclosures that explain the impact of the transition from Canadian GAAP to IFRS on their reported financial position, financial performance and cash flows. On the other hand, the Q1 2011 report could include cross-references to another published document that includes this information.

Illustrative Disclosures:

Extract 20(2) – First-quarter disclosures after adoption of IFRS (conversion from US GAAP)

ThyssenKrupp AG (Interim Report 1ˢᵗ Quarter 2005-2006), pages 18-39

IFRS reconciliations and interim financial statements

IFRS RECONCILIATIONS

First-time adoption of international financial reporting and accounting standards

The Regulation No. 1606/2002 of the European Parliament and the Council concerning the use of International Accounting Standards (IAS) was adopted on July 19, 2002. This regulation requires companies, publicly traded and domiciled in the European Union (eu), to prepare their consolidated financial statements in accordance with International Financial Reporting Standards (IFRS) for fiscal years starting on or after January 01, 2005. Accordingly, ThyssenKrupp AG, as a publicly traded corporation domiciled in Germany, is required to prepare its consolidated financial statements for the fiscal year 2005/2006 under IFRS. ThyssenKrupp ag has decided to adopt the recommendation of the Committee of European Securities Regulators (cesr) to prepare its interim reports in the current fiscal 2005/2006 in accordance with IFRS.

The Group has applied IFRS 1 "First time adoption of International Financial Reporting Standards" to provide a starting point for reporting under International Financial Reporting and Accounting Standards. The date of transition to International Financial Reporting and Accounting Standards was selected as October 01, 2004. An explanation of how the transition to ifrs has affected the reported financial position, financial performance and cash flows of the Group is provided hereafter including reconciliations of equity and profit or loss for comparative periods reported under US GAAP (previous gaap) to those reported under IFRS.

The opening balance sheet has been prepared using the Standards and Interpretations currently issued and expected to be effective as of September 30, 2006. With the exception of the exemptions granted by IFRS 1, the Group expects to adopt these accounting policies when it prepares its first complete set of IFRS consolidated financial statements as of September 30, 2006. A detailed presentation of the applicable accounting policies is provided on page 45 and following. Until September 30, 2006, the opening balance sheet as of October 01, 2004, the consolidated financial statements for the fiscal year ended September 30, 2005, and any interim consolidated financial statements issued for the period between October 01, 2004 and September 30, 2006 should be seen as provisional as the IASB may still enact provisions that could be applied retroactively. Accordingly, neither the opening balance sheet as of October 01, 2004, nor the consolidated financial statements for the fiscal year ended September 30, 2005 have yet been certified under IFRS by the Group's auditor. They form the basis for the first full consolidated financial statements under IFRS for the fiscal year ending September 30, 2006 and will only be certified in conjunction with the audit of these consolidated financial statements. The condensed consolidated interim financial statements have been prepared on the basis of IFRSs in issue that are effective or available for early adoption at the Group's first IFRS annual reporting date, September 30, 2006. Based on these IFRSs, Management has made assumptions about the accounting policies expected to be adopted (accounting policies) when the first IFRS annual financial statements are prepared for the year ended September 30, 2006.

The Group has taken the following exemptions granted by IFRS 1 when preparing its preliminary opening balance sheet:

- **Business combinations**

The Company opted for the retention of the presentation of company acquisitions from the period before October 01, 2004, in place of an accounting treatment in accordance with the provisions of IFRS 3 "Business Combinations". The goodwill arising from those acquisitions contained no intangible assets that should have been shown separately under IFRS and has been taken on to the IFRS opening balance sheet without modifications other than those resulting from the required review of the carrying amounts of goodwill for impairment as of the opening balance sheet date and the required accounting for put options in connection with existing minority interest.

ThyssenKrupp AG (Interim Report 1ˢᵗ Quarter 2005-2006) (continued)

- **Employee benefits**

As of October 01, 2004, all unrecognized actuarial gains and losses that arose in the period from the granting of the entitlement up to the date of transition to IFRS have been recognized directly in retained earnings ("fresh start").

- **Cumulative currency translation gains and losses**

Cumulative currency translation gains and losses resulting from the translation of subsidiary and associated company financial statements up to the date of transition to IFRS have been directly recognized in retained earnings and have not been reported separately in equity. The recognition in retained earnings does not affect the reported equity. Currency translation adjustments arising after the transition are shown separately in equity and are recognized in income when the respective operations are disposed of.

The adoption of International Financial Reporting and Accounting Standards has resulted in the following changes to the Group's significant accounting policies:

Consolidation

Upon acquisition of a subsidiary the interest of minority shareholders under US GAAP is stated at the minority's proportion of the carrying amount of assets and liabilities of the subsidiary at the date of acquisition. Under IFRS, this minority interest is stated at the minority's proportion of fair values of identifiable assets, liabilities and contingent liabilities recognized at the date of acquisition and reported within equity.

Revenue recognition

Under US GAAP, the Group accounted for construction contracts using the percentage-of-completion method of accounting, if the performance of those contracts took place over a period of at least 12 months, beginning from the effective date of the contract to the date on which the contract is substantially completed. In accordance with IFRS, all construction contracts are accounted for using the percentage-of-completion method of accounting regardless the length of the performance period.

Development Costs

Development costs have been expensed as incurred in accordance with US GAAP. IFRS requires the recognition of development costs as an intangible asset, if certain requirements are met.

Components approach

Where under US GAAP no specific rules exist, IFRS requires a "component approach" when accounting for property, plant and equipment. Where fixed assets are comprised of significant parts those parts are accounted for as separate units and are depreciated accordingly.

Investment property

Investments in land and buildings held to earn rental income or for capital appreciation are recorded as part of property, plant and equipment under US GAAP. Those investment properties are shown as a separate line item under non current assets in accordance with IFRS. Furthermore, the fair values of investment properties are included in the Notes to the consolidated financial statements where investment properties are recorded at amortized cost.

Goodwill

Under US GAAP, the Group tested goodwill for impairment on Reporting Unit level which corresponded to the reporting one level below its segments. If the first step of such an impairment test resulted in a carrying value of the reporting unit including goodwill that exceeded the fair value of that unit, the goodwill was deemed to be impaired. In a second step, the fair value of the goodwill was determined and compared with its carrying value which then served as a basis of calculation for the amount to be recorded as impairment charge. IFRS requires testing of goodwill for impairment on Cash Generating Unit (CGU) level. The group of Cash Generating Units to which goodwill has been allocated represents the lowest level within the Group that is monitored for internal management purposes. The IFRS requirement leads to testing levels below the Reporting Unit level in certain segments of the Group. The one-step impairment test under IFRS compares the carrying amount of a CGU including goodwill to its recoverable amount with any excess recorded as impairment charge against goodwill. In cases where the carrying amount of goodwill is less than the determined amount of the impairment charge, the difference is generally allocated proportionally to the remaining non-current assets of the CGU to reduce their carrying amounts accordingly.

ThyssenKrupp AG (Interim Report 1ˢᵗ Quarter 2005-2006) (continued)

Intangible assets, property, plant and equipment and investment property

If facts and circumstances indicate that intangible assets with finite useful lives, property, plant and equipment or investment property may have suffered an impairment loss, US GAAP requires a comparison of the carrying amount of those assets with the sum of undis counted cash flows that are expected to be generated with these assets. If the carrying amount exceeds the sum of undiscounted cash flows, these assets are impaired. The necessary impairment charge is the amount by which the carrying amount of assets exceeds their fair values. Under IFRS, the assets are impaired if the carrying amounts of assets exceed the higher of a fair value less cost to sell or the sum of discounted cash flows that are expected to be generated with these assets (the recoverable amount). The excess carrying amount also represents the necessary impairment charge. Where under US GAAP the impairment creates a new cost basis for the asset, IFRS requires the carrying amount of the asset to be increased to a revised estimate of its recoverable amount if all or a portion of an impairment charge subsequently reverses.

Inventories

US GAAP requires inventories to be stated at the lower of cost or market whereas under IFRS inventories are stated at the lower of cost and net realizable value with a net realizable value being the estimated selling price in the ordinary course of business less estimated costs of completion and selling cost. Where under US gaap the impairment creates a new cost basis for the asset, IFRS requires the carrying amount of the asset to be increased to a revised estimate of its net realizable value if all or a portion of an impairment charge subsequently reverses.

Receivables

Under US GAAP, receivables sold under the "true sale" concept are derecognized from the balance sheet at the time of the sale. In determining whether sold receivables can be derecognized from the balance sheet, IFRS is based primarily on a risk and rewards approach which in certain cases results in a treatment of the sale that differs from the one under US GAAP.

Accrued pension and similar obligations

The measurement date of accrued pension and similar obligations under US GAAP is allowed to differ from the year end balance sheet date of a company. The Group therefore measured its obligations using the assumptions determined as of June 30 of each fiscal year. Under IFRS the measurement date must correspond to a company's year end. Accordingly, the Group measures its obligations using the assumptions determined as of September 30 of each fiscal year.

As of September 30, 2004/October 01, 2004 and September 30, 2005, the following assumptions were used to determine the pension obligations:

| % | Sept. 30, 2004/Oct. 01, 2004 | | | | Sept. 30, 2005 | | | |
| | US GAAP | | IFRS | | US GAAP | | IFRS | |
Weighted-average assumptions:	Germany	Outside Germany	Germany	Outside Germany	Germany	Outside Germany	Germany	Outside Germany
Discount rate	5.50	6.10	5.00	5.53	4.00	5.08	4.00	4.88
Expected return on plan assets	6.00	7.81	6.00	7.57	6.00	7.83	6.00	7.53
Rate of compensation increase	3.00	4.12	3.00	3.76	2.50	2.37	2.50	2.36

As of September 30, 2004/October 01, 2004 and September 30, 2005, the following assumptions were used to determine the health care obligations:

| % | Sept. 30, 2004/Oct. 01, 2004 | | Sept. 30, 2005 | |
| | US GAAP US/ Canadian-plans | IFRS US/ Canadian-plans | US GAAP US/ Canadian-plans | IFRS US/ Canadian-plans |
Weighted-average assumptions:				
Discount rate	6.25	5.75	5.20	5.20
Health care cost trend rate for the following year	10.01	10.01	8.39	8.39
Ultimate health care cost trend rate (expected in 2009)	5.45	5.46	5.44	5.45

When recording an additional minimum pension liability as required under US GAAP, the recognition of an intangible asset is obligatory if certain conditions are met. ifrs has no rules regarding the recognition of an additional minimum pension liability or the related intangible asset.

Starting with balance sheet date September 30, 2005 the Group will no longer apply the corridor approach, but use the so-called "third option" in accordance with IAS 19 amendment (December 2004). Under the provisions of this amendment all actuarial gains and losses are recognized immediately and directly in equity.

ThyssenKrupp AG (Interim Report 1st Quarter 2005-2006) (continued)

The interest cost component and expected rate of return component of pension and health care cost have been included in income from operations under US GAAP. The Group elected to present those components of pension and health care costs within IFRS in net financial income/(expense) for its IFRS reporting.

Share-based compensation

Under US GAAP, the Group had valued its share-based compensation programs using the intrinsic value method until July 01, 2005. Subsequent to the adoption of SFAS 123®) as of July 01, 2005, the Group valued its plans at fair value. Under IFRS, these programs are also recorded at fair value.

Embedded derivative financial instruments

US GAAP requires the recognition of an embedded derivative where parties conclude a contract that is not denominated in the functional currency of one of the parties to the contract. Under IFRS an embedded derivative is not recognized separately if the contract is denominated in a currency that is commonly used in business transactions in the environment in which the transaction takes place.

Discontinued operations

The Group reports the results of a disposal group that qualifies as component of the Group under US GAAP as discontinued operations if its cash flows can be clearly distinguished operationally and for financial reporting from the rest of the Group and the Group does not have significant continuing involvement with the component subsequent to its disposal. In addition to the identification of a component, IFRS requires that the disposed component must also represent a major line of business or all operations within a geographical area. Therefore, certain disposals may qualify as discontinued operations under us gaap but not under IFRS.

Balance Sheet Classification

In previously published consolidated financial statements the balance sheet classification followed the 4th and 7th directive of the EU with additional disclosures required by US GAAP included in the Notes to the consolidated financial statements. Under IFRS, assets and liabilities are classified as current or non-current in the balance sheet.

To simplify the reconciliations of the consolidated balance sheets, the US gaap presentation has been adjusted to the IFRS current/non-current classification.

The effect of the changes to the Group's accounting policies on the reported financial position, results of operations and cash flows of the Group is presented in the following.

RECONCILIATION OF THE CONSOLIDATED OPENING BALANCE SHEET AS OF OCTOBER 01, 2004

ASSETS million €

	Note	US GAAP Sept. 30, 2004	IFRS adjustments	IFRS Oct. 01, 2004
Intangible assets, net	A1, B1, C1	3,554	(385)	3,169
Property, plant and equipment, net	D1, E1, F1, G1	10,574	(1,856)	8,718
Investment property	H1, I1	—	1,618	1,618
Investments accounted for using the equity method	J1	341	(9)	332
Financial assets		679	0	679
Deferred tax assets	K1	1,148	(272)	876
Total non-current assets		16,296	(904)	15,392
Inventories	L1, M1	6,274	(368)	5,906
Trade accounts receivable, net	N1, O1	5,764	653	6,417
Other receivables	P1, Q1	1,049	(75)	974
Current income tax assets		189	0	189
Cash and cash equivalents		1,350	0	1,350
Total current assets		14,626	210	14,836
Assets held for sale	R1, S1	219	37	256
Total assets		31,141	(657)	30,484

ThyssenKrupp AG (Interim Report 1st Quarter 2005-2006) (continued)
EQUITY AND LIABILITIES million €

	Note	US GAAP Sept. 30, 2004	IFRS adjustments	IFRS Oct. 01, 2004
Equity attributable to ThyssenKrupp AG's stockholders		8,327	(1,284)	7,043
Minority interest	A2	—	360	360
Total equity		8,327	(924)	7,403
Minority interest	A2	410	(410)	—
Accrued pension and similar obligations	B2, C2, D2	7,189	1,095	8,284
Other provisions	E2, F2	510	5	515
Deferred tax liabilities	G2	977	(757)	220
Financial liabilities	H2	3,618	60	3,678
Other liabilities	I2	0	42	42
Total non-current liabilities		12,294	445	12,739
Other provisions	J2	1,811	(852)	959
Current income tax liabilities		538	0	538
Financial liabilities	K2	614	238	852
Trade accounts payable	L2	3,644	(13)	3,631
Other liabilities	M2, N2, O2, P2	3,312	831	4,143
Total current liabilities		9,919	204	10,123
Liabilities associated with assets held for sale	Q2	191	28	219
Total liabilities		22,814	267	23,081
Total equity and liabilities		31,141	(657)	30,484

Intangible assets, net

A1 Development costs

Development costs that satisfied the criteria for recognition under IFRS resulted in an increase of intangible assets of €77 million.

B1 Goodwill

The IFRS one-step goodwill impairment test applied on Cash Generating Unit level as of October 01, 2004, resulted in an impairment charge against goodwill in the amount of €437 million.

The recognition of a put option in connection with an existing minority interest of the Dongyang group resulted in an increase of goodwill by €32 million.

C1 Intangible pension asset

The US GAAP intangible pension asset of €53 million was derecognized to account for pension obligations in accordance with IAS 19.

Property, plant and equipment, net

D1 Investment property

Based on the IFRS requirement to present investment property separately in the consolidated balance sheet, property, plant and equipment of €1,688 million were reclassified.

E1 Components approach

Under IFRS, property, plant and equipment is required to be separated into significant accounting parts and depreciated over the expected useful lives of the corresponding units. As a result, the Group recognized an increase of property, plant and equipment of €19 million.

F1 Impairment

The IFRS one-step impairment test of property, plant and equipment based on discounted cash flows resulted in an impairment charge against those assets of €247 million as the corresponding carrying values where no longer supported by the respective recoverable amounts.

ThyssenKrupp AG (Interim Report 1ˢᵗ Quarter 2005-2006) (continued)

G1 Leases

Under US GAAP, the classification of a lease as either operating lease or capital (finance) lease is based on formal criteria. IFRS however, does not use such formal quantitative thresholds to determine the type of a lease. Therefore, the application of IAS 17 "Leases" can result in a different classification of lease transactions. Accordingly, a lease transaction accounted for as an operating lease under US GAAP (whereby the lease payments were expensed as incurred), was accounted for as a finance lease under IFRS (with the related asset and liabilities recognized in the Group's balance sheet). As a result, property, plant and equipment increased by €60 million.

Investment property

H1 Separate balance sheet line item

Based on the IFRS requirement to present investment property separately in the consolidated balance sheet, property, plant and equipment of €1,688 million was reclassified.

I1 Impairment

The IFRS one-step impairment test of investment property based on discounted cash flows resulted in an impairment of €70 million.

Investments accounted for using the equity method

J1 Assets held for sale

Under US GAAP, apart from a disposal group only long-lived assets can be classified as held for sale if certain criteria are met, while under IFRS, all non-current assets can qualify for classification as held for sale. As a result, the Group reclassified an investment accounted for using the equity method in the amount of €9 million in assets held for sale.

Deferred tax assets

K1 IFRS adjustments

Deferred taxes are recognized generally due to different accounting under IFRS/US GAAP and the applicable national income tax calculation methods. As described above, the transition from US GAAP to IFRS accounting resulted in significant changes of various balance sheet items, but the national statutory income tax calculation methods remained unchanged. The transition therefore altered the aforementioned relationship with corresponding impacts on the balance sheet recognition of deferred taxes.

Regulations specifying different rules for the recognition of deferred taxes, under US GAAP and IFRS, as well as goodwill impairment and balance sheet reclassifications (e.g. the reclassification of minority interest to shareholders' equity) did not materially affect deferred taxes.

Compared to US GAAP, there are extended possibilities for balancing deferred taxes at single entity level. Because of this deferred tax assets and liabilities respectively are reduced compared to US GAAP. The netted amount of deferred tax assets and liabilities results in a deferred tax asset under IFRS, while there was a net deferred tax liability under US GAAP. This is in general due to the increased accrued pensions and similar obligations and due to the decreased property, plant and equipment under IFRS.

The IFRS adjustments resulted in a decrease of deferred tax assets of €272 million.

Inventories

L1 Percentage-of-completion method

Under US GAAP, the balance sheet item "Work in progress" included construction contracts accounted for under the percentage-of-completion method. Under IFRS, these construction contracts are included in trade accounts receivable. In this context, €370 million were reclassified.

M1 Lower of cost and net realizable value

The measurement of inventories under IFRS at the lower of cost and net realizable value resulted in an increase of inventories of €2 million.

ThyssenKrupp AG (Interim Report 1ˢᵗ Quarter 2005-2006) (continued)

Trade accounts receivable, net

N1 Percentage-of-completion method

Under US GAAP, the balance sheet item "Work in progress" included construction contracts accounted for under the percentage-of-completion method. Under IFRS, these construction contracts are included in trade accounts receivable. In this context, €370 million were reclassified (ref. l1).

Moreover under IFRS, the percentage-of-completion method is applied to construction contracts which have not been accounted for using the percentage-of-completion method under US gaap due to their performance duration of less than one year resulting in an increase of trade accounts receivable ("Future receivables from construction contracts") of €47 million.

O1 Sale of receivables

Under IFRS, a risks and rewards approach and control are applied to determine whether receivables sold can be derecognized. The application of this approach to receivables sold as of October 01, 2004, under existing programs resulted in an increase of the respective balance sheet caption by €238 million.

Other receivables

P1 Embedded derivatives

Under IFRS, several transactions do not qualify for a separate accounting as an embedded derivative because they are denominated in a currency that is commonly used in such business transactions. As a result, the Group derecognized assets of €3 million.

Q1 Prepaid pension cost

The IFRS pension accounting resulted in a reduction of the prepaid pension cost of €72 million primarily due to different discount rates and different fair values of plan assets as a result of different measurement dates.

Assets held for sale

R1 Additional assets held for sale under IFRS

Under US GAAP, apart from a disposal group only long-lived assets can be classified as held for sale if certain criteria are met, while under IFRS, all non-current assets can qualify for classification as held for sale. As a result, the Group reclassified an investment accounted for using the equity method in the amount of €9 million in assets held for sale (ref. j1).

S1 IFRS adjustments

Under IFRS, assets held for sale increased by €28 million resulting from IFRS adjustments of asset-backed transactions (ref. o1) of €18 million, separate accounting of significant parts (ref. e1) of €1 million and deferred tax assets of (ref. k1) of €8 million. Moreover, the reclassified amount of an investment accounted for using the equity method was increased by €1 million because the basis of presentation of the financial statements of the respective associate has also been changed from US GAAP to IFRS.

Minority interest

A2 Reclassification

Under US GAAP, minority interest is presented as a separate item between equity and liabilities in the consolidated balance sheet. Under IFRS, minority interest is required to be presented as part of equity. This reclassification resulted in an increase of equity of €410 million. Thereof, €50 million refer to ifrs adjustments in the financial statements of the single entities with minority shareholders due to IFRS 1 and the recognition of the put option in connection with the Dongyang group (ref. b1).

Accrued pensions and similar obligations

B2 Pension obligations

A reduced discount rate as of October 01, 2004, compared to the rate used at the early measurement date June 30 under US GAAP, and the allowed recognition of all actuarial gains and losses in equity in the opening balance sheet resulted in an increase of pension obligations by €484 million.

ThyssenKrupp AG (Interim Report 1st Quarter 2005-2006) (continued)

C2 Postretirement obligations other than pensions

A reduced discount rate as of October 01, 2004 compared to the rate used at the early measurement date June 30 under US GAAP and the allowed recognition of all actuarial gains and losses in equity in the opening balance sheet resulted in an increase of health care obligations other than pensions by €540 million.

D2 Voluntary early retirement agreements

Under US GAAP, obligations for voluntary early retirement agreements are only recorded for employees who have actually entered into retirement agreements and are accrued on a pro-rata basis. Under IFRS, obligations for voluntary early retirement benefits are recorded based upon management's best estimate of the number of employees expected to enter into early retirement agreements and are accrued on an actuarial basis. As a result, the provisions increased by €71 million.

Other provisions – non-current –

E2 Employees' anniversary bonuses

Based on the early measurement option of US GAAP, the Group's provisions for anniversary bonuses were calculated using the assumptions as of June 30. Under IFRS, the calculation has to be based on the assumptions as of October 01. Because of the reduced discount rate as of October 01, 2004, the provision for anniversary bonuses increased by €2 million.

F2 Share-based compensation

The IFRS accounting of the Group's cash settled management incentive plans using the fair value method resulted in an increase of the provision of €3 million.

Deferred tax liabilities

G2 IFRS adjustments

Deferred taxes are generally recognized due to different accounting under IFRS/US GAAP and the applicable national income tax calculation methods. As described above, the transition from US GAAP to IFRS accounting resulted in significant changes of various balance sheet items, but the national statutory income tax calculation methods remained unchanged. The transition therefore altered the aforementioned relationship with corresponding impacts on the balance sheet recognition of deferred taxes.

Regulations specifying different rules for the recognition of deferred taxes, under US GAAP and IFRS, as well as goodwill impairment and balance sheet reclassifications (e.g. the reclassification of minority interest to shareholders' equity) did not materially affect deferred taxes.

Compared to US GAAP, there are extended possibilities for balancing deferred taxes at single entity level. Because of this deferred tax assets and liabilities respectively are reduced compared to US GAAP. The netted amount of deferred tax assets and liabilities results in a deferred tax asset under IFRS, while there was a net deferred tax liability under US GAAP. This is in general due to the increased accrued pensions and similar obligations and due to the decreased property, plant and equipment under IFRS.

The IFRS adjustments resulted in a decrease of deferred tax liabilities of €757 million.

Financial liabilities – non-current –

H2 Leases

As described in g1), certain lease contracts that qualified as an operating lease under US GAAP are treated as a finance lease under IFRS. As a result, financial liabilities increased by €60 million.

I2 Other liabilities – non-current –

The accounting for the put option at the Dongyang group (ref. b1) resulted in a recognition of a liability of €42 million.

Other provisions – current –

J2 Reclassification

In previously published consolidated financial statements the balance sheet classification followed the 4th and 7th directive of the EU with additional disclosures required by US GAAP included in the Notes to the consolidated financial statements. Under this classification, certain liabilities were shown as provisions. Under IFRS, €852 million formerly recorded as other provisions are reclassified into other liabilities as they do not fulfill the definition of a provision under IFRS.

ThyssenKrupp AG (Interim Report 1ˢᵗ Quarter 2005-2006) (continued)
Financial liabilities – current –
K2 Sale of receivables

The determination whether receivables sold can be derecognized based on the IFRS risk and reward approach and control (ref. o1) resulted in a corresponding increase of financial liabilities of €238 million.

Trade accounts payable
L2 Percentage-of-completion method

Under IFRS, the percentage-of-completion method is applied on all construction contracts (ref. n1). As a result, the Group reclassified €13 million from trade accounts payable into other liabilities.

Other liabilities
M2 Reclassification

The adoption of the IFRS definitions regarding the classification of provisions and liabilities (ref. j2) resulted in a reclassification of other provisions of €852 million into other liabilities.

N2 Embedded derivatives

Under IFRS, several foreign currency based transactions do not require separate accounting for an embedded derivative component because these transactions are denominated in a currency that is commonly used in such business transactions. As a result, the Group derecognized liabilities of €10 million.

O2 Percentage-of-completion method

Under IFRS, the percentage-of-completion method is applied on all construction contracts (ref. n1). As a result, the Group's other liabilities ("Liabilities from orders in progress (PoC)") increased by €43 million due to excess amounts of advances received or progress billings compared to corresponding attributable revenues.

P2 Sale-and-lease-back transactions

Under US GAAP, gains resulting from sale-and-lease-back transactions are deferred over the contract period. Under IFRS, these gains are recognized immediately on the date of sale if the sale-and-lease-back transaction results in an operating lease and the transaction was established at fair value. This resulted in a decrease of deferred income of €63 million.

Liabilities associated with assets held for sale
Q2 IFRS adjustments

Under IFRS, liabilities associated with assets held for sale increased by €28 million resulting from IFRS adjustments of asset-backed transactions (ref. k2) of €18 million, pension obligations (ref. b2) of €4 million and deferred tax liabilities of (ref. g2) of €6 million.

RECONCILIATION OF EQUITY AS OF OCTOBER 01, 2004

million €	Note	
Stockholders' equity under US GAAP as of Sept. 30, 2004		8,327
Intangible assets, net	A1, B1, C1	(417)
Property, plant and equipment, net	D1, E1, F1, G1	(168)
Investment property	H1, I1	(70)
Deferred tax assets	K1	(272)
Inventories	L1, M1	2
Trade accounts receivable	N1, O1	47
Other receivables	P1, Q1	(75)
Assets held for sale	R1, S1	11
Accrued pensions and similar obligations	B2, C2, D2	(1,095)
Other provisions	E2, F2	(8)
Deferred tax liabilities	G2	757
Financial liabilities	H2	(60)
Other liabilities	N2, O2, P2	33
Liabilities associated with assets held for sale	Q2	(10)
Minority interest	A2	50
Other adjustments		(9)
Equity attributable to ThyssenKrupp AG's stockholders under IFRS as of Oct. 01, 2004		7,043
Minority interest under IFRS as of Oct. 01, 2004		360
Total equity under IFRS as of Oct. 01, 2004		7,403

ThyssenKrupp AG (Interim Report 1ˢᵗ Quarter 2005-2006) (continued)
RECONCILIATION OF THE CONSOLIDATED STATEMENT OF INCOME FOR THE FISCAL YEAR ENDED SEPTEMBER 30, 2005

million €	Note	US GAAP fiscal year ended Sept. 30, 2005	IFRS 5 adjustments	Other IFRS adjustments	IFRS fiscal year ended Sept. 30, 2005
Net sales	A1, B1	42,064	888	(25)	42,927
Cost of sales	C1, D1, E1, F1	(35,063)	(875)	243	(35,695)
Gross margin		7,001	13	218	7,232
Selling expenses	G1, H1	(2,544)	(97)	(4)	(2,645)
General and administrative expenses	I1, J1	(2,360)	(93)	198	(2,255)
Other operating income	H1	259	9	8	276
Other operating expenses	L1, M1	(391)	(32)	(29)	(452)
Gain/(loss) on the disposal of subsidiaries, net		3	14	(1)	16
Income from operations		1,968	(186)	390	2,172
Income from companies accounted for at equity		37	0	0	37
Other financial income/(expense), net		(169)	(4)	(359)	(532)
Financial income/(expense), net	N1	(132)	(4)	(359)	(495)
Income from continuing operations before income taxes		1,836	(190)	31	1,677
Non-recurring losses related to RAG investment		(474)	0	0	(474)
Provisions for income taxes	O1	(735)	10	(12)	(737)
Minority interest	P1	(46)	0	46	—
Income from continuing operations		581	(180)	65	466
Discontinued operations (net of tax)		442	180	(9)	613
Cumulative effects of changes in accounting principles (net of tax)		(4)	0	4	0
Net income		1,019	0	60	1,079
Thereof:					
ThyssenKrupp AG's stockholders		1,019	0	19	1,038
Minority interest		—	0	41	41
Net income		1,019	0	60	1,079
Basic earnings per share					
Income from continuing operations (attributable to ThyssenKrupp AG's stockholders)		1.17	(0.36)	0.04	0.85
Net income (attributable to ThyssenKrupp AG's stockholders)		2.05	0.00	0.03	2.08

IFRS 5 adjustments

Based on the differences in the definition of a discontinued operation under US GAAP and IFRS, the following disposals qualified for reporting as discontinued operations under US GAAP but do not under IFRS:

Segment Steel (structure until September 30, 2005)
• Edelstahl Witten-Krefeld GmbH
• Hoesch Contecna Systembau GmbH
Segment Automotive
• Alu Castings
• European truck spring businesses
• ThyssenKrupp Stahl Company
Segment Technologies
• ThyssenKrupp Stahlbau business
• Turbine components operation group
Segment Services
• Hommel group
• Krupp Druckereibetriebe GmbH

ThyssenKrupp AG (Interim Report 1ˢᵗ Quarter 2005-2006) (continued)

In addition, expenses resulting from disposals of discontinued operations incurred in fiscal year 2003/2004 qualified for reporting as discontinued operations under US GAAP but do not under IFRS.

As a result, only the disposals of the MetalCutting business unit and of the Residential Real Estate business qualify for reporting as discontinued operations under US GAAP and under IFRS as well.

The adjustments to present the disposals as part of continuing operations under IFRS are disclosed in column "IFRS 5 adjustments".

Other IFRS adjustments

These adjustments primarily result from the roll forward of the corresponding adjustments due to the transition from US GAAP to IFRS as of October 01, 2004.

Net sales

A1 Percentage-of-completion method (PoC)

Under IFRS, the percentage-of-completion method is applied to all construction contracts. As a result, the Group's net sales decreased by 8 million mainly due to the fact that part of the result of these contracts has been realized up front in the opening balance sheet as of October 01, 2004 as a result of the extended application of the percentage-of-completion method.

B1 Embedded derivatives

Under IFRS, for several transactions denominated in foreign currencies separate accounting for embedded derivatives is not required because they are denominated in a currency that is commonly used in such business transactions. As a result, net sales decreased by €17 million due to the elimination of the foreign currency embedded derivative effects.

Cost of sales

C1 Percentage-of-completion method (PoC)

Under IFRS, the percentage-of-completion method is applied on all construction contracts. As a result, the Group's cost of sales decreased by €4 million mainly due to the fact that less revenue was recognized in the fiscal year 2004/2005 as a result of the extended application of the percentage-of-completion method.

D1 Embedded derivatives

Under IFRS, for several transactions denominated in foreign currencies separate accounting for embedded derivatives is not required because they are denominated in a currency that is commonly used in such business transactions. As a result, cost of sales decreased by €27 million due to the elimination of the foreign currency embedded derivative effects.

E1 Personnel expenses

Personnel expenses included in cost of sales decreased by €159 million. This was primarily due to the absence of amortization of actuarial losses stemming from pension and other post-retirement benefit plans under IFRS as the result of the application of the fresh start method in the opening balance sheet. Moreover, cost of sales decreased because of the reclassification of pension interest cost to net financial income/(expense). Cost of sales increased by the reclassification of the expected return on plan assets to net financial income/(expense).

F1 Amortization and depreciation

Amortization and depreciation included in cost of sales decreased by €55 million primarily resulting from impairment charges recognized for non-current assets in the IFRS opening balance sheet.

Selling expenses

G1 Personnel expenses

Personnel expenses included in selling expenses decreased by €18 million. This was primarily due to the absence of the amortization of pension and pension-related actuarial losses under IFRS as the result of the application of the fresh start method in the opening balance sheet. Moreover, selling expenses decreased due to the reclassification of pension interest cost to net financial income/ (expense). Selling expenses increased due to the reclassification of the expected return on plan assets to net financial income/(expense).

ThyssenKrupp AG (Interim Report 1ˢᵗ Quarter 2005-2006) (continued)

H1 Other selling expenses

Other selling expenses increased by €9 million. This was due to increased allocations to provisions mainly as a result of the valuation of provisions based on the expected value out of a range of equally probable values.

General and administrative expenses

I1 Personnel expenses

Personnel expenses included in general and administrative expenses decreased by €220 million. This was primarily due to the reversal of amortization of pension and pension-related actuarial losses under IFRS as the result of the application of the fresh start method in the opening balance sheet. Moreover, personnel expenses decreased due to the reclassification of pension interest cost to net financial income/(expense). Personnel expenses increased due to the reclassification of the expected return on plan assets to net financial income/(expense).

J1 Other general and administrative expenses

Other general and administrative expenses increased by €6 million. This is due to increased allocations to provisions mainly as a result of the valuation of provisions based on the expected value out of a range of equally probable values.

Other operating income

K1 Gain from disposal of assets

The increase of miscellaneous other operating income was mainly due to increased gains from disposals as a result of recognized impairment charges in the opening balance sheet.

Other operating expenses

L1 Development costs

The recognition of certain development costs as intangible assets resulted in a reduction of other operating expenses of €20 million.

M1 Costs of voluntary settlements

Additional provisions of €66 million for voluntary settlements were recognized in accordance with the expected claim rate.

Financial income/(expense), net

N1 Accrued pension and similar obligations

Net financial income/(expense) increased by €(359) million primarily due to the recognition of pension interest cost of €(478) million offset by the recognition of the expected return on plan assets of €117 million.

Provisions from income taxes

O1 IFRS adjustments

The increase of provisions from income taxes by €12 million relates to deferred taxes resulting from IFRS adjustments.

Minority interest

P1 Reclassification

Under US GAAP, net income is presented after reduction of minority interest. Under IFRS, net income is inclusive of minority interest. This reclassification resulted in an increase of net income of €46 million.

ThyssenKrupp AG (Interim Report 1st Quarter 2005-2006) (continued) RECONCILIATION OF THE CONSOLIDATED BALANCE SHEET AS OF SEPTEMBER 30, 2005				
ASSETS million €	Note	US GAAP Sept. 30, 2005	IFRS adjustments	IFRS Sept. 30, 2005
Intangible assets, net	A1	4,766	(177)	4,589
Property, plant and equipment, net	B1	9,469	(726)	8,743
Investment property	C1	—	557	557
Investments accounted for using the equity method		329	8	337
Financial assets		190	(9)	181
Deferred tax assets	D1	1,431	(686)	745
Total non-current assets		16,185	(1,033)	15,152
Inventories	E1	7,439	(577)	6,862
Trade accounts receivable, net	F1	5,966	702	6,668
Other receivables		1,172	(39)	1,133
Current income tax assets		270	0	270
Cash and cash equivalents		4,625	0	4,625
Total current assets		19,472	86	19,558
Assets held for sale		582	9	591
Total assets		36,239	(938)	35,301

EQUITY AND LIABILITIES million €	Note	US GAAP Sept. 30, 2005	IFRS adjustments	IFRS Sept. 30, 2005
Equity attributable to ThyssenKrupp AG's stockholders		8,771	(1,282)	7,489
Minority interest		—	389	389
Total equity		8,771	(893)	7,878
Minority interest		481	(481)	—
Accrued pension and similar obligations	A2	7,954	938	8,892
Other provisions		398	19	417
Deferred tax liabilities	B2	1,495	(1,055)	440
Financial liabilities		3,028	57	3,085
Other liabilities	C2	0	207	207
Total non-current liabilities		12,875	166	13,041
Other provisions	D2	2,513	(1,344)	1,169
Current income tax liabilities		459	6	465
Financial liabilities	E2	1,643	130	1,773
Trade accounts payable		3,981	(5)	3,976
Other liabilities	F2	4,931	1,438	6,369
Total current liabilities		13,527	225	13,752
Liabilities associated with assets held for sale		585	45	630
Total liabilities		27,468	(45)	27,423
Total equity and liabilities		36,239	(938)	35,301

A1 Intangible assets, net

Primarily due to the following reasons the amount of negative IFRS adjustments as of September 30, 2005 was reduced by €208 million compared to October 01, 2004:

The recognition of a put option in connection with an existing minority interest of the Howaldtswerke-Deutsche Werft (HDW) and a corresponding reconsideration of the purchase price calculation resulted in an increase of goodwill by €100 million and therefore reduced the amount of negative IFRS adjustments by this amount.

Under US GAAP, an impairment charge against goodwill was recognized in fiscal year 2004/2005 which under IFRS already had been accounted for in the opening balance sheet. As a result, the amount of negative adjustments decreased by €45 million.

Capitalized development cost increased by 15 million and reduced the amount of negative adjustments respectively.

ThyssenKrupp AG (Interim Report 1ˢᵗ Quarter 2005-2006) (continued)

B1 Property, plant and equipment, net

Primarily due to the following reason the amount of negative IFRS adjustments as of September 30, 2005 was reduced by €1,130 million compared to October 01, 2004:

In the opening balance sheet the Group reclassified property from property, plant and equipment into investment property. As a result of the disposal of the Residential Real Estate business in the 2nd quarter ended March 31, 2005 the amount of negative adjustments decreased by €1,061 million.

C1 Investment property

Due to the disposal of the Residential Real Estate business the amount of positive IFRS adjustments as of September 30, 2005 was reduced by €1,061 million compared to October 01, 2004.

D1 Deferred tax assets

Primarily due to the following reason the amount of negative IFRS adjustments as of September 30, 2005 increased by €414 million compared to October 01, 2004:

Compared to US GAAP, there are extended possibilities for balancing deferred taxes at single entity level. Because of this deferred tax assets were reduced compared to US GAAP.

E1 Inventories

Primarily due to the following reason the amount of negative IFRS adjustments as of September 30, 2005 increased by €209 million compared to October 01, 2004:

The necessary reclassification from inventories into trade accounts receivable in connection with the percentage-of-completion method increased by €207 million.

F1 Trade accounts receivable, net

Primarily due to the following reasons the amount of positive IFRS adjustments as of September 30, 2005 increased by €49 million compared to October 01, 2004:

The necessary reclassification from inventories into trade accounts receivable in connection with the percentage-of-completion method increased by €207 million.

Adjustments of asset-backed programs resulted in an increase of derecognized trade accounts receivables of €108 million as of September 30, 2005.

A2 Accrued pension and similar obligations

Primarily due to the following reasons the amount of positive IFRS adjustments as of September 30, 2005 decreased by €157 million compared to October 01, 2004:

Regarding accrued pension obligations the necessary amount of adjustments decreased by €325 million, due to a lesser reduction of the discount rate under US GAAP compared to IFRS as of September 30, 2005.

Regarding post-retirement obligations other than pensions (healthcare obligations) the necessary amount of adjustments increased by €176 million, due to a reduction of the discount rate and resulting actuarial losses in the fiscal year 2004/2005 which were not immediately recognized under US GAAP. Under IFRS, however, the Group opted to apply the so called "third option" of IAS 19 and therefore all actuarial losses resulting from a reduction of the discount rate were recognized and immediately charged against equity.

B2 Deferred tax liabilities

Primarily due to the following reason the amount of negative IFRS adjustments as of September 30, 2005 increased by €298 million compared to October 01, 2004:

Compared to US GAAP, there are extended possibilities for balancing deferred taxes at single entity level. Because of this deferred tax liabilities were reduced compared to US GAAP.

C2 Other liabilities – non current –

Primarily due to the following reason the amount of positive IFRS adjustments as of September 30, 2005 increased by €165 million compared to October 01, 2004:

The recognition of the put option in connection with a minority interest of the Howaldtswerke-Deutsche Werft (HDW) resulted in an increase of liabilities by €160 million.

ThyssenKrupp AG (Interim Report 1ˢᵗ Quarter 2005-2006) (continued)

D2 Other provisions – current –

Primarily due to the following reasons the amount of negative IFRS adjustments as of September 30, 2005 increased by €492 million compared to October 01, 2004:

Under IFRS, the reclassification from provisions into other liabilities increased by €558 million.

Under IFRS, provisions for voluntary early retirement agreements are recorded for upon an expected number of employees entering into early retirement agreements. As a result, in the fiscal year 2004/2005 additional provisions of €66 million were recognized under IFRS only.

E2 Financial liabilities – current –

Adjustments of asset-backed programs resulted in a decrease of current financial liabilities by €108 million as of September 30, 2005.

F2 Other liabilities – current –

Primarily due to the following reason the amount of positive IFRS adjustments as of September 30, 2005 increased by €607 million compared to October 01, 2004:

Under IFRS, the reclassification from provisions into other liabilities increased by €558 million.

RECONCILIATION OF EQUITY AS OF SEPTEMBER 30, 2005

million €	Note	
Stockholders' equity under US GAAP as of Sept. 30, 2005		8,771
Intangible assets, net	A1	(347)
Property, plant and equipment, net	B1	(98)
Investment property	C1	(70)
Deferred tax assets	D1	(686)
Trade accounts receivable	F1	(3)
Other receivables		(42)
Assets held for sale		10
Accrued pensions and similar obligations (w/o reimbursement rights)	A2	(938)
Other provisions	D2	(91)
Deferred tax liabilities	B2	1,055
Financial liabilities		(57)
Other liabilities		(22)
Liabilities associated with assets held for sale		(47)
minority interest		92
Other adjustments		(38)
Equity attributable to ThyssenKrupp AG's stockholders under IFRS as of Sept. 30, 2005		7,489
Minority interest under IFRS as of Sept. 30, 2005		389
Total equity under IFRS as of Sept. 30, 2005		7,878

RECONCILIATION OF THE CONSOLIDATED STATEMENT OF CASH FLOWS FOR 2004/2005

The free cash flow, i.e. the difference between the cash flow from operating activities and the cash flow from investing activities, increased by €126 million. This is due to the recognition of increases or decreases of liabilities resulting from the disposals of trade accounts receivables which are not derecognized from the balance sheet as cash flows from financing activities. As a consequence, the cash inflow resulting from the disposal of a trade account receivable is only recognized in cash flow from operating activities if and at the time the corresponding customer payments are transferred to the bank.

ThyssenKrupp AG (Interim Report 1ˢᵗ Quarter 2005-2006) (continued)
RECONCILIATION OF THE CONSOLIDATED BALANCE SHEET AS OF DECEMBER 31, 2004

ASSETS million €	Note	US GAAP Dec. 31, 2004	IFRS adjustments	IFRS Dec. 31, 2004
Intangible assets, net	A1	3,419	(349)	**3,070**
Property, plant and equipment, net	B1	9,235	(783)	**8,452**
Investment property	C1	—	569	**569**
Investments accounted for using the equity method		295	9	**304**
Financial assets		662	0	**662**
Deferred tax assets	D1	665	(322)	**343**
Total non-current assets		14,276	(876)	**13,400**
Inventories	E1	6,903	(378)	**6,525**
Trade accounts receivable, net	F1	5,516	610	**6,126**
Other receivables		1,352	(80)	**1,272**
Current income tax assets		347	0	**347**
Cash and cash equivalents		854	0	**854**
Total current assets		14,972	152	**15,124**
Assets held for sale		1,639	3	**1,642**
Total assets		30,88	(721)	**30,166**

EQUITY AND LIABILITIES million €	Note	US GAAP Dec. 31, 2004	IFRS adjustments	IFRS Dec. 31, 2004
Equity attributable to ThyssenKrupp AG's stockholders		8,431	(1,171)	**7,260**
Minority interest		—	350	**350**
Total equity		8,431	(821)	**7,610**
Minority interest		402	(402)	**—**
Accrued pension and similar obligations	A2	6,906	1,006	**7,912**
Other provisions		505	2	**507**
Deferred tax liabilities		829	(759)	**70**
Financial liabilities		3,736	59	**3,795**
Other liabilities		0	42	**42**
Total non-current liabilities		11,976	350	**12,326**
Other provisions	B2	1,888	(1,071)	**817**
Current income tax liabilities		528	(1)	**527**
Financial liabilities	C2	567	219	**786**
Trade accounts payable		3,344	(5)	**3,339**
Other liabilities	D2	3,235	1,003	**4,238**
Total current liabilities		9,562	145	**9,707**
Liabilities associated with assets held for sale		516	7	**523**
Total liabilities		22,456	100	**22,556**
Total equity and liabilities		30,887	(721)	**30,166**

A1 Intangible assets, net

Primarily due to the following reasons the amount of negative IFRS adjustments as of December 31, 2004, was reduced by €36 million compared to October 01, 2004:

The amount of additional impairment charges against goodwill in the opening balance sheet was reduced mainly due to changes in currency exchange rates. As a result, the amount of negative adjustments decreased by €29 million.

Capitalized development cost increased by €7 million and reduced the amount of negative adjustments respectively.

B1 Property, plant and equipment, net

Primarily due to the following reason the amount of negative IFRS adjustments as of December 31, 2004 was reduced by €1,073 million compared to October 01, 2004:

In the opening balance sheet the Group reclassified property from property, plant and equipment into investment property. As a result of the classification of the Residential Real Estate business as discontinued operation in the 1st quarter ended December 31, 2004 the amount of reclassification as of December 31, 2004 was recognized in the balance sheet item "Assets held for sale".

ThyssenKrupp AG (Interim Report 1st Quarter 2005-2006) (continued)

C1 Investment property

Due to the reclassification of the Residential Real Estate business into the balance sheet item "Assets held for sale" the amount of positive IFRS adjustments as of December 31, 2004 was reduced by €1,049 million compared to October 01, 2004.

D1 Deferred tax assets

Primarily due to the following reason the amount of negative IFRS adjustments as of December 31, 2005 increased by €50 million compared to October 01, 2004:

Compared to US GAAP, there are extended possibilities for balancing deferred taxes at single entity level. Because of this and due to changes in currency exchange rates deferred tax assets were reduced compared to US GAAP.

E1 Inventories

Due to the necessary reclassification into trade accounts receivable in connection with the percentage-of-completion method the amount of negative IFRS adjustments as of December 31, 2004 increased by €10 million compared to October 01, 2004.

F1 Trade accounts receivable, net

Primarily due to the following reasons the amount of positive IFRS adjustments as of December 31, 2004 decreased by €43 million compared to October 01, 2004:

The necessary reclassification from inventories into trade accounts receivable in connection with the percentage-of-completion method increased by €10 million. At the same time, the adjustments due to the extended application of the percentage-of-completion method decreased by €30 million.

Adjustments of asset-backed programs and changes of exchange rates resulted in an increase of derecognized trade accounts receivables of €19 million as of December 31, 2004.

A2 Accrued pension and similar obligations

Primarily due to the following reasons the amount of positive IFRS adjustments as of December 31, 2004 decreased by €89 million compared to October 01, 2004:

Regarding accrued pension obligations the necessary amount of adjustments decreased by €26 million due to the application of the fresh-start method in the opening balance sheet as of October 01, 2004 and as a result of changes in currency exchange rates.

Regarding postretirement obligations other than pensions (healthcare obligations) the necessary amount of adjustments decreased by €53 million due to the application of the fresh-start method in the opening balance sheet as of October 01, 2004 and as a result of changes in currency exchange rates.

B2 Other provisions – current –

Primarily due to increased reclassification from provisions into other liabilities the amount of negative IFRS adjustments as of December 31, 2004 increased by €219 million compared to October 01, 2004.

C2 Financial liabilities – current –

Adjustments of asset-backed programs and changes in currency exchange rates resulted in a decrease of current financial liabilities by €19 million as of December 31, 2004.

D2 Other liabilities – current –

Primarily due to the following reasons the amount of positive IFRS adjustments as of December 31, 2004 increased by €172 million compared to October 01, 2004:

Under IFRS, the reclassification from provisions into other liabilities increased by €219 million.

The amount of negative IFRS adjustments increased by €23 million as a result of the derecognition of embedded derivatives.

ThyssenKrupp AG (Interim Report 1ˢᵗ Quarter 2005-2006) (continued)
RECONCILIATION OF EQUITY AS OF DECEMBER 31, 2004

million €	Note	
Stockholders' equity under US GAAP as of Dec. 31, 2004		**8,431**
Intangible assets, net	A1	**(372)**
Property, plant and equipment, net	B1	**(144)**
Investment property	C1	**(70)**
Deferred tax assets	D1	**(322)**
Trade accounts receivable	F1	**18**
Other receivables		**(80)**
Assets held for sale		**3**
Accrued pensions and similar obligations	A2	**(1,006)**
Other provisions	B2	**(5)**
Deferred tax liabilities		**759**
Financial liabilities	C2	**(59)**
Other liabilities	D2	**75**
Liabilities associated with assets held for sale		**(7)**
Minority interest		**52**
Other adjustments		**(13)**
Equity attributable to ThyssenKrupp AG's stockholders under IFRS as of Dec. 31, 2004		**7,260**
Minority interest under IFRS as of Dec. 31, 2004		**350**
Total equity under IFRS as of Dec. 31, 2004		**7,610**

RECONCILIATION OF THE CONSOLIDATED STATEMENT OF CASH FLOWS FOR THE 1ST QUARTER ENDED DECEMBER 31, 2004

The free cash flow, i.e. the difference between the cash flow from operating activities and the cash flow from investing activities, increased by €37 million. This is due to the recognition of increases or decreases of liabilities resulting from the disposals of trade accounts receivables which are not derecognized from the balance sheet as cash flows from financing activities. As a consequence, the cash inflow resulting from the disposal of a trade account receivable is only recognized in cash flow from operating activities if and at the time the corresponding customer payments are transferred to the bank.

ThyssenKrupp AG (Interim Report 1st Quarter 2005-2006) (continued)
RECONCILIATION OF THE CONSOLIDATED STATEMENT OF INCOME FOR THE 1ST QUARTER ENDED DECEMBER 31, 2004

million €	Note	US GAAP quarter ended Dec. 31, 2004	IFRS 5 adjustments	Other IFRS adjustments	IFRS quarter ended Dec. 31, 2004
Net sales	A1	9,722	337	29	10,088
Cost of sales	B1, C1	(7,956)	(275)	27	(8,204)
Gross margin		1,766	62	56	1,884
Selling expenses		(631)	(25)	0	(656)
General and administrative expenses	D1	(579)	(35)	62	(552)
Other operating income		58	0	6	64
Other operating expenses	E1	(78)	(4)	8	(74)
Gain/(loss) on the disposal of subsidiaries, net		2	8	0	10
Income from operations		538	6	132	676
Income from companies accounted for at equity		6	0	3	9
Other financial income/(expense), net		(71)	(1)	(83)	(155)
Financial income/(expense), net	F1	(65)	(1)	(80)	(146)
Income from continuing operations before income taxes		473	5	52	530
Non-recurring losses related to RAG investment		0	0	0	0
Provisions for income taxes	G1	(184)	(4)	(20)	(208)
Minority interest	H1	(21)	0	21	—
Income from continuing operations		268	1	53	322
Discontinued operations (net of tax)		7	(1)	3	9
Cumulative effects of changes in accounting principles (net of tax)		0	0	0	0
Net income		275	0	56	331
Thereof:					
ThyssenKrupp AG's stockholders		275	0	34	309
Minority interest		—	0	22	22
Net income		275	0	56	331
Basic earnings per share					
Income from continuing operations (attributable to TK AG's stockholders)		0.54	0.00	0.06	0.60
Net income (attributable to ThyssenKrupp AG's stockholders)		0.55	0.00	0.07	0.62

US GAAP 1st quarter ended December 31, 2004

The originally published US GAAP 1st quarter ended December 31, 2004 has been adjusted to include all discontinued operations of the year ended September 30, 2005. Compared to the originally published figures in the adjusted US GAAP 1st quarter ended December 31, 2004, net sales decreased by €337 million and income from operations decreased by €6 million. Income from continuing operations before income taxes increased by €5 million.

ThyssenKrupp AG (Interim Report 1ˢᵗ Quarter 2005-2006) (continued)

IFRS 5 adjustments

Based on the differences in the definition of a discontinued operation under US GAAP and IFRS, the following disposals qualified for reporting as discontinued operations under US GAAP but do not under IFRS:

Segment Steel (structure until Sept. 30, 2005)

- Edelstahl Witten-Krefeld GmbH
- Hoesch Contecna Systembau GmbH

Segment Automotive

- Alu Castings
- European truck spring businesses
- ThyssenKrupp Stahl Company

Segment Technologies

- ThyssenKrupp Stahlbau business
- Turbine components operation group

Segment Services

- Hommel group
- Krupp Druckereibetriebe GmbH

In addition, expenses resulting from disposals of discontinued operations incurred in fiscal year 2003/2004 qualified for reporting as discontinued operations under US GAAP but do not under IFRS.

As a result, only the disposals of the MetalCutting business unit and of the Residential Real Estate business qualify for reporting as discontinued operations under US GAAP and under IFRS as well.

The adjustments to present the disposals as part of continuing operations under IFRS are disclosed in column "IFRS 5 adjustments".

Other IFRS adjustments

These adjustments primarily result from the roll forward of the corresponding adjustments due to the transition from US GAAP to IFRS as of October 01, 2004.

Net sales

A1 Embedded derivatives

Under IFRS, for several transactions denominated in foreign currencies separate accounting for embedded derivatives is not required because they are denominated in a currency that is commonly used in such business transactions. As a result, net sales increased by €30 million due to the elimination of the foreign currency embedded derivative effects.

Cost of sales

In total, cost of sales was reduced by €27 million due to the following items:

B1 Embedded derivatives

Under IFRS, for several transactions denominated in foreign currencies separate accounting for embedded derivatives is not required because they are denominated in a currency that is commonly used in such business transactions. As a result, cost of sales increased by €23 million due to the elimination of the foreign currency embedded derivative effects.

C1 Personnel expenses

Personnel expenses included in cost of sales decreased by €47 million. This is primarily due to the absence of amortization of actuarial losses stemming from pension and other post-retirement benefit plans under IFRS as the result of the application of the fresh start method in the opening balance sheet. Moreover, cost of sales decreased because of the reclassification of pension interest cost to net financial income/(expense). Cost of sales increased by the reclassification of the expected return on plan assets to net financial income/(expense).

ThyssenKrupp AG (Interim Report 1st Quarter 2005-2006) (continued)

General and administrative expenses

D1 Personnel expenses

Personnel expenses included in general and administrative expenses decreased by €62 million. This is primarily due to the reversal of amortization of pension and pension-related actuarial losses under IFRS as the result of the application of the fresh start method in the opening balance sheet. Moreover, personnel expenses decreased due to the reclassification of pension interest cost to net financial income/(expense). Personnel expenses increased due to the reclassification of the expected return on plan assets to net financial income/(expense).

Other operating expenses

E1 Development costs

The recognition of certain development costs as intangible assets resulted in a reduction of other operating expenses of €7 million.

Financial income/(expense), net

F1 Accrued pension and similar obligations

Net financial income/(expense) increased by €(80) million primarily due to the recognition of pension interest cost of €(106) million offset by the recognition of the expected return on plan assets of €21 million.

Provisions from income taxes

G1 IFRS adjustments

The increase of provisions from income taxes by €20 million relates to deferred taxes resulting from ifrs adjustments.

Minority interest

H1 Reclassification

Under US GAAP, net income is presented after reduction of minority interest. Under IFRS, net income is inclusive of minority interest. This reclassification resulted in an increase of net income of €21 million.

Commentary: This extract consists of a note in the first quarter for the period ended December 31, 2005. The detailed note explains IFRS reconciliations and first-time adoption of IFRS. Note that the company presents one year of comparative financial statements. Consequently, the following dates apply:

- Opening IFRS statement of financial position: October 1, 2004
- Date of transition to IFRS: October 1, 2004
- Date of adoption: October 1, 2005
- First IFRS financial statements: September 30, 2006
- First IFRS reporting period: September 30, 2006

Included in the notes are the following:

- an explanation of how the transition to IFRS has affected the reported financial position, financial performance and cash flows;
- the fact that financial statements are prepared in accordance with standards and interpretations currently issued and expected to be effective as of September 30, 2006 (the current year-end date), except for exemptions granted by IFRS 1;
  - o note that the company specifies that any interim consolidated financial statements issued for the period between October 01, 2004 and September 30, 2006 should be seen as provisional as the IASB may issue new standards;
- the optional exemptions selected under IFRS 1;
- the various reconciliations required by IFRS 1.

Extract 20(3) – Second-quarter disclosures after IFRS adoption (conversion from UK GAAP)

Minster Pharmaceuticals plc (Interim Financial Statements 2007), pages 5 and 6

1. Publication of non-statutory accounts (in part)

i) The interim financial information for the six months ended 30 September 2007 includes the results of Minster Pharmaceuticals plc and its subsidiary Minster Research Limited. The unaudited results for the period have been prepared on the basis of the accounting policies adopted in the audited accounts for the year ended 31 March 2007, as amended as a result of the first time adoption of International Financial Reporting Standards (IFRS) – see notes 2 and 3 below.

2. Basis of preparation

These consolidated interim financial statements are for the six months ended 30 September 2007 and are prepared under the recognition and measurement rules of IFRS 1. They have been prepared in accordance with the requirements of IFRS 1 "First-time Adoption of International Financial Reporting Standards" relevant to interim reports, because they are part of the period covered by the Group's first IFRS financial statements for the year ended 31 March 2008. They do not include all the information required for full annual financial statements, and should be read in conjunction with the consolidated financial statements of the Group for the year ended 31 March 2007.

These consolidated interim financial statements have been prepared in accordance with the accounting policies set out below which are based on the recognition and measurement principles of IFRS 1 in issue as adopted by the European Union (EU) and are effective at 31 March 2008, our first annual reporting date at which we are required to use IFRS accounting standards adopted by the EU.

Minster Pharmaceutical plc's consolidated financial statements were prepared in accordance with United Kingdom Accounting Standards (United Kingdom Generally Accepted Accounting Practice) until 31 March 2007. The date of transition to IFRS was 1 April 2007. The comparative figures in respect of 30 September 2006 and 31 March 2007 have been restated to reflect changes in accounting policies as a result of adoption of IFRS. The revised policies are listed in note 3 below, and their financial effects are listed in note 4 below.

4. Reconciliation of changes to prior periods on adoption of IFRS

As explained in note 2, these are the Group's first interim financial statements prepared in accordance with International Financial Reporting Standards. This has required a reappraisal of the accounting treatment of the formation of the present group structure, which arose on 25 January 2005 with the combination of the Company with its subsidiary.

Previously, under UK Generally Accepted Accounting Practice, the excess of the fair value of the consideration given over the fair value of the net assets acquired was capitalised as goodwill arising on consolidation and amortised on a straight line basis over its estimated useful economic life, which was estimated to be 20 years.

Under IFRS 3, intangible assets acquired as part of that business combination are separately recognised provided they meet the criteria specified in IAS 38, Intangible Assets. In the opinion of the Directors, the excess of the fair value of the consideration given over the fair value of the assets acquired was wholly attributable to the value of intellectual property rights and licences owned by the subsidiary, Minster Research Limited. Under IFRS 38, these assets have been included in the financial statements as intangible assets with effect from the date of formation of the Group.

The Group has adopted a new accounting policy in respect of the amortisation of these intangible assets under which they are amortised over their useful economic lives once such assets are brought into use to generate income for the Group. Up to that point in time, the carrying value of each asset is reviewed annually for impairment.

Minster Pharmaceuticals plc (Interim Financial Statements 2007), pages 5 and 6

The effect of the introduction of IFRS is, therefore, to re-classify goodwill as an intangible asset comprising the value of intellectual property rights and licences, with a consequent write back to reserves of all amortisation previously charged in financial statements up until 31 March 2007, as set out below:

	31 March 2007 £	30 September 2006 £	1 April 2006 £
Equity previously reported under UK GAAP	27,476,450	12,004,204	13,497,738
Write back amortisation of non-current assets	1,297,054	987,110	677,166
Equity as reported under IFRS	28,773,504	12,991,314	14,174,904

	12 months to 31 March 2007 £	6 months to 30 September 2006 £
Loss reported under UK GAAP	(2,590,152)	(1,493,334)
Write back amortisation of non-current assets	619,888	309,744
Loss as reported under IFRS	(1,970,264)	(1,183,590)

Commentary: This extract was obtained from the notes included in the interim financial report for the six months ended September 30, 2007. The company specifies that:

- consolidated interim financial statements were prepared in accordance with IFRS 1 recognition and measurement requirements;
- interim financial statements should be read in conjunction with Minster's consolidated financial statements for the year ended March 31, 2007;
- previous GAAP consisted of United Kingdom accounting standards, which were used until March 31, 2007;
- April 1, 2007 was the date of IFRS adoption;
- comparative figures for September 30, 2006 and March 31, 2007 were restated to reflect changes in accounting policies as a result of IFRS adoption;
- reconciliations were made of changes to prior periods on IFRS adoption, including reclassification of goodwill as an intangible asset comprising the value of intellectual property rights and licences.

Extract 20(4) – Second-quarter disclosures after IFRS adoption (conversion from UK GAAP)

OMG plc (Interim Report 2008), pages 12, 17-20

1. Preparation of the interim financial information

OMG plc will adopt International Financial Reporting Standards (IFRS) for the first time in its financial statements for the year ending 30 September 2008. Therefore the financial information for the six months ended 31 March 2008 has been prepared on the basis of International Financial Reporting Standards (IFRS) and in accordance with IFRS 1, 'First time adoption of International Financial Reporting Standards' as adopted by the European Union. As required by IFRS 1, detailed reconciliations between previously reported amounts under UK Generally Accepted Accounting Principles ('UK GAAP') and restated comparative amounts under IFRS are presented in note 12.

The interim financial information is unaudited and the financial information contained in this report does not constitute statutory accounts within the meaning of the Companies Act 1985. The comparative figures for the year ended 30 September 2007 have been extracted from the Group's financial statements which have been delivered to the Registrar of Companies and have been restated under IFRS.

OMG plc (Interim Report 2008) (continued)
12. Transition from UK GAAP to IFRS
Reconciliation of prior period income statements

	Unaudited six months to 31 March 2007 £'000	Unaudited twelve months to 30 September 2007 £'000
Profit after tax under UK GAAP	**659**	**1,574**
IFRS impacting on operating profit;		
IAS 19 – Employee benefits	(9)	(40)
IFRS 3 – Write back of previously amortised goodwill	64	178
IFRS 3 – Amortisation of intangible asset	-	(15)
IFRS impacting on taxation		
Deferred tax on employee benefits	2	11
Deferred tax on amortisation of intangible asset	-	4
Profit after tax under IFRS	**716**	**1,712**

Reconciliation of prior period equity

	Unaudited at 30 September 2006 £'000	Unaudited at 31 March 2007 £'000	Unaudited at 30 September 2007 £'000
Total shareholders' funds as reported under UK GAAP	10,654	11,301	15,246
IAS 19 – Employee benefits	(117)	(126)	(157)
IFRS 3 – Write back of previously amortised goodwill	-	64	178
IFRS 3 – Amortisation of intangible asset	-	-	(15)
IAS 12 – Deferred tax on employee share options	215	478	437
IAS 12 – Deferred tax liability on intangible asset	-	-	(202)
Total shareholders' funds as reported under IFRS	10,752	11,717	15,487

The tables above set out how the Group's reported opening balance sheet under UK GAAP at 1 October 2006, its financial results for the six months ended 31 March 2007 and financial position at that date and its audited financial results for the year ended 30 September 2007 and financial position at that date would have been reported under IFRS.

The material accounting policy changes resulting from the adoption of IFRS, including the optional exceptions from retrospective application of IFRS that the Group has applied are set out below.

Notes to the reconciliation between previously reported UK GAAP and IFRS

a) Presentation of financial statements

The primary statements have been presented in accordance with the guidelines set out in IAS 1: Presentation of financial statements.

b) First time adoption of International Financial Reporting Standards

IFRS 1: First time adoption of international financial reporting standards, establishes exemptions from the full requirements of IFRS for companies complying with them for the first time. OMG plc has elected to use the following exemptions;

IFRS 3: Business combinations

The Group has elected not to apply IFRS 3 retrospectively to business combinations occurring prior to the transition to IFRS on 1 October 2006.

IAS 21: Cumulative translation differences

The Group has elected to set the cumulative translations differences arising on retranslation of opening net assets of overseas subsidiaries to zero at 1 October 2006. Exchange differences arising since this date are accounted for in a separate reserve within equity.

OMG plc (Interim Report 2008) (continued)

c) Employee benefits

Under UK GAAP no accrual was made by the Group for holiday pay.

IAS 19: Employee benefits requires the expected cost of compensated short term absences (e.g. holidays) to be recognised when the employee rendered the service that increases their entitlement. As a result, an accrual should be made for holidays earned but not taken.

The effect of adopting IAS 19 is to increase operating profit for the period ended 31 March 2008 by £30,000 (30 September 2007: reduction of £40,000, 31 March 2007: reduction of £9,000) and increase profit after tax for the period ended 31 March 2008 by £24,000 (30 September 2007: reduction of £32,000, 31 March 2007: reduction of £7,000). The effect on the balance sheet of adopting IAS 19 was to reduce net assets at 31 March 2008 by £127,000 (30 September 2007: £157,000, 31 March 2007: £126,000).

d) Goodwill and intangible assets

Under IFRS 3: Business combinations, goodwill is carried at cost and subject to an annual impairment review. Previously goodwill was amortised over its useful economic life in accordance with UK GAAP. Under the transitional arrangements of IFRS 1: First time adoption of IFRS, the Group has elected to apply IFRS 3 prospectively from the date of transition to IFRS. Accordingly goodwill is retained at its net book value at that date and subject to an impairment review. However, for acquisitions since 1 October 2006 goodwill amortisation has been written back and the resultant goodwill balance subject to an impairment review under IAS 36: Impairment of assets.

IAS 38: Intangible assets, requires certain intangible assets acquired in business combinations since the date of transition to IFRS to be recognised separately from goodwill. A value of £737,000 has been applied to customer contracts and relationships of Data Collection Limited acquired on 26 July 2007. This is being amortised over a period of eight years.

e) Taxation

Under IAS 12: Income taxes, the Group has elected to recognise in full the potential future corporation tax deductions available in respect of the intrinsic value of unexercised employee share options. The intrinsic value is measured as the difference between the option exercise price and the market value of the shares at each period end. Previously the deferred asset recognised did not take into account the difference between the intrinsic value and the timing difference on the accounting charge. The effect of adopting IAS12 is to increase the deferred tax asset by £182,000 at 31 March 2008 (30 September 2007: £393,000, 31 March 2007: £443,000) with a corresponding credit to shareholders' equity.

Other changes of accounting policy not impacting on previously reported UK GAAP

f) Capitalisation of development costs

External costs are capitalised if the expected future benefits are probable and the costs can be reliably measured. IAS 38 also requires internal development costs to be capitalised when the criteria to do so have been met. This removes the option that existed under UK GAAP to either capitalise or expense such costs.

A review of all major development projects has been made and there have been no additional development costs identified which meet the criteria to capitalise under IAS 38 that have not already been accounted for in this way under UK GAAP.

g) Financial instruments

The Group's policy is to use derivative financial instruments ('derivatives') such as forward currency contracts to hedge risks associated with foreign currency. From 1 October 2006, such derivative financial instruments are initially recognised at fair value on the date on which a derivate contract is entered into and subsequently measured at fair value at each balance sheet date. Derivatives are carried as assets when the fair value is positive and as liabilities when the fair value is negative.

The fair value of forward currency contracts is calculated by reference to current forward exchange rates for contracts with similar maturity profiles.

For those derivatives designated as hedges and for which hedge accounting is desired, the hedging relationship is documented at its inception. This documentation identifies the hedging instrument, the hedged item or transaction, the nature of the risk being hedged and how effectiveness will be measured throughout its duration. Such hedges are expected at inception to be highly effective.

> **OMG plc (Interim Report 2008) (continued)**
>
> For the purposes of hedge accounting, hedges are classified as:
>
> fair value hedges when hedging the exposure to changes in the fair value of a recognised asset or liability; or
>
> cash flow hedges when hedging exposure to variability in cash flows that is either attributable to a particular risk associated with a recognised asset or liability or a highly probable forecast transaction.
>
> Any gains or losses arising from changes in the fair values of derivatives that do not qualify for hedge accounting are taken to the income statement.
>
> This change of accounting policy has had no financial impact.
>
> **h) Government grants**
>
> Under UK GAAP government grants of a revenue nature were credited to the profit and loss account in the same period as the related expenditure. Under IAS 20: Government grants, a grant should not be recognised until there is reasonable assurance that the group will comply with the conditions attached to it and that the grant will be received. This change of accounting policy has had no financial impact.

Commentary: This extract came from the notes included in the interim financial report for the six months ended March 31, 2008. It presents following disclosures related to transition to IFRS:

- first-time adoption of IFRS, including optional elections made by the company;
- reconciliation between IFRS and UK standards; and
- effect of the adoption of various IFRS standards.

First Annual IFRS Financial Statements

The first annual IFRS financial statements must be presented in accordance with IAS 1, *Presentation of Financial Statements* and other relevant standards and interpretations because IFRS 1 provides no relief from presentation and disclosure requirements. Consequently, the first annual IFRS financial statements would comprise:

- three statements of financial position as at January 1, 2010, December 31, 2010 and December 31, 2011;
- two statements of comprehensive income (presented as an all-inclusive statement or two distinct statements) for the periods ended December 31, 2010 and December 31, 2011;
- two statements of cash flows for the periods ended December 31, 2010 and December 31, 2011;
- two statements of changes in equity for the periods ended December 31, 2010 and December 31, 2011; and
- related notes providing comparative information in accordance with IFRS.

Note that the annual financial statements must also provide an explanation of how the transition from Canadian GAAP to IFRS affected reported financial position, financial performance and cash flows. Such an explanation would include:

- reconciliations of equity reported under Canadian GAAP to equity under IFRS both (a) at the date of the opening IFRS statement of financial position and (b) the end of the last annual period reported under Canadian GAAP. For an entity adopting IFRS for the first time for its December 31, 2011 financial statements, the reconciliations would be as of January 1, 2010 and December 31, 2010;
- reconciliations of net income for the last annual period reported under Canadian GAAP to net income under IFRS for the same period;

- an explanation of the material adjustments that were made, in adopting IFRS for the first time, to the statement of financial position, income statement and cash flow statement;

- separate disclosure of any errors in Canadian GAAP financial statements discovered in the course of transition to IFRS;

- disclosure of the recognition or reversal of any impairment losses in preparing the opening IFRS statement of financial position, in accordance with IAS 36, *Impairment of Assets*; and

- appropriate explanations if an entity has availed itself of any of the specific recognition and measurement exemptions permitted under IFRS 1, for instance, if it used fair values as deemed cost.

Illustrative Disclosures:

Extract 20(5) – IFRS adoption – Relevant disclosures

Deutsche Bank Aktiengesellschaft (Annual Review 2007), pages 107-109 and 239-249

[1] SIGNIFICANT ACCOUNTING POLICIES (in part)

TRANSITION TO IFRS

FIRST-TIME APPLICATION OF IFRS

Until December 31, 2006 the Group prepared its consolidated financial statements in accordance with U.S. GAAP. The Group followed the provisions of IFRS 1, "First Time Adoption of IFRS", in preparing its opening IFRS balance sheet as of the date of transition, January 1, 2006. Certain of the Group's IFRS accounting policies used for this opening balance sheet differed from its U.S. GAAP policies applied at the same date. The resulting adjustments arose from events and transactions before the date of transition to IFRS. Therefore, as required by IFRS 1, those adjustments were recognized directly through retained earnings (or another category of equity where appropriate) as of January 1, 2006. This is the effect of the general rule of IFRS 1 which is to apply IFRS retrospectively. There are some exceptions required and some exemptions permitted by IFRS 1. The Group's first time adoption decisions regarding these exemptions are detailed below. Other options available under IFRS 1, which are not discussed here, are not material to the Group's business.

BUSINESS COMBINATIONS: The Group elected not to apply IFRS 3, "Business Combinations", retrospectively to business combinations prior to the date of transition.

FAIR VALUE OR REVALUATION AS DEEMED COST: At transition, the Group took the carrying values of all items of property, plant and equipment on the date of transition under U.S. GAAP as their deemed cost, which is cost less accumulated depreciation.

EMPLOYEE BENEFITS: At transition, the Group recognized all cumulative actuarial gains and losses on defined benefit pension schemes and other post retirement benefits in shareholders' equity.

CUMULATIVE TRANSLATION DIFFERENCES: At transition, the Group elected to reset the cumulative foreign currency translation adjustment arising from the translation of foreign operations to zero.

DESIGNATION OF PREVIOUSLY RECOGNIZED FINANCIAL INSTRUMENTS: At transition, the Group classified certain of its previously recognized financial assets and liabilities at either fair value through profit or loss or as available for sale, as appropriate, under the provisions of IAS 39, "Financial Instruments: Recognition and Measurement".

SHARE-BASED PAYMENT TRANSACTIONS: The Group adopted IFRS 2, "Share-based Payment", with effect from November 7, 2002.

FAIR VALUE MEASUREMENT OF FINANCIAL ASSETS OR FINANCIAL LIABILITIES AT INITIAL RECOGNITION: The Group elected to apply provisions of IAS 39, "Financial Instruments: Recognition and Measurement", which require deferral of trade date profit on financial instruments carried at fair value where the amount is derived from unobservable parameters or prices, from October 25, 2002.

DERECOGNITION OF FINANCIAL ASSETS AND FINANCIAL LIABILITIES: The Group elected only to apply the derecognition provisions of IAS 39, "Financial Instruments: Recognition and Measurement", prospectively for transactions occurring on or after January 1, 2004.

Deutsche Bank Aktiengesellschaft (Annual Review 2007) (continued)

EFFECT OF THE TRANSITION TO IFRS

A description of the differences between the Group's U.S. GAAP and IFRS accounting policies is presented in Note [44]. Reconciliations of the Group's balance sheets prepared under U.S. GAAP and IFRS as of January 1, 2006 and December 31, 2006 are also presented in Note [44]. Reconciliations of the Group's income statements for the year ended December 31, 2006 prepared in accordance with U.S. GAAP and IFRS, as well as a reconciliation of shareholders' equity as of January 1, 2006 and December 31, 2006 prepared under U.S. GAAP and IFRS, are also presented in Note [44]. As the consolidated financial statements for the year ending December 31, 2007 were prepared, a number of adjustments relating to the transition from U.S. GAAP to IFRS were identified and made to the previously unaudited IFRS financial information presented in the Group's Transition Report and subsequent Interim Reports. The effect of these adjustments is included in the reconciliations presented in Note [44].

[44] RECONCILIATION OF IFRS COMPARABLES FROM PREVIOUS GAAP

MAIN POLICY DIFFERENCES BETWEEN U.S. GAAP AND IFRS

Until December 31, 2006, the Group prepared its consolidated financial statements in accordance with U.S. GAAP. The following sets out, by accounting topic, the main differences between the Group's U.S. GAAP accounting policies applied at that date and the IFRS accounting policies set out in Note [1].

U.S. GAAP	IFRS
CONSOLIDATION (A)	
Three models are used to assess consolidation status: voting rights, variable interest entities ('VIEs') and Qualifying Special Purpose Entities ('QSPEs'). Voting rights: Ownership of a majority voting interest (of over 50 %), directly or indirectly, of voting shares leads to consolidation, unless control does not rest with the majority owners. VIEs: VIEs are consolidated by the interest holder that is exposed to the majority of the entity's expected losses or residual returns, that is, the primary beneficiary. QSPE: A special purpose entity ('SPE') that qualifies as a QSPE is not consolidated.	For operating companies, ownership of the majority of voting rights, either directly or indirectly, leads to consolidation. Potential voting rights are considered. A SPE is consolidated by the Group where it is deemed to control it. Indicators of control include the SPE conducting activities on behalf of the Group and/or the Group holding the majority of the risks and rewards of the SPE. There is no concept of a QSPE under IFRS.
LOAN ORIGINATION COSTS (B)	
All cost of the loan origination activities, for example, the costs of evaluating a prospective borrower's financial condition, which are deemed directly attributable to loan origination, using a per unit cost calculation, are deferred regardless of whether they are incremental or not.	Only those costs associated with loan origination activities which are directly attributable and incremental to the origination of a loan are deferred together with the related fees and thus, included in the calculation of the effective yield.

Deutsche Bank Aktiengesellschaft (Annual Review 2007) (continued)	
U.S. GAAP	IFRS
FAIR VALUE OPTION (c)	
The fair value option available in U.S. GAAP was never adopted as a U.S. GAAP policy for the Group reporting under U.S. GAAP.	Financial assets and financial liabilities may be designated as at fair value through profit or loss (the fair value option) on initial recognition/on transition to IFRS where; — a measurement or recognition inconsistency (accounting mismatch) is significantly reduced that would otherwise arise from measuring financial assets or liabilities or recognizing the gains and losses on them on different bases; — they are managed and their performance is evaluated on a fair value basis with a documented risk management or investment strategy and reported to key management personnel on that basis; or — they contain one or more embedded derivatives that significantly modify the cash flows resulting from those financial instruments. Transaction costs in relation to financial assets and financial liabilities designated as at fair value through profit or loss are recognized in the income statement at inception. The decision to classify financial assets or financial liabilities under the fair value option is irrevocable.
EQUITY METHOD INVESTMENTS (D)	
There is specific accounting guidance on limited partnerships and entities of similar nature. A 3-20 % or more interest is required to be accounted for under the equity method of accounting as it is deemed to represent an 'other than minor influence'.	There is no specific guidance on accounting for limited partnerships and similar entities; significant influence is usually demonstrated by a holding of 20-50 % of voting rights including the consideration of potential voting rights.
DEFINITION OF A DERIVATIVE (E)	
Derivative contracts must have a notional and a mechanism to settle net or alternatively the derivative or the underlying asset is readily convertible to cash.	Derivative contracts are not required to have a mechanism to settle net to be classified as derivatives under IFRS.
HEDGE ACCOUNTING (P)	
Under U.S. GAAP, the entire term of the hedged item must be considered when assessing hedge effectiveness, not only for a portion of the hedged item's life. Where hedge accounting is achieved under IFRS but not under U.S. GAAP the hedge accounting has been reversed for U.S. GAAP.	IFRS permits more hedging relationships than U.S. GAAP. Under IFRS it is permitted to designate a derivative as hedging for only a portion of the time period to maturity of a hedged item in a fair value hedge.
LOANS HELD FOR SALE RECLASSIFIED TO TRADING (F)	
Loans held for sale are held at lower of cost or market value. Loan origination fees and costs are recognized upon disposal of the loan. Temporary impairment on loans held for sale under U.S. GAAP is taken through the income statement.	There is no 'loans held for sale' classification. Loans with the intention to sell or securitize in the near term are classified as trading.

Deutsche Bank Aktiengesellschaft (Annual Review 2007) (continued)	
U.S. GAAP	**IFRS**
FINANCIAL ASSETS CLASSIFIED AS AVAILABLE FOR SALE (G)	
EQUITY INVESTMENTS Equity securities that do not have a readily determinable fair value and other non-securitized equity interests are classified as other investments and carried at cost, less any other than temporary impairment.	Non-marketable equity investments and other non-securitized equity interests are classified as financial assets available for sale and are accounted for at fair value unless it can not be reliably determined.
AVAILABLE-FOR-SALE SECURITIES – TREATMENT OF FOREIGN EXCHANGE Changes in the fair value of available for sale debt securities arising from changes in foreign exchange rates are recorded in accumulated other comprehensive income and transferred to income on disposal of the security.	Changes in the fair value of debt instruments classified as available for sale due to changes in foreign exchange rates are reflected in the income statement.
IMPAIRMENT OF ASSETS AVAILABLE FOR SALE Impairments on available for sale debt securities cannot be subsequently reversed if they are no longer considered to be impaired.	Impairments on debt instruments classified as available for sale should be reversed if, in a subsequent period, the fair value increases and the increase can be objectively related to an event occurring after the impairment loss was recognized in the income statement.
INVESTMENT WITH A SALE RESTRICTION In general, investments with a sale restriction of more than one year are classified as other investments and carried at cost, less any other than temporary impairment. When an investment with a sale restriction is held by an entity that is regulated in the U.S. as a broker-dealer then it is carried at fair value with changes through the income statement.	Investments with a restriction on sale are classified as financial assets available for sale with changes through equity.
FINANCIAL ASSET DERECOGNITION (H)	
Derecognition of financial assets is primarily based on control. The relationship between true sale analysis and consolidation generally is that derecognition is considered first and then consolidation. Special rules apply to accounting for repurchase and reverse repurchase agreements – a collateralization close to 100 % is required to preserve financing accounting.	Derecognition is based on risks and rewards. Control is only considered when substantially all risks and rewards have been neither transferred nor retained. The consolidated group has to be determined prior to applying the derecognition criteria. A partial derecognition of transferred financial assets may occur where the Group has a continuing involvement in them.
REAL ESTATE & LEASING (i)	
GAINS ON SALE AND LEASEBACK Gains arising from a sale and operating leaseback transaction are deferred and amortized over the period of the operating lease.	Gains arising from a sale and operating leaseback transaction are recognized immediately in profit or loss provided that the transaction has been entered into at fair value.
CONTINUING INVOLVEMENT IN SALE AND LEASEBACKS Any form of continuing involvement precludes sales accounting.	If continuing involvement exists, this needs to be considered when determining the classification of the lease arrangement.

Deutsche Bank Aktiengesellschaft (Annual Review 2007) (continued)	
U.S. GAAP	**IFRS**
IMPAIRMENT OF INVESTMENT PROPERTIES	
The assessment as to whether an investment property is impaired is calculated by assessing the undiscounted expected future cash flows arising from the property.	The assessment of impairment is performed on a net present value basis, applying a discounting factor to the expected future cash flows.
SHARE-BASED COMPENSATION (J)	
SHARE AWARDS – 'EARLY RETIREMENT'	
Where plan rules allow staff of a certain age and/or service period to retain their awards on leaving, the expense is fully accelerated at the date the employee becomes eligible for early retirement. Early retirement rules were applied prospectively for awards granted after January 1, 2006.	Early retirement rules (accelerated amortization) are applied to all awards granted after November 7, 2002.
SHARE AWARDS – FORFEITURES	
Amortization of the total number of shares expected to vest over the service period (net of expected forfeitures) is required. Forfeitures were no longer accounted for on an actual basis from January 1, 2006.	The rules relating to expected forfeitures apply to all share awards granted after November 7, 2002.
PENSIONS (K)	
PENSIONS – ACCUMULATED ACTUARIAL GAINS AND LOSSES	
From December 31, 2006, any unrecognized gains/losses at yearend are reported as part of accumulated other comprehensive income ('OCI'). The Group used the corridor method whereby actuarial gains and losses exceeding 10 % of the greater of plan assets and plan liabilities are recognized in profit or loss in equal amounts over the remaining service lives of current employees.	On transition the Group recognized all cumulative actuarial gains and losses in shareholders' equity in accordance with the transitional provisions of IFRS 1. Since transition, the corridor approach is used for actuarial gains and losses.
PENSIONS – LONG-TERM EMPLOYEE BENEFITS	
No specific valuation rules apply.	Long-Term Employee Benefits are required to be valued using actuarial methods.
DERIVATIVES ON DEUTSCHE BANK SHARES (L)	
Put and call options indexed to Deutsche Bank shares which are physically settled are classified as derivatives.	Put and call options indexed to Deutsche Bank shares which are physically settled are classified as equity instruments. For the physically settled written put options on Deutsche Bank shares the present value of the redemption amount is recorded as a liability. The liability is accreted over the life of the options to the redemption amount recognizing interest expense in accordance with the effective interest rate method.

Deutsche Bank Aktiengesellschaft (Annual Review 2007) (continued)

U.S. GAAP	IFRS
TAX (O)	

DEFERRED TAX ON SHARE-BASED COMPENSATION

U.S. GAAP	IFRS
If a jurisdiction allows a tax deduction for expenses relating to share-based compensation the permissible amount for the tax deduction might differ from the cumulative remuneration expense recognized in the income statement and/or the deduction might be allowed in a later period (e.g. with delivery of the shares).	
The difference between the tax deductible amount of compensation expense and the cumulative compensation expense recognized for financial reporting (tax benefit/shortfall) has to be recognized only at delivery of the shares to the employees. Benefits are recorded in additional paid-in capital ('APIC'), and shortfalls are recognized through the income statement. Any credit to APIC is conditional upon the tax-paying position of the respective entity/tax group.	In addition to the recognition of excess tax benefits/shortfalls in taxes when shares are delivered the difference between the expected future tax deduction for share awards outstanding and the cumulative compensation expense recognized for financial reporting (tax benefit/shortfall) has to be (i) estimated based on the current share price and (ii) recognized at any reporting date. As IFRS allows for recognition of the expected future tax deduction a credit to APIC would be disallowed only if it is expected that the entity will not be in the position to make use of the excess tax deduction.
Shortfalls can be offset against excess tax benefits recognized in the same accounting period and in prior accounting periods.	Possibilities to offset shortfalls against excess tax benefits are limited.

DEFERRED TAXES AND TAX REVERSAL ON AVAILABLE FOR SALE SECURITIES

U.S. GAAP	IFRS
The impact of changes in tax rate/tax law are included in net income even if the original deferred taxes have been recognized in equity.	Tax rate/tax law changes are accounted for consistently with the accounting for the transaction itself. Therefore, if the underlying temporary difference and related deferred taxes have been recorded in equity, a change due to tax law/tax rates is recorded in equity as well.

The following tables show reconciliations from U.S. GAAP to IFRS for the income statement for the year ended December 31, 2006, the consolidated balance sheets as of January 1, 2006 and December 31, 2006 and the impacts on shareholders' equity as of January 1, 2006 and December 31, 2006.

As the consolidated financial statements for the year ending December 31, 2007 were prepared, a number of adjustments relating to the 2006 transition year were identified and applied to the previously unaudited IFRS financial information that was presented in the Group's Transition Report (which was published on April 19, 2007) and subsequent Interim Reports. These adjustments were limited to the balance sheet and had no effect on net income. These adjustments are indicated below and reflected in the following reconciliation tables. These adjustments should be considered when referring to the Transition Report for interim periods.

— shareholders' equity as of the transition date of January 1, 2006 increased by €91 million;

— total assets and total liabilities each increased by €17.5 billion as of January 1, 2006 and by €12.7 billion as of December 31, 2006, and there were similar effects as of each interim quarter end; and

— several reclassification adjustments between asset and liability categories were made, all of which did not exceed €16 billion in any category or period affected.

Both the gross-up of assets and liabilities and the reclassifications between asset and liability categories were driven by the consolidation of certain securitization vehicles.

Deutsche Bank Aktiengesellschaft (Annual Review 2007) (continued)
INCOME STATEMENT AND BALANCE SHEET RECONCILIATIONS
U.S.GAAP/IFRS RECONCILIATIONS

Consolidated Statement of Income

	U.S. GAAP	Reclassi-fication	Consoli-dation	Loan origina-tion costs	Fair value option	Equity method invest-ments	Definition of a deriva-tive	Hedge Account-ing	Revaluation Loans held for sale re-classified to trading	Revaluation Financial assets avail-able for sale
in € m.			(A)	(B)	(c)	(D)	(E)	(P)	(F)	(G)
Year ended Dec 31, 2006										–
Interest revenues	55,217	572	2,203	91	–	3	–	–	(4)	–
Interest expense	48,298	630	2,245	–	–	–	–	–	(1)	–
Net interest income	**6,919**	**(57)**	**(42)**	**91**	**–**	**3**	**–**	**–**	**(3)**	**–**
Provision for loan losses	330	(330)								
Net interest income after provision for loan losses	**6,589**	**(6,589)**								
Provision for credit losses		268	(3)	–	(1)	–	–	–	–	–
Net interest income after provision for credit losses		**6,594**	**(38)**	**91**	**1**	**3**	**–**	**–**	**(3)**	**–**
Commissions and fees from fiduciary activities	3,995	(3,995)								
Commissions, broker's fees, mark-ups on securities underwriting and other securities activities	5,019	(5,019)								
Fees for other customer services	2,530	(2,530)								
Commissions and fee income		11,123	76	–	–	–	–	–	1	–
Trading revenues, net	8,247	(8,247)								
Net gains (losses) on financial assets/liabilities at fair value through profit or loss		9,061	53	–	(44)	(11)	61	–	(48)	(35)
Net gains on securities available for sale	407	(407)								
Net gains (losses) on financial assets available for sale	–	582	2	–	–	1	(1)	–	–	7
Net income (loss) from equity method investments	512	(53)	(27)	–	–	(19)	–	–	–	–
Other revenues	709	(473)	24	32	85	–	6	–	–	(16)
Total noninterest revenues	**21,419**	**41**	**127**	**32**	**41**	**(29)**	**66**	**–**	**(47)**	**(45)**
Compensation and benefits	12,649	–	–	154	–	–	–	–	–	–
Occupancy expense of premises	1,020	(1,020)								
Furniture and equipment	157	(157)								
IT costs	1,586	(1,586)								
Professional service fees	1,202	(1,202)								
Communication and data services	634	(634)								
Other expenses	2,412	(2,412)								
General and administrative expenses		6,982	57	4	–	–	–	–	–	2
Policyholder benefits and claims		67								
Impairment of intangible assets	31	–	–	–	–	–	–	–	–	–
Restructuring activities	192	–	–	–	–	–	–	–	–	–
Total noninterest expenses	**19,883**	**37**	**57**	**157**	**–**	**–**	**–**	**–**	**–**	**2**
Income before income tax expense	8,125	8	32	(34)	42	(26)	66	–	(50)	(46)
Income tax expense	2,186	–	(10)							
Reversal of 1999/2000 credits for tax rate changes	(1)	–	–							
Cumulative effect of accounting changes, net of tax	46									
Net income	**5,986**	**8**	**41**							
Net income attributable to minority interest	–	9								
Net income attributable to Deutsche Bank's shareholders	5,986	–	41	(34)	42	(26)	66	–	(50)	(46)

Deutsche Bank Aktiengesellschaft (Annual Review 2007) (continued)
INCOME STATEMENT AND BALANCE SHEET RECONCILIATIONS
U.S.GAAP/IFRS RECONCILIATIONS

by accounting topic

in € m.	Financial asset derecog-nition	Real estate & leasing	Share-based compen-sation	Pensions	Derivatives on Deutsche Bank shares	Currency translation adjust-ments	Other	Tax	Total revalua-tion	IFRS
	(H)	(i)	(J)	(K)	(L)	(M)	(N)	(O)		
Year ended Dec 31, 2006										
Interest revenues	132	–	–	–	–	–	28	32	2,486	58,275
Interest expense	64	(1)	–	–	19	–	–	13	2,339	51,267
Net interest income	**68**	**1**	**–**	**–**	**(19)**	**–**	**28**	**19**	**146**	**7,008**
Provision for loan losses										
Net interest income after provision for loan losses										
Provision for credit losses	1	–	–	–	–	–	34	–	30	298
Net interest income after provision for credit losses	**68**	**1**	**–**	**–**	**(19)**	**–**	**(5)**	**19**	**116**	**6,710**
Commissions and fees from fiduciary activities										
Commissions, broker's fees, markups on securities underwriting and other securities activities										
Fees for other customer services										
Commissions and fee income	(4)	–	–	–	–	–	–	–	72	11,195
Trading revenues, net										
Net gains (losses) on financial assets/liabilities at fair value through profit or loss	(65)	–	–	–	(75)	1	(7)	–	(169)	8,892
Net gains on securities available for sale										
Net gains (losses) on financial assets available for sale	–	–	–	–	–	–	–	–	9	591
Net income (loss) from equity method investments	–	–	–	–	–	2	3	–	(40)	419
Other revenues	22	(7)	–	–	–	(1)	11	–	153	389
Total noninterest revenues	**(47)**	**(7)**	**–**	**–**	**(75)**	**2**	**8**	**–**	**26**	**21,486**
Compensation and benefits	–	–	(232)	(73)	–	–	–	–	(151)	12,498
Occupancy expense of premises										
Furniture and equipment										
IT costs										
Professional service fees										
Communication and data services										
Other expenses										
General and administrative expenses	1	11	–	–	–	–	13	–	87	7,069
Policyholder benefits and claims										67
Impairment of intangible assets	–	–	–	–	–	–	–	–	–	31
Restructuring activities	–	–	–	–	–	–	–	–	–	192
Total noninterest expenses	**1**	**11**	**(232)**	**(73)**	**–**	**–**	**13**	**–**	**(63)**	**19,857**
Income before income tax expense	20	(17)	232	73	(94)	2	(11)	19	206	8,339
Income tax expense								84	74	2,260
Reversal of 1999/2000 credits for tax rate changes								1	1	–
Cumulative effect of accounting changes, net of tax	–	–	(68)	(8)	–	–	–	30	(46)	–
Net income								**(37)**	**85**	**6,079**
Net income attributable to minority interest	–	–	–	–	–	–	–	–	–	9
Net income attributable to Deutsche Bank's shareholders	20	(17)	163	65	(94)	2	(11)	(37)	84	6,070

Deutsche Bank Aktiengesellschaft (Annual Review 2007) (continued)
INCOME STATEMENT AND BALANCE SHEET RECONCILIATIONS
U.S.GAAP/IFRS RECONCILIATIONS

Consolidated Statement of Income

in € m.	U.S. GAAP	Gross up	Reclassi-fication	Consoli-dation (A)	Loan origina-tion costs (B)	Fair value option (c)	Equity method invest-ments (D)	Definition of a deriva-tive (E)	Hedge Account-ing (P)	Revaluation — Loans held for sale re-classified to trading (F)
Balance at January 1, 2006										
Cash and due from banks	6,571	–	–	297	–	–	–	–	–	–
Interest-earning deposits with banks	11,963	–	–	160	–	–	–	–	–	–
Central bank funds sold and securities purchased under resale agreements	130,993	35,240	(149,680)	–	–	–	–	–	–	–
Securities borrowed	101,125	16,322	(64,083)	–	–	–	–	–	–	–
Trading assets	448,393		(448,393)							
Financial assets at fair value through profit or loss		313,717	689,321	22,996	–	(163)	1	55	–	44
Securities available for sale	21,675		(21,675)	–	–	–	–	–	–	–
Financial assets available for sale		7	23,536	9,753	–	–	60	–	–	–
Other investments	7,382		(7,382)							
Equity method investments		–	4,607	(60)	–	–	12	–	–	–
Loans	151,355	–	(283)	12,579	(266)	–	–	–	–	–
Premises and equipment	5,079	(97)	(1,798)	44	–	–	–	–	–	–
Goodwill	7,045		(7,045)							
Other intangible assets, net	1,198		(1,198)							
Intangible assets		–	8,340	1	–	–	–	–	–	–
Other assets	99,382	42,676	(29,657)	1,333	(6)	–	–	–	–	–
Income tax assets		–	5,390	119	–	–	–	–	–	–
Total assets	992,161	407,865	–	47,222	(272)	(163)	73	55	–	44
Deposits	380,787	–	(1,089)	(568)	–	–	–	–	–	–
Central bank funds purchased and securities sold under repurchase agreements	143,524	51,561	(108,386)	–	–	–	–	–	–	–
Securities loaned	24,581	–	(411)	–	–	–	–	–	–	–
Trading liabilities	194,347		(194,347)							
Financial liabilities at fair value through profit or loss		314,548	317,117	14,994	–	261	–	63	–	–
Other short-term borrowings	20,549	–	20	23,214	–	–	–	–	–	–
Other liabilities	81,377	41,756	(10,932)	1,055	(12)	(18)	–	1	–	(3)
Provisions		–	2,336	(3)	–	(2)	–	–	–	–
Income tax liabilities		–	6,893	227	–	–	–	–	–	–
Long-term debt	113,554	–	(11,118)	3,726	–	–	–	–	(55)	–
Trust preferred securities	–	–	(706)	4,628	–	–	–	–	–	–
Obligation to purchase common shares	3,506	–	–	–	–	–	–	–	–	–
Total liabilities	962,225	407,865	(623)	47,272	(12)	240	–	63	(55)	(3)
Common shares, no par value, nominal value of € 2.56	1,420	–	–	–	–	–	–	–	–	–
Additional paid-in capital	13,793	–	–	–	–	–	–	–	–	–
Retained earnings	22,628	–	–	(93)	(260)	(285)	12	(8)	55	47
Common shares in treasury, at cost	(3,368)	–	–	–	–	–	–	–	–	–
Equity classified as obligation to purchase common shares	(3,506)	–	–	–	–	–	–	–	–	–
Accumulated other comprehensive income (loss)	(1,031)		1,031							
Net gains (losses) not recognized in the income statement, net of tax		–	(1,031)	42	–	(118)	61	–	–	–
Total shareholders' equity	29,936	–	–	(51)	(260)	(403)	73	(8)	55	47
Minority interest	–	–	624	–	–	–	–	–	–	–
Total equity	29,936	–	624	(51)	(260)	(403)	73	(8)	55	47
Total liabilities and equity	992,161	407,865	–	47,222	(272)	(163)	73	55	–	44

Deutsche Bank Aktiengesellschaft (Annual Review 2007) (continued)
INCOME STATEMENT AND BALANCE SHEET RECONCILIATIONS
U.S.GAAP/IFRS RECONCILIATIONS

by accounting topic

in € m.	Financial assets available for sale	Financial asset derecognition	Real estate & leasing	Share-based compensation	Pensions	Derivatives on Deutsche Bank shares	Currency translation adjustments	Other	Tax	Total revaluation	IFRS
	(G)	(H)	(i)	(J)	(K)	(L)	(M)	(N)	(O)		
Balance at January 1, 2006											
Cash and due from banks	–	–	–	–	–	–	–	–	–	298	6,869
Interest-earning deposits with banks	–	–	–	–		–	–	–	–	160	12,123
Central bank funds sold and securities purchased under resale agreements	–	–	–	–	–	–	–	–	–	–	16,553
Securities borrowed	–	–	–	–	–	–	–	–	–	–	53,364
Trading assets											
Financial assets at fair value through profit or loss	–	1,907	–	–		(357)	–	15	–	24,497	1,027,535
Securities available for sale	–	–	–	–	–	–	–	–	–	–	–
Financial assets available for sale	263	(564)	–	–	–	–	–	1	–	9,513	33,055
Other investments											4,554
Equity method investments	–	–	–	–	–	–	–	(5)	–	(53)	
Loans	(2)	2,094	–	–	–	–	–	(1)	(67)	14,338	165,411
Premises and equipment	–	–	–	–	–	–	–	1	–	44	3,228
Goodwill											
Other intangible assets, net											8,341
Intangible assets	–	–	–	–	–	–	–	–	–	1	
Other assets	–	(595)	(74)	–	(909)	–	–	–	–	(253)	112,148
Income tax assets	–	–	–	–	–	–	–	–	741	860	6,250
Total assets	261	2,842	(74)	–	(909)	(357)	–	11	674	49,405	1,449,431
Deposits	–	4,849	–	–	–	–	–	–	–	4,281	383,979
Central bank funds purchased and securities sold under repurchase agreements	–	–	–	–	–	–	–	–	–	–	86,699
Securities loaned	–	(161)	–	–	–	–	–	–	–	(160)	24,010
Trading liabilities											
Financial liabilities at fair value through profit or loss	–	(407)	–	–	–	(220)	–	–	–	14,688	646,353
Other short-term borrowings	–	(106)	–	–	–	–	–	–	–	23,108	43,677
Other liabilities	–	204	(136)	50	133	–	–	6	–	1,281	113,482
Provisions	2	–	–	–	–	–	–	–	–	(3)	2,333
Income tax liabilities	–	–	–	–	–	–	(36)	–	(460)	(269)	6,624
Long-term debt	–	(1,499)	–	–	–	(1)	–	–	–	2,171	104,606
Trust preferred securities	–	–	–	–	–	–	–	–	–	4,627	3,921
Obligation to purchase common shares	–	–	–	–	–	–	943	–	–	943	4,449
Total liabilities	2	2,880	(136)	50	133	722	(36)	6	(460)	50,667	1,420,133
Common shares, no par value, nominal value of € 2.56	–	–	–	–	–	–	–	–	–	–	1,420
Additional paid-in capital	–	–	–	493	–	(94)	–	–	272	671	14,464
Retained earnings	(2)	(39)	62	(543)	(1,056)	(41)	(1,344)	6	(1,281)	(4,772)	17,856
Common shares in treasury, at cost	–	–	–	–	–	–	–	–	–	–	(3,368)
Equity classified as obligation to purchase common shares	–	–	–	–	(943)	–	–	–	–	(943)	(4,449)
Accumulated other comprehensive income (loss)											
Net gains (losses) not recognized in the income statement, net of tax	261	–	–	–	14	–	1,380	(1)	2,143	3,782	2,751
Total shareholders' equity	259	(39)	62	(50)	(1,042)	(1,078)	36	5	1,133	(1,262)	28,674
Minority interest	–	–	–	–	–	–	–	–	–	–	624
Total equity	259	(39)	62	(50)	(1,042)	(1,078)	36	5	1,133	(1,262)	29,298
Total liabilities and equity	261	2,842	(74)	–	(909)	(357)	–	11	674	49,405	1,449,431

Deutsche Bank Aktiengesellschaft (Annual Review 2007) (continued)
INCOME STATEMENT AND BALANCE SHEET RECONCILIATIONS
U.S.GAAP/IFRS RECONCILIATIONS

Consolidated Statement of Income

in € m.	U.S. GAAP	Gross up	Reclassi- fication	Consoli- dation	Loan origina- tion costs	Fair value option	Equity method invest- ments	Definition of a deriva- tive	Hedge Account- ing	Revaluation — Loans held for sale re- classified to trading
				(A)	(B)	(c)	(D)	(E)	(P)	(F)
Balance at Dec 31, 2006										
Cash and due from banks	7,009	(4)	–	3	–	–	–	–	–	–
Interest-earning deposits with banks	19,470	–	–	(279)	–	–	–	–	–	–
Central bank funds sold and securities purchased under resale agreements	138,763	34,342	(159,532)	–	–	–	–	–	–	–
Securities borrowed	108,266	16,897	(62,220)	–	–	–	–	–	–	–
Trading assets	516,839		(516,839)							
Financial assets at fair value through profit or loss		300,752	778,513	25,590	–	(113)	(10)	89	–	(2)
Securities available for sale	22,054	(22,054)								
Financial assets available for sale		–	28,263	9,355	–	–	89	–	–	–
Other investments	5,357		(5,357)							
Equity method investments		–	2,627	(85)	–	–	(1)	–	–	–
Loans	168,134	–	(7,383)	16,786	(292)	–	–	–	–	(3)
Premises and equipment	4,149	(67)	(886)	45	–	–	–	–	–	–
Goodwill	7,144		(7,144)							
Other intangible assets, net	1,267		(1,267)							
Intangible assets	50	8,561	1	–	–	–	–	–	–	–
Other assets	127,778	53,499	(41,033)	536	(10)	–	–	5	–	(10)
Income tax assets		–	5,751	83	–	–	–	–	–	–
Total assets	1,126,230	405,468	–	52,035	(301)	(113)	78	94	–	(14)
Deposits	408,782	–	(1,252)	(898)	–	–	–	–	–	–
Central bank funds purchased and securities sold under repurchase agreements	187,129	51,239	(136,167)	–	–	–	–	–	–	–
Securities loaned	23,240	–	(669)	–	–	–	–	–	–	–
Trading liabilities	218,854		(218,854)							
Financial liabilities at fair value through profit or loss		300,834	382,803	12,397	–	139	–	34	–	–
Other short-term borrowings	19,793	–	172	28,566	–	–	–	–	–	–
Other liabilities	99,672	53,395	(9,888)	626	(6)	2	–	–	–	(9)
Provisions		–	1,768	(1)	–	(3)	–	–	–	–
Income tax liabilities	–	6,646	158	–	–	–	–	–	–	–
Long-term debt	132,495	–	(24,972)	6,114	–	–	–	–	(55)	–
Trust preferred securities	–	–	(304)	5,075	–	–	–	–	–	–
Obligation to purchase common shares	3,457	–	–	–	–	–	–	–	–	–
Total liabilities	1,093,422	405,468	(717)	52,038	(6)	138	–	34	(55)	(9)
Common shares, no par value, nominal value of € 2.56	1,343	–	–	–	–	–	–	–	–	–
Additional paid-in capital	14,424	–	–	–	–	–	–	–	–	–
Retained earnings	25,069	–	–	(86)	(295)	(250)	(14)	61	55	(3)
Common shares in treasury, at cost	(2,378)	–	–	–	–	–	–	–	–	–
Equity classified as obligation to purchase common shares	(3,457)	–	–	–	–	–	–	–	–	–
Accumulated other comprehensive income (loss)	(2,193)		2,193							
Net gains (losses) not recognized in the income statement, net of tax		–	(2,193)	84	–	(1)	92	–	–	(3)
Total shareholders' equity	32,808	–	–	(2)	(295)	(251)	78	61	55	(6)
Minority interest	–	–	717	–	–	–	–	–	–	–
Total equity	32,808	–	717	(2)	(295)	(251)	78	61	55	(6)
Total liabilities and equity	1,126,230	405,468	–	52,035	(301)	(113)	78	94	–	(14)

Deutsche Bank Aktiengesellschaft (Annual Review 2007) (continued)
INCOME STATEMENT AND BALANCE SHEET RECONCILIATIONS
U.S.GAAP/IFRS RECONCILIATIONS
by accounting topic

in € m.	Financial assets available for sale	Financial asset derecognition	Real estate & leasing	Share-based compensation	Pensions	Derivatives on Deutsche Bank shares	Currency translation adjustments	Other	Tax	Total revaluation	IFRS
	(G)	(H)	(i)	(J)	(K)	(L)	(M)	(N)	(O)		
Balance at Dec 31, 2006											
Cash and due from banks	-	-	-	-	-	-	-	-	-	3	7,008
Interest-earning deposits with banks	-	-	-	-	-	-	-	7	-	(271)	19,199
Central bank funds sold and securities purchased under resale agreements	-	692	-	-	-	-	-	-	-	692	14,265
Securities borrowed	-	-	-	-	-	-	-	-	-	-	62,943
Trading assets											
Financial assets at fair value through profit or loss	-	52	-	-	-	(225)	-	3	-	25,385	1,104,650
Securities available for sale	-	-	-	-	-	-	-	-	-	-	-
Financial assets available for sale	331	-	-	-	-	-	-	-	-	9,775	38,037
Other investments											
Equity method investments	-	-	-	-	-	-	-	-	-	(86)	2,541
Loans	(1)	1,342	-	-	-	-	-	(10)	(50)	17,773	178,524
Premises and equipment	-	-	-	-	-	-	-	-	-	45	3,241
Goodwill											
Other intangible assets, net											
Intangible assets	-	-	-	-	-	-	-	-	-	1	8,612
Other assets	-	(1,582)	(80)	-	(82)	-	-	-	-	(1,224)	139,021
Income tax assets	-	-	-	-	-	-	-	-	618	701	6,452
Total assets	330	504	(80)	-	(82)	(225)	-	-	568	52,795	1,584,493
Deposits	-	5,283	-	-	-	-	-	-	-	4,386	411,916
Central bank funds purchased and securities sold under repurchase agreements	-	-	-	-	-	-	-	-	-	(1)	102,200
Securities loaned	-	(1,396)	-	-	-	-	-	-	-	(1,397)	21,174
Trading liabilities											
Financial liabilities at fair value through profit or loss	-	(1,379)	-	-	-	(209)	-	-	-	10,981	694,619
Other short-term borrowings	-	(98)	-	-	-	-	-	-	-	28,468	48,433
Other liabilities	-	335	(125)	36	86	-	-	6	1	951	144,129
Provisions	3	-	-	-	-	-	-	-	-	-	1,768
Income tax liabilities	-	-	-	-	-	-	(36)	-	(450)	(328)	6,318
Long-term debt	-	(2,220)	-	-	-	-	-	-	-	3,841	111,363
Trust preferred securities	-	-	-	-	-	-	-	-	-	5,075	4,771
Obligation to purchase common shares	-	-	-	-	-	870	-	-	-	870	4,327
Total liabilities	3	525	(125)	36	86	660	(36)	6	(449)	52,846	1,551,018
Common shares, no par value, nominal value of € 2.56	-	-	-	-	-	-	-	-	-	-	1,343
Additional paid-in capital	-	-	344	-	-	(4)	-	-	482	822	15,246
Retained earnings	(56)	(20)	45	(380)	(966)	(32)	(1,328)	(5)	(1,343)	(4,618)	20,451
Common shares in treasury, at cost	-	-	-	-	-	-	-	-	-	-	(2,378)
Equity classified as obligation to purchase common shares	-	-	-	-	-	(850)	-	-	-	(850)	(4,307)
Accumulated other comprehensive income (loss)											
Net gains (losses) not recognized in the income statement, net of tax	383	-	-	-	798	-	1,364	(1)	1,878	4,595	2,403
Total shareholders' equity	327	(20)	45	(36)	(168)	(886)	36	(6)	1,017	(51)	32,758
Minority interest	-	-	-	-	-	-	-	-	-	-	717
Total equity	327	(20)	45	(36)	(168)	(886)	36	(6)	1,017	(51)	33,475
Total liabilities and equity	330	504	(80)	-	(82)	(225)	-	-	568	52,795	1,584,493

Commentary: The above extract is a detailed note disclosure prepared in accordance with IFRS 1. It shows that the bank, which has a calendar year end, adopted IFRS in 2007.

The bank applied IFRS retrospectively, but disclosed that it elected to apply certain optional exemptions as permitted by IFRS 1. It specifies that certain other options available under IFRS 1 were not discussed because they were not material to its business.

The bank also presents the following reconciliations and provides an explanation of material adjustments made in adopting IFRS for the first time (note that no errors were identified):

- reconciliations of equity (in the form of a complete statement of financial position) reported under previous GAAP to IFRS at the beginning (January 1, 2006) and at the end of the comparative period reported (December 31, 2006); and

- reconciliations of net income (in the form of a complete income statement) of the comparative period under previous GAAP with IFRS (December 31, 2006).

By providing reconciliations in the form of complete statements of financial position, the bank effectively presented an opening statement of financial position (as at January 1, 2006) as required by IAS 1.

Disclosures in Periods Subsequent to IFRS Adoption

The accounting policies entities choose when preparing opening IFRS statements of financial position affect not only performance and financial position during the transition periods but also subsequent periods. Consequently, it may be appropriate for entities to continue to disclose in subsequent periods certain optional exemptions initially made during the preparation of the opening IFRS statement of financial position.

Illustrative Disclosures:

Extract 20(6) – Disclosures in years subsequent to transition to IFRS

Alcatel-Lucent (AR 2007 on Form 20-F), pages 156, 157 and 160

NOTE 1 SUMMARY OF ACCOUNTING POLICIES (in part)

c/ Business combinations (in part)

Regulations governing first-time adoption: Business combinations that were completed before January 1, 2004, the transition date to IFRSs, were not restated, as permitted by the optional exemption included in IFRS 1. Goodwill was therefore not recognized for business combinations occurring prior to January 1, 2004, which were previously accounted for in accordance with article 215 of Regulation No. 99-02 of the "Comité de la Réglementation Comptable". According to this regulation, the assets and liabilities of the acquired company are maintained at their carrying value at the date of the acquisition, adjusted for the Group's accounting policies, and the difference between this value and the acquisition cost of the shares is adjusted directly against shareholders' equity.

Business combinations after January 1, 2004: These business combinations are accounted for in accordance with the purchase method required by IFRS 3. Once control is obtained over a company, its assets, liabilities and contingent liabilities are measured at their fair value at the acquisition date in accordance with IFRS requirements. Any difference between the fair value and the carrying value is accounted for in the respective underlying asset or liability, including both the Group interest and minority interests. Any excess between the purchase price and the Group's share in the fair value of such net assets is recognized as goodwill (see intangible and tangible assets).

d/ Translation of financial statements denominated in foreign currencies

The balance sheets of consolidated entities having a functional currency different from the presentation currency of the Group (i.e. euro) are translated into euros at the closing exchange rate (spot exchange rate at the balance sheet date), and the income statements and cash flow statements of such consolidated entities are translated at the average period to date exchange rate. The resulting translation adjustments are included in shareholders' equity under the caption "Cumulative translation adjustments".

Alcatel-Lucent (AR 2007 on Form 20-F) (continued)

Goodwill and fair value adjustments arising from the acquisition of a foreign entity are considered as assets and liabilities of that entity. They are therefore expressed in the entity's functional currency and translated into euros using the closing exchange rate.

Regulations governing first-time adoption: In accordance with the option available under IFRS 1, the accumulated total of translation adjustments at the transition date was deemed to be zero. This amount was reversed against retained earnings, leaving the amount of shareholders' equity unchanged. Translation adjustments that predate the IFRS transition will therefore not be included when calculating gains or losses arising from the future disposal of consolidated subsidiaries or equity affiliates existing as of the IFRS transition date.

k/ Pension and retirement obligations and other employee and post-employment benefit obligations

In accordance with the laws and practices of each country where Alcatel-Lucent is established, the Group participates in employee benefit plans.

For defined contribution plans, the Group expenses contributions as and when they are due. As the Group is not liable for any legal or constructive obligations under the plans beyond the contributions paid, no provision is made. Provisions for defined benefit plans and other long-term employee benefits are determined as follows:

- using the Projected Unit Credit Method (with projected final salary), each period of service gives rise to an additional unit of benefit entitlement and each unit is measured separately to calculate the final obligation. Actuarial assumptions such as mortality rates, rates of employee turnover and projection of future salary levels are used to calculate the obligation;

- the "corridor" method is no longer used from January 1, 2007 (see below).

The service cost is recognized in "income from operating activities" and the interest cost and expected return on plan assets are recognized in "financial income (loss)". In case of plan amendments, the impact is presented on a specific line item of the income statement if material (see note 1p).

Prepaid pension costs cannot exceed the net total present value of any available refund from the plan or reduction in future contributions to the plan. When Alcatel-Lucent expects to use excess pension plan assets to fund retiree healthcare for formerly represented retirees and has the ability to do so, such use is considered as a refund from the related plan. In particular, under Section 420 of the Internal Revenue Code in the United States of America as amended by the Pension Protection Act of 2006, Alcatel-Lucent can use excess pension plan assets applicable to formerly represented retirees to fund the retiree healthcare plan for such retirees until 2013.

As of January 1, 2007, the Group has elected the option provided for in the amendment of IAS 19 "Employee Benefits — Actuarial Gains and Losses, Group Plans and Disclosures" (paragraphs 93A to 93D) that allows for the immediate recognition of actuarial gains and losses and any adjustments arising from asset ceiling limitations, net of deferred tax effects, outside of the income statement in the statement of recognized income and expense. The impact of this change in accounting policy is disclosed in note 4.

Regulations governing first-time adoption: (in part)

In accordance with the option available under IFRS 1, the accumulated unrecognized actuarial gains and losses at the transition date were recorded in shareholders' equity. Before the change in accounting policy disclosed in note 4, which was retrospectively applied from January 1, 2005, the corridor method had been applied starting January 1, 2004.

Commentary: In the above extract, the company describes the optional exemptions it applied when it prepared its opening statement of financial position on January 1, 2004, which relate to:

- business combinations;
- translation adjustments; and
- accumulated unrecognized actuarial gains and losses.

Extract 20(7) – Disclosures in years subsequent to transition to IFRS

British Sky Broadcasting Group plc (AR 2007), pages 55 and 58

1. Accounting policies (in part)

d) Goodwill

Business combinations that have occurred since the Transition Date are accounted for by applying the purchase method of accounting. Following this method, goodwill is initially recognised on consolidation, representing the difference between the fair value cost of the business combination and the fair value of the identifiable assets, liabilities and contingent liabilities assumed. Where a business combination occurs in several stages, as a result of successive share purchases, the goodwill associated with each stage is calculated using fair value information at the date of each additional share purchase.

In respect of business combinations that occurred prior to the Transition Date, goodwill has been included at its deemed cost, as permitted by IFRS 1 "First-time Adoption of International Financial Reporting Standards". Deemed cost represents the goodwill's carrying value under the Group's UK Generally Accepted Accounting Principles ("UK GAAP") accounting policies on the Transition Date. On disposal of a subsidiary, associate or joint venture, the attributable amount of goodwill is included in the determination of profit or loss on disposal, except for goodwill written off to reserves under UK GAAP prior to the Transition Date, which is not reinstated and is not included in determining any subsequent gain or loss on disposal.

Goodwill is stated at cost less any impairment losses and is tested, at least annually, for impairment, based on the recoverable amounts of the cash generating unit to which the goodwill has been allocated. Any impairment identified is recognised immediately in the income statement and is not subsequently reversed. The carrying amount of goodwill in respect of associates and joint ventures is included in the carrying amount of the investment in the associate or joint venture.

n) Employee benefits

Wages, salaries, social security contributions, bonuses payable and non-monetary benefits for current employees are recognised in the income statement as the employees' services are rendered.

The Group provides pensions to eligible employees through defined contribution schemes. The amount charged to the income statement in the year represents the cost of contributions payable by the Group to the schemes in exchange for employee services rendered in that year. The assets of the schemes are held independently of the Group. Termination benefits are recognised as a liability when, and only when, the Group has a demonstrable commitment to terminate the employment of an employee or group of employees before the normal retirement date or as the result of an offer to encourage voluntary redundancy.

The Group issues equity-settled and cash-settled share-based payments to certain employees which must be measured at fair value and recognised as an expense in the income statement, with a corresponding increase in equity in the case of equity-settled payments, and liabilities in the case of cash-settled awards. The fair values of equity-settled payments are measured at the dates of grant using option-pricing models, taking into account the terms and conditions upon which the awards are granted. Cash-settled share-based payments are measured at their fair value as at the balance sheet date. The fair value is recognised over the period during which employees become unconditionally entitled to the awards, subject to the Group's estimate of the number of awards which will lapse, either due to employees leaving the Group prior to vesting or due to non-market based performance conditions not being met. Where an award has market-based performance conditions, the fair value of the award is adjusted for the probability of achieving these via the option pricing model. The total amount recognised in the income statement as an expense is adjusted to reflect the actual number of awards that vest, except where forfeiture is due to the failure to meet market-based performance measures.

In accordance with the transitional provisions in IFRS 1, and IFRS 2, the recognition and measurement principles in IFRS 2 have only been applied to options and awards granted after 7 November 2002 that had not vested by 1 January 2005.

Commentary: Here, the company describes the optional exemptions it applied when it prepared its opening statement of financial position on July 1, 2004, which relate to:

- business combinations; and
- share-based payments.

FUTURE DEVELOPMENTS

IFRS 1, which was first issued in June 2003, has been amended every time a new IFRS was issued. These amendments were required as IFRS 1 generally prohibits first-time adopters from following the transitional provisions included within each individual standard. Consequently, IFRS 1 must be updated to reflect specific requirements whenever new IFRS standards are released.

IFRS 1 became more complex and more confusing with each amendment. This prompted the IASB to propose, as part of its annual improvements project, to change IFRS 1 to make it easier for readers to understand and to design it to better accommodate future changes. The new version of IFRS 1, released on November 27, 2008, presents a restructured standard. It replaces the previous version and is effective for entities applying IFRS for the first time for annual periods beginning on or after July 1, 2009.

The IASB issued an Exposure Draft in September 2008 proposing amendments to IFRS 1 to address three transition issues:

- *Reassessment of accounting under previous GAAP for leases*: The ED proposes that, if a first-time adopter made a determination of whether an arrangement contains a lease under previous GAAP, based on requirements identical to IFRIC 4, *Determining whether an Arrangement contains a Lease*, but at a date other than that required by IFRIC 4, then the first-time adopter need not reassess that determination at its date of transition to IFRS.

- *Cost for oil and gas assets*: The ED proposes an exemption to allow a first-time adopter in the oil and gas industry that used full-cost accounting under its previous GAAP to measure exploration and evaluation (E&E) assets at the amount determined under the entity's previous GAAP at the date of transition to IFRS. In addition, this entity may elect to measure assets in the development or production phases at the amount determined under its previous GAAP, but must allocate this amount on a pro-rata basis to the underlying assets using either reserve volumes or reserve values at the date of transition. The ED does not define full-cost accounting, but explains that, under such accounting, exploration and development costs for properties in development or in production are accounted for in cost centres that include all properties in a large geographical area. The assets to which this exemption is applied must be tested for impairment at the date of transition to IFRS. This impairment test must be conducted in accordance with IFRS 6, *Exploration for and Evaluation of Mineral Resources* for E&E assets, and IAS 36, *Impairment of Assets* for development and production assets. If an entity uses this exemption for oil and gas assets in the development or production phases, the ED proposes that this fact must be disclosed along with the basis on which the carrying amounts determined under previous GAAP were allocated.

- *Cost for property, plant and equipment held for use in operations subject to rate regulation*: The ED proposes an exemption to allow a first-time adopter to use, at the date of transition to IFRS, the carrying amount under its previous GAAP for property, plant and equipment held for use in operations subject to rate regulation. The exemption would only be available, however, if it is otherwise impracticable to identify amounts capitalized under the entity's previous GAAP that would not qualify for capitalization under IFRS. An entity must apply this election on an item-by-item basis. For the purpose of the proposed exemption, rate-regulated operations are operations that provide services or products to customers at prices (i.e., rates) established by legislation, an independent regulator or other authorized body designed to recover the cost of providing the services or products and allowing the entity to earn a determined return on investment. Each item to which this exemption is applied must be tested for impairment in accordance with IAS 36 at the date of transition to IFRS.

COMPREHENSIVE EXAMPLES

This section presents two comprehensive examples. The first illustrates disclosures in various parts of an annual report in the year of transition to IFRS for a European SEC registrant that previously used UK GAAP. The second illustrates disclosures in the annual report and three successive quarterly reports of a Canadian company planning to adopt IFRS early. The second example also provides a brief overview of IFRS-Canadian GAAP differences.

Vodafone Group Plc – All extracts 20(A) were obtained from various parts of the annual report (including financial statements) for the year ended March 31, 2006 (which consists of the first annual IFRS financial statements). In accordance with IFRS, the company presented an opening statement of financial position at April 1, 2004 and comparative figures for the period ended March 31, 2005. The extracts provide various disclosures on: (1) the conversion from UK GAAP to IFRS and (2) differences between IFRS and US GAAP (as the company is an SEC registrant), which may serve as a basis for identifying potential differences between IFRS and Canadian GAAP.

Extract 20(A1) – Vodafone Group Plc, page 2

This extract presents a portion of selected financial data that the company presented in its annual report (outside of the financial statement and the MD&A). The company specifies that it has derived these figures from its consolidated financial statements and that, consequently, these financial highlights should be read in conjunction with the latter, which were prepared in accordance with IFRS.

Note that the amounts presented in the financial highlights are prepared in accordance with (1) IFRS (for year 2006 and 2005, with a convenience translation from £ into US $ for 2006) and (2) US GAAP related to revenues, net losses and equity for all five years. The differences between the amounts reported under IFRS and US GAAP may serve as an indicator of the impact that IFRS adoption could have on the financial position and results of a Canadian company.

Financial Highlights (in part)

The selected financial data set out on the following pages is derived from the Consolidated Financial Statements of the Company on pages 71 to 130 and as such should be read in conjunction with them. Certain trends within the financial data presented below have been impacted by business acquisitions and disposals, the most significant of which are described in "Business Overview – History and Development of the Company".

The Consolidated Financial Statements are prepared in accordance with IFRS, on the basis set out in note 1 to the Consolidated Financial Statements, which differ in certain significant respects from US GAAP. For further details, see note 38 to the Consolidated Financial Statements, "US GAAP information". Solely for convenience, amounts represented below in dollars have been translated at $1.7393: £1, the Noon Buying Rate on 31 March 2006.

	At/year ended 31 March					
	2006 £m	2006 £m	2005 £m	2004 £m	2003 £m	2002 £m
Consolidated Income Statement Data						
IFRS						
Revenue	51,048	29,350	26,678			
Operating (loss)/profit	(24,496)	(14,084)	7,878			
Adjusted operating profit (Non-GAAP measure)[1]	16,348	9,399	8,353			
(Loss)/profit before taxation	(25,833)	(14,853)	7,285			
(Loss)/profit for the financial year from continuing operations	(29,973)	(17,233)	5,416			
US GAAP						
Revenue	41,319	23,756	21,370	19,637	15,487	13,447
Net loss[2][3]	(23,081)	(13,270)	(13,752)	(8,105)	(9,072)	(16,769)
Consolidated Cash Flow Data[4]						
IFRS						
Net cash flows from operating activities	17,723	10,190	9,240			
Net cash flows from investing activities	(11,573)	(6,654)	(4,112)			
Net cash flows from financing activities	(7,896)	(4,540)	(7,242)			
Free cash flow (Non-GAAP measure)[1]	11,163	6,418	6,592			
Consolidated Balance Sheet Data						
IFRS						
Total assets	220,435	126,738	147,197			
Total equity	148,383	85,312	113,648			
Total equity shareholders' funds	148,580	85,425	113,800			
Total liabilities	72,052	41,426	33,549			
US GAAP						
Shareholders' equity	151,291	86,984	107,295	129,141	140,580	141,016

Notes:

(1) Refer to "Non-GAAP Information" on pages 47 to 48 for a reconciliation of this non-GAAP measure to the most comparable GAAP measure and a discussion of this measure.

(2) 2005 net loss includes the cumulative effect of accounting changes related to intangible assets and post employment benefits that increase net loss by £6,372 million or 9.63p per ordinary share. Net loss and shareholders' equity for 2005, 2004, 2003 and 2002 have been restated to give effect to the modified retrospective adoption of SFAS No. 123 (Revised 2004). See note 38 to the Consolidated Financial Statements for further details on these changes in accounting policy.

(3) 2002 net loss includes the cumulative effect of accounting changes related to derivative financial instruments reducing net loss by £17 million or 0.02p per ordinary share.

(4) Amounts reported refer to continuing operations.

Extract 20(A2) – Vodafone Group Plc, pages 25 to 27

In this extract, the company specifies that this financial report has been prepared in accordance with IFRS. It lists certain critical accounting estimates and provides an explanation of certain differences between IFRS and US GAAP (which must be read with "Significant accounting policies" and "Summary of differences between IFRS and US GAAP" provided in the notes to the consolidated financial statements), including:

- impairment reviews;

- business combination (the company specifies that it has used the optional exemption not to apply IFRS 3, *Business Combinations* retrospectively and has recognized an impairment loss).

The company also:

- specifies directors' responsibilities for the preparation of financial statements under IFRS;

- indicates that it has prepared an IFRS/US GAAP reconciliation of revenues, net profit and shareholders' equity; and

- notes that management has discussed its critical accounting estimates and associated disclosures with the company's audit committee.

This extract primarily discusses the differences between IFRS and US GAAP, which may serve as a basis for identifying potential differences between IFRS and Canadian GAAP, since many of the Canadian GAAP requirements are very similar to US GAAP requirements.

Introduction (in part)

The following discussion is based on the Consolidated Financial Statements included elsewhere in this Annual Report.

On 19 July 2002, the European Parliament adopted Regulation No. 1606/2002 requiring listed companies in the Member States of the European Union to prepare their Consolidated Financial Statements in accordance with IFRS from 2005. This is the first time the Company's Annual Report has been prepared under IFRS. Consequently, financial information for the year ended 31 March 2005, presented as comparative figures in this report, has been restated from UK GAAP in accordance with IFRS, as disclosed in note 40 to the Consolidated Financial Statements.

The Consolidated Financial Statements, which are prepared in accordance with IFRS, differ in certain significant respects from US GAAP. Reconciliations of the material differences in the IFRS Consolidated Financial Statements to US GAAP are disclosed in note 38 to the Consolidated Financial Statements, "US GAAP information".

Critical Accounting Estimates (in part)

The Group prepares its Consolidated Financial Statements in accordance with IFRS, the application of which often requires judgements to be made by management when formulating the Group's financial position and results. Under IFRS, the directors are required to adopt those accounting policies most appropriate to the Group's circumstances for the purpose of presenting fairly the Group's financial position, financial performance and cash flows. The Group also prepares a reconciliation of the Group's revenue, net profit and shareholders' equity between IFRS and US GAAP.

In determining and applying accounting policies, judgement is often required in respect of items where the choice of specific policy, accounting estimate or assumption to be followed could materially affect the reported results or net asset position of the Group should it later be determined that a different choice would be more appropriate.

Management considers the accounting estimates and assumptions discussed below to be its critical accounting estimates and, accordingly, provides an explanation of each below. Where it is considered that the Group's US GAAP accounting policies differ materially from the IFRS accounting policy, a separate explanation is provided.

The discussion below should also be read in conjunction with the Group's disclosure of significant IFRS accounting policies, which is provided in note 2 to the Consolidated Financial Statements, "Significant accounting policies" and with the "Summary of differences between IFRS and US GAAP" provided in note 38 to the Consolidated Financial Statements.

Management has discussed its critical accounting estimates and associated disclosures with the Company's Audit Committee.

Impairment reviews

Asset recoverability is an area involving management judgement, requiring assessment as to whether the carrying value of assets can be supported by the net present value of future cash flows derived from such assets using cash flow projections which have been discounted at an appropriate rate. In calculating the net present value of the future cash flows, certain assumptions are required to be made in respect of highly uncertain matters, as noted below.

IFRS requires management to undertake an annual test for impairment of indefinite lived assets, and for finite lived assets, to test for impairment if events or changes in circumstances indicate that the carrying amount of an asset may not be recoverable. Group management currently undertakes an annual impairment test covering goodwill and other indefinite lived assets, and also reviews finite lived assets and investments in associated undertakings at least annually to consider whether a full impairment review is required. In the year to 31 March 2006, the Group has recognised impairment losses amounting to £23,515 million relating to the Group's mobile operations in Germany, Italy and Sweden, of which £23,000 million was recognised following completion of the annual impairment test.

US GAAP (in part)

Under US GAAP, the requirements for testing the recoverability of intangible assets and property, plant and equipment differ from IFRS. US GAAP requires the carrying value of such assets with finite lives to be compared to undiscounted future cash flows over the remaining useful life of the primary asset of the asset group being tested for impairment, to determine if the asset or asset group is recoverable. If the carrying value exceeds the undiscounted cash flows, the carrying value is not recoverable and the asset or asset group is written down to the net present value of future cash flows derived in a manner similar to IFRS.

Business combinations (in part)

IFRS

On transition to IFRS, the Group has elected not to apply IFRS 3, "Business Combinations", retrospectively as the difficulty in applying these requirements to the large number of business combinations completed by the Group from incorporation through to 1 April 2004 exceeded any potential benefits. Goodwill arising before the date of transition to IFRS, after adjusting for items including the impact of proportionate consolidation of joint ventures, amounted to £78,753 million.

If the Group had elected to apply the accounting for business combinations retrospectively, it may have led to an increase or decrease in goodwill and increase in licences, customer bases, brands and related deferred tax liabilities recognised on acquisition.

US GAAP

For acquisitions prior to 29 September 2004, the key difference from IFRS is that for the acquisition of mobile network businesses, the excess of purchase price over the fair value of the identifiable assets and liabilities acquired other than licences ("the residual") was allocated to licences, as opposed to goodwill. However, subsequent to this date and due to the prohibition of this method of accounting following the issuance of EITF Topic D-108 licences are valued using a direct valuation approach, with the residual being allocated to goodwill. For other acquisitions, the residual has been and will continue to be allocated to goodwill.

Extract 20(A3) – Vodafone Group, page 63

In this extract, the company specifies that the remuneration committee has reviewed the impact of the introduction of IFRS on incentive schemes. The idea was to adjust EPS under IFRS to reflect UK GAAP measurement to ensure that EPS performance achievement is measured on a consistent basis and that the adoption of IFRS does not create an advantage or disadvantage for participants.

Board's Report to Shareholders on Directors' Remuneration (in part)

Report on Executive Directors' Remuneration for the 2006 Financial Year and Subsequent Periods (in part)

Measurement of performance under IFRS

From 1 April 2005, the Company has prepared its financial statements under IFRS. The Remuneration Committee has reviewed the impact of the introduction of IFRS for incentive scheme purposes, to ensure that EPS performance achievement is measured on a consistent basis and that the introduction of the new standard does not advantage or disadvantage participants. For the schemes affected, EPS under IFRS is adjusted to reflect UK GAAP measurement so that performance may be measured on a consistent basis. In each case, an independent auditor is requested to review and verify the achievement level.

Extract 20(A4) – Vodafone Group Plc, page 75

This extract comes from the "Basis of Preparation" note in the first annual financial statements presented in accordance with IFRS. The company:

- discloses that the consolidated financial statements have been prepared in accordance with IFRS, which differs in certain material respects from US GAAP (this disclosure is required because the company is an SEC registrant); and

- specifies that certain amounts in relation to the previous financial year have been reclassified to conform the presentation to the new IFRS requirements.

---

1. Basis of preparation (in part)

The Consolidated Financial Statements are prepared in accordance with International Financial Reporting Standards ("IFRS") (including International Accounting Standards ("IAS") and interpretations issued by the International Accounting Standards Board ("IASB") and its committees, and as interpreted by any regulatory bodies applicable to the Group as adopted for use in the European Union ("EU"), the Companies Act 1985 and Article 4 of the IAS Regulations. The Consolidated Financial Statements have been prepared in accordance with IFRS, which differs in certain material respects from US generally accepted accounting principles ("US GAAP") – see note 38.

The preparation of financial statements in conformity with IFRS requires management to make estimates and assumptions that affect the reported amounts of assets and liabilities and disclosure of contingent assets and liabilities at the date of the financial statements and the reported amounts of revenue and expenses during the reporting period. For a discussion on the Group's critical accounting estimates see "Performance – Critical Accounting Estimates" elsewhere in this Annual Report. Actual results could differ from those estimates. The estimates and underlying assumptions are reviewed on an ongoing basis. Revisions to accounting estimates are recognised in the period in which the estimate is revised if the revision affects only that period or in the period of the revision and future periods if the revision affects both current and future periods. Certain amounts in relation to the previous financial year have been reclassified to conform presentation with the requirements of IFRS.

Extract 20(A5) – Vodafone Group Plc, pages 75 to 78

This extract is from the note on significant accounting policies that discloses certain elected IFRS optional exemptions for:

- business combinations (goodwill written off to reserves under UK GAAP prior to 1998 has not been reinstated and is not included in determining any subsequent profit or loss on disposal);

- foreign operations exchange (differences arising before the date of transition to IFRS were deemed to be nil and will be excluded from the determination of any subsequent profit or loss on disposal);

- post-employment benefits (cumulative actuarial gains and losses as at date of transition to IFRS were recognized in the statement of financial position through retained earnings); and

- financial instruments (the company did not elect to use the optional exemption).

---

2. Significant accounting policies (in part)

Intangible assets (in part)

Goodwill (in part)

Goodwill arising before the date of transition to IFRS, on 1 April 2004, has been retained at the previous UK GAAP amounts subject to being tested for impairment at that date. Goodwill written off to reserves under UK GAAP prior to 1998 has not been reinstated and is not included in determining any subsequent profit or loss on disposal.

Foreign currencies (in part)

In respect of all foreign operations, any exchange differences that have arisen before 1 April 2004, the date of transition to IFRS, are deemed to be nil and will be excluded from the determination of any subsequent profit or loss on disposal.

Post employment benefits (in part)

Cumulative actuarial gains and losses as at 1 April 2004, the date of transition to IFRS, have been recognised in the balance sheet.

Financial instruments (in part)

The Group has applied the requirements of IFRS to financial instruments for all periods presented and has not taken advantage of any exemptions available to first time adopters of IFRS in this respect. The Group has early adopted IFRS 7, "Financial Instruments: Disclosures", amendments to IAS 39, "Financial Instruments: Recognition and Measurement" and IFRS 4, "Insurance Contracts", regarding "Financial Guarantee Contracts" and amendments to IAS 39 regarding "The Fair Value Option" and "Cash Flow Hedge Accounting of Forecast Intragroup Transactions" and applied them from 1 April 2004.

Extract 20(A6) – Vodafone Group Plc, pages 122 to 125

This extract illustrates the various disclosures required of an SEC registrant:

- significant differences between IFRS and US GAAP; and

- reconciliations between IFRS and US GAAP (including comparative amounts of net loss for the year and shareholders' equity).

Although these disclosures are not specifically related to the company's IFRS adoption, they may nevertheless serve as a basis for identifying potential differences between IFRS and Canadian GAAP, since many of the requirements under Canadian GAAP are very similar to those under US GAAP.

Note that on December 27, 2007, the SEC adopted final ruling Securities Act Release No 33-8879, *Acceptance from Foreign Private Issuers of Financial Statements prepared in Accordance with International Reporting Standards without Reconciliation to US GAAP* with an effective date of March 4, 2008. Consequently there are no current reconciliations requirements of earnings and equity between IFRS and US GAAP.

38. US GAAP information (in part)

The following is a summary of the effects of the differences between US GAAP and IFRS. The unaudited translation of pounds sterling amounts into US dollars is provided solely for convenience based on the Noon Buying Rate on 31 March 2006 of $1.7393: £1. Amounts at 31 March 2005 and for the year then ended have been restated to give effect to the modified retrospective adoption of SFAS No. 123 (Revised 2004), discussed in (j) below.

Net loss for the years ended 31 March

	Reference	2006 $m	2006 £m	2005 Restated £m
Revenue (IFRS)		51,048	29,350	26,678
Items (decreasing)/increasing revenues:				
Discontinued operations		(1,642)	(944)	(1,108)
Basis of consolidation	a	(10,011)	(5,756)	(5,423)
Connection revenue	b	1,924	1,106	1,223
Revenue (US GAAP)		41,319	23,756	21,370
(Loss)/profit for the financial year (IFRS)		(37,953)	(21,821)	6,518
Items (increasing)/decreasing net loss:				
Investments accounted for under the equity method	c	(2,139)	(1,230)	(5,440)
Connection revenue and costs	b	17	10	16
Goodwill and other intangible assets	d	(24,870)	(14,299)	(15,534)
Impairment losses	e	26,745	15,377	475
Amortisation of capitalised interest	f	(188)	(108)	(105)
Interest capitalised during the year	f	63	36	19
Other	g	(74)	(42)	99
Income taxes	h	15,483	8,902	6,680
Minority interests	i	(165)	(95)	(108)
Cumulative effect of change in accounting principle: post employment benefits	j	–	–	(195)
Cumulative effect of change in accounting principle: intangible assets	j	–	–	(6,177)
Net loss (US GAAP)		(23,081)	(13,270)	(13,752)

Shareholders' equity at 31 March

	Reference	2006 $m	2006 £m	2005 Restated £m
Total equity (IFRS)		148,383	85,312	113,648
Items (decreasing)/increasing shareholders' funds:				
Investments accounted for under the equity method	c	(3,978)	(2,287)	(982)
Connection revenue and costs	b	(9)	(5)	(14)
Goodwill and other intangible assets	d	56,618	32,552	31,714
Capitalised interest	f	2,510	1,443	1,529
Other	g	365	210	104
Income taxes	h	(52,795)	(30,354)	(38,856)
Minority interests	i	197	113	152
Shareholders' equity (US GAAP)		151,291	86,984	107,295

US GAAP condensed consolidated statement of operations

	Reference	2006 $m	2006 £m	2005 Restated £m
Revenue		41,319	23,756	21,370
Cost of sales		(48,920)	(28,126)	(27,803)
Selling, general and administrative expense		(7,552)	(4,342)	(3,779)
Operating loss		(15,153)	(8,712)	(10,212)
Share of results in investments accounted for under the equity method		(1,816)	(1,044)	(2,179)
Non-operating income and expense		(1,151)	(662)	(465)
Loss before income taxes		(18,120)	(10,418)	(12,856)
Income tax benefit		5,614	3,228	4,994
Minority interests		(170)	(98)	(108)
Loss from continuing operations		(12,676)	(7,288)	(7,970)
Discontinued operations, net of taxes		(10,405)	(5,982)	590
Cumulative effect of changes in accounting principles, net of taxes		–	–	(6,372)
Net loss		(23,081)	(13,270)	(13,752)
		Cents	**Pence**	Pence
Basic and diluted loss per share:				
Loss from continuing operations		(20.25)	(11.64)	(12.03)
Discontinued operations		(16.62)	(9.56)	0.89
Cumulative effect of changes in accounting principles		–	–	(9.63)
Net loss	k	(36.87)	(21.20)	(20.77)

Discontinued operations

As discussed in note 29, the Group disposed of its interests in Vodafone Sweden during the year ended 31 March 2006. Vodafone Sweden has been classified as discontinued under US GAAP.

Summary of differences between IFRS and US GAAP

The Consolidated Financial Statements are prepared in accordance with IFRS, which differ in certain material respects from US GAAP. The differences that are material to the Group relate to the following:

a. Basis of consolidation

The basis of consolidation under IFRS differs from that under US GAAP. The Group has interests in several jointly controlled entities, the most significant being Vodafone Italy. Under IFRS, the Group reports its interests in jointly controlled entities using proportionate consolidation. The Group's share of the assets, liabilities, income, expenses and cash flows of jointly controlled entities are combined with the equivalent items in the Consolidated Financial Statements on a line-by-line basis. Under US GAAP, the results and assets and liabilities of jointly controlled entities are incorporated in the Consolidated Financial Statements using the equity method of accounting. Under the equity method, investments in jointly controlled entities are carried in the consolidated balance sheet at cost as adjusted for post-acquisition changes in the Group's share of the net assets of the jointly controlled entity, less any impairment in the value of the investment. The Group's share of the assets, liabilities, income and expenses of jointly controlled entities which are included in the Consolidated Financial Statements are reported in note 13.

b. Connection revenues and costs

Under IFRS and, for transactions subsequent to 30 September 2003, under US GAAP, customer connection revenue is recognised together with the related equipment revenue to the extent that the aggregate equipment and connection revenue does not exceed the fair value of the equipment delivered to the customer. Any customer connection revenue not recognised together with related equipment revenue is deferred and recognised over the period in which services are expected to be provided to the customer.

For transactions prior to 1 October 2003, connection revenue under US GAAP is recognised over the period that a customer is expected to remain connected to a network. Connection costs directly attributable to the income deferred are recognised over the same period. Where connection costs exceed connection revenue, the excess costs were charged in the statement of operations immediately upon connection. The balances of deferred revenue and deferred charges as of 30 September 2003 continue to be recognised over the period that a customer is expected to remain connected to a network.

c. Investments accounted for under the equity method

This line item includes the net effect of IFRS to US GAAP adjustments affecting net loss and shareholders' equity related to investments accounted for under the equity method, other than the cumulative effect of change in accounting principle related to intangible assets, which has been disclosed separately. The differences are:

Adjustment to the share of results in investments accounted for under the equity method

	2006 £m	2005 £m
Goodwill and other intangible assets associated with investments accounted for under the equity method	(7,772)	(8,864)
Impairment loss	3,600	–
Income taxes	2,863	3,362
Other	79	62
Total	(1,230)	(5,440)

Adjustments to the carrying value of investments accounted for under the equity method

	2006 £m	2005 £m
Goodwill and other intangible assets associated with investments accounted for under the equity method	9,539	13,549
Income taxes	(11,997)	(14,615)
Other	171	84
Total	(2,287)	(982)

d. Goodwill and other intangible assets

The differences related to goodwill and other intangible assets included in the reconciliations of net loss and shareholders' equity relate to acquisitions prior to the Group's adoption of SEC guidance issued on 29 September 2004. In determining the value of licences purchased in business combinations prior to 29 September 2004, the Group allocated the portion of the purchase price, in excess of the fair value attributed to the share of net assets acquired, to licences. The Group had previously concluded that the nature of the licences and the related goodwill acquired in business combinations was fundamentally indistinguishable.

Following the adoption of the SEC guidance issued on 29 September 2004, the Group's US GAAP accounting policy for initial and subsequent measurement of goodwill and other intangible assets, other than determination of impairment of goodwill and finite lived intangible assets, is substantially aligned to that of IFRS described in note 2. However, there are substantial adjustments arising prior to 29 September 2004 from different methods of transition to current IFRS and US GAAP as discussed below.

Goodwill arising before the date of transition to IFRS has been retained under IFRS at the previous UK GAAP amounts for acquisitions prior to 1 April 2004. The Group has assigned amounts to licences and customer bases under US GAAP as they meet the criteria for recognition separately from goodwill, while these had not been recognised separately from goodwill under UK GAAP because they did not meet the recognition criteria. Under US GAAP, goodwill and other intangible assets with indefinite lives are capitalised and not amortised, but tested for impairment at least annually. Intangible assets with finite lives are capitalised and amortised over their useful economic lives.

Under IFRS and US GAAP, the purchase price of a transaction accounted for as an acquisition is based on the fair value of the consideration. In the case of share consideration, under IFRS the fair value of such consideration is based on the share price on the date of exchange. Under US GAAP, the fair value of the share consideration is based on the average share price over a reasonable period of time before and after the proposed acquisition is agreed to and announced. This has resulted in a difference in the fair value of the consideration for certain acquisitions and consequently in the amount of goodwill capitalised under IFRS and US GAAP.

The Group's accounting policy for testing goodwill and finite lived intangible assets for impairment under IFRS is discussed in note 2. For the purpose of goodwill impairment testing under US GAAP, the fair value of a reporting unit including goodwill is compared to its carrying value. If the fair value of a reporting unit is lower than its carrying value, the fair value of the goodwill within that reporting unit is compared to its respective carrying value, with any excess carrying value written off as an impairment loss. The fair value of the goodwill is the difference between the fair value of the reporting unit and the fair value of the identifiable net assets of the reporting unit. Intangible assets with finite lives are subject to periodic impairment tests when circumstances indicate that an impairment loss may exist. Where an asset's (or asset group's) carrying amount exceeds its sum of undiscounted future cash flows, an impairment loss is recognised in an amount equal to the amount by which the asset's (or asset group's) carrying amount exceeds its fair value, which is generally based on discounted cash flows.

As a result of the above, there are significant amounts reported as goodwill and not amortised under IFRS which are reported as licences, customers and deferred tax liabilities under US GAAP.

During the year ended 31 March 2005, the Group undertook a number of transactions, including a stake increase in Vodafone Hungary. Under US GAAP, these transactions have resulted in the Group assigning £65 million to intangible assets, of which £21 million was assigned to cellular licences and £20 million to customer bases. A corresponding deferred tax liability of £8 million was recognised. All intangible assets acquired, other than goodwill, are deemed to be of finite life, with a weighted average amortisation period of 8 years, comprising licences of 10 years and customer bases of 5 years.

Finite-lived intangible assets

	2006 £m	2005 £m
Licences		
Gross carrying value	154,135	152,831
Accumulated amortisation	(75,170)	61,188)
	78,965	91,643
Customer bases		
Gross carrying value	1,663	5,952
Accumulated amortisation	(1,071)	(5,333)
	592	619

The total amortisation charge for the year ended 31 March 2006, under US GAAP, was £15,011 million (2005: £15,400 million). The estimated future amortisation charge on finite-lived intangible assets for each of the next five years is set out in the following table. The estimate is based on finite-lived intangible assets recognised at 31 March 2006 using foreign exchange rates on that date. It is likely that future amortisation charges will vary from the figures below, as the estimate does not include the impact of any future investments, disposals, capital expenditures or fluctuations in foreign exchange rates.

Year ending 31 March	£m
2007	15,448
2008	15,362
2009	15,264
2010	12,367
2011	3,754

e. Impairment losses

As discussed in note 10, during the year ended 31 March 2006, the Group recorded impairment losses of £23,000 million in relation to the goodwill of Vodafone Germany and Vodafone Italy under IFRS. Under US GAAP, the Group evaluated the recoverability of the long-lived assets, comprised primarily of licences, in Vodafone Germany and Vodafone Italy using undiscounted cash flows and determined that the carrying amount of these assets was recoverable. As a result, the IFRS impairment losses of £23,000 million related to Vodafone Germany and Vodafone Italy were not recognised under US GAAP.

During the year ended 31 March 2006, the Group also recorded an impairment loss under IFRS of £515 million and £4,900 million in relation to the goodwill of Vodafone Sweden and Vodafone Japan, respectively. Under US GAAP, the Group recognised impairment losses of licences of £883 million and £8,556 million in Vodafone Sweden and in Vodafone Japan. As a result of these impairment losses, the Group released related deferred tax liabilities of £247 million and £3,508 million, which have been included in the adjustment for income taxes. The impairment losses on Vodafone Sweden's and Vodafone Japan's licences have been included in discontinued operations under US GAAP.

Cumulative foreign currency gains and losses arising on the translation of the assets and liabilities into sterling have been included in the carrying value of a discontinued operation when assessing that carrying value for impairment.

f. Capitalised interest

Under IFRS, the Group has adopted the benchmark accounting treatment for borrowing costs and, as a result, the Group does not capitalise interest costs on borrowings in respect of the acquisition or construction of tangible and intangible fixed assets. Under US GAAP, the interest costs of financing the acquisition or construction of network assets and other fixed assets is capitalised during the period of construction until the date that the asset is placed in service. Interest costs of financing the acquisition of licences are also capitalised until the date that the related network service is launched. Capitalised interest costs are amortised over the estimated useful lives of the related assets.

g. Other

Financial instruments

Under IFRS, the equity put rights and similar arrangements are classified as financial liabilities. The liabilities are measured as the present value of the estimated exercise prices of the equity put rights and similar arrangements, which is the fair value of the underlying shares on the date of exercise, with any changes in this estimate recognised in the consolidated income statement each period. Under US GAAP, these equity put rights and similar arrangements are generally classified as derivative instruments. Consequently, this financial liability is eliminated for US GAAP purposes and the equity put rights and similar arrangements are accounted for at fair value.

Pensions

Under both IFRS and US GAAP, the Group recognises actuarial gains and losses as they are incurred. Under IFRS, these gains and losses are recognised directly in equity. These gains and losses are included in the determination of net loss under US GAAP.

Other recognised income and expense

Under both IFRS and US GAAP, the cumulative foreign currency gains and losses arising on the translation of the assets and liabilities of entities with a functional currency other than sterling are reclassified from accumulated other recognised income and expense and included in the determination of profit for the period or net loss on sale or liquidation of a foreign entity. Differences in the amount reclassified arise due to differences in the carrying values of the underlying net assets and because the Group deemed the cumulative translation differences at the date of transition to IFRS to be zero.

During the year ended 31 March 2006, £9 million of foreign currency losses were reclassified from other recognised income and expense and included in the determination of US GAAP net loss as a result of the disposal of Vodafone Sweden. During the year ended 31 March 2005, £63 million of foreign currency losses were reclassified from other recognised income and expense and included in the determination of US GAAP net loss as a result of the partial disposal of Vodafone Egypt. Under IFRS, these gains amounted to £36 million for the year ended 31 March 2006.

h. Income taxes

The most significant component of the income tax adjustment is due to temporary differences between the book basis and tax basis of intangible assets other than goodwill acquired in business combinations prior to 29 September 2004, resulting in the recognition of deferred tax liabilities under US GAAP. This line item also includes the tax effects of the other pre-tax IFRS to US GAAP adjustments described above.

Under IFRS, the Group does not recognise a deferred tax liability on the outside basis differences in its investment in associates to the extent that the Group controls the timing of the reversal of the difference and it is probable the difference will not reverse in the foreseeable future. Under US GAAP, the Group recognises deferred tax liabilities on these differences.

i. Minority interests

Minority interests are reported as a component of total equity under IFRS and, accordingly, profit for the period does not include an adjustment for profit for the period attributable to minority interests. Under US GAAP, minority interests are reported outside of shareholders' equity and the minority interest in the income of consolidated subsidiaries is an adjustment to US GAAP net income.

Extract 20(A7) – Vodafone Group Plc, pages 126 to 130

This extract is the main section covering IFRS 1 requirements, including the following:

- IFRS 1 optional exemptions (business combination, actuarial gains and losses and cumulative translation differences). Some exemptions would not be pertinent in a Canadian context. Note that the company specifies it has not elected to measure any item of property, plant and equipment or intangible asset at the date of transition to IFRS at its fair value.

- Impact of transition to IFRS, including reconciliations, with a description of measurement and recognition differences, presentation differences and other differences with previous GAAP.

40. Transition to IFRS on first-time adoption

Basis of preparation of IFRS financial information

The Group's Annual Report for the year ended 31 March 2006 is the first annual Consolidated Financial Statements that comply with IFRS. The Consolidated Financial Statements have been prepared in accordance with the significant accounting policies described in note 2. The Group has applied IFRS 1, "First-time Adoption of International Financial Reporting Standards" in preparing these statements.

IFRS 1 exemptions

IFRS 1 sets out the procedures that the Group must follow when it adopts IFRS for the first time as the basis for preparing its Consolidated Financial Statements. The Group is required to establish its IFRS accounting policies as at 31 March 2006 and, in general, apply these retrospectively to determine the IFRS opening balance sheet at its date of transition, 1 April 2004. This standard provides a number of optional exemptions to this general principle. These are set out below, together with a description in each case of the exemption adopted by the Group.

Business combinations that occurred before the opening IFRS balance sheet date (IFRS 3, "Business Combinations")

The Group has elected not to apply IFRS 3 retrospectively to business combinations that took place before the date of transition. As a result, in the opening balance sheet, goodwill arising from past business combinations remains as stated under UK GAAP at 31 March 2004.

If the Group had elected to apply IFRS 3 retrospectively, the purchase consideration would have been allocated to the following major categories of acquired intangible assets and liabilities based on their fair values: licence and spectrum fees, brands, customer bases, and deferred tax liabilities. Goodwill would have been recognised as the excess of the purchase consideration over the fair values of acquired assets and liabilities – retrospective application may have resulted in an increase or decrease to goodwill. The fair values of the acquired intangible assets would have been amortised over their respective useful lives.

Employee benefits – actuarial gains and losses (IAS 19, "Employee Benefits")

The Group has elected to recognise all cumulative actuarial gains and losses in relation to employee benefit schemes at the date of transition.

Share-based payments (IFRS 2, "Share-based Payment")

The Group has elected to apply IFRS 2 to all relevant share-based payment transactions granted but not fully vested at 1 April 2004.

Financial instruments (IAS 39, "Financial Instruments: Recognition and Measurement" and IFRS 7, "Financial Instruments: Disclosures")

The Group has applied IAS 32 and IAS 39 for all periods presented and has therefore not taken advantage of the exemption in IFRS 1 that would enable the Group to only apply these standards from 1 April 2005.

Cumulative translation differences (IAS 21, "The Effects of Changes in Foreign Exchange Rates")

The Group has deemed the cumulative translation differences at the date of transition to IFRS to be zero. As a result, the gain or loss of a subsequent disposal of any foreign operation will exclude the translation differences that arose before the date of transition to IFRS.

If the Group had not applied the exemption, the gain or loss on any disposals after the transition date would include additional cumulative transaction differences relating to the businesses disposed of.

Fair value or revaluation as deemed cost (IAS 16, "Property, Plant and Equipment" and IAS 38, "Intangible Assets")

The Group has not elected to measure any item of property, plant and equipment or intangible asset at the date of transition to IFRS at its fair value.

Impact of transition to IFRS

The following is a summary of the effects of the differences between IFRS and UK GAAP on the Group's total equity shareholders' funds and profit for the financial year for the years previously reported under UK GAAP following the date of transition to IFRS.

Total equity shareholders' funds	Note	1 April 2004 £m	31 March 2005 £m
Total equity shareholders' funds (UK GAAP)		111,924	99,317
Measurement and recognition differences:			
Intangible assets	a	(164)	13,986
Proposed dividends	b	728	1,395
Financial instruments	c	385	350
Share-based payments	d	12	63
Defined benefit pension schemes	e	(257)	(361)
Deferred and current taxes	f	(1,011)	(774)
Other		(66)	(176)
Total equity shareholders' funds (IFRS)		111,551	113,800

Profit for the year ended 31 March 2005	Note	£m
Loss on ordinary activities after taxation (UK GAAP)		(6,938)
Measurement and recognition differences:		
Intangible assets	a	14,263
Financial instruments	c	(174)
Share-based payments	d	(91)
Defined benefit pension schemes	e	7
Deferred and current taxes	f	10
Other		(130)
Presentation differences:		
Presentation of equity accounted investments	g	(45)
Presentation of joint ventures	h	(384)
Profit for the financial year (IFRS)		6,518

There were no significant differences between IFRS and UK GAAP on the Group's cash flow statement for the year ended 31 March 2005.

Principal differences between IFRS and UK GAAP
Measurement and recognition differences

a. Intangible assets

IAS 38, "Intangible Assets" requires that goodwill is not amortised. Instead it is subject to an annual impairment review. As the Group has elected not to apply IFRS 3 retrospectively to business combinations prior to the opening balance sheet date under IFRS, the UK GAAP goodwill balance, after adjusting for items including the impact of proportionate consolidation of joint ventures, at 31 March 2004 (£78,753 million) has been included in the opening IFRS consolidated balance sheet and is no longer amortised. Under IAS 38, capitalised payments for licences and spectrum fees are amortised on a straight line basis over their useful economic life. Amortisation is charged from the commencement of service of the network. Under UK GAAP, the Group's policy was to amortise such costs in proportion to the capacity of the network during the start up period and then on a straight-line basis thereafter.

b. Proposed dividends

IAS 10, "Events after the Balance Sheet Date" requires that dividends declared after the balance sheet date should not be recognised as a liability at that balance sheet date as the liability does not represent a present obligation as defined by IAS 37, "Provisions, Contingent Liabilities and Contingent Assets".

c. Financial instruments

IAS 32, "Financial Instruments: Disclosure and Presentation" and IAS 39, "Financial Instruments: Recognition and Measurement" address the accounting for, and reporting of, financial instruments. IAS 39 sets out detailed accounting requirements in relation to financial assets and liabilities.

All derivative financial instruments are accounted for at fair market value whilst other financial instruments are accounted for either at amortised cost or at fair value depending on their classification. Subject to certain criteria, financial assets and financial liabilities may be designated as forming hedge relationships as a result of which fair value changes are offset in the income statement or charged/credited to equity depending on the nature of the hedge relationship.

d. Share-based payments

IFRS 2, "Share-based Payment" requires that an expense for equity instruments granted be recognised in the financial statements based on their fair value at the date of grant. This expense, which is primarily in relation to employee option and performance share schemes, is recognised over the vesting period of the scheme.

While IFRS 2 allows the measurement of this expense to be calculated only on options granted after 7 November 2002, the Group has applied IFRS 2 to all instruments granted but not fully vested as at 1 April 2004. The Group has adopted the binomial model for the purposes of calculating fair value under IFRS, calibrated using a Black-Scholes framework.

e. Defined benefit pension schemes

The Group elected to adopt early the amendment to IAS 19, "Employee Benefits" issued by the IASB on 16 December 2004 which allows all actuarial gains and losses to be charged or credited to equity.

The Group's opening IFRS balance sheet at 1 April 2004 reflects the assets and liabilities of the Group's defined benefit schemes totalling a net liability of £154 million. The transitional adjustment of £257 million to opening reserves comprises the reversal of entries in relation to UK GAAP accounting under SSAP 24 less the recognition of the net liabilities of the Group's and associated undertakings' defined benefit schemes.

f. Deferred and current taxes

The scope of IAS 12, "Income Taxes" is wider than the corresponding UK GAAP standards, and requires deferred tax to be provided on all temporary differences rather than just timing differences under UK GAAP.

As a result, taxes in the Group's IFRS opening balance sheet at 1 April 2004 were adjusted by £1.0 billion. This includes an additional deferred tax liability of £1.8 billion in respect of the differences between the carrying value and tax written down value of the Group's investments in associated undertakings and joint ventures. This comprises £1.3 billion in respect of differences that arose when US investments were acquired and £0.5 billion in respect of undistributed earnings of certain associated undertakings and joint ventures, principally Vodafone Italy. UK GAAP does not permit deferred tax to be provided on the undistributed earnings of the Group's associated undertakings and joint ventures until there is a binding obligation to distribute those earnings.

IAS 12 also requires deferred tax to be provided in respect of the Group's liabilities under its post employment benefit arrangements and on other employee benefits such as share and share option schemes.

Presentation differences

g. Presentation of equity accounted investments

Under IFRS, in accordance with IAS 1, "Presentation of Financial Statements", "Tax on profit" on the face of the consolidated income statement comprises the tax charge of the Company, its subsidiaries and its share of the tax charge of joint ventures. The Group's share of its associated undertakings' tax charges is shown as part of "Share of result in associated undertakings" rather than being disclosed as part of the tax charge under UK GAAP.

In respect of the Verizon Wireless partnership, the line "Share of result in associated undertakings" includes the Group's share of pre-tax partnership income and the Group's share of the post-tax income attributable to corporate entities (as determined for US corporate income tax purposes) held by the partnership. The tax attributable to the Group's share of allocable partnership income is included as part of "Tax on profit" in the consolidated income statement. This treatment reflects the fact that tax on allocable partnership income is, for US corporate income tax purposes, a liability of the partners and not the partnership. Under UK GAAP, the Group's share of minority interests in associated undertakings was reported in minority interests, under IFRS this is reported within investments in associated undertakings.

h. Presentation of joint ventures

IAS 31, "Interests in Joint Ventures" defines a jointly controlled entity as an entity where unanimous consent over the strategic financial and operating decisions is required between the parties sharing control. Control is defined as the power to govern the financial and operating decisions of an entity so as to obtain economic benefit from it.

The Group has reviewed the classification of its investments and concluded that the Group's 76.9% (31 March 2005: 76.8%) interest in Vodafone Italy, classified as a subsidiary undertaking under UK GAAP, should be accounted for as a joint venture under IFRS. In addition, the Group's interests in South Africa, Poland, Kenya and Fiji, which were classified as associated undertakings under UK GAAP, have been classified as joint ventures under IFRS as a result of the contractual rights held by the Group. The Group's interest in Romania was classified as a joint venture until the acquisition of the controlling stake from Telesystem International Wireless Inc. of Canada completed on 31 May 2005. The Group has adopted proportionate consolidation as the method of accounting for these six entities.

Under UK GAAP, the revenue, operating profit, net financing costs and taxation of Vodafone Italy were consolidated in full in the income statement with a corresponding allocation to minority interest. Under proportionate consolidation, the Group recognises its share of all income statement lines with no allocation to minority interest. There is no effect on the result for a financial period from this adjustment.

Under UK GAAP, the Group's interests in South Africa, Poland, Romania, Kenya and Fiji were accounted for under the equity method, with the Group's share of operating profit, interest and tax being recognised separately in the consolidated income statement. Under proportionate consolidation, the Group recognises its share of all income statement lines. There is no effect on the result for a financial period from this adjustment.

Under UK GAAP, the Group fully consolidated the cash flows of Vodafone Italy, but did not consolidate the cash flows of its associated undertakings. The IFRS consolidated cash flow statement reflects the Group's share of cash flows relating to its joint ventures on a line by line basis, with a corresponding recognition of the Group's share of net debt for each of the proportionately consolidated entities.

Other differences

i. Reclassification of non-equity minority interests to liabilities

The primary impact of the implementation of IAS 32 is the reclassification of the $1.65 billion preferred shares issued by the Group's subsidiary, Vodafone Americas Inc., from non-equity minority interests to liabilities. The reclassification at 1 April 2004 was £875 million. Dividend payments by this subsidiary, which were previously reported in the Group's income statement as non-equity minority interests, have been reclassified to financing costs.

j. Fair value of available-for-sale financial assets

The Group has classified certain of its cost-based investments as available-for-sale financial assets as defined in IAS 39. This classification does not reflect the intentions of management in relation to these investments. These assets are measured at fair value at each reporting date with movements in fair value taken to equity. At 1 April 2004, a cumulative increase of £233 million in the fair value over the carrying value of these investments was recognised.

Year ended 31 March 2005

UK GAAP format	UK GAAP £m	Presentation differences £m	Measurement and recognition differences £m	Discontinued operations £m	IFRS £m	IFRS format
Turnover	34,133	–	(60)	(7,395)	26,678	Revenue
Cost of sales	(20,753)	–	(711)	5,664	(15,800)	Cost of sales
Gross profit	13,380	–	(771)	(1,731)	10,878	Gross profit
Selling and distribution costs	(2,031)		(15)	397	(1,649)	Selling and distribution expenses
Administrative expenses	(16,653)	315	12,812	670	(2,856)	Administrative expenses
		404	1,576	–	1,980	Share of result in associated undertakings
		(315)	(160)	–	(475)	Other income and expense
Operating loss	(5,304)	404	13,442	(664)	7,878	Operating profit
Share of result in associated undertakings	1,193	(1,193)				
Exceptional non-operating items	13	(13)				
		8	(2)	(13)	(7)	Non-operating income and expense
		324	(21)	(9)	294	Investment income
Net interest payable and similar items	(604)	(113)	(183)	20	(880)	Financing costs
Loss on ordinary activities before taxation	(4,702)	(583)	13,236	(666)	7,285	Profit before taxation
Tax on loss on ordinary activities	(2,236)	538	265	(436)	(1,869)	Tax on profit
Loss on ordinary activities after taxation	(6,938)	(45)	13,501	(1,102)	5,416	Profit on ordinary activities after taxation from continuing operations
	–	–	–	1,102	1,102	Profit on ordinary activites after taxation from discontinued operations
	(6,938)	(45)	13,501	–	6,518	Profit for the financial year
Minority interest	(602)	45	449	–	(108)	Profit for the financial year attributable to minority interests
Loss for the financial year	(7,540)	–	13,950	–	6,410	Profit for the financial year attributable to equity shareholders

Reconciliation of the UK GAAP consolidated balance sheet to the IFRS consolidated balance sheet
1 April 2004

UK GAAP format	UK GAAP £m	Presentation differences £m	Measurement and recognition differences £m	IFRS £m	IFRS format
Fixed assets:					Non-current assets:
Intangible assets	93,622	–	1,002	94,624	Intangible assets
Tangible assets	18,083	–	(971)	17,112	Property, plant and equipment
Investments in associated undertakings	21,226	–	(800)	20,426	Investments in associated undertakings
Other investments	1,049	–	233	1,282	Other investments
		671	136	807	Deferred tax assets
		221	(9)	212	Trade and other receivables
	133,980	892	(409)	134,463	
Current assets:					Current assets:
Stocks	458	–	10	468	Inventory
Debtors	6,901	(6,901)			
		372	(103)	269	Taxation recoverable
		5,148	305	5,453	Trade and other receivables
Investments	4,381	(4,381)			
Cash at bank and in hand	1,409	4,381	61	5,851	Cash and cash equivalents
	13,149	(1,381)	273	12,041	
Total assets	147,129	(489)	(136)	146,504	Total assets
Capital and reserves:					Equity:
Called up share capital	4,280	–	–	4,280	Called up share capital
Share premium account	52,154	–	–	52,154	Share premium account
Own shares held	(1,136)	–	–	(1,136)	Own shares held
Other reserve	99,640	–	310	99,950	Additional paid-in capital
		–	233	233	Other reserves
Profit and loss account	(43,014)	–	(916)	(43,930)	Retained losses
Total equity shareholders' funds	111,924	–	(373)	111,551	Total equity shareholders' funds
Minority interests	3,007	–	(2,198)	809	Minority interests
	114,931	–	(2,571)	112,360	
Creditors – amounts falling due after more than one year	12,975	(12,975)			Non-current liabilities:
		12,224	1,859	14,083	Long-term borrowings
		3,314	1,421	4,735	Deferred tax liabilities
		(73)	227	154	Post employment benefits
Provisions for liabilities and charges	4,197	(3,858)	5	344	Provisions for liabilities and charges
		751	(449)	302	Trade and other payables
	17,172	(617)	3,063	19,618	
Creditors – amounts falling due within one year	15,026	(15,026)			Current liabilities:
		2,054	788	2,842	Short-term borrowings
		4,275	(356)	3,919	Current taxation liabilities
		8,643	(1,068)	7,575	Trade and other payables
		182	8	190	Provisions for liabilities and charges
	15,026	128	(628)	14,526	
	147,129	(489)	(136)	146,504	Total equity and liabilities

31 March 2005

UK GAAP format	UK GAAP £m	Presentation differences £m	Measurement and recognition differences £m	IFRS £m	IFRS format
					Non-current assets:
Fixed assets:		68,673	12,326	80,999	Goodwill
Intangible assets	83,464	(68,673)	1,358	16,149	Other intangible assets
Tangible assets	18,398	–	(956)	17,442	Property, plant and equipment
Investments in associated undertakings	19,398	–	836	20,234	Investments in associated undertakings
Other investments	852	–	329	1,181	Other investments
		1,084	100	1,184	Deferred tax assets
		12	–	12	Post employment benefits
		613	(28)	585	Trade and other receivables
	122,112	1,709	13,965	137,786	
Current assets:					Current assets:
Stocks	430	–	10	440	Inventory
Debtors	7,698	(7,698)			
		268	(230)	38	Taxation recoverable
		5,049	115	5,164	Trade and other receivables
Investments	816	(816)			
Cash at bank and in hand	2,850	816	103	3,769	Cash and cash equivalents
	11,794	(2,381)	(2)	9,411	
Total assets	133,906	(672)	13,963	147,197	Total assets
Capital and reserves:					Equity:
Called up share capital	4,286	–	–	4,286	Called up share capital
Share premium account	52,284	–	–	52,284	Share premium account
Own shares held	(5,121)	–	–	(5,121)	Own shares held
Other reserve	99,556	–	525	100,081	Additional paid-in capital
		–	1,781	1,781	Accumulated other recognised income and expense
Profit and loss account	(51,688)	–	12,177	(39,511)	Retained losses
Total equity shareholders' funds	99,317	–	14,483	113,800	Total equity shareholders' funds
Minority interests	2,818	–	(2,970)	(152)	Minority Interests
	102,135	–	11,513	113,648	
Creditors – amounts falling due after more than one year	12,382	(12,382)			Non-current liabilities:
		11,613	1,577	13,190	Long-term borrowings
		3,481	1,368	4,849	Deferred tax liabilities
		(171)	307	136	Post employment benefits
Provisions for liabilities and charges	4,552	(4,235)	2	319	Provisions for other liabilities and charges
		797	(359)	438	Trade and other payables
	16,934	(897)	2,895	18,932	
Creditors – amounts falling due within one year	14,837	(14,837)			Current liabilities:
		392	1,611	2,003	Short-term borrowings
		4,759	(406)	4,353	Current taxation liabilities
		9,717	(1,684)	8,033	Trade and other payables
		194	34	228	Provisions for other liabilities and charges
	14,837	225	(445)	14,617	
	133,906	(672)	13,963	147,197	Total equity and liabilities

Thomson Reuters Corporation – Extracts 20(B) were obtained from the MD&A of a Canadian company that plans to adopt IFRS early, in 2010. The extracts were obtained from the MD&A included in the 2007 annual report for year ended December 31, 2007 and following three successive interim reports in 2008:

- Q1 – 2008 (March 31);
- Q2 – 2008 (June 30); and
- Q3 – 2008 (September 30).

Extract 20(B1) – The Thomson Corporation[2] – Annual Report 2007, page 60

This extract is a relatively brief statement that reflects the company's intention to adopt IFRS as soon as permissible under Ontario Securities Commission regulations.

RECENTLY ISSUED ACCOUNTING STANDARDS

In 2006, the CICA announced that it will no longer converge Canadian GAAP with generally accepted accounting principles of the United States (U.S. GAAP). Rather, the CICA will work towards convergence with International Financial Reporting Standards (IFRS) with the expectation that Canadian GAAP will be replaced by IFRS in 2011. As a public company, we are allowed to file our financial statements with the Canadian securities regulatory authorities under either Canadian GAAP or U.S. GAAP. We are also required to file an annual reconciliation of our earnings and shareholders' equity between Canadian GAAP and U.S. GAAP with the U.S. Securities and Exchange Commission (SEC). This reconciliation is presented in note 24 of our financial statements.

We plan to adopt IFRS as soon as permissible under Ontario Securities Commission regulations.

Extract 20(B2) – Thomson Reuters Corporation – First Quarter Report 2008, pages 2 and 24

In this extract, the company presents general information concerning the adoption of IFRS.

OVERVIEW (in part)

Our Business and Strategy (in part)

The primary financial statements for Thomson Reuters shareholders beginning with the six months and quarter ending June 30, 2008 will be the consolidated financial statements of Thomson Reuters Corporation. Those statements, which will account for Thomson Reuters PLC as a subsidiary, will be prepared in accordance with Canadian GAAP and will include a voluntary reconciliation to International Financial Reporting Standards (IFRS) and a reconciliation to US GAAP until no longer required by the Securities and Exchange Commission (SEC). Management intends to present Thomson Reuters Corporation's financial statements in accordance with IFRS as soon as permitted by regulatory authorities in Canada.

RECENTLY ISSUED ACCOUNTING STANDARDS

In 2006, the CICA announced that it will no longer converge Canadian GAAP with generally accepted accounting principles of the United States (U.S. GAAP). Rather, the CICA will work towards convergence with International Financial Reporting Standards (IFRS) such that Canadian GAAP will be replaced by IFRS in 2011. We plan to adopt IFRS as soon as possible under Ontario Securities Commission regulations.

Extract 20(B3) – Thomson Reuters Corporation – Second Quarter Report 2008, pages 3 and 27-31

In this extract, the company presents details on its proposed adoption of IFRS and the estimated impact. Note the following:

- The company presents a statement specifying that the reconciliation presented is not final (i.e., it does not represent an official adoption of IFRS).
- The company:

---

2 The Thomson Corporation acquired in April 2008 Reuters Group PLC, forming Thomson Reuters Corporation. Consequently, the 2007 annual report relates to The Thomson Corporation but, starting the first quarter of 2008, the name of the entity is Thomson Reuters Corporation (i.e., the merged company).

    o   has not quantified the impact of IFRS 1 implementation,

    o   has not definitively concluded if it will elect different policies in selected circumstances under IFRS, and

    o   does not expect the adoption of IFRS to have an impact on the overall revenue and underlying profitability trends of its operating performance.

The company provides:

- a voluntary reconciliation from Canadian GAAP to IFRS (which does not constitute an adoption of IFRS) and describes differences between the two standards;

- its procedures for the initial adoption of IFRS; and

- the anticipated impact of the adoption of IFRS on the financial statements.

OVERVIEW (in part)

Our Business and Strategy (in part)

Consolidated financial statements and accounting standards — Our primary financial statements beginning with the three and six months ended June 30, 2008 are the consolidated financial statements of Thomson Reuters Corporation. Those statements account for Thomson Reuters PLC as a subsidiary and have been prepared in accordance with Canadian GAAP. We are seeking exemptive relief to present Thomson Reuters Corporation's financial statements in accordance with International Financial Reporting Standards (IFRS) in 2009. We have provided a voluntary reconciliation to IFRS in this management's discussion and analysis. See the section entitled "Recently Issued Accounting Standards" for more information.

RECENTLY ISSUED ACCOUNTING STANDARDS

Transition to IFRS from Canadian GAAP

In 2008, the Canadian Accounting Standards Board confirmed that Canadian publicly accountable enterprises will be required to adopt International Financial Reporting Standards (IFRS) by 2011 in replacement of Canadian GAAP. We applied for exemptive relief from the Canadian securities regulatory authorities to adopt IFRS early and our application is currently under review. If permitted by the regulatory authorities, we intend to adopt IFRS in 2009. Comparative periods for 2008 would be restated. The following discussion provides further information about our proposed adoption.

Estimated Impact of IFRS on 2008 Financial Results

IFRS employs a conceptual framework that is similar to Canadian GAAP. In accordance with our agreement with the United Kingdom Listing Authority, we have provided a reconciliation of shareholders equity and net earnings from Canadian GAAP to IFRS as of and for the three and six-month periods ended June 30, 2008 and 2007, respectively in the section entitled "Voluntary reconciliation from Canadian GAAP to IFRS". While this reconciliation does not represent an official adoption of IFRS, it provides an indication of the major differences identified to date, relative to our historical financial statements. With respect to our intended official adoption of IFRS in 2009, we have not quantified the impact that IFRS 1 "First Time Adoption of International Reporting Standards" (IFRS 1) will have on our financial statements, nor have we definitively concluded if we will elect different policies in selected circumstances under IFRS. However, we do not expect the adoption of IFRS to impact the overall revenue and underlying profitability trends of our operating performance.

Voluntary Reconciliation from Canadian GAAP to IFRS

Thomson Reuters consolidated financial statements are prepared in accordance with Canadian GAAP. The following reconciliation presents the material differences between Canadian GAAP and IFRS, relative to our financial statements. However, this reconciliation does not constitute an adoption of IFRS by Thomson Reuters. In preparing the reconciliation, Thomson Reuters applied the principles and elections of IFRS 1, with a transition date of January 1, 2004, consistent with those assumed in its Business Acquisition Report dated May 15, 2008. If we are permitted to adopt IFRS, effective January 1, 2009, we will apply the provisions of IFRS 1 as described under the section entitled "Initial Adoption — IFRS 1", with a January 1, 2008 transition date. We will also apply IFRS standards in effect at December 31, 2009 as required by IFRS 1 and may elect accounting policies which differ from those applied in this reconciliation.

(in millions of US dollars, except per share amounts)	Three Months ended June 30,		Six Months ended June 30,	
	2008	2007	**2008**	2007
Net earnings under Canadian GAAP	**173**	377	**367**	601
Differences in GAAP increasing (decreasing) reported earnings:				
1. Business combinations	**(61)**	—	**(61)**	(1)
2. Employee benefits	**6**	16	**11**	32
3. Stock-based compensation	**(3)**	—	**(16)**	2
4. Impairments of long-term assets	**(17)**	6	**(17)**	(61)
5. Derivative instruments and hedging activities	**—**	(7)	**(2)**	(8)
6. Income taxes	**21**	1	**16**	12
Net earnings under IFRS	**119**	393	**298**	577
Basic earnings per share	**0.15**	0.61	**0.41**	0.90
Diluted earnings per share	**0.15**	0.61	**0.41**	0.89

(in millions of US dollars, except per share amounts)	As at June 30,	
	2008	2007
Shareholders' equity under Canadian GAAP	**21,666**	10,769
Differences increasing (decreasing) reported shareholders' equity:		
1. Business combinations	**(1,083)**	(41)
2. Employee benefits	**(698)**	(458)
3. Stock-based compensation	**(39)**	(15)
4. Impairment of long-term assets	**(17)**	(92)
5. Derivative instruments and hedging activities	**(4)**	(7)
5. Share repurchases	**(21)**	—
6. Income taxes	**228**	188
Shareholders' equity under IFRS	**20,032**	10,344

The following describes the differences presented in the reconciliation of net earnings and shareholders' equity.

1. Business Combinations

Acquisition Cost

Canadian GAAP—Shares issued as consideration are measured at their market price a few days before and after the date the parties reach an agreement on the purchase price and proposed transaction is announced.

IFRS—Shares issued as consideration are measured at their market price on the acquisition closing date.

Contingent Consideration

Canadian GAAP—Contingent consideration is recognized as part of the cost of an acquisition, but only at the point when the amount can be reasonably estimated and the outcome is determined beyond reasonable doubt.

IFRS—Contingent consideration is recognized as part of the cost of an acquisition, at the date of acquisition, if it is probable that the contingency will be met and the amount can be reliably measured at fair value. Changes to the initial amount recognized are recognized through income and discounts on future cash payments are accreted through interest expense.

Acquisition Related Costs

Canadian GAAP—Costs of the acquirer such as (1) exiting an activity, (2) involuntarily terminating an employee, or (3) relocating employees of an acquired company are recognized as part of the cost of an acquisition.

IFRS—These costs are expensed, unless they are part of an existing restructuring by the acquiree, in which case they may be recognized as part of the cost of an acquisition.

2. Employee Benefits

Measurement Date

Canadian GAAP—The measurement date of defined benefit obligations and plan assets may be up to three months prior to the date of the financial statements.

IFRS—The measurement date generally coincides with the date of the financial statements, because the measurement date must not result in a materially different outcome than if the balance sheet date had been used.

Past Service Cost

Canadian GAAP—Past service costs arising from plan amendments are amortized on a straight-line basis over the average remaining service period of active employees expected to benefit from the amendment.

IFRS—These costs are amortized on a straight-line basis over the average period until the benefits become vested. To the extent that the amended benefits are already vested, past service costs are recognized immediately.

Actuarial Gains and Losses

Canadian GAAP—Actuarial gains and losses are recognized on a systematic and consistent basis, subject to a minimum required amortization based on a "corridor" approach. Unrecognized actuarial gains and losses below the corridor are deferred.

IFRS—In accordance with our IFRS 1 election, actuarial gains and losses are recognized immediately into equity.

Fair value of Plan Assets

Canadian GAAP—The expected return on plan assets is calculated using a market-related fair value, which recognizes changes in the fair value of plan assets over a five-year period.

IFRS—The expected return on plan assets is based on market expectations, at the beginning of the period, for returns over the entire life of the related obligation and reflects changes due to actual contributions made and actual benefits paid during the period.

3. Stock-based Compensation

Recognition of expense

Canadian GAAP—The fair value of a stock-based award with graded vesting is recognized on a straight-line basis over the vesting period.

IFRS—Each tranche of an award is considered a separate grant with a different vesting date and fair value, and each is accounted for separately.

Forfeitures

Canadian GAAP—Forfeitures of awards may be recognized as they occur.

IFRS—Forfeiture estimates are recognized in the current period and revised for actual experience in subsequent periods.

Cash-settled share-based payments

Canadian GAAP—The liability for cash-settled share-based payments is accrued based upon the intrinsic value of the award.

IFRS—The liability for cash-settled share-based awards is measured at fair value, using an option pricing model. Changes in fair value are recognized over the remaining vesting period until the liability is settled. Changes in fair value of vested awards are recognized in income immediately.

Recognition of deferred tax assets

Canadian GAAP—Deferred tax asset for share-based awards are based upon the cumulative amount of compensation cost recognized.

IFRS—Deferred tax assets for share-based awards are based upon the estimated tax deduction, which is generally the intrinsic value of the vested award at the balance sheet date. If the estimated deduction exceeds the cumulative compensation expense, the excess is recognized in equity. If no tax deduction is anticipated because the fair value of the shares has declined, then the deferred tax asset is reversed to income or equity as appropriate, depending on how the asset was originally recorded.

Employer Taxes

Canadian GAAP—Employer taxes on share-based compensation are recognized upon exercise of the instrument.

IFRS—Employer taxes on share-based compensation are recognized over the vesting period based upon the fair value of the awards at each balance sheet date.

4. Impairments of Long-Term Assets

Canadian GAAP—Assets held for sale are measured at the lower of their carrying amount or fair value less costs to sell, where the carrying amount for purposes of determining impairment includes cumulative translation adjustments.

IFRS—Assets held for sale are measured at the lower of their carrying amount or fair value less costs to sell, where the carrying amount excludes cumulative translation adjustments.

5. Financial Instruments

Hedge accounting

Canadian GAAP—Effectiveness for compound derivative instruments that hedge currency and interest rate risk is assumed provided the critical terms of the derivative instrument are consistent with the hedged instrument.

IFRS—Effectiveness for compound derivative instruments must be assessed retrospectively and prospectively each reporting period As a result, certain hedge relationships had to be prospectively discontinued as of the date of adoption of IAS 32 and IAS 39.

Share repurchases

Canadian GAAP—An obligation for an entity to purchase its own equity instruments is accounted for as an equity-transaction upon completion of each purchase.

IFRS—A liability must be recognized currently through equity for an obligation when the entity has no discretion to cancel its instructions to repurchase shares. Subsequent adjustments to the present value of the liability are reflected within earnings. If the contract expires without delivery, the liability is reversed against equity.

6. Income Taxes

Intercompany transactions

Canadian GAAP—Prohibits the recognition of deferred tax for a temporary difference arising from intercompany transactions. Further, taxes paid or recovered as a result of an intercompany asset transfer are recorded as an asset or liability and recognized as tax expense when the asset leaves the group or is otherwise utilized.

IFRS—Deferred taxes are recognized for temporary differences arising from intercompany transactions. Taxes paid or recovered as a result of an intercompany asset transfer are recognized in the period incurred.

Business Combinations: Deferred tax assets not previously recognized

Canadian GAAP—Previously unrecognized income tax assets of an acquired company are recognized as part of the cost of the acquisition when such assets are more likely than not to be realized as a result of a business combination. If an unrecognized deferred tax asset becomes realizable subsequent to the acquisition date, such benefit will also be recognized through goodwill. The acquirer recognizes its own tax benefits which become realizable as a result of the acquisition as part of the cost of the acquisition.

IFRS—Previously unrecognized income tax assets of an acquired company are recognized as part of the cost of the acquisition if realization is more likely than not as a result of the business combination. If an unrecognized deferred tax asset becomes realizable subsequent to the acquisition date, the tax benefit is recognized through income, and a corresponding amount of goodwill is written off to operating expense. The acquirer recognizes its own tax benefits which become realizable as a result of the acquisition through income.

Accounting for uncertainty in income taxes in business combinations

Canadian GAAP—Changes to income tax contingencies relating to pre-acquisition periods are adjusted through the purchase price allocation, first reducing goodwill, intangible assets associated with the business combination, and only after exhausting those amounts, reducing income tax expense.

IFRS—Changes to pre-acquisition tax uncertainties beyond twelve months of the acquisition date are recorded to the income statement.

Income tax effect of other reconciling differences between Canadian GAAP and IFRS

Differences from income taxes include the deferred tax effect on earnings of pre-tax differences between Canadian GAAP and IFRS described above. These amounts were $21 million and $1 million for the three-month periods ended June 30, 2008 and 2007, respectively and $16 million and $12 million for the six-month periods ended June 30, 2008 and 2007, respectively.

Initial Adoption of International Accounting Standards

IFRS 1 "First Time Adoption of International Accounting Standards" sets forth guidance for the initial adoption of IFRS. As required, we will restate our comparative 2008 financial statements for annual and interim periods to be consistent with our new IFRS basis. Further, we will reconcile equity and net earnings from the previously reported 2008 Canadian GAAP amounts to the 2008 IFRS amounts.

IFRS 1 generally requires that first-time adopters consistently apply all effective IFRS standards retrospectively from the reporting date. IFRS 1 provides for certain optional exemptions and certain mandatory exceptions to this general principle. While we have not finalized our conclusions with respect to the optional exemptions, we expect to make the following elections:

- **Business combinations**—IFRS 3, Business Combinations, may be applied retrospectively or prospectively. The retrospective basis would require restatement of all business combinations that occurred prior to the transition date. We plan to adopt IFRS 3 on a prospective basis. Further, we do not expect to early adopt IFRS 3 Revised, and will adopt that standard upon its effective date, January 1, 2010.

- **Fair value or revaluation as deemed cost**—IFRS 1 provides a choice between measuring property, plant and equipment at its fair value at the date of transition and using those amounts as deemed cost or using the historical valuation under the prior GAAP. We plan to use our historical bases as deemed cost.

- **Employee benefits**—IAS 19, Employee Benefits allows certain actuarial gains and losses to be either deferred and amortized, subject to certain provisions, or immediately recognized through equity. We expect to elect immediate recognition of actuarial gains and losses as of the transition date and for future periods.

- **Currency translation differences**—IFRS 1 permits cumulative translation gains and losses to be reset to zero at the transition date. Alternatively, IFRS 1 allows translation differences to be recalculated in accordance with IFRS from the date a subsidiary or associate was formed or acquired. We expect to reset cumulative translation gains and losses to zero at the transition date.

- **Share-based payments**—IFRS 2, Share Based Payments, encourages application of its provisions to equity instruments granted on or before November 7, 2002, but permits the application only to equity instruments granted after November 7, 2002 that had not vested by January 1, 2008. We expect to apply IFRS 2 only to equity instruments granted after November 7, 2002 that had not vested by January 1, 2008.

- **Changes in existing decommissioning, restoration and similar liabilities included in the cost of property, plant and equipment**—IFRS 1 allows for either the retroactive adoption or prospective adoption from the transition date of IFRIC 1, Changes in existing decommissioning, restoration and similar liabilities. We plan to prospectively apply this standard.

Further optional exemptions are provided under IFRS 1. However, we do not believe these exemptions will impact our adoption of IFRS.

Hindsight is not permitted to create or revise estimates. The estimates previously made by us under Canadian GAAP will not be revised for application of IFRS except where necessary to reflect any difference in accounting policies.

IFRS Impact on Our Organization

The conversion to IFRS will impact the way we present our financial results. We have obtained an understanding of IFRS from intensive training and preparation of reconciliations of historical Canadian GAAP financial statements to IFRS. Further, our accounting staff includes former Reuters employees who prepared financial statements under IFRS for the past three years.

We are still evaluating the impact of the conversion on our accounting systems. However, based on the differences identified to date, we believe our systems can accommodate the required changes. We believe our internal and disclosure control processes, as currently designed, will not need significant modifications as a result of our conversion to IFRS.

We have assessed the impacts of adopting IFRS on our debt covenants and other contractual arrangements, and have not identified any material compliance issues. We are considering the impacts that the transition will have on our internal planning process and compensation arrangements.

CICA 3064, Goodwill and Intangible Assets

In February 2008, the CICA adopted CICA 3064, Goodwill and Intangible Assets, which replaces CICA 3062 and establishes standards for the recognition, measurement, presentation and disclosure of goodwill and intangible assets. The new standard applies to internally generated intangible assets and rights under licensing agreements and is effective for us in the fourth quarter of 2008. We believe there will not be a significant impact on our financial statements upon adoption.

Extracts 20(B4) – Thomson Reuters Corporation – Third Quarter Report, pages 2 and 28-32

In this extract, the company updates details concerning its proposed adoption of IFRS that were initially disclosed in its previous quarterly report.

OVERVIEW (in part)

Our Business, Strategy and Operating Environment (in part)

Consolidated financial statements and accounting standards—Our financial statements for the three and nine months ended September 30, 2008 are the consolidated financial statements of Thomson Reuters Corporation. Those statements account for Thomson Reuters PLC as a subsidiary and have been prepared in accordance with Canadian GAAP. We have received exemptive relief to present Thomson Reuters Corporation's financial statements in accordance with International Financial Reporting Standards (IFRS) in 2009. We have provided a voluntary reconciliation to IFRS in this management's discussion and analysis. See the section entitled "Recently Issued Accounting Standards" for more information.

RECENTLY ISSUED ACCOUNTING STANDARDS

Transition to IFRS from Canadian GAAP

In 2008, the Canadian Accounting Standards Board confirmed that Canadian publicly accountable enterprises will be required to adopt International Financial Reporting Standards (IFRS) by 2011 in replacement of Canadian GAAP. The Canadian securities regulatory authorities have approved our application to early adopt IFRS in 2009 although we have not yet determined in which quarter we will reflect the adoption. Comparative periods for 2008 would be restated. The following discussion provides further information about our adoption.

Estimated Impact of IFRS on 2008 Financial Results

IFRS employs a conceptual framework that is similar to Canadian GAAP. In accordance with our agreement with the United Kingdom Listing Authority, we have provided a reconciliation of shareholders equity and net earnings from Canadian GAAP to IFRS as of and for the three and nine-month periods ended September 30, 2008 and 2007, respectively, in the section entitled "Voluntary reconciliation from Canadian GAAP to IFRS". While this reconciliation does not represent an official adoption of IFRS, it provides an indication of the major differences identified to date, relative to our historical financial statements. With respect to our official adoption of IFRS in 2009, we have not quantified the impact that IFRS 1, First Time Adoption of International Reporting Standards (IFRS 1), will have on our financial statements, nor have we definitively concluded if we will elect different policies in selected circumstances under IFRS. However, we do not expect the adoption of IFRS to impact the overall revenue and underlying profitability trends of our operating performance.

Voluntary Reconciliation from Canadian GAAP to IFRS

Thomson Reuters consolidated financial statements are prepared in accordance with Canadian GAAP. The following reconciliation presents the material differences between Canadian GAAP and IFRS, relative to our financial statements. However, this reconciliation does not constitute an adoption of IFRS by Thomson Reuters. In preparing the reconciliation, Thomson Reuters applied the principles and elections of IFRS 1, with a transition date of January 1, 2004, consistent with those assumed in its Business Acquisition Report dated May 15, 2008. When we adopt IFRS, effective January 1, 2009, we will apply the provisions of IFRS 1 as described under the section entitled "Initial Adoption—IFRS 1", with a January 1, 2008 transition date. We will also apply IFRS standards in effect at December 31, 2009 as required by IFRS 1 and may elect accounting policies which differ from those applied in this reconciliation.

(in millions of US dollars, except per share amounts)	Three Months ended September 30,		Nine months ended September 30,	
	2008	2007	**2008**	2007
Net earnings under Canadian GAAP	**381**	2,969	**748**	3,570
Differences in GAAP increasing (decreasing) reported earnings:				
1. Business combinations	**(11)**	—	**(72)**	(1)
2. Employee benefits	**5**	46	**16**	78
3. Stock-based compensation	**4**	5	**(12)**	7
4. Impairments of long-term assets	**6**	(18)	**(11)**	(79)
5. Derivative instruments and hedging activities	**(1)**	6	**(3)**	(2)
6. Minority interest in equity of consolidated affiliate	**3**	—	**9**	—
7. Income taxes	**(7)**	(24)	**9**	(12)
Net earnings under IFRS	**380**	2,984	**684**	3,561
Basic earnings per share	**0.46**	4.65	**0.89**	5.55
Diluted earnings per share	**0.45**	4.63	**0.89**	5.52

(in millions of US dollars)	As at September 30,	
	2008	2007
Shareholders' equity under Canadian GAAP	**20,077**	13,584
Differences increasing (decreasing) reported shareholders' equity:		
1. Business combinations	**(1,094)**	(41)
2. Employee benefits	**(529)**	(276)
3. Stock-based compensation	**(38)**	(11)
4. Impairment of long-term assets	**(2)**	(110)
5. Derivative instruments and hedging activities	**(4)**	(1)
6. Minority interest in equity of consolidated affiliate	**69**	—
7. Income taxes	**171**	114
Shareholders' equity under IFRS	**18,650**	13,259

The following describes the differences presented in the reconciliation of net earnings and shareholders' equity.

1. Business Combinations

Acquisition Cost

Canadian GAAP—Shares issued as consideration are measured at their market price a few days before and after the date the parties reach an agreement on the purchase price and proposed transaction is announced.

IFRS—Shares issued as consideration are measured at their market price on the acquisition closing date.

Contingent Consideration

Canadian GAAP—Contingent consideration is recognized as part of the cost of an acquisition, but only at the point when the amount can be reasonably estimated and the outcome is determined beyond reasonable doubt.

IFRS—Contingent consideration is recognized as part of the cost of an acquisition, at the date of acquisition, if it is probable that the contingency will be met and the amount can be reliably measured at fair value. Changes to the initial amount recorded are recognized through income and discounts on future cash payments are accreted through interest expense.

Acquisition Related Costs

Canadian GAAP—Costs of the acquirer such as (1) exiting an activity, (2) involuntarily terminating an employee, or (3) relocating employees of an acquired company are recognized as part of the cost of an acquisition.

IFRS—These costs are expensed, unless they are part of an existing restructuring by the acquiree, in which case they may be recognized as part of the cost of an acquisition.

2. Employee Benefits

Measurement Date

Canadian GAAP—The measurement date of defined benefit obligations and plan assets may be up to three months prior to the date of the financial statements.

IFRS—The measurement date generally coincides with the date of the financial statements, because the measurement date must not result in a materially different outcome than if the balance sheet date had been used.

Past Service Cost

Canadian GAAP—Past service costs arising from plan amendments are amortized on a straight-line basis over the average remaining service period of active employees expected to benefit from the amendment.

IFRS—These costs are amortized on a straight-line basis over the average period until the benefits become vested. To the extent that the amended benefits are already vested, past service costs are recognized immediately.

Actuarial Gains and Losses

Canadian GAAP—Actuarial gains and losses are recognized on a systematic and consistent basis, subject to a minimum required amortization based on a "corridor" approach. Unrecognized actuarial gains and losses below the corridor are deferred.

IFRS—In accordance with our IFRS 1 election, actuarial gains and losses are recognized immediately into equity.

Fair value of Plan Assets

Canadian GAAP—Plan assets are valued using a market-related fair value, which recognizes changes in the fair value of plan assets over a five-year period.

IFRS—Plan assets are valued at fair value at the measurement date.

3. Stock-based Compensation

Recognition of expense

Canadian GAAP—The fair value of a stock-based award with graded vesting is recognized on a straight-line basis over the vesting period.

IFRS—Each tranche of an award is considered a separate grant with a different vesting date and fair value, and each is accounted for separately.

Forfeitures

Canadian GAAP—Forfeitures of awards may be recognized as they occur.

IFRS—Forfeiture estimates are recognized in the current period and revised for actual experience in subsequent periods.

Cash-settled share-based payments

Canadian GAAP—The liability for cash-settled share-based payments is accrued based upon the intrinsic value of the award.

IFRS—The liability for cash-settled share-based awards is measured at fair value, using an option pricing model. Changes in fair value are recognized over the remaining vesting period until the liability is settled. Changes in fair value of vested awards are recognized in income immediately.

Recognition of deferred tax assets

Canadian GAAP—Deferred tax assets for share-based awards are based upon the cumulative amount of compensation cost recognized.

IFRS—Deferred tax assets for share-based awards are based upon the estimated tax deduction, which is generally the intrinsic value of the vested award at the balance sheet date. If the estimated deduction exceeds the cumulative compensation expense, the excess is recognized in equity. If no tax deduction is anticipated because the fair value of the shares has declined, then the deferred tax asset is reversed to income or equity as appropriate, depending on how the asset was originally recorded.

Employer Taxes

Canadian GAAP—Employer taxes on share-based compensation are recognized upon exercise of the instrument.

IFRS—Employer taxes on share-based compensation are recognized over the vesting period based upon the fair value of the awards at each balance sheet date.

4. Impairments of Long-Term Assets Held for Sale

Canadian GAAP—Assets held for sale are measured at the lower of their carrying amount or fair value less costs to sell, where the carrying amount for purposes of determining impairment includes cumulative translation adjustments.

IFRS—Assets held for sale are measured at the lower of their carrying amount or fair value less costs to sell, where the carrying amount excludes cumulative translation adjustments. Upon sale of the assets, the amount of the cumulative translation adjustment is included in the determination of the gain or loss on sale.

5. Financial Instruments

Hedge accounting

Canadian GAAP—Effectiveness for compound derivative instruments that hedge currency and interest rate risk is assumed provided the critical terms of the derivative instrument are consistent with the hedged instrument.

IFRS—Effectiveness for compound derivative instruments must be assessed retrospectively and prospectively each reporting period As a result, certain hedge relationships had to be prospectively discontinued as of the date of adoption of IAS 32 and IAS 39.

6. Minority Interest

Canadian GAAP—Minority interest in the equity of a consolidated affiliate is classified as a separate balance sheet component between liabilities and equity. Minority interest in the profit or loss of a consolidated affiliate is presented as a component of net income.

IFRS—Minority interest in equity of a consolidated affiliate is classified as a component of equity but separate from the equity of the parent. Minority interest in the profit or loss of a consolidated affiliate is presented as an allocation of net income.

7. Income Taxes

Intercompany transactions

Canadian GAAP—The recognition of deferred tax for a temporary difference arising from intercompany transactions is prohibited. Further, taxes paid or recovered as a result of an intercompany asset transfer are recorded as an asset or liability and recognized as tax expense when the asset leaves the group or is otherwise utilized.

IFRS—Deferred taxes are recognized for temporary differences arising from intercompany transactions. Taxes paid or recovered as a result of an intercompany asset transfer are recognized in the period incurred.

Business Combinations: Deferred tax assets not previously recognized

Canadian GAAP—Previously unrecognized income tax assets of an acquired company are recognized as part of the cost of the acquisition when such assets are more likely than not to be realized as a result of a business combination. If an unrecognized deferred tax asset becomes realizable subsequent to the acquisition date, such benefit will also be recognized through goodwill. The acquirer recognizes its own tax benefits which become realizable as a result of the acquisition as part of the cost of the acquisition.

IFRS—Previously unrecognized income tax assets of an acquired company are recognized as part of the cost of the acquisition if realization is more likely than not as a result of the business combination. If an unrecognized deferred tax asset becomes realizable subsequent to the acquisition date, the tax benefit is recognized through income, and a corresponding amount of goodwill is written off to operating expense. The acquirer recognizes its own tax benefits which become realizable as a result of the acquisition through income.

Accounting for uncertainty in income taxes in business combinations

Canadian GAAP—Changes to income tax contingencies relating to pre-acquisition periods are adjusted through the purchase price allocation, first reducing goodwill, intangible assets associated with the business combination, and only after exhausting those amounts, reducing income tax expense.

IFRS—Changes to pre-acquisition tax uncertainties beyond twelve months of the acquisition date are recorded to the income statement.

Income tax effect of other reconciling differences between Canadian GAAP and IFRS

Differences from income taxes include the deferred tax effect on earnings of pre-tax differences between Canadian GAAP and IFRS described above.

Initial Adoption of International Accounting Standards

IFRS 1 sets forth guidance for the initial adoption of IFRS. As required, we will restate our comparative 2008 financial statements for annual and interim periods to be consistent with our new IFRS basis. Further, we will reconcile equity and net earnings from the previously reported 2008 Canadian GAAP amounts to the 2008 IFRS amounts.

IFRS 1 generally requires that first-time adopters consistently apply all effective IFRS standards retrospectively from the reporting date. IFRS 1 provides for certain optional exemptions and certain mandatory exceptions to this general principle. While we have not finalized our conclusions with respect to the optional exemptions, we expect to make the following elections:

- **Business combinations**—IFRS 3, Business Combinations, may be applied retrospectively or prospectively. The retrospective basis would require restatement of all business combinations that occurred prior to the transition date. We plan to adopt IFRS 3 on a prospective basis. Further, we do not expect to early adopt IFRS 3 Revised, and will adopt that standard upon its effective date, January 1, 2010.

- **Fair value or revaluation as deemed cost**—IFRS 1 provides a choice between measuring property, plant and equipment at its fair value at the date of transition and using those amounts as deemed cost or using the historical valuation under the prior GAAP. We plan to use our historical bases as deemed cost.

- **Employee benefits**—IAS 19, Employee Benefits, allows certain actuarial gains and losses to be either deferred and amortized, subject to certain provisions, or immediately recognized through equity. We expect to elect immediate recognition of actuarial gains and losses as of the transition date and for future periods.

- **Currency translation differences**—IFRS 1 permits cumulative translation gains and losses to be reset to zero at the transition date. Alternatively, IFRS 1 allows translation differences to be recalculated in accordance with IFRS from the date a subsidiary or associate was formed or acquired. We expect to reset cumulative translation gains and losses to zero at the transition date.

- **Share-based payments**—IFRS 2, Share Based Payments, encourages application of its provisions to equity instruments granted on or before November 7, 2002, but permits the application only to equity instruments granted after November 7, 2002 that had not vested by January 1, 2008. We expect to apply IFRS 2 only to equity instruments granted after November 7, 2002 that had not vested by January 1, 2008.

- **Changes in existing decommissioning, restoration and similar liabilities included in the cost of property, plant and equipment**—IFRS 1 allows for either the retroactive adoption or prospective adoption from the transition date of IFRIC 1, Changes in existing decommissioning, restoration and similar liabilities. We plan to prospectively apply this standard.

Further optional exemptions are provided under IFRS 1. However, we do not believe these exemptions will impact our adoption of IFRS.

Hindsight is not permitted to create or revise estimates. The estimates previously made by us under Canadian GAAP will not be revised for application of IFRS except where necessary to reflect any difference in accounting policies.

IFRS Impact on Our Organization

The conversion to IFRS will impact the way we present our financial results. We have obtained an understanding of IFRS from intensive training and preparation of reconciliations of historical Canadian GAAP financial statements to IFRS. Further, our accounting staff includes former Reuters employees who prepared financial statements under IFRS for the past three years.

We are still evaluating the impact of the conversion on our accounting systems. However, based on the differences identified to date, we believe our systems can accommodate the required changes. We believe our internal and disclosure control processes, as currently designed, will not need significant modifications as a result of our conversion to IFRS.

We have assessed the impacts of adopting IFRS on our debt covenants and other contractual arrangements, and have not identified any material compliance issues. We are considering the impacts that the transition will have on our internal planning process and compensation arrangements.

CICA 3064, Goodwill and Intangible Assets

In February 2008, the CICA adopted CICA 3064, Goodwill and Intangible Assets, which replaces CICA 3062 and establishes standards for the recognition, measurement, presentation and disclosure of goodwill and intangible assets. The new standard applies to internally-generated intangible assets and rights under licensing agreements and is effective for us as of January 1, 2009. We believe there will not be a significant impact on our financial statements upon adoption.

PLANNING FOR IMPLEMENTATION

The requirements of IFRS 1 are complex and Canadian entities need to perform a careful analysis when planning their conversion from Canadian GAAP to IFRS. Implementing IFRS 1 means that they will have to:

- Prepare an opening statement of financial position at the transition date (i.e., January 1, 2010), which is the starting point for reporting under IFRS. This statement of financial position must be prepared in accordance with IFRS in force at their first reporting date (i.e., December 31, 2011).

- Apply to all periods presented in their first IFRS financial statements the IFRS standards in effect at the first IFRS reporting date (December 31, 2011). This means that there can be no changes in accounting policy in the first IFRS financial statements.

A discussion of some of the IFRS 1 implementation issues follows below.

Opening Statement of Financial Position

A significant portion of the IFRS adoption efforts will be devoted to the preparation of the opening IFRS statement of financial position, which requires the capture of information that was not accumulated under Canadian GAAP.

When preparing its opening statement of financial position, an entity must ensure that it properly applies mandatory exceptions from full restatement. It must also strategically evaluate the voluntary exemptions under IFRS 1 by examining a variety of factors, including the cost of retrospective application, the availability of required information and the conversion elections made by peer companies. For example, for acquisitions made prior to the date of transition, an entity must assess the impact and costs of three options:

- restatement of all historical acquisitions in accordance with the requirements of IFRS 3, *Business Combinations*; or

- no restatement of any historical acquisitions; or

- restatement of all historical acquisitions after a particular date (e.g., the three years prior to the date of transition).

The evaluation of voluntary exemptions is even more important and complex for entities with multiple locations. For them, conversion requires advance planning to coordinate IFRS 1 elections made by subsidiaries with those of the parent.

Additional Disclosures and Dual Reporting

IFRS 1 does not provide significant exemptions for IFRS disclosure requirements. In addition to providing the disclosures required by each IFRS standard, entities have to provide various reconciliations. These disclosures may require the collection of new information and data.

Entities should consider establishing an information system that permits dual reporting for compliance with both Canadian GAAP and IFRS in 2010 to avoid the traditional reconciliation approach. Reporting financial results under both Canadian GAAP and IFRS in 2010 can be a complex undertaking and focusing on streamlined data capture can make the production of multiple financial reports more efficient.

Accounting Policies

An entity that adopts IFRS for the first time has a one-time opportunity to comprehensively reassess and modify its accounting policies. When initially selecting an accounting policy, an entity should carefully consider all implications on future financial statements. Changes to accounting policies after the first-time IFRS adoption need to comply with the requirements of IAS 8, *Accounting Policies, Changes in Accounting Estimates and Errors.*

Keep Posted

Entities should monitor IASB project developments and the status of its standards and interpretations. More specifically, they should:

- assess whether any standards issued but not yet effective on the transition date should be adopted early at the same time as the transition to IFRS to minimize future reporting changes;

- ensure that data requirements for any new IFRS that are issued or about to be issued are incorporated into the IFRS conversion plan so that the relevant financial information, systems and processes are in place when the IFRS become effective; and

- select accounting policies in light of proposed changes to existing IFRS standards to minimize future changes arising from the issue of new standards and/or interpretations effective subsequent to the adoption of IFRS.

Note that the *Roadmap for the Potential Use of Financial Statements Prepared in Accordance with International Financial Reporting Standards by U.S. Issuers*, proposed by the SEC in November 2008, has established ambitious agendas for the FASB and IASB. Companies should expect both standard setters to issue significant new standards, as well as amendments to previously issued standards, over the next few years. This will make the transition to IFRS in Canada a complex undertaking.

IFRS are a moving target. Companies preparing their first IFRS annual financial statements (i.e., for the year ended in December 2011) may need to go back and adjust all periods and the opening IFRS statement of financial position to reflect any new standards that became effective during the transition period leading up to complete IFRS conversion.

Appendix A
IFRS Dealing with Industry Specific Activities

IFRS primarily presents general accounting principles; they provide little industry-specific guidance. However, three IFRS standards cover specific activities or transactions that relate to:

- agriculture (IAS 41, *Agriculture*);
- insurance contracts (IFRS 4, *Insurance Contracts*); and
- exploration and evaluation of mineral resources (IFRS 6, *Exploration for and Evaluation of Mineral Resources*).

The application of IFRS to specific industries is an issue of its own and is not covered in this publication. However, the paragraphs below present a brief overview of the three standards dealing with specific activities.

AGRICULTURE

Agricultural activities are unique because their undertaking results in biological transformations that alter the substance of biological assets (i.e., asset changes through procreation, growth and degeneration; or production of agricultural produce).

IAS 41 establishes the recognition, measurement and disclosure requirements for:

- biological assets;
- agricultural produce at the point of harvest; and
- government grants related to biological assets.

Basically IAS 41 requires that:

- Biological assets are measured at fair value less costs to sell. All gains and losses arising on initial recognition at and from a change in fair value less costs to sell must be recognized in profit or loss. When it is not possible to measure fair value reliably on initial recognition, biological assets are measured at cost.
- Agricultural produce harvested from a biological asset is measured at fair value less costs to sell at the point of harvest. All gains and losses arising on initial recognition at fair value less costs to sell must be recognized in profit or loss.
- Government grants related to biological assets measured at fair value less costs to sell are recognized in profit or loss when they are unconditionally receivable.

Canadian GAAP differs because it does not provide any guidance on accounting for agricultural activities. In practice under Canadian GAAP:

- changes in the fair value of biological assets are not recognized in income until they are sold; and

- government assistance related to biological assets is accounted for in the same way as other government assistance.

Consequently, the significant difference between the requirements under IAS 41 and Canadian GAAP concerns the use of fair value in most cases under the former instead of historical cost. Note that the fair value perspective applies only to biological assets and agricultural produce, as those are the aspects of agriculture that have unique characteristics. Products that are the result of processing after harvest typically represent inventories, which should be accounted for in accordance with IAS 2, *Inventories*. In other words, once a biological asset or agricultural produce has been processed into a product (e.g., when wool is spun into yarn, or trees are cut down and milled into lumber) the specialized accounting principles cease to apply.

INSURANCE CONTRACTS

The IASC started this project to address only the accounting for insurance contracts rather than all the various complex aspects of accounting by insurance companies. Subsequently the IASB published IFRS 4, which became effective for periods beginning in 2005. The IASB issued IFRS 4 as an interim standard while it continues to develop a standard that will provide a basis for consistent accounting for insurance contracts in phase II of the project on insurance contracts. In phase II, the IASB plans to develop guidance for measurement, the applicability of discounting, risk and service adjustments, gain or loss on initial measurement or liability recognition, acquisition costs, participating contracts, and various other relevant topics. In May 2007, the IASB published a Discussion Paper, *Preliminary Views on Insurance Contracts* which proposes that an insurer should measure its insurance liabilities using three building blocks.

The following is a brief summary of certain elements of IFRS 4.

Scope

IFRS 4 specifies the financial reporting for insurance contracts by any entity that issues these contracts (i.e., it is not limited solely to insurance companies). It applies to insurance contracts issued, reinsurance contracts held, and financial instruments issued with a discretionary participation feature. IFRS 4, however, does not apply to other assets and liabilities of issuers of insurance contracts, which are addressed by other IFRS.

Definition of an Insurance Contract

An insurance contract is defined as a contract under which the insurer accepts significant insurance risk from the policyholder by agreeing to compensate the policyholder if the insured event (i.e., a specified uncertain future event) adversely affects the policyholder.

Insurance risk represents any risk, other than a financial risk, transferred from the policyholder to the insurer. Financial risk is the risk of a possible future change in one or more of a specified interest rate, financial instrument price, commodity price, foreign exchange rate, index of prices or rates, credit rating or credit index or other variable (provided in the case of a non-financial variable that the variable is not specific to a party to the contract).

In other words, a contract does not meet the definition of an insurance contract if it exposes one party to financial risk but not insurance risk. Such a contract should be accounted for in accordance with IAS 39, *Financial Instruments: Recognition and Measurement*.

As previously mentioned, IFRS 4 applies to all insurance contracts (including reinsurance contracts). Although the following arrangements may have certain characteristics of insurance contracts, they are excluded from IFRS 4, since they are dealt with under other IFRS standards:

- financial guarantees (including credit insurance);
- product warranties issued directly by a manufacturer, dealer or a retailer;
- employers' assets and liabilities under employee benefit plans;
- retirement benefit obligations reported by defined benefit retirement plans;
- contingent consideration payable or receivable in a business combination;
- direct insurance contracts; and
- contractual rights or contractual obligations that are contingent on the future use of, or right to use, a non-financial item, as well as a lessee's residual value guarantee embedded in a finance lease.

Changes in the Level of Insurance Risk

A contract that qualifies as an insurance contract at inception or later remains an insurance contract until all rights and obligations are extinguished or expire.

Requirements

IFRS 4 allows an insurer to continue to use its existing accounting practices; however, the standard:

- prohibits provisions for possible claims under contracts that are not in existence at the end of the reporting period (i.e., catastrophe and equalisation provisions);
- requires a test for the adequacy of recognized insurance liabilities and an impairment test for reinsurance assets;
- requires an insurer to keep insurance liabilities on its balance sheet until they are discharged or cancelled, or expire, and to present insurance liabilities without offsetting them against related reinsurance assets.

Therefore, a Canadian first-time adopter can continue to account for insurance contracts in accordance with AcG-3, *Financial reporting by property and casualty insurance companies*. AcG-3 has requirements that are similar to IFRS 4, such as the prohibition to recognize provisions for catastrophe and equalisation related to contracts not in existence at the reporting date. However, some of the requirements do differ. For example, under AcG-3:

- reinsurance assets are offset against related life insurance liabilities, and life reinsurance revenues and expenses are offset against expenses and revenues from related life insurance contracts; and
- the term "liability adequacy test" is not used, and instead:
  - o a form of premium deficiency testing is required for property and casualty insurance, and

o life insurance policy liabilities are measured using a prospective cash flow approach, which considers all expected future cash flows using current estimates. This approach meets the liability adequacy test under IFRS 4.

EXPLORATION FOR AND EVALUATION OF MINERAL RESOURCES

IFRS 6 addresses the financial reporting for the exploration for and evaluation of mineral resources (i.e., minerals, oil, natural gas, and similar non-regenerative resources). The IASB issued this standard to provide limited and temporary guidance until it completes its comprehensive review of the accounting for extractive activities.

IFRS 6 limits the need for an entity to change its existing accounting policies for exploration and evaluation assets. Thus, a Canadian first-time adopter may continue to use either:

• *The successful efforts method*: Under this method, costs associated with locating, purchasing, and developing reserves are capitalized on a field-by-field basis. Once the reserves are proven, the capitalized costs are assigned to the discovery. If discovery is not attained, then the expenditures are expensed.

• *The full cost method*: Under this method, costs associated with locating, acquiring and developing reserves are aggregated by large geographic cost centre (i.e., a country or a region) and capitalized.

IFRS 6, however, applies only to expenditures incurred during the exploration and evaluation phase, which starts after the legal right to explore a designated area is obtained, and ends when the technical feasibility and commercial viability of extracting a mineral resource are demonstrable.

This scope limitation creates a particular problem for an entity that has retained its policy to use the full cost method of accounting because it will only be able to apply this method to expenditures incurred during the exploration and evaluation phase. Expenditures incurred before (i.e., in the pre-exploration phase) or after (i.e., in the development phase) must be accounted for using the successful efforts method.

Under Canadian GAAP, an entity is allowed to apply the full cost method to expenditures incurred during all phases (i.e., pre-exploration, exploration, evaluation, and development).

Appendix B

Coverage of Current IFRS Standards and Interpretations

This publication discusses and illustrates the application of all but a few IFRS. The table below summarizes IFRS standards and interpretations with a reference to the chapters of the publication where the issue is covered.

Standards	Coverage Chapter
IFRS 1 – First-time Adoption of International Financial Reporting Standards	20
IFRS 2 – Share-based Payment	16
IFRS 3 – Business Combinations	5
IFRS 4 – Insurance Contracts	Appendix A
IFRS 5 – Non-current Assets Held for Sale and Discontinued Operations	12
IFRS 6 – Exploration for and Evaluation of Mineral Resources	Appendix A
IFRS 7 – Financial Instruments: Disclosures	9
IFRS 8 – Operating Segments	2
IAS 1 – Presentation of Financial Statements	2
IAS 2 – Inventories	11
IAS 7 – Cash Flow Statements	2
IAS 8 – Accounting Policies, Changes in Accounting Estimates and Errors	2
IAS 10 – Events After the Balance Sheet Date	2
IAS 11 – Construction Contracts	11
IAS 12 – Income Taxes	17
IAS 16 – Property, Plant and Equipment	12
IAS 17 – Leases	13
IAS 18 – Revenue	11
IAS 19 – Employee Benefits	16
IAS 20 – Accounting for Government Grants and Disclosure of Government Assistance	19
IAS 21 – The Effects of Changes in Foreign Exchange Rates	10
IAS 23 – Borrowing Costs	19
IAS 24 – Related Party Disclosures	18
IAS 26 – Accounting and Reporting by Retirement Benefit Plans	Not discussed
IAS 27 – Consolidated and Separate Financial Statements	6
IAS 28 – Investments in Associates	7

Standards (continued)	Coverage Chapter
IAS 29 – Financial Reporting in Hyperinflationary Economies	10
IAS 31 – Interests in Joint Ventures	7
IAS 32 – Financial Instruments: Presentation	9
IAS 33 – Earnings per Share	2
IAS 34 – Interim Financial Reporting	2
IAS 36 – Impairment of Assets	4
IAS 37 – Provisions, Contingent Liabilities and Contingent Assets	15
IAS 38 – Intangible Assets	14
IAS 39 – Financial Instruments: Recognition and Measurement	9
IAS 40 – Investment Property	8
IAS 41 – Agriculture	Appendix A
Interpretations	
SIC 7 – Introduction of the Euro	10
SIC 10 – Government Assistance—No Specific Relation to Operating Activities	19
SIC 12 – Consolidation—Special-Purpose Entities	6
SIC 13 – Jointly Controlled Entities—Non-monetary Contributions by Venturers	7
SIC 15 – Operating Leases—Incentives	13
SIC 21 – Income Taxes—Recovery of Revalued Non-depreciable Assets	17
SIC 25 – Income Taxes—Changes in the Tax Status of an Enterprise or Its Shareholders	17
SIC 27 – Evaluating the Substance of Transactions Involving the Legal Form of a Lease	13
SIC 29 – Disclosure—Service Concession Arrangements	11
SIC 31 – Revenue—Barter Transactions Involving Advertising Services	11
SIC 32 – Intangible Assets—Web Site Costs	14
IFRIC 1 – Changes in Existing Decommissioning, Restoration and Similar Liabilities	15
IFRIC 2 – Members' Shares in Cooperative Entities and Similar Instruments	Not discussed
IFRIC 4 – Determining Whether an Arrangement Contains a Lease	13
IFRIC 5 – Rights to Interests Arising from Decommissioning, Restoration and Environmental Rehabilitation Funds	15
IFRIC 6 – Liabilities Arising from Participating in a Specific Market—Waste Electrical and Electronic Equipment	15
IFRIC 7 – Applying the Restatement Approach under IAS 29, Financial Reporting in Hyperinflationary Economies	Not discussed
IFRIC 8 – Scope of IFRS 2	16
IFRIC 9 – Reassessment of Embedded Derivatives	9
IFRIC 10 – Interim Financial Reporting and Impairment	4
IFRIC 11 – IFRS 2: Group and Treasury Share Transactions	16
IFRIC 12 – Service Concession Arrangements	11
IFRIC 13 – Customer Loyalty Programs	11
IFRIC 14 IAS 19—The Limit on a Defined Benefit Asset, Minimum Funding Requirements, and Their Interaction	16
IFRIC 15 – Agreements for the Construction of Real Estate	11
IFRIC 16 – Hedges of a Net Investment in a Foreign Operation	9
IFRIC 17 – Distributions of Non-cash Assets to Owners	6

Exposure Drafts	Coverage Chapter
Group Cash-settled Share-based Payment Transactions (December 2007)	16
Improvements to IFRSs (August 2008)	Various
ED 10 Consolidated Financial Statements (December 2008)	6
State-controlled Entities and the Definition of a Related Party (February 2007)	18
Relationships with the State (December 2008)	18
Discontinued Operations (September 2008)	12
Amendments to IAS 37 Provisions, Contingent Liabilities and Contingent Assets and IAS 19 Employee Benefits (June 2005)	15
ED 9 Joint Arrangements (September 2007)	7
Improving Disclosures about Financial Instruments (October 2008)	9
Embedded Derivatives (December 2008)	9
Investments in Debt Instruments (December 2008)	9
Additional Exemptions for First-time Adopters (September 2008)	20
Simplifying Earnings per Share (August 2008)	2
An Improved Conceptual Framework for Financial Reporting (May 2008)	2
IFRS for Small and Medium-sized Entities (February 2007)	2
Discussion Papers	
Preliminary Views on Amendments to IAS 19 Employee Benefits (March 2008)	16
Preliminary Views on Revenue Recognition in Contracts with Customers (December 2008)	11
Fair Value Measurements (November 2006)	3
Financial Instruments with Characteristics of Equity (February 2008)	9
Reducing Complexity in Reporting Financial Instruments (March 2008)	9
Preliminary Views on Financial Statement Presentation (October 2008)	2
Preliminary Views on an Improved Conceptual Framework for Financial Reporting (May 2008)	2
Management Commentary (October 2005)	2
Preliminary Views on Insurance Contracts (May 2007)	Appendix A

Appendix C
List of Companies

The following table lists the financial reports of the companies from which extracts were used as illustration in this publication. The table also indicates the year end of the financial reports, the set of standards under which the reports were prepared and whether the company is a SEC registrant or not.

Name	Financial Report	Year end	IFRS-IASB/IFRS-EU/IFRS-Other	SEC registrant
A & J Mucklow Group plc	AR 2007	30 June 2007	IFRS-IASB	No
AB Volvo	AR 2007	31 Dec. 2007	IFRS-EU	No
ABB Grain Ltd	Financial Report 2007	30 Sept. 2007	IFRS-Australia	No
ABN AMRO Holding N.V.	AR 2007	31 Dec. 2007	IFRS-IASB	Yes
Acambis plc	AR 2007	31 Dec. 2007	IFRS-EU	No
Acc-Ross Holdings Limited	AR 2007	28 Feb. 2007	IFRS-IASB	No
Acta S.p.A	AR 2007	31 Dec. 2007	IFRS-EU	No
Air France-KLM S.A.	Reference Document 2006-07	31 Mar. 2007	IFRS-EU	Yes
Aker Kvaerner ASA	AR 2007	31 Dec. 2007	IFRS-EU	No
Akzo Nobel N.V.	AR 2007	31 Dec. 2007	IFRS-EU	No
Albidon Limited	AR 2007	31 Dec. 2006	IFRS-IASB	No
Alcatel-Lucent	AR 2006 on Form 20-F	31 Dec. 2006	IFRS-EU	Yes
Alcatel-Lucent	AR 2007 on Form 20-F	31 Dec. 2007	IFRS-IASB	Yes
Alcoa World Alumina and Chemicals	Form 20-F 2006	31 Dec. 2006	US GAAP[1]	Yes
Alma Media Corporation	AR 2007	31 Dec. 2007	IFRS-EU	No
Altana Aktiengesellschaft	AR 2007	31 Dec. 2007	IFRS-IASB	No
Alumina Limited	AR 2006	31 Dec. 2006	IFRS-Australia	Yes
Alumina Limited	Form 20-F 2006	31 Dec. 2006	IFRS-Australia	Yes
Aluminum Corporation of China Limited	Form 20-F 2006	31 Dec. 2006	IFRS-Hong Kong (HKFRS)	Yes
AMG Advanced Metallurgical Group N.V.	AR 2007	31 Dec. 2007	IFRS-EU	No
Andritz AG	AR 2007	31 Dec. 2007	IFRS-EU	No
Ansell Limited	Financial Report 2007	30 June 2007	IFRS-IASB	No
Antofagasta plc	AR 2007	31 Dec. 2007	IFRS-IASB	No
ASOS PLC	AR 2008	31 Mar. 2008	IFRS-EU	No
AstraZeneca PLC	AR & Form 20-F 2006	31 Dec. 2006	IFRS-EU	Yes
AstraZeneca PLC	AR & Form 20-F 2007	31 Dec. 2007	IFRS-IASB	Yes
Astro All Asia Networks plc	AR 2007	31 Jan. 2007	IFRS-IASB	No
Atorka Group hf	AR 2007	31 Dec. 2007	IFRS-EU	No
Atos Origin	AR 2007	31 Dec. 2007	IFRS-EU	No
Auspine Limited	AR 2007	30 June 2007	IFRS-IASB	No
Australian Worldwide Exploration Limited	AR 2007	30 June 2007	IFRS-IASB	No
Aviva plc	AR 2007	31 Dec. 2007	IFRS-IASB	No
BAA Limited	AR 2007	31 Dec. 2007	IFRS-EU	No
Banesto Group	AR 2007	31 Dec. 2007	IFRS-EU	No

Name	Financial Report	Year end	IFRS-IASB/IFRS-EU/IFRS-Other	SEC registrant
Bank of Ireland	Report & Accounts 2007	31 Mar. 2007	IFRS-EU	Yes
Barclays Bank PLC	AR 2007	31 Dec. 2007	IFRS-EU	No
Barclays PLC	AR 2007	31 Dec. 2007	IFRS-EU	Yes
Barloworld Limited	AR 2007	30 Sept. 2007	IFRS-IASB	No
BASF Aktiengesellschaft	AR 2007	31 Dec. 2007	IFRS-IASB	No
Bayer Aktiengesellschaft	AR 2007	31 Dec. 2007	IFRS-EU	No
Beaconsfield Gold NL	Annual Financial Report 2007	30 June 2007	IFRS-IASB	No
Benetton Group SpA	Form 20-F 2006	31 Dec. 2006	IFRS-EU	Yes
BNP Paribas	Registration Document 2007	31 Dec. 2007	IFRS-EU	No
BOC Hong Kong Holdings Limited	AR 2007	31 Dec. 2007	IFRS-Hong Kong (HKFRS)	No
Borealis AG	AR 2007	31 Dec. 2007	IFRS-EU	No
BP p.l.c.	AR 2006	31 Dec. 2006	IFRS-IASB	Yes
British Sky Broadcasting Group plc	AR 2007	30 June 2007	IFRS-IASB	Yes
Brookfield Asset Management Inc.	Interim Report Q2 2008	30 June 2008	Canadian GAAP[1]	Yes
Brookfield Asset Management Inc.	Interim Report Q3 2008	30 Sept. 2008	Canadian GAAP[1]	Yes
BT Group PLC	AR & Form 20-F 2007	31 Mar. 2007	IFRS-IASB	Yes
BT Group PLC	AR & Form 20-F 2008	31 Mar. 2008	IFRS-IASB	Yes
Cadbury Schweppes plc	AR & Acounts 2007	31 Dec. 2007	IFRS-IASB	Yes
Carl Zeiss AG	AR 2007	30 Sept. 2007	IFRS-EU	No
Casino Guichard–Perrachon	AR 2006	31 Dec. 2006	IFRS-EU	No
Centrica plc	AR 2007	31 Dec. 2007	IFRS-EU	No
CEVA Group Plc	AR 2007	31 Dec. 2007	IFRS-EU	No
China Telecom Corporation Limited	AR 2007	31 Dec. 2007	IFRS-IASB	Yes
ClinPhone plc	AR 2007	28 Feb. 2007	IFRS-EU	No
Corporate Express NV	AR 2007	31 Dec. 2007	IFRS-EU	Yes
Corus Group plc	AR 2006	30 Dec. 2006	IFRS-EU	No
CRH public limited company	Form 20-F 2006	31 Dec. 2006	IFRS-EU	Yes
Crucell N.V.	Form 20-F 2006	31 Dec. 2006	IFRS-EU	No
Daejan Holdings PLC	Report & Financial Statements 2007	31 Mar. 2007	IFRS-EU	No
Daimler AG	AR 2007	31 Dec. 2007	IFRS-IASB	Yes
Daimler AG	Form 20-F 2007	31 Dec. 2007	IFRS-IASB	Yes
DaimlerChrysler AG	IFRS Consolidated Financial Statements 2006	31 Dec. 2006	IFRS-IASB	Yes
Danfoss A/S	AR 2007	31 Dec. 2007	IFRS-EU	No
Danisco A/S	AR 2008	30 Apr. 2008	IFRS-EU	No
Delhaize Group SA	AR 2007	31 Dec. 2007	IFRS-EU	Yes
Detica Group plc	AR 2007	31 Mar. 2007	IFRS-EU	No
Deutsche Bank Aktiengesellschaft	Annual Review 2007	31 Dec. 2007	IFRS-IASB	Yes
Deutsche Telekom AG	AR 2007	31 Dec. 2007	IFRS-IASB	Yes
Diageo plc	AR 2007	30 June 2007	IFRS-EU	Yes
Dimension Data Holdings plc	AR 2007	30 Sept. 2007	IFRS-IASB	No
Douglas Holding AG	AR 2007	30 Sept. 2007	IFRS-EU	No
Dragon Mining Limited	AR 2007	31 Dec. 2007	IFRS-IASB	No
Electricité de France S.A.	Financial Report 2007	31 Dec. 2007	IFRS-EU	No
Elisa	AR 2007	31 Dec. 2007	IFRS-EU	No
Enel SpA	AR 2007	31 Dec. 2007	IFRS-EU	No
Eni SpA	AR 2007	31 Dec. 2007	IFRS-EU	Yes

Name	Financial Report	Year end	IFRS-IASB/IFRS-EU/IFRS-Other	SEC registrant
eXpansys PLC	IFRS Restatement Report January 2008	30 Apr. 2008	IFRS-EU	No
Fiat S.p.A.	AR 2007	31 Dec. 2007	IFRS-EU	No
Flaga Group hf.	Consolidated Financial Statements 2007	31 Dec. 2007	IFRS-EU	No
FLSmidth & Co. A/S	AR 2007	31 Dec. 2007	IFRS-EU	No
Fugro N.V.	AR 2007	31 Dec. 2007	IFRS-EU	No
Gecina	AR 2006	31 Dec. 2006	IFRS-EU	No
Gemalto N.V.	AR 2007	31 Dec. 2007	IFRS-EU	No
Givaudan SA	Annual & Financial Report 2007	31 Dec. 2007	IFRS-IASB	No
GlaxoSmithKline	AR 2007	31 Dec. 2007	IFRS-IASB	Yes
Gold Fields Limited	AR 2008	30 June 2008	IFRS-IASB	Yes
Groupe Bruxelles Lambert S.A.	Half-yearly Report June 2008	30 June 2008	IFRS-EU	No
Groupe Danone	Form 20-F 2006	31 Dec. 2006	IFRS-EU	No
Halfords Group plc	AR 2008	28 Mar. 2008	IFRS-EU	No
HEAD N.V.	Form 20-F 2006	31 Dec. 2006	IFRS-EU	Yes
HeidelbergCement Group	AR 2007	31 Dec. 2007	IFRS-EU	No
Heidelberger Druckmaschinen Aktiengesellschaft	AR 2007	31 Mar. 2007	IFRS-EU	No
Heidelberger Druckmaschinen Aktiengesellschaft	AR 2008	31 Mar. 2008	IFRS-EU	No
HELLENIC TELECOMMUNICATIONS ORGANISATION S.A.	AR 2007	31 Dec. 2007	IFRS-EU	Yes
Helphire Group plc	AR 2007	30 June 2007	IFRS-IASB	No
Holcim Ltd	AR 2006	31 Dec. 2006	IFRS-IASB	No
HSBC Holdings plc	Form 20-F 2006	31 Dec. 2006	IFRS-EU	Yes
Informa plc	AR 2007	31 Dec. 2007	IFRS-EU	No
ING Groep N.V.	AR 2007	31 Dec. 2007	IFRS-EU	Yes
Inmet Mining Corporation	AR 2006	31 Dec. 2006	Canadian GAAP[1]	No
Innogenetics NV	Annual Brochure 2006	31 Dec. 2006	IFRS-EU	No
InterContinental Hotels Group PLC	AR 2007	31 Dec. 2007	IFRS-EU	Yes
International Power plc	AR 2007	31 Dec. 2007	IFRS-EU	No
Intrawest Corporation	AR 2006	30 June 2006	Canadian GAAP[1]	No
Italtel Group S.p.A.	AR 2007	31 Dec. 2007	IFRS-EU	No
Kewill Systems PLC	AR 2007	31 Mar. 2007	IFRS-EU	No
Kingfisher plc	AR 2007	3 Feb. 2007	IFRS-EU	No
Koninklijke Ahold N.V.	AR 2007	30 Dec. 2007	IFRS-EU	No
Koninklijke Philips Electronics N.V.	AR 2007	31 Dec. 2007	IFRS-EU	Yes
Lafarge	AR on Form 20-F 2006	31 Dec. 2006	IFRS-EU	No
Lafarge	AR Document de référence 2007	31 Dec. 2007	IFRS-EU	No
Land of Leather Holdings plc	AR 2007	29 July 2007	IFRS-EU	No
Libertas Capital Group plc	AR 2007	31 Dec. 2007	IFRS-EU	No
Lihir Gold Limited	AR 2007	31 Dec. 2007	IFRS-IASB	No
Luminar plc	AR 2007	1 Mar. 2007	IFRS-EU	No
Metso Corporation	AR 2007	31 Dec. 2007	IFRS-EU	No
Minerva plc	AR 2007	30 June 2007	IFRS EU	No
Minster Pharmaceuticals plc	Interim Financial Statements 2007	30 Sept. 2007	IFRS-EU	No
N M Rothschild & Sons Limited	AR 2007	31 Mar. 2007	IFRS-EU	No
National Grid Electricity Transmission plc	AR 2007	31 Mar. 2007	IFRS-EU	No

Name	Financial Report	Year end	IFRS-IASB/IFRS-EU/IFRS-Other	SEC registrant
Nationwide Building Society	AR 2008	4 Apr. 2008	IFRS-EU	No
Nestlé Group	AR 2006	31 Dec. 2006	IFRS-IASB	No
Networkers International PLC	AR 2007	31 Dec. 2007	IFRS-EU	No
Neurochem Inc.	AR 2006	31 Dec. 2006	Canadian GAAP[1]	No
NH Hoteles, S.A.	Consolidated Financial Statements 2006	31 Dec. 2006	IFRS-EU	No
NIREUS AQUACULTURE S.A.	AR 2007	31 Dec. 2007	IFRS-EU	No
Nobel Biocare Holding AG	AR 2007	31 Dec. 2007	IFRS-IASB	No
Nokia Corporation	Form 20-F 2006	31 Dec. 2006	IFRS-EU	Yes
Nokian Tyres plc	AR 2007	31 Dec. 2007	IFRS-EU	No
Norsk Hydro ASA	Conversion to International Financial Reporting Standards 2006	31 Dec. 2006	IFRS-EU	No
Norsk Hydro ASA	AR 2007	31 Dec. 2007	IFRS-EU	No
Northam Platinum Limited	AR 2007	30 June 2007	IFRS-IASB	No
Novartis AG	AR 2006	31 Dec. 2006	IFRS-IASB	Yes
Novo Nordisk A/S	AR 2007	31 Dec. 2007	IFRS-EU	Yes
Nycomed S.C.A. SICAR	AR 2007	31 Dec. 2007	IFRS-EU	No
OAO Baltika Breweries	Financial Statements 2007	31 Dec. 2007	IFRS-IASB	No
Océ N.V.	Financial Statements 2007	30 Nov. 2007	IFRS-EU	No
OMG plc	Interim Report Q2 2008	31 Mar. 2008	IFRS-EU	No
Österreichische Elektrizitätswirtschafts-Aktiengesellschaft	AR 2007	31 Dec. 2007	IFRS-EU	No
Oxford Instruments plc	AR 2007	31 Mar. 2007	IFRS-EU	No
PaperlinX Limited	Full Financial Report 2007	30 June 2007	IFRS-Australia (AASB)	No
Pearson plc	AR 2007	31 Dec. 2007	IFRS-EU	Yes
Pernod Ricard	Financial Report 2007	30 June 2007	IFRS-EU	No
Port Otago Limited	AR 2007	30 June 2007	IFRS-New Zealand	No
PSA Peugeot Citroën	Registration Document 2007	31 Dec. 2007	IFRS-EU	No
Qantas Airways Limited	AR 2007	30 June 2007	IFRS-IASB	No
Quintain Estates and Development PLC	AR 2007	31 Mar. 2007	IFRS-EU	No
Reunert Limited	AR 2007	30 Sept. 2007	IFRS-IASB	No
Ricardo plc	AR 2007	30 June 2007	IFRS-EU	No
Rio Tinto Group	Full Financial Statements 2007	31 Dec. 2007	IFRS-IASB	Yes
Roche Holding Ltd	AR 2006	31 Dec. 2006	IFRS-IASB	No
Roche Holding Ltd	AR 2007	31 Dec. 2007	IFRS-IASB	No
Rockeby biomed Limited	AR 2006	30 June 2006	IFRS-Australia	No
Royal & Sun Alliance Insurance Group plc	AR 2007	31 Dec. 2007	IFRS-EU	No
Royal Ten Cate	AR 2007	31 Dec. 2007	IFRS-EU	No
SABMiller plc	AR 2008	31 Mar. 2008	IFRS-EU	No
Sampo plc	AR 2007	31 Dec. 2007	IFRS-EU	No
Samson Oil and Gas Limited	AR 2007	30 June 2007	IFRS-IASB	No
SAP AG	IFRS Financial Reports 2007	31 Dec. 2007	IFRS-EU	Yes
Sasol Limited	Annual Financial Statements 2007	30 June 2007	IFRS-IASB	Yes
Sasol Limited	Financial Results 2008	30 June 2008	IFRS-IASB	Yes

Name	Financial Report	Year end	IFRS-IASB/IFRS-EU/IFRS-Other	SEC registrant
SGL Carbon Aktiengesellschaft	Form 20-F 2006	31 Dec. 2006	IFRS-IASB	No
Shaftesbury PLC	AR 2007	30 Sept. 2007	IFRS-EU	No
Siemens AG	AR 2007	30 Sept. 2007	IFRS-EU	Yes
Signet Group plc	AR 2007	2 Feb. 2007	IFRS-EU	Yes
Silver Wheaton Corp.	AR 2006	31 Dec. 2006	Canadian GAAP[1]	Yes
Skandinaviska Enskilda Banken AB	AR 2007	31 Dec. 2007	IFRS-EU	No
Skanska AB	AR 2007	31 Dec. 2007	IFRS-EU	No
Smith & Nephew plc	AR 2007	31 Dec. 2007	IFRS-IASB	Yes
Solvay S.A.	AR 2006	31 Dec. 2006	IFRS-EU	No
Solvay S.A.	AR 2007	31 Dec. 2007	IFRS-EU	No
Stagecoach Group plc	AR 2007	30 Apr. 2007	IFRS-IASB	No
Steinhoff International Holdings Limited	AR 2007	30 June 2007	IFRS-IASB	No
Stora Enso Oyj	AR 2007	31 Dec. 2007	IFRS-EU	Yes
Suez	Reference Document 2007	31 Dec. 2007	IFRS-EU	No
Svenska Cellulosa Aktiebolaget SCA	AR 2007	31 Dec. 2007	IFRS-EU	No
Swisscom AG	AR 2006	31 Dec. 2006	IFRS-IASB	No
Swisscom Ltd.	AR 2007	31 Dec. 2007	IFRS-IASB	No
Swiss Post Group	AR 2007	31 Dec. 2007	IFRS-IASB	No
Tadpole Technology plc	AR 2007	30 Sept. 2007	IFRS-EU	No
Telefonaktiebolaget LM Ericsson	AR 2007 on Form 20-F	31 Dec. 2007	IFRS-IASB	No
Telent plc	AR 2007	31 Mar. 2007	IFRS-EU	No
Teleset Networks Public Company Limited	AR 2007	31 Dec. 2007	IFRS-EU	No
TeliaSonera AB	AR 2007	31 Dec. 2007	IFRS-EU	No
Telkom SA Limited	Form 20-F 2008	31 Mar. 2008	IFRS-IASB	Yes
Telstra Corporation Limited	AR 2007	30 June 2007	IFRS-IASB	No
Tesco PLC	AR 2007	24 Feb. 2007	IFRS-EU	No
The Go-ahead Group Plc	AR 2007	30 June 2007	IFRS-EU	No
The Thomson Corporation	AR 2007	31 Dec. 2007	Canadian GAAP[1]	Yes
Thomson	Form 20-F 2006	31 Dec. 2006	IFRS-EU	Yes
Thomson	Form 20-F 2007	31 Dec. 2007	IFRS-IASB	Yes
Thomson Reuters Corporation	First Quarter Report 2008	31 Mar. 2008	Canadian GAAP[1]	Yes
Thomson Reuters Corporation	Second Quarter Report 2008	30 June 2008	Canadian GAAP[1]	Yes
Thomson Reuters Corporation	Third Quarter Report 2008	30 Sept 2008	Canadian GAAP[1]	Yes
Thorntons PLC	AR 2007	30 June 2007	IFRS-EU	No
ThyssenKrupp AG	Interim Report 1st Quarter 2005-06	31 Dec. 2005	IFRS-EU	No
TNT N.V.	AR 2006	31 Dec. 2006	IFRS-EU	No
TNT N.V.	AR 2007	31 Dec. 2007	IFRS-EU	No
TomTom NV	AR 2007	31 Dec. 2007	IFRS-EU	No
Transnet Limited	AR 2008	31 Mar. 2008	IFRS-IASB	No
Transnet Ltd	AR 2007	31 Mar. 2007	IFRS-IASB	No
Ubisoft Entertainment S.A.	AR 2008	31 Mar. 2008	IFRS-EU	No
UBS AG	AR 2007	31 Dec. 2007	IFRS-IASB	Yes
Unibail-Rodamco	AR 2007	31 Dec. 2007	IFRS-EU	No

Name	Financial Report	Year end	IFRS-IASB/IFRS-EU/IFRS-Other	SEC registrant
Unilever	AR on Form 20-F 2006	31 Dec. 2006	IFRS-EU	Yes
Unilever	AR 2007	31 Dec. 2007	IFRS-IASB	Yes
United Utilities PLC	AR 2007	31 Mar. 2007	IFRS-EU	No
Vattenfall AB	AR 2007	31 Dec. 2007	IFRS-EU	No
Vestas Wind Systems A/S	AR 2007	31 Dec. 2007	IFRS-EU	No
Vivendi	AR 2006	31 Dec. 2006	IFRS-EU	No
Vodacom Group Plc	AR 2007	31 Mar. 2007	IFRS-IASB	No
Vodafone Group Plc	AR 2006	31 Mar. 2006	IFRS-IASB	Yes
Vodafone Group Plc	AR 2007	31 Mar. 2007	IFRS-IASB	Yes
Vodafone Group Plc	Form 20-F 2007	31 Mar. 2007	IFRS-IASB	Yes
Vodafone Group Plc	AR 2008	31 Mar. 2008	IFRS-IASB	Yes
voestalpine AG	AR 2008	31 Mar. 2008	IFRS-EU	No
Westpac Banking Corporation	AR 2007	30 Sept. 2007	IFRS-Australia	Yes
Wincanton plc	AR 2007	31 Mar. 2007	IFRS-EU	No
Wolters Kluwer nv	AR 2007	31 Dec. 2007	IFRS-EU	No
Workspace Group PLC	AR 2007	31 Mar. 2007	IFRS-EU	No
WPP Group PLC	AR 2007	31 Dec. 2007	IFRS-IASB	No
Xstrata plc	AR 2006	31 Dec. 2006	IFRS-EU	No
Xstrata plc	AR 2007	31 Dec. 2007	IFRS-EU	No

1   Used only for illustration in one extract.

In the European Union (EU) all listed companies are required by law to prepare their consolidated financial statements in accordance with IFRS as adopted by the EU ("IFRS-EU"). In the current legal framework, the EU has the right to examine each standard or interpretation issued by the IASB ("IFRS-IASB"). Therefore from a practical perspective, IFRS-EU and IFRS-IASB may not be identical at a particular point in time. Consequently any potential difference between IFRS-EU and IFRS-IASB in the extracts is limited to potential temporary differences due to the endorsement process and one very specific difference in hedge accounting, which is only relevant to a limited number of banks. However, all extracts chosen to illustrate any particular standard or interpretation are in accordance with IFRS-IASB.

Appendix D
Abbreviations

The following is a list of abbreviations used in this publication.

Accounting Standards

International Financial Reporting Standards

IAS	International Accounting Standard (issued before April 2001)
IFRIC	International Financial Reporting Interpretations Committee (issued after December 2001)
IFRS	International Financial Reporting Standard (issued after April 2001)
SIC	Standing Interpretations Committee (issued before December 2001)

Canadian GAAP

AcG	Accounting Guideline
CICA (section number)	*CICA Handbook – Accounting* Section (followed by the number of the Section)
EIC	Emerging Issues Committee Abstract

US GAAP

EITF	Emerging Issues Task Force Abstract (issued by FASB)
SFAS	Statement of Financial Accounting Standard (issued by FASB)
FIN	FASB Interpretation
SOP	Statement of Position (issued by AICPA)

Standard-setters

AcSB	Canadian Accounting Standards Board
AICPA	American Institute of Certified Public Accountants
FASB	Financial Accounting Standards Board (US)
IASB	International Accounting Standards Board
ICAEW	Institute of Chartered Accountants in England and Wales

Other Abbreviations

AFS	Available-for-sale
AR	Annual Report
CER	Certified Emissions Reduction
CICA	Canadian Institute of Chartered Accountants
CGU	Cash Generating Unit
CODM	Chief Operating Decision Maker
CSA	Canadian Securities Administrators
CTA	Cumulative Translation Adjustments

Other Abbreviations (continued)

DP	Discussion Paper
E&E	Exploration and Evaluation
EBIDTA	Earnings before Interest, Depreciation, Tax and Amortization
EBIT	Earnings before Interest and Tax
EC	European Commission
ED	Exposure Draft
EPS	Earnings per Share
ETS	Emission Trading Schemes
EU	European Union
FIFO	First-in, First-out
FS	Financial Statements
FVLCTS	Fair Value Less Costs to Sell
GAAP	Generally Accepted Accounting Principles
IAC	IFRS Advisory Committee (Canada)
IPO	Initial Public Offering
IT	Information Technology
IVS	International Valuation Standards
MC	Management Commentary
MD&A	Management Discussion and Analysis
NRV	Net Realizable Value
OIBD	Operating Income before Depreciation
PPE	Property, Plant and Equipment
QSPE	Qualifying Special-purpose Entity
R&D	Research and Development
SEC	Securities and Exchange Commission (US)
SME	Small and Medium-sized Entities
SOCIE	Statement of Changes in Equity (IFRS)
SORIE	Statement of Recognized Income and Expense (IFRS)
SPE	Specific Purpose Entity
UK	United Kingdom
US	United States
VIE	Variable Interest Entity
VIU	Value in Use
WACC	Weighted Average Cost of Capital
WEEE	Waste Electrical and Electronic Equipment

Index

F